STATE TRACTS

SR Scholarly Resources Inc.
Wilmington, Delaware

SCHOLARLY RESOURCES, INC.
1508 Pennsylvania Avenue
Wilmington, Delaware 19806

Reprint edition published in 1973
First published in 1692 by Richard Baldwin,
    London

Library of Congress Catalog Card Number: 72-83171
ISBN: 0-8420-1428-4

Manufactured in the United States of America

STATE TRACTS:

Being a Farther

COLLECTION

OF

Several Choice Treatises

Relating to the

GOVERNMENT.

From the Year 1660, to 1689.

Now Published in a Body, to shew the Necessity, and clear the Legality of the Late REVOLUTION, and Our present Happy SETTLEMENT, under the Auspicious Reign of Their MAJESTIES,

King William and Queen Mary.

LONDON:

Printed, and are to be Sold by RICHARD BALDWIN, near the *Oxford-Arms* in *Warwick-Lane.* MDCXCII.

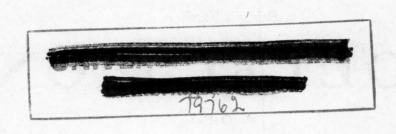

79762

PREFACE to the READER.

THE Main and Principal Design of making this following Collection, was to preserve entire in this Second Volume some other Excellent Tracts, of equal esteem and value with the former, (which made that Book so much obtain among the Learned and Curious, as that the whole Impression of it is already near sold:) And as it cannot but be very entertaining to Us in the reading of them, who do yet so sensibly remember what we then felt, and looked for worse to fall on us every day than other ; so it will certainly be of great Benefit and Advantage to our Posterities in future, who may considerably profit themselves by our Misfortunes.

This is a Collection, that in the general will set forth the true and legal Constitution of our Ancient, Famous English Government, which, ' of all the Countries in Europe, where I was ever ' acquainted, (says the Noble Lord of Argenton) is no where so well managed, the People no ' where less obnoxious to Violence, nor their Houses less liable to the Desolations of War, than in ' England, for there the Calamities fall only upon the Authors.'

Memoirs of Philip de Comines, Kt. lib. 5. cap. 18. p. 334. in Octavo. Printed 1674.

'Twas a true Observation that this Great Man made of the Justice of our Gallant Ancestors in his days ; how miserably the successive Generations have deviated from the virtue of their steps, how much the strict Piety of their Manners, and the noble Bravery of their Spirits, Tempers and Complexions, have been enervated and dissolved by the later looseness, supine carelessness and degeneracy, the present Age hath great reason to bewail ; and, 'tis hoped, that those to come will be hereby cautioned to grow wiser and better by those past Follies and Miscarriages.

In particular, Here will be seen the dangerous Consequences of keeping up a standing Army within these Kingdoms in time of Peace, without consent of Parliament.

The Trust, Power and Duty of Grand Juries, and the great Security of English-men's Lives, in their faithful discharge thereof.

The Right of the Subject to petition their King for Redress of their Wrongs and Oppressions, and that Access to the Sovereign ought not to be shut up in case of any Distresses of his People.

The Spring of all our late private mischievous Councils and Cabals, and the special Tools that were thought fittest for Preferment, to be employed (under a colour of Authority) to put all those concerted Designs in motion and execution.

The Parliament's Care in appointing a Committee to examine the Proceedings of the forward and active Judges upon several Cases that were brought before them of grand importance to the Commonweal, Peace and Safety of the Nation ; and the Resolution of the House of Commons (upon their Report) That the Judges said Proceedings were arbitrary and illegal, destructive to publick Justice, a high and manifest Violation of their Oaths, a Scandal to the Reformation, an Usurpation of the Legislative Power to themselves, and a means to subvert the fundamental Laws of this Kingdom.

And the several Grievances that this Nation hath long been labouring under, for the Advancement of Popery, arbitrary Dominion, and the unmeasurable Growth and Power of France.

There are likewise interspersed in this Volume several Matters of Fact relating to the Male-Administration of Affairs in Scotland, under Duke Lauderdale, and his Favourites, as also a large and faithful Account of the late Earl of Argyle's Tryal, Escape and Sentence, with divers other things for the better clearing of this Case.

In a word, This Collection will discover to us the Mysteries of the Monarchy in the two late Reigns, and the abused Trust of Government in those Princes, by a Dispensing Power both in ecclesiastical and civil Matters, to tyrannize over their Subjects ; who in the mean while were taught, by some Passive-Obedience and Non-Resistance Doctrine-holders, that all their Duty was tamely to submit to, and patiently sigh under their daily Sufferings and Oppressions: and, I think we bore them so long, till we were within one throw more of losing all our good old Laws and Constitutions, and even the Government it self.

Our Miseries were lately so great and many, (as you will find here) that it is impossible for any one better and more fully to express them, than in the words of a very Learned and Judicious Author, who hath thus given us a just and lively Representation of them.

' Our Laws (says he) were trampled under foot, and upon the matter abolished, to set up Will ' and Pleasure in their room, under the Cant and Pretence of Dispensing Power. Our Constitution ' was overthrown by the Trick of new Charters, and by closetting, and corrupting Members of Parliament. Men were required, under pain of the highest Displeasure, to consent, and concur to the ' sacrificing their Religion, and the Liberty of their Country. The worthiest, honestest, and bravest ' Men in England, had been barbarously murthered ; and to aggravate the Injustice which was ' done them, all had been varnished over with a Colour of Law, and the Formality of Tryals ; not ' unlike the Case of Naboth and Ahab. Those whom the Law declared Traytors, were, in defiance of the National Authority, introduced into our Councils, and the Conduct of Affairs put into ' their hands. Our Universities were invaded by open Force ; those who were in the lawful possession of the Government of Colleges, turned out, and Papists sent thither in their room: And if ' that Attempt had thoroughly prospered, the Churches and Pulpits would soon have followed. It ' were vain to go about to enumerate Particulars. In a word, the Nation was undone. All was ' lost. The Judges were suborned, or threatned to declare, that the King was Master of all the Laws ; ' and the Bishops were required to publish this New-created Prerogative in all the Churches of ' England by the Mouths of the Clergy ; which when some of them refused to do, representing ' to the King, with the utmost submission and modesty, that neither Conscience nor Justice permitted ' them to do what he desired, they were prosecuted at Law, as if they had been guilty of some great ' Crime. Letters were written and intercepted, by which it appeared evidently, that the Change of ' our Religion was determined, and that Popery was to be brought in with all speed, lest the op-

Some Considerations about the most proper way of raising Money in the present Conjuncture. Printed Oct. 1691.

' portunity

A 2

' portunity should be lost. And for the better compassing this pious Design, our Civil, and Parlia-
' mentary Rights were to be taken away, in Ordine ad Spiritualia. And when the Nation, and
' those who were concerned for it, being terrified by the greatness of the danger, would have com-
' pounded so far, as to have taken away the penal Laws against Papists, and so have set them upon
' a level with other English Subjects, provided the Test might have been continued, and the Go-
' vernment secured from falling into the hands of that Faction, all such offers were despised and
' rejected with scorn: Nor would any thing content the Bigotry and arbitrary Humour of those
' who were then in the Saddle, less than the total enslaving of the Nation, and the Re-establishment
' of that Idolatrous Religion, from which our Ancestors had freed themselves with so much Bravery
' and Generosity in the beginning of the last Century.

In this deplorable Condition, His then Highness the Prince of Orange found these Kingdoms,
when he came to relieve us from the greatest Oppressions; He heard the Voice of the People, that
earnestly invited him over to their Rescue, and taking it (as undoubtedly it was) for the Voice of
God, complied, and God hath made us All happy with the desired success.

King's Speech
to both Hou-
ses of Parlia-
ment, May 30,
1685.

Had the late King James stuck firmly to the Interests of his People, he would thereby have easily
secured his own; and, if they could have found He had had (what he assured both Houses of Parliament, in a Speech he made to them) ' A true English Heart, as jealous of the Honour of the Na-
' tion, as they themselves could be, he might have carried, by God's Blessing, and their Assistance,
' (as he then said) the Reputation of it yet higher in the World, than ever it had been in the time
' of any of his Ancestors.' He wanted not some about him (at the first especially) that would gladly
have given him faithful Counsel, those that were able to advise him well, and were real Friends to
Him, as they were true to their Religion, and to the Interest of their Country; and, A Wise Man,

Memoirs of
Philip de Co-
mines, lib. 3.
c. 5. p. 159.

says my incomparable Author, in a Prince's Retinue is a great Treasure, and Security to his Master; if one has the Liberty to speak truth, and the other the Discretion to believe him.

But, unhappy Prince! He was resolvedly bent, by the force of his own Superstition, the Power and
Influence of the Priests and Jesuits that continually attended on him, and the Directions from France,
upon the total Destruction of our Reformed Religion, (that Pestilent Northern Heresy) our Liberties
and our Properties, and was upon the point of effecting that tremendous Design; but God in his wise
Providence, with infinite Mercy and Compassion to this almost ruined Land and People, saw it meet
to give check to that Imperial Career, with a hitherto shalt thou come, and no further.

He REMOVETH KINGS, AND SETTETH UP KINGS.

In this Volume, you have a full Account of our late happy Revolution, with almost all the steps
and measures that were taken in it, and a justification of our present Settlement. 'Twas God's doing, and it ought ever to be marvellous in our Eyes.

We have now a King and Queen professing the same Faith with ourselves; who, as He came over
to preserve our dearest Interests, the Protestant Religion, and to restore to Us our invaded Laws
and Liberties, found the Nation generally disposed to receive him, as the Mighty Deliverer, under
God, of this Church and State. The hand of Heaven conducted him with safety up to London, and
all the Kingdom called him Blessed; and in a sense of Joy and Gratitude to Him and His Royal
Consort, The whole Body of the Nation, by their Representatives in Parliament, have recognized
and acknowledged their present Majesties to be their Lawful and Rightful Sovereign Liege Lord
and Lady. And how could we do less than own them for our King and Queen, who by such an a-
mazing turn, have redeemed from Slavery both our Souls and Bodies, if we pretend to any value
for our Holy Religion, or any English Love of Liberty?

We have a King of an extraordinary personal Valour and Conduct, that hath very often already
ventured his Life, and still resolves to despise all difficulties and hazards himself, that his People
may reap the fruit of them in their own Peace and Prosperity, and that the Protestant Religion
may be established to us and our Children to future Generations.

The Queen is as supream in her Virtue as in her Dignity, and hath shewed a most eminent Resolution, as well as a most prudent Care in all the Administrations of the Government, when the Absence of the King hath obliged her to take the Exercise of the Regal Power upon her.

So that the Nation may now hope to enjoy a lasting Felicity from the Royal Protection of both their
Majesties, whose constant endeavours we are assured from themselves, will be employed to procure and
support the Interest and Honour of it, and the Benefit, Safety and Ease of their People; they throughly

Memoirs of
what past in
Christendom,
from the War
begun 1672,
to the Peace
concluded
1679. p. 33,
34.

understanding the Truth of Monf. Gourville's Observation (who had been long enough here in England,
to know the Humour of our Court, and People, and Parliaments, to conclude) Qu'un Roy d'An-
gleterre qui veut estre l'homme de son peuple, est le plus Grand Roy du monde, mais s'il veut
estre quelque chose d'avantage, par Dieu il n'est plus rien, i. e. That a King of England, who
will be the MAN of his People, is the greatest King in the World; but if he will be something more--
he is nothing at all. I may venture therefore to prophesy, that this King and Queen will take the same
care to continue, as they have already done, to make themselves the DARLING of their People; and
no good Englishman can wish for more, but that this King and Queen may long reign, and that the
Tripple Alliance of their Sacred Majesties, their Parliaments, and their People, may never be dissolved.

Little needs be said concerning the Usefulness of such Collections as these, THAT formerly published,
having received sufficient Approbation from Persons of Learning and Knowledge. The benefit of
this is the same with what redounds from a true History, not of Battels and Sieges, Births, Marriages, and Deaths of Princes, which are temporary and momentary things, but of the Legal Government of a Nation, struggling with Arbitrary Power and illegal Proceedings, so far forth as it
was invaded, within the time mentioned in the Title.

A
CATALOGUE
OF THE
TRACTS
Contained in this
Second Volume.

21 *The*

The Contents.

The Contents.

The Contents.

THE
Earl of Clarendon's Speech,
ABOUT
Disbanding the Army.
SEPTEMBER 13, 1660.

My Lords and Gentlemen,

THE King tells you that he hath commanded me to say many particulars to you ; and the truth is, He hath charged me with so many; that I have great reason to fear, that I shall stand in much need of His Mercy, for omitting many things He hath given me in Command ; at least for delivering them in more Disorder and Confusion, than Matters of such Moment and Importance ought to be to such an Assembly, for which the King Himself hath even a kind of Reverence, as well as an extraordinary Kindness. I am to mention some things He hath done already, and many things He intends to do during this Recess, that you may see, how well content soever he is, that you should have Ease, and Pleasure, and Refreshment, he hath designed Work enough for Himself.

The King hath thanked you for the Provision you have made that there may be no free Quarter during the time the Army shall be disbanding, and hath told you what He will do with that Money you have given Him, if there should want wherewithal to disband it ; and now I hope you will all believe, that His Majesty will consent to the disbanding: He will do so ; and yet He does not take it unkindly at their hands, who have thought that his Majesty would not disband this Army ; it was a sober and a rational Jealousy ; No other Prince in *Europe* would be willing to disband such an Army ; an Army to which Victory is entailed, and which, humanly speaking, could hardly fail of Conquest whithersoever He should lead it ; and if God had not restored His Majesty to that rare Felicity, as to be without apprehension of Danger at home or from abroad, and without any Ambition of taking from his Neighbours what they are possessed of ; Himself would never disband this Army ; an Army whose Order and Discipline, whose Sobriety and Manners, whose Courage and Success hath made it famous and terrible over the World ; an Army of which the King and His two Royal Brothers may say, as the noble *Grecian* said of *Æneas*,

———*Stetimus tela aspera contra,*
Contulimusque manus, experto credite, quantus
In clypeum assurgat, quo turbine torqueat hastam.

They have all three in several Countries found themselves engaged in the midst of these Troops, in the heat and rage of Battel, and if any common Soldiers (as no doubt many may) will demand the old *Roman* Privilege for having encountred Princes single, upon my Conscience, he will find both Favour and Preferment: They have all three observed the Discipline, and felt, and admired, and loved the Courage of this Army, when they were the worse for it ; and I have seen them in a season when there was little else of comfort in their view, refresh themselves with joy, that the *English* had done the great Work, the *English* had got the Day, and then please themselves with the Imagination what wonders they should perform in the head of such an Army: And therefore when His Majesty is so entirely possessed of the Affection and Obedience of this Army, and when it hath merited so much from Him, can it be believed, or imagined, that

He

He can without some regret part with them? No: *My Lords and Gentlemen,* He will never part with them, and the only sure way never to part with them, is to disband them; should it be otherwise, they must be exposed to the daily Importunity of His great Neighbours and Allies; and how could he refuse to lend them His Troops, of which He hath no use Himself? His Majesty knows they are too good *English*-men, to wish that a standing Army should be kept in the Bowels of their own Countrey; that they who did but *in Bello pacis gerere negotium,* and who, whilst an Army, lived like good Husbandmen in the Countrey, and good Citizens in the City, will now become really such, and take delight in the Benefit of that Peace they have so honestly and so wonderfully brought to pass: The King will part with them, as the most indulgent Parents part with their Children, for their Education, and for their Preferment; He will prefer them to Disbanding, and prefer them by Disbanding, and will always retain such a Kindness for them, and such a Memory of the Service they have done him, that both Officers and Soldiers, after they are Disbanded, shall always find such countenance, favour, and reward from His Majesty, that He doubts not, but if he should have Occasion to use their Service, they will again resort to Him with the same Alacrity; as if they had never been Disbanded: And if there be any so ill amongst them (as there can be but very few, if any) who will forfeit that Favour and Protection they may have from Him, by any withstanding His Majesty's Commands, and the full and declared Sense of the Kingdom; His Majesty is confident they will be as odious to their Companions, as they can be to any other honest Men.

My Lords and Gentlemen, I am in the next place, by the King's Command, to put you in mind of the Act of Indemnity, not of any Grants or Concessions, or Releases He made to you in that Act, I have nothing of that in charge; no Prince hath so excellent a memory to forget the Favours he doth; but of what he hath done against you in that Act, how you may be undone by that Act, if you are not very careful to perform the Obligations He hath laid upon you in it: the clause I am to put you in mind of, is this, *And to the intent and purpose that all names and terms of Distinction may be likewise put into utter Oblivion, Be it further Enacted by the Authority aforesaid, That if any Person or Persons, within the space of three Years next ensuing, shall presume so maliciously to call or alledge, or object against any other Person or Persons any Name or Names, or other words of Reproach, any way leading to revive the Memory of the late Differences, or the occasion thereof, That then every such Person, so as aforesaid offending, shall forfeit, &c.* It is no matter for the Penalty, it is too cheap a one; the King wishes it had been greater, and therefore hath by His just Prerogative (and 'tis well for us he hath such a Prerogative) added another Penalty more insupportable, even His high Displeasure against all who shall swerve from this Clause in the Act. Give me leave to tell you, that as many Name or Names, or other words of Reproach are expresly against the Letter, and punishable accordingly; so evil and envious looks, murmuring and discontented hearts, are as directly against the Equity of this Statute, a direct breach of the Act of Indempnity, and ought to be punished too; and I believe they may be so. You know Kings are in some sense called Gods, and so they may in some degree be able to look into mens hearts; and God hath given us a King who can look as far into mens hearts as any Prince alive; and he hath great skill in Physiognomy too, you would wonder what Calculations He hath made from thence; and no doubt, if He be provok'd by evil looks, to make a further Enquiry into mens hearts, and finds those corrupted with the Passions of Envy and Uncharitableness, He will never choose those hearts to trust and rely upon. He hath given us a Noble and Princely Example, by opening and stretching His Arms to all who are worthy to be His Subjects, worthy to be thought *Englishmen,* by extending His heart with a pious and grateful joy to find all His Subjects at once in His Arms, and Himself in theirs: and shall we fold our Arms towards one another, and contract our Hearts with Envy and Malice to each other, by any sharp memory of what hath been unneighbourly or unkindly done heretofore? What is this but to rebel against the Person of the King, against the excellent Example and Vertue of the King, against the known Law of the Land, this blessed Act of Oblivion.

My Lords and Gentlemen, The King is a Suitor to you, makes it His Suit very heartily, That you will join with Him in restoring the whole Nation to its primitive Temper and Integrity, to its old good Manners, its old good Humour, and its old good Nature; Good Nature, a Vertue so peculiar to you, so appropriated by God Almighty to this Nation, that it can be translated into no other Language, hardly practised by any other People, and that you will by your Example, by the Candor of your Conversation, by your Precepts, and by your Practice, and by all your Interest,

teach

teach your Neighbours and your Friends, how to pay a full Obedience to this Clause of the Statute, how to learn this excellent Art of Forgetfulness.

Let them remember, and let us remember, how ungracious, how undecent, how ugly the Insolence, the Fierceness, the Brutishness of their Enemies appeared to them; and we may piously and reasonably believe, that God's Indignation against them, for their want of Bowels, for their not being *Englishmen*, (for they had the hearts of Pagans and Infidels) sent a Whirlwind in a moment to blow them out of the World, that is, out of a capacity to do more mischief in the World, except we practise their Vices, and do that ourselves which we pretend to detest them for: Let us not be too much ashamed, as if what hath been done amiss, proceeded from the humour and the temper, and the nature of our Nation. The *Astrologers* have made us a fair excuse, and truly I hope a true one; all the motions of these last twenty Years have been unnatural, and have proceeded from the evil Influence of a malignant Star; and let us not too much despise the Influence of the Stars! And the same *Astrologers* assure us, that the Malignity of that Star is expired; the good *Genius* of this Kingdom is become superiour, and hath mastered that Malignity, and our own good old Stars govern us again, and their Influence is so strong, that with our help, they will repair in a Year, what hath been decaying in twenty; and they only shall have no excuse from the Star, who continue their Malignity, and own all the ill that is past to be their own, by continuing and improving it for the time to come.

If any body here, or any where else, be too much exalted with what he hath done, or what he hath suffered, and from thence thinks himself warranted to reproach others, let him remember the story of *Nicephorus*; it is an excellent story, and very applicable to such Distempers: He was a pious and a religious man, and for his Piety and Religion was condemned to the fire; when he was led to Execution, and when an old Friend who had done him injury enough, fell at his feet and asked him pardon; the poor Man was so elevated with the Triumph he was going unto, with the Glory of Martyrdom, that he refused to be reconciled unto him; upon which he was disappointed of his end: and for this Uncharitableness, the Spirit of God immediately forsook him, and he apostatized from the Faith. Let all those who are too proud of having been as they think less faulty than other Men, and so are unwilling to be reconciled to those who have offended them, take heed of the Apostacy of *Nicephorus*, and that those Fumes of Envy and Uncharitableness, and Murmuring, do not so far transport and intoxicate them, that they fall into those very Crimes, they value themselves for having hitherto declined.

But, *My Lords and Gentlemen*, whilst we conspire together, to execute faithfully this part of the Bill, to put all old Names and Terms of Distinction into utter Oblivion; let us not find new Names and Terms to keep up the same, or a worse Distinction: If the old Reproaches of Cavalier, and Round-head, and Malignant, be committed to the Grave; let us not find more significant and better words, to signify worse things; let not Piety and Godliness grow into terms of Reproach, and distinguish between the Court, and the City, and the Countrey; and let not Piety and Godliness be measured by a morosity in Manners, an affectation of Gesture, a new mode and tone of Speaking; at least, let not our Constitutions and Complexions make us be thought of a contrary Party; and because we have not an affected Austerity in our looks, that we have not Piety in our hearts. Very merry Men have been very godly Men; and if a good *Conscience* be a continual *Feast*, here is no reason but Men may be merry at it.

You, Mr. *Speaker*, have this Day made a noble Present to the King. Do you think if you and your worthy Companions had brought it up with folded Arms, down-cast Looks, with Sighs and other Instances of Desperation, it would not have been a very melancholy Present? Have not your frank and dutiful Expressions, that cheerfulness and vivacity in your Looks, render'd it much more acceptable, much more valuable? No Prince in Christendom loves a cheerful giver so well as *God Almighty* does, and he of all Gifts, a cheerful Heart: and therefore I pray let not a cloudy and disconsolate face be the only, or the best sign of Piety and Devotion in the Heart.

I must ask your Pardon for misplacing much of this Discourse, which I should have mentioned, when I came to speak of the Ministers Bill; they I hope will endeavour to remove these new marks of Distinction and Reproaches, and keep their Auditories from being imposed upon by such Characters and Descriptions. The King hath passed this *Act* very willingly, and done much to the end of this *Act* before; yet hath willingly admitted you to be Sharers and Partners with Him

in

2

in the Obligation : I may say confidently His Majesty hath never denied his Confirmation to any Man in Possession who hath asked it ; and they have all the effect of it, except such who upon Examination and Enquiry, appeared not worthy of it, and such who though they are pardoned, cannot yet think themselves worthy to be preferr'd. His Majesty well knows that by this *Act* he hath gratified and obliged many worthy and pious Men, who have contributed much to His Restauration, and who shall always receive fresh Evidence of His Majesty's Favour and Kindness, but he is not sure that he may not likewise have gratified some who did neither contribute to His coming in, nor are yet glad that he is in ; how comes it else to pass, that he receives such frequent informations of seditious Sermons in the City and the Countrey, in which all Industry is used to alienate the Affections of the People, and to infuse Jealousies into them of the King and His Government ; They talk of introducing Popery, of evil Counsellors, and such other old Calumnies as are pardoned by this Act of Indempnity.

His Majesty told You when he was last here, what Rigour and Severity He will hereafter use, how contrary soever it is to his Nature in these Cases ; and conjured You, *My Lords and Gentlemen,* to concur with him in this just and necessary Severity, which I am sure You will do with Your utmost Vigilance, and that You will believe that too much ill cannot befal those who do the best they can to corrupt His Majesty's Nature, and to extinguish his Mercy.

My Lords and Gentlemen, I told You I was to acquaint you with some things His Majesty intends to do during this Recess, that You may see He will give no intermission to His own Thoughts for the Publick Good, though for a time He dispenses with Your Assistance.

He doth consider the infinite Importance the Improvement of Trade must be to this Kingdom, and therefore His Majesty intends forthwith to establish a Council for Trade, consisting of some principal Merchants of the several Companies ; to which he will add some Gentlemen of Quality and Experience ; and for their greater Honour and Encouragement, some of my Lords of his own Privy Council.

In the next place, His Majesty hopes that by a well-settled Peace, and God's great Blessing upon Him and You, this Nation will in a short time flourish to that Degree, that the Land of *Canaan* did, when *Esau* found it necessary to part from his Brother.————— *For their Riches were more, than that they might dwell together, and the Land wherein they were could not bear them, because of their Cattel :* We have been our selves very near this Pinacle of Happiness, and the Hope and Contemplation that we may be so again, disposes the King to be very solicitous for the Improvement and Prosperity of His Plantations abroad, where there is such large room for the Industry and Reception of such who shall desire to go thither ; and therefore His Majesty likewise intends to erect and establish a Council for those Plantations, in which persons well qualified shall be wholly intent upon the good and advancement of those Plantations.

There are two other particulars, which I am commanded to mention, which were both mentioned and recommended to You by His Majesty in his Declaration from *Breda* ; The one, for the Confirmation of Sales, or other Recompence for Purchasers ; The other, for the composing those Differences and Distempers in Religion, which have too much disturbed the Peace of the Kingdom. Two very weighty particulars, in which His Majesty knows You have spent much time, and concerning which, he should have heard from You before this time, if You had not met with great difficulties in the Disquisition of either.

For the first, His Majesty hath not been without much thought upon the Argument, and hath done much towards the Accommodation of many particular Persons, and You shall not be at Your Journey's end, before His Majesty will put that Business concerning Sale, into such a way of Dispatch, that he doubts not You will find a good Progress made in it before Your coming together again, and I believe the Persons concerned, will be very much to blame, if they receive not good Satisfaction ; and some of You who stay in Town, shall be advised and consulted with on that Settlement.

The other, of Religion, is a sad Argument indeed ; it is a Consideration that must make every religious Heart to bleed, to see Religion, which should be the strongest obligation and cement of Affection, and brotherly Kindness and compassion, made now by the Wranglings of passionate and froward Men, the ground of all

animosity

animosity, hatred, malice, and revenge: And this unruly and unmanly Passion (which no question the Divine Nature exceedingly abhors) sometimes, and I fear too frequently, transports those who are in the right, as well as those who are in the wrong, and leaves the latter more excusable than the former, when men who find their manners and dispositions very conformable in all the necessary obligations of human Nature, avoid one another's Conversation, and grow first unsociable, and then uncharitable to each other, because one cannot think as the other doth: And from this separation we entitle God to the Patronage of, and Concernment in our Fancies and Distinction, and purely for his sake hate one another heartily. It was not so of old, when one of the most ancient Fathers of the Church tells us, *That Love and Charity was so signal and eminent in the* primitive Christians, that it even drew Admiration and Envy from their Adversaries, *Vide, inquiunt, ut invicem se diligunt!* Their Adversaries in that in which they most agreed, in their very prosecution of them, had their Passions and Animosities amongst themselves; they were only Christians, that loved, and cherished, and comforted, and were ready to die for one another: *Quid nunc illi dicerent Christiani, si nostra viderent tempora?* says the incomparable *Grotius:* How would they look upon our sharp and virulent Contentions in the Debates of *Christian Religion,* and the bloody Wars that have proceeded from those Contentions, whilst every one pretended to all the Marks which are to attend upon the true Church, except only that which is inseparable from it, *Charity to one another?*

My Lords and Gentlemen, This Disquisition hath cost the King many a Sigh, many a sad Hour, when he hath considered the almost irreparable Reproach the *Protestant Religion* hath undergone, from the Divisions and Distractions which have been so notorious within this Kingdom. What pains he hath taken to compose them, after several Discourses with learned and pious Men of different Persuasions, you will shortly see, by a *Declaration* He will publish upon that Occasion, by which you will see His great Indulgence to those who can have any Protection from *Conscience* to differ with their Brethren. And I hope God will so bless the Candor of His Majesty in the Condescensions he makes, that the Church, as well as the State, will return to that Unity and Unanimity, which will make both King and People as happy as they can hope to be in this World.

My Lords and Gentlemen, I shall conclude with the King's hearty thanks to you, not only for what you have done towards Him, which hath been very signal, but for what you have done towards each other; for the excellent Correspondence you have maintained; for the very seasonable Deference and Condescension you have had for each other, which will restore *Parliaments* to the Veneration they ought to have. And since His Majesty knows, that you all desire to please him, you have given him ample Evidence, that you do so; He hath appointed me to give you a sure Receipt to attain that good End, it is a Receipt of His own prescribing, and therefore is not like to fail:

Be but pleased your selves, and persuade others to be so; contrive all the ways imaginable for your own Happiness, and you will make Him the best pleased, and the most happy Prince in the World.

C

THE

THE
State of ENGLAND,

Both at HOME and ABROAD,

In Order to

The Designs of France,

CONSIDERED.

To the READER.

THIS *Difcourfe being imaginarily fcened, and yet really performed out of the Trea-fure of a very great Minifter of State's Capacity ; it was thought fit to be Publifhed now, and not before, becaufe that Refpect ought to be payed to the Secret of his Majefty's Affairs, fo as nothing fhould anticipate the King's own Labours, to give the People Satisfaction in his due time touching the tender Care that He is gracioufly pleafed to take of all his Subjects in point of Honour, Safety, Freedom, Union, and Commerce : which nothing could more advance than the Conclufion of the* Treaty *newly made betwixt* England *and the* States *of the* United Provinces ; *which without Flattery may be demon-ftrated to Men of Underftanding to aim at nothing but the Good of his Subjects in general, exempt from all manner of private Intereft whatfoever. Bleffed be God then that it is fo hap-pily concluded ; and that we have a King whom nothing can ever alienate from the true In-terft of his Realms, nor any corrupt Counfellor (let him be thought to be ever fo Powerful or Crafty in order to his own Advantages) prevent the Wifdom and Integrity of fuch a* Prince *from prevailing above the Artifices and Frauds of thofe who would perfuade the Nation, (were they competent Mafters to their Art enough fo to do) that thofe Counfellors who are not inte-refted, can be lefs prudent or fuccefsful than fuch as did make it their Bufinefs to appropriate all to themfelves, and nothing to their Mafter. The* French King *is much commended for his Parts and Activity ; but let us fee him out-do the* King *of* England *in this particular of the* Treaty, *both in Courage and Conduct ; and then I fhall be apt to attribute his Grandeur as much to natural Abilities as extraordinary Fortune, but not before.*

THE

THE

State of England, &c.

THE Adventure which happened unto me lately is of so extraordinary a nature, and contains so many important Discoveries in relation to the publick Good in its Progress, that I should prove defective towards my Countrey, if I did not candidly publish all the
Passages, both touching the Occasion, and Effects of what followed
from this Accident.

Know then that a Peer of the Realm of *England*, and one whose Merit, Quality, and
the Place which he holds in the Administration of the Affairs of the Kingdom are
remarkable; did invite sundry of his Lordship's best Friends to a magnificent Feast,
and amongst the rest he had the kindness not to omit me out of the number: where
the excellence of the Chear which he made to his Guests, after a most noble
manner put the whole Company into such a refined humour of conversing together, that the Entertainment was but one entire pleasing Debate, how to express our compleat enjoying of each other. I was not wanting with the uttermost
of Vigour and Solace to uphold the Genius of this Conference. But as the freest
speakers do commonly come by the worst in Discourse, and are the soonest exposed to interfering lashes; I found my self to be attacqued in so many places
at once with the swiftness of other Mens Reasons and Wits, who held the opposite Arguments, that although I were something heated, yet there remained unto me presence of mind enough (and success of Intervals) to get insensibly
out of the Press, whilst the Disorder and Confusion lasted, (which is usual at
such Meetings) into another room. I retired then, pursuing the Opportunity, into a fair Gallery, which surprised my Eyes with the rich Ornaments wherewith it was furnished; but not without trouble neither, and a Curiosity beyond
the Opticks of the Place, which increased there; so as I was diverted from any
farther Consideration of the Furniture, because the Place seemed to lie too near the
Enemy, to dwell any longer upon those Objects. Wherefore I went into another
Chamber hard by, which instantly filled me with new Apprehensions, by the
means of several large Looking-Glasses hanging on the Walls; which shewed me
my own proper Figure at length on every side, and from thence imprinted in my
wounded Imagination as many Adversaries as there were angular Reflections out of
each Mirrour; that appeared to pursue me so furiously, that I ran on violently with
my head forwards, in order to some Escape, to the door of another Chamber adjoining thereunto, which opened with such Resistance, when I thrust against it,
as if it had been forced with a Petard: And thus falling in the Attempt, I was
so stunned, that it was a good while after before I could come to my self again.
But at last having partly recovered my spirits, I was surprised with a fresh astonish-
ment which as much amazed me, as the former had done that I repeated: for when I
began to open my eyes half way, finding that till then they had been altogether unuseful to me, I attributed the Disorder to want of Sight, often feeling, in regard of
the Darkness of the Room, to try whether they were still in my head or not.
Yet perceiving, betwixt Discerning and Doubting, that all I assayed of this kind
was to no purpose; after having deplored the bitterness of an imaginary Loss, I
groped on more and more in the dark until I chanced to come to an *Alcove*,
where feeling with my hands, I took fast hold upon the *Alcove*, and grasped the
Pillar of a Bed, which had I not lit upon, I must have fallen the second time.
For, thrusting hard against one of the Posts, the Counter-stroak of the Wood threw
me all along into the middle of a Couch, where I remained stretched forth like a Corpse
without any motion, in the same posture of a precipitate Swoon. And then it was that
the Vapours of my Body, which were disturbed by the first Mistake, confusedly did
stir through all the parts in the agitated fluctuancy of a Storm; though by degrees growing to be undeceived, Sleep, which appeaseth all the Mutinies in human Creatures, did naturally and more agreeably seize upon my Faculties, and compose

pose the Tempest with perfect tranquillity of Mind and animal Operations, as if I had never been so discomposed. 'Tis impossible to tell you how long I continued in the State of this *Interregnum* betwixt Life and Death, nor what Care the Company took to learn what was become of me, but in vain ; blaming me for having left them, or rather the War begun, using all sorts of means to find where I was, and bring me back to the Combate.

I shall only tell you by the way, that about Sun-set a great Noise was raised by two of the Servants of the House, who entred suddenly into the Chamber where I lay ; which assured me, as I awaken'd, that I was yet living ; and the blazing of the Wax-tapers, which they set upon the Tables and the Cup-boards, made me extremely joyful at the Restauration of my sight, which in my Opinion till then was absolutely gone from me. But then a third Apprehension seized on my Powers, first, to be catch'd in such a Posture, and exposed to the innocent Jests which might be made by the Guests on the subject of my strange Disorder, and precipitated Flight from them. But as I sought my Eyes once more, to steal away out of this Society for all Night; and not to be seen by any body, another noise obliged me to keep close where I was upon the Bed, and draw the Curtains home, not to be discovered. I was not long in this Concealment, when I saw come into the same Place three Persons, whose Deserts in this Relation must be better known than their Names, and the Importance of their Interest in the State, by what I am going now to say of those particulars, because I am strictly obliged not to reveal them. These strangers the Master of the House did very civily introduce into the Chamber, who without many Compliments sat down on the seats which were prepared for them near the Table. My Sleep had digested those Fumes, and dissipated all the Clouds of my Understanding: therefore judging that the cause that assembled such great Personages together there in this secret Entertainment, could not be but of the highest Importance ; both the Curiosity, and the Shame of having them witnesses to my Disorder, obliged me to keep firm to my Post, within the cover of the Bed, and to lend an attentive ear to all their Discourse. For the Master of the House began the Overture of the Conference in the Terms following.

In that part which we do hold of the Government of the State, it is not enough that a sincere Amity doth link us in one band of Interest and Esteem particularly to each other, if we be not also united in the same Judgment as to all which concerns the Publick Good. In our former Conferences we used to take just Measures how to rectify things within the *Realm* ; but now it rests with us to agree upon some Maxims which are to be maintained in regard of *Foreign Matters*, to the end that in these Rencounters, wherein we are to give Counsel, we may act in all things with a perfect Concert, which no doubt will give a great weight to the Resolutions which shall be formed thereupon, and the present Case ; since never have any Counsellors treated of nicer Points, nor more serious ones than those which are to be debated among us to-day. The fire is already kindled in our Neighbourhood ; the Monarchy of *Spain* is just upon the brink of falling to the ground, if it be not succoured ; and *France* in a condition to avow the vast Design which that Crown hath long meditated, as well against the Peace of *Europe*, as the Commerce of our Navigations, if a powerful Fence be not quickly made, to keep the *French* within their Bounds. Wherefore all the rest of the Forces of *Europe* stand at gaze, expecting the Result of what *England* doth determine herein, considering us the Counter-ballance, which time out of mind hath held the Scales even between those two great Monarchies, for the Safety of all the rest. They wait but our giving of the Sign, to join with us in the common Defence : and the better share of them seek it from *England* ; and the others have their Eyes open towards our Conduct, to take their measures also by no other model but what we shall trace out unto them.

There is no need of a Providence extraordinarily enlightned, to judge which is our true Interest in this Conjuncture ; but the present State of our Affairs doth not leave us the same Facilities to follow it, in which we do abound as to the Knowledge thereof.

Mean while the Mischief presses forwards, and doth not afford Place nor Time sufficient to expect a Benefit of other Vicissitudes, which run sufficiently against us ; nor to regulate our Resolutions by those Events, which take too impetuous a part in the Cause on that side which we ought most to fear. Therefore it is more than season to form our Fundamental Maxim, on which all our Conduct is to move in this present Conjuncture ; and at this very instant decide, whether we will chuse to be simple Spectators, or take some part to act in this Tragedy ; since the Resolution

which

which we shall fix thereupon will be the Center, from whence we must draw all our Lines afterwards. Which is the proper Point that we are to discourse of now among our selves here, before we do give our Opinions on the whole matter to the Publick ; and in which particular I desire the rather to be enlightned by your wise Reasonings, by how much the more I am assured, That the sole Good of the State is the only Rule and Object of all your Counsels.

As soon as ever he had uttered these words, one of the Three, after casting down of his Eyes, and pondering what he was to say to the rest, with having thought before he advised, began his Discourse thus:

If late Experience had not taught us enough to our cost, that it is much easier to begin a War, than successfully to get out of it when once it is commenced, I would enlarge my self on that Subject, to represent unto you piece by piece, the Dangers, Incommodities, and Losses which such a Resolution usually doth carry along with it ; where frequently the Conqueror finds he is more charged with Debts than with Trophies, and the People have always cause to mingle their Acclamations with Tears, in the course of such expensive Triumphs ; since before any Edifice is begun, the Dimensions how to settle a solid Foundation to undertake the War upon, should previously be considered, by measuring our Means and Forces as well as those of the Enemy with whom we are to fight ; and the like touching their Power, whose Interest we intend to embrace.

Our Forces and Means you all know are already exhausted with long and sharp Wars, both at home and abroad ; and by the Hand of God, which hath been heavy upon us in the late *Pestilence*, and in the *Firing* of the City of *London :* wherefore 'tis but now that we begin by the means of Peace to breath again ; which Peace also is not firmly established. Time then is requisite for us to take breath and recover in, after so terrible an Agitation: nor can any thing be so dangerous unto this State as a Relapse in the midst of Amendment. If the noise of our Neighbours doth awaken us, our Weariness likewise invites us to seek some Repose: and in case there be danger to suffer the Growth of a suspected Power, there will not be less peril in the checking of that Power unprepared. You know, as well or better than I can tell you, the Condition of the Revenue, and the excessive Expence of this Realm, which inevitably must carry the War from home, unless we mean supinely to be destroyed: and therefore of necessity must our Wings be suffered to grow again after this clipping, before that we do offer to make a new Flight. You cannot be ignorant too, that Commerce is the Soul and the Life of this Kingdom, which is the Channel from whence the Abundance of it flows: And the Wealth which we formerly enjoyed, and rendred us so considerable in the World, besides the fresh Experiment of the Disorder and Interruption which the War brought into all the Traffick of the Land, hath made us clearly see, that for Merchant-men's Fleets to be changed into Naval Armies, and the *Substance* of the People melted into *Magazines* unusefully, which might more profitably be employed in rich and gainful *Navigations*, cannot be the proper Interest of *England*.

If we consider the present State of *France*, we shall find that all the rest of *Europe* bow under that Power ; and those who are the most concerned to succour *Spain*, bleed at the Nose only, without being able to break the Impostume within. The Intelligences of *France* and their Practices make their way every where, either with Bribes or by Address ; Victory waits still on all their Motions, and by having redressed the Abuses of their Exchequer, they have laid an inexhaustible Foundation of Money within themselves. Over and above that, the *French* are a Nation, or rather a Seminary of Nobility and Soldiers, so versed in the Trade of War, as this Provision puts them in a Posture never to be savingly justled.

I grant, their Designs are vast, and their Pretensions ill grounded ; but how can we take Cognizance of that ? Are we Knights-errant, to expose our Lives in the revenging of other men's Quarrels ; the large Interposition of Sea, which divides us from the rest of the World, may shelter us enough from their Attempts, without founding of our Safety upon the Conservation of our Neighbours.

But suppose we had such an abundance of Charity to spare, as to hazard our own safety in favour of another's ; we should at least be secured before hand, that when we are at a second Charge of succouring them, it might prove profitable unto them, otherwise the Mischief being grown to that point of Extremity where now it rests, all insignificant Remedies of this Nature would but anger them the more to no purpose. And *Spain* being deeply engaged in the War of *Portugal*, which is alone able to give the *Spaniards* work enough, as the *Spanish* Councils stand divided, and according to the slowness of their Operations, their Treasure being likewise exhausted, and

the

the principal Places of *Flanders* in the hands of the *French*, and those which remain unconquered hardly in a Condition to make any Resistance when they shall be attacked, which disposes that Crown to seek a Peace with *France* on any Terms; and the Propositions in order to a League Offensive and Defensive with them, which they make to us, being tendred only to *England* as a wily Lure to oblige the *French* to conclude it the sooner, out of an Apprehension that we may resolve to assist *Spain*; why should we rashly, I pray, thrust our Sickle into this blighted Corn?

Indeed, when Inconveniencies are visible on all sides of the Prospect of such Treaties, the wisest Counsel sure is to suspend the Resolution a while. For on which part can we place our Interest thus, without incurring blame justly? The Party of *Spain* is weak and unlucky; that of *France* is unjust, and contrary to our Good: shall we then sacrifice our selves for *Spain*, which for three Years together hath stood idle, with their Arms folded a-cross, without so much as proffering to help us, whilst three of the greatest Powers of *Christendom* let one another blood, and thus were only passive in our Ruin? Must we then join with *France*, which was so lately combined with our Enemies to destroy us, and that tore the Victory out of our hands when we had it sure? Shall we contribute the Liquor of our Veins to facilitate their Progress, which ought to be so redoubted by this Nation, and so become instrumental towards the erecting a *Colossus* which must certainly tread us under foot with the Weight of it? All these Considerations, which I submit to your Prudence, oblige me to conclude, that there being no part to be taken in this War which is not destructive; the best will be to take no part, but sit still, and observe how the Game is play'd, and in the mean time to provide for the repairing of our Revenues, and quieting of Disorders at home, by conciliating and re-uniting the minds of the People, the re-establishment of Commerce, and to put ourselves into such a Condition, that the Conqueror may not be able to make a wrong use of his Victory to our prejudice. And in the mean time, not to remain altogether idle in the common Danger of *Europe*, we may contribute our endeavours to obtain a Peace, and by a happy Accommodation stop the course of these Conquests, which give us such just Jealousy.

He had scarce made an end of speaking, when a little murmur arose among the rest of the Conferrers, which made me conceive that they did no ways approve of what he did urge. Wherein I found that I was not deceived neither; because he who sat right over against him, answered him presently after this manner.

If Peace were a Benefit which always did depend upon our own Choice, and if War were not, ordinarily speaking, a Mischief as necessary as the other is; the Question which we do treat of now, might easily be resolved, and would not require any longer deliberation. But it is not enough to conserve Peace, to have a pacific Spirit, if our Neighbours likewise be not of the same Disposition towards it; which in effect is to reckon, without the Host, by founding the hopes of our future Quiet, barely on the Promises of our own Moderation; since those which are the most in love with Peace, are oftentimes involved in the opposite Agitation, whether they will or no, by some violent motion of Fortune; and so frequently stumble upon War in the Flight which they make from it, and thus suffocate the Peace by too much avoiding the War.

I do avow that the Reasons which were alledged before could not be answered, if he who did so well deduce them, were able to assure us upon good Grounds, that in keeping ourselves Neuters in this War of the *Low Countries*, we might be sheltered from the Storm of another War, both in the present and future Tense of such Vicissitudes; or peaceably and long enjoy so happy a Tranquillity, which makes him believe that we ought to despise, for that Speculation, all manner of useful Occasions which Fortune doth daily offer unto us. But in truth, my Lord, would you venture to be caution thereupon to the State, and pawn your Faith to the Kingdom, and your Honour concerning the Event? For my own part, I hold you too wise and too quick-sighted, to imagine merely on the Presumption of unsolid Hopes, that there can be the least shadow or colour of Safety remaining for us, if one of these two Monarchies which are at this time engaged in a War, should fall under the absolute Power of the other, or if they do re-unite again by an Agreement, in which possibly, as we have handled the matter, we may very well not be comprehended. In case you'll avow this Truth, which all the World knows to be so, it follows that you must grant, that all those Inconveniences which were already alledged to keep us out of all kinds of Engagement are no longer valid, when there is an indispensable necessity, and the Welfare and the Safety of the State are at stake.

I

I shall not enlarge my self hereon, to represent unto you that our Predecessors ever held this to be a fundamental Maxim of their Conduct, to hold the Balance equal between these two Great Monarchies, and that on which side soever they turned the Scales, Victory did usually follow that Counterpoise, which never failed to put things into that just Temperament that preserves the Health of this Realm. By which means in some sort they made themselves the Arbitrators of Christendom, because by affording their Help unto one of the two Parties, they became in effect Masters over them both, by still keeping one of them at their Devotion, and in our Dependency, through the prospect of those Succours which they do continually need from hence ; and the other, with the apprehension of this Assistance. For thus the *English*, what with the force of their Arms, and the power of Arbitrating in Treaties, have always been the Law-givers to the Success both of their Friends and their Enemies, by holding within the palms of their hands the Results of War and Peace, finding both in the one and the other, those Advantages and Safeties which this Nation most desired.

But laying aside these obsolete Maxims, from which notwithstanding wise men will not willingly depart without the pressure of some invincible Necessity, to come to the Circumstances of the present time ; it is evident that the War of the *Low Countries* cannot possibly terminate otherwise than by the Fall and Oppression of one of the two Parties, or by an Accommodation made betwixt them. If they do agree, and that *England* hath no share in the Treaty, who will assure us that they'll not unite for our Ruin ; or at least *France*, which cannot remain long without War, will not turn their Arms against us? But if *Spain* falls, we shall then be like Dancers of the Ropes that have lost their Counterpoise, and so are ready to tumble down every step they make. What good opinion soever we have of *France*, it cannot be denied, notwithstanding, that in this case, after the *French* have triumphed over *Spain*, they will be Masters over our Fortune too ; and that our being thus, must intirely depend upon their Moderation. For, Gentlemen, do you think that we can take rest securely upon so weak a Foundation as the Giddiness of their Charity is? since 'tis certain that the *most Christian King* hath too much Ardour and Desire of Glory to dwell in Idleness at home, after such a Conquest. And therefore seeing his Dominions and Reputation notably increased, he will form to himself new *Idea's* of enlarging the Bounds of his Empire both by Sea and Land, according to the knowledge which we have of the divers Inclinations to his Court ; whereof some will put him on to become Master of the Commerce of *Europe*, and employ those vast Treasures he hath heaped together in order to that Design this way ; others, to engage him in the finishing of his Conquest over all the *Low Countries* : and some likewise, to begin by us to open the Path to the subduing of all other States which may probably oppose this Design. So that, which Advice soever of these he doth embrace, 'twill be equally dangerous as to us here, and perpetually oblige us to stand upon our Guard, with the Burthen of a continued Expence on our backs, as well as the Incommodities of a War, though we seem to be in peace with him.

On this Position then I say, that the worst Party for *England* that can be taken, whether by choice or necessity, is that of sitting Neuters. By uniting with *Spain* we do follow our ancient Maxim and Interest, which hath ever been successful to this Nation, which is, to be still Masters of the Balance betwixt these two Monarchies, as I urged before. Should we therefore embrace the Party of *France*, we may hope for a considerable portion in the Spoils of *Spain*. And both in the one and the other case we shall find our Surety and other Advantages in the Treaties of Peace which shall be made. But by remaining Neutral we must needs equally offend both ; and so cannot eschew being exposed friendless to the Resentments and the Ambition of the Conqueror, as well as the Scorn and the Reproaches of all the rest of Christendom, for having insipidly abandoned our proper Reason of State, without being either good or wicked in a matter of such universal Concernment, whereby the Name of *Englishmen* will remain so much in the Oblivion of *Europe*, that no body will scarce remember there is such a Nation in the World ; excepting only those who have a mind to conquer us.

I read in the Scripture, so base a Character of none, as of them who are *neither hot nor cold :* And able Statesmen have always reproved this kind of Tepidness or Half-conduct, to be both unuseful and dangerous. *Media via nec Amicos parat, nec Inimicos tollit.* Wherefore *England* must of necessity either preserve the *Low-Countries*, against the Usurpation of the *French*, which is our Bulwark ; or raise a new Fence, that shall shelter us from being conquered.

To

To preferve the firft then, *Spain* muft be affifted from hence; and to make a new Rampart, we muft divide the Spoil with *France*. Experience hath fufficiently fhewn us, that our Ports are not inacceffible; and Reafon demonftrates, that thofe can never be fecure from the like Attempts, but by keeping a powerful Fleet out at Sea, that we may be abfolute Mafters there. 'Tis a Maxim alfo which admits neither of exception nor diminution, That a well-governed Kingdom is obliged to arm when War is kindled in the Neighbourhood. And though we fhould refolve to take part neither with the one Intereft nor the other; yet we muft be in a pofture to hinder the Torrent from coming upon our Land, that fo the Conqueror may not have a mind to extend his Conquefts hitherwards. Here then is the Charge of Arming, which on this Conjuncture is inevitable, the equipping of a Fleet, and raifing of Soldiers to be mutually entertained at the charge of the People, if we do not fpeedily take fome Party; and all this Expence without Glory, or hope to get any fruit by fo unprofitable a Counfel, wherein our Soldiers will never learn the Difcipline of War, or extract any Utility from fuch Prizes, as being uncapable after this manner to fhare in the Booty, or in the Victories and Treaties of Accommodation, according to their feveral events. Whereas by taking part either with *Spain* or *France*, the Charge would be much lefs, becaufe he whom we aid would largely contribute towards it; and the Prizes gotten at Sea might help to difcharge the Expence both of the Naval and the Land-Forces. And thus would our Soldiers be exercifed, and our Nation make a noife again abroad, and regain the Reputation which we have of late but too ignominioufly loft in the World. For when our men fhall be trained up daily in ftrict Difcipline beyond Seas, we fhall by this means eftablifh a Seminary of good and able fighting men at the Coft of others, which will be the firm Pillars of the Party, and render us confiderable in the Eyes of all our Neighbours. Befides, this courfe may be a vent fo to difcharge the Realm of ill humours, and a great company of idle Perfons, which now, being without Employment, are a burthen to the Publick, and who one day may be capable too of difturbing the domeftick Tranquillity of the State: whereas, on the contrary, what Succefs foever this War fhall have, we fhall always find our Accompt in the end of an Accommodation, whereof, being thus prepared, we cannot fail of having the principal benefit and part.

All thefe Confiderations then feem unto me to be fo convincing, that they do oblige me abfolutely to condemn the Opinion of Neutrality, as inconfiftent with our Glory, Safety, and Fundamental Reafons of State; by concluding pofitively, that we ought to lend an ear to thofe Propofitions which fhall be made unto us from all Parties, and embrace thofe which fhall be found to be moft agreeable and convenient to the Intereft of the Kingdom. And in the interim, to be the more confidered by both thefe great Parties, and better affured againft all manner of Attempts; my Advice is, That without any longer lofs of time, a ftrong Fleet fhould be prefently got ready; and that as many days as we have to fpare before the next Campaign, fince now every hour is precious that is not well fpent as to this purpofe, may be employed to render us henceforwards neceffary unto them whofe Caufe we fhall refolve to embrace, and as formidable to thofe againft whom we intend to declare: fo that on both fides we may be the Commanders of the whole Affair, and give it refpite or motion by the fole Rule of the Interefts of *England*.

After that he had fpoken thus, I did obferve by the Countenance of the other two perfons that had not yet fpoken, that this Difcourfe did not difpleafe them; wherefore without any farther Reflection, one of them brifkly began to fpeak to this effect:

Your Reafons, faid he, are fo convincing, that I do not only render my confent unto them without any Reply, but mean to make ufe of them to ferve as the *Bafis* and Foundation of that Edifice which I have a long time meditated upon, in order to the fundamental Maxims of State of this Nation. Therefore, without more ceremony or delay, I fee that we muft act, and take one of the two Parties. For any other Counfel would be dangerous and deftructive, by expofing of us to a thoufand Inconveniencies, which all the human Prudence imaginable cannot be capable of preventing or avoiding in procefs of time. I remain alfo agreed with you, that in the choice of which Party we are to take, we ought not to confider more than juft what our own Intereft properly is, which is the Rule of that conduct of Monarchs, that, as the Soul and the Spirit, vivifying the whole Figure before us, gives it motion in the Body of the State.

It refts then to form the Confequences upon thefe Principles, and decide which of the two Parties is the moft convenient. *France* offers Rofes unto us; *Spain* nothing but Thorns. The firft prefents us with a Scheme of Conquefts without Dangers; the laft

with

with prospect of Dangers without Profit. The one invites us to be their Companions of assured Victories, of which they have already beaten the way; the other doth sollicit us and implore our Aid only to help them out of the mire, without any other Benefit than, as the old Proverb says, *There's your Labour for your pains,* at the price of our Blood and Lives. If we shall engage in the Assistance of *Spain,* in succouring them, we run a *Risco* of being lost our selves, without yet being able to re-establish them : but by joining with *France,* we shall partake of the Spoils with them, which we can never by force be able to take out of their hands; since the Progress of *France* is now arrived at such a point of Effect, that all our Powers combined together are not sufficient to stop it ; and then both our Resistances and Succours will serve but to ruin the *Spaniards* the sooner, and bring the Vengeance of the *French* upon our own heads. And if *Spain* comes to sink under the Weight of the War, all the burthen of that Fall centers upon *England* alone. In fine, 'tis agitated therefore singly as to this particular, Whether we will needs chuse to embark in a Vessel so driven with storms, or in a Ship which sails at ease with full Sails, seconded with the favourable Gales of Fortune.

But in case all these material Objections cannot divert us from engaging in the ill Fortune of the *Spaniards,* let us see on what Terms at least we can assist them usefully. If we shall send Troops into the *Low Countries* to their Aid, 'tis, in effect, to overwhelm them by the very weight and charge of those Succours, and sacrifice so many of our own Subjects to Famine and Misery, as we do thus send Soldiers unto them ; because they have neither Country enough left to lodge them in when they come thither, nor the means to entertain them after once they are there.

If we succour them merely by Sea, that kind of help will not hinder *France* from taking of their Towns in the mean time one by one; and so though we should a little incommode *France,* we shall not ease *Flanders* at all, and such an Assistance will in conclusion prove none, because 'tis an Application of the Plaister too remotely, and on the wrong side of the Wound.

If then the Loss of the *Low Countries* be inevitable, let us do what we can ; were it not much better that we should have our share in the Parcels of so great a Shipwreck, than to suffer *France* to ingross them all to themselves ? Since, supposing that we do divide Booties with the *French* on this Occasion, the Places which by this means must necessarily fall into our hands will be so many new Bulwarks to *England,* which may shelter us for the future against their vast Designs, of which the Partisans of *Spain* make a Chimerical Monster, to intimidate the *English* from taking part with their best and properest Interest in the Case. But when once we are entered into a Communion of Conquests with the *French,* the subduing of *Flanders* will serve us as Ladders to arrive at other Projects by, wherein we may probably hope to find our Profit and Satisfaction mutually together, as well as the Pleasure of a just Revenge. I set aside the Conquest of the *Indies,* which we could not fail to encompass, whilst *France* doth hold all the Forces of *Spain* in play both at Sea and Land, and so occupied, that they'll never be able to retain what they hold in the *New World,* no more than that remainder of Territories which yet they stand possessed of nearer hand.

Wherefore as to what regards the Interest of this Kingdom, what I have last urged methinks might suffice to make you of my Opinion. And if we do impartially consider that of the *Royal Family,* what can be more important and convenient for it, than to have at their devotion a neighbouring Power hard by, which is so formidable, and that is able to protect them in a few hours from all manner of Revolutions, that they may (and perhaps not without cause neither) apprehend at home, by thus commanding both the Treasures and the Armies of *France,* whenever they shall have any need of them, to put a Bridle in the mouths of all such as do seek to check their Authority.

I avow that our properest Interest were to hold the Balance equal between *Spain* and *France,* if we could ; but we should then have thought sooner of that, whilst these matters were in a condition to be disputed : For at present, the Weight of the Case inclining totally to one side, so that we can no longer oppose *France* with *Spain* as a Barricado against their Designs, we must now think how to become our selves the Counterpoise of *France* and the Defence of *Europe,* by establishing of our Power beyond Seas on solid Foundations, that all other Princes may consider us hereafter as the only People who are capable of resisting the Design of the *Universal Monarchy* ; and so as *France* it self may not be able impunitively to thwart *England* in this Resolution, because then our Safety will be much more firmly settled by our

E   own

own Strength than with the Force of others; and all thofe who apprehend the Progrefs of *France* will conjoin with us, and become tyed to the Fortune of *England*, as they would be at this inftant to *Spain*, if they faw that Monarchy in a Condition to be able to maintain them.

So that all thofe Reafons do oblige me to conclude, that we muft no longer hefitate on this point of taking part with *France*, and accept of thofe advantageous Offers which the *French* make unto us, both in refpect of the publick Good of Chriftendom, as well as our own particular Security; fince by being united to them in a Knot of fuch infeparable Conditions, and on fuch a Conjuncture of Affairs, becaufe of which they dare refufe us nothing that we afk, what need we fear from the oppofite Conjunction of any other Parties?

All the Affiftants at this Conference began to exprefs Indignation againft this part of his Difcourfe, and fhewed by their Unquietnefs all the while that he fpake thus, that they had much ado to keep from interrupting of him, or to refrain from anfwering tumultuoufly, before that he had made an end. But as they offered to reply in heat all at once, to deliver their Thoughts on this Subject, the Mafter of the Houfe, who had not yet delivered his fenfe to the Company, broke filence, and with a little fmile, which had fomething in it grave, and fcornful, dexteroufly intermingled together, addreffing himfelf to him who had fpoken with fo much length juft before, held on the Debate as follows.

I know your Prudence, my Lord, too well (fays he), and your Lordfhip's difinterefted Zeal for the good of the State, to believe that you can mean ferioufly what you have urged on the behalf of *France*; but rather am perfuaded, (and that eafily too) that with an ingenious Artifice you have thus difguifed your own true Sentiments of this Cafe, the better to penetrate into the bottom of ours, and fo give Opportunity to fee clearlier through all the Reafons and Doubts which may be formed thereupon, touching this Matter, of which we do now treat; fince the truth of any Argument doth never fo well appear and endure the light, as when it is fifted to the very root, and that the Reflexion thereof is exalted by the Oppofition of the contrary fenfe. So that in combating with your Opinion, I fhall ftill think that we do not difagree, but rather to diffent in the Expofition of a vain Phantafm, which you erected for fport-fake to divert us, and give the Company recreation.

Allow me then to tell you, that this Project, upon which you have thus exercifed the acutenefs of your Wit with fo great a grace, is both unprofitable and chimerical, no lefs than fhameful and unjuft, and ruinous towards *England* to all intents and purpofes whatfoever: whereas the Defign of fuccouring *Spain* is facile, honourable profitable, neceffary, and fuitable to the fundamental Maxims of our State. And if you pleafe to afford me ever fo little attention, it will not be difficult for me to prove unto you very clearly, according to your own Judgment, what I fhall propofe of this nature; that we fhall perfectly accord in one and the fame Refult, and convince you fully of the Truth thereof.

The Defign which you mention, is of the like nature, that it were to demolifh an old ftrong Edifice, to build a new Caftle in the Air; or like his, who, to renew his Youth, confented to be cut into pieces, and put his feveral Members into an Alembick of Glafs. To follow your Counfel then, we muft alter the whole Conftitution of our Politicks, from innovated Interefts and foreign Maxims, by turning all things upfide down, even from the Accidents to the very *Genius* of the Nation, and diftil more modern Blood into the veins of the People, than that which they have hereditarily received from Father to Son. But let us, I befeech you, examine on what ground, and with what Materials this new Edifice is to be raifed. That Earth which you have propofed unto us to make it out of, is a moving fort of Sand, or a floating Ifland, in which we can never fix on any firm bottom. 'Tis upon *France* that you would have us eftablifh our Fortune, to found a Power which one day may counterbalance the Power of the *French*, or at leaft fhelter us from their vaft Defigns. Nay, you will needs have *France* made the Inftrument of a greatnefs in a Neighbour, which they ought to fufpect, if they be not befotted by fo putting *England* into a ftate to be able e'er long to ftop their Progreffes, and erect a Bulwark in us againft themfelves.

As if *France*, that is our *hereditary Enemy*, and hath fo often tried what we are able to do againft the enlarging of their Empire; who have graven deep in their hearts the injury of the Title which (to their fhame) *England* carries in all publick Treaties, and her Trophies in reference to that Crown; this very *France*, which hath no greater defire than to take the Dominion of the Sea from us, and the Precedency in Commerce, will help us (as you believe) to conquer the *Indies*, in which **one third**
part

part of this Realm is interested, and of which they do suck away all the Marrow with the semination of their Baubles, by the ill husbandry of the *Spaniards* ; she who just now comes from joining with our Enemies against us, after she had first contrived how to broach the Quarrel between *England,* and the States of the *United Provinces* under divers false motions ; who snatched the Victory out of our hands, when we were morally certain of beating the *Dutch* ; who reduced the Bishop of *Munster* to a necessity of separating from us in this War, after that he had received our Assistance in large Sums of Money ; debauched *Denmark* from our Party ; hindred the *Swedes* to arm in our favour, and contrived the whole Fabrick of that Affront which we received in the River of *Thames :* Can you, after all these demonstrations of the Rancour which they bear in their hearts against *England,* be so uningenuous as to believe that the *French* will make a Bridge for us on the other side of the Sea, as sincerely intending by this means to make us participate of their Conquests with them, or ever to unite in a sound Amity with our Interests? For God's sake then disabuse your self, as soon as you can, out of this gross Error, if it be so that it hath got the least Fixation in your mind ; since you cannot cordially reason thus, or have the least hope of such an Incongruity in the Reason of State of other Nations, without conceiving at the same time that the *French* have lost both their Wits and Judgment ; of which yet there is no great Reason why we should think, as they have handled us in this matter of Negociations of late : for therein I am sure that we do find them to have more than common Sense.

France indeed will be glad to have us for the Instruments of their Ambition, but never for Companions of their Glory, or Rivals in their Greatness. The *French* do, I confess, seek to make use of us to pull the Chesnut out of the Fire, to save the burning of their Fingers ; but when that is done, the *French* will not endure that we should eat any bit of the Kernel. And the Work which they do now make for us, both at home and abroad, is so incompatible with our Interest and Designs, as well as their own, that their Professions towards us at this time cannot possibly be sincere ; except they be grown so kind on a sudden, as to overthrow all their Fundamental Laws, and in favour of *England* change the whole face of their Designs which they have hitherto been forming upon *Europe.*

They pretend that the *Low-Countries* are entirely fallen to them by the right of Devolution, which *France* hath forged to belong to it self. Then are all those Provinces by consequence united to the *French* Crown, nor can their King divide or alienate any part of them.

If this be true to our advantage, though he would never so fain, but that it must be subject still to return again to their Tribunal, they have annulled the *Renunciation* of the *Infanta* of *Spain,* and thereby have formed a Right to the Succession of that Monarchy, in case the young King should come to fail of a Successor. So that the most Christian King can give us no share in the dismembring of *Spain,* without doing prejudice to a Right which he pretends to be acquired unalienably to his Crown, and whereof he himself may not otherwise dispose.

Next, let us view the Materials which we are to have, to build this new Edifice with. Either we must undertake this War at our own Charge, or at the Expence of *France.* If it be undertaken at the Cost of *France,* we must be their Hirelings (at best) as the *Tartars* be to the *Ottomans,* and cannot move one step beyond What and How they'll have us act : *France,* on these terms, will always hold the Bridle in our Teeth, and the *Cavesson* upon our Noses, to make us stop, turn and wind, in the middle of the Courses, just as they please. From the very first moment that we shall grow burthensome unto them, they have but to withdraw their Supplies, to make us fall headlong to the ground ; and then the Share which we pretend in their Conquests doth purely and arbitrarily depend on their discretion.

But if we shall undertake to carry on this Design out of our own proper Purse, who shall furnish us with the means of doing it? Do you believe that the Parliament and the People will give away their Substance to act against the true Interests of the Realm? and that they'll bleed, to quench the ambitious Thirst of the *French?* or destroy *Spain,* from whence all the abundance of our Commerce is derived ; and which even at this Instant grants unto us such notable Advantages by a Treaty which is solemnly ratified?

The part which *France* doth offer us in the Conquests of *Ostend* and *Neuport* is a vast Liberality indeed, but still of other Folks Goods. It would become them far better to restore back *Dunkirk* to *England,* which they cheated us of by Surprize ; or the Town of *Calais,* which they have dismembred from our ancient Dominion. They take

from

from us what is our own already, and present us with nothing but what is not in their power to give; because they cannot bestow either the Title or the Possession of what they do offer in this Kind upon us; which if we will have, we must gain it by the Point of the Sword. And this Train which they do shew us, is of the same nature with that sort of Temptations with which the Devil tempted our Saviour from the top of the Pinacle. But do not you discover that this is a subtil Artifice to imbroil us again in a new War with the States of the *United Provinces*, who have the Interest to defend these two Places as much as if either *Amsterdam* or *Flushing* were so designed upon? And without an absolute Naval Victory we can never hope to conquer them; and such a Conquest at Sea too, as shall put the *Hollanders* out of all manner of possibility to afford any Succours in this Case. This is a very hard bone which *France* doth cast in for us to gnaw, whilst they eat all the Marrow of it. In fine, when the Arms of *France*, joined to our Forces, shall have put us in possession of these two Places; yet they'll be totally unuseful to *England*, when *France* is possessed of all the rest: Because thus the *French* will shut us quite out of the whole Traffick of the *Low Countries*, and will be always in a Condition to drive the *English* away from thence, unless we do resolve continually to keep a Fleet at Sea for the conserving of them.

If this Design be hollow and visionary, it is not less shameful than airy and full of Injustice. We have no manner of Pretension to the Monarchy of *Spain*, nor is it our *Genius* to whet our Spirits to form Castles in the Clouds of Chimerical Rights. What Glory can it be to our Arms to help to oppress a King in Minority, of six years old, by surprize; only because we find him now to be rudely attacqued and unprovided; on a frivolous Pretext, immediately after the *French* had given the Queen his Mother, and his principal Ministers of State at *Madrid*, such solemn assurances to the contrary, as well as at *Paris*, touching the inviolable continuation of a good Peace and a sincere Friendship? The manner which *Spain* hath held and acted with us newly in relation to *England*, when we were assaulted by three powerful Enemies at one time, ought to oblige us, at least to be deaf to the artificial Allurements of *France*. For although the *French* have tried by all the ways imaginable, and with Offers incomparably more advantageous than those which they do make to us at present, to the end that so they might have gained the Forces of *Spain* to unite with them to our inevitable Oppression; yet was it never in their power to shake the unalterable Amity which the *Spanish* Nation have for us by a kind of natural Sympathy, which one knows not how better to express than by the Immutability of it, whether we do oblige or disoblige them. Would it not then be an Ingratitude totally inconsistent with the Honour and the Hospitality of the *English* Temper, so soon to forget this Kindness; since at the same instant that *Spain* was the deepliest engaged against *Portugal*, they did notwithstanding openly oppose the Designs of *France* which seemed to the prejudice of *England*, by refusing them (in contemplation of us, firmly and with great Resolution) Passage for those Troops of theirs which they sent to ruin the Bishop of *Munster*, our Ally and Confederate then. We cannot complain of any Injury or Attempt wherein the *Spaniards* have tampered against *England*. No League nor ancient Treaty doth oblige us to second the Designs of *France*; and we cannot conclude new Alliances with the *French* to this purpose, without directly contravening that Treaty which we have lately ratified with *Spain*. Let us see then what the Herald is to say to the *Spaniards* that shall be sent to denounce War unto them on this Occasion from *England*; or with what Reasons we shall be able to fill a *Manifesto* which we would offer to the Publick, whereby to justify the Causes of this Rupture. Wherefore I leave the Care, my Lord, to you, being that you seem to be the Author of this Counsel, to found it well in the point of Justice. But pray, see that you perform it better and with more grace than the Writer of the Queen of *France*'s *Pretensions* hath done.

I say farther yet, That this Design is both prejudicial and destructive; and that it carries along with it most pernicious Consequences, as well in the present time as the time to come. For from the very moment that we do break with *Spain*, our Commerce will cease, with the Effects of all those great Advantages which the *Spaniards* have * newly granted unto us: and the Merchants of this Realm, who trade there, will justly be confiscated; since all the Profit that we draw from thence must on these terms infallibly redound in favour of the *Hollanders*, whilest our Arms do busy the *Spaniards* in the *Low Countries*; and the *French*, as they do their utmost against *Spain*, at the same instant will seize their principal Ports into their power, and thus become absolute Masters of the Commerce, by putting themselves into a

* By the Treaty last ratified at *Madrid* by the Earl of *Sandwich*, His Majesty's Embassador there.

Posture

Posture to erect a Dominion over the Sea, which we can never afterwards be able to resist. Not above three Years ago *France* was hardly able to set forth twenty Ships (that is to say, Men of War) now they have sixty large Vessels, ready furnished and well armed, and do apply all their Industry and Pains in every part to augment the number. Could the Ghost of Queen *Elizabeth* return back into the World again, she would justly reproach us who are the Ministers of State here in *England*, for having abandon'd her good Maxims, by tamely suffering before our Eyes a Maritime Power to increase, which she so diligently kept down throughout the whole Course of her Reign. Whereas you are so far from opposing the Growth of this Power, that you rather seem to desire *England* should facilitate the ways to make it grow the faster, and render it yet more formidable than it is, by the Acquisition of the Sea-Ports, which in conclusion must infallibly bring *France* to be Mistress of the Commerce of the *Indies*. All the World knows the vast quantity of Money and Arms which the *French* have accumulated to that end alone out of the richest Purses of that Kingdom. I agree to what hath been said before very prudently in this Conference, that our Power and Greatness doth principally consist in the matter of Commerce; and therefore I conclude even from thence, by an unerrable Consequence, that Commerce ought to be the chief Object of our Jealousy, and that we are bound to be as tender of the Conservation of this Benefit as of the Apples of our Eyes. But then we must look far off, how to prevent whatsoever may hinder the Progress of Trade, or diminish the Abundance of this Commerce. We have nothing to fear in this particular on the account of *Spain*, which applies little towards Traffick, and leaveth almost all the Advantages thereof freely to the *English* in their own proper Ports. But if this Interest should fall into the Power of an industrious and active Nation, and a People covetous of Gain, as the *French* are, we are not to expect any Share of the Utility, or to partake with *France* therein; but rather that they will prescribe the Law of Commerce unto the *English*, according to their own Will and Pleasure. As soon as ever 'tis known that we do treat of Conjunction with *France*, one of these two things must necessarily happen: either that *Spain*, finding it self uncapable to resist the Union of both Forces, will send a Blank to the *French* King to make such Conditions with them as he thinks best, by conceding unto him all their Portion in the *Low Countries*; or that all the rest of the Powers of *Europe*, justly apprehending so terrible an Union, will join with *Spain* to stop the Torrent of our Designs. In the first state of the Case then, we shall quickly find our selves taken for persons deluded in this Negotiation, and *France* only gather all the Fruit of the Cozenage; of which the Shame of having been so grosly cheated can only remain to us, when the whole World discerns that the desire of Prey hath prevailed with *England* above the Faith of those solemn Treaties, which we have made with the Crown of *Spain*: and thus shall we obtain no other Advantage by having made such a false step, than to have facilitated the means for *France* to unite all the *Low Countries* to that Crown without striking one Blow, to the eternal and irreparable Damage of the Crown of *England*. For who can assure us, that from the same instant when we do declare unto *France* our intention to unite with them, the *French*, instead of uniting their Party with *England*, will not rather prevail the sooner in their Pretensions with *Spain*, to make the *Spaniards*, because of this Apprehension, disposed to accord to whatsoever *France* shall demand? which is as the old Proverb says, *To keep the Mule at our Cost*, and hold the stirrup unto the *French*; or play a ridiculous part, in making use only of Scare-crows, and give a false Alarm to favour the Designs of others.

Next, who shall secure us that after *Spain* hath yielded, because of this Apprehension, the *Low Countries* to the Disposition of *France*, That the *Spaniards* and the *French* shall not then streightly unite together, to be revenged of us, and bring us down? The Affinity of Blood, Religion, and the hopes which the *Most Christian King* may found to himself upon the Succession to this Monarchy, (if the *Renunciation* of the Queen once comes to be annulled) are strong Links that may very well unite them together; and the principal of the Division which is at present betwixt them, having no other foundation but reciprocal Jealousy touching the Equality of their Power, this Emulation will expire as soon as ever that *France* doth see *Spain* in a Condition to be no longer able to dispute the Sovereign Arbitrage of *Christendom* with them; and the cause of their Hatred being taken away, all the Effects thereof will cease likewise. And then the common Interests of both will unite them in a Bond which is inseparable any more, from whence our Ruin must infallibly arise: because the Substance and Surety of *England* solely depends upon the Emulation of

F

these

these two Powers, as the Temperament of a human Body consists in the Opposition of the Elementary Qualities.

But what shall we say of the States of the *United Provinces?* Can we reasonably believe that they'll remain without Motion, or that they'll not awaken at the noise only of this Negotiation, which we shall carry on with *France* to the Destruction of *Spain?* Since 'tis evident, they have no other course to take than to prevent us, but by joining themselves with *France* before we have finished this Treaty, or else to bind their Interests fast with the *Spanish* Crown and the Empire on the first Occasion. And then are we excluded from our Pretensions, and all the hopes of our vast Conquests, which we have fancied unto our selves. And in the next place also shall we be replunged into a long and dangerous War; from whence we came but just now, as it were, to escape with so much difficulty and damage. *France* hath yet proposed nothing unto us directly touching the Ports of *Ostend* and *Newport* to be given to the *English*; and 'tis apparent as to *England*, by sundry and authentick Documents, that the *French* have no mind to treat seriously with us on this Point, unless that they do find us disposed to unite with *Spain* and the States of the *United Provinces* for the common Defence. Whereas 'tis no less certain, that the *French* have expresly made the very same Propositions, and more advantageous ones, unto the said States, by soliciting them to re-combine with *France* in order to their old Design of dividing the *Low Countries* mutually between each other, to the entire Exclusion both of us and the *Spaniards*, being fully agreed as to this particular, at the beginning of the War past.

Whereby 'tis clearly to be foreseen, that *France* considers us no farther than as the worst of their Prospects, and that the *French* will always be ready to buy dearer the Amity of the States of the *United Provinces* than ours. Would it not then be a great Imprudence in us, to serve them as Instruments on such disgraceful and disadvantageous Terms, to contribute towards the engaging of the *Hollanders* to their Party? It being out of doubt, that the Jealousy which we should so give them of our Negotiation with *France* would be a powerful Incitement to the States, to put them upon being before-hand with us in this Treaty, and cut the Grass after this manner under our Feet. But admit all this should cease, I do not see what Measures we can take at this time with *France*, nor what Assurances or Precautions the *French* may give us in a Treaty, so as to shelter *England* from the Danger of that known Maxim of theirs, which is, in all Confederations to be bound by no other Rule but their Interest meerly. I avow that the Rupture of the *Pyrenean Treaty* frights me, and the remembrance of their Proceeding held with us heretofore throughout all the Course of our late War with *Holland*, hath made me so incredulous, that they must shew me many Miracles, and evident ones too, before I shall be converted to have the least good Opinion of the Sincerity of their Faith and Dealing.

That which you have alledged touching the Support which the Royal House of *England* may particularly hope for from the Amity of *France*, is both a delicate and a dangerous Stone to stir. The Glory and the Safety of our *King* doth only consist in the Love of his People, and a streight Union betwixt His *Majesty* and his present *Parliament*, since he hath no other sound Interest to rely upon but that of the Kingdom, having need of no other Arms or Assistance. The hearty affections of His Subjects and His own Royal Virtues will be as so many Cittadels erected to maintain His Authority; and any other project is contrary both to His Genius and His admirable Prudence. For all those who shall dare to inspire any other Thoughts into His *Majesty*, will infallibly undergo the Weight of His Displeasure, as Enemies to His Fame and Quiet. But at the bottom of all, what help can He rationally expect from *France*, should He come to need it, (which God defend) after their unworthy abandoning of the *King* His Father in his great Distress, and of the *King* which now is likewise, when the Wheel of *Fortune* ran against them, even to the Extirpation of the Royal Line, had not He by whom Kings reign, wonderfully restored them to the Throne of their Ancestors? It was that shameful Treaty which the *French* ratified with those Usurpers then, that sacrificed *Charles* the First to the Ambition of the Tyrant *Oliver Cromwel*, who had snatched the Scepter from the right Owners and Proprietors thereof. Nay, to such a degree was the Inhospitability of *France* grown at that time, though His Father were thus execrably murthered before the Eyes of the *French*, our King's own Cousin-german refused Him a Retreat that might be secure for His own Person. Therefore 'tis fit that the *English* should be disabused once for all, by being better informed, since *France* is so far from being assisting or useful unto us upon this Conjuncture, that in truth they do seek only to increase our Divisions and Troubles.

For

For 'tis both their Interest and Maxim so to do: which Conduct hath been exactly and hereditarily observed in their Councils for many Ages together, (and newly in the last Civil War here) since all the Baits which they do present unto us are but so many Apples of Discord, which the *French* Emissaries cast up and down among us, purposely to embroil us with our Neighbours, or else with one another.

Next, let us consider at present whether we shall find our Account better with *Spain.* 'Tis evident that solid Reason of State doth totally incline us to leave that other way; and you cannot but all acknowledge this to be our true Fundamental Maxim, whereby we may keep the Balance *in æquilibrio*; and that our Safety doth most consist in such an *æquilibrium*: why then should we swerve from thence out of vain hopes, or quit the Body for the Shadow? The Interest of Commerce no way invites us to take part with *France*: and this Truth is so notorious to all the People of *England*, that there is no Eloquence able to persuade them contrary to their own Experience therein. The Cause is just and favourable: A young * Pupil unworthily oppressed; a Peace so solemnly and piously established as lightly violated by a Process of Cavils and Legerdemain, by a Proceeding thereupon full of Surprisals and Violence, as well as Pretensions unjustly revived after an Authentick † *Renunciation*; are so many Voices which speak to the Root of our Consciences, to call us to that which we owe to Justice, Pity, good Neighbourhood, the publick Cause of Christendom, and our selves. For in this matter is concerned no less than the Case of Royal Successions, which *France* will needs have submitted to the Customs of ordinary Citizens; and the Conservation of that Bulwark which is common to all these parts of *Europe*, against this Torrent which threatens the whole Vicinity with a great Inundation, and the assuring the Tranquillity of the Christian Republick against an unquiet Nation, that will never desist from disturbing of it until their Insolence shall be abated.

The King of Spain.

† Vide *The Buckler of State and Justice*, Art. 4. p. 85, & *seq.*

The Foundation then being so solid, because we shall in this Opposition have to treat with a Nation that makes profession of Honour and Generosity, which hath never yet been accused to be guilty of having violated any Publick Treaty, and that would rather ‖ hazard the loss of their Monarchy than their Reputation; the Advantage is both secure and considerable: whereas on the account of *France* we shall appear but as little Accessories, and the *French* will carry us on as the First Motion, only according to the rapidness of their Progress, by applying us meerly in the course of their Game to their own Ends: and thus shall we become the Ministers of their Ambition, and be made use of like a pair of Stairs, on which they do mean to tread in order to their obtaining the *Universal Monarchy*. In fine, their Interests, if that we are still predestinated to be thus grosly deluded, must be the Rule of ours, and our future Conduct too and Operations. But in taking part with *Spain* we shall be the Arbitrators of Peace and War, and enabled to give the whole weight unto the Resolutions of each Party. Then will *France* consider us with Terror and the Apprehension of what our Arms may do, and *Spain* by the addition of our Succours. If we do desire Conquests, we cannot hope for more lawful ones, nor easier Victories, than to re-unite by this means our ancient Dominions in *France*, which have formerly been dismembred from the Crown of *England*. But if we shall limit our Designs to the sole establishment of a Peace, we can find the Account both of Glory and Safety likewise therein: since it appears by authentick Letters of *Monsieur de Lionn*'s writing, that *France* is resolved to be content with Reason, as soon as ever they do see *England* fixed to join with *Spain* and the States of the *United Provinces*. So that 'tis in our choice whether to make an advantageous War, or procure an honest Peace, at the first appearance of our preparations in Arms. Whereas, on the contrary, 'tis evident by the Interception of the aforesaid Dispatches, that they will despise all manner of Offices and Mediations that are not armed, but rather pursue vigorously their Course whither Fortune shall drive it on, so long as they do meet with no powerful Obstacles in the way.

‖ The remarkable Integrity of *Spain.*

Therefore, because you seem to believe that *Spain* is reduced to so low a Condition, that our Relief would be altogether unuseful to them, and serve for nothing but to bring down the Vengeance of *France* exasperated upon us; for God's sake, cure your self of this pannick Fear as soon as you can. 'Tis *France* endeavours to erect a formidable Power, if she finds no Opposition in the Approaches thereunto; and *Spain* probably must sink under the burthen, unless that Crown be succoured: though it is as true also, that the Mischief is easily to be prevented, if Remedies be applied thereunto in due time, and before that the Inconvenience root it self too deep. All the Advantage which *France* hath gained in this last Campaign, is no more than an effect of their Address, and the over-grown Credulity of *Spain*, rather than of their Valour and

and Power. All the Places which they have conquered in *Flanders*, are but great Country-Towns, where the People being ever the strongest, he that is Master of the Field carries always the Keys of them at his Girdle, to enter when he pleases; and the winning of one Battel recovers them back again.

France hath constantly yielded in every thing where she hath found a real Resistance, without gaining any thing beyond what the fright of an incommodated Multitude hath holpen them to acquire by such a surprising Invasion. *Spain* hath yet great resorts to recur unto, provided only they can gain time, and the means of making them meet together, and thus recover their Spirits. We know that she hath made Contracts for considerable Sums of Money, and that the *Spaniards* are now about to put themselves in a way to be able shortly to withstand the strongest Shocks of the War: and by the little Diversion of the Forces from *France* which we may make without any prejudice to *England*, we can certainly put *Spain* into a Condition of attacquing the *French*, as well as of defending it self, and so shall we reduce *France* into a necessity of demanding Peace. *Spain* is not unprovided of Friends nor Allies. The Emperor doth already make a great step in favour of the Circle of *Burgundy*, by taking of it intirely under his Protection, as a Member of his Body. The States of the *United Provinces* are not asleep, neither as to their own proper Interests upon this Conjuncture, and after having tried in vain the sweeter ways of appeasing the Tempest, they will not abandon themselves on so pressing an Occasion, being that they do see well enough their Safety depends absolutely upon their Resolution. We know that they desire a sincere Alliance with us, and that they would make all the progresses necessary towards it, could they but discern in us any real disposition not to reject the Offer. *Sweden*, which is weary to serve but as an Instrument to the Interests of *France*, to the prejudice of their own Affairs, will no doubt also follow our Motions: and the most part (whom rather Fear than Love doth tye unto the Motions of *France*) will questionless take off the Mask, as soon as ever they shall see a considerable Power on foot to protect them: *France* is a Body replete with ill humours, which will easily degenerate into an universal Corruption, when the *French* are ever so little shaken. The Jealousy alone which our Fleet will give them, must needs oblige them to employ the better part of their Troops to furnish their Maritime Coasts; and consequently render them the weaker every where else. Besides, it is plain that in this last Campaign, in which they thought to swallow all up at a bit, they made all the Force that they were able, and yet were not able notwithstanding to bring into the Field above Forty Thousand Men, after having drawn out of their Garrisons and the Provision of their Towns all the strength almost that they had there, whereby their Frontiers were left naked. Judge then to what point they'll be reduced, when they'll be put both to furnish their Places on all sides, and divide their

or Catalonia. Troops too, in *Alsatia*, *Italy*, the County of * *Rossillon*, and *Flanders*; and that in all these Countries they'll meet with Enemies to fight against, as well as a multitude of Male-contents at home, no less formidable within the Center of their own proper Bowels. For thus they can build no longer upon the strength of their Army, which is destroyed very near already by Labour, Sickness, Diseases, and want of Pay. Wherefore they must begin anew, and with fresh Charges raise more Men, because the ill usage which their Troops have received, doth render them so barren of Soldiers, that they are compelled to seek Recruits, and as it were beg Supplies, with vast Sums of Money, from other States. And this imaginary Fountain of Treasure of theirs, which here is thought to be un-exhaustible, will be found to have a bottom when our Fleet doth disturb their Commerce, the Credit which till then they

Which is the same thing as our Banquer and Farmers of the Customs. may get with the Partisans, by means of oppressing the People, with Tax upon Tax, will fail. The Men of Business and the Natives, being pressed to unsupportable Extremities, will quickly either cast off the yoke, or sink under the burthen and the weight of those Impositions. Their incapacity to hold out any longer, is well enough seen, by the impossibility wherein they now find themselves to make good what they have promised the *Portugueses*, whose Friendship hath been formerly so necessary unto them. And if *Spain*, as 'tis hoped that it may do, once shall take a Resolution to be delivered out of this intestine War with *Portugal* by some Accommodation, the *Spaniards* will soon be in a Condition of being useful to their Allies, and feared by their Enemies. But if we do suffer the Designs of *France* to pass by undiscovered, and impunitively to permit them to conquer the *Low Countries* towards the total oppression of *Spain*; then I cannot but avow that *France* thus will be most terrible unto us. And in case at present we are afraid of drawing their Revenge on our heads, then shall we have much juster cause to apprehend the future effects of their

Am-

Ambition. Wherefore at the Bottom of all these Reasons, it seems to me that by the same Principle of Apprehension which you have of the *French*, we are obliged to oppose these Progresses of theirs, which if not stopped, would yet render them more redoubtable.

If so be that we do fear them in the Field, having so many Friends that do tender their Alliance unto us, our fear were much more justifiable, if after the rejecting of all those Offers, we alone were exposed to their Mercy; or that our Moderation could exempt us from their Outrages, but on the contrary, rather give the *French* better Conveniencies of putting these Violences in execution, should such an insipid Council prevail; for they'll never consider us farther than we do make our selves considerable. They have printed Books of their Pretensions to *England*. Experience teaches us (even to this day) that 'tis enough with them to ground a War, without giving them any other Cause of Hostility, that we have * Kingdoms belonging to this Monarchy which may very well fit their Designs; which is enough to invite the *French* to attack them whilst *England* is weak. *** Scotland and** *Ireland.*

History likewise doth shew us, how that all our Alliances with the House of *Burgundy* have still been glorious and useful, and all those with *France*, unfortunate and prejudicial. 'Tis ever more dangerous to go out of the beaten Road, to travel through By-lanes, unknown, and dark untried Paths.

You'll easily agree with me, that the Union of the *United Provinces* with *France* is the thing of all others which we ought the most to apprehend as fatal to our Crown: and therefore, by consequence, nothing can be more safe for *England* than to disunite them. Heaven furnishes us now with an Occasion of doing that, which we shall never be able to recover again, should it be neglected: and if we do suffer it to slip away, we shall bring that Republick into a necessity of tying this fatal Knot with *France* stronglier than ever it was fastened before. This Union therefore above all others must be the Object of our Care, as it hath of late demonstratively been the Cause of our Misfortunes.

I conclude then upon solid Foundations, without hesitating, that, in the first place, we must necessarily take part in this War, either with *Spain* or *France*; and next, that we must not engage blind-fold, without taking right Measures with those who have the same Interest that *England* hath in the Case: thirdly, that we must knit our Party firmly together, and get all the Advantages we can in this Treaty with *Spain*, as well as all the Security possible with other States; without yet exacting from *Spain* things which are intolerable unto them, whom the loss of the *Low Countries* for fear of being reduced by the Exorbitancy of our Demands, may plunge into a necessity of according to whatever *France* shall require.

This Discourse being ended, I observed by their Countenances, that the two Persons who spake first applauded this Opinion, and that the third man was much shaken. They had some farther Speech together, but so softly, that I cannot well collect the sense of it: after which all the Company embraced, and gave one another their hand, with a reciprocal promise of secresy, as well as an Union in the same Design. And thus they separated each a several way, with evidence of great satisfaction and friendship. And as soon as ever they were gone, I slipped back insensibly again into the former obscurity near the Bed, without being seen by any of the Domesticks. And thus whilst these particulars were fresh in my memory, I did set them down in Paper, and all that I could remember of their Discourse, only to satisfy my own Curiosity, and the Curiousness of my Friends.

G   O F

OF THE
FUNDAMENTAL LAWS,
OR
Politick Conſtitution
OF THIS
KINGDOM.

Fundamental Laws are not (or at leaſt need not be) any written Agreement like Meer-ſtones between King and People, the King himſelf being a part (not party) in thoſe Laws, and the Commonwealth not being like a Corporation treated by Charter, but treating it ſelf. But the Fundamental Law or Laws is a ſettling of the Laws of Nature and common Equity (by common conſent) in ſuch a Form of Polity and Government, as that they may be adminiſtred amongſt us with Honour and Safety. For the firſt of which therefore, we are governed by a King: and for the ſecond, by a Parliament, to overſee and take order that that honourable Truſt that is put into the hands of the King for the Dignity of the Kingdom, be rightly executed, and not abuſed to the alteration of the Politick Conſtitution taken up and approved, or to the deſtruction of that, for whoſe preſervation it was ordered and intended. *A principal part of which honour, is that Royal Aſſent he is to give for the Enacting of ſuch good Laws as the People ſhall chooſe; for they are firſt to conſult their own ſafety and welfare, and then he who is to be intruſted with it, is to give an honourable Confirmation to it, and ſo to put an Impreſs of Majeſty and Royal Authority upon it.*

Fundamental Laws then are not things of Capitulation between King and People, as if they were Foreigners and Strangers one to another, (nor ought they or any other Laws ſo to be, for then the King ſhould govern for himſelf, not for his People) but they are things of Conſtitution, treating ſuch a Relation, and giving ſuch an Exiſtence and Being by an external Polity to King and Subjects, as Head and Members; which Conſtitution in the very being of it is a Law held forth with more Evidence, and written in the very heart of the Republick, far firmlier than can be by Pen and Paper, and in which ſenſe we owe our Allegiance to the King as Head (not only by Power, but Influence) and ſo part of the Conſtitution, not as a party capitulating for a Prerogative againſt or contrary to it ; which whoſoever ſeeks to ſet up, or ſide with, do break their Allegiance, and rebel againſt the State, going about to deprive the King of his juridical and lawful Authority, conferred upon him by the Conſtitution of this State, under the pretence of inveſting him with an illegal and unconſtitutive Power : whereupon may follow this grand Inconvenience, The withdrawment of his People's Allegiance, which, as a Body connexed with the Head by the Conſtitution of this Kingdom, is owing to him ; his Perſon in relation to the Body, as the enlivening and quickning Head thereof, being ſacred and taken notice of by the Laws in that capacity, and under that notion is made inviolate.

And if it be conceived that Fundamental Laws muſt needs be only extant in writing, this is the next way to bring all to confuſion, for then by the ſame Rule the King bids the Parliament produce thoſe Laws that fundamentally give them their being,

ing, privilege and power ; (*Which by the way is not like the Power of inferior Courts, that are Springs of the Parliament, dealing between Party and Party, but is answerable to their trust, this Court being it self Fundamental and Paramount, comprehending Law and Equity, and being intrusted by the whole for the whole, is not therefore to be circumscribed by any other Laws which have their being from it, not it from them, but only by that Law which at first gave its being,* to wit, (*Salus Populi*). By the same Rule I say the Parliament may also intreat the King to produce those Laws that fundamentally give him his Being, Power and Honour. Both which must therefore be determined, not by Laws, for they themselves are Laws, yea the most supreme and fundamental Law, giving Laws to Laws themselves, but by the received Constitution or Polity, which they themselves are ; and the end of their Constitution is the Law or Rule of their Power, to wit, an honourable and safe Regiment of the Common-wealth ; which two whosoever goeth about to divide the one of them from the other, breaks the fundamental constitutive Law or Laws and Polity of this Kingdom, that Ordinance of Man which we are to submit unto ; nor can or ought any Statute or written Law whatsoever, which is of latter Edition and inferior Condition, being but an Off-spring of this Root, be interpreted or brought in plea against this primary and radical Constitution, without Guilt of the highest Treason and destructive Enmity to the Publick-weal and Polity, because by the very Constitution of this Kingdom, all Laws or Interpretation of Laws tending to Confusion or Dissolution, are *ipso facto* void. In this case we may allude and say, That the Covenant which was 400 Years before the Law, an After-Act cannot disannul it.

Ob. *It may be objected, That this Discourse seems to make our Government to be founded in Equity, not in Law, or upon that common Rule of* Salus Populi, *which is alike common to all Nations, as well as any: And so what Difference ?*

Ans. The Fundamental Laws of *England* are nothing but the common Laws of Equity and Nature reduced into a particular way of Policy, which Policy is the ground of our Title to them, and Interest in them: For though it is true, that Nature hath invested all Nations in an equal right to the Laws of Nature and Equity by a common Bounty, without respect of Persons, yet the several Models of external Government and Policy render them more or less capable of this their common Right: For though they have an equal Right in Nature to all the Laws of Nature and Equity, yet having fundamentally subjected themselves by their politick Constitutions unto a Regal Servitude, by Barbarism or the like, they have thereby much disabled and divested themselves of that common Benefit. But on the contrary, where the outward Constitution or Polity of a Republick is purposely framed for the confirming and better conserving this common Right of Nature and Equity (as in ours) there is not only a common Right, but also a particular and lawful Power joined with this Right for its Maintenance and Supportation. For whereas other People are without all supreme Power, either of making Laws or raising Money, both these Bodies of Supremacy being in the arbitrary hands only of the Sovereign Magistrate amongst many Nations, these with us are in the hands of the supreme Government, (not Governor) or Court of Judicature, to wit, the King and Parliament ; here the People (like Freemen) give Money to the King, he doth not take it ; and offers Laws to be enacted, doth not receive them so: Now in such a constituted Kingdom, where the very Constitution it self is the fundamental Law of its own Preservation, as is this mixt Regiment of ours, consisting of King and Parliament, as Head and Body, comprehending Monarchy, Aristocracy, and Democracy ; there the fundamental Laws are like fundamental Truths in these two Properties: First, they are comprehended in a very little room, to wit, Honour and Safety ; and Secondly, they have their influence into all other inferior Laws which are to be subjected to them, and correspondent with them, as lawful Children and natural Branches.

Ob. *But in Process of time there are many written Laws which seem at least to contradict this fundamental Constitution, and are not they binding notwithstanding it ?*

Ans. The Constitution of this Kingdom, which gave its being, and which is the radical and fundamental Law thereof, ought therefore to command in chief, for that it never yields up its Authority to those inferior Laws, which have their being from it, nor ought they which spring from it tend to the Destruction of it, but on the contrary it is to derive its radical Virtue and Influence into all succeeding Laws, and
they

they like Branches are to make the Root flourish, from whence they spring, with exhibiting the lively and fructifying Virtue thereof, according to the Nature and Seasons of succeeding times ; things incident in after-ages not being able to be foreseen, and particularly provided for at the beginning, saving in the fundamental Law of *Salus Populi*, politickly established ; nor can any Laws growing out of that Root, bear any other Fruit, than such as the nature thereof dictates ; for, for a particular branch to ruin the whole Foundation by a seeming sense contrary to it, or differing from it, is very absurd ; for then how can it be said, Thou bearest not the root, but the root thee ? Laws must always relish of, and drink in the Constitution or Polity where they are made ; and therefore with us, the Laws wherein the King is nominated, and so seems to put an absolute Authority into his hands, must never so be construed, for that were with a breath to blow down all the Building at once ; but the King is there comprehended and meant under a two-fold Notion: First, as trusted, being the Head, with that Power the Law conferr'd upon him, for a legal, and not an absolute Purpose, tending to an honourable Preservation, not an unnatural Dissolution. Secondly, as meaning him juridically, not abstractly or personally, for so only the Law takes notice of the King as a juridical Person ; for till the Legislative Power be absolutely in the King, so that Laws come down from him to his People, and go not up from them to him, they must never be so interpreted: for as they have a juridical being and beginning, to wit, in Parliament, so must they have a suitable Execution and Administration, to wit, by the Courts, and legal Ministers, under the King's Authority, which according to the Constitution of this Kingdom, he can no more suspend for the good of his People, than the Courts can theirs ; or if he do, to the publick hazard, then have the Courts this Advantage, that for publick Preservation they may and must provide upon that Principle, *The King can do no wrong, neither in withholding Justice, nor Protection from his People.* So that then *Salus Populi* being so principally respected and provided for, according to the nature of our Constitution and Polity, and so being *Lex legum*, or the Rule of all Laws branching thence, then if any Law do by Variation of Times, Violence of Tyranny, or Misprision of Interpreters, vary there-from, it is a Bastard and not a Son, and is by the lawful Parents either to be reduced or cast out, as gendring into Bondage and Ruin of the Inheritance, by attempting to erect an absolute and arbitrary Government. Nor can this equitable Exposition of particular Statutes taken from the Scope of the politick Constitution be denied without overthrow of just and legal Monarchy, (which ever tends to publick Good and Preservation) and the setting up of an unjust and illegal Tyranny, ruling, if not without Law, yet by abused Laws, turning them as conquered Ordnance upon the People. The very Scripture it self must borrow from its Scope and Principles for Explanation of particular Places, else it will be abused (and as it is through that Default) unto Heresies. See we not how falsely Satan quoted true Scripture to Christ when he tempted him, only by urging the Letter without the Equity, or true Intention or Meaning? We are to know and do things *Verum vere, justum juste*, else we neither judge with righteous Judgment, nor obey with just Obedience.

Ob. *But is not the Parliament guilty of exercising an arbitrary Power, if their Proceedings be not regulated by written Laws, but by* Salus Populi?

Ans. For the Parliament to be bound up by written Laws, is both destructive and absurd.

First, it is destructive, it being the Fundamental Court and Law, or the very *Salus Populi* of *England*, and ordained, as to make Laws, and see them executed, so to supply their Deficiency according to the present Exigency of things for publick Preservation by the Prerogative of *Salus Populi*, which is universally in them, and but particularly in particular Laws and Statutes, which cannot provide against all future Exigents, which the Law of Parliaments doth, and therefore are not they to be limits to this. And it would yet be further destructive, by cutting the Parliament short of half its Power at once, for it being a Court both of Law and Equity (as appears by the Power of making Laws, which is nothing but Equity reduced by common Consent into Polity) when ever it is circumscribed by written Laws, (which only is the Property of inferior Courts) it ceaseth to be supreme, and divests it self of that inherent and uncircumscribed Power which *Salus Populi* comprehends.

Secondly, as it is destructive, so also it is absurd ; for the Legislative Power, which gives Laws, is not to receive Laws, saving from the nature and end of its own Constitution, ftitution, which as they give it a being, fo they endow it with Laws of Prefervation both of it felf and the whole, which it reprefents.

I would not herein be mifunderftood, as if the Parliament, when it only doth the Office of inferior Courts, judging between Party and Party, were not limited by written Laws: there I grant it is, becaufe therein it only deals between *meum* and *tuum*, which particular written Laws can and ought to determine: fo that its fuperlative and uncircumfcribed Power I intend only as relating to the Univerfe, and the Affairs thereof, wherein it is to walk by its fundamental Principles, not by particular Precepts or Statutes, which are made by the Parliament, between King and People, not between People and Parliament: they are ordained to be Rules of Government to the King, agreeing with the Liberty and Property of the People, and Rules of Obedience to the People, without detainment of their Freedom by the Exercife of an illegal, ufurped and unconfented Power, whereunto Kings (efpecially in hereditary Monarchies) are very prone, which cannot be fufpected by a Parliament, which is reprefentatively the Publick, intrufted for it, and which is like to partake and fhare with the Publick, being but fo many private Men put into Authority *pro tempore*, by common Confent, for common Good.

Nor is the Parliament hereby guilty of an arbitrary Government, or is it deftructive to the Petition of Right, when as in providing for Publick-Weal, it obferves not the Letter of the Law; Firft, becaufe as aforefaid, that Law was not made between Parliament and People, but by the People in Parliament, between the King and them; as appears by the whole tenour of it, both in the complaining and praying parts, which wholly relate to the King. Secondly, becaufe of the common Confent, that in the reprefentative Body (the Parliament) is given thereunto, wherein *England* in her Polity imitates Nature in her Inftincts, who is wont to violate particular Principles for publick Prefervation, as when light things defcend, and heavy afcend, to prevent a *Vacuum*: And Thirdly, becaufe of the equitable Power which is inherent in a Parliament, and for publick Good is to be acted above and againft any particular Statute, or all of them: And fourthly, becaufe the end of making that Law, to wit, the publick Prefervation, is fulfilled in the breaking of it, which is lawful in a Parliament that is chofen by the whole for the whole, and are themfelves alfo of the Body, though not in a King; for therein the Law faith, *Better a mifchief than an inconvenience.* But it may be objected, Though it be not arbitrary for the Parliament to go againft written Law, yet it is not fo when they go againft the King's Confent, which the Law, even the fundamental Law, fuppofeth in Parliamentary Proceedings. This hath been anfwered, That the King is juridically, and according to the intention of the Law, in his Courts; fo that what the Parliament confults for the publick Good, that by Oath, and the Duty of his Office, and Nature of this Polity he is to confent unto; and in cafe he do deny it, yet in the Conftruction of the fundamental Law and Conftitutions of this Kingdom, he is conceived to grant it, fuppofing the Head not to be fo unnatural to the Body, that hath chofen it for good, and not for evil.

But it will be anfwered, Where is the King's Negative Voice, if the Parliament may proceed without his Confent? I anfwer, That there is no known nor written Law that gives him any; and things of that nature are willingly believed till they be abufed, or with too much Violence claimed. That his Majefty hath fundamentally a Right of Confent to the Enacting of Laws, is true, which (as aforefaid) is part of that honourable Truft conftituted in him: And that this Royal Affent is an Act of Honour, and not of abfolute and Negative Power or Prerogative, appears by thefe following Reafons;

Firft, by his Oath at the Coronation, mentioned in one of the Parliament's Declarations, where he doth or fhould fwear to confirm and grant all fuch good Laws as his People *fhall choofe* to be obferved, not *hath chofen*; for Firft, The word *concedis* in that Oath were then unneceffary, the Laws formerly enacted being already granted by foregoing Kings, and fo they need no more *Conceffion* or Confirmation; elfe we muft run upon this Shelf, That all our Laws die with the old King, and receive their being a-new, by the new King's Confent. Secondly, hereby the firft and fecond Claufe in that Interrogatory, viz. *Concedis juftas leges & permittas protegendas*, are confounded, and do but *idem repetere*. Thirdly, *Quas Vulgus elegerit*, implies only the Act of the People in a disjunctive fenfe from the Act or Confent of the King, but Laws already made have more than *Quas Vulgus elegerit*, they have alfo the Royal Confent too; fo that that Phrafe cannot mean them, wherein the Act or Confent of the King is already involved.

H

Secondly,

Secondly, by the Practice of requiring the Royal Assent even unto those very Acts of Subsidies which are granted to himself and for his own use, which it is supposed he will accept of, and yet *Honoris gratia* is his Royal Assent craved and contributed thereunto.

Thirdly, by the King's not sitting in Parliament to debate and consult Laws, nor are they at all offered him by the Parliament to consider of, but to consent to, which yet are transmitted from one House to another, as well to consult as consent to, shewing thereby he hath no part in the consultory part of them (for that it belongs only to the People in Parliament to discern and consult their own good,) but he comes only at the time of Enacting, bringing his Royal Authority with him, as it were to set the Seal thereof to the Indenture already prepared by the People; for the King is Head of the Parliament in regard of his Authority, not in regard of his Reason or Judgment, as if it were to be opposed to the Reason or Judgment of both Houses (which is the Reason both of King and Kingdom) and therefore do they as consult, so also interpret Laws without him, supposing him to be a Person replenished with Honour and Royal Authority, not skilled in Laws, nor to receive Information either of Law or Council in Parliamentary Affairs from any, saving from that supreme Court and highest Council of the King and Kingdom, which admits no counterpoise, being intrusted both as the wisest Council and justest Judicature.

Fourthly, either the choice of the People in Parliament is to be the Ground and Rule of the King's Assent, or nothing but his Pleasure; and so all Bills tho' ever so necessary for publick Good and Preservation, and after so much pains and consultation of both Houses, may be rejected, and so they made meer Cyphers, and we brought to that pass, as either to have no Laws, or such only as come immediately from the King (who oft is a Man of Pleasure, and little seen in publick Affairs, to be able to judge) and so the Kingdom's great Council must be subordinated either to his meer Will, and then what Difference between a free Monarchy and an absolute, saving that the one rules without Council, and the other against it? or at the best but to a Cabinet Council consisting commonly of Men of private Interests, but certainly of no publick Trust.

Ob. But if the King must consent to such Laws as the Parliament shall chuse eo nomine, they may then propound unreasonable things to him, as to consent to his own Deposing, or to the lessening his own Revenue, &c.

Ans. So that the Issue is, whether it be fitter to trust the Wisdom and Integrity of our Parliament, or the Will and Pleasure of the King in this case of so great and publick Concernment. In a word, the King being made the Fountain of Justice and Protection to his People by the fundamental Laws or Constitution of this Kingdom, he is therefore to give life to such Acts and Things as tend thereunto, which Acts depend not upon his Pleasure; but though they are to receive their greater Vigour from him, yet are they not to be suspended at pleasure by him: for that which at first was intended by the Kingdom, for an honourable way of Subsistence and Administration, must not be wrested contrary to the nature of this Polity, (which is a free and mixt Monarchy, and not absolute) to its Destruction and Confusion. So that in case the King in his Person should decline his Duty, the King in his Courts is bound to perform it, where his Authority properly resides; for if he refuse that Honour which the Republick by its fundamental Constitution hath conferred upon him, and will not put forth the Acts of it, for the end it was given him, *viz.* for the Justice and Safety of his People; this hinders not but that they, who have as fundamentally reserved a Power of being and well-being in their own hands by the Concurrence of Parliamentary Authority to the Royal Dignity, may thereby provide for their own Subsistence, wherein is acted the King's juridical Authority, though his personal pleasure be with-held; for his legal and juridical Power is included and supposed in the very being, and consequently in the Acts of Courts of Justice, whose being he may as well suspend as their Power of Acting, for that without this is but a Cypher, and therefore neither their being nor their acting so depend upon him, as not to be able to act and execute common Justice and Protection without him, in case he deny to act with them; and yet both so depend upon him, as that he is bound both in Duty and Honour, by the Constitution of this Polity, to act in them, and they for him, so that (according to that Axiom in Law) *The King can do no wrong,* because his juridical Power and Authority is always to controle his personal Miscarriages.

London's Flames Reviv'd:

OR, AN

ACCOUNT

OF

SEVERAL INFORMATIONS

Exhibited to a Committee appointed by

PARLIAMENT,

September the 25th, 1666.

To Enquire into the BURNING of *LONDON*.

WITH

Several other Informations concerning other Fires in *Southwark*, *Fetter-Lane*, and elsewhere.

UPon the Second of September 1666. *the Fire began in* London, *at one* Farriner's House, *a Baker, in* Pudding-Lane, *between the Hours of One and Two in the Morning* ; *and continued burning until the Sixth of* September *following, consuming, as by the Surveyors appears in Print,* Three hundred seventy three Acres within the Walls of the City of London, *and Sixty three Acres and three Roods without the* Walls : *There remains Seventy five Acres and three Roods yet standing within the* Walls, *unburnt.* Eighty nine Parish Churches, *besides Chappels, burnt.* Eleven Parishes within the Walls yet standing. *Houses burnt, Thirteen thousand and two hundred.*

Per ⎨ *Jonas Moore,* *Ralph Gatrix,* ⎬ Surveyors.

UPon the 18th Day of *September*, 1666. the Parliament came together : And upon the 25th of the same Month, the House of Commons appointed a Committee to enquire into the Causes of the late Fire ; before whom the following Informations were given in, and proved before the Committee ; as by their Report will more clearly appear, bearing date the 22d of *January*, 1666. and upon the 8th of *February* following, the Parliament was prorogued, before they came to give their Judgment thereupon.

Die

Die Martis, 25 Septembris 1666. 18 *Car.* 2.

Resolved, &c.

THat a Committee be appointed to enquire into the Causes of the late Fire, and that it be referred to

Sir *Charles Harbord*,	Mr. *Robert Milward*,	Sir *Robert Atkins*,
Mr. *Sandys*,	Sir *William Lowther*,	Sir *Thomas Gower*,
Col. *Birch*,	Sir *Richard Vatley*,	Mr. *Trevor*,
Sir *Robert Brook*,	Sir *Rowland Beckley*,	Sir *Thomas Clifford*,
Sir *Thomas Littleton*,	Sir *Thomas Allen*,	Sir *Henry Cæsar*,
Mr. *Prin*,	Mr. *Whorwood*,	Sir *John Monson*,
Mr. *Jones*,	Mr. *Coventry*,	Sir *John Charleton*,
Sir *Solomon Swale*,	Serj. *Maynard*,	Lord *Ancram*,
Sir *Thomas Tomlins*,	Sir *John Talbot*, .	Mr. *Pepis*,
Mr. *Seymour*,	Mr. *Morley*,	Sir *Richard Everard*,
Mr. *Finch*,	Mr. *Garraway*,	Mr. *Crouch*,
Lord *Herbert*,	Sir *Francis Goodrick*,	Mr. *Merrel*,
Sir *John Heath*,	Col. *Strangeways*,	Sir *William Hickman*,
Mr. *Milward*,	Sir *Edward Massey*,	Sir *Richard Brown*,
Sir *Richard Ford*,	Sir *Edmond Walpool*,	Mr. *Maynard*.

And they are to meet to-morrow, at Two of the Clock in the Afternoon, in the Speaker's Chamber ; and to send for Persons, Papers and Records.

Will. Goldsbrough, Cler. Dom. Com.

October 9. 1666.

Ordered, That these Members following be added to the Committee appointed to enquire into the Causes of the late Fire, *viz.* Sir *John Pelham*, Mr. *Hugh Buscowen*, Mr. *Giles Hungerford*, Sir *William Lewis*, Sir *Gilbert Gerrard*, Sir *John Brampstone*, Mr. *Milward*, Mr. *Buscowen*, and all the Members that serve for the City of *London*.

Will. Goldsbrough, Cler. Dom. Com.

October 16. 1666.

Ordered, That Mr. *Davies*, Sir *Thomas Higgons*, Mr. *St. John*, Sir *Richard Frankling*, Sir *Thomas Tomkins*, Mr. *Devereux*, Mr. *Millard*, Mr. *Lewis*, Mr. *Dodswell*, Sir *James Thyn*, Sir *Edmond Pierse*, Mr. *Coleman*, Sir *Thomas Allen*, Mr. *Giles Hungerford*, Mr. *Churchill*, be added to the Committee appointed to enquire into the Causes of the late Fire.

Will. Goldsbrough, Cler. Dom. Com.

THE Honourable Committee, according to the forementioned Orders of the House, did meet in the Speaker's Chamber ; and having chose Sir *Robert Brook* for their Chairman, proceeded to receive many considerable Informations from divers credible Persons, about the Matter wherewith they were intrusted ; and thereupon did at last agree, that Sir *Robert Brook* should make the ensuing Report to the Honourable House of Commons.

The Report of Sir Robert Brook, *Chair-man to the Committee that was appointed by the House of Commons to Enquire into the Firing of the City of* London; *made the two and twentieth of* January, 1666.

IN a Letter from *Alanson* of the 23d of *August* 1666, *New Stile*, written from one *Dural*, to a Gentleman lodging in the House of one of the Ministers of the *French* Church in *London*, called *Monsieur Herault*, there were these Expressions.

' Pray acquaint me with the truth of certain News which is common in this ' Countrey, That a *Fire from Heaven* is fallen upon a City called *Belke*, situated on ' the side of the River of *Thames*, where a World of People have been killed and ' burnt, and Houses also consumed.' Which seemed a word of *Cabal*, cast out by some that were knowing, and others that might be ignorant of the signification of it.

Mrs. *Elizabeth Styles*, informs, That in *April* last, in an eager Discourse she had with a *French* Servant of Sir *Vere Fan*, he hastily reply'd, *You* English *Maids will like the* Frenchmen *better, when there is not a House left between* Temple-Bar *and* London-Bridge. To which she answered, *I hope your Eyes will never see that.* He reply'd, *This will come to pass between* June *and* October.

William Tisdale informs, That he being about the beginning of *July* at the *Greyhound* in St. *Martin's*, with one *Fitz-Harris*, an *Irish* Papist, heard him say, *There would be a sad Desolation in* September, *in* November *a worse; in* December *all would be united into one.* Whereupon he asked him, where this Desolation would be? He answered, *in London.*

Mr. *Light* of *Ratcliff*, having some Discourse with Mr. *Langhorn* of the *Middle-Temple*, Barister, (reputed a zealous Papist) about *February* 15 last, after some Discourse in Disputation about Religion, he took him by the hand, and said to him, *You expect great things in sixty six, and think that* Rome *will be destroyed, but what if it be* London?

Mr. *Kitely* of *Barkin* in *Essex*, informs, That one Mrs. *Yazly*, a Papist, of *Ilford* in the said County, came unto his House, *August* the 13th, and being in Discourse with his Mother, said, *They say the next* Thursday *will be the hottest Day that ever was in* England. She reply'd, *I hope the hottest Season of the Year is now past.* To which she answered, *I know not whether it be the hottest for Weather or for Action.* This Mrs. *Yazly* coming to the same House the Week after the Fire, Mr. *Kitely* said to her with some trouble, I have often thought of your *Hot Thursday*: to which she reply'd, *It was not indeed upon the* Thursday, *but it happened upon the* Sunday *was sevennight after.* Mrs. *Yazly* hearing this Evidence produced against her, endeavoured to avoid the Words, saying, *That upon the* 13th *of* August *she did tell Mrs.* Kitely, *That they say the next* Thursday *will be the darkest* Thursday *that ever was in* England, but not otherwise; which she affirms to have received from one *Finchman*, an old Woman of *Ilford*; who being examined by a Justice of Peace to discover the Truth thereof, denied that ever she said any such Words to Mrs. *Yazly*, or that she had discoursed with her about any such Matter; and as to the subsequent Words, she saith, Mrs. *Yazly* denies ever to have spoken them: But Mr. *Kitely* offered in her presence (if it should be demanded) to bring his Mother and Wife to testify the same.

William Ducket Esq; a Member of the House, informs, That one *Henry Baker* of *Chippenham* in the County of *Wilts*, coming from Market with one *John Woodman* of *Kelloway*, in the same County; the *Thursday* before the Fire began in *London*, they had some Discourse about the buying of a Yoke of fat Bullocks, wherein they differed, because *Woodman* who was to sell them was desired to keep them a while in his hands: But the said *Woodman* denied so to do, for that, as he alledged, he could not stay in the Country till that time which *Baker* would have them delivered to him in; and being asked whither he was a going, he refused to tell, asking what he had to do to make that Question: But riding a little further, the said *Woodman* expreſt

I

preſt theſe Words, *You have brave Blades at* Chippenham, *you made Bonefires lately for beating the* Dutch ; *but ſince you delight in Bonefires, you ſhall have your Bellies full of them e'er it be long :* Adding, *That if he lived one Week longer, he ſhould ſee* London *as ſad a* London, *as ever it was ſince the World began ; and in ſome ſhort time after, he ſhould ſee as bloody a time as ever was, ſince* England *was* England. This Diſcourſe was not much taken notice of at that time it was ſpoken ; but when the City of *London* was burnt, the ſaid *Henry Baker* gave this Information to the ſaid Mr. *Ducket* ; whereupon he iſſued out his Warrant to apprehend *Woodman*, but he was gone out of the Country, and cannot be heard of ſince.

Robert Hubert of *Roan* in *Normandy*, who acknowledged that he was one of thoſe that fired the Houſe of Mr. *Farryner* a *Baker* in *Pudding-lane*, from whence the Fire had its beginning, confeſſed, that he came out of *France* with one *Stephen Peidloe*, about four Months before the Fire, and went into *Sweden* with him, where he alſo ſtaid with him as his Companion four Months, and then they came together into *England* in a *Swediſh* Ship called the *Skipper*, where he ſtaid on board with the ſaid *Peidloe* till that *Saturday* Night in which the Fire broke out. When *Peidloe* taking him out of the Ship, carried him into *Pudding-lane* ; and he being earneſt to know whither he would carry him, he would not ſatisfy him till he had brought him to the place ; and then he told him, that he had brought three Balls, and gave him one of them to throw into the Houſe. And he would have been further ſatisfied in the Deſign, as he ſaid, before he would execute it : But *Peidloe* was ſo impatient that he would not hear him, and then he did the Fact ; which was, That he put a Fire-ball at the end of a long Pole, and lighting it with a piece of Match, he put it in at a Window, and ſtaid till he ſaw the Houſe in a Flame. He confeſſed, that there were three and twenty Accomplices, whereof *Peidloe* was the Chief.

Mr. *Graves* a *French* Merchant living in St. *Mary Axe*, inform'd this Committee, that he had kown *Hubert* ever ſince he was four Years old, and hath ever obſerved him to be a Perſon of a miſchievous Inclination, and therefore fit for any villainous Enterprize ; and becauſe of his Knowledge he had of him, he went to viſit him in Priſon, where when he ſaw him, he could not but commiſerate the Condition whereinto he had brought himſelf. And for his better Diſcovery of the Fact, he told him, the ſaid *Hubert*, that he did not believe he had done that of which he confeſſed himſelf guilty. To which *Hubert* reply'd, *Yes Sir, I am guilty of it, and have been brought to it, by the inſtigation of Monſieur* Peidloe ; *but not out of any malice to the* Engliſh *Nation, but from a deſire of reward which he promiſed me upon my return into* France.

It is obſervable, That this miſerable Creature who confeſſed himſelf to the Committee to be a *Proteſtant*, was a *Papiſt* ; and died ſo. And as for the aforeſaid *Peidloe*, the ſaid Mr. *Graves* informed, that he had had a full knowledge of him, and knew him to be a very debauch'd Perſon, and apt to any wicked deſign. Moreover, for a clear Conviction of the Guilt of the aforeſaid *Hubert*, Mr. *Lowman*, the Keeper of the *White-Lion* Priſon, was appointed to ſet him upon a Horſe, and to go with him, and ſee if he could find out the place where he threw the *Fire-ball*. Upon which, *Hubert* with more readineſs than they that were well acquainted with the place, went to *Pudding-lane*, unto the very place where the Houſe that was firſt fired, ſtood, ſaying, *Here ſtood the Houſe.* The Jaylor endeavoured to draw him from that belief, and putting him upon ſeeking another place ; but he poſitively perſiſted in what he had firſt ſaid, and affirmed that to have been the ſaid Houſe. It being intimated to the Committee, That notwithſtanding the Confeſſion of the ſaid *Hubert*, it was confidently reported, the Fire in the forementioned *Farryner's* Houſe began by Accident : The Committee therefore ſent for him the ſaid *Farryner* before them, who being examined ſaid, That it was impoſſible any Fire ſhould happen in his Houſe by Accident ; for he had, after Twelve of the Clock that Night, gone through every Room thereof, and found no Fire but in one Chimney, where the Room was paved with Bricks, which Fire he diligently raked up in Embers. He was then aſked, Whether no Window or Door might let in Wind to diſturb thoſe Coals? He affirmed, there was no poſſibility for any Wind to diſturb them ; and that it was abſolutely ſet on fire of purpoſe.

Dawes Weymanſel Eſquire, one of His Majeſty's Juſtices of the Peace, informed, That he ſaw a Man apprehended in the time of the Fire, near the *Temple,*

ple, with his Pockets ſtuft with *Combuſtible Matter*, made of Flax, Tow, and ſuch like Materials.

Doctor *John Packer* informs, That he ſaw a Perſon in the time of the Fire, throw ſome *Combuſtible Matter* into a Shop in the *Old Bailey*, which he thinks was the Shop of an Apothecary ; and that immediately thereupon he ſaw a great ſmoak, and ſmelt a ſmell of *Brimſtone*. The Perſon that did this, immediately run away ; but upon the out-cry of the People he was taken by the Guards.

Mr. *Randal*, Mr. *Haſlam*, Mr. *Humphrey Bowyer*, do all agree, That they ſaw a Perſon flinging ſomething into a Houſe, near St. *Antholin's* Church ; and that thereupon the Houſe was on fire, and the ſmoak thereof infeſted the adjacent Houſes. And when this was done, there was *No fire near the place.*

Mr. *Michael March*, an Officer in the Trained Bands in a Company of Sir *Richard Brown's* apprehended a *Walloon* in the time of the Fire, at the *Nag's-head* in *Leadenhall Street*, with an Inſtrument like a Dark-Lanthorn, made (as is conceived) to lay a Train of Powder, and it was filled with Gun-powder. There were two more of the ſame Nation in his Company. They being asked to what uſe they employed the ſame Inſtrument, would give no Account thereof.

Newton Killingworth Eſq; informed, That he apprehended a Perſon during the Fire, about whom he found much *Combuſtible Matter*, and certain *black things, of a long figure*, which he could not endure to hold in his hand, by reaſon of their extream heat. This Perſon was ſo ſurprized at firſt, that he would not anſwer to any Queſtion ; but being on his way to *White-hall*, he acted the part of a Mad-man, and ſo continued while he was with him.

Sir *John Maynard* a Member of this Houſe affirms, That he had ſome of that *Combuſtible Matter* in his hands ; and though it were in its natural Subſtance, and unfired, yet the heat of it was ſcarcely to be endured by the touch.

Mr. *Freeman* of *Southwark* Brewer, (whoſe Houſe was lately fired) informs, That on the Day his Houſe was fired (about a quarter of an hour before that happened) a Paper with a Ball of Wild-fire, containing near a pound weight wrapt in it, was found in the *Nave of a Wheel*, in a Wheeler's Yard, where lay a great quantity of Timber. How his Houſe was fired, he knoweth not ; but this he affirmed to the Committee, that it could not be by Accident, becauſe there had not been any Candle or Fire in the Houſe where the Hay lay, that whole day ; and that the Hay being laid in very dry, and before *Midſummer*, could not poſſibly be ſet on fire within it ſelf. Moreover, he ſaid, that the Hay-loft was on fire on the top of the Houſe, and that the Fire ſpread from the one end of the Roof to another in an inſtant.

Mr. *Richard Harwood* informs, That being near the *Feathers-Tavern* by St. *Paul's*, upon the fourth of *September*, he ſaw ſomething through a Grate in a Cellar, like Wild-fire ; by the ſparkling and ſpitting of it, he could judge it to be no other; whereupon he gave notice of it, to ſome Soldiers that were near the place, who cauſed it to be quenched.

I had order from the Committee to acquaint you, that we traced ſeveral Perſons upon ſtrong ſuſpicion (during the Fire) to the Guards, but could not make further Diſcovery of them.

Thus far was the Report.

What follows was given into the Committee, but not by them reported to the Houſe at that time.

IN Obedience to an Order directed to me, from the Honourable Committee of the Houſe of Commons, then ſitting in the Speaker's Chamber, on the ſecond of *October*, 1666. I did carry *Robert Hubert* to St. *Katherine's* Tower by Water, to let me know the place where the *Swediſh* Ship lay, that brought him and other *Frenchmen* from *Stockholm*, and he brought me to the Dock over-againſt Mr. *Corſellis* his Brewhouſe, and did then verify to me and Mr. *Corſellis*, that the Ship lay there, until ſuch time as he, with Mr. *Peidloe* and others, did go and ſet fire to a Houſe. And this *Hubert* did then further ſay, That Mr. *Peidloe* did fix two Fire-balls to a long Pole, and put them
into

into a Window, and that he the said *Robert Hubert* did fire one in the same manner, and put it in at the same Window. But with all the inquiry and diligence that I could use, I could neither find nor hear of any such Vessel. And from thence I carried the said *Robert Hubert* to *Tower-hill*, and did then desire him to shew me the House that they did fire, and he said that it was near the Bridge. So we went along *Thames-street* towards the Bridge; but before we came to the Bridge, the said *Robert Hubert* said, that the House was up there (pointing with his hand up *Pudding-lane* :) So I bid him go to the place, and he went along the Bricks and Rubbish, and made a stand. Then I did ask one *Robert Penny*, a Wine-porter, which was the *Baker's* House; and he told me, that was the House where the aforesaid *Robert Hubert* stood. So I went to *Robert Hubert*, and stood by him, and turned my back towards the *Baker's* House, and demanded of him which House it was that he fired, (directing to other Houses contrary to that House) but he turning himself about, said, *This was the House* (pointing to the *Baker's* House) *that was first fired*. Then by reason of his Lameness, I set him on a Horse, and carried him to several other places, but no other place he would acknowledge; but rode back again to the *Baker's* House, and said again, *That was the House*, (pointing to the *Baker's* House.) And this I do humbly certify to this Honourable Committee.

By me *John Lowman*, Keeper of his
Majesty's County-Goal for *Surry*.

S I R,

HEaring that you are Chair-man to the Committee for examining the Fire of *London*, I thought good to acquaint you with this Information that I have received.

William Champneys, a Hatband-maker, now living upon *Horsly-down*, was upon *Tuesday* Morning, *September* the 14th, 1666, in *Shoe-lane*, and there met with a Constable who had apprehended a *Frenchman*, whom he took firing a House there with Fireballs, and charged the said *Champneys* to assist him, who carried the said *Frenchman* to *Salisbury*-Court, hoping there to have found a Justice; but finding that place burning down, returned into *Fleet-street*, who was presently called upon by the Commander of the Life-Guard, to know what the matter was: the Constable told him, he had apprehended a *Frenchman* firing a House in *Shoe-lane*, he examined the Person, and committed him to the Guard, and told the Constable, he would secure him; and carried him along with him. The Constable asked him, whether he should go along with him, to give in his Evidence? He reply'd, that he had done enough; and might go home. But what became of the *Frenchman*, he knoweth not.

Your humble Servant, S. G.

In a Letter directed from *Ipswich*, for the Honourable Sir *Robert Brook*, it is intimated, That about the 30th of *August* 1666, one of the Constables of *Cotton* of *Hartsmer* Hundred, being about the Survey of that Town, about Hearth-money, was told by one Mr. *William Thompson*, a Roman Catholick in that Town, That though times were like to be sad, yet if he found any cause to *change his Religion, he would see he should not want* : And further said to him, *What will you say, if you should hear that* London *is burnt?*

The Affidavits touching a *Frenchman*, that said there were three Hundred of them engaged in Firing the City.

The Informations of Richard Cound *of* St. Giles in the Fields, *Ironmonger*; William Cotes, Samuel Page, Francis Cogny, Edmond Dattins, *and* Richard Pardoe, *taken the 8th day of* September 1666, *by Sir* Justinian Lewen *Knight, one of his Majesty's Justices of the Peace for the County of* Middlesex, *upon* Oath, *as followeth.*

RIchard Cound saith, That upon *Tuesday* Night last about Twelve or One of the Clock, there was a *Frenchman* brought by the Watch to this Informant's Father's House, being at the Sign of the *White-hart* in *King-street*, taken as a suspicious Person: The said Person being questioned by them, whether he was not one of

2
those

those that fired the City, or had any hand therein, or any privity or knowledge of any that had defigned the fame, or words to that effect ; the faid Perfon anfwered a great while in a perverfe manner, quite different from the Queftion. But being further preffed to tell the truth, and being told, that if he were guilty, it would be the only way to fave his Life ; he did at firft obftinately deny, that he knew any thing of any Plot. Whereupon a young Man took the Prifoner afide, to the end of the Room, and after fome private Difcourfe between them, they both returned to this Informant and the reft of the Company, and the faid young Man fpake openly to us, in the hearing of the Prifoner, That the faid *Frenchman* and Prifoner had confeffed, there were *three hundred* Frenchmen *that were in a Plot or Confpiracy to fire the City.* Upon which this Informant and others fpake to the faid *Frenchman* in thefe Words, or to the fame effect : *Well,* Monfieur, *you have done very well to confefs what you have done, and no doubt but you may have your pardon, if you will confefs all you know of this Plot :* And thereupon further afked him, *Are there no more than three hundred Perfons in the faid Plot ?* He anfwered, *There are no more than three hundred Perfons.* Then we enquired who they were, and how he came to know they were *three hundred ?* To which he would give no direct anfwer, but put it off with other extravagant Difcourfe. And being afked why he came to St. *Giles*'s Parifh (where he was apprehended,) he told a Story, that he came from *Iflington-Fields,* where his Mafter's Goods were ; but the Goods were now removed, he could not tell whither ; and that his Mafter bid him go up and down the Fields, but would not declare upon what occafion, or for what end he was fo to do ; and being afked, whether there were *three hundred* Perfons engaged in this Defign or Plot? he reply'd, that there were *three hundred* engaged in it.

The feveral Informations of William Cotes *of* Cow-lane *of* London, *Painter* ; *of* Samuel Page *of* St. Giles *in the Fields, Weaver* ; *of* Edmund Dakins *of* St. Giles *aforefaid, Bookfeller* ; *of* Francis Cogky *of* St. Andrews, Holborn ; *of* Richard Pardoe, *Victualler, taken upon Oath,* &c. *tend to the Confirmation of the foregoing Relation.*

An Extract of a Letter from Hydleburgh *in the* Palatinate, *September* 29. 1666.

SIR,

YOurs *of the fixth current came on* Wednefday *to me, and brought the ill tidings of the burning of* London, *conftantly expected and difcourfed of amongft the* Jefuits *to my knowledge for thefe fifteen Years laft paft, as to happen in this Year. In which they do alfo promife to themfelves and others* Introduction *of the publick Exercife of the Catholick* Religion. *This Letter was fent to Mr.* Alton, *who lives in* New Gravel-lane *in* Shadwel, *who negotiates the Bufinefs of the* Palatinate, *and will produce the Original if there be occafion.*

The Information of John Chifhul, *Schoolmafter in* Enfield.

UPon *Friday, Auguft* 31. Mrs. *St. George,* and her eldeft Daughter *Sufanna St. George,* both *Popifh Recufants,* came to vifit Mrs. *Rebecca Eves,* Widow, at her Houfe in *Enfield* ; where fpeaking concerning the Seffion of Parliament drawing nigh, Mrs. *St. George* told her, that fome would hereafter be called to account for a Plot. Being afked for what ? She told her in her ear, *For burning the City.* Mrs. *Eves* afterwards hearing of the firing of *London,* (and going to a place where fhe might behold it) met with Mrs. *Sufanna St. George,* and (amongft other Difcourfe) told her how much her Mother's words, which fhe fpake the *Friday* before, did run in her thoughts ; which fhe repeated to her Daughter, who made this Reply, That her Mother was very apt to talk, and that fhe had been fain to keep her Mother within doors during the Fire, fearing left fhe fhould talk.

After this (during the Fire) Mrs. *Eves* met with Mrs. *Cook,* another *Popifh Recufant,* and of the fame Family ; to whom fhe alfo related Mrs. *St. George* her Words : who made this return, That fhe was a worthy Woman to keep Counfel !

Alfo the Lady *St. George* at *Enfield,* in the Lord of *Lincoln*'s Houfe, declared to Mrs. *Rebecca Eves* of the faid Town, That within a few Days, the City of *London* would be laid in afhes. This was fpoken about two Days before the Fire happened.

Mrs. Eves *of* Enfield, *her Examination before Mr.* Jolliff *and Mr.* Marvel, December 20, 1666, *concerning Mrs.* St. George.

MRs. *Rebecca Eves* of *Enfield*, three or four Days, or within a Week before the Fire, receiving a Visit in her own House from Mrs. *St. George* (amongst other Discourse) Mrs. *St. George* ask'd her, What News she heard? And if she knew when the Parliament sate? Mrs. *Eves* reply'd, she thought, shortly. The other ask'd, If she heard of any that were to be called in question before the Parliament? Mrs. *Eves* said, *About what?* Mrs. *St. George* said, *About a Plot.* Mrs. *Eves* asked, *What Plot?* Mrs. *St. George* answered, *About firing the City.* Mrs. *Eves* said, *I hope God will preserve the City; but People use not to be questioned before the Fact be committed.* So the Discourse was waved for that time.

At the time of the Fire, Mrs. *Eves* went out to look towards the Fire; and mentioning Mrs. *St. George*, one in the Company reply'd behind her, (but she cannot certainly fix the Person) *A prime Woman to keep Counsel!* After the Fire, Mrs. *St. George*, her Daughter, came to Mrs. *Eves*, who asked her, If she remembred what her Mother had said? She said, *My Mother is such a Woman, she will speak what she thinks.* Afterwards she said, That she had much ado to keep her Mother in at the time of the Fire, left she should speak some things she should be questioned for.

At the first Discourse, Mrs. *Eves*, her Daughter, and others of the Family were present. Mr. *St. George*, his Wife, and Family, have since left *Enfield*. They are all great *Papists*, and there are many more in the Neighbourhood.

A Letter directed, and sent by the Post to Mr. Samuel Thurlton, *in* Leicester-shire, *from a Person unknown, as followeth; dated* October, 1666.

My Friend,

YOur Presence is now more necessary at *London*, than where you are; that you may determine how to dispose of your Estate in *Southwark:* For it is determined by Human Counsel, (if not frustrated by Divine Power) that the Suburbs will shortly be destroyed. Your Capacity is large enough to understand: Proceed as your Genius shall instruct you.

Cave, Cave, Fuge, Vale.

SAturday the first of *September* 1666, the Day before the Fire in *London*, came one *Urmstraw* from *Ireland*, with a Letter from thence, to one Esq; *Holcroft*, at *Eastham* in *Essex*, (being related to that Family by Marriage;) where he supped. After which he asked the Esquire, If he had heard any thing of the firing of *London?* Who answered, *No.* But *Urmstraw* said, he would shortly; for it was, or would be so that Night. The Esquire answered, if it were, he hoped it might be quenched again; as it had been many a time. But *Urmstraw* answered, No, it would not be quenched; for it should be said of it, as of *Troy:* repeating a *Latin* Verse,

Nunc Seges est ubi Troja *fuit.*

Now, Corn grows where Troy-Town *stood.*

This Discourse was managed pleasantly by him; after which, they went to their Beds: And in the Morning, this *Urmstraw* enquires earnestly, Whether they had heard of the firing of *London* that Night? They answered, *No.* But he prayed him to send one of the Family out, to enquire; and, doubtless, they would hear of it. Upon which a Messenger was sent; who brought word from a Man that travelled upon the Road, that it was on fire indeed. After Dinner, this *Urmstraw* desired his Horse to be saddled, that he might be gone. The Esquire intreats him to stay till next Morning: But he answered, *Therefore I would see* London *before it be quite burnt; for I shall never see it more.*

Sunday Morning, the Fire being begun in *London*, a Person coming from *Deptford*, when he came to *Barnaby-street* end in *Southwark*, hears a Woman cry out against a *Frenchman*, for throwing Fire-balls; he runs after him, and lays hold of him. He

asked

asked him, what Commiffion he had for fo doing? He anfwered, That his Commiffion was in his Conftancy. The People coming in, they fearched him, and found Fire-balls in his Pockets. He was delivered to the Guard in *Southwark*, but heard of no more.

A Citizen being fired out of his Houfe, had hired a Lodging in *Queen-ftreet* in *Covent-Garden*; and going up *Holborn*, there being a Crowd of People, fteps in amongft them, and hears a Woman fay, that fhe had a hand in firing the City. The People ask'd her, whether fhe was an *Anabaptift?* She faid, *No.* Are you an Independent? She faid, *No.* Are you a Presbyterian? She faid, *No.* Are you a Roman Catholick? To which fhe would give no anfwer. The Citizen asked her, *But Miftrefs; Had you a hand in burning the City?* She anfwered, *What would you have me to fay? I have confeffed it already, and do deferve to die for it.* This fhe faid, with great trembling; and feemed to be much troubled. The Citizen enquired for a Conftable: The People reply, There was one gone for. But a Gallant comes, and takes her by the Arm, and leads her away; faying, He would have her examined: And forthwith, another Gallant clofeth with him; and they both carried her to the *Griffin-Tavern* in *Holborn.* The Citizen follows them, to fee the Refult of the Bufinefs: But they with the Mafter of the Houfe, fhut out the Company (all but the Citizen, fuppofing him to be one of their own Company,) but asking one the other concerning him, and finding him not of them, put him out again. Whereupon, he goes to the next Company of Soldiers, and enquires for their Captain; who reply'd, He was not there: But told him, *Yonder is my L. C.* Unto whom the Citizen repaired; and acquainted his Lordfhip, That there was a Woman apprehended (and refcued by a Couple of Gallants) that had confeffed fhe had a hand in burning the City; and was at fuch a Tavern. Whereupon the L. C. called to a Captain in the Street, and ordered him to go with that Man, and apprehend the Woman that he fhould direct him to. Whereupon, he goes with the Citizen, and takes her, with the firft Gallant, who ftood up highly in her defence, and carries them both to an Ale-houfe on the other fide of the way. The Citizen perceiving that nothing would be done with her, leaves his Name with the Captain, and where he might be found; but was never called for, to juftify the Words fpoken by her.

A Woman ftanding in *White-Chappel* with a Company about her, was ask'd, what the matter was? She faid, that fhe met two young Men in that place, and asked them how it was with the Fire: They anfwered, *'Tis now almoft out, if it can be kept fo; but the Rogues renew it with their Fire-balls.* As faith another Woman, *Young men, if you have a heart to it, you may be hired to throw them.* It was ask'd her, What was become of the Woman that fpake thus? She anfwered, That fhe had apprehended her, and delivered her to the under Beadle of *White-Chappel* Parifh. The Woman falling under the Accufation (not being able to deny it) there being many Witneffes at that time that heard it; fhe was delivered to Sir *John Robinfon*, but heard of no more.

One from *France* writes to his Correfpondent in *London*, to know the Truth of what was muttered in *Paris*, Whether *London* was laid in Afhes or no: The Letter being dated a Week before the Fire began.

From *Surrey* in or near *Darkin*, a Perfon in ordinary Habit, who was yet obferved to take place of all the Nobility and Gentry among the *Papifts*, feeing the People of *Darkin* mourn for the burning of the City, he fpake flightingly of it, telling them, they fhould have fomething elfe to trouble themfelves for; and that fhortly *Darkin* fhould be laid as low as *London.* Whereupon the People made at him, and one Tr. *H.* a great *Papift* refcues him, and fends him away in his Coach to *London.* This was depofed before Sir *Adam Brown*, a Juftice of Peace, and a Member of Parliament.

Thefe

Thefe following Relations (for fubftance) were delivered to Sir *Robert Brooks*, Chair-man of the Committee, a little before the Prorogation of the Parliament.

A true Relation made by one of the Grand Jury, at Hicks's-Hall, *at a general Quarter-Seffions, prefently after the Fire in* London, *who was upon Trial of fome of thofe that fired the City.*

THat near *Weft-Smithfield* in *Chicklane*, there was a Man taken in the very Act of firing a Houfe, by the Inhabitants and Neighbours ; and carrying him away through *Smithfield*, to have him before a Juftice for the Fact committed, the King's Life-Guard perceiving it, made up unto them, and demanded their Prifoner from them ; but they refufed to let him go. The Life-Guard Men told them, That he was one of the King's Servants, and faid, *We will have him.* And thereupon they drew out their Swords and Piftols, and refcued him out of the People's hands by force of Arms.

A Bill of Indictment was brought againft him, and two or three Witneffes did fwear unto it, and the Bill was found by the Grand-Jury, who did carry it to the *Old Baily*, and prefented it to the Lord Chief Juftice ; but it came to no further Trial, nor was ever feen after at the *Old Baily*, fo far as this Perfon, upon his beft Enquiry, could ever hear, or learn.

Concerning an Houfe-keeper at Soho, *who fired his own Dwelling-houfe.*

FIrft he fecured all his Goods in his Garden, and then went in and fired his Houfe ; which when he had done, he endeavoured to get away out at his Fore-door. A Neighbour demanded of him, Who had fired his Houfe ? He anfwered, *The Devil.* Upon that, his Neighbour bid him ftand, or he would run his Halbert into his Guts. His anfwer was, *If you do, there are enough left behind me to do the Work.* Whereupon, he was fecur'd, and a Bill of Indictment brought againft him, and about three Witneffes did fwear to it : And his Son came in as Witnefs againft him ; who was demanded by the Foreman, What he could fay as to the firing of his Father's Houfe ? He faid, That his Father did fire it with a Fire-ball. It was demanded of him, Whether he did fire it above ftairs, or below ? He anfwered, *Above ftairs.* The Bill was likewife found, but the Petty-Jury did not find him guilty.

A Maid was taken in the Street, with two Fire-balls in her Lap : Some did demand of her, Where fhe had them ? She faid, One of the King's Life-guard threw them into her Lap. She was afked, Why fhe had not caufed him to be apprehended ? She faid That fhe knew not what they were. She was indicted for this, and the Bill found againft her, and turned over to the *Old Baily* ; but no Profecution upon it.

In the time of the Fire, a Conftable took a *Frenchman* firing an Houfe, feized on him ; and going to a Magiftrate with him, met his R. H. the D. Y. who afked the Reafon of the Tumult. One told him, that a *Frenchman* was taken firing a Houfe : His H. called for the Man, who fpake to him in *French* : The D. afked, Who would atteft it ? The Conftable faid, *I took him in the Act, and I will atteft it.* The D. took him into his Cuftody, and faid, *I will fecure him.* But he was heard of no more.

On *Monday* the third of *September*, there was a *Frenchman* taken firing a Houfe ; and upon fearching of him, Fire-balls were found about him. At which time four of the Life-Guards refcued the *Frenchman*, and took him away from the People, after their ufual manner in the whole time of the Fire.

One Mr. *Belland*, a *Frenchman*, living at *Marybone*, who bought great ftore of Pafte-board for a confiderable time before the Fire of the City of *London*, to the Quantity of twenty Grofs in one Shop, and much more elfewhere, was afked by a Citizen, What he did with all that Paft-board ? He anfwered that he made Fire-works for the King's pleafure. The Citizen afked him, *What doth the King give you ?* He replied,

plied, *Nothing, only I have Respect at Court.* The Citizen said, *Take heed, Mr. Belland, you do not expend your Estate, and then lose your Respect at Court, for you are at a great Charge.* Belland answered, *Sir, do you think this a great Matter? I use all this myself; But if you did see all the great Quantities I have made elsewhere in three several Places, three, four, and five miles off, you would say something.* Another time the Stationer, with whom he dealt for the Past-board, being at his House in *Marybone,* and wondring at the many Thousands of Fire-works, that lay piled up of several Sorts, he said, *Sir, do you wonder at this? If you should see the Quantity that I have made elsewhere by other Men, you would wonder indeed.*

The *Sunday* before the Fire began, this *Belland* came to the Shop where he was wont to buy his Past-board, but the Stationer being not there, he desired a Citizen (the Stationer's Neighbour) to speak to him, and to let him know that he had much wronged him in disappointing him of the four Gross of Past-board which he should have had of him, and said, that he should not do his Work by the time; and that if he had it not by *Tuesday* Night, it would come too late, he should have no occasion for it after that, (which was the *Tuesday* Night before the Fire.) Mr. *Belland,* (said the Citizen) *What is the reason of your haste? Have you any Shew suddenly before the King?* At which he blush'd, and would give no Answer. Says the Citizen, *What kind of Fire-works do you make? Only such as will crack and run?* Belland answered, *I make of all Sorts? some that will burn and make no Crack at all, but will fly up in a pure Body of Flame, higher than the Top of Paul's, and waver in the Air.* Says the Citizen, *Mr. Belland, when you make your Shew, shall I see it? Yes,* said *Belland, I promise you,* and gave his Hand upon it. Which Citizen, in the time of the Fire, being upon the *Thames* in a Boat, saw, to his great Amazement, sundry Bodies of Fire, burning above the Fire of the Houses, as high again as *Paul's,* wavering in the Air, directly according to *Belland's* Description.

And after the burning of the City, some Citizens agreed to go to *Marybone,* to speak with this *Belland;* and by the way, met with his two Maids and his Boy; and having some Knowledge of them, asked for young Mr. *Belland:* who told them, he was not at home, neither knew they where he was. But the Citizens observing, that they carried with them Rabbets and Capons ready dressed, concluded they were going to him, and told them so; whereat they were surly, and bid them go look him, for they would not tell them where he was. Upon that, the Citizens resolved to follow them, and did, till they came to *Whitehall.* The Servants went up Stairs, and down Stairs, on purpose to have lost them, but could not, for they kept close to them: And at last, one of the Maids went to a Door, and knocked; crying out, They were dogged by two Men, that they could not be rid of. With that, young Mr. *Belland* opened the Door, saying to one of the Citizens, *Sir, your Servant: How do you do?* One of them answered, *Both I, and many thousand Families more, are the worse for you; for you, under pretence of making Fire-works for the King, have destroyed a famous City, and ruined a noble People.* To which *Belland* replies, *I make nothing but innocent things, that will do no harm; for which I have a Patent from the King.* But the Citizen answered, *If the King gave you a Patent, it was but for yourself.* Who answered, *No.* Said the Citizen, *What made you then to employ so many Men, in so many Places?* No, said *Belland, I set no Man to work; neither know I any Man that makes of them, but myself;* tho' he had often before said otherwise. While they were thus discoursing, old *Belland* looks from under the Hangings; *Sir,* said he, *I hear you charge my Son with Suspicion of burning the City; I pray you, speak lower,* (casting his Eyes about, fearing the Ladies, passing by, might hear;) and said, *My Son doth nothing, but what he hath a Patent from the King for; and shall have an Order to sue any Man, that shall accuse him.* And he said, *My Son is no Prisoner, but lodged here, to prevent him from the Rage of the common People.* Well, said the Citizen, *You must give an Account for what you have done:* And so they shut the Door upon them. The Citizen went, and enquired whose Lodgings they were; and was told, they belonged to a Lady.

The Information of Thomas Middleton *Chirurgeon, late Inhabitant of St.* Brides London.

I The said *Thomas Middleton* do hereby certify, That upon the *Sunday* in the Afternoon (the Day wherein the dreadful Fire broke out in *Pudding-Lane*, which consumed the City) hearing the general Out-cry, that the City was fired by *Papists* and *French*, I repaired to the Top of a Church Steeple, near the *Three Cranes* in the *Vintrey*; where myself, and several others, observ'd the Motion of the Fire for two or three Hours together: And we all took Notice, that the Fire did break forth out of several Houses, when the Houses which were then burning were at a good distance from them every way. And, more particularly, I saw the Fire break out from the Inside of *Lawrence-Poultney* Steeple, when there was no Fire near it. These, and such like Observations, begat in me a Persuasion, that the Fire was maintained by Design. Upon *Monday* I repaired again into the City, and found, as the Day before, that the Fire did break forth in fresh Houses, at a great distance one from another. And as I was returning home, passing through *Watling-Street*, by a Tobacco Merchant's House, I saw the Master of the House come down Stairs, driving a young Fellow before him; saying to him, *You Rogue, do you come to rob me? What did you do in my Garret?* or Words to that purpose; and pushed him out of doors: All which I observed, and he seem'd to be a *Frenchman*; he was a short, black Fellow, of about two and twenty Years of Age. And as soon as he was out of the House, he having a loose Coat on, in a way of Privacy, shuffles something under his Coat; whereupon, I laid hold of him, and said, *Sirrah, What have you there?* The Fellow replied, *What is that to you? the Master of the House knows me.* Upon that, I ask'd the Master of the House, whether he knew the Fellow: He answered, He knew him not. Whereupon I searched the Fellow, and found a Horn of Powder about him; and assoon as the Powder was discovered, he fell a rubbing of his Hands, they being all black with Powder. He had also about him, a Book entitled, *The Jewish Government.* I charged him, that he was a *Frenchman*, because he spake broken *English*; but he denied it, and did much vaunt himself. There coming a Constable by with his Staff, I required him to carry him to Prison, and I would assist him: So we conveyed him to Old *Bridewel*; and by the way, the People were ready to kill him; calling him *French* Rascal. I prayed them to forbear, for Justice would give him Reward. I told the Fellow, he would be hang'd; he made slight of it, saying, *If I die, my Soul shall be saved, but yours shall be damn'd.* And when he was put into *Bridewel*, I desired that he might be secured, and none suffered to speak with him, till he were examined before a Magistrate, because the Tobacco Merchant's House was presently burned upon it. But so it happened on the next Day, that the Fire came on, and consumed my House and Goods; so that I was forced, with my Family, to flee into the Country; and what became of the Fellow, I know not; old *Bridewel* being burnt also. And understanding that the Parliament hath appointed a Committee to enquire after the Actors in, and Fomentors of that terrible Fire; I thought good to inform the Honourable Committee thereof, that they may send for the Keeper of the said *Bridewel*, to know what became of the Fellow, that he might receive Justice according to his Demerit. Thus much I thought myself obliged to do, as in Duty bound to God and my Country; all which I am ready to affirm upon Oath, when I shall be thereunto called.

Tho. Middleton.

IN the Time of the Fire, near *Bridewel*, there was a Man sadly bemoaning the great Loss he was like to sustain (the Fire then being within five or six Houses of him) did beseech the People for God's sake (they having no Goods of their own in danger) to come in and help him to throw out Trunks, Chests, Beds, &c. out at a Window, having procured two Carts or Waggons to carry them away. Whereupon I ran into his House with several others, broke down his Windows, threw out his Goods, and loaded the Carts; and there being some Interval of Time before the Return of the Carts, and seeing a Room wherein were many Books and loose Papers (which seemed to be a Library) I went in and took down a Book, which proved to be *Ovid's Metamorphosis*; and while I was looking upon it, there came into the same Room, an old Man of low Stature, with a white Frock, who looked also on the Book, as it was in my Hand; I took him in my mind to be some Groom come out of a Stable,

and

and thought him to be prefumptuoufly foolifh, fuppofing fuch a mean-like old Man ignorant of that Language in which the Book was written, it being *Latin* ; but I fpoke not to him. In the mean time there brake forth a Fire amongft the Papers which were behind us, there being none in the Room but he and I. Whereupon the reft of the People coming in, cry'd out, *We had fet the Room on fire:* And rufhing in upon us, put out the Fire with their Feet. Whereupon I took hold of the old Man by the Buttons under the Throat, and faid, *How now, Father ! it muft either be you or I that muft fire thefe Papers.* There was a fmall thing of a black matter, which looked like a piece of Link, burning, which queftionlefs fet fire on the Papers, but it was immediately trod out. A Tumult of People thronged in ; and when I faid, *How, now Father !* and took hold on him, *Parce mihi, Domine :* The People which did not underftand it, cried out, He is a *Frenchman*, kill him ; and with pulling of him, his Peruke fell off ; then appeared a bald Skull, and under his Frock he had black Cloaths, I think of Bifhop Sattin ; whereupon he feemed to be a grave Ecclefiaftick Perfon. I had much ado to fave him from the People, but at laft brought him before the D. of *Y.* We found in his Pockets a Bundle of Papers clofed up with Wax like a Packet, which was delivered to the D. of *Y.* I know not what was written in them, neither do I know what Country-man he was ; but methoughts he looked fomething Jefuit-like. This I am certain of, that when I went into the Room, there was no Fire in it, and it was fired when there was none but he and I in it, yet I cannot fay I faw him do it, though I cannot but fufpect he did it ; and the rather, becaufe there were feveral Houfes untouched betwixt this Houfe, and where the Fire was coming on, where the Papers in the Library were thus on fire, as I have related. What became of this Fellow, after we had delivered him to his R. H. I have not heard.

John Stewart.

Thus far concerning the Report and Informations about the Fire : Now follows a true Account of what was reprefented to another Committee of Parliament, touching the In-folency of Popifh Priefts and Jefuites, and the Increafe of Popery, &c.

At the Committee appointed to certify Informations touching the Infolency of Popifh Priefts and Jefuites, and the Increafe of Popery.

Ordered, *That thefe feveral Informations proceeded on, in purfuance of the faid Power of the Committee, be reported to the Houfe in reference to the Infolency of the Popifh Priefts and Jefuites, and the Increafe of Popery.*

AS to the Increafe of Popery, Mr. *Hancock*, Minifter of *Chilmoth* in *Wilts*, informs, That meeting with one Mr. *Thomfon*, about a Month fince, coming from *Mafs*, out of *Somerfet-houfe* Chappel, and difcourfing to him about his Religion, asked him, if there were many lately turned to it ? *Thomfon* anfwered, *Thoufands.* And being de-manded, what Encouragement there was to it ? Replied, *There would be a Change fuddenly.*

Report of his Carriage to the Committee.

Mr. *Thomfon*, being fummoned before the Committee, did behave himfelf very in-folently : They have commanded me to report it. Being asked, Whether he had not a Shop in *Somerfet-houfe* where Popifh Books and Popifh Knacks were fold ? He faid, He had ; and that his Man fold fuch Books and Beads, and other Things. And faid, There was one Crucifix, no Relicks ; but wifhed he had fome good ones. He faid, that he was a *Roman* Catholick, and thanks God for it. He faid, he was no Prieft, but wifhed he were in a Capacity to be one. He faid, he had not taken the Oath of Allegiance and Supremacy, nor would do it. He faid, he would take any Oath that any Chriftian Prince fhould require, but not the Oath of Allegiance, intimating fome Mixture in it. He faid, he had taken the Oath of Allegiance to the King of *Spain*, and was a Subject to the King of *Spain.*

2

One

One Mr. *Aſh* a Miniſter, late of *Capel* in *Surrey*, informed, That being at *Caufield* in *Lancaſhire* this laſt Summer, he ſaw great Reſort on *Sundays* to *Caufield* Houſe, the Houſe of a Papiſt; and asking ſome that were going thither, what the Occaſion was of their Reſort thither, they told him they were going to *Maſs*, and that one Mr. *Robinſon* a Prieſt did ſay *Maſs*.

Mr. *Aſh* did likewiſe inform, that he thought the number of thoſe that went to *Maſs* to that Houſe on *Sundays*, was as great as the Proteſtants that went to the Pariſh Church.

One Mr. *Welden*, Deputy-Ordinary for *Middleſex*, did inform, That in his accuſtomed attendance on the Priſoners at *Newgate*, about the time of Execution, *Romiſh* Prieſts, and particularly one Mr. *Harvy* a Jeſuit, hath conſtantly uſed to reſort to the Priſon at thoſe times, and doth perſuade the Priſoners to become Papiſts; and that divers have been altered in their Religion by them, and turned to Popery.

Mr. *Wootten* informeth, That on *October* 16. he went to *Newgate*, and meeting with one *Howard* an Under-Keeper at the Door, deſired to ſpeak with Mr. *Hubert* the *Frenchman*, who was then condemned: *Howard* told him that he could not ſpeak with him yet, for Mr. *Harvy* the Queen Mother's Confeſſor was in private with him; and ſaid, this *Harvy* uſed frequently to come to the Priſon after Condemnation, and that where one Priſoner died a Proteſtant, many died Papiſts. Mr. *Wootten* ſaid, that after ſome ſtay he ſaw Mr. *Harvy* come out from Mr *Hubert*, and then he was admitted to have Speech with him.

Mr. *Cawdry*, Keeper of *Newgate*, did inform, That Mr. *Harvy* the Jeſuit did frequent the Priſon at *Newgate*, about the times of the Execution upon the pretence of the Queen's Charity, and did ſpend much time with the Priſoners in private, and particularly, did ſo before the laſt Execution, night after night. Mr. *Cawdry* ſaid likewiſe, of the nine that ſuffered, eight died Papiſts, whereof ſome he knew were Proteſtants when they came into the Priſon.

It appeared upon ſeveral Informations, that Mr. *Harvy*, and other Prieſts, did not only reſort to *Newgate* at times of Execution; but likewiſe to the *White-Lion* in *Southwark*, and other places in the Country, and uſed their endeavours to pervert dying Priſoners.

Thomas Barnet, late a Papiſt, informed, That when he was a Papiſt, and reſorted to Gentlemen's Houſes in *Berkſhire* that were *Papiſts*; there was almoſt in every Gentleman's Houſe a Prieſt, and inſtanced in divers private Gentlemen in that County. Others inform the like, in *Surrey*.

Mr. *Cottman* did inform, That one Mr. *Carpenter*, late a Preacher at *Colledge-hill*, did in Diſcourſe tell *Cottman*, 'That the Judgments of God upon this Kingdom by the 'Plague laſt year, and lately by the Fire in *London*, were come upon this Land and 'People, for their forſaking the true *Roman* Catholick Religion, and ſhaking off O-'bedience to the Pope; and that if they would return to the Church of *Rome*, the Pope 'would rebuild the City at his own Charge. *Carpenter* ſaid likewiſe to *Cottman*, 'That 'if he would come and hear him preach the next Sunday at his Houſe in *Queen-ſtreet*, 'he would give twenty Reaſons to prove, that the *Roman* Catholick was the true Reli-'gion, and his the falſe; and that our Bible had a thouſand falſities in it, and that there 'was no true Scripture but at *Rome*, and their Church.'

Carpenter at the Committee confeſſed, that he had formerly taken Orders from the Church of *Rome*, to be a Prieſt; but ſaid he had renounced that Church, and taken Orders in *England*.

The next thing is the Information of their Inſolency, and I ſhall begin with their ſcorning and deſpiſing the Bible.

One *Thomas Williams* an Officer in Sir *William Bowyer's* Regiment, informed, That one *Aſhley* a Papiſt, ſeeing a Woman read in a Bible, asked her why ſhe read in that *damnable Presbyterian Bible*, and ſaid, *A Play-book was as good.*

Thomas Barnet of *Bingfield* in *Berkſhire*, informed, That being at one Mr. *Young's* Houſe in *Bingfield*, at *Bartholomew*-tide laſt, Mr. *Young* ſaid to the Brother of this *Thomas,*

mas, in his hearing, *That within two Years there should not be a Protestant in* England. *Thomas Barnet*, informed further, That being at Mr. *Doncaster's* House in *Bingfield*, one Mr. *Thural*, Son-in-law to Mr. *Doncaster*, (and both Papists) said to this Informer, (who was then likewise a Papist,) *The People take me for a poor Fellow, but I shall find a thousand or two thousand Pounds to raise a party of Horse, to make Mr.* Hathorn's *and Mr.* Bullock's; *fat guts lie on the Ground ; for it is no more Sin to kill an Heretick, than to kill a Grashopper ; and that it was happy for him that he was a Catholick, for by that means he shall be one that shall be mounted.*

Mr. *Linwood* Scrivener in *White-Chapel*, informed, That about the twentieth of *October* last, meeting with one Mr. *Binks* a Papist, and discoursing with him, *Binks* told him, *That there was amongst the Papists, as great a Design as ever was in* England, *and he thought it would be executed suddenly.* Being asked how many Papists there were about *London*, he answered, *About seven thousand, and in* England *an hundred thousand were armed.*

Mr. *Oaks*, a Physician dwelling in *Shadwel*, informed, That a little after the burning of *London*, one Mr. *Carpenter* a Minister, came to his House in *Tower-wharf*, and spake to him to this purpose : *I will not say that I am a Papist, but this I will say, that I had rather die the death of the Papists, and that my Soul should be raised with their Resurrection, than either to be Presbyterian, Independent, or Anabaptist ; and I tell you, the Papists have hitherto been his Majesty's best Fortification ; for when Presbyterians, Independents, and Anabaptists, forsook and opposed him, then they stood by him, and helped him ; and he is now resolved to commit himself into their hands. And take it upon my Word, in a short time the Papists will lay you as low as that House* (pointing to an House that was demolished) *for they are able to raise forty thousand Men, and I believe, the next work will be cutting of Throats.* This was sworn by Mr. *Oaks*, before Sir *John Frederick*, a Member of the House.

Miriam Pilkington, being present when the words were spoken, doth affirm them all, save only those, *That the King is resolved to commit himself into the Papists hands.* Those she doth not remember.

Henry Young, a Distiller of hot Waters, informed, That about *April*, 1661, being in the Jesuits College in *Antwerp*, one *Powel*, an *English* Jesuit, persuaded him to turn a *Roman* Catholick, and said, *That if he intended to save his Life and Estate, he had best turn so, for within seven Years he should see all* England *of that Religion. Young* replied, *That the City of* London *would never endure it. Powel* answered, *That within five or six Years they would break the power and strength of* London *in pieces, and that they had been contriving it these twenty Years ; and that if Young did live, he should see it done.* The said *Young* did likewise inform, That shortly after his coming into *England*, one *Thomson* and *Copervel*, both Papists, did several times say to him, *That within five or six Years at the farthest, the* Roman *Catholick Religion should be all over in this Kingdom.*

Jasper Goodwin of *Darkin*, in the County of *Surrey*, informed, That about a Month since, one *Edward Complin*, a Papist, said to him, *You must all be Papists shortly ; and* that now he was not ashamed to own himself a Roman Catholick, and to own his Priest (naming two that were in *Darkin*, in the houses of two Papists ;) and likewise said, *That in twenty four hours warning, the* Roman *Catholicks could raise thirty thousand Men, as well armed, as any Men in* Christendom.

William Warner of *Darkin*, informed, That the said *Edward Complin* did tell him, *That the* Roman *Catholicks in* England, *could in twenty four hours raise thirty thousand Horse and Arms :* And upon saying so, pulled out his Crucifix and Beads, and said, *He was not ashamed of his Religion.*

John Graunger of *Darkin*, informed, That about a Year since, being in his House, reading the Bible, one *Thomas Collins*, a Papist, said to him, *Are you still a Church-goer? Had you not better turn* Roman Catholick ? *If you stay till you are forced, none will abide you.* And said further, *That there was a Man beyond Sea had prophesied, That in Sixty six, if the King did not settle the* Romish *Religion in* England, *he would be banished out of the Kingdom, and all his Posterity.* And *Collins* further said, *That he being lately turned a* Roman Catholick, *he would not be a* Protestant *for all the World.* He wished *Graunger* again, in the hearing of his Wife, (which he affirmed to the Committee) to turn his Religion ; for all the said Prophecy would come to pass in *Sixty Six*.

M

Robert

Robert Holloway of *Darkin* aforefaid, informed, That one *Stephen Griffin*, a Papift, faid to him, *That all the Blood that had been fhed in the late civil War, was nothing to that which would be fhed this Year in* England. *Holloway* demanded a reafon for thefe words, in regard the Kingdom was in peace, and no likelihood of trouble; and faid, *Do you* Papifts *intend to rife and cut our throats when we are afleep?* Griffin anfwered, *That's no matter, if you live, you fhall fee it.*

Ferdinand de Maffido, a *Portuguefe*, and fome Years fince a *Romifh* Prieft, but turning *Proteftant*, informed, That one Father *Taff* a Jefuit, did the laft Year tell him at *Paris*, *That if all* England *did not return to the Church of* Rome, *they fhould all be deftroyed the next Year.*

Mr. *Samuel Cottman* of the *Middle-Temple*, Barrifter, informed, That about two Years fince, one Mr. *Jevifton*, a *Popifh* Prieft, and called by the Name of Father *Garret*, did perfuade him to turn *Papift*, and he fhould want neither Profit nor Preferment. Mr. *Cottman* objected, that he intended to practife the Law, which he could not do if he turned *Papift*, becaufe he muft take the Oath of *Supremacy* at his being called to the Bar; and if he were a *Papift*, he muft not take it. Mr. *Jevifton* replied, *Why not take the Oath? It is an unlawful Oath, and void* ipfo facto. And after fome paufe, faid further, *Firft take the Oath, and then I will convert you.* He faid further, *The King will not own himfelf to be head of the Church.* And faid further, *You in* England *that fet up the* Dutch *to deftroy our Religion, fhall find that they fhall be the Men to* PULL DOWN YOURS.

Mr. *Stanley*, an Officer to the Duke of *Ormond* in *Ireland*, informed, That coming out of *Ireland* with one *Oriel*, (who owned himfelf of the Order of the *Jefuits*, and commiffioned from the Pope to be Lord Primate of *Ireland*, and Archbifhop of *Armah*) and falling into fome Difcourfe with him, he told him, ' That there had been a ' Difference between him and fome other of the *Jefuits* in *Ireland*, and that part of ' the Occafion was, that one Father *Walfh*, and fome other of the *Jefuits* there, did ' difpenfe with the Papifts in *Ireland*, to take the Oath of *Allegiance* and *Supremacy*, by ' virtue of a ftanding Commiffion from the Pope which he had to do it, during this ' King's Life; and *Oriel* thought they ought not to do it by virtue of the ftanding ' Commiffion, but fhould take a new Commiffion from the Pope every Year to do it. ' And likewife, ' That he brought eight Boys out of *Ireland*, whom he intended to carry ' to *Flanders*, to breed up in fome of the Colleges there. And at his taking Shipping to go for *Flanders*, he fhaked his Foot towards *England*, terming it *Egypt*, and faid, ' He would not return into *England*, till he came with fifty thoufand Men at his heels.

A *French* Merchant being a Papift living in St. *Michael*'s Lane, *London*, writes in a Letter to his Friend, *That a great number of Men and Arms were ready here, if thofe he wrote to were ready there.* He being, upon the Intercepting of this Letter, fearched; forty Fire-locks were found in his Houfe, ready loaden; which were carried to *Fifhmongers* Hall, a Month or two more before the Fire, and he committed to Prifon, but fince releafed.

A poor Woman retaining to one *Belfon*'s Houfe, a Papift, about *Darkin* in *Surrey*, was folicited, that fhe and her Husband would turn *Roman* Catholicks; which if they did voluntarily *Now*, they would be accepted of; but if they ftaid a little longer, they would be forced whether they would or no; and then they would not be efteemed. This was depofed before Sir *Adam Brown*, a Member of Parliament.

A Complaint being made againft a Sugar-Baker at *Vaux-hall*, his Houfe was fearched by Lieutenant Colonel *Luntly*, who found there feveral Guns, with fuch Locks, as no *Englifhman* who was at the taking of them, could difcharge; together with brafs Blunderbuffes and Fire-works, of a furious and burning nature: Trial being made of a fmall part of them, the Materials ware difcerned to be Sulphur, *Aquavitæ*, and Gun-powder, whatever elfe.

In a Letter to Sir *John Frederick*, and Mr. *Nathaniel Heron*, from *Horfham* in *Suffex*, the 8th of *September*, 1666. fubfcribed *Henry Chowne*; wherein is mentioned, that the faid *Henry Chowne* had thoughts to come to *London* that Week, but that they were in Diftraction there concerning the Papifts, fearing they would fhew themfelves all that Day: And that he had been to fearch a *Papift*'s Houfe within fix miles of that place.

place. He, with another Juftice of Peace met the Gentleman's Brother (who is a Prieft) going to *London*, whom they fearched, and found a Letter about him, which he had received that Morning from his Sifter, twenty miles off from him ; wherein is expreffed, *That a great Bufinefs is in hand, not to be committed to Paper, as the times be.*

Your Committee have thought fit to give no Opinion upon thefe Informations ; but leave the matter of Fact to your Judgments.

I am commanded to tell you, That your Committee have feveral other things of this nature under their Inquiry.

AS a further Inftance of the audacious and infolent Behaviour of thefe *Popifh* Recufants, take the following Copy of Verfes made, and then fcattered abroad by fome of their Party in *Weftminfter-hall*, and feveral other places about the City, and elfewhere in the Kingdom:

COvre le feu; *ye Hugonots*
That have fo branded us with Plots ;
And henceforth no more Bonfires make,
Till ye arrive the Stygian *Lake :*
For down ye muft, ye Hereticks,
For all your hopes, in fixty fix.
The hand againft you is fo fteady,
Your Babylon *is fal'n already.*
And if you will avoid that hap,
Return into your Mother's lap ;
The Devil a mercy is for thofe,
That holy Mother-Church oppofe:
Let not your Clergy you betray,
Great Eyes are ope, and fee the way;
Return in time if you will fave
Your Souls, your Lives, or ought you have.
And if you live till fixty feven,
Confefs you had fair Warning given.
Then fee in time, or ay be blind ;
Short time will fhew you what's behind.

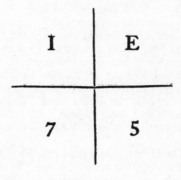

Dated the 5th Day of *November*, in the Year 1666, and the firft Year of the Reftoration of the Church of *Rome* in *England*.

NOt long after the burning of *London*, Mr. *Brook Bridges*, a young Gentleman of the *Temple*, as he was going to attend Divine Service in the *Temple*-Church, in a Pew there, found this following Paper ; which immediately, either by himfelf, or a Relation of his, was delivered to Sir *William Morrice*, one of his Majefty's principal Secretaries of State : The contents of the Paper are as follows.

A *Warning to* Proteftants.

I Who have been a *Papift* from my Infancy, till of late ; and in zeal for their horrid Principles, had too great a fhare in the firing of the City ; and did intend to do further mifchief to the *Proteftants*, of which I am now, and ever fhall be a Member ; do upon Abhorrence of that Villany and Religion that hath moved me to it, declare to all *Proteftants*, the approach of their fudden Ruin, that it may be prevented, if it be not too late.

When I, together with other Papifts, both *French*, *Irifh*, and *Englifh*, fired the City, others were employed to maffacre the *Proteftants*; we thinking thereby to deftroy the Heads of your Religion ; but the Maffacre was difappointed by the Fear of him who was the chief Agent in this Villany. And the Fire not having done all its Work, they

they have often endeavoured to fire the remaining part. They intend likewife to land the *French* upon you, to whofe Affiftance they all intend to come, and for that purpofe are ftored with Arms; and have fo far deceived the King, that they have the Command of moft part of the Army, and the Sea-ports. The *French* intend to land at *Dover,* that Garrifon being moft *Papifts:* And the *Papifts* in *England* have exprefs Command from *Rome,* to haften their Bufinefs before the next Parliament, and to difpatch. Therefore as you love your Lives and Fortunes, prevent your ruin, by difarming all the *Papifts* in *England,* efpecially C. L.——from the *Tower,* and the L. D. ——and all his Adherents and Soldiers from *Dover,* and by difarming all *Papifts.* I have fuch an Abhorrence, that I would willingly undergo any punifhment for it; and declare myfelf openly, were I not affured that I could do you more good in concealing my Name for the prefent. Delay not from following thefe Directions, as you love your Lives; and be not deceived by any pretences whatfoever.

An impartial Account of fome Informations taken before feveral Juftices of the Peace, concerning the feveral Fires happening of late in and near the City of London.

ABout the latter end of *June,* and in *July,* one *Jofeph Harrifon* came feveral times to the *Greyhound-Inn* in *Holborn,* pretending to enquire for Letters for himfelf; and about the beginning of *July,* comes into the faid Inn, and meeting Mr. *Atkins,* the Mafter of the faid Inn, he, the faid *Harrifon,* afked him for a Can of Beer; whereupon Mr. *Atkins* ordered his Man to draw two Cans, drinking one himfelf, and giving the other to *Harrifon:* After which, the faid *Harrifon* took Mr. *Atkins* by the Hand, and led him out of his own Yard into *Holborn,* and by the rails in the Street, the faid *Harrifon* advifed the faid *Atkins* to put off his Houfe and difpofe of his Goods as foon as he could; for within three Weeks or a Month, there would be great and dreadful Fires in and about *London.* Mr. *Atkins* afked him, How he knew fo? The faid *Harrifon* replied, *If you will not believe me, you may chufe:* and fo left him.

On *Monday, July* the 25th, Mr. *Atkins* his Wife hearing of the Fire at the *George-Inn* in *Southwark,* went to her Mother at the *Talbot-Inn* in *Southwark;* the back part of which faid Inn is adjoining to the *George-Inn,* and was likewife on fire; and being there, fhe efpied the aforefaid *Jofeph Harrifon* in the Yard, and remembring the aforefaid Advice to her Husband, defired fome Perfons that were next her, to lay hold on him; which being done, he was conveyed to a Foot-Company that ftood in Arms near the faid Inn, judging that the neareft place to fecure him. After which, Sir *John Smith,* one of the Sheriffs of *London,* was acquainted with the whole matter. Upon which he, with the L. C. went to the faid Company, and in the hearing of feveral, gave charge to the Captain of the faid Company, to keep him fafe, until they had time to examine him. After the Fire was put out, fome went to enquire after the Prifoner, and the Captain told them, *The* L. C. *had difcharged him.*

The next Day being *Tuefday,* a Perfon was informed that the faid *Harrifon* taught School in *Thread-Needle* Street, and that he boafted of his Deliverance; and faid, That the L. C. was pleafed to honour him fo far as to take him in his Barge with him to *White-hall,* and bid him but be patient a while, and he fhould have Satisfaction from the Perfons that had troubled him. But hearing where to find him, endeavours were ufed to retake him, and accordingly was accomplifhed on *Wednefday, July* 27. and had before the worfhipful Sir *John Frederick,* who fent him to *Bifhopfgate,* and ordered him to be brought before the Lord-Mayor and Court of Aldermen the next day to be examined. Before whom, were thefe following things proved againft him upon Oath.

 1. THat he hath had frequent Correfpondency with Jefuits and Papifts.
  2. *That he hath fpoke to feveral of his Acquaintance, to go with him to Popifh Meetings, declaring that he knew of many.*
  3. *That he hath been perfuaded to turn* Mendicant *Friar, and hath been offered a Stipend to turn to the* Romifh *Religion.*
  4. *That he knew there would be divers great and dreadful Fires in and about* London, *within a Month.*

                  5. *That*

5. *That he advised Friends to rid their hands of all their concerns in and about* London, *for there would be a great Consumption of Houses there.*

6. *That when he was in the custody of the Foot Company aforesaid,* Mr. Atkins *aforesaid, affirming to swear the former Article; he threatned him, if he did, it should cost him the best House he had.*

7. *That he said there were forty thousand* French Papists *lately come over, to his knowledge, besides many that were amongst us already.*

8. The Lord Mayor asking him, *Who persuaded him to turn Catholick?* He answered, *The King's Under-Barber,* Phillips.

After which, he told the Court, That when he was apprehended for these things, my *L. C.* discharged him, and took him with him in his Barge to *White-hall.* He further told the Court, That he was some time an Assistant to Mr. *Lovejoy,* School-master at *Canterbury,* and that he had Letters testimonial of his good Behaviour from the Dean of *Canterbury:* Upon which my Lord Mayor remembring that he had seen him with Mr. *Lovejoy,* and said, that Mr. *Lovejoy* told him, *That he was an idle Rogue.* And so he was committed to *Newgate.*

On *Saturday* the 30th of *July,* it was further deposed upon Oath by *Thomas Roe,* before Sir *John Frederick,* as follows.

The Information of Thomas Roe *of* Bernard's-Inn, *Gent. taken the* 3d *of* July, 1670, *by Sir* John Frederick, *Alderman, one of his Majesty's Justices of the Peace, in the City of* London, *upon Oath, as followeth.*

THōmas Roe saith, That he hath, for at least twelve or thirteen Years last past, been acquainted with one *Joseph Harrison,* who was examined lately at the *Guild-hall,* London, before the Honourable the Lord Mayor and Court of Aldermen, upon Suspicion of his being a Conspirator in the firing the City and Suburbs in several parts thereof.

Thomas Roe, and *Joseph Harrison,* having been School-fellows at *Eaton* College, and being thereby acquainted, *Joseph Harrison* hath several times lately been with him, and advised him to withdraw his Concerns, and remove above twenty miles out of the City; for that the City, and twenty miles round, would be suddenly destroyed and laid waste, (or to that purpose.) Whereupon *Thomas Roe* asked him, Whether he were privy to any such Conspiracy, or concern'd in its Agitation? pressing him with divers Arguments to discover what he was acquainted with of that kind. *Harrison* replied, That he had no personal and positive knowledge thereof. *Thomas Roe* demanded upon what ground then he did thus advise him? *Joseph Harrison* replied, That he was sometimes conversant among some *Papists,* and perceived a Plot or Design was carrying on by them against the City of *London,* and the Protestant Religion; which Plot or Design, said he, the Papists call, *The Game of Trap;* or, do you understand *Trap ad Crucem?* which is the Watch-word amongst them. Further, *Joseph Harrison* said, that he was informed of those things, by some *German* Protestants, and that he had offers of fifty Pounds *per annum,* made him by some *Jesuits* and *Papists,* to turn to their Religion; but he had refused it, and would not embrace the *Romish* Religion.

Thomas Roe further saith, That about five Weeks since, he walked through *New Cheap-side,* and from thence into *Mark-lane,* with *Joseph Harrison,* in company with Mr. *Mosely,* (a Gentleman belonging to *Bernard's-Inn* likewise) and one of his Acquaintance, together with another Man, a stranger to *Thomas Roe.* Upon their first associating, *Harrison* said unto him, That he would not discover himself to be an *Englishman,* but pretend himself to be a *German* or *Italian;* (whether of the two he doth not well remember) and that he might not detect himself, spake in the Company as occasion offered, in *Latin.* But leaving the place where they tarried in *Mark-lane,* going towards *Bishopsgate-street,* Mr. *Harrison* told Mr. *Roe* secretly, That he believed that Mr. *Mosely* understood the Game of *Trap,* by some Signs he had observed from him, and that he would try him. Then going all together into a house, about the end of *Threadneedle-street,* Mr. *Harrison* (having by this time discovered himself to be an *Englishman,*) said *Trap,* and made a Cross over his Face with his Finger, directing himself

N

to

to Mr. *Mosely*; whereupon Mr. *Mosely* did also say *Trap*, crossing his Forehead and Face two or three times, and with a quick motion drew his Finger over his own Throat. Upon which Mr. *Roe* asked Mr. *Mosely* what was the meaning of *Trap?* But he refused to tell. Mr. *Roe* urging him again, he replied, he would not; saying, You are not of my Religion. Then Mr. *Mosely* asked Mr. *Harrison* what his Name was? (for he knew him not by Name;) he answered, *Harrison*. Mr. *Mosely* replied, I never saw your Name. Mr. *Harrison* made answer, It is *Don Olanso del Harrisonio*; if so, saith Mr. *Mosely*, I have seen your Name.

After this, Mr. *Mosely* and the other stranger being parted, and Mr. *Roe* and Mr. *Harrison* being alone; said *Harrison*, I told you Mr. *Mosely* did understand *Trap*; you may see there is a List of the *Trap-Gamesters*. Now whether Mr. *Mosely*'s Imitation of Mr. *Harrison* was feigned or real, Mr. *Roe* could not distinguish: But as they two were passing through *Cheapside* homewards, Mr. *Harrison* looking upon the New Buildings, said, To what purpose do they build this poor City, it will be again destroyed; at the same time he pointed at two several Persons, saying, That is a *Trap-Gamester*, and there goes another *Trap-Gamester*.

Mr. *Roe* further informs, That since the last Term, Mr. *Harrison* told him, he would write all the rogueries of the *Trap-Game* and *Gamesters* in a *Play*; and that he would undertake to shew him twenty six Papists Meetings in and about the City and Suburbs of *London*; but said he, some of them are very private, and if you be discovered not to be a Papist, you will peradventure be poisoned or stabb'd.

Mr. *Roe* doth further say, That when the said *Harrison* advised him to remove with all his Concerns about twenty miles from *London*, that the said *Roe* asked him if *Windsor* were not far enough, it being both their native place, and about the distance? The said *Harrison* answered, Not; reflecting upon the Castle. And further, *Harrison* told Mr. *Roe*, That the Jesuits could, by a Composition of Ingredients, make such a matter, the fume of which would corrupt any Man's Intellects; and that he, the said *Harrison*, could do it.

A faithful Account of the apprehending of a Scotsman, *some time since, by* William Colburne, *at the* Cross-Keys *in* Fleet-street, *as followeth.*

A *Scotchman* pretending great respect he had for *William Colburne* aforesaid, came to him, and advised him, That by all means he should remove his Goods out of *London*, and dispose of his House. *William Colburne* asked him, For what reason? The *Scotchman* replied, Because that he, with many others, were employed to set the remainder of *London* on fire; and that they would set it on fire in several places at one time: And *Chancery-lane-end* (which is near the aforesaid *Colburne*'s house) they intended to set first on fire. Upon which, *William Colburne* apprehended him; and being brought to his Trial, he was sentenced to stand in the Pillory; and did accordingly, three times; once at the end of *Chancery-lane*, and twice in, or about the *Old Exchange*.

Much more might be said, but that our aim is, to be as brief as is consistent with the truth of the matter of fact in our Narrative. Therefore we refer any that desire further Satisfaction, in every particular, to *William Colburne* aforesaid, who will fully inform them.

An Account of the firing of Mr. Delanoy's *House, near* Pepper-Alley, *in* Southwark, January 1679-80, *by* John Satterthwait, *a Papist, as appears by the Oath of* Margaret Clarke, *then Servant to Mr.* Delanoy, *who was drawn in by the said* Satterthwait, *to assist him in the burning of her Master's House, and suffered Death for the same.*

I *Margaret Clarke*, being shortly to suffer Death for that which I have deserved, and am much humbled for, and desire to lie low before God, under the sense of my own Guilt, do give the World an Account of the truth of my Case; for I would not be guilty

guilty of a Lye, now I am to appear before my Judge within a few Minutes. Therefore I do say, and shall declare the truth of the matter, as I shall answer it before my Lord and Judge.

Upon the 26th of *January*, 1679-80, *John Satterthwait* came to me, as I was going out of my Master's Gate, and did desire me to tell him whether my Master and Mistress were at home? And I answered him, *No.* And he told me, That he hoped he should have an Opportunity to speak with me, for he had something to say. And I answered him, if he had any thing to say, I should be so civil to give him the hearing when I had time, (for then I was in haste.) Then he came, the next Day, with the same request; and I returned the Answer. Then the third time, being *Wednesday*, he came again, and used great Importunity; and expressed some Kindnesses, as if he had been a Suitor; and prevailed with me to go into the *Burrough* with him to an Ale-house, where were two Men more of his Company: And after some little Discourse, he propounded to me this wicked and horrid Design, which I was to have been engaged in with them; that is, to let them into my Master's house, to set it on fire: And for a Reward, they promised me two thousand Pounds; which Sum I was to receive at the *Fleece*-Tavern in *Holborn*, enquiring for a Room in the said Tavern, called the figure *Nine*. Then coming out of the Alehouse, they would fain have had me away with them, saying, *Come let us take Coach, and go into* Fleet-street; *for,* said they, *there we have a Priest of ours, who lodges at a Grocer's, that shall confess you, and give you the Sacrament.* I told him, I could not possibly go then.

So this *John Satterthwait* went homewards with me, almost to my Master's house; and as we went along, he charged me that I should not divulge it to any Person in the World living; for if I did, I should certainly die for it, (and that quickly) in this World, and be damned in the other.

Then he came on the next Day, and gave me the same Charge to keep it secret.

And then, on *Saturday*, he came and enquired of me, the best time that he might come to do this most horrid and devilish Action; saying, *Would not four or five of the Clock be a good time?* And I said, *Yes.*

Accordingly he came, and conveyed himself into the Dye-house, or thereabouts, while nine or ten of the Clock that Evening; about which time the Fire was discovered.

Whereupon, with the fear and dread he had put upon me, I did deny it to the Company that came in to quench it; but after that, he was there, whom I saw amongst the rest of the Company: But I had much horror upon my Conscience, and after some short time, I confessed the whole Crime, for which I now die. And my Examination before Justice *Reading*, and Justice *Freeman*, was all true.

And this I affirm, and do desire all Protestants to believe, that *John Satterthwait* kindled those three Fires in my Master's House: First, in the Dye-house by the Pump: Secondly, in the Buttery: And, thirdly in the Garret. Which last Fire he kindled, whilst the People were putting out the other.

See the large Account of this, called, *A Warning to Servants, and a Caution to Protestants,* printed in the Year 1680.

An Account of the firing Mr. Robert Bird's *House, in* Fetter-Lane, April *the* 10th, 1679, *by the persuasion of* Nicholas Stubbs, *a Papist.*

ELizabeth Oxley, Servant to Mr. *Robert Bird*, upon her Examination saith, That about *Michaelmas* last, she was acquainted with *Nicholas Stubbs*, who had several times used many persuasions to turn her Papist; and after her shewing a liking to it, and that he supposed she embraced that persuasion, in his Discourse to her at several times, he told her, that before the 28th of *June* next, she should see all the Protestants destroyed that were in *England*; that the Pope should be King over *England*, that all that would turn to the Popish Religion, should live far better than now they did; that all the Land were Hereticks, and it were a meritorious Act to destroy them; and that all such as were Papists, should have Marks upon their Hats, whereby to distinguish them from Protestants, that they might not be destroyed amongst them: Adding, that the Nation do believe that all things will be over before the 23d Day of *June*, but they would be deceived, for all should be destroyed at or before that time. That the D. of Y. was the bravest Prince living, and that he was gone out of the Kingdom, lest the Hereticks should cut off his Head, and he would not return till they

were

were deftroyed ; that the Lords in the *Tower* would not one of them fuffer, for they would come off well enough, being to be tried by the Lords; and that the Scaffolds were fet up for fafhion fake. That fhe telling the faid *Stubbs* that fhe was hired to live with one Mr. *Bird* about the middle of *Fetter-lane*, he ufed perfuafions to her at feveral times to fet fire on her Mafter's houfe ; telling her, if fhe would do it, he would give her 5 *l.* and gave her half a Crown, and faid, he would have other Houfes in *Holborn* fired at the fame time by others : That fhe being with the faid *Stubbs* on *Sunday* before the faid Fire, promifed to fire her Mafter's Houfe on *Thurfday* or *Friday* Night following, and accordingly on *Thurfday* Night, fhe took a Candle and fet fire to her Mafter's Papers in his Study, which were in a kind of a Prefs ; and they being on a light fire, fhe fhut the Doors, and went up Stairs into her own Chamber, in the top of the Houfe, and packed up her own things, and undreffed herfelf, left her Mafter fhould fufpect her, and there ftaid till a great knocking was at the Door, and the Watchmen crying out Fire ; whereupon fhe run down Stairs and cried Fire, and her Mafter gave her the Keys to open the Door ; which done, all hands were employed to quench the Fire. And fhe faith, fhe did not fet fire on her Mafter's houfe out of any Malice to him, nor with Intent to rob him, but meerly to carry on the Defign which *Stubbs* had propofed to her, and out of hopes of his reward.

Nicholas Stubbs, upon his Examination, owns, and fets forth to have ufed Difcourfes to the faid *Elizabeth*, as fhe declareth in her Examinations ; and faith, he did perfuade her to fire her Mafter's houfe, and was to give her five Guineas for doing it, befides half a Crown in hand : And faith, that one Father *Gyfford* a Prieft, and his Confeffor, had put him upon this Bufinefs, and told him it was no fin to fire all the houfes of *Hereticks* and *Hugonots.*

That he acquainted *Flower*, alias *Darby*, and one *Roger*   another *Irifhman* that lodged at the Coach and Horfes in the fame Street. That the faid Father *Gyfford* promifed him 100 *l.* for the fame, and told him he was to have the Money from the Church. That they ufed to meet the faid *Gyfford* and other two Perfons in St. *James's* Fields in the dark of the Evening, and to difcourfe of thefe Matters ; and that the feveral Informations that he had given the faid *Elizabeth Oxley*, he had from the faid Father *Gyfford* ; and faith *Flower* and *Roger*   told the faid *Stubbs*, they would carry on the faid Fire, and that they had Fire-Balls for that purpofe, and that they would fire other Houfes in *Holborn* at the fame time : That he was at the Fire in the *Temple*, but was not engaged to do any thing in it. And faid, that *Gyfford* told him that there were *Englifh, French,* and *Irifh Roman* Catholicks enough in *London*, to make a very good Army ; and that the King of *France* was coming with 60,000 Men, under pretence to fhew the Dauphin his Dominions ; but it was to lay his Men at *Diep, Bulloign, Calais* and *Dunkirk*, to be in an hour's warning landed in *England* ; and he doubted not but it would be by the middle of *June*, and by that time, all the Catholicks here will be in readinefs ; all were to rife in order to bring him in. That the Papifts here were to be diftinguifhed by marks in their Hats ; that the faid Father *Gyfford* doubted not but he fhould be an Abbot or a Bifhop, when the work was over, for the good fervice he hath done. That at their Meeting, Father *Gyfford* ufed to tell them, it was no more Sin to kill a Heretick, than a Dog ; and that they did God good Service, in doing what mifchiefs they could, by firing their houfes. That it was well Sir *Edmondbury Godfrey* was murdered, for he was their devilifh Enemy ; That *Coleman* was a Saint in Heaven for what he had done. And faith, he is fearful he fhall be murdered for this Confeffion ; Father *Gyfford* having fworn him to fecrecy, and told him he fhould be damn'd if he made any Difcovery, and fhould be fure to be killed ; and that he fhould take the Oaths, becaufe he was a Houfe-keeper ; and that it was no Sin. And faith, That *Gyfford* and *Roger*   told him, when their Forces meet, about the middle of *June*, then have at the————

VOTES

VOTES and ADDRESSES

Of the Honourable

Houſe of Commons

ASSEMBLED IN

PARLIAMENT,

Made this preſent Year 1673.

Concerning *Popery* and other *Grievances.*

March 29. 1673.
The Parliament's Addreſs to his Majeſty, for the Removal of Grievances in England *and* Ireland.

WE your Majeſty's moſt loyal Subjects the Commons, in this preſent Parliament aſſembled, conceiving ourſelves bound in neceſſary Duty to your Majeſty, and in diſcharge of the Truſt repoſed in us, truly to inform your Majeſty of the eſtate of your Kingdom : And though we are abundantly ſatisfied that it hath been your royal will and pleaſure that your Subjects ſhould be governed according to the laws and cuſtoms of this Realm, yet finding that, contrary to your Majeſty's gracious Intention, ſome grievances and abuſes are crept in ; We crave leave humbly to repreſent them to your Majeſty's knowledge and deſire.

1. That the impoſition of 12 *d. per* chaldron upon Coals, for the providing of Convoys, by virtue of an order from Council, dated the 15th of *May,* 1672, may be recalled, and all Bonds taken by virtue thereof, cancelled.

2. That your Majeſty's Proclamation of the 24th of *December,* 1672, for preventing of diſorders which may be committed by Soldiers, and whereby the Soldiers now in your Majeſty's Service, are in a manner exempted from the ordinary courſe of Juſtice, may likewiſe be recalled.

3. And whereas great complaints have been made out of ſeveral parts of this Kingdom, of divers abuſes committed in quartering of Soldiers, That your Majeſty would be pleaſed to give order to redreſs thoſe abuſes ; and in particular, that no Soldiers be hereafter quartered in any private Houſes ; and that due Satisfaction may be given to the Inn-keepers or Victuallers where they lie, before they remove.

4. And ſince the continuance of Soldiers in this Nation, will neceſſarily produce many Inconveniences to your Majeſty's Subjects, We do humbly preſent it as our Petition and Advice, that when this preſent War is ended, all your Soldiers which have been raiſed ſince the laſt Seſſion of Parliament, may be disbanded.

5. That your Majeſty would be likewiſe pleaſed to conſider of the irregularities and abuſes in preſſing Soldiers, and to give order for the prevention thereof for the future.

6. And although it hath been the courſe of former Parliaments to deſire redreſs in their grievances before they proceeded to give a ſupply ; yet we have ſo full Aſſurance of your Majeſty's tenderneſs and compaſſion towards your People, that we humbly proſtrate ourſelves at your Majeſty's feet, with theſe our Petitions, deſiring your Majeſty to take them into your princely Conſideration, and to give ſuch Orders for the relief of your Subjects, and the removing theſe preſſures, as ſhall ſeem beſt to your royal Wiſdom.

O   *Addreſs*

Address touching Ireland.

WE Your Majesty's most loyal Subjects, the Commons, in this present Parliament assembled, taking into Consideration the great Calamities which have formerly befallen your Majesty's Subjects of the Kingdom of *Ireland*, from the Popish Recusants there, who for the most part are profest enemies to the Protestant Religion, and the *English* Interest, and how they make use of your Majesty's gracious Disposition and Clemency, are at this time grown more insolent and presumptuous than formerly, to the apparent danger of that Kingdom, and your Majesty's Protestant Subjects there, the Consequence whereof may likewise prove very fatal to this your Majesty's Kingdom of *England*, if not timely prevented : And having seriously weighed what remedies may be most properly applied to those growing Distempers, do in all humility present your Majesty with these our Petitions.

1. That for the establishment and quieting the possessions of your Majesty's Subjects in that Kingdom, your Majesty would be pleased to maintain the Act of Settlement, and explanatory Act thereupon, and to recall the Commission of Enquiry into *Irish* Affairs, bearing date the 17th of *January* last, as containing many new and extraordinary Powers, not only to the prejudice of particular Persons, whose Estates and Titles are thereby made liable to be questioned ; but in a manner to the overthrow of the Acts of Settlement : And if pursued, may be the occasion of great charge and attendance to many of your Subjects in *Ireland*, and shake the peace and security of the whole.

2. That your Majesty would give Order that no Papist be either continued or hereafter admitted to be Judges, Justices of the Peace, Sheriffs, Coroners, or Mayors, Sovereigns, or Portrieves in that Kingdom.

3. That the titular Popish Archbishops, Bishops, Vicars-General, Abbots, and all other exercising ecclesiastical Jurisdiction by the Pope's authority, and in particular *Peter Talbot*, pretended Archbishop of *Dublin*, for his notorious disloyalty to your Majesty, and disobedience and contempt of your Laws, may be commanded by Proclamation forthwith to depart out of *Ireland*, and all other your Majesty's Dominions, or otherwise to be prosecuted according to Law. And that all Convents, Seminaries, and publick Popish Schools may be dissolved and suppressed, and the secular Priests commanded to depart, under the Penalty.

4. That no *Irish* Papist be admitted to inhabit in any part of that Kingdom, unless duly licensed according to the aforesaid Acts of Settlement ; and that your Majesty would be pleased to recall your Letters of the 26th of *February*, 1671. and the Proclamation thereupon, whereby general Licence is given to such Papists as inhabit in Corporations there.

5. That your Majesty's Letters of the 28th of *September* 1672, and the Order of Council thereupon, whereby your Subjects are required not to prosecute any Actions against the *Irish*, for any wrongs or injuries committed during the late Rebellion, may likewise be recalled.

6. That Colonel *Talbot* (who hath notoriously assumed to himself the title of *Agent of the* Roman *Catholicks in* Ireland) be immediately dismissed out of all Command, military and civil, and forbidden access to your Majesty's Court.

7. That your Majesty would be pleased from time to time, out of your princely Wisdom, to give such further order and directions to the Lord Lieutenant, or other Governor of *Ireland*, for the time being, as may best conduce to the Encouragement of the *English* Planters and *Protestant* Interest there, and the suppression of the insolencies and disorders of the *Irish* Papists there.

These our humble Desires we present to your Majesty, as the best means to preserve the peace and safety of that your Kingdom, which hath been so much of late in danger by the practices of the said *Irish* Papists, particularly *Richard* and *Peter Talbot* ; and we doubt not but your Majesty will find the happy effects thereof, to the great satisfaction and security of your Majesty's Person and Government, which of all earthly things is most dear to your Majesty's most loyal Subjects.

Ordered, *October* 20, 1673.

THat an Address be made to his Majesty, by such Members of this House, as are of his Majesty's Privy Council, to acquaint his Majesty, that it is the humble desire of this House, that the intended Marriage of his Royal Highness with the Dutchess of *Modena* be not consummated ; and that he may not be married to any Person, but of the *Protestant* Religion.

And the same Day the Parliament was prorogued till *Monday* next.

The Address of the Parliament to his Majesty.

WE Your Majesty's most humble and loyal Subjects, the Commons, in this present Parliament assembled, being full of Assurance of your Majesty's gracious Intentions to provide for the establishment of Religion, and the preservation of your People in peace and security; and foreseeing the dangerous Consequences which may follow the Marriage of his Royal Highness the Duke of *York* with the Princess of *Modena*, or any other of the *Popish* Religion, we hold ourselves bound in conscience and duty to represent the same to your sacred Majesty; not doubting but these constant testimonies which we have given your Majesty of our true and loyal Affections to your sacred Person, will easily gain a belief, that these our humble Desires proceed from hearts still full of the same Affections toward your sacred Majesty, and with intentions to establish your Royal Government upon those true Supports of the *Protestant* Religion, and the hearts of your People; with all humility desiring your Majesty to take the same into your princely Consideration, and to relieve your Subjects from those fears and apprehensions which at present they lie under from the Progress which hath been made in that Treaty.

We do therefore humbly intreat your Majesty to consider, that if this Match do proceed, it will be a means to disquiet the minds of your *Protestant* Subjects at home, and to fill them with endless jealousies and discontents; and will bring your Majesty into such Alliances abroad, as will prove highly prejudicial, if not destructive to the Interest of the very *Protestant* Religion itself.

And we find by sad experience, that such Marriages have encreased and encouraged Popery in this Kingdom, and given opportunity to Priests and Jesuits to propagate their opinions, and seduce great Numbers of your Majesty's Subjects.

And we do already observe how much the Party is animated with the hopes of this Match, which were lately discouraged by your gracious Concessions in the last meeting in this Parliament.

That we greatly fear this may be an occasion to lessen the affections of the People to his Royal Highness, who is so nearly related to the Crown; and whose Honour and Esteem we desire may always be entirely preserved.

That for another Age more at the least, this Kingdom will be under the continual apprehensions of the growth of Popery, and the danger of the *Protestant* Religion.

Lastly, We consider that this Princess having so near a relation and kindred to many eminent Persons of the Court of *Rome*, may give them great opportunities to promote their Designs, and carry on their Practices among us, and by the same means penetrate into your Majesty's most secret Counsels, and more easily discover the State of the whole Kingdom.

And finding that by the opinions of very learned Men, it is generally admitted that such treaties and contracts by *Proxies* are dissolvable, of which there are several Instances to be produced; We do in all humbleness beseech your Majesty to put a stop to the Consummation of this intended Marriage.

And this we do the more importunately desire, because we have not yet the happiness to see any issue of your Majesty's, that may succeed in the Government of these Kingdoms, which Blessings we most heartily pray Almighty God in his due time to bestow upon your Majesty and these Kingdoms, to the unspeakable joy and comfort of all your Majesty's Subjects, who desire nothing more than to continue under the reigns of your Majesty, and your royal Posterity for ever.

October 30. 1673.

Mr. Secretary *Coventry* brought from his Majesty an Answer to the Address presented to him, touching the Duke of *York*, as followeth.

C. R.

HIS Majesty having received an Address from the House of Commons, presenting their humble desire, that the intended Marriage betwixt his Royal Highness and the Princess of *Modena*, may not be consummated, commanded this Answer to be returned; *That he perceived the House of Commons have wanted a full Information of this matter, the Marriage not being barely intended, but compleated according to the forms used amongst Princes, and by his royal Consent and Authority; nor could he in the least suppose it disagreeable to his House of Commons, his Royal Highness having been in the view of the World for several Months engaged in a treaty of Marriage with another Catholick Princess, and yet a Parliament held during the time, and not the least exception taken at it.*

An

An Addreſs ordered to be preſented to his Majeſty, concerning a Marriage between his Royal Highneſs and the Princeſs of *Modena,* and a Committee appointed for that purpoſe.

A Committee appointed for preparing a Bill for a general Teſt, to diſtinguiſh between *Proteſtants* and *Papiſts*; and thoſe that ſhall refuſe to take it, be incapable to enjoy any Office, military or civil; or to ſit in either Houſes of Parliament, or to come within five miles of the Court.

The Houſe adjourned till *Monday.*

October 31, 1673.

Reſolved, *That the Houſe, conſidering the preſent Condition of the Nation, will not take into any further debate, the conſideration of any aid or ſupplies, or charge upon the Subjects, before the time of payment of the eighteen Months aſſeſſment, granted by a late Act of Parliament, entitled,* An Act for raiſing the Sum of twelve hundred thirty eight thouſand and ſeven hundred and fifty Pounds, for the ſupply of his Majeſty's preſent occaſions, *be expended*; *except it ſhall appear that the obſtinacy of the* Dutch *ſhall render it neceſſary*; *nor before this Kingdom be effectually ſecured from Popery and Popiſh Councils, and the other preſent Grievances be redreſſed.* And

An Addreſs ordered to be preſented to his Majeſty, for a Faſt to be obſerved throughout the Nation, and a Committee appointed for that purpoſe.

A further Addreſs to be preſented to his Majeſty, concerning the Marriage of the Duke of *York,* with the Dutcheſs of *Modena*; and the Privy Counſellors of this Houſe, to attend his Majeſty to know his pleaſure when he will be attended therewith.

And they adjourned till To-morrow in the Afternoon.

November 3. 1673.

A Report from the Committee appointed for that purpoſe was made for an Addreſs to be preſented to his Majeſty, to appoint a general Faſt to be obſerved throughout the Nation, and the Concurrence of the Lords to be deſired thereto.

The ſtanding Army voted a Grievance.

A Committee appointed to prepare an Addreſs to be preſented to his Majeſty, to ſhew how this ſtanding Army is a Grievance; and then adjourned till three of the clock in the Afternoon. Mr. Speaker and the Houſe went to attend his Majeſty at *Whitehall* with the Addreſs; who returning, Mr. Speaker reports, *That it was a matter he would take into his preſent Conſideration, and would return ſpeedily an Anſwer.*

And then the Houſe adjourned till To-morrow morning, at eight of the Clock.

November 4, 1673.

The Houſe of Commons having ordered an Addreſs to be made to his Majeſty, ſhewing that the ſtanding Army was a grievance, and a burden to the Nation; and did intend that Day to wait on his Majeſty to preſent it: But his Majeſty was in his Robes in the Houſe of Peers, and the Lords haſtning to him, the Black Rod being ſent to the Commons Houſe to command the Speaker and the Commons to come to his Majeſty to the Houſe of Peers; but it ſo happened, that the Speaker and the Black Rod met both at the Commons Houſe Door; the Speaker being within the Houſe, the Door was commanded to be ſhut, and they cried to the Chair; others ſaid the Black Rod was at the Door, to command them to wait on the King to the Houſe of Peers: but the Speaker was hurried to the Chair. Then was moved,

1. *That our Alliance with* France *was a Grievance.*
2. *That the evil Counſel about the King, was a Grievance to this Nation.*
3. *That the Lord* Lauderdale *was a Perſon that was a Grievance to this Nation, and not fit to be entruſted or employed in any Office or Place of Truſt, but to be removed.*

Whereupon they cried, *To the Queſtion.* But the Black Rod knocking very earneſtly at the Door, the Speaker roſe out of the Chair, and went away in a confuſion.

A
LETTER
FROM A
PARLIAMENT-MAN to his FRIEND,

Concerning the Proceedings of the

Houfe of Commons

This laft Seffion, begun the 13th of *October*, 1675.

S I R,

I See you are greatly fcandaliz'd at our flow and confufed *Proceedings*. I confefs you have caufe enough, but were you but within thefe walls for one half day, and faw the ftrange make and complexion that this Houfe is of, you would wonder as much that ever you wondered at it: For we are fuch a pied Parliament, that none can fay of what colour we are ; for we confift of old Cavaliers, old Round-heads, indigent Courtiers, and true Country Gentlemen ; the two latter are moft numerous, and would in probability bring things to fome iffue, were they not clogged with the humorous uncertainties of the former. For the old Cavalier grown aged, and almoft paft his Vice, is damnable godly, and makes his doating piety more a plague to the World, than his youthful debauchery was: For he is fo much a Biggot to the Bifhops, that he forces his loyalty to ftrike fail to his Religion, and could be content to pare the Nails a little of the civil Government, fo you would but let him fharpen the ecclefiaftical Talons ; which behaviour of his fo exafperates the Round-head, that he, on the other hand, cares not what encreafes the intereft of the Crown receives, fo he can but diminifh that of the Mitre : fo that the Round-head had rather enflave the Man, than the Confcience ; the Cavalier rather the Confcience than the Man, there being a fufficient ftock of Animofity, as proper matter to work upon.

Upon thefe therefore the Courtier mutually plays : For if any anticourt Motion be made, he gains the Round-head either to oppofe or abfent, by telling them, *If they will join him now, he will join with them for Liberty of Confcience.* And when any Affair is ftarted on the behalf of the Country, he affures the Cavaliers, *If they will then ftand by him, he will then join with them in promoting a Bill againft the Fanaticks.* Thus play they on both hands, that no motion of a publick nature is made, but they win upon the one or other of them ; and by this art gain a Majority againft the Country Gentlemen, which otherwife they would never have : Wherefore it were happy that we had neither Round-head nor Cavalier in the Houfe ; for they are each of them fo prejudicate one againft the other, that their fitting here fignifies nothing but their foftering their old Venom, and lying at catch to fnap every Advantage to bear down each other, though it be in the deftruction of their Country.

For if the Round-heads bring in a good Bill, the old Cavalier oppofes it, for no other reafon, but becaufe they brought it. So that as the poor *Englifh* Silk-weavers are fain to hire a *Frenchman* to fell their Ribbons, fo are the Round-heads a Cavalier, to move for thofe Bills they defire fhould pafs ; which fo fowers the Round-head, that he revenges that carriage upon any Bill the Cavalier offers, and the rage and the paffion of the one and the other, are fo powerful, that it blinds them both, that neither perceives

P
ceives

ceives the advantage they give the Courtier, to abuse both them and their Country too: so that if either of them do any good, it is only out of pure envy against the other. Thus you see how we are yoked, and seeing this, you may cease your Admiration that we offer at all, and do just nothing.

Nor is this Division alone of the House, all we have to lament, (for Death, that common Cure, does now every day lessen this evil) but that which is more our Misery, is, that those Gentlemen who are truly for the good of their Country, will not be persuaded to stand upon the sure basis of rational Principles (like Workmen too presumptive of their Judgments, that will not build by rule) but rather affect the most loose standing, on the sandy Foundation of Heat and Humour: By reason of which, they often do as much harm as good, and yet perceive it not; this is the sore evil we are under. For I would not doubt the Country's carrying it from the Court in every Vote, let the Courtiers use all the Art they could, would the Country Gentlemen but give themselves the trouble to inform their Understandings a little, and not suffer themselves to be hurried by a heedless inadvertency into vulgar Notions. Which, if well examined, are directly contrary to their honest Intentions; for lack of which, they totally mistake their Interests, fall foul on their Friends, support their Enemies, and carry on the designs of the Court, whilst they aim at the service of their Country. For if they would take the pains but to think what is the greatest Enemy in the World, *English* Law and Liberty always had, still hath, and ever must have; it may be the result of such a thought would say, it was encroaching Prerogative. Well, if then they would but beg from themselves but so much seriousness, as to think this second thought, to check this Prerogative, which is so dangerous an enemy to our Laws and Liberties, peradventure that thought would answer, *In suppressing all they could, its Creatures and Dependants, and supporting such, whose Interest it is to keep Prerogative within its just bounds.* Now could they but be prevailed with to think a third thought, it would land them at the full and satisfactory Solution of the Question, and will hold in every thing. But I will put it in a case wherein we are most apt to err, and wherein we reckon it no less than piety to play the fool, to the end you may see how miserably we are cheated and abused, by sucking in the untried notions that Education, the arts of others, or our own ignorance have imposed upon us.

The third Thought therefore shall be this: *Which are most the creatures and supporters of boundless Prerogative, Prelates or dissenting Protestants?* The answer to which must, and can be no otherwise, *The Prelates.* Well then, if we would now reduce this to Practice, and say, *The greatest friends to Prerogative are the Prelates, the greatest Enemies to our Laws and Liberties is Prerogative.* The only way therefore to restrain Prerogative, is to do, *What?* To fortify and strengthen the Yoke of the Prelates over the neck of the People? *No:* (Surely this were an odd and a barbarous kind of reasoning) *But to give liberty to dissenting Protestants, as the best means to keep up the ballance against boundless Prerogative.* For these must, and never can be otherwise (unless by accident, and by mistake) than Friends to Liberty: But the Prelates neither are, nor can be otherwise than Creatures to Prerogative, for all their Promotions, Dignities, and Domination depends upon it.

The same might be said concerning the only ancient and true strength of the Nation, the legal Militia, and a standing Army. The Militia must, and can never be otherwise than for *English* Liberty, because else it doth destroy itself; but a standing Force can be for nothing but Prerogative, by whom it hath its idle living and subsistance. I could instance also in many other particulars, but our inadvertency in this, is demonstration enough how much we are cheated by the common and hackney Notions imposed upon us? and this is almost the cause of all the Error we commit. For missing our true footing, you see we have run in the mistaken Notion of being for the Church so long, till we have almost destroyed the State, and advanced Prerogative so much by suppressing Nonconformity, that it's well nigh beyond our reach or power to put a check to it; and had not Time, and but an indifferent Observation, shewed us how much we were abused in this matter; and that a Lay-Conformist and a Fanatick, can live as quietly and neighbourly together (would the Prelates but suffer them) as any in the world; we had ruined ourselves past all recovery. For by our buoying up the Bishops in their harsh and irreconcileable Spirit, instead of healing we have so fed and nourished the Discontents throughout the Kingdom, that I think nothing keeps the Fire from flaming out afresh in another intestine War, but the bare circumstance of opportunity only; and how long that will be able to restrain Passions that are made wild by oppression, is worthy a very serious Consideration. And therefore there is hardly any thing more a wonder to wise men, than to see the Clergy

run

run at this rate upon the Diffenters: Wherefore fince the Nonconformifts have given fo large and ample a teftimony of their willingnefs to live peaceably, if yet notwith-standing the Clergy will not fuffer them to be quiet in their Families and their Hou-fes, I doubt, they may at one time or other, drive them into the Field, and then it may exceed their divine art to conjure them down again ; for he fees but little, that fees not the *Englifh* temper is better to be led than driven. And therefore I think it would not be more a vanity, to compel the Ladies to wear Queen *Elizabeth's* Ruff, than to force the Nonconformifts to be dreft in her Religion.

Nor yet are thefe all the Arts we are under: For we have a gang that huff, and bear themfelves high on the Country fide, but earn only for the Court ; thefe lay out their Craft in putting the Houfe upon little trifling things, and fpend and wafte the Mettle thereof, upon fuch pitiful piccadilloes, as 'tis next to fhame for an *Englifh* Parliament fo much as to mention. Thefe ftart a fierce Difpute about fome little matter, and keep a blufter as if none were fuch faithful Patriots as they, when they do it on purpofe only to while out the time, and thin the Houfe, by tiring the honeft Country Gentry in fo tedious, fruitlefs and trifling attendance. Do but move things worthy a Parliament ; as that *we may have our old known Rights of annual Parliaments afcertained:* That *none that are or fhall be bribed by any Place or Office, fhall ever fit in this Houfe:* That *Parliaments ought not to be prorogued, adjourned, or diffolved, till all Petitions are heard, and the Grievances of the People redreffed* ; with many things more of as great importance: O then, forfooth, their pretended Loyalty (which in plain *Englifh* is eafily underftood) will not abide fuch unmannerly and clownifh Debates as thefe, and twenty fuch little fhreds of Nonfenfe are impertinently urged inftead of Argument.

But further, thefe Country-Court Engines, after they have taken the meafures of the Houfe, at the opening of every Seffion, by our thanks for the gracious Speech, which being the true pulfe of the Houfe, if it happen to come fo hard as fpeaks us but faint and cool to the one thing neceffary, (*the matter of Money*) then they know what will follow, that the Court will get no Grift that Seffions ; and though the Court in Indignation could turn them home on the morrow, yet it muft confult its Reputation a little, reftrain its Refentments, and fuffer them to fit about fix Weeks, or two Months, and then they affure the Court, fince they can get no good by them, they fhall take no harm ; and therefore to ftop them from fome worthy Undertaking, they by their feigned zeal againft Court-Corruptions, put them upon impeaching fome Treafurer, Counfellor, or Minifter of State ; and having fpent half our time about this, the reft is fpent for the Clergy upon Church-work; which we have been fo often put upon, and tired with, thefe many Seffions: Though Partiality unbecomes a Parliament, who ought to lay the whole Body that we reprefent alike eafy, Nonconformifts, as well as Conformifts, for we were chofen by both, and with that Intention, that we fhould opprefs neither. To lay one part therefore of the Body on a Pillow, and the other on a Rack, forts our Wifdom little, but our Juftice worfe. You now fee all our Shapes, fave only the Indigents, concerning whom I need fay but little, for their Votes are publickly faleable for a Guinea, and a Dinner every Day in the Week, unlefs the Houfe be upon Money or a Minifter of State: For that is their harveft ; and then they make their Earnings fuit the Work they are about, which inclines them moft conftantly as fure *Clients* to the Court. For what with gaining the one and faving the other, they now and then adventure a Vote on the Country fide ; but the dread of diffolution makes them ftrait tack about. The only thing we are obliged to them for, is, that they do nothing *Gratis,* but make every Tax as well chargeable to the Court, as burthenfome to the Country, and fave no Man's Neck, but they break his Purfe. And yet when all is faid, did but the Country Gentry rightly underftand the Intereft of Liberty, let the Courtiers and Indigents do what they could, they might yet at laft deferve the Name of a worthy *Englifh* Parliament ; which that we may do, is not more paffionately your Defire, than it alfo is of,

S I R,

Your moft humble

Servant,

T. E.

A

A
SPEECH
MADE BY
Sir William Scrogg,
ONE OF HIS

𝕸𝖆𝖏𝖊𝖘𝖙𝖎𝖊𝖘 𝕾𝖊𝖗𝖏𝖊𝖆𝖓𝖙𝖘 𝖆𝖙 𝕷𝖆𝖜.

To the Right Honourable the

Lord High Chancellor
Of *ENGLAND*;
AT HIS

Admiſſion to the Place of One of His Majeſty's Juſtices of the Court of *Common-Pleas.*

My Lord,

THAT the King's Favour is the Effect of the Duty I have paid him, (which your Lordſhip is pleaſed to call Service) is the moſt welcome and pleaſing part of his kindneſs; and I truſt we ſhall ſtill ſee ſuch Times, that no Man ſhall hope to have it, or keep it on any other account. The right application of rewards and puniſhments, is the ſteady juſtice of a Nation; where though the rewards of Kings exceed what a Subject can merit, they ſhould never reach him that demerits. To return good for evil may be an obligation of Charity, it is never of Bounty. And the taking off (as they call it) of an ambitious, and therefore a factious Man, by favours, is the worſt way to ſtop or open his Mouth; for he will whiſper one way louder, than he will ſpeak the other: And when you think you gain one Enemy, you make many.

On ſuch an occaſion as this, I think it very proper to give your Lordſhip ſome Account what Conſiderations I have had, in order to the diſcharge of my Duty in this Place, ſince the King's firſt intimations of his Pleaſure.

And that reſpects matters, either as they ſtand betwixt the King and his People, or betwixt Man and Man.

As for the firſt, I know that the Law gives ſuch Prerogatives to the King, that to endeavour more were to deſire worſe; and it gives to the People ſuch Liberties, that more would be licentious.

What then hath a Man to do that hath courage enough to be honeſt, but to apply his underſtanding to the miniſtration of thoſe Laws juſtly to both: wherein I may ſay, that the caſes will be rare that will be difficult in themſelves. They

may

may be made to from finifter caufes; when Men thinking to ferve a turn, or like *Pilate*, to pleafe the People, deliver up that which is right, to be crucified. Then they are fain to rack their fancies, to make good their faults. This makes fuch nice Diftinctions, and fuch ftrained Conftructions, till they leave nothing plain in the World. Whereas in truth, the Duty we owe to the King and his People, is like the Duty we owe to God, not hard to underftand, whatever it is to practife.

This Court, *My Lord,* 'tis true, is properly a Court of *Meum* and *Tuum*; where Prerogative and Liberty are feldom Plaintiffs or Defendants, but yet 'tis certain, that even in private caufes, matter of Government many times intervenes, and the Publick is concerned by confequence. And therefore I think it fair, and like *Englifh* honefty and plainnefs, fomething to unveil one's felf in that particular, that Men may know before-hand what they may expect. And herein I do declare, I would no more wrong or leffen the People's Liberties, than I would facrifice up my Son. But then I will no more derogate from the King's Prerogative, than I would betray my Father.

My Lord, In time when Faction is fo bold as to be bare-fac'd, and falfe and feditious News is openly talk'd, and greedily embraced; when the King's reafonable Demands are difputed, and turned into cavils, and thofe that oppofe them talk confidently; and thofe that fhould maintain them fpeak fearfully and tenderly; when the Reverence we owe to the King is paid to the People; the Government is befet, the King is in danger, and there is nothing wanting but Opportunity.

But when, to prevent that Opportunity, Men are afraid, and hold it dangerous to avoid the danger; when we dare not call a Crime by its right name; and for fome, find none; and a Mifchief muft be effected, before we will think it one: When dangerous Attempts are minc'd, and by fome trivial difference, Treafon is diftinguifhed into a Trefpafs; when Men are forward and ventrous enough in what thwarts the Government, but in fupporting it, feem grave and cautious, nice and timorous, and fo fill'd with Prudentials, till they are as wife as fear can make them: The Law is enervated, and becomes ufelefs to its greateft end, which is, the Prefervation of the whole.

'Tis true, in publick Caufes, the fame integrity is neceffary as in private; but that is but part of a Judge's Duty. He muft be magnanimous as well as virtuous. And I acknowledge it to be a main and principal part of my Duty, as it relates to the King and his People, with hearty Refolution to fupprefs all open Force and private Confederacies; not thinking any thing little that attempts the Publick Safety; for when the Motives are fmall, the Danger is greater; when Difcontents exceed their Caufes.

And for the Difcharge of my Duty betwixt Party and Party, it is impoffible to be performed without thefe two Cardinal Virtues, [Temper] and [Cleannefs of Hands.] Temper comprehends Patience, Humility, and Candor. It feems to me that faying, *Be quick to hear, and flow to fpeak,* was made on purpofe for a Judge. No direction can be apter, and no Character becomes him better: and he that would not be faid to have but one Ear, methinks fhould be afhamed to have none. And I appeal to your Lordfhips Experience, if a patient Attention, accompanied with indifferent Parts, and a Competency in the Law, with a Mind fairly difpofed for Information or Conviction, will not, as to Ufe and common Benefit, exceed the profoundeft Knowledge, and moft towering Underftanding, that is attended with an impetuous hafte, either out of a glory of fpeaking, or too great a fulnefs of himfelf.

And for Humility, though I will not fay that every impatient Man is proud; (becaufe that may arife from other Caufes) yet every proud Man is impatient, fometimes of Information, always of Contradiction; and he muft be violent to maintain his own imperioufnefs.

Harfhnefs is a needlefs and unbecoming Provocation: It makes Men hate where they fhould fear and reverence: And yet by Gentlenefs I underftand not Tamenefs, but Moderation; not without Rebukes, but without Taunts.

For Corruption, that perverter of Law and Deftruction of Property, that leaves in the World neither *Bonum* nor *Equum*; for when he does Right, he does not Juftice; and he that fells Juftice, will fell Injuftice: 'Tis not only to be avoided, but abhorred; and not alone in its direct Approaches, but in Relatives and Servants, thofe By-ways of Bribery; and it becomes every Man fo manifeftly to deteft it, that it may fcare even the Attempt: For no Man is fufficiently fafe, unlefs to his power he avoids the Sufpicion as well as the Fault. Practice does

one

one, and that which makes me fpeak this, a publick Profeffion againft it, is the way to do the other.

And where Gifts prevail not ; yet if Fear, Relation or Popularity fway,'tis the fame thing. If there be a byafs put to a Man, it matters not of what 'tis made. Nay, thefe are worfe than corruption by money ; for there both fides may have the fame Tools, when a Man cannot make himfelf a-kin, nor his caufe popular.

And now give me leave, *my Lord,* to fhew why I thought it fit, nay extremely neceffary to fay fomething on the particulars I have mentioned.

Firft, To fatisfy your Lordfhip and the World, I undertake not this place without due confiderations of the duty belonging to it. Next, it is fome tie upon a Man not to commit thofe errors he hath in publick declaimed againft : for he muft add impudence to his crime, to have his own words fly in his face, with which every Man will upbraid, and no Man can excufe him.

My Lord, In a difcourfe on fuch an occafion as this, where Men are concerned in point of Intereft, (for fo they are when a Judge is made) my aim is not to fay what will pleafe their Humours, but what fhould fatisfy their Minds : Neither am I fo vain as to think I fhall do that with all ; nor much concerned though it fall out fo. If Reputation and a good Name can be got by doing my Duty, 'tis welcome ; but if it muft be fought by other arts, I will be no feeker : efpecially confidering that the applaufe of the Multitude, that contingent judge of good and bad, rather attends the Vain than the Virtuous, and is oftner fought by fuch too. The approbation of the Wife, which are the few, and of the Honeft, by which I intend, Men heartily affected to the Government, I acknowledge I earneftly covet : For them that are otherwife, I court not their good opinion, becaufe I fear not their bad ; and would not draw that Sufpicion upon my felf, that Men may fay, What ill has he done, that thofe Men fpeak fo well of him ? I never was of their party, nor never will be ; and to be even with them, I think as meanly of them, as they do of Loyalty ; whofe misfortunes are more to be efteemed than their triumphs. The good words of fuch as truely love their Country, (which no man ever did, that does not love his Prince) indeed I highly prize, and will endeavour to deferve ; though your Lordfhip at this time has been beforehand with me in that particular, by beftowing them upon me firft ; and fo many, that I am afhamed I have been no better to have made them good : But becaufe your Lordfhip is willing and able to render any Man much better than he is, they ought to be efteemed as the proceed of a generous Nature, and an indulgent Prudence ; which by telling me what I am, does but kindly infinuate what I fhould be.

My Lord, I will wafte no more of your time, though I omit thofe ufual returns of formal Thanks ; for they are of courfe ; or extreme wondring at the great Surprizals of the King's favour ; and thofe humble, yet high debafements of one's felf, which look like Modefty, but is a fort of Bravery.

My thanks fhall be paid in (what the KING likes beft) fervice to his People. The wonder will ceafe by that time I get to the Bench ; and my Defects are beft confeft by endeavouring to amend them.

A

A
DISCOURSE
UPON THE
Designs, Practices & Counsels
OF
FRANCE.

SIR,

YOU gave me a brief, and a pertinent Deduction, the other day, of the *French* Practices and Designs ; the progress of their Arms, and the methods of their Proceedings : Together with a Scheme of the inevitable ruin and slavery that threatens *Europe*, with a speedy and a powerful Conjunction against them.

After this general contemplation of the present state of *Christendom*, you were pleased to take a particular prospect of the interest of this Nation, and how far we are to reckon ourselves concerned in the common Calamity : Coming at last to this conclusion, That *England cannot reasonably expect to stand long, after the loss of* Holland *and* Flanders. For the support of this opinion, (besides the force of your own reasoning) you referr'd me to several historical and political Treatises upon the Subject ; which I have diligently examin'd, and made use of, in this following discourse ; wherein I take the freedom to give you my thoughts upon the whole matter.

Your first charge upon the *French*, was, Breach of Faith ; and you pitch'd upon the Cases of *Spain* and *Portugal*, the barbarous usage of the Duke of *Lorrain*, and the nulling of the most *Christian Queen*'s Renunciation upon Marriage, (which was the very foundation of the *Pyrenean Treaty*) by a pretended devolution of the *Spanish Netherlands*, in the right of that Match : Their under-hand tampering with *Denmark* and *Sweden*, to draw the one from us, and hinder the other from joining with us ; the influence they had upon our disgrace at *Chatham*, their playing booty on both sides, betwixt *England* and *Holland* in the *Dutch War* : And to these instances, (which are all so notorious that they need no expounding) you might have added a thousand more of the like quality. But these may suffice for a seasonable and a necessary caution, and without the helps of aggravation and clamour ; especially that extraordinary Action of destroying the *Queen's Renunciation*, and then invading the *Spanish Netherlands* upon it : An Action hardly to be parallel'd in the story of the whole World, for a concurrence of so many enormous Circumstances. There was in it, *The publick Faith of the two Crowns*, which is the only security of Government, and the bond of human Society : There was in it, *The solemnity of an Oath at the very Altar*, which is the most sacred tie of a *Christian* : There was also, *The highest Profession, and Assurance of Friendship imaginable*, which is accounted one of the most binding obligations betwixt Man and Man : And then there was a *Brother, a Cousin, and an Infant in the case* ; which makes it matter of humanity and honour. And yet all these cords were as easily broken as Bulrushes. This single precedent may serve, however, for a warning to all Princes and States, not to leave themselves at the mercy of Men of such Principles. But his most Christian Majesty is not the only Prince that has been abused by corrupt and ambitious Ministers.

Your next observation was, That they are the greatest intermeddlers in the World, in other People's Affairs, that they embroil all wherever they come ; and that there's hardly any Rebellion, but they are in the bottom of it. For their Money walks in all the Courts and Councils of *Christendom* ; nay, and beyond it too : For 'tis said that the

last

†

last *Grand Visier* was their Pensioner. Was it not *France* that debauched *Scotland* first ; and afterwards *England* into the late Rebellion ? Nay, did they not stand still, and look on, to see the crowning of the Work which they themselves began, in the execrable Murder of the late King ? And did they not refuse to our gracious and persecuted Sovereign————even a Retreat in their Dominions ? How did they prolong the War in *Portugal* ? What havock have they made in *Poland*, and what work in *Hungary* ? And are they not this Day in Council with the Port against the Empire, and undermining the bulwark of *Christendom* ? How have they dashed *England* against *Holland* ; blinded the Eyes of several Princes of the Empire ; and baffled all Mediations towards a general Peace ? Did they not formerly, under the colour of protecting *Germany*, cut off *Alsatia* from the Empire ? And in a word, this has been their Practice wheresoever they have come : *They covet Harbours in* Spain, (says the admirable *Baron del' Isola*) *Leagues in the Empire, Factions in* Poland, *Wars in* England *and* Holland, *Passes into* Italy, *and the sovereign Arbitrage every where: Their quiet consists in the trouble of all others, and their advantage is in the publick Calamities.* Nor have they any other way, than by dividing, and weakening of the parts, to master the whole, which is the capital Design. And if so, there's no Fence against a common Enemy, but a common Union.

It is already made appear, by what is above said, how dangerous they are to Mankind. The next hint you gave me, was to consider on't, whether the *English* may reasonably expect any better quarter from them, than other People : In which point, I shall only lay the matter before you, and leave you the judge on't.

The four main Interests of a Nation, are Religion, Reputation, Peace, and Trade. For the first of these ; we shall neither fare the better, nor the worse ; but lose just as much for being of another Communion, as his *Catholick Majesty* gets by being of the same. The Question now on foot, is a Communion of State, not of Faith. The *Alcoran* and the *Gospel* go hand in hand ; and at the same time, the *Protestants* are protected in *Hungary*, and persecuted in *France*. To say nothing of the Encouragements they give there to the *Jansenists*, which may, for aught we know, prove the greatest Blow to the Church of *Rome*, that ever it received since the Reformation. But what do I talk of Religion, in a cause that is dipped in Christian Blood, and in the Tears of Widows and Orphans ? A Cause that is propagated by Sacrilege, Rapes, Depopulation, Slavery, Oppression, and at least a Million of Lives sacrificed to it already ? The very thought of it is enough to strike the Soul of any Man with Horror and Indignation.

If you would see how tenderly they have handled us in the Business of Reputation ; pray do but cast an Eye upon the Character of an *Englishman*, in their *Politique de France.*

Quant a ce qui est des Anglois, ils n'ont aucuns Amis, ce sont des gens sans Foy, sans Religion, sans Probité, sans Justice aucune, defians, legers au dernier point, Cruels, Impatiens, Gourmands, Superbes, Audacieux, Avares, Propres pour les coups de main, et pour une promte execution, mais incapables de conduire une Guerre avec jugement. Leur pais est assez bon pour vivre, mais il n'est pas assez riche pour leur fournir les moyens de sortir, & de faire aucune conqueste : aussi n'ont ils jamais rien conquis, excepte l'Irlande, dont les babitans sont foibles, & mauvais Soldats, &c. i. e. *As for the* English, *they are a People without Friends, without Faith, Religion, Honesty, or Justice ; Distrustful, and fickle to the highest degree imaginable : Cruel, Impatient, Gluttonous, Proud, and Audacious ; they will do well enough for a Rubber at Cuffs, or a sudden Exploit, but they understand nothing at all of the Government of a War. The Country is passable enough for them to live in ; but not rich enough to offer at any Conquest abroad ; nor did they ever make any, but upon the* Irish, *which are a weakly People, and ill Soldiers.*

I think it were not amiss in this Place, to desire our impertinent Undertaker to turn back to the History of *Philip de Valois*, and he shall there find that our *Edward* the IIId. made a shift with one Army to beat 60,000 *French*, and leave betwixt thirty and forty Thousand of them upon the Place ; and with another Army in the Bishoprick of *Durham*, to defeat as many *Scots*, and cut off 15000 of them too. And it must not be here omitted, that this *Scotch* Army was also animated by *French* Counsels. I would not willingly run out a Letter into a Volume ; so that all other Reflections apart, I shall only add, that if the *English* had not once recovered the Field, and another time made it good in two of the greatest Actions of late, that have yet passed betwixt the *Imperialists* and the *French*, 'tis the Opinion of wise Men, that the latter would not have had much to brag of upon the Success of this War. And this in some degree is acknowledged by the Author of a *French Relation of the Actions betwixt the two Armies in*

2

1675.

1675, 1676, and 1677, (how Romantical soever in other Cases.) Speaking of the Battle under the Command of the *Count de Lorge,* after the Death of the *Vicount Turenne,* these are his words, *Et à rendre justice aux* Anglois, & *aux* Irlandois, *on peut dire, qu'on leur doit une bonne partie de cette victoire :* That is to say, *And to give the* English *and* Irish *their due,* France *is indebted to them in a large measure for this Victory.* But now to our Politician again : *Ils se haïssent les uns les autres, & sont en division continuelle, soit pour la Religion, soit pour le Gouvernment. The* English, says he, *hate one another, and are still quarrelling, either about Religion or Government.*

These Indecencies would almost make a Man call them Names ; but let us pass without one angry Word, from the Interest of our *Reputation,* to that of our *Peace,* and enquire how they stand affected to us upon that point. To say, that *England* has not for a long time had any Troubles either at home or abroad, which the *French* have not promoted, or improv'd to their own Advantage ; is to say no more than that they deal with *us,* as they do with *all the World beside ;* so that we must e'en have recourse again to their *Politicks* for some particular Mark of their Favour, where you shall find that our State-Mountebank has not yet shewn all his Tricks, but puts himself with a very grave and fore-casting Countenance upon the very Project of our Ruin : *Une Guerre de France de trois ou quatre ans contre eux, les ruinera entierement, ainsi il semble qu'il ne faut point faire de paix avec eux qu'a des Conditions qui nous soient tres avantageuses. A War* (says he) *of three or four Years with* France, *would absolutely destroy the* English *; so that methinks we should not entertain any Peace with them, but upon very profitable Terms.* And then a little after : *In fine,* says he, *the way to undo the* English, *is to make them keep an Army on foot; and there's no fear of their Landing in* France, *but to their certain destruction, unless they should be invited by a Rebellion ; without which, their Troops will in a short time most undoubtedly fall foul one upon another. To keep them upon continual Expence,'tis but giving them the Alarm upon the Isles of* Jersey, *and* Guernsey, Wight *and* Man, Ireland *and the* Cinque Ports *; by which means they will be put upon the Charge of Fortifications and Garrisons, which will perswade the People that the King intends to set up a Standing Army, and an Arbitrary Government. So long as this holds, the Nation will never be at quiet, but torment themselves with Fears and Jealousies, which may be easily fomented by Letters in Cypher, to such or such particular Persons ; and in such sort to be intercepted, as shall be found convenient. These Letters may give a Hint of a Descent in* Ireland, *and elsewhere, which would dispose the* Irish, *who mortally hate the* English, *to a Revolt ; and among the suspicious Multitude they would pass for Gospel. This Contrivance would make the* Scots *also to bethink themselves of recovering their Liberty ; where there must be Parties made, and the Sects encourag'd one against another; especially the* Roman Catholicks *must be fairly handled, and private Assurance given (in the Name of the King of* England) *to the* Benedictins, *(who are easy enough to be imposed upon) that they shall be restor'd to all their former Benefits, according to the Printed* Monasticon; *which will presently make the* Roman Catholicks *declare themselves; and the Monks will move Heaven and Earth for the bringing of matters about : But then Care must be taken to carry on the Report, that the King is of the* Romish *Religion ; which will distract the Government, and throw all into an Absolute Confusion.*

From hence we may gather : First, What Opinion the *French* have of us. Secondly, That it is not only their Desire and Study, but a formed Design to embroil us. Thirdly, That they will stick at nothing neither, to compass that End, be it never so foul. Fourthly, This Libeller has trac'd us out the very Methods of their working: As by amusing the People with forged Letters of Intelligence, where the first Author of the Plot must miraculously discover it. By filling the Peoples Heads with Fears and Jealousies, and leaving no Stone unturn'd in *England, Scotland* and *Ireland,* to stir up a Rebellion. Why has he not advis'd the Poysoning of all our Fountains too ? which would have been a Course of as much Christianity and Honour. But that this Trifler may not glorify himself too much in his wondrous Speculations, take notice, that he is only the Transcriber, not the Author of this goodly Piece, for the Original was betwixt *Richlieu* and *Mazarine* ; and it amounts to no more in effect, than an imperfect History of the *French* Dealings with us for a long time, and particularly in our late Troubles.

To come now from his most unmannerly Malice, to his Reason of State ; if I am not mistaken : England *might longer subsist in a War with* France, *than* France *could in a Peace within itself,* (the heaviest of all Judgments, when a Nation must be wicked upon necessity.) And again, when he says, That England *cannot hurt* France *by a Descent, unless call'd in by a Rebellion.* He never considers, That if *England* had an Army a-foot, and stood inclin'd to make use of it that way, we should not be long without an Invitation. For we see what the *Bourdelois,* &c. did upon their own Bottom, and without any Foreign En-

R   En-

Encouragement ; and the whole Business miscarried only for want of a vigorous Second. Lastly, Give me leave to say, that he has extreamly over-shot himself in one thing more ; for tho' this has been really the Practice of the *French*, and is at this Day the very Model and Rule by which their Emissaries govern themselves ; it should yet have been kept as the greatest Secret in the World : for the owning of these inglorious Artifices in Publick, makes it one of the grossest Libels that ever was written against the *French Government* ; to say nothing of his Oversight in disobliging the *Roman Catholicks*, and laying Snares to trepan them.

The Question of *Trade* has been so beaten already, that there remains little to be added to it : Nor in truth needs it, since it is agreed on all hands, that the *French* set up for an *Universal Commerce*, as well as for an *Universal Monarchy*. And in effect, the one is but a necessary Consequent upon the other. Nor is it enough, it seems, for us to be design'd upon by them, without lending them our Hands towards the cutting of our own Throats : *For upon a sober and judicious Estimate, we are Losers by our Trade with* France, *at least a Million and an half* per Annum. I shall conclude this Head with one Passage more out of our *Politiques of France* : (And you'll say 'tis a pleasant one too, but it must be under the Rose.) Upon a pre-supposal of Mischief that's a brewing in *England* : Now, says he, *it will be our Business to renew our Alliance with* Holland *; we can wheedle them into an Opinion, that they are the only Men that understand the Knack of Trade, so that they shall have that to themselves* : *The Talent of the* French, *alas ! lies another way ; and there's no forcing of any thing against Nature ; and that now's the nick of Time to crush their Competitors for the Northern Seas.* So that we are all of us to be served with the same Sauce ; but 'tis some Degree of Honesty yet, when they tell the World what they are to trust to.

Now to sum up all that's said, If the *French* can dispense with *Oaths*, and *Solemn Contracts* ; if it be their *Custom*, and a Branch of their *Policy*, to *fish in troubled Waters* ; if they *hate* us as *English-men*, and are not for us as *Reformed Catholicks* ; if they do all they can to wound us in our *Reputation*, our *Peace*, and our *Trade*, we may take for granted, that they will destroy us to all purposes, if they can ; which naturally leads me to an Enquiry, how far we are in their Power, or likely so to be, that we may take our Measures accordingly.

It will not stand with the Brevity I propose in this Paper, to give you a *Geographical*, or an *Historical* Account of Places or Actions : But in as few Words as I can, I am to present you with a general View of the present State of *Christendom*, with a regard to the Power of *France* ; and then to consider how far *England* may be concern'd in the Common Fate. Here it was that you and I brake off in our last Discourse ; so that in the Prosecution of it, I must try to walk without leading, (saving only the Helps that I have gathered from certain Tracts which I have read, upon his Recommendation) wherein I shall steer a middle Course, betwixt some that over-value the Strength of *France*, and others that will have it to be less than indeed it is.

That the Arms of *France* are at this Day formidable to all *Christendom*, is not to be denied, and *Tacitus* gives you the Reason of it, in the Case of the *Romans* and the *Britains* ; *Rarus* (says he) *ad propulsandum commune periculum conventus : ita, dum singuli pugnant, universi vincuntur.* There must be a common Force to oppose a common Danger ; they struggled one by one, till they were all destroyed. The French (no doubt of it) are a Wealthy, a Populous, and a Military Nation. But it must be allowed, that they are more indebted for their Greatness, to the Slips and Oversights of others, (and this without Disparagement too) than they are to their proper Conduct and Valour. The Advance they made into *Flanders* in 1667, was introduced by the *Spaniards* trusting to their Assurances of Friendship, and rather imputable to an Excess of Charity, than any want of Precaution ; though it seemed not very likely, that they should march with Horse, Foot, and Cannon, only to go a Birding. Through these and the like Arts they have rais'd themselves to that dangerous Height where now we behold them ; taking all Advantages of the unsettled Condition of *Spain* ; the Divisions of the Empire, and the Factions in *Holland*, and of all other Mistakes in point of Fore-sight and Resolution elsewhere. You know very well, the Conquests they have made upon the *United Provinces*, the *Spanish Netherlands*, a considerable part of *Germany* ; with the Terror and Devastation that accompanies them every-where : The Progress of their Arms in *Catalonia*, *Sicily*, the *West-Indies*, &c. Now what may be the Consequences of this over-growing Power, and how to prevent them, is the Matter in question.

2

A S

AS it is without dispute, that the *French* aim at *Universal Dominion*, (which is only a more plausible Cover for that *Universal Slavery* which must create it) so is it accounted as indubitable a Principle, that the Conquest of *Flanders* must be the Foundation of it. And according to this Maxim it is, that they take their Measures ; for they have made themselves Masters of the Out-works already in *Valenciennes, Cambray* and *St. Omer* ; three Places of very great Strength and Importance : And it is generally believ'd by the recalling of their Troops from the *Rhine*, and bending the Flower of their Force that way, that they will push for the rest this Campaign. If they carry it, (as probably they will, without the speedy Addition of some powerful Alliance) take notice, I beseech you, of that which naturally follows. In the first place, the Charge and the Hazard of that War is over, which in Garrisons, and in the Field, has put his *most Christian Majesty* to the Expence of keeping near 100000 Men in Pay, (which will then be at liberty to fall in upon the Empire :) Beside, what has been expended in *Management*, as the *French* call it, which in honest *English* is downright *Corruption*. Secondly, This Acquisition will furnish the *French* King with Men and Monies, for an Army of Fifty thousand Men, (and no better Soldiers in *Europe*.) Thirdly, what will become of the Duke of *Brandenburg*, if the *French* should fall into *Cleves*, and *Mark*, with a matter of Forty or Fifty thousand Men more, and from thence into *Pomeren* and *Prussia* ? Fourthly, the whole Patrimony of the Empire, from the *Rhine* to the Frontiers of *France*, fall by an inevitable Consequence into the hands of the *French*, as they have already swallowed the three Bishopricks of *Metz, Toul* and *Verdun*. So that the *Imperial* Army will be forced over the *Rhine*, and there probably kept in play, and upon the bare *Defensive*, by the Princes of the *French* Interest ; while in the mean time, the Princes of *Westphalia* will be reduc'd to an absolute Necessity of ranging themselves under the *French* Protection and changing their Party. And what can then be expected from *Holland*, after what they have suffered already, and under their present Despairs, but to content themselves with such Conditions as *France* will give them ? For after the Loss of *Cleves* and *Flanders*, their Case is wholly desperate, unless *England* should vigorously interpose to their Relief. And the State of the *Empire* is neither better nor worse than that of their Neighbours ; for they must all submit their Necks to the same Yoke. When matters are brought to this pass, they have before them, *England, Spain* and *Italy* ; the Cloud is gathered already, and it is wholly at their Choice where it shall break.

There are a great many People, I know, that promise themselves mighty Things from the Event of another Campaign, for want, I fear, of consulting the Chart ; and the almost insuperable Difficulties that lie in the way : The Means they propose are either by carrying the War into *France*, by way of *Revulsion*, or by forcing the *French* upon a Capital Battle ; the former Proposition seems first very impracticable ; and Secondly, of little or no Advantage, if it could be effected. It must be considered that beyond *Mentz, Coblentz* and *Treves*, the *Imperialists* have no Magazine at all beside that betwixt *Treves* and *France* (a part of *Luxenburg* excepted) is absolutely in the Enemies power. Now how should an Army subsist there, that must over and above, pass through a Country of about twenty Leagues, that is wholly laid waste, and in ashes, and without any Cattle in it, or any other sort of necessary Provision ?

Put the Case now, that the *Imperialists* should break through all these Difficulties, and carry an Army even into *Lorrain* it self, the Country of *Metzin* or *Burgundy*, (which would take them up the best part of the Summer too)all the Strong-Holds are in the hands of the *French*, and the Country laid so desolate, that there's no living for an Army there. When 'tis come to this, they must resolve either upon a Battle or Siege. If the former, the *French* are at liberty whether they will fight or no, and there's no compelling of them, for they are among their Strong-Holds ; and all's their own both behind them, and on each Side, and the Country either burnt or deserted. But carry it farther yet, and suppose the *French* forc'd upon the Risque of a Battle, First, the *Imperialists* are not sure to get the better of it. And Secondly, What if they should ? Nay to the Degree of an entire *Victory* ? All that would be expected more for that Year, would be only to take in some considerable Post, and make good the Ground they had gotten for the next Campaign : For it would be a Madness to pursue their Victory into the Heart of an Enemy's Country, and leave so many Garrisons upon their Backs, which would undoubtedly cut off all their Convoys and starve them.

But this is still the supposing of a Thing not to be supposed ; for the *French*, in this Case, would stand upon the Defensive, and not come to a Battle. Or in case they should, and be worsted ; they have Men enough in Garrison for Recruits, that would immediately reinforce them.   Now

Now on the other side, what if the *Imperialists* should chance to be routed? The Garrisons which the *French* hold in *Lorrain*, *Burgundy* and *Alsatia*, would in such Case totally destroy that broken Army, and cut out such work in *Germany*, as has not been known in the *Empire* for many Ages.

In this extremity, let us suppose that the *Empire* should yet bring another Army into the Field; and try the Issue of a second Battle, and miscarry: And that the disaffected Princes of the *Empire* should declare themselves for the Enemy; all that part of *Germany* that lies within two or three Days Journey of the *Rhine*, would be irrecoverably lost; a great part of it being so harrassed already, that 'tis not able so much as to furnish an Army upon a March, much less for a Winter Quarter.

Now to the Business of a Siege, the *French* have taught us, by *Philipsburg* and *Mastricht*, that they want neither Skill to fortify a Place, nor Courage to defend it. So that without a great loss of Time and Men, it cannot be expected that the Imperialists should make themselves Masters of any considerable Place: and when they shall have carried it; what will a Town in *Lorrain*, or *Burgundy*, signify to the saving of the *Spanish Netherlands*, which if once lost, are hardly ever to be retriev'd?

Now taking this for granted; if *England* does not step in with all the Speed and Vigour imaginable, see what will be the End on't: First, That the *French*, being Masters of all the Posts, Passes and Strong-Holds in *Lorrain* and *Burgundy*, may dodge and trifle the Imperialists at pleasure; and make them spend out the Year without any Advantage to the *Netherlands*. The way would have been for the *Imperialists* to have prest with an Army of 50000 Men directly into the Body of *France*, and the *Confederate* Troops in the *Low Countries*, to have made another Inroad by the way of *Picardy* or *Bologne*; but since the taking of *Valenciennes*, *Cambray* and *St. Omer*, there's no possibility of piercing *France* that way, so that a very small Army now upon the *Spanish Netherlands*, with the help of the *French* Garrisons, is sufficient to amuse and tire out the whole Force of *Spain*, and *Holland* upon that Quarter.

Secondly, *France* being thus secured on that side, will unquestionably fall in with all their Power upon the *Empire*; unless diverted by the Alarm they have now received from *England*. Now admitting this to be the Condition of *France*, let any Man of Sense judge what Good the *Imperial Army* can do to the *Netherlands*, (upon which single point depends the Fortune of *Christendom*.) What if they should march up to the Borders of *France* with 50000 Men? Will not the *French* encounter them there with as many, or more? And with this odds too, that the *Imperialists* suffer a thousand Incommodities in their March through a ruin'd Country; Whereas the *French* have good Quarters, and plenty of all Things at hand, watching the others Motions, and improving all Advantages against them.

Thirdly, In this Posture of Affairs, the *Confederates* must never expect to do any great Matter upon the *French*, in these Provinces, unless they do very much outnumber them.

And it is likewise to be considered, that these Troubles falling out in the Minority of his *Catholick Majesty*, the Distractions of that Government, the Revolt of *Sicily*, and great Disorders upon the Frontiers of *Spain*; the *Netherlands* have been much neglected, till the Elevation of his Highness *Don John* of *Austria* to the Dignity of *Prime Minister*. And that it is not possible for him, by reason of the many Exigencies of that Crown nearer home, to send any considerable Succour to the *Low Countries*, otherwise than by Supplies of Money: So that by that time the *Imperialists* and the *Hollanders* are got into their Winter-Quarters, or at least, before they take the Field again, the *French* from time to time will be ready with fresh Troops out of their Garrisons to prosecute their Conquests; which by degrees must needs break the Hearts of the poor Inhabitants, when they find that neither their Faith, nor their Courage, is able any longer to protect them. And when that Day comes, what by their Armies, and what by other Influences, the *French* will have as good as subjected two thirds of *Europe*. And there will also occur these farther Difficulties: First, No body knows where the *French* will begin their Attack; which will oblige the *Spaniard* and *Hollander* to strengthen all their Garrisons as far as their Men will reach. Secondly, When the *Spanish* and *Holland* Troops shall be so dispersed, wheresoever the *French* sit down, they must then give themselves for lost, for want of an Army to relieve them; beside their furious and obstinate manner of Assault, for they care not how many Men they lose, so they carry the place. (And then most of the Men too are made Prisoners of War.) Nor is the Season of the Year any Discouragement to them neither; witness their first Irruption into *Burgundy*, and the restless Activity of their Troops even at this Instant.

I

So soon as their work in *Flanders* is over (which only *England* under Heaven, is able to prevent or check) the *French* will have an Army of at least 50000 Men about *Lorain*, *Luxenburg* and *Burgundy* to face the *Imperialists*, and at the same time with as many more perhaps they will seize upon the Dutchy of *Juliers*, and of *Cleves*, and from thence pass the *Rhine*, to countenance those that are of the *French Cabal*, on the side of *Westphalia* ; and so in due time, several other Princes of the *Empire*. It is remarkable that in Three Years War against the *Confederates*, his most *Christian Majesty* has not only stood his ground, without losing so much as one Inch of his Ancient Patrimony, but actually and almost without Opposition, taken several Towns, and some entire Provinces, from the Principals of the *Confederacy*; and made himself almost as considerable at Sea, as he is at Land ; not only in the *Mediterranean*, and upon the Coasts of *Spain* and *Italy*, but in *America* too : where he has laid a Foundation of great Mischief both to *England* and *Holland*, in the point of Commerce ; if not timely prevented. And he does little less by his Money, than by his Arms ; for he pays all, and with *French* Money, under pretext of Neutrality, maintains considerable Armies in the very heart of the Empire ; which, 'tis feared, will be ready enough upon any disaster, to join with the Common Enemy. It is the *French* Court that manages the Counsels of *Poland*, and they govern the *Swiss* no less ; who by the Conquest of the *Franche County* are made little better than Slaves. And yet by a fatal Blindness that *Republick* still furnishes the *French* with the best of their Soldiers, and helps forward the Destruction of *Europe*, never dreaming that they themselves are to be undone too at last.

But it is no great matter, you'll say, to impose upon the *Swiss* (which are a heavy and phlegmatick People) but the *French* Charms have betwitch'd even *Italy* it self, though a Nation the most clear-sighted, and suspicious of all others. For their *Republicks* lie as quiet, as if they were asleep ; though the Fire is already kindled in *Sicily*, and the Danger brought home to their own Doors. It is a wonder, that they lay things no more to heart, considering, First, the Passages the *French* have to favour their Entry. Secondly, That they are many and small States, weak, and easily to be corrupted, if not so already. Thirdly, that though they have been formerly very brave, and many particulars remain so still, yet in the generality they are soft and effeminate. And Fourthly, that the *French* is there the Master of the Seas. These Reflections methinks might convince any Man of the Condition they are in. And certainly they that were not able to defend themselves against *Charles* the Eighth, will be much less able to encounter *Lewis* the Fourteenth. Or if he gets in, to drive him out again, as they did the other. For they must do it wholly upon their own Strength, having only the *Turk* in Condition to help them : For *Germany* and *Spain* are sunk already ; and the *Swiss* will neither dare to venture upon't, nor are they able to do it, if they had a mind to't.

As for *Spain*, it is neither Populous, nor fortify'd, and perhaps want of Provisions may keep it from an Invasion. And yet for all that, with a Body of Thirty or Forty Thousand Men by the way of *Fontaraby*, and as many by *Catalonia*, the *French* may (if they please) in two Campaigns make themselves Masters of *Navarre*, *Arragon*, *Catalonia*, and *Valencia* ; and then it is but fortifying the Frontiers, and making his *Catholick Majesty* a Tributary in *Castile* ; who must content himself to take what they please to give him, over and above, in consideration of his Dominions in *Italy*, and the *Spanish Indies* : *A Possibility that* England *and* Holland *shall do well to think of* ; *for when he has the* Mines *in his Power, and* Europe *under his Feet, there will be no contending*.

After this, they have only the *Swiss* or the *English*, to fall upon next : For the former, they are neither fortify'd nor united in Affections or Religion.

As for *England* ; They are a People not naturally addicted to the *French*, sensible of their Honour, and of their Interest, and the whole World is convinced of their Courage. They are united under the Government of a Gracious Prince ; and their Concerns are at this Instant lodged in the hands of the most Loyal and Publick-spirited Representatives that ever acted in that Station ; beside the Strength of the Island by Situation : So that the *French* would find it a hard matter, either to make a Conquest here, or if they should surprize it, to keep it. But yet they have finer Ways to Victory than by Force of Arms ; and their *Gold* has done them better Service than their *Iron*.

What have we now to do then, but in a Common Cause, to arm against Common Oppression ? This is the time, or never, for *Italy* to enter into a League for their common Safety, and not only keep, but, if possible, to force the *French* from their Borders ; while the *Imperial* Army holds the Capital Power of *France* in play ?

S

And

And this is the time too, for the *Swiss* to recall all their Troops out of the *French* Service, and to strike a general League also for the Recovery of *Burgundy*, the only Outwork of their Liberties, and to expel the *French* Garrisons, and deliver the places into the hands of the Right Owners.

And will it not concern *Poland* as much as any of the rest? that stands and falls with the *Empire*, as the Defence of *Christendom* against the *Turks*, and whose turn is next.

This Alarm methinks should call off the Princes from the Acquisitions they have made upon part of the *Swedes* Possessions in the Empire, to the Assistance of the *Spanish Netherlands*; and make all the *French* Mercenaries in the Empire, to bethink themselves of returning from the Delusions which either the *French* Artifice or Money has imposed upon them. He that has no Regard for the Head, will have less for the Dependences, when he has them at his mercy.

Nay, the very *French* themselves should do well to contemplate the Slavery that is now prepar'd for them. Their Laws and Liberties are trampled upon; and *till the* French *Government be reduc'd to the Bounds of its Ancient Constitution, neither the People, nor their Neighbours, can ever be secure.*

In this dangerous Crisis of Affairs, it has pleas'd Divine Providence to leave *England* the Arbitress of the Fate of *Europe*; and to annex such advantages to the Office, that the Honour, the Duty, and Security of this Nation seem to be wrapt up together. In the Point of Honour, what can be more generous, than to succour the Miserable and the Oppress'd, and to put a stop to that Torrent that threatens *Christendom* with an Universal Deluge? Beside the Vindication of our selves for those Affronts and Indignities, both Publick and Private, that we have suffer'd upon our own Account. And then in matter of Duty: It is not only Christendom, but *Christianity* itself, that lies at stake. For in the Ruin of the *Empire*, the *Turk's* work is done to his hand, by breaking down the only Fence that has preserv'd us all this while from the Incursions of the *Ottoman* Power. Now as nothing can be more glorious than at all hazards to hinder the effusion of more Christian Blood, and to save Christendom itself from Bondage; it is so much our Interest too, that we our selves are lost without it. And as the Obligation is reciprocal, so the Resolution is necessary: The Choice we have before us being only this, *Either to unite with our Neighbours for a common Safety, or to stand still and look on, the tame Spectators of their Ruin, till we fall alone.* This is so demonstrative, that if we do not by a powerful Alliance and Diversion, prevent the Conquest of *Flanders* (which lies already a gasping) we are cut off from all Communication with the rest of *Europe*, and coop'd up at home, to the irrecoverable loss of our Reputation and Commerce; for *Holland* must inevitably follow the Fate of *Flanders*, and then the *French* are Masters of the Sea; ravage our Plantations, and infallibly possess themselves of the *Spanish Indies*, and leave us answerable for all those Calamities that shall ensue upon it: which, as yet, by God's Providence, may be timely prevented. But *he that stills the raging of the Sea, will undoubtedly set Bounds to this overflowing Greatness*: having now, (as an Earnest of that Mercy) put it into the Hearts of our Superiours to provide seasonably for the common Safety, and in proportion also to the Exigence of the Affair; knowing very well, that things of this Nature are not to be done by halves.

We have to do with a Nation of a large Territory, abounding in Men and Money; their Dominion is grown absolute, that no Man there can call any Thing his own, if the Court says *Nay* to't. So that the sober and industrious part, are only Slaves to the Lusts and Ambition of the Military. In this Condition of Servitude, they feel already what their Neighbours fear, and wish as well to any Opportunity, either of avoiding, or of casting off the Yoke: which will easily be given by a Conjunction of *England* and *Holland* at Sea; and almost infallibly produce these effects: *First*, It will draw off the Naval Force of *France* from *Sicily*, *America*, and elsewhere, to attend this Expedition. *Secondly*, The Diversion will be an Ease to the *Empire* and *Confederates*, from whence more Troops must be drawn to encounter this Difficulty, than the *French* can well spare. *Thirdly*, It will not only encourage those Princes and States that are already engag'd, but likewise keep in awe those that are disaffected, and confirm those that waver.

'Tis true, this War must needs be prodigiously expensive; but then in probability it will be short: And in Cases of this Quality, People must do as in a Storm at Sea, rather throw part of the Lading over-board, than founder the Vessel. I do not speak this, as supposing any difficulty in the Case, for the very Contemplation of it has put fire into the Veins of every true *English-man*; and they are moved as by a sacred impulse, to the necessary, and the only means of their Preservation. And that which crowns our Hopes, is, that these generous Inclinations are only ready to execute what the

the Wifdom of their Superiors fhall find reafonable to command. I need not tell you how jealous the People of *England* are of their Religion and Liberties ; to what degree they have contended, even for the fhadow of thefe Interefts ; nor how much Blood and Treafure they have fpent upon the Quarrel. Could any Impofture work fo much ; and can any Man imagine that they will be now lefs fenfible, when they fee before their Eyes a manifeft Plot upon their Religion ; their Liberties invaded, their Traffick interrupted ; the Honour and the very Being of their Country at ftake ; their Wives and Children expos'd to Beggary and Scorn ; and in conclufion, *The Privilege of a Free-born* Englifh-man *exchang'd for the Vaffalage of* France ?

An ANSWER *to a* LETTER *written by a Member of Parliament in the Country, upon the occafion of his Reading of the* Gazette *of the* 11th *of* December, 1679 ; *wherein is the Proclamation for further Proroguing the Parliament, till the* 11th *of* November *next enfuing.*

SIR,

I Received your Letter, when I was engaged in much other Bufinefs, which will excufe me that I have not returned an Anfwer fooner, and that it is done no better now : You defire me to let you know what that Judgment is which my Lord Chancellor acquainted my Lord Mayor and his Brethren with, and what my thoughts are upon it : And that I may obey you in both, I will firft tranfcribe that Cafe, as it is reported by Juftice *Crook,* that being already put into *Englifh,* whereas the Cafe in *Moor* is in *French.*

MEmorandum, That by Command from the King, all the Juftices of *England,* with divers of the Nobility, *viz.* The Lord *Ellefmere* Lord-Chancellor, the Earl of *Dorfet* Lord-Treafurer, Vifcount *Cranbourn* Principal Secretary, the Earl of *Nottingham* Lord Admiral, the Earls of *Northumberland, Worcefter, Devon,* and *Northampton,* the Lords *Zouch, Burghley,* and *Knowles,* the Chancellor of the *Dutchy,* the Archbifhop of *Canterbury,* the Bifhop of *London, Popham* Chief Juftice, *Bruce* Mafter of the Rolls, *Anderfon, Gawdy, Walmefley, Fenner, Kingfmil, Warburton, Savel, Daniel, Yelverton* and *Snigg,* were affembled in the *Star-Chamber,* where the Lord Chancellor, after a long Speech made by him concerning Juftices of the Peace, and his Exhortation to the Juftices of Affize, and a Difcourfe concerning Papifts and Puritans, declaring how they both were Difturbers of the State, and that the King intending to fupprefs them, and to have the Laws put in execution againft them, demanded of the Juftices their Refolutions in three things : Firft, Whether the Deprivation of Puritan-Minifters by the High Commiffioners, for refufing to conform themfelves to the Ceremonies appointed by the laft Canons, was lawful ? Whereto all the Juftices anfwered, That they had conferred thereof before, and held it to be lawful, becaufe the King hath the Supreme Ecclefiaftical Power, which he hath delegated to the Commiffioners, whereby they had the Power of Deprivation by the Canon-Law of the Realm. And the Statute of 1 *Eliz.* which appoints Commiffioners to be made by the Queen, doth not confer any new Power, but explain and declare the Ancient Power. And therefore they held it clear, *That the King without Parliament might make Orders and Conftitutions for the Government of the Clergy, and might deprive them if they obeyed not. And fo the Commiffioners might deprive them.* But they could not make any Conftitutions without the King : And the divulging of fuch Ordinances by Proclamation is a moft gracious Admonition : And forafmuch as they have refufed to obey, they are lawfully deprived by the Commiffioners *ex Officio,* without Libel, *Et ore tenus convocati.* Secondly, Whether a Prohibition be

Cro. Ja. f.37.
Nov. 100.
Moor 755.

grantable

grantable against the Commiſſioners upon the Statute of 2 *H.* 5. if they do not deliver the Copy of the Libel to the Party : Whereto they all anſwered, That that Statute is intended where the Eccleſiaſtical Judge proceeds *ex Officio & ore tenus.* Thirdly, Whether it were an Offence puniſhable, and what Puniſhment they deſerved, who framed Petitions, and collected a multitude of Hands thereto, to prefer to the King in a publick cauſe, as the Puritans had done, with an Intimation to the King, That if he denied their Suit, many thouſands of his Subjects would be diſcontented ? Whereto all the Juſtices anſwered, That it was an Offence finable at Diſcretion, and very near to *Treaſon and Felony in the Puniſhment :* For they tended to the raiſing of Sedition, Rebellion, and Diſcontent among the People. To which Reſolution all the Lords agreed. And then many of the Lords declared, That ſome of the Puritans had raiſed a falſe Rumour of the King, how he intended to grant a Toleration to Papiſts : Which Offence the Juſtices conceived to be heinouſly finable by the Rules of the Common Law, either in the King's Bench, *or by the King and his Council* ; or now, ſince the Statute of 3 *H.* 7. in the Star-Chamber. And the Lords ſeverally declared how the King was diſcontented with the ſaid falſe Rumour, and had made but the Day before a Proteſtation unto them, that he never intended it, and that he would ſpend the laſt drop of Blood in his Body before he would do it ; and pray'd, that before any of his Iſſue ſhould maintain any other Religion than what he truly profeſſed and maintained, that God would take them out of the World.

I doubt not but yourſelf, and every *Engliſh* Proteſtant, will join with this Royal Petitioner, and will heartily ſay *Amen.*

But you deſire to know if I think the Reſolution of the Judges in this caſe ought to deter us from humbly Petitioning his Majeſty, that this Parliament may effectually ſit on the 26*th* day of *January* next. In order to this, give me leave to obſerve to you, As it is moſt certain, that a great Reverence is due to the Unanimous Opinion of all the Judges, ſo there is a great difference to be put between the Authority of their Judgments when ſolemnly given in Caſes depending before them, and their ſudden and extrajudicial Opinions. The Caſe of Ship-money itſelf is not a better proof of this, than that which you have now read, as you will ſee, if you conſider diſtinctly what they ſay to the ſeveral Queſtions propoſed to them.

As to their Anſwer to the firſt Queſtion, it much concerns the Reverend Clergy to enquire whether they did not miſtake in it ? And whether the King, by his Proclamation, can make new Conſtitutions, and oblige them to obedience under the Penalty of Deprivation ? Should it be ſo, and ſhould this unhappy Kingdom ever ſuffer under the Reign of a Popiſh Prince, he might eaſily rid himſelf of ſuch obſtinate Hereticks, and leave his Eccleſiaſtical Preferments open for Men of better Principles : He will need only to publiſh a Proclamation, that Spittle and Salt ſhould be uſed in Baptiſm, that Holy-water ſhould be uſed, and Images ſet up in Churches ; and a few more ſuch things as theſe, and the Buſineſs were effectually done. But if you will believe my Lord Chief Juſtice *Coke,* he will tell you that it was agreed by all the Judges upon Debate, *Hill. 4to Jacobi,* that the King cannot change his Eccleſiaſtical Law ; and you may eaſily remember ſince the whole Parliament declared, That he could not alter or ſuſpend them.

12. Co. 19.
12. Co. 49.

Co. Mag.
Char. 616.

I have the uniform Opinion of all the Judges given upon great Deliberation, *Mich. 4to. Jac.* to juſtify me, if I ſay that our Judges here were utterly miſtaken in the Anſwer which they gave to the ſecond Queſtion ; I will not cite the numerous ſubſequent Authorities, ſince every Man knows that it is the conſtant Practice of *Weſtminſter-Hall* at this day to grant Prohibitions, upon a refuſal to give a Copy of Articles, where the Proceedings in the Eccleſiaſtical Courts are *ex Officio.*

You ſee there was a kind of ill Fate upon the Judges this day, as uſually there was when met in the Star-Chamber, and that they were very unfortunate in anſwering two of the three Queſtions propoſed to them ; let us go on to conſider what does principally concern us at preſent, their Anſwer to the laſt Queſtion.

You have juſt done reading it, and therefore I need not repeat to you either the Doubt or the Solution of it ; but one may be allowed to ſay modeſtly, that it was a ſudden Anſwer : 'Tis poſſible the Lords then preſent were well enough inform'd, when they were told that ſuch kind of Petitioning was an Offence next to Treaſon and Felony ; but I dare be ſo bold as to ſay, That at this Day, not a Lawyer in *England* would be the wiſer for ſuch an Anſwer ; they would be confounded, and not know whether it were Miſpriſion of Treaſon, which ſeems an Offence neareſt to Treaſon, or Petty-Larceny, which ſeems neareſt to Felony.

You will be apt to tell me that I miſtake my Lords the Judges, and they ſpoke not the nature of the Crime, but the manner of the Puniſhment ; but this will mend the

2   matter

matter but little; for since the Punishments of those two Crimes are so very different, you are still as much in the dark as ever, what these ambiguous Words mean.

Well, but we will agree, that the Crime about which the Enquiry was made, was a very great one. When Men arrive to such Insolence, as to threaten their Prince, it will be but little excuse to them to call their Menaces, by the soft and gentle Name of Petitions.

But you would know for what, and in what manner we are at present to petition; and I will give you a plain and infallible Rule. It is the Statute 13 *Car*. 2. *c*. 5.   13 *Car*. 2. *c*. 5.

Be it enacted, &c. that no Person or Persons whatsoever, shall solicit, labour, or procure the getting of hands, or other consent of any Persons above the number of twenty, or more, to any Petition, Complaint, Remonstance, Declaration, or other Addresses to the King, or both, or either Houses of Parliament, for alteration of matters established by law in Church or State, unless the matter thereof have been first consented to, and ordered by three or more Justices of the County, or by the major part of the Grand Jury of the County, or Division of the County, where the same matter shall arise at their publick Assizes, or general Quarter-Sessions, or if arising in *London*, by the Lord-Mayor, Aldermen, and Commons in Common Council assembled; and that no Person or Persons whatsoever shall repair to his Majesty, or both, or either of the Houses of Parliament, upon pretence of presenting or delivering any Petition, Complaint, Remonstrance, or Declaration, or other Addresses, accompanied with excessive numbers of People, not at any one time with above the number of ten Persons, upon the pain of incurring a Penalty, not exceeding the Sum of 100 *l*. in Money, and three Months imprisonment, without Bail or Mainprize for every Offence; which Offence to be prosecuted at the Court of *King's-bench*, or at the Assizes, or general Quarter-Sessions, within six Months after the Offence committed, and proved by two or more credible Witnesses.

Here you observe the Parliament, who set themselves directly to obviate all the Inconveniences which might arise to the Government from tumultuous petitioning, will not allow that great numbers should join in Petitions, for alteration of the Laws (because it is possible ill Men should abuse such Liberty) unless the matter of the Petition be consented to in such a manner as the Act directs; but in all other Cases, they leave the Subjects to their undoubted Liberty, as well knowing that from thence there could arise no possible Inconvenience; but on the contrary, that to bar the People of that humble way of making their Wants known, might force them upon worse ways of doing it.

And therefore I must tell you, that you do my Lord Chancellor great Injustice if you think his Speech tends to deter Men from all manner of petitioning: No, that wise and eloquent Lord, who receives every day so many Petitions, will I suppose be content the King should receive some too. It never yet was thought * seditious or tumultuous in any Government, for the Subjects in an humble manner to beg, That he who has the only Power to do it, would redress their Grievances: 'Tis the way by which we apply ourselves to the King of Heaven, who knows all our Wants, and yet expects from us that we should daily express them to him in humble Petitions. And the Wisdom of the Church, which has appointed Liturgies, and Forms of Common-Prayer, seems to instruct us, that God is pleased when huge Numbers join in the same Petition. Why should not then suppliant Subjects, with like Humility, and in like manner address themselves to the God on Earth? Especially since Kings cannot know our Desires, or our Grievances, till we ourselves inform them what they are. I remember some wicked Counsellors of *Darius* did once obtain a Law to be made, that none should petition any one but the King for thirty days; but there never yet was found so absurd a Statesman as to advise a Law, that Subjects should not supplicate their Prince. 'Tis probable it would be well for some Favourites, who are near a King, if such a Right could be taken from the People, for then all their false Suggestions and Informations might pass undiscovered; but 'tis impossible that a King should long be safe in such a Condition. I will suppose a malicious Statesman, intending to raise a jealousy in the mind of the Sovereign, should inform him in dangerous times, that he was not beloved by his People, and that he was not to trust them: How could the Subjects in such a Case recover the Prince's good Opinion, in the absence of a legal Representative, but by humble and affectionate Addresses? Or suppose some good Protestant Prince should be so unfortunate, as to have some Counsellors near him who are conceal'd; and others, whose Crimes make them fear Parliaments; it is easy to sup-

* It is the Right of all People that apprehend themselves aggriev'd, to approach his Majesty by Petition. Mr. *Finch's* Argument in the Trial of the seven Bishops. *f.* 105. The Subjects have a Right to petition the King in all their Grievances; so say all our Books of Law, and so says the Statute 13 *Car*. 2. Serjeant *Levinz* in the same Trial, *fol.* 121.

It was one Article against the Earl of *Strafford*, That he issued out a Proclamation and Warrant of Restraint, to inhibit the King's Subjects to come to the Fountain, their Sovereign, to deliver their Complaints of their Wrongs and Oppressions. *Rushw.* in his Trial 721.

poſe, that the one ſort will be filling his ears with Stories, that a great part of his King-dom are inclin'd to Popery ; and the other ſort, that the beſt of his Subjects are quite out of love with Parliaments, as factious and ſeditious Aſſemblies : Into what unfor-tunate Circumſtances, would ſuch a Prince be apt to fall, if his People were precluded from addreſſing themſelves, and opening their Deſires to him ?

I might go on to trouble you with infinite Inſtances of this nature, but there is no want of any in ſo plain a Caſe : 'Tis the Doctrine of our Church, that the only Arms of Subjects, are Prayers, Petitions, Supplications, and Tears ; and they are no Friends either to the King or Church, who would diſarm us of theſe. My Lord Chief Juſtice *Hobbart* tell us, That it is lawful for any Subject to petition the King for Re-dreſs in an humble and modeſt Manner ; for (ſays he) Acceſs to the Sovereign muſt not be ſhut up in caſe of the Subjects Diſtreſſes. It was one of the Crimes for which the *Spencers* were baniſhed by Parliament, that they hindred the King from receiving and anſwering Petitions from great Men, and others.

Nob. 220.
Wrenham's
Caſe.
Vet. Magn.
Chart. Exil.
Hug. De Spen-
cer. 51.

And as it is our unqueſtionable Right, ſo in all Ages the Uſage has been by Petition, to inform our King of our Grievances. In the Reign of King *Ed.* II. and *Ed.* III. Pe-titions were frequent for Redreſs of publick Grievances, and for Parliaments, eſpecially out of *Ireland,* (though that is a conquered Nation) as may be ſeen in the Cloſe Rolls of the Reigns of thoſe two Kings. One Inſtance I will give you for your Satisfaction. but I will tire you with no more, for that would be endleſs.

Be the Right
of the Subject
never ſo clear,
manifeſt, and
acknowledg-
ed by all ;
yet if his own
be detained

from him by the King, he hath no other Writ or Account to recover, but a mere Petition, *Supplicare Celſitudini,* &c. A learned Judge's Argument about Impoſitions. Printed, 1641. *p.* 26.

Clauſ. 10E. 2.
M.28.intusPro
communita-
te Hiberniæ.

'Tis *Clauſ.* 10 Ed. 2. M. 28. *Intus pro Communitate Hiberniæ. Rex. Dilect. & fide-liter ſuis Juſt. Cancellar. & Theſaur. ſuis Hib. ſalutem, ex parte populi noſtri terræ prædict. per Petitionem ſuam coram nobis & Concilio noſtro exhibitum nobis eſt cum inſtantia ſuppli-care, quod cum,* &c.

Cook's Juriſ-
diction of
Courts, p. 79.
Burnet's Hiſ-
tory of the
Reformation,
Pag. 231.
Procl. Dat. 7.
Feb. 11 Jac.

In the 5th Year of King *Richard* II. the whole Body of the Realm petitioned, that the moſt wiſe and able Men within the Realm might be choſen Chancellors.

King *Henry* VIII. told his Subjects then in Arms againſt him in *Yorkſhire,* that they ought not to have rebelled, but to have applied themſelves to him by Petition.

King *James,* by a Proclamation publiſhed in the 12th Year of his Reign, begins thus : 'The Complaints lately exhibited to us by certain Noblemen, and others of our 'Kingdom of *Ireland,* ſuggeſting Diſorders and Abuſes, as well in the Proceedings of 'the late begun Parliament, as in the martial and civil Government of the Kingdom, 'We did receive with extraordinary Grace and Favour.

Procl. 12 Jac.

And by another Proclamation in the 12th Year of his Reign, he declares, That it was the Right of his Subjects to make their immediate Addreſſes to him by Petition ; and in the 19th Year of his Reign he invites his Subjects to it.

Procl. Dat.
10 July, 19
Jac.
Procl. Dat.
14 Feb. 20,
Jac.

And in the 20th Year of his Reign, he tells his People, that his own, and the Ears of his Privy Council, did ſtill continue open to the juſt Complaints of his People ; and that they were not confined to Times and Meetings in Parliament, nor reſtrained to particular Grievances ; not doubting but that his loving Subjects would apply themſelves to his Majeſty for Relief ; to the utter aboliſhing of all thoſe private Whiſperings and cauſleſs Rumors, which without giving his Majeſty any Opportunity of Reformation by particular knowledge of any Fault, ſerve to no other Purpoſe but to occaſion and blow abroad Diſcontentment.

Lords Journ.
Anno 1640.

It appears, that the Houſe of Lords, both Spiritual and Temporal, *Nemine Contradi-cente,* voted Thanks to thoſe Lords who petitioned the King at *York,* to call a Parlia-ment.

Declar. 1644.

And the King by his Declaration printed in the ſame Year, declares his royal Will and Pleaſure, That all his loving Subjects who have any juſt Cauſe to preſent or com-plain of any Grievances or Oppreſſions, may freely addreſs themſelves by their hum-ble Petitions to his ſacred Majeſty, who will graciouſly hear their Complaints.

Temp. Car. 2.

Since his Majeſty's happy Reſtauration, the Inhabitants of the County of *Bucks* made a Petition, That their County might not be over-run by the King's Deer ; and the ſame was done by the County of *Surrey,* on the ſame Occaſion.

'Tis time for me to conclude your trouble : I ſuppoſe you do no longer doubt but that you may join in Petition for a Parliament, ſince you ſee it has been often done heretofore ; nor need you fear how many of your honeſt Countrymen join with you, ſince you hear of Petitions by the whole Body of the Realm ; and ſince you ſee, both by the Opinions of our Lawyers, by the Doctrine of our Church, and by the Declara-tions of our Kings, That it is our undoubted Right to petition. Nothing can be more abſurd

:bſurd than to ſay, That the number of the Supplicants makes an innocent Petition an Offence ; on the contrary, if in a thing of this publick Concernment, a few only ſhould addreſs themſelves to the King, it would be a thing in itſelf ridiculous ; the great End of ſuch Addreſſes being to acquaint him with the general Deſires of his People, which can never be done unleſs multitudes join. How can the Complaints of the diffuſive Body of the Realm reach his Majeſty's ears in the abſence of a Parliament, but in the actual Concurrence of every individual Perſon in petition? for the perſonal Application of multitudes is indeed unlawful and dangerous.

Give me leave, ſince the *Gazette* runs ſo much in your mind, to tell you (as I may modeſtly enough do, ſince the Statute directs me) what anſwer the Judges would now give if ſuch another Caſe were put to them, as was put to the Judges 2 *Jacobi*. *Stat.*13 *Car.*
2.*c.*5.

Suppoſe the Nonconformiſts at this day, (as the Puritans then did) ſhould ſolicite the getting of the hands of Multitudes to a Petition to the King, for ſuſpending the Execution of the penal Laws againſt themſelves ; the preſent Judges would not tell you that this was an Offence next to Treaſon or Felony, nor that the Offenders were to be brought to the Council-board to be puniſhed : but they would tell you plainly and diſtinctly, That if the hands of more Perſons than twenty were ſolicited or procured to ſuch a Petition, and the Offenders were convicted upon the Evidence of two or more credible Witneſſes upon a Proſecution in the King's-bench, or at the Aſſizes or Quarter-Seſſions, within ſix Months, they would incur a Penalty not exceeding 100 *l*. and three Months impriſonment, becauſe their Petition was to change a matter eſtabliſh'd by Law. But I am ſure you are a better Logician than not to ſee the Difference which the Statute makes between ſuch a Petition, which is to alter a thing eſtabliſhed by Law, and an innocent and humble Petition : That a Parliament may meet according to Law, in a time when the greateſt Dangers hang over the King, the Church, and the State.

The Right Honourable the Earl of Shaftſbury's *Speech in the* Houſe of Lords, March 25, 1679.

My Lords,

YOU are appointing of the Conſideration of the State of *England*, to be taken up in a Committee of the whole Houſe, ſome Day next Week. I do not know how well what I have to ſay may be received, for I never ſtudy either to make my Court well, or to be popular ; I always ſpeak what I am commanded by the Dictates of the Spirit within me.

There are ſome other Conſiderations that concern *England* ſo nearly, that without them you will come far ſhort of Safety and Quiet at home : *We have a little Siſter, and ſhe hath no Breaſts, what ſhall we do for our Siſter in the day when ſhe ſhall be ſpoken for? If ſhe be a Wall, we will build on her a Palace of Silver ; if ſhe be a Door, we will incloſe her with Boards of Cedar.* We have ſeveral little Siſters without Breaſts, the *French* Proteſtant Churches, the two Kingdoms of *Ireland* and *Scotland* ; the foreign Proteſtants are a Wall, the only Wall and Defence to *England* ; upon it you may build Palaces of Silver, glorious Palaces. The protection of the Proteſtants abroad, is the greateſt Power and Security the Crown of *England* can attain to, and which can only help us to give check to the growing Greatneſs of *France*. *Scotland* and *Ireland* are two Doors, either to let in Good or Miſchief upon us ; they are much weakened by the Artifice of our cunning Enemies, and we ought to encloſe them with boards of Cedar.

Popery and *Slavery*, like two Siſters, go hand in hand, ſometimes one goes firſt, ſometimes the other in a-doors, but the other is always following cloſe at hand.

In *England*, *Popery* was to have brought in *Slavery* ; in *Scotland*, *Slavery* went before, and *Popery* was to follow.

I do not think your Lordſhips or the Parliament have Juriſdiction there. It is a noble and ancient Kingdom ; they have an illuſtrious Nobility, a gallant Gentry, a learned Clergy, and an underſtanding, worthy People : but yet we cannot think of *England* as we ought, without reflecting on the Condition therein. They are under the ſame Prince, and the Influence of the ſame Favourites and Councils ; when
they

they are hardly dealt with, can we that are the richer expect better Usage? for 'tis certain, that in all absolute Governments, the poorest Countries are always most favourably dealt with.

When the ancient Nobility and Gentry there cannot enjoy their Royalties, their Shrevaldoms, and their Stewardries which they and their Ancestors have possessed for several hundreds of years; but that now they are enjoined by the Lords of the Council to make Deputations of their Authorities to such as are their known Enemies:

Can we expect to enjoy our *Magna Charta* long under the same Persons, and Administration of Affairs? If the Council-table there can imprison any Nobleman or Gentleman for several Years, without bringing him to Trial, or giving the least Reason for what they do; can we expect the same Men will preserve the Liberty of the Subject here?

I will acknowledge, I am not well vers'd in the particular Laws of *Scotland*; but this I do know, that all the *Northern* Countries have, by their Laws, an undoubted and inviolable Right to their Liberties and Properties; yet *Scotland* hath out-done all the *Eastern* and *Southern* Countries, in having their Lives, Liberties, and Estates subjected to the arbitrary Will and Pleasure of those that govern. They have lately plundered and harrassed the richest and wealthiest Countries of that Kingdom, and brought down the barbarous *Highlanders* to devour them; and all this without almost a colourable pretence to do it: Nor can there be found a Reason of State for what they have done; but that those wicked Ministers designed to procure a Rebellion at any Rate, which, as they managed, was only prevented by the miraculous Hand of God, or otherwise all the Papists in *England* would have been armed, and the fairest Opportunity given in the just time for the execution of that wicked and bloody Design the Papists had; and it is not possible for any Man that duly considers it, to think other, but that those Ministers that acted that, were as guilty of the Plot, as any of the Lords that are in question for it.

My Lords, I am forced to speak this the plainer, because, till the Pressure be fully and clearly taken off from *Scotland*, 'tis not possible for me, or any thinking Man to believe that good is meant us here.

We must still be upon our Guard, apprehending that the Principle is not changed at Court, and that these Men that are still in Place and Authority, have that Influence upon the mind of our excellent Prince, that he is not, nor cannot be that to us, that his own Nature and Goodness would incline him to.

I know your Lordships can order nothing in this, but there are those that hear me, can put a perfect Cure to it; until that be done, the *Scottish Weed* is like Death in the Pot, *Mors in Olla*: but there is something too, now I consider, that most immediately concerns us; their Act of twenty two thousand Men to be ready to invade us upon all Occasions. This, I hear, that the Lords of the Council there have treated as they do all other Laws, and expounded it into a standing Army of six thousand Men. I am sure we have Reason and Right to beseech the King, that that Act may be better considered in the next Parliament there. I shall say no more for *Scotland* at this time, I am afraid your Lordships will think I have said too much, having no Concern there: But if a *French* Nobleman should come to dwell in my House and Family, I should think it concerned me to ask what he did in *France?* for if he were there a Felon, a Rogue, a Plunderer, I should desire him to live elsewhere; and I hope your Lordships will do the same thing for the Nation, if you find the same cause.

My Lords, give me leave to speak two or three Words concerning our other Sister *Ireland*: Thither, I hear, is sent *Douglas's* Regiment, to secure us against the *French*. Besides, I am credibly informed, that the Papists have their Arms restored, and the Protestants are not many of them yet recovered from being the suspected Party; the Sea-towns as well as the In-land, are full of Papists: That Kingdom cannot long continue in the *English* Hands, if some better care be not taken of it. This is in your power, and there is nothing there, but is under your Laws; therefore I beg that this Kingdom at least may be taken in consideration, together with the State of *England*: For I am sure there can be no Safety here, if these Doors be not shut up and made sure.

THE

THE
INSTRUMENT
OR
𝕎riting of Association,
THAT THE
True Proteſtants of ENGLAND enter'd into,
IN THE
Reign of Q. Elizabeth.

Foraſmuch as Almighty God hath ordained *Kings, Queens* and *Princes,* to have Dominion and Rule over all their Subjects, and to preſerve them in the Poſſeſſion and Obſervation of the true Chriſtian Religion, according to his holy Word and Commandment: And in like ſort, that all Subjects ſhould *Love, Fear* and *Obey* their Sovereign Princes, being *Kings* or *Queens,* to the utmoſt of their Power; at all times to withſtand, purſue and ſuppreſs all manner of Perſons that ſhall by any means intend and attempt any thing dangerous or hurtful to the Honour, States, or Perſons of their Sovereigns.

Therefore we, whoſe Names are or ſhall be ſubſcribed to this Writing, *being Natural born Subjects of this Realm of* England, and having ſo gracious a Lady, our Sovereign *Elizabeth,* by the Ordinance of God, our moſt rightful Queen, reigning over us theſe many Years with great Felicity, to our ineſtimable Comfort: And finding lately by divers *Depoſitions, Confeſſions,* and ſundry *Advertiſements out of Foreign Parts, from credible Perſons,* well known to her Majeſty's Council, and to divers others; that for the Furtherance and Advancement of ſome pretended Title to the Crown, it hath been manifeſted that the Life of our gracious Sovereign Lady Queen *Elizabeth,* hath been moſt dangerouſly to the Peril of her Perſon; if Almighty God, her perpetual Defender, of his Mercy had not revealed and withſtood the ſame; by whoſe Life we and all other her Majeſty's true and loyal Subjects, do enjoy an ineſtimable Benefit of Peace in this Land; do for the Reaſons and Cauſes before alledged, not only acknowledge our ſelves moſt juſtly bound with our Lives and Goods for her Defence, in her Safety, to proſecute, ſuppreſs and withſtand all ſuch Intenders, and all other her Enemies, of what Nation, Condition and Degree whatſoever they ſhall be, or by what Council or Title they ſhall pretend to be her Enemies, or to attempt any Harm upon her Perſon; but do further think it our bounden Duties for the great Benefit of Peace, Wealth, and Godly Government, we have more plentifully received theſe many Years, under her Majeſty's Government, than any of our Forefathers have done in any longer time of any other Progenitors, Kings of this Realm:

Do declare, and by this Writing make manifeſt, our bounden Duties to our ſaid Sovereign Lady for her Safety. *And to that end, We, and every of us, firſt calling to Witneſs the Name of Almighty God, do voluntarily and moſt willingly bind our ſelves, every one of us to the other, jointly and ſeverally in the Band of one firm and loyal Society: And do hereby vow and promiſe by the MAJESTY OF ALMIGHTY GOD, That with our whole Powers, Bodies, Lives and Goods, and with our Children and Servants, We,*

and

and every of us, will faithfully ſerve and humbly obey our ſaid Sovereign Lady Queen Elizabeth, *againſt all States, Dignities and Earthly Powers whatſoever* ; and will as well with our joint and particular Forces during our Lives, withſtand, offend, and purſue, as well by Force of Arms, as by all other means of Revenge, all manner of Perſons of what State ſoever they ſhall be, and their Abbettors, that ſhall attempt any Act, Council, or Conſent to any thing that ſhall tend to the Harm of her Majeſty's Royal Perſon ; and will never deſiſt from all manner of Forcible Purſuit againſt ſuch Perſons, to the utter Extermination of them, their Counſellors, Aiders and Abettors.

And if any ſuch wicked Attempt againſt her moſt Royal Perſon, ſhall be taken in hand, or procured, whereby any that have, may or ſhall pretend Title to come to this Crown, by the untimely Death of her Majeſty ſo wickedly procured (which God for his Mercy ſake forbid) may be avenged ; *We do not only bind our ſelves both jointly and ſeverally never to allow, accept, or favour any ſuch pretended Succeſſor, by whom, or for whom any ſuch deteſtable Act ſhall be attempted or committed, as unworthy of all Government in any Chriſtian Realm or Civil State:*

But do alſo further vow and proteſt, as we are moſt bound, and that in the *Preſence of the Eternal and Everlaſting God*, to proſecute ſuch Perſon and Perſons to Death with our joint or particular Forces, and to act the utmoſt Revenge upon them that by any means we or any of us can deviſe and do, or cauſe to be deviſed and done for their utter Overthrow and Extirpation.

And to the better *Corroboration* of this our *Loyal Band and Aſſociation*, We do alſo teſtify by this Writing, that we do confirm the Contents hereof by our *Oaths* corporally taken upon the *Holy Evangeliſts*, with this expreſs Condition, That no one of us ſhall for any reſpect of *Perſons* or *Cauſes*, or for *Fear or Reward*, ſeparate our ſelves from this *Aſſociation*, or fail in the Proſecution thereof, *during our Lives*, upon pain of being by the reſt of us proſecuted, *and ſuppreſt as perjur'd Perſons, and as publick Enemies to God, our Queen, and to our Native Country*. To which Puniſhment and Pains we do voluntarily ſubmit our ſelves, and every of us, without Benefit of any Colour or Pretence.

In Witneſs of all which Premiſes to be inviolably kept, we do to this Writing put our Hands and Seals ; and ſhall be moſt ready to accept and admit any other hereafter, to this Society and Aſſociation.

The ACT of Parliament of the 27th *of Queen* Elizabeth *in Confirmation of the ſame.*

FOraſmuch as the Good, Felicity and Comfort of the whole Eſtate of this Realm conſiſteth only (next under God) in the Surety and Preſervation of the *Queen's* moſt excellent Majeſty : And for that it hath manifeſtly appeared, that ſundry wicked Plots and Means have of late been deviſed and laid as well in Foreign Parts beyond the Seas, as alſo within this Realm, to the great indangering of her Highneſs's moſt Royal Perſon, and to the utter Ruin of the whole Commonweal, if by God's merciful Providence the ſame had not been revealed : Therefore for preventing of ſuch great Perils as might hereafter otherwiſe grow, by the like deteſtable and deviliſh Practices, at the humble Suit and earneſt Petition and Deſire of the Lords Spiritual and Temporal, and the Commons in this preſent Parliament aſſembled, and by the Authority of the ſame Parliament, Be it Enacted and Ordained, if at any time after the End of this preſent Seſſion of Parliament, any open Invaſion or Rebellion ſhall be had or made, into or within any of her Majeſty's Realms or Dominions, or any Act attempted, tending to the hurt of her Majeſty's moſt Royal Perſon *by or for* any Perſon that ſhall or may petend any Title to the Crown of this Realm, after her Majeſty's Deceaſe ; or if any thing ſhall be compaſſed or imagined, tending to the hurt of her Majeſty's Royal Perſon, by any Perſon, or with the *Privity* of any Perſon that ſhall or may pretend Title to the Crown of this Realm ; that then by Her Majeſty's Commiſſion under Her Great Seal, the Lords and other of Her Highneſs's *Privy Council*, and ſuch other Lords of Parliament to be named by her Majeſty, as with the ſaid *Privy Council* ſhall make up the Number of Four and twenty at the leaſt, having with them for their Aſſiſtance in that behalf ſuch of the Judges of the Courts of

Re-

Record at *Weſtminſter*, as Her Highneſs ſhall for that purpoſe aſſign and appoint, or the more part of the ſame Council, Lords and Judges, ſhall by virtue of the Act, have Authority to examine all and every the Offences aforeſaid, and all Circumſtances thereof, and thereupon to give Sentence or Judgment, as upon good Proof of the matter ſhall appear unto them : And that after ſuch Sentence or Judgment given, and Declaration thereof made and publiſhed by Her Majeſty's Proclamation under the Great Seal of *England*, all Perſons againſt whom ſuch Sentence or Judgment ſhall be ſo given and publiſhed, ſhall be *excluded and diſabled for ever to* have or claim, *or to* pretend to have or claim the Crown of this Realm, or of any Her Majeſty's Dominions, any former Law or Statute whatſoever to the contrary in any wiſe notwithſtanding : And that thereupon *All Her Highneſs's Subjects* ſhall and may lawfully, by virtue of this Act, and Her Majeſty's Direction in that behalf, by forcible and poſſible means purſue to death every ſuch wicked Perſon, by whom, or by whoſe means aſſent or privity, any ſuch Invaſion or Rebellion ſhall be in Form aforeſaid denounced to have been made, or ſuch wicked Act attempted, or other thing compaſſed or imagined againſt Her Majeſty's Perſon, and all their Aiders, Comforters and Abettors.

And if any ſuch deteſtable Act ſhall be executed againſt her Highneſs's moſt Royal Perſon, whereby Her Majeſty's Life ſhall be taken away (which God of his great mercy forbid ;) that then every ſuch perſon, by or for whom any ſuch Act ſhall be executed, and their Iſſues being any wiſe aſſenting or privy to the ſame, ſhall by virtue of this Act be excluded and diſabled for ever to have or claim, or pretend to have or claim the ſaid Crown of this Realm or of any other her Highneſs's Dominions, any former Law or Statute whatſoever to the contrary in any wiſe notwithſtanding. And that all the Subjects of this Realm, and all other her Majeſty's Dominions, ſhall and may lawfully by virtue of this Act, by all forcible and poſſible means purſue to death every ſuch wicked Perſon, by whom, or by whoſe means, any ſuch deteſtable Fact ſhall be in Form hereafter expreſſed denounced to have been committed, and alſo their Iſſues being any way aſſenting or privy to the ſame, and all their Aiders, Comforters, and Abettors in that behalf.

And to the end that the Intention of this Law may be effectually executed, if Her Majeſty's Life ſhall be taken away by any violent or unnatural means (which God defend ;) Be it further Enacted by the Authority aforeſaid, That the Lords and others which ſhall be of her Majeſty's Privy Council at the time of ſuch Her Deceaſe, or the more part of the ſame Council, joining unto them for their better Aſſiſtance five other Earls, and ſeven other Lords of Parliament at the leaſt, (foreſeeing that none of the ſaid Earls, Lords or Council be known to be perſons that may make any Title to the Crown,) thoſe perſons which were Chief Juſtices of either Bench, Maſter of the Rolls, and Chief Baron of the Exchequer at the time of Her Majeſty's Death, or in default of the ſaid Juſtices, Maſter of the Rolls, and Chief Baron, ſome other of thoſe which were Juſtices of ſome of the Courts of Records at *Weſtminſter*, at the time of Her Highneſs's Deceaſe, to ſupply their Places, or any Four and twenty or more of them, whereof Eight to be Lords of the Parliament, not being of the Privy Council, ſhall to the uttermoſt of their Power and Skill examine the cauſe and manner of ſuch Her Majeſty's Death, and what Perſons ſhall be any way guilty thereof, and all Circumſtances concerning the ſame, according to the true meaning of this Act, and thereupon ſhall by open Proclamation publiſh the ſame, and without any delay by all forcible and poſſible means proſecute to death, all their Aiders and Abettors : And for the doing thereof, and for the withſtanding and ſuppreſſing of all ſuch Power and Force, as ſhall any way be levied or ſtirred in Diſturbance of the due Execution of this Law, ſhall by virtue of this Act, have Power and Authority not only to raiſe and uſe ſuch Forces as ſhall in that behalf be needful and convenient, but alſo to uſe all other means and things poſſible and neceſſary for the maintenance of the ſame Forces, and proſecution of the ſaid Offenders. And if any ſuch Power and Force ſhall be levied or ſtirred in Diſturbance of the due Execution of this Law, by any perſon that ſhall or may pretend any Title to the Crown of this Realm, whereby this Law may not in all things be fully executed, according to the effect and true meaning of the ſame ; that then every ſuch perſon ſhall by virtue of this Act be therefore excluded and diſabled for ever to have or claim, or to pretend to have or claim the Crown of this Realm, or of any other Her Highneſs's Dominions, any former Law or Statute whatſoever to the contrary notwithſtanding.

And be it further Enacted by the Authority aforeſaid, That all and every the Subjects of all Her Majeſty's Realms and Dominions, ſhall to the uttermoſt of their Power, aid and aſſiſt the ſaid Council and all other the Lords and other Perſons to be adjoined

joined to them for Aſſiſtance, as is aforeſaid, in all things to be done, and executed according to the effect and intention of this Law: And that no Subject of this Realm ſhall in any wiſe be impeached in Body, Lands or Goods, at any time hereafter, for any thing to be done or executed according to the Tenour of the Law, any Law or Statute heretofore made to the contrary in any wiſe notwithſtanding.

And whereas of late many of Her Majeſty's good and faithful Subjects have in the Name of God, and with the Teſtimonies of good Conſciences, by one Uniform manner of Writing under their Hands and Seals, and by their ſeveral Oaths voluntarily taken, joined themſelves together in one Bond and Aſſociation to withſtand and revenge to the uttermoſt all ſuch malicious Actions and Attempts againſt Her Majeſty's moſt Royal Perſon: Now for the full explaining of all ſuch Ambiguities and Queſtions as otherwiſe might happen to grow by reaſon of any ſiniſter or wrong Conſtruction or Interpretation to be made or inferred, of or upon the words or meaning thereof; Be it declared and enacted by the Authority of this preſent Parliament, That the ſame Aſſociation and every Article and Sentence therein contained, as well concerning the diſallowing, excluding or diſabling any Perſon that may or ſhall pretend any Title to come to the Crown of this Realm, as alſo for the purſuing and taking Revenge of any Perſon for any ſuch wicked Act or Attempt as is mentioned in the ſame Aſſociation, ſhall and ought to be in all things expounded and adjudged according to the true intent and meaning of this Act, and not otherwiſe, nor againſt any other Perſon or Perſons.

A Word without Doors concerning the Bill *for* Succession.

SIR,

I AM very ſenſible of the great Honour you were pleaſed to do me in your laſt, which I received immediately after our late unhappy Diſſolution; but could have wiſhed you would have laid your Commands on ſome more able Perſon, to have given you Satisfaction in the matter you there propoſe relating to the Duke, who, you ſeem to inſinuate, was like (if the Parliament had continued) to have received hard meaſure. I muſt ingenuouſly confeſs to you, I was not long ſince perfectly of your Opinion, and thought it the higheſt Injuſtice imaginable, for any Prince to be debar'd of his Native Right of Succeſſion upon any pretence whatſoever. But upon a more mature Deliberation and Enquiry, I found my Error proceeded principally from the falſe Notions I had took up of Government it ſelf, and from my Ignorance of the Practices of all Communities of Men in all Ages, whenever Self-preſervation and Neceſſity of their Affairs obliged them to declare their Opinion in Caſes of the like Nature: To the knowledge of all which, the following Accident I ſhall relate to you, did very much contribute.

My Occaſions obliging me one day to attend the coming of a Friend in a Coffee-houſe near *Charing-Croſs*, there happened to ſit at the ſame Table with me two ingenious Gentlemen, who according to the Frankneſs of Converſation now uſed in the Town, began a Diſcourſe on the ſame Subject you deſire to be more particularly informed in; and having extolled the late Houſe of Commons as the beſt number of Men that had ever ſat within theſe Walls; and that no Houſe had ever more vigorouſly maintained and aſſerted *Engliſh* Liberty and Proteſtant Religion, than they had done, as far as the nature of the things that came before them, and the Circumſtances of time would admit (to all which I very readily and heartily aſſented;) they then added, That the great Wiſdom and Zeal of that Houſe had appeared in nothing more, than in ordering a Bill to be brought in for debarring the Duke of *Y.* from inheriting the Crown. A Law they affirmed to be the moſt juſt and reaſonable in the World, and the only proper Remedy to eſtabliſh this Nation on a true and ſolid Intereſt, both in relation to the preſent and future Times.

To which I could not but reply, That I beg'd their Pardon if I differed from them in Opinion; and did believe, that how honeſtly ſoever the Houſe of Commons might intend in that matter, yet that the point of Succeſſion was ſo ſacred a thing, and of ſo high a Nature, that it was not ſubjected to their Cognizance: That Monarchy was of

Di-

Divine Right: That Princes ſucceeded by Nature and Generation only, and not by Authority, Admiſſion, or Approbation of the People ; and conſequently, that neither the Merit or Demerit of their Perſons, nor the different Influences from thence upon the People, were to be reſpected or had in conſideration ; but the Common-wealth ought to obey and ſubmit to the next Heir, without any further Inquiſition ; and if he proved a worthy, virtuous and juſt Prince, it was a great Happineſs ; if unjuſt, barbarous and tyrannical, there was no other Remedy, but Prayer, Patience and an intire Submiſſion to ſo difficult a Diſpenſation of God's Providence.

I had no ſooner ended my Diſcourſe, but one of the Gentlemen (that was the moſt ſerious in the Company) ſeeing me a young Man, gravely replied, That he could not but be extreamly concerned to hear that ſuch pernicious Notions, againſt all lawful Government, had been taught in the World ; that he believed they were in me purely the Effects of an Univerſity-Education ; and that it had been my Misfortune to have had a very high Church-man for my Tutor, who had endeavoured (as it was their conſtant Practice to all young Gentlemen under their Care) to debauch me with ſuch Principles as would enſlave my Mind to their Hierarchy, and the Monarchical part of the Government, without any Regard at all to the Ariſtocratical and Popular ; and that fat Parſonages, Prebendſhips, Deaneries, and Epiſcopal Sees, were the certain and conſtant Rewards of ſuch Services ; that the Place we were in, was a little too publick for Diſcourſes of this nature ; but if I would accept of a Bottle of Wine at the next Tavern, he would undertake to give me juſter meaſures ; adding, it was pity ſo hopeful a Gentleman ſhould be tainted with bad Principles. My Friend coming in at the ſame time, proved to be one of their particular Acquaintance ; and both he and I readily complied with ſo generous a Motion.

We had no ſooner drank a Glaſs round, but the old Gentleman was pleaſed to renew his Diſcourſe, and ſaid it was undoubtedly true, that the Inclination of Mankind to live in Company (from whence come Towns, Cities, and Common-wealths) did proceed of Nature, and conſequently of God the Author of Nature : So likewiſe Government and the Juriſdiction of Magiſtrates in general (which does neceſſarily flow from the living together in Society) is alſo of Nature, and ordained by God for the common Good of Mankind ; but that the particular Species and Forms of this or that Government, in this or that manner ; to have many, few, or one Governour ; or that they ſhould have this or that Authority, more or leſs, for a longer, or a ſhorter time ; or whether ordinarily by Succeſſion or by Election : All theſe things (he ſaid) are ordained and diverſified by the particular poſitive Laws of every Country, and are not eſtabliſh'd either by Law Natural or Divine, but left by God unto every Nation and Country, to pitch upon what Form of Government they ſhall think moſt proper to promote the common Good of the whole, and beſt adapted to the Natures, Conſtitutions, and other Circumſtances of the People ; which accordingly for the ſame Reaſons may be altered or amended in any of its parts, by the mutual Conſent of the Governours and Governed, whenever they ſhall ſee reaſonable Cauſe ſo to do ; all which appears plainly, both from the diverſity of Governments extant in the World, and by the ſame Nations living ſometimes under one ſort of Government, and ſometimes under another. So we ſee God himſelf permitted his peculiar People the *Jews* to live under divers Forms of Government ; as firſt, under Patriarchs, then under Captains, then under Judges, then under High-Prieſts, next under Kings, and then under Captains and High Prieſts again, until they were conquered by the *Romans*, who themſelves alſo firſt lived under Kings, and then Conſuls, whoſe Authority they afterwards limited by a Senate, by adding Tibunes of the People ; and in extraordinary Emergencies of the Commonwealth, they were governed by Dictators, and laſt of all by Emperors. So that 'tis plain no Magiſtrate has his particular Government, or an Intereſt of Succeſſion in it, by any Inſtitution of Nature, but only by the particular Conſtitution of the Commonwealth within it ſelf. And as the kinds of Government are different, ſo alſo are the meaſures of Power and Authority in the ſame kind, in different Countries.

I ſhall begin, (ſaid he) with that of the *Roman* Empire, which though it be the firſt in Dignity among Chriſtian Princes, yet it is ſo reſtrained and limited by the particular Laws of the Empire, that he can do much leſs in his State, than other Kings in theirs. He can neither make War, nor exact any Contribution of Men or Money, but by the Conſent of all the States of the *German* Diet : And as for his Children and Relations, they have no Intereſt or Pretence to ſucceed, but only by Election, if they ſhall be thought worthy. Nay, the chiefeſt Article the Emperor ſwears to keep at his Admiſſion to that Honour, is, That he ſhall never endeavour to make the Dignity of the Empire hereditary to his Family. X In

In *Spain* and in *France*, the Privileges of Kings are much more eminent, both in Power and Succeſſion ; their Authority is more abſolute, every Order of theirs having the Validity of a Law, and their next of Blood does ordinarily inherit, though in a different manner.   In *Spain* the next Heir cannot ſucceed but by the Approbation of the Nobility, Biſhops, and States of the Realm.   In *France* the Women are not admitted to ſucceed, let them be ever ſo lineally deſcended.   In *England* our Kings are much more limited and confined in their Power, than either of the two former ; for here no Law can be made but by Conſent and Authority of Parliament ; and as to the Point of Succeſſion, the next of Kin is admitted, unleſs in extraordinary Caſes, and when important Reaſons of State require an Alteration : And then the Parliaments of *England* (according to the ancient Laws and Statutes of the Realm) have frequently directed and appointed the Succeſſion of the Crown in other manner than in courſe it would have gone ; of which I ſhall give you ſome Examples in Order.

But firſt let us look abroad, and ſee how things have been carried as to this Point in other Countries.

Amongſt the *Jews* the Law of Succeſſion did ordinarily hold ; and accordingly *Reboboam* the lawful Son and Heir of *Solomon*, after his Father's Deceaſe, went to *Sichem* to be crowned and admitted by the People ; and the whole Body of the People of *Iſrael* being there gathered together, did (before they would admit him their lawful King) make unto him certain Propoſitions for taking away ſome heavy Taxes that had been impoſed on them by his Father *Solomon*, which he refuſing to gratify them in, and following the Advice of young Men, ten of the twelve Tribes immediately choſe *Jeroboam*, a Servant of *Reboboam*'s, a meer Stranger and of mean Parentage, and made him their King ; and God approved thereof, as the Scriptures in expreſs Words do teſtify : For when *Reboboam* had raiſed an Army of One hundred and fourſcore thouſand Men, intending by force of Arms to have juſtified his Claim, God appeared unto *Semaiah*, and commanded him to go to *Reboboam*, and to the Houſe of *Judah* and *Benjamin*, ſaying, *Return every Man to his Houſe, for this thing is of me, ſaith the Lord.*   So that ſince God did permit and allow this in his own Commonwealth, which was to be the Pattern for all others, no doubt he will approve the ſame in other Kingdoms, whenever his Service and Glory, or the Happineſs of the Weal-publick ſhall require it.

The next inſtance, I ſhall give you, ſhall be in *Spain*, where *Don Alonſo de la Cerda* having been admitted Prince of *Spain* in his Father's Life-time (according to the Cuſtom of that Realm) married *Blancha* Daughter of *Lewis* the firſt King of *France*, and had by her two Sons named *Alonſo* and *Hernando de la Cerda* ; but their Father (who was only Prince) dying before *Alonſo* the Ninth, then King, he recommended them to the Realm as lawful Heirs apparent to the Crown : But *Don Sancho* their Father's younger Brother, who was a great Warrior, and Sirnamed *El Bravo*, was admitted Prince, and they put by, in their Grandfather's Life-time, by his and the States conſent ; and this was done at a Parliament held at *Segovia*, in the Year 1276.   And in the Year 1284, (*Alonſo* the Ninth being dead) *Don Sancho* was acknowledg'd King, and the two Princes impriſoned ; but at the Mediation of *Philip* the third, King of *France*, their Uncle, they were ſet free, and endowed with conſiderable Revenues in Land, and from them do deſcend the Dukes *De Medina Celi* at this day ; and the preſent King of *Spain* that is in Poſſeſſion, deſcendeth from *Don Sancho*.

In *France*, *Lewis* the Fourth had two Sons, *Lothairin*, who ſucceeded him, and *Charles* whom he made Duke of *Lorrain*.   *Lothairin* dying, left an only Son nam'd *Lewis*, who dying without Iſſue after he had reigned two Years, the Crown was to have deſcended on his Uncle *Charles* Duke of *Lorrain*.   But the States of *France* did exclude him, and choſe *Hugo Capetus*, Earl of *Paris*, for their King ; and in an Oration made by their Embaſſador to *Charles* of *Lorrain*, did give an Account of their Reaſons for ſo doing, as it is related by *Belforeſt* a *French* Hiſtorian, in theſe very Words :

Every Man knoweth (Lord *Charles*) *that the Succeſſion of the Crown and Kingdom of* France, *according to the ordinary Rights and Laws of the ſame, belongeth unto you, and not unto* Hugh Capet, *now our King : But yet the ſame Laws which do give unto you ſuch Right of Succeſſion, do judge you alſo unworthy of the ſame, for that you have not endeavoured hitherto to frame your Life according to the Preſcript of thoſe Laws, nor according to the Uſe and Cuſtom of the Kingdom of* France, *but rather have allied your ſelf to the* Germans, *our old Enemies, and have accuſtomed your ſelf to their vile and baſe Manners. Wherefore ſince you have abandoned and forſaken the ancient Virtue, Amity and Sweetneſs of your Country, your Country has alſo abandoned and forſaken you ; for we have choſen* Hugh Capet *for our King, and have put you by, and this without any Scruple in our Conſciences at all ; eſteeming it far*

better

better and more juft to live under Hugh Capet, *the poffeffor of the Crown, with enjoying the ancient ufe of our Laws, Cuftoms, Privileges, and Liberties, than under the next Heir by Blood, in Oppreffions, ftrange Cuftoms and Cruelty : For, as they who make a Voyage in a Ship on a dangerous Sea, do not fo much refpeft whether the Pilot claims Title to the Ship or no, but rather, whether he be skilful, valiant, and like to bring them in fafety to their way's end; even fo our principal Care is, to have a good Prince, to lead and guide us happily in this way of Civil and Politick Life; which is the end for which Princes are appointed.* And with this Meffage ended his Succeffion and Life, he dying not long after in Prifon.

And now I fhall come home, and give you an Inftance or two in *England,* fince the Conqueft, and fo conclude.

William Rufus, fecond Son of *William the Conqueror,* by the affiftance of *Lanfrank,* Archbifhop of *Canterbury,* who had a great Opinion of his Virtue and Probity, was admitted King by the confent of the Realm, his elder Brother *Robert* Duke of *Normandy* being then in the War at *Jerufalem: William* dying, his younger Brother *Henry,* by his Ingenuity and fair Carriage, and by the affiftance of *Henry* Earl of *Warwick,* who had greateft Intereft in the Nobility, and *Maurice* Bifhop of *London,* a leading Man amongft the Clergy, obtained alfo the Crown : And *Robert* Duke of *Normandy* was a fecond time excluded. And though this King *Henry* could pretend no other Title to the Crown than the Election and Admiffion of the Realm, yet he defended it fo well, and God profpered him with Succefs, that when his elder Brother *Robert* came to claim the Kingdom, by force of Arms, he beat him in a pitch'd Battle, took him Prifoner, and fo he died miferable in Bonds.

King *Henry* had one only Daughter, named *Maud,* or *Matilda,* who was married to the Emperor, and he dying without Iffue, fhe was afterwards married to *Geofry Planta-genet* Earl of *Anjou* in *France,* by whom fhe had a Son named *Henry,* whom his Grand-father declared Heir-apparent to the Crown in his Life-time ; yet after his Death, *Henry* was excluded, and *Stephen* Earl of *Bulloine,* Son of *Adela,* Daughter of *William the Conqueror,* was by the States thought more fit to govern than Prince *Henry,* who was then but a Child. And this was done by the perfuafion of *Henry* Bifhop of *Winchefter,* and at the folicitation of the Abbot of *Glaftenbury,* and others, who thought they might do the fame lawfully, and with a good Confcience, for the publick Good of the Realm.

But the Event did not prove fo well as they intended ; for this occafioned great Factions and Divifions in the Kingdom ; for the quieting of which, there was a Par-liament held at *Wallingford,* which paffed a Law, That *Stephen* fhould be King only during his Life, and that Prince *Henry* and his Off-fpring fhould fucceed him ; and by the fame Law debarred *William,* Son of King *Stephen,* from inheriting the Crown, and only made him Earl of *Norfolk.*

Thus did the Parliament difpofe of the Crown in thofe Days, which was in the year 1153 ; which fufficiently proves what I have afferted.

The fum of all I have faid amounts to this, That Government in general is by the *Law of Nature,* and confequently the Ordinance of God ; but that the different Forms of Government, whether to refide in One, Few, or Many ; or whether it fhall be continued by Succeffion or by Election, together with the different meafures and li-mitations of Power and Authority in Governours of the fame kind in feveral Countries ; all thefe things, I fay, are ordained by, and purely depend upon pofitive and human Laws: From whence it will neceffarily follow, That the fame human Authority (refiding in King, Lords and Commons, here in *England*) which gave being to thofe Laws for the good of the Community, is Superintendant over them, and both may and ought to make any Addition to, or Alteration of them, when the publick Good and Welfare of the Nation fhall require it ; unlefs you will admit, That an Human Authority eftablifhing any thing, intentionally for the common good of the Society, which in tract of Time, by reafon of unforefeen Circumftances and Emergencies, proves deftructive of it, has by that Act concluded it felf, and made that accidental Evil moral and un-changeable, which to affirm is fenflefs and repugnant.

And now, Sir, I hope, by this time (faid the old Gentleman) you begin to think that the Bill for difabling the Duke, was not fo unjuft and unreafonable as was pretended ; and that the courfe of Succeffion (being founded upon the fame bottom with other Ci-vil Conftitutions) might likewife as juftly have been altered by the King, Lords and Commons, as any other Law or Cuftom whatever.

And here I might conclude ; but becaufe a late *Penfionary Pen* has publickly arraign'd the Wifdom, Loyalty and Juftice of the Honourable Houfe of Commons, on the ac-count of this Bill, I will *ex abundanti* add a Word or two more to that particular.

Where-

I

Whereupon he pluck'd a Paper out of his Pocket, intituled, *Great and weighty Considerations relating to the Duke and Successor of the Crown, &c.* Which as soon as he had read unto us, You see here (said he) the true Temper of those Men, of whom I first gave you Caution: There never was an Endeavour (though in a Legal and Parliamentary way) after any Reformation either in Church or State, but the Promoters of it were sure to be branded by them with the odious Imputations of *Fanaticism* and *Faction.* Nay, if the Country-Electors of Parliament-men, will not pitch upon such Rake-hells of the Nation as are usually proposed by them, but, on the contrary, make use of their Freedom and Consciences in chusing able, upright, and deserving Persons ; and if good Men thus chosen, do but (according to their Duty in the House) enquire into publick Grievances, pursue in a legal Course notorious Offenders, and consult and advise the Security of the Government and Protestant Religion, the high Church-man immediately swells, and in a Passion tells you, That all this proceeds from the old *Fanatick Leven*, not yet worn out amongst the People ; that we are going back again to Forty-One, and acting over afresh the Sins of our Forefathers.

Thus ignorantly do they compliment the Times and Persons they endeavour to expose, by appropriating to them such Virtues as were common to good Men in all Ages. But enough of this.

In the next place, pray observe how hypocritically the *Considerer* puts this Question, *viz.*

Whether Protestant Religion was not settled in this Nation by the same mighty hand of God, that establish'd Jeroboam *in the Kingdom of* Israel ? (And then adds) *Whether we (like that wicked King) should so far despair of God's Providence in preserving the work of his own Hands, as never to think it safe, unless it be establish'd on the Quick-sands of our own wicked Inventions ?* (viz. the Bill against the Duke.)

And throughout his whole Discourse, he frequently calls all Care of preserving our Religion, a Mistrust of God's Providence ; and on that score calls out to the Nation, *O ye of little Faith, &c.* Now I will allow him, That the least Evil is not to be done, that the greatest and most important Good may ensue : But that the Bill for disabling the Duke is highly justifiable both by the Laws of God and Constitution of our Government, I think, by my former Discourse, I have left no room to doubt : And the *Considerer* having scarce attempted to prove the contrary, 'tis preposterously done of him to give us his Use of Reproof before he has clear'd his Doctrine.

However, I owe him many thanks for putting me in mind how Protestant Religion was first establish'd here in *England* ; it was indeed by the mighty Hand of God, influencing the publick Councils of the Nation, so that all imaginable care was taken, both by Prince and People, to rescue themselves from under the Popish Yoke ; and accordingly most excellent Laws were made against the usurpation and tyranny of that Man of Sin. Our noble Ancestors, in those days, did not palliate a want of Zeal for their Religion, with a lazy pretence of trusting in God's Providence ; but, together with their Prayers to, and Affiance in Heaven, they joined the Acts of their own Duty, without which (they very well knew) they had no Reason to expect a Blessing from it.

But now be pleased to take notice of the Candor of this worthy *Considerer* ; nothing less will serve his turn, than the proving all the Voters for the Bill guilty of the highest Perjury : *For* (says he) *they have all sworn in the Oath of Allegiance to bear Faith and true Allegiance to his Majesty, his Heirs and Successors ; but the Duke is Heir,* ergo, *&c.* A very hopeful Argument indeed ! But what if it should happen, (as it is neither impossible nor very improbable to imagine it) that the next Heir to the Crown should commit Treason, and conspire the Death of the present Possessor, and for this Treason should not only be attainted by Parliament, but executed too : Pray, Mr. *Considerer*, would the Parliament in this Case be guilty of Murder and Perjury ? I am confident you will not say it. If therefore the next Heir become obnoxious to the Government, in a lower degree, why may not the same Authority proportion the Punishment, and leave him his Life, but debar him the Succession ? This I say only to shew the absurdity of his Argument.

My Answer is this : No Man can bear Allegiance to two persons at the same time; nor can Allegiance be ever due to a Subject, and therefore my Obligation by the Word (*Heir*) in the Oath, does not commence till such Heir has a present Right to, or actual Possession of the Crown ; which if he never attains, either by reason of Death, or any other Act that incapacitates and bars him, then can my Obligation to him by the Word *Heir* in the Oath, never have a beginning.

But

But befides all this, it cannot be denied but Mr. *Confiderer*'s Doctrine does bring great Inconveniencies on Succeffion; for the next Heir (by his way of arguing) is let loofe from all the Reftrictions and Penalties of Human Laws; and has no other ties upon him, not to fnatch the Crown out of the Hands of the Poffeffor, than purely thofe of his own Confcience, which is worthy Mr. *Confiderer*'s higheft Confideration.

I fhall only take notice of one Objection more, and then conclude, (fearing I have too much trefpaffed on your Patience already.)

'Tis very hard (fays he) *that a man fhould lofe his Inheritance, becaufe he is of this or that Perfuafion in matters of Religion.*

And truly, Gentlemen, were the Cafe only fo, I fhould be entirely of his mind: But alas! Popery (whatever Mr. *Confiderer* is pleas'd to infinuate) is not an harmlefs innocent Perfuafion of a Number of Men, differing from others in matters relating to Chriftian Religion; but is really and truly a different Religion from Chriftianity it felf. Nor is the Inheritance he there mentions, an Inheritance only of *Black-Acre* and *White-Acre*, without any Office annexed, which requires him to be *par Officio*: But the Government and Protection of feveral Nations, the making War and Peace for them, the Prefervation of their Religion, the Difpofal of Publick Places and Revenues, the Execution of all Laws, together with many other things of the greateft Importance, are in this Cafe claimed by the Word *Inheritance*; which if you confider, and at the fame time reflect upon the enflaving and bloody Tenets of the Church of *Rome*, more particularly the hellifh and damnable Confpiracy thofe of that Communion are now carrying on againft our Lives, our Religion, and our Government; I am confident you will think it as proper for a Wolf to be a Shepherd, as it is for a Papift to be the *Defender of our Faith*, &c.

The old Gentleman had no fooner ended his Difcourfe, but I returned him my hearty Thanks, for the Trouble he had been pleafed to give himfelf on this Occafion; and I could not but acknowledge he had given me great Satisfaction in that Affair; what it will give thee, *Charles*, I know not, I am fure I parted from him very melancholy for having been a Fool fo long. *Adieu*,

I am thy affectionate,

I. D.

A

Collection of Speeches,

IN THE

House of Commons,

In the Year 1680.

The Lord L. *Speech.*

My Lords,

MAny have been the Defigns of the Papifts to fubvert this poor Nation from the Proteftant Religion to that of the See of *Rome*, and that by all the undermining Policies poffibly could be invented, during the Recefs of Parliament, even to the cafting the Odium of their moft damnable Defigns on the Innocency of his Majefty's moft loyal Subjects. We have already had a tafte of their Plottings in *Ireland*, and find how many unaccountable *Irifh* Papifts daily arrive, which we have now under Confideration. My Lord *Dunbarton*, a great *Romanift*, has petitioned for his ftay here, alledging feveral Reafons therein, which in my Opinion make all for his fpeedy Departure; for I can never think his Majefty and this Kingdom fufficiently fecure, till we are rid of thofe *Irifh* Cattle, and all others befides; for I durft be bold to fay, that whatfoever they may pretend, there is not one of them but have a deftructive Tenet, only they want Power, not Will to put it in force.

Y   I

I would not have fo much as a Popifh Man nor a Popifh Woman to remain here, nor fo much as a Popifh Dog, or a Popifh Bitch, no not fo much as a Popifh Cat that fhould pur or mew about the King. We are in a Labyrinth of Evils, and muft carefully endeavour to get out of them ; and the greateft Danger of all amongft us are, our conniving Proteftants, who notwithftanding the many Evidences of the Plot, have been induftrious to revile the King's Witneffes ; and fuch an one is *R——L'E——* who now difappears, being one of the greateft Villains upon the Earth, a Rogue beyond my Skill to delineate, has been the Bugbear to the Proteftant Religion, and traduced the King and Kingdom's Evidences by his notorious fcribling Writings, and hath endeavoured as much as in him lay, to eclipfe the Glory of the *Englifh* Nation ; he is a dangerous rank Papift, proved by good and fubftantial Evidence, for which, fince he has walked under another Difguife, he deferves of all Men to be hanged, and I believe I fhall live to fee that be his State. He has fcandalized feveral of the Nobility, and detracted from the Rights of his Majefty's great Council the Parliament, and is now fled from Juftice, by which he confeffes the Charge againft him, and that fhows him to be guilty.

My humble Motion is, that this Houfe addrefs to his Majefty, to put him out of the Commiffion of Peace, and all other publick Employments for ever.

Speeches in the Honourable Houfe of Commons.

Mr. Speaker,

IN the Front of *Magna Charta* it is faid, *nulli negabimus, nulli differimus Juftitiam,* we will defer or deny Juftice to no Man ; to this the King is fworn, and with this the Judges are intrufted by their Oaths. I admire what they can fay for themfelves : if they have not read this Law, they are not fit to fit upon the Bench ; and if they have, I had almoft faid, they deferve to lofe their Heads.

Mr. Speaker, The State of the poor Nation is to be deplored, that in almoft all ages, the Judges, who ought to be Prefervers of the Laws, have endeavoured to deftroy them ; and that to pleafe a Court-Faction, they have by Treachery attempted to break the Bonds afunder of *Magna Charta*, the great Treafury of our Peace ; it was no fooner paffed ; but a Chief Juftice in that day perfuades the King he was not bound by it, becaufe he was under Age when it was paffed. But this fort of Infolence the next Parliament refented, to the ruin of the pernicious Chief Juftice. In the time of *Richard* the Second, an unthinking diffolute Prince, there were Judges that did infinuate into the King, that the Parliament were only his Creatures, and depended on his Will, and not on the Fundamental Conftitutions of the Land ; which treacherous Advice proved the Ruin of the King, and for which all thofe evil Inftruments were brought to Juftice. In his late Majefty's Time, his Misfortunes were occafioned chiefly by the Corruptions of the long Robe ; his Judges by an extrajudicial Opinion give the King Power to raife Money upon an extraordinary Occafion without Parliament, and made the King Judge of fuch Occafions. Charity prompts me to think, they thought this a Service to the King, but the fad Confequences of it may convince all Mankind, that every illegal Act weakens the Royal Intereft ; and to endeavour to introduce Abfolute Dominion in thefe Realms, is the worft of Treafons, becaufe, whilft it bears the Face of Friendfhip to the King, and defigns to be for his Service, it never fails of the contrary effect.

The two great Pillars of the Government are Parliaments and Juries ; it is this gives us the Title of Free-born *Englifh-men* : for my Notion of free *Englifh-men* is this, that they are ruled by Laws of their own making, and tried by Men of the fame Condition with themfelves. The two great and undoubted Privileges of the People have been lately invaded by the Judges that now fit in *Weftminfter-Hall* ; they have efpoufed Proclamation againft Law ; they have difcountenanced and oppofed feveral legal Acts, that tended to the fitting of this Honourable Houfe ; they have grafped the Legiflative Power into their own Hands, as in that Inftance of Printing ; the Parliament was confidering that matter, but they in the interim made their private Opinion to be Law, to fuperfede the Judgment of this Houfe ; they have difcharged Grand Juries on purpofe to quell their Prefentments, and fhelter great Criminals from Juftice ; and when Juries have prefented their Opinion for the fitting of this Parliament, they have in difdain thrown them at their feet, and told them, they would be no Meffengers to carry fuch Petitions ; and yet in a few days after have encouraged all that would fpit their Venom againft the Government ; they have ferved an ignorant and arbitrary Faction, and been the Meffengers of Abhorrences to the King.

Mr.

Mr. Speaker, What we have now to do, is to load them with fhame, who have bid defiance to the Law ; they are guilty of Crimes againſt Nature, againſt the King, againſt their Knowledge, and againſt Poſterity. The whole Frame of Nature doth loudly and daily petition to God their Creator ; and Kings, like God, may be addreſſed to in like manner by Petition, not Command. They likewiſe knew it was lawful to petition ; Ignorance can be no Plea, and their Knowledge aggravates their Crimes. The Children unborn are bound to curſe ſuch Proceedings ; for 'twas not petitioning, but Parliaments they abhor'd. The Atheiſt pleads againſt a God, not that he diſbelieves a Deity, but would have it ſo. *Trefilian* and *Belknap* were Judges too, their Learning gave them Honour, but their Villanies made their *Exit* by a Rope. The end of my Motion therefore is, That we may addreſs warmly to our Prince againſt them, let us ſettle a Committee to enquire into their Crimes, and not fail of doing Juſtice upon them that have perverted it ; let us purge the Fountain, and the Streams will iſſue pure.

November *the 17th, being appointed for Conſideration of His Majeſty's Meſſage, the Order being read, it was moved by a worthy Member,*

THAT as long as *Popery* hangs over us, we could do nothing, and we ought to repreſent our Condition to the King ; and then, when we had ſecured our Religion and Property, we ſhould be ready to do any thing that might make the King happy and great.

A Second. I am ſorry that *Tangier* (that is, a Supply) is moved for, at ſo unſeaſonable a time ; I confeſs *Tangier* is of great moment, but we have now in hand that which is of greater moment than ten *Tangiers* put together. The Conſideration of that, before we are ſecure in our Religion at home, is as when an Enemy was landed we ſhould afterwards go to fortify the Coaſts of *Kent.* And being told us by his Majeſty, we ſhould ſecure our ſelves againſt Popery, by all ways but meddling with the Succeſſion, and ſhould reſt there, we are prevented of what is our Preſervation : And the providing for *Tangier* now, will be the weakening of our Security. When *Tangier* was put into the Hands of the *Engliſh* firſt, there was an Article that there ſhould continue a Popiſh Church, and the Religion that belonged to it, to continue their Lives, but not to be repleniſh'd with new. And if it be enquired into, I believe it will be found the number of them is not yet decreaſed.' It is not long ſince there was a Popiſh Governour there, many Papiſts and Soldiers gone thither lately from *Ireland.* It is not a little Sum that will do what is needful there ; and if it ſhould be a conſiderable one that ſhould be given for it, it may be made uſe of to raiſe an Army there ; ſo that we run into a great Inconveniency by providing for it ; I think we ought to conſider well of it before we do : And yet I am not for ſullenly ſaying, we will raiſe no Money, but for clearly ſtating the Caſe by an Addreſs to the King.

A Third. I am only to acquaint you, That *Tangier* is not to be maintained without your Support.

A Fourth. All things are to be conſidered comparatively, and if it be made an Argument againſt the Duke's Bill, that he is at the Head of an Army in *Scotland,* and that in *Ireland* there are ten Papiſts to one Proteſtant, his great Intereſt in the Fleet, and being Admiral, and *Tangier* being a Seminary of Papiſts ; then ſure you have a ſpecial Argument to take *Tangier* into your Coſideration, and Money may be for that Service. But then this Parliament do not aſk Petitions of Grace, but of Right. And will you part with your Money without any Security ? You have often done ſo, and what are you the better for it ? I long for the Time when we may give Money to make the King great ; but if things muſt go on as they do, I am for a plain Bargain, to know what we ſhall have for our Money. For my part, I only deſire our Security ; but if we ſhould give Money, I ſuppoſe you will take care what hands we put it in, and there ought to be a Truſt : Let us addreſs his Majeſty.

A Fifth. We are told *Tangier* is of Importance, it is a Nurſery of Papiſts : And we are likewiſe told, the *Iriſh* ſent thither a part of the *Iriſh* Army, and they take the Oath, that is no Security : Was not the Lord *Bellaſis* Governour of *Tangier* and *Hull,* and the Penſioners Captain, all at a time, and took the Oaths ? Thoſe Soldiers, for ought I know, may be brought hither, and the aſking for a Supply for it at this time, is very unreaſonable, becauſe Parliaments have been put off two or three Years ; and whilſt there are People that dare make a difference between the King and this Houſe, we ſhall never be ſafe. Let us repreſent our Condition as boldly as may ſtand with

good

I

good manners. It is not to be endured, to fee the Duke preferred before the King, as he was ; as if Arguments of his Greatnefs and Power were Arguments ftrong enough to hinder the Bill : He hath violated the Law, and we needed not to have gone this way to work, if we could have had Juftice againft him ; but he is too great for that, let us addrefs his Majefty.

A Sixth. If *Tangier* be wholly under the Duke's Care and Protection, and fuch a Seminary for Papifts as hath been reprefented, I think any Motion to have a Supply for it is unfeafonable, and am againft it ; order the bringing in the ftate of it.

A Seventh. I fpoke the fenfe of the City formerly, and do fo now again, and in the name of the greateft part of the Commonalty of the City of *London* ; and we do declare, That we are ready to give Money, half we have, nay all, and be content to fet up again, and get new Eftates, if we can but be fecured. The burning of *London*, juftly laid upon the Papifts, and keeping Watch fince the Plot, hath coft the City above 100000 *l.* The City of *London* is the Bulwark of our Religion : And is it not faid, the Duke is at the head of 30 or 40000 Men ? The Lieutenancy and Juftices, how are they molded for his turn ! And if you do nothing now in this Houfe, we muft all, without any more ado, try to make a Peace with him as well as we can, I'll never do it : And will you, for the fake of one Man, deftroy three Kingdoms ?

An Eighth. He moved, that the Reprefentation might declare, That we fee no Security, but removing the Duke of *York*.

A Ninth. We difcourfing of *Tangier* at this time, is like *Nero*'s Fiddling whilft *Rome* was confuming by Fire : If it be in a good condition, we cannot help it ; if in a bad one, we are not in a pofture to do it. Pray confider the condition by what's paft, when King *Henry* the Eighth was for Supremacy, the Kingdom was for it. When King *Henry* the Eighth was againft it, the Kingdom was againft it. When King *Edward* the Sixth was a Proteftant, the Kingdom was fo ; when Queen *Mary* was a Papift, the Kingdom was fo ; when Queen *Elizabeth* was a Proteftant, the Kingdom fo again ; *Regis ad exemplum,* &c. And I believe, even in King *Edward* the Sixth's time, the Bifhops themfelves would not have been for throwing out fuch a Bill as this. And if King *Edward* had promifed any thing for the prefervation of the *Proteftant Religion*, fo that *Mary* might fucceed, the Pope would no way have contrived fo great a Favour. The bidding us prevent *Popery*, and the letting alone a *Popifh* Succeffor, is as if a Phyfician fhould come to a man in a *Pleurify*, and tell him he may make ufe of any Remedies but letting of blood ; the Party muft perifh, that being the only Cure. I am not at prefent for giving of Money, that being to the State as Food to the Stomach ; if that be clean, Meat turns to good Nourifhment ; but if it be out of order, it breeds Difeafes : And fo it is in the State, if that be not in order too. We have been often deceived, and by the fame men again. Was not 200000 *l.* given for the Fleet in 74, and was any of it employed that way ? Money given for an actual War with *France*, employed for a difhonourable Peace. Never fo many Admirals, and fo few Ships to guard us ; never more Commiffioners of the Treafury, and fo little Money ; never fo many Counfellors, and fo little Safety : Let us addrefs his Majefty.

A Tenth. I'll never be for giving of Money for promoting Popery, and a Succeffor a publick Enemy to the Kingdom, and a Slave to the Pope : Whilft he hath 11 to 7 in the Council, and 63 to 31 in the Houfe of Lords, we are not fecure. And if my own Father had been one of the 63, I fhould have voted him an Enemy to the King and Kingdom ; and if we cannot live Proteftants, I hope we fhall die fo.

The Eleventh. Redrefs our Grievances firft, and then, and not till then, Money. *Tangier* never was, nor will be a place of Trade. *Tetuan* and *Sallee* fo near, they will never trade with us to deftroy themfelves, and can never be for our Advantage. And I have many years wonder'd at the Council that have been for the keeping of it ; and am of Opinion, that *Popery* may be aim'd at by it, and that our Councils are managed at *Rome*, from whence I faw a Letter from a Friend, dated the 21ft of *October*, with the Heads of the King's Speech in it, to this effect, That his Majefty would command them not to meddle with the Succeffion ; That he would ask no Money ; That he would ftand upon the Confirmation of the Lord *Danby*'s Pardon ; and, That the keeping of *Tangier* was to draw on Expences, and was it not, would be for blowing of it up.

Twelfth. I am for a Reprefentation.

Thirteenth. I remember, before the laft Seffion of Parliament, there was a Council held at *Lambeth*, and there hatched a Bill againft Popery. It was for the breeding of Children of a Popifh Succeffor, which admitted the thing ; and it was called a Bill againft Popery, but we called it the Popifh Bill. I am for the Church of *England*, but

not

Mr. Speaker, What we have now to do, is to load them with shame, who have bid defiance to the Law; they are guilty of Crimes against Nature, against the King, against their Knowledge, and against Posterity. The whole Frame of Nature doth loudly and daily petition to God their Creator; and Kings, like God, may be addressed to in like manner by Petition, not Command. They likewise knew it was lawful to petition; Ignorance can be no Plea, and their Knowledge aggravates their Crimes. The Children unborn are bound to curse such Proceedings; for 'twas not petitioning, but Parliaments they abhor'd. The Atheist pleads against a God, not that he disbelieves a Deity, but would have it so. *Tresilian* and *Belknap* were Judges too, their Learning gave them Honour, but their Villanies made their *Exit* by a Rope. The end of my Motion therefore is, That we may address warmly to our Prince against them, let us settle a Committee to enquire into their Crimes, and not fail of doing Justice upon them that have perverted it; let us purge the Fountain, and the Streams will issue pure.

November the 17th, being appointed for Consideration of His Majesty's Message, the Order being read, it was moved by a worthy Member,

THAT as long as *Popery* hangs over us, we could do nothing, and we ought to represent our Condition to the King; and then, when we had secured our Religion and Property, we should be ready to do any thing that might make the King happy and great.

A Second. I am sorry that *Tangier* (that is, a Supply) is moved for, at so unseasonable a time; I confess *Tangier* is of great moment, but we have now in hand that which is of greater moment than ten *Tangiers* put together. The Consideration of that, before we are secure in our Religion at home, is as when an Enemy was landed we should afterwards go to fortify the Coasts of *Kent.* And being told us by his Majesty, we should secure our selves against Popery, by all ways but meddling with the Succession, and should rest there, we are prevented of what is our Preservation: And the providing for *Tangier* now, will be the weakening of our Security. When *Tangier* was put into the Hands of the *English* first, there was an Article that there should continue a Popish Church, and the Religion that belonged to it, to continue their Lives, but not to be replenish'd with new. And if it be enquired into, I believe it will be found the number of them is not yet decreased. It is not long since there was a Popish Governour there, many Papists and Soldiers gone thither lately from *Ireland.* It is not a little Sum that will do what is needful there; and if it should be a considerable one that should be given for it, it may be made use of to raise an Army there; so that we run into a great Inconveniency by providing for it; I think we ought to consider well of it before we do: And yet I am not for sullenly saying, we will raise no Money, but for clearly stating the Case by an Address to the King.

A Third. I am only to acquaint you, That *Tangier* is not to be maintained without your Support.

A Fourth. All things are to be considered comparatively, and if it be made an Argument against the Duke's Bill, that he is at the Head of an Army in *Scotland,* and that in *Ireland* there are ten Papists to one Protestant, his great Interest in the Fleet, and being Admiral, and *Tangier* being a Seminary of Papists; then sure you have a special Argument to take *Tangier* into your Cosideration, and Money may be for that Service. But then this Parliament do not ask Petitions of Grace, but of Right. And will you part with your Money without any Security? You have often done so, and what are you the better for it? I long for the Time when we may give Money to make the King great; but if things must go on as they do, I am for a plain Bargain, to know what we shall have for our Money. For my part, I only desire our Security; but if we should give Money, I suppose you will take care what hands we put it in, and there ought to be a Trust: Let us address his Majesty.

A Fifth. We are told *Tangier* is of Importance, it is a Nursery of Papists: And we are likewise told, the *Irish* sent thither a part of the *Irish* Army, and they take the Oath, that is no Security: Was not the Lord *Bellasis* Governour of *Tangier* and *Hull,* and the Pensioners Captain, all at a time, and took the Oaths? Those Soldiers, for ought I know, may be brought hither, and the asking for a Supply for it at this time, is very unreasonable, because Parliaments have been put off two or three Years; and whilst there are People that dare make a difference between the King and this House, we shall never be safe. Let us represent our Condition as boldly as may stand with

good

I

good manners. It is not to be endured, to see the Duke preferred before the King, as he was ; as if Arguments of his Greatness and Power were Arguments strong enough to hinder the Bill : He hath violated the Law, and we needed not to have gone this way to work, if we could have had Justice against him ; but he is too great for that, let us address his Majesty.

A Sixth. If *Tangier* be wholly under the Duke's Care and Protection, and such a Seminary for Papists as hath been represented, I think any Motion to have a Supply for it is unseasonable, and am against it ; order the bringing in the state of it.

A Seventh. I spoke the sense of the City formerly, and do so now again, and in the name of the greatest part of the Commonalty of the City of *London* ; and we do declare, That we are ready to give Money, half we have, nay all, and be content to set up again, and get new Estates, if we can but be secured. The burning of *London*, justly laid upon the Papists, and keeping Watch since the Plot, hath cost the City above 100000 *l.* The City of *London* is the Bulwark of our Religion : And is it not said, the Duke is at the head of 30 or 40000 Men ? The Lieutenancy and Justices, how are they molded for his turn ! And if you do nothing now in this House, we must all, without any more ado, try to make a Peace with him as well as we can, I'll never do it : And will you, for the sake of one Man, destroy three Kingdoms ?

An Eighth. He moved, that the Representation might declare, That we see no Security, but removing the Duke of *York*.

A Ninth. We discoursing of *Tangier* at this time, is like *Nero*'s Fiddling whilst *Rome* was consuming by Fire : If it be in a good condition, we cannot help it ; if in a bad one, we are not in a posture to do it. Pray consider the condition by what's past, when King *Henry* the Eighth was for Supremacy, the Kingdom was for it. When King *Henry* the Eighth was against it, the Kingdom was against it. When King *Edward* the Sixth was a Protestant, the Kingdom was so ; when Queen *Mary* was a Papist, the Kingdom was so ; when Queen *Elizabeth* was a Protestant, the Kingdom so again ; *Regis ad exemplum*, &c. And I believe, even in King *Edward* the Sixth's time, the Bishops themselves would not have been for throwing out such a Bill as this. And if King *Edward* had promised any thing for the preservation of the *Protestant Religion*, so that *Mary* might succeed, the Pope would no way have contrived so great a Favour. The bidding us prevent *Popery*, and the letting alone a *Popish* Successor, is as if a Physician should come to a man in a *Pleurisy*, and tell him he may make use of any Remedies but letting of blood ; the Party must perish, that being the only Cure. I am not at present for giving of Money, that being to the State as Food to the Stomach ; if that be clean, Meat turns to good Nourishment ; but if it be out of order, it breeds Diseases : And so it is in the State, if that be not in order too. We have been often deceived, and by the same men again. Was not 200000 *l.* given for the Fleet in 74, and was any of it employed that way ? Money given for an actual War with *France*, employed for a dishonourable Peace. Never so many Admirals, and so few Ships to guard us ; never more Commissioners of the Treasury, and so little Money ; never so many Counsellors, and so little Safety : Let us address his Majesty.

A Tenth. I'll never be for giving of Money for promoting Popery, and a Successor a publick Enemy to the Kingdom, and a Slave to the Pope : Whilst he hath 11 to 7 in the Council, and 63 to 31 in the House of Lords, we are not secure. And if my own Father had been one of the 63, I should have voted him an Enemy to the King and Kingdom ; and if we cannot live Protestants, I hope we shall die so.

The Eleventh. Redress our Grievances first, and then, and not till then, Money. *Tangier* never was, nor will be a place of Trade. *Tetuan* and *Sallee* so near, they will never trade with us to destroy themselves, and can never be for our Advantage. And I have many years wonder'd at the Council that have been for the keeping of it ; and am of Opinion, that *Popery* may be aim'd at by it, and that our Councils are managed at *Rome*, from whence I saw a Letter from a Friend, dated the 21st of *October*, with the Heads of the King's Speech in it, to this effect, That his Majesty would command them not to meddle with the Succession ; That he would ask no Money ; That he would stand upon the Confirmation of the Lord *Danby*'s Pardon ; and, That the keeping of *Tangier* was to draw on Expences, and was it not, would be for blowing of it up.

Twelfth. I am for a Representation.

Thirteenth. I remember, before the last Session of Parliament, there was a Council held at *Lambeth*, and there hatched a Bill against Popery. It was for the breeding of Children of a Popish Successor, which admitted the thing ; and it was called a Bill against Popery, but we called it the Popish Bill. I am for the Church of *England*, but not

not for the Church-men. The late Bishop of *St. Asaph*, on his Death-bed, good man, could hardly forbear declaring himself, which his Epitaph did *(Ora pro Anima)* ordered to be written upon his Tomb. We are told the other day, we ought to make the Duke a Substantive to stand by himself; That there was less danger of a General without an Army, than an Army without a General. And I have read in *Pliny* which was most to be feared, an Army of Lyons with a Hare to their General, or an Army of Hares with a Lyon to their General? and it was concluded, that an Army of Hares with a Lyon to their General, was most to be feared of the two. His Majesty is inclosed by a sort of Monsters, who endeavour to destroy, and I hope to move against them before we rise; and though we have lost our last Bill, we have not lost our Courage and Hearts.

Fourteenth. His Majesty desires your Advice and Assistance, it is seldom, which is very kind; and though you shall think fit not to give the latter, 'tis but mannerly to give the first. And I hope you will not resent any Injury, if any there were done by the House of Lords on the King, who though he cannot cure all ill in one day, he can ruin all. And I acquaint you, there is a very great Weight laid upon this Session of Parliament, and upon the agreeing of the King with the People, on which depends the Welfare of the Protestants abroad, and hope you will not go about to remonstrate now.

Fifteenth. If you had sent the Duke's, Lord *Craven*'s, and *Mulgrave*'s Regiment to *Tangier*, it would supply the Place with Men, and disband the Lord *Oxford*'s Regiment, and the Money on those employed, would bear much of the share of this.

Then the House resolved to appoint a Committee to draw up an Address upon the Debate of this House, to represent to his Majesty the State and Condition of the Kingdom, in Answer to his Majesty's Message about Tangier.

The SPEECHES of several Learned and Worthy Members of the Honourable House of Commons, for Passing the Bill against the Duke of York.

Mr. Speaker,

THE Gentleman that spoke last, seems to intimate that we ought to have a due regard to the King's Brother, and consider what infinite disadvantages will accrue to us, if we are too hasty in our Resolutions; as before the Duke is found guilty, to proceed to pass a Bill for Exclusion; for that nothing but War and Bloodshed can be expected from it; and therefore he says we ought to be moderate, and find out a Medium to secure the Protestant Religion, notwithstanding the Duke may be a Papist. Now Gentlemen, I give you the Dictates of my Heart, without either Passion or Prejudice, and should be as willing as any Person to agree with what that Gentleman hath proposed, if any such Reason can be brought to enforce it. For my part, I think it absolutely impossible that this Kingdom can be safe, or the Protestant Religion succeed under a Popish Successor; for do but review the Ancient and Modern Histories, and you shall find how Protestants have lived under a Popish King: Have they not been massacred, butchered and enslaved in *Germany*, *France*, and in our own Countries, notwithstanding all the Laws, Vows and Promises to the contrary? Are not the Tenets of the Papists destructive to the Protestant Religion, which is Heresy, and that Faith is not to be kept with such? See the barbarous Usage of the Protestants in *Piedmont*, and in Queen *Mary*'s Time; how then can we expect any better Success? For by how much a Popish Prince seems to be Religious, by so much ought he to be look'd upon desperately dangerous; for since the Papists make such Plotting and Designing to subvert our Religion under a Protestant Prince, how much more will they act against us under a Popish Successor? For to think to restrain a Prince under the Power of a penal Law, thereby to secure Religion, is no more than to tye *Sampson* with Cords; for will not the Courtiers be flattered by their Prince, to imitate the same Religion with him? and then will not we Protestants be discountenanced, and none but Priests and Jesuites have Dominion over us? For my part, if you pass not this Bill, we shall all agree to have our Throats cut; and I have no patience at all for that: you see how the Duke of *York* being a Papist, they have all the dependency on him, and hope

Z   to to perfect their Villanies. Therefore take away this General, and this Army may be secured ; and then being united at home, we need not fear what all the Papists in the World can do unto us, when we fight for the maintenance of our Laws and Religion by Exclusion of a Popish Prince, and rather withstand any Violence that shall be brought against us, than be in danger every day to have our Throats cut by those that are amongst us. One Gentleman was pleased to say, that it was a Papist Jesuits Bill, and that which they brand the Papists withal, (*viz.*) Deposing of Princes. I do say as to that, That we do not depose *James* D. of *Y.* but as being a Papist, considering the sad Consequence that will ensue ; for should we admit a Papist, we should give away the Crown, for he would only have the Title, the Pope would be our Sovereign. And we ought to prevent any such Usurpers, who no doubt would make havock of our Estates, if he spares us our Lives. To tell us that Exclusion will cause a Civil War, I am of the contrary Opinion ; for it will be more conducing to the Preservation of the King's Person and Government, our Laws, Lives and Religion, to be unanimous. Whereas Oppression, Fire and Faggot, might cause People to rebel and be mutinous, when the other would be a means to unite us. As I will give you a Reason why we cannot restrain him otherwise, or use Moderation towards him ; for suppose I were riding a full speed on the Road on a secure Horse, a Gentleman passing by, desired me to be moderate, for that I would kill my Horse, when at the same time he knows that if I slacken my pace, I shall have my Throat cut by thieves that are swiftly pursuing me ; therefore I cannot be moderate in this case, unless I will fling away my Life. And I will lay down another Similitude, that is, if I were sailing to the *East Indies*, and passing the Equinoctial Line, most of the Seamen were distempered through Heat, and on their sick Beds, but it being told them, that the Ship is in danger of sinking, for there springs a Leak, upon which they all arise, and instantly fall to pump ; but the Chirurgeon acquaints them, that if they do not work more moderately, they will get the Calenture, and so destroy themselves ; but they give him only the Hearing, knowing that if they cease ever so little, they are all drowned in the Deep : Therefore in this case there can be no Moderation. And to give an Instance in Holy Writ, *Moses* was a meek and mild Man, and a moderate Man, but seeing an *Egyptian* and an *Israelite* fighting, he immediately slew the *Egyptian*, for he knew it was to no purpose to be moderate with him ; and afterwards seeing two *Israelites* fighting, endeavoured to part them, telling them, they were Brethren, and ought to be moderate ; so we must place it upon the right Object, and not suffer ourselves and Posterity to be irrecoverably undone.

Another Speech by a Worthy Gentleman.

Mr. Speaker,

NO Man hath a greater Veneration for the Royal Family than my self, to which I am obliged both in gratitude and duty, I am bold to say that I have a great esteem and honour for the D. of *Y.* Yet I must before the passing of this Bill (to dissent from that worthy Gentleman that thought it a Bill of Rigour, for it is as I conceive, a Bill of Grace and Mercy) Vote for it, as a Favour for the D. I am sure it is so to the Royal Family, they cannot be safe till the Bill be passed ; in tenderness to one Branch we must not endanger the whole.

That worthy Gentleman that moved last, seems to intimate, that the passing this Bill is against our Oaths of Allegiance and Supremacy : I admire his Mistake, and it is the first Time I ever heard the Protestant Oaths cited to justify a Popish Successor ; it is urged we are sworn to the King, his Heirs and lawful Successors ; it is true, we are so, but not obliged to any in the King's life-time but himself, for that were Treason : He has no Heirs or Successors by Law during his own Life, *Non est Hæres viventis.* We are likewise told, we are designing a Bill to UNITE the Protestant Interest, but will divide it, because many true Protestants are for the true Heir, and for the D. of *Y.* if he be so, which may occasion the Effusion of much Blood amongst us.

Mr. Speaker,

UNITY is desired by all, yet let us be glad to divide from such Men, for when the Bill is passed, their false Loyalty will be a Crime, and we know not what Character to give it, and what Punishment to assign them ; LOYALTY is a Correspondency and Submission to the Law, it is that surrounds the King, and makes his Person Sacred.

It is hinted that we must impeach the Duke, I should be for that if he did not withdraw,

draw, I will not fay fly from Juftice ; if we impeach him being abfent, we can only Attaint him; and fhould he furvive the King, and be then lawful Heir, the Defcent of the Crown takes off all Attainders, and fuch Proceedings were only an Illufion, and would indeed involve us in Blood.

Let us difable him, 'tis abfolutely neceffary; without, 'tis impoffible to falve. I perceive no Gentleman here has confidence to deny the Loyalty of the Fact, or excufe the black Crimes that appear before us. Why do they not anfwer the Evidence that is now come in? If it be falfe, contradict it ; if true, what is the Reafon of this Debate ? Is not the King alive ? Is not all Loyalty due to him ? Love hates a Competitor, much more a Crown.

A Speech fpoke by the fame Worthy Member, upon the Irifh *Informations, given in at the Bar in Writing.*

THIS is not fo much a *Difcovery* as a *Confirmation* of the *Difcovery* of the Plot, although fome inconfiderate Men are apt to give credit to the dying Words of fome Men. This agrees exactly with *Oates* his firft *Difcovery*. It adds to the ftrength of what *Coleman's* Letters imported ; but fo deplorable is our Condition, we are in danger, we fee the Knife is even at our Throats, but *none feeks to take it out of our Enemies Hand.*

You have Witneffes againft a great Perfon, one before; another now ; he is a Lord, a Privy Counfellor, and fits in Council ftill : My Lord of *Tyrone*, he is in the *Gate-houfe*, but not fecured : There is one *Informant* tells you they received Encouragement from the D. of *Y*. and that he promifed them Affiftance : I call not the Truth of this in queftion, but we fee they make ufe of thefe great Names ; fo that even in this King's time, we are not fecure a day without the Bill. They have reafon to believe that a Po-pifh Succeffor will affift them in their Rebellion.

Now we fee why our Minifters made a Peace ; we thought our Security to be in the *French* King's being involved in a War : Now I fay, the reafon of the *Nimeguen* Ple-nipotentiaries making a Peace is feen, to have the *French* King be at liberty to fend Men into *Ireland*. Here you have a full Confirmation of this Evidence ; we fee our danger both at home and abroad, and what pofture we are in, if any means be left for our Security.

Let thefe *Depofitions* be printed, that the Country may fee our Danger : if we will not impeach the Earl of *Tyrone* prefently ; if he fhould write into *Ireland*, I am afraid he will find too much Favour there: confider the Cafe of this Lord the Privy Coun-fellor ; he is a great Man, and a Lawyer; if I thought we could not reach him, we would not go about to impeach him. Agree with the Lords in their Vote, and defire them to agree with you, that the Papifts may not draw their Encouragement from a Popifh Succeffor.

Another Speech by a Perfon of Honour.

Mr. Speaker,

I Have not hitherto troubled you, and am fo fenfible of my own Inabilities in compa-rifon of fo many wifer and abler Men in this Houfe, that 'tis with great unwilling-nefs, I rife up to fpeak ; but when I hear the Honour and Juftice of this Houfe call'd in queftion, as it was by that Honourable Member which fpake laft ; I cannot I con-fefs bear it with patience, but muft (as I think it my Duty) endeavour to vindicate the Juftice of the Houfe: for I muft profefs, Sir, that in my Judgment this Bill is fo far from an unjuft thing, that it is rather a Favour to him, fince if he were proceeded againft by Impeachment for the Crimes he is accufed of by feveral Witneffes, he might perhaps forfeit more than a Crown ; which for our Safeties only we go about to exclude him from enjoying: And fince it is undoubtedly in the power of Parliament to difpofe of fuch Succeffions, it feems very hard with me to tax this Houfe with Unjuftice for fo doing, upon fo great reafon and neceffity as now requires it.

I will not, Sir, at all deny the many great Services (mentioned by that Honourable Member,) the Duke has done the Nation at Sea, nor will I fay any thing at all in De-rogation of any one of them ; but yet I do not think he fought for us when he was afleep.

There

I

There are several things, Sir, wherein this Nation hath been betray'd, I will not lay any of them directly upon him, but when I think of some of them, I am very much startled, and know not well what to believe; for when I consider that in the Fire of *London,* there were several outlandish Men taken in the very act of Firing a House, and being delivered to the Guard, were presently set at liberty by the Officer that commanded it, and that such a Man should ever since not only continue, but increase in the Duke's Favour to the greatest degree imaginable, I must confess I do not like it, and I think it looks very ill.

When I also think of the general Design which plainly appears to have been carried on all along, to destroy the People and to weaken the Nation as much as possible, as appears by the Treachery was used at *Chatham,* and the *French's* standing still while the *Dutch* and we cut one another's Throats; this also in my Judgment is very ill; nor doth it appear better that it was taken ill, that the D. of *Monmouth* when he was sent into *Scotland,* did not cut those poor miserable Peoples Throats. (But that Prince had too much Humanity and Discretion than to do it.) But I do not particularly charge any Person with these.

There are many things, Sir, spoken of by the Witnesses you have heard relating to the Duke, as also several things in the Letters you have heard read, I shall not repeat any of them: I will only tell you a Passage comes into my mind, and I do not tell it for the sake of the Story, but that it appears to me by it, that the Duke was either somewhat concerned in the Plot, or at least to hinder the discovery of it; for the D. speaking publickly to all that were round him of one *Le Faire* that was accused by Mr. *Bedloe,* to have been one of Sir *E. B. Godfrey's* Murderers, and one of the Queen's Servants, he said that could not be, because there was no such Man as *Le Faire* about the Queen; but yet it so fell out, they say, that in some little time after there was a Bond found, under this Man's own hand, and he proved to be one of the Queen's Servants, and run away upon this Business.

Now, Sir, if this were so, 'tis impossible the other should be true; and if a Prince, or any Man speaks an untruth, it is a fault so hateful to me, that I must confess I know not what to call it, nor what Name to give it, (it is the Devil.)

I shall trouble you, Sir, with one thing more which comes into my mind, and if true, is as bad as any thing can be: There was, Sir, a *French* Protestant came over to the King to make Proposals for the Interest of the Protestant Religion ———

Here a Person of Honour standing up, said, He never heard a Prince so reflected upon in his life. *Upon which the House cried,* Go on, Go on: *The Gentleman answered,*

Mr. Speaker,

I wonder that Noble Lord should thus interrupt me, for I have not positively affirmed any thing at all of the Duke, though I have said nothing but what in my Judgment I thought might be truth, and I shall not change my mind for his being displeased at it; but however I am very well satisfied to say no more, but only, that I remember that Honourable Person by the Bar, told us, he would not speak to the prudential part against the Bill, and truly, Sir, I think he has kept his Word very exactly; and that, whereas another Member before him objected, *That it was possible the Duke might turn Protestant,* I would only answer, that I do not think it possible, that any Person that has been bred up in the Protestant Religion, and hath been weak enough (for so I must call it) to turn Papist, should ever after (in that respect) be wise enough to turn Protestant; and therefore, Sir, upon the whole matter, my humble Motion is, *That the Bill may pass.*

Debates *in the House of Commons,* Jan. 7. 1680. *upon his Majesty's Message.*

The First Speech by an Honourable Gentleman.

HIS Majesty relies not only on the Dictates of his own Judgment, but is confirmed by the Judgment of the House of Lords; but many of them have gained their Honour by Interest rather than Merit. His Majesty hath given no Answer to several of your Addresses; when you say nothing can secure you but this Bill, that he should propose other means; but if we have not the Bill, we are deprived of the means to preserve His Majesty's Life, Person and Government. I never knew that *Tangier* was more considerable than all the Three Kingdoms: Is it time to be silent, or not? Why is all this stir for a Man that desires the Throne before His Majesty is dead? He is in all the Plot, either at one end or other: Who took evidence of *London* Fire? Arbitrary Power was at the end; and no Religion like Popery to set up. That I will pay the Duty and Allegiance of an *Englishman*, to an *English* Prince: But Popery and Arbitrary Power must be rooted out. Can you hope for any Good while this Man is Heir, an Apostate from his Religion; his Government is the most dangerous: Our Ministers of State give us little hopes from *Whitehall*; I hope they will be named: First set a Brand on all them that framed the Answer, and all them that shall lend Money by way of Anticipation; desire him to take Advice of his Parliament, rather than private Men, or to let us go home, and attend his Service when he shall again call for us.

The Second Speech by another Person of Honour.

I am afraid we are lost, we have done our Parts, shewed ourselves good Subjects; but some stand between the King and us to promote the Duke of *York's* Interest; Those that advised the King not to pass the Bill, deserve to be branded.

The Third Speech by an Honourable Gentleman.

We have made the modestest Request that ever People did in such a time of Danger: we have neither passed a Bill, nor obtained a kind Answer; our Trust must be in our Votes. When the King bids us look into the Plot, like well-meaning Country-Gentlemen, we looked into the *Tower*; we should have looked into *Whitehall*, there the Plot is hatched, cherished and brought up: It would be well, if all against the Bill were put out of Council, and all of this House were put out of Commission that were for it: I had rather the *Moors* had *Tangier*, the *French* King *Flanders*, than the *Pope* had *England*.

The Fourth Speech by a Person of Honour.

I think the Debate is upon a Message from the King; and the most especial part is about the Bill; I concur with that noble Person, rather than with all the rest; But begin with the first, his Majesty hath suffered us twice to address upon the Bill; yet the Lords have not admitted one Conference; I believe every man came unwillingly into this Bill; have any that were against it proposed any thing for our Security? if they will, let them stand up, and I will set down: I have advised with Men that know the Laws, Religion and Government; they say, if you will preserve this Government, this Law, this Bill must pass: We have received no expedient from the Lords; the State of the Nation lies at their Door: they sit to hear Causes, they mind you of Mr. *Seymour*, but say nothing of the Bills. In *Richard* the Second his Time, some Lords were said to be Lords in the King's Pocket, but had no Shoulders to support him. It's plain our Evil comes from evil Ministers. There are some that will have a Prince of one Religion on the Throne, to rule the People of another; a Popish Prince and a Protestant Kingdom: will any Minister of Parts, unless they have an Indifferency of Religion, think this consistent? I dedicate my Allegiance to the King, they to another Person, so the Kingdom must be destroy'd, either this limited Monarchy must stand, or come to Blood. On the other side the Water, *Monarchy* is absolutely supported by little Men of no Fortune, and he that takes mean and low Men to make Ministers of, sets up for *Popery* and *Arbitrary* Government: The King hath Counsels born; if you have a Popish Prince, and a Protestant Parliament, will the King ever concur with them in matters of Religion and Property, are not your Estates sprinkled with *Abbey-Lands*? If he asks Money, will you trust him? must Foreigners comply with a Prince that in effect hath no People? We must be overcome with *France* and *Popery*, or the Body will get a new Head, or the Head a new Body.

The Fifth Speech by a Person of Honour.

The House was unwilling at first to enter into a Debate about Expedients, and I am not prepared to propound them; any thing you have heard proposed by the King in *Print*, if you had them they will do you no harm: One Day you say the King had been a good Prince, if he had good Company and good Councils; no great Complement to the King: he offers you any thing but the Bill, I humbly make my motion to try it.

A a

The

The Sixth Speech by an Honourable Gentleman.

I think it becomes that Gentleman very well to be of the Opinion he is, though no Man else in this House. I wish the D. was of that Opinion his Father desired him. The Lords rejected the Bill, but I am afraid the King sollicited, or else they would not; it's some Men's *Interest* to be for the D. but while they are at Court, we shall never have it: Foreign Persons have given Influence at Court, the *French* Ministers access to Court, inclines me to believe somebody is paid for it: The Court is a Nursery of Vice; they transmit them into the Country, and none but such Men are imployed.

The Seventh Speech by an Honourable Gentleman.

The Question now before you is, *Whether any other Means be effectual besides the Bill*; I have heard none proposed in this Parliament; the last Parliament thought not fit to debate them, they were so weak, but hath this Plot been no longer than 1678. We gave 250,000 *l.* to fight the *Dutch,* and assist them that had a Design to subdue us, and the *Protestant* Religion, which is not well settled. Have all the Laws been put in Execution against the *Papists?* But a few Apprentices going to pull down a Bawdy-house, with a Red Cloth on a Pole, was made Treason; but what hath been done with the Plot in the intervals of Parliament? The Lords have confirmed the King in his Opinion; but did not the *Proviso* for the D. come from the Lords House? I believe the Lords do not fear him; but I believe the Plot is more dangerous than ever. To rely upon any Remedy but this Bill, will expose your Selves and your Religion.

The Eighth Speech by an Honourable Gentleman.

You have heard several Propositions, but first make an end of one. It is long since we thought in this House we were not secure without the Bill, some have not yet considered of it, and I think we never shall. To make an *Act of Association* against the D. is to say, *Let him be lawful King, and then fight against him.* Another way is *Banishment*; if it be during the King's Life, truly you run into more Dangers, rather than remove them; if you talk of *Banishment* during the D. Life, that is *Exclusion:* if the D. be a *Papist,* exclude all *Papists* from inheriting. Some talk if an Act pass, they would not satisfy their Consciences, I am sure a Vote to *Exclude* him will not. *Popery* encreases upon hopes the D. may come to the Crown? we ought to take care of this *Presumption*; Will not *Papists* expect to have their Religion established when the D. is next? I wonder Men will pretend to plead for Loyalty to one, that they may never come to use it; some say, *Cannot the D. change his Religion?* Must not the Two Houses join? Did not Queen *Mary* do it, *Regis ad Exemplum,* most will conform. To make Arguments of this Bill is to lessen it; the King bids you go on to other Things; let's declare *all other Things are ineffectual without this Bill*; We cannot think our selves safe; to rely on any thing else, is not only insufficient but dangerous.

The Ninth Speech by an Honourable Gentleman.

Now I see the House is full, so considerate, I am bound to give my Thoughts. The Reason, the Verity of the Bill hath formerly been debated, and Precedents are Printed to shew it hath been done. *It will be a Reproach to us when dead in our Graves, if we do not whatever any Parliament did to preserve Religion.* When we received the King's Message, I was persuaded he was over-ruled by other Men; for he saith, *What shall come in a Parliamentary Way*; how comes the King to know what's done in Parliament? When *Clifford* set up bare-fac'd for *Popery,* he brought the King to come frequently to the House of Lords. *Cranmer* saith, That King *Henry* the Eighth passed the Act of 6 *Articles* in an Un-Parliamentary Way, *by the King's coming and solliciting. Henry* the Fourth in a Record called, *The Indempnity of the Peers and Commons,* the King being in haste for Money, sends a Message, desires he may debate the matter with them; they return Answer, *Parliaments ought to debate free.* It's entred into the Rolls, *That the King shall neither come to one House or other: Danby's* solliciting could not move them, the King comes and he prevails: Some Lords have little Estates, some little Consciences, some less Religion. The King calls it *an Opinion,* and tells you *he is confirmed in it by the House of Lords*; he may come to take up other Resolutions, if the Parliament go away and leave this Work undone: The King is in the highest Danger, though some Men think they shall be accounted Loyal for opposing an *Act of Parliament*; it is but a

Nick-

Nick-name. King *James* in his Speech, 1603, thought it his Security to comply with his Parliament : Nay, *He would betray his Country and Posterity in not doing it.* Remember what care the last King took *to have his Posterity maintain the Protestant Religion.* Remember Queen *Mary* broke her Word for *Conscience sake every day* ; a Security would draw me from the Bill. Queen *Elizabeth*'s Association against the Queen of *Scots* in the *Act of Parliament* was an *Exclusion,* she was but a Woman, but had wise Councellors ; Prelates *then did not fear the Frown of a Prince.* Surely when the King sees so many Gentlemen of this House so firm, he will take their Advice, and prorogue them, and then pass the Bill. I find not a Man that hath understanding, but saith, *We are undone without it* ; We have not compounded yet for our Throats, as some at *Whitehall* have done, there is no next best ; the only way to preserve the *Protestant* Religion is to pass the Bill : what is as secure as this, must be amounting to *Exclusion.* We can't save his Personal Dignity, but with the loss of our Laws and Lives too. I would to God the King knew how well this House doth love him.

The Tenth Speech by an Honourable Gentleman.

Consider whether the Dis-inheriting of a lawful Prince be Injustice or not ; or whether we ought not rather to trust to the Providence of Almighty God.

The Eleventh Speech by an Honourable Gentleman.

I should be glad the last Gentleman would make it good, that we are to trust to the Providence of Almighty God, rather than do, as he supposes, an unlawful Act ; but can he prove it unlawful ? can the King, Lords and Commons do an unlawful Act ? Must we not have a Supream Power ? But to hint it to something, is to say, it is not Supream ; was there not *Machinations* every Year against Queen *Elizabeth,* but she took away the *Scotch* Queen. I wonder we have this Answer, till I consider who is at the King's Ear, and have had an Interest carried on so long. The denial of this, is the denial of every thing ; you see where there are divers Medicines, yet but one conducing to the end ; you shall have a *Popish* King, if that be allowed, with Power to compel and corrupt you, you shall have what you will to protect you, but you shall be under the Power of one to destroy you. *The Frogs must have a Government, but they must have a Stork for their King. Samson's Locks will be grown again by that time he comes in ; There is a Lion in the Lobby, keep him out say I ; no say some, open the Door, we will chain him when he's come in.* Would you have a King that would neither court you nor protect you ? You would have a Parliament to make Judges and Bishops, then sure the *Long-House* will be *Jure divino* ; you can have no Security under the Copes of Heaven without this Bill.

A Copy of the Duke of YORK's Bill.

WHereas *James* Duke of *York* is notoriously known to have been perverted from the *Protestant* to the *Popish* Religion ; whereby not only great Encouragement hath been given to the *Popish* Party to enter into, and carry on most Devilish and Horrid Plots and Conspiracies for the Destruction of His Majesty's Sacred Person and Government, and for the Extirpation of the True Protestant Religion : But also if the said Duke should succeed to the Imperial Crown of this Realm ; nothing is more manifest than that a Total Change of Religion within these Kingdoms would ensue. For the Preservation whereof, *Be it Enacted* by the King's Most Excellent Majesty, by, and with the Advice and Consent of the Lords Spiritual and Temporal, and the Commons in this present Parliament Assembled, and by the Authority of the same ; That the said *James* Duke of *York* shall be, and is, by the Authority of this present Parliament, Excluded, and made for ever uncapable to Inherit, Possess or Enjoy the Imperial Crown of this Realm, and of the Kingdoms of *Ireland,* and the Dominions and Territories to them, or either of them belonging ; or to have, exercise or enjoy any Dominion, Power, Jurisdiction or Authority in the same Kingdoms, Dominions, or any of them. *And be it further Enacted* by the Authority aforesaid, That if the said *James* Duke of *York* shall at any time hereafter, challenge, claim, or attempt to possess, or enjoy, or shall take upon him to use or exercise any Dominion, Power, or Authority, or Jurisdiction within the said Kingdoms,

or

or Dominions, or any of them, as King or Chief Magiſtrate of the ſame ; That then he the ſaid *James* Duke of *York*, for every ſuch Offence, ſhall be deemed and adjudged guilty of High Treaſon, and ſhall ſuffer the Pains, Penalties and Forfeitures as in caſe of High Treaſon: *And further*, That if any Perſon or Perſons whatever ſhall aſſiſt or maintain, abett, or willingly adhere unto the ſaid *James* Duke of *York*, in ſuch Challenge, Claim or Attempt ; or ſhall of themſelves attempt, or endeavour to put or bring the ſaid *James* Duke of *York* into the Poſſeſſion or Exerciſe of any Regal Power, Juriſdiction or Authority within the Kingdoms and Dominions aforeſaid ; or ſhall by Writing or Preaching, adviſedly publiſh, maintain or declare, That he hath any Right, Title or Authority to the Office of King or Chief Magiſtrate of the Kingdoms and Dominions aforeſaid, that then every ſuch Perſon ſhall be deemed and adjudged guilty of High Treaſon ; and that he ſuffer and undergo the Pains, Penalties and Forfeitures aforeſaid.

And be it further Enacted by the Authority aforeſaid, That he the ſaid *James* Duke of *York* ſhall not at any time, from, and after the Fifth of *November* 1680, return or come into, or within any of the Kingdoms or Dominions aforeſaid ; *And* then he the ſaid *James* Duke of *York* ſhall be deemed and adjudged guilty of High Treaſon ; and ſhall ſuffer the Pains, Penalties and Forfeitures as in caſe of High Treaſon. *And further*, That if any Perſon or Perſons whatſoever ſhall be aiding or aſſiſting unto ſuch Return of the ſaid *James* Duke of *York*, that then every ſuch Perſon ſhall be deemed and adjudged guilty of High Treaſon ; and ſhall ſuffer as in Caſes of High Treaſon.

And be it further Enacted by the Authority aforeſaid, That he the ſaid *James* Duke of *York*, or any other Perſon being guilty of any of the Treaſons aforeſaid, ſhall not be capable of, or receive Benefit by any Pardon, otherwiſe than by Act of Parliament, wherein they ſhall be particularly named ; and that no *Noli proſequi*, or Order for ſtay of Proceedings, ſhall be received or allowed in, or upon any Indictment for any of the Offences mentioned in this Act.

And be it further Enacted and Declared ; and it is hereby Enacted and Declared, That it ſhall and may be lawful to, and for any Magiſtrates, Officers and other Subjects whatſoever of theſe Kingdoms and Dominions aforeſaid ; and they are hereby enjoined and required to apprehend and ſecure the ſaid *James* Duke of *York*, and every other Perſon offending in any of the Premiſes, and with him or them in caſe of Reſiſtance to fight, and him or them by Force to ſubdue : For all which Actings, and for ſo doing, they are, and ſhall be by virtue of this Act ſaved harmleſs and indemnified.

Provided, and it is hereby Declared, That nothing in this Act contained ſhall be conſtrued, deemed or adjudged to diſenable any other Perſon from inheriting and enjoying the Imperial Crown of the Realms and Dominions aforeſaid, (other than the ſaid *James* Duke of *York*.) But that in caſe the ſaid *James* Duke of *York* ſhould ſurvive his now Majeſty, and the Heirs of his Majeſty's Body ; the ſaid Imperial Crown ſhall deſcend to, and be enjoyed by ſuch Perſon or Perſons ſucceſſively during the Life of the ſaid *James* Duke of *York*, as ſhould have inherited and enjoyed the ſame in caſe the ſaid *James* Duke of *York* were naturally dead, any thing contained in this Act to the contrary notwithſtanding.

And be it further Enacted, by the Authority aforeſaid, That during the Life of the ſaid *James* Duke of *York*, this Act ſhall be given in charge at every Aſſizes and General Seſſions of the Peace within the Kingdoms, Dominions and Territories aforeſaid ; and alſo ſhall be openly read in every Cathedral Church, and Pariſh Church, and Chappels within the aforeſaid Kingdoms, Dominions and Territories, by the ſeveral reſpective Parſons, Vicars, Curates, and Readers thereof, who are hereby required immediately after Divine Service in the Fore-noon to read the ſame twice in every Year, that is to ſay, on the 25*th* of *December*, and upon *Easter-day*, during the Life of the ſaid *James* Duke of *York*.

This BILL was read Three Times, and Paſſed, and ſent up to the Lords for their Concurrence.

Some

Some particular Matters of Fact relating to the Administration of Affairs in *Scotland* under the Duke of *LAUDERDALE*.

Humbly offered to Your Majesty's Consideration, in Obedience to Your Royal Commands.

1. THE Duke of *Lauderdale* did grosly misrepresent to your Majesty the Condition of the Western Countries, as if they had been in a State of Rebellion, though there had never been any Opposition made to your Majesty's Authority, nor any Resistance offered to your Forces, nor to the Execution of the Laws. But he purposing to abuse your Majesty, that so he might carry on his sinistrous Designs by your Authority, advised your Majesty to raise an Army against your peaceable Subjects; at least did frame a Letter, which he sent to your Majesty, to be signed by your Royal Hand to that effect; which being sent down to your Council, Orders were thereupon given out for raising an Army of Eight or Nine thousand Men, the greatest part whereof were *Highlanders*; and notwithstanding that, to avert threatning, the Nobility and Gentry of that Country did send to *Edinburgh*, and for the Security of the Peace did offer to engage, that whatsoever should be sent to put the Laws in Execution, should meet with no Affront; and that they would become Hostages for their Safety: yet this Army was marched and led into a peaceable Country, and did take *free Quarters* according to their Commissions, and in most Places levied great Sums of Money, under notion of dry Quarters, and did plunder and rob your Subjects; of which no Redress could be obtained, though Complaints were frequently made: all which were expresly contrary to the Laws of the Kingdom.

2. In their Quarters it was apparent that Regard was only had to the Duke's private Animosities; for the greatest part of those Places that were most quartered on and destroyed, had not been guilty of the Field-Conventicles complained of, and many of the Places that were most guilty were spared upon private Considerations.

3. The Subjects at that time were required to subscribe an exorbitant and illegal Bond, which was impossible to be performed by them; that they, their Wives and Children and Servants should live orderly according to Law, nor go to Conventicles, or entertain vagrant Preachers, with several other Particulars; by which Bond, those that signed it were made liable for every Man's Fault that lived upon their Ground.

4. Your Majesty's Subjects were charged with Labourers, denounced Rebels; and Captions were issued out for seizing their Persons upon their refusing to sign the aforesaid Bond: and the Nobility and Gentry there, who have ever been faithful to your Majesty, and had appeared in Arms for suppressing the last Rebellion, were disarmed upon Oath. A Proclamation was also issued, forbidding them upon great Penalty to keep any Horses above four Pounds ten Groats Price.

5. The Nobility and Gentry of the Shire of *Ayre* were also indicted at the Instance of your Majesty's Advocate of very high Crimes and Misdemeanors: whereof some did import Treason. These Indictments were delivered them in the Evening, to be answered by them the next Morning upon Oath: and when they did demand two or three Days time to consider of their Indictments, and crave the Benefit of Lawyers to advise with in matters of so high Concernment; and also excepted to their being put to swear against themselves in matters that were Capital, which was contrary to all Law and Justice; those their Desires were rejected, though the like had never been done to the greatest Malefactor in the Kingdom. And it was told them, they must either swear instantly, or they would repute them Guilty, and proceed accordingly.

6. The Noblemen and Gentlemen knowing themselves innocent of all that had been surmised against them, did purge themselves by Oath of all the Particulars that were objected to them, and were thereupon acquitted. And though the Committee of the Council used the same manner of Enquiry to discover any seditious or treasonable Designs, which were pretended as the Grounds of leading in that Army into those Countries; yet nothing could ever be proved: so false was that Suggestion concerning a Rebellion then designed that was offered to your Majesty, and prevailed with you for sending the aforementioned Letter.

7. The Oppressions and Quarterings still continued. The Noblemen and Gentry of those Countries went to *Edinburgh* to present to your Council the heavy

Pressure

Preffure that they and their People lay under, and were ready to offer to them all that in Law or Reafon could be required of them for fecuring the Peace. The Council did immediately upon their appearing there, fet forth a Proclamation requiring them to depart the Town within three Days upon all higheft Pains: and when the Duke of *Hamilton* did petition for leave to ftay two or three Days longer for fome very urgent Affairs, that was refufed him.

8. When fome Perfons of Quality had declared to the Duke of *Lauderdale* that they would go to reprefent their Condition to your Majefty, if they could not have Juftice from your Minifters; for preventing that, a Proclamation was fet forth, forbidding all the Subjects to depart the Kingdom without Licenfe; that fo your Majefty might not be acquainted with the faid Condition of your Subjects from making their Application to your Majefty, no lefs contrary to your Majefty's true Intereft (who muft always be the Refuge of his People) than to the natural Right of the Subject.

The former Particulars relate to the Invafion of the Rights of great Numbers of your Subjects all at once. What follow, have indeed only fallen on fome fingle Perfons; yet are fuch, that your whole People apprehend they may be all upon the flighteft Occafions brought under the like Mifchiefs.

1. The Council hath upon many Occafions proceeded to a new kind of Punifhment, of declaring Men uncapable of all publick Truft; concerning which your Majefty may remember what Complaints the faid Duke made, when during the Earl of *Middleton*'s Adminiftration, he himfelf was put under, and incapacitated by an Act of Parliament. The Words of his Paper againft the Earl of *Middleton* are [*Uncapacitating Ways*] to whip with Scorpions, a Punifhment to rob Men of their Honour, and to lay a lafting Stain upon them and their Pofterity. And if this was complained of, when done by the higheft Court of Parliament, your Majefty may eafily conclude, it cannot be done in any lower Court. But yet notwithftanding it is become of late Years an ordinary Sentence in Council, when the leaft Complaints are brought againft any, with whom the Duke of *Lauderdale* and his Brother are offended.

Inftances of this are:

The declaring Thirteen worthy Citizens of *Edinburgh* uncapable of publick Truft, againft whom no Complaint was ever made to this Day, as your Majefty will perceive by a Paper more fully concerning that Affair. The true Caufe of it was, that thofe Men being in the Magiftracy, that Duke and his Brother could not get a vaft Bribe from them out of the Town's-money, which was afterwards obtained when they were removed.

The Provoft of *Glafcow*, *Aberdeen* and *Jadburgh* were put under the fame Sentence, for figning a Letter to your Majefty in the Convention of the Burroughs with the reft of that Body, which Letter was advifed by him who is now your Majefty's Advocate, as that which had nothing in it which could bring them under any Guilt; and yet thofe three were fingled out of the whole Number, and incapacitated, befides an high Fine and long Imprifonment, as to your Majefty will more fully appear by another Paper.

Sir *Patrick Holme* of *Polworth* being fent by the Shire of *Berwick* to complain of fome illegal Proceedings; and to obtain a legal remedy to them, which he did only in the common Form of Law, was alfo declared uncapable of publick Truft, befides many Months Imprifonment.

The Provoft of *Linlythgo* being complained of for not furnifhing fome of your Forces with Baggage Horfes, was called before the Council; and becaufe he faid they were not bound in Law to furnifh Horfes in fuch manner, he was immediately declared incapable of publick Truft, and was both fined and imprifoned.

There are alfo fifty of the Town of *St. Johnftons* incapacitated upon a very flight Pretence, fo that it's very impoffible for them to find a fufficient Number of Citizens for the Magiftracy of that Town.

2. Your Subjects are fometimes upon flight, and fometimes upon no Grounds imprifoned, and often kept Prifoners many Months and Years, nothing being objected to them, and are required to enter themfelves Prifoners; which is contrary to Law. It was in the former Article expreffed, that many of thefe Perfons declared incapable of publick Truft, did alfo fuffer Imprifonment; and befides thefe Inftances, Lieutenant General *Drummond* (whofe eminent Loyalty and great Services are well known to your Majefty,) was required to enter himfelf Prifoner in the Caftle of *Dunbarton*, where he was kept one Year and a half; and was made a clofe Prifoner for nine Months of that time, and yet nothing was ever objected to him to this Day to juftify that Ufage.

The

The Lord *Cardrofs* was for his Lady's keeping two Conventicles in her own Houfe (at which he was not prefent) fined 110 *l.* and hath now been kept Prifoner four Years in the Caftle of *Edinburgh*, where he ftill remains, although he hath often petitioned for his Liberty ; and Sir *Patrick Holme* hath been now a fecond time almoft one Year, and nothing is yet laid to his Charge.

Befides thefe illegal Imprifonments, the Officers of your Ma'efty's Forces frequently carry Warrants with them for apprehending Perfons that are under no legal Cenfure, nor have been fo much as cited to appear ; which hath put many of your Subjects under great Fears, efpecially upon what was done in Council three Years ago ; Captain *Carftairs* (a Man now well enough known to your Majefty) did intrap one *Kirkton*, an outed Minifter, into his Chamber at *Edinburgh*, and did violently abufe him ; and defigned to have extorted fome Money from him. The Noife of this coming to the Ears of one *Baily*, Brother-in-law to the faid *Kirkton*, he came to the Houfe, and hearing him cry Murder, Murder, forced open the Chamber-door, where he found his Brother-in-law and the Captain grappling ; the Captain pretended to have a Warrant againft *Kirkton*, and *Baily* defired him to fhew it, and promifed, that all Obedience fhould be given to it : But the Captain refufing to do it, *Kirkton* was refcued. This was only delivering a Man from the Hands of a Robber, which Nature obligeth all Men to do; efpecially when joined with fo near a Relation. The Captain complained of this to the Council, and the Lord *Hatton* with others were appointed to examine the Witneffes : And when it was brought before the Council, the Duke of *Hamilton*, Earls of *Moreton*, *Dumfrize* and *Kinkarden*, the Lord *Cocheren*, and Sir *Archibald Primrofe*, then Lord Regifter, defired, that the Report of the Examination might be read ; but that not ferving their Ends, was denied. And thereupon thofe Lords delivered their Opinion, that fithence *Carftairs* did not fhew any Warrant, nor was cloathed with any publick Character, it was no oppofing of your Majefty's Authority in *Baily*, fo to refcue the faid *Kirkton*; yet *Baily* was for this fined in 6000 Marks, and kept long a Prifoner.

Thofe Lords were upon that fo reprefented to your Majefty, that by the Duke of *Lauderdale*'s Procurement they were turned out of the Council, and all command of the Militia. And it can be made appear, that the Captain had at that time no Warrant at all againft *Kirkton*, but procured it after the Violence committed : And it was ante-dated, on defign to ferve a turn at that time. This manner of Proceedings hath ever fince put your Subjects under fad Apprehenfions.

There is one Particular further offered to your Majefty's Confideration, concerning their Way of ufing Prifoners.

There were 14 Men taken at a Field Conventicle, who without being legally convict of that or any other Crimes, were fecretly and in the Night taken out of Prifon upon a Warrant figned by the Earl of *Linlythgo*, and the Lord *Hatton* and *Collington*, and were delivered to Captain *Maitland*, who had been Page to the Duke of *Lauderdale*, but was then a *French* Officer, and was making his Levies in *Scotland*, and were carried over to the Service of the *French* King in the Year 1676.

3. The Council hath, upon many Occafions, proceeded to moft unreasonable and Arbitrary Fines, either for flight Offences, or for Offences where the Fine is regulated by Law, which they have never confidered, when the Perfons were not acceptable to them : So the Lord *Cardrofs* was fined in 1111 *l.* for his Lady's keeping two Conventicles in his Houfe, and chriftning a Child by an outed Minifter without his Knowledge. The Provoft formerly mentioned, and *Baily* with many more, were alfo fined without any regard to Law.

The Council hath at feveral times proceeded to the taking of Gentlemens Dwelling-houfes from them, and putting Garrifons in them, which in time of Peace is contrary to Law. In the Year 75, it was defigned againft twelve of your Majefty's Subjects, and was put in Execution in the Houfes of the Earl of *Calendar*, the Lord *Cardrofs*, the Lady *Lumfden*, &c. and was again attempted in the Year 78, the Houfes belonging to the Lairds of *Cofnock*, *Blagan*, and *Rowal*, and were poffeffed by Soldiers, and declared Garrifons. Nor did it reft there, but Orders were fent from the Council, requiring the Countries about thofe Houfes, to furnifh them for the Soldiers Ufe, and to fupply them with Neceffaries, much contrary to Law. It was againft this, that Sir *Patrick Holme* came to defire a Remedy ; and common Juftice being denied him, he ufed a legal Proteftation in the ordinary Form of Law, and was thereupon for many Months kept a Prifoner, and declared incapable of all publick Truft, &c.

There is another Particular, which becaufe it is fo odious, is unwillingly touched : yet it is neceffary to inform your Majefty about it ; for thereby it will appear, that the

the Duke of *Lauderdale* and his Brother have in a moſt ſolemn manner broken the publick Faith that was given in your Majeſty's Name.

One *Mitchel* being put in Priſon upon great Suſpicion of his having attempted to murder the late Arch-Biſhop of *St. Andrews*, and there being no Evidence againſt him, Warrant was given by the Duke of *Lauderdale* (then your Majeſty's Commiſſioner) and your Council, to promiſe him his Life if he would confeſs: Whereupon he did confeſs, and yet ſome Years after, that Perſon, who indeed deſerved many Deaths, if there had been any other Evidence againſt him, was upon that confeſſion convicted of the Crime, and the Duke of *Lauderdale* and his Brother being put to it by him, did ſwear, that they never gave or knew of any Aſſurance of Life given him: And when it was objected, that the Promiſe was upon Record in the Council-books, the Duke of *Lauderdale* did in open Court, where he was preſent only as a Witneſs, and ſo ought to have been ſilent, threaten them, if they ſhould proceed to the Examination of that Act of Council, which, as he then ſaid, might infer Perjury on them that ſwore: and ſo did cut off the Proof of that Defence, which had been admitted by the Court as good in Law, and ſufficient to ſave the Priſoner, if proved. Thus was that Man hanged upon that Confeſſion only, though the Promiſe that drew it from him, doth appear upon Record, and can be proved by good and clear Evidence. And from this your Majeſty may judge, what Credit may be given to ſuch Men.

We do not at preſent enlarge on other Particulars, though of great Importance; ſuch as Monopolies, ſelling Places of ·Honours, turning Men of known Integrity out of their Imployments, to which they had a good and juſt Right during their Lives: the Profits of one of the moſt conſiderable of theſe, being ſequeſtred for ſome time, and applied for the Dutcheſs of *Lauderdale*'s Uſe: the treating about, and receiving of great Bribes by the Duke and Dutcheſs of *Lauderdale*, and the Lord *Hatton*, and particularly from the Towns of *Edinburgh*, *Aberdeen*, *Linlythgo*, and many others, for procuring from your Majeſty Warrants for illegal Impoſitions within theſe Towns: the manifeſt and publick perverting of Juſtice in the Seſſion: beſides the moſt ſignal Abuſes of the Mint and Copper Coin, that are moſt grievous to all your Subjects. But the Number of theſe is ſo great, and they will require ſo many Witneſſes to be brought hither for proving them, that we fear it would too much trouble your Majeſty now to examine them all: But your Majeſty ſhall have a full Account of them afterwards.

One thing is humbly offered to your Majeſty, as the Root of theſe and many other Oppreſſions, which is, that the Method of governing that Kingdom for ſeveral Years hath been, That the Lord *Hatton* and his Adherents frame any Letter that they deſire from your Majeſty to your Council, and ſend it to the Duke of *Lauderdale*, who returns it ſigned; and this is brought to the Council: upon which, if at any time a Debate ariſeth concerning the matter of this Letter, as being againſt or with Law; and when it is propoſed, that a Repreſentation of that ſhould be made to your Majeſty; then the Lord *Hatton*, in his inſolent way, calls to have it put to the Queſtion, as if it were a Crime to have any Warrant either debated or repreſented to your Majeſty, which is procured by the Duke of *Lauderdale* or himſelf; and this is ecchoed by his Party, and by this means any further debating is ſtopped.

There are ſome other Particulars relating to theſe Heads, that are to be offered to your Majeſty in other Papers, which are not added here, left your Majeſty ſhould now be troubled with too long a Paper.

The Impeachment of the Duke and Dutcheſs of Lauderdale, *with their Brother my Lord* Hatton, *Preſented to His Majeſty by the City of* Edinburgh. *The matters of Fact particularly relating to the Town of* Edinburgh, *humbly offered for your Majeſty's Information. Before the Matter of Fact be ſpoken to, it is neceſſary that your Majeſty be informed of one Thing upon which this whole Affair hath moved.*

THE City of *Edinburgh* had at ſeveral times given conſiderable Sums of Money to the Duke of *Lauderdale*, amounting to upwards of Twelve Thouſand Pound *Sterling*, and the Lord *Hatton*, Brother to the ſaid Duke, being inraged by that their former Practice, and being arrived to great Height and Influence in the Adminiſtration of Your Majeſty's Affairs in *Scotland*, did thereupon reſolve on a Deſign of getting
Money

Money for himself also from them, as will appear to your Majesty by the following Narration; but the Magistrates at that time, and such others as then had the Principal Influence in the Administration of Affairs in that Town, being honest Men of good Fortunes, and not to be thought to comply with his Design, he bethought himself of all Ways to vex them; and knowing they did much value the Prosperity of the Town, he thought that the first means for promoting that his Design, was to have them threatned with removing your Majesty's *Publique Judicatures* from that City to *Sterlin*, and perswaded his Brother the Duke of *Lauderdale* of move Your Majesty to that purpose; but being disappointed of that Project by Your Majesty's Royal Wisdom, Your Majesty looking upon it as if it were to declare to the World that You were jealous of so great a Part of that Your Ancient Kingdom, he bethought himself of new Ways to accomplish his Design, for which he judged nothing so proper and effectual, as to disturb them in the choice of their Magistrates and Town-Council; and by all means possible to get some of his own chusing, fit for his own Ends, brought into the Administration of the Affairs of that City. In order to which, being impatient of any longer delay, he laid hold of what follows, being the first occasion that offered, though a very frivolous one.

At *Michaelmas* 1674, the said City of *Edinburgh* being to go about the Election of their Magistrates for the ensuing Year, there was procured a Letter from Your Majesty to Your Privy Council, commanding them to forbid the Magistrates and Town-Council to proceed in their Elections, but to continue the Magistrates that then were, till Your Majesty's further Pleasure should be known; the Reason suggested to Your Majesty for it, was taken from this Circumstance, That the Election ought to be made upon the *Tuesday* after *Michaelmas*, and (it happening this Year that *Michaelmas* fell to be on a *Tuesday*) they were resolved to proceed to their Elections upon *Michaelmas*-day.

Though this was a very small Matter, and upon very good and prudent Considerations resolved, as will afterwards appear, yet was it represented to Your Majesty as a factious Design, and an Innovation of dangerous Consequence, tending to create and maintain Faction in that City, contrary to Your Majesty's Service. Your Majesty's foresaid Letter being intimated to the Magistrates and Town-Council, they did immediately give exact Obedience to the same.

They did also represent to Your Majesty's Privy Council, the Rights that they had for chusing their own Magistrates, which had been granted to them by many of Your Majesty's Royal Ancestors, and confirmed by many Parliaments; by virtue of which they humbly conceived they ought to be suffered to proceed in their Elections.

They did also represent to your Majesty's Privy Council, the Reasons which had moved them to resolve of making their Elections on the said *Tuesday*, being *Michaelmas* Day, which in short were, that by their Constitution they were obliged upon the *Friday* before *Michaelmas* to make the List out of which the Magistrates are to be chosen; after the doing of which, there is a Surcease and Vacation of all ordinary Courts of *Judicature* within the Town, and the whole Time is spent by the common People and Tradesmen of the Town, in Rioting and Drinking, until the Elections be finished, which in this case would have been twelve Days; which they did in Prudence think they ought to shorten, not conceiving it contrary in the least to the established Rules of their Election.

2. On these things they did humbly crave Your Majesty's Privy Council would be pleased to represent to your Majesty, that thereby they might be freed from the suspicion of any Factious Design, with which they were charged by the said Letter.

This being, through the influence of the Lord *Hatton*, refused by the Privy Council, they dispatched a Gentleman to the Duke of *Lauderdale*, with Letters and Instructions full of Respect and Submission to his Grace.

The Gentleman at his first arrival found Duke *Lauderdale* very kind, and was made believe he should be quickly dispatched with Answers according to his Desire; but some Delays having fallen in, the Duke of *Lauderdale* fell likewise upon thoughts of getting Money from the Town upon this occasion, and therefore pretending still more and more Kindness to the said Gentleman; he did first by some Insinuations let fall to him his Expectation, and at last flatly asked him if he had brought a heavy Purse with him; which when he understood, he was not to expect, he changed his Method, and grew harsher; and having detained him five or six Weeks, he the said Duke entered into Consultation with his old Friend Sir *Andrew Ramsey*, how to order the Affair. By his Advice he did write a Letter, and sent Proposals to the said Town, That they should give Bond and Security, that the Townsmen

C c

men

men should live regularly as to all matters Ecclesiastical in the largest extent, as the same is determined in the late Acts of Parliament; and to keep the Town free of all sorts of Tumults either of Man or Woman : Judging that this was impossible for them to perform, and unfavourable to attempt, and that therefore it would oblige them to make offers of Money.

This Letter was all the Gentleman could obtain, and having got back to *Scotland* and delivered it to the Magistrates, they were so far from being carried in the Design, that they were glad of that Opportunity to witness their Zeal to serve Your Majesty ; for they did very heartily comply with what was proposed concerning the Bonds and Securities demanded ; and immediately urged that Your Majesty's Officers and Lawyers would cause draw such Bonds and Securities as was fit for the purpose, offering good Security for great Sums of Money for the Performance. But this not being the Thing truly intended, their ready Compliance with it, set them yet farther off from their desired Settlement, and served for no other Intent than to cause the Lord *Hatton* to double his Diligence to find out new Means to molest them ; to which end it was alledged by him, that they had of old forfeited their Privileges and Liberties by some great Misdemeanour, and that therefore they had not right to chuse their own Magistrates, for which he would needs have their Records searched ; and accordingly they themselves, with their Books and Records, were in a most unusual manner brought often before him and his Friends, though they had not Authority for it, to the great Disturbance and Annoyance of the Citizens, who being abundantly jealous of their Liberties, were with no small care kept within the due Bounds of Moderation, by the Loyalty and Vigilancy of their Magistrates.

They the said Magistrates, finding how they were used at home by the Lord *Hatton*, did again apply themselves to the Duke of *Lauderdale*, both by private Letters to the Duke of *Lauderdale* and his Dutchess, from some of the most eminent of them, full of Assurances of particular Respect to their Graces, and by a publick Letter to him from the whole Town-Council, offering Bond and Security to him in the Terms proposed by his fore-mentioned Letter. But this could not prevail, it being objected to them, from some frivolous Things the Lord *Hatton* had scraped together out of their old Records, that they had lost their Liberties, and that the right of chusing their Magistrates did no more belong to them.

Then did they produce their Charters, and did convincingly clear all Mistakes, and evidently make appear that the right of chusing their own Magistrates did remain to them undoubtedly and intirely.

All these things being cleared and open, they expected to be restored to the free Exercise of their Election in their accustomed manner. They were still kept off with Delays, until the Lord *Hatton*, in pursuance of his Design, fell a practising with some few of themselves, who did undertake with his assistance, to get such elected as were fit for his ends ; whereupon he writes to his Brother the Duke of *Lauderdale* to move Your Majesty for a Letter, and accordingly the Letter was procured from your Majesty upon the Seventh of *August*, 75 ; wherein Your Majesty after reciting Your former Orders in that Affair, did declare, that You were well informed of their Obedience to Your Commands, and of their dutiful Carriage in Your Concerns ; and therefore ordained them, the next Day after the Receipt of the Letter, to convene their whole Council, after their accustomed Manner, and out of the Lists already made, to Elect the Lord Provost, Bailies, and other Officers.

According to which Letter, they did the next Day proceed to their Elections, but instead of those whom the Lord *Hatton* expected they would have chosen, they did elect some Men of good Fortunes and Integrity, not at all fit for his Purpose (those who had ingaged to him not being Men of that esteem or influence as to be able to carry his Design as they had undertaken.)

The new Magistrates and Council did immediately after their Election, acquaint Your Majesty with their Proceedure, and gave Your Majesty great Acknowledgments and Assurances of their care of the Peace of the Town, and of Your Majesty's Service in all Matters, both Ecclesiastical and Civil.

The said Lord *Hatton* being exceedingly enraged at this Act of theirs, did by Advice of Sir *George Mackenzie*, now Your Majesty's Advocate, send a Letter to the Duke of *Lauderdale* ; to which he procured Your Majesty's Hand upon the 25th of the same Month of *August*, by which your Majesty ordered Your Privy Council to intimate to the Magistrates and Town-Council, that it was Your Royal Pleasure that there should be turned out of the Town-Council and declared incapable of any publick Trust in the said Town, twelve of the most eminent of

the

the same Men with whom Your Majesty had expressed Your self so well pleased, and whose Actings Your Majesty had approv'd, by Your Letter of the Seventh of the said Month.

This was accordingly executed by the Privy Council, without ever so much as calling before them the said Persons, though great Crimes were laid to their Charge, as being Factious Persons, and mis-representing Your Majesty's Proceedings, without mentioning any particular Fact of theirs which could import any such Crime. And though they be threatned by the said Letter to be pursued for these great Crimes, and that Your Majesty's Advocate is commanded in the same to insist against them, yet could they never obtain from Your Majesty's Privy Council that they should be try'd for these things, though by a Petition signed by the whole Twelve, they did represent the great Prejudice they sustained both in their Reputation and Trade, by being kept under such Threatnings; and therefore did humbly offer themselves to the strictest and severest Trial. To which Petition they never received any answer.

To make appear to Your Majesty that these Things were done for private and sinistrous Designs, and not upon account of the Ill-affectedness, or factious Dispositions of the Men, as was pretended; Your Majesty is humbly pray'd to take notice of these Particulars following:

First, There are three of the most considerable of these very Persons who had been charged with so great Crimes, admitted since that Time, by bribing the Dutchess of *Lauderdale*, into a Trust in Your Majesty's Affairs in *Scotland*, more eminent and considerable than any Trust the Town of *Edinburgh* can confer, *viz.* The paying off Your Majesty's Forces, and bringing in Your Majesty's Excises.

Secondly, No sooner were these twelve Men turned out of the Town-Council, but after many great and essential Informalities, (with the recital of which it is needless to trouble Your Majesty) they elected for Magistrates, Men of no Reputation either for Parts, Estate, or Honesty: And though these Bonds and Securities, which had been demanded from the others, and consented to by them, was formerly pretended to be of great importance for your Majesty's Service, yet they were not so much as once demanded, either by the Duke of *Lauderdale*, or the Lord *Hatton*, from these Men who were now chosen.

Thirdly, These new Magistrates were not long in their Seats, when off comes the Mask, and the true Design of getting Money appears. For by an Act of the Town-Council there is about 5000 *l.* Sterling disposed of amongst their nameless Friends, which were the Duke of *Lauderdale*, the Lord *Hatton*, and some other of their Friends. A great Sum to be got from that City, considering that the Duke of *Lauderdale* had got before that about 12000 *l.* Sterling from them.

The Dutchess of *Lauderdale* did also, since that time, endeavour to get more Money from them, and did with great Wrath threaten the Magistrates in plain Terms for not giving her a Present, notwithstanding all the Good she said she had done for them, reckoning the Favours Your Majesty hath at any time been pleased to bestow upon them, as done by herself.

Thus hath that poor Town been abused, and doth now lie, having Magistrates without either Conduct or Courage, in a time when the Disorders of that Nation doth require Persons to be employ'd there of eminent Fidelity and Capacity to serve Your Majesty.

His Majesty's Declaration for the Dissolution of his late Privy Council, and for constituting a new one, made in the Council-Chamber at White-Hall, April *the twentieth,* 1679.

By His Majesty's Special Command.

My Lords,

HIS Majesty hath called you together at this time, to communicate unto you a Resolution he hath taken in a matter of great Importance to his Crown and Government, and which he hopes will prove of the greatest Satisfaction and Advantage to his Kingdoms in all Affairs hereafter, both at home and abroad; and therefore he doubts not of your Approbation, however you may seem concerned in it.

In

In the first place, His Majesty gives you all Thanks for your Service to him here, and for all the good Advices you have given him, which might have been more frequent, if the great Number of this Council had not made it unfit for the Secrecy and Dispatch that are necessary in many great Affairs. This forced him to use a smaller Number of you in a foreign Committee, and sometimes the Advices of some few among them (upon such Occasions) for many Years past. He is sorry for the ill Success he has found in this Course, and sensible of the ill Posture of Affairs from that, and some unhappy Accidents, which have raised great Jealousies and Dissatisfactions among his good Subjects, and thereby left the Crown and Government in a Condition too weak for those Dangers we have Reason to fear both at home and abroad.

These his Majesty hopes may be yet prevented by a Course of wise and steady Counsels for the future, and these Kingdoms grow again to make such a Figure as they have formerly done in the World, and as they may always do, if our Union and Conduct were equal to our Force. To this end he hath resolved to lay aside the Use he may have hitherto made of any single Ministry or private Advices, or foreign Committees for the general Direction of his Affairs; and to constitute such a Privy Council, as may not only by its Number be fit for the Consultation and Digestion of all Business both Domestick and Foreign, but also by the Choice of them out of the several Parts this state is composed of, may be the best informed in the true Constitutions of it, and thereby the most able to counsel him in all the Affairs and Interests of this Crown and Nation. And by the constant Advice of such a Council, his Majesty is resolved hereafter to govern his Kingdoms; together with the frequent Use of his Great Council of Parliament, which he takes to be the true ancient Constitution of this State and Government.

Now for the greater Dignity of this Council, his Majesty resolves their constant Number shall be limited to that of Thirty. And for their greater Authority, there shall be fifteen of his Chief Officers who shall be Privy Counsellors by their Places. And for the other Fifteen, he will choose ten out of the several Ranks of the Nobility, and five Commoners of the Realm, whose known Abilities, Interest and Esteem in the Nation, shall render them without all suspicion of either mistaking or betraying the true Interests of the Kingdom, and consequently of advising him ill.

In the first place therefore, and to take care of the Church, his Majesty will have the Archbishop of *Canterbury*, and Bishop of *London* for the time being; and to inform him well in what concerns the Laws, the Lord Chancellor, and one of the Lord Chief Justices; for the Navy and Stores (wherein consists the chief Strength and Safety of the Kingdom) the Admiral and Master of the Ordnance; for the Treasury, the Treasurer and Chancellor of the Exchequer (or whenever any of these Charges are in Commission, then the first Commissioner to serve here in their room) the rest of the Fifteen, shall be the Lord Privy-Seal, the Master of the Horse, Lord Steward and Lord Chamberlain of his Houshold, the Groom of the Stole, and the two Secretaries of State. And these shall be all the Offices of his Kingdom, to which the Dignity of Privy-Counsellor shall be annexed. The others his Majesty has resolved, and hopes he has not chosen ill. His Majesty intends besides, to have such Princes of his Blood as he shall at any time call to this Board, being here in Court. A President of the Council whenever he shall find it necessary, and the Secretary of *Scotland*, when any such shall be here. But these being uncertain, he reckons not of the constant Number of Thirty, which shall never be exceeded.

To make way for this new Council, his Majesty has now resolved to dissolve this old one, and does hereby dissolve it, and from this time excuses your farther Attendance here, but with his repeated Thanks for your Service hitherto, and with the Assurance of his Satisfaction in you so far, that he should not have parted with you but to make way for this new Constitution, which he takes to be, as to the Number and Choice, the most proper and necessary for the Uses he intends them. And as most of you have Offices in his Service, and all of you particular Shares in his Favour and good Opinion, so he desires you would continue to exercise and deserve them, with the same Diligence and good Affections that you have hitherto done, and with Confidence of his Majesty's Kindness to you, and of those Testimonies you shall receive of it upon other Occasions.

There-

Therefore upon the prefent Diffolution of this Council, his Majefty appoints and commands all thofe Officers he hath named, to attend him here to-morrow at nine in the Morning, as his Privy-Council, together with thofe other Perfons he defigns to make up the Number, and to each of whom he has already figned particular Letters to that purpofe; and commands the Lord Chancellor to fee them iffued out accordingly, which is the Form he intends to ufe, and that hereafter they fhall be figned in Council, fo that nothing may be done unadvifedly in the Choice of any Perfon to a Charge of fo great Dignity and Importance to the Kingdom.

Names of the Lords of His Majefty's moft Honourable Privy-Council.

HIS Highnefs Prince *Rupert.*
William Lord Archbifhop of *Canterbury.*
Heneage Lord *Finch,* Lord Chancellor of *England.*
Anthony Earl of *Shaftsbury,* Lord Prefident of the Council.
Arthur Earl of *Anglefey,* Lord Privy-Seal.
Chriftopher Duke of *Albemarle.*
James Duke of *Monmouth,* Mafter of the Horfe.
Henry Duke of *Newcaftle.*
John Duke of *Lauderdale,* Secretary of State for *Scotland.*
James Duke of *Ormond,* Lord Steward of the Houfhold.
Charles Lord Marquis of *Winchefter.*
Henry Lord Marquis of *Worcefter.*
Henry Earl of *Arlington,* Lord Chamberlain of the Houfhold.
James Earl of *Salisbury,*
John Earl of *Bridgewater.*
Robert Earl of *Sunderland,* one of his Majefty's Principal Secretaries of State.
Arthur Earl of *Effex,* firft Lord Commiffioner of the Treafury.
John Earl of *Bath,* Groom of the Stole.
Thomas Lord Vifcount *Falconberg.*
George Lord Vifcount *Halifax.*
Henry Lord Bifhop of *London.*
John Lord *Roberts.*
Denzil Lord *Holles.*
William Lord *Ruffel.*
William Lord *Cavendifh.*
Henry Coventry, Efq; one of his Majefty's Principal Secretaries of State.
Sir *Francis North* Knt. Lord Chief Juftice of the Common Pleas.
Sir *Henry Capell,* Knight of the *Bath,* firft Commiffioner of the Admiralty.
Sir *John Ernle,* Knt. Chancellor of the Exchequer.
Sir *Thomas Chicheley,* Knt. Mafter of the Ordnance.
Sir *William Temple,* Bart.
Edward Seymour, Efq;
Henry Powle, Efq;

Whitehall, April 11. 1679.

HIS Majefty being this Day in Council, did caufe fuch of the aforementioned Lords, and others, who were then prefent, to be fworn Privy Councellors; which being done, they took their Places accordingly.
His Majefty was alfo pleafed to declare, that he intended to make
Sir *Henry Capell,* Knight of the *Bath,*
Daniel Finch, Efq;
Sir *Thomas Lee,*
Sir *Humphrey Winch,* } Baronets.
Sir *Thomas Meers,*
Edward Vaughan,
    and } Efquires.
Edward Hales,
Commiffioners for the Execution of the Office of Lord High Admiral of *England.*
And his Majefty being afterwards come into the Houfe of Peers in his Royal Robes, and the Houfe of Commons attending, his Majefty was pleafed to make this Speech.

My Lords and Gentlemen,

I Thought it requisite to acquaint you with what I have done now this Day; which is, That I have established a new Privy-Council, the constant Number of which shall never exceed thirty.

I have made choice of such Persons as are worthy and able to advise Me, and am resolved in all my Weighty and Important Affairs, next to the Advice of my Great Council in Parliament (which I shall very often consult with) to be advised by this Privy-Council.

I could not make so great a Change without acquainting both Houses of Parliament.

And I desire you all to apply your selves heartily, as I shall do, to those things which are necessary for the Good and Safety of the Kingdom, and that no time may be lost in it.

The Message of the King, by Mr. Secretary Jenkins *to the Commons, on the* 9th *of* November 1680.

CHARLES R.

HIS Majesty desires this House, as well for the Satisfaction of his People, as of Himself, to expedite such matters as are depending before them, relating to Popery, and the Plot; and would have them rest assured, that all Remedies they can tender to his Majesty, conducing to those Ends, shall be very acceptable to him, provided they be such as may consist with preserving the Succession of the Crown in its due and legal Course of Descent.

The Address to his Majesty from the Commons, Saturday November 13. 1680.

May it please your most Excellent Majesty,

WE, Your Majesty's most Loyal and Obedient Subjects, the Commons in this present Parliament assembled, having taken into our most serious Consideration Your Majesty's most gracious Message brought unto us the ninth Day of this instant *November*, by Mr. Secretary *Jenkins*, do with all Thankfulness acknowledge Your Majesty's Care and Goodness in inviting us to expedite such matters as are depending before us relating to Popery and the Plot. And we do, in all Humility, represent to Your Majesty, that we are fully convinced that it is highly incumbent upon us, in discharge both of our Duty to Your Majesty, and of that great Trust reposed in us, by those whom we represent, to endeavour, by the most speedy and effectual Ways, the Suppression of Popery within this Your Kingdom, and the bringing to publick Justice all such as shall be found Guilty of the horrid and damnable Popish Plot. And though the time of our Sitting (abating what must necessarily be spent in the choosing and presenting a Speaker, appointing Grand Committees, and in taking the Oaths and Tests enjoin'd by Act of Parliament) hath not much exceeded a Fortnight; yet we have in this Time not only made a considerable Progress in some things which to us seem, and (when presented to Your Majesty in a Parliamentary way) will, we trust, appear to Your Majesty, to be absolutely necessary for the Safety of Your Majesty's Person, the effectual Suppression of Popery, and the Security of the Religion, Lives, and Estates of your Majesty's Protestant Subjects. But even in relation to the Trials of the five Lords impeached in Parliament for the execrable Popish Plot, we have so far proceeded, as we doubt not but in a short time we shall be ready for the same. But we cannot (without being unfaithful to Your Majesty, and to our Country, by whom we are entrusted) omit, upon this Occasion, humbly to inform Your Majesty, that our Difficulties, even as to these Trials, are much encreased by the evil and destructive Counsels of those Persons who advised Your Majesty, first, to the Prorogation, and then, to the Dissolution of the last Parliament; at a time when the Commons had taken great pains about, and were prepared for those Trials. And by the like pernicious Counsels of those who advised the many and long Prorogations of the present Parliament, before the same was permitted to sit; whereby by ſome of the Evidence which was prepared in the laſt Parliament may poſſibly (during ſo long an Interval) be forgotten or loſt, and ſome Perſons, who might probably come in as Witneſſes, are either dead, have been taken off, or may have been diſcouraged from giving their Evidence. But of one miſchievous Conſequence of thoſe dangerous and unhappy Counſels we are certainly and ſadly ſenſible, namely, That the Teſtimony of a material Witneſs againſt every of thoſe five Lords (and who could probably have diſcovered and brought in much other Evidence about the Plot in general, and thoſe Lords in particular) cannot now be given *vivâ voce*.   Foraſmuch as that Witneſs is unfortunately dead between the Calling and the Sitting of this Parliament: To prevent the like or greater Inconveniences for the future, We make it our moſt humble Requeſt to Your Excellent Majeſty, that as You tender the Safety of Your Royal Perſon, the Security of Your Loyal Subjects, and the Preſervation of the True Proteſtant Religion, You will not ſuffer Your Self to be prevailed upon by the like Counſels to do any thing which may occaſion in conſequence (though we are aſſured, never with your Majeſty's Intention) either the deferring of a full and perfect Diſcovery and Examination of this moſt wicked and deteſtable Plot, or the preventing the Conſpirators therein from being brought to ſpeedy and exemplary Juſtice and Puniſhment. And we humbly beſeech you Majeſty to reſt aſſured (notwithſtanding any Suggeſtions which may be made by Perſons, who, for their own wicked purpoſes, contrive to create a diſtruſt in your Majeſty of your People,) That nothing is more in the Deſires, and ſhall be more the Endeavours of us Your faithful and loyal Commons, than the promoting and advancing of your Majeſty's true Happineſs and Greatneſs. ·

The Addreſs of the Commons in Parliament to his Majeſty, to remove Sir George Jeffreys *out of all publick Offices.*

WE your Majeſty's moſt Dutiful and Loyal Subjects the Commons in Parliament aſſembled, having received a Complaint againſt Sir *George Jeffreys,* Knight, your Majeſty's Chief Juſtice of *Cheſter,* and heard the Evidence concerning the ſame, and alſo what he did alledge and prove in his Defence: And being thereupon fully ſatisfy'd, that the ſaid Sir *George Jeffreys* well knowing that many of your Loyal Proteſtant Subjects, and particularly thoſe of your Great and Famous City of *London,* out of Zeal for the Preſervation of the Proteſtant Religion, your Majeſty's Royal Perſon and Government, and in hopes to bring the Popiſh Conſpirators to ſpeedy Juſtice, were about to petition your Majeſty in an Humble, Dutiful and Legal Way, for the Sitting of this Parliament; the ſaid Sir *George Jeffreys,* not regarding his Duty to your Majeſty, or the welfare of your People, did on purpoſe to ſerve his own private Ends, and to create a Miſ-underſtanding between your Majeſty and your Good Subjects, though diſguiſed with pretence of Service to your Majeſty, maliciouſly declare ſuch Petitioning, ſometimes to be Tumultuous, Seditious and Illegal, and at other times did preſume publickly to inſinuate and aſſert, as if your Majeſty would deprive your Citizens of *London* of their Charters, and divers other Privileges, Immunities and Advantages, and alſo of your Royal Favour, in caſe they ſhould ſo petition; and alſo did publickly declare, That in caſe they ſhould ſo petition, there ſhould not be any Meeting or Sitting of Parliament: thereby traducing your Majeſty, as if you would not purſue your Gracious Intentions, the rather becauſe they were grateful to your good Subjects; do, in moſt humble manner, beſeech your Majeſty to remove the ſaid Sir *George Jeffreys* out of the ſaid Place of Chief Juſtice of *Cheſter,* and out of all other publick Offices and Employments under your Majeſty.

His Majeſty by Mr. Secretary *Jenkins* was pleaſed to return Anſwer to this Addreſs, That he would conſider of it.

His

His Majesty's Message to the Commons in Parliament, relating to Tangier.

CHARLES REX.

HIS Majesty did in his Speech, at the opening of the Session, desire the Advice and Assistance of his Parliament, in relation to *Tangier*: The Condition and Importance of the Place obliges his Majesty to put this House in mind again, that He relies upon them for the Support of it, without which it cannot be much longer preserved. His Majesty does therefore very earnestly recommend *Tangier* again to the due and speedy Consideration and Care of this House.

The Humble Address of the Commons in Parliament assembled, presented to his Majesty, Monday 29th *Day of* November, 1680. *in answer to that Message.*

May it please your most Excellent Majesty,

WE Your Majesty's most Obedient and Loyal Subjects, the Commons in Parliament assembled, having with all Duty and Regard taken into our serious Consideration your Majesty's late Message relating to *Tangier*, cannot but account the present Condition of it, as Your Majesty is pleased to represent in Your said Message, (after so vast a Treasure expended to make it useful) not only as one Infelicity more added to the afflicted Estate of Your Majesty's faithful and loyal Subjects, but as one Result also of the same Counsels and Designs which have brought Your Majesty's Person, Crown and Kingdoms into those great and imminent Dangers, with which at this Day they are surrounded; and we are the less surprised to hear of the Exigencies of *Tangier*, when we remember that since it became a part of Your Majesty's Dominions, it hath several times been under the Command of Popish Governors, (particularly for some time under the Command of a Lord Impeached, and now Prisoner in the *Tower* for the Execrable and Horrid Popish Plot) That the Supplies sent thither have been in great part made up of Popish Officers and Soldiers, and that the *Irish* Papists amongst the Soldiers of that Garrison, have been the Persons most countenanced and encouraged.

To that Part of Your Majesty's Message which expresses a Reliance upon this House for the Support of *Tangier*, and a Recommendation of it to our speedy care, We do with all Humility and Reverence give this Answer, That although in due Time and Order we shall omit nothing incumbent on Us for the Preservation of every Part of Your Majesty's Dominions, and advancing the Prosperity and flourishing Estate of this Your Kingdom; yet at this Time, when a Cloud which has long threatned this Land is ready to break upon our Heads in a Storm of Ruin and Confusion, to enter into any further Consideration of this Matter; especially to come to any Resolutions in it, before we are effectually secured from the imminent and apparent Dangers arising from the Power of Popish Persons and Councils, We humbly conceive will not consist either with our Duty to Your Majesty, or the Trust reposed in Us by those we represent.

It is not unknown to Your Majesty how restless the Endeavours, and how bold the Attempts of the Popish Party, for many Years last past have been, not only within this, but other your Majesty's Kingdoms, to introduce the *Romish*, and utterly to extirpate the true Protestant Religion. The several Approaches they have made towards the compassing this their Design (assisted by the Treachery of perfidious Protestants) have been so strangely successful, that it is matter of Admiration to Us, and which we can only ascribe to an Over-ruling Providence, that Your Majesty's Reign is still continued over Us, and that we are yet assembled to consult the Means of our Preservation: This bloody and restless Party not content with the great Liberty they had a long time enjoy'd to exercise their own Religion privately among themselves, to partake of an equal Freedom of their Persons and Estates, with your Majesty's Protestant Subjects, and of an Advantage above them in being excused from chargeable Offices and Employments, hath so far prevailed as to find Countenance for an open and avowed Practice of their Superstition and Idolatry, without controul, in several Parts of this Kingdom. Great Swarms of Priests and Jesuits have resorted hither, and have here exercised their Jurisdiction rifdiction, and been daily tampering to pervert the Consciences of your Majesty's Subjects. Their Opposers they have found means to disgrace, and if they were Judges, Justices of the Peace, or other Magistrates, to have them turned out of Commission: And in contempt of the known Laws of the Land, they have practised upon People of all Ranks and Qualities, and gained over divers to their Religion; some openly to profess it, others secretly to espouse it, as most conduced to the service thereof.

After some time they became able to influence matters of State and Government, and thereby to destroy those they cannot corrupt. The continuance or prorogation of Parliaments has been accommodated to serve the purposes of that Party. Money raised upon the People to supply your Majesty's extraordinary Occasions, was by the prevalence of Popish Counsels employ'd to make War upon a Protestant State, and to advance and augment the dreadful power of the *French* King, though to the apparent hazard of this, and all other Protestant Countries. Great Numbers of your Majesty's Subjects were sent into, and continued in the service of that King, notwithstanding the apparent Interest of your Majesty's Kingdoms, the Addresses of the Parliament, and your Majesty's gracious Proclamations to the contrary. Nor can we forbear to mention, how that at the beginning of the same War, even the Ministers of *England* were made Instruments to press upon that State, the acceptance of one demand, among others, from the *French* King for procuring their peace with him, that they should admit the publick exercise of the Roman Catholick Religion in the United Provinces, the Churches there to be divided, and the Romish Priests maintained out of the publick Revenue.

At home, if Your Majesty did at any time by the Advice of your Privy-Council, or of Your two Houses of Parliament, command the Laws to be put in execution against Papists, even from thence they gained advantage to their Party, while the Edge of those Laws was turned against Protestant Dissenters, and the Papists escaped in a manner untouch't. The Act of Parliament enjoining a Test to be taken by all Persons admitted into any publick Office, and intended for a security against Papists coming into Employment, had so little effect, that either by Dispensations, obtained from *Rome,* they submitted to those Tests, and held their Offices themselves, or those put in their places, were so favourable to the same Interests, that Popery itself has rather gain'd than lost ground since that Act.

But that their business in hand might yet more speedily and strongly proceed, at length a Popish Secretary (since executed for his Treasons) takes upon him to set afoot and maintain correspondencies at *Rome* (particularly with a Native Subject of your Majesty's promoted to be a Cardinal) and in the Courts of other foreign Princes (to use their own form of Speech) for the subduing that Pestilent Heresy, which has so long domineer'd over the Northern World; that is, to root the Protestant Religion out of *England,* and thereby to make way the more easily to do the same in other Protestant Countries.

Towards the doing this great Work, (as Mr. *Coleman* was pleased to call it) Jesuits (the most dangerous of all Popish Orders to the Lives and Estates of Princes) were distributed to their several Precincts within this Kingdom, and held joint Councils with those of the same Order in all Neighbour Popish Countries: Out of these Councils and Correspondencies was hatcht that damnable and hellish Plot, by the good Providence of Almighty God brought to light above two Years since, but still threatning us; wherein the Traitors impatient of longer delay, reckoning the prolonging of your sacred Majesty's Life (which God long preserve) as the great Obstacle in the way to the Consummation of their hopes, and having in their prospect a proselyted Prince immediately to succeed in the Throne of these Kingdoms, resolved to begin their Work with the Assassination of your Majesty, to carry it on with armed Force, to destroy Your Protestant Subjects in *England,* to execute a second Massacre in *Ireland,* and so with ease to arrive at the suppression of our Religion, and the subversion of the Government.

When this accursed Conspiracy began to be discovered, they began the smothering it with the barbarous Murder of a Justice of the Peace, within one of Your Majesty's own Palaces, who had taken some Examinations concerning it.

Amidst these distractions and fears, Popish Officers, for the command of Forces were allowed upon the Musters by special Orders (surreptitiously obtained from Your Majesty) but counter-signed by a Secretary of State, without ever passing under the Tests prescribed by the aforementioned Act of Parliament. In like manner above fifty new Commissions were granted about the same time to known Papists, besides a great number of desperate Popish Officers, though out of Command,

E e

mand, yet entertained at half pay. When in the next Parliament the House of Commons were prepared to bring to a legal Trial the principal Conspirators in this Plot, that Parliament was first prorogued, and then dissolved. The Interval between the Calling and Sitting of this Parliament was so long, that now they conceive Hopes of covering all their past Crimes, and gaining a seasonable time and advantages of practising them more effectually.

Witnesses are attempted to be corrupted, and not only promises of a Reward, but of the Favour of your Majesty's Brother, made the Motives to their Compliance. Divers of the most considerable of your Majesty's Protestant Subjects have Crimes of the highest nature forged against them, the Charge to be supported by Subornation and Perjury, that they may be destroy'd by Forms of Law and Justice.

A Presentment being prepared for a Grand Jury of *Middlesex*, against your Majesty's said Brother the Duke of *York*, (under whose Countenance all the rest shelter themselves) the Grand Jury were in an unheard of and unprecedented and illegal manner discharged; and that with so much haste, and fear left they should finish that Presentment, that they were prevented from delivering many other Indictments by them at that time found against other Popish Recusants. Because a Pamphlet came forth weekly, called, *The Weekly Pacquet of Advice from* Rome, which exposes Popery (as it deserves) as ridiculous to the People, a new and arbitrary Rule of Court was made in your Majesty's Court of King's Bench (rather like a Star-Chamber than a Court of Law) That the same should not for the future be printed by any Person whatsoever.

We acknowledge your Majesty's Grace and Care in issuing forth divers Proclamations since the Discovery of the Plot, for the banishing Papists from about this great City, and Residence of your Majesty's Court, and the Parliament; but with trouble of Mind we do humbly inform your Majesty, That notwithstanding all these Prohibitions, great Numbers of them, and of the most dangerous Sort, to the Terrour of your Majesty's Protestant Subjects, do daily resort hither, and abide here. Under these and other sad Effects and Evidences of the prevalency of Popery, and its Adherents, We Your Majesty's faithful Commons found this your Majesty's distressed Kingdom, and other parts of your Dominions labouring, when we assembled.

And therefore from our Allegiance to Your Majesty, our Zeal to our Religion, our Faithfulness to our Country, and our Care of *Posterity*, we have lately, upon mature Deliberation, proposed one Remedy of these great Evils without which (in our Judgments) all others will prove vain and fruitless, and (like all deceitful Securities against certain Dangers) will rather expose your Majesty's Person to the greatest hazard, and the People, together with all that's valuable to them as Men or Christians, to utter Ruin and Destruction. We have taken this occasion of an Access to your Majesty's Royal Presence, humbly to lay before your Majesty's great Judgment and gracious Consideration this most dreadful Design of introducing Popery, and, as necessary Consequences of it, all other Calamities, into your Majesty's Kingdoms. And if after all this, the private Suggestions of the subtile Accomplices of that Party and Design should yet prevail, either to elude or totally obstruct the faithful endeavours of Us your Commons for an happy Settlement of this Kingdom, we shall have this remaining comfort, That we have freed our selves from the Guilt of that Blood and Desolation which is like to ensue. But our only Hope, next under God, is in your Sacred Majesty, that by your great Wisdom and Goodness we may be effectually secured from Popery, and all the Evils that attend it; and that none but persons of known Fidelity to Your Majesty and sincere Affections to the Protestant Religion, may be put into any Employment, Civil or Military; that whilst we shall give a Supply to *Tangier*, we may be assured we do not augment the Strength of our Popish Adversaries, nor encrease our own Dangers. Which Desires of your faithful Commons, if your Majesty shall graciously vouchsafe to grant, We shall not only be ready to assist your Majesty in the Defence of *Tangier*, but do whatsoever else shall be in our power to enable your Majesty to protect the Protestant Religion and Interest, at home and abroad, and to resist and repel the Attempts of your Majesty's and the Kingdom's Enemies.

The

The Humble Address of the House of Commons presented to his Majesty upon Tuesday *the* 21st *Day of* December, 1680. *In Answer to his Majesty's Gracious Speech to both Houses of Parliament, upon the* 15th *Day of the same* December.

May it please Your most Excellent Majesty,

WE Your Majesty's most dutiful and loyal Subjects, the Commons in this present Parliament Assembled, have taken into our serious Consideration Your Majesty's Gracious Speech to both Your Houses of Parliament, on the 15th of this Instant *December*; and do with all the grateful Sense of faithful Subjects and sincere Protestants, acknowledge Your Majesty's great Goodness to us, in renewing the Assurances You have been pleased to give us, in your readiness to concur with us in any means for the Security of the Protestant Religion, and Your Gracious Invitation of us to make our Desires known to Your Majesty.

But with grief of Heart we cannot but observe, that to these Princely Offers Your Majesty has been advised (by what secret Enemies to Your Majesty and your People, we know not) to annex a Reservation, which if insisted on, in the Instance to which alone it is applicable, will render all Your Majesty's other gracious Inclinations of no effect or advantage to us. Your Majesty is pleased thus to limit your Promise of Concurrence in the Remedies which shall be proposed, that they may consist with preserving the Succession of the Crown in its due and legal Course of Descent. And we do humbly inform Your Majesty, that no Interruption of that Descent has been endeavoured by us, except only the Descent upon the Person of the Duke of *York*, who by the wicked Instruments of the Church of *Rome*, has been manifestly perverted to their Religion. And we do humbly represent to your Majesty, as the Issue of our most deliberate Thoughts, and Consultations, that for the Papists to have their hopes continued, that a Prince of that Religion shall succeed to the Throne of these Kingdoms, is utterly inconsistent with the Safety of your Majesty's Person, the Preservation of the Protestant Religion, and the Prosperity, Peace and Welfare of your Protestant Subjects.

That Your Majesty's Sacred Life is in continual danger, under the prospect of a Popish Successor, is evident, not only from the Principles of those devoted to the Church of *Rome*, which allow that an Heretical Prince (and such they term all Protestant Princes) excommunicated and deposed by the Pope, may be destroy'd and murthered; but also from the Testimonies given in the prosecution of the horrid Popish Plot, against divers Traitors attainted for designing to put those accursed Principles into practice against Your Majesty.

From the Expectation of this Succession, has the Number of Papists in Your Majesty's Dominions so much encreased within these few Years, and so many been prevailed with to desert the true Protestant Religion, that they might be prepared for the Favours of a Popish Prince as soon as he should come to the possession of the Crown: and while the same Expectation lasts, many more will be in the same danger of being perverted.

This it is that has hardned the Papists of this Kingdom, animated and confederated by their Priests and Jesuits, to make a common Purse, provide Arms, make Application to foreign Princes, and solicite their Aid for imposing Popery upon us; and all this even during your Majesty's Reign, and while Your Majesty's Government and Laws were our Protection.

It is Your Majesty's Glory and true Interest, to be the Head and Protector of all *Protestants*, as well abroad as at home: But if these Hopes remain, what Alliance can be made for the Advantage of the Protestant Religion and Interest, which shall give Confidence to your Majesty's Allies, to join so vigorously with Your Majesty, as the State of that Interest in the World now requires, while they see this *Protestant Kingdom* in so much danger of a *Popish Successor*; by whom at the present, all their Councils and Actions may be eluded, as hitherto they have been, and by whom (if he should succeed) they are sure to be destroy'd?

We

We have thus humbly laid before your Majesty, some of those great Dangers and Mischiefs which evidently accompany the expectation of a *Popish Successor*. The certain and unspeakable Evils which will come upon Your Majesty's *Protestants Subjects* and their posterity, if such a Prince should inherit, are more also than we can well enumerate.

Our Religion, which is now so dangerously shaken, will then be totally overthrown: Nothing will be left, or can be found to protect or defend it.

The execution of old Laws must cease, and it will be vain to expect new ones. The most sacred Obligations of Contracts and Promises (if any should be given) that shall be judged to be against the Interest of the *Romish Religion*, will be violated; as is undeniable not only from Argument and Experience elsewhere, but from the sad experience this Nation once had on the like occasion.

In the Reign of such a Prince, the Pope will be acknowledged Supream (though the Subjects of this Kingdom have sworn the contrary) and all Causes, either as Spiritual, or in order to Spiritual Things, will be brought under his Jurisdiction.

The Lives, Liberties and Estates of all such *Protestants*, as value their Souls and their Religion more than their secular Concernments, will be adjudged forfeited.

To all this we might add: That it appears in the discovery of the Plot, that foreign Princes were invited to assist in securing the Crown to the Duke of *York*; with Arguments from his great Zeal to establish Popery, and to extirpate Protestants (whom they call *Hereticks*) out of his Dominions; and such will expect performance accordingly.

We further humbly beseech Your Majesty, in Your great Wisdom to consider, Whether in case the Imperial Crown of this Protestant Kingdom, should descend to the Duke of *York*; the opposition which may possibly be made to his possessing it, may not only endanger the further descent in the Royal Line, but even Monarchy itself.

For these Reasons we are most humble Petitioners to your most sacred Majesty, That in tender commiseration of your poor Protestant People, your Majesty will be graciously pleased to depart from the Reservation in Your said Speech; and when a Bill shall be tendered to your Majesty in a Parliamentary way, to disable the Duke of *York* from inheriting the Crown, Your Majesty will give your Royal Assent thereto; and as necessary to fortify and defend the same, that your Majesty will likewise be graciously pleased to assent to an Act whereby your Majesty's Protestant Subjects may be enabled to associate themselves for the defence of your Majesty's Person, the Protestant Religion, and the Security of Your Kingdoms.

These Requests we are constrained humbly to make to your Majesty, as of absolute Necessity, for the safe and peaceable enjoyment of our *Religion*.

Without these things the Alliances of *England* will not be valuable, nor the People encouraged to contribute to your Majesty's Service.

As some farther means for the Preservation both of our *Religion* and *Propriety*; We are humble Suiters to your Majesty, that from henceforth such Persons only may be *Judges* within the Kingdom of *England* and Dominion of *Wales*, as are Men of Ability, Integrity, and known Affection to the *Protestant Religion*; and that they may hold both their Offices and Salaries, *Quam diu se bene gesserint*. That (several Deputy-Lieutenants and Justices of the Peace fitly qualified for those Imployments, having been of late displaced, and others put in their room, who are Men of Arbitrary Principles and Countenancers of *Papists* and Popery) such only may bear the Office of a Lord-Lieutenant, as are Persons of Integrity and known Affection to the *Protestant Religion*. That Deputy-Lieutenants and Justices of the Peace may be also so qualify'd, and may be moreover Men of Ability, of Estates and Interest in their Country.

That none may be employ'd as Military Officers, or Officers in your Majesty's Fleet, but Men of known Experience, Courage and Affection to the *Protestant Religion*.

These our humble Requests being obtained, we shall on our part be ready to assist your Majesty for the Preservation of *Tangier*, and for putting your Majesty's Fleet into such a Condition, as it may preserve your Majesty's *Sovereignty* of the Seas, and be for the Defence of the Nation.

If your Majesty hath or shall make any necessary Alliances for defence of the *Protestant Religion*, and Interest and Security of this Kingdom, this House will be ready to assist and stand by Your Majesty in the support of the same.

After

After this our humble Anſwer to Your Majeſty's Gracious Speech, we hope no evil Inſtruments whatſoever ſhall be able to leſſen your Majeſty's Eſteem of that Fidelity and Affection we bear to your Majeſty's Service ; but that your Majeſty will always retain in your Royal Breaſt, that Favourable Opinion of us your Loyal *Commons*, That thoſe other good Bills which we have now under Conſideration, conducing to the Great Ends we have before mentioned, as alſo all Laws for the Benefit and Comfort of your People, which ſhall from time to time be tendred for Your Majeſty's Royal Aſſent, ſhall find acceptance with Your Majeſty.

The Report of the Committee of Commons appointed to examine the Proceedings of the Judges, &c.

THis Committee being informed that in *Trinity-Term* laſt, the Court of *King's-Bench* diſcharged the Grand Jury, that ſerved for the Hundred of *Oſſulſton*, in the County *Middleſex*, in a very unuſual manner ; proceeded to enquire into the ſame, and found by the Information of *Charles Umfrevil*, Eſq; Foreman of the ſaid Jury, *Edward Proby*, *Henry Gerard*, and *John Smith*, Gentlemen, alſo of the ſaid Jury, that on the 21ſt of *June* laſt, the Conſtables attending the ſaid Jury, were found defective, in not preſenting the *Papiſts* as they ought, and thereupon were ordered by the ſaid Jury to make further Preſentments of them on the 26th following, on which Day the *Jury* met for that purpoſe ; when ſeveral Peers of this Realm, and other Perſons of Honour and Quality, brought them a Bill againſt *James* Duke of *York*, for not coming to Church: But ſome exceptions being taken to that Bill, in that it did not ſet forth the ſaid Duke to be a *Papiſt*, ſome of the *Jury* attended the ſaid Perſons of Quality to receive Satisfaction therein. In the mean time, and about an Hour after they had received the ſaid Bill, ſome of the *Jury* attended the Court of *King's-Bench*, with a Petition, which they deſired the Court to preſent in their Name unto his Majeſty for the Sitting of this *Parliament*. Upon which the Lord Chief Juſtice *Scroggs* raiſed many Scruples, and on pretence that they were not all in Court (though twenty of the *Jury* had ſubſcribed the Petition) ſent for them, ſaying, he would diſpatch them preſently. The *Jury* being come, and their Names called over, they renewed their Deſire that the Court would preſent their Petition: But the Chief Juſtice asked, if they had any Bills ? they anſwered, They had, but the Clerks were drawing them into Form: Upon which the Chief Juſtice ſaid, They would not make two Works of one Buſineſs: and the Petition being read, he ſaid, This was no Article of their Charge, nor was there any Act of Parliament that required the Court to deliver the Grand *Jury's* Petitions: That there was a *Proclamation* about them ; and that it was not reaſonable the Court ſhould be obliged to run on their Errands: And he thought it much that they ſhould come with a Petition to alter the King's Mind declared in the News-Books. The *Jury* ſaid, They did it not to impoſe on the Court, but (as other *Juries* had done) with all Submiſſion they deſired it : But the Court refuſed, bidding the Cryer return them their Petition: And Mr. Juſtice *Jones* told them, They had meddled with matters of State, not given them in Charge, but preſented no Bills of the matters given in Charge. They anſwered as before, They had many before them, that would be ready in due time. Notwithſtanding which, the ſaid Juſtice *Jones* told them, They were diſcharged from further Service. But *Philip Ward*, (the Clerk that attended the ſaid *Jury*) cry'd out, No, No, they have many Bills before them ; for which the Court underſtanding (as it ſeems to this Committee) a ſecret Reaſon, which the Clerk did not, reproved him, asked if he or they were to give the Rule there? The Cryer then told the Court They would not receive their Petition ; the Chief Juſtice bid them let it alone ; ſo it was left there, and the *Jury* returned to the Court-Houſe, and there found ſeveral Conſtables, with Preſentments of *Papiſts* and other Offenders, as the *Jury* had directed them on the 21ſt before, but could not now receive the ſaid Preſentments, being diſcharged. Whereby much Buſineſs was obſtructed, though none of the ſaid Informants ever knew the ſaid Jury diſcharged before the laſt Day of the Term, which was not till four Days after. And it further appeared to the Committee, by the Evidence of *Samuel Aſtrey*, *Jaſper Waterhouſe*, and *Philip Ward*, Clerks, that have long ſerved in the ſaid Court, That they were much ſurpriſed at the ſaid diſcharging of the *Jury*, in that it was never done in their Memory before ; and the rather, becauſe the ſaid

Waterhouse, as Secondary, conftantly enters on that *Grand Jury's* Paper that the laft day of the Term is given them to return their Verdict on, as the laft day but one is given to the other Two Grand *Juries* of that County, which Entry is as followeth:

Trinit. 32 Car. 2.

Juratores habent diem ad Verediclum fuum reddendum ufque diem Mercurii proxime poft tres Septimanas, fanéte Trinitatis.

Being the laft day of the Term, and fo in all the other Terms the laft day is given; which makes it appear to this Committee, That they were not in truth difcharged for not having their Prefentments ready, fince the Court had given them a longer day, but only to obftruct their further proceedings: And it appeareth by the Evidence aforefaid to this Committee, that the four Judges of that Court were prefent at the Difcharging of the faid *Jury,* and it did not appear that any of them did Diffent therein; upon Confideration whereof, the Committee came to this Refolution.

Refolved, That it is the Opinion of this Committee, That the Difcharging of the Grand *Jury* of the Hundred of *Offulfton,* in the County of *Middlefex,* by the Court of *King's-Bench* in *Trinity*-Term laft, before the laft day of the Term, and before they had finifh'd their Prefentments, was Illegal, Arbitrary, and an High Mifdemeanour.

This Committee proceeded alfo to inquire into a Rule of the Court of *King's-Bench,* lately made againft the publifhing a Book called, *The weekly Pacquet of Advice from* Rome; or, *The Hiftory of* Popery: and *Samuel Aftrey* Gent. examined thereupon, inform'd this Committee, that the Author of the faid Book *Henry Carr,* had been informed againft for the fame, and had pleaded to the Information: But before it was tryed, a Rule was made on a Motion, as he fuppofeth, againft the faid Book: All the Judges of that Court (as he remembers) being prefent, and none diffenting. The Copy of which Rule he gave into this Committee, and is as followeth.

Die Mercurij proxime poft tres Septimanas, fanéte Trinitatis. Anno 32
Car. 2. *Regis.*

Ordinatum eft quod liber intitulat. The Weekly Pacquet of Advice from *Rome,* or, The Hiftory of *Popery, non ulterius imprimatur vel publicetur per aliquam Perfonam quamcunque. Per Cur.*

And this Committee admiring that Proteftant Judges fhould take offence againft a Book whofe chief defign was to expofe the Cheats and Foppery of Popery, enquired further into it, and found by the Evidence of *Jane Curtis,* that the faid Book had been Licens'd for feveral for Months, that her Hufband paid for the Copy, and enter'd it in the Hall-Book of the Company: But for all this, fhe could not prevail by thefe Reafons with the Lord Chief Juftice *Scroggs* to permit it any longer; who faid, 'Twas a Scandalous Libel, and againft the King's Proclamation, and he would ruin her if ever fhe printed it any more: and foon after fhe was ferved with the faid Rule, as the Author and other Printers were; and by the Author's Evidence it appears, That he was taken and brought before the faid Chief Juftice by his Warrant above a year fince, and upon his owning he writ part of that Book, the Chief Juftice called him Rogue, and other ill names; faying, he would fill all the Goals in *England* with fuch Rogues, and pile them up as men do Faggots: and fo committed him to prifon, refufing fufficient Bayl, and faying, he would goal him, to put him to charges; and his Lordfhip obferved his word punctually therein, forcing him to his *Habeas Corpus,* and then taking the fame Bayl he refufed before. Upon which, this Committee came to this Refolution;

Refolved, That it is the opinion of the Committee, that the Rule made by the Court of *King's-Bench* in Trinity Term laft, againft printing a Book called, *The Weekly Pacquet of Advice from* Rome, is Illegal and Arbitrary.

And the Committee proceeded further, and upon Information that a very great latitude had been taken of late by the Judges, in impofing Fines on the perfons found Guilty before them, caufed a Tranfcript of all the Fines impofed by the *King's-Bench* fince Eafter-Term in the 28th of His Majefty's Reign, to be brought
before

before them from the said Court by *Samuel Aftrey* Gent. by perufal of which, it appear'd to this Committee, That the quality of the Offence, and the Ability of the perfon found guilty, have not been the Meafures that have determined the quantity of many of thefe Fines, which being fo very numerous, the Committee refer themfelves to thofe Records as to the general, inftancing in fome particulars, as followeth.

Upon *Joseph Brown* of *London* Gent. on an Information for publifhing a printed Book called, *The Long Parliament Diffolved*; in which is fet forth thefe words: *Nor let any man think it ftrange, that we account it Treafon for you to fit and act contrary to our Laws: for if in the firft Parliament of* Richard *the fecond,* Grimes *and* Weston *for lack of Courage only were adjudged guilty of High Treafon for furrendring the places committed to their truft; how much more you, if you turn Renegadoes to the people that intrufted you; and as much as in you lie furrender not a little pitiful Caftle or two, but all the legal defence the people of* England *have for their Lives, Liberties, and Properties, at once. Neither let the vain perfuafion delude you, That no precedent can be found, that one Englifh Parliament hath hang'd up another; tho' peradventure even that may be proved a miftake; for an unprecedented Crime calls for an unprecedented punifhment; and if you fhall be fo wicked to do the one, or rather endeavour to do (for now you are no longer a Parliament) what ground of confidence you can have that none will be found fo worthy to do the other, we cannot underftand; and do faithfully promife, if your unworthinefs provoke us to it, that we will ufe our honeft and utmoft endeavours (whenever a new Parliament fhall be called) to chufe fuch as may convince you of your miftake: the old and infallible Obfervation, That Parliaments are the pulfe of the people, fhall lofe its efteem; or you will find, that this your prefumption was over-fond; however it argues but a bad mind, to fin, becaufe it's believ'd it fhall not be punifhed.* The Judgment was, That he be fin'd 1000 Marks, be bound to the good behaviour for feven years, and his name ftruck out of the Roll of the Attorneys, without any offence alledged in his faid Vocation. And the publifhing this Libel confifted only in fuperfcribing a Pacquet, with this inclofed, to the *Eaft Indies.* Which Fine he not being able to pay (living only upon his practice) he lay in prifon for three years, till his Majefty gracioufly pardon'd him, and recommended him to be reftored to his place again of Attorney, by His Warrant dated the 15. of *Decem.* 1679. Notwithftanding which, he has not yet obtained the faid Reftauration from the Court of King's Bench. Trinit. 29. Car. 2.

Upon *John Harrington* of *London,* Gent. for fpeaking thefe words in *Latin* thus: *Quod noftra Gubernatio de tribus ftatibus confiftebat, & fi Rebellio eveniret in regno, & non accideret contra omnes tres ftatus, non eft Rebellio;* a Fine of 1000 *l.* Sureties for the Good Behaviour for feven years, and to recant the words in open Court: which Fine he was in no capacity of ever paying. Hill. 29 & 30. Car. 2.

Upon *Benjamin Harris* of *London,* Stationer, on an Information for printing a Book call'd, *An Appeal from the Countrey to the City,* fetting forth thefe words: *We in the Countrey have done our parts, in chufing for the generality good Members to ferve in Parliament: but if (as our two laft Parliaments were) they muft be diffolved or prorogued whenever they come to redrefs the grievances of the Subject, we may be pitied, not blam'd, if the Plot takes effect; and in all probability it will. Our Parliaments are not then to be condemn'd, for that their not being fuffer'd to fit, occafion'd it.* Judgment to pay 500 *l.* Fine, ftand on the Pillory an hour, and give Sureties for the good behaviour for three years. And the faid *Benj. Harris* inform'd this Committee, That the Lord Chief Juftice *Scroggs* preft the Court then to add to this Judgment his being publickly whipt; but Mr. Juftice *Pemberton* holding up his hands in admiration at their feverity therein, Mr. Juftice *Jones* pronounc'd the Judgment aforefaid; and he remains yet in prifon, unable to pay the faid Fine. Hill. 31 & 39. Car. 2.

Notwithftanding which Severity in the cafes forementioned, this Committee has obferved the faid Court has not wanted in other cafes an extraordinary Compaffion and Mercy, though there appear'd no publick reafon judicially in the Trial; as in particular,

Upon *Thomas Knox* Principal, on an Indictment of Subornation and Confpiracy againft the Teftimony and Life of Dr. *Oats* for Sodomy; and alfo againft the Teftimony of *William Bedloe*; a Fine of 200 Marks, a year's Imprifonment, and to find Sureties for the good behaviour for three years. Hill. 31 & 32. Car. 2.

Upon *John Lane,* for the fame offence, a Fine of 100 Marks, to ftand in the Pillory for an hour, and to be imprifon'd for one year. Eod. Ter.

Upon

4

Pan.32.Car.2. Upon *John Tasborough* Gent. on an Indictment for Subornation of *Stephen Dugdale*, tending to overthrow the whole Discovery of the Plot: The said *Tasborough* being affirmed to be a Person of good Quality, a Fine of 100 *l.*

Eod. Ter. Upon *Ann Price* for the same offence, 200 *l.*

Trin.32.C.2. Upon *Nathaniel Thompson* and *William Badcock*, on an Information for Printing and Publishing weekly a Libel, call'd *The true Domestick Intelligence*, or *News from both City and Country*, and known to be Popishly affected, a Fine of 3, 6, 8, on each of them.

Eod. Ter. Upon *Matthew Turner*, Stationer, on an Information for vending and publishing a Book, call'd *the Compendium*, wherein the Justice of the Nation in the late Tryals of the Popish Conspirators, even by some of these Judges themselves, is highly arraign'd; and all the Witnesses for the King horribly asperst: and this being the common notorious Popish Book-seller of the Town, Judgment to pay a Fine of 100 Marks, and is said to be out of Prison already.

Trin.32.C.2. Upon   *Loveland*, on an Indictment for a Notorious Conspiracy and Subornation, against the Life and Honour of the Duke of *Buckingham*, for Sodomy, a Fine of 5 *l.* and to stand an hour in the Pillory.

Mich.32.C.2. Upon *Edward Christian*, Esq; for the same offence, a Fine of 100 Marks, and to stand an hour in the Pillory. And upon *Arthur Obrian*, for the same offence, a Fine of 20 Marks, and to stand an hour in the Pillory.

Upon Consideration whereof, this Committee came to this Resolution;

Resolv'd, That it is the Opinion of this Committee, That the Court of *King's-Bench* (in the Imposition of Fines on Offenders of late years) hath acted Abitrarily, Illegally and Partially, favouring Papists, and Persons Popishly affected, and excessively oppressing His Majesty's Protestant Subjects.

And this Committee being inform'd, That several of His Majesty's Subjects had been committed for Crimes bailable by Law, although they then tendred sufficient Sureties, which were refus'd, only to put them to vexation and charge, proceeded to enquire into the same, and found that not only the fore-mention'd *Henry Carr* had been so refus'd the common Right of a Subject, as is above-said; but that *George Broome*, being a Constable last year in *London*, and committing some of the Lord Chief Justice *Scroggs*'s Servants for great Disorders, according to his Duty, he was in few days arrested by a Tipstaff, without any *London* Constable, and carried before the said Chief Justice by His Warrant, to answer for the committing of those Persons above-said; but being there, was accused of having spoken irreverently of the said Chief Justice; and an *Affidavit* read to him to that purpose, which was falsly (as the said *George Broome* affirms) sworn against him by two persons that use to be common Bail in that Court, and of a very ill Reputation. Upon which he was committed to the *King's-Bench*, though he then tendred two able Citizens and Common-Councilmen of *London* to be his Bail: And was forc'd to bring his *Habeas Corpus*, to his great Charge, before he came out: When the Marshal, Mr. *Cooling*, exacted 5 *l.* of him, of which he complain'd to the Chief Justice, but had no other Answer, but he might take his Remedy at Law. But the said Marshal, fearing he should be questioned, restor'd him two Guineas of it.

And further this Committee was inform'd by *Francis Smith*, Bookseller, That about *Michaelmas* was Twelve-month he was brought before the said Chief Justice by his Warrant, and charged by the Messenger, *Robert Stephens*, That he had seen some parcels of a Pamphlet call'd *Observations on Sir* George Wakeman*'s Tryal*, in his Shop: Upon which the Chief Justice told him, he would make him an Example, use him like a Boar in *France*, and pile him and all the Booksellers and Printers up in Prison, like Faggots; and so committed him to the *King's-Bench*, swearing and cursing at him in great fury. And when he tendred Three sufficient Citizens of *London* for his Bail, alledging Imprisonment in his circumstances would be his utter ruin; the Chief Justice replied, The Citizens lookt like sufficient persons, but he would take no Bail; and so he was forc'd to come out by *Habeas Corpus*, and was afterwards inform'd against in the same matter, to his great charge and vexation. And a while after *Francis* (the Son of the said *Francis Smith*) was committed by the said Chief Justice, and Bail refus'd, for selling a Pamphlet, call'd, *A New-year's Gift* for the said Chief Justice, to a Coffee-house; and he declared to them he would take no Bail, for he would ruin them all.

And

And further it appear'd to this Committee, that the said Chief Justice (about *October* was Twelve-month) committed in like manner *Jane Curtis*, she having a Husband and Children, for selling a Book call'd, *A Satyr against Injustice*, which his Lordship call'd a Libel against him ; and her Friends tendring sufficient Bail, and desiring him to have mercy on her Poverty and Condition, he swore by the Name of God she should go to Prison ; and he would shew no more Mercy than they could expect from a Wolf that came to devour them ; and she might bring her *Habeas Corpus*, and come out so : Which she was forc'd to do ; and after inform'd against and prosecuted to her utter Ruin, four or five Terms after.

In like manner it appeared to this Committee, that about that time also, *Edward Berry*, (Stationer of *Gray's-Inn*) was committed by the said Chief Justice, being accus'd of selling *The Observations on Sir* George Wakeman's *Tryal* ; and though he tendered 1000 *l*. Bail, yet the Chief Justice said, he would take no Bail ; he should go to Prison, and come out according to Law. And after he with much Trouble and Charge got out by *Habeas Corpus*, he was forc'd by himself, or Attorney, to attend five Terms before he could be discharg'd, though no Information was exhibited against him in all that time. In Consideration whereof, and of others of the like Nature, (too tedious here to relate) this Committee came to this Resolution :

Resolved,
That it is the Opinion of this Committee, That the refusing sufficient Bail in these Cases, wherein the Persons committed were bailable by Law ; was Illegal, and a high Breach of the Liberty of the Subject.

And this Committee being informed of an extraordinary kind of a Charge, given at the last Assizes at *Kingston* (in the County of *Surrey*) by Mr. Baron *Weston*, and proceeding to examine several Persons then and there present : It was made appear to this Committee, by the Testimony of *John Cole*, *Richard Mayo*, and *John Pierce*, Gentlemen, and others (some of whom put down the said Baron's Words in Writing immediately) that part of the said Charge was to this effect : He inveighed very much against *Farel*, *Luther*, *Calvin*, and *Zuinglius*, condemning them as Authors of the Reformation : Which was against their Princes minds, and then adding to this purpose ; *Zuinglius set up his Fanaticism, and* Calvin *built on that blessed Foundation : And to speak Truth, all his Disciples are seasoned with such a sharpness of Spirit, that it much concerns Magistrates to keep a strait Hand over them. And now they are restless, amusing us with Fears, and nothing will serve them but a Parliament : For my part, I know no Representative of the Nation but the King ; all Power centers in him. 'Tis true, he does intrust it with his Ministers, but he is the sole Representative ; and i-faith, he has Wisdom enough to intrust it no more in these Men, who have given us such late Examples of their Wisdom and Faithfulness.* And this Committee taking the said matter into their Consideration, came to this Resolution :

Resolved,
That it is the Opinion of this Committee, That the said Expressions in the Charge given by the said Baron *Weston*, were a Scandal to the Reformation, in derogation of the Rights and Privileges of Parliaments, and tending to raise Discord between his Majesty and his Subjects.

And this Committee being informed by several Printers and Booksellers, of great Trouble and Vexation given them unjustly by one *Robert Stephens*, (called a Messenger of the Press) the said *Stephens* being examined by this Committee, by what Authority he had proceeded in that manner, produced two Warrants under the Hand and Seal of the Chief Justice *Scroggs*, which were *in hæc verba*:

Angl. ff. **W**HEREAS *There are divers ill-disposed Persons who do daily Print and Publish many Seditious and Treasonable Books and Pamphlets, endeavouring thereby to dispose the Minds of his Majesty's Subjects to Sedition and Rebellion : And also infamous Libels reflecting upon particular Persons, to the great Scandal of his Majesty's Government ; for Suppressing whereof, his Majesty hath lately issued out his Royal Proclamation : And for the more speedy suppressing the said seditious Books, Libels and Pamphlets, and to the end that the Authors and Publishers thereof may be brought to their Punishment :*
These are to will and require you, and in His Majesty's Name to charge and command you, and every of you, upon Sight hereof, to be Aiding and Assisting unto Robert Stephens, *Messenger of the Press, in the seizing on all such Books and*

Pam-

and Pamphlets as aforesaid, as he shall be informed of, in any Booksellers or Printers Shops or Warehouses, or elsewhere whatsoever, to the end they may be disposed as to Law shall appertain: Also if you shall be informed of the Authors, Printers, or Publishers of such Books or Pamphlets as are above-mentioned, you are to apprehend them, and have them before one of His Majesty's Justices of the Peace, to be proceeded against according to Law. Dated this 29th Day of November, 1679.

To *Robert Stephens* Messenger of
  the Press, and to all Mayors,
  Sheriffs, Bailiffs, Constables, and
  all other Officers and Ministers
  whom these may concern.

WILLIAM SCROGGS.

Angl. ss. **Whereas** *The King's Majesty hath lately issued out his Proclamation for Suppressing the Printing and Publishing Unlicensed News-Books, and Pamphlets of News: Notwithstanding which, there are divers Persons who do daily Print and Publish such Unlicensed Books and Pamphlets:*
  These are therefore to Will and Require you, and in his Majesty's Name to Charge and Command You, and every of You, from Time to Time, and at all Times; so often as You shall be thereunto required, to be Aiding and Assisting to Robert Stephens, Messenger of the Press, in the Seizing of all such Books and Pamphlets as aforesaid, whereof you shall be informed of, in any Bookseller's Shop, or Printer's Shop or Warehouses, or elsewhere whatsoever, to the end they may be disposed of as to Law shall appertain. Likewise, if You shall be informed of the Authors, Printers, or Publishers of such Books and Pamphlets, You are to apprehend them, and have them before Me, or one of His Majesty's Justices of the Peace, to be proceeded against as to Law shall appertain. Dated this 28th Day of May, Anno Dom. 1680.

To all Mayors, Sheriffs, Bailiffs,
  Constables, and all other Officers and Ministers whom these
  may concern.

WILLIAM SCROGGS.

To *Robert Stephens*, Messenger of the Press.

Upon view whereof this Committee came to this Resolution:
  Resolved, *That it is the Opinion of this Committee, That the said Warrants are Arbitrary and Illegal.*
And this Committee being informed of certain scandalous Discourses, said to be uttered in publick Places by the Lord Chief Justice *Scroggs*, proceeded to examine Sir *Robert Atkins*, late one of the Justices of the Common Pleas, concerning the same; by whom it appears, That at a Sessions-Dinner at the *Old-Baily* (in the Mayoralty of Sir *Robert Clayton*) who was then present, the said Chief Justice took occasion to speak very much against petitioning, condemning it as resembling 41, as Factious and tending to Rebellion, or to that effect; to which the said Sir *Robert Atkins* made no Reply, suspecting he waited for some Advantage over him: But the Chief Justice continuing and pressing him with the said Discourse, he began to justify petitioning as the Right of the People, especially for the sitting of a Parliament, which the Law requires, if it be done with Modesty and Respect. Upon which the Chief Justice fell into a great Passion; and there is some Reason to believe, that soon after he made an ill Representation of what the said Sir *Robert* had then spoke unto his Majesty. And this Committee was further informed, That the said
Sir

Sir *Robert Atkins* being in Circuit with the said Chief Justice at Summer Assizes was Twelve-month, at *Monmouth*, (Mr. *Arnold*, Mr. *Price*, and Mr. *Bedlow* being then in company) the Chief Justice fell severely in publick upon Mr. *Bedlow*, taking off the Credit of his Evidence, and alledging he had over-shot himself in it, or to that Effect; very much to the Disparagement of his Testimony: And the said Sir *Robert* defending Mr. *Bedlow*'s Evidence and Credit, he grew extreme Angry and Loud, saying to this Effect, *That he verily believed* Langhorn *died innocently*. To which the said Sir *Robert* replied, He wondred how he could think so, who had condemned him himself, and had not moved the King for a Reprieve for him. All which matters of Discourse this Committee humbly submit to the Wisdom and Consideration of this House, without taking upon them to give any Opinion therein.

And this Committee proceeded further to inquire into some Passages that happened at *Lent Assizes* last for the County of *Somerset*, at the Trial of *Thomas Dare*, Gent. there, upon an Indictment for saying falsly and seditiously, *That the Subjects had but two means to redress their Grievances, one by Petitioning, the other by Rebellion:* And found, that though by his other Discourse, when he said so, that it appeared plainly he had no rebellious Intent, in that he said, *Then God forbid there should be a Rebellion, he would be the first Man to draw his Sword against a Rebel;* yet he was prosecuted with great Violence: And having pleaded *Not Guilty*, he moved Mr. Justice *Jones* (who then sate Judge there) that he might try it at the next *Assizes*, for that Mr. *Searle* (who was by at the speaking of the Words, and a material Witness for his Defence) was not then to be had, and an *Affidavit* to that purpose was made and received. But the said Justice *Jones* told him, that was a Favour of the Court only, and he had not deserved any Favour, and so forc'd him to try it presently. But the Jury, appearing to be an extraordinary one, provided on purpose, being all of Persons that had highly opposed Petitioning for the Sitting of this Parliament, he was advised to withdraw his Plea; and the said Justice *Jones* encouraging him so to do, he confest the Words, denying any evil Intention, and gave the said Justice an Account in writing of the Truth of the whole matter, and made a Submission in Court, as he was directed by the said Justice: who promis'd to recommend him to His Majesty, but imposed a Fine of 500 *l.* on him, and to be bound to the good Behaviour for three Years; declaring also, That he was turned out from being a Common-Counsellor of the Corporation of *Taunton* in the said County, on pretence of a Clause in their *Charter*, giving such a Power to a Judge of *Assize*. And the said *Thomas Dare* remains yet in Prison for the said Fine; in which matter of the Tryal aforesaid, this Committee desireth to refer it self to the Judgment of this House.

The Resolutions of the House of Commons upon the said Report.

I.

THAT it is the Opinion of this House, that the Discharging of the Grand Jury of the Hundred of *Oswalston*, in the County of *Middlesex*, by the Court of *King's-Bench* in *Trinity Term* last, before the last Day of the Term, and before they had finished their Presentments, was Arbitrary and Illegal, destructive to publick Justice, a manifest Violation of the Oaths of the Judges of that Court, and a means to subvert the Fundamental Laws of this Kingdom, and to introduce Popery.

II.

That it is the Opinion of this House, That the Rule made by the Court of *King's-Bench* in *Trinity Term* last, against printing of a Book, called, *The Weekly Pacquet of Advice from* Rome, is Illegal and Arbitrary; thereby usurping to themselves Legislative Power, to the great Discouragement of the Protestants, and for the countenancing of Popery.

III.

That it is the Opinion of this House, That the Court of *King's-Bench* in the Impositions of Fines on Offenders, of late Years, have acted Arbitrarily, Illegally, and Partially, favouring Papists and Persons popishly affected, and excessively oppressing His Majesty's Protestant Subjects.

IV. That

IV.

That it is the Opinion of this House, That the refusing sufficient Bail in these Cases, wherein the Persons committed were bailable by Law, was Illegal, and a high Breach of the Liberties of the Subject.

V.

That it is the Opinion of this House, That the said Expressions in the Charge given by the said Baron *Weston*, were a Scandal to the Reformation, and tending to raise Discord between his Majesty and his Subjects, and to the Subversion of the Ancient Constitution of Parliaments, and of the Government of this Kingdom.

VI.

That it is the Opinion of this House, That the said Warrants are Arbitrary and Illegal.

The Resolutions of the Commons, *for the Impeachment of the said Judges.*

Resolved,

THAT Sir *William Scroggs*, Knight, Chief Justice of the Court of *King's-Bench*, be impeached upon the said Report, and the Resolutions of the House thereupon.

Resolved,

That Sir *Thomas Jones*, one of the Justices of the said Court of *King's-Bench*, be impeached upon the said Report, and Resolutions of the House thereupon.

Resolved,

That Sir *Richard Weston*, one of the Barons of the Court of *Exchequer*, be impeached upon the said Report, and Resolutions of the House thereupon.

Ordered,

That the Committee appointed to prepare an Impeachment against Sir *Francis North*, Chief Justice of the Court of *Common-Pleas*, do prepare Impeachments against the said Sir *William Scroggs*, Sir *Thomas Jones*, and Sir *Richard Weston*, upon the said Report and Resolutions.

Ordered,

That the said Report, and several Resolutions of this House thereupon, be printed ; and that Mr. Speaker take care in the Printing thereof apart from this Day's other Votes.

The Report from the Committee of the Commons *in Parliament, appointed by the Honourable the* House of Commons, *to consider the Petition of* Richard Thompson *of Bristol,* Clerk ; *and to Examine Complaints against him. And the Resolution of the* Commons *in Parliament upon this Report, for his Impeachment of high Crimes and Misdemeanours.* Friday, Decemb. 24. 1680.

At the Committee *appointed to take into Consideration the Petition of* Richard Thompson, Clerk, *and to examine the Complaints against him.*

In the First Place,

THE *Committee* read unto the said *Thompson*, the Heads of the Complaint against him ; which (for the most part) he denying, desired to have his Accusers brought Face to Face: Whereupon the *Committee* proceeded to the Examination of Witnesses, to prove the said Complaint.

The Firſt Witneſs examined, ſaith,

That there being a great Noiſe and Rumour, that Mr. *Thompſon* had prepared a Sermon to be preached on the *Thirtieth of January*, 1679. the ſaid Witneſs went to the ſaid Sermon, and did hear Mr. *Thompſon* publickly declare, that the *Presbyterians* were ſuch Perſons, as the very *Devil* bluſh'd at them ; and that the Villain *Hamden* grudged, and made it more ſcruple of 'Conſcience, to give Twenty Shillings to the KING, for ſupplying his Neceſſities (by Ship-Money and Loan) which was his Right by Law, than to raiſe Rebellion againſt him : And that the *Presbyterians* are worſe (and far more intolerable) than either *Prieſts* or *Jeſuits*.

The Second ſaith,

That hearing a great Talk and Noiſe ſpread of a Sermon to be preached by Mr. *Thompſon*, on the *Thirtieth of January*, 1679. was minded to hear the ſame, and accordingly did ; at which he writ ſome Notes ; amongſt which, he ſaith, That Mr. *Thompſon* openly preached, that the *Devil* bluſh'd at the *Presbyterians* ; and that the Villain *Hamden* grudged more to give the KING Twenty Shillings, which was his juſt Due by Law, (Ship-money and Loan) than to raiſe Rebellion againſt Him ; and that a *Presbyterian*-Brother, *qua talis*, was as great a Traitor by the Statute, as any *Prieſt* or *Jeſuite* whatſoever.

That he heard, that Mr. *Thompſon* ſaid ; That he hoped the *Presbyterians* would be pulled out of their Houſes, and the Goals filled with them : and wiſh'd their Houſes burnt.

The Third ſaith,

That he was cited to the Biſhop's Court, to receive the Sacrament laſt *Eaſter* ; but being out of Town that time, did receive it at a Place called *Purl* in *Wiltſhire* ; and that a Month after he came home, was again cited to the ſaid Court ; and he did accordingly appear, and told the Court, That he hoped his Abſence and Buſineſs might be accepted for a lawful Excuſe. Upon which, Mr. *Thompſon* immediately ſaid, That they would proceed to Excommunicate him. Upon which, this Informant produced his Certificate, of which the Chancellor approved, and ſaid, It was lawful. Hereupon Mr. *Thompſon* ſaid, That his receiving the Sacrament from any other Miniſter, than the Miniſter of the Pariſh wherein he dwelled, was Damnation to his Soul : and that he would maintain this Doctrine.

The Fourth ſaith,

That being at *Briſtol*-Fair, he heard a great Talk and Noiſe of a Satyr-Sermon prepared, and deſigned to be preached by Mr. *Thompſon* againſt the Presbyterians, on the *Thirtieth of January*, 1679 ; and that very many reſorted to hear him : In which Sermon, the ſaid Mr. *Thompſon* declared and ſaid, That there was a great Talk of a Plot : but (ſays he) a Presbyterian is the Man : And further added, That the Villain *Hamden* ſcrupled to give the King 20 s. upon Ship-money and Loan, which was his due by Law, but did not ſcruple to raiſe Rebellion againſt him.

The Fifth ſaith,

That Mr. *Thompſon* in a Sermon preached the *Thirtieth of January*, 1679. did ſay, That the Presbyterians did ſeem to out-vie *Mariana*, and that *Calvin* was the firſt that preached the *King-killing Doctrine* ; and that after he had quoted *Calvin* often, ſaid, If this be true, then a Presbyterian-Brother, *qua talis*, is as great a Traitor as any Prieſt or Jeſuit ; and that then he condemned all the Proceedings of Parliaments.

The Sixth ſaith,

That the ſaid Mr. *Thompſon* had utter'd many ſcandalous Words concerning the Act for *Burying in Woollen* ; affirming, That the makers of that Law, were a Company of *old Fools and Fanaticks, and that he would bring a School-Boy ſhould make a better Act than that, and conſtrue it when he had done.*

The Seventh faith,

That Mr. *Thompson* in a Sermon by him preached (while Petitions for the fitting of this Parliament were on foot) fpeaking of a fecond Rebellion by the *Scotch,* who had framed a formidable Army, and came as far as *Durham* to deliver a Petition forfooth; and that they feemed rather to *command,* than *petition* their Sovereign to grant: And comparing that Petition with the then Petition on foot, greatly inveigh'd againft it, and fcoffed much at it.

The Eighth faith,

That Mr. *Thompson* (when the Petition was on foot for the fitting of this Parliament) ufed at the Funeral Sermon of one Mr. *Wharton* thefe Words, (pointing at the Deceafed) That he was no Schifmatical Petitioning Rebel; and that by his Inftigations, the Grand-Jury of *Briftol* made a Prefentment of their Deteftation againft petitioning for the fitting of the Parliament: that he faid Mr. *Thompson* had told him, that he was Governour to Mr. *Narbor,* when he was beyond Sea; and faid, that he had been very often (and above one hundred times) at Mafs, in the great Church at *Paris,* and ufually gave half a Crown to get a Place to hear a certain Doctor of that Church, and that he was like to be brought over to that Religion; and that when he went beyond Sea, did not know but that he might be of that Religion before his return. That he is very cenforious, and frequently cafts evil Afperfions againft feveral Divines at *Briftol* of great Note, *viz.* Mr. *Chetwind,* Mr. *Standfaft,* Mr. *Crofman,* Mr. *Palmer* and others, faying, That fuch as went to their Lectures, were the Brats of the Devil.

The 9th, That Mr. *Thompson* in his preaching inveighed bitterly againft fubfcribing Petitions for Sitting of this Parliament, faying, That it was the Seed of Rebellion, and like to Forty-one; and that the Devil fet them on work, and the Devil would pay them their Wages: faying, That before he would fet his Hand to fuch Petitions, he would cut it off, yea and cut them off.

The 10th faith, That about two Years fince, being in the Chancel of *St. Thomas's* Church in *Briftol,* where Queen *Elizabeth's* Effigies is, Mr. *Thompson* pointing his Finger to it, faid, That fhe was the worft of Women, and a moft lewd and infamous Woman: Upon which this Informant replied, He never heard any fpeak ill of her; thereupon Mr. *Thompson* faid, She was no better than a Church-Robber, and that *Henry* the 8th begun it, and that fhe finifh'd it.

The 11th, *Rowe,* faith, That in the Year 1678, he waited on the Mayor to Church, and that Mr. *Thompson* who was there, railed at *Henry* the Eighth, faying, He did more hurt in robbing the Abby-Lands, than he did good by the Reformation. That after Dinner Mr. *Thompson* comes to this Informer, and claps his Hands on his Shoulders, faying, Hah Boy, had Queen *Elizabeth* been living, you needed not to have been Swordbearer of *Briftol.* The faid *Rowe* asked him why? He replied, She loved fuch a lufty Rogue (fo well) as he was; and he would have been very fit for her Drudgery at *White-hall.*

The 12th faith, That he heard a great Noife of a Sermon to be preached by Mr. *Thompson* on the 30th of *January,* 1679, to the fecond part of the fame Tune: And that he was prefent at the fame Sermon, in which Mr. *Thompson* faid, There was a great Noife of a Popifh Plot, but, fays he, Here is nothing in it but a Presbyterian Plot; for here they are going about to petition for the fitting of the Parliament, but the end of it will be to bring the King's Head to the Block, as they have done his Father.

The 13th faith, That in *January* laft, or thereabouts, there was a Petition going about for the fitting of this Parliament; when Mr. *Thompson* in *Redcliff* Church, in his Sermon, faid, It was a feditious and rebellious Petition, and rather than he would fign it, his Hand fhould be cut off.

The 14th faith, The eighth day of *April,* he going to pay Mr. *Thompson* his Dues, fpeaking concerning the Meeters in private; Mr. *Thompson* faid, He would hall them out, and fill the Goals with them, and hoped to fee their Houfes afire about their Ears in a fhort time; and this he the faid *Thompson* doubled again and again.

The 15th faith, That about *December* 1679, Mr. *Thompson* came to vifit his Mother, being fick, and difcourfing of Religion, the faid *Thompson* faid, If he were as well fatisfied of other things, as he was of Juftification, Auricular Confeffion, Penance, Extreme Unction, and Crifme in Baptifm, he would not have been fo long feparated from the Catholick Church. And further affirmed, That the Church of *Rome* was the True Catholick Church. He further endeavoured to prove Extreme Unction, and Auricular Confeffion, as well as he could, out of the Epiftles. Further, he hath heard him fay,

The

The King was a Perſon of mean and ſoft Temper, and could be led eaſily to any thing, but yet a *Solomon* in Vices; but that the Duke of *York* was a Prince of a brave Spirit, would be faithful to his Friends, and that it was our own faults that he was a Roman Catholick, in that we forc'd him to fly into *France*, where he imbraced that Religion. About the ſame time, he the ſaid *Thompſon*, ſaid the Church would be Militant, but greatly commended the Decency of Solemnizing the Maſs in *France*; and that it was performed with much more Reverence and Devotion than any other Religion doth uſe. He further heard him ſay in a Sermon, about the time of Petitioning, he would rather cut off his Hand than ſign it, and had many bad Expreſſions of it; that it was the Seed of Rebellion, and like 40 and 41: And further, the ſaid Mr. *Thompſon* at one *Sandford*'s Shop-door at *Briſtol*, ſpeaking of *Bedloe*, ſaid, That he was not to be believ'd, becauſe *Bedloe* had ſaid he, meaning Mr. *Thompſon*, was at *St. Omers*, where Mr. *Thompſon* ſaid he was not; and that *Bedloe* was of a bad Life, and in many Plots, and not to be credited in any thing he ſaid. And that in another Diſcourſe he commended the Romiſh Clergy for their ſingle Life, and is himſelf ſo; and did at the ſame time vilify and rail at the Engliſh Clergy for marrying; ſaying, It was better for a Clergy-man to be gelt, than to marry; and that the *Calviniſts* in *France* were leacherous Fellows, and could ſcarce be two Years a Prieſt without a Wife. About the time and after the Election of Sir *John Knight* to this Parliament, Mr. *Thompſon* ſaid, he was not fit to be believ'd, and as bad as any Fanatick. He further ſaid in the Pulpit at *St. Thomas's*, that after Excommunication by the Biſhop, without Abſolution from the Spiritual Court, ſuch a one was ſurely damned; and he would pawn his Soul for the Truth of it.

Mr. *Thompſon*, after the Evidence given by every particular Perſon Face to Face, was asked to every one, If he had any Queſtions to ask, before they called another? Who anſwer'd, he ſhould not ſay any thing at preſent. When the Witneſſes before-mentioned were all examined, Mr. *Thompſon* being deſit'd to make his Defence, and declare whether he were guilty of the Matters laid to his charge; did for the greateſt part confeſs Words ſpoken to that effect; and in other things endeavoured to turn the Words with more Favour towards himſelf; but the Witneſſes being of great Credit, and many more being ready to have made good the ſame things, the Committee look'd upon the Buſineſs to be of a high Nature, and therefore ordered the matter to be reported ſpecially; leaving it to the Wiſdom of the Houſe.

The Reſolutions of the Houſe of Commons upon the ſaid Report.

Reſolved, *Nemine contradicente,*

THAT *Richard Thompſon* Clerk, hath publickly defamed his Sacred Majeſty, preached Sedition, vilified the Reformation, promoted Popery, by aſſerting Popiſh Principles, decrying the Popiſh Plot, and turning the ſame upon the Proteſtants; and endeavoured to ſubvert the Liberty and Property of the Subject, and the Rights and Privileges of Parliament; and that he is a Scandal and Reproach to his Function.

And that the ſaid *Richard Thompſon* be impeached upon the ſame Report and Reſolution of the Houſe. And a Committee is appointed to prepare the ſaid Impeachment, and to receive further Inſtructions againſt him; and to ſend for Perſons, Papers, and Records.

Articles of Impeachment of Sir William Scroggs, *Chief Juſtice of the Court of* King's-Bench, *by the* Commons *in this preſent Parliament Aſſembled, in their own Name, and in the Name of all the* Commons *of England, of High-Treaſon; and other great Crimes and Miſdemeanors.*

i.

THAT he the ſaid Sir *William Scroggs*, then being Chief Juſtice of the Court of *King's-Bench*, hath traitorouſly and wickedly endeavoured to ſubvert the Fundamental Laws and the Eſtabliſh'd Religion and Government of this Kingdom of *England*; and inſtead thereof, to introduce *Popery*, and an Arbitrary and Tyrannical Government, againſt

against Law, which he has declared by divers traiterous and wicked Words, Opinions, Judgments, Practices and Actions.

II.

That he, the said Sir *William Scroggs*, in *Trinity Term* last, being then Chief Justice of the said Court, and having taking an Oath duly to administer Justice, according to the Laws and Statutes of this Realm, in pursuance of his said traiterous Purposes, did, together with the rest of the said Justices of the same Court, several days before the end of the said Term, in an Arbitrary manner discharge the Grand Jury which then served for the Hundred of *Oswaldston* in the County of *Middlesex*, before they had made their Presentments, or had found several Bills of Indictment, which were then before them; whereof the said Sir *William Scroggs* was then fully informed: and that the same would be tendered to the Court upon the last day of the said Term, which day then was, and by the known Course of the said Court, hath always heretofore been given unto the said Jury for the delivering in of their Bills and Presentments, by which sudden and illegal Discharge of the said Jury, the Course of Justice was stopt maliciously and designedly, the Presentments of many *Papists* and other Offenders were obstructed; and in particular, a Bill of Indictment against *James* Duke of *York*, for absenting himself from Church, which was then before them, was prevented from being proceeded upon.

III.

That whereas one *Henry Carr*, had for some time before publish'd every Week a certain Book, intituled, *The Weekly Packet of Advice from Rome: or, The History of Popery*; wherein the Superstitions and Cheats of the Church of *Rome* were from time to time exposed; he the said Sir *William Scroggs*, then Chief Justice of the Court of *King's-Bench*, together with the other Judges of the said Court, before any legal Conviction of the said *Carr* of any Crime, did in the same *Trinity Term*, in a most illegal and arbitrary manner, make, and cause to be entred, a certain Rule of that Court, against the printing of the said Book, *in hæc verba:*

Dies Mercurii proxime post tres Septimanas Sanctæ Trinitatis, Anno 32 Car. II. *Regis.*

ORdinatum est quod Liber intitulat' The weekly Packet of Advice from *Rome*: or, The History of Popery, *Non ulterius imprimatur vel publicetur per aliquam personam quamcunque.*

Per Cur'

And did cause the said *Carr*, and divers Printers, and other Persons to be served with the same; which said Rule and other Proceedings were most apparently contrary to all Justice, in condemning not only what had been written without hearing the Parties, but also all that might for the future be written on that Subject; a manifest countenancing of *Popery*, and discouragement of *Protestants*; an open Invasion upon the Right of the Subject, and an encroaching and assuming to themselves a Legislative Power and Authority.

IV.

That he the said Sir *William Scroggs*, since he was made Chief Justice of the *King's-Bench*, hath, together with the other Judges of the said Court, most notoriously departed from all Rules of Justice and Equality, in the Imposition of Fines upon Persons convicted of Misdemeanours in the said Court; and particularly in the Term of *Easter* last past, did openly declare in the said Court, in the Case of one *Jessop*, who was convicted of publishing false News, and was then to be fined, That he would have regard to Persons and their Principles in imposing of Fines, and would set a Fine of 500*l.* on one Person for the same Offence, for the which he would not fine another 100*l.* And according to his said unjust and arbitrary Declaration, he the said Sir *William Scroggs*, together with the said other Justices, did then impose a Fine of 100*l.* upon the said *Jessop*, although the said *Jessop* had before that time proved one *Hewit* to be convicted as the Author of the said false News; and afterwards, in the same Term, did fine the said *Hewit* upon his said Conviction, only

only five Marks. Nor hath the said Sir *Will. Scroggs*, together with the other Judges of the said Court, had any regard to the Nature of the Offences, or the Ability of the Persons, in the imposing of Fines: but have been manifestly partial and favourable to Papists, and Persons affected to, and promoting the Popish Interest, in this time of imminent Danger from them: And at the same time have most severely and grievously oppressed his Majesty's Protestant Subjects, as will appear upon view of the several Records of Fines set in the said Court: By which arbitrary, unjust, and partial Proceedings, many of his Majesty's Liege People have been ruined, and Popery countenanced under colour of Justice; and all the Mischiefs and Excesses of the Court of *Star-Chamber*, by Act of Parliament suppressed, have been again, in direct opposition to the said Law, introduced.

V.

That he the said Sir *Will. Scroggs*, for the further accomplishing of his said traitorous and wicked Purposes, and designing to subject the Persons as well as the Estates of his Majesty's Liege People to his lawless Will and Pleasure, hath frequently refused to accept of Bail, though the same were sufficient, and legally tendered unto him by many Persons accused before him, only of such Crimes for which by Law Bail ought to have been taken; and divers of the said Persons being only accused of Offences against himself: declaring at the same time, That he refused Bail, and committed them to Goal only to put them to Charges; and using such furious Threats as were to the Terrour of his Majesty's Subjects, and such scandalous Expressions as were a Dishonour to the Government, and to the Dignity of his Office. And particularly, That he the said Sir *Will. Scroggs* did, in the Year 1679, commit and detain in Prison, in such unlawful manner, among others, *Henry Carr*, *George Broome*, *Edw. Berry*, *Benj. Harris*, *Francis Smith*, Sen. *Francis Smith*, Jun. and *Jane Curtis*, Citizens of *London*: Which Proceedings of the said Sir *Will. Scroggs*, are a high Breach of the Liberty of the Subject, destructive to the Fundamental Laws of this Realm; contrary to the Petition of Right, and other Statutes; and do manifestly tend to the introducing of Arbitrary Power.

VI.

That he the said Sir *Will. Scroggs*, in further Oppression of his Majesty's Liege People, hath since his being made Chief Justice of the said Court of *King's-Bench*, in an arbitrary manner, granted divers general Warrants for Attaching the Persons and Seizing the Goods of his Majesty's Subjects, not named or described particularly in the said Warrants: By means whereof, many of his Majesty's Subjects have been vexed, their Houses entered into, and they themselves grievously oppressed, contrary to Law.

VII.

Whereas there has been a Horrid and Damnable Plot, contrived and carried on by the *Papists*, for the Murthering the King, the Subversion of the Laws and Government of this Kingdom, and for the Destruction of the *Protestant* Religion in the same; all which the said Sir *William Scroggs* well knew, having himself not only tried, but given Judgment against several of the Offenders: nevertheless, the said Sir *Will. Scroggs* did at divers times and places, as well sitting in Court, as otherwise, openly defame and scandalize several of the Witnesses, who had proved the said Treasons against divers of the Conspirators, and had given Evidence against divers other Persons, who were then untried, and did endeavour to disparage their Evidence, and take off their Credit; whereby, as much as in him lay, he did traitorously and wickedly suppress and stifle the Discovery of the said *Popish* Plot, and encourage the Conspirators to proceed in the same, to the great and apparent Danger of his Majesty's Sacred Life, and of the well-established Government and Religion of this Realm of *England*.

VIII.

Whereas the said Sir *William Scroggs* being advanced to be Chief Justice of the Court of *King's-Bench*, ought by a sober, grave, and vertuous Conversation, to have given a good Example to the King's Liege People, and to demean himself answerable to the Dignity of so eminent a Station; yet he, the said Sir *William Scroggs*, on the contrary, by his frequent and notorious Excesses and Debaucheries, and his prophane and atheistical Discourses, doth daily affront Almighty God, dishonour

I i

his Majesty, give countenance and incouragement to all manner of Vice and Wickedness, and bring the highest Scandal on the publick Justice of the Kingdom.

All which Words, Opinions, and Actions of the said Sir *William Scroggs*, were by *him* spoken and done, traitorously, wickedly, falsly and maliciously, to alienate the Hearts of the King's Subjects from his Majesty, and to set a Division between him and them, and to subvert the Fundamental Laws, and the Establisht Religion and Government of this Kingdom, and to introduce *Popery*, and an arbitrary and tyrannical Government, and contrary to his own Knowledge, and the *known Laws* of the *Realm* of *England*: and thereby he the said Sir *William Scroggs* hath not only broken his own Oath, but also as far as in him lay, hath broken the King's Oath to his People; whereof he the said Sir *William Scroggs* representing his Majesty in so high an Office of Justice, had the Custody, for which the said *Commons* do impeach him the said Sir *William Scroggs* of the High Treason against our Sovereign Lord the King, and his Crown and Dignity, and other the High Crimes and Misdemeanors aforesaid.

And the said *Commons* by Protestation saving to themselves the Liberty of exhibiting at any time hereafter, any other Accusation or Impeachment against the said Sir *William Scroggs*, and also of replying to the Answer that he shall make thereunto, and of offering Proofs of the Premises, or of any other Impeachments or Accusations that shall be by them exhibited against him as the Case shall (according to the Course of *Parliament*) require; Do pray that the said Sir *Will. Scroggs*, Chief Justice of the Court of *King's-Bench*, may be put to answer to all and every the Premises, and may be committed to safe Custody: and that such Proceedings, Examinations, Trials, and Judgments, may be upon him had and used, as is agreeable to Law and Justice, and the Course of Parliaments.

Resolved, *That the said Sir* William Scroggs *be impeached upon the said Articles.*

The Humble Petition of the Right Honourable the Lord Mayor, Aldermen, and Commons of the City of London, *in Common-Council Assembled, on the Thirteenth of* January, 1680. *to the King's Most Excellent Majesty, for the Sitting of this present Parliament, Prorogu'd to the Twentieth Instant. Together with the Resolutions, Orders, and Debates of the said Court.*

Commune Concil' tent' in Camera Guildhall *Civitatis* London, *Die Jovis decimo tertio die* Januarii *Anno Domini* 1680. *Annoque Regni Domini nostri* Carol' *Secundi nunc Regis* Angl' &c. *Tricesimo secundo, coram* Patient' Ward *Mil' Major' Civitatis* London, Thoma Aleyn *Mil' & Bar'*, Johanne Frederick *Mil'*, Johanne Lawrence *Mil'*, Georgio Waterman *Mil'*, Josepho Sheldon *Mil'*, Jacobo Edwards *Mil'*, & Roberto Clayton *Mil'*, *Aldermannis,* Georgio Treby *Ar' Recordatore dictæ Civit.* Johanne Moore *Mil'*, Willielmo Pritchard *Mil'*, Henrico Tulse *Mil'*, Jacobo Smith *Mil'*, Roberto Jeffery *Mil'*, Johanne Shorter *Mil'*, Thoma Gould *Mil'*, Willielmo Rawsterne *Mil'*, Thoma Beckford *Mil'*, Johanne Chapman *Mil'*, Simone Lewis *Mil'*, Thoma Pilkington *Ar' Ald'ris,* & Henrico Cornish *Ar' Ald'ro ac unum Vicecom' dictæ Civitatis, necnon major' parte Comminarior' dictæ Civitatis in Communi Concil' tunc & ibidem Assemblat'.*

THIS Day the Members that serve for this City in Parliament, having communicated unto this Court a Vote or Resolution of the Honourable House of Commons, whereby that House was pleased to give Thanks unto this City for their manifest Loyalty to the King, their Care, Charge, and Vigilance for the Preservation of his Majesty's, Person, and of the Protestant Religion : This Court is greatly sensible of the Honour thereby given to this City ; and do declare, That it is the fix'd and uniform Resolution of this City to persevere in what they have done, and to contribute their utmost Assistance for the Defence of the Protestant Religion, His Majesty's Person, and the Government Established.

It was now unanimously Agreed and Ordered by this Court, That the Thanks of this Court be given to the Members that serve for this City in Parliament, for their good Service done this City, and their Faithfulness in discharging their Duties in that honourable and great Assembly.

Upon a Petition now presented by divers Citizens and Inhabitants of this City; representing their Fears from the Designs of the Papists and their Adherents, and praying this Court to acquaint his Majesty therewith, and to desire, That the Parliament may sit from the Day to which it stands prorogued, until they have sufficiently provided against Popery and Arbitrary Power : This Court, after some Debate and Consideration had thereupon, did return the Petitioners Thanks for their Care and good Intention herein ; and did thereby nominate and appoint Sir *John Lawrence*, Sir *Robert Clayton*, Knights and Aldermen, Mr. *Recorder*, Sir *Thomas Player* Kt. Mr. *John Du Bois*, *John Ellis* Esq; and Mr. *Michael Godfrey*, Commoners, to withdraw, and immediately to prepare a Petition to his Majesty upon the Subject Matter of the said Petition ; who accordingly withdrawing, after some time returned again to this Court, and then presented the Draught of such a Petition to his Majesty. The Tenor whereof followeth, *viz.*

To the King's most Excellent Majesty, &c.

After reading whereof, It is agreed and ordered by this Court (*Nemine Contradicente*,) That the said Petition shall be presented to his Majesty this Evening, or as soon as conveniently may be. And the Right Honourable the Lord Mayor is desired to present the same, accompanied with Sir *John Lawrence*, Sir *Joseph Sheldon*, Sir *James Edwards*, Knights, and Aldermen, Mr. *Recorder*, Deputy *Hawes*, Deputy *Daniel*, *John Nichols*, *John Ellis*, Esquires, Mr. *Godfrey*, and Capt. *Griffith*, Commoners, who are now nominated and appointed to attend upon his Lordship at the presenting thereof.

Ward Mayor.

Commune Concil' tent' 13 Januarii 1680. Annoq; Regis *Car.*II. 32.

IT is *Agreed and Ordered by this Court,* (Nemine Contradicente) *That the Humble Petition to his Majesty from this Court, now read and agreed upon, shall be presented to His Majesty this Evening, or as soon as conveniently may be. And the Right Honourable the Lord Mayor is desired to present the same, accompanied with* Sir John Lawrence, Sir Joseph Sheldon, *and* Sir James Edwards, *Knights and Aldermen,* Mr. Recorder, Deputy Hawes, Deputy Daniel, John Nichols, John Ellis, *Esquires,* Mr. Godfrey, *and* Capt. Griffith, *Commoners, who are now nominated and appointed to attend upon his Lordship at the presenting thereof.*

Wagstaffe.

To the KING's *most Excellent Majesty,*

The Humble Petition of the Lord Mayor, Aldermen, and Commons of the City of London, *in Common Council Assembled,*

Most Humbly sheweth,

THAT Your Majesty's great Council in Parliament, having in their late Session, in pursuance of Your Majesty's Direction, entred upon a strict and impartial Inquiry into the horrid and execrable Popish Plot, which hath been for several Years last past, and still is, carried on for destruction of Your Majesty's Sacred Person
and

and Government, and extirpation of the Proteſtant Religion, and the utter ruin of your Majeſty's Proteſtant Subjects; and having ſo far proceeded therein, as juſtly to attaint upon full Evidence, one of the five Lords, impeached for the ſame, and were in further Proſecution of the remaining four Lords, and other Conſpirators therein.

And as well the Lords Spiritual and Temporal, as the Commons in Your ſaid Parliament aſſembled having declared, That they are fully ſatisfied, that there now is, and for divers Years laſt paſt, hath been a horrible and treaſonable Plot and Conſpiracy, contrived and carried on by thoſe of the Popiſh Religion in *Ireland*, for maſſacring the *Engliſh*, and ſubverting the Proteſtant Religion, and the ancient eſtabliſhed Government of that Kingdom.

And Your ſaid Commons having impeached the Earl of *Tyrone*, in order to the bringing him to Juſtice for the ſame; and having under Examination other Conſpirators in the ſaid *Iriſh* Plot.

And Your ſaid Commons having likewiſe impeached Sir *William Scroggs*, Chief Juſtice of Your Majeſty's Court of *King's-Bench*, for Treaſon and other great Crimes and Miſdemeanors, in endeavouring to ſubvert the Laws of this Kingdom by his arbitrary and illegal Proceedings; and having voted Impeachments againſt ſeveral other Judges for the like Miſdemeanors.

Your Petitioners conſidering the continual Hazards to which Your Sacred Life, and the Proteſtant Religion, and the Peace of this Kingdom are expoſed, while the Hopes of a Popiſh Succeſſor, gives Countenance and Encouragement to the Conſpirators in their wicked Deſigns: And conſidering alſo the diſquiet and dreadful Apprehenſions of Your good Subjects, by reaſon of the Miſeries and Miſchiefs which threaten them on all Parts; as well from Foreign Powers, as from the Conſpiracies within Your ſeveral Kingdoms, againſt which no ſufficient Remedy can be provided but by Your Majeſty and Your Parliament, were extremely ſurprized at the late Prorogation, whereby the Proſecution of the publick Juſtice of the Kingdom, and the making the Proviſions neceſſary for the Preſervation of Your Majeſty, and Your Proteſtant Subjects, hath received an Interruption. And they are the more affected herewith, by reaſon of the Experience they have had of the great Progreſs, which the emboldned Conſpirators have formerly made in their Deſigns, during the late frequent Receſſes of Parliament. But that which ſupports them againſt Deſpair, is the Hopes they derive from Your Majeſty's Goodneſs, That Your Intention was, and does continue by this Prorogation, to make way for Your better Concurrence with the Counſels of Your Parliament.

And Your Petitioners humbly hope, That Your Majeſty will not take Offence, that Your Subjects are thus zealous, and even impatient at the leaſt Delay of the long hoped for Security, whilſt they ſee your precious Life invaded, the true Religion undermined, their Families and innocent Poſterity likely to be ſubjected to Blood, Confuſion, and Ruin; and all theſe Dangers encreaſed, by reaſon of the late Endeavours of Your Majeſty, and Your Parliament, which have added Provocation to the Conſpirators, but have had little or no Effect towards ſecuring againſt them: And they truſt Your Majeſty will graciouſly accept this Diſcovery and Deſire of their Loyal Hearts to preſerve Your Majeſty, and whatever elſe is dear to them, and to ſtrengthen Your Majeſty againſt all Popiſh and Pernicious Counſels, which any ill-affected Perſons may preſume to offer.

> They do therefore moſt humbly pray, That Your Majeſty would be graciouſly pleaſed (as the only means to quiet the Minds, and extinguiſh the Fears of Your Proteſtant People, and prevent the imminent Dangers which threaten Your Majeſty's Kingdoms, and particularly this Your Great City, which hath already ſo deeply ſuffered for the ſame) to permit Your ſaid Parliament to ſit, from the Day to which they are prorogued, until by their Counſels and Endeavours thoſe good Remedies ſhall be provided, and thoſe juſt Ends attained, upon which the Safety of Your Majeſty's Perſon, the Preſervation of the Proteſtant Religion, the Peace and Settlement of Your Kingdoms, and the Welfare of this Your Ancient City, do ſo abſolutely depend. For the purſuing and obtaining of which good Effects, Your Petitioners unanimouſly do offer their Lives and Eſtates.

And ſhall ever Pray, &c.

Vox Patriæ: *Or, the Resentments and Indignation of the Free-born Subjects of* England, *against Popery, Arbitrary Government, the Duke of* York, *or any Popish Successor; being a true Collection of the Petitions and Addresses lately made from divers* Counties, Cities, *and* Boroughs *of this Realm, to their respective Representatives, chosen to serve in the* Parliament *held at* Oxford, March 21, 1680.

HE was certainly no Fool, that first said, *Parliaments were the Pulse of the People:* 'Tis from thence wise State-Physicians take their Diagnosticks. What Sentiments our late Parliament had of our modern Affairs, is obvious in their *Printed Votes and Addresses.* Nor will it be less plain, what is the *common Sense* of the Body of the People in this Juncture of imminent Danger, if the unanimous Addresses from so many considerable parts of *England* be regarded.

No sooner was the late Parliament surprizingly prorogued, *Jan.* 10. 168½, in the very Crisis of Business, and when they had so many excellent Bills before them, and had made so hopeful a Progress in unveiling the horrid Popish Plot (which still, like an *ill Spright*, haunts and *night-mares* us) and in bringing Criminals to Justice, but presently the whole Nation was startled, and forthwith (as Convulsions are first perceived in the *Head*) the same Day a considerable Number of eminent Citizens of *London* presented the following Address to their Mayor.

To the Right Honourable Sir Patience Ward, *Knight, Lord-Mayor of the City of* London.

WE the Citizens of the said City (on behalf of our selves and others our Fellow-Citizens) being very apprehensive of the great and imminent Dangers that this *Metropolis*, and the whole *Protestant Interest* are expos'd to, by the horrid and devilish Designs of the *Papists* and their Adherents: And being sensible that they are increas'd and heightned by the *surprizing Prorogation* of this present *Parliament*, do most humbly recommend to your Lordship the Particulars hereunder-mentioned.

I. That your Lordship will be pleased to cause the several Watches of this City to be doubled this Night, and so to continue, and cause some House-keepers to watch in person, and a sufficient Ward to be kept by Day.

II. To cause the several Chains in the several Streets of this City to be put up this Night, and so to continue.

III. That your Lordship will be pleased to keep the Keys of the several Gates of this City this Night, and so to continue.

IV. To cause the several Gates of this City to be kept lock'd up every Lord's Day, and permit the several Wicket-Doors only to be opened.

V. That your Lordship will not permit any Body of armed Soldiers, greater or less (other than the trained Bands of this City) to march through any part of the same.

VI. That your Lordship will forthwith order a Meeting of the Common-Council of this City.

Which his Lordship was pleased favourably to receive and read, and then gave the Gentlemen answer, *That he was very apprehensive of the Danger of this City, and had done something already to have full Watches, and intended to go out himself to see that they were kept; and assured them, that he would seriously consider their Desires, and take all the care that lay in him, to prevent the Danger that so threatned them.*

The very same Day, and before it was possible, the News, or Thoughts of any Prorogation could reach so far, the *Grand-Jury of* Shropshire, in the name and behalf of themselves and that whole County, thought fit to express their hearty Concurrence with, and Thanks to the then House of Commons for their zealous Proceedings against the most dangerous Popish Interest in the Terms following:

K k

To

To the Honourable Ric. Newport, *Esq; and Sir* Vincent Corbet, *Bar. Knights of the Shire in this present Parliament for the County of* Salop, Jan. 10. 1680.

WHereas the Honourable the Commons in this Parliament assembled, have, to the great satisfaction of the Nation, caused their Votes to be published, thereby letting the Kingdom know the Candour and Integrity of their Proceedings, which they desire may be examined in the face of the Sun : but fully satisfying us with what Wisdom, Constancy and Courage in this time of imminent danger, they have endeavoured to secure our King, our Religion, the Government and our Liberties : We the *Grand-Jury* impannelled for the Body of this County of *Salop*, being extreamly sensible how worthily you have discharged the Trust reposed in you, and finding our Opinions therein seconded *by the unanimous Resolution of the rest of our County*, do believe our selves in all Justice obliged, humbly to testify unto you, how much *we rejoice in the Proceeding you have made*, how easily we concur with your wise Resolutions, and how earnestly we desire they may be brought to perfection, and in particular the Bill to *exclude the D. of York*. That so we and our Posterity may be delivered from the apparent Danger of *Popery*, and the necessary Consequences thereof, *Tyranny* and *Oppression*, and remain *Free Protestant* Subjects ; to acknowledge evermore the Service and *Obligation* we owe to Patriots that have serv'd us so faithfully.

   Signed by all the Members of the Grand Jury ; *being* 17 *of the most considerable Gentlemen of the County.*

   January, 13. 168⁴⁄₁. A Common Council being held at *Guild-Hall*, several eminent Citizens presented the following Petition.

To the Right Honourable Sir Patience Ward, *Kt. Lord Mayor of the City of* London, *and the Right Worshipful the Aldermen and Commons in Common-Council assembled.*

The humble Petition of the Citizens and Inhabitants of the said City,

   Sheweth,

THat we being deeply sensible of Evils and Mischiefs hanging over this Nation in general, and this City in particular, in respect of the danger of the King's Person, the Protestant Religion, and our well-establish'd Government, by the continued hellish and damnable Designs of the Papists and others their Adherents: And, knowing no way (under heaven) so effectual to preserve His Royal Majesty (and us) from the utter ruin and destruction threatned ; as by the speedy sitting of this present Parliament, the surprising Prorogation of which greatly adds to, and increases the just fears and jealousies of your Petitioners minds :

   We your Petitioners do therefore beseech your Lordship, and this Honourable Court, to acquaint His Majesty with these our fears and apprehensions ; and that it is our humble and earnest desire, (as well as yours) that His Majesty would be pleased (for the utter defeating the wicked and bloody purposes of our Enemies) to permit this present Parliament, which stands prorogued to the 20th of this instant *January*, then to assemble and continue to sit until they have effectually secured us against Popery, and arbitrary Power, and redressed the manifold Grievances which at present we groan under ; and for our immediate security, that you will be pleased to order whatsoever else shall be thought necessary and expedient by your Lordship and this Honourable Court, in this time of imminent danger, for the safety of this great City.

       And your Petitioners shall ever Pray, &c.

The

The Address of the Freeholders of the County of Middlesex, *to Sir* William Roberts *Knight*, *and* Nicholas Raynton *Esq;* Knights of the Shire.

WE the Freeholders of this County, have (in great Confidence of your Integrity, Wisdom and Courage) now chosen you to represent us in the next Parliament, to be holden at *Oxford*, on the 21st Day of this present *March.* And although we do not in the least question your Faithfulness to the true Interest of this Nation, nor your Prudence in the management thereof; yet esteeming it greatly our Duty, in this unhappy Juncture, wherein our Religion, Lives, Liberties, Properties, and all that is dear unto us, are in such imminent danger, to signify our pressing Dangers unto you: And accordingly we do request, that in the next Parliament, wherein we have chose you to sit, and act, You will with the greatest Integrity, and most undaunted Resolution, join with, and assist the other worthy Representatives and Patriots of this Nation, in the searching into, and preventing the horrid and hellish Villanies, Plots and Designs of that wicked and restless sort of People the *Papists*, both in this, and the neighbouring Kingdoms; and making some honourable Provision for the discovery thereof.

In securing to us the Enjoyment of the true *Protestant Religion*, and the well established Government of this Kingdom. In promoting the happy, and long prayed for Union among all His Majesty's *Protestant Subjects*. In repealing the 35th of *Elizabeth*, the *Corporation-Act*, and all other Acts, which upon experience have proved injurious to the true *Protestant* Interest. In asserting the People's unquestionable Rights of Petitioning. In removing our just Fears, by reason of the great Forces in this Kingdom, under the Name of Guards, which the Law hath no knowledge of. In preventing the Misery, Ruin, and utter Destruction, which unavoidably must come upon this and the neighbouring Nation, if *James* Duke of *York*, or any other *Papist*, shall ascend the royal Throne of this Kingdom. And lastly, in securing to us our legal Right of annual Parliaments; which (under God) will unquestionably prove the highest security of all that is good and desirable to us and our Posterity after us. Always assuring our selves, that you will not in any wise consent unto any Money-Supply, until we are effectually secured against *Popery* and *Arbitrary Power*.

And particularly we desire you to give the most hearty Thanks of this County to that Noble Peer, the Earl of *Essex*, and by him to the rest of those Noble and Renowned Peers, who were pleased lately, and so seasonably, to offer their Petition and Advice to His Majesty. In the pursuance of all which needful, worthy and excellent Ends, we shall, as in duty bound, stand by you with our Lives and Fortunes.

A Letter of Thanks from the Grand-Jury *of the County of* Worcester, *to the Knights of this Shire;* Dated, Jan. 12. 1680.

Honoured Sirs,

WE the *Grand-Jury* of the County of *Worcester*, at the general Quarter Sessions of the Peace held for the said County the 11th day of *Jan.* in the 32d year of the King's Majesty's Reign, do hereby, in the behalf of our selves and the County for which we serve, return you our most hearty Thanks for your constant and unwearied Attendance upon the Service of His Majesty and your Country in this present Parliament, in a Time of such imminent danger: And especially of your concurrence in those Methods that have been taken for the Security of His Majesty's Sacred Person, the Protestant Religion, and the Properties of His Majesty's Subjects, against the *hellish Plots* of the *Papists* and their Adherents. And we do humbly request your continuance therein, and shall ever pray for the preservation of the Person of our most gracious

Sovereign,

Sovereign, and that God will direct and unite his Councils; and upon all Occaſions teſtify that we are,

Honoured Sirs, *Your very Humble, Obliged, and Thankful Servants.*

This was ſigned by all the ſaid *Grand-Jury*, and directed, to the Honourable Colonel *Samuel Sandys*, and *Thomas Foley* Eſquires, Members of this preſent Parliament.

A Letter from the Antient and Loyal Borough of North-Allerton in Yorkſhire, dated Jan. 14. 1680. to their Burgeſſes in Parliament.

Honoured Sirs,

THe unexpected and ſudden News of this Day's Poſt, preventing us from ſending thoſe due Acknowledgments which the greatneſs of your Services for the publick Good have merited from us, we have no better way (now left us) to expreſs our Gratitude, and the higheſt Reſentments of your Actions before, and in your laſt Seſſions of Parliament, than to manifeſt our Approbation thereof, by an Aſſurance, that if a Diſſolution of this preſent Parliament happen, ſince you have evidenced ſo ſufficiently your Affections to His Majeſty's Royal Perſon, and Endeavours for the preſerving the Proteſtant Religion, our Laws and Liberties, we are now reſolved, if you are pleaſ'd to continue with us, to continue you as our Repreſentatives: And do therefore beg your Acceptance thereof; and farther, that you will continue your Station during this Prorogation: faithfully aſſuring you, that none of us deſire to give, or occaſion you the expence or trouble of a Journey in order to your Election (if ſuch happen) being ſo ſenſible of the too great Expence you have been at already, in ſo carefully diſcharging the Truſt and Confidence repoſed in you, by Gentlemen,

Your obliged and faithful Friends and Servants.

Signed by the Burgeſſes and Electors of *North-Allerton*, and directed to Sir *Gilbert Gerrard*, and Sir *Henry Calverly*, Burgeſſes for the Borough of *North-Allerton* in *Yorkſhire.*

The ſame day the *Grand-Jury* of *Reading* preſented the following Paper to the Mayor of that Town.

Berkſhire ſſ. The Petition of the Grand-Jury of the Borough of Reading, at the Seſſions holden at the ſaid Borough, Jan. 14. 1680.

To the Right Worſhipful the Mayor and Aldermen of the Town and Borough of *Reading*;

The Humble Petition of the Grand-Jury *of the ſaid Town, in behalf of themſelves and others the Inhabitants of the ſame;*

Sheweth,

THat your Petitioners are deeply ſenſible of the great and imminent Dangers and Miſchiefs that threaten us, as well as the whole Nation, by the implacable Malice and Endeavour of our Enemies, to introduce *Popery* and *Arbitrary Government*, to ſubvert the *Proteſtant Religion*, and our well-eſtabliſh'd Laws, and to deprive us of our undoubted Rights and Liberties.

We therefore humbly entreat you, that you would take it into your conſideration, that no Perſon whatſoever may be imployed, encouraged, or empowered to
act

act in any wife in this *Corporation*, that hath been voted and deemed in *Parliament* a *Betrayer of the Rights of the People of* England.

And your Petitioners shall pray, &c.

Soon after the amazing Diffolution happened, and His Majefty having then declared his pleafure to fummon and hold the next Parliament, not at *Weftminfter*, which in all Ages has been generally the ufual place of convening thofe Affemblies (as being moft conveniently fituate near the *Metropolis* of the Kingdom, where all Perfons may be much better accommodated than elfewhere) but at the City of *Oxford*; feveral noble Lords thought it their Duty humbly to reprefent the Inconveniencies which in their apprehenfions would attend fuch chargeable Removal, and fubmiffively to offer their Advice to His Majefty, to alter that Refolution, in the following Petition; which being prefented to His Majefty by that noble Peer, of approved Loyalty and Prudence, the Right Honourable the Earl of *Effex*, His Lordfhip being accompanied with feveral other Lords at the Delivery thereof, thus expreffed himfelf.

The Earl of *Effex*'s Speech, at the Delivering of the following Petition to His moft Sacred Majefty, *Jan.* 25. 1680.

May it pleafe your Majefty,

THE *Lords here prefent, together with divers other Peers of the Realm, taking notice that by your late Proclamation, Your Majefty has declared an intention of calling a* Parliament *at* Oxford; *and obferving from Hiftory and Records, how unfortunate many Affemblies have been, when called at a Place remote from the capital City; as particularly the Congrefs in* Henry *the Second's time at* Clarendon; *Three feveral Parliaments at* Oxford *in* Henry *the Third's time, and at* Coventry *in* Henry *the Sixth's time; with divers others, which proved very fatal to thofe Kings, and have been followed with great mifchief on the whole Kingdom: And confidering the prefent pofture of affairs, the many jealoufies and difcontents, which are amongft the People, we have great caufe to apprehend, that the confequences of a Parliament now at* Oxford *may be as fatal to Your Majefty and the Nation, as thofe others mentioned have been to the then reigning Kings: And therefore we do conceive that we cannot anfwer it to God, to Your Majefty, or to the People, if we being Peers of the Realm, fhould not on fo important an Occafion humbly offer our Advice to Your Majefty; that, if poffible, Your Majefty may be prevailed with, to alter this (as we apprehend) unfeafonable Refolution. The Grounds and Reafons of our Opinion, are contained in this our Petition, which we humbly prefent to Your Majefty.*

To the King's moft Excellent Majefty, *The Humble Petition and Advice of the Lords under-named, Peers of the Realm;*

Humbly Sheweth,

THat whereas Your Majefty hath been pleafed, by divers Speeches, and Meffages to Your Houfes of Parliament, rightly to reprefent to them the Dangers that threatned Your Majefty's Perfon, and the whole Kingdom, from the mifchievous and wicked Plots of the *Papifts*, and the fudden Growth of a Foreign Power, unto which, no ftop or remedy could be provided, unlefs it were by Parliament, and an Union of Your Majefty's *Proteftant* Subjects, in one Mind, and one Intereft.

And the Lord *Chancellor*, in purfuance of Your Majefty's Commands, having more at large demonftrated the faid Dangers to be as great, as we in the midft of our Fears could imagine them; and fo preffing, that our Liberties, Religion, Lives, and the whole Kingdom would be certainly loft, if a fpeedy provifion were not made againft them.

And Your Majefty, on the 21ft of *April*, 1679, having called unto your Council, many Honourable and Worthy Perfons, and declared to them and the

L l   whole

whole Kingdom, That being sensible of the evil Effects of a single Ministry, or private Advice, or foreign Committee, for the general Direction of your Affairs; your Majesty would, for the future, refer all Things unto that Council, and by the constant Advice of them, together with the frequent use of your great Council, the *Parliament*, Your Majesty was hereafter resolved to govern the Kingdoms; we began to hope we should see an end of our Miseries.

But to our unspeakable Grief and Sorrow, we soon found our Expectations frustrated. The *Parliament*, then subsisting, was prorogued and dissolved, before it could perfect what was intended for our Relief and Security; and though another was thereupon called, yet by many Prorogations it was put off till the 21st of *October* past; and notwithstanding Your Majesty was then again pleased to acknowledge, that neither your Person, nor your Kingdom could be safe, till the Matter of the Plot was gone thorow, it was unexpectedly prorogued on the 10th of this *Month*, before any sufficient Order could be taken therein; all their just and pious Endeavours to save the Nation were overthrown; the good Bills they had been industriously preparing to unite all your Majesty's *Protestant* Subjects brought to nought; the discovery of the *Irish* Plot stifled; the Witnesses that came in frequently more fully to declare that, both of *England* and *Ireland*, discouraged. Those foreign Kingdoms and States, who by a happy conjunction with us, might give a check to the *French* Power disheartned, even to such a despair of their own Security against the growing greatness of that Monarch, as we fear may induce them to take new Resolutions, and perhaps such as may be fatal to us: The Strength and Courage of our Enemies both at home and abroad increased; and our selves left in the utmost danger of seeing our Country brought into utter Desolation.

In these *Extremities*, we had nothing under God to comfort us, but the Hopes, that your Majesty (being touched with the Groans of your perishing People) would have suffered your Parliament to meet at the day unto which it was prorogued: and that no further interruption should have been given to their Proceedings, in order to their saving of the Nation. But that failed us too: For then we heard that your Majesty, by the private suggestion of some *wicked Persons, Favourers of Popery*, Promoters of *French Designs*, and *Enemies* to your Majesty and the Kingdom (without the Advice, and, as we have good reason to believe, against the opinion, even of your *Privy-Council*) had been prevailed with to *dissolve it*, and to call another to meet at *Oxford*, where neither Lords nor Commons can be in safety, but will be daily exposed to the Sword of the *Papists*, and their Adherents, of whom too many are crept into Your Majesty's *Guards*. The Liberty of speaking according to their Consciences, will be thereby destroyed, and the validity of all their Acts and Proceedings consisting in it, left disputable. The Straitness of the Place, no ways admits of such a concourse of Persons, as now follows every Parliament; the *Witnesses* which are necessary to give Evidence against the Popish Lords, such Judges, or others whom the Commons have impeached, or had resolved to impeach, can neither bear the *Charge* of going thither, nor trust themselves under the Protection of a Parliament, that is it self evidently under the power of *Guards* and *Soldiers*.

The Premises considered, we Your Majesty's *Petitioners*, out of a just Abhorrence of such a dangerous and pernicious Counsel, (which the Authors have not *dared* to avow) and the direful Apprehensions of the Calamities and Miseries, that may ensue thereupon; do make it our most humble Prayer, and Advice, that the *Parliament* may not sit at a Place, where it will not be able to act with that *Freedom*, which is necessary; and especially, to give unto their Acts and Proceedings, that Authority which they ought to have amongst the People, and have ever had, unless impaired by some Awe upon them, (of which there wants no Precedents:) And that Your Majesty would be graciously pleased, to order *It* to sit at *Westminster* (it being the usual Place, and where they may consult and act with Safety and Freedom.)

And your Petitioners shall ever pray, &c.

Monmouth,		Salisbury,		Shaftsbury,		Grey,
Kent,		Clare,		Mordant,		Herbert,
Huntington,		Stanford,		Evers,		Howard,
Bedford,		Essex,		Paget,		Delamer.

The

The Counties and Corporations throughout *England*, were generally so well satisfied with the Proceedings of the Honourable House of *Commons* in the last Parliament, that as soon as they heard of the *Dissolution*, they resolved to chuse the very same respective Persons again, and contriv'd to make their Elections, without putting the Gentlemen chosen to any *Charge*; thereby to crush that *pernicious Custom* of over-ruling *Debauchery*, at *Choice of Members*, which had not only scandaliz'd the Nation, but almost poison'd and destroyed the very Constitution of our Parliaments.

A Letter from the famous Town of Kingston *upon* Hull, *to Sir* Michael Wharton *Kt. and* William Gee *Esq;* Burgesses *for that Town in the late Parliament.*

Worthy Gentlemen,

WE understand you have signified to our Magistrates your willingness to represent them in the ensuing Parliament, and that they have gratefully accepted of your generous Offer, which if they had communicated to us, our joint compliance would have been readily manifested: for we are so sensible of your Integrity in the late Parliament, by your indefatigable care and pains, in endeavouring the security of His Majesty's Sacred Person, as also our Religion and Property, that we cannot but rejoice that you are pleased again to offer us that kindness, which your former good Service hath engaged us to become Suitors for. We do therefore return you our hearty thanks, and you may be confident, without your appearance, or the least charge, to have all our Suffrages *Nemine contradicente*; and will, as our Obligations bind us, stand by your Proceedings, as becomes loyal Subjects and true *Englishmen*; subscribing our selves,

> *Your obliged and affectionate Friends and Servants,* &c.

Which was subscribed by *Matthew Johnson* Esq; Sheriff of the said Town, and 122 more of the most eminent Burgesses and Electors.

Another Letter from *Lewis* in *Sussex* on the like Occasion.

To their late *Worthy Representatives* Richard Bridger *and* Thomas Pelham, *Esquires.*

Gentlemen,

WE are sensible of the great trouble and charge you have been at, as our Representatives, and of your great care and constancy; for which we return you our hearty Thanks; with our earnest Request, that you would be pleased once more to favour us in the same capacity: And you will thereby much oblige

> *Your faithful Friends and Servants.*

This was subscribed by near 150 of the Inhabitants of *Lewis* aforesaid.

On the 4th of *February*, the *City of London* assembled in *Common-Hall*, consisting of several thousand *Livery-Men*, having by an *unanimous Voice*, elected their old Representatives, returned them their Thanks in a *Paper* there *publickly read*, and approved of with a general Consent.

The

The Addreſs of the City of *London.*

To the Honoured Sir Robert Clayton, *Knight,* Thomas Pilking-ton, *Alderman, Sir* Thomas Player, *Knight, and* William Love, *Eſq; late (and now choſen) Members of Parliament for this Honourable City of* London.

WE the Citizens of this City in *Common-Hall* aſſembled, having experienced the great and manifold Services of you our *Repreſentatives* in the *two laſt Parliaments,* by your moſt faithful and unwearied Endeavours to ſearch into and diſcover the depth of the horrid and helliſh *Popiſh Plots,* to preſerve His Majeſty's Royal Perſon, the Proteſtant Religion, and the well eſtabliſhed Government of this Realm; to ſecure the meeting and ſitting of frequent *Parliaments,* to aſſert our undoubted Rights of *petitioning,* and to puniſh ſuch who would have *betrayed* thoſe Rights, to promote the happy and long-wiſhed for Union amongſt all His Majeſty's Proteſtant Subjects, to repeal the 35th of *Elizabeth,* and the *Corporation-Act;* and eſpecially for what Progreſs hath been made towards the Excluſion of all *Popiſh Succeſſors,* and particularly of *James Duke of York,* whom the Commons of *England* (in the two laſt Parliaments) have declar'd, and we are greatly ſenſible is, *the principal Cauſe of all the Ruin and Miſery impending theſe Kingdoms in general, and this City in particular.* For all which, and other your conſtant and faithful Management of our Affairs in Parliament, we offer and return to you our moſt hearty *Thanks,* being confidently aſſur'd that you will not conſent to the granting any *Money-Supply,* until you have effectually ſecur'd us againſt *Popery* and *Arbitrary Power;* reſolving (by Divine Aſſiſtance) in purſuance of the ſame Ends, to ſtand by you with our Lives and Fortunes.

And likewiſe there was offered another Paper directed to the Sheriffs, purporting their Thanks to the ſeveral *Noble Peers* for their *late Petition and Advice to His Majeſty*; which was as followeth:

To the Worſhipful Slingsby Bethel *and* Henry Corniſh *Eſquires, Sheriffs of the City of* London *and* Weſtminſter.

WE the Citizens of the ſaid City, in *Common-Hall* aſſembled, having read, and diligently peruſ'd the late Petition and Advice of ſeveral noble Peers of this Realm to His Majeſty, whoſe Counſels we humbly conceive are (in this unhappy Juncture) highly ſeaſonable, and greatly tending to the Safety of theſe Kingdoms: We do therefore make it our moſt hearty Requeſt, that you (in the Name of this Common-Hall) will return to the Right Honourable the Earl of *Eſſex,* and (by him) to the reſt of thoſe noble Peers, the grateful Acknowledgment of this Aſſembly.

Which being read, and approved of by a general Acclamation, the Sheriffs promiſed to give their Lordſhips the Thanks of the Common-Hall, in purſuance of their Requeſt.

The

The Address of the City of *Westminster,* Febr. 10. 168⅞.

To the Honoured Sir William Poultney, *and Sir* William
Waller, *Knights, Unanimously Elected Members of the ensuing Parliament for the Ancient City of* Westminster.

WE the Inhabitants of this City and the Liberties thereof, assembled, retaining a most grateful and indelible Sense of your prudent Zeal in the late
Parliament, in searching into the depth of the horrid and hellish Plots of
the Papists against His Majesty's Royal Person, the Protestant Religion, and the
Government of the Realm, and in endeavouring to bring the Authors of *Wicked Counsels* to condign punishment: And remembring also your faithful discharge of that
great Trust reposed in you, in vindicating our undoubted Right of *Petitioning* His
Majesty, That Parliaments may sit for the Redress of our Grievances, which Hereditary Privilege some *Bad Men* would have wrested out of our Hands ; upon whom
you have set such a just *Brand of Ignominy*, as may deter them from the like Attempts
for the time to come : And further reflecting upon your vigorous Endeavours to secure to us and our Posterity the Profession of the *True Religion*, by those Just, Legal
and Necessary Expedients, which the great Wisdom of the two last Parliaments
fixed upon, and adhered to ; Do find our selves obliged to make our open Acknow-
ledgement of, and to return you our hearty Thanks for your eminent Integrity and
Faithfulness, your indefatigable Labour and Pains in the Premises, not once question-
ing but you will maintain the same good Spirit and Zeal to secure His Majesty's Royal Person, and to preserve to us the Protestant Religion (wherein all good Subjects
have an Interest) against the secret and subtil Contrivances and open Assaults of the
Common Enemy ; as also our Civil Rights and Properties against the Incroachments
of *Arbitrary Power*. In pursuance of which Great and Good Ends, we shall always
be ready, as we are obliged, to adhere to you our Honoured Representatives, with
the utmost hazard of our Persons and Estates.

City of Chichester, *the same Day*.

After the Unanimous Choice of *John Braman* and *Richard Farington* Esquires,
(who serv'd for that City in the late Parliament) they had the Sense of that Eminent
City delivered to them by a Worthy Person, in the Name, and by the Consent of
the rest, in the following Speech:

Gentlemen,

THe Faithful discharge of the like high Trust we formerly gave you, is the true
Inducement of our chusing you again: And as we heartily thank you for
your past worthy Behaviour in Parliament, and in a particular manner, for your
being for the Bill of Exclusion ; for the Bill of Uniting all His Majesty's Subjects,
for Vindicating our (almost lost) Right of Petitioning for frequent Parliaments,
and for your endeavour to call those wretched Pensioners to an Account, that betray'd the Nation in the late Long Parliament: So we pray you to persevere in
your faithful Service of us, until the Nation be thoroughly secured against Popery and
Arbitrary Power. And since that Famous and Renowned Bulwark of the Protestant
Religion, the ever-to-be-honoured City of *London*, have commanded their Sheriffs
to present their Thanks to the true *English* and Noble Earl of *Essex*, and by
him to the rest of those Right Honourable Peers, for their late Excellent Petition
and Advice to His Majesty ; so we being willing to imitate so Good and Great an
Example, do desire you in our names, to present in like manner, our humble and
hearty Thanks to the said Earl, and those Noble Lords.

Borough of Colchester, February 15. 1680-81.

After the Election made, a great Number of the Free-Burgesses of this Corporation agreed upon the following Address to be presented to their Representatives.

To the Honourable Sir Harbottle Grimston Baronet, and Samuel Reynolds Esq; now chosen Burgesses for our Corporation of Colchester, in the County of Essex.

WE the Free-Burgesses of the said Corporation, being deeply sensible of the unspeakable danger threatning His Majesty's Life, and the Protestant Religion, and the well established Government of this Kingdom, from the Hellish Designs of the Papists, and their wicked Adherents: And that our Religion and Liberties can only, under God, be secured to us and our Posterity, by wholesome Advice in Parliament; have now chosen you to represent us there; in confidence of your Intergity and Courage, to discharge so great a Trust in this Time of Imminent Danger. And we do desire you to allow us to speak our stedfast Resolution (with utmost hazard of our Lives and Fortunes) to shew our Approbation of what shall be resolved in Parliament, for maintaining the Protestant Religion and our Liberties, against Popery, and Arbitrary Government. And we hope you will endeavour, to the utmost of your power, to disable *James* Duke of *York*, and all other Popish Pretenders, from Inheriting the Imperial Crown of this Realm: And we shall pray for your good success.

Here we cannot but inform the Reader, That the Notorious *Thompson* in his *Popish Intelligence* of the 15th of *March*, would insinuate as if there were no such Address, by Printing a Story, That the Mayor, Aldermen, and some others of this Town, being assembled on *February* 28. 1680-81, a Printed Paper purporting to be the manner of the Election, and containing also an Address made to the Members, *&c.* was read amongst them, and that none of the Assembly would own his Consenting to or making that Paper or Address. Touching which, it must be Noted, 1. That the Mayor, and several of these Gentlemen, were disobliged by being Out-Voted, and much offended, because they could not carry it for their Friend Sir *Walter Clarges* ; and so had no Reason to address to the Members duly and fairly Elected, because they had vigorously appeared for a contrary Party. 2. That there are in that Pamphlet in relating the manner of the Election some galling Truths, or if you please Reflections, which possibly had better been spared, and therefore no wise man would own the making it. But for the Address it self 'tis certain, That it was agreed upon, consented unto, and will be justified by the far greater part of the Electors of this Antient and Eminently Loyal Borough ; of which 'twas thought fit here to give this brief Account, for obviating any slanderous Objection that might be made on that occasion.

The Address of the Gentlemen and Free-holders of *Bedford*.

To the Right Honourable the Lord Russel, and Sir Humphrey Munnox, Elected Knights for the Shire, on the 14th. of February, 168$\frac{0}{1}$.

WHen it pleased His Majesty to summon His Peers and Commons of this His Realm to meet Him, at *Westminster*, in the last Parliament, we accordingly then chose You to act on our behalf. And being abundantly satisfied, not only in Your Courage, Integrity and Prudence in general; but also in Your particular Care, and faithful conscientious Endeavours: (1.) To assert our Right of Legal Petitioning for Redress of our just Grievances, and to punish those who were studious to betray it: (2.) To secure the Meeting and Sitting of frequent Parliaments (already by Law provided for) for the preservation of our Lives, Liberties and Estates ; and for the support of His Sacred Majesty ; and even of the Government it self : (3.) To Repeal the Act of the 35th of *Elizabeth*, whereby all true Protestants might

possibly,

possibly, in case of a Popish Successor (from which God of his infinite Mercy defend us) be liable to utter Ruin, Abjuration, and perpetual Banishment. (4.) To secure his Majesty's Royal Person, the Protestant Religion, and well-established Government of this Realm. (5.) To destroy and root out Popery. (6.) To use the most effectual means conducing to so good an End ; *viz.* The Exclusion of a Popish Successor, both by name, and otherwise. We have therefore now chosen you again to represent us in like manner in this Parliament called to be held at *Oxford*, in full Trust and Confidence, that with the same Courage and Integrity you will persevere in the same good Endeavours, pursuing all things that (by joint consent of your Fellow-Members) shall be found for our publick Good and Safety. And in full assurance that you will not consent to the disposal of any of our Moneys, till we are effectually secured against Popery, and Arbitrary Power, do resolve (by Divine Assistance) to stand by you therein.

The Address of the Gentry and Free-holders of the County of Suffolk, *to their Representatives chosen the 14th of* February, 168⅞, *presented to them by Sir* Philip Skippon, *in the name and by consent of the rest of the Electors.*

To the Honourable Sir Sam. Barnardiston, *and Sir* Will. Spring, *Baronets, Knights of the Shire for the County of* Suffolk.

Gentlemen,

WE the Free-holders of this County having chosen you our Representatives in the last Parliament, in which we had satisfactory Demonstration of your Zeal for the Protestant Religion, of your Loyalty to his Majesty's Person and Government, and of your faithful Endeavours for the Preservation of the Laws, our Rights and Properties ; we now return you our most hearty Thanks, and have unanimously chosen you to represent this County at the Parliament to be holden at *Oxford* the 21st of *March* next : And though we have not the least distrust of your Wisdom to understand, or of your Integrity and Resolution to maintain and promote our common Interests now in so great hazard, yet we think it meet (at this time of imminent Danger to the King and Kingdom) to recommend some things to your Care : And particularly we do desire,

1. That (as hitherto you have, so) you will vigorously prosecute the Execrable Popish Plot, now more fully discovered and proved by the Trial of *William* late Viscount *Stafford.*

2. That you will promote a Bill for excluding *James* D. of *York*, and all Popish Successors from the Imperial Crown of this Realm ; as that which under God may probably be a present and effectual means for the preservation of his Majesty's Life, (which God preserve) the Protestant Religion, and the well-established Government of this Kingdom.

3. That you will endeavour the frequent meetings of Parliaments, and their sitting so long as it shall be requisite for the dispatch of those great Affairs for which they are convened, as that which is our only Bulwark against *Arbitrary Power.*

4. That you will endeavour an happy and necessary Union amongst all his Majesty's Protestant Subjects, by promoting those several good Bills which were to that end before the last Parliament.

And that till these things be obtained, which we conceive necessary even to the Being of this Nation, you will not consent to bring any Charge upon our Estates : And we do assure you, that we will stand by you with our Lives and Fortunes in Prosecution of the good Ends before recited.

The

The Addreſs of the Town of Hertford, *February* 21. 168$\frac{0}{1}$.

To the Right Worſhipful Sir William Cooper, *Baronet,* and Sir Thomas Byde *Knight.*

WE the Free-men and Inhabitants of the Borough of *Hertford,* in the County of *Hertford,* having unanimouſly choſen You our Repreſentatives to ſit in the next enſuing Parliament to be holden at *Oxford* the 21ſt of *March* next, cannot but with all Thankfulneſs acknowledge your moſt faithful Endeavours, and unwearied Pains in ſerving us in the laſt Parliament, ſearching into and diſcovering the late damnable Helliſh Popiſh Plot ; the preſervation of His Majeſty's Perſon, the Proteſtant Religion, and the well-eſtabliſhed Government of the Realm ; to ſecure the Meeting and Sitting of frequent Parliaments ; to aſſert our undoubted Right of Petitioning, and to puniſh ſuch who would have betrayed thoſe Rights ; to promote a happy Union amongſt all His Majeſty's Proteſtant Subjects ; to Repeal the Act of the 35th of Queen *Elizabeth,* and the Corporation Act ; and particularly for what Progreſs hath been made in the Bill of Excluſion of all Popiſh Succeſſors, the principal Cauſe of all the Miſeries and Ruin impending on theſe Kingdoms in general ; beſeeching You as now our Repreſentatives, to proſecute the ſame good Ends and Purpoſes, until the Nation ſhall be thoroughly ſecured againſt Popery and Arbitrary Power, both in Church and State. And further, in imitation of the ever renowned City of *London,* We requeſt You on our behalf, to preſent our humble Acknowledgements to the Right Honourable the Earl of *Eſſex,* and by him to all the reſt of thoſe Right Honourable Peers, for their late Excellent Petition and Advice to His Majeſty ; and for all the reſt of their Faithful Service and Endeavours they have performed for the Proteſtant Intereſt of the Nation.

The Addreſs of the Gentry and Freeholders of the County of Eſſex.

To Sir Henry Mildmay *and* John Lemot Honeywood Eſq; *Unanimouſly Re-elected Knights for the Shire,* Feb. 22. 168$\frac{0}{1}$.

Gentlemen,

THe faithful Diſcharge of that Truſt we formerly gave You, is the true Inducement of our chuſing You again to be our Repreſentatives, being abundantly ſatiſfied not only in your Care and Prudence in general, but alſo in Your Particular Care and Unwearied Diligence in your Conſcientious Endeavours to ſecure His Majeſty's Royal Perſon, the Proteſtant Religion, and Government of the Realm ; to Unite all his Majeſty's Proteſtant Subjects ; to Repeal the Act of the 35th of *Elizabeth* ; to Aſſert our juſt and ancient Rights and Privileges, and particularly that of *Petitioning* ; and to puniſh thoſe who were ſtudious to betray them : For your two excellent Addreſſes, and Publiſhing your Votes ; Endeavouring to ſecure the Meeting and Sitting of Frequent Parliaments ; to deſtroy and root out *Popery,* by ſecuring us againſt all Popiſh Succeſſors, and particularly by paſſing a Bill againſt *James* Duke of *York,* without which, we are highly ſenſible, that all other means will be ineffectual, and the Peace and Safety of the Kingdom and Government (it ſelf) left in great danger ; it being inconſiſtent with our Oath, by which we ſwear againſt the *Pope's Supremacy,* whilſt a Popiſh King himſelf owns it ; and it being againſt the Eſſence of Government, that People ſhould obey him, who by his Principles, (as a *Papiſt*) is bound to deſtroy them.

And as we do heartily thank You for Your paſt worthy Behaviour herein, ſo we have choſen You to act on our behalf in the next Parliament to be holden at *Oxford,* in full truſt and confidence, that with Courage and Integrity, You will perſevere in the ſame good Endeavours, purſuing all things that ſhall be found for our Publick Good and Safety.

And

And in full Affurance that You will not confent to the difpofal of any of our Moneys, till we are effectually fecured againft *Popery* and *Arbitrary Power* ; and until the Fleet and Garifons are fettled in the hands of fuch as are Perfons of known Loyalty and Fidelity to the King and Kingdom, and true Zeal and Affection for the Proteftant Religion ; and we do refolve (by the divine Affiftance) to ftand by You therein with our Lives and Fortunes.

'Tis obfervable, That this Addrefs being openly read to their Reprefentatives, and confirm'd by the unanimous and loud Acclamations of the Free-holders, for further demonftration that it was the Senfe of each individual perfon of that Numerous Affembly, it was offered, that fo many as agreed to it, fhould fay *Ay* ; upon which, they all cried out *Ay, Ay.* And if any were otherwife minded, they were defired to exprefs their Diffent by faying *No :* At which there was *Altum Silentium,* not one to be heard faying *No.*

The Addrefs of the Gentry and other Free-holders of the County of Surrey, *being in number about* 2000, Feb. 23. 168 9/4/.

To Arthur Onflow *and* George Evelin *Efqs; elected Knights for this County, in the enfuing Parliament, whofe Seffion is appointed at* Oxon, *the 21ft of the following Month.*

WE the Free-holders of the County of *Surrey,* having in the two former Parliaments chofen you to be our Reprefentatives, and being fully fatisfied in your Faithfulnefs and Care to preferve the Proteftant Religion, His Majefty's Royal Perfon, the good Government of the Nation by Law, and in fecuring our Rights and Liberties ; for your real Endeavours herein, we jointly return our hearty Thanks, and have now chofen you again, to be our Reprefentatives in this Parliament. And though we have not the leaft Sufpicion or Doubt of your Wifdom, and Integrity, in acting for our Common Good (now, as we apprehend, in great danger) yet we judge it expedient to difcover our Minds and hearty Defires, in the Particulars following, (*viz.*)

I. That you will continue vigoroufly to profecute the horrid Popifh Plotters, and endeavour they may be brought to condign punifhment, efpecially all *Sham-Plotters,* which we efteem the worft of Villains.

II. That you will infift on a Bill for excluding all Popifh Succeffors to the Crown, which (we believe) an effectual Means (under God) for preferving the Proteftant Religion, His Majefty's Life and Tranquillity, with the well eftablifhed Government of the Kingdom, and fecuring it to our Pofterity.

III. That you endeavour paffing a Bill for Regulating Elections, and the Frequency of Parliaments (for difpatch of thofe weighty Affairs of the Nation, that fhall from time to time be before them) which we judge the beft prevention of an Arbitrary Power.

IV. That you perfevere in Afferting our Right of Legal Petitioning, for removing our juft Grievances, and pafs a Bill (if there be no Law) to punifh fuch that fhall obftruct it.

V. That you will ufe your utmoft Endeavours to bring in a Bill againft Pluralities of Church-Livings, Non-refidency, and Scandalous Minifters, of which there are too many in moft Counties.

VI. That you will endeavour to preferve His Majefty's Perfon, to root out Popery, and prevent Arbitrary Government, and ufe your utmoft Endeavours to unite His Majefty's Proteftant Subjects.

VII. Laftly, That you will not confent to any Money-Bill, till the forefaid Particulars be effected ; and in fo doing, we hereby promife to ftand by you with our Lives and Fortunes.

The Address of the Free-holders of the County of Leicester.

To the Right Honourable Bennet *Lord* Sherrard, *and Sir* John Hartopp *Baronet*; *as it was audibly read in Court by the Sheriff, and unanimously approved of by the said Free-holders, immediately after their Election,* 24 *Febr.* 168⅞.

WE the Free-holders of the County of *Leicester*, having chosen you to be our Representatives in the Two last Parliaments, being highly sensible of the care you have taken to secure his Majesty's Royal Person, the Protestant Religion, our Liberties and Properties; as also your endeavours further to discover and prosecute the horrid Popish Plot spread over the Realm of *England*, and others of his Majesty's Dominions, with your zealous promoting an happy Union of all good Protestants in this Land, not only by good and wholesome Laws for that End, but by Repealing those which were destructive to it; and especially for your *persisting in the Exclusion of* James *Duke of* York, and all other Popish Successors from inheriting the Imperial Crown of *England*; which we esteem the *only Security under God*, of His Majesty's Person and Dominions; likewise, your Vindicating our fundamental Right of Petitioning His Majesty for frequent sitting of Parliaments, by your particular Marks of Displeasure laid upon the Opposers of it: For all which, and other good Laws you were about to make, we give you most hearty *Thanks*. And having now again Unanimously chosen you for the ensuing Parliament, if you shall continue the prosecution of the aforementioned *absolutely necessary Things*, we shall stand by you with our Lives and Fortunes.

The Address of the Gentry and Free-holders of the County of York, *publickly read in Court, and fully consented to by the whole Assembly, by a general Acclamation at their Election,* March 2.

To the Right Honourable Charles *Lord* Clifford, *and* Henry *Lord* Fairfax.

May it please your Lordships,

THe Assurance we had of your Fidelity and Activity, for the Service of our King and Country, in the Parliament which began at *Westminster* the 6th of *March* 1678, was the only Reason of our Choice of you to Represent us in the last Parliament; and our experience of your Faithfulness and Diligence in the same Service the last Parliament, is the only Ground of our uncontradicted Choice of you again this Day into the same Trust, for the ensuing Parliament, appointed to meet at *Oxford* the 21st instant. And we judge it our Duty, as good Protestants, Loyal Subjects, and True *Englishmen*, not only to express our hearty Concurrence with you in, but also to return you our real and publick Thanks for the many *good Things* you did, and *were about to do* in both the last Parliaments; and more especially, for your seasonable Addresses to His Majesty, your Necessary Votes, Resolutions, Orders, and Bills; whereby you have endeavoured,

1. To preserve the Protestant Religion, His Majesty's Person, and the Kingdoms of *England* and *Ireland* from the many Dangers which threaten them.

2. To Exclude *a Popish Successor.*

3. To *Unite* all His Majesty's Protestant Subjects.

4. To purge out the Corruptions which abound in Elections of Members to serve in Parliament. And,

5. To secure us for the future against Popery and Arbitrary Power.

And we intreat you to proceed in a Parliamentary way to the Accomplishment of these *Excellent Things*; and we assure you, that *these things being done*, we shall
with

with great chearfulness be willing to supply His Majesty (to the utmost of our Ability) *with Money*, for the securing of His Interest and Honour, both at home and abroad.

A Letter agreed upon by the Mayor and Inhabitants of the Borough of Bridgwater, *to be sent to their Burgesses chosen on the* 26th *of* February.

Sir *Halswel Tynt*, and Sir *John Malet*,

WE greet you both with our most humble and hearty Service, and by these inform you, that on *Saturday* the 26th past, with all becoming Calmness and Fairness, we elected you to be our Burgesses and Representatives in the ensuing Parliament.

We do also Unanimously approve of that great Care and indefatigable Industry which the last Parliament took, in and toward the securing of the Protestant Religion (than which nothing is more dear to us,) His Majesty's Sacred Person and Government, together with the Vindication and Preservation of our Native Rights, Liberties and Privileges: For their utmost Endeavour to bring the *Betrayers* of the same, together with all the principal Conspirators in that most damnable and hellish Popish Plot, to condign punishment, not omitting our grateful Acknowledgments of those many *Good Bills* which they had prepared: And moreover, for all those worthy Votes, Resolutions and Orders made and past in that *most Loyal*, and never-to-be-forgotten Parliament, whereof one of you in the last, and both of you in former Parliaments (to our great comfort and encouragement) approved your selves faithful Members.

We do also humbly and heartily desire and petition you to follow their good Precedent and Example in this ensuing Parliament, to do your utmost to secure the King's Person with the Protestant Religion (which we apprehend, with deep sense of mind, to be in imminent Danger) from all Popish Attempts and Conspiracies whatsoever: As also to take Care for the *Exclusion* and Prevention of any Popish Successor from inheriting the Imperial Crown of this Realm.

In the firm and faithful Discharge of that great Trust we have reposed in you (whereof we do not in the least doubt) withal confidently believing, That you will not *charge our Estates, till we are effectually secured* from Popery and Arbitrary Government; We do assure you, That we will stand by you with our Lives and Fortunes: And we shall ever pray for your good Success.

The Sense of the Gentry and Free-holders of the County of Nottingham, *to Sir* Scroop How *and* John White, *elected Knights of the Shire there,* Febr. 22. *as it was delivered in the following Speech made by a worthy Gentleman, in the Name, and by and with the Consent and Approbation of the whole Company of Electors.*

Gentlemen,

WE give you hearty Thanks for your good Service in the late Parliaments, and for accepting the same Trust again: And we desire you to persevere in the same steps you have before made for the Preservation of His Majesty's Royal Person, against the wicked Attempts of the Hellish Plotters; and for the Defence of Religion and Property, against Popery and Arbitrary Power; and that you would be *sparing of our Money*, until those things are effectually secured, and a sure Foundation laid of an happy Union between the King and his People, by the removal of *those evil Instruments*, who through private Interest and Ambition, make it their business to divide their Affections.

The

The Berkſhire *Addreſs, to the Gentlemen Unanimouſly Elected to ſerve for that County,* Feb. 28. 168⅞.

To the Worſhipful William Barker, *and* Richard Southby *Eſqs; now choſen to be the Repreſentatives of the County of* Berks.

WE the Free-holders of this County being abundantly ſatisfied of your faithful Diſcharge of the great Truſt we repoſed in you in the laſt Parliament, in your Care and conſtant Attendance, is the true Inducement of our Chuſing you again this Day to be our Repreſentatives in this Parliament to be holden at *Oxford*, and do return you our hearty Thanks,

1. That you have aſſerted our Right of the Legal Petitioning for Redreſs of our juſt Grievances, and puniſhing thoſe who labour to betray it.

2. For endeavouring to preſerve his Majeſty's Royal Perſon, the Proteſtant Religion, and the Eſtabliſhed Government of this Realm.

3. In uſing the moſt effectual Means conducing to ſo good an End, (*viz.*) the Excluding of *James* Duke of *York*, or any Popiſh Succeſſor, from ever Inheriting this Crown, being the only way (as we imagine) under God, to deſtroy and root Popery out of this Realm.

4. For endeavouring the frequent Meeting and Sitting of Parliaments (already by Law provided,) for the preſervation of our Lives, Liberties, and Eſtates, for the ſupport of his Majeſty and the Government it ſelf.

5. For Repealing the 35th of Queen *Elizabeth*, whereby all true Proteſtants might not be liable to utter Ruin, and perpetual Baniſhment.

6. For your Inſpection into the Illegal and Arbitrary Proceedings of the Courts in *Weſtminſter-Hall*, as deſtructive to publick Juſtice, and violating the Rights of the Subjects; and in effect to ſubvert the Ancient Conſtitution of Parliaments, and the Government of this Kingdom.

7. That you laboured for an Happy and Neceſſary Union amongſt all his Majeſty's Proteſtant Subjects, as being the ſureſt way to defend the true Religion from all the evil Attempts of our Popiſh Adverſaries.

8. For Repealing the Corporation-Act.

And now our Requeſt is, That you will not conſent to any Money-Bill, till the aforeſaid Particulars be throughly effected; and in ſo doing, we do hereby engage to ſtand by you with our Lives and Fortunes.

The Addreſs of the Town of Dover.

To Thomas Papillon, *and* William Stokes *Eſqs; the late and now new elected Members to ſerve in Paliament, for the Town and Port of* Dover *in the County of* Kent.

WE the Mayor, Jurats, and Commonalty of the ſaid Town of *Dover*, having duly conſidered the good Abilities, and great Faithfulneſs of you who have been our Repreſentatives in the two preceding Parliaments, and have therein given demonſtration of your Loyalty to his Majeſty, and for the Security of his Majeſty's Kingdoms, do with all gratefulneſs return you our hearty thanks; and do pray that in purſuance of the Truſt we have now again repoſed in you, you will, with the ſame Candor and Faithfulneſs, endeavour the Security of his Majeſty's Perſon, the Proteſtant Religion, and his Majeſty's Proteſtant Subjects, by your utmoſt endeavours for the perfecting of thoſe good Bills that were before you in the laſt Parliament; in proſecution of which we will ſtand by you with our Lives and Fortunes.

The

The Addreſs of the Borough of New-Caſtle under Line, *as it was read in the* Town-Hall *by the Recorder, and fully con-ſented to by the Inhabitants,* March *the* 3d.

To the Right Worſhipful Sir Thomas Bellot, *Bar. and* William Leveſon Gower, *Eſq; now choſen Burgeſſes for the Borough of* New-Caſtle under Line.

WE the Mayor, Aldermen, and Free-Burgeſſes, Inhabitants of the aforeſaid Borough, being deeply ſenſible of your faithful Diſcharge of the great Truſt repoſed in you the two laſt Parliaments, and of the unſpeakable Danger threatning his Majeſty's Life, the Proteſtant Religion, and the well eſtabliſhed Government of this Kingdom, from the Helliſh Deſigns of the Papiſts, and their Adherents: And that our Religion and Liberties can only (under God) be ſecured to us and our Poſterities by the wholeſome Advice of Parliaments, have now choſen you again to repreſent us in the next enſuing Parliament to be held at *Oxford,* March 21ſt inſtant, in confidence of your continued Faithfulneſs, Integrity and Courage ſtill to diſcharge ſo great a Truſt, eſpecially in this time of ſo imminent Danger.

And we do hereby declare, That to our utmoſt power (though with the hazard of our Lives and Fortunes) we will maintain and approve of what ſhall be reſolved in Parliament for the maintaining the Proteſtant Religion againſt Popery and Arbitrary Government.

And we alſo (having already had ſuch Experience of your Affections to the Kingdom's Intereſt) hope that you will *not conſent to the Diſpoſal of any of our Moneys* till we are effectually ſecured againſt Popery, and *then* a Charge upon us *to the half of* what we enjoy will be chearfully accepted by us.

And, we hope, that you will alſo endeavour, to the utmoſt of your power, to diſable *James* Duke of *York,* and all other Popiſh Pretenders, from Inheriting the Imperial Crown of this Realm. And thereby you will lay a firm Obligation upon us; who will heartily and unfeignedly pray for your good Succeſs in ſo weighty an undertaking.

Signed *Ralph Wood,* Mayor, *Nath. Beard,* and *Will. Middleton,* Juſtices, and by the Aldermen, and Capital Burgeſſes, and above 200 more of the Chief Inhabitants with their own hands.

The Addreſs of the Gentry and other Free-holders of the County of Suſſex.

To Sir Will. Thomas, *and Sir* John Fagg, *preſented them upon their being elected Knights of the County, at* Lewis, March *the* 3d.

Gentlemen,

HAd we not heard well of Your Fidelity in diſcharging former Publick Truſts, we had not this day called You to the ſame Imploy; for they that betray, or neglect our ſervice once, ſhall never receive our Truſt again: And though we have no intention to limit or circumſcribe the Power we have laid in You, yet we muſt deſire, (and with that earneſtneſs as becometh thoſe that beg for no leſs than the Life of their King, Government, Religion, Laws, Liberties and Properties, yea the very Lives and Beings of all the Proteſtants in the World,) That you would pleaſe as our Repreſentatives, to have an eſpecial regard to theſe particulars following.

O o

1. That

1. That you would effectually secure His Majesty's Royal Life, and the Lives of all His Majesty's Protestant Subjects, by a firm and legal Association.

2. That you would repeat the Endeavours of the Two former Worthy Parliaments, in barring the Door against all Popish Successors to the Crown; in particular against *James* Duke of *York*, and Arbitrary Government.

3. That You would be incessant in your Endeavours for uniting His Majesty's Protestant Subjects.

4. That you would further search into the bottom of those Damnable and Hellish Plots of the *Papists*, that have been laid against His Majesty's Life, the Protestant Religion and Government, and to bring those Horrid Criminals to Justice.

5. That You would not forget those Execrable Villains, that by receiving Pensions, betrayed their Trusts, and our Liberties in the late Long Parliament; but do such Exemplary Justice on them, that all others for the future may fear, and do no more so wickedly.

And in doing these Great things, and all others that You shall judge necessary for the Peace, Safety and Prosperity of the Nation, we shall not only stand by you as Thankful Acknowledgers of Your Service, but reckon it our Duty (if any hazard threaten you) to defend You as Worthy Patriots, with our Lives and Fortunes.

The *Cheshire* Address.

To the Honourable Henry Booth *Esq*; *and Sir* Robert Cotton, Kt. *and Bar. being chosen Knights for that County,* March *the* 7*th : Immediately after their Election, the Right Honourable the Lord* Colchester, *and the Lord* Brandon, *presented them a Paper, containing the Sentiments and Desires of the Gentry and Freeholders, in these words :*

WE the Gentry and Freeholders of the County Palatine of *Chester*, who have by a free and unanimous Consent *Re-elected* You to be our Representatives in Parliament, do thankfully acknowledge Your joint Integrity and Concurrence with the Worthy and Eminent Members of the *Last*, who in so *Signal* (and never to be forgotten) a manner of *Petitioning*, promoted the Union, Support and Growth of the True Protestant Religion Established by Law : And the only Expedient (we think) to perpetuate these to our Posterity, is to *adhere* to what the late Parliament designed *relating to the Duke of* York, and all Popish Successors; to provide for the Defence and Safety of his Majesty's Person; vigorously to pursue the Discovery of the horrid Popish Plot; and to punish all Sham-plotters, whom we esteem the worst of Villains, without which His Majesty can neither be easy, nor secure. These, with those great and Excellent things then under their Considerations, make us confident of Your Sincerity and Proceedings; which that they may be successful, is our prayer, and will be the *support* of all those who wish the happiness of His Majesty, and these distressed Kingdoms. We likewise desire the Votes may continue to be *Printed*, that till the effects of your endeavours (on which depends the happiness both of Church and State) are accomplished, we may be truly acquainted with your proceeding.

The

The Northamptonſhire *Addreſs,* March *the* 8*th.*

To John Parkhurſt *and* Miles Fleetwood, *Eſqs; then elected Knights for that County.*

Gentlemen,

THat we are extreamly ſatisfied of Your faithful and honeſt diſcharge of the great Truſt repoſed in You by this County of *Northampton* in the laſt Parliament, is moſt evident, by our hearty Thanks we now return You, and by our Unanimous Electing of you again, to ſerve for us in the next Parliament to be holden at *Oxford.*

Gentlemen, We find by Experience, you ſo well judge of the ſenſe of our Country, that we need not tender You our Thoughts in many Particulars. Only, as the Preſervation of His Majeſty's Sacred Perſon, the Proteſtant Religion, and our Properties, are of the greateſt Concern, and moſt dear unto us ; ſo more eſpecially we recommend them unto you, deſiring You to uſe Your utmoſt Endeavours,

1. That there may be a more full and perfect Diſcovery of that moſt Helliſh Popiſh Plot, and all other Sham-Plots.
2. That we may be ſecured againſt a Popiſh Succeſſor.
3. That there may be found means of Uniting His Majeſty's Proteſtant Subjects, againſt the Common Enemy.

Gentlemen, In purſuance of theſe good Ends, and ſuch others, as you ſhall think conducing to the happineſs of the King and Kingdom, We ſhall ſtand by You with our Lives and Fortunes.

The Addreſs of the Town of Taunton, March 11*th.*

To Edmund Prideaux *and* John Trenchard, *Eſqs;*

Worthy Sirs,

WE do moſt heartily acknowledge Your great Wiſdom, Courage, and Faithfulneſs in the Diſcharge of the Truſt, by Us repoſed in You, as Members of the late diſſolved Parliament, whoſe worthy Endeavours for the Happineſs of the King and Kingdom, exceedingly rejoiced the hearts of True *Engliſh* and *Proteſtant* Spirits, and will make them famous to Poſterity.

And now, Sirs, having a full aſſurance of Your Perſeverance in the ſame good Works, we have preſumed again to make choice of You, as our Repreſentatives in the enſuing Parliament, deſiring your Acceptance of that great Truſt. And begging You, as that wherein the Glory of God, the Intereſt of the *Proteſtant Religion,* the Safety and Welfare of the King and Kingdom is highly concerned, to proſecute (as ſhall be guided by the Wiſdom of that Honourable Houſe,) theſe following Particulars, *viz.*

1. That ſome effectual courſe may be taken for the Safety of His Majeſty's Sacred Perſon and Government, which have been and ſtill are in extreme danger, by the abominable Plots and Attempts of Papiſts.
2. That further Search be made into the Horrid Popiſh Plot, and the Plotters and Abettors thereof brought to condign Puniſhment.

3. That

3. That You will join with the reft of that Honourable Houfe (whereof You are now chofen to be Members) in repeating the Endeavours of the Two laft Worthy Parliaments, to bar all Papifts (and efpecially *James* Duke of *York*) from the exercife of the Royal Authority of this Kingdom.

4. That You will with all diligence endeavour the Uniting of His Majefty's Proteftant Subjects, and the Repealing thofe fevere Laws that are obftructive thereof.

5. That all good Endeavours be ufed for the fecuring of our Religion and Property, and the juft Rights and Privileges of the Subject.

6. That fome Law may be made for the preventing of the Exceffes and Exorbitances in the Elections of Members of Parliament, and of undue Returns ; and that fome effectual Provifion may be made for the meeting of frequent Parliaments, and for their fitting to redrefs Grievances, and to make fuch wholefome Laws as fhall be neceffary for the welfare of this Nation.

7. That fome effectual courfe be taken to give a check to Prophanenefs and Debauchery, which threaten Ruin, or at leaft exceeding great Prejudice to the Kingdom.

In profecuting of all which worthy Acts, we fhall endeavour your Defence with our Lives and Fortunes.

The Humble Address of the Young Men of the Borough of Taunton.

To Edmund Prideaux *and* John Trenchard *Efqs; who were Unanimoufly chofen by the Inhabitants, to be the Reprefentatives of the faid Borough, to ferve in this Parliament, which is to fit at* Oxford, *March* 21, 168$\frac{0}{1}$.

SIRS,

THough we are not immediately concern'd in the *Electing* Members to ferve in Parliament ; yet being deeply fenfible that we fhall bear an equal fhare with others in the fame common *Danger*, and univerfal Slavery, which *Hell* and *Rome* have been, and ftill are with joint and unwearied Endeavours attempting to involve thefe Proteftant Nations in ; we cannot without charging our felves with unparallell'd Ingratitude, omit the returning you our hearty Thanks for that good and eminent Service you did both us and the Nation in the late diffolved Parliament ; That you did with fuch inflamed Zeal, with fuch undaunted Courage and Refolution, endeavour the Security of our *Religion, Liberty* and *Property*, againft that curfed Popifh Faction, who were the *Invaders* of them ; particularly we deem our felves infinitely obliged for the great Care you manifefted in the prefervation of His Majefty's Sacred Perfon, in your ftrenuous profecution of the Horrid and Damnable *Popifh Plot*, and in that your Attempts were fo Brisk and Vigorous for the preventing of an Arbitrary and Tyrannical Power (which we cannot but Unanimoufly abhor) Liberty and Property being an Inheritance, which as *Englifhmen*, we are born unto. And above all, we commend your Courage and Prudence in profecuting the happy Expedient of Excluding a *Popifh Succeffor*. from Inheriting the Imperial Crown of this Realm ; without which we judge it utterly impoffible, that the *Proteftant Religion* can be fecured to us, or our Necks can be long free from that *Romifh Yoke*, which neither we nor our Fathers were able to bear : And now fince it hath pleafed our Gracious King to iffue forth His Royal Proclamation, fignifying His pleafure to meet His People again in Parliament, We cannot but addrefs our felves to you the Reprefentatives of this Borough, humbly requefting, That you would, according to the Truft repofed in you, vigoroufly profecute thofe Counfels that have a Tendency to an happy Settlement of both in Church and State ; particularly, our Unanimous Requeft to you is,

1. That forafmuch as the late Horrid and Hellifh Plot hath according to the Votes of the preceding Parliaments, received Life and Countenance from *James* Duke of
York,

York, you would expedite a Bill for the utter incapacitating him ever to fway the Scepter of thefe Kingdoms, and that the Bill of *Affociation* may be annexed, whereby all his Majefty's Subjects may be enabled to *oppofe* him or any of his Accomplices, in cafe he fhould attempt to poffefs himfelf of the fame.

2. To take fuch Meafures as your Wifdom fhall agree upon for the *uniting* of the Proteftant Intereft in thefe Nations.

3. That the *Artillery* and *Militia* of the Nation be fettled in the hands of Men of known Integrity, Courage and Conduct; and that all Papifts and Popifhly affected Perfons now in Places of *publick* Truft, be difcharged (which if effected) may be a means to prevent thofe great *Fears* and *Jealoufies* which are apt otherwife to be nourifhed amongft us.

4. That you proceed to the Trial of the *Popifh Lords*, together with all other criminal Offenders, and go on fifting to the bottom of that execrable Plot, which hath been, and we muft fear *ftill* is carried on, to take away his Majefty's Life (whom God long preferve) to root out the Fundamental Laws of this Realm, as alfo to introduce Popery into the Church, and Tyranny into the State.

5. That you take Cognizance of the Illegal and Arbitrary Proceedings of Courts, as well *Ecclefiaftical* as *Civil*, as you have begun, that fo the *Laws* may not be wrefted againft the Proteftant Diffenters, nor ftretched in favour of *Popifh Recufants*: As alfo to confider the unprecedented *Finings* and *Imprifonings*, whereby many of his Majefty's truly loyal Subjects have been grievoufly oppreffed.

6. That you would fpeedily think of fome good Expedient for the regulating of Elections, as alfo for removing of thofe Oaths and Tefts, which have proved no fmall hinderance to divers worthy Proteftants, from being ufeful Inftruments in ferving their King and Country in *Church* and *State*.

Thefe things, worthy Sirs, we humbly offer to your Confiderations, not as *Directors*, but *Remembrancers*, out of a principle of loyal Zeal for his Majefty's Security and our Country's Tranquillity: And affure your felves in the Profecution of thefe truly noble Defigns, we will defend you with our Lives and Fortunes; accounting our deareft Blood a Tribute due to the Safety of our King and Country, when called for, in their Defence.

The Addrefs of the Ancient Town of Winchelfea, *(a Branch of the* Cinque-Ports,)

To their Barons Sir Stephen Lenord *and* Crefwel Draper *Efquire, elected in their Abfence, March 4. and ordered by the Mayor and Jurates to be prefented to them; the faid Mr.* Draper *ferving for them in the laft Parliament.*

Mr. *Draper*,

YOU may affure your felf, That we are very highly fatisfied with your unwearied Pains; as alfo, of your honeft Difcharge of the great Truft we repofed in you in the laft Parliament, by our hearty Thanks we now return you, and by our unanimous electing you again to ferve for us in the next Parliament to be holden at *Oxford*.

And

And Gentlemen, as for you both,

WE know you are ſo ſenſible of our Condition, that we need not tender you our Thoughts in many Particulars; only the Preſervation of his Sacred Majeſty's Perſon, our Religion, and Properties, which are of the greateſt Concern, and moſt dear unto us: And eſpecially in order thereunto, we commend unto you, and deſire you to uſe your utmoſt Endeavours,

1. That there may be a full and perfect Diſcovery of that moſt Helliſh and Damnable *Popiſh Plot* in *England* and *Ireland*, and all other *Sham-Plots,* which have been wickedly contriving and acting for many Years paſt.

2. That effectual Means be uſed for *uniting* all his Majeſty's Proteſtant Subjects againſt the common Enemy, both at home and abroad.

3. That all effectual Means and Ways may be provided to ſecure us againſt a *Popiſh Succeſſor* : and particularly againſt *James* Duke of *York.*

4. That you will endeavour, as far as in you lies, That a Law may be made for putting out *Free-Lands* and *Houſes* under a *voluntary Regiſter,* that thereby this Kingdom may be a juſt and honourable *Fund,* whereby Moneys may be taken up upon all urgent Occaſions, and ſo prevent the great Ruins we now lie under, for want thereof.

5. That you will uſe your utmoſt Endeavours to put a Brand upon thoſe abominable *Monſters,* which were the *Penſioners* in the late long *Parliament* ; that thereby the Generations to come may be deterr'd from attempting the like unheard of Villany.

6. That you will vigorouſly and carefully repreſent to the reſt of your *Fellow Members,* the preſent Condition of the *Royal Navy,* as alſo of the *Stores, Caſtles* and *Forts,* which are, under God, the Bulwarks of *England* ; and that ſuch effectual Ways and Means may be found out and proſecuted for the better ſecuring and improving the Navy ; as alſo, That none may be imployed therein, but ſuch Perſons who are of known Integrity and Loyalty both to the King and Nation ; and that all debauch'd and unskilful Perſons now employed, may be removed, and Men fearing God, loving Truth, and hating Covetouſneſs, may be put into their Places ; that ſo our preſent Fears may be abated, and thereby the dreadful growing Power of *France* may be timely check'd.

Gentlemen, In the purſuance of theſe good Ends, and ſuch other as you ſhall think conducing to the Happineſs of the King and Kingdom, we ſhall ſtand by you with our Lives and Fortunes.

There were many more Addreſſes *of like Nature and Purport, made from divers other Parts of the Realm ; true Copies of which are not come to our Hands: But, indeed, the Re-election of ſo many of the former Members, is it ſelf a* general Addreſs, *and loudly ſpeaks it the Voice of the People, which we truſt, will be ratified by the Voice of Heaven,* No Popiſh Succeſſor, *no* French Slavery

THE

THE
SPEECH

Of the Honourable

Henry Booth, Esq;

Spoken in *Chester*, *March* 2. 168⅘, at his being Elected one of the Knights of the Shire for that County, to serve in the Parliament, Summon'd to meet at *Oxford* the Twenty first of the said Month.

Gentlemen and Countrymen,

I Must acknowledge that God hath been good unto me from my Cradle to this Moment, and of all his Providences to me, there is none for which I have greater reason to bless his Holy Name, than that he hath enabled me to govern my self and Actions so, as to gain your good Opinion and Kindness ; and I cannot but own I have your favour accompanied with all the obliging Circumstances imaginable : for the first time that you were pleased to command my Service was in the Eighteen Years Parliament, upon the death of Sir *Foulk Lucy*, who had served you faithfully in that Parliament ; and though I was raw and unacquainted with those Affairs, and without any Tryal of my Integrity, you ventured all you had in my Hands at a time when *England* was in danger to be lost for want of a Vote : For that Parliament chiefly consisted of such as sold their Country for private Advantage, and would have sold their King too, if they could have made a better Market ; I served you some time in that Parliament, at last it was dissolved, and a new one called, and then as if you had approved of what I did, you thought fit to employ me again in that Service ; though you laid him aside who had been my Collegue. That Parliament continued not long, but was dissolved, and a new one called ; and then again a third time you thought me fit to represent you in Parliament, though, as you had done before, you set him aside whom you had sent along with me, and chose a new one in his room ; but why you did me so singular an Honour as to continue me in your Service two Parliaments together, and did not the like to the other Gentlemen, it is not for me to give the Reasons of it, those are best known to your selves. This is now the fourth time that I have waited on you on the like Occasion, and it is not a lessening of your former Kindness, that you have not changed my former Partner ; but rather a Confirmation of it, because that the first time you have continued him is when he appears to be of my Opinion ; and that which still adds weight to your Kindness is, that notwithstanding all this Stir, this Bustle, this unnecessary Charge and Expence, all the Stories by which I have been traduced, you have not prevailed upon to withdraw or diminish your Favour.

Gentlemen, I humbly beg your Patience to speak a few Words in answer to what they say of me, lest by Silence I may seem to cry Amen to their Reports and Stories. The first thing they reported, was, that I would not stand again, but would

decline

decline your Service: but withal they give no reason for it, only it is so because they said it; but what reason there is to contradict them now who said so the last time, and how true it was, you well remember. So that this being the second time that they have told you the self-same Falshoods, I hope for the future that others will believe them as little as you have done. It was reported that I was killed without giving any Reasons or Circumstances, and that to this also they expected an implicit Belief; I wish they are not for an implicit Faith in all things. It was truly an excellent Artifice to threap you out of your Votes; yet had I been kill'd, had it been for your Service, I should have thought myself well bestowed, and rather meet than avoid the Occasion of my Death. They tell you also that I am very obnoxious to the King, but they do not tell you that I am restored to my former Station of my Commission of the Peace, without seeking or desiring it; it cannot be imagined that his Majesty would be so gracious to a Man of whom he hath an ill Opinion, and it is a Reflection on his Majesty to think he will do a thing of that nature, out of any regard whatsoever, but when a thing carries its Weight and Reasons with it: so that by this you may discern how all their Reports are grounded, being rather the effects of their Desires than that the thing is truly so.

It seems the Gentlemen are much displeased that this County have frequently commanded those of my Family to serve them in Parliament, they call it an entailing upon the Family, but they are not pleased to vouchsafe the Reasons why the Son may not be imployed as well as the Father, in case he proves as fit for it; but the truth is, they would govern you, and are angry that you will be your own chusers; yet whether in this they design to serve you or their own ends, I submit to your Judgment: but as to my own particular, they think the County highly —— that I have served you in several Parliaments. Alas, Gentlemen, I know I am much inferiour in Parts and Learning to a great many, but in Faithfulness to your Interest, I will submit to no Man; but if you would observe it, they would impose that upon you which they would not have done to themselves. If they have a Servant who hath served them faithfully, they would not take a new one in his room because they have entertained him several Years; but you must change your Members as oft as you have new Parliaments, though they serve you well, and you ought to hate them because they would have it so; for they give no better Reasons for it; but whether they seek your Good or their private Regard, I leave to you to determine.

A reverend Gentleman at *Northwich* was pleased to tell you, that you must not chuse the same Members again, for if you did, the King and Parliament would not agree. I wonder how long he hath been one of the King's Cabinet Council, that he can tell so well before; if we may believe the greatest Ministers, they say otherwise, and that the King out of his gracious Disposition to the People will deny himself in that which is most dear, rather than break with his People: so that either he or they are out; and I am not convinc'd that he is infallible, and am apt to believe that he is in the wrong, since I have observed that they are for the most part mistaken, who take upon them to judge of matters when they are at so great a distance from *White-hall*, though it may be remembred that this Gentleman hath an Affair at *London*, that requires his Presence much oftner than he is pleased to afford it; and but that great Wits are unhappy in short Memories, that Gentleman could not have forgot that if the Parliament had continued, one of his Cloth had been severely reproved for meddling with matters not belonging to his Function, I mean Mr. *Thompson* of *Bristol*. And I hear there is so great a Number of the last House chosen, and like to be chosen, that his Fault will be remembred; which by the way, Gentlemen, is the Judgment of you in your Choice of me, you doing that which the rest of the Nation hath done; and where any change is, it is only to reject those who were Pensioners, or else vehemently suspected to be Mercenaries. But I could wish it were not the Opinion of too many, that the way to recommend themselves as true Sons of the Church, is to preach seldom, and meddle with State-Affairs much.

I hear some have taken Offence, because at *Northwich* I did commend the last House of Commons; truly, Gentlemen, I only gave it as my Opinion, and till the contrary doth appear, I must believe that for Riches, Integrity, Learning, Experience, and all things that are expedient for Members of that House, *England* never had

had a better; and why the Parliament was diſſolved I know not, for they who adviſed it, have neither dared to own it, nor the reaſons for it. There is one thing I could not but take notice of, in the Oppoſition that hath been made againſt me. If you will obſerve, they are the Perſons that were moſt inveterate one againſt another in the Diſpute between Sir *Philip Egerton* and my Couſin *Cholmondley*, but to oppoſe me they are united as one Man. If their new-made Friendſhip be ſincere, and they have this way to do it, I am very glad I have been the Occaſion of their Reconciliation; but if in this matter alone they are cemented, then it doth diſcover upon what Principles they act, and they are to be blamed, and not the Gentlemen who were ſet up to oppoſe me; for I believe them both to be very worthy Men; one of them is my Neighbour, and I will do him what Service I can; and for the other, he ſhall find me a Gentleman if he hath occaſion to uſe me.

Gentlemen, I have as well as I can repeated the particular Charges againſt me: I had but a ſhort time to recollect my ſelf; there remains yet a general Charge which I deſire to ſpeak to; and truly it is an heavy Charge, a Charge not to be born if I were guilty of it. They ſay I am an evil man as to the King and Church; I wiſh my Accuſers had either ſo much Power or Will to ſerve the King or Church as I have; and becauſe I do not know my ſelf to be guilty as to either of them, I hold my ſelf obliged to ſay ſomething in my Vindication.

I know not where I ever gave my Vote to impair the King's Prerogative; for this is my Principle, and ever hath been my Opinion, that the King's Prerogative, when rightly uſed, is for the Good and Benefit of the People; and the Liberties and Properties of the People are for the Support of the Crown and King's Prerogative, when they are not abuſed; but this bleſſed Harmony may ſometimes be diſordered either by the influence of ſome ill Counſel about the King, who to obtain their own Ends, do not care to ruin their King and Maſter; or elſe from the reſtleſs Spirits of ſome ambitious Men of broken Fortunes, who hope to repair them out of other Men's Eſtates. But it ſeems that I and the Houſe of Commons are much to blame, becauſe by one of our Votes we forbid the People to lend Money upon the Revenue by way of Anticipation: I never knew it was a Crime to paſs a Vote the Law had juſtified, for the Law will maintain every part of that Vote; and therefore I need ſay no more of it, and beſides this is not a Place to argue it in. As for my part, I'll do my beſt to preſerve the King's Prerogative, and the way to do it is neither to add nor to diminiſh; for to make a King abſolute, is not to ſupport, but pull down his Prerogative, for the King holds his Prerogative by the Law, and if that be deſtroy'd, the Title is to be diſputed by the Sword, and he that hath the ſharpeſt will prove to have the beſt Right. As to the Church I am for it as it is now eſtabliſhed under Epiſcopacy, but I would have them be ſuch as St. *Paul* to *Tim.* in his firſt Book and 3 *Chap.* deſcribes; and when they live accordingly, I have as great a Reverence for them as any Man; but when they live otherwiſe, they prove to be ——— and a Ruin to the Church, and ought to be abhorr'd of all true Chriſtians. And for Ceremonies, I take them not to be neceſſary to Salvation, but for Decency and Order ſake; and I conceive, this Ceremony is ſo much the more neceſſary, as it tends to the more effectual uniting of Proteſtants, and to preſerve Peace and Concord in the Church. I am of opinion the Church is in danger, and I'll do my beſt to ſupport it, and as the caſe ſtands we muſt either bring in Proteſtants or Papiſts; I am for bringing in Proteſtants, and that is my Crime; but you are pleaſed to judge me to be in the right. Now I will no longer doubt of my Opinion, I am ſure he that is againſt bringing in Proteſtants, is for bringing in Papiſts; and whether it be more profitable to ſupport the Church by uniting of thoſe who differ in Ceremonies, or thoſe who differ in Fundamentals, I think is very plain. Is he as the Man who, if his Houſe be falling, by reaſon of too much Weight upon the top, will lay more upon it, rather than prop it up and take off ſome of the Weight? So they who take the Church to conſiſt of Ceremonies, muſt pardon me that I am not of their opinion, ſince the Word of God warrants no ſuch thing, and my Reaſon tells me that they are too much intereſted in the cauſe to be fit Judges: for with them he is accounted a good Son of the Church, who keeps a great ſtir about Ceremonies, though he live ever ſo ill a Life, and perhaps is drunk when he performs his Devotion: but if a Man ſeem to be indifferent as to Ceremonies, and make

Q q   them

them no more than indeed they be, yet in Practice conforms more than he that makes a great noise about them, though he live never so Godly a Life, and as near as he can to the rule of God's Word, yet he is a Fanatick and an Enemy to the Church; but God Almighty tells us he will have Mercy and not Sacrifice.

Gentlemen, They who accuse me for an Enemy to the King and Church, have left you out of the Story; but I hope I shall not forget you, but remember on whose Errand I am sent: and as I have hitherto stuck to your Interest, I hope nothing will draw me aside from it, and if I know my own Heart, I am persuaded that neither Rewards, Threats, Hopes nor Fears will prevail upon me. I desire nothing but to promote God's Glory and the Interest of the King and People; and if it shall please God to let me see the Protestant Religion and Government established, I shall think I have lived long enough, and I shall be willing at that instant to resign my Breath. Gentlemen, I thought good to say this to you, and I thank you for your Patience, and hope I shall so behave myself in your Service, that I shall make it appear I am sensible of the Honour you have done me.

I humbly thank you all.

An Account of the Proceedings at the Sessions for the City of Westminster, *against* Thomas Whitfield, *Scrivener*; John Smallbones, *Woodmonger; and* William Laud, *Painter; for Tearing a Petition prepared to be presented to the King's Majesty, for the Sitting of the Parliament. With an Account of the said Petition, presented on the* 13*th instant, and His Majesty's Gracious Answer.*

Vide the Resolutions of the Law, Coke. Jurisdict. of Courts 79. Hobart. 220. Vel Magna Chart. Ex l. Spencer 51. Vide the Proclamations of K. Charles I.

IT being the undoubted Right of the Subjects of *England*, and warranted by the Law of the Land, and the general Practice of all former Times, in an humble manner to apply themselves to His Majesty, in the Absence of Parliaments, *by Petition; for the Redress of their Grievances, and for the obtaining such things as they apprehend necessary or beneficial, to the safety and well-being of the Nation:* And it being their Duty to which they are bound, by the express words of the Oath of Allegiance,

* I do Swear from my Heart, That I will bear Faith and true Allegiance to His Majesty, His Heirs, and Successors, and Him and Them will defend to the uttermost of my Power against all Conspiracies and Attempts whatsoever, which shall be made against His or Their Persons, Their Crown and Dignity. And will do my best endeavour to disclose and make known unto His Majesty, His Heirs and Successors, all Treasons and Traitorous Conspiracies, which I shall know or hear of, to be against Him or any of Them.

* to represent to him any danger which they apprehend Threatening His Royal Person or His Government; divers Persons in and about the City of *Westminster*, considering the too apparent and unspeakable Danger His Majesty and His Kingdoms are in, from the hellish Plots and villainous Conspiracies of the *Bloody Papists and their Adherents*; and conceiving no sufficient (or at least so fit) Remedy could be provided against it, but by the Parliament, by whom alone several Persons accused of these accursed Designs, can be brought to Trial, did prepare and sign a Petition; humbly representing to His Majesty, the imminent Danger His Royal Person, the Protestant Religion, and the Government of this Nation were in, from that most damnable and hellish Popish Plot, *branched forth into several the most horrid Villanies*; for which several of the principal Conspirators stand impeached by Parliament: and thereby humbly praying that the Parliament might sit upon the 26th of *January, to try the Offenders, and to redress the important Grievances, no otherwise to be redressed.* Of which *Thomas Whitfield, John Smallbones, and William Laud,* Inhabitants in *Westminster,* taking notice, upon the 20th day of *December* last, they sent to Mr. *William Horsley,* who had signed and promoted the Petition, and in whose custody it was, to bring or send it to them, for that they desired to sign it. And thereupon Mr. *Horsley* attended them, and producing the Petition, in which many Persons had joined, he delivered it at their request to be by them read and signed; but Mr. *Whitfield* immediately tore it in pieces, and threw
it

it towards the Fire; and *Smallbones* catching it up, said, That he would not take 10 s. for the Names: and then they declared that they sent for it for that very purpose, and owned themselves all concerned in the Design.

Upon Mr. *Horsley*'s complaint hereof to a Justice of the Peace, a Warrant was granted against them, and they being taken thereupon, after examination of the matter, were bound to appear and answer it at the next Quarter Sessions of the Peace for the City of *Westminster*; and upon *Friday* the 9th of *January* instant the Sessions being holden, and there being present several Justices of the Peace that are eminent Lawyers, the matter was brought before them, and the Grand Jury indicted the said *Whitfield*, *Smallbones*, and *Laud* as followeth, (*viz.*)

The City, Borough, *and* Town *of* Westminster *in the County of* Middlesex.

" THE Jurors for our Sovereign Lord the King, *upon their Oath do present, that*
" *whereas the Subjects and Liege People of the Kings and Queens of this Realm of*
" England, *by the Laws and Customs of the Realm, have used and been accustomed to re-*
" *present their Publick Grievances by Petition, or by any other submissive way:* And that
" the 20th. day of *December* in the one and thirtieth Year of the Reign of our Sovereign
" Lord *Charles* the Second, by the Grace of God, of *England, Scotland, France* and
" *Ireland* King, Defender of the Faith, &c. at the Parish of *St. Martin*'s in the *Fields*,
" within the Liberty of the Dean and Chapter of the Collegiate Church of St.
" *Peter*, of the City, Borough and Town of *Westminster* in the County of *Middle-*
" *sex*; a *Petition* written in Paper, *was prepared and subscribed* with the Hands of
" divers the said King's Subjects and Liege People, (to the Jury unknown) and to
" our said Sovereign Lord King *Charles* the Second directed, and to our said Sove-
" reign Lord the King to be presented and delivered; *by which Petition it was*
" *shown, that whereas there had been and was a most damnable Plot against the Royal Per-*
" *son of our said Sovereign Lord the King, the Protestant Religion, and well-established*
" *Government of this Realm; for which Plot several of the Principal Conspirators were*
" *impeached by Parliament, and whereby it was humbly prayed that the Parliament which*
" *was prorogued to the 26th day of* January *next ensuing in the said Year, might then*
" *sit to try the Offenders, and to redress the pressing Grievances not otherwise to be redressed.*
" And that *Thomas Whitfield*, late of the said Parish of *St. Martin*'s in the *Fields*, in
" the Liberty aforesaid, and the County aforesaid, Yeoman; *John Smallbones*, late
" of the said Parish, within the Liberty aforesaid, in the County aforesaid, Wood-
" monger; and *William Laud*, late of the Parish aforesaid, in the County afore-
" said, Yeoman; *being Persons ill-affected, and Contriving*, Devising and Intending, as
" much as in them lay, *to hinder the sitting of the said Parliament, as was prayed by the*
" *said Petition, and also to hinder the Trial of the said Offenders, and redressing the said*
" *Grievances*, the said 20th day of *December* in the said one and thirtieth Year of the
" Reign of our said Sovereign Lord the King, as Rioters and Disturbers of the
" Peace of our Sovereign Lord the King, for the disturbing of the Peace of our
" said Sovereign Lord the King, with Force and Arms at the said Parish within the
" Liberty aforesaid, in the County aforesaid, Unlawfully and Riotously did assem-
" ble themselves; and being so then and there assembled, with Force and Arms then
" and there *unlawfully, riotously and injuriously, the said Petition* being delivered by one
" *William Horsley* to them, the said *Thomas Whitfield, John Smallbones* and *William Laud*
" at their request, and for the subscribing their Names thereunto if they should think
" fit, *did tear in pieces, in contempt of our said Sovereign Lord the King*, and of his Laws,
" to the evil Example of all others in the like Cases offending, and against the Peace
" of our said Sovereign Lord the King, his Crown and Dignity.

The

The Names of the *Grand-Jury* that found the Bill, are thefe,

William Jacob,	*Edward Whitefoot*,
Thomas Trevor,	*John Gentle*,
Erafmus Browne,	*Thomas Harris*,
Henry Dugley,	*William Fortune*,
Richard Streete,	*Roger Higdon*,
John Henly,	*James Harrold*,
John Wefton,	*Cornelius Rickfield*,
Martin Frogg,	*George Wright*, Apothecary,
John Pierce,	*Walter Wright*,
Robert Binke,	*Adam Langley*.
Nathaniel Wilkinfon,	

Upon *Wednefday* the 7th of this inftant *January*, many Gentlemen and eminent Citizens, who had been concerned for managing the Petition for the fitting of the Parliament, upon the 26th inftant, met together, and agreed upon the method of finifhing the fame, and of nominating fit Perfons for the prefenting it to His Majefty, which being accordingly done; thefe Gentlemen following, *(viz.)*

Sir *Gilbert Gerrard*, Baronet, Son in Law to the late Bifhop of *Durham*,

Francis Charlton, Efq;	*Ellis Crifpe*, Efq;
John Ellis, Efq;	*Anthony Selby*, Efq;
John Smith, Efq;	*Henry Afhurft*, Efq;
Johnfon of *Stepney*, Efq;	*Tho. Smith*, Efq;

Gentlemen of good Worth and Eftates, and feveral of whom have been eminent Sufferers for His Majefty, did this 13th of *January*, attend His Majefty with it at *Whitehall*; when being introduced into his Royal Prefence, Sir *Gilbert Gerrard* kneeling, prefented this Petition;

To the King's moft Excellent Majefty,

The humble Petition of Your Majefty's moft Dutiful and Loyal Subjects, Inhabitants in and about the City of London, *whofe Names are hereunder fubfcribed;*

Sheweth,

" THAT whereas there has been, and ftill is a moft damnable and hellifh *Popifh*
" *Plot*, branched forth into the moft horrid Villanies againft Your Majefty's
" moft Sacred Perfon, the *Proteftant* Religion, and the well-eftablifh'd Government
" of this Your Realm, for which feveral of the principal Confpirators ftand now im-
" peached by Parliament:
" Therefore in fuch a time, when Your Majefty's Royal Perfon, as alfo the *Pro-*
" *teftant* Religion, and the Government of this Nation, are thus in moft imminent
" Danger:

We Your Majefty's moft Dutiful and Obedient Subjects, in the deepeft fenfe of our Duty, and Allegiance to Your Majefty, do moft humbly and earneftly pray, That the Parliament, which is prorogued until the 26th day of *January*, may then fit, to try the Offenders, and to redrefs all our moft important Grievances, no otherways to be redreffed.

And your Petitioners fhall ever pray for Your
Majefty's long and profperous Reign.

And
4

And expreſſed himſelf to this effect, Sir, *I have a Petition from many thouſands of your Majeſty's Dutiful and Loyal Subjects, in and about your City of* London, *which I humbly preſent in their Names, and deſire your Majeſty would be pleaſed to read it.*

To which His Majeſty gave this gracious Anſwer, *I know the Subſtance of it already, I am Head of the Government, and will take care of it*; and then received the Petition, it being a great Roll of above 100 Yards in length, and carried it away in his Hand.

The Judgment and Decree of the Univerſity of Oxford, *paſs'd in their* Convocation, July 21. 1683. *againſt certain pernicious Books and damnable Doctrines, deſtructive to the ſacred Perſons of Princes, their State and Government, and of all Human Society.*

Publiſhed by Command.

ALtho' the barbarous Aſſaſſination lately enterprized againſt the Perſon of his ſacred Majeſty and his royal Brother, engage all our Thoughts to reflect with utmoſt Deteſtation and Abhorrence of that execrable Villainy hateful to God and Man; and pay our due Acknowledgments to the Divine Providence, which by extraordinary Methods brought it to paſs, that the *Breath of our Noſtrils, the Anointed of the Lord*, is not taken in the Pit which was prepared for him; and that under his Shadow we continue to live, and injoy the Bleſſings of his Government: Yet, notwithſtanding we find it to be a neceſſary Duty at this time to ſearch into and lay open thoſe impious Doctrines, which having of late been ſtudiouſly diſſeminated, gave riſe and growth to thoſe nefarious Attempts: and paſs upon them our ſolemn publick Cenſure and Decree of Condemnation.

Therefore to the Honour of the holy and undivided Trinity, the preſervation of catholick Truth in the Church; and that the King's Majeſty may be ſecur'd from the Attempts of open and bloody Enemies, and the Machinations of treacherous Hereticks and Schiſmaticks: We the Vice-Chancellor, Doctors, Proctors, and Maſters Regent and not Regent, met in Convocation in the accuſtom'd manner, Time and Place, on *Saturday* the 21 of *July* in the Year 1683. concerning certain Propoſitions contained in divers Books and Writings publiſhed in *Engliſh*, and alſo in the *Latin* Tongue, repugnant to the holy Scriptures, Decrees of Councils, Writings of the Fathers, the Faith and Profeſſion of the Primitive Church; and alſo deſtructive of the kingly Government, the ſafety of his Majeſty's Perſon, the publick Peace, the Laws of Nature, and Bonds of human Society: By our unanimous Aſſent and Conſent have decreed and determin'd in manner and form following:

Propoſition 1. All Civil Authority is derived originally from the People.

2. There is a mutual Compact, tacit or expreſs, between a Prince and his Subjects; and that if he perform not his Duty, they are diſcharg'd from theirs.

3. That if lawful Governors become Tyrants, or govern otherwiſe than by the Laws of God and Man they ought to do, they forfeit the Right they had unto their Government.

　Lex Rex. Buchanan de Jure Regni. Vindiciæ contra tyrannos. Bellarmine de Conciliis, de Pontifice. Milton. Goodwin. Baxter, H. C.

R r

4. The

4. The Sovereignty of *England* is in the three Estates, *viz.* King, Lords, and Commons. The King has but a co-ordinate Power, and may be over-ruled by the other two.

    Lex Rex. Hunton of a limited and mix'd Monarchy. Baxter H. C. Polit. Catech.

5. Birthright and proximity of Blood give no title to Rule or Government, and it is lawful to preclude the next Heir from his Right of Succession to the Crown.

    Lex Rex. Hunt's Postscript. Doleman. History of Succession. Julian the Apostate. Mene Tekel.

6. It is lawful for Subjects, without the Consent, and against the Command of the supreme Magistrate, to enter into Leagues, Covenants, and Associations, for defence of themselves and their Religion.

    Solemn League and Covenant. Late Association.

7. Self-preservation is the fundamental Law of Nature, and supersedes the Obligation of all others, whenever they stand in competition with it.

    Hobbs de Cive. Leviathan.

8. The Doctrine of the Gospel concerning patient suffering of Injuries, is not inconsistent with violent resisting of the higher Powers in case of Persecution for Religion.

    Lex Rex. Julian Apostat. Apolog. Relat.

9. There lies no Obligation upon Christians to *Passive Obedience*, when the Prince commands any thing against the Laws of our Country: And the Primitive Christians chose rather to die than resist, because Christianity was not yet settled by the Laws of the Empire.

    Julian Apostate.

10. Possession and Strength give a right to govern, and Success in a Cause or Enterprize proclaims it to be lawful and just; to pursue it, is to comply with the Will of God, because it is to follow the Conduct of his Providence.

    Hobbs. Owen's Sermon before the Regicides, Jan. 31. 1648. *Baxter, Jenkin's Petition,* Octob. 1651.

11. In the State of Nature there is no difference between good and evil, right and wrong; the State of Nature is a State of War, in which every Man hath a right to all Things.

12. The Foundation of civil Authority is this natural Right, which is not given, but left to the supreme Magistrate upon Men's entring into Societies, and not only a foreign Invader, but a domestick Rebel, puts himself again into a State of Nature, to be proceeded against, not as a Subject but an Enemy: And consequently acquires by his Rebellion the same right over the Life of his Prince, as the Prince for the most heinous Crimes has over the Life of his own Subjects.

13. Every Man, after his entring into a Society, retains a right of defending himself against Force, and cannot transfer that right to the Commonwealth, when he consents to that Union whereby a Commonwealth is made; and in case a great many Men together have already resisted the Commonwealth, for which every one of them expecteth Death, they have Liberty then to join together to assist and defend one another. Their bearing of Arms subsequent to the first Breach of their Duty, though it be to maintain what they have done, is no new unjust Act; and if it be only to defend their Persons, is not unjust at all.

14. An Oath superadds no Obligation to Pact, and a Pact obliges no further than it is credited: And, consequently, if a Prince gives any Indication that he does not believe the Promises of Fealty and Allegiance, made by any of his Subjects, they

are

are thereby freed from their Subjection; and, notwithstanding their Pacts and Oaths, may lawfully rebel against, and destroy their Sovereign.
Hobbs de Cive. Leviathan.

15. If a People that by Oath and Duty are oblig'd to a Sovereign shall sinfully dispossess him, and, contrary to their Covenants, chuse and covenant with another; they may be obliged by their latter Covenant, notwithstanding their former.
Baxter H. C.

16. All Oaths are unlawful, and contrary to the Word of God.
Quakers.

17. An Oath obliges not in the Sense of the Imposer, but the Takers.
Sheriffs Case.

18. Dominion is founded in Grace.

19. The Powers of this World are Usurpations upon the Prerogative of Jesus Christ, and it is the Duty of God's People to destroy them, in order to the setting Christ upon his Throne.
Fifth-Monarchy Men.

20. The Presbyterian Government is the Scepter of Christ's Kingdom, to which Kings as well as others are bound to submit; and the King's Supremacy in Ecclesiastical Affairs asserted by the Church of *England* is injurious to Christ, the sole King and Head of his Church.
Altare Damascenum. Apolog. relat. Hist. Indulgen. Cartwright. Travers.

21. It is not lawful for Superiors to impose any thing in the Worship of God that is not antecedently necessary.

22. The Duty of not offending a weak Brother is inconsistent with all human Authority of making Laws concerning indifferent Things.
Protestant Reconciler.

23. Wicked Kings and Tyrants ought to be put to death, and if the Judges and inferior Magistrates will not do their Office, the Power of the Sword devolves to the People; if the major Part of the People refuse to exercise this Power, then the Ministers may excommunicate such a King, after which it is lawful for any of the Subjects to kill him, as the People did *Athaliah*, and *Jehu Jezabel.*
Buchanan. Knox. Goodman. Gilby. Jesuits.

24. After the sealing of the Scripture-Canon, the People of God in all Ages are to expect new Revelations for a rule of their Actions*; and it is lawful for a private Man, having an inward Motion from God, to kill a Tyrant†.
* *Quakers and other Enthusiasts.* † *Goodman.*

25. The Example of *Phineas* is to us instead of a Command; for what God has commanded or approved in one Age, must needs oblige in all.
Goodman. Knox. Naphtali.

26. King *Charles* the First was lawfully put to death, and his Murtherers were the blessed Instruments of God's Glory in their Generation.
Milton. Goodwin. Owen.

27. King *Charles* the First made War upon his Parliament; and in such a Case the King may not only be resisted, but he ceaseth to be King.
Baxter.

We

We decree, judge and declare all and every of these Propositions to be false, seditious and impious; and most of them to be also Heretical and Blasphemous, infamous to Christian Religion, and destructive of all Government in Church and State.

We farther decree that the Books which contain the foresaid Propositions and impious Doctrines, are fitted to deprave good Manners; corrupt the Minds of unwary Men, stir up Seditions and Tumults, overthrow States and Kingdoms, and lead to Rebellion, Murder of Princes, and Atheism it self: And therefore we interdict all Members of the University from the reading the said Books, under the Penalties in the Statutes exprest.

We also order the before recited Books to be publickly burnt, by the Hand of our Marshal in the Court of our Schools.

Likewise we order that in perpetual Memory hereof, these our Decrees shall be entred into the Registry of our Convocation, and that Copies of them being communicated to the several Colleges and Halls within this University, they be there publickly affixt in the Libraries, Refectories, or other fit Places, where they may be seen and read of all.

Lastly, We command and strictly enjoin all and singular Readers, Tutors, Catechists and others, to whom the care and trust of Institution of Youth is committed, that they diligently instruct and ground their Scholars in that most necessary Doctrine, which in a manner is the Badge and Character of the Church of *England*, of submitting to every Ordinance of Man for the Lord's sake, whether it be to the King as Supreme, or unto Governors as unto them that are sent by him, for the Punishment of evil Doers, and for the Praise of them that do well: Teaching that this Submission and Obedience is to be clear, absolute and without exception of any State or Order of Men: Also that all Supplications, Prayers, Intercessions and giving of Thanks be made for all Men, for the King and all that are in Authority, that we may lead a quiet and peaceable Life in all Godliness and Honesty; for this is good and acceptable in the Sight of God our Saviour. And in especial manner that they press and oblige them humbly to offer their most ardent and daily Prayers at the Throne of Grace for the Preservation of our Sovereign Lord King *Charles*, from the Attempts of open Violence, and secret Machinations of perfidious Traitors: That he the Defender of the Faith, being safe under the defence of the most High, may continue his Reign on Earth, till he exchange it for that of a late and happy Immortality.

THE
4

The Cafe of the Earl of Argyle : *or, An exact and full Account of his Trial, Efcape, and Sentence. As likewife a Relation of feveral Matters of Fact, for better clearing of the faid Cafe.*

Edinburgh, 30. *May,* 1682.

SIR,

THE Cafe of the late Earl of *Argyle*, which, even before the Procefs laid againft him, you was earneft to know, was at firft, I thought, fo plain, that I needed not, and grew afterwards fo exceedingly myfterious, that I could not, for fome time, give you fo perfect an Account of it, as I wifhed: But this Time being ftill no lefs proper, the exactnefs of my Narrative will, I hope, excufe all Delays.

The defign againft him being now fo clear, and the Grounds founded on it fo flender, that to fatisfy all unbyafs'd Perfons of his Integrity, there needs no more, but barely to reprefent Matter of Facts; I fhould think fhame to fpend fo many Words, either on Arguments, or Relation, were it not left to Strangers fome Myftery might be fufpected to remain concealed: And therefore to make plain what they can hardly believe, though we clearly fee it.

At his Royal Highnefs's Arrival in *Scotland*, the Earl was one of the firft to wait upon him, and until the Meeting of our laft Parliament, the World believed, the Earl was as much in his Highnefs's favour, as any intrufted in his Majefty's Affairs, in this Kingdom.

When it was refolved, and His Majefty moved to call the Parliament, the Earl was in the Country, and at the opening of it, he appeared as forward as any in His Majefty's and his Highnefs's Service; but it had not fat many Days when a Change was noticed in his Highnefs, and the Earl obferved to decline in his Highnefs's favour.

In the beginning of the Parliament, the Earl was appointed one of the *Lords of the Articles*, to prepare Matters for the Parliament, and named by his Highnefs to be one of a *Committee of the Articles* for Religion, which, by the cuftom of all *Scots* Parliaments, and His Majefty's Inftructions to his Commiffioners, at this time, was the firft thing treated of: In this Committee there was an Act prepared for fecuring the Proteftant Religion; which Act did ratify the Act approving the *Confeffion of Faith*, and alfo the Act containing the *Coronation Oath*, appointed by feveral ftanding Acts of Parliament, to be taken by all our Kings, and Regents, before their entry to the Exercife of the Government.

This Act was drawn fomewhat lefs binding upon the Succeffor, as to his own Profeffion, but full as ftrictly tying him to maintain the Proteftant Religion, in the publick Profeffion thereof, and to put the Laws concerning it in Execution, and alfo appointing a further Teft, befide the former, to exclude Papifts from places of publick Truft; and becaufe the Fines of fuch as fhould act, without taking the *Teft*, appeared no better than difcharged, if falling in the Hands of a Popifh Succeffor, and *fome* accounting any Limitation worfe than an Exclufion, and all being content to put no Limitation on the Crown, fo it might confift with the Safety, and Security of the Proteftant Religion; it was ordained, that all fuch Fines and Forfaultures fhould appertain the one half to the Informers, and the other half fhould be beftowed on pious Ufes, according to certain Rules expreffed in the Act.

But this Act being no wife pleafing to *fome*, it was laid afide, and the Committee difcharged any more to meet; and inftead of this Act, there was brought into the Parliament, at the fame time, with the *Act of Succeffion*, a fhort Act, ratifying all former Acts made for the Security of the Proteftant Religion, which is the firft of the printed Acts of this Parliament.

At the paffing of this Act, the Earl propofed that thefe Words, *And all Acts againft Popery*, might be added, which was oppofed by the Advocate, and fome of the Clergy, as unneceffary; but the Motion being feconded by Sir *George Lockhart*, and the then Prefident of the Seffion, now turned out, it was yielded to, and added without a Vote: and this Act being ftill not thought fufficient, and feveral Members defiring other additions, and other Acts, a promife was made by his Royal Highnefs, in open Parliament, that Time and Opportunity fhould be given, to bring in any other Act, which fhould be thought neceffary for further fecuring the Proteftant Religion. But though feveral Perfons, both before and after paffing the Act for the *Teft* (here fubjoined) did give in Memorials, and Overtures; yet they were never fuffered to be read, either in *Articles*, or *Parliament*, but in place of all, this Act for the *Teft* was ftill obtruded, and nothing

S f

of

of that nature fuffered to be heard, after once that Act paft, though even at paffing it the Promife was renewed.

As for the *Teft*, it was firft brought into the Parliament without mentioning the *Confeffion of Faith*, and after feveral hours debate, for adding the *Confeffion of Faith*, and many other Additions and Alterations, it was paft at the firft prefenting, albeit it was earneftly preft by near half the Parliament, that it might be delayed till next Morning; the Draught being fo much changed and interlined, that many, even of the moft engaged in the Debate, did not fufficiently underftand it, and though they took Notes, knew not precifely how it ftood. And this was indeed the Earl's Cafe in particular, and the caufe why in voting, he did forbear either to approve, or difapprove.

His Part in the debate was, that in the entry of it, he faid, that he thought as few Oaths fhould be required as could be, and thefe as fhort and clear as poffible: That it was his humble Opinion, that a very fmall Alteration in thefe Acts, which had been ufed thefe twenty Years, might ferve, for it was manifeft, and he attefted the whole Parliament upon it, *That the Oath of Allegiance and Declaration* had effectually debarred all Fanaticks from getting into places of Truft all that time: It was true, fome Papifts had fwallowed the Oath of Allegiance, and therefore a word or two only of Addition, to guard againft them, was all he judged neceffary.

And thereafter, where in the clofe of the Act, *The King's Sons, and Brothers*, were intended to be difpenfed with from taking the *Teft*, he oppofed the Exception, and faid, it was our Happinefs that King and People were of one Religion, and that they were fo by Law: That he hoped the Parliament would do nothing to loofe what was faft, nor open a gap for the royal Family to differ in Religion, their Example was of great confequence, one of them was as a thoufand, and would draw the more Followers, if once it appeared to the People that it were honourable, and a Privilege to be of another Religion: And therefore he wifhed if any Exception were, it might be particular for his Royal Highnefs; but his Highnefs himfelf oppofing this, the Earl concluded with his fear, that if this Exception did pafs, it would do more hurt to the Proteftant Religion than all the reft of that Act, and many other Acts could do good.

Whilft thefe Acts about Religion were in agitation, his Highnefs told the Earl one day in private, to beware of himfelf, for the Earl of *Errol*, and others, were to give in a Bill to the Parliament, to get him made liable to fome Debts they pretended to be Cautioners in for his Father, and thofe that were moft forward in His Majefty's Service muft be had a care of. The Earl faid, he knew there was no Ground for any *fuch Bill*, and he hoped neither the Earl of *Errol*, nor any other fhould have any advantage of him, upon any Head relating to His Majefty's Service. His Highnefs told others likewife, he had given the Earl good Advice.

But fhortly after the above-mentioned Debates, there were two *Bills* given into the Meeting of the *Articles* againft the Earl; one by the Earl of *Errol*, the other by his Majefty's Advocate, who alledged he did it by Command, for otherwife he acknowledged it was without his Line. The Earl of *Errol's* Claim was, that the Earl of *Argyle* might be declared liable to relieve him and others of a Debt, wherein they alledged, they ftood bound as Cautioners, for the late Marquefs of *Argyle*, the Earl's Father. To which the Earl anfwered, that he had not got his Father's whole Eftate, but only a Part of it, and that exprefly burdened with all the Debts he was liable to pay; whereof this pretended Debt was none, and that the Marquefs of *Huntly*, who at that time was owing to the Marquefs of *Argyle* 35000 *l.* Sterl. had got 4000 *l.* Sterl. of yearly Rent, out of the Marquefs of *Argyle's* forfaulture, without the burden of any Debt; fo that both by Law, and Equity, the Earl could not be liable, the Marquefs of *Huntly*, and not he having got that which fhould bear *this Relief*, and which fhould indeed have paid the far greateft part of the Marquefs of *Argyle's* Debt, the fame having been undertaken for *Huntly* by *Argyle*, either as Cautioner for *Huntly*, or to raife Money to pay his Debt: Befides that the Earl of *Errol* can never make it appear, that he, or his Predeceffors, were bound for the Marquefs of *Argyle* in the third part of the Sums he acclaims; yet fome were much inclined to believe *Errol* on his bare Affertion.

His Majefty's Advocate's claim was, to take from the Earl *his heritable Offices of Sheriff*, &c. efpecially that of *Juftice-General of Argyle-Shire*, the Ifles, and other Places, which laft is neverthelefs only a part of the general Jufticiary of all *Scotland*, granted to his Predeceffors, fome hundred of Years ago, for honourable, and onerous caufes, and conftantly enjoyed by them until exprefly furrendered, in his late Majefty's hands, for a new Grant of the above-mentioned *Jufticiary of Argyle*, &c. And this *new Grant* was alfo confirmed by many Acts of Parliament, and particularly by his Majefty's Royal Father, of bleffed Memory, in the Parliament holden by him *Anno* 1633. As likewife by his Majefty that now is (whom
God

God long preserve) his *new Gift and Charter*, after several Debates before him in *Anno* 1663. and 1672. Which *new Gifts and Charters* were again ratified by a special Instruction from His Majesty in the Parliament 1672. So that albeit several *late Gifts of Regality* granted to the Marquess of *Athol*, Marquess of *Queensberry*, and others, may be questioned, because granted since the Acts of Parliament discharging all *such Gifts* in time coming; yet the Earl of *Argyle*'s Rights are good, as being both of a far different nature, and granted long before the said Acts of Parliament, and in effect the Earl his Rights are rather confirmed by these prohibitive Acts, because both anterior to, and excepted from them, as appears by the Act *Salvo Jure* 1633. wherein the Earl's Rights are particularly and fully excepted in the body of the printed Act.

When these things appeared so plain as not to be answered, it was alledged that upon the forfaulture of the late Marquess of *Argyle*, his Estate *was annexed* to the Crown, and so could not be gifted to the Earl by his Majesty, (wherein they soon discovered a design to forfault him, if any Pretence could be found.) But the *Act of Forfaulture* being read, and containing no such thing, but on the contrary a clear Power left to his Majesty to dispose of the whole, and the Earl telling them plainly, that these that were most active to have his Father forfaulted, were very far from desiring his Estate *to be annexed* to the Crown, seeing it was in expectation of *Gifts* out of it they were so diligent, that pretence of the *Annexation* was past from, but yet the Design was no wise given over, for there was a Proposition made, and a Vote carried in the *Articles*, that a *Committee* should be appointed with parliamentary Power, to meet in the Intervals of Parliament, to determine all Controversies could be moved against any of the Earl's Rights; which was a very extraordinary Device, and plainly carried by extraordinary Influences.

Upon this the Earl applyed to the Parliament, where this Vote was to be brought, and having informed the Members of his Right, and the consequences of such a new Judicature, he had good hope to get the Vote reversed, when his Royal Highness on second Thoughts judged it fit to put a stop to it, and excused himself, saying, it was his not being acquainted, and but lately in Affairs, had made him go along with it; for he found it did plainly impugn His Majesty's Prerogative, and might be of ill consequence, and indeed it is plain enough. It would have exposed the Marquess of *Huntly*'s Gift, which proceeded on the same Forfaulture, as well as the Earl of *Argyle*'s to the same, and far greater Hazard, as some came to be sensible when they heard all. You see here at what rate the Earl was pursued, and on what Grounds, before his taking of the Test came in hand.

After the Parliament was adjourned, there was a new Design to apply to His Majesty for a *Commission* of the same nature, for reviewing all the Earl's Rights, and to deprive him of his heritable Offices, and, if possible, to burden him with more Debts than his Estate was worth.

Upon which, the Earl waited on his Highness, and informed him more particularly, offering to make it appear, by unquestionable Rights and Evidences, that his Estate was not subject to any such Review, as was intended, and that it might breed the Earl great trouble, but could have no effect in Law. To which his Highness *answered*, That a review could do no hurt. The Earl *said*, if a Commission for a review were granted, something must be intended, and something must be done, and it was very like that some of these put into such a Commission would be his Enemies, at least small Friends, and therefore intreated that if any intended to quarrel his Rights, they and he and all their Debates might be remitted to the *ordinary Judicatories*: And indeed he had reason to desire, it might be so, the *ordinary Judicatories* being established by the ancient Laws of the Kingdom, not in order nor with respect to particular Causes and Persons, but for the general, equal and impartial Administration of Justice to all. Whereas the granting particular *Commissions*, for trying and judging such and such Cases, and Persons, cannot but expose to the just contrary Inconveniences; there being certainly a vast difference betwixt a Man's *finding* a Judge indifferently constitute, and his *having* one expresly and particularly appointed, for his single Affair, who might possibly think himself commissionate, rather to serve a turn in an arbitrary way, than to administer fair Justice: But all this prevailed not. Only *his Highness said*, the Commission should not be expede until the Earl knew the Names of the Persons insert in it. Whereunto the *Earl answered*, that there might be many Persons, against whom he could make no legal Exception, whom yet he might have very good Reason to decline to be his particular Judges, and to have his Rights taken from the ordinary Judges, and committed to their Examination, and all he might possibly gain *by excepting* would be to irritate; *adding*, that as to his heritable Offices, he had undoubtedly right to them, and they were rather honourable, than of advantage, that his Family had them for faithful services to the Crown; and because they had served more faithfully than their Neighbours, and been more useful than others, in keeping the

Country

4

Country in Peace, from Thieves and Robbers, therefore all the *broken Men* and their *Patrons* were Enemies to him, and his Family, and defirous to have thefe Offices out of his hand ; but he refolved to do as he had always done, to put himfelf in *His Majefty's Will*, and if His Majefty were refolved to have back all heritable Offices, and fhould think fit after hearing him to have back his, His Majefty fhould have them, either freely or for a juft value: For though they rendered the Earl no free yearly Rent, as the Earl ufed them, yet he might be a Sufferer in the want of them, if the Country were left open to Thieves and Robbers, which he hoped His Majefty would repair. His Rights (as he had faid in Parliament) were unqueftionable, and oftentimes confirmed : Yet he was willing to furrender them all on his Knee to His Majefty, but was not willing to have them torn from him with an Affront by any other.

Upon this, his Highnefs was pleafed to allow the Earl a time to go to the Country, to bring his Papers, and he was put in hopes no *Commiffion* fhould pafs till his Return, which was indeed obferved.

In the mean time, the Earl did write to the *Earl of Murray*, His Majefty's Secretary, that he might have leave to wait upon His Majefty, which His Majefty did gracioufly and readily grant ; the Earl purpofing at his return to *Edinburgh*, to beg the fame Favour of his Highnefs. But he found this Motion more fatal to him than he could have at firft expected fo innocent a Defign could prove: For it was at firft told him, he could not have Accefs to kifs His Majefty's Hand without taking the *Teft* ; then it dropt out, that it was ill taken, His Majefty's was at all addreffed to, for leave to kifs his Hand: And at length it became plain, that taking the *Teft* would not clear the way.

As the Earl was on his return to *Edinburgh*, to wait upon his Highnefs, and come the length of *Glafgow*, he got the news, that the late Prefident of the Seffion, and he, were both turned out of it; and at his Arrival at *Edinburgh*, feveral Meetings of Council were appointed only to occafion his taking of the *Teft* : But the Earl having gone fome Miles out of Town, was not prefent. At laft a Meeting of the Council was appointed *exprefly*, and one of the Clerks ordered to warn the Earl particularly to be prefent ; whereof the Earl being advertifed before the Clerk came to him, he waited on his Highnefs, and had the honour of an opportunity after Supper, to fpeak to his Royal Highnefs, in his Bed-chamber. The *Earl told* his Highnefs he was now returned, to make good his Word, and to fhew thofe *Writs and Rights* he had promifed: But Sir (*faid the Earl*) I have heard by the way of Alterations, and that I am turn'd out of the Seffion. His *Highnefs faid*, it was fo. The Earl *afked* what next? His *Highnefs faid*, he knew no more. The *Earl faid*, he had never fought that, nor any Place, and he knew that Place was at His Majefty's difpofe, and it might foon be better filled: But *faid the Earl*, if it be to exprefs a Frown, it is the firft I have had from His Majefty this Thirty Years ; I know I have Enemies, but they fhall never make me alter my Duty, and Refolution to ferve His Majefty ; I have ferved His Majefty in Arms, and in his Judicatures, when I knew I had Enemies on my right Hand, and on my left, and I will do fo ftill. But if any have power to render His Majefty or your Highnefs jealous of me, it will make my Service the more ufelefs to both, and the lefs comfortable to my felf. His *Highnefs faid*, he knew no more than what he had faid. The *Earl then faid*, it was late, and he would wait on his Highnefs fome other time, about thefe Matters: But the thing that at prefent preffes (*fays the Earl*) is, That I hear one of the Clerks of Council is appointed to tell me to be at the Council to-morrow, I conceive, to take the *Teft* ; pray, what is the hafte? May not I, with your Highnefs's Favour, have the *time allowed* by the Act of Parliament? His *Highnefs faid*, No. The *Earl urged it* again, but in vain : And all the delay he could obtain, was till *Thurfday* the Third of *November*, the next Council-Day in courfe. The *Earl faid* he was the lefs fond of the *Teft*, that he found that fome that refufed it were ftill in Favour, and others that had taken it turned out, as the *Regifter* ; at which His *Highnefs only laught*. But Sir, [faid the Earl] how comes your Highnefs to prefs the *Teft* fo haftily? Sure there are fome Things in it your Highnefs doth not over-much like: Then *faid his Highnefs, angerly, and in a paffion* ; Moft true, that *Teft* was brought into the Parliament, *without the Confeffion of Faith*: But the late Prefident caufed put in the Confeffion, which makes it *fuch as no honeft Man can take it*. The *Earl faid*, he had the more reafon to advife: Whereby you may fee, whether his Highnefs then thought, the *Confeffion* was to be fworn to in the *Teft*, or not.

After this the Earl waited feveral times on his Highnefs, and made new Attempts for the favour of a delay, but with no fuccefs: What paffed in private, fhall not be repeated except fo far as is abfolutely neceffary to evince the Earl his Innocency, and to fhew that in what he did he had no ill Defign, nor did in the leaft prevaricate, or give any offence willingly, but was ready to comply, as far as he could, with a good Confcience: It was in this Interval, that the Earl fpoke with the Bifhop of *Edinburgh*, and faw his

Vin-

Vindication of the *Test*, and all the *Explanations* I here send you, only the Council's Explanation was not yet thought on: And that all the Bishop did then urge the Earl with, beyond what is in his *Vindication*, was to have a care of a noble Family, and to tell him, *that the opposing the exception of the King's Sons, and Brothers, from taking the Test, had fired the Kiln.*

At the last, upon *Wednesday,* the second of *November,* late, the Earl waited on his Highness, and did in the most humble, and easy Expressions he could devise, decline the present taking of the *Test*; but if his Highness would needs have a present Answer, *he beg'd* his Favour, that he would accept of his refusing it in private; which was denied again. Then, *he said,* if his Highness would allow him time to go home and consider, he would either give Satisfaction, or the Time prescribed by the Act of Parliament would elapse, and so he would go off in course, and without noise. But this also *his Highness absolutely refused:* Upon which the *Earl asked,* what good his appearing in Council, to refuse there, would do? *His Highness was pleased to answer,* that he needed not appear, but to employ some Friend to speak for him; and his Highness himself named one. This the Earl yielded to, as the best of a bad choice, *and said,* he should either use the Person named by his Highness, or some other Relation that were a Counsellor; and in Town: And, in compliance with his Highness's Pleasure, the next Morning, the Earl drew a Letter, for a Warrant to the same Person his Highness had named, for declaring his Mind in Council; wherein he exprest his constant Resolution to continue a true Protestant, and loyal Subject, which were the true Ends of the *Test*: But the Letter concluding on a delay of taking the Oath, and his Highness having given some Indication, how little pleasing that Office was to him, neither that Friend, nor any other would, by any means, accept of it.

Upon this the Earl drew a second, and shorter Letter, to any that should that day preside in Council; but after much Discourse, it being suggested, that an Explanation would be allowed, but the shorter the better, the Earl first drew one, suitable to his own thoughts; and it being thought too long, did instantly shorten it, and put it into his Pocket, but withal *said* he would not offer it, till he knew his Highness's Pleasure, lest his Highness might take it ill that any had prevailed more with him, than himself; and therefore the Earl did refuse to go to the Council, or out of his Chamber, till he had his Approbation. A little after a Coach was sent for the Earl, and it was told him, in the Room without the Council-Chamber, that the Bishop of *Edinburgh* had spoke to his Highness, and signified to him, that the Earl was willing to take the *Test,* with an *Explanation,* and that the Bishop *said, it would be very kindly accepted.* These were the express Words, and then (and not till then) the Earl went into the Council, and delivered (that is pronounced) his *Explanation* close by his Highness, and directly towards him; so loud, and audible, that some in the furthest Corner of the Room acknowledged they heard it: Whereupon the Oath was administred, and the Earl took it; and his Highness with a well-satisfied Countenance, and the honour of a Smile, *commanded* him to take his Place: And while he sat by his Highness (which was his Honour to do that Day) his Highness spake several times privately to him, and always very pleasantly.

And the Earl hath since protested to his Friends, that he thinks his Highness was, at the time, well pleased, though some others that wish'd the Earl out of the Council, appeared surprized, and in some Confusion.

The first Thing came to be treated of in Council, after the Earl had taken his Seat, was the Council's *Explanation,* at that time intended, and resolved to be allowed to the *Clergy only,* and no other, and withal not to be printed: To which the Earl refused to Vote, which was afterwards made a Ground of Challenge. A little after, it being the Post-Night, the Earl stept out and went to his Lodging, and though he acknowledges, he did not decline to give some Friends an Account of what had past, yet he was so far from spreading Copies of his *Explanation,* at taking the Oath, that he flatly refused to give a kind, and discreet Friend, then in his Chamber, a Copy of it, lest it might go abroad: And the Words being few, and publickly spoke, it is not strange they might be almost perfectly repeated, as it's known, the Clerks pretended to do; but the King's Advocate having past from the Accusation of *Spreading,* this is only mentioned to evidence how singly studious the Earl was to satisfy his own Conscience, and how tender of giving Offence, for *I can say* truly for him, he was never heard to dissuade any to take the *Test,* nor to disparage it, after it past in an Act; only he refused to take it himself, *without an Explanation,* hich to stretch to a Crime, is beyond all Example. I confess, he never cry'd it up as *super-excellent,* or divine, as some have done that can alter their tone, and decry it as much, whenever there shall be occasion.

The next morning the Earl waited on his Highness, expecting yesternight's Countenance, and indeed nothing less than what he met with; for beginning to speak with his Highness in private, his *Highness interrupted him,* and said he was not pleased with his *Explanation.*

The

The *Earl said*, he did not presume to give it till his Highness allowed him: *His Highness acknowledged*, that the Bishop of *Edinburgh* had told him, that the Earl intended an Explanation: *But (says his Highness)* I thought it had been some short one, like Earl *Queensburries*. *The Earl answered* that his Highness heard what he said: *His Highness said*, he did, but he was surprized. Then the *Earl said*, he had said the same thing, in private, to his Highness, wherewith he, at that time, appeared satisfied: And *the Earl* being about to *say more*, in his own vindication, his *Highness interrupting* him *said, well it is past with you, but it shall pass so with no other*; which words the Earl thought, did both confirm the Council's *acceptance*, and his *explanation*, and sufficiently clear him of all *offence*, if he had incurred any.

And whatever hath been his Highness resolution, or the Earl's misfortune since, the Earl is perswaded that his Highness was resolved then to push the Affair no further; for though some had still the same Animosities, and Prejudices against the Earl, yet hitherto they had not adventured to undertake to extract, and forge such Crimes, out of his words, as afterwards they did: And it was not, till private Suggestions were made, that Advocates were asked (as they were) if these words could be stretched to Treason; and that (when the ablest denied) the King's Advocate complied, and was ordered to draw the Indictment, and some Judges were engaged, and secured about it, as will appear, whenever His Majesty thinks it his Interest to take an exact Trial of that whole Affair.

The Earl did think (as I just now said) his Highness saying, *it was past as to him*, was enough; he was resolved to say no more for justifying himself, but seeing he is so hardly pressed, and his Life, and Honour at the stake, it is hoped his Highness will not disown what the Earl hath hitherto so respectfully concealed, and is now no less necessary to be spoke out for his Vindication. And that is, that besides that his Highness did allow the Earl to explain, and did hear his explanation in Council, and approve it; the Earl did twice in private, once before, and once after his Oath in Council, repeat to his Highness, the same words, that the Treason is so founded on: (*viz.*) *That the Earl meant not to bind up himself, to wish, and endeavour, in a lawful way, and in his Station, any Alteration, he thought to the advantage of Church and State, not repugnant to the Protestant Religion, and his Loyalty*; and that his Highness was so far from charging them with Treason, that *he said*, plainly, both times, *the Earl's scruples were unnecessary, and that the Test did not bind him up as he imagined; adding further, the last time, that the Earl had cheated himself, for notwithstanding the explanation, he had taken the Test*. To which *the Earl only answered, that then his Highness should be satisfied*. Now, after all this, that Treason should be so earnestly searched for, and so groundlessly found, in those words, is it not strange beyond all Example? Could it be Treason for the Earl to say, *He will not bind up himself*, where his Highness says so oft, and so plainly, *It was not intended that he, or any Man, should be bound up?*

What past the next day, after the Earl had taken the *Test*, and was received by the Council, is also proper for you to know. The Earl, being to take it as one of the *Commissioners of the Treasury*, it was commonly thought that he, and the other *Commissioners*, were to take it in the Exchequer; but after Ten of the Clock, about two hours after the Earl had parted from his Highness, one told him there was a Design upon him, to make him swear once more before the Council: And accordingly, at Twelve, there was an extraordinary *Council* called in the *Abbey*, and there it was found, that the *Commissioners of Treasury, as Officers of the Crown*, were to take the *Test* before the Council; and it was told the Earl, that the *Exchequer* could not, that day, sit without him. And to make the Matter more solemn, it was resolved that the Council should meet that Afternoon, and that his Highness should be present: So soon as they were met, the Oath was tendered, and the Earl offering to take it, and saying only these words, *as before*, the Earl of *Roxburgh*, never heard to speak in Council till then, stood up behind his Highness Chair, and with Clamour, asked *what was said*: To whom his Highness was pleased to turn and inform him; upon which *Roxburgh*, prepared for the purpose, desired, that what the Earl of *Argyle* had said, the day before, might be repeated: Which the Earl, seeing a design upon him, did at first decline, till he was peremptorily put to it by his Highness, and he being Ingenuous, and thinking no course more proper to prevent mistakes of words, *he said* he had a *Note* of what he had said in his Pocket, which his Highness called for very earnestly, and *commanded* him to produce; which being done, and the Paper read, so secure was the Earl of his Innocency, that he was willing, upon the first motion, to sign it: But the then new President of the Session, now Chancellor, and the new Register, could not agree, whether it was fit, or not, the Treason not yet appearing, when read in Council, as when they had talked of it in private; so the Earl was removed, and then called in, and after *these two* had whetted, and adjusted their Inventions, he was desired positively to sign the Paper he had given in. To which he answered, he meant well, and truly did see no ill in the Paper, why he might not; and if the words did please them then, as they did when they were first pronounced, he would do it: But, if they found the least matter of

Displeasure

Difpleafure in them, he would forbear. Whereupon being again removed, and called in, he was told, he had not given the Satisfaction required by the Act of Parliament, in taking the *Teft*: And fo could not fit in the Council, and fomewhat more was added, as if the Matter drew deeper, but the particular words I do not know. To which *the Earl faid*, that he judged, all the Parliament meant was to exclude Refufers of the *Teft* from Places of truft: And if he were judged a Refufer, he fubmitted, but could conceive no greater danger in the Matter, for he had ferved His Majefty faithfully within doors, and was refolved to do fo without doors; and fo he made his obeyfance, and went out. Next morning, being *Saturday, November 5.* the Earl waited on his Royal Highnefs, and amongft other things, told his Highnefs, he was ftrangely furprized, that the faying, *He could not bind up himfelf in his Station and in a lawful way, &c.* as was contained in that Paper, was lookt on as a Crime, feeing he had faid the fame words to his Highnefs formerly in private, without any offence, to which *His Highnefs* gave no anfwer, but held his peace; which made the Earl make bold, to put him to remember his own words, and to afk him, what he had faid, when the Earl formerly fpoke to him. Then *His Highnefs* was pleafed *to fay*, he had forgot what he had faid: To which the *Earl anfwered, the worfe indeed for me.* But, Sir, here are the fame words, I formerly faid, without offence, what fays your Highnefs now? What ill is in them? Let me know, and I will vindicate my felf. And all his Highnefs at this fecond time *faid*, was, what hath been above remarked, *That they were unneceffary words, that the Earl fcrupled needlefly, that he was not tyed up by that Oath, as he imagined*; and after a paufe added, *As I have already told you, Well, you have cheated your felf, you have taken the Teft:* To which the Earl replied, he hoped then his Highnefs was fatisfied, (as above.) His Highnefs then *began to complain*, that the Earl, the little while he fat in Council, after he had taken the Oath, had not gone along to approve the Council's explanation: *The Earl faid* he had not heard the debate; and therefore, it was reafonable, to excufe him from voting. *His Highnefs returned*, a little warmly, that the Earl knew the Cafe well enough, (which indeed was not unlike, and yet not at all ftrange, that the Earl could not vote, for that explanation, feeing he could not but know, the Parliament did intend *the Confeffion* fhould be fworn: And that he himfelf had taken it in that Senfe, as all others had done, before that explanation paft in Council) but the Earl replying nothing, his Highnefs *continued, that the Earl, and others had defigned to bring trouble upon an handful of poor Catholicks, that would live peaceably, however they were ufed, but it fhould light upon others.*

A little after, *his Highnefs commanded* the Earl not to go out of Town, till he waited on him, which the Earl faid he fhould obey: But notwithftanding thereof, one of the Clerks of the Council was fent to the Earl, that fame Night, late, to intimate to him, not to go out of Town, till the Council fhould fit, upon the *Tuefday* thereafter.

Upon *Monday* the Seventh of *November*, the Earl waited on his Highnefs again, and told him, he was furprized to get fuch a Meffage from the Council, after his Highnefs had laid his own Commands upon him, and afked what the Council's meaning could be: His Highnefs was pleafed to fay, he knew nothing, but referred all to themfelves, at their Meeting.

Upon *Tuefday*, the Eighth of *November*, when the Council met, without ever calling the Earl, an Order was fent to him, by one of their Clerks, to enter himfelf Prifoner in the Caftle of *Edinburgh*, before Twelve of the Clock the next Day, with a Warrant to the *Deputy Governor*, to keep him Prifoner, wherein the word *Sure-firmance* was ftruck in it, which appeared to have been fairly writ. This Order the Earl received, and obeyed it, with great Submiffion, entering all alone in an Hackney-Coach: And when fome of his Relations, and Perfons of Quality, offered to go along with him, he refufed, *faying*, that if he were purfued at the Inftance of any other, he would accept of their civility; but feeing he was purfued, at the Inftance of his Majefty's Advocate, he would go, in the moft humble way that he could think on, and have no body concerned but himfelf.

But all this did not hinder the Council, to write to his Majefty the Letter hereafter infert, giving Judgment before Tryal, without any hearing, and feeking leave to proceed to a Procefs, which they likewife proceeded in, before any return came; as likewife, about the very Date of this Letter, they emitted their Explanation of the *Teft*: Albeit in their Letter, they affert, *That they had been very careful not to fuffer any to take the Teft with Gloffes and Explanations.*

The Earl fome days after his entering Prifoner into the Caftle of *Edinburgh*, did write a Letter to his Royal Highnefs, *telling him*, that he had obeyed his Highnefs, and the Council's Order, in entering Prifoner in that Place; that he had not written fooner, left he might be thought too impatient of his Punifhment, which appeared to be the Effects of an high Difpleafure, which, he hoped, he no wife deferved; that he

was

4

was refolved to continue in all duty, and obedience to his Majefty, and his Royal Highnefs, and never to fail in any profeffion thereof he had made; and begged to know what Satisfaction was expected, and where, and how he might live with his Highnefs's Favour.

This Letter at firft feemed to pleafe, and the *Earl heard* it did, but the only Anfwer, directly returned, was *Summonds* charging the Earl *with leafing-making, and depraving of Laws*, before any return from His Majefty: And after a *Return*, came another *Summonds*, with Sound of Trumpet, containing *Perjury and Treafon*, added to the former Crimes. Notwithftanding all which, fair Weather was made, and it was given out, and likewife intimated to the Earl, by a particular Meffage from one of the *Club*, that no more was defigned, but to humble the Earl, and to take his heritable and other Offices from him, and his Family; and when his Highnefs was told *it was hard Meafure*, by fuch a Procefs, and on fuch Pretenfions, to threaten *Life and Fortune*, his Highnefs faid, *Life and Fortune! God forbid.*

What happened after thefe Things, and how the Procefs was carried on, follows now in order: And for your more clear and diftinct Information, I have fent you feveral very neceffary and ufeful *Papers*, with *Indexes* on the Margin, pointing at fuch Paffages, as more remarkably concern this Affair.

The TEST, containing the Oath to be taken by all Perfons in publick Truft.

I Solemnly fwear, in the prefence of the eternal God, whom I invoke as Judge, and Witnefs of the fincere Intention of this my Oath, that I own, and fincerely profefs the true Proteftant Religion, *contained in the* **Confeffion of Faith**, Recorded in the firft Parliament of King *James the VI*, and that *I believe the fame* to be founded on, and agreeable to the written Word of God. And I promife and fwear, that I fhall adhere thereunto, during all the Days of my Life-time; and fhall endeavour to educate my Children therein; *And fhall never confent to any Change or Alteration contrary thereto, and that I difown and renounce all fuch Principles, Doctrines, or Practices, whether Popifh, or Fanatical, which are contrary unto, and inconfiftent with the faid Proteftant Religion, and* **Confeffion of Faith**. And for Teftification of my Obedience to my moft gracious Sovereign *Charles the II.* I do affirm, and fwear by this my folemn Oath, that the King's Majefty is the only fupreme Governor of this Realm, over all Perfons, and in all Caufes, as well Ecclefiaftical as Civil; and that no Foreign Prince, Perfon, Pope, Prelate, State or Potentate, hath, or ought to have any Jurifdiction, Power, Superiority, Preheminency, or Authority, Ecclefiaftical or Civil, within this Realm. And therefore I do utterly renounce, and forfake all Foreign Jurifdictions, Powers, Superiorities, and Authorities: And do promife, that from henceforth I fhall bear Faith, and true Allegiance to the King's Majefty, his Heirs and lawful Succeffors; and to my power fhall affift, and defend all Rights, Jurifdictions, Prerogatives, Privileges, Preferments and Authorities belonging to the King's Majefty, his Heirs and lawful Succeffors; and I further affirm and fwear by this my folemn Oath, that I judge it unlawful for Subjects, upon pretence of Reformation, or any other Pretence whatfoever, to make all Covenants or Leagues, or to convocate, conveen, or affemble in any other Conventions or Affemblies, to treat, confult, or determine in any matter Civil or Ecclefiaftick, without His Majefty's fpecial Command, or exprefs Licence had thereto; or to take up Arms againft the King, or thofe commiffionate by him. And that I fhall never fo rife in Arms, or enter into fuch Covenants or Affemblies: And that there lies no Obligation on me from the national Covenant, or the folemn League and Covenant (commonly fo called) or any other manner of way whatfoever, to endeavour *any Change or Alteration* in the Government, either in Church or State, as it is now eftablifhed by the Laws of this Kingdom. And I promife and fwear, that I fhall, with my utmoft power, defend, affift and maintain His Majefty's Jurifdiction forefaid againft all Oppofers. And I fhall never decline His Majefty's Power and Jurifdiction, as I fhall anfwer to God. And finally, I affirm and fwear, that this my folemn Oath is given in the plain, genuine Senfe, and meaning of the Words, without any Equivocation, mental Refervation, or any manner of Evafion whatfoever; and that I fhall not accept or ufe any Difpenfation from any Creature whatfoever; *So help me God.*

The

The Bishop of Aberdeen, *and the Synod's Explanation of the* Test.

WE do not hereby swear to all the particular Assertions and Expressions of the *Confession of Faith*, mentioned in the *Test*, but only tö the uniform Doctrine of the reformed Churches contained therein.

II. We do not hereby prejudge the Church's Right to, and Power of making any alteration *in the said Confession, as to the ambiguity and obscure expressions thereof*, or of making a more unexceptionable frame.

III. When we swear, That the King is Supreme Governor over all Persons, and in all Causes, as well Ecclesiastick as Civil, and when we swear to assert and defend all His Majesty's Rights and Prerogatives, this is reserving *always the intrinsick unalterable Power of the* Church, immediately derived from Jesus Christ; to wit, the power of the Keys consisting in the preaching of the Word, administration of the Sacraments, ordaining of *Pastors, exercise of Discipline, and the holding of such Assemblies as are necessary for preservation of Peace and Unity*, Truth and Purity in the Church; and withal, we do hereby think, that the King has a power to alter the Government of the Church at his pleasure.

IV. When we swear, That it is unlawful for Subjects to meet or convene, to treat or consult, &c. about matters of State, Civil and Ecclesiastick, this is excepting meetings for Ordination, publick Worship and Discipline, and such meetings as are necessary for the conservation of the Church, and true Protestant Religion.

V. When we swear, There lies no obligation on us, &c. to endeavour any change or alteration in Government, either in Church or State, *we mean by Arms, or any seditious way.*

VI. When we swear, That we take the *Test* in the plain and genuine sense of the words, &c. *we understand it only in so far as it does not contradict these Exceptions.*

The Explanation of the Test, *by the Synod and Clergy of* Perth.

BEcause our Consciences require the publishing and declaring, of that express meaning we have in taking the *Test*, that we be not mis-interpreted to swear it in these Glosses which men uncharitable to it, and enemies to us, are apt to put upon it; and because some men, ill-affected to the Government, who are daily broachers of odious and calumnious Slanders against our Persons and Ministry, are apt to deduce inferences and conclusions from the *alledged ambiguity of some Propositions of the* Test, *that we charitably and firmly do believe were never intended by the Imposers, nor received by the Takers*: Therefore to satisfy our Consciences, and to save our Credit from these unjust imputations, we expresly declare, That we swear the *Test* in this following meaning.

I. By taking the *Test*, we do not swear to every Proposition and Clause contained in the *Confession of Faith*, but only to the true Protestant Religion, founded upon the Word of God, contained in that *Confession*, as it is opposed to Popery and Fanaticism.

II. By swearing the Ecclesiastick Supremacy, we swear it as we have done formerly, without any reference to the assertory Act. We also reserve intire unto the Church, its own intrinsick and unalterable Power of the Keys, as it was exercised by the Apostles, and the pure primitive Church, for the first three Centuries.

III. By swearing, That it is unlawful to convocate, convene or assemble in the Council, Conventions or Assemblies, to treat, consult, &c. in any matter of State, Civil or Ecclesiastick, as we do not evacuate our natural Liberty, whereby we are in freedom, innocently without reflection upon, or derogating to Authority, or persons intrusted with it, to discourse in any occasional meeting of these things; so we exclude not those other meetings which are necessary for the Well-being and Discipline of the Church.

IV. By our swearing it unlawful to endeavour any change or alteration in the Government, either of Church or State, we mean, that it is *unlawful for us to endeavour the alteration of the specifick Government of Monarchy, in the true and lineal Descent, and Episcopacy.*

V. When we swear in the genuine and literal sense, &c. we understand *it so far as it is not opposite, or contradictory to the foresaid exceptions.*

They were allow'd to insert after the Oath, before the Subscriptions, these words, or to this purpose:

U u

We

4

We under-written do take this Oath, according to the Explanation made by the Council, approved by his Majesty's Letter; and we declare, we are no further bound by this Oath.

EDINBURGH.

The Sederunt of the Council.

Sederunt vigesimo secundo Die Septembris, 1681.

His Royal Highness, &c.

Montrose,	Roxburgh,	Rosse,
Errol,	Queensberry,	Dalziel,
Marshall,	Airley,	Treasurer Deputy *Præses,*
Marr,	Kintore,	Advocate,
Glencarne,	Breadalbane,	Justice *Clerk,*
Winton,	Lorne,	Collintoun,
Linlithgow,	Levingston,	Tarbet,
Perth,	Bishop of *Edinburgh,*	Haddo,
Strathmore,	Elphinston,	Lundie.

This day the *Test* was subscribed by the above-written Privy-Counsellors, and by the Earl of *Queensberry,* who coming in after the rest had taken it, declared that he took it with the Explication following.

The Earl of Queensberry's *Explanation of the* Test *when he took it.*

HIS Lordship declared, that by that part of the *Test, That there lies no obligation-- to endeavour any change, or alteration in the Government,* &c. he did not understand himself to be obliged against *Alterations,* in case it should please His Majesty to make alterations of the Government of Church or State.

HALYRUDEHOUSE.

Sederunt vigesimo primo Die Octobris, 1681.

His Royal Highness, &c.

Winton,	Airley,	Treasurer Deputy *Præses,*
Perth,	Lorne,	Register,
Strathmore,	Levingston,	Advocate,
Queensberry,	Bishop of *Edinburgh,*	Collintoun.
Ancram,		

This day the Bishop of *Edinburgh* having drawn up a long Explication of the *Test,* to satisfy the many Objections and Scruples moved against it, especially by the conformed Clergy, presented it to the Council for their Lordships Approbation, which was ordered to be read; but the Paper proving prolix, and tedious, his Highness, after reading of a few Leaves, interrupted, saying very wittily, and pertinently, *That the first Chapter of* John *with a Stone will chase away a Dog,* and so brake it off. Yet the Bishop was afterward allowed to print it, if he pleased.

Sederunt quarto Die Novembris, 1681.

His Royal Highness, &c.

Montrose *Præses,*	Winton,	Linlithgow,
Perth,	Strathmore,	Roxburgh,
Ancram,	Airley,	Balcaras,
Levingston,	Bishop of *Edinburgh,*	Elphinstoun,
President of *Session,*	Treasurer Deputy,	Register.
Advocate,	Lundie.	

This day the Earl of *Argyle* being about to take the *Teft*, as a Commiffioner of the Treafury, and having upon Command produced a Paper bearing the fenfe in which he took the *Teft*, the preceding day, and in which he would take the fame, as a Commiffioner of the Treafury: Upon confideration thereof it was refolved, that he cannot fit in Council, not having taken the *Teft*, in the fenfe and meaning of the Act of Parliament, and therefore was removed.

The Earl of Argyle's *Explication of the* Teft *when he took it.*

I Have confidered the Teft, and I am very defirous to give obedience as far as I can. I'm confident the Parliament never intended to impofe contradictory Oaths: Therefore I think no Man can explain it but for himfelf. Accordingly I take it, as far as it is confiftent with it felf and the Proteftant Religion: And I do declace, That I mean not to bind up my felf in my ftation and in a lawful way, to wifh and endeavour any alteration I think to the advantage of Church or State, not repugnant to the Proteftant Religion and my Loyalty. And this I underftand as a part of my Oath.

But the Earl finding, as hath been narrated, this his Explication though accepted, and approven by his Highnefs and Council the day before, to be this day carped and offended at, and advantages thereupon fought and defigned againft him, did immediately draw up the following Explanation of his Explication, and for his own vindication did firft communicate it to fome privately, and thereafter intended to have offered it at his Trial for clearing of his defences.

The Explanation of his Explication.

I Have delayed hitherto to take the Oath, appointed by the Parliament to be taken, by the firft of January next: But now being required, near two Months fooner, to take it, this day peremptorily, or to refufe; I have confidered the Teft, and have feen feveral Objections moved againft it, efpecially by many of the Orthodox Clergy, notwithftanding whereof, I have endeavoured to fatisfy my felf with a juft Explanation, which I here offer, that I may both fatisfy my Confcience, and obey Your Highnefs, and Your Lordfhips commands in taking the Teft; though the Act of Parliament do not fimply command the thing, but only under a Certification which I could eafily fubmit to, if it were with Your Highnefs favour, and might be without offence: But I love not to be fingular, and I am very defirous to give obedience in this and every thing, as far as I can, and that which clears me is, that I am confident whatever any Man may think, or fay, to the prejudice of this Oath, the Parliament never intended to impofe contradictory Oaths. And becaufe their fenfe, (they being the framers and impofers) is the true fenfe, and that this Teft injoined is of no private interpretation, nor are the King's Statutes to be interpreted but as they bear, and to the intent they are made; therefore I think no Man, that is, no private Perfon, can explain it for another, to amufe or trouble him with (may be) miftaken Gloffes: But every Man, as he is to take it, fo is to explain it for himfelf, and to endeavour to underftand it, (notwithftanding all thefe exceptions) in the Parliament's, which is its true and genuine fenfe. I take it therefore notwithftanding any fcruple made by any as far as it is confiftnet with it felf, and the Proteftant Religion, which is wholly in the Parliament's fenfe and their true meaning; which (being prefent) I am fure, was owned by all to be the fecuring of the Proteftant Religion, founded on the Word of God, and contained in the Confeffion of Faith recorded J. 6. p. 1. c. 4. And not out of fcruple as if any thing in the Teft did import the contrary, but to clear my felf from all cavils; as if thereby I were bound up further than the true meaning of the Oath. I do declare that by that part of the Teft, that there lies no obligation on me, &c. I mean not to bind up my felf, in my ftation, and in a lawful way, ftill difclaiming all unlawful endeavours, to wifh and endeavour any alteration I think, according to my confcience, to the advantage of Church, or State, not repugnant to the Proteftant Religion, and my Loyalty. And by my Loyalty, I underftand no other thing than the words plainly bear, to wit, the duty and allegiance of all Loyal Subjects. And this Explanation I underftand as a part not of the Teft or Act of Parliament, but as a qualifying part of my Oath that I am to fwear, and with it I am willing to take the Teft, if Your Royal Highnefs and Your Lordfhips allow me; or otherwife, in fubmiffion to Your Highnefs, and the Council's pleafure, I am content to be held as a refufer at prefent.

The

4

The Council's Letter to His Majesty, concerning their having committed the Earl of Argyle.

May it please your Sacred Majesty,

THE laft Parliament having made fo many and fo advantageous Acts, for fecuring the Proteftant Religion, the Imperial Crown of this Kingdom, and Your Majefty's Sacred Perfon, (whom God Almighty long preferve) and having for the laft, and as the beft way for fecuring all thefe, appointed a *Teft* to be taken by all who fhould be entrufted with the Government; which bears exprefly, That the fame fhould be taken in the plain and genuine fenfe and meaning of the words: *We were very careful not to fuffer any to take the faid* Oath *or* Teft, *with their own Gloffes or Explications.* But the Earl of *Argyle* having, after fome delays, come to Council, to take the faid Oath, as a Privy-Counfellor, fpoke fome things which were not then heard, nor adverted to, and when his Lordfhip at his next offering to take it in Council, as one of the Commiffioners of Your Majefty's Treafury, was commanded to take it fimply, he refufed to do fo; but gave in a Paper, fhewing the only fenfe in which he would take it, which Paper we all confidered, *as that which had in it grofs and fcandalous Reflections upon that excellent Act of Parliament, making it to contain things contradictory and inconfiftent; and thereby depraving Your Majefty's Laws, mifreprefenting Your Parliament, and teaching Your Subjects to evacuate and difappoint all Laws and Securities that can be enacted for the prefervation of the Government;* fuitable to which his Lordfhip declares in that Paper, *That he means not to bind up himfelf from making any alterations he fhall think fit, for the advantage of Church or State;* and which Paper he defires may be looked upon as a part of his Oath, as if he were the Legiflator, and able to add a part to the Act of Parliament. Upon ferious perufal of which Paper, we found our felves obliged to fend the faid Earl to the Caftle of *Edinburgh,* and to tranfmit the Paper to Your Majefty, being exprefly obliged to both thefe by Your Majefty's exprefs Laws. And we have commanded your Majefty's Advocate to raife a purfuit againft the faid Earl, for being Author, and having given in the faid Paper: And for the further profecution of all relating to this Affair, we expect Your Majefty's Commands, which fhall be moft humbly and faithfully obeyed by

Your Majefty's moft Humble,
moft Faithful,
and moft Obedient
Subjects and Servants.

Edinburgh, *Nov.* 8. 1681.   Sic Subfcribitur,
Glencairne, Winton, Linlithgow, Perth,
Roxburgh, Ancram, Airlie, Levingftoun,
Jo. Edinburgen. Rofs, Geo. Gordon,
*Ch. Maitland, G. M*c*kenzie, Ja. Foulis,*
J. Drumond.

Nov. 15. 1681.

The King's Anfwer to the Council's Letter.

C. R.

MOft dear, *&c.* Having in one of your Letters directed unto us, on the 8th. Inftant, received a particular account of the Earl of *Argyle's* refufing to take the *Teft* fimply, and of your proceedings againft him, upon the occafion of his giving in a Paper fhewing the only fenfe in which he will take it, which had in it grofs and fcandalous Reflections upon that excellent late Act of our Parliament there, by which the faid *Teft* was enjoined to be taken; we have now thought fit to let you know, that as we do hereby approve thefe your Proceedings, particularly your fending the faid Earl to our Caftle of *Edinburgh*; and your commanding our Advocate to raife a Purfuit againft him for being Author of, and having given in the faid Paper; fo we do alfo authorize you to do all things that may concern the further profecution of all relating to this Affair. Neverthelefs, it is our exprefs Will and Pleafure, That before any Sentence fhall be pronounced againft him, at the Conclufion of the *Procefs* you fend us a particular account of what he fhall be found guilty of, to the end that, after our being fully informed thereof, we may fignify our further pleafure in this matter. For doing whereof, *&c.*

But

But as notwithſtanding the Council's demanding by their Letter His Majeſty's allowance for proſecuting the Earl, they before any return cauſed His Majeſty's Advocate to exhibit an Indictment againſt him, upon the points of ſlandering and depraving, as hath been already remarked ; ſo after having received His Majeſty's anſwer, the deſign grows, and they thought fit to order a new Indictment, containing beſide the former points, the Crimes of *Treaſon* and *Perjury*, which accordingly was exhibited, and is here ſubjoined, the difference betwixt the two Indictments being only in the particulars above noted.

The Copy of the Indictment againſt the Earl of Argyle.

Archibald Earl of *Argyle*,

YOU are Indicted and Accuſed, That albeit by the Common Law of all well-govern'd Nations, and by the Municipal Laws and Acts of Parliament of this Kingdom ; and particularly, by the 21ſt, and by the 43d Act, Par. 2 *James* 1. and by the 83d Act, Par. 6. *James* 5. and by the 34th Act, Par. 8. *James* 6. and the 134th Act, Par. 8. *James* 6. and the 205th Act, Par. 14. *James* 6. all Leaſing-makers, and tellers of them, are puniſhable with tinſel of Life and Goods ; like as by the 107th Act, Par. 7. *James* 1. it is ſtatuted, That no man interpret the King's Statutes otherwiſe than the Statute bears, and to the intent and effect that they were made for, and as the makers of them underſtood ; and whoſo does in the contrary, to be puniſhed at the King's will. And by the 10th Act, Par. 10. *James* 6. it is ſtatuted, That none of His Majeſty's Subjects preſume or take upon him publickly to declare, or privately to ſpeak or write any purpoſe of reproach or ſlander of His Majeſty's Perſon, Eſtate or Government, or to deprave his Laws, or Acts of Parliament, or miſconſtrue his Proceedings, whereby any miſtaking may be moved betwixt his Highneſs, his Nobility, and loving Subjects, in time coming, under pain of death, certifying them that do in the contrary, they ſhall be reputed as ſeditious and wicked Inſtruments, enemies to his Highneſs and to the Commonwealth of this Realm, and the ſaid pain of death ſhall be executed againſt them with all rigour, to the example of others : And by the ſecond Act, Seſ. 2. Par. 1. *Car.* 2. it is ſtatuted, That whoſoever ſhall by Writing, Libelling, Remonſtrating, expreſs, publiſh, or declare any words or ſentences to ſtir up the people to the diſlike of His Majeſty's Prerogative and Supremacy, in Cauſes Eccleſiaſtick, or of the Government of the Church by Archbiſhops and Biſhops, as it is now ſettled by Law, is under the pain of being declared incapable to exerciſe any Office, Civil, Eccleſiaſtick, or Military, within this Kingdom, in any time coming. Like as by the fundamental Laws of this Nation, by the 130th Act, Par. 8. *James* 6. it is declared, That none of His Majeſty's Subjects preſume to impugn the Dignity or Authority of the three Eſtates, or to procure innovation or diminution of their Power and Authority, under the pain of Treaſon. And that it is much more Treaſon in any of His Majeſty's Subjects to preſume to alter Laws already made, or to make new Laws, or to add any part to any Law by their own Authority, that being to aſſume the Legiſlative Power to themſelves, with His Majeſty's higheſt, and moſt incommunicable Prerogative. Yet true it is, that albeit His Sacred Majeſty did not only beſtow on you the ſaid *Archibald* Earl of *Argyle*, thoſe vaſt Lands, Juriſdictions and Superiorities, juſtly forfaulted to His Majeſty by the Crimes of your deceaſed Father, preferring your Family to thoſe who had ſerved His Majeſty againſt it, in the late Rebellion ; but alſo pardoned and remitted to you the Crimes of Leaſing-making, and miſconſtruing His Majeſty's and his Parliament's Proceedings againſt the very Laws above-written, whereof you were found guilty, and condemned to die therefore, by the High Court of Parliament, the 25th of *Auguſt*, 1662. and raiſed you to the Title and Dignity of an Earl, and being a Member of all His Majeſty's Judicatures. Notwithſtanding of all theſe, and many other favours, you the ſaid *Archibald* Earl of *Argyle*, being put by the Lords of His Majeſty's Privy-Council to take the *Teſt*, appointed by the Act of the laſt Parliament to be taken by all perſons in publick Truſt, you, inſtead of taking the ſaid *Teſt*, and ſwearing the ſame in the plain genuine ſenſe and meaning of the words, without any equivocation, mental reſervation, or evaſion whatſoever, you did declare againſt, and defame the ſaid Act ; and having, to the end you might corrupt others by your pernicious ſenſe, drawn the ſame in a Libel, of which Libel you diſperſed, and gave abroad Copies, whereby ill impreſſions were given of the King and Parliament's Proceedings, at a time eſpecially when His Majeſty's Subjects were expecting what ſubmiſſion ſhould be given to the ſaid *Teſt* ; and being deſired the next day to take the ſame, as one of the Commiſſioners of His Majeſty's Treaſury, you did give into the Lords of His Majeſty's Privy-Council, and owned twice, in plain judgment before them, the ſaid defamatory Libel againſt the ſaid *Teſt* and Act of Parliament, declaring, That you *had conſidered the ſaid* Teſt, *and was deſirous to give obedience as far as you could* ; whereby you clearly inſinuated, that you was not able to give full obedience. In the ſecond Article of which Libel you declare, That you were *confident the Parliament never intended to impoſe con-*

tradictory Oaths, thereby to abuse the people with a belief, that the Parliament had been so impious, as really and actually to have imposed contradictory Oaths; and so ridiculous, as to have made an Act of Parliament (which should be most deliberate of all human Actions) quite contrary to their own intentions; after which you subsumed, contrary to the nature of all Oaths, and to the Acts of Parliament above cited, *that every man must explain it for himself, and take it for his own sense,* by which not only that excellent Law, and the Oath therein specified, which is intended to be a Fence to the Government, both of Church and State, but all other Oaths and Laws shall be rendred altogether useless to the Government. If every man take the Oaths imposed by Law in his own sense, then the Oath imposed is to no purpose, for the Legislator cannot be sure that the Oath imposed by him will bind the takers according to the design and intent for which he appointed it, and the Legislative Power is taken from the Imposers, and settled in the taker of the Oath, and so he is allowed to be the Legislator, which is not only an open and violent depraving of his Majesty's Laws and Acts of Parliament, but is likewise a settling of the Legislative Power on private Subjects, who are to take such Oaths. In the third Article of that Paper you declare, That you *take the* Test *in so far only as it is consistent with it self, and the Protestant Religion;* by which you maliciously intimate to the people, That the said Oath is inconsistent with it self, and with the Protestant Religion; which is not only a downright depraving of the said Act of Parliament, but is likewise a misconstruing of His Majesty's and the Parliament's proceedings, and misrepresenting them to the people in the highest degree, and in the tenderest points they can be concerned; and implying, that the King and Parliament have done things inconsistent with the Protestant Religion, for securing of which that *Test* was particularly intended. In the Fourth Article you do expresly declare, that you *mean not* by taking the said *Test, to bind up your self from wishing and endeavouring any alteration in a lawful way that you shall think fit, for advancing of Church and State;* whereby also it was designed by the said Act of Parliament and Oath, That no man should make any alteration in the Government of Church and State, as it is now established; and that it is the Duty of all good Subjects, in humble and quiet manner, to obey the present Government. Yet you not only declare your self, but by your example you invite others to think themselves loosed from that Obligation, and that it is free for them to make any alteration in either, as they shall think fit, concluding your whole Paper with these words, (*And this I understand as a part of my Oath*); which is a treasonable invasion upon the Royal Legislative Power, as if it were lawful for you to make to your self an Act of Parliament, since he who can make any part of an Act, may make the whole, the Power and Authority in both being the same. Of the which Crimes above-mentioned, you the said *Archibald* Earl of *Argyle* are Actor, Art and Part; which being found by the Assize, you ought to be punished with the pains of Death, forfaulture and escheat of Lands and Goods, to the terror of others to commit the like hereafter.

An Abstract of the several Acts of Parliament upon which the Indictment against the Earl of Argyle *was grounded.*

Concerning raisers of Rumours betwixt the King and his People, Chap. 20. 1. *Statutes of King* Robert 1.

IT is defended and forbidden, That no man be a Conspirator, or Inventer of Narrations or Rumours by the which occasion of discord may arise betwixt the King and his People. And if any such man shall be found, and attainted thereof, incontinent he shall be taken and put in Prison, and there shall be surely keeped up; ay, and while the King declare his will anent him.

Act 43. *of Par.* 2. *King* James 1. March 11. 1424. *Leasing-makers forfault Life and Goods.*

Item, It is ordained by the King and whole Parliament, that all Leasing-makers and tellers of them, which may engender discord betwixt the King and his people, wherever they may be gotten, shall be challenged by them that power has, and tine Life and Goods to the King.

Act 83. *Par.* 6. James 5. Dec. 10. 1540. *Of Leasing-makers.*

Item, Touching the Article of Leasing-makers to the King's Grace of his Barons, great Men, and Lieges, and for punishment to be put to them therefore, the King's Grace, with advice of his three Estates, ratifies and approves the Acts and Statutes made thereupon before, and ordains the same to be put in execution in all points; and also statutes and ordains, That if any manner of person makes any evil Information of his

his Highneſs to his Barons and Lieges, that they ſhall be puniſhed in ſuch manner, and by the ſame puniſhment as they that make Leaſings to his Grace of his Lords, Barons, and Lieges.

Act 134. *Par.* 8. James 6. *May* 22. 1584. *Anent Slanderers of the King, his Progenitors, Eſtate and Realm.*

FOraſmuch as it is underſtood to our Sovereign Lord, and his three Eſtates aſſembled in this preſent Parliament, what great harm and inconveniency has fallen in this Realm, chiefly ſince the beginning of the Civil Troubles occurred in the time of his Highneſs *minority,* through the wicked and licentious, publick and private ſpeeches, and untrue calumnies of divers of his Subjects, to the diſdain, contempt and reproach of His Majeſty, his Council and Proceedings, and to the diſhonour and prejudice of his Highneſs his Parents, Progenitors and Eſtate, ſtirring up his Highneſs's Subjects thereby to miſliking, ſedition, unquietneſs, and to caſt off their due obedience to His Majeſty, to their evident peril, tinſil and deſtruction ; his Highneſs continuing always in love and clemency toward all his good Subjects, and moſt willing to ſeek the ſafety and preſervation of them all, which wilfully, needleſsly, and upon plain malice, after his Highneſs's mercy and pardon oft-times afore-granted, has procured themſelves, by their treaſonable deeds, to be cut off as corrupt Members of this Commonwealth. Therefore it is ſtatute and ordained by our Sovereign Lord, and his three Eſtates in this preſent Parliament, that none of his Subjects, of whatſoever Function, Degree or Quality, in time coming ſhall preſume, or take upon hand, privately or publickly, in Sermons, Declamations, and familiar Conferences, to utter any falſe, ſlanderous, or untrue Speeches, to the diſdain, reproach, and contempt of His Majeſty, his Council and Proceedings, or to the diſhonour, hurt or prejudice of his Highneſs, his Parents and Progenitors, or to meddle in the Affairs of his Highneſs, and his Eſtate preſent, by-gone, and in time coming, under the pains contained in the Acts of Parliament anent makers and tellers of Leaſings, certifying them that ſhall be tried contraveners thereof, or that hear ſuch ſlanderous Speeches, and reports not the ſame with diligence, the ſaid pain ſhall be executed againſt them with all rigour, in example of others.

Act 205. *Par.* 14. King James 6. *June* 8. 1594. *Anent Leaſing-makers, and Authors of Slanders.*

OUR Sovereign Lord, with advice of his Eſtates in this preſent Parliament, ratifies, approves, and for his Highneſs and Succeſſors, perpetually confirms the Act made by his Noble Progenitors, King *James* the Firſt, of worthy Memory, againſt Leaſing-makers, the Act made by King *James* the Second, entituled, *Againſt Leaſing-makers, and tellers of them* ; the Act made by King *James* the Fifth, entituled, *Of Leaſing-makers* ; and the Act made by his Highneſs's ſelf, with advice of his Eſtates in Parliament, upon the 22d day of *May,* 1584. entituled, *For the puniſhment of the Authors of Slanders, and untrue Calumnies againſt the King's Majeſty, his Council and Proceedings, to the diſhonour and prejudice of his Highneſs, his Parents, Progenitors, Crown and Eſtate* ; as alſo the Act made in his Highneſs's Parliament holden at *Linlithgow,* upon the 10th of *December,* 1585. entituled, *Againſt the Authors of ſlanderous Speeches or Writs* ; and ſtatutes and ordains all the ſaid Acts to be publiſhed of new, and to be put in execution in the time coming, with this addition, That whoever hears the ſaid Leaſings, Calumnies or ſlanderous Speeches or Writs to be made, and apprehends not the Authors thereof, if it lies in his power, and reveals not the ſame to his Highneſs or one of his Privy Council, or to the Sheriff, Steward or Bailiff of the Shire, Stewards in Regality or Royalty, or to the Provoſt, or any of the Bailiffs within Burgh, by whom the ſame may come to the knowledge of his Highneſs, or his ſaid Privy-Council, wherethrough the ſaid Leaſing-makers, and Authors of ſlanderous Speeches may be called, tried and puniſhed according to the ſaid Acts : The hearer, and not apprehender, (if it lie in his power) and concealer, and not revealer of the ſaid Leaſing-makers, and Authors of the ſaid ſlanderous Speeches or Writs, ſhall incur the like pain and puniſhment as the principal Offender.

Act 107. *Par.* 7. King James 1. *March* 1. 1427. *That none interpret the King's Statutes wrongouſly.*

ITem, the King by deliverance of Council, by manner of Statute, forbids, That no man interpret his Statutes otherwiſe than the Statutes bear, and to the intent and effect that they were made for, and as the maker of them underſtood ; and whoſo does in the contrary, ſhall be puniſhed at the King's will.

Act

4

Act 10. *Par.* 10. *King James* 6. *Dec.* 10. 1585. *Authors of slanderous Speeches or Writs should be punished to the Death.*

IT is statuted and ordained by our Sovereign Lord and three Estates, that all his Highness's Subjects content themselves in quietness and dutiful obedience to his Highness and his Authority, and that none of them presume, or take in hand publickly to declaim, or privately to speak or write any purpose of reproach or slander of His Majesty's Person, Estate, or Government, or to deprave his Laws and Acts of Parliament, or misconstrue his Proceedings, whereby any misliking may be moved betwixt his Highness and his Nobility, and loving Subjects in time coming, under the pain of Death; certifying them that do in the contrary, they shall be reputed as seditious and wicked Instruments, enemies to his Highness, and the Commonwealth of this Realm, and the said pain of Death shall be executed upon them with all rigour, in example of others.

Act for preservation of His Majesty's Person, Authority and Government, May 1662.

——And further it is by His Majesty and Estates of Parliament declared, statuted and enacted, That if any person or persons shall by writing, printing, praying, preaching, libelling, remonstrating, or by any malicious or advised speaking, express, publish or declare any words or sentences, to stir up the people to the hatred or dislike of His Majesty's Royal Prerogative and Supremacy, in Causes Ecclesiastical, or of the Government of the Church by Archbishops and Bishops, as it is now settled by Law——That every such person or persons so offending, and being legally convicted thereof, are hereby declared incapable to enjoy or exercise any place or employment, Civil, Ecclesiastick, or Military, within this Church and Kingdom, and shall be liable to such further pains as are due by the Law in such Cases.

Act 130. *Par.* 8. *James* 6. *May* 22. 1584. *Anent the Authority of the three Estates of Parliament.*

THE King's Majesty considering the Honour and the Authority of his Supreme Court of Parliament, continued past all memory of Man unto their days, as constitute upon the free Votes of the three Estates of this ancient Kingdom, by whom the same under God, has ever been upholden, Rebellious and Traitorous Subjects punished, the Good and Faithful preserved and maintained, and the Laws and Acts of Parliament (by which all Men are governed) made and established. And finding the Power, Dignity and Authority of the said Court of Parliament, of late years, called in some doubt, at least, some curiously travelling to have introduced some Innovation thereanent, His Majesty's firm will and mind always being as it is yet, That the Honour, Authority, and Dignity of his said three Estates shall stand and continue in their own Integrity, according to the ancient and laudable custom by-gone, without any alteration or diminution : Therefore it is statuted and ordained, by our said Sovereign Lord, and his said three Estates in this present Parliament, That none of his Lieges or Subjects presume, or take upon hand to impugn the Dignity and Authority of the said three Estates, or to seek or procure the innovation or diminution of the Power and Authority of the same three Estates, or any of them in time coming, under the pain of Treason.

The Earl of Argyle's *first Petition for Advocates, or Council to be allowed him.*

To his Royal Highness, His Majesty's High Commissioner, and to the Right Honourable the Lords of His Majesty's Privy-Council,

The Humble Petition of Archibald *Earl of* Argyle,

SHEWETH,

THat your Petitioner being criminally indicted before the Lords Commissioners of Justiciary, at the instance of His Majesty's Advocate, for Crimes of an high Nature : And whereas in this Case no Advocate will readily plead for the Petitioner, unless they have your Royal Highness's and Lordships special Licence and Warrant to that effect, which is usual in the like Cases :

It is therefore humbly desired, that Your Royal Highness and Lordships would give special Order and Warrant to Sir George Lockhart, *his ordinary Advocate, to consult and plead for him in the foresaid Criminal Process, without incurring any hazard upon that account; and your Petitioner shall ever pray.*

Edin-

Edinburgh, Nov. 22. 1681.

The Council's Answer to the Earl of Argyle's first Petition, about his having Advocates allowed him.

HIS Royal Highness, his Majesty's High Commissioner, and Lords of Privy-Council do refuse the desire of the above-written Bill, but allows any Lawyers the Petitioners shall employ, to consult and plead for him in the Process of Treason, and other Crimes, to be pursu'd against him at the instance of his Majesty's Advocate. Extr. By me,

Will. Paterson.

The Earl of Argyle's second Petition for Council to be allow'd him.

To His Royal Highness, His Majesty's High Commissioner, and to the Right Honourable the Lords of His Majesty's Privy-Council;

The humble Petition of Archibald *Earl of* Argyle,

SHEWETH,

THat your Petitioner having given in a former Petition, humbly representing, That he being criminally indicted before the Lords Commissioners of Justiciary, at the Instance of his Majesty's Advocate, for Crimes of an high nature; and therefore desiring that Your Royal Highness, and Lordships, would give special warrant to Sir *George Lockhart*, to consult and plead for him: Whereupon your Royal Highness and Lordships, did allow the Petitioner to make use of such Advocates as he should think fit to call. Accordingly your Petitioner having desired Sir *George Lockhart* to consult and plead for him, he hath as yet refused your Petitioner. And by the 11th Parliament of King *James* the VI. *Chap.* 38. as it is the undeniable Privilege of all Subjects, accused for any Crimes, to have liberty to provide themselves of Advocates, to defend their Lives, Honour and Lands, against whatsoever Accusation; so the same Privilege is not only by Parliament 11. King *James* VI. *Chap.* 90. farther asserted and confirmed, but also it is declared, That in case the Advocates refuse, the Judges are to compel them, lest the Party accused should be prejudged. And this being an Affair of great Importance to your Petitioner, and Sir *George Lockhart* having been not only still his ordinary Advocate, but also by his constant converse with him is best known to your Petitioner's Principles; and of whose eminent abilities and fidelity your Petitioner (as many others have) hath had special Proof all along in his Concerns, and hath such singular confidence in him, that he is most necessary to your Petitioner on this occasion.

> *May it therefore please your Royal Highness and Lordships to interpose your Authority, by giving a special Order and Warrant to the said Sir* George Lockhart, *to consult and plead for him in the said Criminal Process, conform to the Tenor of the said Acts of Parliament, and constant known Practice in the like Cases; which was never refused to any Subject of the meanest Quality, even to the greatest Criminals. And your Royal Highness's and Lordships Answer is humbly craved.*

Edinburgh, Nov. 24. 1681.

The Council's Answer to the Earl of Argyle's second Petition.

HIS Royal Highness, his Majesty's High Commissioner, and Lords of Privy Council, having considered the foresaid Petition, do adhere to their former Order, allowing Advocates to appear for the Petitioner in the Process foresaid, Extr. By me,

Will. Paterson.

The Earl of Argyle's Letter of Attorney, constituting Alex. Dunbar his Procurator for requiring Sir George Lockhart to plead for him.

WE Archibald Earl of *Argyle*, do hereby substitute, constitute and ordain *Alexander Dunbar*, our Servitor, to be our Procurator, to pass and require Sir *George Lockhart* Advocate to consult, and plead for us in the Criminal Process intended against us, at the instance of his Majesty's Advocate; and to compear with us, before the Lords Com-

missioners

missioners of Justiciary, upon the 12*th* of *December* next, conform to an Act of Council, dated the 22*d* of *Nov.* instant, allowing any Lawyers that we should employ, to consult and plead for us in the said Process; and to another Act of Council of the 24*th* of *Novemb.* instant, relative to the former, and conform to the Acts of Parliament. In witness whereof, we have subcribed these Presents, at *Edinburgh-Castle, Nov.* 26. 1681. before these Witnesses, *Duncan Campbell* Servitor to *James Glen* Stationer in *Edinburgh*, and *John Thom*, Merchant in the said Burgh.

ARGYLE.

Duncan Campbel, }
John Thom, } Witnesses.

An Instrument whereby the Earl of Argyle *required Sir* George Lockhart *to appear and plead for him.*

Apud Edinburgum vigesimo sexto die Mensis Novembris, *Anno Domini millesimo sexcentesimo octuagesimo primo, & Anno Regni* Car. 2. *Regis trigesimo tertio.*

THE which Day in presence of me Notar publick, and Witnesses under subscribed, compeared personally *Alexander Dunbar*, Servitor to a Noble Earl, *Archibald* Earl of *Argyle*, as Procurator, and in name of the said Earl, conform to a Procuration subscrib'd by the said Earl at the Castle of *Edinburgh*, upon the 21*st* Day of *November*, 1681. making and constituting the said *Alexander Dunbar* his Procurator, to the effect under-written: and past to the personal presence of Sir *George Lockhart* Advocate, in his own Lodgings in *Edinburgh*, having and holding in his hands an Act of his Majesty's Privy Council of the date the 22*d* of *November*, 1681. instant, proceeding upon a Petition given in by the said Earl of *Argyle*, to the said Lords, shewing, that he being criminally indicted before the Lords Commissioners of Justiciary, at the instance of his Majesty's Advocate, for Crimes of an high nature; and whereas in that Case no Advocates would readily plead for the said Earl, unless they had your Royal Higness's and their Lordships special Licence and Warrant to that effect, which is usual in the like Cases: And by the said Petition humbly supplicated, that his Highness and the Council would give special Order and Command to the said Sir *George Lockhart*, the said Earl's ordinary Advocate, to consult and plead for him in the foresaid Criminal Process, without incurring any hazard upon that account: His Royal Highness, and Lords of the said Privy Council, did refuse the desire of the said Petition, but allowed any Lawyers the Petitioner should employ to consult and plead for him in the Process of Treason and other Crimes to be pursued against him, at the instance of his Majesty's Advocate. And also the said *Alexander Dunbar* having, and holding in his hands another Act of the said Lords of Privy Council, of the date the 24*th* of the said Month, relative to, and narrating the said first Act, and proceeding upon another Supplication given in by the said Earl to the said Lords, craving, That his Royal Highness and the said Lords would interpose their Authority, by giving a positive and special Order and Warrant to the said Sir *George Lockhart*, to consult and plead with him in the foresaid Criminal Process, conform to the tenor of the Acts of Parliament mentioned and particularized in the said Petition, and frequent and known practice in the like Cases, which was never refused to any Subject of the meanest Quality. His Royal Highness, and Lords of Privy Council, having considered the foresaid Petition, did by the said Act adhere to their former Order, allowing Advocates to appear for the said Earl in the Process foresaid, as the said Acts bear, and produced the said Acts and Procuratory foresaid to the said Sir *George Lockhart*, who took the same in his hands, and read them over *successivè*; and after reading thereof, the said *Alexander Dunbar* Procurator, and in name and behalf foresaid, solemnly required the said Sir *George Lockhart*, as the said Noble Earl's ordinary Advocate, and as a Lawyer and Advocate, upon the said Earl's reasonable expence, to consult and advise the said Earl's said Process, at any time and place the said Sir *George* should appoint to meet thereupon, conform to the foresaid two Acts of Council, and Acts of Parliament therein mentioned, appointing Advocates to consult in such Matters; which the said Sir *George Lockhart* altogether refused: Whereupon the said *Alexander Dunbar*, as Procurator, and in Name foresaid, asked and took Instruments, one or more, in the hands of me Notary Publick under-subscribed. And these things were done within the said Sir *George Lockhart's* Lodging, on the South-side of the Street of *Edinburgh*, in the *Lane-Market*, within the Dining-room of the said Lodging, betwixt four and five hours in the Afternoon, Day, Month, Year, Place, and of his Majesty's Reign, *respectivè* foresaid, before *Robert Dickson*, and *John Lesly*,

4

Lesly, Servitors to *John Campbell*, Writer to his Majesty's Signet and *Dowgal Mc Alester*, Messenger in *Edinburgh*, with divers others called and required to the Premisses.

Ita esse Ego Johannes Broun, *Notarius publicus, in Premissis requisitus, Attestor, Testantibus his meis signo & subscriptione manualibus solitis & consuetis.*

Robert Dickson,
Dowgall Mc Alester, } Witnesses.
John Lesly,

Broun.

December 5. 1682.

The Opinion of divers Lawyers concerning the Case of the Earl of Argyle.

WE have considered the Criminal Letters, raised at the Instance of his Majesty's Advocate against the Earl of *Argyle*, with the Acts of Parliament contain'd and narrated in the same Criminal Letters, and have compared the same with a Paper, or Explication, which is libelled to have been given in by the Earl to the Lords of his Majesty's Privy Council, and own'd by him, as the sense and explication in which he did take the Oath imposed by the late Act of Parliament: Which Paper is of this tenor ; *I have considered the* Test, *and am very desirous to give obedience as far as I can*, &c. And having likewise considered that the Earl, after he had taken the Oath, with the explication and sense then put upon it, it was acquiesced to by the Lords of Privy-Council, and he allowed to take his Place, and to sit and vote. And that, before the Earl's taking of the Oath, there were several Papers spread abroad, containing objections, and alledging inconsistencies and contradictions in the Oath, and some whereof were presented by Synods and Presbyteries of the Orthodox Clergy, to some of the Bishops of the Church: It is our humble Opinion, that seeing the Earl's design and meaning in offering the said Explication was allenarly for the clearing of his own Conscience, and upon no factious or seditious design ; and that the matter and import of the said Paper is no contradiction of the Laws and Acts of Parliament, it doth not at all import any of the Crimes libelled against him, *viz.* Treason, Leasing-making, depraving of his Majesty's Laws, or the Crime of Perjury, but that the glosses and inferences put by the Libel upon the said Paper are altogether strain'd and unwarrantable, and inconsistent with the Earl's true design, and the sincerity of his meaning and intention, in making of the said Explication.

Wednesday the 12th of *December*, the day of compearance assign'd to the Earl being now come, he was brought by a Guard of Soldiers from the Castle to the place appointed for the Trial, and the Justice Court being met and fenced, the Earl, now Marquis of *Queensberry*, then Justice-General, the Lords *Nairn, Collingtoun, Forret, Newton* and *Kirkhouse*, the Lords of Justiciary sitting in Judgment, and the other formalities also perform'd, the Indictment above set down *Num.* 24. was read, and the Earl spoke as follows.

The Earl of Argyle's *Speech to the Lord Justice-General and the Lords of the Justiciary, after he had been arraign'd, and his Indictment read.*

My Lord Justice-General, &c.

I Look upon it as the undeniable Privilege of the meanest Subject to explain his own Words in the most benign sense ; and even when Persons are under an ill Character, the misconstruction of words in themselves not ill can only reach a presumption or aggravation, but not any more.

But it is strange to alledge, as well as, I hope, impossible, to make any that know me believe, that I could intend any thing but what was honest and honourable, suitable to the Principles of my Religion and Loyalty, tho' I did not explain myself at all.

My Lord, I pray you be not offended that I take up a little of your time, to tell you I have from my youth made it my business to serve his Majesty faithfully, and have constantly to my power appeared in his Service ; especially in times of difficulty, and have never join'd, nor complied with any Interest or Party, contrary to his Majesty's Authority, and have all along served him in his own way, without a frown from his Majesty these thirty Years.

As soon as I pass'd the Schools and Colleges, I went to travel to *France* and *Italy*, and was abroad 1647, 1648, and till the end of 1649.

My first Appearance in the World, was to serve his Majesty as Colonel in his Foot-Guards ; and tho' at that time all the Commissions were given by the then Parliament, yet

I

I would not serve without a Commission from his Majesty, which I have still the Honour to have by me.

After the misfortune of *Worcester*, I continued in Arms for his Majesty's Service, when *Scotland* was over-run with the Usurpers, and was alone with some of my Friends in Arms in the Year 1652. and did then keep up some appearance of opposition to them : And General Major *Dean* coming to *Argyleshire*, and planting several Garisons, he no sooner went away, but we fell upon the Garisons he had left, and in one Day took two of them, and cut off a considerable Part of a third, and carried away in all about three hundred Prisoners. And in the end of that Year I sent Capt. *Shaw* to his Majesty, with my humble Opinion how the War might be carried on, who returned to me with Instructions and Orders which I have yet lying by me.

After which, I joined with those his Majesty did commissionate, and stood out till the last, that the Earl of *Middleton*, his Majesty's Lieutenant General, gave me Orders to capitulate, which I did without any other Engagements to the Rebels, but allowing Persons to give Bail for my living peaceably, and did at my Capitulating relieve several Prisoners by exchange, whereof my Lord *Granard*, out of the Castle of *Edinburgh*, was one.

It is notarly known that I was forefaulted by the Usurpers, who were so jealous of me, that contrary to their Faith within eight Months after my Capitulation, upon pretence I kept Horses above the value, they seiz'd on me, and kept me in one Prison after another, till his Majesty's happy Restauration; and this only becuase I would not engage not to serve his Majesty, tho' there was no Oath required.

I do with all gratitude acknowledge his Majesty's goodness, bounty, and royal favours to me, when I was pursued before the Parliament in the year 1662. His Majesty was graciously pleased not to send me here in any opprobrious way, but upon a bare verbal Parole; upon which I came down Post, and presented my self a fortnight before the Day. Notwithstanding whereof, I was immediately clapt up in the Castle, but having satisfy'd his Majesty at that time of my entire Loyalty, I did not offer to plead by Advocates. And his Majesty was not only pleased to pardon my Life, and to restore me to a Title and Fortune, but to put me in his Service, in the most eminent Judicatories of this Kingdom, and to heap Favours upon me far beyond what ever I did or can deserve, tho' I hope his Majesty hath always found me faithful and thankful, and ready to bestow all I have, or can have for his Service : And I hope never hath had, nor never shall have ground to repent any Favour he hath done me. And if I were now really guilty of the Crimes libelled, I should think my self a great Villain.

The next occasion I had to shew my particular zeal to his Majesty's Service, was in *Anno* 1666, when the Insurrection was made that was represt at *Pentland-Hills*. At the very first, the intercourse betwixt this place and me was stopt, so that I had neither Intelligence nor Orders from the Council, nor from the General; but upon a Letter from the now Archbishop of *St. Andrews*, telling me there was a Rebellion like to be in the three Kingdoms, and bidding me beware of *Ireland* and *Kintyre*, I brought together about two thousand men; I seiz'd all the Gentlemen in *Kintyre* that had not taken the Declaration, tho' I found them peaceable: And I sent a Gentleman to General *Dalziel*, to receive his Orders, who came to him just as they were going to the Action at *Pentland*, and was with him in it, and I kept my men together till his return. And when I went with considerable trouble from my Neighbours, rebelliously in Arms, and had Commissions both on publick and private accounts, have I not carried dutiful to his Majesty, and done what was commanded with a just moderation; which I can prove under the hands of my enemies, and by many infallible demonstrations?

Pardon me a few Words: Did I not in this present Parliament shew my readiness to serve his Majesty and the Royal Family, in asserting vigorously the lineal legal Succession of the Crown, and had a care to have it exprest in the Commissions of the Shires and Burghs I had interest in? Was I not for offering proper Supplies to his Majesty and his Successor ? And did I not concur to bind the Landlords for their Tenants, altho' I was mainly concerned? And have I not always kept my Tenants in obedience to his Majesty ?

I say all this, not to arrogate any thing for doing what was my Honour and Duty to his Majesty ; but if after all this, upon no other ground but words that were spoken in absolute innocence, and without the least design, except for clearing my own Conscience, and that are not capable of the ill sense wrested from them by the Libel, I should be further troubled, what assurance can any of the greatest Quality, Trust or Innocence have that they are secure? Especially considering that so many Scruples have been started, as all know, not only by many of the Orthodox Clergy, but by whole Presbyteries, Synods, and some Bishops, which were thought so considerable, that an eminent Bishop took the pains to write a Treatise that was read over in Council, and allow'd to be printed, and a Copy given to me, which contains all the Expressions I am charged for, and many more that may be stretched to a worse sense.   Have

Have I not shewed my zeal to all the ends of the *Test* ? How then can it be imagin'd that I have any *finifter* defign in any thing that I have faid ? If I had done any thing contrary to it in all the courfe of my Life, which I hope fhall not be found, yet one Act might pretend to be excufed by a habit. But nothing being queftioned but the fenfe of words mifconftrued to the greateft height; and ftretched to imaginary infinuations, quite contrary to my fcope and defign, and fo far contrary, not only to my Senfe, but my Principles, Intereft and Duty, that I hope my Lord Advocate will think he hath gone too far on in this Procefs, and fay plainly what he knows to be truth by his acquaintance with me, both in publick and private, *viz.* That I am neither Papift nor Fanatick, but truely loyal in my principles and practices.

The hearing of this Libel would trouble me beyond moft of the fufferings of my Life, if my innocence did not fupport me, and the hopes of being vindicated of this and other Calumnies before this publick and noble Auditory.

I leave my Defences to thefe Gentlemen that plead for me, they know my innocence, and how groundlefs that Libel is.

I fhould only fay, As my Life hath moft of it been fpent in ferving and fuffering for his Majefty, fo whatever be the event of this Procefs, I refolve, while I breath, to be loyal and faithful to his Majefty. And whether I live publickly or in obfcurity, my head, my heart, nor my hand, fhall never be wanting where I can be ufeful to his Majefty's Service. And while I live, and when I die, I fhall pray, That God Almighty would blefs his Majefty with a long, happy, and profperous Reign ; and that the lineal legal Succeffors of the Crown may continue Monarchs of all his Majefty's Dominions, and be defenders of the true Primitive, Chriftian, Apoftolick, Catholick, Religion, while Sun and Moon endure.

God fave the King.

The King's own Letter to this Nobleman when he was Lord Lorn.

Collogne, December 20. 1654.

My Lord *Lorn,*

I Am very glad to bear from Middleton, *what affection and zeal you fhew to my Service, how conftantly you adhere to him in all his diftreffes, and what good Service you have performed upon the Rebels. I affure you, you fhall find me very juft, and kind to you in rewarding what you have done and fuffered for me ; and I hope you will have more Credit and Power with thofe of your Kindred, and Dependants upon your Family, to engage them with you for me, than any body elfe can have to feduce them againft me ; and I fhall look upon all thofe who fhall refufe to follow you as unworthy of any protection hereafter from me, which you will let them know. This honeft Bearer, M--- will inform you of my Condition and Purpofes, to whom you will give Credit ; and he will tell you, That I am very much*

Your very affectionate Friend,

C. R.

General Middleton's Order to the Earl of Argyle, who was then Lord Lorn, for capitulating with the English, wherein he largely expreffeth his Worth and Loyalty.

John Middleton, *Lieutenant General, next and immediate under his Majefty, and Commander in chief of all the Forces raifed, and to be raifed, within the Kingdom of* Scotland.

SEeing the Lord *Lorn* hath given fo fingular proofs of clear and perfect Loyalty to the King's Majefty, and of pure and conftant affection to the good of his Majefty's affairs, as never hitherto to have any ways comply'd with the enemy, and to have been principally inftrumental in the enlivening of this late War, and one of the chief and firft movers in it, and hath readily, chearfully and gallantly engaged, and refolutely and conftantly continued active in it, notwithftanding the many powerful diffuafions, difcouragements, and oppofitions he hath met with from divers hands ; and hath in the carrying on of the Service fhewn fuch fignal Fidelity, Integrity, Generofity, Prudence, Courage and Conduct, and fuch high Virtue, Induftry, and Ability, as are fuitable to the Dignity of his Noble Family, and the Truft his Majefty repofed in him, and hath not only ftood out

Z z   againft against all temptations and enticements, but hath moſt nobly croſſed and repreſſed deſigns and attempts of deſerting the Service, and perſiſted loyally and firmly in it to the very laſt, through exceſſive toil and many great difficulties, miſregarding all perſonal Inconveniencies, and chuſing the loſs of Friends, Fortune, and all private Concernments, and to endure the utmoſt extremities rather than ſwerve in the leaſt from his Duty; or taint his Reputation with the meaneſt ſhadow of diſloyalty and diſhonour. I do therefore hereby teſtify and declare, That I am perfectly ſatisfy'd with his whole Deportments, in relation to the Enemy, and this late War; and do highly approve them, as being not only above all I can expreſs of their worth, but almoſt beyond all parallel. And I do withal hereby both allow, and moſt earneſtly deſire, and wiſh him, to loſe no time in taking ſuch courſe for his ſafety and preſervation by Treaty, and Agreement, or Capitulation, as he ſhall judge moſt fit and expedient for the good of his Perſon, Family and Eſtate, ſince inevitable and invincible neceſſity hath forced us to lay aſide this War. And I can now no other way expreſs my reſpects to him, nor contribute my endeavour to do him Honour and Service. In teſtimony whereof, I have ſigned and ſealed theſe Preſents at *Dunveagave*, the laſt day of *March*, 1655.

JOHN MIDDLETON.

Another Letter from the Earl of Middleton, *to the ſame purpoſe.*

Paris, April 17. 1655.

My Noble Lord,

I Am hopeful, that the Bearer of this Letter will be found one who has been a moſt faithful Servant to your Lordſhip and my kind Friend, and a ſharer in my Troubles. Indeed I have been ſtrengthened by him to ſupport and overcome many difficulties. He will acquaint you with what hath paſt, which indeed was ſtrange to both of us, but your own Re-encounters will leſſen them. My Lord, I ſhall be faithful in giving you that Character which your Worth and Merit may juſtly challenge. I profeſs it is, next to the ruin of the Service, one of my chiefeſt Regrets that I could not poſſibly wait upon you before my going from *Scotland*, that I might have ſettled a way of Correſpondence with you, and that your Lordſhip might have underſtood me better than yet you do; I ſhould have been plain in every thing, and indeed have made your Lordſhip my Confeſſor, and I am hopeful the Bearer will ſay ſomewhat for me, and I doubt not but your Lordſhip will truſt him. If it ſhall pleaſe God to bring me ſafe from beyond Sea, your Lordſhip ſhall hear from me by a ſure hand. Sir *Ro. M.* will tell you a way of correſponding. So that I ſhall ſay no more at preſent, but that I am without poſſibilty of change,

My Noble Lord,
Your Lordſhip's moſt Faithful,
and moſt Humble Servant,
JO. MIDDLETON.

A Letter from the Earl of Glencairn, *teſtifying his Eſteem for this Noble Perſon, and the ſenſe he had of his Loyalty to the King, when few had the Courage to own him.*

My Lord,

LEſt it may be my misfortune, in all theſe great Revolutions, to be miſrepreſented to your Lordſhip, as a perſon unworthy of your favourable Opinion (an Artifice very frequent in theſe times) I did take occaſion to call for a Friend and Servant of yours, the Laird of *Spanie*, on whoſe diſcretion I did adventure to lay forth my heart's deſire, to obviate in the bud any of theſe miſunderſtandings: Your Lordſhip's true worth and zeal to your Country's happineſs being ſo well known to me, and confirmed by our late ſuffering acquaintance. And now finding how much it may conduce to theſe great ends we all wiſh that a perfect Unity may be among all good and honeſt-hearted *Scotchmen*, tho' there be few more inſignificant than my ſelf; yet my zeal for thoſe ends obliges me to ſay, that if your Lordſhip's health and affairs could have permitted you to have been at *Edinburgh* in theſe late times, you would have ſeen a great inclination and deſire amongſt all here of a pefect Unity, and of a mutual reſpect to your Perſon, as of chief eminence and worth. And I here ſhall ſet it under my hand to witneſs againſt all my Informers, that none did

with

4

with more passion, nor shall with more continued zeal, witness themselves to be true Honourers of you, than he who desires infinitely to be esteemed,

My Lord,

Your most Humble Servant,

GLENCAIRN.

What I cannot well write I hope this discreet Gentleman will tell you in my Name: and I shall only beg leave to say, that I am your most Noble Lady's Humble Servant.

After the reading of which Order and Letters, which yet the Court refused to record, the Earl's Advocate or Council, Sir *George Lockhart*, said in his defence as follows.

Sir George Lockhart's *Argument and Plea for the Earl of* Argyle.

SIR *George Lockhart* for the Earl of *Argyle* alledgeth, That the Libel is not Relevant, and whereupon he ought to be put to the knowledge of an Inquest. For,

It is alledged in the general, That all Criminal Libels, whereupon any Person's Life, Estate and Reputation can be drawn in question, should be founded upon clear, positive, and express Acts of Parliament, and the matter of Fact, which is libell'd to be the Contravention of those Laws, should be plain, clear and direct Contraventions of the same, and not argued by way of Implications and Inferences. Whereas in this Case, neither the Acts of Parliament founded upon, and libelled, can be in the least the foundation of this Libel; nor is the Explication which is pretended to be made by the Pannel, at the time of the taking of his Oath (if considered,) any Contravention of those Laws; which being premised, and the Pannel denying the Libel, as to the whole Articles and Points therein contained, it is alledged in special,

That the Libel, in so far as it is founded upon the 21*st Chap. Stat.* 1. *Robert* 1. and upon 8 3*d. Act, Par.* 6. *James* 5. the 43*d. Act, Par.* 2. *James* 1. and upon the 8 3*d. Act, Par.* 10. *James* 5. and upon the 8 4*th Act, Par.* 8. *James* 6. and upon the 10*th Act, Par.* 10. *James* 6. and upon the 2*d. Act, Par.* 1. *Sess.* 2. of his sacred Majesty, and inferring thereupon, That the Pannel, by the pretended Explication given in by him to the Lords of his Majesty's Privy Council, as the sense of the Oath he had taken, doth commit the Crime of Leasing-making, and depraving his Majesty's Laws: The inference and subsumption is most unwarrantable, and the Pannel, tho' any such things were acknowledged or proved, can never be found guilty of contravening these Acts of Parliament. In respect it is evident, upon perusal and consideration of these Acts of Parliament, that they only concern the Case of Leasing-making tending to Sedition, and to beget discord betwixt his Majesty and Subjects, and the dislike of his Majesty's Government, and the reproach of the same: And the said Laws and Acts of Parliament were never understood or libelled upon in any other sense. And all the former Acts of Parliament, which relate to the Crime of Leasing-making in general terms, and under the qualification foresaid, as tending to beget discord betwixt his Majesty and his Subjects, are explained, and fully declared, as to what is the true meaning and import thereof, by the 134*th Act, Par.* 8. *James* 6. which relates to the same Crime of Leasing-making, and which is expresly described in these Terms, To be wicked and licentious, publick and private Speeches, and untrue calumnies, to the disdain and contempt of his Majesty's Council and Proceedings, and to the dishonour and prejudice of his Highness and his Estate, stirring up his Highness's Subjects to misliking, and Sedition and unquietness; which being the true Sense and Import of the Acts of Parliament made against Leasing-makers, there is nothing can be inferred from the Pannel's alledged Explication, wrested or construed to be a contravention of these Laws: In respect,

First, It is known by the whole tenor of his Life, and graciously acknowledged by his Sacred Majesty, by a Letter under his Royal Hand, that the Pannel did ever most zealously, vigorously, and faithfully promote and carry on his Majesty's Service and Interest, even in the worst and most difficult times: Which is also acknowledg'd by a Pass under the Earl of *Middleton*'s hand, who had then a special Commission from his Majesty, for carrying on his Majesty's Service in this Kingdom, as Lieutenant General under his Majesty; and by a Letter under the Earl's hand, of the date. Both which do contain high expressions of the Pannel's loyalty, and of the great services he had perform'd for his Majesty's Interest, and his Majesty, as being conscious thereof, and perfectly knowing the Pannel's loyalty, and his zeal, and faithfulness for his Service, did think fit to entrust the Pannel in Offices and Capacities of the greatest trust of the Kingdom. And it is a just and rational presumption, which all Laws make and infer, That the words and expressions of persons, who by the tenor and

course

courfe of their Lives have expreffed their Duty and Loyalty to his Majefty's Intereft, are ever to be interpreted and underftood *in meliorem partem.* And by way of Implication and Inference, to conclude and infer crimes from the fame, which the ufer of fuch words and expreffions never mean'd nor defigned, is both unreafonable and unjuft.

2. As the forefaid Acts of Parliament made againft Leafing-makers, and depravers of his Majefty's Laws, only proceed in the terms aforefaid, where the words and fpeeches are plain, tending to beget difcord between the King and his Subjects, and to the reproach and diflike of the Government, and when the fame are fpoke and vented in a fubdolous, pernicious and fraudulent manner: So they never were, nor can be underftood to proceed in the cafe of a perfon offering in the prefence of a publick Judicature, (whereof he had the honour to be a Member) his fincere and plain meaning and apprehenfion of what he conceived to be the true fenfe of the Act of Parliament impofing and enjoyning the *Teft*: There being nothing more oppofite to the Acts of Parliament made againft Leafing-making, and venting and fpreading abroad the fame upon feditious defigns, than the forefaid plain and open declaration of his fenfe and apprehenfion, what was the meaning of the faid Act of Parliament. And it is of no import to infer any Crime, and much lefs any of the crimes libelled, albeit the Pannel had erred and miftaken in his apprehenfion of the Act of Parliament. And it were a ftrange extenfion of the Act of Parliament made againft Leafing-makers, requiring the qualifications forefaid, and the Acts againft depraving his Majefty's Laws, to make the Pannel, or any other perfon guilty upon the miftakes and mifapprehenfions of the fenfe of the Laws, wherein men may miftake and differ very much, and even eminent Lawyers and Judges. So that the Acts of Parliament againft Leafing-making, and depraving his Majefty's Laws, can only be underftood in the exprefs terms and qualifications forefaid. Like as it neither is libell'd nor can be proven, that the Pannel, before he was call'd and required by the Lords of his Majefty's Privy-Council to take Oath, did ever, by word or practice, ufe any reproachful fpeeches of the faid Act of Parliament or of his Majefty's Government: But being required to take the Oath, he did humbly with all fubmiffion, declare what he apprehended to be the fenfe of the Act of the Parliament, enjoining the *Teft*, and in what fenfe he had freedom to take the fame.

3. The Act of Parliament enjoining the *Teft* does not enjoin the fame to be taken by all perfons whatfoever, but only prefcribes it as a qualification without which perfons could not affume or continue to act in publick Truft: Which being an Oath to be taken by fo folemn an invocation in the Name of Almighty God, is not only allowable by the Laws and cuftoms of all Nations, and the opinion of all Divines and Cafuifts, Popifh or Proteftant, but alfo commended, that where a Party has any fcrupulofity, or unclearnefs in his Confcience, as to the matter of the Oath, that he fhould exhibit and declare the fenfe and meaning in which he is willing and able to take the Oath. And it is not at all material, whether the fcruples of a man's confcience, in the matter of an Oath, be in themfelves juft or groundlefs, it being a certain *maxim*, both in Law and Divinity, that *Confcientia etiam erronea ligat*: and therefore tho' the Pannel had thought it fit, for the clearing and exoneration of his own confcience, in a matter of the higheft concern to his peace and repofe, to have expreft and declared the exprefs fenfe in which he could take the Oath, whether the faid fenfe was confiftent with the Act of Parliament or not, yet it does not in the leaft import any matter of reproach or reflection upon the Juftice or Prudence of the Parliament in impofing the faid Oath; but allenarly does evince the weaknefs and fcrupulofity of a man's confcience, who neither did, nor ought to have taken the Oath but with an explanation that would have faved his confcience to his apprehenfion. Otherwife he had grofly finned before God, even tho' it was *Confcientia errans.* And this is allowed and prefcribed by all Proteftant Divines, as indifpenfibly neceffary, and was never thought to import any crime, and is alfo commended even by popifh Cafuifts themfelves, who tho' they allow, in fome cafes, of mental refervations and equivocations, yet the exprefs declaration of the fenfe of the Party is allowed and commended, as much more ingenuous: and *tutius Remedium Confcientiæ ne illaqueatur*, as appears by *Bellarmine de Juramento*, and upon the fame Title *de Interpretatione Juramenti*; and *Leffius*, that famous Cafuift, *de Juftitia & Jure, Dubitatione 8, 9. utrum fi quis falvo animo aliquid Juramento promittat obligetur, & quale peccatum hoc eft.* And which is the general opinion of all Cafuifts and all Divines, as may appear by *Amefius*, in his Teatife *de confcientia, Sanderfon de Juramento, Prælectione fecunda.* And fuch an exprefs Declaration of the fenfe and meaning of any party, when required to take an Oath, for no other end but for the clearing and exoneration of his own Confcience, was never in the opinion of any Lawyer, or any Divine, conftrued to be the Crime of Leafing-making, or of defamatory Libels, or depraving of publick Laws, or reproaching or mifconftruing of the Government: but on the contrary, by the univerfal fuffrage of all Proteftant Divines, there is exprefly required,

red, in Cases of a scrupulous Conscience, an abhorrence and detestation of all reserved senses, and of all *Amphibologies* and Equivocations, which are in themselves unlawful and reprobate, upon that unanswerable Reason, that *Juramentum* being the highest Act of Devotion and Religion, *in eo requiritur maxima simplicitas*; and that a party is obliged, who has any scruples of Conscience, publickly and openly to clear and declare the same.

4. Albeit it is not controverted, but that a Legislator, imposing an Oath, or any publick Authority, before whom the Oath is taken, may, after hearing of the Sense and Explication which a Person is willing to put upon it, either reject or accept of the same, if it be conceived not to be consistent with the genuine sense of the Oath: Yet, tho' it were rejected, it was never heard of, or pretended, that the offering of a sense does import a Crime, but that notwithstanding thereof, *Habetur pro Recusante*, and as if he had not taken the Oath, and to be liable to the Certification of Law, as if he had been a Refuser.

5. The Pannel having publickly, and openly declared the sense in which he was free to take the Oath, it is offered to be proved that he was allowed, and did accordingly proceed to the taking of the Oath, and did thereafter take his place, and sit and vote, during that *Sederunt* of the Privy Council. So as the pretended Sense and Explication, which he did then emit and give, can import no Crime against him.

6. It is also offered to be proved, that before the Pannel was required to take the Oath, or did appear before his Royal Highness, and Lords of the Privy-Council, to take the same, there were a great many Papers spread abroad from Persons and Ministers of the Orthodox Clergy; and as the Pannel is informed, some thereof presented to the Bishops of the Church, in the name of Synods and Presbyteries, which did, in downright terms, charge the *Test* and Oath with alledged contradictions and inconsistencies. And for satisfaction whereof some of the Learned and Reverend Bishops of the Church did write a learned and satisfying Answer, called, *A Vindication of the* Test, *for clearing the Scruples, Difficulties and Mistakes that were objected against it.* And which Vindication and Answer was exhibited, and read before the Lords of his Majesty's Privy Council, and allowed to be printed, and from which the Pannel argues,

1. That it neither is, nor can be pretended in this Libel, that the alledged Explication, wherein he did take the Oath, does propose the scruples of his Conscience in these terms, which were proposed by the Authors of these Objections, which do flatly and positively assert, that the Oath and *Test* do contain matters of Inconsistency and Contradiction; whereas all that is pretended in this Libel, with the most absolute violence can be put upon the words, is arguing from Implications and Inferences, which neither the words are capable to bear, nor the sincerity of the Earl's intention and design, nor the course of his by-past life, can possibly admit of. And yet none of the persons who were the Authors of such papers were ever judged or reputed Criminal or Guilty, and to be prosecuted for the odious and infamous Crimes libelled, of *Treason, Leasing-making, Perjury,* and the like.

2. The Pannel does also argue from the said matter of Fact, that the alledged Explication libelled, can neither in his intention and design, nor in the Words, infer or import any Crime against him, because, before his being required, or appearing to take the Oath, there were spread abroad such Scruples and Objections, by some of the Orthodox Clergy and others, so that the Earl can never in any sense be construed in his Explication wherein he took the Oath, to have done it *animo infamandi*, and to declaim against the Government; for the Scruples and Objections that were spread abroad by others, were a fair and rational occasion why the Earl in any sense or explication which he offered might have said, that he was confident the Parliament never intended to impose contradictory Oaths: and this is so far from importing the insinuation and inference made by the Libel, that thereby the Parliament were so impious as to impose contradictory Oaths, as on the contrary, considering the circumstances fore-mentioned, that there were papers spread abroad, insinuating, That there were inconsistencies and contradictions contained therein, the said expression was an high Vindication of the Honour and Justice of the Parliament, against the Calumnies and Mis-representations which were cast upon it, and was also a just Rise for the Pannel, for the clearing and exoneration of his own Conscience, in the various senses and apprehensions which he found were going abroad as to the said *Test*, humbly to offer his sense, in which he was clear and satisfied to take the Oath.

7. To the Libel, in so far as it is founded upon the Act of Parliament, viz. *Act* 130. *Par.* 8. *James* 6. declaring, That none should presume to impugn the Dignity or Authority of the three Estates of Parliament, or procure any Invasion or Diminution thereof, under the pain of Treason; as also in so far as it is pretended in the Libel,

That

That the Pannel by offering the sense and explication libelled, has assumed the Legislative power, which is incommunicable, and has made a Law, or a part of a Law.

It is answered, The Libel is most groundless and irrelevant, and against which the Act of Parliament is opponed, which is so plain and evident upon the reading thereof, that it neither is, nor can be subject to the least cavillation: And the plain meaning whereof is nothing else but to impugn the Authority of Parliaments, as if the King and Parliament had not a Legislative Power, or were not the highest Representative of the Kingdom; or that any of the three Estates were not essentially requisite to constitute the Parliament. And besides, there is nothing more certain, than that the occasion of the said Act its being made was in relation to the Bishops and Clergy; and there is nothing in the pretended Explanation, that can be wrested to import the least Contravention of the said Act, or to be an impugning of the three Estates of Parliament, or a seeking any innovation therein. And it is admired, with what shadow of Reason it can be pretended, that the Pannel has assumed a Legislative Power, or made a part of a Law, seeing all that is contained in the alledged Explication libelled, is only a Declaration of the Earl's sense in which he was satisfied to take the Oath, and so respected none but himself, and for the clearing of his own Conscience, which justly indeed the Word of God calls a Law to himself, without any incroaching upon the Legislative Power. And where was it ever debated, but that a man in the taking of an Oath, if, as to his Apprehensions he thought any thing in it deserv'd to be clear'd, might declare the same, or that his exhibiting, at the time of the taking of the Oath, his sense and explication wherein he did take it, was ever reputed or pretended to be the assuming of the Legislative Power, it being the universal practice of all Nations to allow this liberty; and which sense may be either rejected or accepted, as the Legislature shall think fit, importing no more but a Party's private sense, for the exoneration of his own Conscience? And as to that Member of the Libel founded upon *Act* 19. *Par.* 3. Queen *Mary*, it contains nothing but a Declaration of the pain of Perjury, and there is nothing in the Explication libelled, which can in the least be inferred as a Contravention of the said Act, in respect if it should be proved, That the Pannel, at the time of the taking of the Oath, did take it in the Words of the said Explication, as his sense of the Oath, it is clear that the sense being declared at the time of taking the Oath, and allowed as the sense wherein it was taken, the Pannel can only be understood to have taken it in that sense. And although publick Authority may consider whether the sense given by the Pannel does satisfy the Law or not, yet that can import no more though it was found not to satisfy, but to hold the Pannel as a Refuser of the Oath; but it is absolutely impossible to infer the Crimes of Perjury upon it, being as is pretended by the Libel, the Pannel did only take it with the Declaration of the Sense and Explication libelled.

8. As the Explication libelled does not at all import all, or any of the Crimes contained in the said Libel, so by the common principles of all Law, where a person does emit words for the clearing and exoneration of his own Conscience, altho' there were any ambiguity, or unclearness, or involvedness, in the tenor or import of the expressions or words, yet they are ever to be interpreted, *Interpretatione benigna & favorabili, according to the general Principles of Law and Reason.* And it never was, nor can be refused to any person to interpret, and put a congruous Sense upon his own words, especially the Pannel being a person of eminent Quality, and who hath given great demonstration, and undeniable Evidences of his fixt and unalterable Loyalty to his Majesty's Interest and Service; and, at the time of emitting the said Explication, was invested and entrusted in publick Capacities. And it is a just and rational interpretation and caution which *Saunderson*, that judicious and eminent Casuist gives, *Prælect.* 2. That *dicta & facta principum, parentum, rectorum,* are ever to be look'd upon as *benignæ Interpretationis,* and that *Dubia sunt interpretanda in meliorem partem.* And there is nothing in the Explication libelled, which, without detortion and violence, and in the true sense and design of the Pannel, is not capable of this benign Interpretation and Construction, especially respect being had to the Circumstances wherein it was emitted and given, after a great many Objections, Scruples, and alledged Inconsistencies, were owned, vented and spread abroad, which was a rise to the Earl for using the expressions contained in the pretended Declaration libelled.

10. These words whereby it is pretended the Pannel declares, *he was ready to give obedience as far as he could,* first, do not in the least import, That the Parliament had imposed any Oath which was in itself unlawful, but only the Pannel's scrupulosity and unclearness in matter of Conscience. And it is hoped it cannot be a Crime, because all men cannot go the same length. And if any such thing were argued, it might be argued ten times more strongly from a simple refusing of the Oath, as if any thing were enjoined which were so hard that it is not possible to comply with it: And yet such implications are most irrational and inconsequential, and neither in the case of a
simple

simple and absolute refusing of the Oath, nor in the case of an Explication of the party's sense, wherein he is willing to take the Oath, is there any impeachment of the Justice, and Prudence of the Legislator, who imposeth this Oath, but singly a declaration of the scrupulosity and weakness of the party, why he cannot take the Oath in other terms; and such Explications have been allowed by the Laws and Customs of all Nations, and are advised by all Divines, of whatsoever Principles, for the solace and security of a Man's Conscience.

2. As to that point of the Explication libelled, *That I am confident the Parliament never intended to impose contradictory Oaths*; it respects the former answer, which, considering the plain and downright Objections that were spread abroad, and made against the Oath, as containing Inconsistencies and Contradictions, was an high Vindication of the Justice and Prudence of the *Parliament*.

3. As to these words, *And therefore I think No-body can explain it but for himself*; the plain and clear meaning is nothing else, but that the Oath being imposed by Act of Parliament, it was of no private Interpretation; and that therefore every Man who was to take it, behooved to take it in that sense which he apprehended to be the genuine sense of the Parliament: And it is impossible, without impugning common sense, that any Man could take it in any other sense, it being as impossible to see with another Man's eyes, as to see with his private Reason. And a Man's own private sense, and apprehension of the genuine Sense, was the only proper way wherein any Man could rationally take the Oath.

And as to these words, *That he takes it as far it is consistent with itself and the Protestant Religion*; the Pannel neither intended nor expressed more, but that he did take it as a true Protestant, and he hopes all Men have taken it as such.

And as to that Clause, wherein the Pannel is made to declare, *That he does not bind up himself in his Station, in a lawful way, to wish and endeavour any alteration he thinks to the advantage of Church or State, not repugnant to the Protestant Religion and his Loyalty:* It is answered, There is nothing in this Expression that can import the least Crime or give the least umbrage for any Mistake. For,

1. It is most certain, it is impossible to elicite any such thing from the Oath, but that it was the Intention of the Parliament, That Persons, notwithstanding of the Oath, might concur in their Stations, and in a lawful way, in any Law, to the advantage of Church and State. And no rational Man ever did, or can take the Oath in other terms, that being contrary to his Allegiance and Duty to his sacred Majesty and Prince.

2. There is nothing in the said Expression, which does touch in the least point at any alteration in the fundamentals of Government, either in Church or State, but on the contrary, by the plain and clear words and meaning, rather for its perpetuity, stability, and security. The Expression being cautioned to the utmost scrupulosity, as that it was to be done in a lawful manner; that it was to be to the advantage of Church or State; that it was to be consistent with the Protestant Religion, and with his Loyalty, which was no other but the Duty and Loyalty of all faithful Subjects; and which he has signally and eminently expressed upon all Occasions. So that how such an Expression can be drawn to import all or any of the Crimes libelled, passeth all natural Understanding.

And as to the last words, *And this I understand as a part of my Oath*, which is libelled to be a treasonable Invasion, and assuming of the legislative Power: It is answered, it is most unwarrantable; and a party's declaring the Sense and Meaning, in which he was free to take an Oath, does not at all respect or invade the legislative Power, of which the Pannel never entertained a thought, but has an absolute abhorrence and detestation of such Practices. But the plain and clear meaning is, That the Sense and Explication was a part of his Oath, and not of the Law imposing the Oath, these being as distant as the two Poles; and which sense was taken off the Earl's hands, and he accordingly was allowed to take his place at the Council-board, and therefore repeats the former general Defences.

And to convince the Lords of Justiciary, that there is nothing in the pretended Explication libelled, which can be drawn to import any Crime, even of the lowest size and degree, and that there is no Expression therein contained, that can be detorted or wrested to import the same, is evident from the learned Vindication published and spread abroad by an eminent Bishop, and which was read in the face of the Privy-Council, and does contain Expressions of the same nature, and to the same import contained in the pretended Explication, libelled as the Ground of this Indictment libelled against the Pannel. And it is positively offered to be proven, That these terms were given in, and read, and allowed to be printed, and (without taking notice of the whole tenor of the said Vindication, which the Lords of Justiciary are humbly desired to peruse, and consider,

I der,

der, and compare the fame with the Explication libelled) the fame acknowledgeth, that Scruples had been raifed and fpread abroad againft the Oath ; and alfo acknowledgeth, that there were Expreffions therein that were dark and obfcure ; and likewife takes notice, that the Confeffion ratified *Par. 1. James 6.* to which the Oath relates, was haftily made, and takes notice of that Authority that made it, and acknowledges in plain terms, that the Oath does not hinder any regular endeavour to regulate or better the eftablifhed Government, but only prohibits irregular Endeavours and Attempts to invert the Subftance or Body of the Government ; and does likewife explain the Act of Parliament anent his Majefty's Supremacy, that it does not reach the alteration of the external Government of the Church. And the Pannel and his Proctors are far from infinuating in the leaft, that there is any thing in the faid Vindication, but what is confiftent with the exemplary Loyalty, Piety, and Learning of the Writer of the fame. And tho' others perhaps may differ in their private Opinion, as to this Interpretation of the Act of Parliament anent the King's Supremacy, yet it were moft abfurd and irrational to pretend that whether the Miftake were upon the Interpretation of the Writer, or the fenfe of others, as to that point, that fuch Miftakes or Mifapprehenfions, upon either hand, fhould import or infer againft them the Crimes of Leafing-making, or depraving his Majefty's Laws: For if fuch Foundations were laid, Judges and Lawyers had a dangerous employment, there being nothing more ordinary than to fall into differences and miftakes of the fenfe and meaning of the Laws and Acts of Parliament. But fuch Crimes cannot be inferred, but with and under the Qualifications above-mentioned, of malicious and perverfe defigns, joined with licentious, wicked, and reproachful Speeches fpread abroad, to move Sedition and Diflike of the Government. And the faid Laws were never otherwife interpreted, nor extended in any cafe. And therefore the Explication libelled, neither as taken complexly, nor in the feveral Expreffions thereof, nor in the defign of the ingiver of the fame, can in Law import againft him all or any of the Crimes libelled.

In like manner the Pannel conjoins with the grounds above-mentioned, the Proclamation iffued forth by his Majefty's Privy-Council, which acknowledges and proceeds upon a Narrative, that fcruples and jealoufies were raifed and fpread abroad againft the Act of Parliament enjoining the *Teft.* For clearing and fatisfaction whereof, the faid Proclamation was iffued forth, and is fince approved by his facred Majefty.

The King's Advocate's Argument and Plea againft the Earl of Argyle.

HIS Majefty's Advocate, for the foundation of his debate, does reprefent, That his Majefty, to fecure the Government from the rebellious Principles of the laft Age, and the unjuft Pretexts made ufe of in this, from Popery and other Jealoufies ; as alfo to fecure the Proteftant Religion, and the Crown, called a Parliament ; and that the great fecurity refolved on by the Parliament was this excellent *Teft,* in which, that the old juggling Principles of the Covenant might not be renewed, wherein they ftill fwore to ferve the King in their own way, the Parliament did pofitively ordain, That this Oath fhould be taken in the plain genuine meaning of the words, without any evafion whatfoever. Notwithftanding whereof, the Earl of *Argyle,* by this Paper, does invent a new way, whereby no man is at all bound to it : For how can any Perfon be bound, if every Man will only obey it as far as he can, and as far as he conceives it confiftent with the Proteftant Religion, and with itfelf, and referve to himfelf, notwithftanding thereof, to make any alteration that he thinks confiftent with his Loyalty? And therefore his Majefty's Advocate defires to know, to what the Earl of *Argyle,* or any Man elfe, can be bound by this *Teft?* What the Magiftrate can expect, or what way he can punifh his Perjury? For if he be bound no farther than he himfelf can obey, or fo far as this Oath is confiftent with the Proteftant Religion, or itfelf, *quomodo conftat,* to whom or what is he bound? And who can determine that? Or againft what alteration is the Government fecured, fince he is Judge of his own alteration? So that that Oath, that was to be taken without any evafion, is evaded in every fingle word or letter ; and the Government as infecure as before the Act was made, becaufe the taker is no farther bound than he pleafes. From which it cannot be denied, but his Interpretation deftroys not only this Act, but all Government, fince it takes away the fecurity of all Government, and makes every Man's Confcience, under which Name there goes ordinarily in this Age, Humour and Intereft, to be the rule of the taker's obedience. Nor can it be conceived to what purpofe Laws, but efpecially Oaths, needed to be made, if this were allowed ; or how this cannot fall under the 197th *Act, Par. 7. James 6.* whereby it is ftatuted, *That no Man interpret the Statutes otherwife than the maker underftood.* For what can be more contrary to the taking of them in the maker's

fenfe,

sense, than that every man should obey as far as they can, and be allowed to take them in a general sense, so far as they are consistent with themselves, and the Protestant Religion, without condescending wherein they do not agree with the Protestant Religion? and that they are not bound not to make any Alteration which they think good for the States? For all these make the rule of obedience in the taker, whereas the positive Law makes it to be in the maker. Or how could they be punished for Perjury after this Oath? For when he were quarrelled for making alterations against this Oath; and so to be perjured, he might easily answer, That he took this Oath only in so far as it was consistent with the Protestant Religion, and with a *Salvo,* that he might make any alteration that he thought consistent with his Loyalty. And as to these Points, upon which he were to be quarrelled, he might say, he did not think them to be inconsistent with his Loyalty, think we what we pleased, and so needed not to be perjured, except he pleased to decide against himself, for in these Generals he reserves to himself to be still Judge. And this were indeed a fine security for any Government. And by the same rule that it looses this Oath, it shews a way of loosing all Oaths and Obedience, and consequently strikes at the root of all Laws, as well as this; whereas to shun all this, not only this excellent Statute 107, has secured all the rest, but this is common Reason: And in the opinion of all Divines, as well as Lawyers in all Nations, *Verba juramenti intelliguntur secundum mentem & intentionem ejus, cui fit juramentum.* Which is set down as the grand position, by *Sanderson* (whom they cite *pag.* 137. and is founded upon that Mother-Law, *Leg.* 10. *Cui interrogatus f. f. de interrogationibus in Jure faciendis ;* and without which no Man can have sense of Government in his head, or practise it in any Nation. Whereas on the other hand there is no danger to any tender Conscience; since there was no force upon the Earl to take the Oath, but he took it for his own advantage, and might have abstained.

2. It is inferred from the above written matter of Fact, that the Earl is clearly guilty of contravention of the 10 *Act, Parl.* 10. *James* VI. whereby the Lieges are commanded not to write any purpose of Reproach of his Majesty's Government, or misconstrue his proceedings, whereby any misliking may be raised betwixt his Highness, his Nobility, or his People. And who can read this paper, without seeing the King and Parliament reproached openly in it? For who can hear, that the Oath is only taken as far as it is consistent with itself and the Protestant Religion, but must necessarily conclude, that in several things it is inconsistent with itself, and the Protestant Religion? For if it were not inconsistent with itself and the Protestant Religion, why this Clause at all, but it might have been simply taken? For the only Reason of hindering it to be taken simply, was because of the inconsistency: *ergo,* there behooved necessarily to be an inconsistency. And if there be any inconsistency with the Protestant Religion, or any contradiction in the Oath itself, can there be any thing a greater reproach on the Parliament, or a greater ground of mislike to the people? And whereas it is pretended, That all Laws and Subsumptions should be clear, and these are only Inferences: It is answered, That there are some things which the Law can only forbid in general; and there are many inferences which are as strong and natural, and reproach as soon, or sooner, than the plainest defamations in the world do; for what is openly said of reproach to the King, does not wound him so much as many seditious insinuations have done in this Age and the last: So that whatever was the Earl's design (albeit it is always conceived to be unkind to the Act, against which himself debated in Parliament) yet certainly the Law in such cases is only to consider what effect this may have amongst the people; and therefore the Acts of Parliament, that were to guard against the misconstruing of his Majesty's Government, do not only speak of what was designed, but where a misliking may be caused, and so judgeth *ab effectu :* And, consequentially to the same emergent Reason, it makes all things tending to the raising of dislike, to be punishable by the *Act* 60. *Parl.* 6. Q. *Mary ;* and the 9 *Act, Parl.* 20. *James* VI. So that the Law designed to deter all men by these indefinite and comprehensive Expressions: And both in this and all the Laws of Leasing-making, the Judges are to consider what falls under these general and comprehensive words. Nor could the Law be more special here, since the makers of Reproach and Slander are so various that they could not be bound up, or exprest in any Law : But as it evidently appears, that no man can hear the Words exprest, if he believe this paper, but he must think the Parliament has made a very ridiculous Oath, inconsistent with itself and the Protestant Religion, the words allowing no other sense, and having that natural tendency ; even as if a Man would say, I love such a man only in so far as he is an honest man, he behooved certainly to conclude, that the man was not every way honest: So if your Lordships will take measures by other Parliaments, or your Predecessors, ye will clearly see, That they thought less than this a defaming of the Government, and misconstruing his Majesty's Proceedings. For in *Balmerino's*

merino's Case, the Justices find an humble Supplication made to the King himself to fall under these Acts now cited. Albeit as that was a Supplication, so it contained the greatest expressions of Loyalty, and offers of Life and Fortune that could be exprest ; yet because it infinuates darkly, That the King in the preceding Parliament had not favoured the Protestant Religion, and they were sorry he should have taken Notes with his own Hand of what they said, which seems to be most innocent, yet he was found guilty upon those same very Acts: And the Parliament 1661, found his Lordship himself guilty of Leasing-making, tho' he had only written a Letter to a private Friend, which requires no great Care nor Observation, (but this paper which was to be a part of his own Oath does) because after he had spoken of the Parliament in the first part of this Letter, he thereafter added, *That the King would know their Tricks* ; which words might be much more applicable to the private persons therein designed, than that the words now insisted on can be capable of any such Interpretation. And if either Interpretations, upon pretext of exonering Conscience, or otherwise, be allowed, a man may easily defame as much as he pleases. And have we not seen the King most defamed by Covenants entred into upon pretence to make him great and glorious, by Remonstrances made to take away his Brother and best Friend, upon pretence of preserving the Protestant Religion, and his Sacred Person? And did not all who rebelled against him in the last Age declare, That they thought themselves bound in duty to obey him, but still as far as that could consist with their respect to the Protestant Religion, and the Laws and Liberties, which made all the rest ineffectual? And whereas it is pretended, That by these Words, *I take the same as far as it is consistent with itself and the Protestant Religion*, nothing more is meant; but that he takes it as a true Protestant : His Majesty's Advocate appeals to your Lordships, and all the Hearers, if upon hearing this expression they should take it in this sense, and not rather think that there is an inconsistency. For if that were possible to be the sense, what need he say at all, *As far as it is consistent with itself?* Nor had the other part, *As far as it is consistent with the Protestant Religion*, been necessary ; for it is either consistent with the Protestant Religion, or otherwise they were Enemies to the Protestant Religion, that made it. Nor are any Lawyers or others in danger, by pleading or writing, for these are very different from, and may be very easily pleaded without defaming a Law, and an Oath, when they go to take it. But if any Lawyer should say, in pleading or writing, That the *Test* was inconsistent ; or, which is all one, that it were not to be taken by any man, but so far as it was consistent with it self and the Protestant Religion, no doubt this would be a crime even in pleading, tho' pleading has a greater allowance than deliberate swearing has. And as there is nothing wherein there is not some inconveniency, so the inconveniency of defaming the Government, is much greater than that of any private man's hazard, who needs not err except he please.

Whereas it is pretended, That before the Earl gave in this Explication, there were other Explications spread abroad, and Answers read to them in Council, and that the Council itself gave an Explication : It is answered, That if this paper be Leasing-making, or misconstruing his Majesty's proceedings, and Treasonable, as is contended, then a thousand of the like offences cannot excuse it. And when the King accused Noblemen, Ministers and others, in the year 1661, for going on in the Rebellions of that Age, first with the Covenanters, and then with the Usurpers, it was found no Defence, That the Nation was over-grown with those Crimes, and that they were thought to be duties in those days. Yea, this were to invite men to offend in multitudes. And albeit sometimes these who follow the examples of multitudes, may thereby pretend this as an excuse to many ; yet this was never a formal defence against Guilt, nor was ever the chief of the Offenders favourable on that Head. And it is to be presumed, That the Earl of *Argyle* would rather be followed by others, than that he would follow any Example. But his Majesty's Advocate does absolutely decline to debate a point that may defame a constant and standing Act of Parliament, by leaving upon record a memory of its being opposed. Nor were this Relevant, except it could be said, the Council had allowed such Explications which reflected upon the King and the Government: For the writing an answer is no Allowance, but a condemning ; nor can the Council allow any more than they can remit : And tho' it may justly be denied that the Council heard even the Earl's own Explanation, yet the hearing or allowing him to sit is no Relevant Plea, because they might very justly have taken a time to consider how far it was fit to accuse upon that Head. And it is both just and fit for the Council to take time, and by express Act of Parliament, the negligence of the King's Officers do not bind them. For if this were allowed, Leading Men in the Council might commit what Crimes they pleased in the Council, which certainly the King may quarrel many years after. And tho' all the Council had allowed
lowed

lowed him that day, any one Officer of State might have quarrelled it the next day. As to the Opinion of *Bellarmine, Sanderfon,* and others, it is ever contended, that the principles of the Covenant agree very well with thofe of the Jefuits, and both do ftill allow Equivocations and Evafions: But no folid Orthodox Divine ever allowed, That a Man who was to fwear without any Evafion, fhould fwear fo as he is bound to nothing, as it is contended the Earl is not, for the Reafons reprefented: And as they ftill recommend, That when Men are not clear, they might abftain, as the Earl might have done in this cafe, fo they ftill conclude, that Men fhould tell in clear terms what the fenfe is by which they are to be bound to the State: Whereas the Earl here tells only in the general, and in moft ambiguous terms, That he takes it as far as he can obey, and as far as it is confiftent with the Proteftant Religion, and that he takes it in his own fenfe, and that he is not bound by it from making alterations, but as far as he thinks it for the advantage of Church or State; which fenfe is a thoufand times more doubtful than the *Teft,* and is in effect nothing but what the taker pleafes himfelf.

As to the Treafon founded on, his Majefty's Advocate founds it firft upon the fundamental and common Laws of this and all Nations, whereby it is Treafon for any Man to make any alteration he fhall think for the advantage of Church or State, which he hopes is a Principle cannot be denied in the general. And whereas it is pretended, That this cannot be underftood of mean alterations, and of alterations to be made in a lawful way: It is anfwered, That as the thing itfelf is Treafon, fo this Treafon is not taken off by any of thefe qualifications, becaufe he declares, he will wifh and endeavour any alterations he thinks fit; and any alteration comprehends all alterations that he thinks fit: *Nam propofitio indefinita æquipollet univerfali.* And the word *any* is general in its own nature, and is in plain terms a referving to himfelf to make alterations, both great and fmall. And the reftriction is not all alterations that the King fhall think fit, or are confiftent with the Laws and Acts of Parliament; but he is ftill to be Judge of this, and his Loyalty is to be the Standard. Nor did the Covenanters in the laft Age, nor do thefe who are daily executed, decline that they are bound to obey the King, fimply, but only that they are bound to obey him no otherwife than as far as his Commands are confiftent with the Law of God, of Nature, and of this Kingdom, and with the Covenant: And their Treafon lies in this. And when it is asked them, Who fhall be judge in this, they ftill make themfelves Judges. And the reafon of all Treafon being, that the Government is not fecure, it is defired to be known, what way the Government can be fecured after this Paper, fince the Earl is ftill Judge how far he is obliged, and what is his Loyalty. And if this had been fufficient, the Covenant had been a very excellent Paper, for they are there bound to endeavour, in their feveral ftations, to defend the King's Perfon; but when the King challenged them, how they came to make War againft him, their great Refuge was, That they were themfelves ftill Judges as to that. And for illuftrating this Power, the Lords of Jufticiary are defired to confider, *Quid Juris,* if the Earl, or any Man elfe, fhould have referved to himfelf, in this Oath, a liberty to rife in Arms, or to oppofe the lineal Succeffion, tho' he had added, *In a lawful manner*; for the thing being in itfelf unlawful, this is but fham, and *Proteftatio contraria facto.* And if thefe be unlawful, notwithftanding of fuch Addition, fo much more muft this general refervation, *of making any alterations,* likewife be unlawful, notwithftanding of thefe additions. For he that referves the general Power of making any alteration, does, *a fortiori,* referve Power to make any alteration, tho' never fo fundamental. For all particulars are included in the general; and whatever may be faid againft the particulars, may much more ftrongly be faid againft the general.

2. The 130 *Act, Par.* 8. *James* VI. is exprefly founded on, becaufe nothing can be a greater diminution of the Power of the Parliament, than to introduce a way or means whereby all their Acts and Oaths fhall be made infignificant and ineffectual, as this Paper does make them, for the Reafons reprefented. Nor are any of the Eftates of Parliament fecure at this rate, but that they who referved a general Power to make all alterations, may, under that general, come to alter any of them.

3. What can be a greater impugning of the Dignity and Authority of Parliaments, than to fay, That the Parliament has made Acts for the fecurity of the Kingdom, which are in themfelves ridiculous, inconfiftent with themfelves and the Proteftant Religion?

And as to what is anfwered againft invading the King's Prerogative, and the Legiflative Power in Parliaments, in adding a part to an Oath or Act, is not relevantly inferred, fince the fenfe of thefe words, *And this I underftand as a part of my Oath,* is not to be underftood as if any thing were to be added to the Law, but only to the Oath, and to be an Interpretation of the Oath. It is replied, That after this, no Man needs to add a Caution to the Oath in Parliament. But when he comes to take the Oath, do the Parliament what they please, he will add his own Part. Nor can this part be looked upon as a sense, for if this were the sense before this Paper, he needed not understand it as a part of it, for it wanted not that part. And in general, as every Man may add his own part, so the King can be secure of no part. But your Lordships of Justiciary are desired to consider, how dangerous it would be in this Kingdom, and how ill it would sound in any other Kingdom, That Men should be allowed to reserve to themselves liberty to make any alteration they thought fit in Church or State, as to the legality of which, they were themselves to be Judges; and how far, from degree to degree, this at last may come to absolute Anarchy, and how scandalous a thing, as well as unsecure, this new way may look in an Age, wherein we are too much tracing the steps of our rebellious Progenitors in the last, whose great defection and error was, That they thought themselves, and not the King, the Authors of Reformation in Church and State. And no Man ever was barred by that, that the way he was upon was not a lawful way; for if it be allowed to every Man to take his own way, every Man will think his own way to be the lawful way.

As to the Perjury, it is founded on this, First, That Perjury may be committed, not only by breaking an Oath, but even in the swearing of it, *viz.* To swear it with such Evasions as make the Oath ineffectual; for which *Sanderson* is cited, *pag.* 138. *Alterum Perjurii genus est novo aliquo excogitato Commento Juramenti vim declinare, aut eludere, & Jurans tenetur sub pœna* Perjurii *implere secundum Intentionem deferentis*; both which are here. For the Earl being bound by the very Oath, to swear in the genuine meaning, without any evasion, he has sworn so as he has evaded every word, there being not one word to which it can be said particularly he is bound, as is said. And it is undeniable, that he has not sworn in the sense of the makers of the Law, but in his own sense, which is Perjury, as is said. And consequentially, whatever sense may be allowed in ambiguous Cases, yet there can be none where the Paper clearly bears Generals: And where he declares, That he takes it in his own sense, his Majesty's Advocate declares, he will not burden himself, that Copies were dispersed, tho' it is certain, since the very Paper itself by the giving in is chargeable with all that is above charged upon it.

Sir John Dalrymple's *Defence and Plea for the Earl of* Argyle, *by way of Reply upon the King's Advocate.*

SIR *John Dalrymple* replies for the Pannel, That since the solid grounds of Law adduced in the Defences have received no particular Answers in relation to the common consent of all Casuists, *viz.* That a party who takes an Oath is bound in Conscience to clear and propose the terms and sense in which he does understand the Oath; nor in relation to the several Grounds adduced concerning the legal and rational Interpretation of dubious Clauses: And since these have received no Answers, the Grounds are not to be repeated. But the Proctors for the Pannel do farther insist on these Defences.

1. It is not alledged, That any Explanation was given in by the Pannel to any Person, or any Copy spread, before the Pannel did take the *Test* in Council: So that it cannot be pretended, That the many Scruples that have been moved concerning the *Test*, did arise from the Pannel's Explication: But on the contrary, all the Objections that are answered, and obviated in the Pannel's Explication, were not only privately muttered, or were the thoughts of single or illiterate Persons, but they were the Difficulties proposed by Synods and Presbyteries, long before the Pannel came from home, or was required to take the *Test*: So that the general terms of the Acts of Parliament founded upon in the Libel are not applicable to this Case. For as these Laws, in relation to Leasing-makers, are only relative to atrocious wilful Insinuations, or Misconstructions of his Majesty's Person or Government, or the open depraving of his Laws; so the restrictive Clause, *whereby Sedition or Misconstructions may be moved, raised, or engendered betwixt his Majesty and his Lieges*, cannot be applied to this Case, where all these Apprehensions and Scruples were on foot, and agitated long before the Pannel's Explanation.

As it cannot be pretended, That any new Dust was raised by the Pannel's Explanation, so it is positively offered to be proved, That there is not one word contained in this Explanation, but that either these individual words, or much worse, had been publickly proposed, and *verbatim* read in Council, without the least discouragement, or the least Objection made by any Member of the Council. And where a writing *ex proposito* read in so high a Court, was universally agreed upon, without the alteration

of

of a Syllable, how can it be pretended, that any Perfon thereafter ufing the faid individual terms in any Explanation, and far eafier terms, that they fhall incur the high and infamous Crimes libelled? And the queftion is not here, whether the Council was a proper Judicature to have propofed, or impofed a fenfe, or allowed any Explanation of the *Teft* to be publifhed ; but that it is impoffible that a fenfe they allowed, or being publickly read before them, and which the King's Advocate did not controul, that this fhould import Treafon, or any Crime : And tho' the Pannel's Advocate will not purfue or follow the Reply that has been made to this point, yet certainly no Man of fober fenfe will think that it is fit to infinuate that fo high a Judicature might have authorized or acquiefced in fuch Explanations as the Lieges thereafter fhould be entrapped to have ufed.

If the Pannel had officioufly or ulteroneoufly offered a Senfe or Explanation of His Majefty's Laws, which the Laws themfelves could not have born, it might juftly have been alledged, that he was *extrà ordinem*, and meddling in a matter he was not concerned in ; but where the Act of Council did enjoin, and he was required and cited to that effect, it could neither be conftructed as Oftentation, or to move or encourage Scruples or Refiftance, but it was abfolutely neceffary, either for to have refufed the *Teft*, or elfe to have declared what he thought to be the true and genuine meaning of it. And there being fo many Objections publickly moved and known, his Explanation was nothing elfe but to clear, That he did not look upon thefe Scruples and Objections moved by others, as well founded and rational in themfelves ; and therefore he was able to take the *Teft* in that fenfe the Council had heard or allowed. And it is not controverted, that the fenfe of the Legiflator is the genuine fenfe both of Laws and Oaths : And if a Perfon were only interpreting the meaning of either a Law or an Oath impofed, he fhould deprave and mifconftruct the Law and Oath, if he rendered it wittingly and willingly in terms inconfiftent with the meaning of the Impofer. But there is a great difference betwixt taking of Oaths, and interpreting Oaths : For when a Man comes to take an Oath, except his particular fenfe did agree with the genuine meaning of the Impofer, he cannot take that Oath, tho' he may very well interpret and declare what is the fenfe of the Legiflator, which he may know, and yet perhaps not be able to take the Oath.

And therefore when there is any doubtfulnefs in an Oath, and a party is bound to take it, if then he gives in an Explication of the fenfe which in his private judgment he doth apprehend to be the genuine meaning, if that private Senfe be difconform to the Legiflator's Senfe in the Oath, then the Impofer of the Oath, or he that has power to offer it to the party, if he confiders the party's fenfe difconform, he ought to reject the Oath, as not fulfilling the Intent of the Law impofing it.

But it is impoffible to ftate that as a Crime, That a Party fhould neither believe what is propofed in the Oath, nor be able to take it : And he can run no farther hazard, but the Penalty impofed upon the Refufer. And therefore in all Oaths there muft be a concourfe both of the fenfe impofed by Authority, and of the private Senfe, Judgment, or Confcience of the Party. And therefore if a Party fhould take an Oath in the Senfe propofed by Authority, contrary to his own Senfe, he were perjured. Whereby it is evident that the Senfe of Authority is not fufficient, without the acquiefcence and confent of the private Perfon. And therefore it is very ftrange, why that part of the Pannel's Explanation fhould be challenged, that he takes it in his own Senfe, the *pofterior* words making it as plain as the light, that that Senfe of his own is not what he pleafes to make of the Oath, for it bears exprefly, that no-body can explain it but for himfelf, and reconcile it as it is genuine, and agrees in its own Senfe : So that there muft be a Reconciliation betwixt his own Senfe and the genuine Senfe, which upon all hands is acknowledged to be the Senfe of Authority. And if the Pannel had been of thefe lax and debauched Principles, that he might have evaded the meaning and energy of the Oath, by impofing upon it what Senfe he pleafed, certainly he would have contented himfelf in the general refuge of Equivocation, or mental Refervation, and he would never have expofed his Senfe to the World, in which he took this Oath, whereby he became abfolutely fixed and determined to the Oath, in that particular Senfe, and fo had no latitude of fhuffling off the Energy or Obligation of the Oath. And it is likewife acknowledged, That the Cafes alledged in the Reply are true, *viz.* That the Perfon is guilty of Perjury, *fi aliquo novo Commento* he would elude his Oath, or who doth not fulfil the Oath in the Senfe of the Impofer. But that does not concern this Cafe : For in the aforefaid Citation, a Perfon, after he has taken an Oath, finding out fome new conceit to elude it, he is perjured : But in this Cafe the Pannel did at, and before his taking the *Teft*, declare the terms in which he underftood it ; fo that this was not *novo aliquo commento* to elude it. And the other Cafe, where a Party takes it in the Senfe of Authority, but has fome Subterfuge, or concealed Explanation, it is acknowledged to be perjury. But in this Cafe there was no concealed Explanation, but it was publickly expreffed, and an Explanation given, which the Pannel defigned, and underftood as the meaning of Authority, and had ground to believe he was not miftaken, fince upon that Explanation he was received and allowed to fit and vote in Council.

And as to that part of the Reply, that explains the Treafon, there can be no Treafon in the Pannel's Cafe, becaufe the exprefs Act of Parliament founded upon doth relate only to the Conftitution of the Parliament: And I am fure His Majefty's Advocate cannot fubfume in thefe Terms. And therefore in the Reply he recurs to the general Grounds of the Law, that the ufurping of his Majefty's Authority, in making a part of the Law ; and to make alterations in general, and without the King, are high and treafonable words or defigns, and fuch as the party pleafes, and fuch Defigns as have been practiced in the late times. And that even the adjection of fair and fafe words, as in the Covenant, does not fecure from treafonable Defigns ; and that it was fo found in *Balmerino's* Cafe, tho' it bear a fair Narrative of an humble Supplication.

It is replied, That the Ufurpation of making of Laws is undoubtedly treafonable ; but no fuch thing can be pretended or fubfumed in this Cafe : For albeit the Pannel declares his Explanation to be a part of his Oath, yet he never meaned to impofe it as even a part of the Law, or that his Explanation fhould be a thing diftinct, or a feparate part of his Oath. For this Explanation being but *exegetick* of the feveral parts of the Oath, it is no diftinct thing from the Oath, but declared to be a part of the Oath *de natura rei*. And it was never pretended, that he that alledged any thing to be *de natura rei*, did fay, That that was diftinct and feparate, which were a Contradiction. And therefore the Argument is retorted, the Pannel having declared, this Explanation was *de natura rei*, implied in the Oath, he necessarily made this Explanation no addition or extenfion of the Oath. So that for all this Explanation, the Oath is neither broader nor longer than it was.

And as to thefe Words, *I do not mean to bind up myfelf in my ftation, and in a lawful way, to wifh and endeavour any alteration I think to the advantage of Church or State, not repugnant to the Proteftant Religion, and my Loyalty* ; it is a ftrange thing how this Claufe can be drawn in queftion as treafonable, when it may with better Reafon be alledg'd, that there is not a good Subject but is bound to fay it. And albeit the words *to endeavour in my ftation*, be words contained in the Covenant, yet that is no Reafon, why two words in the Covenant may not be made ufe of in another very good and loyal fenfe. And there is no Man that fhall have the honour either to be entrufted by his Majefty in his Council, or any other Judicature, or to be a Member of Parliament, but he is bound by his Loyalty to fay the fame thing. And there was never a Claufe more cautiously expreffed, for the words run ; *to endeavour any alteration I fhall think to the advantage of Church and State.* And tho' that was fufficient, yet the Claufe is fo cautioufly conceived, that it contains another Reftriction, *not repugnant to Religion and his Loyalty.* So that except it could be alledged, that a Man by lawful means, to the advantage of Church and State, confiftent with his Religion and Loyalty, could make treafonable Alterations, and Invafions upon the Government and Monarchy, which are the higheft Contradictions imaginable, there can be nothing againft the Pannel. And albeit, the Claufe, *any Alterations,* might, without the Reftrictions and Qualifications aforefaid, be generally extended, yet the preceding words of *lawful way,* and the rational Interpretation of the emiffion of words, efpecially before a folemn Judicatory, leaves no Place or Shadow to doubt, that thefe alterations were no fundamental or treafonable alterations, but fuch as the frailty of human Affairs and Conftitutions, and Viciffitude of things and Circumftances do conftantly require in the moft exact Conftitutions under Heaven. And the Claufe does not fo much as import, that there is a prefent neceffity of alteration, but it was a neceffary and rational Profpect, That albeit at prefent all things under Heaven had been done to fecure the Religion and Government, yet there might occur Cafes that would require new helps, alterations, and remedies. And it is not pretended in this Cafe for the Pannel, that he defires to alleviate, or take off words truly treafonable, or having an ill Defign, by the mixing of fair and fafe, dutiful and fubmiffive Expreffions, which indeed are Proteftations *contrariæ facto.* For there is nothing in his Explanation, that either in his Defign, or in the words themfelves, being rationally and naturally interpreted, can infer the Crimes libelled, or any of them. And the Pannel's known Principles, and known Practices, do not only clear that Loyalty that he has profeft before the Lords of Jufticiary, and inftructed by unqueftionable Documents, but they put him far from the Sufpicion of thefe damnable Principles related in the Reply, of which the whole tract of his Life hath been an entire Evidence of his *Abhorrency* and *Deteftation.* And in the laft place, it is thought ftrange, why that fhould be reprefented as an affront or difgrace to the Government, That the Parliament impofed a *Teft* which the Pannel is not able to take fimply. And it is not pretended, That he hath

defamed,

defamed, written or spoken against the *Test* itself, or for the inconvenience of it ; but only that he hath not been able to see the good Ground upon which it may be simply taken. And this were to condemn him for want of sight or sense, when the Law hath punished no Man for not taking the *Test*, but only turned him out of the Government. And it is as strange an Inference, That because the Pannel declares, he believes the Parliament meaned no Contradiction and would take the *Test*, in as far as it is consistent ; that therefore he said the Parliament imposed Contradictions : Which is so far from a rational Induction, that the Contradiction of these Subsumptions, in all congruity of Language and Sense, is necessarily true. And therefore the last part of that Clause, *in so far as it is consistent*, is a Consequence inferred upon the former : *viz.* I believe the Parliament designed to impose no Contradictions ; *ergo*, I take the *Test* as consistent, and in so far as it must be consistent, if the Parliament did not impose Contradictions, as certainly they have not ; and to convince the World, that in this sense this Explanation is receivable, it was proposed in Council, and allowed, and therefore, without the highest reflection, it cannot now be quarrelled.

Sir George Lockhart's *second Plea for the Earl of* Argyle, *by way of Reply upon the King's Advocate.*

SIR *George Lockhart* duplies, That the Defender repeats and oppones his former Defences, which are no ways eluded, nor satisfied by the Reply made by his Majesty's Advocate. And altho' it be easy for the King's Advocate, out of his zeal, to pretend and argue Crimes of the highest nature, upon Inferences and Consequences neither consistent with the Pannel's designs nor with his words and expressions, yet there cannot be a more dangerous foundation laid, for the security and interest of the Government, and the security and protection of the Subjects, than that Crimes should be inferred but from clear, evident, and express Laws, and plain palpable Contravention of these Laws ; it being both against the Laws of God and Man, that a Man should be made an Offender for a word, and especially expressions which according to Sense and Reason, and considering the time and place where they were spoken by the Pannel, *viz.* as a Member of his Majesty's Privy Council, and in presence of his Royal Highness, and the Members of Council, and when required to take the *Test*, were safe and innocent : and it were against all Law and Reason, to suppose that the Pannel either did, or designed to do any thing which may, or did import the Crimes libelled against him. And whereas it is pretended, That the Oath required and imposed by Act of Parliament was for the security of the Government ; and that the Pannel by his Explanation does evade the Oath, by taking it only so far as it is consistent with the Protestant Religion, and his own Loyalty, whereof he was Judge : It is answered, That the pretence is most unwarrantable, and the Security of his Majesty's Government is not at all endangered (as God forbid it should,) tho' the Pannel and a thousand more had simply refused the *Test*, or had taken it in a sense which does not satisfy the Law ; it being competent to publick Authority to consider, whether the Pannel's Oath, in the terms of the Explication wherein he did take it, does satisfy the Act of Parliament or not ; and if not, there can be no rational consequence inferred thereupon, but that he is holden as a Refuser of the Oath, and liable to the Certification of the Act of Parliament, of not assuming and continuing in any publick Trust : And no more was intended or designed by the Act of Parliament itself, than strictly to make the Oath in the true and genuine sense and meaning of the Parliament, an indispensible qualification of persons admitted to publick Trust. So that it is not at all material to dispute, whether the Pannel's Explication can be looked upon as a full satisfaction of the Act, which whether it should or not, it can import no Crime against him, it not being consistent with Sense and Reason, that a Person who absolutely refuseth the *Test*, upon the scrupulosity of his Conscience, albeit he be not capable of publick Trust, should be, notwithstanding, looked upon as guilty of no Crime ; and yet another, who was willing to go a greater length, albeit he did demur and scruple as to the full length, that he should be reputed criminal and guilty of a Crime.

2. The Pannel repeats and conjoins with this the grounds above mentioned, contained in his Defences, *viz.* That neither the Crimes libelled, nor any other Crime, were ever pretended or made use of against any others, who did spread abroad Objections of an high nature, which yet were so favourably looked upon, as to be construed only to proceed from scrupulosity of Conscience; as also the satisfaction endeavoured is in such terms, and by such condescensions, as do take in, and justify the whole terms of the Explication libelled.

It

It is of great moment, and whereof the Lords of Justiciary are desired to take special notice, both for clearing the absolute innocence of the Pannel's meaning and intention, and to take off all possible misconstruction that can be wrested or detorted from the tenor and expressions of the libelled Explication, That the Pannel was put to, and required to take the Oath, before the Lords of his Majesty's Privy-Council did pass and publish their Proclamation explaining the Oath, and declaring the genuine sense and meaning thereof, namely, That it did not tye to the whole Articles of the *Confession of Faith*, ratified by Act of Parliament, *James* 6. and which, as to several Articles thereof, had occasioned the scruples, and difficulties, and alledged inconsistency and contradiction betwixt the last part of the Oath and the said *Confession*, and betwixt some of the Articles, and the Current of the Protestant Doctrine, received and contained in the *Syntagma* of the Protestant Confessions. And therefore if the Pannel at that time did think fit, for the clearing and exoneration of his own Conscience, to use the expressions in the Explication libelled, and yet with so much duty and confidence of the Parliament's Justice, as to their meaning and intention, *That the Parliament never intended to impose contradictory Oaths*; and that he *did take it so far as it was consistent with itself, and the Protestant Religion*, not knowing then, whether the whole *Confession* was to be reputed a part of the Oath, and doubting there-anent; and which the Lords of his Majesty's Privy Council, and his Sacred Majesty by his approbation since, have thought a difficulty of so great moment as it was fit to clear the same by a publick Proclamation: how now is it possible, that any Judicatory under Heaven, which proceeds upon the solid grounds of Law and Reason, and who (it cannot be doubted) will have a just regard to the intrinsick Principles of Justice, and to all mens security; that they can now believe all, or any of the Crimes libelled, should be in the least inferred from all, or any of the expressions contained in the said Explication? But that on the contrary it was a warrantable allowance, and Christian practice, condemned by the Law and Custom of no Nation, That having scruples in the matter of an Oath, which should be taken in *Truth, Judgment and Righteousness*, and upon full deliberation, and with a full assurance and sincerity of mind, That he did plainly, openly, and clearly declare the sense in which he was willing to take it; and if Authority did allow it as the genuine sense of the Oath, the Pannel to be holden as a Taker of the Oath: And if upon farther Consideration, Authority think not, that *habetur pro Recusante*, and a Refuser of the Oath, but no ways to be looked upon as a criminal or guilty person.

And the Pannel repeats and conjoins with this Point of the Reply, that Point in his Defence, whereby he positively offers to prove, 1. That his Explication, and the sense wherein he took the Oath, was heard, and publickly given and received in Council, and the Pannel thereafter allowed to take his place, and sit and vote in that *Sederunt.*

2. The Pannel also offers positively to prove, That the tenor and terms of his Sense and Explication wherein he did take the Oath, is contained in that Solid, Learned, and Pious Vindication, written by the Bishop of *Edinburgh*, in answer to the Objections and alledged Inconsistencies and Contradictions in the Oath, and which Vindication was publickly read in Council; and so far approved, that it was allowed to be printed and published, and was accordingly dispersed and spread abroad. And it is not of the least import, that the Proclamation of the Lords of Privy Council, altho' it does oft allow the same to be taken by the Clergy, yet at the same time very expresly declare the genuine sense and meaning of the Parliament not to comprehend the whole Articles of the *Confession*, which was not cleared before the Pannel's taking his Oath.

And whereas it is pretended, That the Acts of Parliament libelled upon, against Leasing-makers, Depravers of his Majesty's Laws, do obtain and take place, wherever there are any words or expressions that have a tendency in themselves, or by a natural consequence, and rational inferences, to reflect upon the Government, or misconstrue his Majesty's Proceedings; and that the Explication libelled is such, and that it was found so in the Case of *Balmerino*, albeit it was drawn up by way of humble Petition and Address to his Majesty, and with great Protestations and Expressions of Loyalty: It is answered, The Acts of Parliament libelled upon, are opposed, and the 43d *Act*, Par. 8. *James* 6. and the other Acts, making the depraving of his Majesty's Laws to be Crimes, do expresly require, that Speeches so judged be perverse and licentious Speeches *ex natura sua probrosa*, and reproachful, and spoke *animo defamandi*, and which could not receive any other rational Construction, which cannot in the least be applied to or subsumed upon the Words, or Explication given in by the Pannel. And Law and Reason never infers or presumes a Crime, where the thing is capable of a fair and rational Construction, and where it was done *palam* and publickly, and in

pre-

prefence of his Majefty's High Commiffioner, and Lords of his Majefty's Privy Council, whereof the Pannel had the honour to be a Member: Perfons committing and
defigning to commit Crimes, making ufe of Times, and Places and Companies of a-
nother nature, on whom their fuggeftions and infinuations may prevail. But it is a
violence to the common Reafon of mankind, to pretend, that a perfon of the Pannel's
Quality, having the honour to ferve his Majefty in moft eminent Capacities, and devoted to his Majefty's Intereft and Service, beyond the ftricteft ties of Duty and Allegiance, by the tranfcendent Favours he had received, that the Pannel in thofe Circumftances, and in prefence of his Royal Highnefs and Lords of Privy Council, fhould
defign to declaim, and *de facto* declaim againft, and defame his Majefty's Government:
To fuppofe this, is abfolutely contradictory to the common Principles and Practices of
Law, and common Topicks of Reafon.

And as to *Balmerino's* Cafe, it is anfwered, That the Lords of Jufticiary are humbly
defired to call for, and perufe the faid Petition, and Books of Adjournal, which was
certainly a defamatory Libel of his Majefty's Father, of bleffed Memory, and of the
States of Parliament in the higheft degree; being exprefly, that there was nothing defigned but an Innovation of the Proteftant Religion, and the fubverfion and overturning the Liberties and Privileges of the Parliament, and the Conftitutions of the Articles, and other things of that kind; which made certainly of itfelf a moft villanous
and execrable Libel, containing the higheft Crimes of *Treafon* and *Perduellion*, and was
not capable of any good fenfe or interpretation, but was abfolutely pernicious and deftructive: So that it is in vain to pretend, that the faid Libel did contain Prefaces and
Proteftations of Loyalty, which no Law regards, even *in fimplici injuria & maledicto*,
tho' committed by a private Perfon, *cum præfatione falvo honore*, or the like, and
which were certainly ridiculous to fuftain in a Libel concerning Crimes of Treafon.

And whereas it is pretended, That tho' others were guilty of thefe Crimes, it does
not excufe the Earl: That the Lords of Privy-Council cannot remit Crimes; and the
negligence of the King's Officers cannot prejudge his Intereft: It is anfwered, the
Pannel is very confident, that neither the Lords of his Majefty's Privy-Council, confifting of Perfons of eminent Loyalty and Judgment, nor his Majefty's Officers, were
capable of any fuch efcape as is pretended. And if the tenor of the Pannel's Explication
did in the leaft import the high and infamous Crimes libelled, as beyond all peradventure it does not, it were ftrange, how the fame being contained in the aforefaid Vindication, and the whole Claufes thereof juftified, that this fhould have been looked on as
no crime, and allowed to be publifhed. And the Pannel neither does, nor needs to
make farther ufe thereof, but to convince all dif-interefted Perfons, that his Explication
can import no Crime.

And whereas it is pretended, That the crime of Treafon is inferred from the fundamental Laws of the Kingdom, and from that Claufe of the Pannel's Explication, whereby
he declares, *He is not bound up by any thing in this Oath not to endeavour any alteration in a
lawful way*; which being an indefinite Propofition, is equipollent to an univerfal, and
is upon the matter coincident with a Claufe, which was rebellious in its confequences, contained in the folemn League and Covenant: It is anfwered, that it is ftrange, how fuch
a plain and innocent Claufe, whereby, beyond all queftion, he does exprefs no more
than was natural, fhould import the crime of Treafon; which no Lawyer ever allowed, except where it was founded upon exprefs Law, *& Luce Meridiana clarior*: And indeed
if fuch ftretches and inferences can make men guilty of Treafon, no Man can be fecure. And the words in the Pannel's Declaration, are plain and clear (yet *non funt
cavillanda*) and import no more, but that, in his ftation, and in a lawful way, and confiftent with the Proteftant Religion, and his Loyalty, he might endeavour any alteration to the advantage of Church and State. And was there ever any loyal or rational
Subject, that does, or can doubt, that this is the natural import of the Oath? And
indeed it were a ftrange Oath, if it were capable of another fenfe, and being defigned
for the fecurity of the Government, fhould bind up men's hands to concur for its advantage. And how was it poffible that the Pannel, or any other in the capacity of a Privy-Counfellor, or a Member of the Parliament, would have fatisfied his Duty and
Allegiance in other terms? And whereas it is pretended, that there was the like cafe
in the pretended League and Covenant, it is anfwered, The affertion is evidently a
Miftake; and tho' it were, the Argument is altogether inconfequential: For that
League and Covenant was treafonable in itfelf, as being a Combination entered into
without his Majefty's Authority, and was treafonable in the Gloffes that were put upon
it, and was impofed by abfolute violence on the Subjects of this Kingdom. And how
can the Pannel be in the leaft fuppofed to have had any refpect to the faid League and
Covenant, when he had fo often taken the Declaration, difowning and renouncing it,

as an unlawful and finful Oath, and concurred in the many excellent Laws and Acts of Parliament made by his Majefty, condemning the fame as feditious and treafonable? And whereas it is pretended, That the Pannel is guilty of Perjury, having taken the Oath in another fenfe than was confiftent with the genuine fenfe of the Parliament, and that by the Authority cited he doth *commento eludere Juramentum*, which ought always to be taken in the fenfe of him that impofeth the Oath: It is anfwered, The Pretence is moft groundlefs, and Perjury never was, nor can be inferred, but by the commiffion or omiffion of fomething directly contrary to the Oath. And altho' it is true, That where an Oath is taken, without any Declaration of the exprefs fenfe of the perfons who take it, it obliges *fub pœna Perjurii*, in the fenfe, not of the taker, but of the impofer of the Oath, becaufe expreffing no Senfe, Law, and Reafon, prefumes there is a full acquiefcence in the fenfe and meaning of the impofer of the Oath; and then if an Oath be not fo taken, he that takes it is guilty of Perjury: Yet there was never Lawyer, nor Divine, Popifh or Proteftant, but agree in this, that whatever be the tenor of the Oath, if before the taking thereof, the party in exprefs terms does publickly and openly declare the fenfe in which he takes it, it is impoffible he can infer the Crime of Perjury againft him in any other fenfe, this not being *Commentum excogitatum*, after the taking of the Oath. And if this were not fo, how is it poffible in Senfe and Reafon, that ever any Explication or Senfe could folve the Scruples of a Man's Confcience? For it might be always pretended, That notwithftanding of the exprefs fenfe wherein he took it, he fhould be guilty of Perjury from another fenfe. And that this is the irrefragable Opinion of all Divines, of whatever perfuafion, is not only clear from the Authority above-mentioned, even thofe who allow of referved fenfes, but more efpecially by the univerfal fuffrage of all Proteftant Divines, who tho' they do abominate all thoughts of Subterfuges or Evafions, after taking of the Oath, yet they do always allow and advife for the fafety and fecurity of a doubting and fcrupulous Confcience, that they fhould exprefs and declare, before the taking of the Oath, the true fenfe and meaning wherein they have freedom to take it; and for which *Sanderfon de Juramento* is cited, *Prælect.* 6. *Sect.* 10. *pag.* 75. where his words are, *Sanè ut inter Jurandum omnia rectè fiant, expedit ut de verborum fenfu inter omnes partes quarum intereft liquido conftet, quod veteribus dictum, liquido jurare.* And an Oath being one of the higheft Acts of Devotion, containing *Cultum Latriæ*, there is nothing more confonant to the nature of all Oaths, and to that Candor, Ingenuity, and Chriftian Simplicity, which all Law and Religion requires in fuch Cafes.

The King's Advocate's Third Plea againft the Earl of Argyle.

HIS Majefty's Advocate conceives he has nothing to anfwer as to depraving, leafing-making, and mif-interpreting, &c. fave that this Oath was only defigned to exclude Recufants; and confequently, the *Pannel* may thereby be debarred from his Offices, but not made guilty of a Crime. To which he triplies, 1. If ever the Earl had fimply refus'd, that had been true, but that did not at all excufe from defaming the Law; for a Defamer is not punifhed for refufing, but for defaming.

2. If he had fimply refufed, the Government had been in no more hazard, but if Men will both retain their Places, and yet take the fame in fuch words as fecure not the Government, it were ftrange to think, that the defign of the Law being to fecure againft Men's poffeffing who will not obey, that yet it fhould allow them poffeffion who do not obey. Nor is the Refufer here in a better cafe than the Earl, and others, who offered to obey, becaufe it is the defaming the Law, as ridiculous, and inconfiftent with the Proteftant Religion; and Leafing-making betwixt the King, the Nobility, and the People, the mif-conftruing, and mif-reprefenting, as hath been formerly urg'd, that puts the Earl in a worfe condition. And all thofe arguments might be as well urged for any who had uncontrovertedly contravened thefe Acts, as for the *Pannel*.

Whereas it is pretended, That the King emitted a Proclamation to fatisfy Diffenters; it is anfwered, That the Proclamation was defigned for none who had been Members of Parliament, and fo fhould have known the fenfe; but it was defign'd for mere Ignorants, not for fuch as had defamed the Law, which is ftill here charged upon the *Pannel*.

As to the Article of Treafon, it is conceived, That it is unanfwerably founded upon the Common Law, difcharging all Men to make alteration of the Government; as to which there needs no exprefs Statute, that being the very effence of Government, and needing no Laws. Like as it falls pofitively under all the Laws that difcharge the affuming the Royal or Legiflative Power; for to alter the Government, is infeparably
united

united to the Crown : Like as the Subfumption is as clear, the exprefs words not bearing, That the Earl referves to himfelf a Power to propofe to his Majefty any alterations or to concur to ferve his Majefty in making alterations ; but owning in moft general and arbitrary terms, to wifh and endeavour any alteration he fhould think fit, for the advantage of Church or State, and not determining any thing that could bind him otherwife than according to his own pleafure ; for the word *(lawful)* is ftill fubjected to himfelf, and has fubjoined to it, *as he fhould think fit*, which governs the whole propofition : and in that fenfe, and as the words are here fet down, the greateft Rebel in *Scotland* will fubfcribe that Explanation, for there is no Man but will reftrict himfelf to a lawful Obedience, provided he be judge of the lawfulnefs. And feeing all Oaths propofed for the fecurity of Government, require a certain depending upon the Legiflator, and not upon the Taker, it is impoffible that that end could be attained by any qualification, how fpecial foever, which is made to depend abfolutely upon the Taker, and not upon the Legiflator. And we have often feen, how little fecurity there is in thofe fpecious words, the very Covenant itfelf having not only the very words above-repeated, but attefting all the world to be witneffes to their Loyalty and Sincerity. And as to the former inftances, *viz.* Rifing in Arms, or oppofing the lawful Succeffor, there is no Covenanter in *Scotland* but will fay, he will do neither, but in a lawful way, and in his ftation, and in a way confiftent with his Loyalty, for a man were mad to fay otherwife ; but yet when they come to explain this, they will only do it as they think fit, and will be Judges themfelves, and then will tell us, That defenfive Arms are lawful, and that no Popifh Succeffor fhould fucceed, nor no Succeffor unlefs he fubfcribe the Covenant. And whereas it is pretended, That no Claufe in the *Teft* does exclude a man from making alterations, it is anfwered, That the alterations which the *Teft* allows are none at all, but in fubordination to Authority. And as to the two points above mentioned, it excludes all Alterations as to thefe points. And as to the making fundamental Alterations, this refervation allows to make any alteration, and confequently fundamental alterations ; to preclude which Libertinifm, this excellent Law was invented.

Whereas it is pretended, That the Pannel defigns not to add any thing as a part of the Law, but as a part of his Oath, it is duplied, Since the Oath is a part of the Law, whoever adds to the Oath, adds to the Law.

Whereas it is pretended, That the Crime of Perjury cannot be inferred here, becaufe as Divines allow, That the Taker of an Oath is ftill allowed to declare in what fenfe he takes the Oath ; and that this is clear from *Sanderfon*, p. 175. It is triplied, That where there are two dubious fenfes, Lawyers and Divines allow, that the taker fhould clear himfelf, which of the two he fhould take ; which is very juft, becaufe to which foever of the two he determines himfelf, the Legiflature in that cafe is fure of him. But here it is not pretended, That there are two fenfes ; nor does the Pannel declare in which of the two he takes it, or in what clear fenfe at all he takes it, which is indeed *liquido Jurare*. But here the Pannel neither condefcends, what particular Claufe of the Teft is unclear ; nor after he has condefcended upon the Articles, does he condefcend upon the fenfe, but in general myfterious Words, where he can neither be followed or found out ; he only takes it, in fo far as it is confiftent with itfelf, and the Proteftant Religion, referving the fquaring all by his own Loyalty, as he did in the beginning declare, That he took it in his own fenfe, by which general fenfe, neither is the Government fecure of any thing it does enjoin, nor could he be punifhed if he tranfgreffed. Nor can it be doubted, but Perjury may be inferred by any equivocal or evading fenfe, *inter Jurandum*, as well as by breaking an Oath afterwards ; which is very clear from *Sanderfon*, p. 138. the words whereof are *alterum perjurii genus eft inter Jurandum detorquere verba* ; and which is farther clear by the 28 *page* ; but above all, from the principles of Reafon, and the neceffity of Commerce and Government : For if Men may adhibit fuch Gloffes, even whilft they fwear, as may make the Oath ufelefs, what way will either Government or Commerce be maintained ? And he deceives as much that deceives in fwearing *falvis verbis*, as he who after he has fworn, does break the Oath. Nay, and more too, becaufe the breaking may come from forgetfulnefs, or other Accidents, but the evading by general Claufes, which bind no man, does from the firft inftance originally make all Oaths ufelefs and dangerous ; and that this interpretation eludes the Oath abfolutely, is very clear from what hath been formerly debated. For it may be argued, That the Earl broke the Oath in fo far, as the firft day he fwears the Oath, which bears to be without any evafion, (and muft be fo, notwithftanding of whatever he could fay :) And the next day he gives in this evafion, which is a down-right violation of that Oath, and inconfiftent with it. Nor was this Oath forced, but voluntarily emitted, to keep his

own

own places. And it was the greater Crime that it was done in the Council, because that was to make it the more publick, and consequently, the more to mis-represent the Government.

After this Debate, which, according to the custom of the Court, was *verbatim* dictated by the Advocates of either side, and written by the Clerk, and so took up much time ; and the Court having sat, at least twelve hours, without intermission, it adjourned till the next day, being *Tuesday* the 13th of *December*, at two of the Clock in the Afternoon : And then the Earl being again brought to the Bar, the following *Interloquutor* (that is, Judgment and Sentence) of the *Lords of Justiciary*, on the foregoing Debate, was read, and pronounced in open Court.

Edinburgh, December 12. 1681.

The Interloquutor of the Lords of Justiciary.

THE Lords, Justice-General, and Commissioners of the Justiciary, having considered the Libel and Debate, they sustain the Defence proponed for the Earl of *Argyle*, the Pannel, in relation to the Perjury libelled, viz. *That he emitted this Explanation at, or before his taking the* Test, *first before his Royal Highness, his Majesty's High Commissioner, and the Lords of his Majesty's Privy-Council, relevant*, to elude that Article of the Libel.

The Lords sustain the Libel, as being founded upon the Common Law, and Explication libelled, and upon *Act*. 130. *Parl.* 8. *James* VI. to infer the pain of *Treason*.

They likewise sustain the Libel, as founded upon the 10. *Act. Parl.* 10. *James* VI. to infer the pain of Death ; and likewise sustain that part of the Libel anent *Leasing-making*, and *Leasing-telling*, to infer the particular pains mentioned in the several Acts libelled.

And repel the whole other *defences, duplies,* and *quadruplies,* and remits the Libel, with the defences anent the Perjury, to the knowledge of an Assize.

Thereafter the *Assize*, that is the *Jury*, being constitute and sworn, *viz.*

List of the Assizers,

Marquis Montrose,	*E. Roxburgh, P. C.*	*Lord Bruntisland,*
E. Middleton,	*E. Dumfries,*	*Laird of Gosfoord,*
E. Airlie,	*E. Linlithgow, P. Cr.*	*Laird of Claverhouse,*
E. Perth, P. Cr.	*Lord Lindoors,*	*Laird of Balnamoon,*
E. Dalhousie,	*Lord Sinclare,*	*Laird of Park Gordon.*

HIS Majesty's Advocate adduced four Witnesses, to prove the points of the Indictment, remitted to the knowledge of the *Assize*, viz. *John Drummond* of *Lundie,* then Governor of the Castle of *Edinburgh*, now Treasurer-Deputy : Sir *William Paterson,* and Mr. *Patrick Menzies,* Clerks of the Privy Council ; and *H. Stevenson* their Under-Clerk. Who deponed, *That on the 5th of* November, *the Earl did give in an unsubscribed Explanation of the* Test, *which he refused to sign:* One of the Witnesses also adding, *That he heard him make the same Explanation, the day before, in Council, and that it was there accepted:*

Then his Majesty's Advocate asked, if the Earl would make use of his *Exculpation* for eliding the Perjury libelled, *to wit,* That he had emitted the same Explanation, before taking the *Test,* in presence of his royal Highness and the Council. To which the Earl answered, That seeing they had sustain'd the Libel, as to the *alledged Treason,* he would not trouble them about the *Perjury* ; especially the matter of Fact, inferred by the *Interloquutor* to his probation, being of itself so clear and notour.

But the truth is, the *Interloquutor* pronounced was so amazing, that both the Earl and his Advocates were struck with deep silence ; for they plainly perceived that, after such a *Judgment* in the case, all further endeavours would be in vain, it being now manifest, that seeing the Earl's Innocence had so little availed, as that his plain and honest words, purely uttered for the necessary satisfaction of his own conscience, and clearing of his loyalty, had been construed, and detorted, to infer *Leasing-making, Depraving,* and *Treason* ; the tongues of Men and Angels (as some of his Advocates also said) could not do any good ; and therefore neither did the Earl, nor they object any thing, either against the *Assizers* or *Witnesses,* though liable to obvious, and unanswerable Exceptions : Nor did the Earl's Advocates say any thing to the *Assize,* as the custom is, and as in this case they might well have done to take off the force of the *Evidence,* and to demonstrate that the Depositions, instead of proving the Indictment, did rather prove the Earl's defences. But, as I have said, they now plainly saw that all this had been unnecessary work, and, in effect, were of opinion, that after so black and dreadful a sense, put

upon

upon what the Earl had ſpoke and done, in ſuch fair, and favourable circumſtanᵉes, there could be nothing ſaid, before *ſuch a Court*, which might not expoſe themſelves to the like hazard, and more eaſily be made liable to the ſame miſ-conſtruction.

But, upon this ſilence, the Advocate, taking Inſtruments, proteſts (whether in form only, or from a real fear, let others judge) for an *Aſſize of Error*, in caſe the *Aſſizers* ſhould *aſſoil* or acquit: Whereupon the *Aſſize* removing was incloſed, and, after ſome time, returned *their Verdict*, which was read in open Court of this tenor:

The Verdict of the Aſſize.

THE *Aſſize having elected, and choſen the Marquiſs of* Montroſe *to be their Chancellor, they all in one voice find the Earl of* Argyle *guilty, and culpable of the Crimes of Treaſon, Leaſing-making, and Leaſing-telling. And find, by plurality of Votes, the ſaid Earl innocent, and not guilty of Perjury.*

And then the Court again adjourned: And the Privy Council wrote the following Letter to his Majeſty.

Halyrude-Houſe, December 14, 1681.

The Council's Letter to the King, deſiring leave to pronounce Sentence againſt the Earl of *Argyle.*

May it pleaſe your ſacred Majeſty,

IN *obedience to your Majeſty's Letter, dated the* 15th *of* November *laſt, we ordered your Majeſty's Advocate to inſiſt in that Proceſs, raiſed at your Inſtance, againſt the Earl of* Argyle: *And having allowed him a long time for his appearance, and any Advocates he pleaſed to employ, and Letters of Exculpation, for his defence; he, after full Debate, and clear Probation, was found guilty of Treaſon, Leaſing-making betwixt your Majeſty, your Parliament, and your People, and the reproaching of your Laws, and Acts of Parliament. But becauſe of your Majeſty's Letter, ordaining us to ſend your Majeſty a particular account of what he ſhould be found guilty of, before the pronouncing of any Sentence againſt him, we thought it our duty to ſend your Majeſty this account of our, and your Juſtices Proceedings therein: And to ſignify to your Majeſty, with all Submiſſion, That it is uſual, and moſt fit for your Majeſty's Service, and the advantage of the Crown, that a Sentence be pronounced, upon the Verdict of the Aſſize, without which the Proceſs will be ſtill imperfect. After which, your Majeſty may, as you in your royal Prudence and Clemency ſhall think fit, ordain all farther execution to be ſiſted, during your Majeſty's Pleaſure: Which ſhall be dutifully obey'd, by*

Your MAJESTY's

Moſt humble,

Moſt faithful,

And moſt obedient

Subjects and Servants,

Sic Subſcribitur,

Alex. St. And.	*Roxburgh,*	*Dalziell,*
Athol,	*Dumfries,*	*Geo. Gordon,*
Douglas,	*Strathmore,*	*Ch. Maitland,*
Montroſe,	*Airlie,*	*Geo. Mᶜ. kenzie,*
Glencairn,	*Ancram,*	*G. Mᶜ. kenzie,*
Wintoun,	*Livingſtoun,*	*Ramſay,*
Linlithgow,	*Jo. Edinburgenſ.*	*J. Drummond.*
Perth,	*Elphingſtoun,*	

THE Earl, as well as the Lords of Privy-Council, waited ſome days for the anſwer of this Letter: But the Earl making his Eſcape a day or two before it came, I ſhall take occaſion to entertain you, in the mean time, with an account of ſome thoughts that the Earl had ſet down in writing, in order to ſome diſcourſe he intended to have made to the Lords of Juſticiary, before their pronouncing Sentence. And then I ſhall ſubjoin the Motives and Arguments, which (as he hath ſince informed ſome of his Friends) did induce him to make his eſcape: Which, with what I have ſaid before, will give you a full account of all matters, till his Majeſty's return came, and the Sentence paſt.

And

And firft, he takes notice, That on *Monday* the twelfth of *December*, the day of his Arraignment, the *Court* adjourned, before he was aware : And it being then late, about nine of the Clock, and after a *Sederunt* of twelve hours, he did not imagine, they would have proceeded further that night ; but only heard afterwards that they fat it out till two or three after midnight : And was furpirzed the next Morning, to underftand, that without calling him again, or asking at him, or hearing, or confidering his own fenfe of his own words, they had not only found the Libel relevant, but repelled his defences, and with one breath rejected all his moft material reafons of *Exculpation*, root and branch. This feemed hard, tho' the words had been worfe, and no way capable of a favourable conftruction, (which none, no not the Judges themfelves, can be fo void of fenfe, as to think really they were not) and this was fo far beyond all imagination, that, neither the Earl, nor his Advocates did ever dream it could fall out, tho' all was not faid that might have been faid ; nor what was faid, fo fully enforced as the Earl's Advocates could eafily have done, if the cafe had not been thought fo very clear, and the Earl's Innocence fo obvious and apparent, and they unwilling unneceffarily to irritate many concern'd.

This great hafte, and ftrange Proceeding, did fo furprize and aftonifh him (as I have faid) that it caufed him, the next day when the Sentence was read, to keep deep filence, and fuffer the *Interloquutor* to be pronounced, the *Affizers* chofen, and fworn, and the *Witneffes* received, and examined, without once offering to fay, or object any thing, or fo much as enquiring, at either *Affizers* or *Witneffes*, whether they had not been tampered with, and practiced by Promifes and Threatnings ; or whether fome of them had not previoufly, and publickly declared themfelves in the cafe, and others of them had not partially advifed, and folicited againft him ; which, as they are juft, and competent Exceptions, fo he was able to have proven them, againft moft of them, inftantly, and fully.

And indeed, as to fuch of the *Affizers* as were *Counfellors*, (whom, for your better Information, I have marked in the Lift of *Affizers* thus, *P. Cr.*) and had firft ordered his Imprifonment ; next, figned the Letter to his Majefty, and then ordered the *Procefs*, and therein manifeftly fore-ftall'd their own judgment (had they done no more) it was a wonder, beyond parallel, That, neither their own honour, nor the common decency of Juftice, nor even his Majefty's Advocate's Intereft, did prevent their being impannelled on that Affize.

But the truth is, the Earl did fo far neglect and abandon himfelf, and give way to the Court, that he did not fo much as open his Mouth, to clear himfelf of the Perjury laid to his charge, which yet God Almighty was pleafed to do, by the plurality of voices of the fame Affize, who it appears plainly did bear him little kindnefs : For whereas Affizers do ufually return their Verdict, *Proven, or not Proven*, rather than *Guilty or not Guilty*, and ought always to do fo, where the relevancy is *in dubio*, and efpecially in a cafe of this nature, in which the alledged Treafon is no overt Act, and indeed no Act, nor fo much as a real ground of offence ; but plainly fuch a fubtil, chimerical, and nonfenfical confequence, that the finding it doth quite furpafs the comprehenfion of all unbyaffed men ; it might have been expected that Perfons of their quality would have chofen the more *moderate Form of proven or not proven*, and not involv'd themfelves unneceffarily upon Oath in adjudging the relevancy of a guilt, which fo few are able to imagine, and none will ever make out ; yet you fee in their Verdict, that all in one voice they did find the Earl *Guilty*, in the moft pofitive and ftrong form ; adding, for fuperabundance, *culpable*, forfooth, the better to demonftrate their good will. Nor is it unworthy of remark, that when fuch of the Affizers as were prefent at the Council, declared the Earl innocent of the Perjury (which his Majefty's Advocate did only pretend to infer from the Earl's alledged filence, or not fpeaking loud enough, the firft day, when he figned the Teft) becaufe they heard him, at the fame time, pronounce his Explanation ; yet fome other Affizers that were no Counfellors, and knew nothing of the matter of fact, but by hear-fay, without all regard to the witneffing of thefe Counfellors, their fellow Affizers, voted him *Guilty*: And fo took it formally on their Confciences, that he had faid nothing in the Council, at his taking the *Teft*, albeit all the Council knew the contrary ; (by which they are clearly perjured.) Nay, fuch was the earneftnefs of fome (who thought it fcarce poffible to carry the Treafon upon words fo fafe and innocent) to have the Earl found guilty of Perjury, that it was particularly recommended to his Majefty's Advocate to get him made guilty of that point, to render him for ever uncapable of publick employment. And the Clerk of the Affize was fo concerned in it, that he twice mifreckon'd the Votes, before he would yield that the Earl was affoil'd, or acquit of the Perjury. And this, among other things, may ferve to clear, how that whole matter was influenc'd and manag'd : For, as the Earl cannot be charg'd with Perjury the fecond day, becaufe he fwore none at all ; fo as little the firft day, feeing whether he took the *Teft* with an Explanation (as certainly he did)

or

or simply without saying any thing, it is equally apparent, there was no *Perjury* in the case: But it appears, their *Assizers* were of the Opinion, that the *Indictment* or *Libel* alone (as it was indeed the only evidence) was a sufficient proof of the Earl his being guilty of *Perjury.* And indeed for any other Rule or Reason that occurs, they might as well have found him *guilty* of the *Perjury* as of the *Treason.* But the *Assizers* that were *Counsellors* being under a particular check, apprehending they might be found perjur'd themselves, if they had not acknowledg'd the hearing of the words, that all others present could have attested to have been audibly spoken, and some of themselves have confessed to have heard, before they knew the tenor of the *Libel* ; and the great Crime of *Treason* being sufficient to do the *Jobb,* it is like they judged it advisable to give this insignificant *Absolution from Perjury,* that their *Verdict of Treason* might have the greater colour, and shew of candor and sincerity. However it seems to be without measure hard to prosecute with such a *deadly Dilemma* of either *Treason or Perjury* ; for you see, in their account, if the Earl swear with an *Explanation,* his *Life* is knockt down by *Treason* ; and if without an *Explanation, his Honour,* which is dearer to him than his *Life,* is run thorow with *Perjury.* But, to compleat a fancy beyond *Bedlam,* the *Advocate* urges, and several *Assizers* agree, at the same time, to condemn the Earl as *perjured,* for not *explaining* ; and *for Treason,* for explaining. *Quis talia fando ?* ———

In the next place, the Earl's Papers contain some *thoughts,* and *endeavours,* to remove certain mistakes, which, he had good ground to believe, did so much prompt, and precipitate the Judges to pronounce so important a Sentence against him, upon so weak and sandy foundations, and which were indeed either meer fancies, or so frivolous, that tho' they were true, they could never excuse them before men, far less exoner them before God Almighty. Where, laying down a true ground, that *nunquam concluditur in criminalibus, &c.* and withal representing, how *his Advocates* were questioned, in so extraordinary a manner, for *signing their Opinion* (which you have above, *Num.* 32. where you may see how fair, just, and safe it was) that now they dare no more plead for him ; *He says,* He cannot be denied to plead for himself, as he best may.

The first ground of mistake then that he was to represent, was, that he knew it had been told them, it was very much *His Majesty's Interest,* and necessary for *the support of the Government,* to divest and render him uncapable of publick Trust : Which words had been oft said, and said to himself, to persuade him that there was no further rigour intended : But as he is very confident our gracious King will never, upon any such pretence, allow any innocent Person to be condemned, far less to be destroyed, in a pique or frolick, where his Majesty can reap no Advantage ; so he is persuaded, his Majesty hath no design to render him miserable, far less to cut him off, without a cause. And therefore concludes, it is only his misfortune, in his present circumstances, never having access to, nor being heard by his Majesty, nor the Case perfectly understood by him, that hath made his Majesty give so much as way to *a Process to be raised or led,* far less to a *Sentence* to be pronounced against him. But in effect, as this Affair hath been managed all along, and *so many* engaged, in so extraordinary ways, to act, and write against him, first and last, nothing should appear strange or surprising : However, as their own Consciences, and God Almighty knows how they have been brought to meddle, and act, as they have done ; so, one day or other, the World may likewise know it.

A second ground of mistake, which, he says, may impose upon them, is a confidence of his Majesty's *Pardon* intended for him, a pretence only given out to render the *Condemnation* more easy ; yet indeed least wished for by those who were readiest to spread the report, and whereof the Earl had indeed more confidence than any that talked of it, if his Majesty were left to himself, and had the Case fully and truly represented to him : but as his Majesty needs not this false occasion to make his clemency appear, which is so well known over all his Dominions, by far more true and genuine discoveries ; so it were the heighth of injustice in their *Lordships of the Justiciary* to proceed to sentence against him, upon such *Apprehensions,* in case in their hearts they believe him innocent, (as he certainly knows they do :) besides, they cannot but see their acting, upon so unjust a ground, will not only stain their names and memories ; but instead of alleviating, rather aggravate their guilt, both in their own Consciences, when they reflect on it *in cold blood,* and in the sight of God Almighty : And if his Majesty on *importunity and a third Application,* should give way to *Execution,* as he hath already given way, first to the *Process* and then to the *Sentence* ; or if, (as some may design) *Execution* should be adventured on, without the formality of a *new Order* (as the Process was at first commenced, before his Majesty's return, and so is not impossible) would not their Lordships be as guilty of his blood, as if they had cut his throat ?

And in effect, these are the *Grounds* and *Excuses* pretended at this day, *in private,* by such of his *Judges,* for their proceedure, who are not yet come to have the confidence, at all Occasions, to own directly what they have done.

A

A third Reafon why *his Exculpation* was not allowed, *he fays,* might be, becaufe the fuftaining of it might have brought other *Explanations* above-board, and difcover both thofe
who had made, and thofe who had accepted them, and perhaps not have left *their own
Bench* untouched.   But as this Artifice will not keep up *the Secret* ; and as this way *of
fhifting* is neither juft nor equal ; fo to all interefted it is the meaneft of Securitys ; for his
Majefty's Advocate hath already told us, that his Majefty's *Officers* can never wrong
him : And although the *Lords* and *He* fhould conceal what others had done, it might
make themfelves more guilty, but not prove any *Exoneration* to thofe concerned, without a down-right *Remiffion :* Whereas it is manifeft, That if *their Lordfhips* had admit-
ed the Earl's *Exculpation,* upon the fure and evident grounds therein contained, it would
not only have anfwered the *Juftice* of this Cafe, but vindicated all concerned.

And laftly, he was to tell them, that poffibly they might be inclined to go on, becaufe
they were already fo far engaged, as they knew not how to retreat with their honour : but
as there can be no true honour where there is manifeft wrong, and injuftice ; fo, in the
frail and fallible condition of human things, there can be no delufion more dangerous
and pernicious than this, that *unum fcelus eft alio fcelere tegendum.* And here the Earl
thought to lay before them very plainly and pertinently, fome remarkable and excellent Rules, whereby the *L. Chief Juftice Hales,* a renowned Judge of our Neighbour
Nation, tells, he did govern himfelf in all Criminal Cafes ; which (adds the Earl) if
they took a due impreffion, would certainly give them peace, and joy, when all the vain
Confiderations that now amufe, will avail them nothing.

The Rules are thefe,

I. *Not to be rigid in matters purely confcientious, where all the harm is diverfity of Judgment.*

II. *That Popular,* or Court-applaufe, or diftafte, *have no influence on any thing is to be
done, in point of diftribution of Juftice.*

III. *In a criminal Cafe, if it be a* meafuring caft, *then to incline to mercy and acquittal.*

IV. *In criminal things, that confift only of* words, *where no harm enfues, moderation is
then no injuftice.*

V. *To abhor all private* Sollicitations, *of what kind foever, and by whomfoever.*

VI. *In matters depending, not to be follicitous what men will fay or think, fo long as the
rule of Juftice is exactly kept.*

VII. *And laftly, Never to engage themfelves in the beginning of a Caufe, but referve themfelves* unprejudged, *till the whole Bufinefs be heard.*

Then the Earl *goes on,* and makes notes, for *Additional Defences,* reducible to
thefe Heads :

I. *The absolute innocence of his* Explication, *in its true and genuine meaning, from all*
crime or offence, *far more from the horrible* Crimes libelled.

II. *The impertinency and abfurdity of his Majefty's Advocate's* Arguings, *for inferring
the* Crimes libelled, *from the Earl's* words.

III. *The reafonablenefs of the* Exculpation.

IV. *The Earl's* Anfwers *to the Advocate's* groundlefs Pretences *for aggravating of his Cafe.*

As to the firft, the Earl waving what hath been faid from common Reafon, and Humanity itfelf, and from the whole tenour and circumftances of his Life, comes clofe to
the point, by offering that juft and genuine *Explanation* of his *Explication* which you
have above, *Num.* 21.

*I have delayed hitherto to take the Oath appointed by the Parliament to be taken, betwixt and
the firft of* January *next : But now being required, near two Months fooner, to take it this day
peremptorily, or to refufe* ; I have confidered the Teft, *and have feen feveral Objections moved against it, especially by many of the Orthodox Clergy ; notwithftanding whereof I have endeavoured to fatisfy my felf with a juft Explication, which I here offer, that I may both fatisfy
my Confcience, and obey your Highnefs, and your Lordfhips Command in taking the* Teft, *though
the Act of Parliament doth not fimply command the thing, but only under a certification, which I
could eafily fubmit to, if it were with your Highnefs's favour, and might be without offence : But
I love not to be fingular* ; and I am very defirous to give obedience *in this, and every thing,
as far as I can* ; and that which clears me, is, *that* I am confident, *whatever any Man may
think or fay to the Prejudice of this Oath,* the Parliament never intended to impofe contradictory Oaths ; and becaufe their fenfe, *(they being the Framers and Impofers) is the
true fenfe, and this* Teft enjoined, *is of no private interpretation, nor are the King's Statutes
to be interpreted, but as they bear, and to the intent they are made* ; therefore I think no
man, *that is, no private Perfon,* can explain it *for another, to amufe or trouble him with (it
may be) miftaken gloffes : But every man, as he is to take it, fo is to explain it* for himfelf, *and
to endeavour to underftand it, notwithftanding all thefe Exceptions in the Parliament's, which is
its true and genuine fenfe ; I take it therefore, notwithftanding any fcruple made by any,* as far as
it

it is confiftent with it felf, and the Proteftant Religion, *which is wholly in the Parliament's fenfe, and their true meaning; which (being prefent) I am fure, was owned by all to be the fecuring of the Proteftant Religion, founded on the Word of God, and contained in the Confeffion of Faith recorded,* J. 6. p. 1. c. 4. *And not out of Scruple, as if any thing in the Teft did import the contrary. But to clear my felf from Cavils, as if thereby I were bound up further than the true meaning of the Oath;* I do declare, *that by that part of the Teft, that there lies no obligation on me,* &c. I mean not to bind up my felf in my ftation, and in a lawful way ; *ftill difclaiming all unlawful endeavours,* to wifh and endeavour any alteration, I think, *according to my Confcience,* to the advantage of the Church or State, *not repugnant to the Proteftant Religion,* and my Loyalty : *And by my Loyalty I underftand no other thing than the words plainly bear, to wit, the duty and allegiance of all Loyal Subjects;* and this Explanation I underftand as a part, *not of the Teft, or Act of Parliament, but as a qualifying part of my Oath that I am to fwear;* and with it I am willing to take the Teft, if your Royal Highnefs and your Lordfhips allow me. Or otherwife in fubmiffion to your Highnefs and the Council's pleafure, I am content to be held as a Refufer, at prefent.

Which Explanation doth manifeftly appear to be fo juft and true, without violence or ftraining ; fo clear and full, without the leaft impertinency ; fo notour and obvious to common fenfe, without any Commentary ; fo loyal, and honeft, without ambiguity; and laftly, fo far from all, or any of the *Crimes libelled,* that it moft evidently evinceth, that the words thereby explained are altogether innocent : And therefore it were loft time to ufe any Arguments to enforce it.

Yet feeing this is no trial of wit, but to find out common fenfe ; let us examine the Advocate's fantaftical Paraphrafe, upon which he bottoms all the alledged Crimes, and fee whether it agrees in one jot, with the true and right meaning of the Earl's words ; and (as you may gather from the Indictment) it is plainly thus.

I have confidered the Teft; which ought not to be done, *and am very defirous to give obedience, as far as I can,* but am not willing to give full obedience: *I am confident the Parliament never intended to impofe contradictory Oaths;* that is, I am confident they did intend to impofe contradictory Oaths ; *and therefore I think no man can explain it but for himfelf:* that is to fay, every man may take it in any fenfe he pleafes to devife, and thereby render this Law, and alfo all other Laws, tho' not at all concerned in this Affair, ufelefs ; and fo make himfelf a Legiflator, and ufurp the fupreme Authority. *And I take it in fo far as it is confiftent with it felf, and the Proteftant Religion,* whereby I fuppofe that it is not at all confiftent with either ; nor was ever intended by the Parliament it fhould be confiftent : *And I declare, that by taking this Teft, I mean not to bind up my felf in my ftation, and in a lawful way, to wifh or endeavour any alteration, I think, to the advantage of Church or State, not repugnant to the Proteftant Religion, and my Loyalty:* Whereby I declare my felf, and all others, free from all oppofition to the Government, either of Church or State, as by Law eftablifhed, and from the duty and loyalty of good Subjects ; refolving of my felf to alter all the Fundamentals, both of Law and Religion, as I think fit. *And this I underftand as a part of my Oath:* that is, as a part of the Act of Parliament, by which I take upon me, and ufurp the Royal Legiflative Power.

Which fenfe and explanation, as it confifts of the Advocate's own words, and was indeed, every word, neceffary to infer thefe horrible Crimes contained in the Indictment; fo, to fpeak with all the modefty that truth will allow, I am fure it is fo *violent, falfe, and abfurd,* that the greateft difficulty muft be to believe that any fuch thing was alledged, far more received, and fuftained in judgment, by Men profeffing only Reafon, far lefs Religion.

But thirdly, If neither the Earl's true, genuine, and honeft fenfe, nor this violent, corrupt, and falfe fenfe, will fatisfy ; let us try what tranfprofing the Earl's Explanation will do, and fee how the juft contrary will look.——And it muft be thus.

I *Have confidered the Teft, nor am I defirous to give obedience, fo far as I can; I am confident the Parliament intended to impofe contradictory Oaths; and therefore I think every man can explain it for others, as well as for himfelf, and take it without reconciling it either to it felf, or his own fenfe of it: And I do take it, tho' it be inconfiftent with it felf and the Proteftant Religion. And I declare, that I mean thereby to bind up my felf never (either in my ftation, or in any lawful way whatfoever) to wifh, or endeavour in the leaft any alteration, tho' to the advantage of Church or State, and tho never fo fuitable, and no way repugnant to the Proteftant Religion, and my Loyalty: And tho' this be the exprefs quality of my Swearing, yet I underftand it to be no part of my Oath.*

Now whether this contradictory Converfion be not Treafon, or highly criminal, at beft, I leave all the World to judge ; and to make both fides of a contradiction, that is, both the Affirmative and Negative of the fame Propofition, Treafon, is beyond ordinary Logick. *Efcobar* finds two contrary ways may both be probable and fafe ways to go to Heaven; but neither he, nor the Devil himfelf, have hitherto adventured to declare two contradictory

F f f

Propofitions,

Propositions, both damnable, and either of them a juſt Cauſe to take away Men's Lives, Honours and Fortunes.

But where the Diſeaſe is in the Will, it is loſt labour to apply Remedies to the Underſtanding; and muſt not this be indeed, either the oddeſt Treaſon, or ſtrangeſt Diſcovery that ever was heard of? The Biſhop of *Edinburgh* ſees it not, witneſs his Vindication, ſaying the ſame, and more; nor many of the orthodox Clergy, witneſs their Explanations; nor his Royal Highneſs in private; nor at firſt in Council, nor all the Counſellors, when together at the Council-board; nor the Preſident of the Council, nor the then Preſident of the Seſſion (now Chancellor) though he roſe from his Seat, to be ſure to hear; nor any of the moſt learned Lawyers, witneſs their ſigned Opinion; nor the moſt learned of the Judges on the Bench; nor the generality of the knowing Perſons, either in *Scotland* or *England:* Wonderful Treaſon, one day ſeen by none, another day ſeen by ſo many! A Stander-by hearing the Trial, and the Sentence, ſaid, he believed the Earl's Words were by Popiſh Magick *tranſubſtantiate,* for he ſaw them the ſame as before; another anſwered, that he verily thought it was ſo; for he was confident, none could ſee Treaſon in the Words that would not, when-ever it was a proper time, readily alſo profeſs his belief of *Tranſubſtantiation*; but he believed many that profeſſed both, believed neither.

The ſecond Head of the Earl's Additional Defence, contains the Impertinencies and Abſurdities of the Advocate's Arguings. And here you muſt not expect any ſolid Debate: For as there is no diſputing with thoſe that deny Principles, ſo as little with thoſe who heap up phantaſtical and inconſequential Inferences, without all Shadow of Reaſon. If a Stone be thrown, though it may do hurt, yet having ſome Weight, it may be thrown back with equal or more force: But if a Man trig up a Feather, and fling it, it is in vain to throw it back; and the more ſtrength, the leſs ſucceſs: It ſhall therefore ſerve, by a curſory Diſcourſe, to expoſe his Arguments, which are in effect eaſier anſwered than underſtood; and without any ſerious Arguing, which they cannot bear, rather leave him to be wiſe in his own Eyes, than by too much empty talk hazard to be like him.

He alledges firſt, that *the Earl inſtead of taking the Teſt in its plain and genuine meaning, as he ought, doth declare againſt, and defame the Act that enjoined it,* which is certainly a great Crime: But now, *inaſmuch,* ſays the Advocate, *as he tells us that he had conſidered the Teſt;* which I have indeed heard ſay was his greateſt Crime; and that he ought to have taken it *with a profound and devout Ignorance,* as ſome of our moſt inventive Politicians boaſted they have done. But the Earl ſays, *that he was deſirous to give Obedience as far as he could; whereby,* ſays the Advocate, *he inſinuates that he was not able to give full Obedience.* This is not the meaning; but what if it were, and that indeed he could not? Have not thouſands given no Obedience, yet even in Law are guiltleſs? And ought not that to pleaſe his Highneſs, and the Council, that is accepted of God Almighty, and is all any Mortal can perform? *But the Earl,* ſays the Advocate, *goes on, that he was confident the Parliament never intended to impoſe contradictory Oaths; whereby,* ſays the Advocate, *he abuſes the People with a Belief that the Parliament did intend to impoſe ſuch.* Wonderful reaſoning! All Men know that Parliaments neither are nor pretend to be infallible: And in our preſent Caſe, hundreds of loyal Subjects complain of Contradictions and Inconſiſtencies, ſome way or other, crept into this Oath; and even the Council have yielded ſo far to their Exceptions, as to make an Alteration upon it, for ſatisfying thoſe Scruples, far beyond any thing the Earl ſaid; and ſuch an Alteration, as I believe few dreamed of; and I am certain none durſt have attempted without their expreſs Command and Authority: and yet in the midſt of all this, the Earl's charitable and honeſt Opinion, in the behalf of the Parliament's good Intentions, muſt be perverted to a direct ſlander. But the Earl ſays, *that every man muſt explain it for himſelf*; and ſo, no doubt he muſt, if the Teſt be either in it ſelf, or in his apprehenſion, ambiguous; otherwiſe how can he ſwear in Judgment? But this the Advocate will have to be a man's own ſenſe, and thereupon runs out, *that hereby this Law and Oath, and all Laws and Oaths are rendred uſeleſs, and to no purpoſe: and further, the legiſlative Power is taken from the Impoſer, and ſettled in the Taker of the Oath,* which certainly is a moſt treaſonable preſumption. But firſt, although there be no reaſon to ſtrain, or miſtake the Expreſſion, yet the Earl did not ſay, *that every man muſt take the Teſt in his own ſenſe.*

II. The Council hath now explained the Teſt for the Clergy: Might not then the Earl before their Explanation was deviſed, ſay, by the Council's Allowance, which he had, *that he might explain it for himſelf?* For if an ambiguous Propoſition (*the Teſt for example*) may be reconciled to it ſelf two different ways; muſt not the Taker reconcile it, as in his own ſenſe he thinks it doth beſt agree with the genuine meaning of the words themſelves, and with the ſenſe he conceives was intended by the Parliament that formed it, eſpecially before the Parliament emit their own Explanation? And is it not juſter to do it ſo, than in any other man's ſenſe, which he thinks agrees leſs with the words, albeit they may be thought by others to be reconcileable another way?

III. All this looks like deſigned Miſtakes and Traps; for ſhould any man ſwear, unleſs
he

he understand? And where an Oath is granted to be ambiguous, can any man understand, unless in want of the Imposer's help, he explain it for himself?

IV. Was ever a Man's explaining an Oath for himself, before taking it, far less his bare saying that he must explain it, before he take it, alledged to be, *the overturning of all Laws and Oaths, and the usurping of the legislative Power, and making of new Laws?* Certainly to offer to answer such things, were to disparage common Reason.

And lastly, this is strange Doctrine from the Advocate, who himself in Council did allow not only the Earl his Explanation, but that Explanation to the Clergy, contrary, as appears by their Scruples, to what they that took it thought either the Parliament's design, or the plain words of the Test could bear, and certainly different from the sense many had already taken it in, and wherein others were commanded to take it. And whatever the Advocate may cavil to insnare the Earl, sure he will not allow that by his explaining this Oath he himself hath taken on him the legislative Power of the Parliament, far less, though he should acknowledge it, will any believe that he hath, or could thereby *make all Laws or Oaths useless?* By this you see what strange stuff he pleads; which deserves no Answer.

But says the Advocate, the Earl affirms, *he takes the Test, only as far as it consists with it self, and with the Protestant Religion; by which he most maliciously insinuates, that it is inconsistent with both.* But first, this *only* is not the Earl's, but the Advocate's addition. Secondly, I would soberly ask the Advocate, or any Man, whether the Test, as it includes the Confession in general, and consequently all contained in it, was not either really, or at least might not have been apprehended to be inconsistent with it self? Else what was the use or sense of the Council's explanation, wherein it is declared, that Men do not swear to every proposition of the Confession, but only to the Protestant Religion therein contained? And if it was either inconsistent, or apprehended to be so, how could the Earl or any honest Man swear it in other terms, with a safe Conscience? But thirdly, If Parliaments be fallible, and this Oath, as being ambiguous, needed the Council's explanation to clear it from inconsistencies, must the Earl's words, when he was to swear, *that he took it in so far as it was consistent,* be in this Case understood as spoken maliciously, and with a criminal intent, when all Sense, Reason, and Religion, made this caution his duty? And if it be so criminal for one going to swear, to suppose a possibility of inconsistencies in it, is it not manifestly more criminal in others, plainly to confess and grant that there are inconsistencies in it, *after they have swallowed it in gross,* without any explanation whatsoever?

But says the Advocate, *the Earl hath invented a new way, whereby no Man is at all bound to the Test; for how can any Man be bound, if he will obey only as far as he can?* And yet it will be hard, even for the Advocate, tho' he sometimes attempts indeed, more than he and all the World with him can do, to tell how a man can obey farther: And I am sure, that in a matter of this kind, *viz.* the free tender of an Oath, all discreet men will judge the Earl's offer both frank and obliging. Then he asks, *to what the Earl is bound, if he be bound no further than he himself can obey?* Manifest confusion! and never either spoke by the Earl, nor at all pertinent to his case; besides he freely acknowledges, that all men are bound to more than they can do; *or so far as the Test is consistent with it self, and the Protestant Religion* (a strange doubting *or!* yet, I dare say, imports as much as His Majesty expects of any, and more than the Advocate will ever perform.) But says the Advocate, *who can determine to what the Earl is bound?* which says plainly, that either the Test agrees with it self, and the Protestant Religion *in nothing,* or that *the Protestant Religion is nothing,* both which the Earl thinks far from truth. But the Advocate's reasoning reflects far more on the Council's Explanation, where it is plainly said, *that the Confession is not sworn to in the Test, but only the Protestant Religion contained in the Confession;* so that the *Protestant Religion* indefinitely is that which is said to be sworn to. Now pray, is it not much worse for a Man to say, *that by taking the Test he swears only to the Confession as it contains or agrees with the Protestant Religion* (which is in effect to set the Protestant Religion at variance with its own Confession, and so to reproach and ranverse the standard, and make void the very security that the Parliament intended) than to say, *that he swears the Test as it agrees with it self and the Protestant Religion,* which imports no such insinuation? But from these pleasant Principles, he jumps into this fantastick Conclusion, *that therefore it cannot be denied but the Earl's interpretation destroys, not only this Act, but all Government, and makes every Man's Conscience or Humour the rule of his Obedience.*

But first, as to the whole of his arguing, the Earl neither invents, says, nor does any thing, except that he offered his Explanation to the Council, which they likewise accepted. Secondly, What mad Inferences are these! *You say, you will explain this Oath for your self, therefore you overturn all Government, and what not!* Whereas it is manifest on the other hand, that if the Earl apprehending, as he had reason, the Oath to be ambiguous, and in some things inconsistent, had taken it without explaining it for himself, or respect to its inconsistency, it might have been most rationally concluded, that in so doing he was both

impious

impious and perjured. Thirdly, It is false, that the Earl doth make his Conscience any other way the rule of his obedience, than as all honest men ought to do: that is, as they say, *To be Regula regulata*, in conformity to the undoubted *Regula regulans, the eternal rules of truth and righteousness*, as is manifest by his plain words. As for what the Advocate insinuates of *Humour* instead of *Conscience*, it is very well known to be the ordinary Reproach, whereby men that have no *Conscience* endeavour to defame it in others.

But the Advocate is again at it, and having run himself out of all consequences, he insists and inculcates, that the Earl had sworn nothing. But it is plain, that to swear nothing, is none of the crimes libelled. Secondly, The Earl swears positively to the Test *as it is consistent with it self and the Protestant Religion*, which certainly is something; unless the Advocate prove, as he insinuates, that there is nothing in the Test consistent with either. And 3dly, If the Protestant Religion, and the Earl his reference to it, be nothing, then is not only the Council sadly reproached, who in their Explanation declare this to be the only thing sworn to in the first part of the Test, but our Religion quite subverted, as far as this Test can do it.

But next for the Treason, the Advocate says, *that the Earl expresly declares, he means not by the Test to bind up himself from wishing, or endeavouring in his station, and in a lawful way, any alteration he shall think for the advantage of Church or State*; *whereby*, says he, *the Earl declares himself, and others, loosed from any obligation to the Government, and from the duty of all good Subjects, and that they may make what alterations they please.* A direct contrariety, instead of a just consequence; as if to be tied to Law, Religion, and Loyalty, were to be loosed from all three; can there be a flatter and more ridiculous contradiction? Next, the Advocate pretends to found upon the fundamental Laws of this, and all Nations, *Whereby it is Treason for any Man to make any alterations he thinks fit for the advantage of Church or State.* But first, The Earl is not, nor cannot be accused of so much as wishing, much less endeavouring or making any alteration, either in Church or State, only he reserves to himself the same freedom, for wishing which he had before his Oath, and that all that have taken it do in effect say they still retain. 2dly, For a man to endeavour *in his station, and in a lawful way, such alterations in Church or State, as he conceives to their advantage, not repugnant to Religion and Loyalty*, is so far from being Treason, that it is the duty of every Subject, and the sworn duty of all His Majesty's Counsellors, and of all Members of Parliament: But the Advocate by fancying and misapplying *Laws of Nations*, wresting Acts of Parliament adding, taking away, chopping and changing words, thinks to conclude what he pleases. And thus he proceeds, *that the Treason of making Alterations, is not taken off by such qualifications, of making them in a lawful way in one's station, to the advantage of Church or State, and not repugnant to Religion or Loyalty.* But how then? Here is a strange matter! *Hundreds of Alterations* have been made within these few years, in our Government, and in very material Points; and the King's best Subjects, and greatest Favourites have both endeavoured, and effectuate them: And yet, because the things were done according to the Earl's qualifications, instead of being accounted Treason, they have been highly commended and rewarded. The Treasury hath been sometimes in the hands of a Treasurer, sometimes put into a Commission, backward and forward: And the Senators of the College of Justice (the right of whose places was thought to be founded on an Act of Parliament, giving His Majesty the prerogative only of presenting) are now commissioned by a Patent under the great Seal, both which are considerable alterations in the Government, which some have opposed, others have wished and endeavoured, and yet without all fear of Treason on either hand; only because they acted according to these qualifications, *in a lawful way, and not repugnant to Religion and Loyalty.* But that which the Advocate wilfully mistakes, for it is impossible he could do it ignorantly) is, that he will have the *endeavouring of alterations* in general, not to be of it self a thing indifferent, and only determinable to be good or evil by its qualifications (as all men see it plainly to be) but to be forsooth in this very generality *intrinsically evil*; a Notion never to be admitted on Earth, in the frail and fallible condition of human Affairs. And then he would establish this wise Position by an example he adduces, *that rising in Arms against the King* (for so sure he means, it being otherwise certain that rising in Arms in general is also a thing indifferent, and plainly determinable to be either good or evil, as done with or against the King's Authority) *is Treason*; and says, *if the Earl had reserved to himself a liberty to rise in Arms against the King, tho' he had added in a lawful manner, yet it would not have availed, because* (and he says well) *this being in it self unlawful, the qualification had been but shams and contrariæ facto.* But why then doth not his own reason convince him where the difference lies? *viz.* That rising in Arms against the King, is in it self unlawful; whereas endeavouring alterations is only lawful or unlawful, as it is qualified; and if qualified in the Earl's Terms, can never be unlawful. But says the Advocate, *the Earl declares himself free to make all alterations*, and so he would make Men believe that the Earl is for making all or any, without any reserve; whereas the Earl's words are most express, that he is *neither for making all or any, but only for wishing and endeavouring for such as are good and lawful, and in a lawful way*; which no Man can disown, without denying common reason; nor no sworn Counsellor disclaim, without mani-

manifeſt Perjury. But the Advocate's laſt conceit is, *That the Earl's reſtriction is not as the King ſhall think fit, or as is conſiſtent with the Law, but that himſelf is ſtill to be judge of this, and his Loyalty to be the ſtandard.* But firſt, The Earl's reſtriction is expreſly *according to Loyalty,* which in good ſenſe is the ſame with *according to Law,* and the very thing that the King is ever ſuppoſed to think. Secondly, As neither the Advocate, nor any other hitherto, have had reaſon to diſtinguiſh the exerciſe and actings of the Earl's Loyalty, from thoſe of His Majeſty's beſt Subjects; ſo, is it not a marvellous thing, that the Advocate ſhould profeſs to think (for in reality he cannot think it) the Earl's words, *His Loyalty,* which all men ſee to be the ſame with his Duty and Fidelity, or what elſe can bind him to his Prince, capable of any quibble, far more to be a ground of ſo horrid an accuſation? And whereas the Advocate ſays, *The Earl is ſtill to be judge of this*; it is but an inſipid calumny, it being as plain as any thing can be, That the Earl doth no-wiſe deſign *His thinking* to be the Rule of Right and Wrong; but only mentions it as the neceſſary application of theſe excellent and unerring Rules of Religion, Law, and Reaſon; to which he plainly refers, and ſubjects both his thinking and himſelf, to be judged accordingly. By which it is evident, that the Earl's reſtriction is rather better, and more dutiful than that which the Advocate ſeems to deſiderate: And if the Earl's reſtrictions had not been full enough, it was the Advocate's part, before adminiſtrating the Oath, to have craved what more he thought neceſſary, which the Earl, in the Caſe, would not have refuſed. But it is believed, the Advocate can yet hardly propoſe reſtrictions more full and ſuitable to Duty than the fore-mentioned of Religion, Law and Reaſon, which the Earl did of himſelf proffer. As for what His Majeſty's Advocate adds, *That under ſuch profeſſions and reſerves, the late Rebellions and Diſorders have all been carried on and fomented,* it is but a meer vapour; for no Rebellion ever was, or can be, without a breach of one or other of the Earl's qualifications; which doth ſufficiently vindicate that part of the Earl's Explanation.

The Advocate inſiſts much, that *Any* is equivalent to *All*; and that *All* comprehends *Every* particular under it; which he would have to be the deadly Poiſon in the Earl's words: And yet the Earl may defy him and all his detracters, to find out a Caſe of the leaſt Undutifulneſs, much leſs of Rebellion, that a Man can be guilty of while he keeps within the excellent Rules and Limitations wherewith his words are cautioned. I could tell you further, that ſo imaginary, or rather extravagant, and ridiculous is this pretended Treaſon, that there is not a perſon in *Scotland,* either of who have refuſed, or who by the Act are not called to take the Teſt, that may not upon the ſame ground and words be impeach'd, *viz. That they are not bound* (and ſo without doubt both may and do ſay it) *by the Teſt, in their ſtation,* &c. *to wiſh and endeavour any alteration,* &c. Nay, I deſire the Advocate to produce the Man, among thoſe that have taken the Teſt, that will affirm, that by taking it he hath bound himſelf never to wiſh or endeavour any alteration, *&c.* according to the Earl's qualifications, and I ſhall name Hundreds (to whom his Highneſs, as you have heard, may be added) that will ſay they are not bound up.

So that by this concluſion, if it were yielded, all *Scotland* are equally guilty of Treaſon, the Advocate himſelf, to ſay nothing of His Royal Highneſs, not excepted: Or if he ſtill think he is, I wiſh he would teſtify under his hand to the World, that, *by his Oath he is bound up never to wiſh, nor endeavour any alteration he thinks to the advantage of Church or State, in a lawful way, nor in his ſtation, though neither repugnant to the Proteſtant Religion, nor his Loyalty.* And if this he do, he does as a Man, if not of Senſe, at leaſt of Honour; but if not, I leave a blank for his Epithets.

But that you may ſee that this whole affair is a deep Myſtery, pray, notice what is objected againſt the laſt part of the Explanation: *This I underſtand as a part of my Oath. Which,* ſays the Advocate, *is a Treaſonable Invaſion upon the Royal Legiſlative Power, as if the Earl could make to himſelf an Act of Parliament, ſince he who can make any part of an Act, may make the whole.* And then ſay I, farewel all Takers of the Teſt with an Explanation, whether the Orthodox Clergy, or Earl *Queensberry* (tho' himſelf Juſtice General) who were allowed by the Council ſo to do; ſeeing that whether they hold their Explanation for a part of their Oath or not, yet others may; and in effect all Men of ſenſe do underſtand it ſo: And thus, in the Advocate's Opinion, they have *Treaſonably invaded the Legiſlative Power, and made an Act of Parliament to themſelves.* Neither, in that Caſe, can the Council's allowance excuſe them, ſeeing not only the Earl had it as well as they, but even the Council it ſelf cannot make an Act of Parliament, either for themſelves, or others. But Sir, I proteſt, I am both aſhamed and wearied of this trifling; and therefore to ſhut up this Head, I ſhall only give a few remarks: Firſt, you may ſee, by the Acts of Parliament upon which the Advocate founds his Indictment, That as to *Leaſing-making* and *depraving* Laws, all of them run in theſe plain and ſenſible terms; *The inventing of Narrations, the making and telling of Lyes, the uttering of wicked and untrue Calumnies, to the ſlander of King and Government, the depraving of his Laws, and miſconſtruing his Proceedings, to the engendering of diſcord, moving and raiſing of hatred and diſlike betwixt the King and his People.* And, as to the Treaſon, in theſe yet more poſi-

Ggg

tive

tive terms; *That none impugn the dignity and authority of the Three Estates, or seek, or procure the innovation, or diminution thereof.* Which are things so palpable, and easily discerned, and withal so infinitely remote both from the Earl's words and intentions, or any tolerable construction can be put on either, that I confess, I never read this Indictment, but I was made to wonder that its forger and maker was not, in looking on it, deterred by the just apprehensions he might have, not only to be sometime accused as a manifest depraver of all Law, but to be for ever accounted a gross and most disingenuous perverter of common sense. The Earl's words are sober, respectful, and dutifully spoken, for the exoneration of his own Conscience, without the least insinuation of either *reflection* or *slander*, much less the *impugning of the Authority of Parliament*, as the Earl may appeal, not only to His Majesty's true and royal sense, but to the most scrupulous and nice affecters of the exactest discerning; besides that they were first formally tendered in Council, for their approbation, and by them directly allowed: How then can any Man think, that they could be charged with the greatest and vilest of crimes, *Leasing-making, Depraving, Perjury, and Treason?* But the Advocate tells us, *That there are some things which the Law commonly forbids in general, and that some inferences are as natural and strong, and reproach as soon or sooner than the plainest defamations.* But what of all this? Must therefore such generals be left to the phantastick application of every wild imagination, to the confounding of the use of Speech, and subverting of human Society, and not rather be still submitted to the judgment of common sense, for their true and right understanding, and the deducing thence these strong and natural inferences talk'd of? Of which good sense, if the Advocate do but allow a grain weight, it is evident that the inferences he here libels against the Earl, must infallibly be cast, and by all rational unbiassed Men be found strange, unnatural, and monstrous.

For, Sir, Secondly, pray observe these rational and sound Maxims he founds his Inferences on, and they are manifestly these: First, *That he who says he will only obey as far as he can, invents a new way whereby no man is at all bound to obey.* 2dly, *That he who in the midst of Hundreds of exceptions and contradictions, objected against an Oath injoined by Act of Parliament, and still unanswered, says, That he is confident the Parliament never intended to impose contradictory Oaths, reproaches the Parliament.* 3dly, *That he that says he must explain an ambiguous Oath for himself, before he take it, renders all Laws and Oaths useless, and makes himself the Legislator.* 4thly, *That he that says that he takes this Oath, as far as it is consistent with it self, and the Protestant Religion, swears nothing.* 5thly, *That he that declares himself not tied up by the Test from endeavouring, in a lawful way, such alterations as he thinks to the advantage of Church and State, consistent with Religion and Loyalty, declares himself and all others loosed from the Government, and all duty to it, and free to make any, and all alterations that he pleases.* And 6thly, *That he that takes the Test with an Explanation, and holds it to be a part of his Oath, invades the Legislative Power, and makes Acts of Parliament.*

Upon which rare and excellent Propositions, I dare say, The Earl is content, according to the best Judgment that you and all unbiassed Men can make, either of their Truth, or of my ingenuity in excerping them, to be adjudged Guilty or not Guilty, without the least fear or apprehension of the issue.

And in the third and last place, I shall only intreat you to try how the Advocate's reasoning will proceed in other Cases, and what brave work may be wrought by so useful a Tool. Suppose then a Man refuse the Test simply, or falls into any other kind of Nonconformity, either Civil or Ecclesiastick, or pays not the King's Custom or other dues; or lastly, understands an Act otherwise than the Advocate thinks he should; Is not his Indictment already formed, and his Process as good as made? viz. *That he regards not the Law, That he thinks it is unjustly or foolishly enacted; That he will only obey as far as he can, and as he pleases, and thereby render all Laws useless, and so reproaches the King and Parliament, and impugns their Authority, and assumes to himself the Legislative Power;* and therefore *is guilty of Leasing-making, Depraving His Majesty's Laws, and of Treason, of which crimes above-mentioned, or one or other of them, he is Actor, Art and Part: Which being found by an Assize, he ought to be punished with the pains of Death, Forfaulture and Escheat of Lands and Goods, to the terror of others to do or commit the like hereafter.* And if there be found a convenient Judge, the poor Man is undoubtedly lost.

But, Sir, having drawn this Parallel, rather to retrieve the Earl's Case, than to make it a precedent, which I hope, it shall never be, and chusing rather to leave the Advocate than follow him in his follies, I forbear to urge it further.

These things considered, must it not appear strange, beyond expression how the Earl's Explanation, such as it is, did fall under such enormous and grievous misconstructions: For, setting aside the Council's allowance and approbation (which comes to be considered under the next Head) suppose the Earl, or any other person called before the Council, and there required to take the Test, had, in all due humility, said, either that he could not at all take it, or, at least not without an Explanation; because the Test did contain such things, as, not only he, but many other, and those the best of the Loyal and Orthodox

dox

dox Clergy, did apprehend to be Contradictions, and Inconsistencies : And thereupon had proponed one or two such as the Papers above set down do plainly enough hold out, and the Bishop in his Explanation rather evades than answers ; would it not be hard, beyond all the measures of Equity, and Charity, to look upon this as a designed Reflection, far more a malicious and wicked Slander, and the blackest Treason ? We see the Act of Parliament doth not absolutely injoin the taking of the Test, but only proposeth it to such as are intrusted in the Government, with the ordinary certification, either of losing, or holding their Trusts, at their option. We know also, that in Cases of this nature, it is far more suitable both to our Christian Liberty, and the respect we owe to a Christian Magistrate, to give a reason of our conscientious non-compliance, with meekness, and fear, than by a mute compearance, to fall under the censure of a stubborn obstinacy. And lastly, It is certain, and may be safely affirmed, without the least reproach, that *Parliaments are not infallible* ; as witness the frequent changes, and abrogations of their own Acts, and their altering of Oaths imposed by themselves ; and even of this Oath, after it was presented, which the Earl was not for altering, so much as it was done, as I told you before. How then can it be, that the Earl appearing before a Christian Council, and there declaring in terms, at the worst a little obscure, because too tender, and modest, his Scruples at an Oath presented to him, either to be freely taken, or refused, should fall under any Censure ? If the Earl had, in this occasion, said, he could not take the Test, unless liberty were given him first to explain himself, as to some Contradictions and Inconsistencies, which he conceived to be in it, tho' he had said far more than is contained in his controverted Explanation, yet he had said nothing but what Christian Liberty hath often freely allowed ; and Christian Charity would readily construe for an honest expression of a commendable tenderness, without any imputation of reproach against either King or Parliament. How much more then is his part clear and innocent, when albeit so many thought the Contradictions to be undeniable, yet such was his well-tempered respect, both to God and Man, to his own Conscience, and His Majesty's Authority, that before and not after, the taking of this Oath, to clear himself (in the midst of the many Exceptions and Scruples raised) of all ambiguities in swearing, he first applies himself, for a satisfying Explanation, to the Parliament, the prime Imposers, their true intentions and genuine meaning ; and then gathering it very rationally, from the Oath's consistency with it self, and with the Protestant Religion, the Parliament's aim and scope, and so asserting the King and Parliament's truth, and honour, he places the relief and quiet of his own Conscience in his taking the Test with this Explanation, and in declaring its congruity with his Oath, and duty of Allegiance.

The third Head of the Earl's additional Defences, is the further clearing and improving of his grounds of Exculpation, above adduced, and repelled : Which were, first, that before the Earl did offer his Explanation to the Council, a great many Papers were spread abroad by some of the Orthodox Clergy, charging the Test with Contradictions and Inconsistencies. 2dly, That there was a Paper penned by a Reverend Bishop, and presented and read in Council, and by them allowed to be printed, which did contain the same, and far more important things than any can be found in the Earl's Explanation : And consequently, far more obnoxious to all His Majesty's Advocate's Accusations. 3dly, That the Explanation upon which he was indicted was publickly by himself declared in Council, and by the Council allowed ; so that the Oath was administrat to him, and he received to sit in Council, and vote, by his Highness, and the rest of the Members, with, and under this express qualification.

But, to all urged for the Earl's Exculpation, the Advocate makes one short Answer, *viz. That if the Earl's Paper did infer the Crimes charged on it, a thousand the like offences cannot excuse it : And His Majesty is free to pursue the Offenders, when and in what order, he thinks fit.* Which Answer doth indeed leave the Council, and all concerned, in His Majesty's Mercy : But that it doth no way satisfy the Earl's Plea, is manifest : For, the first ground of Exculpation, *viz.* That before the Earl did offer his Explanation, a great many Papers, writ by the Orthodox Clergy and others, were abroad, charging the Test with Contradictions, &c. was not alledged by the Earl merely to justify his Explanation by the multitude of the like Papers, and so to provide for an escape in the croud : But, the Earl having most rationally pleaded, that his Explanation was given in by him, after these many Scruples and Objections raised by others were abroad, it was a good Plea, from a most pregnant circumstance, clearing both the design, and sense of his words, from the foul aspersions of reproaching, and depraving, thrown upon them : Seeing the words spoken by him under the motive of such a circumstance, by all fair rules of interpretation, instead of being judged misconstruing and depraving, could only be understood as a seasonable asserting of the Integrity of the Parliament's Intentions, and the uprightness of the Earl's Conscience. Which Argument being in reason unanswerable, it necessarily follows, that the Advocate's return to the first ground was neither sufficient, nor pertinent, and that therefore the Exculpation was justly repelled. But next, The second ground of Exculpation is so far from being answered by the Advocate, that it does not appear it was so much as understood: For, the Earl's Argument being, That words allowed and approven by the Council, can never fall under the Accusation, either of Leasing-making, or slandering His Majesty's Proceedings, or depraving Laws and Acts of Parliament, as is evident in it self, and granted by the Advocate, where he says that an Explanation, tho' reflecting on the King and Government (which the Earl's was not) yet, if allowed by the Council, is to be sustained. But so it is, that the Council hath allowed the words contained in this Explanation controverted, both in themselves, and also in their equivalent, and far more important Expressions: As for instance, not only by accepting the Earl's Explanation (as shall be cleared in the next place) but by giving warrant for the publication of the Bishop of *Edinburgh* his Vindication; wherein first, for obviating the contradictions objected from the Confession of Faith, he positively asserts, that by the Test men do not swear to own every Article of that Confession; and yet the Test binds expresly to believe *that Confession to be founded on, and agreeable to the Word of God, and never to consent to any alteration contrary thereto, or inconsistent therewith:* So that he gives both the Test and the Parliament the Lye. And then, for removing another Scruple, he tells us, That *by the Test men are not bound up from regular endeavours to rectify or better the Established Government, both of Church and State,* which is clearly the same thing (but not so well cautioned) with that which in the Earl's Case is made a ground of Treason: From which it unquestionably follows, that the Earl's words, *having been allowed, and approved by the Council,* could never, in Law, or Reason, be thereafter made a ground of accusation, by any, much less by themselves. Now I desire to know where the Advocate, in all his Plea, doth so much as notice, far less answer, this Defence; or what his telling us, *A thousand Offences of the like nature doth not excuse one,* either doth or can signify? seeing this Argument for the Earl, instead of pleading excuses, doth justify the matter, and for ever purge all shadow of offence or ground of quarrel, which will be yet more apparent, when you shall add to this the third ground of the Earl's Exculpation, *viz.* That the Explanation, whereupon the Earl was indicted, was publickly by himself declared in Council, and by the Council allowed and accepted: Insomuch as after he had given his Explanation as the sense wherein he was free to swear the Test, the Oath was thereupon administrate to him, and he received to sit, and vote as a Counsellor. Whereby it is evident, That, by this allowance, and acceptance, the Earl's Explanation became the Council's, as much as if, after the Earl's pronouncing the words, they had *verbatim* repeated them, and told him, they were satisfied he should swear the Test in these terms: And whether this ought not to be a sufficient exoneration to the Earl, let all men judge. The Advocate makes a noise, *That in the case of an Oath required, the Taker ought to swear it in the sense of the Imposer,* (which none doubts) and then runs out, *That the Earl in place of taking it in the Imposer's sense, did unwarrantably intend a sense of his own, to the eluding and frustrating of the obligation of this, and all other Oaths.* But all this is nothing to the purpose; for waving that in the Earl's Case it is most impertinent to talk of his obtruding of a sense, to the eluding, and frustrating of the obligation of his Oath, seeing his Oath was not then given, or at all in being; it is expresly alledged by the Earl, and notour, that the Explanation tendered by him, when called to take the Test, was accepted by the Council, and the Oath thereupon administrated, and so the Earl freely joins issue with the Advocate, and acknowledging that the Taker of the Oath ought to swear in the sense of the Imposer, subsumes *in terminis* that he himself did swear so, and not otherwise, inasmuch as he did swear in a sense accepted by the Council, before he gave his Oath; as is evident, 1. By their commanding him to sit after he had sworn; and 2. In that neither the Advocate, nor any other, had ever the confidence to quarrel his sitting, as a breach of the Law, which no doubt they had done, if not convinced that by taking the Oath he had satisfied the Act of Parliament; which things, in true dealing, and the construction of all honest men, are the same as if the Oath had been required of him by the Council, in the very sense and words of this Explanation. Neither is it material whether the Explanation, offered by the Earl, doth deserve (as certainly it doth not) these many ill names, which the Advocate would fix upon it; because, though it had been much worse than it is, yet being offered to the Council, and submitted to their judgment, and they having accepted of it, the thing became *quasi res judicata,* and cannot be retracted, without subverting the surest Rules, both of Truth and Government. The Advocate indeed tells us, 1. *That the Council heard not the Earl's Explanation:* But I have already told you, they did hear it, and the Earl is still ready to prove it. And suppose some say they did not hear it distinctly; (as what thing spoken in Council is distinctly heard and considered by all?) Yet it being certain that they did all approve it, it is sufficient to the Earl: And it is only their concern, whether in approving what they did not hear, they observed their Oath *De fideli, &c.* or not. His Highness, who the Earl was most concerned should hear, did certainly hear, as himself afterwards acknowledged. 2. The Advocate says, *That the hearing and allowing the Earl to sit, is no relevant Plea; yea further, though all the Council had allowed him that day, yet any of his Majesty's Officers might have quarrled with him the*

next

next day. But firft, I would gladly know, upon what head ? For if upon obtruding a fenfe of his own, it is undeniable that whatever the fenfe was, the obtruding of it was purged by the Council's acceptation, and it became theirs, and was no more his. But if the Advocate doth think, that even the matter of the Explanation, though allowed and accepted, may ftill be quarrelled ; then, 1. I hope, he will confider in what terms he doth it ; for if he charge it after it becomes the Council's (as in truth he hath done already) with the fame liberty wherewith he treats it as the Earl's, he runs fair to make himfelf the *arranteft Defamer* and *Slanderer* of the King and Council that ever yet attempted it. But 2*dly,* It merits a worfe name than I am free to give it, to fay, That an Explanation allowed by the Council, in the adminiftrating of an Oath proper to be adminiftrat by them, doth not fecure the Takers as to that fenfe, both in Law, and Confcience ; feeing in effect this quite takes away the beft grounds of affurance among men, and turns their greateft fecurity to their greateft fnare. And 3*dly,* if this be found Doctrine, it is worth the enquiring, what fecurity the Clergy, to whom the Council, as you have heard, did indulge an Explanation, have thereby obtained : For as to fuch Laicks as did only at their own hand take hold of, and fnatch at this Indulgence, not provided for them by the Council's Act, it is clear their doom is dight. It is not here debated how far that Explication of the Council's may fatisfy, and quiet Confcience, let fuch concerned fee to it. Some pleafe themfelves with a general notion, That if the fenfe given by the Adminiftrator be found, then it is alfo fafe, whether it be agreeable to the plain and genuine meaning of the Oath, or not ; nay, whether it be agreeable to the fenfe of the firft Impofers, or not : But others, who confider more tenderly what it is to fwear in Truth, and in Judgment, think it rather a prophanation, and a finful preferring of the Credit of Men to the Glory of the Almighty, to offer to fmooth an Oath by a difagreeable interpretation, when in effect the Oath it felf ought to be changed : But the thing in queftion *is about the fecurity of life and fortune* ; for feeing the Council's Explanation is, at leaft, to fay no worfe, liable enough to the Calumnies of the inventive malice, and the Advocate telleth us, *Though all the Council had allowed a man to fwear with an Explanation,* yet any of *His Majefty's Officers may the next day quarrel him* ; it is evident that this allowance can afford him no fecurity. It is true, the Advocate may alledge, and poffibly find a difference betwixt the Council's *emitting,* and their *accepting* of an Explanation. But as in truth there is none, more than betwixt a *Mandat* and a *Ratihabition* ; fo I am confident, if ever the thing come to be queftioned, this Pretence will evanifh, and come to nothing.

It is likewife to be remembred, That when the Earl, the next day after he took the Teft, was queftioned for the Explanation he had made, and required to exhibit a Copy (which was afterwards made the ground of his Indictment) fo foon as he obferved that fome began to carp, he refufed to fign it, demanded it back, and would have deftroyed it, as you have heard, which were all clear Acts of difowning, and retracting, for eviting offence, and of themfelves fufficient to have prevented any further enquiry ; there being nothing more juft and humane, than that words, though at the firft hearing offenfive, yet if inftantly retracted, when queftioned, fhould be paft : But this, as well as other things, muft in the Earl's Cafe be fingular ; and whether he plead the *Council's allowing,* or his own *difowning* (as in effect he doth both) it is equally to no purpofe, the thing determined muft be accomplifhed. You heard before, how that a Reverend Bifhop, and many of the Orthodox Clergy, did take a far greater liberty of Explanation than the Earl pretended to ; you fee alfo that firft the Council allows his words, whereupon he refts : And when he finds that they begin to challenge, he is willing to difown : And withal, it is undeniable, and acknowledged by the Council themfelves, that the Teft, as it ftands in the Act of Parliament, is ambiguous, and needs to be explained. And the Earl may confidently aver, that of all the Explanations that have been offered (even the Council's not excepted) his is the moft fafe, found, and leaft difagreeable to the Parliament's true fenfe and meaning. And yet, when others efcape, he alone muft be feized ; and for a thing fo openly innocent, clearly juftifiable, and undeniably allowed, found guilty of the worft of Crimes, even *Leafing-making, Leafing-telling, Depraving of Laws, and Treafon* ; but all thefe things God Almighty fees, and to him the Judgment yet belongs.

And thus I leave this Difcourfe, fhutting it up with the Cafe of Archbifhop *Cranmer,* plainly parallel to the Earl's, to fhew how much he was more favourably dealt with by the King, and Government, in thofe days, than the Earl now is, though he live under a much more merciful, and juft Prince, than that worthy Prelate did ; for *Cranmer* being called and promoted by *Henry* VIII. of *England* to be Archbifhop of *Canterbury,* and finding an Oath, was to be offered to him, which, in his apprehenfion, would bind him up from what he accounted his duty, he altogether declined the Dignity and Preferment, unlefs he were allowed to take the Oath with fuch an Explanation as he himfelf propofed, for falving of his Confcience ; and tho' this Oath was no other than the Statute, and folemn Oath, that all his Predeceffors in that See, and all the mitred Clergy in *England,* had fworn, yet he was admitted to take it, as you fee in *Fuller's* Church Hift. of *Britain,* lib. 5. p. 185, and 186. with this formal Proteftation.

H h h

In

4

In nomine Domini, Amen. Coram vobis, &c. Non est, aut erit meæ voluntatis, aut intentionis, per hujusmodi juramentum vel juramenta, qualitercunque verba in ipsis posita sonare videbuntur me obligare ad aliquid, ratione eorundem, posthac dicendum, faciendum, aut attentandum, quod erit, aut esse videbitur, contra Legem Dei, vel contra illustrissimum Regem nostrum Angliæ, Legesve, aut Prærogativas ejusdem: Et quod non intendo, per hujusmodi juramentum vel juramenta, quovis modo me obligare qui minus libere loqui, consulere, aut consentire valeam, in omnibus & singulis Reformationem Religionis Christianæ, Gubernationem Ecclesiæ Anglicanæ, & Prærogativam Coronæ ejusdem Reipublicæ vel commoditatem earundem, quoquo modo concernentibus; & ea ubique exequi, & reformare, quæ mihi in Ecclesia Anglicana reformanda videbuntur: Et secundum hanc interpretationem & intellectum hunc, & non aliter, nequa alio modo, dictum juramentum me præstiturum protestor, & profiteor.

That is to say. In the name of God, Amen. Before you, &c. *It neither is, nor shall be, my will or meaning, by this kind of Oath, or Oaths, and however the words of themselves shall seem to sound or signify, to bind up my self, by virtue hereof, to say, or endeavour any thing, which shall really be, or appear to be, against the Law of God, or against our most Illustrious King of* England, *or against his Laws and Prerogatives: And that I mean not, by this my Oath, or Oaths, any way to bind up my self from speaking, consulting, and consenting freely, in all, and every thing in any sort concerning the Reformation of the Christian Religion, the Government of the Church of* England, *and the Prerogative of the Crown of the Commonwealth thereof, or their advantage; and for executing, and reforming such things as I shall think need to be reformed in the Church of* England: *And according to this Explanation, and Sense, and not otherwise, nor in any other manner, I do protest, and profess, that I am to take, and perform this Oath.*

Nor did that excellent Person, says Mr. *Fuller,* smother this privately in a corner, but publickly interposed it three several times; once in the *Charter-house,* before authentick Witnesses; again upon his bended knees, before the high Altar, in view and hearing of many People, and Bishops beholding him, when he was consecrated; and the third time, when he received the Pall, in the same place.

Now would it not be very strange if the like liberty should not be allowed to the Earl, under His Majesty, in reference to the Test, which *Henry* the VIIIth, a Prince that stood as much on his Prerogative as ever any, did vouchsafe to this *Thomas Cranmer,* who as another Historian observes, *acted fairly, and above-board:* But there wanted then the high and excellent Designs of the great Ministers, the rare Fidelity of Counsellors, sound Religion and tender Piety of Bishops, solid Law and Learning of Advocates, incorruptible Integrity of Judges, and upright Honesty of Assizers, that now we have, to get Archbishop *Cranmer* accused, and condemned, for *Leasing-making, depraving Laws, Perjury,* and *Treason,* to which Accusation his Explanation was certainly no less obnoxious than the Earl's.

But I hasten to the fourth and last Head of the Earl's Additional Defences, *viz.* The removing certain groundless Pretences, alledged by the Advocate for aggravating the Earl's Offence: As 1. *That the Earl, being a Peer, and a Member of Parliament, should have known the sense of the Parliament, and that neither the Scruples of the Clergy, nor the Council's Proclamation, designed for meer Ignorants, could any way excuse the Earl for offering such an Explanation.* But first, the Advocate might have remembred, that in another Passage he taxes the Earl as having debated in Parliament against the Test, whereby it is easy to gather, that the Earl having been in the matter of the Test a dissenter, this quality doth rather justify than aggravate the Earl's Scrupling. 2*dly,* If the Proclamation was designed for the meer Ignorants of the Clergy, as the Advocate calls them, who knew nothing of what had past in Parliament, an Explanation was far more necessary for the Earl, who knows so little of what the Advocate alledges to have past in Parliament, *viz. That the Confession of Faith was not to be sworn to as a part of the Test,* that of necessity (as I think) he must know the contrary; inasmuch as, first, this is obvious from the express tenor of the Test, which binds *to own, and profess the true Protestant Religion, contained in the Confession of Faith, and to believe the same to be agreeable to the Word of God; as also to adhere thereto, and never to consent to any change contrary to, or inconsistent with the said Protestant Religion, and Confession of Faith:* Which to common sense appears as plain, and evident, as can be contrived, or desired. But 2*dly,* It is very well known, that it was expresly endeavoured, and carried in Parliament, that the *Confession of Faith* should be a part of the Test and Oath: For the *Confession of Faith* being designed to be sworn to, by an Act for securing the Protestant Religion (which you have heard was prepared in the Articles, but afterwards thrown out) when this Act for the Test was brought into the Parliament, some days after, by the Bishop of *Edinburgh,* and others, the *Confession* was designedly left out of it: But it being again debated that the bare naming of the Protestant Religion, without condescending on a Standard for it, was not sufficient, the *Confession of Faith* was of

new

new added: And, after the affirmative Clause for owning it, and adhering to it was infert, upon a new motion, the negative, *never to consent to any alteration, contrary to, or inconsistent with the said Protestant Religion,* and *Confession of Faith,* was also subjoined: But not without a new debate and opposition made against the words, *And Confession of Faith,* by the Bishop of *Edinburgh,* until at length he also yielded; all which, it is hoped, was done for some purpose: And if at that time, any had doubted of the thing, he had certainly been judged most ridiculous; for it was by that addition concluded by all, That the *Confession* was to be sworn. And further, it appears plainly, by the Bishop of *Edinburgh his Vindication,* that, when he wrote it, he believed the *Confession* was to be sworn to, for he takes pains to justify it (though calumniously enough) alledging, *That it was hastily compiled, in the short space of four days, by some Barons and Ministers in the infancy of our Reformation.* Where, by the by, you see that he makes no reckoning of what the Act of Parliament, to which the Test refers, expresly bears, viz. *That that second Ratification,* 1567. which we only have recorded, *was no less than seven years after this Confession was first exhibited, and approven Anno* 1560. But moreover he tells us, *That the Doctors of* Aberdeen *who refused the* Covenant, *were yet willing not only to subscribe, but to swear this* Confession of Faith. Which again, to answer the Bishop's Critick of *Four days,* was more than 70 years after it was universally received. It's true, that, when the Bishop finds himself straitned how to answer Objections, he is forced to make use of the new Gloss (I shall not call it of *Orleans*) whereby the Protestant Religion is made to be sworn to only as far as every Man pleases to interpret, and as far as may be consistent with any new principles of State. But the Parliament certainly (I do not speak Ironically) did intend by this Test, to swear and assert the *True Protestant Religion, and the said Confession of Faith,* whatever may be now pretended. The Earl could not also but very well remember what his Highness had said to himself, about the inserting of the *Confession*; and no doubt, the Advocate, if ingenuous, knows all this: For the thing was at that time matter of common talk, and indeed, till Papers objecting contradictions, and inconsistencies betwixt the *Confession* and the rest of the *Test,* began to be so numerous (which was about the end of *October*) that there was no possibility left to answer them, but by alledging, *That in the* Test, *men do not swear to every article and proposition of the Confession, but only the Protestant Religion therein contained,* this point was never doubted. And whether this answer be true, and a solid Vindication, consonant to the words of the Test, or a circulating evasion enervating all its force, let others judge. But the Advocate says, *When it was moved in Parliament to read the Confession, it was waved:* Most true; and the reason given by the Bishops for it was, *That it was notour, they knew it, and it was already insert in the Acts of Parliament:* And, the truth was, the reading of it would have spent more time than was allowed on examining the whole Test. It was likewise late, after a long *Sederunt,* and it was resolved to have the Act passed that night, and so it went on: But it was moved *to read the Covenant, seeing it was to be disclaimed,* and was flatly refused. And will the Advocate thence infer, That by the *Test* the *Covenant* is not abjured, albeit it be most certain, that many in the Parliament, at that time, had never read the one or the other? But to follow the Advocate's excursions, and answer them more particularly: The motion for reading the *Confession* being made on this very occasion, *Because it was to be insert in the* Test *and sworn to,* concludes enough against him; for no body can be so effrontted as to say, it was used in Parliament, as an argument not to read it, because it was not to be sworn to, but (though it cost a debate) it was plainly agreed to be sworn to, and therefore insert, 2dly, Can any man doubt the *Confession* was to be Sworn to, when it is notour that severals who were members of Parliament, and by reason of offices they enjoyed, were called to swear the *Test,* pretending, with reason, tenderness of an Oath, did, before swearing, make a fashion at least of reading and studying the *Confession,* to satisfy themselves how far they might swear it. And that this was done by an Hundred, I can attest themselves. Lastly, It is certain that, when, in the end of *October,* the Bishop of *Edinburgh* did quarrel Sir *George Lockhart,* for causing the *Confession* to be insert in the *Test,* and he answered that without it a *Turk* might sign the *Test,* it was not then pretended by the Bishop that the *Confession* was not to be sworn to, and therefore he at that time had no reply.

But this is a debate, I confess, not altogether necessary for my present task, only thereby you may see ground enough for the Earl to believe the *Confession* was sworn to: And all that did swear, before the Council's Explanation, having sworn in that sense, and, for aught I know, all (except the Clergy) being by the Council's Act still bound to do so, it was not strange the Earl might be of this Opinion. And seeing that many of the Contradictions were alledged to arise hence, and the Earl being a Dissenter, it was yet less strange that the Earl did scruple; nor is it unreasonable that his modest Explanation should have a most benign acceptance.

This second pretence of aggravation is, *That His Majesty did not only bestow on the Earl his Lands and Jurisdictions, fallen into His Majesty's hands by the forfaulture of his Father, but also pardon him the crimes of Leasing-making and Misconstruing, whereof he was found guilty by the Parliament* 1662. *And raifed him to the title and dignity of an Earl, and to be a member of all His Majefty's Judicatories.* All which the Earl, as he hath ever, doth ftill moft thankfully acknowledge. But feeing the Advocate hath no warrant to upbraid him with His Majefty's Favours, and that thefe things are now remembred with a manifeft defign to raife duft, and blind ftrangers, and to add a very ill thing, Ingratitude, to the heap of groundlefs calumnies caft upon him ; I muft crave leave to anfwer a little more particularly, and refute this new *Tout* (as the *Scots* Proverb is) *in an old Horn.* This old *Leafing-making* is then now brought in ferioufly after it hath been treated in ridicule for Eighteen years, by the very Actors who did never pretend to defend it in cold blood : And, were it not to digrefs too much, I could name the perfons, and make them (if capable) think fhame of their falfhood and prevarications in that, and of their abufing His Majefty, and proftrating Juftice ; but I forbear.

The Advocate, in his Book of Pleadings, makes this a *Stretch,* and fays, *His Majefty refcinded it.* And His Majefty himfelf hath feveral times exprefs'd his fenfe of the *ftretches* made by fome againft the Earl, at that time. It is well known the Family of *Argyle* is both Ancient and Honourable, and hath been Loyal and Serviceable to the Crown for feveral Hundreds of years ; but they muft now be deftroyed, for having done, and being able, as they fay, to do too much, which others neither can nor will do.

Neither is the Advocate ignorant that the only failing that Familiy hath been charged with in all that long tract of time, was a compliance of the late Marquefs of *Argyle,* the Earl's Father, in the time of the late Ufurpation, by fitting in the then Parliament of *England,* fome years after all the ftanding Forces of the Kingdom were broken, His Majefty beyond Sea, the whole Country over-run, the Ufurpers univerfally acknowledged, and neither probability of refiftance, nor poffiblility of fhelter left to any that were moft willing to ferve His Majefty, as the Advocate himfelf hath publifhed in his printed Pleadings, in which he likewife lays out the fpecial and extraordinary Circumftances whereby the Marquefs was neceffitate to do what he did. And the compliance charged on him was fo epidemick, that all others were pardoned for the fame, except he alone, though none had fuch favourable Arguments to plead, and though he pleaded the fame Indemnity that faved others. And feeing he fubmitted, and delivered up himfelf, and loft his Life, and feeing at the fame time of the Compliance that he fuffered for, the Earl his Son was actually ferving and fuffering for His Majefty, as you find in the former part of this Letter, the Earl's Reftitution was no lefs than He and his Family might well expect of His Majefty's Goodnefs and Juftice. It is true, The Earl was again accufed and condemned (which may appear indeed ftrange to fuch as know not all particulars) upon the fame old Acts of *Leafing-making,* and with as little ground (if poffible) as now, and was pardoned by His Majefty, for which he hath often, and doth always acknowledge, that he owes to his Majefty both his Life and Fortune : But upon this occafion, and being baited as he is, he hopes His Majefty will not take it ill that he fay, That His Majefty's Mercy was in this cafe determined by Juftice : And for proof that His Majefty did then know him to be innocent, did not His Majefty then fay, *It was impoffible to take a Man's Life upon fo fmall an account ?* Though neverthelefs it had been done, if His Majefty had not interpofed and pardoned him. Did not the Chancellor *Clarendon* (who was Patron to the moft confiderable of the Earl's purfuers) hearing of his Condemnation, *blefs God, he lived not in a Country where there were fuch Laws ?* (*He fhould have faid, fuch Judges.*) And I believe many more will fay the fame now. Did it not plainly appear, at that time, that his principal purfuers were very bitter, malicious, and unjuft to him? For the Earl had not only ferved His Majefty in that troublefome and hazardous appearance in the Hills, but he had been particularly ufeful to Earl *Middleton,* then His Majefty's Lieutenant General, and had ftood by him, when thefe deferted him, whom notwithftanding he took afterwards by the hand, when he was His Majefty's Commiffioner in the year 1661. and then defigned new Interefts and new Alliances, whereof fome did hold, and fome never held. And then indeed it was, that he and others thought it proper for them to deftroy the Family of *Argyle,* to make their own Fortunes ; but it pleafed God and His Majefty to difpofe otherwife : Then it was that the Earl was fo hotly purfued for his Life ; having at that time no Fortune, all being in His Majefty's hands. Then was the accufation of Treafon likewife urged by the fame perfons, and muft have carried, but it was not found neceffary, *Leafing-making* being fufficient to take his Life ; and, as it falls out, when any Game is ftarted, and the Hounds in chafe, all the little Curs run along, fo the Earl wanted not then many purfuers that are now fcarce to be heard of. And further, fome of the parties themfelves confeffed the particulars to the Earl afterwards, who yet now return to act their former parts, and that they had then laid down a refolution to intrap him, *per fas, aut nefas ;* but notwithftanding all this ill humour and violence, all the ground they could get for a quarrel, in two years time, was one fingle Letter, among

many

many they intercepted, the occasion and import whereof was as follows: About a Twelvemonth after the death of the late Marquess of *Argyle*, the Earl his Son being, by the loss of his Estate, and burden of his Debts, brought into straits, a Friend from *Edinburgh* wrote to him, then at *London*, to do what he could for himself at Court, and the sooner the better ; for he needed neither expect Favour nor Justice from some in *Scotland* ; and if matters were delayed, his Father's whole Estate would be begg'd away in parcels. His Friend likewise complained, that the Earl did not write to inform his Friends in *Scotland* ; and on this he insisted several post-days, which, at last, drew an answer from the Earl, that he had been to wait upon His Majesty, and had found him both just and kind to him, and doubted not the effects of his Royal Favour ; that he was sensible of his loss by delay, yet must proceed discreetly, and not press to give His Majesty trouble, but must take His Majesty's method, and wait his time ; That he judged, much of what his Friend told him was true, but he must have patience : It was his misfortune that some took pains to make His Majesty believe, that the Parliament was his Enemy, and the Parliament to believe the King was his Enemy ; and by such informations he was like to be a sufferer, but he hoped in God all should be well. *This blast must blow out, and will blow over: The King will see their tricks.* And upon this Letter, specially those last words, the Earl was accused of *Leasing-making betwixt the King and Parliament, and that he expected changes* ; and so had a great deal of the same stuff laid to his charge, as now you have heard : And if the now Register will produce the Earl's principal Letter, and the Paper the Earl gave in to the Parliament, these two would clear all ; the Case then, and now, as you may see, *Mutatis Mutandis*, being much the same, and some of the same Tools used. But to go on, The Earl's words in that Letter being clear and plain, *viz. That he complained of others that reported Lyes to the King and Parliament, but did himself report none to either* ; he acknowledged the Letter, which could never have been proven to be his ; and as soon as he heard that it was intercepted, did render himself to His Majesty before he was call'd for : But, which very much troubled him, had not access. Yet His Majesty was so gracious, that instead of sending him Prisoner to *Scotland* with a Guard (as was much pressed) he allowed him to go down on a Verbal Bail : And His Majesty was pleased to say, *That he saw nothing in the Earl's Letter against His Majesty or the Parliament ; but believed the Earl did design to reflect on the Earl of Middleton.* The Earl came to *Edinburgh*, a fortnight before the day appointed by His Majesty, and thought to have the liberty of the City, till that day should come ; but was sent to the Castle the next day after his arrival : Upon which he advertised His Majesty of his condition, who would hardly believe they would take his Life, till it was told plainly it was designed, and if he died it lay at His Majesty's door ; upon which His Majesty was graciously pleased to send immediately an Order to the Earl of *Middleton*, not to proceed to Execution against him. Yet the Sentence of Death was pronounced, and the Day of Execution remitted by the Parliament to the Earl of *Middleton* : Which he accepted of, albeit he had no particular instruction for it from His Majesty, which, before a year went about, Earl *Middleton* found could not be justified by him, and some of the Earl's chief accusers were declared by His Majesty to be themselves *Leasing-makers* ; and then the Earl, by his Majesty's favour and goodness, was restored to a part of his Predecessors Estate and Titles, which he took as thankfully, as if a new Estate, and new and greater Honours had been conferred upon him. And though His Majesty was pleased, at the granting of these Titles, to say, *He could help them when he pleased* ; yet His Majesty knows, that the Earl never troubled him about any such matter, nor solicited him now these eighteen years, for any Title, Office, or Imployment, (though he confesses he had of all sorts) nor hath he been burthensome to His Majesty's Exchequer (500 *l*. yearly, for four or five years that the Earl served in the Treasury, being all that ever he touched of His Majesty's Money) albeit few attended more, and none so much that lived at his distance. He was also twice at *London*, to kiss his Majesty's Hand, but still on his own Charges : which things are not said to lessen his Majesty's bounty and goodness, whereof the Earl still retains all just and dutiful impressions ; but to answer the Advocate, and to teach others to hold their peace, that cannot say so much.

His Life is known to have been True, Honest, and of a piece, and all along he hath walked with that straitness, that he can compare his Integrity with all that now attack him.

By all which it is apparent, That what the Advocate here pretends for an aggravation, may well be accounted a *Second part of the Earl's Persecutions* ; but cannot, in the least, impair either his Innocence, or his Honour.

Seeing therefore the ground of the Earl's present accusation, with all he either designed, said, or did, in this matter, was only that, when called, nay required to take the Test, and after leave first obtained from his Highness and Council, he did in their presence, before the giving of his Oath, declare, and propose to them the sense wherein he was willing

ling

ling to take it ; That this his sense neither contains, nor insinuates, the least slander, reproach or reflection, either upon the King, the Parliament, or any Person whatsomeever ; but, on the contrair, is in effect tenfold more agreeable to the words of the Test, and meaning of the Parliament that framed it, than the Explanation emitted by the Council ; and was also most certainly, the first day, by them accepted ; and, when the next day challenged, by him offered to be retracted, and refused to be signed : That the whole Indictment, and more especially that part of it about the Treason, is a meer Rhapsody of the most irrational, absurd, and pernicious consequences, that ever the Sun beheld, not only forcing the common Rules of Speech, Charity, and Humanity, but ranversing all the Topicks of Law, Reason, and Religion, and threatning no less, in the Earl's person, than the ruin of every Man's Fortune, Life, and Honour : That the Earl's Defences, and grounds of Exculpation, were most pregnant, and unanswerable, and either in themselves notour, or offered to be instantly verified. And lastly, That the aggravations pretended against him do either directly make for him, or most evidently discover the restless malice of some of his implacable Enemies. Shall our Gracious King, who not only clearly understands Right, and hates Oppression, but also, to all his other excellent qualities, hath by his Gentleness and Clemency, even towards his Enemies, added that great Character of Goodness, upon vain and false insinuations, and unreasonable and violent stretches, not only take away the Life of an innocent person, but of one who himself, and his Family (be it said without disparagement) have, for a longer time, and more faithfully, and signally served His Majesty and the Crown, than any Person, or Family of his degree and quality, of all his Persecutors can pretend to ? Shall his numerous Family, hopeful Children, his Friends and Creditors, all be destroyed ? Shall both former Services be forgot, Innocence oppressed, and all Rules of Justice, and Laws of Society and Humanity for his sake overturned ? Shall not only the Earl be cut off, and his noble and ancient Family extinguished, but his Blood and Memory tainted with as black and horrible a stain, as if he had conspired with *Jacques Clement, Ravillack,* the Gun-powder Miscreants, the Bloody *Irish* Rebels, and all the other most wicked and heinous Traytors of that Gang ? And all this for a meer imaginary Crime, whereof it is most certain, that no Man living hath, or can have, the least real conviction, and upon such frivolous allegations as all men see to be, at the top, meer Moon-shine ; and at the bottom, Villany unmixed.

After clearing these things, the Earl, it seems, intended to have addressed himself to His Majesty's Advocate in particular, and to have told him, that he had began very timeously in Parliament to fall first on his heritable Jurisdictions, and then upon his Estate, and that now he was fallen upon his Life and Honour, whereby it was easy to divine that more was intended from the beginning, than the simple taking away of his Offices : seeing that some of them, on his refusing the Test, were taken away by the Certification of the Act of Parliament, and that those that were heritable he offered, in Parliament, to present and surrender to His Majesty on his knee, if His Majesty, after hearing him, should think it fit ; only he was not willing to have them torn from him, as hath been said ; and if that were all were designed, as was at first given out, the Advocate need not have set him on high, as *Naboth,* and accuse him as a Blasphemer of God and the King.

Then turning his Speech to the Lords of Justiciary, he thought to have desired that they would yet seriously consider his words, in their true sense and circumstances, his own Explanation of his Explication, and especially the foregoing matter of Fact to have been laid before them, with his defences and grounds of Exculpation ; as also to have told them, That they could not but observe how that he was singled out amongst Thousands, (against whom much more than all he is charged with could be alledged) and that they must of necessity acknowledge (if they would speak out their own Conscience) that what he had said was spoke in pure innocence, and duty, and only for the exoneration of himself, as a Christian, and one honoured to be of His Majesty's Privy Council (where he was bound, by his Oath, to speak truth freely) and not to throw the smallest reproach on either person or thing : Adding, That he was loth to say any thing that looks like a reflection upon His Majesty's Privy Council ; but if the Council can wrong one of their own number, he thought he might demand, If he had not met with hard measure ? For first he was pressed, and persuaded to come to the Council ; then they receive his Explanation, and take his Oath, then they complain of him to His Majesty, where he had no access to be heard ; and by their Letter, under their hands, affirm, That they had been careful not to suffer any to take the Test with their own Explanations, albeit they had allowed a thing very like it, first to Earl *Queensberry,* then to the Clergy : And the President, now Chancellor, had permitted several Members of the College of Justice to premise, when they swear the Test, some one sense, and some another, and some nonsense, as one saying he took it, *in sano sensu* ; another making a Speech that no Man understood ; a third, all the time of the reading, repeating, *Lord, have mercy upon me, miserable sinner.* Nay, even an Advocate, after being debarred a few days, because caufe albeit no Clerk, yet he would not take it without the *benefit of his Clergy, viz.* the *Council's Explanation,* was yet thereafter admitted without the *Warrant of the Council's Act*; but all this in the Cafe of fo many other was right and good. Further, the Council exprefly declare the Earl to be guilty, before he had ever faid one word in his own defence. Thereafter fome of them become his Affizers, and others of them witnefs againft him; and after all, they do of new concern themfelves, by a Second Letter to His Majefty (*wherein they affert, that after full debate, and clear probation, he was found guilty of Treafon,* &c.) to have a fentence paft againft him, and that of fo high a nature, and fo dreadful a confequence, as fuffers no perfon to be unconcerned, far lefs their Lordfhips his Judges; who upon grounds equally juft, and which is more, already predetermined by themfelves, may foon meet with the fame meafure, not only as Concealers of Treafon, but upon the leaft pretended difobedience, or non-compliance with any Act of Parliament: and, after all, muft infallibly render an account to God Almighty. He bids them therefore *lay their hands to their hearts,* and whatever they fhall judge, he is affured that God knows, and he hopes all un-biaffed men in the World will, or may know, he is neither guilty of Treafon, nor any of the Crimes libelled. He fays he is glad how many out-do him in afferting the true Proteftant Religion, and their Loyalty to His Majefty; only he adds, If he could juftify himfelf to God, as he can to His Majefty, he is fure he might account himfelf the happieft man alive. But yet, feeing he hath a better hope in the mercy of God through Jefus Chrift he thereupon refts, whether he finds Juftice here on Earth, or not. He fays, he will add nothing to move them either to tendernefs or pity; he knows that not to be the place, and pretends to neither from them; he pleads his Innocence, and craves Juftice, leaving it to their Lordfhips to confider not fo much his particular Cafe, as what a Preparative it may be made, and what may be its Confequences: And if all he hath faid, do neither convince, nor perfuade them to alter their judgment, yet he defires them to confider, whether the Cafe do not, at leaft, deferve to be more fully reprefented, and left to His Majefty's wifdom and juftice, feeing that if once the matter pafs upon record for Treafon, it is undoubted, that hundreds of the beft, and who think themfelves moft innocent, may, by the fame methods, fall under the like Condemnation, whenever the King's Advocate fhall be thereto prompted.

And thus you have a part of what the Earl intended to have faid, before pronouncing Sentence, if he had not made his Efcape before the day: Yet fome things I perceive by his Notes are ftill in his own breaft, as only proper to be faid to His Majefty. I find feveral Quotations out of the Advocate's printed Books, that, it feems, he was to make fome ufe of; but feeing it would have been too great an interruption to have applied them to the places defigned, I have fubjoined them together, leaving them to the Advocate's own and all mens confideration.

It was by fome remarked, That when the Lords of Jufticiary, after the ending of the firft day's debate, refolved that fame night to give judgment upon it, they fent for the Lord *Nairn,* one of their number, an old and infirm man, who being alfo a Lord of the Seffion, is fo decayed through age, that he hath not for a confiderable time been allowed to take his turn, in the Outer-houfe (as they call it) where they judge leffer Caufes alone: But notwithftanding both his age, and infirmity, and that he was gone to bed, he was raifed, and brought to the Court, to confider a Debate, a great deal whereof he had not heard, in full Court; and withal, as is informed, while the Clerk was reading fome of it, fell of new afleep.

It was alfo remarked, that the Lords of Jufticiary being, in all, five, *viz.* the Lord *Nairn* above-mentioned, with the Lords, *Collintoun, Newtoun, Kirkhoufe,* and *Forret,* the Libel was found relevant only by the odds of three to two, *viz.* the Lord *Nairn* aforefaid, the Lord *Newtoun,* fince made Prefident of the Seffion, and the Lord *Forret,* both well enough known, againft the Lord *Collintoun,* a very ingenious Gentleman, and a true old Cavalier, and the Lord *Kirkhoufe,* a learned and upright Judge: As for the Lord Juftice General, who was alfo prefent, and prefided, his Vote, according to the conftitution of the Court, was not afked.

But to return to my Narrative, the Earl, as I have already told you, did not think fit, for reafons that you fhall hear, to ftay till His Majefty's return came to the Council's laft Letter, but, taking his opportunity, made his efcape out of the Caftle of *Edinburgh,* upon *Tuefday* the Twentieth of *December* about eight at night, and in a day or two after, came His Majefty's Anfwer here fubjoined.

The King's Answer to the Council's Letter.

December 18. 1681.

C. R.

MOST dearly, &c. *having this day received your Letter of the 14th inftant, giving an account, that our Advocate having been ordered by you to infift in that Procefs raifed at our inftance againft the Earl of* Argyle, *he was, after full debate, and clear probation, found guilty of* Treafon, *and* Leafing-making *betwixt us, our Parliament, and our People ; and the* reproaching *our Laws and Acts of Parliament : We have now thought fit, notwithftanding of what was ordered by us in our Letter to you of the 15th of* November *laft, hereby to authorize you to grant a Warrant to our Juftice-General, and the remanent Judges of our Juftice Court, for proceeding to pronounce a Sentence, upon the Verdict of the Jury, againft the faid Earl ; neverthelefs it is our exprefs pleafure, and we do hereby require you, to take care, that all execution of the Sentence be ftopped, until we fhall think fit to declare our further pleafure in this Affair : For doing whereof, &c.*

Which Anfwer being read in Council on the *Thurfday*, and the Court of Jufticiary, according to its laft Adjournment, as fhall be told you, being to meet upon the *Friday*, after a little hefitation in Council whether the Court of Jufticiary could proceed to the Sentence of Forfaulture againft the Earl, he being abfent, it was refolved in the affirmative ; and what were the grounds urged, either of hefitation or refolution, I cannot precifely fay, there being nothing on record that I can learn. But that you may have a full, and fatisfying account, I fhall briefly tell you what was ordinarily difcourfed, a part whereof I alfo find in a Petition given in by the Countefs of *Argyle* to the Lords of Jufticiary, before pronouncing fentence, but without any anfwer or effect. It was then commonly faid, that by the old Law, and Cuftom, the Court of Jufticiary could no more in the cafe of Treafon, than of any other Crime, proceed further. againft a Perfon not compearing, and abfent, than to declare him Out-Law, and Fugitive : And that, albeit it be fingular, in the Cafe of Treafon, that the Trial may go on, even to a final Sentence, though the Party be abfent, yet fuch Trials were only proper to, and always referved for Parliaments : And fo it had been conftantly obferved until after the Rebellion in the Year 1666. But there being feveral Perfons notourly engaged in that Rebellion, who had efcaped, and thereby withdrawn themfelves from Juftice, it was thought, that the want of a Parliament, for the time, ought not to afford them any immunity ; and therefore it was refolved by the Council, with advice of the Lords of Seffion, that the Court of Jufticiary fhould fummon, and proceed to trial, and fentence, againft thefe Abfents, whether they compeared or not, and fo it was done : Only becaufe the thing was new, and indeed an innovation of the old Cuftom, to make all fure, in the firft Parliament held thereafter, in the Year 1669, it was thought fit to confirm thefe Proceedings of the Jufticiary, in that point, and alfo to make a perpetual Statute, in the cafe of *open Rebellion, and Rifing in Arms* againft the King and Government, the Treafon, in all time coming, might by an Order of His Majefty's Council be tried, and the Actors proceeded againft by the Lords of the Jufticiary, even to final fentence, whether the Traytors compeared, or not. This being then the prefent Law, and Cuftom, it is apparent in the firft place, that the Earl's Cafe, not being that of an *open Rebellion*, and *Rifing in Arms*, is not at all comprehended in the Act of Parliament ; fo that it is without queftion, that, if in the beginning he had not entered himfelf Prifoner, but abfented himfelf, the Lords of Jufticiary could not have gone further, than, upon a citation, to have declared him *Fugitive*. But others faid, that the Earl having both entered himfelf Prifoner, and compeared, and after debate having been found guilty, before he made his efcape, the cafe was much altered. And whether the Court could, notwithftanding of the Earl's intervening efcape, yet go on to fentence, was ftill debatable : for it was alledged for the affirmative, that feeing the Earl had twice compeared, and that after debate, the Court had given judgment, and the Affize returned their Verdict, fo that had nothing remained but the pronouncing of Sentence, it was abfurd to think that fhould be in the power of the Party, thus accufed, and found guilty, by his efcape to fruftrate Juftice, and withdraw himfelf from the punifhment he deferved. But on the other hand it was pleaded for the Earl ; That firft, It was a fundamental Rule, *That until once the Caufe were concluded, no Sentence could be pronounced* : Next, that it was a fure Maxim in Law, that in *Criminal Actions there neither is, or can be any other conclufion of the caufe of the Party's prefence and filence.* So that, after all that had paft, the Earl had ftill freedom to add what he thought fit, in his own defence, before pronouncing fentence ; and therefore the Lords of Jufticiary could no more proceed to fentence againft him, being efcaped, than if he had been abfent from the beginning, the Caufe being in both cafes equally not concluded,

cluded, and the principle of Law uniformly the fame, *viz. That in Criminals* (except in cafes excepted) *no final fentence can be given in abfence* : For, as the Law, in cafe of abfence from the beginning, doth hold that juft temper, as neither to fuffer theContumacious to go altogether unpunifhed, nor, on the other hand, finally to condemn a party unheard ; and therefore do only declare him Fugitive, and there ftops : So in the cafe of an Efcape, before Sentence, where it cannot be faid the Party was fully heard, and the Caufe concluded, the Law doth not diftinguifh, nor can the parity of Reafon be refufed. Admitting then that the Caufe was fo far advanced, againft the Earl, that he was found guilty ; yet, 1. This is a declaring of what the Law doth as plainly prefume againft the Party abfent from the beginning, and confequently, of it felf can operate no further. 2*dly,* The finding of a Party guilty is no conclufion of the Caufe. And 3*dly,* As it was never feen, nor heard, that a Party was condemned in abfence, (except in excepted Cafes) whereof the Earl's is none ; fo he having efcaped, and the Caufe remaining thereby unconcluded, the general rule did ftill hold, and no fentence could be given againft him.

It was alfo remembred, that the Dyets and Days of the Juftice Court are peremptour ; and that in that cafe, even in Civil, far more in Criminal Courts and Caufes, a Citation to hear Sentence is conftantly required ; which induced fome to think, that at leaft the Earl fhould have been lawfully cited to hear Sentence, before it could be pronounced. But it is like this courfe, as confeffing a difficulty, and occafioning too long a delay, was therefore not made ufe of. However, upon the whole, it was the general Opinion, That feeing the denouncing the Earl Fugitive would have wrought much more in Law, than all that was commonly faid, at firft, to be defigned againft him ; and that his Cafe did appear every way fo favourable, that impartial men ftill wondered how it came to be at all queftioned : it had been better to have fifted the Procefs, with his Efcape, and taken the ordinary courfe of Law, without making any more ftretches.

But as I have told you, when the *Friday* came, the Lords of Jufticiary, without any refpect, or anfwer given to the Petition above-mentioned, given in by the Countefs of *Argyle* to the Court for a ftop, pronounced Sentence, firft in the Court, and then caufed publifh the fame, with all folemnity, at the *Mercat-Crofs at* Edinburgh.

FOrafmuch as it is found by an *Affize,* That Archibald *Earl of* Argyle, *is guilty and culpable of the Crimes of Treafon, Leafing-making and Leafing-telling, for which he was detained within the Caftle of* Edinburgh, *out of which he has now fince the faid Verdict made his Efcape : Therefore the Lords Commiffioners of Jufticiary decern and adjudge the faid* Archibald, *Earl of* Argyle, *to be execute to the death, demained as a Traytor, and to underly the pains of Treafon, and other punifhments appointed by the Laws of this Kingdom, when he fhall be apprehended, at fuch a time, and place, and in fuch manner as his Majefty in his Royal Pleafure fhall think fit to declare and appoint : And his Name, Memory, and Honours, to be extinct ; and his Arms to be riven forth, and delete out of the Books of Arms, fwa that his Pofterity may never have place, nor be able hereafter to bruick or joyfe any Honour, Offices, Titles, or Dignities, within this Realm in time coming ; and to have forfaulted, amitted, and tint, all and fundry his Lands, Tenements, Annual-Rents, Offices, Titles, Dignities, Tacks, Steedings, Rowmes, Poffeffions, Goods, and Geere whatfumever pertaining to him, to our Sovereign Lord, to remain perpetually with his Highnefs in property. Which was pronounced for Doom*—23 Dec. 1681.

After the reading (and publifhing) whereof, the Earl's Coat of Arms, by order of the Court, was alfo torn, and ranverfed, both in the Court, and at the *Mercat-Crofs.* Albeit fome thought that this was rather a part of the Execution, which His Majefty's Letter difcharges, than a neceffary Solemnity, in the Publication : and the Advocate himfelf fays, *p.* 61. of his printed Criminals, That it fhould be only practifed in the Crime of *Perduellion,* but not in other Treafons.

The Reafons and Motives of the Earl's Efcape, with the Conclufion of the whole Narrative.

THE Earl's Efcape was at firft a great furprize, both to his Friends and Unfriends ; for, as it is known that his Procefs, in the beginning, did appear, to the lefs concerned, more like a piece of pageantry, than any reality ; and even by the more concerned was accounted but a politick Defign, to take away his Offices, and leffen his Power and Intereft : So neither did any of his Friends fear any greater hazard, nor did moft of his Unfriends imagine them to be more apprehenfive. Whereby it fell out, that upon report of his Efcape, many, and fome of his Well-wifhers, thought he had too lightly abandoned a fair Eftate, and the probable expectation he might have had of His Majefty's favour : As alfo fome, that were judged his greateft Adverfaries, did appear very angry, as if the Earl had taken that courfe, on purpofe to load them with the odium of a defign againft his Life. And truly, I am apt to think, it was not only hard and uneafy for others to believe, that a Perfon of the Earl's quality, and character, fhould, upon fo flender a pretence, be deftroyed, both as to life,

life,

life, and fortune, but alſo that he himſelf was ſlow enough to receive the impreſſions neceſſary to ripen his Reſolution ; and that if a few Accidents, as he ſays himſelf, happening a little before his eſcape, had not as it were opened his eyes, and brought back, and preſented to him ſeveral things paſt, in a new light, and ſo made all to operate to his final determination, he had ſtayed it out to the laſt.

Which that you may the better underſtand, you may here conſider the ſeveral Particulars, that, together with what he himſelf hath ſince told ſome Friends, apparently occurred to him in theſe his ſecond thoughts, in the following order.

And firſt you have heard, in the beginning of this Narrative, what was the firſt occaſion of the Earl his declining in his Highneſs's favour : You may alſo remember, that his Majeſty's Advocate takes notice, that he debated againſt the Act enjoining the Teſt, in the Parliament : And, as I have told you, he was indeed the Perſon that ſpoke againſt excepting the King's Brothers, and Sons, from the Oath then intended for ſecuring the Proteſtant Religion, and the Subjects Loyalty, not thinking it fit to complement with a Privilege, where all poſſible caution appears rather to be neceſſary : And this a Reverend Biſhop told the Earl afterwards had downright fired the kiln. What thereafter happened in Parliament, and how the Earl was always ready to have laid all his Offices at his Majeſty's feet ; and how he was content, in Council, to be held a Refuſer of the Teſt, and thereby incur an intire deprivation of all publick Truſt, is above fully declared ; and only here remembred, to ſhew what reaſon the Earl had, from his firſt coming to *Edinburgh*, in the end of *October*, to think that ſomething elſe was intended againſt him than the ſimple diveſting him of his Employments and Juriſdictions. And yet ſuch was his aſſurance of his Innocence, that when ordered by the Council to enter his Perſon in Priſon under the pain of Treaſon, he entered freely, in an Hackney Coach, without either heſitation or noiſe, as you have heard.

2*dly*, The ſame day of the Earl's Commitment, the Council met, and wrote (as I have told you) their Letter to his Majeſty, above ſet down, Num. 22. Wherein they expreſly charge him with reproaching, and depraving ; but yet neither with Perjury nor Treaſon. And a few days after, the Earl wrote a Letter to his Highneſs, wherein he did endeavour to remove his Offence, in terms that, it was ſaid, at firſt had given ſatisfaction : But yet the only return the Earl had, was a Criminal Summons containing an Indictment, and that before any Anſwer was come from His Majeſty. And then, ſo ſoon as his Majeſty's Anſwer came, there was a new Summons ſent him, with a new Indictment, adding the Crimes of Treaſon and Perjury to thoſe of Reproaching and Depraving, which were in the firſt Libel, as you have heard above ; whereby you may perceive, how early the Deſign againſt the Earl began to grow, and how eaſily it took encreaſe, from the leaſt encouragement.

3*dly*, When the Earl petitioned the Council for Advocates to plead for him ; albeit he petitioned twice, and upon clear Acts of Parliament, yet he had no better Anſwer than what you have above ſet down. And when the Earl's Petition, naming Sir *George Lockhart* as his ordinary Advocate, was read in Council, his Highneſs openly threatned, that in caſe Sir *George* ſhould undertake for the Earl, he ſhould never more plead for the King, nor him. But the Earl taking Inſtruments upon Sir *George* his refuſal, and giving out, that he would not anſwer a word at the Bar, ſeeing the benefit of Lawyers, according to Law, was denied him ; Sir *George*, and other Lawyers, were allowed to aſſiſt him, but ſtill with a grudge. Likewiſe afterwards, they were queſtioned and convened before the Council, for having, at the Earl's deſire, ſign'd their poſitive Opinion of the Caſe. At which time it was alſo ſaid in Council by his Highneſs, That their fault was greater than the Earl's : However, we ſee that as he was the occaſion of the anger, ſo he hath only found the ſmart of it.

4*thly*, The whole Proceſs, with the Judgement of the Lords of Juſticiary, and Verdict of the Aſſize, whereby the Earl was found guilty, as you have ſeen (notwithſtanding of what hath ſo plainly appeared, and was ſo ſtrongly pleaded in his behalf) of Leaſing-making, Depraving, and Treaſon, is of it ſelf a clear demonſtration, that either the higheſt puniſhment was intended for ſo high a guilt ; or that, at leaſt, it was no ſmall humiliation that ſome deſigned for him : It being equally againſt reaſon, and prudence, ſetting aſide the Intereſt of Juſtice, to ſtrain things of this nature beyond the ends truly purpoſed, and which, in effect, are only the more to be ſuſpected, the more they are concealed.

5*thly*, The Proceſs being carried on to the Verdict of the Aſſize, and the Council being tied up by His Majeſty's Letter, *before pronouncing Sentence, to ſend a particular account to His Majeſty of what the Earl ſhould be found guilty of, for His Majeſty's full information* ; the Council doth indeed diſpatch away a new Letter immediately, for His Majeſty's leave to proceed : but inſtead of that particular account required by His Majeſty, for his full information, all the information was ever heard of to be ſent by the Council, was what is contained in the body of the Letter, wherein they, briefly, but poſitively, affirm, *That after full debate, and clear probation, he was found guilty of Treaſon.* Which, all men muſt ſay, was far better contrived to prompt his Majeſty to a ſpeedy allowance, than to give him that particular information of the caſe which His Majeſty's Letter expreſly requires, and the Earl expected ſhould have been performed.

But

But further, the Council was commanded to sign this Letter, not simply in the ordinary form, but by a special Command laid on every Member, and the Clerk appointed to go about and get their Subscriptions, telling them *they were Commanded*; and complaining to the Duke when any scrupled to do it. The strictness of which Orders is apparent enough from the very Subscriptions, where you may not only read the names of Bishops subscribing *in causa sanguinis*, but some of the Earl's Friends and Relations who wanted Courage to refuse; and, in effect, how many of all the Members did it willingly, is hard to say, seeing generally they excuse the deed in private.

6thly, About a week or two before the Trial, the Earl had notice, that at a *close Juncto*, where were Persons of the greatest eminency, it was remembered by one present, how that *Anno* 1663, the Earl had been pardoned by His Majesty, after he had been found guilty by the Earl of *Middleton* and that Parliament. And that then it was looked on as an Error in the Earl of *Middleton*, that he had not proceeded to Execution, albeit His Majesty had given command to the contrary, because (as it was said) it would have been but the same thing to him. *But now*, adds this kind Remembrancer, *the case is much more easy: Now his Royal Highness is on the Throne: It might have cost Earl* Middleton *a frown, but now it can signify nothing, but will rather be commended in his Royal Highness, as acting freely like himself. The stop of the sentence looks like a distrust ; but this will vindicate all, and secure all.* And as the first part of the Story the Earl remembered well he had heard from the same Person, *An.* 1664. and had reported it to the Duke of *Lauderdale* a little after ; so the second part being of a very well known dialect, could not but give the Earl the deeper impressions. It was further told the Earl, at the same time when the Council's Letter to obtain His Majesty's assent to the pronouncing Sentence, and leaving all to discretion, was sent, that it was thought fit that nothing should appear but fair weather till the very close. Yet was the Earl so confident of his own Innocence, and His Majesty's Justice, that he did not doubt but His Majesty, seeing the Process, would at least put a stop to the Sentence. But after the Council's Letter was gone, in such terms as you have seen, to seek Liberty from His Majesty to proceed to Sentence (without either double, or abbreviate of the Process sent with it) and no doubt smooth insinuations made with it, that all designed was to *humble the Earl, or clip his wings*; and that this Letter was hasted away by a fleeing Pacquet, to prevent the Earl's Application, which it could not but do; and so could not but have weight, and prevail with His Majesty, (to whom the Earl's Petition, as coming too late, was indeed never presented) then, and not till then, the Earl began to have new thoughts.

7thly, The Earl's Trial having been upon *Monday* and *Tuesday*, the 12th and 13th of *December*; upon the 14th, the Council's Letter was dispatched; and upon the 15th, the Earl intreated, by a friend, for liberty to speak to his Royal Highness, whose Answer was, *That it was not ordinary to speak to Criminals, except with Rogues on some Plot, where discoveries might be expected:* yet his Highness said, he would advise upon it. But upon *Friday* the 16th, he did refuse it. Yet the Earl did renew his suit, and urged, That he had sent a Petition to His Majesty, which was the first he had sent upon that occasion ; and that before the return should come, he was desirous to have his Highness's Answer, that he might owe some part of the favour he expected, to his Highness.

But on *Monday* morning, the 19th, the Earl was told, he was not like to have any access; and in the afternoon, he heard that the return of the Council's Express was looked for, on *Thursday* the 22d, being the Council-day. And further, That the Justice Court (which, according to its custom, had sat the same *Monday*, and, in course, should have adjourned till *Monday* the 26th of *December*, or, because of *Christmass*, to the first *Monday* of *January*) was, for the Earl's sake, adjourned till *Friday* the 23d ; to the end, that immediately upon the King's return, they might pronounce Sentence. He was moreover informed, that his Royal Highness was heard to say, That if the Express returned not timously, he would take upon himself what was to be done. Which being general, and dark, was the more to be suspected. All this, the Earl told, made him the same *Monday* late, cast in his thoughts whether it were not fit for him to attempt an escape; but his doubtings were so many, he could resolve nothing, that night, except to put off till *Wednesday*. Yet on *Tuesday* morning he began to think, if he did at all design to escape, he had best do it that same evening. However he was, even then, not fully resolved, nor had he as yet spoke one word of it to any mortal. But about Ten of the clock this *Tuesday*, his Highness absolute refusal to suffer the Earl to see him, until His Majesty's Return came, was confirmed: And about Noon the Earl heard that some Troops, and a Regiment of Foot were come to Town ; and that the next day he was to be brought down from the Castle to the Common Goal (from which Criminals are ordinarily carried to Execution) and then he resolved to make his escape that very Night, and yet did not conclude it thoroughly till five of the clock in the Evening ; at which time he gave directions about it, not thinking to essay it, till near Ten. But at Seven, one coming up from the City, and telling him that new Orders were privately given for further securing of him ; That the Castle-Guards were

doubled,

4

doubled, and none fuffered to go out without fhowing their faces, and that fome Ladies had been already put to do it, and therefore diffuading him to attempt any efcape, becaufe it was impoffible: The Earl faid, *No, then it is full time.* And fo he made hafte, and within half an hour after, by God's bleffing, got fafe out, queftioned pretty warmly by the firft Centry, but not at all by the Main-guard; and then, after the great Gate was opened, and the lower Guard drawn out double, to make a Lane for his Company, one of the Guard who open'd the Gate, took him by the Arm, and viewed him; but it pleafed God he was not difcerned. When he was out, he was not fully refolved whither to go. Home he had judged fafeft; but he thought it might breed Miftakes and Trouble that he defigned not: So he refolved to go for *England,* and to take the Road, that by Poft he might be His Majefty's firft informer of his efcape. But being difappointed of Horfes that he expected, he found that the notice of his efcape was got before him; and foon after, as he came the length of *Newcaftle,* heard that His Majefty had given way to pronounce Sentence againft him, according as he had apprehended from the circumftances and other grounds I have told you; which made him judge, it would be an undifcreet prefumption, in that ftate, to offer himfelf to his Majefty, while he knew none durft addrefs him, and fo he rather chufed to fhift in the wide World, till his Majefty might be at fome greater freedom both to underftand his Cafe, and apply fuitable Remedies. His Majefty's clear and excellent underftanding, and gracious benign difpofition, do fully affure him, that His Majefty doth not, in his thoughts, charge him with the leaft Difloyalty, and that he hath no Complacence in his ruin. But if His Majefty do, at prefent, lie under the preffure of fome unlucky influences, not fo eafy to his Royal Inclination, the Earl, it feems, thinks it reafonable to wait patiently for a better opportunity. It may indeed appear ftrange, that Innocence and Honour oppreffed in his Perfon, almoft beyond a parallel, fhould not, e'er now, have conftrained him to fome publick Vindication; efpecially when to the horrid Sentence given againft him, his Adverfaries have further prevailed to caufe His Majefty to difpofe, not only of his Heritable Offices and Jurifdictions (the pretended eye-fore;) but alfo upon his whole Eftate and Fortune, with as little confideration of the Earl's perfonal Intereft, as if he had fallen for the blackeft Treafon, and moft atrocious *Perduellion.* But, befides that fome things are of themfelves fo abfurdly wicked, that all palliating pretences do only render them the more hateful; and the very fimple hearing doth ftrike with an horrour, not to be heightned by any reprefentations, next, that the Earl being fo aftonifhingly overtaken for words, as fairly and honeftly uttered as he could poffibly devife, doth, with reafon, apprehend that there is nothing he can fay in this matter, though with the ferenefl mind, and in the greateft truth and fobriety, that may not be conftrued to flow from a defign to lay blame where hitherto he hath been tender to give any ground of offence: I fay (befides thefe things) he is withal (I know) moft firmly perfuaded, That, if ever he fhall have the happinefs to be once heard by His Majefty, and in his prefence allowed to explain a few Particulars, in Duty here omitted, His Majefty's Juftice and Goodnefs will quickly difpel all the Clouds that now hang over him, and reftore him to that favour wherein he hath fometime reckoned himfelf very happy, and which he will ever be moft ready to acknowledge. And therefore all that in the mean time he judged neceffary, or would give way to, was, that for preferving the remembrance of fo odd a Tranfaction, until a more feafonable juncture, fome Memorial fhould be drawn, and depofited in fure keeping; which being grown under my hand unto this Narrative, I thought I could not better obferve his Order, than by tranfmitting it to your faithful cuftody. I have carefully therein obferved the Truth, in point of fact, avouching nothing but upon the beft and cleareft evidence can poffibly be expected; nor have I, as to the manner, licenfed or indulged my felf in any feverity of expreffion, which I thought could be juftly, in fuch a cafe, omitted, without betraying the Caufe. Yet if you now, or any other hereafter, fhall judge, that I do fometime exceed, let it not be imputed to him; for as he did indeed charge me to guard againft any more warm or vehement expreffion, than the merit and exigence of the fubject do indifpenfibly require; fo I am affured that he filently and patiently waits on the Lord, committing his way to him, and trufting in him, that he may bring it to pafs; and that *He fhall bring forth his righteoufnefs as the light, and his judgement as the noon-day.*

P O S T S C R I P T.

S I R,

HAving in this Narrative fometimes adduced, as you have feen, the Advocate's own Authority, *ad hominem;* I fhall here, as I promifed, fubjoin fuch paffages out of his Printed Book, as, though they deferved not a place above, may yet make a pertinent *Poftfcript.*

And,

And, omitting what in that Book, called, *The Laws and Cuftoms of* Scotland *in Matters Criminal*, he frequently repeats, from the known grounds of Law, of the nature of Crimes, and the defign of Criminal Laws ; *viz.* ' That as there can be no Crime ' without a fraudulent purpofe, either apparent or proven ; fo it was the defign of Law- ' givers, only to punifh fuch Acts as are defignedly malicious.' I defire you only to confider the particulars following : And,

1. Pag. 11. l. 7. of his *Book of Criminals*, having made the queftion, ' Whether what ' tends to a Crime, not perfected, doth fall under the Statute, or Law, by which that ' Crime to which it approaches is punifhed ; he inftances in the Crime of Mifconftruing ' His Majefty's Government, and Proceedings, or depraving his Laws, which, as he fays, ' is punifhable by death, *Ja.* 6. Par. 10. Act 10. And then further moves, Whether ' Papers, as tending to mifconftrue His Majefty's Proceedings, and Government, or bear- ' ing infinuations which may raife in the people jealoufy againft the Government, be pu- ' nifhed by that Law ?' Which being one of the great Crimes pretended and libelled a- gainft the Earl, I fhall here (omitting his Reafons in the affirmative, which have not the leaft ground in the Earl's Cafe, as you have heard) reprefent to you, how exactly he him- felf, and others, have acted for the Earl's overthrow, all thefe dangerous and pernicious things, from which he argues in the Negative. His words then are thefe :

' And that fuch infinuations and tendencies are not punifhed criminally, he fays, 1. ' It is the intereft of mankind to know exprefly what they are to obey, efpecially where ' fuch great Certifications are annexed, as in Crimes. 2. The Law, having taken ' under its confideration this guilt, has punifhed the actual mifconftruing, or depraving ; ' but has not declared fuch infinuations or tendencies punifhable : *Et in ftatutis cafus omif- ' fus habetur pro omiffo.* 3. This would infallibly tend to render all Judges arbitrary ; for ' tendencies and infinuations are in effect the product of conjecture, and Papers may feem ' Innocent, or Criminal, according to the zeal, or humour, as well as malice of Judges ; ' Men being naturally prone to differ in fuch confequential inferences, and too apt to ' make conftructions in fuch, according to the favour or malice they bear to the Perfon ' or Caufe : Are not fome men apt to conftruct that to tend to their difhonour, which ' was defigned for their honour ? and to think every thing an innovation of Law or Pri- ' vilege, which checks their inclination and defign ? Whereas fome Judges are fo violent ' in their Loyalty, as to imagine the meaneft miftakes do tend to an oppofition againft ' Authority ; and thus Zeal, Jealoufy, Malice, or Intereft, would become Judges. 4. ' Men are fo filly, or may be in fuch hafte, or fo confounded, (and the beft are fubject to ' fuch miftakes) as that no Man could know when he were innocent ; fimplicity might ' oft times becomes a Crime, and the fear of offending might occafion offence ; and how ' uncomfortably would the people live, if they knew not how to be innocent ?

2*dly*, P. 47. l. 9. of the fame Book, he fays, ' That the eighth point of Treafon is ' to impugn the Dignity and Authority of the three Eftates, or to feek, and procure ' the innovation and diminution of their Power and Authority, Act 103. *Ja.* 6. *p.* 6.' Now this being another of the Crimes charged upon the Earl, hear how the Advocate there underftands it. ' But this (he adds immediately) is to be underftood of a (N. B) di- ' rect impugning of their Authority ; as if it were contended, that Parliaments were not ' neceffary, or that one of the three Eftates might be turned out.' Which, how vaftly dif- ferent from his indirect, forced and horrible inferences, in the Earl's Cafe, is plain and obvious.

3*dly*, Ibid. p. 58. l. 2. after having faid, ' That, according to former Laws, no fort ' of Treafon was to be purfued in abfence before the Juftices ; and urging it to be reafon- able, he adds, ' Nor is it imaginable, but if it had been fafe, it had been granted former- ly. And *l.* 31. he fays. ' The Juftices are never allowed, even by the late Act of Par- ' liament, to proceed to fentence againft Abfents, but fuch as are purfued for Rifing in ' Arms againft the King. The true reafon whereof, he tells us, is, that the Law is not ' fo inhuman as to punifh equally prefumed and real guilt : And that it hath been often ' found, that men have abfented themfelves, rather out of fear of a prevailing Faction, ' or corrupt Witneffes, *&c.* than out of confcioufnefs of guilt :' Reafons which albeit neither true nor juft, (feeing that the Law punifhes nothing even in cafe of abfence, but either manifeft Contumacy, or Crimes fully proven : And that the only reafon why it allows no other Crime fave *Perduellion* to be proceeded againft in abfence, is becaufe it judges no other Crime *tanti*) yet you fee how this whole paffage quadrats with the Earl's Cafe ; who being neither purfued for *Perduellion*, nor prefent at giving Sentence, was yet fentenced in abfence, as a moft defperate Traytor.

4*thly*, Ibid. p. 60. l. 24. fpeaking of the Solemnities ufed in Parliament, at the pro- nouncing Sentences for Treafon, *viz.* That the Pannel receives his Sentence kneeling ; and that after the doom of Forfaulture pronounced againft him, the Lyon and his Bre- thren the Heralds in their Formalities, come and tear his Coat of Arms at the Throne ; and thereafter hang up his Efcutcheon ranverfed upon the Mercat-Crofs : He adds,

' But

'But this, I think, should only hold in the Crime of *Perduellion* ; and then goes on to
'add, that the Children of the Delinquent are declared incapable to bruik any Office
'or Estate, is another Specialty introduced in the punishment of *Perduellion* only.' And
yet both these terrible Solemnities were practised against the Earl, even by a Court of
Justiciary, and not in Parliament ; albeit he was not accused of *Perduellion*, nor be in
deed more guilty of any Crime than all the World sees.

5thly, Ibid, *page* 303. *ult.* he says, 'That verbal Injuries are these that are committed
'by unwarrantable expressions, as to call a Man a Cheat, a Woman Whore : But be-
'cause expressions may vary, according to the intention of the Speaker ; therefore ex-
'cept the words can allow of no good sense, as Whore or Thief, or that there be strong
'presumptions against the Speaker, the *injuriandi animus*, or design of injuring, as well
'as the injuring words, must be proven ; and the speaker will be allowed to purge his
'guilt by declaring his intention ; and his declaration, without an Oath, will be suffi-
'cient. 2dly, The pursuer should libel the design, and prove it, except the words clearly
'infer it. 3dly, The pursuer is presently to resent the injury ; and if, at first, the words be
'taken for no injury, they cannot afterward become such.' Which things, being applied
to the Earl's words, do evidently say, That unless his words could allow of no good sense,
or that there were strong presumptions against him, or that he could not purge his guilt,
by declaring his intention, or that his words did clearly infer the guilt, there could be no
Crime of Slandering, Reproaching or Depraving, charged against him, except the *injuriandi animus*, as well as the words, had been both libelled, and proven. But so it is that his
words do manifestly allow of a good sense, that there is not the least presumption of injury can be alledged against him ; That he did most plainly purge himself of all supicion
of guilt, by declaring his sound and upright intention ; and that his words do not infer,
either clearly, or unclearly, the smallest measure of guilt ; and withal neither was the
injuriandi animus at all proven : But on the contrary, the words at first were taken for no
injury ; so that they could not afterward become such, as is above fully cleared : *Ergo*, Even the Advocate being Judge, the Earl is no Slanderer.

6thly, If it were necessary, I could further tell you several things that he alledges to
be sufficient for purging a Man of any Criminal Intention : As, where he says, *Ibid. p.*
563. *l.* 2. 'That in matters of fact, persons, even judicious, following the Faith of
'such as understand, are to be excused. And *l.* 30. 'That if it appear, by the mean-
'ness of the Crime (he should say the smallness of the deed : And what can be less than
'the uttering of a few words in the manner that the Earl spoke them ?) that there was
'no design of transgression ; and that the committer designed not, for so small a matter
'to commit a Crime (much less such horrid ones as Depraving and Treason.) In that case,
'the meanness of transgression (or deed) ought to defend against the relevancy, &c.'
But to give you one instance for all, how much the Advocate may, one day or other,
be obliged to plead the innocence of his intentions, to free himself of words downright
in themselves slanderous and depraving an Act of Parliament, much better nor he understands it, and in fresh and constant observance ; *Ibid p.* 139. towards the middle, speaking of the 151 Act, *Ja.* 6. p. 12. whereby it is statute : 'That seeing divers excep-
'tions and objections rises upon criminal Libels, and parties are frustrate of Justice by
'the alledged irrelevancy thereof, That in time coming all Criminal Libels shall con-
'tain, that the persons complained on are *Art* and *Part* of the Crimes libelled ; which
'shall be relevant to accuse them thereof ; swa that no exception, or objection take away
'that part of the Libel in time coming : He says, he finds no Act of Parliament more
'unreasonable ; for the Statutory part of that Act, committing the Tryal of Art and
'Part to Assizers, seems most unjust ; seeing in committing the greatest questions of
'the Law to the most ignorant of the Subjects, it puts a sharp Sword into the hands of
'blind men. And the reason of this Act specified in the Narrative, is likewise most
'inept, and no ways illative, &c.' What Reproaches ! What Blasphemies ! The Earl
said not one word against any Act of Parliament : But on the contrary, That he was
confident the Parliament intended no contradiction ; and that he was willing to take the
Test in the Parliament's sense. But here the Advocate both says and prints it, That *an
Act of Parliament is most unreasonable, and most unjust, and it's reason most inept, and that
it puts a sharp Sword in the hands of blind men.* Whereof the smallest branch is infinitely
more reproachful than all can be strained out of the Earl's words. But, Sir, Speculation
is but Speculation ; and if the Advocate, when his day comes, be as able to purge himself of Practical Depravations, as I am inclined to excuse all his Visionary Lapses, notwithstanding of the famous Title, *Quod quisque juris in alterum statuerit, ut ipse eodem jure
utatur*, he shall never be the worse of my censure.

Murther will out: *Or, the King's Letter, justifying the Marquess of* Antrim; *and declaring, That what he did in the* Irish *Rebellion, was by Direction from his Royal Father and Mother, and for the service of the Crown.*

Ireland, Aug. 22. 1663.

Ever honoured Sir,

LAST *Thursday* we came to Trial with my Lord Marquess of *Antrim*; but according to my Fears (which you always surmised to be in vain) he was by the King's Extraordinary and Peremptory *Letter of Favour*, restored to his Estate, as an Innocent Papist. We proved Eight Qualifications in the *Act of Settlement* against him, the least of which made him uncapable of being restored as Innocent.

We proved, 1. *That he was to have a hand in surprizing the Castle of* Dublin, *in* 1641.

2. *That he was of the Rebels Party before the* 15th *of* September, 1643, *which we made appear by his hourly and frequent intercourse with* Renny O Moore, *and many others; being himself the most notorious of the said Rebels.*

3. *That he entered into the Roman-Catholick Confederacy before the Peace in* 1643.

4. *That he constantly adhered to the Nuncio's Party, in opposition to his Majesty's Authority.*

5. *That he sate from time to time in the Supream Council of* Kilkenny.

6. *That he signed that execrable Oath of Association.*

7. *That he was commissioned, and acted as Lieutenant-General, from the said Assembly at* Kilkenny.

8. *That he declared by several Letters of his own penning, himself in conjunction with* Owen Ro Oneale, *and a constant Opposer of the several Peaces, made by the Lord Lieutenant with the* Irish.

We were seven hours by the Clock in proving our Evidence against him, but at last the King's Letter being opened, and read in Court, *Rainsford,* one of the Commissioners, said to us, *That the King's Letter on his behalf was Evidence without Exception,* and thereupon declared him to be an Innocent Papist.

This Cause, Sir, hath (tho' many Reflections hath passed upon the Commissioners before) more startled the Judgments of all men, than all the Tryals since the beginning of their sitting; and it is very strange and wonderful to all the Long Robe, that the King should give such a Letter, having divested himself of that Authority, and reposed the Trust in the Commissioners for that purpose: And likewise it is admired, that the Commissioners having taken solemn Oaths, *To execute nothing but according to, and in pursuance of the Act of Settlement,* should, barely upon his Majesty's Letter, declare the Marquess innocent.

To be short; There never was so great a Rebel, that had so much favour from so good a King: And it is very evident to me, though young, and scarce yet brought upon the stage, that the consequence of these things will be very bad; that if God of his extraordinary mercy do not prevent it, War, and (if possible) greater Judgments, cannot be far from us: Where Vice is pattroniz'd, and *Antrim,* a Rebel upon Record, and so lately and clearly proved one, should have no other colour for his Actions but the King's own Letter; which takes all Imputations from *Antrim,* and lays them totally upon his own Father.

Sir, I shall by the next, if possible, send you over one of our Briefs against my Lord, by some Friend: It's too large for a Pacquet, it being no less in bulk than a Book of Martyrs. I have no more at present, but refer you to the King's Letter, hereto annexed.

CHARLES R.

RIght Trusty and Well-beloved Cousins and Counsellors, *&c.* We greet you well. How far we have been from interposing on the behalf of any of our *Irish* Subjects, who by their miscarriages in the late Rebellion in that Kingdom of *Ireland,* had made themselves unworthy of our Grace and Protection, is notorious to all men; and We were so jealous in that particular, that shortly after our return into this our Kingdom, when the Marquess of *Antrim* came hither to present his duty to Us, upon the Information We received from those Persons who then attended Us, by a Deputation from Our Kingdom of *Ireland,* or from those who at that time owned our Authority there, that the Marquess of *Antrim* had so misbehaved himself towards Us, and Our late Royal Father of blessed memory, that he was in no degree worthy of the least Countenance from Us, and that they had manifest and unquestionable Evidence of such his guilt: Whereupon We refused to admit the said Marquess so much as into Our Presence; but on the contrary, committed him Prisoner to our Tower of *London,* where after he had continued several Months under a strict restraint, upon the continual Information of the said Persons, We sent him into *Ireland,* without interposing the least on his behalf, but left him to undergo such a Tryal and Punishment, as by the Justice of that Our Kingdom should be found due to his Crime; expecting still that some heinous Matter would be objected and

proved

proved againſt him, to make him uncapable, and to deprive him of that Favour and Protection from Us, which we knew his former Actions and Services had merited. After many months attendance there, and (We preſume) after ſuch Examinations as were requiſite, he was at laſt diſmiſſed without any Cenſure, and without any tranſmiſſion of Charge againſt him to Us, and with a Licence to tranſport himſelf into this Kingdom ; We concluded that it was then time to give him ſome inſtance of Our Favour, and to remember the many Services he had done, and the Sufferings he had undergone, for his Affections and Fidelity to Our Royal Father, and Our ſelf, and that it was time to redeem him from thoſe Calamities, which yet do lie as heavy upon him ſince, as before Our happy Return: And thereupon We recommend him to You Our Lieutenant, that you ſhould move Our Council there, for preparing a Bill to be tranſmitted to Us, for the Re-inveſting him the ſaid Marqueſs, into the poſſeſſion of his Eſtate in that Our Kingdom, as had been done in ſome other Caſes. To which Letter, you Our ſaid Lieutenant returned us anſwer, That you had informed Our Council of that Our Letter, and that you were, upon conſideration thereof, unanimouſly of Opinion, that ſuch a Bill ought not to be tranſmitted to Us, the Reaſon whereof would forthwith be preſented to Us from our Council. After which time We received the incloſed Petition from the ſaid Marqueſs, which We referred to the conſiderations and examinations of the Lords of Our Privy Council, whoſe Names are mentioned in that Our Reference, which is annexed to the ſaid Petition, who thereupon met together, and after having heard the Marqueſs of *Antrim*, did not think fit to make any Report to Us, till they might ſee and underſtand the Reaſons which induced you not to tranſmit the Bill We had propoſed, which Letter was not then come to Our Hands. After which time We have received your Letter of the 18th of *March*, together with ſeveral Petitions which had been preſented to you, as well from the Old Soldiers and Adventurers, as from the Lady Marchioneſs of *Antrim*, all which We likewiſe tranſmitted to the Lords Referrees. Upon a ſecond Petition preſented to Us by the Lord Marqueſs, which is here likewiſe encloſed, commanding Our ſaid Referrees to take the ſame into their ſerious conſideration, and to hear what the Petitioner had to offer in his own Vindication, and to report the whole matter to Us, which upon a third Petition herein likewiſe incloſed, We required them to expedite with what ſpeed they could. By which deliberate Proceedings of ours, you cannot but obſerve, that no importunity, how juſt ſoever, could prevail with Us to bring Our Self to a Judgment in this Affair, without very ample Information. Our ſaid Referrees, after ſeveral Meetings, and peruſal of what hath been offered to them by the ſaid Marqueſs, have reported unto Us, That they have ſeen ſeveral Letters, all of them the hand-writing of Our Royal Father to the ſaid Marqueſs, and ſeveral Inſtructions concerning his treating and joining with the *Iriſh*, in order to the King's Service, by reducing to their Obedience, and by drawing ſome Forces from them for the Service of *Scotland*. That beſides the Letters and Orders under His Majeſty's Hand, they have received ſufficient Evidence and Teſtimony of ſeveral private Meſſages and Directions ſent from Our Royal Father, and from Our Royal Mother, with the privity, and with the Directions of the King Our Father, by which they are perſuaded, that whatever Intelligence, Correſpondence or Actings, the ſaid Marqueſs had with the Confederate *Iriſh* Catholicks, was directed or allowed by the ſaid Letters, Inſtructions and Directions ; and that it manifeſtly appears to them, that the King our Father was well pleaſed with what the Marqueſs did, after he had done it, and approved the ſame.

This being the true ſtate of the Marqueſs his Caſe, and there being nothing proved upon the firſt Information againſt him, nor any thing contained againſt him in your Letter of *March* 18th, but that you were informed, he had put in his Claim before the Commiſſioners appointed for executing the *Act of Settlement*; and that if his Innocency be ſuch as is alledged, there is no need of tranſmitting ſuch a Bill to us as is deſired ; and that if he be nocent, it conſiſts not with the Duty which you owe to Us, to tranſmit ſuch a Bill, as if it ſhould paſs into a Law, muſt needs draw a great prejudice upon ſo many Adventurers and Soldiers, which are, as is alledged, to be therein concerned: We have conſidered of the Petition of the Adventurers and Soldiers, which was tranſmitted to Us by you, the Equity of which conſiſts in nothing, but that they have been peaceably in poſſeſſion for the ſpace of ſeven or eight years, of thoſe Lands which were formerly the Eſtate of the Marqueſs of *Antrim*, and others, who were all engaged in the late *Iriſh* Rebellion ; and that they ſhall ſuffer very much, and be ruined, if thoſe Lands ſhould be taken from them. And we have likewiſe conſidered another Petition from ſeveral Citizens of *London*, near ſixty in number, directed to our Self, wherein they deſire, That the Marqueſs his Eſtate may be made liable to the payment of his juſt Debts, that ſo they may not be ruined in the favour of the preſent Poſſeſſors, who (they ſay) are but a few Citizens and Soldiers, who have disburſed very ſmall Sums thereon. Upon the whole matter, no man can think We are leſs engaged by Our *Declaration*, and by the *Act of Settlement*, to protect thoſe who are *Innocent*, and who have faithfully endeavoured to ſerve the *Crown*, how unfortunate ſoever,

than

than to expose to Justice those who have been really and maliciously *guilty*. And therefore we cannot in Justice, but, upon the *Petition* of the *Marquess* of *Antrim*, and after the serious and strict Inquisition into his Actions, declare unto you, That We do find him innocent from any Malice, or rebellious Purpose against the Crown ; and that what he did by way of Correspondence or Compliance with the *Irish* Rebels, was in order to the Service of Our Royal Father, and warranted by his Instructions, and the Trust reposed in him ; and that the benefit thereof accrued to the Service of the Crown, and not to the particular advantage and benefit of the Marquess. And as we cannot in justice deny him this Testimony, so we require You to transmit Our Letter to Our Commissioners, that they may know our Judgment in this Case of the Lord of *Antrim*, and proceed accordingly. And so we bid you heartily farewel.

Given at our Court at White-Hall, July 10th, *in the* 15*th Year of Our Reign* 1663.

To Our Right Trusty and Right entirely Well-beloved Cousin and Counsellor, James Duke of Ormond, *Our Lieutenant-General, and General Governor of Our Kingdom of* Ireland ; *and to the Lords of Our Council of that Our Kingdom.*

By His Majesty's Command,

HENRY BENNET.

Entered at the Signet-Office, *July* 13, 1663.

Vox Populi : *or, The People's Claim to their Parliament's Sitting, to redress Grievances, and to provide for the Common Safety, by the known Laws and Constitutions of the Nation.*

SInce the wonderful Discovery, and undeniable Confirmation of that horrid Popish Plot, which designed so much ruin and mischief to these Nations, in all things both Civil and Sacred ; and the unanimous Sense and Censure of so many Parliaments upon it, together with so many publick Acts of Justice upon so many of the Traytors ; it was comfortably hoped before thirty Months should have past over, after the detection thereof, some effectual Remedies might have been applied to prevent the further Attempts of the Papists upon us, and better to have secured the Protestants in their Religion, Lives and Properties. But by sad experience we have found, that notwithstanding the vigorous Endeavours of three of our Parliaments to provide proper and wholesome Laws to answer both ends : Yet so prevalent has this Interest been, under so potent a Head the D. of Y. as to stifle in the birth all those hopeful Parliament-Endeavours ; by those many surprizing and astonishing Prorogations and Dissolutions which they have procured, whereby our Fears and Dangers have manifestly increased, and their Spirits heightned and encouraged to renew and multiply fresh Plottings and Designs upon us.

But that our approaching Parliament may be more successful for our Relief before it be too late, by being permitted to sit to redress our Grievances, to perfect those Good Bills which have been prepared by the former Parliaments to this purpose ; these following Common-Law Maxims respecting King and Parliament, and the Common and Statute Laws themselves (to prevent such unnatural Disappointment and Mischiefs) providing for the sitting of Parliaments till Grievances be redress'd, and publick Safety secured and provided for, are tendered to consideration.

Some known Maxims, taken out of the Law-Books.

1. Respecting the King.

That the Kings of England *can do nothing as Kings, but what of right they ought to do.*
That the King can do no wrong, nor can he die.
That the King's Prerogative and the Subject's Liberty are determined by Law.
That the King hath no Power but what the Law gives him.
That the King is so called from Ruling well, Rex à bene Regendo *(viz. according to Law) Because he is a King whilst he Rules well, but a Tyrant when he Oppresses.*
That Kings of England *never appear more in their glory, splendor, and Majestick Sovereignty, than in Parliaments.*
That the Prerogative of the King cannot do wrong, nor be a Warrant to do wrong to any. Plowd. Comment. *fol.* 246.

2. Respecting the Parliament.

That Parliaments constitute, and are laid in the Essence of the Government.
That a Parliament is that to the Commonwealth, which the Soul is to the Body, which is only able to apprehend and understand the Symptoms of all Diseases which threaten the Body-politick.

That

That a Parliament is the Bulwark of our Liberty, the Boundary which keeps us from the In-undation of Tyranical Power, arbitrary and unbounded Will-Government.

That Parliaments do make new, abrogate old Laws ; reform Grievances in the Commonwealth, settle the Succession, grant Subsidies ; and in sum, may be called the great Physicians of the Kingdom.

From whence it appears, as is self-evident, if Parliaments are so absolutely necessary in this our Constitution, That they must then have their certain stationary times of Session, and continuance, for providing Laws essentially necessary for the being, as well as the well-being of the People ; and redressing all publick Grievances, either by the want of Laws, or of the undue Execution of them in being, or otherwise : And suitable hereunto are those Provisions made by the Wisdom of our Ancestors, as recorded by them both in the Common and Statute-Law.

First, What we find hereof in the Common-Law.

Coke, *lib.* 7. **Rep.** *p.* 12, 13. — *The Common-Law* (saith my Lord *Coke*) *is that which is founded in the immutable Law and Light of Nature, agreeable to the Law of God, requiring Order, Government, Subjection and Protection, &c. Containing ancient Usages, warranted by Holy Scripture ; and because it is generally given to all, it is therefore called* Common.

Lib. 9. Preface. — And further saith, *That in the Book called* The Mirror of Justice, *appeareth the whole frame of the ancient Common Laws of this Realm from the time of K.* Arthur, 516. *till near the Conquest ; which treats also of the Officers, as well as the diversity and distinction of the Courts of Justice* (which are Officinæ Legis) *and particularly of the High Court of Parliament by the name of Council-General, or Parliament ; so called from* Parler-là-ment, *speaking judicially his mind : And amongst others gives us the following Law of King* Alfred, *who reigned about* 880.

Mirror of Justice. Ch. 1. Sect. 3. — ' *Le Roy* Alfred *ordeigna pur usage perpetuel que a deux foits per lan ou plus sovene pur mi-stier in temps de peace se assembler a* Londres, *pur Parliamenter sur le guidement del people de dieu comment gents soy garderent de pechers, viverent in quiet, receiverent droit per certain usages & saints Jugements.*

' King *Alfred* ordaineth for a usage perpetual, that twice a Year, or oftner if need be, in ' time of peace, they shall assemble themselves at *London,* to treat in Parliament of the Go-' vernment of the People of God, how they should keep themselves from Offences, should ' live in quiet, and should receive right by certain Laws and holy Judgments.

Lord *Coke's* **Comment upon it.** — ' And thus (saith my Lord *Coke*) you have a Statute of King *Alfred,* as well concerning ' the holding of this Court of Parliament twice every year at the City of *London,* as to ma-' nifest the threefold end of this great and honourable Assembly of Estates : As,

' *First,* That the Subject might be kept from offending ; that is, that Offence might be ' prevented both by good and provident Laws, and by the due Execution thereof.

' *Secondly,* That Men might live safely, and in quiet.

' *Thirdly,* That all Men might receive Justice by certain Laws, and holy Judgments ; that ' is, to the end that Justice might be the better administred, that Questions and Defects ' in Law might be by the High Court of Parliament planed, reduced to certainty and ad-' judged. And further tells us, That this Court being the most Supream Court of this ' Realm, is a part of the frame of the Common Laws, and in some cases doth proceed le-' gally, according to the ordinary course of the Common-Law, as it appeareth, 39 *E.* 3. f. *Coke Inst. ch.* 29. *fol.* 5. To be short, of this Court it is truely said, *Si vetustatem spectes est antiquissima, si dignitatem est honoratissima, si jurisdictionem est capacissima.* If you regard Anti-quity, it is the most Ancient ; if Dignity, the most Honourable ; if Jurisdiction, the most sovereign.

And where questions have been made, whether this Court continued during the Heptar-chy, let the Records themselves make answer, of which he gives divers Instances in the times of King *Ina, Offa, Ethelbert.* After the Heptarchy, King *Edward,* Son of *Alfred,* King *Ethelston, Edgar, Ethelred, Edmond, Canutus.* All which (he saith) and many more, are ex-tant, and publickly known ; proving by divers Arguments, that there were Parliaments unto which the Knights and Burgesses were summoned, both before, in, and after the Reign of the Conqueror, till *Hen.* 3d's time ; and for your further satisfaction herein, see 4 *E.* 3. 25. 49 *Ed.* 3. 22, 23. 11 *H.* 4. 2. *Little. lib.* 2. *chap.* 20.

Whereby we may understand,

1. That Parliaments are part of the frame of the Common Law, [which is laid in the Law and Light of Nature, right Reason and Scripture.]

2. That according to this Moral Law of Equity and Righteousness, Parliaments ought frequently to meet for the common Peace, Safety and Benefit of the People, and Sup-port of the Government.

3. That Parliaments have been all along esteemed an essential part of the Government, as being the most ancient, honourable and sovereign Court of the Nation, who are fre-quently and perpetually to sit, for the making and abolishing Laws, redressing of Grie-vances, and to see the due Administration of Justice.

4. That

4. That as to the Place of Meeting, it was to be at *London* the Capital City, the Eye and Heart of the Nation, as being not only the Regal Seat, but the principal place of Judicature, and residence of the chief Officers, and Courts of Justice, where also the Records are kept, as well as the principal Place of Commerce and Concourse in the Nation, and to which the People may have the best recourse, and where they may find the best accommodation.

5. The Antiquity of Parliaments in this Nation, which have been so ancient, that no Record can give any account of their Beginning; my Lord *Coke* thus tracing them from the *Britains*, through the *Saxons*, *Danes* and *Normans*, to our days.

So that not to suffer Parliaments to sit, to answer the great ends for which they were instituted, is expresly contrary to the Common-Law, and so consequently of the Law of God as well as the Law of Nature; and thereby Violence is offered to the Government it self, and Infringement of the People's fundamental Rights and Liberties.

Secondly, What we find hereof in the Statute-Law.

The Satute-Laws are the Acts of Parliament which are (or ought to be) only Declaratory of the Common-Law, which, as you have heard, is founded upon rightReason and Scripture; for we are told, that if any thing is enacted contrary thereto, it is void and null: As *Coke Inst.* l. 2. c. 29. f. 15. *Finch* p. 3. 28 *H.* 8. c. 27. *Doct. and Stud.*

The first of these Statutes, which require the frequentMeeting and Sitting of Parliaments, agreeable to the Common-Law, we find to be in the time of *Ed.* 3. viz. 4 *Ed.* 3. & *ch.* 14. In these Words.

' Item, *It is accorded that a Parliament shall be held every year once, or more often, if need be.* The next is the 36 of the same K. *Ed.* 3. c. 10. viz.

' Item, *For the maintenance of the said Articles and Statutes, and redressing of divers Mis-* ' *chiefs and Grievances which daily happen; a Parliament shall be holden every year, as at* ' *another time was ordained by a Statute.* viz. his aforementioned, in 14th year. And agreeable hereto are those Statutes upon the Rolls, *viz.* 5. *Ed.* 2.---1 *R.* N°. 95.

By which Statutes it appeareth, ThatParliaments ought annually to meet, to support the Government, and to redress the Grievances which may happen in the Interval of Parliaments; that being the great End proposed in their said Meetings. Now, for Parliaments to meet annually, and not suffered to sit to answer the Ends, but to be prorogued or dissolved before they have finished their Work, would be nothing but a deluding of the Law, and a striking at the Foundation of the Government it self, and rendring Parliaments altogether useless; for it would be all one to have no Parliaments at all, as to have them turned off by the Prnice before they have done that they were called and entrusted to do. For by the same Rule whereby they may be so turned off one Session, they may be three Sessions, and so to threescore, to the breaking of the Government, and introducing Arbitrary Power. To prevent such intolerable Mischiefs and Inconveniencies are such good Laws as these made in this King's time, and which were so sacredly observed in after times, That it was a Custom, especially in the Reigns of *H.* 4. *H.* 5. *H.* 6. to have a Proclamation made in *West-minster-Hall* before the end of every Session, * ' *That all those who had any matter to pre-* ' *sent to theParliament, should bring it in before such a day, for otherwise the Parliament at that* ' *day should determine.'* Whereby it appears, that People were not to be eluded, or disappointed by surprising Prorogations and Dissolutions, to frustrate and make void the great ends of Parliaments.

An honest and a necessary Proclamation to be made every Parliament.

And to this purpose, saith a late learned Author, ' *That if there was no Statute, or any thing* ' *upon record extant, concerning the Parliament's sitting to redress grievances, yet I must believe,* ' *that it is so by the fundamental Law or Government, which must be lame and imperfect without* ' *it; [For otherwise the Prince and his Ministers may do what they please, and their Wills may* ' *be their Laws.]*

' *Therefore it is provided for in the very Essence and Constitution of the Government itself; and* ' *this* (saith our Author) *we may call the Common-Law, which is of as much value (if not more)* ' *than any Statute, and of which all our good Acts of Parliament and Magna-Charta itself is but* ' *Declaratory; so that tho' the King is intrusted with the formal part of summoning and pronouncing* ' *the Dissolution of Parliaments, which is done by Writ; yet the Laws which oblige him (as well* ' *as us) have determined how, and when he shall do it: which is enough to shew, that the King's* ' *Share in the Sovereignty, that is, in the Parliament, is cut out to him by Law, and not left at* ' *his disposal.*

The next Statute we shall mention to enforce this fundamental Right and Privilege, is the 25th *Ed.* 3. *ch.* 23. called the *Statute of Provisors*, which was made to prevent and cut off the Incroachments of the Bishops of *Rome*, whose Usurpations in disposing of Benefices occasioned intolerable Grievances, wherein, in the Preamble of the said Statute, it is expressed as followeth:

25Ed.3.c.23 Statute of Provisors.

' *Where*

'*Whereupon the Commons have pray'd our said Sovereign Lord the King, that sith the Right of the*
'*Crown of* England, *and the Law of the said Realm is such, that upon the Mischiefs and Damage*
'*which happeneth to his Realm, he ought, and is bounden of the accord of his said People in his*
'*Parliament, thereof to make Remedy and Law, in avoiding the Mischiefs and Damage which*
'*thereof cometh ; that it may please him thereupon to provide remedy.* Our Sovereign Lord
'*the King seeing the Mischiefs and Damages before-named, and having regard to the said Sta-*
'*tute made in the Time of his said Grand-father, and the causes contained in the same, which*
'*Statute holdeth always his force, and was never defeated or annul'd in any point, and by so much*
'*is bound by his Oath to do the same to be kept as the Law of the Realm, tho' that by Sufferance*
'*and Negligence it hath since been attempted to the contrary : And also having regard to the*
'*grievous Complaint made to him by his People in divers Parliaments holden heretofore, Willing*
'*to ordain Remedy for the great Damages and Mischiefs which have happened, and daily do*
'*happen by the said Causes,* &c. *By the Assent of all the Great Men and Commonalty of his*
'*said Realm, hath ordained and established,* &c.

In which preamble of the Statute we may observe, (1) The intolerable grievance and
burden which was occasion'd by the illegal Incroachments of the See of *Rome*. (2.) The
many Complaints the People had made, who in those dark times under Popery were sensible of groaning under their Burdens. (3.) The Endeavours used in vain by former
Parliaments to redress the same, and to bring their Laws in being, to have their Force
and Effect. (4.) The Acknowledgment of the King and Parliament, that the Obligation
hereto was upon the King,

(1.) From the Right of the Crown, which obliged every King to pass good Laws.
(2.) The Statute in force. (3.) The King's Oath to keep the Old, and pass New Laws
for his People's safeguard, which they should tender to him. (4.) From the sense of the
People, expressed in their Complaints ; and, (5.) From the Mischief and Damage which
would otherwise ensue.

And therefore by the desire and accord of his People, He passes this famous Law ; the
Preamble whereof is here recited.

Another Statute to the same purpose you find 2 R. 2. N°. 28. '*Also the Commons in*
'*Parliament pray, That forasmuch as the Petitions and Bills presented in Parliament by divers*
'*of the Commons, could not heretofore have their respective Answers ; That therefore both their*
'*Petitions and Bills in this present Parliament, as also others which shall be presented in any fu-*
'*ture Parliament, may have a good and gracious Answer, and Remedy obtained thereupon, be-*
'*fore the departing of every Parliament : And that to this purpose, a due Statute be ensealed*
'*[or enacted] at this present Parliament, to be and remain in force for all times to come.*
To which the King reply'd :

The King's Answer.

*T*H E *King is pleased that all such Petitions delivered in Parliament, of things* (or matters)
*which cannot otherwise be determined ; a good and reasonable Answer shall be made and
given before the departure of Parliament.*

In which excellent Law we may observe, (1.) A Complaint of former Remissness, their
Bills having aforetime been pass'd by, their Grievances unredress'd, by unreasonable dissolving of Parliaments, before their Laws could pass. (2.) That a Law might pass in that
very Parliament to rectify that Abuse for the future : And, (3.) That it should not pass
for a temporary Law, but for perpetuity, being of such absolute Necessity, that before the
Parliaments be dismiss'd, Bills of common Right might pass.

And the King agreed hereto.

Suitable hereto, we have my Lord Chief Justice *Coke*, that great Oracle of the Law, in
his *Instit.* 4. *B.* p. 11. asserting, '*Petitions being truly preferr'd* (tho' very many) *have been*
'*answered by the Law and Custom of Parliament, before the end Parliament.*

This appears, saith he, by the ancient Treatise, *De Modo tenendi Parliamentum*, in these
Words faithfully translated, *The Parliament ought not to be ended while any Petition dependeth
undiscussed, or at the least to which a determinate Answer is not made.* Rot. Par. 17 E. 3. N°.
60. 25 E. 3. N°. 60. 50 E. 3. N°. 212. 2 R. 2. 134. 2 R. 2. N°. 38. 1 H. 4. 132. 2 H. 4. 325. 113.
'*And that one of the principal ends of calling Parliaments is for redressing Grievances that*
'*daily happen.* 36 E. 3. c. 10. 18 E. 3. c. 14. 50 E. 3. N°. 17. *Lyon's Case*, Rot. Par.
1 H. 5. N°. 17. 13 H. 4. N°. 9.

And that as concerning the departing of Parliaments, *It ought to be in such a manner,* saith
Modus Tenendi, viz. *To be demanded, yea and publickly proclaimed in the Parliament, and within the Palace of the Parliament, whether there be any that hath delivered a Petition to the Parliament, and hath not received Answer thereto ; if there be none such, it is to be supposed, that
every one is satisfy'd, or else answered unto at the least, so far forth as by the Law he may be.
And which custom was observed in* After-Ages, *as you have heard before.*

Con-

Concerning the Antiquity and Authority of this ancient Treatise, called, *Modus tenendi Parliamentum* (saith my Lord *Coke*) whereof we make often use in our Institutes ; certain it is, *that this Modus was rehearsed and declared before the Conqueror at the time of his Conquest, and by him approved for* England ; *and accordingly he, according to* Modus, *held a Parliament for* England, *as appears* 21 E. 3. fol. 60.

Whereby you clearly perceive, that these wholesome Laws are not only in full agreement with the Common Law, and declarative thereof, but in full accord with the Oath and Office of the Prince, who has that great trust by the Law, lodged with him for the good and benefit, not hurt and mischief of the People, *viz.*

First, These Laws are very suitable to the Duty and Office of a Ruler, and the end for which he was instituted by God himself, who commands him to do Judgment and Justice to all, especially to the Oppressed ; and not to deny them any request for their relief, protection or welfare, 2 *Sam.* 22. 3. 1 *Chron.* 13. 1, to 5. 2 *Chron.* 9. 8. 19. 5, &c. *Esth.* 1. 13. Our Law-Books enjoining the same, as *Bracton,* Lib. 1. c. 2. Lib. 3. c. 9. fol. 107, &c. *Fortescue,* ch. 9. *fol.* 15. *c.* 7. *fol.* 5. 11. *Coke* 7. Book Reports, *Calvin's* Case, *f.* 11.

Secondly, They are also in full Harmony with the King's Coronation-Oath solemnly made to all his Subjects, *viz. To grant, fulfil and defend all the rightful Laws which the Commons of the Realm shall choose, and to strengthen and maintain them after his power.*

Thirdly, these Laws are also in full agreement, and oneness with *Magna Charta* it self, that ancient fundamental Law, which hath been confirmed by at least forty Parliaments, *viz. We shall deny, We shall defer to no Man Justice and Right ;* much less to the whole Parliament and Kingdom, in denying or deferring to pass such necessary Bills which the Peoples Needs call for.

Object. But to all this which hath been said, it may be objected, That several of our Princes have otherwise practised, by dissolving, or [as latterly used, by] proroguing Parliaments at their pleasures, before Grievances were redressed, and publick Bills of common Safety pass'd, and that as a privilege belonging to the Royal Prerogative.

Answ. To which it is answered, That granting they have so done ; First, It is most manifest, that doth not therefore create a right to them so to do ; according to that known Maxim, à facto ad jus non valet consequentia, *especially when such Actions are against so many express and positive Laws, such principles of common Right and Justice, and so many particular Tyes and Obligations upon themselves to the contrary.*

Secondly, But if it had been so, yet neither can Prerogative be pleaded to justify such Practices, because the King has no Prerogative, but what the Law gives him ; and it can give none to destroy it self, and those it protects, but the contrary. *Bracton,* in his Comments, *pag.* 487. tells us, ' *That although Common-Law doth allow many Prerogatives to the* *Bracton.* ' *King, yet it doth not allow any, that he shall wrong, or hurt any by his Prerogative.*' There- P. 487. fore 'tis well said by a late worthy Author on this point, *That what Power or Prerogative the Kings have in them, ought to be used according to the true and genuine intent of the Government ; that is, for the Preservation and Interest of the People ; and not for the disappointing the Counsels of a Parliament, towards reforming Grievances and making provision for the future Execution of the Laws ; and whenever it is applied to frustrate those Ends, it is a Violation of Right, and Infringement of the King's Coronation-Oath, who is obliged to pass or confirm those Laws his People shall chuse.* And tho' he had such a Prerogative by Law, yet it should not be so used, especially in time of imminent danger and distress. The late King in his Advice to his Majesty that The late now is, in his Ἐικὼν Βασιλικη 239. *tells him, That his Prerogative is best shewed, and exercised,* King's Ad- *in remitting, rather than exacting the rigor of the Laws, there being nothing worse than legal Tyranny.* vice to His

Nor would he have him entertain any aversion or dislike of Parliaments, which in their right Majesty. *Constitution with freedom and honour, will never injure or diminish his Greatness, but will rather be as interchanging of Love, Loyalty and Confidence between the Prince and his People.*

'Tis true some Flatterers and Traytors have presum'd, in defiance to their Country's Rights, to assert that such a boundless Prerogative belongs to Kings ; as did Chief Justice *Treslian,* &c. in R. 2's time ; *Advising him, that he might dissolve Parliaments at pleasure ; and that no Member should be called to Parliament, nor any Act pass'd in either House, without his Approbation in the first place ;* and, *that whosoever advised otherwise, were Traytors.* But this Advice, you read, was no less fatal to himself, than pernicious to his Prince. *Baker's Chron.* p. 147, 148, and 159.

King James, *in his Speech to the Parliament* 1609, *gives them assurance, That he never meant to govern by any Law, but the Law of the Land ; tho' it be disputed among them, as if he had an intention to alter the Law, and govern by the absolute Power of a King ; but to put them out of doubt in that matter, tells them, That all Kings who are not Tyrants, or perjured, will bound themselves within the limits of their Laws. And they that perswade the contrary, are Vipers and Pests, both against them and the Commonwealth.* Wilson's *K. J.* p. 46.

Nnn

The

The Conclusion.

1. IF this be so, that by so great Athority (*viz.* so many Satutes in force, the Fundamentals of the Commnc-Law, the Essentials of the Government it self, *Magna Charta*, the King's Coronation-Oath, so many Laws of God and Man ;) the Parliament ought to sit to redress Grievances, and provide for Common Safety, especially in times of Common Danger : (And that this is eminently so, who can doubt, that will believe the King ; so many Parliaments, the Cloud of Witnesses, the Publick Judicatures, their own sense and experience of the manifold Mischiefs which have been acted, and the apparent Ruin and Confusion that impends the Nation, by the restless Attempts of a bloody Interest, if a speedy Remedy is not applied:)

Then let it be queried, Whether the People having thus the Knife at the Throat, Cities and Habitations fired, and therein their Persons fried, Invasions and Insurrections threatned to destroy the King and Subjects, Church and State ; and as so lately told us, (upon Mr. *Fitz-Harris*'s Commitment) the present Design on foot was to depose and kill the King ; and their only remedy hoped for, under God, to give them Relief thus from time to time cut off, *viz.* Their Parliaments, who with so much care, cost and pains, are elected, sent up, and intrusted for their help, turned off *re infecta*, and rendred so insignificant by those frequent Prorogations and Dissolutions.

Are they not therefore justify'd in their important Cries, in their many humble Petitions to their King, fervent Addresses to their Members, earnest Claims for their Birthright here pleaded, which the Laws of the Kingdom consonant to the Laws of God and Nature, have given them ?

2. If so, what shall be said to those who advise to this high Violation of their Country's Rights, to the infringing so many just Laws, and exposing the Publick to those desperate hazards, if not a total Ruin.

If King *Alfred* (as *Andrew Horne* in his *Mirrour of Justice* tells us) hanged *Darling*, *Segnor*, *Cadwine*, *Cole*, and forty Judges more, for judging contrary to Law ; and yet all those false Judgments were but in particular and private Cases : What Death do those Men deserve, who offer this Violence to the Law it self, and all the sacred Rights of their Country ? If the Lord Chief Justice *Thorp*, in *Ed. 3d*'s time, for receiving the Bribery of one hundred Pounds, was adjudged to be hanged as one that had made the King break his Oath to the People ; how much more guilty are they of making the King break his Coronation-Oath, that persuade him to act against all the Laws for holding Parliaments, and passing Laws therein, which he is sworn so solemnly to do? And if the Lord Chief Justice *Tresilian* was hanged, drawn and quartered, for advising the King to act contrary to some Statutes only : What do those deserve that advise the King to act not only against some, but against all those ancient Laws and Statutes in his Realm ?

And if *Blake*, the King's Council, but for assisting in the matter, and drawing up Indictments by the King's Command contrary to Law, tho' it is likely he might plead the King's Order for it, yet if he was hanged, drawn and quartered, for that ; what Justice is due to them that assist in the Total Destruction of all the Laws of the Nation, and, as much as in them lies, their King and Country too ? And if *Usk*, the Under-Sheriff (whose Office is to execute the Laws) for but endeavouring to aid *Tresilian*, *Blake*, and their Accomplices against some of the Laws, was also, with five more, hanged, drawn and quartered ; what Punishment may they deserve that aid and endeavour the Subversion of all the Laws of the Kingdom ? And if *Empson* and *Dudley* in *Henry* the Eighth's time, tho' two of the King's Privy Council, were hanged for procuring and executing an Act of Parliament contrary to the Fundamental Laws of the Kingdom, and to the great vexation of the People ; so that tho' they had an Act of Parliament of their side, yet the Act being against the known Laws of the Land, were hanged as Traitors for putting the Statute in Execution : Then what will become of them who have no such Act to shelter themselves under, and who shall act not only contrary to, but to the Destruction of the fundamental Laws of the Kingdom ? And how Harmonious such Justice will be, the Text tells us, *Deut.* 27. 17. *Cursed be he that removeth his Neighbour's Land-mark : and all the People shall say* Amen.

That this present Session may have a happy Issue, to answer the great Ends of Parliaments, and therein our present Exigencies and Necessities, is the incessant Cry and longing Expectation of all the Protestants in the Land.

The

The Security of Engliſhmen*'s Lives; or, the Truſt, Power, and Duty of the* Grand Jurys *of* England. *Explained according to the Fundamentals of the* Engliſh *Government, and the Declarations of the ſame made in Parliament by many Statutes.*

THE principal Ends of all Civil Government and of Human Society, were the Security of Men's Lives, Liberties and Properties, mutual aſſiſtance and help each unto other, and proviſion for their common benefit and advantage ; and where the fundamental Laws and Conſtitution of any Government have been wiſely adapted unto thoſe ends, ſuch Countries and Kingdoms have encreaſed in Virtue, Proweſs, Wealth and Happineſs, whilſt others thro' the want of ſuch excellent Conſtitutions, or neglect of preſerving them, have been a Prey to the Pride, Luſt and Cruelty of the moſt Potent ; and the People have had no aſſurance of Eſttates, Liberties or Lives, but from their Grace and Pleaſure. They have been many times forced to welter in each other's Blood in their Maſters quarrel for Dominion, and at beſt they have ſerved like Beaſts of burthen, and by continual baſe ſubſerviency to their Maſters Vices, have loſt all ſenſe of true Religion, Virtue and Manhood.

Our Anceſtors have been famous in their Generations for Wiſdom, Piety and Courage, in forming and preſerving a Body of Laws to ſecure themſelves and their Poſterities from Slavery and Oppreſſion, and to maintain thir Native Freedoms ; to be ſubject only to the Laws made by their own Conſent in their General Aſſemblies, and to be put in execution chiefly by themſelves, their Officers and Aſſiſtants ; to be guarded and defended from all Violence and Force, by their own Arms, kept in their own hands, and uſed at their own charge under their Prince's Conduct ; entruſting nevertheleſs an ample Power to their Kings, and other Magiſtrates, that they may do all the good, and enjoy all the happineſs that the largeſt Soul of Man can honeſtly wiſh ; and carefully providing ſuch means of correcting and puniſhing their Miniſters and Counſellors, if they tranſgreſſed the Laws, that they might not dare to abuſe or oppreſs the People, or deſign againſt their freedom or welfare.

This Body of Laws our Anceſtors always eſteemed the beſt Inheritance they could leave to their Poſterities, well knowing that theſe were the ſacred Fence of their Lives, Liberties and Eſtates, and an unqueſtionable Title whereby they might call what they had their own, or ſay they were their own Men: The ineſtimable value of this Inheritance mov'd our Progenitors with great reſolution bravely from Age to Age to defend it ; and it now falls to our lot to preſerve it againſt the dark Contrivances of a Popiſh Faction, who would by Frauds, Sham-plots and infamous Perjuries, deprive us of our Birth-rights, and turn the points of our Swords (our Laws) into our own Bowels. They have impudently ſcandalized our Parliaments with Deſigns to overturn the Monarchy, becauſe they would have excluded a Popiſh Succeſſor, and provided for the Security of the Religion and Lives of all Proteſtants : They have cauſed Lords and Commons to be for a long time kept in Priſons, and ſuborned Witneſſes to ſwear matters of Treaſon againſt them ; endeavouring thereby, not only to cut off ſome who had eminently appeared in Parliament for our ancient Laws, but through them to blaſt the Repute of Parliaments themſelves, and to leſſen the People's Confidence in thoſe great Bulwarks of their Religion and Government.

The preſent purpoſe is to ſhew, how well our worthy Fore-fathers have provided in our Law for the ſafety of our Lives, not only againſt all attempts of open Violence, by the ſevere puniſhment of Robbers, Murderers, and the like ; but the ſecret poiſonous Arrows that fly in the dark, to deſtroy the Innocent by falſe Accuſations and Perjuries. Our Law-makers foreſaw both their dangers from the Malice, and Paſſions, that might cauſe ſome of private conditions to accuſe others falſely in the Courts of Juſtice, and the great hazards of worthy and eminent Men's Lives from the Malice, Emulations and ill Deſigns of corrupt Miniſters of State, or otherwiſe potent, who might commit the moſt odious of Murders in the form and courſe of Juſtice ; either by corrupting of Judges, as depending upon them for their Honour and great Revenue, or by bribing and hiring Men of depraved Principles, and deſperate Fortunes, to ſwear falſely againſt them ; doubtleſs they had heard the Scriptures, and obſerved that the great Men of the *Jews* ſought out many to ſwear Treaſon and Blaſphemy againſt *Jeſus Chriſt* : They had heard of *Ahab*'s Courtiers and Judges, who, in the courſe and form of Juſtice, by falſe Witneſſes, murdered *Naboth, becauſe he would not ſubmit his Property to an Arbitrary Power.* Neither were they ignorant of the ancient *Roman* Hiſtories, and the peſtilent falſe Accuſers that abounded in the Reign of ſome of thoſe Emperors, under whom the greateſt of Crimes was, to be virtuous : Therefore, as became good Legiſlators, they made a prudent Proviſion, as perhaps any Country in the World enjoys, for equal and impartial Adminiſtration of Juſtice in all the concerns of the People's Lives ; that every

Man,

Man, whether Lord or Commoner, might be in safety, whilst they lived in due obedience to the Laws.

For this purpose it is made a Fundamental in our Government, that unless it be by Parliament, no Man's Life should be touched for any Crime whatsoever, save by the Judgment of at least 24 Men ; that is, 12 or more, to find the Bill of Indictment, whether he be Peer of the Realm, or Commoner ; and 12 Peers, or above, if a Lord ; if not, 12 Commoners to give the Judgment upon the general Issue of Not guilty joined. Of these 24, the first 12 are called the Grand Inquest, or the Grand Jury, for the extent of their Power, and in regard that their number must be more than 12, sometimes 23, or 25, never were less than 13. twelve whereof at least must agree to every Indictment, or else it is no legal Verdict ; if 11 of 21, or of 13, should agree to find a Bill of Indictment, it were no Verdict. The other twelve, in Commoners Cases, are called the Petit-Jury, and their number is ever twelve ; but the Jury for a Peer of the Realm may be more in number, though of like Authority. The Office and Power of these Juries is *Judicial*, they only are the Judges, from whose Sentence the Indicted are to expect Life or Death : upon their Integrity and Understanding, the Lives of all that are brought into Judgment do ultimately depend ; from their Verdict there lies no Appeal, by finding Guilty or not Guilty ; they do complicately resolve both Law and Fact.

As it hath been the Law, so it hath been always the Custom and Practice of these Juries, upon all general Issues, pleaded in Cases Civil as well as Criminal, to judge both of the Law and Fact. So it is said in the Report of the Lord Chief Justice *Vaughan*, in *Bushel's* Case, That these Juries determine the Law in all matters where Issue is joined and tried, in the principal Case, whether the Issue be about Trespass, or a Debt, or Disseizin in Assizes, or a Tort, or any such like; unless they should please to give a special Verdict, with an implicite faith in the Judgment of the Court, to which none can oblige them against their wills.

These last 12 must be Men of equal condition with the Party indicted, and are called his Peers ; therefore if it be a Peer of the Realm, they must be all such, when indicted at the Suit of the King ; and in the case of Commoners, every Man of the 12 must agree to the Verdict freely, without compulsion, fear or menace, else it is no Verdict. Whether the Case of a Peer be harder, I will not determine. Our Ancestors were careful, that all Men of the like condition, and quality, presumed to be sensible of each other's Infirmity, should mutually be Judges each of other's Lives, and alternately taste of Subjection and Rule ; every Man being equally liable to be accused, or indicted, or perhaps to be suddenly judg'd by the Party, of whom he is at present Judge, if he be found innocent. Whether it be Lord or Commoner that is indicted, the Law intends (as near as may be) that his Equals that judge him, should be his Companions, known to him, and he to them, or at least his Neighbours, or Dwellers near about the Place where the Crime is supposed to have been committed, to whom something of the Fact must probably be known ; and though the Lords are not appointed to be of the Neighbourhood to the indicted Lord, yet the Law supposes them to be Companions, and personally well known each unto other, being presumed to be a small number (as they have anciently been) and to have met yearly, or oftener in Parliament, as by the Law they ought, besides their other meetings, as the hereditary Counsellors of the Kings of *England*. If time hath altered the case of the Lords as to the number, indifferency, and impartiality of the Peers, it hath been, and may be worthy of the Parliament's consideration ; and the greater duty is incumbent upon grand Juries to examine with the utmost Diligence the Evidence against Peers, before they find a Bill of Indictment against any of them, if in truth it may put their Lives in greater danger.

It is not designed at this time to undertake a Discourse of Petit-Juries, but to consider the Nature and Power of Grand Inquests ; and to shew how much the Reputation, the Fortunes, and the Lives of *Englishmen*, depend upon the conscientious performance of their Duty.

It was absolutely necessary for the support of the Government, and the safety of every Man's Life and Interest, that some should be trusted to enquire after all such, as by Treasons, Felonies, or lesser Crimes, disturb'd the peace, that they might be prosecuted, and brought to condign punishment ; and it was no less needful for every man's quiet and safety, that the trust of such Inquisitions should be put into the hands of persons of understanding, and integrity, indifferent and impartial, that might suffer no man to be falsly accused, or defamed ; nor the Lives of any to be put in jeopardy, by the malicious Conspiracies of great or small, or the perjuries of any profligate Wretches : For these necessary, honest Ends, was the institution of Grand Juries.

Our Ancestors thought it not best to trust this great concern of their Lives and Interests in the hands of any Officer of the King's, or in any Judges named by him, nor in any certain number of men during life, lest they should be awed or influenced by great men, corrupted by Bribes, Flatteries, or love of Power, or become negligent, or partial to Friends and Relations,

Margin notes:

See Ld. *Coke's Inst.* 3d part, p. 40.

See *Mag. Chart. Coke's* 2d part of *Instit.* p. 50, 51.

See the Reports of the Ld Chief Justice *Vaughan*, p. 150, 151.

lations, or pursue their own Quarrels or private Revenges; or connive at the Conspiracies of others, and indict thereupon. But this trust of enquiring out, and indicting all the Criminals in a County, is placed in men of the same County, more at least than Twelve of the most honest, and most sufficient for knowledge, and ability of Mind and Estate, to be from time to time at the Sessions and Assizes, and all other Commissions of *Oyer* and *Terminer*, named and returned by the chief sworn Officer of the County, the Sheriff, (who was also by express Law anciently chosen annually by the People of every County) and trusted with the Execution of all Writs and Processes of the Law, and with the Power of the County to suppress all Violences, unlawful Routs, Riots, and Rebellions: Yet our Laws left not the Election of these Grand Inquests absolutely to the Will of the Sheriffs, but have described in general their Qualifications, who shall enquire and indict either Lord or Commoner: They ought, by the old Common-Law, to be lawful Liege People, of ripe Age, not over-aged or infirm, and of good Fame amongst their Neighbours, free from all reasonable Suspicion of any design for himself or others upon the Estates or Lives of any suspected Criminals, or quarrel or controversy with any of them: They ought to be indifferent and impartial, even before they are admitted to be sworn, and of sufficient Understanding and Estate for so great a Trust. The ancient Law-book, called *Briton*, of great Authority, says, The Sheriffs *See* Brit. p. 9. Bailiffs ought to be sworn to return such as know best how to enquire, and discover all *and* 10. Breaches of the Peace; and lest any should intrude themselves, or be obtruded by others, they ought to be returned by the Sheriff, without the denomination of any, except the Sheriff's Officers. And agreeable hereunto was the Statute of 11 *H.* 4. in these Words : *See* 11Hen. 4.
' *Item*, Because of late, Inquests were taken at *Westminster* of Persons named to the
' Justices, without due Return of the Sheriff, of which Persons some were outlawed, &c.
' and some fled to sanctuary for Treason and Felony, &c. by whom, as well many Of-
' fenders were indicted, as other lawful Liege People of the King not guilty; by Conspi-
' racy, Abetment, and false Imagination of others, &c. against the force of the Common-
' Law, &c. It is therefore granted, for the Ease and Quietness of the People, that the
' same Indictment, with all its Dependences, be void, and holden for none for ever;
' and that from henceforth, no Indictment be made by any such Person, but by
' Inquest of the King's Liege People, in the manner as was used, &c. returned by the
' Sheriffs, &c. without any denomination to the Sheriffs, &c. according to the Law of *See* Coke's
' *England*; and if any Indictment be made hereafter in any point to the contrary, the Instit. 3*d part*,
' same be also void, and holden for none for ever.' See also the Statute of *Westm.* 2d. fol. 33.
cap. 38. and *Articul. super Chartas*, cap. 9.

So careful have our Parliaments been, that the Power of Grand Inquests might be placed in the hands of good and worthy Men; that if one Man of a Grand Inquest, though they be Twenty three or more, should not be *Liber et Legalis Homo*, or such as the Law requires, and duly returned without denomination to the Sheriff; all the Indictments found by such a Grand Jury, and the Proceedings upon them, are void and null. So it was adjudged in *Scarlet*'s Case.

I know too well, that the Wisdom and Care of our Ancestors, in this Institution of Grand Juries, hath not been of late considered as it ought; nor the Laws concerning them duly observed; nor have the Gentlemen, and other Men of Estates, in the several Counties, discerned how insensibly their Legal Power and Jurisdiction in their Grand and Petit Juries is decayed, and much of the means to preserve their own Lives and Interests taken out of their hands. 'Tis a wonder that they were not more awakened with the Attempt of the late L. Ch. J. who would have usurped a Lordly Dictatorian Power over the Grand Jury of *Somersetshire*, and commanded them to file a Bill of Indictment for Murther, for which they saw no Evidence; and upon their refusal, he not only threatned the Jury, but assumed to himself an arbitrary Power to fine them.

Here was a bold Battery made upon the ancient Fence of our Reputations and Lives: If that Justice's Will had passed for Law, all the Gentlemen of the Grand Juries must have been the basest Vassals to the Judges, and have been penally obliged *jurare in Verba Magistri*, to have sworn to the Directions or Dictates of the Judges: But thanks be to God, the late long Parliament (tho' filled with Pensioners) could not bear such a bold Invasion of the *English* Liberty; but upon the Complaint of one Sir *Hugh Windham*, Foreman of the said Jury, and a Member of that Parliament, the Commons brought the then Chief Justice to their Bar, to acknowledge his Fault, whereupon the Prosecution ceased.

The Trust and Power of Grand Juries is, and ought to be accounted amongst the greatest and of most concern, next to the Legislative. The Justice of the whole Kingdom, in Criminal Cases, almost wholly depending upon their Ability and Integrity, in the due execution of their Office: Besides, the Concernments of all Commoners, the Honour, Reputation, Estates and Lives of all the Nobility of *England*, are so far submitted to their Censure, that they may bring them into question for Treason, or Felony, at their discretion; their Verdict must be entred upon Record, against the greatest Lords, and process must legally

gally go out against them thereupon, to imprison them if they can be taken, or to outlaw them, as the Statutes direct ; and if any Peer of the Realm, though innocent, should justly fear a Conspiracy against his Life, and think fit to withdraw ; the direction of the Statutes, in proceeding to the Outlawry, being rightly pursued, he could never reverse the Outlawry, as the Law now stands, save by Pardon, or Act of Parliament. Hence it appears, that in case a Grand Jury should be drawn to indict a Noble Peer unjustly, either by means of their own Weakness, or Partiality, or a blind Submission to the Direction or Opinion of Judges ; one such failure of a Jury may occasion the Ruin of any of the best or greatest Families in *England :* I mention this extent of the Grand Jury's Power over all the Nobility, only to shew their joint Interest and Concern with the Commons of *England* in this ancient Institution.

The Grand Juries are trusted to be the principal means of preserving the Peace of the whole Kingdom, by the terror of executing the Penal Laws against Offenders, by their Wisdom, Diligence, and Faithfulness in making due Inquiries after all Breaches of the Peace, and bringing every one to answer for his Crime, at the peril of his Life, Limb, and Estate ; that every Man, who lives within the Law, may sleep securely in his own House.

'Tis committed to their Charge and Trust, to take care of bringing capital Offenders to pay their Lives to Justice, and less Criminals to other Punishments, according to their several demerits. The Courts, or Judges, or Commissioners of *Oyer* and *Terminer,* and of Goal-Delivery, are to receive only from the Grand Inquest, all Capital Matters whatsoever, to be put in issue, tried and judged before them by the Petit Juries. The whole stream of Justice, in such cases, either runs freely, or is stopped and disturbed, as the Grand Inquests do their Duties, either faithfully and prudently, or neglect or omit them.

And as one part of their Duty is to indict Offenders, so another part is to protect the Innocent, in their Reputations, Lives and Interests, from false Accusers, and malicious Conspirators : They are to search out the Truth of such Informations as come before them, and to reject the Indictment, if it be not sufficiently proved ; and farther, if they have reasonable suspicion of Malice, or wicked Designs against any Man's Life or Estate by such as offer a Bill of Indictment ; the Laws of God, and of the Kingdom, bind them to use all possible means to discover the Villany ; and if it appear to them (whereof they are the legal Judges) to be a Conspiracy, or malicious Combination against the Accused, they are bound by the highest Obligations upon Men and Christians, not only to reject such a Bill of Indictment, but to indict forthwith all the Conspirators, with their Abettors and Associates.

Doubtless there hath been Pride and Covetousness, Malice, and Desire of Revenge in all Ages, from whence have sprung false Accusations and Conspiracies ; but no Age before us ever hatched such Villanies, as our Popish Faction have contrived against our Religion, Lives and Liberties. No History affords an Example of such Forgeries, Perjuries, Subornations and Combinations of infamous Wretches, as have been lately discovered amongst them, to defame loyal, innocent Protestants, and to shed their guiltless Blood in the Form and Course of Justice, and to make the King's most faithful Subjects appear to be the vilest Traitors unto him. In this our miserable State, Grand Juries are our only security, inasmuch as our Lives cannot be drawn into jeopardy, by all the malicious Crafts of the Devil, unless such a number of our honest Countrymen shall be satisfied in the Truth of the Accusations. For prevention of such Plotters of wickedness as now abound, was that Statute made in

See the Stat. 42 E. 3. 3. the 42 of *E. 3. 3.* in these Words : ' To eschew the Mischiefs and Damage done to divers ' of the Commons by *False Accusers,* which oft-times have made the Accusations more ' for Revenge and singular Benefit, than for the Profit of the King, or of his People ; ' which accused Persons, some have been taken, and sometimes caused to come before ' the King's Council by Writ, and otherwise, upon grievous Pain, against the Law ; It ' is assented and accorded for the good Government of the Commons, That no Man be ' put to answer without presentment before Justices, or matter of Record, *&c.* according to the old Law of the Land, and if any thing be done to the contrary, it shall ' be void in Law, *&c.*' And (saith the Statute of the 25 of *E. 3. 4.*) ' None shall be ' taken by Petition, or Suggestion made to the King, or his Council, unless it be by ' Indictment, or Presentment of good and lawful People of the same Neighbourhood ' where such deeds be done, *&c.* that is to say, by a Grand Jury.'

All our Lives are thus by Law trusted to the care of our Grand Inquests, that none may be put to answer for their Lives, unless they indict them. If a causeless Indictment of any Man should carelesly pass from them, his guiltless Blood, or what Prejudice soever the Accused should thereby suffer, must rest upon them, who by Breach of their Trust were the occasions of it ; their Fault cannot be excused by the prosecution of an Attorney, or Sollicitor General, or any other Accuser, if it were in their power to be more truly informed in the Case. Whosoever presents not an Evil when he may, consents to it.

Now

NOW to oblige these Juries to the more conscientious care, to indict all that shall appear to them Criminals, and to save every Innocent, if it may be, from unjust Vexation, and Danger, by Malice and Conspiracy, our Ancestors appointed an Oath to be imposed upon them, which cannot be altered, except by Act of Parliament: Therefore every Grand-Jury-Man is sworn as the Foreman, in the Words following, *viz.*

You shall diligently enquire, and true Presentment make of all such Articles, Matters and Things as shall be given you in charge; and of all other matters and things as shall come to your own knowledge, touching this present Service. The King's Counsel, your Fellows, and your own, you shall keep secret: You shall present no Person for Hatred or Malice; neither shall you leave any one unpresented for Favour or Affection, for Love or Gain, or any hopes thereof; but in all things you shall present the Truth, the whole Truth, and nothing but the Truth, to the best of your knowledge; so help you God. The Tenor of the Oath is plain, saving in these words, *All such matters and things as shall be given you in charge:* But whensoever a general Commission of *Oyer* and *Terminer* is issued, all Capital Offences are always the principal matters given in charge to the Grand Jury, which is enough for the present discourse of their duty: Hence then it evidently appears, that every Grand Jury is bound to enquire diligently after the Truth of every thing, for which they shall indict or present any Man: They are not only bound by the eternal Law of loving their Neighbour, to be as tender of the Life and good Name of every Man, as of their own, and therefore to take heed to the Truth in accusing or indicting any Man; but their express Oath binds them to be diligent in their Enquiries, that is, to receive no suggestion of any Crime for Truth, without examining all the Circumstances about it, that fall within their knowledge; they ought to consider the first Informers, and enquire as far as they can into their Aims and Pretences in their prosecutions: if Revenge or Gain should appear to be their ends, there ought to be the greater suspicion of the Truth of their Accusations, the Law intending all Indictments to be for benefit of the King and of his People, as appears by the Stat. of 42 *E.* 3. 3. Next, the Jury are bound to enquire into the matters themselves, whereof any Man is accused, as to the Time, Place, and all other Circumstances of the Fact alledged. There have been false Informers, that have suggested things impossible; for instance, That Thirty Thousand Men in Arms were kept in readiness for an Exploit, in a secret place, as if they could have been hid in a Chamber, or a Cabinet. The Jury ought also to enquire after the Witnesses, their Condition and Quality, their Fame and Reputation, their Means of Subsistence, and the Occasion whereby the Facts, whereof they bear witness, came to their Knowledge. Sometimes Persons of debauched Lives, and low Condition, have deposed Discourses and Treasonable Councils again Persons of Honour and Virtue, so unlikely to come to their knowledge, (if such things had been) that their Pretence of being privy to them, was a strong Evidence that their whole story was false and feigned. It is also agreeable unto our ancient Law and Practice, and of great consequence in cases of Treason or Felony, that the Jury enquire after the time, when first the matters deposed came to the Witnesses knowledge, and whether they pursued the directions of the Law in the immediate discovery and pursuit of the Traitor or Felon, by Hue and Cry, or otherwise, or how long they concealed the same; their Testimony being of little or no value, if they have made themselves partakers of the Crime by their voluntary Concealment.

Neither may the Jury lawfully omit to enquire concerning the Parties accused, of their Quality, Reputation, and the Manner of their Conversation, with many other Circumstances; from whence they may be greatly helped to make right Inferences of the Falshood or Truth of the Crimes whereof any Man shall be accused. The Jury ought to be ignorant of nothing whereof they can enquire, or be informed, that may in their understandings enable them to make a true Presentment or Indictment of the matters before them.

When a Grand Jury is sworn to enquire diligently after all Treasons, *&c.* 'tis natural and necessary to their Business, to think of whom they should enquire; and 'tis plainly and easily resolved, that they ought to enquire of every Man that can or will inform them; and if any kind of Treason be suggested to them, to have been done by any Man, or number of Men, their Duty is the same in that particular, as it was in the general; that is, to seek diligently to find the Truth. 'Tis certainly inconsistent with their Oaths, to shut their Ears against any lawful Man that can tell them any thing relating unto a crime in question before them: No Man will believe, nor can they themselves think that they desire to find and present the Truth of a Fact, if they shall refuse to hear any Man who shall pretend such knowledge of it, or such material Circumstances, as may be useful to discover it; whether that which shall be said by the pretenders will answer the Jury's expectations, must rest in their Judgments, when they have heard them. It seems therefore, from the words of the Oath, that there is no bound or limit set (save their own Understanding or Conscience) to restrain them to any number or sort of Persons of whom they are bound to enquire;

they

they ought firſt and principally to enquire of one another mutually, what knowledge each of them hath of any matters in queſtion before them ; the Law preſumes that ſome at leaſt of ſo many ſufficient Men of a County, muſt know or have heard of all notable things done there againſt the publick Peace : for that end the Juries are by the Law to be of the Neighbourhood to the Place where the Crimes are committed. If the Parties, and the Facts whereof they are accuſed, be known to the Jury, or any of them, their own Knowledge will ſupply the room of many Witneſſes. Next, they ought to enquire of all ſuch Witneſſes as the Proſecutors will produce againſt the Accuſed ; they are bound to examine all fully and prudently to the beſt of their Skill ; every Jury-man ought to ask ſuch Queſtions (by the Foreman at leaſt) as he thinks neceſſary to reſolve any doubt that may ariſe in him, either about the Fact, or the Witneſſes, or otherwiſe : if the Jury be then doubtful, they ought to receive all ſuch further Teſtimony as ſhall be offered them, and to ſend for ſuch as any of them do think able to give Teſtimony in the Caſe depending.

If it be asked how, or in what manner the Juries ſhall enquire ; the Anſwer is ready, According to the beſt of their Underſtandings. They only, not the Judges, are ſworn to ſearch diligently to find out all Treaſons, &c. within their charge, and they muſt and ought to uſe their own diſcretion in the way and manner of their Enquiry : No directions can legally be impoſed upon them by any Court or Judges. An honeſt Jury will thankfully accept good Advice from Judges, as they are Aſſiſtants ; but they are bound by their Oaths to preſent the Truth, the whole Truth, and nothing but the Truth, to the beſt of their own, not the Judge's, knowledge : Neither can they, without breach of that Oath, reſign their Conſciences, or blindly ſubmit to the Dictates of others ; and therefore ought to receive, or reject ſuch Advices, as they judge them good or bad.

If the Jury ſuſpect a Combination of Witneſſes againſt any Man's Life, (which perhaps the Judges do not diſcern) and think it needful to examine them privately and ſeparately, the diſcretion of the Juries in ſuch a caſe, is their only beſt and lawful Guide, tho' the Example of all Ages and Countries, in examining ſuſpected Witneſſes privately and ſeparately, may be a good direction to them.

Nothing can be more plain and expreſs, than the Words of the Oath are to this purpoſe : The Jurors need not ſearch the Law-Books, nor tumble over heaps of old Records for the Explanation of them. Our greateſt Lawyers may from hence learn more certainly our ancient Law in this caſe, than from all the Books in their Studies. The Language wherein the Oath is penned, is known and underſtood by every Man, and the Words in it have the ſame ſignification, as they have whereſoever elſe they are uſed. The Judges (without aſſuming to themſelves a Legiſlative Power) cannot put a new Senſe upon them, other than according to their genuine, common meaning. They cannot magiſterially impoſe their Opinions upon the Jury, and make them forſake the direct Words of their Oath, to purſue their gloſſes. The Grand Inqueſt are bound to obſerve alike ſtrictly every part of their Oath ; and to uſe all juſt and proper ways which may enable them fully to perform it ; otherwiſe it were to ſay, that after Men had ſworn to enquire diligently after the Truth, according to the beſt of their knowledge, they were bound to forſake all the natural and proper means which their Underſtandings ſuggeſt for the Diſcovery of it, if it be commanded by the Judges.

And therefore if they are jealous of a Combination of the Witneſſes, or that Corruption or Subornation hath been made uſe of, they cannot be reſtrained from asking all ſuch Queſtions, as may conduce to the ſifting out of the Truth, nor from examining the *Fort. de Laud.* Witneſſes privately and ſeparately ; leſt (as *Forteſcue* ſays) the ſaying of one ſhould pro-
Leg Ang. cap. voke or inſtruct others to ſay the like.
26.
Nor are the Jury tied up to enquire only of ſuch Crimes as the Judges ſhall think fit to give them directly in charge, much leſs of ſuch Bills only as ſhall be offered to them ; but their Enquiry ought to extend to *All other matters and things that ſhall come to their Knowledge, touching the preſent Service.* If they have ground to ſuſpect that any Accuſation before them proceeds from a Conſpiracy, they are obliged by their Oath, to turn the Enquiry that way ; and if they find cauſe, not only to reject the Bills offered upon ſuch Teſtimonies, but to indict ſuch Witneſſes, and all the Abetters of their Villany.

They are carefully to examine what ſort of Men the Witneſſes are ; for 'tis a Rule in all Laws, That *Turpes à Tribunalibus arcentur*, Vile Perſons ought to be rejected by Courts of Juſtice. Such Witneſſes would deſtroy Juſtice inſtead of promoting it. And the Grand Jury are to take care of admitting ſuch : They may and ought (if they have no certain knowledge of them) to ask the Witneſſes themſelves of their Condition, and way of living, and all other Queſtions, which may beſt inform them what ſort of Men they are. 'Tis true, it may be lawful for the Witneſſes, in many caſes, to refuſe to give anſwer to ſome demands which the Jury may make ; as where it would be to accuſe themſelves of Crimes : but yet that very Refuſal, or avoiding to give direct Anſwers, may be of great
uſe

ufe to the Jury, whofe only Bufinefs is to find out the Truth; and who will be in a good meafure enabled to judge of the Credit of fuch Witneffes, as dare not clear themfelves of Crimes, which common Fame, or the Knowledge of fome of the Grand Inqueft has charged them with?

If the Witneffes which come before the Grand Jury upon an Indictment for Treafon, fhould difcover upon their Examination, that they concealed it a long time without juft Impediment; the prefumption of Law will be ftrong againft them, that no fenfe of Honefty or of their Duty brought them at laft to reveal it.

It appears by *Bracton*, that ancient Writer of our Laws, that in Cafes of Treafon the Juries were in his days advifed (as now they ought) to be fo fevere in their Enquiry within what time the Witneffes difcovered the Treafon after it came to their knowledge; that if it were not evident that they revealed it with as much expedition as was well poffible for them, they were not by Law to be heard as Witneffes: It was fcarce permitted them (faith he) *to look back* in their going; fuch ought to be their fpeed to make known the Treafon. Or if in cafe they be otherways openly flagitious, though they be not legally infamous, or if they are Men of defperate Fortunes, fo that the temptation of want is manifeftly ftrong upon them, and the reftraint of Confcience can be fuppofed to be little or none at all; whatever they fay is (at leaft) to be heard with extraordinary caution, if not totally rejected. In *Scotland* fuch a degree of Poverty, that a Witnefs cannot fwear himfelf to be worth Ten pounds, is fufficient to lay him afide wholly in thefe high Concernments of Criminal Cafes: And in fome other Kingdoms, to be a loofe liver, is an Objection of the fame force, againft any produced for Witneffes.

Brac. L. 3. c. 3.
Non morari debet, &c. nec debet ad aliqua negotia, quamvis urgentiffima, fe convertere, quia vix permittitur ei quod retro afpiciat, &c. Si poft intervallum accufare velit, non erit de Jure audiendus.
S. G. Mackenzy, Crim. Law, lib. 26. 3.

And for the better difcovery of the Truth of any Fact in queftion, the Credit of the Witneffes, and the Value of the Teftimonies, it is the duty of the Grand Inqueft to be well informed concerning the Parties indicted; of their ufual Refidence, their Eftates and Manner of living; their Companions and Friends with whom they are accuftomed to converfe; fuch Knowledge being neceffary to make a good Judgment upon moft Accufations; but moft of all in Sufpicions, or Indictments of fecret Treafons, or treafonable Words, where the Accufers can be of no Credit, if it be altogether incredible that fuch things as they teftify fhould come to their Knowledge.

Sometimes the Quality of the accufed Perfon may fet him at fuch a diftance from the Witneffes, that he cannot be fuppofed to have converfed with them familiarly, if his Wifdom and Conduct has been always fuch, that it is not incredible he would truft Men fo inconfiderable, or meer Strangers to him, and fuch as are wholly uncapable to affift in the Defign which they pretend to difcover.

Can the Grand Inqueft believe fuch Teftimony to be of any Value? Or can they avoid fufpecting Malice, Combination, and Subornation in fuch a Cafe? Or can they fhew themfelves to be juft, and confcientious in their Duty, if they do not fufpend their Verdict until further Enquiry, and write *Ignoramus* upon the Bill?

It is undoubtedly Law, which we find reported in *Stiles*, That *though there be Witneffes who prove the Bill, yet the Grand Inqueft is not bound to find it, if they fee caufe to the contrary.*

Stiles, Report 11.

Now to make their Enquiry more inftrumental and advantageous to the Execution of Juftice, they are enjoined by their Oath to keep fecret the *King's Counfel, their Fellows, and their own.* Perhaps 'tis not fufficiently underftood or confidered, what Duty is enjoined to every Man of a Grand Inqueft by this Claufe of their Oath, being feldom (if ever) explained to them in their general Charge of the Judges at Seffions or Affizes: But it is neceffary that they fhould apprehend what Counfel of the King is trufted with them. Certainly there is or ought to be much more of it communicated to them, than is commonly thought, and in things of the greateft confequence. To them ought to be committed in the feveral Counties where any Profecutions are begun, the firft Informations and Sufpicions of all Treafons, Murders, Felonies, Confpiracies, and other Crimes, which may fubvert the Government, endanger, or hurt the King, or deftroy the Lives or Eftates of the innocent People, or any way difquiet or difturb the common Peace. Our Law intends the Counfels of the King to be continually upon the protection and fecurity of the People, and prevention of all their mifchiefs and dangers by wicked, lawlefs, and injurious Men. And in order thereunto to be advifing how to right his wronged Subjects in general, if the publick Safety be hazarded by Treafons of any kind; or their Relations fnatcht from them by Murderers, or any way deftroy'd by malicious Confpirators in form of Law; or their Eftates taken away by Robbery and Thieves, or the Peace broken. And for thefe ends to bring to exemplary Juftice all Offenders, to deter others from the like wickednefs. And until thefe Counfels of the King come to the Grand Jury, he can bring no fuch Criminals to judgment, or to anfwer the Accufations and Suggeftions againft them. Hence it becomes unavoidably neceffary to reveal to the Grand Juries all that hath been difcover'd to the King or any of his Minifters, Judges, or Juftices, concerning any Treafons, or other Offences,

P p p

Offences, whereof any Man is accuſed. And where ſuſpicion has cauſed any to be impriſoned, all the Grounds of their ſuſpicions ought to be opened, concerning the Principals and Acceſſories, as well before as after the Fact, all the Circumſtances and Preſumptions that may induce a Belief of their Guilt, and all notices whatſoever, which may enable the Jury to make a more exact and effectual Enquiry, and to preſent the whole Truth. They themſelves will not only be offenders againſt God by reaſon of their Oath, but ſubject to legal Puniſhments, if they knowingly conceal any Criminals, and leave them unpreſented ; and none can be innocent, who ſhall conceal from them any thing that may help and aſſiſt them in their Duty.

The firſt notices of Crimes or Suſpicions of the Criminals, by whomſoever brought in, and the Intentions of ſearching them out, and proſecuting them legally, are called the King's Counſel, becauſe the principal care of executing Juſtice is entruſted to him, and they are to be proſecuted at his Suit, and in his Name ; and ſuch Proceedings are called Pleas of the Crown. From hence may be eaſily concluded, that the King's Counſel, which by the Oath of the Grand Inqueſt is to be kept ſecret, includeth all the Perſons offered to them to be indicted, and all the matters brought in Evidence before them, all Circumſtances whatſoever, whereof they are informed, which may any way conduce to the diſcovery of Offences ; all Intimations given them of Abettors and Encouragers of Treaſons, Felonies, or Perjuries and Conſpiracies, or of the Receivers, Harbourers, Nouriſhers, and Concealers of ſuch Criminals.

Likewiſe the Oath which enjoins the Counſel of their Fellows, and their own, to be kept, implies that they ſhall not reveal any of their perſonal Knowledge concerning Offences or Offenders ; nor their Intentions to indict any Man thereupon ; nor any of the Propoſals and Advices amongſt them of ways to enquire into the Truth of any matter before them, either about the Crimes themſelves, or the Accuſers and Witneſſes, or the Party accuſed, nor the Debates thereupon amongſt themſelves, nor the diverſity of Opinions in any caſe before them.

Certainly this Duty of ſecrecy concerning the King's Counſel was impoſed upon the Grand Inqueſt with great reaſon, in order to the publick Good. It was intended that they ſhould have all the Advantages which the ſeveral caſes will afford, to make effectual Enquiries after Criminals, to offer them to Juſtice. If packs of Thieves, private Murderers, ſecret Traitors, or Conſpirators and Suborners, can get intelligence of all that is known of their Villanies, all the Parties concerned may conſult together, how to hide their Crimes, and prevent ſuch further Enquiries as can be made after them ; they may form Sham-Stories by agreement, that may have appearance of Truth to miſlead and delude the Jury in their Examination, and avoid contradicting each other ; they may remove or conceal all ſuch things as might occaſion a fuller diſcovery of their Crimes, or become circumſtantial Evidences againſt any of their Aſſociates, if one or more of them be known or taken, or is to be indicted. There have been Confederates in high Crimes, who have ſecured themſelves from the Juſtice done upon ſome of their Companions, by their confident appearance and denial of the Fact, having been emboldened therein from the knowledge of all the grounds of Suſpicion, and all the Witneſſes examined about them, and the matter of their Teſtimonies. 'Tis too well known what helps of diſcovering the whole Popiſh Plot were loſt, thro' the want of keeping ſecret the King's Counſel therein, before the matter was brought either to the Parliament, or to any Grand Inqueſt ; and thereby they were diſabled for the effectual execution of their Offices, and could never ſearch into the Bowels of that dangerous Treaſon in any County. But our Law having placed this great truſt of Enquiry in the Prudence and Faithfulneſs of the Grand Inqueſt, was careful that they might not diſable themſelves for their own Truſt, by the Indiſcretion or worſe Fault of any of their own Number, in revealing the King's Counſel or their own.

And as it was intended hereby to preſerve unto them all reaſonable helps for their bringing to light the hidden Miſchiefs that might diſturb the common Peace ; ſo it was neceſſary to prevent the Flight of Criminals ; if the Evidence againſt one that is accuſed ſhould be publickly known, whether it ſhould be ſufficient for an Indictment of him, and how far it extends to others ; his Confederates and Accomplices might eaſily have notice of their Danger, and take Opportunity to eſcape from Juſtice.

Yet the reaſon will be ſtill more manifeſt for keeping ſecret the Accuſations and the Evidence by the Grand Inqueſt, if it be well conſidered, how uſeful and neceſſary it is for diſcovering Truth in the Examinations of Witneſſes in many, if not in moſt Caſes that may come before them ; when if by this privacy Witneſſes may be examined in ſuch manner and order, as Prudence and Occaſion direct ; and no one of them be ſuffered to know who hath been examined before him, nor what queſtions have been asked him, nor what anſwers he hath given, it may probably be found out whether a Witneſs hath been biaſſed in his Teſtimony by Malice or Revenge, or the Fear or Favour of Men in Power, or the

Love

Love or Hopes of Lucre and Gain in prefent or future, or Promifes of impunity for fome enormous Crime.

The fimplicity of Truth in a Witnefs may appear by the natural plainnefs, eafinefs, and directnefs of his Anfwers to whatfoever is propounded to him, by the equality of his Temper, and fuitablenefs of his Anfwers to queftions of feveral kinds, and perhaps to fome that may be asked for trial fake only of his uprightnefs in other matters. And the Falfenefs, Malice, or ill Defign of another, may be juftly fufpected from his ftudioufnefs and difficulty in anfwering; his Artifice and Cunning in what he relates, not agreeable to his way of Breeding and Parts; his referved, indirect, and evafive Replies to eafy Queftions; his pretences of doubtfulnefs, and want of remembring things of fuch fhort dates, or fuch Notoriety, that 'tis not credible he could be ignorant or forgetful of them. In this manner the Truth may be evidenced to the fatisfaction of the Jurors Confciences, by the very demeanor of the Witnefles in their private Examinations, inafmuch as the greateft certainty doth often arife from the careful obfervation and comparing of fuch minute Matters; of which a diftinct Account is not poffible to be given to a Court: And for that Reafon (among others) the Juries are made the only abfolute Judges of their Evidence.

Yet further, Their private Examination may difcover Truth out of fome difagreement of the Witnefles, when feparately interrogated, and every of the Grand Inqueft ask them Queftions for his own Satisfaction about the matters which have come to his particular Knowledge; and this freely, without Awe or Controul of Judges, or diftruft of his own Parts, or fear to be checked for asking impertinent Queftions.

Confpiracies againft the Lives of the Innocent in a form of Juftice, have been frequently detected by fuch fecret and feparate Examination of Witnefles. The Story of *Sufanna* is famous; that two of their Elders and Judges of great Credit and Authority, teftified in the open Affembly a malicious Invention againft her, with all the folemnity ufed in capital Cafes, and Sentences of Death paffed upon her, and was ready to be executed, had not wife *Daniel* cried out in her Behalf: *Are ye fuch Fools, O Ifraelites, that without examination, or knowledge of the Truth, ye have condemned a Daughter of Ifrael? Return* (faid he) *again to judgment, and put thefe two one far from another, and I will examine them.* And being asked feparately (tho' in publick, the Teftimony having been fo given before) concerning the Place of the Fact then in queftion, they had not agreed upon that Circumftance, as they had upon their Story; and fo their Falfhood became manifeft, one faying, *the Adultery was committed under a Lentisk Tree,* the other, *it was under a Pine Tree:* And upon that conviction of the falfe Witnefles, the whole Affembly cried with a loud Voice, and praifed God. Thefe falfe Witnefles were put to death, as the Law required.

Note, That the Teftimony given in the Affembly without feparating the Witnefles, and trying the Truth by Circumftances, was efteemed no Examination, or knowledge of the Truth.

We have alfo a late Inftance of the Ufefulnefs of private and feparate Examinations, in the Cafe of the Lord *Howard,* againft whom the Attorney-General profecuted an Accufation of Treafon, the laft *Midfummer* Term, before the Grand Inqueft for *Middlefex.* Mrs. *Fitz-Harris,* and *Terefa Peacock* her Maid, fwore words of Treafon againft him pofitively, and agreed in every Point whilft they were together: But by the prudence of the Inqueft, being put afunder, and the Miftrefs asked how her Maid came to be admitted to the knowledge of fuch Matters; fhe had an Evafion ready, pretending her Maid to have craftily hearkened behind a Wainfcot Door, and fo heard the Treafon. But the Maid not fufpecting what her Miftrefs had faid, continued her firft Story, that fhe heard the Treafon from the Lord *Howard* himfelf, and was as much trufted by him as her Miftrefs: By this Circumftance the Falfhood and Perjury (which Mrs. *Fitz-Harris* hath fince acknowledged) was difcovered, and the Snare for the Life of the injured Lord was broken, as is manifeft by his Liberty now obtained by Law.

Witnefles may come prepared, and tell plaufible Stories in open Court, if they know from the Profecutor to what they muft anfwer; and have agreed and acquainted each other with the Tales they will tell; and have refolved to be careful, that all their Anfwers to crofs Interrogatories, may be conformable to their firft Stories: And if thefe relate only to Words fpoken at feveral times in private to diftinct Witnefles, in fuch a cafe, Evidence, if given in open Court, may feem to be very ftrong againft the Perfon accufed, though there be nothing of Truth in it. But if fuch Witnefles were privately and feparately examined by the Grand Inqueft, as the Law requires, and were to anfwer only fuch Queftions as they thought fit, and in fuch order as was beft in their Judgments, and moft natural to find out the Truth of the Accufation, fo that the Witnefles could not guefs what they fhould be asked firft, or laft, nor one conjecture what the other had faid, (which they are certain of, when they know beforehand what the Profecutor will ask in Court of every of them, and what they have refolved to anfwer) if the Inqueft fhould put them out of their Road, and then compare all their feveral Anfwers together, they might poffibly difcern marks enough of Falfhood, to fhew that their Teftimonies ought not to be depended upon, where Life is in queftion.

By

By what is now faid, the reafonablenefs of this Inftitution of Secrecy may be difcerned in refpect to the difcovery of Truth, and the protection of the Innocent from malicious Combinations and Perjuries. Yet the fame Secrecy of the King's Counfel is no lefs neceffary to referve the guilty for punifhment; when the Evidence againft any party accufed is not manifeft and full, it may be kept without prejudice under Secrecy until further enquiry; and if fufficient proof can afterwards be made of the Offence, an Indictment may be found by a Grand Inqueft, and the Party brought to anfwer it: But when the Examinations are in open Court, or the King's Counfel any other way divulged, and the Evidence is weak, and lefs than the Law requires, 'tis not probable that it will be more or ftronger; and fhould an Indictment be found, and the Party tried by a Petit Jury, whilft the Evidence is not full, they muft and ought to acquit him, and then the further profecution for the fame Offence is for ever barred, though his guilt fhould afterwards be manifeft, and confeffed by himfelf.

From hence may certainly be concluded, That Secrecy in the Examinations and Enquiries of Grand Juries is in all refpects for the intereft and advantage of the King. If he be concerned to have fecret Treafon, Felonies, and all other Enormities brought to light, and that none of the Offenders fhould efcape Juftice; if the gain of their Forfeitures be thought his Intereft (which God forbid) then the firft notices of all dangerous Crimes, and wicked Confederacies ought to be fecretly and prudently purfued and fearch'd into by the Grand Inqueft; the Accufers and Witneffes ought not to publifh in a Court before a multitude what they pretend to know in fuch Cafes, until the difcretion of fo many honeft Men of the Neighbourhood hath firft determined whether their Teftimony will amount to fo good and full Evidence, that it may be made publick with fafety to the King and People in order to Juftice. Elfe they are obliged by Oath to lock up in their own Breafts all the Circumftances and Prefumptions of Crimes, until they, or fuch as fhall fucceed in the fame Truft, fhall have difcovered (as they believe) Evidence enough to convict the Accufed; and then, and not before, they are to accufe the Party upon Record, by finding the Bills, (as it's ufually called.) But when Bills are offered without fatisfactory Evidence, and they neither know, nor can learn any more, they ought for the King's fake to indorfe *Ignoramus* upon them, left his Honour and Juftice be ftained, by caufing or permitting fuch Profecution of his People in his own name, and at his Suit, as fhall appear upon their Tryal and Acquittal to have been frivolous, or elfe malicious defigns upon their Lives and Fortunes.

If it fhould be faid, That whatfoever Reafons there are for this Oath of Secrecy, yet it cannot deprive the King of the benefit of having the Evidence made publick, if he defires it; and that the Grand Jury do not break their Oaths, when the King, or the Profecutor for him, will have it fo: 'Tis not hard to fhew, that fuch Notions have no foundation in Law or Reafon, and feem to come from Men who have not well ftudied the firft Principles of the *Englifh* Government, or of True Religion.

Whofoever hath learnt that the Kings of *England* were ordained for the good Government of the Kingdom in the Execution of the Laws, muft needs know, that the King cannot lawfully feek any other benefit in judicial Proceedings, than that common Right and Juftice be done to the People according to their Laws and Cuftoms. Their Safety and Profperity are to be the Objects of his continual Care and Study, that being the higheft concern. The Greatnefs and Honour of a Prince confifts in the Virtue, Multitude, Wealth and Prowefs of his People; and the greateft Glory is, by the excellency of his Government fo to have encouraged Virtue and Piety, that few or no Criminals are to be found in his Dominions. Thofe who have made this their principal aim, have in fome places fo well fucceeded, as to introduce fuch a Difcipline and Rectitude of Manners, as rendred e-
Gar. de la very man a Law unto himfelf. As it is reported in the Hiftory of *Peru*, that though the
Veg. Hift. de Laws were fo fevere as to make very fmall Crimes capital, yet it often fell out, that not
los Incas. one man was put to death in a year, within the whole compafs of that vaft Empire.

The King's only benefit in finding out and punifhing Offenders by Courts of Juftice, are the prefervation and fupport of the Government, the protection of the Innocent, revenging their wrongs, and preventing further mifchiefs by the terrors of exemplary Punifhments.

The King is the head of Juftice in the efteem of our Laws, and the whole Kingdom is to expect right to be done them in his feveral Courts inftituted by Law for that purpofe. Therefore Writs iffue out in his name in all cafes where relief is fought by the Subject; and the wrongs done to the Lives or Limbs of the People, are faid to be done againft the Peace of the King, his Crown and Dignity; reckoning it a difhonour to him and his Government, that Subjects fhould not, whilft they live within the Law, enjoy Peace and Security. It ought to be taken for a fcandal upon the King, when he is reprefented in a Court of Juftice as if he were partially concerned, or rather inclined to defire, that a Party accufed fhould be found guilty, than that he fhould be declared innocent, if he be fo in truth. Doubtlefs the
King

King ought to wish in all Enquiries made after Treason, Felonies, &c. that there were none to be found in his Kingdom ; and that whosoever is accused, might be able to answer so well and truly for himself, as to shew the Accusation to be erroneous or false, and to be acquitted of it. Something of this appears in the common Custom of *England*, that the Clerks of the King's Courts of Justice, when any man hath pleaded Not guilty to an Indictment, pray forthwith that God would send him a good deliverance.

The destruction of every Criminal is a loss to a Prince, and ought to be grievous to him, in the common regard of humanity, and the more particular relation of his Office, and the name of Father. The King's Interest and Honour is more concerned in the protection of the Innocent, than in the punishment of the Guilty. This Maxim can never run them into excesses ; for it hath ever been lookt upon as a mark of great Wisdom and Vertue in some Princes and States, upon several occasions to destroy all Evidences against Delinquents ; and nothing is more useful than to compose the most dangerous Distempers of Nations by Acts of general Amnesty, which were utterly unjust, if it were as great a Crime to suffer the Guilty to escape, as to destroy the Innocent. We do not only find those Princes represented in History under odious Characters, who have basely murthered the Innocent, but such as by their Spies and Informers were too inquisitive after the Guilty ; whereas none was ever blamed for Clemency, or for being too gentle Interpreters of the Laws. Tho' *Trajan* was an excellent Prince, endowed with all heroical Virtues; yet the most Eloquent Writers, and his best Friends, found nothing more to be praised in his Government, than that in his time, all men might think what they pleased, and every man speak what he thought ; and he had no better way of distinguishing himself from his wicked Predecessors, than by hanging up the Spies and Informers, whom they had employed for the discovery of Crimes. But if the punishment of Offenders were as universally necessary as the protection of the Innocent, he were as much to be abhorred as *Nero* ; and that Clemency which is so highly praised, were to be lookt upon as the worst of Vices ; and those who have hitherto been taken for the best of Princes, were altogether as detestable as the worst. *Tacit.* lib. i. Hist.

Moreover, all human Laws were ordained for the preservation of the Innocent; and for their sakes only are punishments inflicted ; that those of our own Country do solely regard this, was well understood by *Fortescue*, who saith, *Indeed I could rather wish Twenty Evildoers to escape death through pity, than one man to be unjustly condemned. Such Blood hath cried to Heaven for Vengeance against Families and Kingdoms, and their utter destruction hath ensued. If a Criminal should be acquitted by too great lenity, caution, or otherwise, he may be reserved for future Justice from Man or God, if he doth not repent ; but 'tis impossible that satisfaction or reparation should be made for innocent Bloodshed, in the forms of Justice* *Fort.* deLaud. Leg. Ang ch. 27.

Without all question, the King's only just Interest in the Evidence given against the Party accused and in the manner of taking it, is to have the truth made manifest, that Justice may thereupon be done impartially : And if Accusations may be first examined in secret more strictly and exactly, to prevent Fraud and Perjury, than is possible to be done in open Court, (as hath before appeared) then it is for the King's benefit to have it so. And nothing done in, or by a Court, about the Trial of the Accused, is for the King, (in the sense of our Law) unless it some way conduce to Justice in the case. The Witnesses which the Prosecutor brings, are no further for the King, than they tell the truth, and the whole truth impartially ; and by whomsoever any others may be called, upon the Enquiry, or the Trial, to be examined, if they sincerely deliver the truth of the matters in question, they are therein the King's Witnesses, though the Accused be acquitted by reason of their Testimonies. If such as are offered by the Attorney-General to prove Treason against any man, shall be found to swear falsly, maliciously, or for Reward or Promises, though they depose positively Facts of Treason against the Accused, yet they are truly and properly Witnesses against the King, by endeavouring to prevent Justice, and destroy his Subjects : Their Malice and Villany being confessed or proved, the King's Attorney ought (*ex Officio*) to prosecute them in the King's Name, and at his Suit, for their Offences against him in such Depositions pretended to have been for him ; and the legal Form of the Indictment ought to be for their swearing falsly and maliciously against the Peace of the King, his Crown and Dignity. The Prosecutors themselves, notwithstanding their big words, and assuming to themselves to be for the King, if their Prosecution shall be proved to be malicious, or by Conspiracy against the Life or Fortune of the Accused, they are therein against the King, and ought to be indicted at the King's Suit, for such Prosecutions done against his Crown and Dignity. And if an Attorney-General should be found knowingly guilty of abetting such a Conspiracy, his Office could not excuse or legally exempt him from suffering the villanous Judgment to the destruction of him and his Family. 'Tis esteemed in the Law one of the most odious Offences against the King, to attempt in his Name to destroy the Innocent, for whose Protection he himself was ordained. Queen *Elizabeth* had the true sense of our Law, when

Q q q

4

Co. Inſt. 3d
part, p. 79. when the Lord *Burleigh,* upon Sir *Edward Coke* her then Attorney's coming into her preſence, told her, This is he who proſecutes *pro Domina Regina,* for our Lady the Queen ; and ſhe ſaid ſhe would have the form of the Records altered ; for it ſhould be *Attornatus Generalis qui pro Domina veritate ſequitur.* The Attoney-General who proſecutes for our Lady the Truth. Whoever is truſted in that employment, diſhonours his Maſter and Office, if he gives occaſion to the Subjects to believe that his Maſter ſeeks other profits or advantages by Accuſations, than the common Peace and Welfare : He ought not to excite a jealouſy in any of their minds, that Confiſcations of Eſtates are deſigned or deſired by any of the King's Miniſters ; whoſoever makes ſuch advantages to the Crown, their principal aim in accuſing, are either Robbers and Murtherers, (in the Scripture-ſenſe) in ſeeking innocent Blood for gain ; or in the mildeſt Conſtruction, (ſuppoſing the Accuſation to be on good grounds) they ſhew themſelves to be of corrupt minds, and a ſcandal to their Maſter, and the Government: Profit or loſs of that kind ought to have no place in judicial proceedings againſt ſuſpected Criminals, but truth is only to be regarded ; and for this reaſon the Judgments given in Court of human Inſtitution, are in Scripture called, the Judgments of God, who is the God of truth.

Yet further, if any benefit to the King could be imagined by making the Evidence to the Grand Jury publick, it could not come in competition with the Law expreſſed in their Oath ; which by conſtant and uninterrupted uſage, for ſo many Ages, hath obtained the force of Law. *Bracton* and *Britton* in their ſeveral Generations bear witneſs, that it was then practiſed ; and greater proof of it needs not be ſought, than the Diſputes that appear by the Law-Books to have been amongſt the ancient Lawyers, whether it was Treaſon or Felony for a Grand Jury to diſcover, either who was indicted, or what Evidence was given them. The Truſt of the Grand Juries was thought ſo ſacred in thoſe Ages, and their ſecrecy of ſo great concern to the Kingdom, that whoſoever ſhould break their Oath there-

Co. Inſtit. 3d
part, p. 107.
Roll's Indic.
771. in, was by all thought worthy to die ; only ſome would have had them ſuffer as Traytors, others as Felons. And at this day it is held to be a high Miſpriſion, puniſhable by Fine and Impriſonment. The Law then having appointed the Evidence to be given to Grand Juries in ſecret, the King cannot deſire to have it made publick. He can do no wrong, ſaith the old Maxim, that is, he can do nothing againſt the Law ; nor is any thing to be judged for his benefit that is not warranted by Law : His Will, Commands, and Deſires, are therein no otherwiſe to be known. He cannot change the legal Method or Manner of enquiring by Juries, nor vary in any particular caſe from the cuſtomary and general Forms of judicial proceedings ; he can neither abridge nor enlarge the power of Juries, no more than he can leſſen the legal Power, of the Sheriffs or Judges, or by ſpecial Direction order the one how they ſhall execute Writs, and the other how they ſhall give Judgments, though theſe made by himſelf.

'Tis criminal, no doubt, for any to ſay, that the King deſires a Court of Juſtice or a Jury, to vary from the direction of the Law, and they ought not to be believed therein: If Letters, Writs, or other Commands ſhould come to the Judges for that purpoſe, they are bound by their Oaths not to regard them, but to hold them for null ; the Statutes of 2 *E.* 3. 8. and 20 *E.* 3. 1. are expreſs, That if any Writs, or Commandments come to the Juſtices in diſturbance of the Law, or the Execution of the ſame, or of right to the Parties, they ſhall proceed as if no ſuch Letters, Writs, or Commands were come to them : And the ſubſtance of theſe and other Statutes is inſerted into the Oath taken by every Judge ; and if they be under the moſt ſolemn and ſacred Tye in the Execution of Juſtice, to hold for nothing or none, the Commands of the King under the Great Seal, ſurely the Word, or Deſire of an Attorney-General, in the like caſe, ought to be leſs than nothing.

Beſides, they are ſtrangely miſtaken, who think the King can have an Intereſt different from, or contrary unto that of the Kingdom, in the proſecution of Accuſed Perſons : His Concernments are involved in thoſe of his People ; and he can have none diſtinct from them. He is the Head of the Body Politick ; and the legal Courſe of doing Juſtice, is like the orderly Circulation of the Blood in the Natural Bodies, by which both Head and Body are equally preſerved, and both periſh by the interruption of it.

The King is obliged to the utmoſt of his Power, to maintain the Law, and Juſtice in its due courſe, by his Coronation-Oath, and the Truſt thereby repoſed in him. In former Ages he was conjured not to take the Crown, unleſs he reſolved punctually to obſerve *Brom.*p.1159
Mat. Paris,
p. 153. it. *Bromton* and others, ſpeaking of the Coronation of *Richard* the firſt, delivered it thus ; That having firſt taken the Oath, *deinde indutus Mantello, ductus eſt ad Altare, & conjuratus ab Archiepiſcopo, & prohibitus ex parte Dei ne hunc Honorem ſibi aſſumat, niſi in mente habeat tenere Sacramenta & Vota quæ ſuperius fecit. Et ipſe reſpondit, ſe per Dei auxilium omnia ſupradicta obſervaturum bona fide. Deinde cepit Coronam de Altari, & tradidit eam*

Archie-

Archiepiscopo, qui posuit eam super caput Regis ; & sic Coronatus Rex, ductus est ad sedem suam. Afterward clothed with the Royal Robe, he is led to the Altar, and conjured by the Archbishop, and forbid in the Name of God, not to assume that Honour, unless he intended to keep the Oaths and Vows he had before made ; and he answered, By God's help he would faithfully observe all the Premises : and then he took the Crown from off the Altar, and delivered it to the Archbishop, who put it upon the King's Head, and the King thus crowned, is led unto his Seat. The violation of which Trust cannot but be as well a wound unto their Consciences, as bring great Prejudice upon their Persons and Affairs.

The Common-Law that exacts this, doth so far provide for Princes, That having their minds free from cares of preserving themselves, they may rest assured, that no Acts, Words, or Designs, that may bring them into danger, can be concealed from the many Hundreds of Men, who by the Law are appointed in all parts of the Kingdom, watchfully to take care of the King ; and are so far concerned in his safety, that they can hope no longer to enjoy their own Lives and Fortunes in Peace, than they can preserve him, and the good Order which according to the Laws he is to uphold.

It is the joint Interest of King and People, that the ancient Rules of doing Justice be held sacred and inviolable ; and they are equally concerned in causing strict enquiries to be made into all Evidence given against suspected or accused Persons, that the Truth may be discovered ; and such as dare to disturb the Publick Peace, by breaking the Laws, may be brought to punishment. And the whole course of Judicial Proceedings in Criminal Causes, shews that the People are therein equally concerned with the King, whose name is used. This is the ground of that distinction which Sir *Ed. Coke* makes between the Proceedings in Pleas of the Crown, and Actions for wrongs done to the King himself. *In Pleas of the Crown, or other common Offences, Nusances, &c. principally concerning others, or* Co. 3d. Inst. *the Publick, there the King by Law must be apprised by Indictment, Presentment, or other* pag. 136. *matter of Record ; but the King may have an Action for such wrong as is done to himself, and whereof none other can have an Action but the King, without being apprised by Indictment, Presentment, or other matter of Record, as a* Quare impedit, Quare incumbravit, *a Writ of Attaint, of Debt, Detinue of Ward, Escheat, Scire fac. pur repealer patent, &c. unto* which every Man must answer : But no Man can be brought to answer for Publick Crimes at the King's Suit, otherwise than by Indictment of a Grand Jury

The whole Course of doing Justice upon Criminals, from the beginning of the Process, unto the Execution of the Sentence, is, and ever was esteemed to be the Kingdom's concernment, as is evidenced by the frequent Complaints made in Parliament, that Capital Offenders were pardon'd to the People's damage and wrong. In the 13 *Rich.* 2. it is said, that the King hearing the grievous complaints of his Commons in Parliament, of the outrageous mischiefs which happened unto the Realm, for that Treasons, Murders, and Rapes of Women be commonly done, and committed, and the more, because Charters of Pardon had been easily granted, in such Cases ; and thereupon it was enacted, That no Pardon for such Crimes should be granted, unless the same were particularly specified therein ; and if a Pardon were otherwise granted for the Death of a Man, the Judges should notwithstanding enquire by a Grand Jury, of the Neighbourhood, concerning the Death of every such Person, and if he were found to have been wilfully murthered, such Charter or Pardon to be disallowed ; and provisions were made by imposing grievous Fines upon every person, according to his Degree and Quality, or Imprisonment, who should presume to sue to the King for any Pardons of the aforesaid Crimes, and that such persons might be known to the whole Kingdoms, their Names were to be upon several Records. The like had been done in many Statutes made by several Parliaments, as in the 6 *Ed.* 1. 9. the 2 *Ed.* 3. 2. the 10 *Ed.* 3. 2. and the 14 *Ed.* 3. 15. where it was acknowleged by the King in Parliament, *That the Oath of the Crown had not been kept, by reason of the Grant of Pardons contrary to the aforesaid Statutes ; and Enacted, that any such Charter or Pardon, from thenceforth granted against the Oath of his Crown, and the said Statutes, the same should be holden for none.* In the 27 *Edw.* 3. 2. it is further provided, for preventing the People's damage by such Pardons, *That from thenceforth in every Charter of Pardon of Felony, which shall be granted at any man's suggestion, the said suggestion, and the name of him that maketh the suggestion, shall be comprised in the same Charter ; and if after the same suggestion be found untrue, the Charter shall be disallowed and holden for none : And the Justices before whom such Charter shall be alledged, shall enquire of the same suggestion, and that as well of Charters granted before this time, as of which shall be granted in time to come ; and if they find them untrue, then they shall disallow the Charter so alledged, and shall moreover do as the Law demandeth.*

Thus have Parliaments from time to time declared, that the Offences against the Crown are against the publick welfare, and that Kings are obliged by their Oath and Office to

cause

4

9 Hen. 3. 29. cauſe Juſtice to be done upon Traytors and Felons for the Kingdom's ſake; according to the ancient Common-Law, declared by *Magna Charta* in theſe words: *Nulli nega-bimus, nulli vendemus, nulli differemus Juſtitiam.* We will ſell to no Man, we will not deny or defer to any Man either Juſtice or Right.

And as the Publick is concerned, that the due and legal Methods be obſerved in the Proſecution of Offenders, ſo likewiſe doth the ſecurity of every ſingle Man in the Nation depend upon it : No Man can aſſure himſelf he ſhall not be accuſed of the higheſt crimes. Let a Man's Innocence and Prudence be what it will, yet his moſt inoffenſive Words and Actions are liable to be misconſtrued ; and he may, by Subornation and Conſpiracy, have things laid to his charge, of which he is no ways guilty. Who can ſpeak to carry himſelf with that circumſpection, as not to have his harmleſs Words or Actions wreſted to ano-ther ſenſe than he intended ? Who can be ſecure from having a Paper put into his Pockets, or laid in his Houſe, of which he ſhall know nothing till his Accuſation ? Hiſtory affords many Examples of the deteſtable Practices in this kind of wicked Court-Paraſites, among

Polyb. *lib.* 5. which one may ſuffice for Inſtance, out of *Polybius,* an approved Author: *Hermes,* a power-ful Favourite, under *Antiochus* the younger, but a Man noted to be a favourer of Lyars, was made uſe of againſt the innocent and brave *Epigenes:* ' He had long watch'd to kill him, ' for that he found him a Man of great Eloquence and Valour, having alſo Favour and ' Authority with the King : He had unjuſtly, but unſucceſsfully, accuſed him of Treaſon ' by falſe gloſſes put upon his faithful Advice given to the King in open Council ; this not ' prevailing, he by artifice got him put out of his Command, and to retire from Court, ' which done, he laid a Plot againſt him, with the help and Council of (one of his Com-' plices) *Alexis,* and writing Letters as if they had been ſent from *Molon,* (who was ' then in open Rebellion againſt his Prince for fear, amongſt other Reaſons, of the Cruelty ' and Treachery of *Hermes*) and corrupted one of *Alexis*'s Servants with great Promiſes, ' who went to *Epigenes,* to thruſt the Letters ſecretly among his other Writings ; which ' when he had done, *Alexis* came ſuddenly to *Epigenes,* demanding of him if he had re-' ceived any Letter from *Molon :* And when he ſaid he had none, the other ſaid, he was ' confident he ſhould find ſome ; wherefore entering the Houſe to ſearch, he found the ' Letters, and taking this occaſion, ſlew him, (leſt if the Fact had been duly exami-' ned, the Conſpiracy had been diſcovered.) Theſe things happening thus, the King ' thought that he was juſtly ſlain ; in this manner the worthy *Epigenes* ended his days : ' But this great Man's deſigns did not reſt here ; for within a while, heightned with ſuc-' ceſs, he ſo arrogantly abuſed his Maſter's Authority, as he grew dangerous to the King ' himſelf, as well as to thoſe about him ; inſomuch as *Antiochus* was forced, for that he ' hated and feared *Hermes,* to take away his Life by Stratagem, thereby to ſecure himſelf.' By theſe and a thouſand other ways, the moſt unblemiſh'd Innocence may be brought into the greateſt danger. Since then every Man is thus eaſily ſubject to queſtion, and what is one Man's Caſe this day, may be another Man's to-morrow, it is undoubtedly every Man's concern, to ſee (as far as in him lies) in every caſe, that the accuſed Perſon may have the benefit of all ſuch proviſions, as the Law hath made for the defence of In-nocence and Reputation.

Now to this end there is nothing ſo neceſſary as the ſecret and ſeparate examination of Witneſſes, though perhaps (as hath been already obſerved) it may be no very diffi-cult thing for ſeveral perſons, who are permitted to diſcourſe with each other freely, and to hear, or be told what each of their fellows had been asked and anſwered, to agree in one ſtory, eſpecially if the Jury may not ask what queſtions they ſhall think fit for the ſatisfaction of their own Conſciences ; but that they ſhall be ſo far under the correction and cenſure of the Judges, as to have the queſtions which they put, called by them trifles, impertinent, and unfit for the Witneſſes to ſpeak to ; yet if they be examined apart, with that due care of ſifting out all the Circumſtances which the Law requires, where every Man of the Jury is at full liberty to enquire into any thing for his clearer Information, and that with what deliberation they think fit, and all this be done with that ſecrecy which the Law commands ; it will be almoſt impoſſible for a Man to ſuffer under a falſe Accuſation.

Nor has the Law been leſs careful for the Reputation of the Subjects of *England,* than for their Lives and Eſtates, and this ſeems to be one reaſon why in criminal Caſes, a Man ſhall not be brought to an open legal Tryal by a Petit Jury, till the Grand Jury have firſt found the Bill : The Law having entruſted the Grand Inqueſt in a ſpecial manner with their good names ; they are therefore not only to enquire whe-ther the fact that is laid, was done by the party accuſed, but into the circumſtances there-of too, whether it was done Traitorouſly, Feloniouſly, or Maliciouſly, *&c.* according to the manner charged ; which Circumſtances are not barely matter of form, but do conſtitute
the

the very essence of the Crime ; and lastly into the Credit of the Witnesses, and that of the Party accused, and unless they find both the Fact proved upon him, and strong presumptions of such aggravating circumstances attending it, as the Law requires in the specification of such Crime, and likewise are satisfied in the credibility of the Witnesses ; they ought not to expose the Subject to an open Trial in the face of the County, to a certain loss of his Reputation, and hazard of his Life and Estate. Moreover, should this practice of publick Examination prevail, and the Jurors Oath of Secrecy continue, how partial and unequal a thing would it be to declare that to all the World, which will blast a Man's good name, and religiously conceal what they may know tending to his Justification : To examine Witnesses (perhaps suborned) certainly prepared, and have Evidence dressed up with all the advantages that Lawyers wits can give it, of the foulest Crimes a Man can be guilty of, and this given before some thousands against him, and yet for the same Court to swear those, whom the Law makes Judges in the Case, not to reveal one word of those reasons, which have satisfied their Consciences of his Innocence ; what is this, but an Artifice of slandering men (it may be) of the most unspotted Conversation, and of abusing Authority, not so much to find Men guilty, as to make them infamous ? After this Ignominy is fixed, what Judgment can the Auditors (and from them the World) make, but of high probability of guilt in the party accused, and Perjury in the Jury.

This course, if it should be continued, must needs be of most dangerous consequence to all sorts of Men ; it will both subject every one without relief to be defamed, and fright the best and most conscientious Men, from serving on Grand-Juries, which is a most necessary part of their duty. Now since there is in our Government (as in every one that is well constituted there ought to be) great liberty of Accusation, that no Man may be encouraged to do ill through hopes of impunity, if by this means a Method be opened, for the blasting the most innocent Man's honour, and deterring the most honest from being his Judges ; what remains, but that every Man's Reputation, which is most dear unto such as are good, is held precariously, and it will be in the power of great Men to pervert the Laws, and take away whose Life and Estate they please, or at least to fasten imputations of the most detested Crimes upon any, whom, for secret reasons, they have a mind to defame. The consequences of which scandal, as they are very mischievous to every Man, so in a Trading Country in a more especial manner, to all who live by any vocation of that kind.

The greatest part of Trade is driven upon credit, most Men of any considerable Employment, dealing for much more than they are truly worth, and every Man's credit depends as well upon his behaviour to the Government he lives under, as upon his private honesty in his transactions between Man and Man : so that the suspicion only of his being obnoxious to the Government is enough to set all his Creditors upon his back, and put a stop to all his Affairs, perhaps to his utter ruin. What expedition and violence will they all use to recover their debts, when he shall be publickly charged with such Crimes as forfeit Life and Estate ? Though there should not be one word of the Accusation true, yet they knowing the Charge and the seeming proofs in the Court, and the Consequences of it, and not being acquainted with the truth, as it appears to the Jury, self-interest will make his Creditors to draw in their effects, which is no more than a new contrivance, under colour of Law, of undoing honest Men.

If to prevent any of these mischiefs the Jury should discover their fellows and their own Counsel, as the Court by publick Examination doth, it would not only be a wilful breach of their Oath, but a betraying of the trust which the Law has reposed in them, for the security of the Subject : For to subject the reasons of their Verdicts upon Bills to the censure of the Judges, were to divest themselves of the Power which the Law has given them, for most important Considerations, without account or controul, and to interest those in it, whom the Law has not in this case trusted ; and so by degrees, the course of Justice in one of the most material parts may be changed, and a fundamental security of our Liberty and Property insensibly lost. On the other hand, if for fear of being unworthily reproached as *Ignoramus* Jury-Men, obstinate Fellows, that obstruct Justice, and disserve the King, the Grand-Jury shall suffer the Judges, or the King's Counsel to prevail with them to indorse *Billa vera*, when their Consciences are not satisfied in the truth of the Accusation, they act directly against their Oaths, oppress the Innocent, whom they ought to protect ; as far as in them lies, subject their Country, themselves, and posterity to arbitrary Power, pervert the Administration of Justice, and overthrow the Government, which is instituted for the obtaining of it, and subsists by it.

This seems to be the greatest Treason, that can be committed against the whole Kingdom, and threatens ruin unto every Man in private in it. None can be safe against

authorized

authorized Malice, and notwithstanding the care of our Anceftors, Rapine, Murther, and the worft of Crimes may be advanced by the formality of Verdicts, if Grand-Juries be overawed, or not fuffered to enquire into the Truth, to the fatisfaction of their Confciences. Every Man whilft he lives innocently, doth, under God, place his hopes of fecurity in the Law, which can give no protection, if its due courfe be fo interrupted, that frauds cannot be difcovered; Witneffes may as well favour Offenders, as give falfe teftimony againft the guiltlefs; and if they, by hearing what each other faith, are put into a way of concealing their villainous defigns, there can be no legal Revenge of the crimes already committed. Others by their impunity will be encouraged to do the like: And every quiet-minded Perfon will be equally expofed unto private injuries, and fuch as may be done unto him, under the colour of Law. No man can promife unto himfelf any fecurity for his Life or Goods, and they who do not fuffer the utmoft violences in their own perfons, may do it in their Children, Friends, and neareft Relations, if he be deprived of the remedies that the Law ordains, and forced to depend upon the Will of a Judge, who may be, and (perhaps we may fay) are too often corrupted, or fwayed by their own Paffions, Interefts, or the impulfe of fuch as are greater than they. This mifchief is aggravated by a commonly received Opinion, that whofoever fpeaks againft an accufed perfon is the King's Witnefs; and the worft of men, in their worft defigns, do ufually fhelter themfelves under that name, whereas he only is the King's Witnefs, who fpeaks the truth, whether it be for or againft him that is accufed. As the Power of the King is the Power of the Law, he can have no other intention than that of the Law, which is to have Juftice impartially adminiftred; and as he is the Father of his People, he cannot but incline ever to the gentleft fide, unlefs it be poffible for a Father to delight in the deftruction, or defire to enrich himfelf by the confifcation of his Childrens Eftates. If the moft wicked Princes have had different thoughts, they have been obliged to diffemble them. We know of none worfe than *Nero*, but he was fo far from acknowledging, that he defired any Man's condemnation, the he looked upon the neceffity of figning Warrants for the Execution of * Malefactors, as a burden, and rather wifhed he had not learnt to write, than to be obliged to do it. They who by fpreading fuch barbarous errors, would create unto the King an intereft different from that of his People which he is to preferve, whilft they pretend to ferve him in deftroying of them, they deprive him of his honour and dignity; Juftice is done in all places, in the name of the chief Magiftrate, it being prefumed, that he doth embrace every one of his Subjects with equal tendernefs, until the Guilty are by legal proofs difcriminated from the Innocent, and amongft us the King's name may be ufed in civil cafes as well as criminal: But it is as impoffible for him rightly to defire I fhould be condemned for killing a Man whom I have not killed, or a Treafon that I have not committed, as that my Land fhould be unjuftly taken from me by a judgment in his Bench, or I fhould be condemned to pay a debt that I do not owe.

In both Cafes we fue unto him for Juftice, and demand it as our right. We are all concerned in it, publickly and privately, and the King as well as all the Officers of Juftice, are by their feveral Oaths obliged in their refpective capacities to perform it. They are bound to give their affiftance to find out Offenders, and the King's Attorney is by his Oath to profecute them if he be required; and he is not only the King's fervant in fuch cafes, but the Nation's; or rather cannot otherwife ferve the King, than by feeing Juftice done in the Nation. Whenfoever any Man receives an injury in his Perfon, Wife, Children, Friends, or Goods, the King is injured, in as much as he is by his Office to prevent fuch mifchiefs, and ought to be concerned in the Welfare of every one of his Subjects; but the parties to whom the injuries are done, are the immediate fufferers, and the profecution is principally made, that they may be repaired or revenged, and other innocent perfons fecured by the punifhment of Offenders, in which the King can be no otherwife concerned, than as he is to fee his Office faithfully perform'd, and his People protected. The King's fuit therefore is in the behalf of his People, yet the Law leaves unto every man a Liberty, in cafe of Treafons, Murthers, Rapes, Robberies, &c. to fue in the King's name, and crave his aid, or by way of appeal in his own; the fame Law looks upon Felons, or Traitors as publick Enemies, and by authorizing every one to purfue or apprehend them, teacheth us, that every man in his place ought to do it. The fame Act whereby one or a few are injured, threatneth all, and every Man's private intereft fo concurs with that of the publick, that all depends upon the exact prefervation of the Method prefcribed by the Law, for the impartial inquifition after fufpected Offenders, and moft tender care of preferving fuch as are innocent. As this cannot poffibly be effected without fecret and feparate examinations, the forbidding them is no lefs, than to change

the

* Suet. Vit. Ner. *Utinam nefcirem litteras.*

the Courſe which is enjoined by Law, confirmed by cuſtom, and grounded upon Reaſon and Juſtice.

If on the other ſide any man believe, that ſuch as in the King's name proſecute ſuſpected Delinquents, ought only to try how they may bring them to be condemned, he
may be pleaſed to conſider, that all ſuch perſons ought, according unto Law, to produce no Witneſs whom they do not think to be true ; no Evidence which they do
not believe good, nor can conceal any thing that may juſtify the accuſed. No trick
or Artifice can be lawfully uſed to deceive a Grand-Jury, or induce them to find or reject a Bill, otherwiſe than as they are led by their own Conſciences. All Lawyers
were anciently ſworn to put no deceit upon the Courts for their Clients ſake, and
there are Statutes ſtill in force to puniſh them if they do it ; but there is an eternal
obligation upon ſuch as are of Counſel againſt perſons accuſed of Crimes, not to uſe
ſuch Arts as may bring the Innocent to be condemned, and thereby pervert that which
is not called the Judgment of Man but of God, becauſe Man renders it in the ſtead,
and by the commandment of God ; ſuch practices exalt not the Juriſdiction of Tribunals, but infect and pollute them with that innocent Blood, which will be their overthrow : And leaſt of all, can it be called a Service to the King, ſince none could ever
ſtand againſt the cry of it. This is neceſſarily implyed in the Attorney General's
Oath, to ſerve the King in his Kingly Office, wherein the Law preſumes he can do no
wrong. But the greateſt of all wrongs, and that which hath been moſt deſtructive
unto Thrones, is by Fraud to circumvent and deſtroy the Innocent: This is to turn a
Legal King into a *Nimrod*, a Hunter of Men : This is not to act the part of a Father
or a Shepherd, who is ready to lay down his Life for his Sheep, but ſuch as the Pſal-
miſt complains of, who eat up the People as if they eat Bread. *Jezebel* did perhaps
applaud her own Wit, and think ſhe had done a great Service to the King, by finding
out Men of *Belial*, Judges and Witneſſes to bring *Naboth* to be ſtoned ; but that unre-
garded Blood was a Canker, or the Plague of Leproſy in his Throne and Family,
which could not be cured but by its overthrow and extinction. But if the Attorney General cannot ſerve the King by abuſing Juries, and ſubverting the Innocent, he can as
little gain an advantage to himſelf by falſifying his Oath, by the true meaning whereof he is to proſecute Juſtice impartially, and the Eternal Divine Law would annul any
Oath or Promiſe that he ſhould have taken to the contrary, even though his Office had
obliged him unto it.

The like Obligation lies upon Jurors not to ſuffer themſelves to be deluded, or perſuaded that the Judges, King's Council, or any others can diſpenſe with that Oath,
or any part of it, which they have taken before God unto the whole Nation ; nor to
think that they can ſwerve from the Rules ſet by the Law without a damnable breach
of it. The power of relaxing or diſſolving conſcientious Obligations, acknowledged
in the Pope, makes a great part of the *Roman* Superſtition ; and that grand Impoſtor
could never corrupt Kingdoms and Nations to their deſtruction, and the eſtabliſhment
of his Tyranny, until he had brought them to believe he could diſpenſe with Oaths, taken by Kings unto their Subjects, and by Subjects to their Kings ; not impoſe ſo extravagant an Error upon either, until he had perſuaded them he was in the place of
God. It is hard to ſay how the Judges or King's Council can have the ſame Power,
unleſs it be upon the ſame Title ; but we may be ſure they may as well diſpenſe with
the whole Oath as any part of it, and can have no pretence to either, unleſs they have
the Keys of Heaven and Hell in their keeping. It is in vain to ſay, the King as any o-
ther man may remit the Oath taken unto and for himſelf ; he is not a Party for himſelf,
but in the behalf of his People, and cannot diſpoſe of their Concernments without their
Conſent, which is given only in Parliament.

The King's Council ought to remember, they are in criminal Caſes of Council unto
every man in the Kingdom ; it is no ways referr'd unto the Direction of the Judges,
or unto them, whether that ſecrecy enjoined by Law, be profitable unto the King or
Kingdom : They muſt take the Law as it is, and render Obedience unto it, until it be
altered by the Power that made it. To this end the Judges by Acts of Parliament,
viz. 18 *Ed. 3. cap.* 8. and 20 *Ed. 3. cap.* 1. are ſworn to ſerve the People, *Ye ſhall ſerve
our Lord the King and his People in the Office of Juſtice,* &c. *Ye ſhall deny to no man common Right by the King's Letters, nor no other man's, nor for no other cauſe ; and in default
thereof in any point, they are to forfeit their Bodies, Lands, and Goods.* This proves
them to be the People's Servants as well as the King's.

Further by the expreſs words of the Commiſſions of Oyer and Terminer, they are required to *aſſiſt every man that ſuffers injury, and make diligent inquiſition after all manner of
falſhoods, deceits, offences, and wrongs done to any man, and thereupon to do Juſtice according to the Law:* So that in the whole proceedings in order unto Trial, and in the Trials
them-

themselves, the Thing principally intended, which several persons are severally in their capacities obliged to pursue, is the discovery of Truth: The Witnesses are to depose *the Truth, the whole Truth, and nothing but the Truth*: Thereupon the Council for the King are to prosecute: The Grand-Jury to present; and the Petit Jury to try. These are several Offices, but all to the same End; 'tis not the Prisoner, but the Crime that is to be pursued: This primarily, the Offender but by consequence; and therefore such Courses must be taken, as may discover that, and not such as may ensnare him. When the Offence is found, the impartial Letter of the Law gives the Doom; and the Judges have no share in it, but the pronouncing of it: Till then the Judges are only to preside, and take care, that every man else, who is employed in this necessary Affair, do his duty according to Law. So that upon result of the whole Transaction impartial Justice may be done, either to the acquittal or condemnation of the Prisoner.

Hereby it is manifest why the Judges are obliged by Oath, to *serve the People as well as the King*: And by Commission, to *serve every one that suffers Injuries*. As they are to see that Right be done to the King, and his injur'd Subjects in discovering of the Delinquent; so they are to be of Counsel with the Prisoner, whom the Law supposeth may be ignorant as well as innocent; and therefore has provided, that the Court shall be of Council for him, and as well inform him of what legal advantages the Law allows him, as to resolve any point of Law when he shall propose it to them. And it seems to be upon the presumption of this steady impartiality in the Judges, (thus obliged by all that is held sacred before God and Man to be unbyassed) that the Prisoner hath no Council; for if the Court faithfully perform their duty, the Accused can have no wrong or hardship, and therefore needs no Adviser.

Now suppose a man perfectly innocent, and in some measure knowing in the Law, should be accused of Treason or Felony: If the Judges shall deny unto the Grand Jury the liberty of examining any Witnesses, except in open Court, where nothing shall be offered that may help to clear the Prisoner, but every Thing aggravated, that gives colour for the Accusation; such Persons only produced, as the King's Council, or the Prosecutors shall think fit to call, of whose Credit also the Jury must not inquire, but shall be controll'd and brow-beaten in asking Questions, of such unknown Witnesses, for their own Satisfaction, if they have any Tendency to discover the Infamy of these Witnesses, or the Falshood of their Testimony: How can Innocence secure any Man from being arraigned?

And if the Oath of the Judges should be as much forgotten in the further Proceedings upon the Trial, where in Cases of Treason the Prisoner shall have all the King's Council (commonly not the most unlearned) prepared with studied Speeches, and Arguments, to make him black and odious, and to strain all his words, and to alledge them for Instances of his Guilt: If then all his private Papers, and Notes to help his Memory in his Plea and Defence, shall be taken from him by the Goaler, or the Court, and given to his Prosecutors: And all Advice and Assistance from Counsel, or Friends, and his nearest Relations shall be denied him, and none suffered by word or writing to inform him of the indifferency, or honesty, or the partiality or malice of the Pannels returned (whom the Law allows him to challenge or refuse, either peremptorily, or for good Reasons offered;) should he be thus deprived of all the good provisions of the Law for his safety, to what Frauds, Perjuries, and Subornations is not he, and every man exposed, who may be accused? What Deceits may there not be put upon Juries? and what Probability is there of finding Security in Innocence? What an admirable Execution would this be of their Commission, to *make diligent Inquisition after all manner of Falshoods, Deceits, Wrongs and Frauds, and thereupon to do Justice according to Law?* When at the same time, if so managed, a Method would be introduced of ruining and destroying any Man in the form of Justice. Such practices would be the highest dishonour to the King imaginable, whose name is used, and so far misrepresent the Kingly Office, as to make that appear, to have been erected to vex and destroy the People, which was intended, and ordained to help and preserve them.

The Law so far abhors such proceedings, that it intends, that every Man should be strictly bound, to be exactly just in their several Imployments, relating to the Execution of Justice. The Serjeant of the King's Council (Sir *George Jeffreys*, among the rest) who prosecute in the King's name, and are consulted in the forming Bills of Indictment, and advise about the Witnesses and their Testimonies against the Accused; These (if they would remember it) when they are made Serjeants, take an Oath (*Coke*'s 2d Institute, Pag. 214.) *as well and truly to serve the People* (whereof the party accused is one) *as the King himself, and to minister the King's matters duly and truly after the course of the Law to their Cunning*: Not to use their Cunning and Craft to hide the Truth, and destroy the accused if they can.

They

They are also obliged by the Statute of *Weſtm. 1. Cap. 29.* to put no manner of Deceit or Colluſion upon the King's Court, nor ſecretly to conſent to any ſuch Tricks as may abuſe or beguile the Court, or the Party, be it in Cauſes Civil or Criminal: And it is ordained, that if any of them be convicted of ſuch practices, he ſhall be impriſoned for a year, and never be heard to plead again in any Court; and if the miſchievous conſequence of their Treacheries be great, they are ſubject to further and greater puniſhments. Our ancient Law-Book called *the Mirror of Juſtice, Cap. 2. Sect. 4.* ſays, *That every Serjeant Pleader is chargeable by his Oath, not to maintain or defend any Wrong or Falſhood to his knowledge, but ſhall leave his Client when he ſhall perceive the wrong intended by him: Alſo that he ſhall not move or proffer any falſe Teſtimony, nor conſent to any Lyes, Deceits, or Corruptions whatſoever in his Pleadings.*

As a further Security unto the People againſt all Attempts upon their Laws, Exemplary Juſtice hath been done, in ſeveral Ages, upon ſuch Judges, and Juſticiaries, as through Corruption, Submiſſion unto unjuſt Commands, or any other ſiniſter Conſideration, have dared to ſwerve from them: The puniſhments of theſe wicked Men remain upon Record, as Monuments of their Infamy to be a Terror unto all that ſhall ſucceed them. In the Reign of the *Saxons* the moſt notable Example was given by King *Alfred,* who cauſ'd above forty Judges to be hanged in a ſhort ſpace, for ſeveral wrongs done to the People, as is related in *the Mirror of Juſtice:* Some of them ſuffered for impoſing on Juries, and forcing them to give Verdicts according to their will; and one, as it ſeems, had taken the Confidence to examine a Jury, that he might find which of them would ſubmit to his Will, and ſetting aſide him who would not, condemned a Man upon the Verdict of Eleven.

Since the Coming of the *Normans,* our Parliaments have not been leſs ſevere againſt ſuch Judges, as have ſuffered the Courſe of Juſtice to be perverted, or the Rights and Liberties of the People to be invaded: In the time of *Edward* the 1ſt, *Anno* 1289, the Parliament finding, that all the Judges (except two) had ſwerv'd from their duty, condemned them to ſeveral puniſhments according unto their Crimes, as Baniſhment, *Ex Chron.* perpetual Impriſonment, or the loſs of all their Eſtates, *&c.* Their particular Offen- *Anno. 10. Ed.* ces are ſpecified in a Speech made by the Arch-Biſhop of *Canterbury* in Parliament. *1. ad finem.* They had broken *Magna Charta*; incited the King againſt his People; violated the Laws under pretence of expounding them; and impudently preſumed to prefer their own Councils to the King, before the Advices of Parliament, as appears by the Speech, *&c.* hereunto annext.

The like was done in *Ed.* the 2d's Time, when *Hugh De Spencer* was charged for having prevailed with the King to break his Oath to the People, in doing Things againſt the Law by his Authority.

In *Edward* the 3d's Time, Judge *Thorpe* was hang'd for having in the like manner brought the King to break his Oath: And the happy Reign of that great King affords *Dan. Hiſtory.* many Inſtances of the like nature, amongſt which, the puniſhment of Sir *Henry Green* *p. 260, 261.* and Sir *William Skipwith,* deſerve to be obſerved and put into an equal Rank with thoſe of his brave and victorious Grand-father.

In *Richard* the Second's Time, Eleven of the Judges, forgetting the dreadful Puniſh- See all the ments of their Predeceſſors, ſubſcrib'd malicious Indictments againſt Law, and gave *Engliſh* Hiſto- falſe Interpretations of our ancient Laws to the King, thereby to bring many of his moſt ries of *Wal-* eminent, and worthieſt Subjects, to ſuffer as Traytors at his Will: Subjected the Au- *ſingham, Fa-* thority, and very Being of Parliaments to his abſolute pleaſure, and made him believe, *bian, Speed,* that all the Laws lay in his own breaſt: Hereupon ſentence of death paſſed upon them; &c. in the 11 and tho' upon their repentance, and confeſſing, they had been ſwayed by fear, and and 12 years threatnings from the King, two only were executed, all the others were for ever ba- of *Richard* niſhed, as unworthy to enjoy the benefit of that Law, which they had ſo perfidiouſly, II. and baſely betrayed.

It were an endleſs Work to recite all the Examples of this kind that are found in our Hiſtories and Records; but that of *Empſon* and *Dudley* muſt not be omitted: They had craftily contriv'd to aboliſh Grand-Juries, and to draw the Lives and Eſtates of the People into queſtion, without Indictments by them; and by ſurprize, and other wicked practices, they gained an Act of Parliament for their countenance: Hereupon falſe Accuſations followed without number; Oppreſſion and Injuſtice broke forth like a Flood, and to gain the King's Favour, they fill'd his Coffers: The Indictments againſt them mentioned in *Anderſon's* Reports, p. 156, 157, are worth reading; whereby they are charged *with Treaſon, for ſubverting the Laws, and Cuſtoms of the Land, in their proceedings without Grand-Juries, and procuring the murmuring and hatred of the People againſt the King, to the great danger of him, and the Kingdom.* Nothing could ſatisfy the Kingdom, tho' the King was dead, whom they had flattered, and ſerved, but ſuch Juſtice

done

done upon them, and many of their Inftruments, and Officers, as may for ever make the Ears of Judges to tingle.

And it is not to be forgotten, that the Judges in Queen *Eliz.* time, in the Cafe of *R. Cavendifh* in *Anderfon*'s Reports, p. 152, and 155. *were* (as they told the Queen, and her Counfellors) *by the punifhment of former Judges, efpecially of* Empfon *and* Dudley, *deterred from obeying her illegal Commands*: The Queen had fent feveral Letters under her Signet ; Great Men preffed them to obey her Patent under the Great Seal, and the Reafons of their difobedience being requir'd ; they anfwered, *That the Queen her felf, and the Judges alfo, had taken an Oath to keep the Laws: And if they fhould obey her Commands, the Laws would not warrant them, and they fhould therein break their Oath, to the Offence of God, and their Country, and the Commonwealth wherein they were born: And, fay they, if we had no fear of God, yet the Examples, and Punifhments of others before us, who did offend the Laws, do remember, and recall us from the like Offences.*

Whofoever being in the like places may defign, or be put upon the like practices, will do well to confider thefe Examples, and not to think that he, who obliquely endeavours to render Grand-Juries ufelefs, is lefs Criminal, than he, that would abfolutely abolifh them : That which doth not act according to its Inftitution, is, as if it were not in being : And whoever doth without prejudice confider this matter, will fee that it is not lefs pernicious to deny Juries the ufe of thofe Methods of difcovering Truth which the Law hath appointed, and fo by degrees turn them into a meer matter of form, than openly, and avowedly to deftroy them.   Surely fuch a gradual Method of deftroying our native Right is the moft dangerous in its confequence.   The fafety, which our Fore-fathers, for many hundred of years, enjoyed under this part of the Law efpecially, and have tranfmitted to us, is fo apparent to the meaneft Capacity, that whoever fhall go about to take it away, or give it up, is like to meet with the fate of *Ifhmael*, to have every man's hand againft him, becaufe he is againft every Man.   Artifices of this kind, will ruin us more filently, and fo with lefs oppofition, and yet as certainly, as the other more moved oppreffion : This only is the difference, that one way we fhould be flaves immediately, and the other infenfibly ; but with this further difadvantage too, that our flavery fhould be the more unavoidable, and the fafter riveted upon us, becaufe it would be under colour of Law, which Practice in time would obtain.

Few men at firft fee the danger of little changes in Fundamentals, and thofe, who defign them, ufually act with fo much craft, as befides the giving fpecious Reafons, they take great care, that the true Reafon fhall not appear : Every defign therefore of changing the Conftitution ought to be moft warily obferved, and timely oppofed : Nor is it only the Intereft of the People, that fuch Fundamentals fhould be duly guarded, for whofe Benefit they were at firft fo carefully laid, and whom the Judges are fworn to ferve ; but of the King too, for whofe fake thofe pretend to act, who would fubvert them.

Our Kings as well as Judges are fworn to maintain the Laws ; they have themfelves in feveral Statutes required the Judges, at their peril, to adminifter equal Juftice to every Man, notwithftanding any Letters, or Commands, *&c.* even from themfelves to the contrary : And when any failure hath been, the greateft, and moft powerful of them have ever been the readieft to give Redrefs.   It appears by the Preface to the Statutes of 20th *Ed. 3.* that the Judicial Proceedings had been perverted, that Letters, Writs and Commands had been fent from the King, and great Men to the Juftices, and that Perfons belonging to the Court of the King, the Queen, the Prince of *Wales* had maintained, and abetted Quarrels, *&c.* whereby the Laws had been violated, and many wrongs done : But the King was fo far from juftifying his own Letters, or thofe illegal practices, that the preamble of thofe Statutes faith, they were made for the relief of the People in their fufferings by them.   That brave King, in the height of his glory and vigor of his Age, chofe rather to confefs his Error, than to continue in it, as is evidently by his own words: Edward, *by the Grace of God,* &c. *Becaufe by divers Complaints made unto us, we have perceived that the Law of the Land, which we by our Oath are bound to maintain, is the lefs well kept, and Execution of the fame difturbed many times by maintenances and procurements, as well in the Court as the Country, we greatly moved of Confcience in this matter, and for this Caufe, defiring as much for the pleafure of God, and eafe and quietnefs of our Subjects, as to fave our Confcience, and to fave and keep our faid Oath, by the Affent,* &c. Enact, *That Judges fhall do Juftice, notwithftanding Writs, Letters or Commands from himfelf,* &c. *and that none of the King's Houfe, or belonging to the King, Queen, or Prince of* Wales, *do maintain Quarrels,* &c.

King *James* in his Speech to the Judges in the *Starchamber, Anno.* 1616. told them ; *That he had after many years refolved to renew his Oath, made at his Coronation, concerning*

Juftice

4

Juſtice, and the promiſe therein contained for maintaining the Law of the Land. And in the next Page ſave one ſays, *I was ſworn to maintain the Law of the Land, and therefore had been perjured, if I had broken it ; God is my Judge I never intended it.* And His Majeſty, that now is, hath made frequent Declarations, and Proteſtations of his being far from all thoughts of deſigning an arbitrary Government, and that the Nation might be confident, he would rule by Law.

Now if after all this, any Officer of the King ſhould pretend Inſtructions from his Maſter, to demand ſo material an alteration of proceedings, in the higheſt Caſes againſt Law, as are above mentioned, and the Court (who are required to ſlight and reject the moſt ſolemn Commands under the great Seal, if contrary to Law) ſhould upon a verbal Intimation allow of ſuch a Demand, and ſo break in upon this Bulwark of our Liberties, which the Law has erected ; might it not give too juſt an occaſion to ſuſpect, that all the legal Securities of our Lives and Properties are unable to protect us ? And may not ſuch fears rob the King of his greateſt Treaſure and Strength, the People's hearts, when they dare not rely upon him in his Kingly Office, and truſt for ſafety and protection by the Laws ? Our *Engliſh* Hiſtory affords many inſtances of thoſe that have pretended to ſerve our King in this manner, by undermining the People's Rights and Liberties, whoſe practices have ſometimes proved of fatal conſequence to the Kings themſelves, but more frequently ended in their own deſtruction.

But after all, imagining it could be made out, that this Method of private Examinations by a Grand-Jury (which from what has been ſaid before, hath appeared to be ſo extremely neceſſary for the publick good, and to every private man's ſecurity) were inconvenient or miſchievous, and therefore fit to be changed ; yet being ſo eſſential a part of the common Law, it is no otherwiſe alterable than by Parliament. We find by Precedents, that the bare Forms of Indictments could not be reformed by the Judges : The words *Depopulatores agrorum, Inſidiatores viarum, Vi & Armis, Baculis, Cultellis, Arcubus & Sagittis,* could not be left out, but by advice of the Kingdom in Parliament. A writ iſſued in the time of K. *Ed.* 3. giving power to hear and determine Offences, and all the Juſtices reſolved, (*Cok.* 4. Inſt. Pag. 164.) *That they could not lawfully act, having their Authority by Writ, where they ought to have had it by Commiſſion ; tho' it was in the form and words, that the legal Commiſſion ought to be.* John Knivett *Chief Juſtice, by Advice of all the Judges, reſolved that the ſaid Writ was* contra Legem : *And where divers Indictments were before them found againſt* T. S. *the ſame, and all that was done by colour of that Writ, was damned.*

If in ſuch ſeeming little Things as theſe, and many others, that may be inſtanced, the Wiſdom of the Nation hath not thought fit to intruſt the Judges, but reſerved the Conſideration of them to the legiſlative Power ; it cannot be imagined, that they ſhould ſubject to the diſcretion and pleaſure of the Judges, thoſe important Points, in the eſtabliſhed Courſe of the adminiſtring Juſtice, whereupon depends the ſafety of all the Subjects Lives and Fortunes. If Judges will take upon themſelves to alter the conſtant practice, they muſt either alter the Oath of the Grand-Jury, or continue it : If they ſhould alter it, ſo as to make it fail with any ſuch new Method, and thus in appearance charitably provide, that the Grand-Jury ſhould not take a mock Oath, or forſwear themſelves ; they then make an incroachment upon the Authority of Parliaments, who only can make new, or change old legal Oaths, and all the proceedings thereupon would be void.

If they ſhould continue conſtantly to impoſe the ſame Oath, as well when they have notice from the King, that the Jury ſhall not be bound to keep his Secrets, and their own, as when they have none ; they muſt aſſume to make the ſame form of Law to be of force, and no force ; and the ſame words to bind the Conſcience, as they will have them ; whereby they would prophane the natural Religion of an Oath, and bring a foul ſcandal upon Chriſtianity, by trifling worſe than Heathens in that ſacred matter : and whilſt the Judges find themſelves under the neceſſity of adminiſtring the Oath unto Grand-Juries, and not ſuffer them to obſerve it according unto their Conſciences, they would confeſs the illegality of their own Proceedings, and can never be able to repair the Breaches, by pretending a tacite Implication, if the King will, but muſt unavoidably fall under that approved Maxim of our Law, *Maledicta eſt Interpretatio quæ corrumpit Textum* ; it is a curſed Interpretation that diſſolves the Text.

Theſe are two vulgar Errors concerning the Duty of Grand-Juries, which if not removed, will in time deſtroy all the benefit we can expect from that Conſtitution, by turning them into a meer matter of form, which were deſigned for ſo great Ends. Many have of late thought, and affirmed it for Law, that the Grand-Jury is neither to make ſo ſtrict inquiry into matters before them, nor to look for ſo clear Evidence of the Crime, as the Petit Jury ; but that of their Preſentments, being to paſs a ſecond Examination, they ought to indict upon a ſuperficial Inquiry, and bare Probabilities :

Whereas

Whereas should either of these Opinions be admitted, the prejudice to the Subject would be equal to the total laying aside Grand-Juries; there being in truth no difference between arraigning without any Presentment from them at all, and their Presenting upon slight grounds.

For the first, that Grand-Juries ought not to make so strict Inquiry, it were to be wish'd, that we might know how it comes to pass, that an Oath should be obligatory unto a Petit Jury, and not unto the Grand: Or in what Points they may lawfully and with good Conscience omit that Exactness, whether in relation to the Witnesses, and their credibility: Or the fact and all its circumstances: Or the Testimony and its weight: Or lastly, in reference to the Prisoner, and Probability of his guilt: And withal, upon what grounds of Law, or Reason, their Opinion is founded. On the contrary, he that will consider either the Oath they take, or the Commission, where their duty is described, will find in all Points, that there lies an equal Obligation upon them, and the Petit Juries.

They swear diligently to inquire, and true Presentment make, &c. and to present the Truth, the whole Truth, and nothing but the Truth, &c. And in the Commission of *Oyer* and *Terminer* their Duty (with that of the Commissioners) is thus described: *Ad Inquirendum per Sacramentum proborum & legalium hominum, &c. per quos rei veritas melius sciri poterit, de quibuscunque proditionibus, &c. confœderationibus, falsis Allegantiis, nec non Accessoriis eorundem, &c. per quoscunque & qualitercunque habit. fact. perpetrat. sive commiss. Et per quos, et per quem, cui vel quibus, quando, qualiter, vel quomodo, & de aliis articulis & circumstantiis præmis. & eorum aliquod. vel aliqua qualitercunque concernent. To inquire by the Oath of honest and lawful Men, &c. by whom the Truth of the matter may be best known, of all manner of Treasons, &c. Confederacies, false Testimonies, &c. As also the Accessories, &c. by whomsoever, or howsoever, done, perpetrated, or committed, by whom, or to whom, how, in what way, or in what manner. And of other Articles and Circumstances premised, and of any other Thing or Things howsoever concerning the same.* Now for any Man, after this to maintain, that Grand-Juries are not to inquire, or not carefully, is as much as in plain terms to say they are bound to act contrary to the Commission, and their Oath: And to affirm that they can discharge their duty according to the Obligations of Law and Conscience which they lie under, without a strict Inquiry into particulars, is to affirm that the End can be obtained without the Means necessary unto it.

The truth is, that Grand-Juries have both a larger field for their Inquiry, and are in many respects better capacitated to make a strict one, than the Petit Juries: These last are confined as to the Person and the Crime, specified in the Indictment; but they are at large obliged to search into the whole matter, that any ways concerns every Case before them, and all the Offences contained in it, all the criminal Circumstances whatsoever, and into every thing, howsoever concerning the same. They are bound to enquire whether their Information of suspected Treasons or Felonies, brought by Accusers, be made by Conspiracy, or Subornation; who are the Conspirators, or false Witnesses: By whom abetted, or maintained: Against whom, and how many the Conspiracy is laid; when, and how, and in what course it was to have been prosecuted.

But none of these most intricate matters (which need the most strict and diligent Inquiries) can come under the Cognisance of the Petit Jury; they can only examine so much as relates to the Credit of those Witnesses brought to prove the Charge against the Parties indicted; wherein also they have neither Power, nor convenient Time to send for Persons, or Papers, if they think them needful, nor to resolve any doubts of the Lawfulness and Credibility of the Testimonies.

Yet further, if the Crimes objected are manifest, 'tis then the Grand Jury's duty to inquire after all the Persons any ways concerned in them, and the several kinds of Offences, whereof every one ought jointly, or separately, to be indicted, as they shall discover them to have been Principals, or Accessories, parties or privy thereunto, or to have comforted, or knowingly relieved, either the Traitors or Felons, or conceal'd the offences of others: But the Inquisition into all these matters, which require all possible strictness in searching, as being of the highest importance unto the publick Justice and safety, is wholly out of the Power and Trust of the Petit Juries. The guilt or innocence of the Parties put upon their Trials, and the Evidence thereof given, is the only Object of their Inquiries. It is not their work, nor within their Trust to search into all the guilt or crimes of the Parties whom they try; they are bound to move within the Circle of the Indictment made by the Grand-Jury, who are to appoint and specify the offences for which the Accused shall be tried by the Petit Jury.

When a Prosecutor suggests that any Man is criminal, and ought to be indicted, it belongs

longs to the Grand-Jury to hear all the proof he can offer, and to use all other means they can, whereby they may come to understand the truth of the suggestion, and every thing or circumstance that may concern it: Then they are carefully to examine the nature of the Facts, according unto the Rules of the common Law, or the express words of the Statutes, whereby offences are distinguished, and punishments allotted unto each of them: 'Tis true, that upon hearing the Party, or his Witnesses, the Petit Jury may acquit or judge the Facts in the Indictment to be less heinous, or malicious than they were presented by the Grand-Jury, but cannot aggravate them; which being considered, it will easily appear by the intent and nature of the Powers given unto Grand-Juries, that they are by their Oaths obliged, and their instruction, to keep all injustice from entering the first gates of Courts of Judicature, and to secure the innocent not only from punishment, but from all disgrace, vexation, expence, or danger.

To understand our Law clearly herein, the Jurors must first know the lawful grounds whereupon they may and ought to indict, and then what truly and justly ought to be taken for the ground of an Indictment. The principal and most certain is the Jurors personal knowledge, by their own eyes or ears, of the Crimes whereof they indict; or so many pregnant concurring Circumstances, as fully convince them of the guilt of the Accused: When these are wanting, the Depositions of Witnesses and their Authority are their best Guides in finding Indictments. When such Testimonies make the charge manifest and clear to the Jury, they are called Evidence, because they make the guilt of Criminals evident, and are like the light that discovers what was not seen before: All Witnesses for that reason are usually called the Evidence, taking their name from what they ought to be. Yet Witnesses may swear directly and positively to an Accusation, and be no evidence of its truth to the Jury; sometimes such remarks may be made upon the Witnesses, as well in relation to their Reputation and Lives, as to the Matter, Manner, and Circumstance of their Depositions, that from thence the falshood may appear, or be strongly suspected: It is therefore necessary to know what they mean by a probable Cause or Evidence, who say that our Law requires no more for an Indictment.

Probable, is a logical Term, relating to such propositions, as have an appearance, but no certainty of Truth, shewing rather what is not, than what is the matter of Syllogisms: These may be allowed in Rhetorick, which worketh upon Passions, and makes use of such Colours as are fit to move them, whether true or false; but not in Logick, whose Object is Truth; as it principally intends to obviate the Errors that may arise from the credit given unto appearances, by distinguishing the uncertain from the certain, *verisimile a vero*, it cannot admit of such Propositions, as may be false as well as true, it being as impossible to draw a certain conclusion from uncertain premises, as to raise a solid Building upon a tottering or sinking foundation. This ought principally to be considered in Courts of Justice, which are not erected to bring men into Condemnation, but to find who deserves to be condemned; and those Rules are to be followed by them, which are least liable to deception. For this reason the Council of the *Areopagites*, and some others of the best Judicatures that have been in the World, utterly rejected the use of Rhetorick, looking upon the Art of perswading by uncertain probabilities, as little differing from that of deceiving, and directly contrary to their ends, who by the knowledge of truth desired to be led into the doing of Justice: But if the Art that made use of these probabilities was banished from uncorrupted Tribunals, as a hindrance unto the discovery of Truth, they that would ground Verdicts totally upon them, declare an open neglect of it; and as it is said, that *uno absurdo dato, mille sequuntur*, if Juries were to be guided by probabilities, the next question would be concerning the more or less probable, or what degree of probability is required to perswade them to find a Bill: This being impossible to fix, the whole Proceedings would be brought to depend upon the Fancies of Men, and as nothing is so slight but it may move them, there is no security that innocent Persons may not be brought every day into danger and trouble. By this means certain mischiefs will be done, whilst it is by their own confession uncertain whether they were any ways deserved by such as suffer them, to the utter overthrow of all Justice.

If the word *Probable* be taken in a common, rather than a nice logical Sense, it signifies no more than likely, or rather likely than unlikely: When a Matter is found to be so, the Wager is not even, there is odds upon one side, and this may be a very good ground for betting in a Tennis-Court, or at a Horse-race, but he that would make the Administration of Justice to depend upon such Points, seems to put a very small value upon the fortunes, liberties and reputations of men; and to forget that those who sit in Courts of Justice, have no other business there than to preserve them.

This continues in force, though in a Dialogue between a Barrister and a Grand-Jury Man, published under the Title of the Grand-Jury Man's Oath and Office, it be said, p. 8. and 9. *That their work is no more than to present Offences fit for a Trial, and for that*

Reafon, give in only a verifimilar or probable Charge ; and others have affirmed, that a far lefs Evidence will warrant a Grand-Jury's Indictment, than a Petit Jury's Verdict. For nothing can be more oppofite to the juftice of our Laws, than fuch Opinions: All Laws in doubtful Cafes direct a fufpenfion of Judgment, or a Sentence in favour of the accufed perfon. But if this were hearkened unto, Grand-Juries fhould upon their Oaths affirm, they judge him criminal, when the Evidence is upon fuch uncertain grounds that they cannot but doubt, whether he is fo or not.

It cannot be hereupon faid, that no Evidence is fo clear and full, but it may be falfe, and give the Jury occafion of doubts, fo as all Criminals muft efcape, if no Indictment ought to be found unlefs the proofs are abfolutely certain; for it is confefs'd, that fuch Cafes are not capable of an infallible Mathematical demonftration : but a Jury that examines all the Witneffes, that are likely to give any light concerning the bufinefs in queftion, and all Circumftances relating to the fact before them, with the Lives and Credit of thofe that teftify it, and of the Perfon accufed, may and do often find that which in their Confciences doth fully perfuade them, that the accufed Perfon is guilty : This is as much as the Law, or their Oath doth require, and fuch as find Bills, after having made fuch a Scrutiny, are blamelefs before God and Man, if through the fragility infeparable from human Nature, they fhould be led into Error? For they do not fwear that the Bill is true, but that they in their Confciences believe that it is fo ; and if they write *Ignoramus* upon the Bill, it is not thereby declared to be falfe, nor the Perfon accufed acquitted, but the matter is fufpended, until it can be more clearly proved, as in doubtful Cafes, it always ought to be.

Our Anceftors took great care that fufpicious and probable Caufes fhould not bring any Man's Life and Eftate into danger ; for that reafon, it was ordain'd by the Stat. *37. Ed.3.* Cap. 18. *That fuch as made fuggestions to the King, fhould find furety to purfue and incur the fame pain, that the other fhould have had if he were attainted, in cafe their fuggeftion be not found evil, and that then procefs of the Law fhould be made againft the Accufed.*

This manner of Proceeding hath its roots on eternal and univerfal Reafon : The Law given by God unto his People, *Deut.* 19. allotted the fame Punifhment unto a falfe Witnefs, as a Perfon convicted. The beft-difciplined Nations of the world, learnt this from the *Hebrews*, and made it their Rule, in the adminiftration of Juftice. The *Grecians* generally obferved it, and the *Romans*, according to their *Lex Talionis*, did not only punifh death with death, but the intention of committing Murther by falfe Accufations, with the fame feverity, as if it had been effected by any other means. This Law was inviolably obferved as long as any thing of regularity or equity remained amongft them ; and when through the wickednefs of fome of the Emperors, or their Favourites, it came to be overthrown, all Juftice perifhed with it. A Crew of falfe Informers brake out to the deftruction of the beft men, and never ceas'd until they had ruined all the moft eminent and ancient Families ; circumvented the Perfons, that by their Reputation, Wealth, Birth or Virtue deferved to be diftinguifhed from the common fort of People, and brought defolation upon that victorious City. *Tacitus* complains of this, as the caufe of all the mifchiefs fuffered in his Time and Country.

Tac. Ann. 4.

By their means the moft favage Cruelties were committed under the name of Law, which thereby became a greater Plague, than formerly had been : No remedy could be found, when thofe *Delatores*, whom he calls, *genus hominum publico exitio repertum,*

Tac. Ann. 3. *& pænis quidem nunquam fatis coercitum,* were invited by impunity, or reward; and the miferable People groaned under this calamity, until thofe inftruments of iniquity were, by better Princes, put to the moft cruel, tho' well-deferved deaths.

The like hath been feen in many places, and the domeftick quiet, which is now enjoyed in the principal Parts of *Europe*, proceeds chiefly from this, that every man knows the fame Punifhment is appointed for a falfe Accufation, and proved Crime.

It is hardly feven years fince Monfieur *Courboyer*, a man of quality in *Brittany*, fuborned two of the King of *France* his Guards, to fwear treafonable Defigns againft *La Motte*, a *Norman* Gentleman ; the matter being brought to Monfieur *Colbert*, he caus'd the accufed Perfon and the Witneffes to be fecured, until the fraud was difcovered by one of them, whereupon he was pardoned ; *La Motte* releafed ; *Courboyer* beheaded, and the other falfe Witnefs hanged by the Sentence of the Parliament of *Paris.* Though this Law feems to be grounded upon fuch foundation, as forbids us to queftion the equity of it, our Anceftors (for Reafons beft known unto themfelves) thought fit to moderate its Severity, by the Statute of 38 *Ed.3.* Cap. 9. yet then it was enacted, and the Law continues in force unto this day ; *That whofoever made complaints to the King, and could not prove them againft the Defendant,* by the procefs of Law limited in former Statutes, which is firft by a Grand-Jury, *he fhould be imprifoned until he had made gree to the Party of his damages, and of the flander he fuffered by fuch occafion, and after fhall make fine and ranfom to the King* ; which is for the common damage, that the King and his

his People suffer by such a false accusation and defamation of any Subject: And in the 42 *Ed.* 3. *Cap.* 3. *To eschew the Mischiefs and Damage done by false Accusers,* 'tis enacted, That *no man be put to answer such* Suggestions *without presentment before the Justices, i.e.* by the Grand-Jury. It cannot surely be imagined, that the Suggestions made to the King and his Council, had no probability in them. Or that there was no colour, cause, or reason for the King to put the party to answer the Accusation; but the grievance and complaint was, that the People suffered certain damage, and vexation upon untrue, and at best, uncertain accusations, and that therein the Law was perverted by the King and his Council's taking upon them, to judge of the Certainty, or Truth of them, which of right belonged to the Grand-Jury only, upon whose Judgment and Integrity our Law doth wholly rely, for the indemnity of the Innocent, and the punishment of all such as do unjustly molest them.

Our Laws have not thought fit so absolutely to depend upon the Oaths of Witnesses, as to allow, that upon two, or ten men's swearing positively Treason or Felony against any Man, before the Justices of Peace, or all the Judges, or before the King and his Council, that the party accused, be he either Peer of the Realm, or Commoner, should without further Inquiry be thereupon arraigned, and put upon his Trial for his Life: Yet none can doubt but there is something of probability in such depositions; nevertheless the Law refers those matters unto Grand-Juries, and no man can be brought to Tryal, until upon such strict Inquiries, (as is before said) the Indictment be found. The Law is so strict in these Inquiries, that tho' the Crime be never so notorious, nay if Treason should be confessed in writing under Hand and Seal, before Justices of Peace, Secretaries of State, or the King and Council; yet before the party can be arraigned for it, the Grand-Jury must inquire, and be satisfied, whether such a Confession be clear and certain; whether there was no collusion therein; or the party induced to such confession by promise of pardon; or that some pretended partakers in the Crime may be defamed, or destroyed thereby: they must inquire, whether the Confession was not extorted by fear, threatnings, or force, and whether the party was truly *Compos mentis,* of sound Mind and Reason at that time.

The *Stat.* 5 *Eliz. Cap.* 1. declares the ancient common Law concerning the Trust and Duty of Juries, and enacts that none should *be indicted for assisting, aiding, comforting, or abetting* Criminals in the Treasons therein made and declared, *unless he, or they, be thereof lawfully accused by such good and sufficient Testimony or Proof, as by the Jury, by whom he shall be indicted, shall be thought good, lawful, and sufficient to prove him, or them guilty of the said Offences.* Herein is declared, the only true Reason of Indictments, *i. e.* the Grand-Jury's Judgment, that they have such Testimonies as they esteem sufficient to prove the party indicted guilty of the Crimes whereof he is accused; and whatsoever the Indictment doth contain, they are to present no more, or other Crimes, than are proved to their satisfaction, as upon Oath they declare it is, when they present it. This exactness is not only required in the Substance of Crimes, but in the Circumstances; and any doubtfulness, or uncertainty in them makes the Indictment, and all proceedings upon it by the Petit Jury, to be insufficient, and void, and holden for none, as appears by the following Cases.

In *Young's* Case in the Lord *Coke's* Reports, *Lib.* 4. *Fol.* 40. an Indictment for Murther was declared void for its incertainty, because the Jury had not laid certainty, in what part of the body the mortal wound was given, saying only, that 'twas about his breast: the words were *Unam Plagam mortalem circiter pectus.* In like manner in *Vaux* Case, *Coke's* Rep. *Lib.* 4. *Fol.* 44. he being indicted for poisoning *Ridley,* the Jury had not plainly and expresly averred that *Ridley* drank the Poison, tho' other words imply'd it, and thereupon the Indictment was judged insufficient; *for* (saith the Book) *the matter of an Indictment ought to be full, express, and certain, and shall not be maintained by argument or implication, for that the Indictment is found by the Oath of the Neighbourhood.* In the 2d part of *Roll's* Reports, *p.* 263. *Smith* and *Mall's* Case, the Indictment was quashed for incertainty, because the Jury had averred that *Smith* was either a Servant or Deputy, *Smith existens servus sive deputatus,* are the words: It was doubtless probably enough proved to the Jury, that he was either a Deputy, or Servant; but because the Indictment did not absolutely and certainly aver his condition either of Servant, or Deputy, it was declared void. If there be any defect of certainty in the Grand-Jury's Verdict, no Proof or Evidence to the Petit Jury can supply it, so it was judged in *Wrote* and *Wig's* Case, *Coke* 4. Rep. *Fol.* 45, 46, 47. It was laid, that *Wrote* was killed at *Shipperton,* but did not aver that *Shipperton* was within the *Verge,* tho' in truth it was; and no Averment or Oath to the Petit Jury, could supply that small failure of certainty to support the Indictment: and the reason is rendered in these words, *viz. The Indictment being Veredictum, id est dictum Veritatis, a Verdict,* (that is, *a saying of Truth and matter of Record) ought to contain the whole Truth which is requisite by the Law; for when it doth not appear, 'tis the same, as if it were not, and every material part of the Indictment ought to be found upon the Oath of the Indicters, and cannot be supplied by the Averment of the Party.* The Grand-Jury's Verdict is the foundation of all judicial proceeding against capital Offenders (at the King's suit ;) if that fail in any point of certainty, both convictions and acquittals thereupon are utterly void, and the proceedings against both may begin again, as if they had never been tried, as it appears in the Case last cited, *Fol.* 47.

Now as the Law requires from the Grand-Jury particular, certain, and precise affirmations of Truth, so it expects that they should look for the like, and accept of no other from such as bring accusations to them. For no Man can certainly affirm that which is uncertainly delivered unto him, or which he doth not firmly believe. The Witnesses that they receive for good, are to depose only absolute certainties about the Facts committed, that is, what they have seen, or heard from the accused parties themselves, not what others have told of them ; they are not to be suffered to make probable arguments, and infer from thence the guilt of the accused : Their depositions ought to be positive, plain, direct, and full : The Crime is to be sworn without any doubtfulness or obscurity ; not in words qualified, and limited to belief, conceptions, or apprehensions. This absolute certainty required in the deposition of the Witnesses, is one principal ground of the Jury's most rational assurance of the Truth of their Verdict : The credit also of the Witnesses ought to be free from all blemish, that good and conscientious Men may rationally rely upon them, in matters of so great moment, as the blood of a Man. It must also be certainly evident, that all the matters which they depose, are consistent with each other, and accompanied with such Circumstances, as in their Judgment render it credible : All just Indictments must be built upon these moral assurances, which the wisdom of all Nations hath devised as the best, and only way of deciding Controversies ; neither can a Grand-Jury Man, who swears to present nothing but the Truth, be satisfied with less.

'Tis scarce credible that any learned in our Laws, should tell a Grand-Jury that a far less Evidence will warrant their Indictment (being but an Accusation) than the Petit Jury ought to have for their Verdict. Both of them do in like manner plainly and positively affirm upon their Oaths, the Truth of the Accusation ; their Verdicts are indeed one and the same in substance, and sense, tho' not in words. There is no real difference between affirming in writing, that an Indictment of Treason is true, as is the practice of Grand-Juries, and saying that the party tried thereupon is guilty of the Treason whereof he is indicted, as is the course of Petit Juries : They are both upon their Oaths ; they are equally obligatory unto both, the one therefore must expect the same proof, for their satisfaction, as the other ; and as clear Evidence must be required for an Indictment, as for a Verdict : It is unreasonable to think that a slighter proof should satisfy the Consciences of the greater Jury, than is requisite to convince the less ; and uncharitable to imagine, that those should not be as sensible as the others of the sacred Security they have given by Oath, to do nothing in their Offices but according to truth.

If there ought to be any difference in the Proceedings of the Grand and Petit Juries, the greater exactness and diligence seems to be required in the Grand : For as the same work of finding out the truth in order to the doing of Justice is allotted unto both, the greatest part of the burthen ought to lie upon them that have the best opportunities of performing it. The invalidity, weakness, or defects of the Proofs may be equally evident to either of them : But if there be deceit in stifling true Testimonies, or malice in suborning wicked Persons, to bring in such as are false, the Grand-Jury may most easily, nay probably, can only discover it. They are not straitned in time ; they may freely examine in private, without interruption from the Council, or Court, such Witnesses as are presented unto them, or they shall think fit to call ; they may jointly or severally enquire of their Friends or Acquaintance after the Lives and Reputations of the Witnesses, or the accused Persons, and all circumstances relating unto the matter in question, and consult together under the Seal of Secrecy : On the other side, the Petty Jury being charged with the Prisoner, acts in open Court under the awe of the Judges, is subject to be disturb'd, or interrupted by Counsel ; deprived of all opportunity of consulting one another until the Evidence be summ'd up, and not suffered to eat or drink until they bring in a Verdict ; so it is almost impossible for them thus limited to discover such evil practices as may be used for, or against the Prisoner, by Subornation or Perjury to pervert Justice : if therefore the Grand-Jury be not permitted to perform this part of their duty, it is hard to imagine how it should be done at all. And it is much more inconceivable, how they can satisfy their Consciences, if they so neglect, as to find a Bill upon an imperfect Evidence, in the absence of the Prisoner,

soner, in expectation that it will be supplied at the Bar: It concerns them therefore to remember, that if they proceed upon such uncertainties, they will certainly give incurable wounds into their Neighbours Reputations, in order unto the destruction of their Persons.

Whatever grounds this Doctrine of Indicting upon slight proofs may have got in our days, it is (as we have seen) both against Law and Reason, and contrary to the practice of former times. My Lord *Coke* in his *Comment on Westm.* 2d. tells us, *That in those days (and as yet it ought to be) Indictments taken in the Absence of the Party were formed upon plain and direct Proofs, and not upon Probabilities and Inferences.* Herein we see, that the practice of our Forefathers, and the opinion of this great and judicious Lawyer, were directly against this new Doctrine, and some that have carefully looked backward, observed, that there are very few Examples of men acquitted by Petit Juries, because Grand-Juries of old were so wary in canvasing every thing narrowly, and so sensible of their Duty, in proceeding according unto truth upon satisfactory Evidence, that few or none were brought unto Trial till their guilt seemed evident.

It is therefore a great mistake to think that the second Juries were instituted for the hearing of fuller proofs, that was not their work, but to give an opportunity to the accused persons to answer for themselves, and make their defence, which cannot be thought to strengthen the Evidence, unless they be supposed to play booty against their own Lives. By way of answer, the Prisoner may avoid the Charge: He is permitted to take exceptions; he may demur or plead to the Indictments in points of Law: Herein the Judges ought to assist him, and appoint Counsel if he desire it: He may shew that the Indictors, *i. e.* the Grand-Jury, or some of them, are not lawful men, or not lawfully returned by the Sheriffs; embracery or practice may be proved in the packing of the Jury: A Conspiracy or Subornation may be discovered; falshood may be found out in the Witnesses, by questions about some circumstances that none could have asked, or imagined, except the Party accused: And besides doing right to the Indicted, in these and many other things, 'tis the People's due to have all the Evidence first taken in private, to be afterwards made publick at the Trial, that the Kingdom may be satisfied in the equal administration of Justice, and that the Judgments against Criminals may be of greater terrour, and more useful to preserve the common peace.

If any object that this Doctrine would introduce double Trials for every offence, and all the delays that accompany them, it may be answered, that *Nulla unquam de morte hominis cunctatio longa est.* Ju. Sat. No delay is to be esteemed long, when the life of a man is in question. The punishment of an Offender that is a little deferred, may be compensated by its severity; but blood rashly split cannot be gathered up, and a Land polluted by it, is hardly cleansed. Wise and good men in matters of this nature have ever proceeded with extreme caution, whilst the swift of foot are in the Scripture represented under an ill Character, and have been often found in their haste to draw more guilt upon themselves, than what they pretended to chastize in others. To avoid this mischief, in many well polished Kingdoms, several Courts of Justice are instituted, who take cognizance of the same facts, but so subordinate to one another, that in matters of life, limb, liberty, or other important cases, there is a right of appeal from the inferior, before which it is first brought, to the superior; where this is wanting, means have been found to give opportunity unto the Judges to reflect upon their own sentences, that if any thing had been done rashly, or through mistake, it might be corrected; man, even in his best estate, seeming to have need of some such helps. *Tiberius Cæsar* was never accused of too much lenity, but when he heard that *Lutorius Priscus* had been accused of Treason before the Senate, condemned, and immediately put to death, *Tam præcipites deprecatus est pœnas,* he desired that such sudden punishment might for the future be forborn; and a Law was thereupon made, *That no Decree of the Senate should in less than ten days be transmitted to the Treasury,* before which time it could not be executed, *Tac. An.* 3. Matters of this nature concerning every man in *England,* it is not to be doubted but our Ancestors consider'd them, and our Constitutions, neither admitting of subordinate Judicatures, from whence Appeals may be made, nor giving opportunities unto Juries to re-examine their Verdicts, after they were given, they could not find a way more suitable to the Rules of Wisdom, Justice, and Mercy, than to appoint two Juries with equal care, according unto different methods, the one in private, and at leisure, the other publickly in the presence of the Party, and more speedy to pass upon every man, so as none can be condemned, unless he be thought guilty by them both; and it cannot be imagined that so little time, as is usually spent in Trials at the Bar, before a Petit Jury, should be allowed unto one that pleads for his life, or unto them who are to be satisfied in their Consciences, unless it were presumed that the Grand-Jury had so well examined, prepared, and digested the matter, that the other may proceed more succinctly, without danger of error.

Therefore

Therefore let the Grand-Juries faithfully perform their high Trust, and neither be cheated, nor frighted from their Duty: Let them pursue the good old way, since no Innovation can be brought in, that will not turn to the prejudice of the accused Persons, and themselves: Let them not be deluded with frivolous Arguments, so as to invalidate a considerable part of our Law, and render themselves insignificant cyphers, in expectation that Petit Juries will repair the faults they commit, since that would be no less than to slight one of the best fences that the Law provides for our Lives and Liberties, and very much to weaken the other.

When a Grand-Jury finds a Bill against any person, they do all that in them lies to take away his Life, if the crime be capital; and it is ridiculous for them to pretend they rely upon the virtue of the Petit Jury, if they shew none themselves. They cannot reasonably hope the other should be more tender of the Prisoner's concernments, more exact in doing Justice, or more careful in examining the Credit of the Witnesses, when they have not only neglected their duty of searching into it, but added strength unto their Testimony by finding a Bill upon it.

They cannot possibly be exempted from the blame of consenting (at the least) unto the mischiefs that may ensue, unless they use all the honest care that the Law allows to prevent them; nor consequently avoid the stain of the blood that may be shed by their omission, since it could not have been, if they had well performed their part before they found the Indictment, whereby the party is exposed to so many disadvantages, that it is hard for the clearest Innocence to defend it self against them.

But when the one and the other Jury act as they ought, with courage, diligence, and indifference, we shall have just reason, with the wise Lord Chancellor *Fortescue,* to celebrate that Law that instituted them. To congratulate with our Countrymen *Fort. de Laud.* the happiness we enjoy, whilst our Lives lie not *at the mercy of unknown Witnesses, hired,* *Leg. Ang.* cap. *poor, uncertain, whose Conversation or Malice we are strangers to, but Neighbours of Sub-* 26. *stance, of honest report, brought into Court by an honourable sworn Officer; men who know the Witnesses, and their Credit, and are to hear them, and judge of them: that want no means for disclosing of Truth, and from whom nothing can be hid, which can fall within the compass of human Knowledge.*

Ex chronico ab Anno 1272. 1. Ed. 1. ad An. 1317. 10 Ed. 2. Miss. An. Dom. 1289. Annoq; Regni Regis Ed. 1. 18.

Certe scimus quam plurimos eorum qui judiciis sub Ed. 1. præfuere viros quidem maximos, & ævo in illo Jurisconsultos celeberrimos, repetundarum & quod lites suas fecerant aliosq; præter Ministros forenses aliquot merito damnatos multos, exitio & carcere punitos. Ex Selden. ad Fletam dissertat. p. 548.

POstquam Rex per spatium trium Annorum & amplius in partibus transmarinis remansisset,& de partibus Vasconiæ & Franciæ in Angliam rediisset, valde anxiatus & conturbatus fuit per quotidianum clamorem tam Clericorum quam Laicorum petentium ab eo congruum remedium apponi versus Justiciarios, & alios Ministros suos, de multimodis oppressionibus & gravaminibus contra bonas leges & consuetudines regni illis factis; super quo Dominus Edvardus Rex, per regale scriptum Vicecomitibus Angliæ præcipit quod in omnibus Comitatibus, Civitatibus, & Villis mercatoriis, publice proclamari facerent, quod omnes qui sese sentient gravari venirent apud Westm. ad proximum Parliamentum, & ibi querimonias suas monstrarent, ubi tam majores quam minores opportunum remedium & celerem justitiam recuperent, sicut Rex vinculo juramenti die Coronationis suæ astrictus fuit: Ac jam adest magnus dies & judiciarius, Justiciorum & aliorum Ministrorum Concilii Regis, quem nulla tergiversatione, nullo munere, nulla arte vel ingenio placitandi valent eludi. Coadunatis itaque Clero & Populo & in magno Palatio Westmonasterii consessis, Archiepiscopus Cantuariensis (vir magnæ pietatis & columna quasi sanctæ Ecclesiæ & Regni) surrexit in medio, & ab alto ducens

After that the King, for the space of three Years and more, had remained beyond Sea, and returned out of Gascoign *and* France *into* England, *he was much vexed and disturbed by the continual clamour both of the Clergy and Laity, desiring to be relieved against the Justices, and other His Majesty's Ministers, of several oppressions and injuries done unto them, contrary to the good Laws and Customs of the Realm; whereupon King* Edward, *by his Royal Letters to the several Sheriffs of* England, *commanded, that in all Counties, Cities, and Market-Towns, a Proclamation should be made,that all who found themselves aggrieved should repair to* Westminster *at the next Parliament, and there shew their Grievances, where as well the great as the less should receive fit Remedies and speedy Justice, according as the King was obliged by the Bond of his Coronation Oath: And now that great day was come, that day of judging, even the Justices and the other Ministers of the King's Council, which by no Collusion or Reward, no Argument or Art of Pleading, they could elude or avoid: The Clergy therefore and the People being gathered together, and seated in the great Palace of* Westminster, *the Archbishop of* Canterbury *(a man of eminent Piety, and as it were a Pillar of the holy Church and the King-*

cens   dom)

cens fufpiria, Noverit univerfitas veftra (ait) quod convocati fumus de magnis & arduis negotiis regni (heu nimis perturbati & his diebus enormiter mutilati) unanimiter, fideliter, & efficaciter fimul cum Domino Rege ad tractandum & ordinandum, audiviftis etiam univerfi querimonias graviffimas fuper intolerabilibus injuriis & oppreffionibus & quotidianis defolationibus, tam fanctæ Ecclef. quam Reg. factis per hoc iniquum Concilium Domini Regis contra magnas Chartas tot, toties & multoties emptas & redemptas, conceffas & confirmatas per tot & talia Juramenta Domini Regis nunc, & Dominorum Henrici & Johannis, ac per terribiles fulminationes Excommunicationis fententiæ in transgreffores communium libertatum Angliæ, quæ in chartis prædictis continentur corroboratas, & cum fpes præconcepta de libertatibus illis obfervandis fideliter ab omnibus putaretur ftabilis & indubitata, Rex conciliis malorum Miniftrorum præventus & feductus eafdem infringendo contravenire non formidavit, credens deceptive pro munere abfolvi à transgreffione quod effet manifeftum regni exterminium.

Aliud etiam nos omnes angit intrinfecus quod Jufticiarii fubtiliter ex malitia fua ac per diverfa argumenta avaritiæ, & intolerabilis fuperbiæ Regem contra fideles fuos multipliciter provocaverunt & incitaverunt, fanoque & falubri confilio Ligeorum Angliæ contrarium reddiderunt, confilia fua vana impudenter præponere & affirmare non erubuerunt feu formidaverunt, ac fi plus habiles effent ad confulendam & confervandam Rempublicam quam tota Univerfitas Regni in unum collecta. Ita de illis poffit vere dici, viri qui turbaverunt terram & concufferunt Regnum fub fuco gravitatis totum populum graviter opprefferunt, prætextuq; folummodo exponendi veteres Leges, novas (non dicam Leges) fed malas confuetudines introduxerunt & vomuerunt, ita quod per ignorantiam nonnullorum ac per partialitatem aliorum qui vel per munera vel timorem aliquorum potentum innodati fuerunt, nulla fuit ftabilitas Legum nec alicui de populo Juftitiam dignabantur exhibere, opera eorum funt opera nequitiæ, & opus iniquitatis in manibus, pedes eorum ad malum currunt & feftinant, ac viam recti nefcierunt. Quid dicam? non eft judicium in greffibus fuis.

Quam plurimi liberi homines terræ noftræ fideles Domini Regis quafi viles ultimæ fervi conditionis diverfis Carceribus fine culpa commiferunt, ibidem carcerandi quorum nonnulli in carcere fame, mœrore & vinculorum pondere defecerunt, extorquerunt pro Arbitrio infuper infinitam pecu-

Vide Fletâ Cap. 17. p. 18, 19. *Authoritas & Officium ordinarii Concilii Regis.*

dom) *rising from his Seat, and fetching a profound figh, spoke in this manner: Let this Assembly know that we are called together concerning the great and weighty Affairs of the Kingdom (too much alas of late disturbed, and still out of order) unanimously, faithfully, and effectually with our Lord the King to treat and ordain: Ye have all heard the grievous complaints of the most intolerable injuries and oppressions of the daily desolations committed both on Church and State, by this corrupt Council of our Lord the King, contrary to our great Charters, so many and so often, purchased and redeemed, granted and confirmed to us by the several Oaths of our Lord the King that now is, and of our Lords King Henry and John, and corroborated by the dreadful thundrings of the sentence of Excommunication against the Invaders of our common Liberties of England in our said Charters contained; and when we had conceived firm and undoubted hopes, that these our Liberties would have been faithfully preserved by all men, the King circumvented and seduced by the Counsels of evil Ministers, hath not been afraid to violate it by infringing them, falsly believing that he could for Rewards be absolved from that offence, which would be the manifest destruction of the Kingdom.*

There is another thing also that grieves our Spirits, that the Justices subtilly and maliciously, by diverse Arguments of covetousness and intolerable pride, have the King against his faithful Subjects sundry ways incited and provoked, counselling him contrary to the good and wholesome Advice of all the Liegemen of England, and have not blushed nor been afraid, impudently to assert and prefer their own foolish Counsels, as if they were more fit to consult and preserve the Commonwealth, than all the Estates of the Kingdom together assembled; so that it may be truly said of them, they are the men that troubled the Land, and disturb'd the Nation under a false colour of gravity, have the whole People grievously opprest, and under pretence of expounding the ancient Laws, have introduced new (I will not say Laws, but) evil Customs; so that through the Ignorance of some, and Partiality of others, who for reward or fear of great Men have been engaged, there was no certainty of Law, and they scorned to administer Justice to the people, their deeds are deeds of wickedness, and the work of iniquity is in their hand, their feet make haste to evil, and the way of truth have they not known; what shall I say? there is no Judgment in their paths.

How many Free-men of this Land, faithful Subjects of our Lord the King, have like the meanest Slaves of lowest condition, without any fault been cast into Prison, where some of them by hunger, grief, or the burden of their chains have expired; they have also extorted at their pleasure infinite sums of money

pecuniam ab eisdem pro redemptione sua, crumenas aliorum ut suas impregnarent tam à divitibus quam pauperibus exhauserunt, ratione quorum incurriverunt odium inexorabile & formidabile imprecationes omnium, quasi tale incommunicabile privilegium, *per Chartam detestabilem* de non obstante obtinuerunt & perquiviserunt, ut à lege divina humanaque quasi ad libitum immunes essent.

Gravamen insuper solitum adhuc sive aliquo modo sævit, omnia sunt venalia si non quasi furtiva, proh dolor.

——Quid non mortalia pectora cogit Auri sacra fames?——

Ex ore meo contra vos, O Impii, tremebunda cœli decreta jam auditis. Agnitio vultuum vestrorum accusat vos, & peccatum vestrum quasi Sodoma prædicavistis nec abscondistis; væ animæ vestræ, væ qui condunt leges & scribentes injustitiam scripserunt, ut opprimerent in judicio pauperes, & vim facerent causæ humilium populi, ut essent viduæ præda eorum, & pupillos diriperent; væ qui ædificant domum suam injustitia & cœnacula sua non in Judicio, væ qui concupiverunt agros & violenter tulerunt & rapuerunt domos, & oppresserunt virum & domum ejus, imo virum & hæreditatem suam; væ Judices qui sicut Lupi vespere non relinquebant ossa in mane; Justus Judex adducit Consiliarios in stultum finem & Judices in stuporem, mox alta voce justum Judicium terræ recipietis.

Vide Mat. West. Anno 1289. p. 376. li. 13. His auditis omnium aures tinniebant totaque Communitas ingemuerunt, dicentes heu nobis, heu, ubi est Angliæ toties empta, toties concessa, toties scripta, toties jurata Libertas?

Anno vero 1290. (18. Ed. 1.) deprehensis omnibus Angliæ Justiciariis de repetundis (præter Jo. Metingham, & Eliam de Alii de Criminalibus sese à visibus populi subtrahentes in locis secretis cum amicis tacite latitaverunt, alios protulerunt in medium unde merito fere omnes ab officiis depositi & amoti, unus à terra exulatus, alii perpetuis prisonis incarcerati, alii que gravibus pecuniarum solutionibus juste adjudicati fuerunt.

Bleckingham quos honoris ergo nominatos volui) judicio Parliamenti vindicatum est in alios, atque alios carcere, exilio, fortunarumque omnium dispendio, in singulos mulcta gravissima & amissione officii. Spelman's Glossary, p. 1. co. 1. 416.

money for their ransoms; the Coffers of some, that they might fill their own, as well from the rich as the poor, they have exhausted, by reason whereof they have contracted the irreconcileable hatred and dreadful imprecations of all men, as if they had purchas'd and obtain'd such an incommunicable privilege, by their detestable Charter of Non Obstante, that they might at their own lust be free from all Laws both human and divine.

Moreover, there is another more than ordinary grievance, which hitherto hath, and in some measure doth still rage among us: All things are expos'd to sale, if not as it were to plunder and theft. Alas! how great power hath the love of mony in the breasts of Men? Hear therefore, O ye wicked, from my mouth the dreadful decree of Heaven; the dejection of your countenances accuseth you, and like the men of Sodom, ye have not hidden but proclaimed the sin; woe be to your souls, woe be to them that make Laws, and writing, write injustice, that they may oppress the poor in Judgment, and injure the cause of the humble; that Widows may become their Prey, and that they might destroy the Orphan. Woe be to those that build their Houses in injustice, and their Tabernacles in unrighteousness: Woe be to them that covet large possessions, that break open Houses and destroy the Man and his Inheritance; woe be to such Judges who are like Wolves in the Evening, and leave not a bone till the morning. The righteous Judge will bring such Counsellors to a foolish end, and such Judges to confusion: ye shall all presently with a loud cry, receive the just sentence of the Land.

At the hearing of these things all Ears tingled, and the whole Community, lifted up their Voice, and mourned, saying, Alas, alas for us! what is become of that English Liberty which we have so often purchased, which by so many Concessions, so many Statutes, so many Oaths have been confirmed to us.

Hereupon several of the Criminals withdrew into secret places, being concealed by their friends; some of them were brought forth into the midst of the People, and deservedly turned out of their Offices; one was banished the Land, and others were grievously fined, or condemned to perpetual Imprisonment.

This is confirmed by Spelman, An. 1290. *An. 18. Ed. 1. All the Justices of England, saith he, were apprehended for corruption, except John Metingham, and Elias Bleckingham, whom I name for their honour; and by Judgment of Parliament condemned, some to Imprisonment, others Banishment, or Confiscation of their Estates, and none escaped without grievous Fines, and the loss of their Offices.*

THE

The Speech and Carriage of

STEPHEN COLLEDGE,

Before the Caſtle at *Oxford,* Wedneſday, *Aug.* 31. 1681. Taken exactly from his Mouth at the Place of Execution.

Mr. High-Sheriff.   **M**R. Colledge, *It is deſired, for ſatisfaction of the World, becauſe you have profeſt your ſelf a Proteſtant, that you would tell what Judgment you are of.*

Dear People, dear Proteſtants, and dear Country-men,

Colledge.   **I** Have been accuſed and convicted for Treaſon, the Laws adjudge me to this Death, and I come hither willingly to ſubmit to it. I pray God forgive all thoſe perſons that had any hand in it. I do declare to you, whatever has been ſaid of me, that I was never a Papiſt, or ever that way inclined ; they have done me wrong : I was ever a Proteſtant, I was born a Proteſtant, I have lived ſo, and ſo by the Grace of God I will die, of the Church of *England,* according to the beſt Reformation of the Church from all Idolatry, from all Superſtition, or any thing that is contrary to the Goſpel of our bleſſed Lord and Saviour. I do declare, I was never at any Popiſh Service, Prayers, or Devotions in my life, ſave one time about ſeventeen or eighteen years ago, as near as I remember, I was out of a Curioſity one afternoon at St. *James*'s Chappel, the Queen's Chappel at St. *James*'s ; except that one time, I never did hear any Popiſh Service, any thing of the Church of *Rome,* Maſs or Prayers, or any thing elſe, private or publick.

I know you expect that I ſhould ſay ſomething as to what I die for. It has been charged upon me : when I was apprehended and brought before the Council, ſome of the Council, the Secretary, and my Lord *Killingworth,* and Mr. *Seymour,* they told me there was Treaſon ſworn againſt me ; truly they ſurprized me when they ſaid ſo : for of all things in the World, I thought my ſelf as free from that as any man. I aſked them if any man living had the confidence to ſwear Treaſon againſt me ? They ſaid ſeveral, three or four, as I remember. Then they told me, it was ſworn againſt me, that I had a deſign to pull the King out of *White-hall,* and to ſerve him as his Father was ſerved, or to that purpoſe, the Loggerhead his Father, or that kind of Language. I did deny it then, and do now deny it upon my Death. I never was in any manner of Plot in my days, neither one way nor another, never knew any ſuch perſons, nor ever had ſuch Communication with any man hitherto. I know of no Plot in the World but the Popiſh Plot, and that every man may know as much as I. If I had had ſuch a deſign as theſe men have ſworn againſt me, to have ſeiz'd his Majeſty either at *London,* or this place at *Oxford* ; I take God to witneſs, as I'm a dying man, and upon the terms of my Salvation, I know not any one man upon the face of the Earth that would have ſtood by me ; and how likely it was that I ſhould do ſuch a thing my ſelf, let the whole World judge.

Dugdale ſwears, that I ſpoke Treaſon to him, treaſonable Words in the Coffee-houſe, and in the Barber's ſhop by the *Angel,* even he could not pretend to ſee me any where elſe ; but it is falſe, and a very unlikely thing, that I ſhould ſpeak Treaſon to him. I muſt confeſs, I was in his company at the Coffee-houſe and that Barber's ſhop, before I went out of Town, but there could be no Communication between us ; for he was writing at one end of the Room and eating a piece of bread, and I lighted a Pipe of Tobacco at the other end, and took it, till Sir *Tho. Player* and Sir *Rob. Clayton* came to me, and we went to my Lord *Lovelace*'s out of Town that night : ſo when they came, we took horſe and went out of Town with the reſt.

For my part, I can't ſum up my Witneſſes. I was under moſt ſtrange Circumſtances as ever any man was ; I was kept Priſoner ſo cloſe in the *Tower,* that I could have no Converſation with any, though I was certain the Popiſh Lords had it every day there, but I could have none : I could not tell the Witneſſes that were to ſwear againſt me ; I could not tell what it was they ſwore againſt me, for I could have no Copy of the Indictment, nor no way poſſible to make any preparation to make my Defence, as I ought to have done, and might have done by Law ; I had no Liberty to do any thing, as I am a dying man.

And as to what *Dugdale, Smith, Turberville,* and *Heyns* ſwore againſt me, they did ſwear ſuch Treaſon, that nothing but a mad man would ever have truſted any body

with,

with, and leaſt of all to Papiſts; every one of them that had been concerned with Plots and Treaſons among their own party, and under the greateſt Tyes and Obligations of Damnation, and to be Sainted if they kept it ſecret, and to be damned if they revealed it. If theſe men will not keep things ſecret for their own Party, how could I truſt them? I take God to witneſs, and do freely acknowledge, I have ſought my God with Tears ſeveral times, to inform me if ſo be I had with any word tranſgreſſed at any time. I knew not of any part of what they ſwore againſt me, till ſuch time as I heard it ſwore againſt me at the Bar. This is very hard, Gentlemen, but this is the Truth.

And there be a great many other ſtrange Reports that I have heard ſince I have been a Priſoner, that I ſhould be a means to convert the Counteſs of *Rocheſter*, by bringing one *Thompſon* a Prieſt to her. Truly all that I was concerned in was, ſome fifteen or ſixteen years ago I lodged at Col. *Vernon*'s that married my Lady *Brookes*: The Family were Papiſts, the *Brookes* were Papiſts, and there was this *Thompſon*; and I did ſuppoſe him a Prieſt in the Houſe, though I never ſaw him at Popiſh Service or Worſhip, though I was there half a year; but coming afterwards to my Lord *Rocheſter*'s about ſome buſineſs I had to do for him and ſeveral other perſons of Quality, he ſent for me one afternoon from the Parſonage in *Adderbury* to his Houſe, and his Lady and he ſtood together: He ſent to me, and aſk'd me if my Horſe were at home: ſaid he, I would have you carry this Letter to Mr. *Thompſon*, if you are at leiſure this afternoon. My Lord, I am at leiſure to ſerve you. So I took a Letter from his hand, and his Lady's too, as I remember (he made an offer that way) ſealed with his own Seal, and carried it to *Thompſon*, and delivered it to him; and he told me that he would wait upon my Lord, for it was for ſome Lands my Lord did offer to raiſe Money for ſome occaſions. This is the Truth of that Scandal.

It is ſaid, that I had a Prieſt ſeveral years in my Houſe, *viz. Serjeant* that came over from *Holland* to diſcover: About ſome ten years ago, that very ſame man came to me, but was a ſtranger to me, and he came to me by the name of Dr. *Smith* a Phyſician; and there was an Apothecary in the *Old-baily*, and a Linnen-draper within *Ludgate*, that came with him: they brought him thither and took a Chamber, and lay about half a year or three quarters, at times, by the name of Dr. *Smith*, and as a Phyſician. This is the Truth of that, and no otherwiſe. This is the Entertainment of *Serjeant*.

So the occaſion of my coming to *Oxford*, I do ſay, was voluntary. The Parliamentmen laſt Parliament at *Weſtminſter*, and ſeveral Lords, dined together the day before they ſate: the laſt Seſſions of Parliament at *Weſtminſter* they ſent for me to the Sun-Tavern behind the *Exchange*; and when I came, the Duke of *Monmouth* and ſeveral Lords were together, and I believe above a hundred Parliament-men of the Commons. The Duke of *Monmouth* called me to him, and told me, he had heard a good Report of me, and that I was an honeſt man, and one that may be truſted; and they did not know but their Enemies the Papiſts might have ſome deſign to ſerve them as they did in King *James*'s time, by Gun-powder, or any other ways: And the Duke, with ſeveral Lords and Commons, did deſire me to uſe my utmoſt ſkill in ſearching all places ſuſpected by them; which I did perform, and from thence I had, as I think, the popular name of the *Proteſtant Joyner*, becauſe they had intruſted me before any man in *England* to do that Office.

The ſame *Haynes*, one of them that ſwore againſt me, had diſcovered to me and ſeveral others, as to *Macknamar* and his Brother, and this *Ivy*, who are now all of another Stamp, that the Parliament was to be deſtroyed at *Oxford*; and that there was a deſign to murther my Lord *Shaftſbury* by *Fitzgerald* and his Party; and that they did endeavour to bring *Macknamar* over to him, and ſaid, then it would be well with him; and they would not be long before they had *Shaftſbury*'s life. And he made Depoſitions of this to Sir *Geo. Treby*, as I heard afterwards; for I was not with him when it was ſworn. I wiſh the Commons of *England* as well as I wiſh my own heart; and I did not underſtand, but when I ſerv'd the Parliament, I ſerv'd his Majeſty too: and let them be miſerable that make the Difference between them; for my part I never did.

I came to *Oxford* with my Lord *Howard*, whom I look upon to be a very honeſt worthy Gentleman, my Lord *Clare*, my Lord *Paget*, and my Lord *Huntingdon*; and this Capt. *Brown* and Don *Lewis* were in my Company, and came along with us as they were my Lord *Howard*'s Friends. *Brown* I have known, I believe, two or three months, but *Lewis* I never ſaw before that day; they ſaid they came with my Lord *Howard*. I take God to witneſs, I never had one ſixpence or any thing elſe, to carry on any deſign; and if it were to ſave my life now, I can't charge any man in the world with any deſign againſt the Government, as God is my witneſs, or againſt his Majeſty, or any other perſon.

As for what Arms I had, and what Arms others had, they were for our own defence, in caſe the Papiſts ſhould make any attempt upon us by way of Maſſacre, or any Invaſion or Rebellion, that we ſhould be ready to defend our ſelves. God is my witneſs this is all I know: If this be a Plot, this I was in; but in no other. But never knew of any

numbers

numbers or times appointed for meeting; but we said one to another, that the Papists had a Design against the Protestants, when we did meet, as I was a man of general Conversation; and in case they should rise, we were ready: but then they should begin the Attempt upon us. This was my business, and is the business of every good Subject that loves the Laws of his Country and his King: For *England* can never hope to be happy under those blood-thirsty men, whose Religion is Blood and Murther; which I do with all my Soul, and did ever since I knew what Religion was, abhor and detest, *viz.* the Church of *Rome*, as pernicious and destructive to human Societies, and all Government.

I beseech God, that every Man of you may unite together as Protestants against this common Foe. *Gentlemen*, it is my sense, and I do in that believe I am as certainly murthered by the hands of the Papists as Sir *Edmondbury Godfrey* himself was, though the thing is not seen. These Witnesses certainly are mercenary men, and I beseech God Almighty to have mercy upon their Souls, and forgive them; and either by his Judgments or Mercies reclaim them, that they shed no more innocent blood: There is not a man of them that I know of, that ever heard me say or do any bit of Treason in my life. This is (the first I mayn't say it is) but almost the twentieth Sham-Plot that they have endeavoured to put upon the Nation, to delude the People, and put off their own damnable Plot. This is not the first, but I think the sixteenth or seventeenth; I pray God that my Blood may be the last. I pray God defend every man's Blood, and all Protestants in *England*, from the hand of these bloody Papists, by whose means I die this Death; and if they shall go on in this nature, I hope the good God will open every man's eyes to see it before he feels it: And I beseech you, if you have any love for your King, your Country, and the Protestants, unite together, if you are Protestants. I pray God, those that deserve the name, let them be called how they will, either Dissenters, or Church of *England* men, that they may unite together like men, like Christians, against the common Foe, who will spare neither the one side nor the other, but beat you one against another like two Pitchers, the last that stands they will certainly destroy if they can. This is my sense, and God is my witness, I speak my Conscience. I do not know, Mr. *Sheriff*, whether there be any thing else I have to say, or no. We have a good God, and I beseech every man that hears me this day (for we live in a sinful Age, good People, and it behoveth every one of you, it cannot be long before all that look upon me in this condition, must lie down in the Dust, and God knows, must come into an eternal estate either for Mercy or Judgment) I beseech you in the name of God, he is a God of Mercy, and a God of Patience, and Long-suffering, that you would break off your Sins by Repentance, and serve a good God, who must be your Friend at last, or else you are lost to Eternity.

O Lord, how ungrateful wretches are we, that have a God of such infinite Mercy and Goodness, that affords us our Life, our Health, and a thousand Mercies every day; and we like ungrateful People, not deserving the name of Men or Christians, live riotous Lives, in Debauchery and Swearing, in Malice, and the Lord knows how many Evils. I beseech God that I may be this day a means in the hand of God to bring some of their Souls over to him. I beseech you remember what I say. Indeed I do not know, I have been so strangely used since I have been a Prisoner, what to say, being brought from one Affliction to another, that my Body is worn out, and my Memory and Intellects have failed me much, to what they were; I can't remember what I have to say more, but that the Lord Jesus Christ would bless my Country, and preserve it from Popery; and in mercy bless his Majesty: good God be merciful to him, make him an instrument in thy hands to defend his Protestant Subjects; Lord, in mercy defend him from his Enemies; good God bless this People; good Lord continue the Gospel of Jesus Christ, thy Gospel in its purity, to us and our Posterity, as long as the Sun and Moon endureth. O Lord, save all that call upon thee, be merciful to all thy Servants, all thy People that put their trust in thee, good Lord deliver them from the hands of their Enemies: good Lord, let their Lives, and Bodies, and Souls, be all precious in thy sight. O merciful God, put a stop to these most wicked Conspiracies of thy Enemies, and the Nation's Enemies, the Papists; let no more Protestant Blood be shed but this of mine, I beseech thee, O my God. O Lord look upon me; O Lord bless me, O good God, receive me into thy blessed presence by Jesus Christ my alone Saviour and Redeemer, in whom alone I put my trust for Salvation: It is thee, O God, that I trust in, thou righteous Judge of Heaven and Earth. All Popery, all Pardons, all Popes and Priests, all Dispensations I disown, and will not go out of the World with a lye in my mouth. From the sincerity of my heart, I declare again, that what I've said to you, is the very Sentiments of my Soul, as God shall have mercy upon me, and to the best of my knowledge.

I desire the Prayers of you, good People, whilst I am here: and once more I beseech you to think upon Eternity, every one of you that hear me this day; the Lord turn

your

your Hearts and Souls, if you have been wicked livers, if you do live wicked lives, the Lord in mercy convert you, and shew you your danger: for I as little thought to come to this, as any man that hears me this day, and I bless God, I have no more deserved it from the hands of men, than the Child that sucks at his Mother's breast, I bless my God for it. I do say, I have been a sinner against my God, and he hath learned me Grace ever since I have been a Prisoner. I bless my God for a Prison; I bless my God for Afflictions: I bless my God that ever I was restrain'd; for I never knew my self till he had taken me out of the World. Therefore you that have your liberties, time, and precious opportunities, be up, and be doing for God and for your Souls, every one of you.

To his Son. Where is my dear Child?

Mr. Sheriff. *I made one request to you, you gave me an imperfect Answer; you said you were of the best reformed Church in the world, the Church of* England, *according to the best Reformation in the world. I desire you, for the satisfaction of the world, to declare what Church that is, whether Presbyterian, or Independent, or the Church of* England, *or what.*

Colledge. Good Mr. Sheriff, for your satisfaction, for 20 years and above I was under the Presbyterian Ministry, till his Majesty's Restauration; then I was conformable to the Church of *England*, when that was restored, and so continued till such time as I saw Persecution upon the dissenting People, and undue things done in their Meeting-places; then I went among them to know what kind of people those were, and I take God to witness, since that time I have used their Meetings, *viz.* the Presbyterians, others very seldom, and the Church of *England.* I did hear Dr. *Tillotson* not above three weeks before I was taken. I heard the Church of *England* as frequently as I heard the Dissenters, and never had any prejudice, God is my witness, against either, but always heartily desired that they might unite, and be Lovers and Friends, and I had no prejudice against any man; and truly I am afraid that it is not for the Nation's good, that there should be such Heart-burnings between them: That some of the Church of *England* will preach, that the Presbyterians are worse than the Papists. God doth know that what I say, I speak freely from my heart, I have found many among them truly serving God, and so I have of all the rest that have come into my company; Men without any manner of Design but to serve God, serve his Majesty, and keep their Liberties and Properties; Men that I am certain are not of vicious lives: I found no Dammers or those kind of People amongst them, or at least few of them.

To his Son, kissing him several times with great passion. Dear Child, farewel, the Lord have mercy upon thee. Good people, let me have your Prayers to God Almighty to receive my Soul.

And then he prayed, and as soon as he had done, spake as followeth:

The Lord have mercy upon my Enemies, and I beseech you, good People, whoever you are, and the whole World that I have offended, to forgive me; whomever I have offended in word or deed, I ask every man's pardon, and I forgive the World with all my soul, all the Injuries I have received; and I beseech God Almighty forgive those poor Wretches who have cast away their souls, or at least endangered them, to ruin this body of mine: I beseech God that they may have a sight of their Sins, and that they may find mercy at his hands: Let my blood speak the justice of my Cause.

I have done: And God have mercy upon you all.

To Mr. *Crosthwait.* Pray, Sir, my Service to Dr. *Hall*, and Dr. *Reynall*, and thank them for all their Kindnesses to me; I thank you, Sir, for your Kindness: The Lord bless you all. Mr. *Sheriff*, God be with you: God be with you all, good People.

The Executioner Ketch *desired his pardon; and he said,* I do forgive you. The Lord have mercy on my Soul.

The SPEECH of the late Lord RUSSEL, to the SHERIFFS.

Together with the PAPER deliver'd by him to them, at the place of Execution, on July 21. 1683.

Mr. SHERIFF,

I Expected the Noise would be such, that I could not be very well heard: I was never fond of much speaking, much less now: Therefore I have set down in this Paper, all that I think fit to leave behind me. God knows how far I was always from Designs against the King's Person, or of altering the Government; and I still pray for the Preservation of both, and of the Protestant Religion.

I am told, that Captain *Walcot* has said some things concerning my knowledge of the

Plot:

Plot: I know not whether the Report is true or not, I hope it is not: For to my knowledge, I never ſaw him, or ſpake with him in my whole Life; and in the Words of a dying Man, I profeſs I know of no Plot, either againſt the King's Life, or the Government. But I have now done with this World, and am going to a better. I forgive all the World, and I thank God I die in Charity with all Men; and I wiſh all ſincere Proteſtants may love one another, and not make way for Popery by their Animoſities.

The PAPER *deliver'd to the* SHERIFFS.

I Thank God, I find my ſelf ſo compoſed and prepared for death, and my Thoughts ſo fixed on another World, that I hope in God I am now quite weaned from ſetting my heart on this. Yet I cannot forbear now, in ſetting down in Writing a fuller Account of my Condition, to be left behind me, than I'll venture to ſay at the place of Execution, in the noiſe and clutter that is like to be there. I bleſs God heartily for thoſe many Bleſſings, which he in his infinite Mercy has beſtowed upon me, through the whole courſe of my Life: That I was born of worthy good Parents, and had the Advantages of a religious Education, which I have often thank'd God very heartily for, and look'd upon as an invaluable Bleſſing; for even when I minded it leaſt, it ſtill hung about me, and gave me checks, and has now for many years ſo influenced and poſſeſſed me, that I feel the happy Effects of it in this my extremity, in which I have been ſo wonderfully (I thank God) ſupported, that neither my impriſonment, nor the fear of Death, have been able to diſcompoſe me to any degree; but on the contrary, I have found the Aſſurances of the Love and Mercy of God, in and through my bleſſed Redeemer, in whom only I truſt: and I do not queſtion, but that I am going to partake of that fulneſs of Joy which is in his preſence, the hopes thereof does ſo wonderfully delight me, that I reckon this as the happieſt time of my Life, tho' others may look upon it as the ſaddeſt.

I have lived, and now die of the reformed Religion, a true and ſincere Proteſtant, and in the Communion of the Church of *England*, though I could never yet comply with, or riſe up to all the heights of many People. I wiſh with all my Soul, all our unhappy Differences were removed, and that all ſincere Proteſtants would ſo far conſider the danger of Popery, as to lay aſide their Heats, and agree againſt the common Enemy; and that the Church-men would be leſs ſevere, and the Diſſenters leſs ſcrupulous: For I think Bitterneſs and Perſecution are at all times bad, but much more now.

For Popery, I look on it as an idolatrous and bloody Religion, and therefore thought my ſelf bound in my ſtation, to do all I could againſt it. And by that I foreſaw I ſhould procure ſuch great Enemies to my ſelf, and ſo powerful ones, that I have been now for ſome time expecting the worſt: And bleſſed be God, I fall by the Axe, and not by the fiery Tryal. Yet, whatever apprehenſions I had of Popery, and of my own ſevere and heavy ſhare I was like to have under it, when it ſhould prevail, I never had a thought of doing any thing againſt it baſely, or inhumanly, but what could well conſiſt with the Chriſtian Religion, and the Laws and Liberties of this Kingdom. And I thank God I have examin'd all my actings in that matter, with ſo great care, that I can appeal to God Almighty, who knows my heart, that I went on ſincerely, without being moved, either by Paſſions, By-ends, or ill Deſign. I have always loved my Country much more than my Life; and never had any Deſign of changing the Government, which I value and look upon as one of the beſt Governments in the World, and would always have been ready to venture my life for the preſerving it, and would have ſuffered any Extremity, rather than have conſented to any Deſign to take away the King's Life: Neither ever had Man the impudence to propoſe ſo baſe and barbarous a thing to me. And I look on it as a very unhappy and uneaſy part of my preſent Condition, that in my Indictment there ſhould be ſo much as mention of ſo vile a Fact; tho' nothing in the leaſt was ſaid to prove any ſuch Matter; but the contrary, by the Lord *Howard*: Neither does any body, I am confident, believe the leaſt of it. So that I need not, I think, ſay more.

For the King, I do ſincerely pray for him, and wiſh well to him, and to the Nation, that they may be happy in one another; that he may be indeed the Defender of the Faith, that the Proteſtant Religion, and the Peace and Safety of the Kingdom may be preſerved, and flouriſh under his Government; and that he in his Perſon may be happy both here, and hereafter.

As for the ſhare I had in the Proſecution of the Popiſh Plot, I take God to witneſs, that I proceeded in it in the ſincerity of my heart, being then really convinced (as I am ſtill) that there was a Conſpiracy againſt the King, the Nation, and the Proteſtant Religion: And I likewiſe profeſs, that I never knew of any thing, either directly, or indirectly, of any Practice with the Witneſſes; which I look upon as ſo horrid a thing, that I could never have endured it. For, I thank God, Falſhood and Cruelty were never in my Nature, but always the fartheſt from it imaginable. I did believe, and do ſtill, that Popery

pery is breaking in upon the Nation : and that those who advance it, will ſtop at nothing, to carry on their Deſign ; I am heartily ſorry that ſo many Proteſtants give their helping hand to it. But I hope God will preſerve the Proteſtant Religion, and this Nation : Though I am afraid it will fall under very great Tryals, and very ſharp Sufferings. And indeed the Impiety and Prophaneneſs that abounds, and appears ſo ſcandalouſly bare-fac'd every where, gives too juſt reaſon to fear the worſt things which can befall a People. I pray God prevent it, and give thoſe who have ſhew'd Concern for the Publick Good, and who have appear'd heartily for the true Intereſt of the Nation, and the Proteſtant Religion, Grace to live ſo, that they may not caſt a reproach on that which they endeavour to advance ; which (God knows) has often given me many ſad thoughts. And I hope ſuch of my Friends as may think they are touch'd by this, will not take what I ſay in ill part, but endeavour to amend their ways, and live ſuitable to the Rules of the true reformed Religion, which is the only thing can adminiſter true Comfort at the latter end, and revive a man when he comes to die.

As for my preſent Condition, I bleſs God, I have no repining in my heart at it. I know for my Sins I have deſerved much worſe at the hands of God ; ſo that I chearfully ſubmit to ſo ſmall a Puniſhment, as the being taken off a few years ſooner, and the being made a Spectacle to the World. I do freely forgive all the World, particularly thoſe concerned in taking away my life : and I deſire and conjure my Friends to think of no Revenge, but to ſubmit to the holy Will of God, into whoſe Hands I reſign my ſelf entirely.

But to look back a little, I cannot but give ſome touch about the Bill of Excluſion, and ſhew the Reaſons of my appearing in that Buſineſs, which in ſhort is this : That I thought the Nation was in ſuch danger of Popery, and that the expectation of a *Popiſh Succeſſor* (as I have ſaid in Parliament) put the King's life likewiſe in ſuch danger, that I ſaw no way ſo effectual to ſecure both, as ſuch a Bill. As to the Limitations which were propoſed, if they were ſincerely offered, and had paſs'd into a Law, the Duke then would have been excluded from the power of a King, and the Government quite alter'd, and little more than the name of a King left. So I could not ſee either Sin or Fault in the one, when all People were willing to admit of t'other : but thought it better to have a King with his Prerogative, and the Nation eaſy and ſafe under him, than a King without it, which muſt have bred perpetual Jealouſies, and a continual ſtruggle. All this I ſay only to juſtify my ſelf, and not to enflame others : Though I cannot but think my Earneſtneſs in that matter has had no ſmall influence in my preſent Sufferings. But I have now done with this World, and am going to a Kingdom which cannot be moved.

And as to the Conſpiring to ſeize the Guards, which is the Crime for which I am condemned, and which was made a conſtructive Treaſon for taking away the King's Life, to bring it within the Statute of *Ed.* the 3 *d* ; I ſhall give this true and clear account. I never was at Mr. *Shepherd*'s with that Company but once, and there was no undertaking then of ſecuring or ſeizing the Guards, nor none appointed to view, or examine them : Some Diſcourſe there was of the feaſibleneſs of it, and ſeveral times by accident in general Diſcourſe elſewhere, I have heard it mention'd, as a thing might eaſily be done, but never conſented to as fit to be done. And I remember particularly at my Lord *Shaftſbury*'s there being ſome general Diſcourſe of this kind, I immediately flew out, and exclaim'd againſt it, and aſk'd, if the thing ſucceeded, what muſt be done next, but maſſacring the Guards, and killing them in cold Blood ? Which I look'd upon as ſo deteſtable a thing, and ſo like a Popiſh Practice, that I could not but abhor it. And at the ſame time the Duke of *Monmouth* took me by the hand, and told me very kindly, My Lord, I ſee you and I are of a Temper, did you ever hear ſo horrid a thing ? And I muſt needs do him that Juſtice to declare, that I never obſerved in him but an abhorrence to all baſe things.

As to my going to Mr. *Shepherd*'s, I went with an intention to taſte *Sherry*, for he had promiſed me to reſerve for me the next very good piece he met with, when I went out of Town ; and if he recollects, he may remember I aſk'd him about it, and he went and fetch'd a Bottle ; but when I taſted it, I ſaid 'twas hot in the mouth, and deſired that whenever he met with a choice Piece, he would keep it for me, which he promiſed. I enlarge the more upon this, becauſe Sir *George Jefferies* inſinuated to the Jury, as if I had made a ſtory about going thither ; but I never ſaid, that was the only Reaſon : And I will now truly and plainly add the reſt.

I was the day before this Meeting, come to Town for two or three days, as I had done once or twice before ; having a very near and dear Relation lying in a very languiſhing and deſperate Condition : And the Duke of *Monmouth* came to me, and told me, he was extremely glad I was come to Town ; for my Lord *Shaftſbury*, and ſome hot Men would undo us all. How ſo, my Lord, I ſaid ? Why (anſwered he) they'll certainly do
                                                                        ſome

fome diforderly thing or other, if great Care be not taken ; and therefore for God's fake ufe your Endeavours with your Friends to prevent any thing of this kind. He told me there would be Company at Mr. *Shepherd*'s that Night, and defired me to be at home in the Evening, and he would call me ; which he did : And when I came into the Room, I faw Mr. *Rumfey* by the Chimney ; though he fwears he came in after ; and there were things faid by fome with much more Heat than Judgment, which I did fufficiently difapprove, and yet for thefe things I ftand condemned. But I thank God, my part was fincere, and well meant. It is, I know, inferr'd from hence, and was preffed to me, that I was acquainted with thefe Heats and ill Defigns, and did not difcover them. But this is but Mifprifion of Treafon at moft. So I die innocent of the Crime I ftand condemn'd for, and I hope no body will imagine that fo mean a Thought could enter into me, as to go about to fave my felf, by accufing others. The part that fome have acted lately of that kind, has not been fuch as to invite me to love Life at fuch a rate.

As for the Sentence of Death paffed upon me, I cannot but think it a very hard one. For nothing was fworn againft me (whether true or falfe, I will not now examine) but fome Difcourfes about making fome Stirs. And this is not levying War againft the King, which is Treafon by the Statute of *Edward* the Third, and not the confulting and difcourfing about it, which was all that was witneffed againft me. But, by a ftrange fetch, the Defign of feizing the Guards was conftrued a defign of killing the King ; and fo I was in that caft.

And now I have truly and fincerely told what my part was in that, which cannot be more than a bare Mifprifion ; and yet I am condemned as guilty of a Defign of killing the King. I pray God lay not this to the charge, neither of the King's Counfel, nor Judges, nor Sheriffs, nor Jury : And for the Witneffes, I pity them, and wifh them well. I fhall not reckon up the particulars wherein they did me wrong ; I had rather their own Confciences fhould do that, to which, and the Mercies of God, I leave them. Only I ftill aver, that what I faid of my not hearing Col. *Rumfey* deliver any Meffage from my Lord *Shaftsbury*, was true ; for I always detefted Lying, tho' never fo much to my advantage. And I hope none will be fo unjuft and uncharitable, as to think I would venture on it in thefe my laft Words, for which I am fo foon to give an account to the great God, the Searcher of Hearts, and Judge of all Things.

From the time of chufing Sheriffs, I concluded the Heat in that Matter would produce fomething of this kind ; and I am not much furprized to find it fall upon me. And I wifh what is done to me, may put a ftop, and fatiate fome People's Revenge, and that no more innocent Blood be fhed ; for I muft and do ftill look upon mine as fuch, fince I know I was guilty of no Treafon : and therefore I would not betray my Innocence by Flight, of which I do not (I thank God) yet repent (tho' much preffed to it) how fatal foever it may have feem'd to have proved to me ; for I look upon my Death in this manner (I thank God) with other eyes than the World does. I know I faid but little at the Trial, and I fuppofe it looks more like Innocence than Guilt. I was alfo advis'd not to confefs Matter of Fact plainly, fince that muft certainly have brought me within the Guilt of Mifprifion. And being thus reftrained from dealing frankly and openly, I chofe rather to fay little, than to depart from that Ingenuity, that by the Grace of God, I had carried along with me in the former parts of my Life, and fo could eafier be filent, and leave the whole Matter to the Confcience of the Jury, than to make the laft and folemneft part of my Life fo different from the Courfe of it, as the ufing little Tricks and Evafions muft have been. Nor did I ever pretend to a great readinefs in fpeaking : I wifh thofe Gentlemen of the Law, who have it, would make more Confcience in the Ufe of it, and not run Men down, and by ftrains and fetches impofe on eafy and willing Juries, to the ruin of innocent Men : For to kill by forms and fubtilties of Law, is the worft fort of Murther. But I wifh the rage of hot Men, and the partialities of Juries, may be ftopp'd with my Blood, which I would offer up with fo much the more Joy, if I thought I fhould be the laft were to fuffer in fuch a way.

Since my Sentence, I have had but few Thoughts, but preparatory ones for Death : Yet the importunity of my Friends, and particularly of the beft and deareft Wife in the World, prevail'd with me to fign Petitions, and make an Addrefs for my Life: To which I was very averfe. For (I thank God) tho' in all refpects I have lived one of the happieft and contented'ft Men of the World (for now very near fourteen years) yet I am fo willing to leave all, that it was not without difficulty, that I did any thing for the faving of my Life, that was begging. But I was willing to let my Friends fee what Power they had over me, and that I was not obftinate, nor fullen, but would do any thing that an honeft Man could do, for their Satisfaction. Which was the only Motive that fway'd, or had any weight with me.

And now to fum up all : As I never had any Defign againft the King's Life, or the Life of any Man whatfoever ; fo I never was in any Contrivance of altering the Government.

ment. What the Heats, Wickedneſs, Paſſions, and Vanities of other men have occaſioned, I ought not to be anſwerable for ; nor could I repreſs them, though I now ſuffer for them. But the Will of the Lord be done ; into whoſe Hands I commend my Spirit ; and truſt that thou, O moſt merciful Father, haſt forgiven me all my Tranſgreſſions ; the Sins of my Youth, and all the Errors of my paſt Life ; and that thou wilt not lay my ſecret Sins and Ignorances to my charge, but wilt graciouſly ſupport me during that ſmall part of my Time now before me, and aſſiſt me in my laſt Moments, and not leave me then to be diſorder'd by Fear, or any other Temptations ; but make the Light of thy Countenance to ſhine upon me, for thou art my Sun and my Shield : And as thou ſupporteſt me by thy Grace, ſo I hope thou wilt hereafter crown me with Glory, and receive me into the Fellowſhip of Angels and Saints, in that bleſſed Inheritance purchaſed for me by my moſt merciful Redeemer ; who is, I truſt, at thy right Hand, preparing a place for me, and is ready to receive me : into whoſe Hand I commend my Spirit.

To the KING's Moſt Excellent Majeſty,
The Humble Petition of Algernon Sidney, *Eſquire* ;

SHEWETH,

THat your Petitioner, after a long and cloſe Impriſonment, was on the 7th day of this Month, with a guard of Soldiers, brought into the *Palace-yard,* upon an *Habeas Corpus* directed to the Lieutenant of the *Tower,* before any Indictment had been exhibited againſt him : But while he was there detain'd, a Bill was exhibited, and found ; whereupon he was immediately carried to the *King's-Bench,* and there arraign'd. In this ſurprize he deſir'd a Copy of the Indictment, and leave to make his Exceptions, or to put in a ſpecial Plea, and Counſel to frame it ; but all was deny'd him. He then offer'd a ſpecial Plea ready ingroſs'd, which alſo was rejected without reading : And being threatned, that if he did not immediately plead *Guilty* or *Not Guilty,* Judgment of High Treaſon ſhould be entred, he was forc'd, contrary to Law (as he ſuppoſes) to come to a general Iſſue in pleading *Not Guilty.*

Novemb. 21. He was brought to his Tryal, and the Indictment being perplexed and confuſed, ſo as neither he nor any of his Friends that heard it, could fully comprehend the ſcope of it, he was wholly unprovided of all the helps that the Law allows to every man for his Defence. Whereupon he did again deſire a Copy, and produc'd an Authentick Copy of the Statute of 36 *Ed.* 3. whereby it is enacted, That every man ſhall have a Copy of any Record that touches him in any manner, as well that which is for or againſt the King, as any other Perſon ; but could neither obtain a Copy of his Indictment, nor that the Statute ſhould be read.

The Jury by which he was try'd, was not (as he is inform'd) ſummon'd by the Bailiffs of the ſeveral Hundreds, in the uſual and legal manner, but names were agreed upon by Mr. *Graham,* and the Under-Sheriff, and directions given to the Bailiffs to ſummon them : And being all ſo choſen, a Copy of the Pannel was of no uſe to him. When they came to be call'd, he excepted againſt ſome for being your Majeſty's Servants, which he hoped ſhould not have been return'd, when he was proſecuted at your Majeſty's Suit ; many others for not being Freeholders, which Exceptions he thinks were good in Law ; and others were lewd and infamous perſons, not fit to be of any Jury : But all was over-rul'd by the Lord Chief Juſtice, and your Petitioner forc'd to challenge them peremptorily, whom he found to be pick'd out as moſt ſuitable to the Intentions of thoſe who ſought his Ruin ; whereby he loſt the Benefit allow'd him by Law of making his Exceptions, and was forc'd to admit of mechanick Perſons utterly unable to judge of ſuch a matter as was to be brought before them. This Jury being ſworn, no Witneſs was produc'd, who fixed any thing beyond Hearſay upon your Petitioner, except the Lord *Howard,* and them that ſwore to ſome Papers ſaid to be found in his Houſe, and offer'd as a ſecond Witneſs, and written in an Hand like to that of your Petitioner.

Your Petitioner produced ten Witneſſes, moſt of them of eminent Quality, the others of unblemiſh'd Fame, to ſhew the Lord *Howard's* Teſtimony was inconſiſtent with what he had declared before (at the Tryal of the Lord *Ruſſel*) under the ſame religious Obligation of an Oath, as if it had been legally adminiſtred.

Your Petitioner did further endeavour to ſhew, that beſides the Abſurdity and Incongruity of his Teſtimony, he being guilty of many Crimes which he did not pretend your Petitioner had any knowledge of, and having no other hope of Pardon, than by the *drudgery* of *Swearing* againſt him, he deſerv'd not to be believ'd. And ſimilitude of Hands could be no Evidence, as was declared by the Lord Chief Juſtice *Keiling,* and the whole Court in the Lady *Carr's* Caſe ; ſo as that no Evidence at all remain'd againſt him.

That

That whofoever wrote thofe Papers, they were but a fmall part of a polemical Difcourfe, in anfwer to a Book written about thirty years ago, upon general Propofitions, apply'd to no Time, nor any particular Cafe; that it was impoffible to judge of any part of it, unlefs the whole did appear, which did not: That the fenfe of fuch parts of it as were produced, could not be comprehended, unlefs the whole had been read, which was denied: That the Ink and Paper fhew'd them to be writ many years ago: That the Lord *Howard* not knowing of them, they could have no concurrence with that your Petitioner is faid to have defign'd with him and others: That the Confufion and Errors in the writing fhew'd they had never been fo much as review'd, and being written in an Hand that no man could well read, they were not fit for the Prefs, nor could be in fome Years, though the Writer of them had intended it, which did not appear. But they being only the prefent crude and private thoughts of a man, for the exercife of his own underftanding in his Studies, and never fhewed to any, or applied to any particular Cafe, could not fall under the Statute of 25 *Ed.* 3. which takes cognizance of no fuch matter, and could not by Conftruction be brought under it; fuch matters being thereby referved to the Parliament, as is declared in the Provifo, which he defired might be read, but was refufed.

Several important points of Law did hereupon emerge, upon which your Petitioner, knowing his own weaknefs, did defire that Counfel might be heard, or they might be referr'd to be found Specially. But all was over-rul'd by the violence of the Lord Ch. Juftice, and your Petitioner fo frequently interrupted, that the whole method of his Defence was broken, and he not fuffered to fay the tenth part of what he could have alledged in his defence. So the Jury was hurried into a Verdict they did not underftand.

Now forafmuch, as no man that is oppreffed in *England*, can have Relief, unlefs it be from your Majefty, your Petitioner humbly prays, that the Premifes confidered, your Majefty would be pleas'd to admit him into your prefence; and if he doth not fhew, that 'tis for your Majefty's Intereft and Honour to preferve him from the faid Oppreffion, he will not complain though he be left to de deftroy'd.

The very Copy of a Paper delivered to the Sheriffs, upon the Scaffold on Tower-Hill, *on* Friday December 7. 1683. *By* Algernon Sidney, *Efq; before his Execution ther e.*

Men, Brethren, and Fathers; Friends, Countrymen, and Strangers:

IT may be expected that I fhould now fay fome great Matters unto you, but the Rigour of the Seafon, and the Infirmities of my Age, encreafed by a clofe Imprifonment of above five Months, doth not permit me.

Moreover, we live in an Age that maketh Truth pafs for Treafon: I dare not fay any thing contrary unto it, and the Ears that are about me will probably be found too tender to hear it. My Trial and Condemnation doth fufficiently evidence this.

Weft, Rumfey, and *Keyling,* who were brought to prove the Plot, faid no more of me, than that they knew me not; and fome others equally known unto me, had ufed my Name, and that of fome others, to give a little Reputation unto their Defigns. The Lord *Howard* is too infamous by his Life, and the many Perjuries not to be denied, or rather fworn by himfelf, to deferve mention; and being a fingle Witnefs, would be of no value, though he had been of unblemifh'd Credit, or had not feen and confeffed that the Crimes committed by him would be pardoned only for committing more; and even the Pardon promifed could not be obtained till the Drudgery of Swearing was over.

This being laid afide, the whole matter is reduc'd to the Papers faid to be found in my Clofet by the King's Officers, without any other proof of their being written by me, than what is taken from the fuppofitions upon the Similitude of an Hand that is eafily counterfeited, and which hath been lately declared in the Lady *Car's* Cafe to be no lawful Evidence in criminal Caufes.

But if I had been feen to write them, the matter would not be much altered. They plainly appear to relate unto a large Treatife written long fince in anfwer to *Filmer's* Book, which by all intelligent Men is thought to be grounded upon wicked Principles, equally pernicious unto Magiftrates and People.

If he might publifh unto the World his Opinion, that all Men are born under a neceffity derived from the Laws of God and Nature, to fubmit to an abfolute kingly Government, which could be reftrained by no Law, or Oath; and that he that hath the power, whether he came unto it by Creation, Election, Inheritance, Ufurpation, or any other way, had the Right; and none muft oppofe his Will, but the Perfons and Eftates of his Subjects muſt be indiſpenſably ſubject unto it. I know not why I might not have publiſhed my Opinion to the contrary, without the breach of any Law I have yet known.

I might as freely as he, publickly have declared my Thoughts, and the Reaſons upon which they were grounded, and I perſwaded to believe, that God had left Nations unto the Liberty of ſetting up ſuch Governments as beſt pleaſed themſelves.

That Magiſtrates were ſet up for the good of Nations, not Nations for the honour or glory of Magiſtrates.

That the Right and Power of Magiſtrates in every Country, was that which the Laws of that Country made it to be.

That thoſe Laws were to be obſerved, and the Oaths taken by them, having the force of a Contract, between Magiſtrate and People, could not be violated without danger of diſſolving the whole Fabrick.

That Uſurpation could give no Right, and the moſt dangerous of all Enemies unto Kings were they, who raiſing their Power to an exorbitant Height, allowed unto Uſurpers all the Rights belonging unto it.

That ſuch Uſurpations being ſeldom compaſſed without the Slaughter of the Reigning Perſon, or Family, the worſt of all Villanies was thereby rewarded with the moſt glorious Privileges.

That if ſuch Doctrines were received, they would ſtir up Men to the Deſtruction of Princes with more Violence than all the Paſſions that have hitherto raged in the Hearts of the moſt Unruly.

That none could be ſafe, if ſuch a Reward were propoſed unto any that could deſtroy them.

That few would be ſo gentle as to ſpare even the beſt, if, by their deſtruction, of a vile Uſurper he could become God's Anointed ; and by the moſt execrable Wickedneſs inveſt himſelf with that Divine Character.

This is the Scope of the whole Treatiſe ; the Writer gives ſuch Reaſons as at preſent did occur unto him to prove it. This ſeems to agree with the Doctrines of the moſt Reverenced Authors of all Times, Nations and Religions. The beſt and wiſeſt Kings have ever acknowledged it. The preſent King of *France* hath declared that Kings have that happy want of Power, that they can do nothing contrary unto the Laws of their Country, and grounds his Quarrel with the King of *Spain, Anno* 1667, upon that Principle. King *James* in his Speech to the Parliament, *Anno* 1603. doth in the higheſt degree aſſert it : The Scripture ſeems to declare it. If nevertheleſs the Writer was miſtaken, he might have been refuted by Law, Reaſon, and Scripture ; and no man for ſuch matters was ever otherwiſe puniſhed, than by being made to ſee his Error, and it hath not (as I think) been ever known that they had been referred to the Judgment of a Jury, compoſed of Men utterly unable to comprehend them.

But there was little of this in my Caſe ; the extravagance of my Proſecutors goes higher : The above-mentioned Treatiſe was never finiſhed, nor could be in many years, and moſt probably would never have been. So much as is of it, was written long ſince, never reviewed nor ſhewn unto any man ; and the fiftieth part of it was produced, and not the tenth of that offer'd to be read. That which was never known unto thoſe who are ſaid to have conſpired with me, was ſaid to be intended to ſtir up the People in proſecution of the Deſigns of thoſe Conſpirators.

When nothing of particular Application unto Time, Place, or Perſon could be found in it, (as hath ever been done by thoſe who endeavour'd to raiſe Inſurrections) all was ſupplied by *Innuendo's.*

Whatſoever is ſaid of the Expulſion of *Tarquin,* the Inſurrection againſt *Nero ;* the Slaughter of *Caligula,* or *Domitian ;* the Tranſlation of the Crown of *France* from *Merovius* his Race unto *Pepin ;* and from his Deſcendants unto *Hugh Capet,* and the like, applied by *Innuendo* unto the King.

They have not conſidered, that if ſuch Acts of State be not good, there is not a King in the World that has any Title to the Crown he bears ; nor can have any, unleſs he could deduce his Pedigree from the Eldeſt Son of *Noah,* and ſhew that the Succeſſion had ſtill continued in the Eldeſt of the Eldeſt Line, and been ſo deduced to him.

Every one may ſee what advantage this would be to all the Kings of the World ; and whether that failing, it were not better for them to acknowledge they had received their Crowns by the Conſent of willing Nations ; or to have no better Title unto them than Uſurpation and Violence, which by the ſame ways may be taken from them.

But I was long ſince told that I muſt die, or the Plot muſt die.

Left the means of deſtroying the beſt Proteſtants in *England* ſhould fail, the Bench muſt be filled with ſuch as had been Blemiſhes to the Bar.

None

None but such as these would have advised with the King's Council, of the means of bringing a Man to Death; suffered a Jury to be packed by the King's Sollicitors, and the Under-Sheriff; admit of Jury-men who are not Freeholders; receive such Evidence as is above-mentioned: Refuse a Copy of an Indictment, or to suffer the Statute of 46 *Ed.* 3. to be read, that doth expresly Enact, it should in no Case be denied unto any Man upon any occasion whatsoever; over-rule the most important Points of Law without hearing. And whereas the Stat. 25 *Ed.* 3. upon which they said I should be tried, doth reserve unto the Parliament all Constructions to be made in Points of Treason; they could assume unto themselves not only a Power to make Constructions, but such Constructions as neither agree with Law, Reason, or common Sense.

By these means I am brought to this place. The Lord forgive these Practices, and avert the Evils that threaten the Nation from them. The Lord sanctify these my Sufferings unto me; and tho' I fall as a Sacrifice unto Idols, suffer not Idolatry to be established in this Land. Bless thy People, and save them. Defend thy own Cause, and defend those that defend it. Stir up such as are faint; direct those that are willing; confirm those that waver; give Wisdom and Integrity unto all. Order all things so, as may most redound unto thine own Glory. Grant that I may die glorifying thee for all thy Mercies; and that at the last thou hast permitted me to be singled out as a Witness of thy Truth; and even by the confession of my Opposers; for that *OLD CAUSE* in which I was from my Youth engaged, and for which thou hast often and wonderfully declared thy self.

CHAP. I.
Of MAGISTRACY.

I. **R**ELATION is nothing else but that State of mutual Respect and Reference which one Thing or Person has to another.

II. Such are the Relations of Father and Son, Husband and Wife, Master and Servant, Magistrate and Subject.

III. The Relations of a Father, Husband and Master, are really distinct and different; that is, one of them is not the other: for he may be any one of these, who is none of the rest.

IV. This Distinction proceeds from the different Reasons, upon which these Relations are founded.

V. The Reason or Foundation, from whence arises the Relation of a Father, is from having begotten his Son, who may as properly call every old Man he meets his Father, as any other Person whatsoever, excepting him only who begat him.

VI. The Relation of an Husband and Wife is founded in Wedlock, whereby they mutually consent to become one Flesh.

VII. The Relation of a Master is founded in that Right and Title which he has to the Possession, or Service, of his Slave or Servant.

VIII. In these Relations, the Name of Father, Husband and Master, imply Sovereignty and Superiority, which varies notwithstanding, and is more or less absolute, according to the Foundation of these several Relations.

IX. The Superiority of a Father is founded in that Power, Priority and Dignity of Nature, which a Cause hath over its Effect.

X. The distance is not so great in Wedlock, but the Superiority of the Husband over the Wife, is like that of the right Hand over the left in the same Body.

XI. The Superiority of a Master, is an absolute Dominion over his Slave, a limited and conditionate Command over his Servant.

XII. The Titles of *Pater Patriæ*, and *Sponsus Regni*, Father of the Country, and Husband of the Realm, are Metaphors and improper Speeches: For no Prince ever begat a whole Country of Subjects; nor can a Kingdom more properly be said to be married, than the City of *Venice* is to the *Adriatique Gulph.*

XIII. And to shew further that Magistracy is not paternal Authority, nor Monarchy founded in Fatherhood; it is undeniably plain, that a Son may be the natural Sovereign Lord of his own Father, as *Henry* the second had been of *Jeffrey Plantagenet*, if he had been an *Englishman*; which, they say, *Henry* the Seventh did not love to think of, when his Sons grew up to Years. And this Case alone is an eternal Confutation of the Patriarchate.

XIV. Neither is Magistracy a martial Power, for the Husband may be the obedient Subject of his own Wife, as *Philip* was of Queen *Mary*.

XV. Nor

XV. Nor is it that Dominion which a Master has over his Slave, for then a Prince might lawfully sell all his Subjects, like so many head of Cattle, and make Money of his whole stock whenever he pleases, as a Patron of *Algiers* does.

XVI. Neither is the Relation of Prince and Subject the same with that of a Master and hired Servant, for he does not hire them; but, as St. *Paul* saith, *They pay him Tribute,* in consideration of his continual *Attendance* and *Imployment* for the publick Good.

XVII. That publick Office and Imployment is the Foundation of the Relation of King and Subject, as many other Relations are likewise founded upon other Functions and Administrations, such as *Guardian* and *Ward,* &c.

XVIII. The Office of a King is set down at large in the XVII. Chap. of the Laws of King *Edward* the Confessor, to which the succeeding Kings have been sworn at their Coronation: and it is affirmed in the Preambles of the Statutes of (*a*) *Marlbridge,* and of the Statute of *Quo Warranto,* made at (*b*) *Gloucester,* that the Calling of Parliaments to make Laws for the Estate of the Realm, and the more full Administration of Justice, *belongeth to the Office of a King.* But the fullest account of it in few words, is in Chancellor *Fortescue,* Chap. XIII. which Passage is quoted in *Calvin's* Case, *Coke* VII. Rep. Fol. 5. *Ad Tutelam namque Legis Subditorum, ac eorum Corporum & Bonorum Rex hujusmodi erectus est, & ad hanc potestatem à populo effluxam ipse habet, quo ei non licet potestate alia suo populo dominari.* For such a King, (*that is, of every political Kingdom, as this is*) is made and ordained for the Defence or *Guardianship* of the Law of his Subjects, and of their Bodies and Goods, whereunto he receiveth power of his People, so that he cannot govern his People by any other power.

Corollary 1. A Bargain's a Bargain.

2. *A Popish Guardian* of Protestant Laws is such an Incongruity, and he is as unfit for that Office, as Antichrist is to be Christ's Vicar.

(a) Prout Regalis Officii exposcit utilitas.

(b) sicome le profit de Office Demaunde. The Kingly or Regal Office of this Realm. 1°. Mar. Sess. 3. Cap. 1.

CHAP. II.

Of Prerogatives by Divine Right.

I. GOvernment is not matter of Revelation; if it were, then those Nations that wanted Scripture, must have been without Government; whereas Scripture it self says, that Government is *the Ordinance of Man,* and of human Extraction. And King *Charles* the First says of this Government in particular, *that it was* moulded *by the Wisdom and Experience of the People.* Answ. to XIX. Prop.

II. All just Governments are highly beneficial to Mankind, and *are of God,* the Author of all Good; they are his *Ordinances* and *Institutions,* Rom. 13. 1, 2.

III. Plowing and Sowing, and the whole business of preparing Bread-Corn, is absolutely necessary to the subsistence of Mankind; *This also cometh forth from the Lord of Hosts, who is wonderful in Counsel, and excellent in Working,* Isa. 28. from 23. to 29*th* Verse.

IV. Wisdom saith, *Counsel is mine, and sound Wisdom, I am Understanding; I have strength: By me Kings reign, and Princes decree Justice: By me Princes rule, and Nobles, even all the Judges of the Earth,* Prov. 8. 14.

V. The Prophet, speaking of the Plowman, saith, *His God doth instruct him to discretion, and doth teach him,* Isa. 28. 26.

VI. Scripture neither gives nor takes away Men's Civil Rights, but leaves them as it found them, and (as our Saviour said of himself) is no Divider of Inheritances.

VII. Civil Authority is a Civil Right.

VIII. The Law of *England* gives the King his Title to the Crown. For, where is it said in Scripture, that such a Person or Family by Name shall enjoy it? And the same Law of *England* which has made him King, has made him King according to the *English* Laws, and not otherwise.

IX. The King of *England* has no more right to set up a *French* Government, than the *French* King has to be King of *England,* which is none at all.

X. *Render unto* Cæsar *the things which are* Cæsar's; neither makes a *Cæsar,* nor tells who *Cæsar* is, nor what belongs to him; but only requires Men to be just, in giving him those supposed Rights, which the Laws have determined to be his.

XI. The Scripture supposes Property, when it forbids Stealing; it supposes Men's Lands to be already butted and bounded, when it forbids removing the antient Land-marks: And as it is impossible for any Man to prove what Estate he has by

Scripture

Scripture, or to find a Terrier of his Land there; so it is a vain thing to look for Statutes of Prerogative in Scripture.

XII. If *Mishpat Hamelech*, the manner of the King, 1 *Sam.* 8. 11. be a Statute of Prerogative, and prove all those particulars to be the Right of the King, then *Mishpat Haccohanim* the Priest's custom of Sacrilegious Rapine, *Chap.* 2. 13. proves that to be the Right of the Priests, the same word being used in both places.

XIII. It is the Resolution of all the Judges of *England*, that even the known and undoubted Prerogatives of the *Jewish* Kings, do not belong to our Kings, and that it is an absurd and impudent thing to affirm they do. *Coke* 11. *Rep.* p. 63. *Mich.* 5 *Jac.*

Give us a King to judge us. 1 Sam. 8. 5, 6, 20.

' Note, upon *Sunday* the Tenth of *November*, in this same Term, the King upon Complaint made to him by *Bancroft*, Archbishop of *Canterbury*, concerning Prohibitions, ' was informed, that when Question was made of what matters the Ecclesiastical Judges ' have Cognizance, either upon the Exposition of the Statutes, concerning Tythes, ' or any other Thing ecclesiastical, or upon the Statute of 1 *Eliz.* concerning the High ' Commission, or in any other Case, in which there is not express Authority by Law, ' the King himself may decide it in his Royal Person; and that the Judges are but the ' Delegates of the King, and that the King may take what Causes he shall please to determine from the Determination of the Judges, and may determine them himself. And the ' Archbishop said, *That this was clear in Divinity, That such Authority belongs to the King, by the Word of God in Scripture.* ' To which it was answered by me, in the presence, ' and with the clear consent of all the Justices of *England*, and Barons of the *Exchequer*, ' That the King in his own person cannot adjudge any Case, either Criminal, as Treason, ' Felony, &c. but this ought to be determined and adjusted in some Court of Justice, ' according to the Law and Custom of *England.* And always Judgments are given, ' *Ideo consideratum est per Curiam*, so that the Court gives the Judgment:——And it ' was *greatly marvelled*, that the Archbishop *durst* inform the King, that such absolute ' power and authority, as is aforesaid, belonged to the King, *by the Word of God.*

CHAP. III.
Of OBEDIENCE.

I. NO Man has any more Civil Authority than what the Law of the Land has vested in him; nor is he one of St. *Paul's* higher Powers any farther, or to any other purposes than the Law has impower'd him.

II. An usurped, illegal and arbitrary Power, is so far from being the Ordinance of God, that it is not the Ordinance of Man.

III. Whoever opposes an usurped, illegal and arbitrary Power, does not oppose the Ordinance of God, but the Violation of that Ordinance.

IV. The 13th of the *Romans* commands Subjection to our Temporal Governors, because their Office and Employment is for the publick Welfare, *For he is the Minister of God to thee for Good.* *Verse 4.*

V. The 13th of the *Hebrews* commands Obedience to Spiritual Rulers, *Because they watch for your Souls.* *Verse 17.*

VI. But the 13th of the *Hebrews* did not oblige the Martyrs and Confessors in Queen *Mary's* Time, to obey such blessed Bishops as *Bonner* and the Beast of *Rome*, who were the perfect Reverse of St. *Paul's* Spiritual Rulers, and *whose practice was murthering of Souls and Bodies*, according to the true Character of *Popery* which was given it by the Bishops who compiled the Thanksgiving for the Fifth of *November*; but Archbishop *Laud* was wiser than they, and in his time blotted it out.

The Prayer formerly run thus: *To that end, strengthen the Hands of our Gracious King, the Nobles and Magistrates of the Land, to cut off these workers of Iniquity (whose Religion is Rebellion, whose Faith is Faction, whose Practice is murthering of Souls and Bodies) and to root them out of the Confines of this Kingdom.*

VII. All the Judges of *England* are bound by their Oath, and by the duty of their place, to disobey all Writs, Letters, or Commands which are brought to them, either under the little Seal, or under the great Seal, to hinder or delay common Right. Are the Judges all bound in an Oath, and by their places, to break the 13th of the *Romans*? *18 Edw. III. 20 Edw. III. Cap. 1, 2.*

VIII. The Engagement of the Lords attending upon the King at *York*, June 13, 1642, which was subscribed by the Lord Keeper, and thirty nine Peers besides, the Lord Chief-Justice *Banks*, and severl others of the Privy-Council, was in these words:

We

We do engage our selves not to obey any Orders or Commands whatsoever, not warranted by the known Laws of the Land. Was this likewise an Association against the 13th of the *Romans?*

IX. A *Constable* represents the King's Person, and in the Execution of his Office is within the purview of the 13th of the *Romans*, as all Men grant; but in case he so far pervert his Office, as to break the Peace, and commit Murther, Burglary, or Robbery on the Highway, he may, and ought to be resisted.

X. The Law of the Land is the best Expositor of the 13th of the *Romans, Here*; and in *Poland,* the Law of the Land *There.*

XI. The 13th of the *Romans* is receiv'd for Scripture in *Poland*, and yet this is *expressed* in the Coronation-Oath in that Country; *Quid si Sacramentum meum violavero, Incolæ Regni nullam nobis Obedientiam præstare tenebuntur.* And if I shall violate my Oath, the Inhabitants of the Realm shall not be bound to yield me any Obedience.

XII. The Law of the Land, according to *Bracton,* is the highest of all the Higher Powers mentioned in this Text; for it is superior to the King, and made him King, (*Lib.* 3. *Cap.* 26. *Rex habet superiorem Deum, item Legem, per quam factus est Rex, item Curiam suam, viz. Comites & Barones*) and therefore by this Text we ought to be subject to it in the first place. And according to *Melancthon, It is the Ordinance of God, to which the Higher Powers themselves ought to be subject.* Vol. 3. In his Commentary on the Fifth Verse, (*Wherefore ye must needs be subject, not only for Wrath, but also for Conscience sake.*) he hath these words, *Neque vero hæc tantum pertinent ad Subditos, sed etiam ad Magistratum, qui cum fiunt Tyranni, non minus dissipant Ordinationem Dei, quam Seditiosi. Ideo & ipsorum Conscientia fit rea, quia non obediunt Ordinationi Dei, id est, Legibus, quibus debent parere. Ideo Comminationes hic positæ etiam ad ipsos pertinent. Itaque hujus mandati severitas moveat omnes, ne violationem Politici status putent esse leve peccatum.* Neither doth this place concern Subjects only, but also the Magistrates themselves, who when they turn Tyrants, do no less overthrow the Ordinance of God than the Seditious; and therefore their Consciences too are guilty, for not obeying the Ordinance of God, that is, the Laws which they ought to obey: So that the Threatnings in this place do also belong to them; wherefore let the Severity of this Command deter all men from thinking the Violation of the Political Constitution to be a light Sin.

Corollary. To destroy the Law and legal Constitution, which is the *Ordinance of God,* by false and arbitrary Expositions of this Text, is a greater Sin than to destroy it by any other means; for it is *Seething the Kid in his Mother's Milk.*

CHAP. IV.
Of LAWS.

I. THere is no natural Obligation, whereby one Man is bound to yield Obedience to another, but what is founded in paternal or patriarchal Authority.

II. All the Subjects of a patriarchal Monarch are Princes of the Blood.

III. All the People of *England* are not Princes of the Blood.

IV. No Man, who is naturally Free, can be Bound, but by his own Act and Deed.

V. Publick Laws are made by publick Consent, and they therefore bind every man, because every man's consent is involved in them.

VI. Nothing but the same Authority and Consent which made the Laws, can repeal, alter, or explain them.

VII. To judge and determine Causes against Law, without Law, or where the Law is obscure and uncertain, is to assume legislative Power.

VIII. Power assumed, without a Man's consent, cannot bind him as his own Act and Deed.

IX. The Law of the Land is all of a piece, and the same Authority which made one Law, made all the rest, and intended to have them all impartially executed.

X. Law on *One Side,* is the Back-Sword of Justice.

XI. The best Things, when corrupted, are the worst; and the wild Justice of a State of Nature, is much more desirable than Law perverted, and over-rul'd, into *Hemlock* and Oppression.

Copies

Copies of Two Papers written by the Late King CHARLES II.

Published by His MAJESTY's Command.　Printed in the Year 1686.

The First Paper.

THE Discourse we had the other day, I hope satisfied you in the main, that Christ can have but one Church here upon Earth, and I believe that it is as visible as that the Scripture is in Print, That none can be that Church, but that, which is called the *Roman Catholick Church.* I think you need not trouble your self with entring into that Ocean of particular Disputes, when the main, and, in truth, the only Question is, Where that Church is, which we profess to believe in the two Creeds? We declare there to believe *one Catholick and Apostolick Church,* and it is not left to every phantastical man's head to believe as he pleases, but to the Church to whom Christ left the power upon Earth to govern in matters of Faith, who made these Creeds for our Directions. It were a very irrational thing to make Laws for a Country, and leave it to the Inhabitants, to be the Interpreters and Judges of those Laws; for then every man will be his own Judge, and by consequence no such thing as either right or wrong. Can we therefore suppose that God Almighty would leave us at those uncertainties, as to give us a Rule to go by, and to leave every man to be his own Judge? I do ask any ingenuous man, whether it be not the same thing to follow our own Fancy, or to interpret the Scripture by it? I would have any man shew me, where the power of deciding matters of Faith is given to every particular man. Christ left his power to his Church even *to forgive Sins in Heaven,* and left his Spirit with them, which they exercised after his Resurrection: First by his Apostles in these Creeds, and many years after by the Council at *Nice,* where that Creed was made that is called by that name; and by the power which they had received from Christ, they were the Judges even of the Scripture it self, many years after the Apostles, which Books were Canonical and which were not. And if they had this power then, I desire to know how they came to lose it, and by what Authority men separate themselves from that Church? The only pretence I ever heard of, was, because the Church has fail'd in wresting and interpreting the Scripture contrary to the true sense and meaning of it, and that they have imposed Articles of Faith upon us, which are not to be warranted by God's word? I do desire to know who is to be Judge of that, whether the whole Church, the Succession whereof has continued to this day without Interruption, or particular men who have raised Schisms for their own advantage?

This is a true Copy of a Paper I found in the late King my Brother's Strong Box, *written in his own Hand.*

JAMES R.

The Second Paper.

IT is a sad thing to consider what a world of Heresies are crept into this Nation: Every man thinks himself as competent a Judge of the Scriptures as the very Apostles themselves; and 'tis no wonder that it should be so, since that part of the Nation which looks most like a Church, dares not bring the true Arguments against the other Sects, for fear they should be turned against themselves, and confuted by their own Arguments. The Church of *England* (as 'tis call'd) would fain have it thought, that they are the Judges in matters Spiritual, and yet dare not say positively that there is no Appeal from them; for

either

either they muſt ſay, that they are infallible (which they cannot pretend to) or confeſs that what they decide in matters of Conſcience, is no further to be followed, than it a-grees with every man's private Judgment. If Chriſt did leave a Church here upon Earth, and we were all once of that Church, how, and by what Authority, did we ſeparate from that Church? If the power of interpreting of Scripture be in every man's brain, what need have we of a Church or Church-men; to what purpoſe then did our Saviour, after he had given his Apoſtles power to *Bind and Looſe in Heaven and Earth,* add to it, *that he would be with them even to the end of the World?* Theſe words were not ſpoken parabolically, or by way of Figure. Chriſt was then aſcending into his Glory, and left his Power with his Church even *to the end of the World.* We have had theſe hun-dred years paſt, the ſad effects of denying to the Church that Power in matters Spiri-rual, without an Appeal. What Country can ſubſiſt in peace or quiet, where there is not a ſupream Judge from whence there can be no Appeal? Can there be any Juſtice done where the Offenders are their own Judges, and equal Interpreters of the Law, with thoſe that are appointed to adminiſter Juſtice? This is our Caſe here in *England* in Mat-ters Spiritual; for the Proteſtants are not of the Church of *England,* as 'tis the true Church from whence there can be no Appeal; but becauſe the Diſcipline of that Church is conformable at that preſent to their fancies, which as ſoon as it ſhall contradict or vary from, they are ready to embrace or join with the next Congregation of People, whoſe Diſcipline and Worſhip agrees with their Opinion at that time; ſo that accord-ing to this Doctrine, there is no other Church nor Interpreter of Scripture but that which lies in every man's giddy brain. I deſire to know therefore of every ſerious Conſiderer of theſe things, whether the great work of our Salvation ought to depend upon ſuch a ſandy Foundation as this? Did Chriſt ever ſay to the Civil Magiſtrate (much leſs to the People) *that he would be with them to the end of the World?* Or, did he give them the Power *to forgive Sins?* St. *Paul* tells the *Corinthians, Ye are God's Huſ-bandry, ye are God's Building; we are Labourers with God.* This ſhews who are the *La-bourers,* and who are the *Husbandry* and *Building:* And in this whole Chapter, and in the preceding one, St. *Paul* takes great pains to ſet forth that they, the Clergy, *have the Spirit of God, without which no man ſearcheth the deep things of God;* and he concludeth the Chapter with this Verſe, *For who hath known the mind of the Lord, that he may inſtruct him? But we have the mind of Chriſt.* Now if we do but conſider in human probability and reaſon, the powers Chriſt leaves to his Church in the Goſpel, and St. *Paul* explains ſo diſtinctly afterwards, we cannot think that our Saviour ſaid all theſe things to no pur-poſe; and pray conſider on the other ſide, that thoſe who reſiſt the Truth, and will not ſubmit to his Church, draw their Arguments from Implications, and far-fetch'd Inter-pretations, at the ſame time that they deny plain and poſitive words; which is ſo great a Diſingenuity, that 'tis not almoſt to be thought that they can believe themſelves. Is there any other foundation of the Proteſtant Church, but that if the Civil Magiſtrate pleaſe, he may call ſuch of the Clergy as he thinks fit for his turn at that time; and turn the Church either to *Presbytery, Independency,* or indeed what he pleaſes? This was the way of our pretended Reformation here in *England;* and by the ſame Rule and Au-thority it may be altered into as many more Shapes and Forms as there are Fancies in men's Heads.

This is a true Copy of a Paper written by the late King my Brother in his own Hand, which I found in his Cloſet.

JAMES R.

A LETTER, *containing ſome Remarks on the Two Papers, writ by His late Majeſty King* CHARLES II. *concerning Religion.*

S I R,

I Thank you for the two Royal Papers that you have ſent me; I had heard of them before, but now we have them ſo well atteſted, that there is no hazard of being deceived by a falſe Copy: you expect that in return, I ſhould let you know what im-preſſion they have made upon me. I pay all the reverence that is due to a crowned Head, even in Aſhes; to which I will never be wanting: far leſs am I capable of ſuſ-pecting the Royal Atteſtation that accompanies them; of the truth of which I take

it

it for granted no man doubts ; but I muſt crave leave to tell you, that I am confident, the late King only copied them, and that they are not of his compoſing : for as they have nothing of that free Air, with which he expreſſed himſelf ; ſo there is a Con-texture in them, that does not look like a Prince ; and the beginning of the firſt ſhews it was the effect of a Converſation, and was to be communicated to another ; ſo that I am apt to think they were compoſed by another, and were ſo well reliſhed by the late King, that he thought fit to keep them, in order to his examining them more particularly ; and that he was prevailed with to copy them, leſt a Paper of that nature might have been made a Crime, if it had been found about him written by another hand : and I could name one or two Perſons, who as they were able enough to compoſe ſuch Papers, ſo had power enough over his Spirit to engage him to copy them, and to put themſelves out of danger by reſtoring the Original.

You ought to addreſs your ſelf to the learned Divines of our Church; for anſwer to ſuch things in them as puzzle you, and not to one that has not the honour to be of that Body, and that has now carried a Sword for ſome time, and employs the leiſure that at any time he enjoys, rather in Philoſophical and Mathematical Enquiries than in mat-ters of Controverſy. There is indeed one Conſideration that determined me more eaſily to comply with your deſires, which is, my having had the honour to diſcourſe copi-ouſly of thoſe matters with the late King himſelf : and he having propoſed to me ſome of the particulars that I find in thoſe Papers, and I having ſaid ſeveral things to him, in anſwer to thoſe Heads, which he offered to me only as Objections, with which he ſeemed fully ſatisfied, I am the more willing to communicate to you, that which I took the liberty to lay before His late Majeſty on ſeveral occaſions: The particulars on which he inſiſted in diſcourſe with me, were the " uſeleſsneſs of a Law without a Judge, " and the neceſſity of an infallible Tribunal to determine Controverſies, to which he " added, the many Sects that were in *England*, which ſeemed to be a neceſſary conſe-" quence of the Liberty that every one took to interpret the Scriptures: and he often " repeated that of the Church of *England*'s arguing, from the obligation to obey the " Church, againſt the Sectaries, which he thought was of no force, unleſs they allowed " more Authority to the Church than they ſeemed willing to admit, in their Diſputes " with this Church of *Rome*." But upon the whole matter I will offer you ſome Re-flections, that will, I hope, be of as great weight with you, as they are with myſelf.

I. All Arguments that prove upon ſuch general Conſiderations, that there ought to be an infallible Judge named by Chriſt, and cloathed with his Authority, ſignify no-thing, unleſs it can be ſhewed us, in what Texts of Scripture that Nomination is to be found ; and till that is ſhewed, they are only Arguments brought to prove that *Chriſt ought to have done ſomewhat that he has not done.* So theſe are in effect ſo many Ar-guments againſt Chriſt, unleſs it appears that he has authoriſed ſuch a Judge ; there-fore the right way to end this Diſpute, is, to ſhew where ſuch a Conſtitution is autho-riſed : So that the moſt that can be made of this, is, that it amounts to a favourable preſumption.

II. It is a very unreaſonable thing for us to form Preſumptions, of what is, or ought to be, from Inconveniences that do ariſe, in caſe that ſuch things are not : for we may carry this ſo far, that it will not be eaſy to ſtop it. It ſeems more ſuitable to the infi-nite Goodneſs of God, to communicate the knowledge of himſelf to all Mankind, and to furniſh every Man with ſuch aſſiſtances as will certainly prevail over him. It ſeems alſo reaſonable to think, that ſo perfect a Saviour as Jeſus Chriſt was, ſhould have ſhewed us a certain way, and yet conſiſtent with the free Uſe of our Faculties, of avoid-ing all Sin : nor is it very eaſy to imagine, that it ſhould be a reproach on his Goſpel, if there is not an infallible Preſervative againſt Error, when it is acknowledged, that there is no infallible Preſervative againſt Sin : for it is certain, that the one damns us more infallibly, than the other.

III. Since Preſumptions are ſo much inſiſted on, to prove what things muſt be ap-pointed by Chriſt ; it is to be conſidered, that it is alſo a reaſonable Preſumption, that if ſuch a Court was appointed by him, it muſt be done in ſuch plain terms that there can be no room to queſtion the meaning of them: and ſince this is the hinge upon which all other matters turn, it ought to be expreſſed ſo particularly, in whom it is veſted, that there ſhould be no occaſion given to diſpute, whether it is in one Man or in a Body ; and if in a Body, whether in the Majority, or in the Two thirds, or in the whole Body unanimouſly agreeing ; in ſhort, the chief thing in all Governments being the Nature and Power of the Judges, thoſe are always diſtinctly ſpecified ; and therefore if theſe things are not ſpecified in the Scriptures, it is at leaſt a ſtrong Preſumption, that Chriſt did not intend to authoriſe ſuch Judges.

IV. There

IV. There were several Controversies raised among the Churches to which the Apostles writ, as appears by the Epistles to the *Romans, Corinthians, Galatians,* and *Colossians,* yet the Apostles never make use of those Passages that are pretended for this Authority to put an end to those Controversies; which is a shrewd Presumption, that they did not understand them in that sense in which the Church of *Rome* does now take them. Nor does St. *Paul* in the Directions that he gives to the Church-men in his Epistles to *Timothy* and *Titus,* reckon this of submitting to the directions of the Church for one, which he could not have omitted, if this be the true meaning of those disputed Passages: and yet he has not one word sounding that way, which is very different from the directions which one possessed with the present view that the Church of *Rome* has of this matter must needs have given.

V. There are some things very expresly taught in the *New Testament,* such as the *Rules of a good Life, the Use of the Sacraments, the addressing of our selves to God, for Mercy and Grace,* thro' the Sacrifice that Christ offered for us on the Cross, and the worshipping him as God, the Death, Resurrection and Ascension of *Jesus Christ,* the Resurrection of our Bodies, and Life everlasting; by which it is apparent, that we are set beyond doubt in those matters: if then there are any other Passages more obscure concerning other matters, we must conclude, that these are not of that consequence, otherwise they would have been as *plainly* reveal'd as others are. But above all, if the Authority of the *Church* is delivered to us in *disputable terms,* that is a just prejudice against it, since it is a thing of such consequence, that it ought to have been revealed in a way so very clear and past all dispute.

VI. If it is a *Presumption* for particular Persons to judge concerning *Religion,* which must be still referred to the Priests and other Guides in sacred Matters, this is a good Argument to oblige all Nations to continue in the *Established Religion,* whatever it may happen to be; and above all others, it was a convincing Argument in the Mouths of the *Jews* against our *Saviour.* He pretended to be the *Messias,* and proved it both by the *Prophecies* that were accomplished in him, and by the *Miracles* that he wrought: as for the *Prophecies,* the Reasons urged by the Church of *Rome* will conclude much stronger, that such dark Passages as those of the Prophets were, ought not to be interpreted by *particular Persons,* but that the Exposition of these must be referred to the *Priests* and *Sanhedrim,* it being expresly proved in their Law (Deut. 17. 8.) *That when Controversies arose, concerning any cause that was too intricate, they were to go to the place which God should chuse, and to the Priests of the Tribe of* Levi, *and to the Judge in those days, and that they were to declare what was right, and to their decision all were obliged to submit, under pain of Death:* So that by this it appears, that the *Priests* in the *Jewish Religion* were authorized in so extraordinary a manner, that I dare say, the Church of *Rome* would not wish for a more formal Testimony on her behalf: As for our *Saviour*'s Miracles, these were not sufficient neither, unless his *Doctrine* was first found to be good: since *Moses* had expresly warned the People (Deut. 13. 1.) *That if a Prophet came and taught them to follow after other Gods, they were not to obey him, tho' he wrought Miracles to prove his Mission, but were to put him to death:* So a *Jew* saying, that *Christ,* by making himself one with his Father, brought in the worship of another God, might well pretend that he was not *oblig'd* to yield to the Authority of our *Saviour's Miracles,* without taking cognizance of his *Doctrine,* and of the Prophecies concerning the *Messias,* and in a word, of the whole matter. So that if these *Reasonings* are now good against the *Reformation,* they were as strong in the Mouths of the *Jews* against our *Saviour:* and from hence we see, that the Authority that seems to be given by *Moses* to the *Priests,* must be understood with some Restrictions; since we not only find the Prophets, and *Jeremy* in particular, opposing themselves to the whole body of them, but we see likewise, that for some considerable time before our *Saviour's* days, not only many ill-grounded Traditions had got in among them, by which the vigour of the moral Law was much enervated, but likewise they were universally possessed with a false notion of their *Messias;* so that even the Apostles themselves had not quite shaken off those Prejudices at the time of our Saviour's Ascension. So that here a Church, that was still the Church of God, that had the appointed means of the Expiations of their Sins, by their Sacrifices and *Washings,* as well as by their Circumcision, was yet under great and fatal Errors, from which particular Persons had no way to extricate themselves, but by examining the Doctrine and Texts of Scripture, and by judging of them according to the Evidence of Truth, and the force and freedom of their Faculties.

VII. It seems evident, that the passage (*Tell the Church*) belongs only to the *reconciling of Differences:* that of *binding and loosing,* according to the use of those terms among

among the *Jews* fignifies only an *Authority* that was given to the *Apoftles* of giving Precepts, by which men were to be obliged to fuch Duties, or fet at liberty from them: and (*the Gates of Hell not prevailing againft the Church*) fignifies only, that the *Chriftian* Religion was never to come to an end, or to perifh; and that of (*Chrift's being with the* Apoftles ● *the end of the* world) imports only a fpecial conduct and protection which the *Church may always* expect: but as the promife, *I will not leave thee nor forfake thee*, that belongs to every *Chriftian*, does not import an *Infallibility*, no more does the other. And for thofe paffages concerning (*the Spirit* of God *that fearches all things*) it is plain, that in them St. *Paul* is treating of the Divine *Infpiration*, by which the *Chriftian* Religion was then opened to the World, which he fets in oppofition to the Wifdom or Philofophy of the *Greeks*; fo that as all thofe paffages come fhort of proving that for which they are alledged, it muft at laft be acknowledged, that they have not an Evidence great enough to prove fo important a truth, as fome would evince by them; fince 'tis a matter of fuch vaft confequence, that the proofs for it muft have an undeniable Evidence.

VIII. In the matters of *Religion* two things are to be confidered; firft, the *Account* that we muft give to God, and the *Rewards* that we expect from him: and in this every man muft anfwer for the fincerity of his Heart, in *examining* Divine Matters, and the following what (upon the beft Enquiries that one could make) appeared to be true: and with relation to this, there is no need of a Judge; for in that Great Day every one muft *anfwer* to God according to the Talents that he had, and all will be faved according to their fincerity; and with relation to that Judgment, there is no need of any other Judge but God. A fecond view of *Religion*, is as it is a Body united together, and by confequence brought under fome Regulation: and as in all States, there are fubaltern Judges, in whofe decifions all muft at leaft acquiefce, tho' they are not *infallible*, there being ftill a fort of an Appeal to be made to the Sovereign or the Supream Legiflative Body, fo that the Church has a fubaltern Jurifdiction: but as the Authority of inferior Judges is ftill regulated, and none but the Legiflators themfelves have an Authority equal to the Law; fo it is not neceffary for the prefervation of Peace and Order, that the Decifions of the Church fhould be *infallible*, or of equal *Authority* with the *Scriptures*. If Judges do fo manifeftly abufe their Authority, that they fall into Rebellion and Treafon, the Subjects are no more bound to confider them; but are obliged to refift them, and to maintain their Obedience to their Sovereign; tho' in other matters their Judgment muft take place, till they are reverfed by the Sovereign. The cafe of *Religion* being then this, *That Jefus Chrift is the Sovereign of the Church*; the Affembly of the *Paftors* is only a fubaltern Judge: if they manifeftly oppofe themfelves to the *Scriptures*, which is the *Law of Chriftians*, particular perfons may be fuppofed as competent *Judges* of that, as in civil Matters they may be of the Rebellion of the Judges, and in that cafe they are bound ftill to maintain their Obedience to *Jefus Chrift*. In matters indifferent, Chriftians are bound, for the prefervation of Peace and Unity, to acquiefce in the Decifions of the Church, and in Matters juftly doubtful, or of fmall confequence, tho' they are convinced that the *Paftors* have erred, yet they are obliged to be filent, and to bear tolerable things, rather than make a Breach; but if it is vifible, that the *Paftors* do rebel againft the *Sovereign of the Church*, I mean *Chrift*, the people may put in their Appeal to that great Judge, and there it muft lie. If the Church did ufe this Authority with due Difcretion, and the people followed the Rules that I have named with Humility and Modefty, there would be no great danger of many Divifions; but this is the great Secret of the Providence of God, that men are ftill men, and both Paftors and People mix their Paffions and Interefts fo with matters of Religion, that as there is a great deal of Sin and Vice ftill in the World, fo that appears in the Matters of Religion as well as in other things: but the ill Confequences of this, tho' they are bad enough, yet are not equal Effects that ignorant Superftition and obedient Zeal have produced in the World, witnefs the Rebellions and *Wars* for eftablifhing the Worfhip of Images; the *Croifades* againft the *Saracens*, in which many Millions were loft; thofe againft Hereticks, and Princes depofed by Popes, which lafted for fome Ages; and the Maffacre of *Paris*, with the Butcheries of the Duke of *Alva* in the laft Age, and that of *Ireland* in this: which are, I fuppofe, far greater Mifchiefs than any that can be imagined to arife out of a fmall Diverfion of *Opinions*: and the prefent State of this Church, notwithftanding all thofe unhappy Rents that are in it, is a much more defirable thing, than the grofs Ignorance and blind Superftition that reigns in *Italy* and *Spain* at this day.

IX. All thefe reafonings concerning the Infallibility of the Church fignify nothing, unlefs we can certainly know, whither we muft go for this Decifion: for while one
Party

Party ſhews us, that it muſt be in the *Pope*, or is no where; and another Party ſays it cannot be in the *Pope*, becauſe as many *Popes* have erred, ſo this is a Doctrine that was not known in the Church for a thouſand Years, and that has been diſputed ever ſince it was firſt aſſerted, we are in the right to believe both ſides; firſt, that if it is not in the *Pope*, it is now here; and then, that certainly it is not in the *Pope*; and it is very incongruous to ſay, that there is an infallible Authority in the Church, and that yet it is not certain where one muſt ſeek for it; for the one ought to be as clear as the other: and it is alſo plain, that what Primacy ſoever St. *Peter* may be ſuppoſed to have had, the Scripture ſays not one word of his Succeſſors at *Rome*; ſo at leaſt this is not ſo clear, as a matter of this conſequence muſt have been, if Chriſt had intended to have lodged ſuch an Authority in that See.

X. It is no leſs incongruous to ſay, that this Infallibility is in a General Council; for it muſt be ſomewhere elſe, otherwiſe it will return only to the Church by ſome ſtarts, and other long intervals: and as it was not in the Church, for the firſt Three Hundred and Twenty Years, ſo it has not been in the Church theſe laſt 120 Years. It is plain alſo, that there is no Regulation given in the Scriptures, concerning this great Aſſembly, who have a right to come and Vote, and what forfeits this right, and what numbers muſt concur in a Deciſion, to aſſure us of the Infallibility of the Judgment. It is certain, there was never a General Council of all the Paſtors of the Church: for thoſe of which we have the Acts, were only the Council of the *Roman* Empire, but for thoſe Churches, that were in the South of *Afric*, or the Eaſtern parts of *Aſia*, beyond the bounds of the *Roman* Empire, as they could not be ſummoned by the Emperor's Authority, ſo it is certain none of them were preſent; unleſs one or two of *Perſia* at *Nice*, which perhaps was a Corner of *Perſia* belonging to the Empire; and unleſs it can be proved, that the Pope has an abſolute Authority to cut off whole Churches from their right of coming to Councils, there has been no General Council theſe laſt 700 Years in the World, ever ſince the Biſhops of *Rome* have excommunicated all the *Greek* Churches upon ſuch trifling Reaſons, that their own Writers are now aſhamed of them; and I will ask no more of a Man of a competent Underſtanding, to ſatisfy him, that the Council of *Trent* was no General Council, acting in that Freedom that became Biſhops, than that he will be at the pains to read Card. *Pallavicin*'s Hiſtory of that Council.

XI. If it is ſaid, that this Infallibility is to be ſought for in the Tradition of the Doctrine in all Ages, and that every particular Perſon muſt examine this: here is a Sea before him, and inſtead of examining the ſmall Book of the *New Teſtament*, he is involv'd in a ſtudy that muſt coſt a Man an Age to go thro' it; and many of the Ages, thro' which he carries this Enquiry, are ſo dark, and have produced ſo few Writers, at leaſt ſo few are preſerved to our days, that it is not poſſible to find out their Belief. We find alſo Traditions have varied ſo much, that it is hard to ſay that there is much weight to be laid on this way of Conveyance. A Tradition concerning Matters of Fact that all People ſee, is leſs apt to fall than a Tradition of Points of Speculation: and yet we ſee very near the Age of the Apoſtles, contrary Traditions touching the Obſervation of *Eaſter*, from which we muſt conclude, that either the Matter of Fact of one ſide, or the other, as it was handed down, was not true, or at leaſt that it was not rightly underſtood. A Tradition concerning the Uſe of the Sacraments, being a viſible thing, is the more likely to be exact, than a Speculation concerning their Nature; and yet we find a Tradition of giving Infants the Communion, grounded on the indiſpenſible neceſſity of the Sacrament, continued 1000 years in the Church. A Tradition on which the Chriſtians founded their Joy and Hope, is leſs like to be changed, than a more remote Speculation, and yet the firſt Writers of the Chriſtian Religion had a Tradition handed down to them by thoſe who ſaw the Apoſtles, of the Reign of Chriſt for a Thouſand Years upon Earth; and if thoſe who had Matters at ſecond hand from the Apoſtles, could be thus miſtaken, it is more reaſonable to apprehend greater Errors at ſuch a diſtance. A Tradition concerning the Book of the Scriptures is more like to be exact, than the Expoſitions of ſome paſſages in it; and yet we find the Church did unanimouſly believe the Tranſlation of the 70 Interpreters to have been the effect of a miraculous Inſpiration, till St. *Jerome* examined this matter better, and made a new Tranſlation from the *Hebrew* Copies. But which is more than all the reſt, it ſeems plain, that the Fathers before the Council of *Nice* believed the Dignity of the Son of God to be in ſome ſort inferior to that of the Father, and for ſome Ages after the Council of *Nice*, they believed them indeed both equal, but they conſidered theſe as two different Beings, and only one in Eſſence, as, three men have the ſame human Nature in common among them; and that as one Candle lights another, ſo the one flowed from another: and after the fifth Century the Doctrine

trine of one individual Essence was received. If you will be farther informed concerning this, *Father Petau* will satisfy you as to the first Period before the Council of *Nice*, and the learned Dr. *Cudworth* as to the second. In all which particulars it appears, how variable a thing Tradition is. And upon the whole matter, the examining Tradition thus, is still a searching among Books, and here is no living Judge.

XII. If then the Authority that must decide Controversies, lies in the Body of the Pastors scattered over the World, which is the last retrenchment, here as many and as great Scruples will arise, as we found in any of the former Heads. Two difficulties will appear at first view, the one is, How can we be assured that the present Pastors of the Church are derived in a just Succession from the Apostles: There are no Registers extant that prove this: So that we have nothing for it but some Histories, that are so carelesly writ, that we find many mistakes in them in other matters; and they are so different in the very first Links of that Chain, that immediately succeeded the Apostles, that the utmost can be made of this, is, that here is an Historical Relation somewhat doubtful; but here is nothing to found our Faith on: So that if a Succession from the Apostles times, is necessary to the Constitution of that Church, to which we must submit our selves, we know not where to find it; besides that, the Doctrine of the necessity of the Intention of the Minister to the Validity of a Sacrament, throws us into inextricable Difficulties. I know they generally say, that by the Intention they do not mean the inward Acts of the Minister of the Sacrament, but only that it must appear by his outward deportment, that he is in earnest going about a Sacrament, and not doing a thing in jest; and this appeared so reasonable to me, that I was sorry to find our Divines urge it too much: till turning over the Rubricks that are at the beginning of the Missal, I found upon the head of the Intention of the Minister, that if a *Priest* has a number of *Hosties* before him to be consecrated, and intends to consecrate them all, except one, in that case that vagrant Exception falls upon them all: it not being affixed to any one, and it is defined that he consecrates none at all. Here it is plain, that the secret *Acts* of a Priest can defeat the Sacrament; so this overthrows all certainty concerning a Succession: But besides all this, we are sure, that the *Greek Churches* have a much more uncontested Succession than the *Latins*: So that a Succession cannot direct us. And if it is necessary to seek out the Doctrines that are universally received, this is not possible for a private Man to know. So that in ignorant Countries, where there is little Study, the People have no other certainty concerning their Religion, but what they take from their Curate and Confessor: since they cannot examine what is generally received. So that it must be confessed, that all the Arguments that are brought for the necessity of a constant *infallible Judge*, turn against all those of the Church of *Rome*, that do not acknowledge the *Infallibility* of the *Pope*: for if he is not *infallible*, they have no other *Judge* that can pretend to it. It were also easy to shew, that some Doctrines have been as universally received in some Ages, as they have been rejected in others; which shews, that the Doctrine of the present Church is not always a sure measure. For five Ages together, the Doctrine of the Pope's Power to *depose Heretical Princes* was received without the least Opposition; and this cannot be doubted by any that knows what has been the State of the Church, since the end of the eleventh Century: and yet I believe few Princes would allow this, notwithstanding all the concurring Authority of so many Ages to fortify it. I could carry this into a great many other Instances, but I single out this, because it is a point in which Princes are naturally extream sensible.

Upon the whole matter, it can never enter into my mind, that God, who has made Man a Creature, that naturally enquires and reasons, and that feels as sensible a pleasure when he can give himself a good account of his Actions, as one that sees, does perceive, in comparison to a blind Man that is led about; and that this God that has also made Religion on design to perfect this Human Nature, and to raise it to the utmost height to which it can arrive, has contrived it to be dark, and to be so much beyond the penetration of our Faculties, that we cannot find out his mind in those things that are necessary for our Salvation: and that the *Scriptures*, that were writ by plain men, in a very familiar Stile, and addrest without any Discrimination to the Vulgar, should become such an unintelligible Book in these Ages, that we must have an *infallible Judge* to expound it: and when I see not only *Popes*, but even some Bodies that pass for General Councils, have so expounded many Passages of it, and have wrested them so visibly, that none of the modern Writers of that *Church* pretend to excuse it; I say, I must freely own to you, that when I find that I need a Commentary on dark passages, these will be the last persons to whom I will address my self for it. Thus you see how fully I have opened my mind to you in this matter; I have gone over a great deal of

ground

ground in as few words as is possible, because hints I know are enough for you ; I thank God, these Considerations do fully satisfy me, and I will be infinitely joyed, if they have the same effect on you.

I am yours.

THis Letter came to *London* with the return of the first Post after his late Majesty's Papers were sent into the Country ; some that saw it, liked it well, and wished to have it publick, and the rather, because the Writer did not so entirely confine himself to the Reasons that were in those Papers, but took the whole Controversy to task in a little compass, and yet with a great variety of Reflections. And this way of examining the whole matter, without following those Papers word for word, or the finding more fault than the common concern of this Cause required, seemed more agreeing to the respect that is due to the Dead, and more particularly to the Memory of so great a Prince ; but other considerations made it not so easy nor so adviseable to procure a Licence for the printing this Letter, it has been kept in private hands till now: those who have boasted much of the Shortness of the late King's Papers, and of the Length of the Answers that have been made to them, will not find so great a disproportion between them and this Answer to them.

A Brief Account of Particulars occurring at the happy Death of our late Sovereign Lord King Charles II. in regard to Religion ; faithfully related by his then Assistant, Mr. Jo. Hudleston.

UPON *Thursday* the Fifth of *February* 1685, between Seven and Eight a-clock in the Evening, I was sent for in haste to the Queen's Back-stairs at *Whitehall*, and desired to bring with me all things necessary for a dying Person. Accordingly I came, and was order'd not to stir from thence till further notice ; being thus obliged to wait, and not having had time to bring along with me the Most Holy Sacrament of the Altar, I was in some anxiety how to procure it : In this Conjuncture (the Divine Providence so disposing) Father *Bento de Lemos* a *Portugueze* came thither, and understanding the circumstance I was in, readily proffer'd himself to go to *St. James's*, and bring the Most Holy Sacrament along with him.

Soon after his departure I was call'd into the King's Bed-Chamber, where approaching to the Bed-side, and kneeling down, I in brief presented his Majesty with what Service I could perform for God's honour, and the happiness of his Soul at this last Moment on which Eternity depends. The King then declared himself, that he desired to die in the Faith and Communion of the Holy Roman Catholick Church, that he was most heartily sorry for all the Sins of his Life past, and particularly for that he had deferred his Reconciliation so long ; that through the Merits of Christ's Passion he hoped for Salvation, that he was in Charity with all the World ; that with all his heart he pardon'd his Enemies, and desired Pardon of all those whom he had any wise offended, and that if it pleased God to spare him longer life, he would amend it, detesting all Sin.

I then advertis'd his Majesty of the benefit and necessity of the Sacrament of Penance, which Advertisement the King most willingly embracing, made an exact Confession of his whole Life, with exceeding Compunction and Tenderness of Heart ; which ended, I desired him, in farther sign of Repentance and true Sorrow for his Sins, to say with me this little short Act of Contrition.

O my Lord God, with my whole Heart and Soul I detest all the Sins of my Life past for the Love of Thee, whom I love above all things, and I firmly purpose by thy Holy Grace never to offend thee more, *Amen*, Sweet Jesus, *Amen*. Into thy Hands, Sweet Jesus, I commend my Soul ; Mercy, Sweet Jesus, Mercy. This he pronounced with a clear and audible Voice ; which done, and his Sacramental Penance admitted, I gave him Absolution.

After some time thus spent, I asked his Majesty, if he did not also desire to have the other Sacraments of the Holy Church administred unto him ? He reply'd, By all means, I desire to be Partaker of all the Helps and Succours necessary and expedient for a Catholick Christian in my condition. I added, And doth not your Majesty also desire to receive the precious Body and Blood of our dear Saviour Jesus Christ in the Most Holy Sacrament of the Eucharist ? His Answer was this: If I am worthy, pray fail not to let me have it. I then told him, it would be brought to him very speedily, and desired his Majesty, that in the interim he would give me leave to proceed to the Sacrament

crament of Extreme Unction ; he replied, with all my heart. I then Anoiled him, which as soon as perform'd I was call'd to the door, whither the Blessed Sacrament was now brought and delivered to me.

Then returning to the King, I entreated His Majesty that he would prepare and dispose himself to receive. At which the King raising up himself, said, let me meet my Heavenly Lord in a better Posture than in my Bed. But I humbly begg'd His Majesty to repose himself: God Almighty, who saw his Heart, would accept of his good Intention. The King then having again recited the fore-mentioned Act of Contrition with me, he received the most Holy Sacrament for his Viaticum, with all the Symptoms of Dvotion imaginable. The Communion being ended, I read the usual Prayers, termed the Recommendation of the Soul, appointed by the Church for Catholicks in his Condition. After which, the King desired the Act of Contrition : O my Lord God, &c. to be repeated ; this done, for his last Spiritual Encouragement I said,

Your Majesty hath now received the Comfort and Benefit of all the Sacraments, that a good Christian (ready to depart out of this World) can have or desire. Now it rests only, that you think upon the Death and Passion of our Dear Saviour Jesus Christ, of which I present unto you this Figure (shewing him a Crucifix) lift up therefore the Eyes of your Soul, and represent to your self your sweet Saviour here crucified : Bowing down his Head to kiss you : His Arms stretched out to embrace you : His Body and Members all bloody and pale with Death to redeem you : And as you see him dead and fixed upon the Cross for your Redemption ; so have his Remembrance fixed and fresh in your Heart : Beseech him with all Humility, that his most precious Blood may not be shed in vain for you : And that it will please him by the Merits of his bitter Death and Passion to pardon and forgive you all your Offences, and finally to receive your Soul into his Blessed Hands ; and when it shall please him to take it out of this transitory World, to grant you a joyful Resurrection, and an eternal Crown of Glory in the next. In the Name of the Father, and of the Son, and of the Holy Ghost : *Amen*.

So recommending his Majesty on my Knees, with all the Transport of Devotion I was able, to the Divine Mercy and Protection, I withdrew out of the Chamber.

In Testimony of all which, I have hereunto subscribed my Name,

JO. HUDLESTON.

Some REFLECTIONS on His Majesty's Proclamation of the Twelfth of February 1686-7, for a Toleration in Scotland ; together with the said Proclamation.

I. THE Preamble of a Proclamation is oft writ in haste, and is the flourish of some wanton Pen : but one of such an extraordinary nature as this is, was probably more severely examined ; there is a new designation of his Majesty's Authority here set forth of his *Absolute Power*, which is so often repeated, that it deserves to be a little searched into. Prerogative Royal, and Sovereign Authority, are Terms already received and known ; but for this *Absolute Power*, as it is a new Term, so those who have coined it, may make it signify what they will. The Roman Law speaks of *Princeps Legibus solutus*, and *Absolute* in its natural signification, importing the being without all Ties and Restraints ; then the true meaning of this seems to be, that there is an inherent Power in the King, which can neither be restrained by Laws, Promises, nor Oaths ; for nothing less than the being free from all these, renders a Power *Absolute*.

II. If the former Term seemed to stretch our Allegiance, that which comes after it, is yet a step of another nature, tho' one can hardly imagine what can go beyond *Absolute Power* : and it is in these Words, *Which all our Subjects are to obey without reserve*. And this is the carrying Obedience many sizes beyond what the Grand Seignior ever yet claimed : For all Princes, even the most violent Pretenders to *Absolute Power*, 'till *Lewis* the Great's time, have thought it enough to oblige their Subjects to submit to their Power, and to bear whatsoever they thought good to impose upon them ; but till the Days of the late Conversions by the Dragoons, it was never so much as pretended, that Subjects were bound to *obey* their Prince *without reserve* ; and to be of his Religion, because he would have it so. Which was the only Argument that those late Apostles made use of ; so it is probable this qualification of the Duty of Subjects was put in here, to prepare us for a terrible *le Roy le veut* ; and in that case we are told here, that we muſt *obey without reſerve* ; and when thoſe ſevere Orders come, the Privy-Council, and all ſuch as execute this Proclamation, will be bound by this Declaration to ſhew themſelves more forward than any others, *to obey without reſerve:* and thoſe poor pretenſions of Conſcience, Religion, Honour, and Reaſon, will be then reckoned as *Reſerves* upon their Obedience, which are all now ſhut out.

III. Theſe being the grounds upon which this Proclamation is founded, we ought not only to conſider what Conſequences are now drawn from them, but what may be drawn from them at any time hereafter ; for if they are of force, to juſtify that which is inferred from them, it will be full as juſt to draw from the ſame premiſes an Abolition of the Proteſtant Religion, of the Rights of the Subjects, not only to Church-Lands, but to all Property whatſoever. In a word, it aſſerts a Power to be in the King, to command what he will, and an Obligation in the Subjects, to obey whatſoever he ſhall command.

IV. There is alſo mention made in the Preamble of the *Chriſtian Love and Charity,* which his Majeſty would have eſtabliſhed among Neighbours ; but another daſh of a Pen, founded on his *Abſolute Power,* may declare us all Hereticks ; and then in wonderful Charity to us, we muſt be told, that we are either to obey without reſerve, or be burnt without reſerve. We know the Charity of that Church pretty well : It is indeed fervent and burning ; and if we have forgot what has been done in former Ages, *France, Savoy,* and *Hungary* have ſet before our Eyes very freſh Inſtances of the Charity of that Religion. While thoſe Examples are ſo green, it is a little too impoſing on us, to talk to us of *Chriſtian Love and Charity.* No doubt His Majeſty means ſincerely, and his Exactneſs to all his Promiſes, chiefly to thoſe made ſince he came to the Crown, will not ſuffer us to think an unbecoming Thought of his Royal Intentions ; but yet after all, tho' it ſeems by this Proclamation, that we are bound to *obey without reſerve,* it is hardſhip upon hardſhip to be bound to *believe without reſerve.*

V. There are a ſort of People here tolerated, that will be hardly found out : and theſe are the Moderate Presbyterians. Now, as ſome ſay, that there are very few of thoſe People in *Scotland* that deſerve this Character, ſo it is hard to tell what it amounts to ; and the calling any of them Immoderate, cuts off all their ſhare in this Grace. Moderation is a quality that lies in the Mind, and how this will be found out, I cannot ſo readily gueſs. If a Standard had been given of Opinions or Practices, then one could have known how this might have been diſtinguiſhed ; but as it lies, it will not be eaſy to make the Diſcrimination ; and the declaring them all immoderate, ſhuts them quite out.

VI. Another Foundation laid down for repealing all Laws made againſt the Papiſts, is, that they were enacted in King *James* the Sixth's Minority : with ſome harſh Expreſſions, that are not to be inſiſted on, ſince they ſhew more the heat of the Penner, than the Dignity of the Prince, in whoſe name they are given out. But all theſe Laws were ratified over and over again by King *James,* when he came to be of full Age ; and they have received many Confirmations by King *Charles* the Firſt, and King *Charles* the Second, as well as by his preſent Majeſty, both when he repreſented his Brother in the Year 1681, and ſince he himſelf came to the Crown : ſo that whatſoever may be ſaid concerning the firſt Foundation of thoſe Laws, they have received now for the courſe of a whole hundred Years, that are lapſed ſince King *James* was of full Age, ſo many Confirmations, that if there is any thing certain in human Government, we might depend upon them ; but this new coined *Abſolute Power* muſt carry all before it.

VII. It is alſo well known, that the whole Settlement of the Church Lands and Tythes, with many other things, and more particularly the Eſtabliſhment of the Proteſtant Religion, was likewiſe enacted in King *James's* Minority, as well as thoſe Penal Laws : ſo that the Reaſon now made uſe of, to annul the penal Laws, will ſerve full as well for another Act of this *Abſolute Power,* that ſhall aboliſh all thoſe : and if Maxims that unhinge all the Securities of human Society, and all that is ſacred in Government, ought to be look'd on with the juſteſt and deepeſt prejudices poſſible, one is tempted to loſe the reſpect that is due to every thing that carries a Royal Stamp upon it, when he ſees ſuch grounds made uſe of, as muſt ſhake all Settlements whatſoever ; for if a Preſcription of 120 Years, and Confirmations reiterated over and over again theſe 100 Years paſt, do not purge ſome Defects in the firſt Formation of thoſe Laws, what can make us ſecure ? But this looks ſo like a fetch of the *French* Prerogative Law, both in their Proceſſes with relation to the Edict of *Nantes,* and thoſe concerning Dependencies at *Mets,* that this ſeems to be a Copy from that famous Original.

VIII.

VIII. It were too much ill-nature to look into the History of the last Age, to examine on what grounds those Characters of *Pious* and *Blessed* given to the Memory of Q. *Mary* are built; but since K. *James*'s Memory has the Character of *Glorious* given to it, if the Civility of the Fair Sex makes one unwilling to look into one, yet the other may be a little dwelt on. The peculiar Glory that belongs to K. *James*'s Memory, is, that he was a Prince of great Learning, and that he employed it chiefly in writing for his Religion: of the Volume in Folio in which we have his Works, two thirds are against the Church of *Rome*, one part of them is a Commentary on the Revelation, proving that the Pope is Antichrist; another part of them belonged more naturally to his Post Dignity; which is the warning that he gave to all the Princes and States of *Europe*, against the treasonable and bloody Doctrines of the Papacy. The first Act he did when he came of Age, was to swear in Person with all his Family, and afterwards with all his People of *Scotland*, a Covenant, containing an Enumeration of all the points of Popery, and a most solemn Renunciation of them, somewhat like our Parliament Test: his first Speech to the Parliament of *England* was copious on this Subject; and he left a Legacy of a Wish on such of his Posterity as should go over to that Religion, which in good manners is suppressed. It is known, K. *James* was no Conqueror, and that he made more use of his Pen than his Sword; so the Glory that is peculiar to his Memory, must fall chiefly on his learned and immortal Writings: and since there is such a Veneration expressed for him, it agrees not ill with this, to wish, that his Works were more studied by those who offer such Incense to his *glorious* Memory.

IX. His Majesty assures his People of *Scotland*, upon a certain Knowledge and long Experience, that the Catholicks, as they are good Christians, so they are likewise dutiful Subjects: but if we must believe both these equally, then we must conclude severely against their being good Christians; for we are sure they can never be good Subjects, even to a *Roman* Catholick Prince, if he does not extirpate Hereticks; for their beloved Council of the Lateran, that decreed Transubstantiation, has likewise decreed, that if a Prince does not extirpate Hereticks out of his Dominions, the Pope must depose him, and declare his Subjects absolved from their Allegiance, and give his Dominions to another: so that even his Majesty, how much soever he may be a zealous Catholick, yet he cannot be assured of their fidelity to him, unless he has given them secret assurances, that he is resolved to extirpate Hereticks out of his Dominions; and that all the Promises which he now makes to these poor wretches, are no other way to be kept, than the Assurances which the great *Lewis* gave to his Protestant Subjects, of his observing still the Edict of *Nantes*, even after he had resolved to break it, and also his last Promise made in the Edict, that repealed the Edict of *Nantes*, by which he gave Assurances that no violence should be used to any for their Religion, in the very time that he was ordering all possible Violences to be put in execution against them.

X. His Majesty assures us, that on all occasions the Papists have shewed themselves good and faithful Subjects to him and his royal Predecessors; but how *absolute* soever the King's *Power* may be, it seems his Knowledge of History is not so absolute, but it may be capable of some Improvement. It will be hard to find out what Loyalty they shewed on the Gunpowder Plot, or during the whole progress of the Rebellion of *Ireland*; if the King will either take the words of King *James* of *glorious* Memory, or K. *Charles* the first, that was indeed of *pious* and *blessed* Memory, rather than the penners of this Proclamation, it will not be hard to find Occasions where they were a little wanting in this their so much boasted Loyalty: and we are sure, that by the Principles of that Religion, the King can never be assured of the Fidelity of those he calls his Catholick Subjects, but by engaging them to make his heretical Subjects sacrifices to their Rage.

XI. The King declares them capable of all the Offices and *Benefices* which he shall think fit to bestow on them, and only restrains them from invading the Protestant Churches by force; so that here a door is plainly opened for admitting them to the exercise of their Religion in Protestant Churches, so they do not break into them by force; and whatsoever may be the Sense of the term *Benefice* in its ancient and first signification, now it stands only for Church-Preferments; so that when any Churches, that are in the King's Gift, fall vacant, here is a plain intimation, that they are to be provided to them; and then it is very probable, that all the Laws made against such as go not to their parish Churches, will be severely turned upon those that will not come to Mass.

XII. His Majesty does in the next place, in the virtue of his *absolute Power*, annul a great many Laws, as well those that established the Oaths of Allegiance and Supremacy, as the late Test, enacted by himself in person, while he represented his Brother: upon which he gave as strange an Essay to the World of his absolute Justice in the Attainder

4

tainder of the late Earl of *Argyle*, as he does now of his *absolute Power* in condemning the Teft it felf; he alfo repeals his own Confirmation of the Teft, fince he came to the Crown, which he offered as the cleareft Evidence that he could give of his Refolution to maintain the Proteftant Religion, and by which he gained fo much upon that Parliament, that he obtained every thing from them that he defired of them; till he came to try them in the Matters of Religion. This is no extraordinary Evidence to affure his People, that his Promifes will be like the Laws of the *Medes* and *Perfians*, which alter not; nor will the difgrace of the Commiffioner that enacted that Law, lay this matter wholly on him; for the Letter, that he brought, the Speech that he made, and the Inftruction, which he got, are all too well known to be fo foon forgotten; and if Princes will give their Subjects reafon to think, that they forget their Promifes, as foon as the turn is ferved for which they were made, this will be too prevailing a Temptation on the Subjects to mind the Prince's promife as little as it feems he himfelf does, and will force them to conclude, that the Truth of the Prince, is not fo abfolute as it feems he fancies his Power to be.

XIII. Here is not only a repealing of a great many Laws, and eftablifhed Oaths and Tefts, but by the Exercife of the *abfolute Power*, a new Oath is impofed, which was never pretended to by the Crown in any former time; and as the Oath is created by this *abfolute Power*, fo it feems the *abfolute Power* muft be fupported by this Oath: fince one branch of it, is an Obligation to maintain his Majefty and his lawful Succeffors in the Exercife of this their *abfolute Power* and *Authority* againft all deadly, which I fuppofe is *Scotch* for Mortals. Now to impofe fo hard a yoke as this *abfolute Power* on the Subject, feems no fmall ftretch; but it is a wonderful exercife of it to oblige the Subjects to defend this; it had been more modeft, if they had been only bound to bear it, and fubmit to it: but it is a terrible thing fo far to extinguifh all the remnants of natural Liberty, or of a legal Government, as to oblige the Subjects by Oath to maintain the Exercife of this, which plainly muft deftroy themfelves: for the fhort execution of the Bow-ftrings of *Turkey*, or by fending Orders to Men to return in their Heads, being an Exercife of this *abfolute Power*, it is a little too hard to make men fwear to maintain the King in it; and if that Kingdom has fuffered fo much by the many Oaths that have been in ufe among them, as is marked in his Proclamation, I am afraid this new Oath will not much mend the matter.

XIV. Yet after all, there is fome Comfort; his Majefty affures them, he will ufe no Violence nor Force, nor any *invincible Neceffity*, to any man on the account of his perfwafion: It were too great a want of refpect to fancy, that a time may come, in which even this may be remembred, full as well, as the promifes that were made to the Parliament after his Majefty came to the Crown; I do not, I confefs, apprehend that; for I fee here fo great a Caution ufed in the choice of thefe words, that it is plain, very great Severities may very well confift with them: It is clear, that the general words of Violence and Force are to be determined by the laft *invincible Neceffity*, fo that the King does only promife to lay no *invincible Neceffity* on his Subjects; but for all Neceffities that are not invincible, it feems they muft bear a large fhare of them; Difgraces, want of Imployments, Fines and Imprifonments, and even Death it felf are all vincible things to a man of a firmnefs of mind: fo that the Violences of Torture, the Furies of Dragoons, and fome of the Methods now practifed in *France*, perhaps may be included within this Promife; fince thefe feem almoft *invincible* to human Nature, if it is not fortified with an extraordinary meafure of Grace: but as to all other things, his Majefty binds himfelf up from no part of the Exercife of his *abfolute Power* by this Promife.

XV. His Majefty orders this to go immediately to the Great Seal, without paffing through the other Seals: now fince this is counter-figned by the Secretary in whofe hands the Signet is, there was no other ftep to be made but through the Privy Seal; fo I muft own I have a great Curiofity of knowing his Character in whofe hands the Privy Seal is at prefent; for it feems his Confcience is not fo very fupple, as the Chancellor's and the Secretaries are; but it is very likely, if he does not quickly change his Mind, the Privy Seal at leaft will quickly change his Keeper; and I am forry to hear, that the Lord Chancellor and Secretary have not another Brother to fill this poft, that fo the guilt of the ruin of that Nation, may lie on one fingle Family, and that there may be no others involved in it.

XVI. Upon the whole matter many fmaller things being waved, it being extream unpleafant to find fault, where one has all poffible difpofitions to pay all refpect; we here in *England* fee what we muft look for. A Parliament in *Scotland* was try'd, but it proved a little ftubborn; and now *abfolute Power* comes to fet all right; fo when the Clofetting has gone round, fo that Nofes are counted, we may perhaps fee a Parliament here; but if it chances to be untoward, and not to *Obey without Referve,* then

our

our reverend Judges will copy from *Scotland*, and will not only tell us of the King's imperial Power, but will difcover to us this new Myftery of *abfolute Power*, which we are all bound *to Obey without Referve.*

Thefe Reflections refer in fo many places to fome words in the Proclamation, that it was thought neceffary to fet them near one another, that the Reader may be able to judge, whether he is deceived by any falfe Quotations or not.

By the King, A PROCLAMATION.

JAMES R.

JAMES the *Seventh, by the Grace of God,* King of *Scotland, England, France* and *Ireland,* Defender of the Faith, *&c.* To all and fundry our good Subjects, whom thefe Prefents do or may concern, *Greeting.* We have taken into our royal Confideration the many and great inconveniencies which have happened to that our ancient Kingdom of *Scotland* of late years, through the different perfwafions in the Chriftian Religion, through the great Heats and Animofities amongft the feveral Profeffors thereof, to the ruin and decay of Trade, wafting of Lands, extinguifhing of Charity, contempt of the royal Power, and converting of true Religion, and the Fear of God, into Animofities, Names, Factions, and fometimes into Sacrilege and Treafon. And being refolved, as much as in us lies, to unite the Hearts and Affections of our Subjects, to GOD in Religion, to Us in Loyalty, and to their Neighbours in *Chriftian Love and Charity,* have therefore thought fit to grant, and by our Sovereign Authority, Prerogative Royal, and *abfolute Power, which all our Subjects are to obey without Referve ;* do hereby give and grant our Royal Toleration, to the feveral Profeffors of the Chriftian Religion after named, with, and under the feveral Conditions, Reftrictions, and Limitations after-mentioned. In the firft place, we allow and tolerate the moderate Prefbyterians to meet in their private Houfes, and there to hear all fuch Minifters, as either have, or are willing to accept of our Indulgence allanerly, and none other, and that there be not any thing faid or done contrary to the Well and Peace of our Reign, Seditious or Treafonable, under the higheft Pains thefe Crimes will import ; nor are they to prefume to build Meeting-Houfes, or to ufe Out-Houfes or Barns, but only to exercife in their private Houfes, as faid is. In the mean time, it is our Royal Will and Pleafure, that Field-Conventicles, and fuch as preach, or exercife at them, or who fhall any ways affift or connive at them, fhall be profecuted according to the utmoft Severity of our Laws made againft them; feeing from thefe Rendezvoufes of Rebellion, fo much Diforder hath proceeded, and fo much Difturbance to the Government, and for which after this our Royal Indulgence for tender Confciences there is no Excufe left. In like manner, we do hereby tolerate Quakers to meet and exercife in their Form, in any place or places appointed for their Worfhip. And confidering the fevere and cruel *Laws* made againft *Roman Catholicks* (therein called *Papifts*) in the Minority of our Royal Grand-Father of * *Glorious* Memory, without his Confent, and contrary to the Duty of good Subjects, by his Regents, and other Enemies to their lawful Sovereigns our Royal Great Grand-Mother Queen *Mary* of *Bleffed* and *Pious* Memory, wherein, under the pretence of Religion, they cloathed the worft of Treafons, Factions, and Ufurpations, and made thefe *Laws,* not as againft the Enemies of GOD, but their own ; which *Laws* have ftill been continued of courfe without defign of executing them, or any of them, *ad terrorem* only, on Suppofition, that the *Papifts* relying on an external Power, were incapable of Duty, and true Allegiance to their natural Sovereigns, and rightful Monarchs ; We of our certain Knowledge, and long Experience, knowing that the *Catholicks,* as it is their Principle to be good *Chriftians,* fo it is to be dutiful Subjects ; and that they have likewife on all Occafions fhewn themfelves good and faithful Subjects to Us, and our Royal Predeceffors, by hazarding, and many of them actually lofing their Lives and Fortunes, in their Defence (though of another Religion) and the Maintenance of their Authority againft the Violences and Treafons of the moft violent Abetters of thefe *Laws* ; do therefore, with Advice and Confent of our Privy Council, by our Sovereign Authority, Prerogative Royal, and *Abfolute Power,* aforefaid, fufpend, ftop, and difable all Laws or Acts of Parliament, Cuftoms or Conftitutions, made or executed againft any of our *Roman Catholick* Subjects, in any time paft, to all intents and purpofes, making void all Prohibitions therein mentioned, pains or penalties therein ordain'd to be inflicted; fo that they fhall in all things be as free in all Refpects whatfoever, not only to exercife their Religion, but to enjoy all *Offices, Benefices,* and others which we fhall think fit to beftow upon them in all time coming: Neverthelefs, it is our Will and Pleafure, and we do hereby command all *Catholicks* at their higheft Pains, only to exercife their religious Worfhip in Houfes or Chappels ; and that they prefume not to preach in the open Fields, or to invade the Proteftant Churches by force,

under

under the pains aforesaid, to be inflicted upon the Offenders respectively; nor shall they presume to make publick Processions in the High-Streets of any of our Royal Burghs, under the Pains above mentioned. And whereas the Obedience and Service of our good Subjects is due to Us by their Allegiance, and our Sovereignty, and that no Law, Custom, or Constitution, difference in Religion, or other Impediment whatsoever, can exempt or discharge the Subjects from their native Obligations and Duty to the Crown, or hinder us from protecting and employing them, according to their several Capacities, and our Royal Pleasure; nor restrain Us from conferring heretable Rights and Privileges upon them, or vacate or annul these Rights Heretable, when they are made or conferred: And likewise considering, that some Oaths are capable of being wrested by men of sinistrous Intentions, a practice in that Kingdom fatal to Religion as it was to Loyalty: Do therefore, with Advice and Consent aforesaid, Cass, Annul and Discharge all Oaths whatsoever, by which any of our Subjects are incapacitated, or disabled from holding Places, or Offices in our said Kingdom, or enjoy their hereditary Right and Privileges, discharging the same to be taken or given in any time coming, without our special Warrant and Consent, under the pains due to the Contempt of our Royal Commands and Authority. And to this effect, we do by our Royal Authority aforesaid, Stop, Disable, and Dispense with all *Laws* enjoining the said *Oaths, Tests,* or any of them, particularly the first Act of the first Session of the first Parliament of King *Charles* the Second; the eleventh Act of the foresaid Session of the foresaid Parliament, the sixth Act of the third Parliament of the said King *Charles*; the twenty first and twenty fifth Acts of that Parliament, and the thirteenth Act of the first Session of * Our late Parliament, in so far allanerly as concerns the taking the *Oaths or Tests* therein prescrib'd, and all others, as well not mentioned as mentioned; and that in place of them, all our good Subjects, or such of them as We or our Privy Council shall require so to do, shall take and swear the following Oath allanerly.

I A. B. do acknowledge, testify and declare, that JAMES *the Seventh, by the Grace of God, King of* Scotland, England, France *and* Ireland, *Defender of the Faith,* &c. *is rightful King and supream Governour of these Realms, and over all persons therein; and that it is unlawful for Subjects, on any pretence, or for any cause whatsoever, to rise in Arms against Him, or any commissionated by Him; and that I shall never so rise in Arms, nor assist any who shall so do; and that I shall never resist his Power or Authority, nor ever oppose his Authority to his Person, as I shall answer to God: but shall to the utmost of my Power assist, defend, and maintain Him, his Heirs and lawful Successors, in the Exercise of their absolute Power and Authority against all Deadly.* So help me God.

And seeing many of our good Subjects have before our Pleasure in these Matters was made publick, incurred the Guilt appointed by the Acts of Parliament abovementioned, or others; We, by our Authority, and *absolute Power* and Prerogative Royal above-mentioned, of our certain Knowledge, and innate Mercy, give our ample and full Indemnity to all those of the *Roman Catholick* or *Popish Religion,* for all things by them done contrary to our Laws, or Acts of Parliament, made in any time past, relating to their Religion, the Worship and Exercise thereof, or for being Papists, Jesuits, or Traffickers, for hearing, or saying of Mass, concealing of Priests or Jesuits, breeding their Children Catholicks at home or abroad, or any other thing, Rite or Doctrine, said, performed, or maintained by them, or any of them: And likewise, for holding or taking of Places, Employments, or Offices, contrary to any Law or Constitution, Advices given to Us, or our Council, Actions done, or generally any thing perform'd or said against the known Laws of that our ancient Kingdom: Excepting always from this our Royal Indemnity, all Murthers, Assassinations, Thefts, and such like other Crimes, which never used to be comprehended in our general Acts of Indemnity. And we command and require all our Judges, or others concerned, to explain this in the most ample Sense and Meaning, Acts of Indemnity at any time have contained: Declaring this shall be as good to every one concerned, as if they had our Royal Pardon and Remission under our great Seal of that Kingdom. And likewise indemnifying our Protestant Subjects from all pains and penalties due for hearing or preaching in Houses; providing there be no treasonable Speeches uttered in the said Conventicles by them, in which case the Law is only to take place against the Guilty, and none other present; providing also, that they reveal to any of our Council the Guilt so committed: As also, excepting all Fines, or Effects of Sentences already given. And likewise indemnifying fully and freely all Quakers, for their Meetings and Worship, in all time past, preceding the publication of these presents. And we doubt not but our Protestant Subjects will give their Assistance and Concourse hereunto, on all Occasions, in their respective Capacities. In consideration whereof, and the ease those of our Religion, and others may have hereby, and for the Encouragement of our Protestant Bishops

Bifhops, and the Regular Clergy, and fuch as have hitherto lived orderly, We think fit to declare, that it never was Our Principle, nor will We ever fuffer Violence to be offered to any Man's Confcience, nor will We ufe Force, or *invincible Neceffity* againft any Man on the account of his Perfwafion, nor the Proteftant Religion, but will protect Our Bifhops and other Minifters in their Functions, Rights and Properties, and all Our Proteftant Subjects in the free Exercife of their Proteftant Religion in the Churches. And that We will, and hereby promife, on Our Royal Word, to maintain the Poffeffors of Church Lands formerly belonging to Abbeys, or other Churches of the Catholick Religion, in their full and free Poffeffion and Right, according to Our Laws and Acts of Parliament in that behalf in all time coming. And We will imploy indifferently all Our Subjects of all Perfwafions, fo as none fhall meet with any Difcouragement on the account of his Religion, but be advanced, and efteemed by Us, according to their feveral Capacities and Qualifications, fo long as we find Charity and Unity maitained. And if any Animofities fhall arife, as we hope in God there will not, We will fhew the fevereft Effects of Our Royal Difpleafure againft the Beginners or Fomenters thereof, feeing thereby Our Subjects may be deprived of this general Eafe and Satisfaction, We intend to all of them; whofe Happinefs, Profperity, Wealth and Safety, is fo much Our Royal Care, that We will leave nothing undone which may procure thefe Bleffings for them. And laftly, to the end all our good Subjects may have Notice of this Our Royal Will and Pleafure, We do hereby command, Our *Lyon* King at Arms, and his Brethren Heraulds, Macers, Purfevants and Meffengers at Arms, to make timeous Proclamation hereof at the Mercat-Crofs of *Edinburgh*; and befides the printing and publifhing of this Our Royal Proclamation, it is our exprefs Will and Pleafure, that the fame *be paffed under the Great Seal of that Our Kingdom, per faltum*, * without paffing any other Seal or Regifter. In order whereunto, this fhall be to the Directors of Our Chancellary, and their Deputies for writing the fame, and to Our Chancellor for caufing our Great Seal aforefaid, to be appended thereunto, a fufficient Warrant.

Given at Our Court at Whitehall *the twelfth Day of* Feb. 1686. *and of Our Reign the third Year.*

By His Majefty's Command,

MELFORT.

God fave the King.

His Majefty's Gracious DECLARATION *to all his Loving Subjects for Liberty of Confcience.*

JAMES R.

IT having pleafed Almighty God not only to bring Us to the Imperial Crown of thefe Kingdoms through the greateft Difficulties, but to preferve Us by a more than ordinary Providence upon the Throne of Our Royal Anceftors, there is nothing now that we fo earneftly defire as to eftablifh our Government on fuch a Foundation, as may make our Subjects happy, and unite them to Us by Inclination as well as Duty; which We think may be done by no Means fo effectually, as by granting to them the free Exercife of their Religion for the time to come, and add that to the perfect Enjoyment of their Property, which has never been in any cafe invaded by Us fince Our coming to the Crown: which being the two things Men value moft, fhall ever be preferved in thefe Kingdoms, during our Reign over them, as the trueft Methods of their Peace and Our Glory. We cannot but heartily wifh, as it will eafily be believed, That all the People of Our Dominions were Members of the Catholick Church; yet we humbly thank Almighty God, it is, and hath of long time been Our conftant Senfe and Opinion (which upon diverfe Occafions We have declared) That Confcience ought not to be conftrained, nor People forced in Matters of meer Religion: It has ever been directly contrary to Our Inclination, as We think it is to the Intereft of Government, which it deftroys by fpoiling Trade, depopulating Countries, and difcouraging Strangers; and finally, that it never obtained the End for which it was employ'd: And in this We are the more confirmed, by the Reflections We have made upon the Conduct of the four laft Reigns. For after all the frequent and preffing Endeavours that were ufed in each of them, to reduce this Kingdom to an exact Conformity in Religion, it is vifible the Succefs has not anfwered the Defign, and that the Difficulty is invincible. We therefore out of Our Princely Care and Af-

fection

fection unto all Our Loving Subjects, that they may live at Eafe and Quiet, and for the increafe of Trade, and encouragement of Strangers, have thought fit by virtue of Our Royal Prerogative, to iffue forth this Our Royal Declaration of Indulgence; making no doubt of the Concurrence of our two Houfes of Parliament, when We fhall think it convenient for them to meet.

In the firft place we do declare, That we fhall protect and maintain Our Arch Bifhops, Bifhops, and Clergy, and all other our Subjects of the Church of *England*, in the free Exercife of their Religion, as by Law eftablifhed, and in the quiet and full Enjoyment of all their Poffeffions, without any Moleftation or Difturbance whatfoever.

We do likewife declare, That it is our Royal Will and Pleafure, that from henceforth the Execution of all and all manner of Penal Laws in Matters Ecclefiaftical, for not coming to Church, or not receiving the Sacrament, or for any other Non-conformity to the Religion eftablifhed, or for or by reafon of the Exercife of Religion in any manner whatfoever, be immediately fufpended; and the further Execution of the faid Penal Laws and every of them is hereby fufpended.

And to the end that by the Liberty hereby granted, the Peace and Security of Our Government in the Practice thereof may not be endangered, We have thought fit, and do hereby ftraitly charge and command all Our Loving Subjects, That as we do freely give them leave to meet and ferve God after their own Way and Manner, be it in private Houfes or in Places purpofely hired or built for that Ufe; fo that they take efpecial Care, that nothing be preached or taught among them which may any ways tend to alienate the Hearts of Our People from Us or Our Government; and that their Meetings and Affemblies be peaceably, openly, and publickly held, and all Perfons freely admitted to them; and that they do fignify and make known to fome one or more of the next Juftices of the Peace what place or places they fet apart for thofe Ufes.

And that all our Subjects may enjoy fuch their Religious Affemblies with greater Affurance and Protection, We have thought it requifite, and do hereby command, that no difturbance of any kind be made, or given to them, under pain of our Difpleafure, and to be further proceeded againft with the utmoft Severity.

And for as much as we are defirous to have the Benefit of the Service of all Our Loving Subjects, which by the Law of Nature is infeparably annexed to, and inherent in Our Royal Perfon; and that none of Our Subjects may for the future be under any Difcouragement or Difability (who are otherwife well inclined and fit to ferve Us) by reafon of fome Oaths or Tefts, that have been ufually adminiftred on fuch Occafions: We do hereby further declare, that it is our Royal Will and Pleafure, that the Oaths commonly called, *The Oaths of Supremacy and Allegiance*, and alfo the feveral Tefts and Declarations mentioned in the Acts of Parliament made in the 25th and 30th Years of the Reign of our late Royal Brother King *Charles* the Second, fhall not at any time hereafter be required to be taken, declared or fubfcribed by any perfon or perfons whatfoever, who is, or fhall be employ'd in any Office or Place of Truft, either Civil or Military, under Us, or in Our Government. And We do further declare it to be Our Pleafure and Intention from time to time hereafter, to grant Our Royal Difpenfations under Our Great Seal to all Our loving Subjects fo to be employ'd, who fhall not take the faid Oaths, or fubfcribe or declare the faid Tefts or Declarations in the abovementioned, Acts and every of them.

And to the End that all Our Loving Subjects may receive and enjoy the full Benefit and Advantage of Our Gracious Indulgence hereby intended, and may be acquitted and difcharged from all Pains, Penalties, Forfeitures, and Difabilities by them or any of them incurred or forfeited, or which they fhall or may at any time hereafter be liable to, for or by reafon of their Non-conformity, or the Exercife of their Religion, and from all Suits, Troubles or Difturbances for the fame: We do hereby give Our free and ample pardon unto all Non-conformifts, Recufants, and other Our Loving Subjects, for all Crimes and Things by them committed, contrary to the Penal Laws formerly made relating to Religion, and the Profeffion or Exercife thereof; hereby declaring, That this Our Royal Pardon and Indempnity fhall be as good and effectual to all intents and purpofes, as if every individual Perfon had been therein particularly named, or had particular Pardons under Our Great Seal, which We do likewife declare fhall from time to time be granted unto any Perfon or Perfons defiring the fame: Willing and requiring Our Judges, Juftices, and other Officers, to take notice of, and obey our Royal Will and Pleafure herein before declared.

And although the Freedom and Affurance We have hereby given in relation to Religion and Property, might be fufficient to remove from the Minds of Our Loving Subjects all Fears and Jealoufies in relation to either; yet We have thought fit farther

ther to declare, That we will maintain them in all their Properties and Possessions, as well of Church and Abby Lands, as in any other their Lands and Properties whatsoever.

> *Given at our Court at* Whitehall, *the fourth Day of* April, 1687. *In the third Year of Our Reign.*

𝕭𝖞 𝕳𝖎𝖘 𝕸𝖆𝖏𝖊𝖘𝖙𝖞'𝖘 𝕾𝖕𝖊𝖈𝖎𝖆𝖑 𝕮𝖔𝖒𝖒𝖆𝖓𝖉.

A LETTER, containing some Reflections on his Majesty's Declaration for Liberty of Conscience, dated the fourth of April, 1687.

SIR,

I. I Thank you for the Favour of sending me the late *Declaration* that his Majesty has granted for *Liberty of Conscience.* I confess I longed for it with great impatience, and was surprised to find it so different from the *Scotch* pattern; for I imagined, that it was to be set to the second part of the same tune: nor can I see why the Penners of this have sunk so much in their stile; for I suppose the same Man penned both. I expected to have seen the imperial Language of *Absolute Power, to which all the Subjects are to obey without reserve; and of the Casting, Annulling, the Stopping, and Disabling of Laws,* set forth in the Preamble and Body of this *Declaration;* whereas those dreadful words are not to be found here: for instead of *Repealing the Laws,* his Majesty pretends by this only to *Suspend them;* and though in effect this amounts to a *Repeal,* yet it must be confessed that the Words are softer. Now since the *Absolute Power,* to which his Majesty pretends in *Scotland,* is not founded on such poor things as *Law;* for that would look as if it were the Gift of the People; but on the Divine Authority, which is supposed to be delegated to his Majesty, this may be as well claimed in *England* as it was in *Scotland:* and the pretensions to *Absolute Power,* is so great a thing, that since his Majesty thought fit once to claim it, he is little beholden to those that make him fall so much in his Language, especially since both these *Declarations* have appeared in our *Gazettes;* so that as we see what is done in *Scotland,* we know from hence what is in some People's Hearts, and what we may expect in *England.*

II. His Majesty tells his People, that *the perfect enjoyment of their Property has never been in any Case invaded by him since his coming to the Crown.* This is indeed matter of great Encouragement to all good Subjects; for it lets them see that such Invasions as have been made on *Property,* have been done without his Majesty's knowledge: so that no doubt the continuing to levy the *Customs* and the *Additional Excise,* (which had been granted only during the late King's Life) before the Parliament could meet to renew the Grant, was done without his Majesty's knowledge; the many Violences committed not only by *Soldiers,* but *Officers,* in all the Parts of *England,* which are severe Invasions on *Property,* have been all without his Majesty's knowledge; and since the first Branch of *Property* is the Right that a Man has to his Life, the strange Essay of *Mahometan Government* that was shewed at *Taunton,* and the no less strange Proceedings of the present Lord Chancellor, in his Circuit after the Rebellion (which are very justly called his Campaign, for it was an open Act of Hostility to all Law) and for which and other Services of the like nature, it is believed he has had the reward of the Great Seal; and the Executions of those who have left their Colours, which being founded on no Law, are no other than so many Murders: all these, I say, are, as we are sure, invasions on Property. But since the King tells us, that no such Invasions have been made, since he came to the Crown, we must conclude that all these things have fallen out without his privity. And if a standing Army, in time of Peace, has been ever lookt on by this Nation as an Atempt upon the whole Property of the Nation in gross, one must conclude, that even this is done without his Majesty's knowledge.

III. His Majesty expresses his Charity for us in a kind wish, that we were all Members of the Catholick Church; in return of which, we offer up daily our most earnest Prayers for him, that he may become a Member of the true Catholick Church: for Wishes and Prayers do no hurt on no side. But his Majesty adds, that it has ever been his Opinion, that Conscience ought not to be constrained, nor People forced in matters of meer Religion. We are very happy if this continues to be always his Sense: but we are sure in this he is no obedient Member of that which he means by the Catholick Church: for it has over and over again decreed the Extirpation of Hereticks. It encourages Princes to it, by the Offer of Pardon of their Sins; it threatens them to

it,

it, by denouncing to them not only the Judgments of God, but that which is more sensible, the loss of their Dominions: and it seems they intend to make us know that part of their Doctrine even before we come to feel it, since tho' some of that Communion would take away the horror which the fourth Council of the *Lateran* gives us, in which these things were decreed, by denying it to be a General Council, and rejecting the Authority of those Canons; yet the most learned of all the *Apostates* that has fallen to them of our Church, has so lately given up this Plea, and has so formally acknowledged the Authority of that Council, and of its Canons, that it seems they think they are bound to this piece of fair dealing, of warning us before hand of our Danger. It is true, *Bellarmine* says, " That the Church does not always execute the Power of " Deposing Heretical Princes, tho' she always retains it: one Reason that she assigns, is, " because she is not at all times able to put it in execution:" so the same Reason may perhaps make it appear unadviseable to extirpate Hereticks, because that at present it cannot be done; but the Right remains entire, and is put in execution in such a relenting manner in all places where that Religion prevails, that it is a very ill Grace, to see any Member of that Church speak in this strain; and when neither the Policy of *France,* nor the Greatness of their Monarch, nor the Interests of their Emperor, joined to the Gentleness of his own Temper, could withstand these bloody Councils, that are indeed parts of that Religion, we can see no reason to induce us to believe that a Toleration of Religion is proposed with any other Design but either to divide us, or lay us asleep till it is time to give us the Alarm for destroying us.

VI. If all the Endeavours that had been used in the last four Reigns for bringing the Subjects of this Kingdom to an Unity in Religion have been ineffectual, as his Majesty says; we know to whom we owe the first beginnings, and the progress of the Divisions among our selves; the gentleness of Queen *Elizabeth*'s Government, and the numbers of those that adhered to the Church of *Rome,* made it scarcely possible to put an end to that party during her Reign; which has been ever since restless, and has had Credit enough at Court during the three last Reigns, not only to support it self, but to distract us, and divert us from apprehending the danger of being swallowed up by them, by fomenting our own Differences, and by setting on either a Toleration or a Persecution, as it has happened to serve their Interests. It is not so very long since, that nothing was to be heard at Court but the supporting of the Church of *England,* and the Extirpating all the Nonconformists: and it were easy to name the Persons, if it were decent, that had this in their mouths; but now all is turned round again, the Church of *England* is in Disgrace; and now the Encouragement of Trade, the Quiet of the Nation and Freedom of Conscience are again in vogue, that were such odious things but few Years ago, that the very mentioning of them was enough to load any Man with suspicions as backward in the King's Service; while such Methods are used, and the Government is in an Ague, divided between hot and cold fits, no wonder if the Laws so unsteadily executed have failed of their effect.

V. There is no good reserve here left for Severity, when the proper Opportunity to set it on presents it self: for his Majesty declares himself only against the forcing of Men in matters of meer Religion, so that whensoever Religion and Policy come to be so interwoven, that meer Religion is not the Case, and that publick Safety may be pretended, then this Declaration is to be no more claimed: So that the fastning any thing upon the Protestant Religion, that is inconsistent with the publick Peace, will be pretended, to shew that they are not persecuted for meer Religion. In *France,* when it was resolved to extirpate the Protestants, all the Discourses that were written on that Subject were full of the Wars occasioned by those of Religion in the last Age, tho' as these were the happy occasions of bringing the House of *Bourbon* to the Crown, they had been ended above 80 Years ago, and there had not been so much as the least Tumult raised by them these 50 Years past: So that the *French* who have smarted under this Severity, could not be charged with the least Infraction of the Law; yet Stories of a hundred years old were raised up to inspire into the King those Apprehensions of them, which have produced the terrible effects that are visible to all the World. There is another Expression in this Declaration, which lets us likewise see with what Caution the offers of favour are now worded, that so there may be an Occasion given, when the Time and Conjuncture shall be favourable, to break through them all. It is in these Words; " So that they take special Care that nothing be preached or " taught amongst them, which may any ways tend to alienate the Hearts of the People " from Us or Our Government." This in it self is very reasonable; and could admit of no Exception, if we had not to do with a Set of Men, who to our great misfortune have so much Credit with his Majesty, and who will be no sooner lodged in the Power to which they pretend, than they will make every thing that is preached against Popery pass for that which may in some manner alienate the Subjects from the King.

VI.

VI. His Majesty makes no doubt of the Concurrence of his two Houses of Parliament, when he shall think it convenient for them to meet. The Hearts of Kings are unsearchable, so that it is a little too presumptuous to look into his Majesty's secret Thoughts: but according to the Judgments that we would make of other Men's Thoughts by their Actions, one would be tempted to think, that his Majesty made some doubt of it, since his Affairs both at home and abroad could not go the worse, if it appeared that there was a perfect understanding between him and his Parliament, and that his People were supporting him with fresh Supplies; and this House of Commons is so much at his devotion, that all the World saw how ready they were to grant every thing that he could desire of them, till he began to lay off the Mask with relation to the Test; and since that time the frequent Prerogations, the closetting, and the pains that has been taken to gain Members by Promises made to some, and the Disgraces of others, would make one a little inclined to think, that some doubt was made of their Concurrence. But we must confess, that the depth of his Majesty's Judgment is such, that we cannot fathom it, and therefore we cannot guess what his Doubts or his Assurances are. It is true, the words that come after unriddle the Mystery a little, which are, when his Majesty shall think it convenient for them to meet: for the meaning of this seems plain, that his Majesty is resolved that they shall never meet, till he receives such Assurances, in a new round of Closetting, that he shall be put out of doubt concerning it.

VII. I will not enter into the Dispute concerning Liberty of Conscience, and the Reasons that may be offered for it to a Session of Parliament; for there is scarce any one point, that either with relation to Religion, or Politicks, affords a greater variety of matter for Reflection: and I make no doubt to say, that there is abundance of Reason to oblige Parliaments to review all the Penal Laws, either with relation to Papists or to Dissenters: but I will take the boldness to add one thing, that the King's Suspending of Laws strikes at the Root of this whole Government, and subverts it quite: for if there is any thing certain with relation to *English* Government, it is this, that the executive Power of the Law is entirely in the King; and the Law, to fortify him in the Management of it, has cloathed him with a vast Prerogative, and made it unlawful on any pretence whatsoever to resist him: whereas on the other hand, the *Legislative Power* is not so entirely in the King, but that the Lords and Commons have such a share in it, that no Law can either be made, repealed, or, which is all one, suspended, but by their consent; so that the placing this *Legislative Power* singly in the King, is a subversion of the whole Government, since the Essence of all Governments consists in the Subjects of the Legislative Authority. Acts of Violence or Injustice, committed in the Executive Part, are such things that all Princes being subject to them, the peace of mankind were very ill secured, if it were not unlawful to resist upon any pretence taken from any ill Administrations, in which as the Laws may be doubtful, so the Facts may be uncertain, and at worst the publick Peace must always be more valued than any private Oppressions or Injuries whatsoever. But the total Subversion of a Government, being so contrary to the Trust that is given to the Prince who ought to execute it, will put Men upon uneasy and dangerous Inquiries: which will turn little to the advantage of those that are driving matters to such a doubtful and desperate Issue.

VIII. If there is any thing in which the Exercise of the *Legislative Power* seems indispensable, it is in those Oaths of Allegiance and Tests, that are thought necessary to qualify Men either to be admitted to enjoy the protection of the Law, or to bear a share in the Government; for in these the security of the Government is chiefly concerned: and therefore the total Extinction of these, as it is not only a Suspension of them, but a plain repealing of them, so it is a subverting of the whole Foundation of our Government: for the Regulation that King and Parliament had set both for the Subjects having the protection of the State by the Oath of Allegiance, and for a share in the places of trust by the Tests, is now pluckt up by the roots; when it is declared, That these shall not at any time hereafter be required to be taken or subscribed by any Persons whatsoever: for it is plain, that this is no Suspension of the Law, but a formal Repeal of it, in as plain words as can be conceived.

IX. His Majesty says, that the Benefit of the Service of all his Subjects is by the Law of Nature inseparably annexed to and inherent in his sacred Person. It is somewhat strange, that when so many Laws, that we all know are suspended, the Law of Nature, which is so hard to be found out, should be cited; but the Penners of this Declaration had best let that Law lie forgotten among the rest; and there is a scurvy Paragraph in it concerning Self-Preservation, that is capable of very unacceptable

Glosses.

Glosses. It is hard to tell what Section of the Law of Nature has markt either such a Form of Government, or such a Family for it. And if his Majesty renounces his Pretensions to our Allegiance as founded on the Laws of *England*; and betakes himself to this Law of Nature, he will perhaps find the Counsel was a little too rash: but to make the most that can be, the Law of Nations or Nature does indeed allow the Governour of all Societies a Power to serve themselves of every Member of it in the cases of Extream Danger; but no Law of Nature that has been yet heard of will conclude, that if by special Laws, a sort of Men have been disabled from all Employments, that a Prince who at his Coronation swore to maintain those Laws, may at his pleasure extinguish all these Disabilities.

X. At the end of the Declaration, as in a Postscript, his Majesty assures his Subjects, that he will maintain them in their Properties, as well in Church and Abby-Lands, as other Lands: but the chief of all their Properties being the share that they have by their Representatives in the *Legislative Power*; this Declaration, which breaks through that, is no great Evidence that the rest will be maintained: and to speak plainly, when a Coronation-Oath is so little remembered, other Promises must have a proportioned degree of Credit given to them. As for the Abby-Lands, the keeping them from the Church is according to the Principles of that Religion, Sacrilege; and that is a mortal Sin, and therefore can no *Absolution* be given to any who continue in it: and so this Promise being an obligation to maintain Men in a mortal Sin, is null and void of it self: *Church-Lands* are also according to the Doctrine of their Canonists, so immediately God's Right, that the Pope himself is the only Administrator and Dispenser, but is not the Master of them; he can indeed make a truck for God, or lett them so low, that God shall be an easy Landlord: but he cannot alter God's Property, nor translate the Right that is in him to Sacrilegious Laymen and Hereticks.

XI. One of the Effects of this Declaration, will be the setting on foot a new run of Addresses over the Nation: for there is nothing, how impudent and base soever, of which the abject flattery of a slavish Spirit is not capable. It must be confest, to the Reproach of the Age, that all those strains of flattery among the *Romans*, that *Tacitus* sets forth with so much just scorn, are modest things, compared to what this Nation has produced within these seven Years: only if our Flattery has come short of the Refinedness of the *Romans*, it has exceeded theirs as much in its loathsome Fulsomeness. The late King set out a Declaration, in which he gave the most solemn Assurances possible of his adhering to the Church of *England*, and to the Religion established by Law, and of his Resolution to have frequent Parliaments; upon which the whole Nation fell as it were into raptures of Joy and Flattery: but though he lived four Years after that, he called no Parliament, notwithstanding the Law for Triennial Parliaments: and the manner of his Death, and the Papers printed after his Death in his Name, having sufficiently shewed that he was equally sincere in both those Assurances that he gave, as well in that relating to Religion, as in the other relating to frequent Parliaments, yet upon his Death a new Set of Addresses appeared, in which all that Flattery could invent was brought forth in the Commendations of a Prince, to whose Memory the greatest kindness can be done, is to forget him; and because his present Majesty upon his coming to the Throne, gave some very general Promises of maintaining the Church of *England*, this was magnified in so extravagant a strain, as if it had been a security greater than any that the Law could give: tho' by the regard that the King has both to it and to the Laws, it appears that he is resolved to maintain both equally. Since then the Nation has made it self sufficiently ridiculously both to the present and to all succeeding Ages; it is time, that at last Men should grow weary, and become ashamed of their Folly.

XII. The *Non-conformists* are now invited to set an Example to the rest: and they who have valued themselves hitherto upon their Opposition to Popery, and that have quarrelled with the Church of *England*, for some small Approaches to it, in a few Ceremonies, are now solicited to rejoice, because the Laws, that secure us against it, are all pluckt up: since they enjoy at present, and during pleasure, leave to meet together. It is natural for all Men to love to be set at ease, especially in the matter of their Consciences; but it is visible, that those who allow them this favour, do it with no other design, but that under pretence of a General Toleration, they may introduce a Religion which must persecute all equally: It is likewise apparent how much they are hated, and how much they have been persecuted by the Instigation of those who now court them, and who have now no game that is more promising, than the engaging them and the Church of *England* into new Quarrels: and as for the Promises now made to them, it cannot be supposed that they will be more lasting
ing

ing than those that were made some time ago to the Church of *England*, who had both a better Title in Law, and greater Merit upon the Crown, to assure them that they should be well used, than these can pretend to. The Nation has scarcely forgiven some of the Church of *England*, the Persecution into which they have suffered themselves to be cosened; though now they see Popery barefaced, the Stand that they have made, the vigorous Opposition that they have given to it, is that which makes all Men willing to forget what is past, and raises again the Glory of a Church that was not a little stained by the Indiscretion and Weakness of those that were too apt to believe and hope, and so suffer themselves to be made a Property to those who would make them a Sacrifice. The Sufferings that the *Nonconformists*, and the Fury that the Popish Party expressed against them, had recommended them so much to the Compassion of the Nation, and had given them so just a pretension to favour in a better time, that it will look like a Curse of God upon them, if a few men, whom the Court has gained to betray them, can have such an ill Influence upon them, as to make them throw away all that Merit, and those Compassions which their Sufferings have procured them; and to go and court those who are only seemingly kind to them, that they may destroy both them and us. They must remember that as the Church of *England* is the only Establishment that our Religion has by Law; so it is the main Body of the Nation, and all the Sects are but small and straggling parties: and if the legal Settlement of the Church is dissolved, and that body is once broken, these lesser bodies will be all at mercy: and it is an easy thing to define what the Mercies of those of *Rome* are.

XIII. But tho' it must be confessed, that the *Nonconformists* are still under some Temptations, to receive every thing that gives them present ease, with a little too much kindness; since they lie exposed to many severe Laws, for which they have of late felt the weight very heavily, and as they are Men, and some of them as ill-natured Men as other People, so it is no wonder if upon the first surprises of the Declaration, they are a little delighted to see the Church of *England*, after all its Services and Submissions to the Court, so much mortify'd by it; so that taking all together, it will not be strange if they commit some Follies upon this occasion. Yet on the other hand it passes all Imagination to see some of the Church of *England*, especially those whose Natures we know are so particularly sharpened in the point of Persecution, chiefly when it is levell'd against the Dissenters, rejoice at this Declaration, and make Addresses upon it. It is hard to think that they have attained to so high a pitch of Christian Charity, as to thank those who do now *despitefully use them*, and that as an earnest that within a little while they will *persecute* them. This will be an Original, and a Master-piece in Flattery, which must needs draw the last Degrees of Contempt on such as are capable of so abject and sordid a Compliance, and that not only from all the true Members of the Church of *England*, but likewise from those of the Church of *Rome* it self; for every Man is apt to esteem an Enemy that is brave even in his Misfortunes, as much as he despises those whose Minds sink with their Condition. For what is it that these Men would address the King? Is it because he breaks those Laws that are made in their favour, and for their Protection: and is now striking at the Root of all legal Settlement that they have for their Religion? Or is it because that at the same time that the King professes a Religion that condemns his Supremacy, yet he is not contented with the Exercise of it as it is warranted by Law, but carries it so far as to erect a Court contrary to the express words of a Law so lately made: That Court takes care to maintain a due proportion between their Constitution and all their Proceedings, that so all may be of a piece, and all equally contrary to Law. They have suspended one Bishop, only because he would not do that which was not in his power to do: for since there is no Extrajudiciary Authority in *England*, a Bishop can no more proceed to the Sentence of Suspension against a Clergyman without a Trial, and the hearing of Parties, than a Judge can give Sentence in his Chamber without an Indictment, a Trial, or a Jury; and because one of the greatest Bodies of *England* would not break their Oaths, and obey a *Mandate* that plainly contradicted them, we see to what a pitch this is like to be carried. I will not anticipate upon this illegal Court, to tell what Judgments are coming; but without carrying our Jealousies too far, one may safely conclude, that they will never depart so far from their first Institution, as to have any regard either to our Religion, or our Laws, or Liberties, in any thing they do. If all this were acted by avowed Papists, as we are sure it is projected by such, there were nothing extraordinary in it: but that which carries our Indignation a little too far to be easily governed, is to see some pretended Protestants, and a few Bishops, among those that are the fatal Instruments of

pulling

pulling down the Church of *England*, and that those Mercenaries sacrifice their Religion and their Church to their ambition and interests; this has such peculiar Characters of misfortune upon it, that it seems it is not enough if we perish without pity, since we fall by that hand that we have so much supported and fortified, but we must become the Scorn of all the World, since we have produced such an unnatural Brood, that even while they are pretending to be the Sons of the Church of *England*, are cutting their Mother's throat: And not content with *Judas's* Crime, of saying, *Hail Master*, and *kissing* him, while they are betraying him into the hands of others; these carry their Wickedness further, and say, *Hail Mother*, and then they themselves murder her. If after all this we are called to bear this as Christians, and to suffer it as Subjects, if we were required in patience to possess our own Souls, and to be in Charity with our Enemies; and, which is more, to forgive our false Brethren who add treachery to their hatred; the Exhortation were seasonable, and indeed a little necessary: for Human Nature cannot easily take down things of such a hard digestion. But to tell us that we must make Addresses, and offer Thanks for all this, is to insult a little too much upon us in our Sufferings: and he that can believe that a dry and cautiously worded Promise of maintaining the Church of *England*, will be religiously observed, after all that we have seen, and is upon that carried so far out of his Wits, as to Address and give Thanks, and will believe still, such a Man has nothing to excuse him from believing Transubstantiation it self; for it is plain, that he can bring himself to believe even when the thing is contrary to the clearest Evidence that his Senses can give him.

Si populus hic vult decipi, decipiatur.

POSTSCRIPT.

THese Reflections were writ soon after the Declaration came to my hands; but the Matter of them was so tender, and the Conveyance of them to the Press was so uneasy, that they appear now too late to have one Effect that was designed by them, which was the diverting Men from making Addresses upon it; yet if what is here proposed makes Men become so far wise as to be ashamed of what they have done, and is a Means to keep them from their Courtship further than good Words, this Paper will not come too late.

A
LETTER
TO A
DISSENTER,

Upon occasion of His MAJESTY's late Gracious DECLARATION of *INDULGENCE*.

SIR,

SInce Addresses are in fashion, give me leave to make one to you. This is neither the Effect of Fear, Interest, or Resentment; therefore you may be sure it is sincere: and for that reason it may expect to be kindly received. Whether it will have Power enough to convince, dependeth upon the Reasons, of which you are to judge; and upon your preparation of Mind, to be perswaded by truth, whenever it appeareth to you. It ought to be the less welcome, for coming from a friendly hand, one whose kindness to you is not lessened by difference of Opinion, and who will not let his Thoughts for the Publick be so tyed or confined to this or that Subdivision of Protestants, as to stifle the Charity, which, besides all other Arguments, is at this time become necessary to preserve us.

I

I am neither surprised nor provoked, to see that in the Condition you were put into by the Laws, and the ill Circumstances you lay under, by having the Exclusion and Rebellion laid to your charge, you are desirous to make your selves less uneasy and obnoxious to Authority. Men who are sore, run to the nearest Remedy with too much haste, to consider all the Consequences: Grains of allowance are to be given, where Nature giveth such strong Influences. When to Men under Sufferings it offereth Ease, the present Pain will hardly allow time to examine the Remedies; and the strongest Reasons can hardly gain a fair Audience from our Mind, whilst so possessed, till the smart is a little allayed.

I do not know whether the Warmth that naturally belongeth to new Friendships, may not make it a harder Task for me to persuade you. It is like telling Lovers in the beginning of their Joys, that they will in a little time have an end. Such an unwelcome Style doth not easily find Credit: but I will suppose you are not so far gone in your new Passion, but that you will hear still; and therefore I am under the less Discouragement, when I offer to your Consideration two things. The *first* is, the Cause you have to suspect your new Friends. The *second*, the Duty incumbent upon you, in Christianity and Prudence, not to hazard the publick Safety, neither by desire of Ease nor of Revenge.

To the *First*, Consider that notwithstanding the smooth Language which is now put on to engage you, these new Friends did not make you their Choice, but their Refuge: They have ever made their first Courtships to the Church of *England*, and when they were rejected there, they made their Application to you in the second place. The Instances of this, might be given in all times. I do not repeat them, because whatsoever is unnecessary, must be tedious; the Truth of this Assertion being so plain, as not to admit a Dispute. You cannot therefore reasonably flatter your selves, that there is any Inclination to you. They never pretended to allow you any Quarter, but to usher in Liberty for themselves under that Shelter. I refer you to Mr. *Coleman's Letters,* and to the *Journals* of *Parliament,* where you may be convinced, if you can be so mistaken, as to doubt; nay, at this very Hour, they can hardly forbear, in the height of their Courtship, to let fall hard Words of you. So little is Nature to be restrained; it will start out sometimes, disdaining to submit to the Usurpation of Art and Interest.

This Alliance, between *Liberty* and *Infallibility,* is bringing together the two most contrary Things that are in the World. The Church of *Rome* doth not only dislike the allowing Liberty, but by its Principles it cannot do it. Wine is not more expresly forbidden to the *Mahometans,* than giving Hereticks Liberty is to *Papists:* They are no more able to make good their Vows to you, than a Man married before, and his Wife alive, can confirm his Contract with another. The continuance of their Kindness would be a Habit of Sin, of which they are to repent; and their Absolution is to be had upon no other Terms, than their Promises to destroy you. You are therefore to be hugg'd now, only that you may be the better squeez'd at another time. There must be something extraordinary, when the Church of *Rome* setteth up Bills, and offereth Plaisters for tender Consciences: By all that hath hitherto appeared, her Skill in Chirurgery lieth chiefly in a quick Hand, to cut off Limbs; but she is the worst at Healing, of any that ever pretended to it.

To come so quick from another Extream, is such an unnatural Motion, that you ought to be upon your Guard; the other Day you were *Sons of Belial,* now, you are *Angels of Light.* This is a violent Change, and it will be fit for you to pause upon it, before you believe it: If your Features are not altered, neither is their Opinion of you, whatever may be pretended. Do you believe less than you did, that there is Idolatry in the Church of *Rome?* sure you do not. See then, how they treat both in Words and Writing, those who entertain that Opinion. Conclude from hence, how inconsistent their Favour is with this single Article, except they give you a Dispensation for this too, and by a *Non-Obstante,* secure you that they will not think the worse of you.

Think a little how dangerous it is to build upon a Foundation of Paradoxes. Popery now is the only Friend to Liberty, and the known Enemy to Persecution: The Men of *Taunton* and *Tiverton,* are above all other eminent for Loyalty. The *Quakers,* from being declared by the *Papists* not to be Christians, are now made Favourites, and taken into their particular Protection; they are on a sudden grown the most accomplished Men of the Kingdom, in good Breeding, and giving Thanks with the best Grace, in double-refined Language. So that I should not wonder, though a Man of that Perswasion, in spight of his Hat, should be Master of the Ceremonies. Not to say harsher Words, these are such very new things, that it is impossible not to suspend our Belief, till by a little more Experience we may be informed whether they are Realities or Apparitions: We have been under shameful Mistakes, if these Opinions are true; but for the present, we are apt to be incredulous; except we could be convinced, that the Priests Words, in this Case too, are able to make such a sudden, and effectual Change; and that their Power is not limited to the Sacrament, but that it extendeth to alter the Nature of all other things, as often as they are so disposed.

Let

Let me now speak of the Instruments of your Friendship, and then leave you to judge, whether they do not afford matter of Suspicion. No Sharpness is to be mingled where Healing only is intended; so nothing will be said to expose particular Men, how strong soever the Temptation may be, or how clear the Proofs to make it out. A word or two in general, for your better Caution, shall suffice: Suppose then, for argument's sake, that the Mediators of this new Alliance, should be such as have been formerly imployed in Treaties of the same kind, and there detected to have acted by Order, and to have been impowered to give Encouragements and Rewards: Would not this be an Argument to suspect them?

If they should plainly be under Engagements on the one side, their Arguments to the other, ought to be received accordingly; their fair Pretences are to be looked upon as part of their Commission, which may not improbably give them a Dispensation in the case of Truth, when it may be a prejudice upon the Service of those by whom they are imployed.

If there should be Men, who having formerly had Means and Authority to perswade by secular Arguments, have, in pursuance of that Power, sprinkled Money amongst the dissenting Ministers; and if those very Men should now have the same Authority, practice the same Methods, and disburse, where they cannot otherwise perswade: It seemeth to me to be rather an Evidence, than a Presumption of the Deceit.

If there should be Ministers among you, who, by having fallen under Temptation of this kind, are in some sort engaged to continue their Frailty, by the Awe they are in, lest it should be exposed; the Perswasions of these unfortunate Men must sure have the less Force, and their Arguments, though never so specious, are to be suspected, when they come from Men who have mortgaged themselves to severe Creditors, that expect a rigorous Observation of the Contract, let it be never so unwarrantable.

If these, or any others, should at this time preach up Anger and Vengeance against the Church of *England*; may it not without Injustice be suspected, that a thing so plainly out of season, springeth rather from Corruption than Mistake; and that those who act this cholerick part, do not believe themselves, but only pursue higher Directions, endeavour to make good that part of their Contract which obligeth them, upon a Forfeiture, to make use of their inflaming Eloquence? They might apprehend their Wages would be retrenched, if they should be moderate: And therefore whilst Violence is their Interest, those who have not the same Arguments, have no reason to follow such a partial Example.

If there should be Men, who by the Load of their Crimes against the Government, have been bowed down to comply with it against their Conscience; who by incurring the want of a Pardon, have drawn upon themselves the necessity of an intire Resignation: such Men are to be lamented, but not to be believed. Nay, they themselves, when they have discharged their unwelcome Task, will be inwardly glad that their forced Endeavours do not succeed, and are pleased when Men resist their Insinuations; which are far from being voluntary or sincere, but are squeezed out of them by the weight of their being so obnoxious.

If in the height of this great Dearness, by comparing things, it should happen, that at this Instant, there is much a surer Friendship with those who are so far from allowing Liberty, that they allow no Living to a Protestant under them: Let the Scene lie in what part of the World it will, the Argument will come home, and sure it will afford sufficient Ground to suspect. Apparent Contradictions must strike us; neither Nature nor Reason can digest them: Self-flattery, and the desire to deceive our selves, to gratify a present Appetite, with all their Power, which is great, cannot get the better of such broad Conviction, as some things carry along with them. Will you call these vain and empty Suspicions? Have you been at all times so void of Fears and Jealousies, as to justify your being so unreasonably Valiant in having none upon this Occasion? Such an extraordinary Courage at this unseasonable time, to say no more, is too dangerous a Virtue to be commended.

If then, for these and a thousand other Reasons, there is cause to suspect, sure your new Friends are not to dictate to you, or advise you; for instance, the Addresses that fly abroad every Week, and murther us with *another to the same*; the first Draughts are made by those who are not very proper to be Secretaries to the Protestant Religion; and it is your Part only to write them out fairer again. Strange! that you who have been formerly so much against *set Forms*, should now be content the Priests should indite for you. The Nature of Thanks is an unavoidable Consequence of being pleased or obliged; they grow in the Heart, and from thence shew themselves either in Looks, Speeches, Writing, or Action: No Man was ever thankful, because he was bid to be so, but because he had, or thought he had some Reason for it. If then there is cause in this Case to pay such extravagant Acknowledgments, they will flow naturally, without taking such pains to procure them, and it is unkindly done to tire all the Post-Horses with carrying circular Letters to sollicit that which would be done without any trouble or constraint. If it is really in it self such a Favour, what needeth so much pressing Men to be thankful, and with such eager Circumstances, that where Perswasions cannot delude, Threatnings are employed to fright them into Compliance? Thanks must be voluntary, not only unconstrained, but unsolicited, else

they

they are either Trifles or Snares, they either fignify nothing, or a great deal more than is intended by thofe that give them. If an inference fhould be made, that whofoever thanketh the King for his Declaration, is by that engaged to juftify it in point of Law; it is a greater ftride than, I prefume, all thofe care to make who are perfwaded to addrefs. If it fhall be fuppofed, that all the Thankers will be Repealers of the *TEST*, when ever a *Parliament* fhall meet: Such an Expectation is better prevented before, than difappointed afterwards; and the fureft way to avoid the lying under fuch a fcandal, is not to do any thing that may give a colour to the Miftake. Thefe befpoken Thanks are little lefs improper than Love-Letters that were folicited by the Lady to whom they are to be directed: So, that befides the ground there is to give them, the manner of getting them, doth extremely leffen their Value. It might be wifhed that you would have fuppreffed your impatience, and have been content for the fake of Religion, to enjoy it within your felves, without the Liberty of a publick Exercife, till a Parliament had allowed it: but fince that could not be, and that the Artificers of fome amongft you have made ufe of the well-meant Zeal of the Generality to draw them into this miftake; I am fo far from blaming you with that fharpnefs which, perhaps, the Matter in ftrictnefs would bear, that I am ready to err on the fide of the more gentle Conftruction.

There is a great difference between enjoying quietly the advantages of an Act irregularly done by others, and the going about to fupport it againft the Laws in being: The Law is fo facred, that no Trefpafs againft it is to be defended; yet Frailties may in fome meafure be excufed, when they cannot be juftified. The defire of enjoying a Liberty from which men have been fo long reftrained, may be a Temptation that their Reafon is not at all times able to refift. If in fuch a cafe, fome Objections are leapt over, indifferent men will be more inclined to lament the Occafion, than to fall too hard upon the Fault, whilft it is covered with the Apology of a good intention; but where to refcue your felves from the feverity of one Law, you give a blow to all the Laws, by which your Religion and Liberty are to be protected; and inftead of filently receiving the benefit of this Indulgence, you fet up for Advocates to fupport it; you become voluntary Aggreffors, and look like Counfel retained by the Prerogative againft your old Friend *Magna Charta*, who hath done nothing to deferve her falling thus under your Difpleafure.

If the cafe then fhould be, that the Price expected from you for this Liberty, is giving up your Right in the Laws, fure you will think twice, before you go any further in fuch a lofing Bargain. After giving Thanks for the breach of one Law, you lofe the right of complaining of the breach of all the reft; you will not very well know how to defend your felves, when you are preffed; and having given up the Queftion, when it was for your advantage, you cannot recall it, when it fhall be to your prejudice. If you will fet up at one time a Power to help you, which at another time by Parity of Reafon fhall be made ufe of to deftroy you, you will neither be pitied, nor relieved againft a Mifchief you draw upon your felves, by being fo unreafonably thankful. It is like calling in Auxiliaries to help, who are ftrong enough to fubdue you: In fuch a cafe your Complaints will come too late to be heard, and your Sufferings will raife Mirth inftead of Compaffion.

If you think, for your excufe, to expound your thanks fo as to reftrain them to this particular cafe, others, for their ends, will extend them further; and in thefe differing Interpretations, that which is back'd by Authority will be the moft likely to prevail; efpecially when by the advantage you have given them, they have in truth the better of the Argument, and that the Inferences from your own Conceffions are very ftrong and exprefs againft you. This is fo far from being a groundlefs Suppofition, that there was a late inftance of it, the laft Seffion of Parliament, in the Houfe of Lords, where the firft Thanks, though things of courfe, were interpreted to be the Approbation of the King's whole Speech, and a Reftraint from the further Examination of any part of it, though never fo much difliked; and it was with difficulty obtained, not to be excluded from the Liberty of objecting to this mighty Prerogative of Difpenfing, meerly by this innocent and ufual piece of good Manners, by which no fuch thing could poffibly be intended.

This fheweth, that fome bounds are to be put to your good Breeding, and that the Conftitution of *England* is too valuable a thing to be ventured upon a Complement. Now that you have for fome time enjoyed the benefit of the End, it is time for you to look into the Danger of the Means: The fame Reafon that made you defirous to get Liberty, muft make you folicitous to preferve it; fo that the next thought will naturally be, not to engage your felf beyond Retreat, and to agree fo far with the Principles of all Religions, as not to rely upon a Death-bed Repentance.

There are certain periods of Time, which being once paft, make all Cautions ineffectual, and all Remedies defperate. Our Underftandings are apt to be hurried on by the firft heats; which if not reftrained in time, do not give us leave to look back, till it is too late. Confider this in the Cafe of your Anger againft the Church of *England*, and take warning by their Miftake in the fame kind, when after the late King's Reftauration, they preferved

fo

so long the bitter taste of your rough usage to them in other times, that it made them forget their Interest, and sacrifice it to their Revenge.

Either you will blame this Proceeding in them, and for that reason not follow it, or if you allow it, you have no reason to be offended with them ; so that you must either dismiss your Anger, or lose your Excuse ; except you should argue more partially than will be supposed of Men of your Morality and Understanding.

If you had now to do with those rigid Prelates, who made it a Matter of Conscience to give you the least Indulgence ; but kept you at an uncharitable distance, and even to your more reasonable Scruples continued stiff and inexorable, the Argument might be fairer on your side : but since the common Danger hath so laid open that Mistake, that all the former Haughtiness towards you is for ever extinguish'd, and that it hath turned the Spirit of Persecution, into a Spirit of Peace, Charity and Condescension ; shall this happy Change only affect the Church of *England?* And are you so in love with Separation, as not to be moved by this Example? It ought to be followed, were there no other reason than that it is a Virtue ; but when besides that, it is become necessary to your preservation, it is impossible to fail the having its Effect upon you.

If it should be said, that the Church of *England* is never humble, but when she is out of Power, and therefore loseth the Right of being believed when she pretendeth to it ; the Answer is, *First*, it would be an uncharitable Objection, and very much miss-timed ? an unseasonable Triumph, not only ungenerous, but unsafe : So that in these respects it cannot be urged without scandal, even though it could be said with Truth. *Secondly*, This is not so in Fact, and the Argument must fall, being built upon a false Foundation ; for whatsoever may be told you, at this very hour, and in the heat and glare of your present sun-shine, the *Church* of *England* can in a moment bring Clouds again ; and turn the royal Thunder upon your Heads, blow you off the Stage with a Breath, if she would give but a Smile or a kind Word ; the least Glimpse of her Compliance, would throw you back into the state of Suffering, and draw upon you all the arrears of Severity, which have accrued during the time of this kindness to you; and yet the *Church* of *England*, with all her Faults, will not allow her self to be rescued by such unjustifiable means, but chuseth to bear the weight of Power, rather than lie under the burthen of being Criminal.

It cannot be said, that she is unprovoked ; Books and Letters come out every day, to call for Answers, yet she will not be stirred. From the supposed Authors and the Stile one would swear they were Undertakers, and had made a Contract to fall out with the *Church* of *England*. There are Lashes in every Address, challenges to draw the Pen in every Pamphlet; in short, the fairest occasions in the World given to quarrel; but she wisely distinguisheth between the Body of Dissenters, whom she will suppose to act, as they do, with no ill intent ; and these small Skirmishers pickt and sent out to picqueer, and to begin a Fray amongst the Protestants, for the entertainment, as well as the advantage of the *Church* of *Rome*.

This Conduct is so good, that it will be scandalous not to applaud it. It is not equal dealing, to blame our Adversaries for doing ill, and not commend them when they do well.

To hate them because they persecuted, and not to be reconciled to them when they are ready to suffer, rather than receive all the Advantages that can be gained by a criminal Compliance, is a principle no sort of Christians can own, since it would give an Objection to them never to be answered.

Think a little, who they were that promoted your former Persecutions, and then consider how it will look to be angry with the Instruments, and at the same time to make a League with the Authors of your Sufferings.

Have you enough considered what will be expected from you ? Are you ready to stand in every Borough by virtue of a *Conge d'Eslire*, and instead of Election, be satisfied if you are return'd ?

Will you in *Parliament*, justify the Dispensing Power, with all its consequences, and repeal the *Test*, by which you will make way for the repeal of all the Laws, that were made to preserve your Religion, and to enact others that shall destroy it ?

Are you disposed to change the Liberty of Debate, into the Merit of Obedience, and to be made Instruments to repeal or enact Laws, when the *Roman Consistory* are *Lords of the Articles?*

Are you so linked with your new Friends, as to reject any Indulgence a *Parliament* shall offer you, if it shall not be so Comprehensive as to include the *Papists* in it ?

Consider that the implied Conditions of your new Treaty are no less, than that you are to do every thing you are desired, without examining, and that for this pretended Liberty of Conscience, your real Freedom is to be sacrificed : Your former Faults hang like Chains still about you, you are let loose only upon Bayl ; the first Act of Non-compliance, sendeth you to jail again.

You may see that the Papists themselves do not rely upon the Legality of this Power, which you are o justify, since they being so very earnest to get it establish'd by a Law, and
the

the doing such very hard things in order, as they think, to obtain it, is a clear Evidence, that they do not think, that the single Power of the Crown is in this Case a good Foundation; especially when this is done under a Prince, so very tender of all the Rights of Sovereignty, that he would think it a diminution to his Prerogative, where he conceiveth it strong enough to go alone, to call in the Legislative Help to strengthen and support it.

You have formerly blamed the *Church of England*, and not without reason, for going so far as they did in their Compliance; and yet as soon as they stopped, you see they are not only deserted, but prosecuted: Conclude then from this Example, that you must either break off your Friendship, or resolve to have no Bounds in it. If they do not succeed in their Design, they will leave you first; if they do, you must either leave them, when it will be too late for your Safety, or else after the Squeeziness of starting at a Surplice, you must be forced to swallow Transubstantiation.

Remember that the other day those of the Church of *England* were *Trimmers* for enduring you, and now by a sudden Turn, you are become the Favourites; do not deceive your selves, it is not the nature of lasting Plants thus to shoot up in a Night; you may look gay and green for a little time, but you want a Root to give you a continuance. It is not so long since, as to be forgotten, that the *Maxim* was, *It is impossible for a Dissenter, not to be a REBEL.* Consider at this time in *France*, even the new Converts are so far from being imployed, that they are disarmed: Their sudden Change maketh them still to be distrusted, notwithstanding that they are reconciled: What are you to expect then from your dear Friends, to whom, whenever they shall think fit to throw you off again, you have in other times given such Arguments for their excuse?

Besides all this, you act very unskilfully against your visible Interest, if you throw away the Advantages, of which you can hardly fail in the next probable Revolution. Things tend naturally to what you would have, if you would let them alone, and not by an unseasonable Activity lose the Influences of your good Star, which promiseth you every thing that is prosperous.

The *Church* of *England*, convinced of its Error in being severe to you; the *Parliament*, whenever it meeteth, sure to be gentle to you; the next Heir bred in the Country which you have so often quoted for a Pattern of Indulgence; a general Agreement of all thinking Men, that we must no more cut our selves off from the Protestants abroad, but rather inlarge the Foundations upon which we are to build our Defences against the common Enemy; so that in truth, all things seem to conspire to give you ease and satisfaction, if by too much haste to anticipate your good Fortune, you do not destroy it.

The Protestants have but one Article of human Strength, to oppose the Power which is now against them; and that is, not to lose the advantage of their Numbers, by being so unwary as to let themselves be divided.

We all agree as in our Duty to our Prince, our Objections to his Belief do not hinder us from seeing his Virtues; and our complying with his Religion, hath no effect upon our Allegiance; we are not to be laughed out of our Passive Obedience, and the Doctrine of Non-Resistance, tho' even those who perhaps owe the best part of their Security to that Principle, are apt to make a Jest of it.

So that if we give no advantage by the fatal Mistake of misapplying our Anger, by the natural course of things, this Danger will pass away like a shower of Hail; fair weather will succeed, as lowring as the Sky now looketh, and all by this plain and easy Receipt. Let us be still, quiet and undivided, firm at the same time to our Religion, our Loyalty, and our Laws, and so long as we continue this method, it is next to impossible, that the odds of two hundred to one should lose the Bett, except the Church of *Rome*, which hath been so long barren of Miracles, should now in her declining Age, be brought a-bed of one that would out-do the best she can brag of in her *Legend*.

To conclude, the short Question will be, whether you will join with those who must in the end run the same fate with you. If Protestants of all sorts, in their Behaviour to one another, have been to blame, they are upon the more equal terms, and for that very reason it is fitter for them now to be reconciled. Our Dis-union is not only a Reproach, but a Danger to us; those who believe in modern Miracles, have more right, or at least more excuse, to neglect all secular Cautions: but for us, it is as justifiable to have no Religion, as wilfully to throw away the human Means of preserving it. I am,

Dear SIR,

Your most Affectionate
Humble Servant,

T. W.

H h h h

The ANATOMY of an EQUIVALENT.

I. THE World hath of late years never been without some extraordinary *Word* to furnish the Coffee-houses, and fill the Pamphlets. Sometimes it is a *new* one invented, and sometimes an *old* one revived. They are usually fitted to some present purpose, with Intentions as differing as the various Designs several *Parties* may have, either to delude the People, or to expose their Adversaries: They are not of long continuance, but after they have passed a little while; and that they are grown nauseous by being so often repeated, they give place to something that is newer. Thus, after *Whig*, *Tory*, and *Trimmer*, have had their Time, now they are dead and forgotten, being supplanted by the word *Equivalent*, which reigneth in their stead.

The Birth of it is in short this: After many repeated Essays to dispose Men to the repeal of Oaths and Tests, made for the security of the *Protestant Religion*, the general aversion to comply in it was found to be so great, that it was thought advisable to try another manner of attempting it, and to see whether by putting the *same thing* into *another Mould*, and softning an *harsh Proposition* by a *plausible Term*, they might not have better success.

To this end, instead of an *absolute quitting* of these Laws, without any Condition, which was the *first* Proposal; now it is put into gentler Language, and runneth thus; *If you will take away the* Oath *and* Tests, *you shall have as good a thing for them.* This, put into the fashionable Word, is now called an *Equivalent*.

II. So much to the Word it self. I will now endeavour in short to examine and explain, in order to the having it fully understood,

First, What *is* the nature of a true *Equivalent*; and

In the next place, what things *are not* to be admired under that denomination.

I shall treat these as general Propositions; and tho' I cannot undertake how far they may be *convincing*, I may safely do it, that they are *Impartial*; of which there can be no greater evidence than that I make neither Inference, nor Application, but leave that part intirely to the Reader, according as his own Thoughts shall direct and dispose him.

III. I will first take notice, that this Word, by the Application which hath been made of it in some modern instances, lieth under some *Disadvantage*, not to say some *Scandal*. It is transmitted hither from *France*; and if, as in most other things that we take from them, we carry them beyond the Pattern, it should prove so in this, we should get into a more *partial* Stile than the Principles of *English* Justice will I hope ever allow us to be guilty of.

The *French* King's *Equivalents* in *Flanders* are very *extraordinary Bargains*; his manner of proposing and obtaining them, is very differing from the usual methods of *equal* dealing. In a later Instance, *Denmark*, by the encouragement as well as by the example of *France*, hath propos'd things to the Duke of *Holstein*, which are called *Equivalents*; but that they are so, the World is not yet sufficiently convinc'd, and probably the Parties concern'd do not think them to be so, and consequently do not appear to be at all disposed to accept them. Princes enjoin and prescribe such things when they have *Strength* and *Power* to supply the want of *Arguments*; and according to practice in these Cases, the weaker are never thought to have an *ill Bargain*, if they have *any thing* left them. So that the first Qualification of an *Equivalent*, must be, that the Appraisers be *indifferent*, else it is only a *Sound*, there can be nothing *real* in it: For, where the same party that *proposeth* a Bargain, claimeth a Right to set the *Value*; or, which is worse, hath *power* too to make it good; the other may be forced to *submit* to the Conditions, but he can by no means ever be perswaded to *treat* upon them.

IV. The next thing to be considered is, that to make an *Equivalent* in reality an equal thing, in the Proposer, it must be a *better* thing than that which is required by him; *just as good* is subject to the hazard of not being *quite so good*: It is not easy to have such an even Hand, as to make the Value exactly equal; besides, according to the Maxim in Law, *Melior conditio possidentis*, the Offer is not fair, except the thing offered is better in value than the thing demanded. There must be Allowance for removing what is fixed, and there must be something that may be a Justification for *Changing*. The value of Things very often dependeth more upon other Circumstances, than upon what is meerly intrinsick to them; therefore the Calculation must be made upon that foot, perhaps in most Cases; and particularly the *Want* which one of the Parties may have of the Thing he requireth, maketh it more valuable to *him* than it is in *it self*. If the Party *proposing* doth not want the Thing he would have in Exchange; his requiring it is *impertinent*: If he doth, his want of it must go *into* the Appraisement; and by consequence every Proposer of an *Equivalent* must offer a *better* Thing, or else he must not take it unkindly to be refused, except the other Party hath an *equal Want* of the *same* Thing, which is very improbable, since naturally he that wanted most, will speak first.

V. Another

V. Another thing neceſſary to the making a fair Bargain is, that let the Parties who treat, be they ever ſo unequal in themſelves, yet as to the particular thing propoſed, there muſt be an *exact* Equality, as far as it relateth to the full Liberty of *taking* or *refuſing*, *concurring* or *objecting*, without any conſequence of Revenge, or ſo much as Diſſatisfaction; for it is impoſſible to *treat* where it is an affront to *differ:* in that Caſe there is no mean between the two Extreams, either an open Quarrel, or an intire Submiſſion; the *way* of *Bargaining* muſt be equal, elſe the Bargain *it ſelf* cannot be ſo : For example, the *Propoſer* is not only to uſe *equal* Terms as to the *Matter*, but *fair* ones in the *Manner* too. There muſt be no Intimations of *Anger* in caſe of *Refuſal*, much leſs any open *Threatning.* Such a Stile is ſo ill ſuited to the uſual way of Treating, that it looketh more like a Breach of the *Peace*, than the making a Bargain. It would be yet more improper, and leſs agreeing with the Nature of an *Equivalent*, if, whilſt two Men are a chaffering about the *Price*, one of them ſhould actually *take* the thing in queſtion at his *own rate*, and afterwards deſire to have his *Poſſeſſion* confirmed by a formal Agreement; ſuch a *Proceeding* would not only *deſtroy* that *particular Contract*, but make it impoſſible to have any *other*, with the *Party* that could be guilty of ſuch a *Practice.*

VI. *Violence* preceding, deſtroyeth all Contracts, and even though the Party that offereth it ſhould have a right to the thing he ſo taketh, yet it is to be obtained by *legal* Means, elſe it may be *forfeited* by his *Irregularity* in the purſuit of it : The *Law* is ſuch an Enemy to *Violence*, and ſo little to be reconciled to it, that in the caſe of a *Rape*, the Puniſhment is not taken off, tho' the Party injured afterward conſenteth. The Juſtice of the Law hath its Eye upon the firſt Act, and the Maxim of *Volenti non fit injuria*, doth not in this Caſe help the Offender; it being a Plea *ſubſequent* to the Crime, which maketh it to be rejected as a thing wrong dated, and out of time.

In taking away Goods or Money, it is the ſame thing. The Party robbed, by giving them afterwards to the Taker, does not exempt him from the Puniſhment of the *Violence* : Quite contrary, the Man from whom they were taken is puniſhable, if he doth not *proſecute.* If the Caſe ſhould be, that a Man thus taking away a thing without Price, claimeth a Right to take it; then whether it is well or ill founded is not the Queſtion; but ſure, the Party from whom it is ſo taken, whilſt he is treating to *ſell* or *exchange* it, can never make a Bargain with ſo *arbitrary* a Chapman, there being no room left after that to talk of the Value.

VII. To make an equal Bargain there muſt be a Liberty of *differing*, not only in every thing that is *really Eſſential*, but in every thing that is *thought ſo* by *either Party*, and moſt eſpecially by him who is in *Poſſeſſion* of the thing demanded : His *Opinion* muſt be a *Rule* to him, and even his *Miſtake* in the Value, though it may not convince the Man he hath to deal with, yet he will be juſtified for not accepting what is offered, till that *Miſtake* is fairly rectified and over-ruled.

When a *Security* is deſired to be *changed*, that Side which *deſireth* it muſt not pretend to *impoſe* upon the other, ſo as to dictate to them, and tell them without debate, that they are *ſafe* in what is propoſed, ſince of that the Council on the *other Side* muſt certainly be the moſt *competent Judges.* The *Hand* it cometh from is a great Circumſtance, either to invite or diſcourage in all Matters of Contract : the Qualifications of the *Party offering*, muſt ſuit with the *Propoſition* it ſelf, elſe let it ever be ſo fair, there is ground for *Suſpicion.*

VIII. What Men are of a Temper, that they think they have *wrong* done them, if they have not always the *better* ſide of a *Bargain :* If they happen to be ſuch, as by Experience have been found to have an *ill Memory* for their *Word :* If the Character they bear, doth not recommend their *Juſtice*, where-ever their *Intereſt* is concern'd : In theſe Caſes, thinking Men will avoid Dealing, not only to prevent *Surprize*, but to cut off the occaſions of *Difficulty* or *Diſpute.*

It is yet *more diſcouraging*, when there are, either a *precedent Practice*, or *ſtanding* Maxims *of groſs Partiality*, in aſſuming a Privilege of *Exemption* from the uſual Methods of *equal* Dealing.

To illuſtrate this by an Inſtance : Suppoſe that in any Caſe, the Church of *Rome* ſhould have an *Intereſt* to promote a Bargain; let her *way of Dealing* be a little examin'd, which will direct thoſe with whom ſhe treateth, how far they are to rely upon what *ſhe propoſeth* to them. We may begin with the Quality in the World, the leaſt conſiſting with equal Dealing, *viz.* An incurable *Partiality to herſelf*; which, that it may arrive to its full Perfection, is crowned with *Infallibility.* At the firſt ſetting out, ſhe maketh herſelf uncapable of dealing upon Terms of *Equality*, by the Power ſhe claimeth of *Binding* and *Looſing*, which hath been ſo often applied to *Treaties*, as well as to *Sins.*

If the Definition of *Juſtice* is to deal *equally*, ſhe cannot be guilty of it without *betraying* her *Prerogative*; and according to her Principles, ſhe giveth up the Superiority derived to her by *Apoſtolical Succeſſion*, if ſhe degradeth her ſelf ſo as to be judged by the Rules of *common Right*; eſpecially if the Bargain ſhould be with *Hereticks*, who in her Opinion have *forfeited* the Claim they might otherwiſe have had to it.

IX. Be-

4

IX. Befides, her Tafte hath been fo fpoiled by *unreasonable Bargains*, that fhe can never bring down her Palate to any thing that is *fair* or *equal*. She hath not only judg'd it an *Equivalent*, but a *great Bargain* for the other fide, to give them *Abfolutions* and *Indulgences* for the *real Payment* of great Sums, for which fhe hath drawn Bills to have them repayed with Intereft in *Purgatory*.

This *fpiritual Bank* hath carried on fuch a Trade upon thefe *advantageous Terms*, that it can never fubmit to the fmall Profits an *ordinary Bargain* would produce.

The feveral Popes have in exchange for the *Peter-Pence*, and all their other *Rents* and *Fines* out of *England*, fent *fanctified Rofes*, *Reliques*, and other fuch wonder-working Trifles. And by virtue of their Character of *holy Fathers*, have ufed Princes like *Children*, by fending them fuch *Rattles* to play with, which they have made them buy at extravagant Rates ; befides which, they were to be thankful too, into the bargain.

A Chip of the Crofs, a piece of St. *Laurence*'s Grid-iron, a Hair of St. *Peter*, have been thought *Equivalents* for much more *fubftantial* things. The Popes being Mafters of the Jewel-Houfe, have fet the *Rates* upon them, and they have paffed ; though the whole Shop would not take up the value of a Bodkin in *Lombard-Street* upon the credit of them.

They are *unconfcionable Purchafers*, for they get all the Money from the *Living*, by praying for them when they are *dead*. And it is obfervable, that the northern Part of *Chriftendom*, which beft underftandeth *Trade*, were the firft that *refufed* to make any more Bargains with them ; fo that it looketh as if the chief Quarrel to the *Hereticks* was not as they were *ill Chriftians*, but as they were *unkind Merchants* ; in fo difcourteoufly rejecting the Commodities of the Growth of *Rome*.

To conclude this Head, There is no bartering with *Infallibility*, it being fo much *above Equality*, that it cannot bear the Indignity of a *true Equivalent*.

X. In all Bargains, there is a Neceffity of looking back, and reflecting how far a *prefent Propofal* is reconcileable with a *former Practice*: For example, if at any time a thing is offered, quite *differing* from the *Arguments* ufed by the *Propofer*, and inconfiftent with the *Maxims* held out by him at other times: Or in a publick Cafe, if the *fame* Men who promote and prefs a thing with the *utmoft Violence*, do in a little time after with *as much Violence* prefs the *contrary*, and profefs a *Deteftation* of the *very thing*, for which they had before imployed *all* their *Intereft* and *Authority*: Or if in the Cafe of a Law *already* made, there fhould be a Privilege claimed to *exempt* thofe from the Obligation of obferving it, who yet fhould *afterwards defire* and *prefs* to have a *new Law* made in exchange for the *old* one, by which they would not be bound ; and that they fhould propofe a *Security* by a thing of the very fame *Nature* as that which they did *not* allow to be any *before*: Thefe *Incoherences* muft naturally have the Effect of raifing *Sufpicion*, or rather they are a *certain Proof*, that in fuch Circumftances it is *irrational* for Men to expect an *effectual Equivalent*.

XI. If whatfoever is more than *ordinary* is *fufpicious*, every thing that is unnatural is more fo : It is not only *unneceffary*, but *unnatural* too to *perfwade* with *Violence* what it is *Folly* to refufe ; to *pufh* Men with Eagernefs into a *good Bargain* for *themfelves*, is a Stile very much unfuitable to the *nature* of the thing. But it goeth further, and is yet more abfurd, to grow *angry* with Men for not receiving a *Propofal* that is for their *Advantage*: Men ought to be content with the Generofity of *offering* good Bargains, and fhould give their *Compaffion* to thofe who do *not underftand* them : but by carrying their Good-nature fo far as to be *Cholerick* in fuch a Cafe, they would follow the Example of the *Church of Rome*, where the Definition of *Charity* is very extraordinary. In her Language, the Writ *de Hæretico Comburendo* is a *Love-Letter*, and *burning* Men for differing with them in Opinion, howfoever mifcalled *Cruelty*, is, as they underftand it, the *Perfection* of *flaming Charity*.

When *Anger* in thefe Cafes lafteth *long*, it is moft probable that it is for our *own fakes* ; Good-nature for *others* is one of thofe Difeafes that is *cured* by *Time*, and efpecially where it is *offered* and *rejected* ; but for our felves it *never faileth*, and cannot be extinguifhed but with our Life. It is fair, if Men can believe that their Friends love them *next* to themfelves, to love them *better* is too much ; the Expreffion is fo *unnatural*, that it is *cloying*, and Men muft have no *Senfe*, who in this cafe have no *Sufpicion*.

XII. Another Circumftance neceffary to a *fair Bargain*, is, that there muft be *Opennefs* and *Freedom* allowed, as the Effect of that *Equality* which is the Foundation of Contracting. There muft be full Liberty of *Objecting*, and making *Doubts* and *Scruples*: If they are fuch as can be *anfwered*, the *Party* convinced is fo much the more *confirmed* and *encouraged* to deal, inftead of being hindred by them ; but if inftead of an *Anfwer* to fatisfy, there is nothing but *Anger* for a Reply, it is impoffible not to conclude that there is never a good one to give ; fo that the Objection *remaining*, without being fully *confuted*, there is an abfolute *Bar* put to any further Treaty.

There can be no Dealing where one fide affumeth a Privilege to *impofe*, fo as to make an *Offer*, and not bear the *Examination* of it ; this is giving *Judgment*, not making a *Bargain*. Where

it

4

it is called *unmannerly* to *object*, or *criminal* to *refuse*, the sureſt way is for Men to ſtay where they are, rather than treat upon ſuch Diſadvantages.

If it ſhould happen to be in any Country where the governing Power ſhould allow Men *Liberty of Conſcience* in the Choice of their *Religion*, it would be ſtrange to deny them *Liberty of Speech* in making a *Bargain*. Such a Contradiction would be ſo diſcouraging, that they muſt be *unreaſonably ſanguine*, who in that caſe can entertain the Hopes of a *fair Equivalent*.

XIII. An *equal* Bargain muſt not be a *Myſtery* nor a *Secret*, the Purchaſer or Propoſer is to tell *directly* and *plainly*, what it is he intendeth to give in exchange for that which he requireth. It muſt be *viewed* and *conſidered* by the other *Party*, that he may judge of the Value ; for without knowing what it is, he cannot determine whether he ſhall *take* or *leave* it. An Aſſertion in *general*, that it ſhall be *as good*, or a *better* thing, is not in this a *ſufficient* Excuſe for the miſtake of dealing upon ſuch uncertain Terms. In all things that are dark, and not enough explained, *Suſpicion* naturally followeth : A *Secret* generally implieth a *Defect* or a *Deceit* ; and if a *falſe Light* is an Objection, *no Light* at all is yet a greater. To pretend to give a *better* thing, and to refuſe to ſhew it, is very near ſaying, it is *not ſo good* a one ; at leaſt ſo it will be taken in common conſtruction. A *Myſtery* is yet a more diſcouraging thing to a *Proteſtant*, eſpecially if the Propoſition ſhould come from a *Papiſt* ; it being one of his great Objections to that Church, that there are ſo many of them *Inviſible* and *Impoſſible*, which are ſo violently thruſt upon their Underſtandings, that they are overlaid with them. They think that *rational Creatures* are to be convinced only by *Reaſon*, and that *Reaſon* muſt be *viſible* and *freely expoſed* ; elſe they will think themſelves uſed with *Contempt*, inſtead of *Equality*, and will never allow ſuch a *ſuſpected Secrecy* to be a fit Preface to a *real Equivalent*.

XIV. In Matters of Contract, not only the preſent Value, but the *Contingencies* and *Conſequences*, as far as they can be fairly ſuppoſed, are to be conſidered. For example, if there ſhould be a *Poſſibility*, that one of the Parties may be ruined by *Accepting*, and the other only *diſappointed* by his *Refuſing* ; the Conſequences are ſo *extremely unequal*, that it is not imaginable a Man ſhould take that for an *Equivalent*, which hath ſuch a *fatal Impoſſibility* at the heels of it.

If it ſhould happen in a *publick* Caſe, that ſuch a *Propoſal* ſhould come from the *minor Part* of an Aſſembly or Nation, to the *greater* ; it is very juſt, that the *Hazard* of ſuch a *Poſſibility* ſhould more or leſs likely fall upon the *leſſer Part*, rather than upon the *greater* ; for whoſe Sake and Advantage, things are and muſt be calculated in all *publick Conſtitutions*. Suppoſe in any mixed Government, the *chief Magiſtrate* ſhould propoſe upon a *Condition*, in the *Senate*, *Diet*, or other *ſupreme Aſſembly*, either to enact or abrogate one or more Laws, by which a *Poſſibility* might be let in of *deſtroying* their *Religion* and *Property*, which in other Language ſignifieth no leſs than *Soul* and *Body* ; where could be the *Equivalent* in the Caſe, not only for the *real Loſs*, but even for the *fear of loſing* them ? Men can fall no lower than to *loſe all*, and if *loſing all* deſtroyeth them, the *venturing all* muſt fright them.

In an Inſtance when Men are ſecure, that how far ſoever they may be over-run by *Violence*, yet they can never be undone by *Law*, except they give their Aſſiſtance to make it poſſible ; tho' it ſhould neither be likely, nor intended, ſtill the *Conſequence* which may happen is too big for any preſent thing to make amends for it. Whilſt the word *Poſſible* remaineth, it muſt *forbid* the Bargain. Where-ever it falleth out therefore, that in an Example of a publick nature, the changing, enacting, or repealing a Law, *may naturally* tend to the *miſplacing* the Legiſlative Power in the hands of thoſe who have a *ſeparate Intereſt* from the Body of a People, there can be no Treating, till it is demonſtrably made out, that ſuch a Conſequence ſhall be *abſolutely impoſſible* : for if that ſhall be *denied* by thoſe who make the Propoſal, if it is becauſe they *cannot* do it, the Motion at firſt was very *unfair*. If they *can* and *will not*, it would be yet leſs reaſonable to expect that ſuch *partial* Dealers would ever give an *Equivalent* fit to be *accepted*.

XV. It is neceſſary in all Dealings to be *aſſured*, in the firſt place, that the *Party propoſing* is in a Condition to *make good* his Offer ; that he is neither under any *former Obligations* or *pretended Claims*, which may render him uncapable of performing it ; elſe he is ſo far in the Condition of a *Minor*, that whatever he diſpoſeth by Sale or Exchange, may be afterwards reſumed, and the Contract become void, being *originally defective*, for want of *ſufficient* legal *Power* in him that made it.

In the Caſe of a ſtrict Settlement, where the Party is only *Tenant* for *Life*, there is no poſſibility of treating with one under ſuch Fetters ; no Purchaſe or Exchange of Lands, or any thing elſe can be good, where there is ſuch an *Incapacity* of making out a Title ; the Intereſt veſted in him being ſo *limited*, that he can do little more than pronounce the Words of a Contract, he can by no means perform the *Effect* of it.

In

In more *publick* Inſtances, the *Impoſſibility* is yet more expreſs ; as ſuppoſe in any King-dom, where the *People* have ſo much Liberty left them, as that they may make Contracts with the *Crown*, there ſhould be ſome *peculiar Rights* claimed to be ſo *fixed* to the royal Function, that no King for the time being could have Power to *part* with them, being ſo *fundamentally* tied to the Office, that they can never be *ſeparated*. Such *Rights* can upon no occaſion be received in *exchange* for any thing the Crown may deſire from the People: That can never be *taken* in Payment, which cannot lawfully be *given*, ſo that if they ſhould part with that which is required upon thoſe Terms, it muſt be a *Gift*, it cannot be a *Bargain*.

There is not in the whole *Dictionary* a more untractable Word than *Inherent*, and leſs to be reconciled to the Word *Equivalent.*

The Party that will contract in ſpight of ſuch a Claim, is content to *take* what is im-*poſſible* to grant ; and if he complaineth of his Diſappointment, he neither *can have* Reme-dy, nor *deſerveth* it.

If a Right ſo claimed happeneth to be of ſo *comprehenſive* a Nature, as that by a clear Inference it may extend to *every thing elſe*, as well as to the *particular* Matter in queſtion, as often as the ſupream Magiſtrate ſhall be ſo diſpoſed, there can in that caſe be no *treat-ing* with a Prerogative that ſwalloweth all the Right that People can pretend ; and if they have no Right to any thing of which they are poſſeſſed, it is a *Jeſt* and not a *Bargain*, to obſerve any Formality in parting with it.

A Claim may be ſo ſtated, that by the *Power* and *Advantage of Interpreting*, it ſhall have ſuch a murthering Eye, that if it looketh upon a Law, like a *Baſiliſk*, it ſhall ſtrike it dead: Where is the poſſibility of Treating, where *ſuch a Right is aſſumed?* Nay, let it be ſuppoſed, that ſuch a Claim is *not well founded* in *Law*, and that upon a free Diſ-quiſition it could *not be made out* ; yet even in this Caſe, none that are well adviſed, will conclude a Bargain till it is fully *ſtated* and *cleared*, or indeed, ſo much as *engage* in a *Trea-ty*, till by way of preliminary all *poſſibility* ſhall be *remov'd* of any Trouble or Diſpute.

XVI. There is a collateral Circumſtance in making a Contract, which yet deſerveth to be conſidered, as much as any thing that belongeth to it ; and that is the *Character* and *Figure* of the *Parties* contracting, if they treat only by themſelves ; and if by others, the *Qualifications* of the *Inſtruments* they employ.

The *Propoſer* eſpecially, muſt not be ſo *low*, as to want *Credit*, or ſo raiſed, as to carry him *above* the Reach of *ordinary Dealing*. In the firſt, there is *Scandal*; in the other, *Dan-ger*. There is no Rule without ſome Exception, but generally ſpeaking, the *Means* ſhould be ſuited to the *End* ; and ſince all Men who treat, pretend an *equal Bargain*, it is deſira-ble that there may be *Equality* in the *Perſons*, as well as in the *Thing*.

The *Manner* of doing things hath ſuch an Influence upon the *Matter*, that Men may gueſs at the *End* by the *Inſtruments* that are uſed to obtain it, who are a very good *Di-rection* how far to rely upon, or ſuſpect the *Sincerity* of that which is propoſed. An Abſur-dity in the way of *carrying on* a Treaty in any *one* Circumſtance, if it is very groſs, is e-nough to perſwade a thinking Man to break off, and take warning from ſuch an *ill Ap-pearance*. Some things are ſo glaring, that it is impoſſible to ſee, and conſequently not to *ſuſpect* them ; as ſuppoſe in a private Caſe there ſhould be a Treaty of *Marriage* between two honourable Families, and the propoſing ſide ſhould think fit to ſend a *Woman* that had been *carted* to perſwade the *young Lady* to an Approbation and Conſent ; the unfit-neſs of the *Meſſenger* muſt naturally diſpoſe the other Party to *diſtruſt* the *Meſſage*, and to reſiſt the Temptation of the *beſt Match* that could be offered, when conveyed by that *Hand*, and uſhered in by ſuch a *diſcouraging Preliminary.*

In a *publick* Inſtance, the Suſpicion ariſing from *unfit Mediators*, ſtill groweth more rea-ſonable in proportion, as the *Conſequence* is much *greater* of being deceived. If a *Jew* ſhould be employed to ſollicit all ſorts of *Chriſtians* to *unite* and *agree* ; the *Contrariety* of his *Profeſſion*, would not allow Men to ſtay till they heard his Arguments, they would conclude from his *Religion*, that either the *Man himſelf* was mad, or that he thought *thoſe* to be ſo, whom he had the Impudence to endeavour to perſwade.

Or ſuppoſe an *Adamite* ſhould be very ſollicitous and active, in all places, and with all ſorts of Perſons, to ſettle the *Church of England* in particular, and a fair *Liberty of Con-ſcience* for all Diſſenters ; though nothing in the World has more to be ſaid for it than *naked Truth*, yet if ſuch a Man ſhould run up and down without Cloaths, let his Argu-ments be ever ſo good, or his Commiſſion ever ſo authentick, his *Figure* would be ſuch a *Contradiction* to his *Buſineſs*, that how ſerious ſoever that might be in it ſelf, *his Interpoſi-tion* would make a Jeſt of it.

Though it ſhould not go ſo far as this, yet if Men have *Contrarieties* in their *way of Liv-ing*, not to be reconciled ; as if they ſhould pretend infinite *Zeal* for *Liberty*, and at that time be in great *Favour*, and *employed* by thoſe who will not *endure* it.

If they are effectually *ſingular*, and conform to the Generality of the World in *no one* thing, but in playing the *Knave*.

If

If *Demonstration* is a familiar Word with them, moſt eſpecially where the thing is *impoſſible.*

If they quote *Authority* to ſupply their Want of *Senſe,* and juſtify the value of their Arguments, not by *Reaſon,* but by their being *paid* for them (in which, by the way, thoſe who pay them have probably a very *melancholly Equivalent.*) If they brandiſh a *Prince's Word* like a Sword in a Crowd, to make way for their own *Impertinence*; and in a diſpute, as Criminals formerly fled to the *Statue* of the Prince for Sanctuary ; if they ſhould now, when baffled, creep under the Protection of a King's *Name,* where out of reſpect they are no farther to be purſued.

In theſe Caſes, though the Propoſitions ſhould be *really* good, they will be corrupted by paſſing through ſuch *Conduits,* and it would be a ſufficient *Miſtake* to enter into a *Treaty*; but it would be little leſs than *Madneſs* from ſuch Hands to expect an *Equivalent.*

XVII. Having touched upon theſe Particulars as neceſſary in order to the ſtating the Nature of an *equal Bargain,* and the Circumſtances belonging to it, let it now be examined in two or three Inſtances, what things are not to be admitted by way of Contract, to paſs under the Name of an *Equivalent.*

Firſt, Though it will be allowed, that in the general Corruption of Mankind, which will not admit *Juſtice* alone to be a ſufficient Tye to make good a Contract, that a *Puniſhment* added for the breach of it, is a *fitting,* or rather a *neceſſary* Circumſtance ; yet it does not follow, that in *all* Caſes, *a great Penalty* upon the Party offending, is an *abſolute* and *entire Security.* It muſt be conſidered in every particular Caſe, how far the *Circumſtances* may rationally lead a Man to *rely more* or *leſs* upon it.

In a private Inſtance, the *Penalty* inflicted upon the breach of Contract muſt be, *Firſt,* ſuch a one as the Party injured *can enforce*; and *Secondly,* ſuch a one as he *will enforce,* when it is in his power.

If the *offending Party* is in a capacity of *hindring* the other from bringing the Vengeance of the Law upon him : If he hath *Strength* or *Privilege* ſufficient to *over-rule* the Letter of the Contract ; in that Caſe a *Penalty* is but a *Word,* there is no Conſequence belonging to it. *Secondly,* The *Forfeiture* or *Puniſhment* muſt be ſuch, as the Man aggrieved will *take :* For example, if upon a Bargain, one of the Parties ſhall ſtipulate to ſubject himſelf, in caſe of his *Failure* to have his *Ears cut,* or his *Noſe ſlit* by the other, with *Security given,* that he ſhall not be proſecuted for *executing* this part of the Agreement, the *Penalty* is heavy enough to diſcourage a Man from breaking his Contract ; but on the other ſide it is of *ſuch a kind,* that the other, how much ſoever he may be provoked, will not in cold Blood care to inflict it. Such an extravagant Clauſe would ſeem to be made only for Shew and Sound, and no Man would think himſelf ſafer by a thing which one way or other is ſure to prove *ineffectual.*

In a publick Caſe, ſuppoſe a Government ſo conſtituted, that a *Law* may be made in the Nature of a *Bargain,* it is in it *ſelf* no more than a *dead Letter,* the Life is given to it by the *Execution* of what it containeth ; ſo that let it in it ſelf be ever ſo perfect, it dependeth upon thoſe who are intruſted with ſeeing it *obſerved.*

If it is in any Country where the *chief Magiſtrate* chuſeth the *Judges,* and the *Judges* interpret the *Laws* ; a *Penalty* in any one particular Law can have no effect but what is *precarious.* It may have a *loud Voice* to threaten, but it has not a *Hand* to give a Blow ; for as long as the governing Power is in poſſeſſion of this Prerogative, let who will chuſe the *Meat,* if they chuſe the *Cooks,* it is they that will give the *taſte* to it. So that it is clear, that the *Rigour* of a *Penalty* will not in all caſes *fix* a *Bargain,* neither is it univerſally a true Poſition, that the Increaſe of *Puniſhment* for the breach of a *new Law,* is an *Equivalent* for the Conſent to part with an *old* one.

XVIII. In moſt Bargains there is a Reference to the *time to come,* which is therefore to be conſidered, as well as that which cometh within the Compaſs of the *preſent* Valuation.

Where the *Party contracting* hath not a *full Power* to diſpoſe what belongeth to him or them in *Reverſion,* who ſhall ſucceed after him in his Right ; he cannot make any part of what is ſo *limited* to be the *Condition* of the Contract. Further, he cannot enjoin the *Heir* or *Succeſſor* to forbear the Exerciſe of any Right that is inherent to him, as he is a Man : neither can he *reſtrain* him without his own Conſent, from doing any Act, which in it ſelf is lawful, and liable to no *Objection.* For example, a *Father* cannot ſtipulate with any other Man, that in Conſideration of ſuch a thing done, or to be done, his *Son* ſhall *never marry* ; becauſe Marriage is an Inſtitution eſtabliſhed by the Laws of God and Man, and therefore no body can be ſo reſtrained by any Power from doing ſuch an Act, when he thinketh fit, being warranted by an Authority that is not to be controuled.

XIX. Now as there are *Rights inherent* in Men's Perſons in their *ſingle Capacities,* there are *Rights* as much fixed to the *Body Politick,* which is a Creature that never dieth. For inſtance, there can be no Government without a *ſupreme Power,* that Power is not always in the ſame Hands, it is in *different* Shapes and Dreſſes, but ſtill where-ever it is lodged, it muſt be *unlimited :* It hath a Juriſdiction over every thing *elſe* ; but it cannot have it above it felf. *Supreme Power* can be no more *limited* than *Infinity* can be *meafured*; becaufe it ceafeth to be the thing, its very being is diffolved, when any bounds can be put to it.

Where this fupreme Power is *mixed*, or *divided*, the *fhape* only *differeth*, the *Argument* is ftill the fame.

The prefent State of *Venice* cannot reftrain thofe who fucceed them in the fame power, from having an entire and unlimited Sovereignty; they may indeed make *prefent Laws* which fhall retrench their *prefent Power*, if they are fo difpofed, and thofe *Laws* if not *repealed* by the *fame Authority* that enacted them, are to be *obferved* by the fucceeding Senate till they think fit to abrogate them, and no longer: for if the fupreme Power fhall ftill refide in the Senate, perhaps compofed of *other* Men, or of *other* Minds (which will be fufficient) the neceffary confequence is, that *one* Senate muft have as much right to *alter* fuch a Law, as *another* could have to *make* it.

XX. Suppofe the *fupreme Power* in any State fhould make a *Law*, to enjoin all fubfequent Law-makers to take an *Oath* never to *alter it*, it would produce thefe following Abfurdities.

Firft, All *fupreme Power* being inftituted to promote the *fafety* and *benefit*, and to prevent the *prejudice* and *danger* which may fall upon thofe who live under the *protection* of it; the *confequence* of fuch an *Oath* would be, that all Men who are fo trufted, fhall take God to witnefs, that fuch a Law once made, being judged *at the time* to be *advantageous* for the publick, though *afterwards* by the viciffitude of times, or the variety of accidents or interefts, it fhould plainly appear to them to be *deftructive*, if they will fuffer it to have its courfe, and will never repeal it.

Secondly, If there could in any Nation be found *a Set of Men*, who having *a part* in the *fupreme* legiflative *Power*, fhould, as much as in them lieth, betray their Country by fuch a criminal engagement, fo *directly oppofite to the nature* of their *Power*, and to the *Truft* repofed in them: If thefe Men have their power only for *life*, when they are dead fuch an Oath can operate *no further*; and though that would be *too long* a Leafe for the Life of fuch a *Monfter* as an *Oath fo compofed*, yet it muft *then* certainly give up the Ghoft. It could bind none but the *firft* makers of it, *another* generation would never be tied up by it.

Thirdly, In thofe Countries where the *fupreme Affemblies* are not conftant *ftanding* Courts, but called together upon *occafions*, and compofed of fuch as the People chufe for *that time* only, with a Truft and Character that remaineth no longer with them than that Affembly is *regularly diffolved*; fuch an Oath taken by the Member of a Senate, Diet, or other Affembly fo chofen, can have very little effect, becaufe at the *next meeting* there may be quite *another Set of Men* who will be under *no Obligation* of that kind. The Eternity intended to that Law by thofe that made it will be cut off by *new Men* who fhall fucceed them in their power, if they have a *differing Tafte*, or another *Intereft*.

XXI. To put it yet further, fuppofe a Claufe in fuch a Law, that it fhall be *criminal* in the laft degree for any Man chofen in a fubfequent Affembly, to *propofe* the *repealing* it; and fince nothing can be *enacted* which is not yet firft *propofed*, by this means it feemeth as if a Law might be created which fhould *never die*. But let this be examined.

Firft, Such a Claufe would be fo *deftructive* to the *being* of fuch a Conftitution, as that it would be as reafonable to fay, that a King had right to *give* or *fell* his Kingdom to a *Foreign Prince*, as that any number of Men who are *intrufted* with the fupreme Power, or any part of it, fhould have a right to *impofe* fuch fhackles upon the Liberty of thofe who are to *fucceed* them in the *fame Truft*. The ground of that *Truft* is, that every Man who is chofen into fuch an Affembly, is to do all that in him lieth for the *good* of thofe who *chofe* him. The *Englifh* of fuch a Claufe would be, that he is *not* to do his *beft* for thofe that *chofe* him, becaufe though he fhould be *convinc'd* that it might be very *fatal* to *continue* that *Law*, and therefore very *neceffary* to *repeal* it, yet he muft not repeal it, becaufe it is made a *Crime*, and attended with a *Penalty*.

But fecondly, to fhew the *emptinefs* as well as *injuftice* of fuch a Claufe, it is clear, that although fuch an Invafion of Right fhould be impofed, it will never be obeyed: There will only be *Deformity* in the *Monfter*, it will neither *fting* nor *bite*. Such *Law-givers* would only have the honour of attempting a *contradiction* which can never have any fuccefs; for as fuch a *Law* in it felf would be a *madnefs*, fo the *Penalty* would be a *jeft*; which may be thus made out.

XXII. A Law that carrieth in it felf *Reafon* enough to *fupport* it, is fo far from wanting the *protection* of fuch a Claufe, or from *needing* to take fuch an *extraordinary receipt* for long Life, that the *admitting* it muft certainly be the *likelieft* and the *fhorteft* way to *deftroy* it; fuch a Claufe in a Law muft imply an opinion that the *greateft* part of Mankind is *againft* it, fince it is impoffible fuch an exorbitance fhould be done for its *own fake*; the end of it muft be to *force* Men by a *Penalty*, to that which they could *not* be *perfwaded* to, whilft their Reafon is left at *liberty*. This Pofition being granted, which I think can hardly be denied, put the cafe that a Law fhould be made with this *imaginary* Claufe of

Immortality,

Immortality, after which another *Assembly* is chosen ; and if the Majority of the *Electors* shall be *against* this Law, the greater part of the *Elected* must be *so* too, if the choice is fair and regular ; which must be presumed, since the supposition of the contrary is not to come within this Argument. When these Men shall meet, the *Majority* will be visible before-hand of those who are *against* such a Law, so that there will be no *hazard* to any single Man in proposing the *Repeal* of it, when he cannot be *punished* but by the *Majority*, and he hath such a kind of assurance as cometh near to a Demonstration, that the *greater Number* will be of his mind, and consequently, that for their own sakes they will *secure* him from any danger.

For these Reasons, where-ever, in order to the making a Bargain, a Proposition is advanc'd to make a *new Law*, which is to tie up those who neither *can* nor *will be bound* by it, it may be a good *Jest*, but it will never be a good *Equivalent*.

XXIII. In the last place, let it be examined how far a *Promise* ought to be taken for a *Security* in a Bargain.

There is a great variety of Methods for the *Security* of those that deal, according to their *Dispositions* and *Interests* ; some are *binding*, others *inducing* circumstances, and are to be so distinguished.

First, *Ready Payment* is without exception, so of that there can be no dispute ; in default of that, the *good Opinion* Men may have of one another, is a great ingredient to supply the want of *immediate* Performances. Where the Trust is grounded upon *Inclination* only, the Generosity is not always *return'd* ; but where it springeth from a *long Experience* it is a better foundation, and yet that is not always *secure*. In ordinary dealing, *one Promise* may be an *Equivalent* to *another*, but it is not so for a thing *actually* granted or conveyed ; especially if the thing required in exchange for it, is of great *value*, either in it *self* or in its *consequences*. A *bare* Promise as a *single Security* in such a case is not an *equal* proposal ; if it is offered by way of *Addition*, it generally giveth cause to doubt the Title is crazy, where so *slender* a thing is brought in to be a *supplement*.

XXIV. The *Earnest* of making good a Promise, must be such a behaviour *preceding* as may encourage the party to whom it is made to depend upon it : Where instead of that, there hath been *want of kindness*, and, which is worse, an *Invasion* of *Right*, a Promise hath no perswading force ; and till the *Objection* to such a proceeding is *forgotten* (which can only be the work of time) and the Skin is a little grown over the tender part, the wound must not be touch'd. There must be some *Intermission* at least to abate the smart of *unkind usage*, or else a Promise in the eye of the party injur'd is so far from *strengthening* a Security, that it raiseth more *doubts*, and giveth more justifiable cause to *suspect* it.

A *Word* is not like a Bone, that being broken and well set again, is said to be sometimes stronger in that part: It is far from being so in a *word* given and *not made good*. Every single Act either *weakeneth* or *improveth* our Credit with other Men ; and as an Habit of being *just* to our Word will *confirm*, so an Habit of too freely *dispensing* with it must necessarily *destroy* it. A *Promise* hath its effect to perswade a man to lay some weight upon it, where the *Promise* hath not only the *power*, but may reasonably be supposed to have the *will* of performing it ; and further, that there be no *visible Interest* of the party promising to excuse himself from it, or to evade it.

All Obligations are *comparative*, and where they seem to be opposite, or between the greater and the lesser, which of them ought to have precedence in all respects, every man is apt to be his *own Judge*.

XXV. If it should fall out that the *Promiser* with full *intent* at the *time* to perform, might by the interposition of *new Arguments*, or *differing Advice*, think himself oblig'd to turn the matter of Conscience on the *other* side, and shou'd look upon it to be much a *greater* fault to *keep* his word than to *break* it ; such a Belief will *untye* the *strictest Promise* that can be made, and though the Party thus absolving himself should do it *without* the mixture or temptation of *private Interest*, being moved to it meerly by his *Conscience*, as then informed ; yet how far soever that might diminish the *Fault* in him, it would in no degree lessen the *inconveniences* to the *party* who is *disappointed*, by the breach of an engagement upon which he relied.

XXVI. A *Promise* is to be understood in the *plain* and *natural* sense of the words, and to be sure not in his *who made* it, if it was given as part of a Bargain. That would be like giving a Man power to *raise* the *value* of his Money in the payment of his *Debt*, by which though he paid but half or less, he might pretend according to the letter to have made good the contract.

The *power* of *interpreting* a Promise intirely taketh away the *virtue* of it. A Merchant who should once assume that privilege, would save himself the trouble of making any more Bargains.

It is still worse if this *Jurisdiction* over a Man's *Promise*, should be *lodg'd* in hands that have Power to support such an *extraordinary Claim* ; and if in *other* Cases, forbearing to deal upon those terms is *advisable*, in this it becometh absolutely *necessary*.

XXVII. There must in all respects be a full liberty to *claim* a Promise, to make it reasonable to *take* it in any part of payment ; else it would be like agreeing for a *Rent*, and at the same time making it *criminal* to *demand* it.

A *Superiority* of *Dignity* or *Power* in the Party promising, maketh it a more *tender* thing for the other party to treat upon that security. The first maketh it a *nice* thing to *claim*, the latter maketh it a *difficult* thing to *obtain*.

In some cases, a *Promise* is in the nature of a *Covenant*, and then between *equal* Parties the breach of it will bear a *suit* ; but where the *greatness* of the Promiser is very much raised above the Level of *equality*, there is no Forfeiture to be taken. It is so far from the party grieved his being able to *sue* or *recover* Damages, that he will not be allow'd to *explain* or *expostulate*, and instead of his being *relieved* against the breach of Promise, he will run the hazard of being *punished* for breach of good Manners. Such a difficulty is putting all or part of the Payment in the Fire, where Men must burn their Fingers before they can come at it.

That cannot properly be called *good Payment*, which the party to whom it is due, may not receive with *ease* and *safety*. It was a King's Brother of *England* who refused to lend the Pope money, for this reason, *that he would never take the bond of one, upon whom he could not distrain*.

The Argument is still *stronger* against the validity of a Promise, when the Contract is made between a *Prince* and a *Subject*. The very offering a King's Word in Mortgage, is rather a *threatning* in case of Refusal, than an *inducing* Argument to accept it ; it is *unfair* at *first*, and by that giveth greater cause to be cautious, especially if a thing of that *value* and *dignity* as a King's Word ought to be, should be put into the hands of *State-brokers* to strike up a Bargain with it.

XXVIII. When God Almighty maketh a Covenant with Mankind, *his Promise* is a *sufficient Security*, notwithstanding his *Superiority* and his *Power* ; because, first, he can neither *err* nor do *injustice*. It is the *only* Exception to his Omnipotence, that by the Perfection of his *being* he is incapacitated to do *wrong*. Secondly, at the *instance* of *his Promise*, by the extent of his Foresight which cannot fail, there is no room left for the possibility of any thing to *intervene*, which might *change* his mind. Lastly, he is above the receiving either *Benefit* or *Inconvenience*, and therefore can have no *Interest* or *Temptation* to vary from his Word, when once he hath granted it.

Now though Princes are God's Vicegerents, yet their Commission not being so *large* as that *these Qualifications* are devolved to them, it is quite another case ; and since the *offering* a Security implieth it to be *examined* by the party to whom it is proposed, it must not be taken ill that Objections are made to it, even though the Prince should be the *immediate Proposer*.

Let a familiar Case be put ; Suppose a Prince, tempted by a Passion too strong for him to resist, should descend, so as to promise Marriage to one of his Subjects ; and as Men are naturally in great haste upon such occasions, should press to take possession before the *necessary Forms* could be complied with ; would the poor *Lady's Scruple* be called *Criminal*, for not taking the Security of the royal Word? Or would her *Allegiance* be tainted, by her *resisting* the sacred Person of her Sovereign, because he was impatient of delay? *Courtesy* in this case might perswade her to *accept* it, if she was so disposed ; but sure the *just exercise* of Power can never *claim* it.

XXIX. There is one Case where it is more particularly a *Duty* to use very *great caution* in accepting the Security of a Promise, and that is, when Men are *authorized* and *trusted* by *others* to act for them. This putteth them under much *greater restraints*, than those who are at liberty to treat for *themselves*. It is *lawful*, though it is not *prudent*, for any man to make an *ill Bargain* for *himself* ; but it is neither the one nor the other, where the party contracting treateth on behalf of *another*, by whom he is *intrusted*. Men who will unwarily accept an *ill Security*, if it is for *themselves*, forfeit their own discretion, and undergo the Penalty, but they are not responsible to any body else. They lie under the mortification and the loss of committing the error, by which though they may expose their *Judgment* to some *censure*, yet their *Morality* suffers no *reproach* by it.

But those who are *reputed* by *others* to treat for them, upon terms of *best advantage*, though the *Confidence* placed in them should prevent the putting any *limits* to the power in their Commission, yet the *Condition implied*, if not *expressed*, is, that the Persons so trusted shall neither make an *ill Bargain*, nor accept a *slight Security*.

The Obligation is yet *more* binding when the Trust is of a *publick* nature. The aggravation of disappointing a *Body* of Men that *rely* upon them, carrieth the Fault as *high* as it can go ; and perhaps no Crime of any kind can outdo such a *deliberate Breach of Trust*, or would more justly make Men *forfeit* the protection of *human Society*.

XXX. I

XXX. I will add one thing more upon this Head, which is, that it is not *always* a *true Proposition*, that 'tis safe to rely upon a Promise, if at the time of making it, it is the *Interest* of the *Promiser* to make it good. This, though many times it is a good *Inducement*, yet it hath these Exceptions to it. First, if the proposer hath at other times gone plainly *against* his *visible Interest*, the Argument will turn the other way, and his *former Mistakes* are so many *Warnings* to others, not to come within the danger any more: let the Inducements to those Mistakes be never so great and generous, that does not alter the nature, they are *Mistakes* still.

Interest is an uncertain thing, it goeth and cometh, and varieth according to times and circumstances; as good build upon a *Quick-sand*, as upon a presumption that Interest shall not alter. Where are the Men so distinguished from the rest of Mankind, that it is impossible for them to mistake their Interest? Who are they that have such an Exemption from human Frailty, as that it can never happen to them not to see their Interest for want of Understanding, or not to leap over it by excess of Zeal.

Above all, *Princes* are most liable to mistake; not out of any *defect* in their Nature, which might put them under such an unfortunate distinction; quite contrary, the blood they derive from great and wise Ancestors, does rather distinguish them on the better side; besides that their great Character and Office of Governing, giveth a noble Exercise to their Reason, which can very hardly fail to raise and improve it. But there is one Circumstance annexed to their glorious Calling, which in this respect is sufficient to outweigh all those Advantages; it is, that Mankind, divided in most things else, agree in this, to conspire in their Endeavours to deceive and mislead them, which maketh it above the Power of human Understanding, to be so exactly guarded, as never to admit a Surprize; and the highest Applause that could ever yet be given to the greatest Men that ever wore a Crown, is, that they *were no oftner deceived*.

Thus I have ventured to lay down my Thoughts of the *Nature* of a *Bargain*, and the *due Circumstances* belonging to an *Equivalent*, and will now conclude with this short Word: " Where *Distrusting* may be the cause of provoking *Anger*, and *Trusting* may " be the cause of bringing *Ruin*, the Choice is too easy to need the being explained.

A

LETTER

From a Gentleman in the City, to his Friend in the Country. Containing his Reasons for not Reading the Declaration.

SIR,

I Do not wonder at your Concern for finding an Order of Council published in the *Gazette* for reading the King's Declaration for Liberty of Conscience in all Churches and Chappels in this Kingdom. You desire to know my Thoughts about it, and I shall freely tell them; for this is not a time to be reserved. Our Enemies who have given our gracious King this Counsel against us, have taken the most effectual way, not only to ruin us, but to make us appear the Instruments of our own Ruin, that what Course soever we take, we shall be undone; and one side or other will conclude, that we have undone our selves, and fall like Fools.

To lose our Livings and Preferments, nay, our Liberties and our Lives in a plain and direct Opposition to Popery, as suppose for refusing to read Mass in our Churches, or to swear to the *Trent*-Creed, is an honourable way of falling, and has the divine Comforts of suffering for Christ and his Religion; and I hope there is none of us but can chearfully submit to the Will of God in it. But this is not our present Case; to read the Declaration,

tion, is not to read the Mass, nor to profess the *Romish* Faith; and therefore, some will judge that there is no hurt in reading it, and that to suffer for such a Refusal, is not to fall like Confessors, but to suffer as Criminals for disobeying the lawful Commands of our Prince. But yet we judge, and we have the concurring Opinions of all the Nobility and Gentry with us, who have already suffered in this Cause, that to take away the Test and penal Laws at this time, is but one step from the introducing of Popery; and therefore to read such a Declaration in our Churches, though it do not immediately bring Popery in, yet it sets open our Church-Doors for it, and then it will take its own time to enter: So that should we comply with this Order, all good Protestants would despise and hate us, and then we may be easily crushed, and shall soon fall with great dishonour, and without any pity. This is the difficulty of our Case; we shall be censured on both sides, but with this difference: We shall fall a little sooner by not reading the Declaration, if our gracious Prince resent this as an Act of an obstinate and peevish, or factious Disobedience, as our Enemies will be sure to represent it to him; we shall as certainly fall not long after, if we do read it, and then we shall fall unpitied and despised, and it may be with the Curses of the Nation, whom we have ruined by our Compliance; and this is the way never to rise more: And may I suffer all that can be suffered in this World, rather than contribute to the final Ruin of the best Church in the World.

Let us then examine this Matter impartially, as those who have no mind either to ruin themselves, or to ruin the Church: I suppose no Minister of the Church of *England* can give his Consent to the Declaration. Let us then consider, whether reading the Declaration in our Churches be not an interpretative Consent, and will not with great reason be interpreted to be so: For,

First, By our Law all ministerial Officers are accountable for their Actions: The Authority of Superiors, though of the King himself, cannot justify inferior Officers, much less the Ministers of State, if they should execute any illegal Commands; which shews that our Law does not look upon the Ministers of Church or State to be meer Machines and Tools, to be managed wholly by the Will of Superiors, without exercising any Act of Judgment or Reason themselves; for then inferior Ministers were no more punishable, than the Horses are, which draw an innocent Man to *Tyburn:* and if inferior Ministers are punishable, then our Laws suppose that what we do in obedience to Superiors, we make our own Act by doing it, and I suppose that signifies our Consent, in the eye of the Law, to what we do. It is a Maxim in our Law, *that the King can do no wrong*; and therefore if any Wrong be done, the Crime and Guilt is the Ministers who do it: for the Laws are the King's publick Will, and therefore he is never supposed to command any thing contrary to Law; nor is any Minister, who does an illegal Action, allowed to pretend the King's Command and Authority for it: and yet this is the only Reason I know, why we must not obey a Prince against the Laws of the Land, or the Laws of God, because what we do, let the Authority be what it will that commands it, becomes our own Act, and we are responsible for it; and then, as I observed before, it must imply our own Consent.

Secondly, The Ministers of Religion have a greater Tye and Obligation than this, because they have the Care and Conduct of Men's Souls, and therefore are bound to take care that what they publish in their Churches, be neither contrary to the Laws of the Land, nor to the Good of the Church: For the Ministers of Religion are not look'd upon as common Cryers, but what they read, they are supposed to recommend too, though they do no more than read it; and therefore to read any thing in the Church, which I do not consent to and approve, nay, which I think prejudicial to Religion, and the Church of God, as well as contrary to the Laws of the Land, is to misguide my People, and to dissemble with God and Men; because it is presum'd, that I neither do, nor ought to read any thing in the Church, which I do not in some degree approve. Indeed, let Men's private Opinions be what they will, in the nature of the thing, he that reads such a Declaration to his People, teaches them by it: For is not reading teaching? Suppose then I do not consent to what I read, yet I consent to teach my People what I read: and herein is the evil of it; for it may be it were no fault to consent to the Declaration; but if I consent to teach my People what I do not consent to my self, I am sure that is a great one. And he who can distinguish between consenting to read the Declaration, and consenting to teach the People by the Declaration, when reading the Declaration is teaching it, has a very subtile distinguishing Conscience. Now if consenting to read the Declaration be a Consent to teach it my People, then the natural Interpretation of reading the Declaration is, that he who reads it in such a solemn teaching Manner, approves it. If this be not so, I desire to know, why I may not read an Homily for Transubstantiation, or Invocation of Saints, or the Worship of Images, if the King sends me such good Catholick Homilies,

milies, and commands me to read them? And thus we may inftruct our People in all the points of Popery, and recommend it to them with all the Sophiftry and Artificial Infinuations, in obedience to the King, and a very good Confcience; becaufe without our Confent. If it be faid, this would be a Contradiction to the Doctrine of our Church by Law eftablifhed; fo I take the Declaration to be: And if we may read the Declaration contrary to Law, becaufe it does not imply our Confent to it; fo we may Popifh Homilies, for the bare Reading them will not imply our Confent, no more than the reading the Declaration does: But whether I confent to the Doctrine or no, it is certain I confent to teach my People this Doctrine, and it is to be confidered, whether an honeft Man can do this.

Thirdly, I fuppofe no Man will doubt but the King intends that our Reading the Declaration fhould fignify to the Nation our Confent and Approbation of it; for the Declaration does not want Publifhing, for it is fufficiently known already: but our Reading it in our Churches muft ferve inftead of Addreffes of Thanks, which the Clergy generally refufed, tho' it was only to thank the King for his Gracious Promifes renewed to the Church of *England,* in his Declaration, which was much more innocent, than to publifh the Declaration it felf in our Churches. This would perfwade one, that the King thinks our Reading the Declaration, to fignify our Confent, and that the People will think it to be fo. And he that can fatisfy his Confcience, to do an Action without Confent, which the Nature of the Thing, the Defign, and Intention of the Command, and the Senfe of the People expound to be a Confent, may, I think, as well fatisfy himfelf with Equivocations and mental Refervations.

There are two things to be anfwered to this, which muft be confidered.

I. That the People underftand our Minds, and fee that this is Matter of Force upon us, and meer Obedience to the King. To which I anfwer,

1. Poffibly the People do underftand that the Matter of the Declaration is againft our Principles: But is this any Excufe, that we read that, and by Reading, recommend that to them, which is againft our own Confciences and Judgments? Reading the Declaration would be no Fault at all, but our Duty, when the King commands it, did we approve of the Matter of it; but to confent to teach our *People* fuch Doctrines as we think contrary to the Laws of God, or the Laws of the Land, does not leffen, but aggravate the Fault, and the *People* muft be very good-natured to think this an Excufe.

2. It is not likely that all the *People* will be of a mind in this Matter: fome may excufe it; others, and thofe it may be the moft, the beft, and the wifeft Men, will condemn us for it; and then how fhall we juftify our felves againft their Cenfures? When the World will be divided in their Opinions, the plain way is certainly the beft, to do what we can juftify our felves, and then let Men judge as they pleafe. No Man in *England* will be pleafed with our Reading the Declaration, but thofe who hope to make great Advantage of it againft us, and againft our Church and Religion; others will feverely condemn us for it, and cenfure us as falfe to our Religion and as Betrayers both of Church and State: and befides that, it does not become a Minifter of Religion, to do any thing, which in the Opinion of the moft charitable Men can only be excufed; for what needs an Excufe, is either a Fault, or looks very like one. Befides this, I fay, I will not truft Men's Charity; thofe who have fuffered themfelves in this Caufe, will not excufe us for fear of fuffering; thofe who are inclined to excufe us now, will not do fo when they confider the thing better, and come to feel the ill Confequences of it: when our Enemies open their Eyes, and tell them what our Reading the Declaration fignify'd, which they will then tell us we ought to have feen before, tho' they were not bound to fee it; for we were to guide and inftruct them, not they us.

II. Others therefore think that when we read the Declaration, we fhould publickly profefs, that it is not our Judgment, but that we only read it in obedience to the King, and then our reading it cannot imply our Confent to it. Now this is only *Proteftatio contra factum,* which all People will laugh at, and fcorn us for: for fuch a folemn Reading it, in time of Divine Service, when all Men ought to be moft grave and ferious, and far from diffembling with God or Men, does in the nature of the thing imply our Approbation; and fhould we declare the contrary, when we read it, what fhall we fay to thofe who ask us, why then do you read it? But let thofe who have a mind to try this way, which, for my part, I take to be a greater and more unjuftifiable Provocation to the King, than not to read it; and, I fuppofe thofe who do not read it, will be thought plainer and honefter Men, and will efcape as well as thofe who read it and proteft againft it: and yet nothing lefs than an exprefs Proteftation againft it will falve this matter; for only to fay, they read it meerly in Obedience to the King, does not exprefs their Diffent: It fignifies indeed, that they would not have read it, if the King had not commanded it; but thefe Words do not fignify, that they difapprove of the Declaration, when their Reading it, though only in O-

bedience

bedience to the King, fignifies their Approbation of it, as much as Actions can fignify a Confent: let us call to mind how it fared with thofe in King *Charles* the Firft's Reign, who read the *Book of Sports*, as it was called, and then preached againft it.

To return then to our Arguments; if reading the Declaration in our Churches be in the Nature of the Action, in the Intention of the Command, in the Opinion of the People, an interpretative Confent to it; I think my felf bound in Confcience not to read it, becaufe I am bound in Confcience not to approve it.

It is againft the Conftitution of the Church of *England*, which is eftablifhed by Law, and to which I have fubfcribed; and therefore am bound in Confcience to teach nothing contrary to it, while this Obligation lafts.

It is to teach an unlimited and univerfal Toleration, which the Parliament in 72 declared illegal, and which has been condemned by the Chriftian Church in all Ages.

It is to teach my People, that they need never come to Church more, but have my Leave, as they have the King's, to go to a Conventicle or Mafs.

It is to teach the Difpenfing Power, which alters, what has been formerly thought the whole Conftitution of this Church and Kingdom; which we dare not do, till we have the Authority of Parliament for it.

It is to recommend to our People, the Choice of fuch Perfons to fit in Parliament, as fhall take away the *Teft* and *Penal Laws*, which moft of the Nobility and Gentry of the Nation have declared their Judgment againft.

It is to condemn all thofe great and worthy Patriots of their Country, who forfeited the deareft thing in the World to them, next a good Confcience, *viz.* The Favour of their Prince, and a great many honourable and profitable Employments with it, rather than confent to that Propofal of taking away the *Teft* and *Penal Laws*, which they apprehend deftructive to the *Church of England* and the *Proteftant Religion*; and he who can in Confcience do all this, I think need fcruple nothing.

For let us confider further, what the effects and confequences of our Reading the Declaration are likely to be; and I think they are Matter of Confcience too, when they are evident and apparent.

This will certainly render our Perfons and Miniftry infinitely contemptible, which is againft that apoftolical Canon, *Let no Man defpife thee*, Titus 2. 15: That is, fo to behave himfelf in his Minifterial Office, as not to fall under Contempt; and therefore this obliges the Confcience, not to make our felves ridiculous, nor render our Miniftry, our Counfels, Exhortations, Preaching, Writing, of no effect, which is a thoufand times worfe than being filenced. Our Sufferings will preach more effectually to the People, when we cannot fpeak to them: but he who for Fear or Cowardife, or the Love of this World, betrays his Church and Religion by undue Compliances, and will certainly be thought to do fo, may continue to preach, but to no purpofe; and when we have rendered our felves ridiculous and contemptible, we fhall quickly fall, and fall unpitied.

There is nothing will fo effectually tend to the final Ruin of the Church of *England*, becaufe our Reading the Declaration will difcourage, or provoke, or mifguide all the Friends the Church of *England* has: can we blame any Man for not preferving the Laws and Religion of our Church and Nation, when we our felves venture nothing for it? Can we blame any Man for confenting to repeal the *Teft* and *Penal Laws*, when we recommended it to them by the Reading the Declaration? Have we not reafon to expect, that the Nobility and Gentry, who have already fuffered in this Caufe, when they hear themfelves condemned for it in all the Churches of *England*, will think it time to mend fuch a Fault, and reconcile themfelves to their Prince? and if our Church fhould fall this way, is there any reafon to expect it fhould ever rife again? Thefe Confequences are almoft as evident as Demonftrations, and let it be what it will in itfelf, which I forefee will deftroy the *Church of England* and the *Proteftant Religion* and *Intereft*, I think I ought to make as much Confcience of doing it, as of doing the moft immoral Action in nature.

To fay that thefe mifchievous Confequences are not abfolutely neceffary, and therefore do not affect the Confcience, becaufe we are not certain they will follow, is a very mean Objection; Moral Actions indeed have not fuch Confequences, as natural Caufes have neceffary Effects, becaufe no moral Caufes act neceffarily: Reading the Declaration, will not as neceffarily deftroy the Church of *England*, as Fire burns Wood; but if the Confequence be plain and evident, the moft likely thing that can happen, if it be unreafonable to expect any other, if it be what is plainly intended and defigned,
either

either I muſt never have any regard to Moral Conſequences of my Actions, or if ever they are to be conſidered, they are in this caſe.

Why are the Nobility and Gentry ſo extreamly averſe to the Repeal of the Teſt and Penal Laws? Why do they forfeit the King's Favour, and their Honourable Stations, rather than comply with it? If you ſay, that this tends to deſtroy the Church of *England* and the Proteſtant Religion, I ask whether this be the neceſſary conſequence of it? whether the King cannot keep his promiſe to the Church of *England* if the Teſt and Penal Laws be repealed? We cannot ſay but this may be: And yet the Nation does not think fit to try it; and we commend thoſe great Men who deny it; and if the ſame queſtions were put to us, we think we ought in Conſcience to deny them our ſelves. And are there not as high probabilities, that our Reading the Declaration will promote the Repeal of the Teſt and Penal Laws, as that ſuch a Repeal will ruin our Conſtitution, and bring in Popery upon us? Is it not as probable, that ſuch Compliance in us will oblige all the Nobility and Gentry, who have hitherto been firm to us, as that when the power of the Nation is put into Popiſh Hands by the Repeal of ſuch Teſts and Laws, the Prieſts and Jeſuits may find ſome *ſalvo* for the King's Conſcience, and perſwade him to forget his Promiſe to the Church of *England*? And if the probable ill conſequences of the Repealing the Teſt and Penal Laws, be a good reaſon not to comply with it, I cannot ſee but that the probable ill conſequences of Reading the Declaration, is a good reaſon not to read it.

The moſt material Objection is, That the Diſſenters, whom we ought not to provoke, will expound our Reading it, to be the effect of a perſecuting Spirit: Now I wonder Men ſhould lay any weight on this, who will not allow the moſt probable conſequences of our Actions, to have any influence upon Conſcience: For if we muſt compare conſequences, to diſoblige all the Nobility and Gentry by reading it, is likely to be much more fatal, than to anger the Diſſenters; and it is more likely, and there is much more reaſon for it, that one ſhould be offended than the other: For the Diſſenters, who are wiſe in conſidering, are ſenſible of the ſnare themſelves; and though they deſire Eaſe and Liberty, they are not willing to have it with ſuch apparent hazard of Church and State: I am ſure that though we were ever ſo deſirous that they might have their Liberty, (and when there is opportunity of ſhewing our inclinations without danger, they may find that we are not ſuch Perſecutors as we are repreſented) yet we cannot conſent that they ſhould have it this way, which they will find the deareſt Liberty that ever was granted.

This Sir, is our Caſe in ſhort, the Difficulties are great on both ſides, and therefore now if ever we ought to beſiege Heaven with our Prayers for Wiſdom, and Counſel, and Courage; that God would protect his Church and Reformed Chriſtianity, againſt all the Devices of their Enemies: Which is the daily and hearty Prayer of,

S I R,

Your Friend and Brother.

May 22. 1688.

POSTSCRIPT.

I Have juſt now ſeen H. Care's Paper call'd, The publick Occurrences, *which came out to-day, and cannot but ſet you right as to his News about the Reading of the Declaration on* Sunday : *He tells you,* 'That ſeveral Divines of the Church of England, *in and about* 'this City, eminent for their Piety and Moderation, *did yeſterday read his Majeſty's Declara-* 'tion in their Churches, *according to the Order in that behalf ; but ſome (to the great ſurprize* 'of their Pariſhioners) were pleaſed to decline it.' *You in the Country are from this Account to believe, that it was read here by the generality of the Clergy, and by the eminent Men among them : But I can and do aſſure you, that this is one of the moſt impudent Lyes that ever was printed. For as to this City, which hath above a Hundred Pariſhes in it, it was read only in four or five Churches ; all the reſt, and beſt of the Clergy, refuſing it every where. I will ſpare their Names who read it ; but ſhould I mention them, it would make you, who know this City, a little heartily to deride* H. C's *Account of them. And for the ſurprize he talks of, the contrary of it is ſo true, that in* Woodſtreet, *where it was read by Dr.* M. *the People generally went out of the Church. This I tell you, that you may be provided for the future againſt ſuch an impudent Lyar, who, for bread, can vouch and put about the Nation, the falſeſt of things.*

I am Yours.

AN

AN
ANSWER

To the City Minister's LETTER, *from his Country Friend.*

SIR,

IT is not for me now to acknowledge my private Debt to you for the favour of your Letter, since the Publick is as much concerned in it as I: and if I may judge of all by the compass of my Neighbourhood and Acquaintance, I may assure you they are not insensible of your Obligation, though they are ignorant of the Author.

The Country, as far as my Intelligence reaches, has followed the Example of the City, and refus'd to read the Declaration of Indulgence according to a certain Order said to be the King's, which we in the Country can scarce believe to be his. For it has neither been signify'd to the Ordinaries according to the usual manner, nor could those that dispersed it give any account whence it came to them. I have heard indeed that an Act of Council concerning it has been published in the *Gazette*, which I never saw; and if I had, I should scarce have thought Authentick: For I always took that Paper, as for its Authority, to have been all of a piece, and that we were no more bound to take notice of any Order published there under any penalty, than we are to believe all the News from *Poland* or *Constantinople*. Nay, tho' this Order had come to us in due form, yet had we had great reason to suspect something of surreption and surprize upon his Majesty in this matter, and that it could not proceed from his Majesty's full and free consent; for we cannot yet forget his repeated professions of kindness to us, and of satisfaction in our Principles and Duty: and having done nothing since which might forfeit his good Opinion, we are unwilling to believe that it is his Majesty's own mind and pleasure to load us with such an Order, as we cannot execute with any congruity, safety, or good conscience.

I. As to his Majesty's Declaration, we of all his Majesty's Subjects are the least concerned in it; and with all Duty be it spoken, we cannot see, that our legal Establishment receives any Addition by this Declaration. For there are yet, thanks be to God, no Penal Laws to which our Congregations are obnoxious, and therefore we do not stand in need of any Toleration: Yet it is upon us only that the Reading of it is imposed. An Act which cannot well be construed otherwise than as a soliciting and tempting our own People to forsake our Communion. If this Declaration must needs be read in any Religious Assemblies, in reason surely it should be in those, who wholly owe their subsistence to it. It would better have become the *Roman* than the *Protestant* Chappels. But in the *Roman* Church *Indulgence* hath another signification; and belongs to those only who frequent their Churches, but not to such as leave them: for with them this is the only sin that is not capable of Indulgence. But the Priests desire to be excused, lest while they proclaim Toleration to others they bring an Interdict upon themselves. Or why I pray was not Father *Pen* ordered to publish it in his Meetings? Or the worthy Mr. *Lob*, the reputed Father of this Project; why had not he the benefit of his own Invention, and a Patent for being the sole Publisher of it within his own Pound? Or why was not my *Lord Mayor*'s private and select Congregation thought worthy of so great a grace? Surely it is not to draw upon us the envy of the Dissenters, that the honour of publishing this Declaration is imposed upon us alone, when it belongs to all other Communions in the Kingdom, except our own: And if we refuse it, I hope it will be imputed to our Modesty, for we are not ambitious of being impertinent or busy-bodies in other Men's matters.

A certain Person much greater than he deserves, but perhaps not so high, is said to have used the Words of *Rabshaketh* upon this occasion, *That the Church of* England *Clergy should eat their own Dung.* Isa. 36. 12. This sentence might better have become a Messenger of the King of *Assyria*, than a pretended Counsellor of our own Prince, though some make a question to which King he belongs: But God be thanked, we are not yet so straitly besieg'd as to be reduced to that extremity; and tho' by the permission of God, we should be reduced to so miserable a Condition, we should, I hope, by the Grace of God, be content to endure that

and

4

and worfe extremities if poffible, rather than betray or furrender the City of God. But before that comes, it is poffible that the Mouth that belch'd out this Nafty Infolence, may be ftopp'd with fomething which it cannot fwallow.

II. Befides, there are fome paffages in the Declaration, which in Confcience we cannot read to our People, though it be in the King's Name; for among others we are to read thefe Words: *We cannot but heartily wifh, as will eafily be believed, that all the People of our Dominions were Members of the Catholick Church.* Our People know too well the *English* of this, and could not but be ftrangely furprized to hear us tell them, that it would be an acceptable thing to the King, that they fhould leave the Truth and our Communion, and turn Papifts. The Wifh of a King, when folemnly declared, is no light infignificant thing, but has real influence and effect upon the Minds of Men. It was but a Wifh of *Henry* the Second that cut off *T. Becket,* then Archbifhop of *Canterbury.* Councils and Courts of Juftice too often bend to a King's Wifhes, though againft their own Inclinations, as well as againft their Rule: And can we imagine that they can have no force at all upon the common People? Therefore we cannot in confcience pronounce thefe words in the ears of the people whofe fouls are committed to our Charge. For we fhould hereby lay a Snare before them, and become their Tempters inftead of being their Inftructers; and in very fair and reafonable Conftruction we fhall be underftood to folicite them to Apoftacy, to leave the Truth of the Gofpel, for Fables, and the Miftakes of Men; a reafonable and decent Worfhip, for Superftition and Idolatry; a true Chriftian Liberty, for the moft intolerable Bondage both of Soul and Body. If any will forfake our Doctrine and Fellowfhip, which yet is not ours but Chrift's, at their own peril be it: But as for us, we are refolved by the Grace of God, to lay no ftumbling-block in their way, nor to be acceffary to their ruin, that we may be able to declare our integrity with St. *Paul,* That *we are pure from the blood of all Men.*

III. In the next place, we are to declare in the King's Name, *That from henceforth the Execution of all, and all manner of Penal Laws, in matters Ecclefiaftical, for not coming to Church, or not receiving the Sacrament, or for any other Nonconformity to the Religion eftablifhed, or for, or by reafon of the Exercife of Religion, in any manner whatfoever, be immediately fufpended, and the farther Execution of the faid Penal Laws, and every of them, is hereby fufpended.* What! *All,* and *all Manner of Laws, in Matters Ecclefiaftical?* What, the Laws againft Fornication, Adultery, Inceft? for thefe are in Ecclefiaftical Matters. What! All Laws againft Blafphemy, Prophanenefs, open Derifion of Chriftian Religion? Yet thefe Crimes are punifhable by no other Laws here, than fuch as have been made in favour of the eftablifhed Religion. How fhall the Lord's Day be obferved? What fhall hinder covetous Men to plow and cart, and follow their feveral Trades upon that Day? fince all the Laws that fecure this obfervance, and outward countenance of refpect to the Chriftian Religion, are by this general Expreffion laid afide: Befides thefe Words, *For not coming to Church, or not receiving the Sacrament, or for any other Nonconformity to the Religion eftablifhed,* cannot in Confcience be read by us in our Churches, becaufe they may be a Temptation to young unguided People to neglect all manner of Religious Worfhip, and give them occafion of depriving themfelves of fuch opportunities of grace and falvation, as thefe Penal Laws did often oblige them to ufe. For being difcharged attendance on our Service, they are left at liberty to be of any Religion, or none at all: Nay, Chriftian Religion is by thefe general terms left at difcretion, as well as the Church of *England.* For Men may forfake us, to become Jews or Mahometans, or Pagan Idolaters, as well as to be Papifts or Diffenters, for any care taken in this Declaration to prevent it. And even of fuch as pretend to be Chriftians, there either are or may be fuch blafphemous Sects, fo difhonourable to our Common Lord and Mafter, as are incapable of all publick encouragement and allowance; for that would involve the Government in the Imputation of thofe Blafphemies, and the whole Nation in that Curfe and Vengeance of God, which fuch Provocations may extort. Wherefore it is not out of any unreafonable opinion of our felves, nor difaffection to Proteftant Diffenters, that we refufe to publifh this Indulgence, but out of a tender care of the Souls committed to us, efpecially thofe of the weaker fort, to whom we dare not propofe an Invitation to Popery, and much lefs any thing that may give countenance or encouragement to Irreligion. It is faid indeed, that we are not required to approve, but to read it: To this, Sir, you have very well anfwered, that Reading was Teaching it; or if it be not fo abfolutely in the nature of the thing, yet in common Conftruction, I am afraid it would have been underftood. But we do not ftand in need of this Excufe, for if there be any paffages in it, that are plain Temptations to Popery or Licentioufnefs; it cannot confift with our duty either to God or the Church, to read them before our People.

As for the difpenfing Power, and the Oaths and Tefts required to qualify Men for Offices Military and Civil, I muft leave them to the Confideration of thofe who are nearer concerned, and therefore reafonably prefum'd to underftand them better. Nor do I envy his Ma-

M m m m

jefty

jefty the ufe of his Popifh Subjects, tho' I do not know what fervice they may be capable of doing more than other Men. This Nation has for fome time made hard fhift to fubfift without much of their Aid, and againft the wills of feveral of them: But now they are become the only neceffary Men, and feem to want nothing but Number to fill all Places Military and Civil in the Kingdom; in the mean time, the Odioufnefs of their Perfons, and the Infolence of their Behaviour, with their way of menacing ftrange things, makes fome abatement of the merit of their fervice.

Laftly, The refpect which we have for his Majefty's Service, will not permit us to read the Appendix to the Declaration: where the flower of the Nobility and Gentry of this Kingdom are fomething hardly reflected on, as Perfons *that will not contribute to the Peace and Honour of the Nation*; becaufe they would not confent to the taking away the Laws againft Papifts, that they be put in a Condition to give us Laws. The Perfons here reflected on, we know to be the chief for Ability and Intereft, and Inclination to ferve the King, and therefore cannot do his Majefty that differvice as to be publifhers of their Difgrace, and make our felves the Inftruments of alienating from his Majefty the Affections of his beft Subjects. Nay, we find in our felves a ftrange difficulty to believe that this could come from his Majefty, who has experienced their faithfulnefs upon fo many and preffing Occafions. This could not well proceed from any but a Stranger to thofe Honourable Perfons and the Nation, and a greater Stranger to Shame and Good Manners; and what have we to do to publifh the Venom and Virulency of a Jefuit?

A Letter from a Gentleman in Ireland, *to his Friend in* London; *upon occafion of a Pamphlet, entituled,* A Vindication of the prefent Government of Ireland, *under his Excellency,* Richard Earl of Tyrconnel.

SIR,

AS foon as the Letter, entituled, *A Vindication of the prefent Government of* Ireland, *&c.* came to my hands, I fet upon Anfwering it with the fame expedition, and plainnefs of Style, as ufes to accompany naked Truth; which needs not the cloathing of fophiftical Arguments, or florid Expreffions, to recommend it to the unprejudiced part of Mankind: And indeed upon the very firft reading of every Paragraph of it, the Slightnefs of the Arguing, or the notorious Falfhood of the Matter of Fact, did fo evidently appear, that a Man of ordinary Capacity needs not put his Natural Talent on the Rack to refute them.

The very firft Pofition of the paper, viz. [That *Ireland* is in a better way of Thriving under the Government of a *Native* than an *Englifhman*;] (by which, I fuppofe, you mean one not barely fo by Birth, but by Inclination, Intereft, Education, Religion, *&c.*) is fo falfe, that it contradicts the Experience and Reafon of Mankind, and difgufts one fo much in the front of the Letter, that I was tempted to fling it away unread, judging it not worth the lofs of fo much time, if the reft fhould prove of the fame kind, (as indeed I found it upon perufal;) but having ventured through it, I looked upon my felf obliged to fay fomething by way of Anfwer, fince in the opinion of fome fort of Men, the not Anfwering (though even the moft trifling Pamphlet) is given out to be the inability of the party to reply to the weight of fuch arguments as are contained in it.

I will not infift upon the conftant practice of all the Predeceffors of our *Englifh* Kings, and their Counfellors ever fince the Conqueft of *Ireland*, who made it an eftablifhed Maxim, in relation to that Kingdom, That none but an *Englifhman* fhould be Chief Governour; infomuch that (till within thefe two Years) that practice gave occafion to the common erroneous opinion, That a Man born in *Ireland*, however otherwife qualified, was thereby incapacitated from being Lord Deputy: It is certain, That long before the Reformation, when Matters of Religion made no diftinction between the Natives of each Country, this was the fettled and unaltered Rule. Have we any reafon then to alter it, (now that Religion is put into the Scale, and become the additional weight, which never fails giving the advantage to the fide it efpoufes and adheres to) or rafhly to condemn the wife proceedings of the Anceftors of our Kings, and (contrary to the opinion of the World) judge our Author's *Irifh* Underftanding, better than all the *Englifh* ones that have been heretofore?

Our Author will certainly allow *Ireland* to be a conquered Country, and confequently, that the Conquerors have Right to eftablifh Laws with fuch Reftrictions and Limitations, as shall seem fitting and convenient towards the keeping *it in their* hands, and the Welfare of the Inhabitants ; which are of two sorts, the *British Planters*, and the *Natives*. I shall prove, that it has been, and still is, the Advantage of both these, that *Ireland* should be governed by an *Englishman*.

By the way, I would have it understood that I do not pretend to put these two Interests into any Ballance : I know the *British* Interests do so far outweigh the other, that it were a Wrong done it, to bring them into any competition ; more than two parts of three of the Lands of *Ireland*, being (by the several Rebellions of the *Irish*) in *British* Hands ; and for the Quality, Temper, Industry, &c. there is no Comparison : besides, that if one of two Parties is to be pleased (though by the Detriment of the other) 'tis but just that the Conquerors (who have Right to give Law) should be indulged ; how much more when it is consistent with the Welfare of the *Irish* themselves, if they understood their own Good ?

I am convinced, that whatever has been done in favour of the Natives, is pure Grace, and cannot be claimed as a just Debt, any otherwise than since it has been confirm'd by our Laws, and Acts of Parliament : He that reflects on 1641. will readily assent to this, which makes me admire at the Pertness of our Author, in Capitulating, as if we stood upon even Ground with them ; but 'tis plain he considers the Intreest but of one Party in that Kingdom, and though he names *Ireland* often, he means the native *Irish* Papists only. But I proceed ;

To prove that it is the Interest of the *British*, that *Ireland* should be governed by an *Englishman*, I need say no more, than that they all ardently desire it ; and People are the best Judge of their own Necessities : The common Maxim, *That Interest will not lye*, holds good here to some purpose. The ill Effects the contrary Method has had on their Persons and Estates, are but too visible. Whosoever had seen *Ireland* four Years ago, and would compare its Condition with what it is now, from the most thriving and flourishing *Country* of *Europe*, from a place of the briskest Trade and best-paid Rents in Christendom, it has fallen in one Year and a half's time to Ruin and Desolation : in the most frequented *Cities*, empty Houses, and melancholly *Countenances* ; in the best peopled *Counties*, unmanur'd neglected Fields, and Solitariness : Such a one, I say, might justly exclaim, *Heu ! Quantum mutatus ab illo*. But it would be impertinent to insist any longer on this. I must now prove, That it is the Advantage of the very Natives themselves (who have long been uneasy under the *English* Government, and often endeavoured to shake it off) to be ruled and guided by that Nation they hate so much. They are beholden to us for reducing them from a State of Barbarity, which left but little difference between them and the Brutes : We taught them to Live, to Eat, Drink, and Lodge like human *Creatures* ; (if they esteem' this any Advantage, and do not really prefer their Native Wildness to all the Benefits of Civil Society, Trade, Agriculture, Merchandizing, Learning, &c.) and if the Gentleness of the *English* Government could have had any influence upon them, they had no reason to be discontented at it : They had the equal Protection of the Laws in relation to their Estates and Persons : They bore but their just Proportion in all Taxes and Cesses : Their Lands improved in Value by the Means of their *British* Neighbours, and their Rents were much better paid than formerly whilst themselves were Masters of the whole Island : They had a large Connivance for the Exercise of their Religion, and were even allowed to hold a National Synod of their own *Clergy* in *Dublin*, *Anno* 1666. The poor Natives were not oppressed, when their severe Landlords, the *Irish* Gentry, by their *cruel Extortions*, *Cashierings*, *Duty* and *Days-Labour* ruined them ; who as soon as the *English* Manner prevailed among them (as they were introduced with Difficulty enough, there was need of the Authority of Acts of Parliament to constrain them for their own Good) lived plentifully, and in convenient Houses, had their share of the current Coin, and all other Necessaries, to the Life, and Well-being of Man, which now they want ; insomuch that several of them have been heard to curse my Lord *Tyrconnel* ; for to his Government they attribute their Misery, and acknowledge they never lived so well as under the Direction of the *English* Rulers, nor expected to do so again, till they were restored to the Helm. See the Force of Truth, which compels the Confession of it even from the Mouths of its Adversaries !

One may easily perceive by our Author's manner of arguing, where the Shoe pinches ; he is really concerned that *Ireland* is not altogether an independent Kingdom, and in the hands of its own Natives : he longs till the Day, when the *English* Yoak of Bondage shall be thrown off. Of this he gives us broad Hints, when he tells us, That [*England* is the only Nation in the World that impedes their Trade :] That [a Man of *English* Interest will never Club with them (as he phrases it) or project any thing which may tend to their Advantage, that will be the least bar or prejudice to the Trade of *England*.] Now, why a Man of *English* Interest (unless he will allow none of that Nation to be an able and just Minister to his Prince) should be partial, to ruin one Kingdom (to avoid the least inconveniency

niency of the other] contrary to the positive Commands of his King, I cannot imagine: For since [it is the Governour's Duty to rule by Law, and such Orders as he shall receive from his Majesty;] I know no Grounds for our Author's arraigning the whole *English* Nation, in saying, that no one Man among them, of what Perswasion soever, will be true, either to the Laws, or his Majesty's positive Orders, which shall seem repugnant to the smallest Conveniencies of *England*. This is a glory reserved only (as it seems) for his Hero, my Lord *Tyrconnel*.

The Imbargo upon the *West-India* Trade, and the Prohibition of *Irish* Cattel, are the two Instances given.

It were to be wished indeed, for the Good of that Kingdom, that both were taken off; and I question not but to see a Day wherein it shall seem proper to the King and an *English* Parliament, to repeal those Laws; a Day wherein they will consider us as their own Flesh and Blood, a Colony of their Kindred and Relations, and take care of our Advantages with as little Grudging and Repining (I am sure they have the same, and no stronger Reason) as *Cornwal* does at *Yorkshire*: There are Instances in several Islands in the *East-Indies*, as far-distant as *Ireland* is from *England*, that make up but one Kingdom, and govern'd by the same Laws; but the Wisdom of *England* will not judge it time fitting to do this, till we of *Ireland* be one Man's Children, either in Reality or Affection; we wish the latter, and have made many Steps and Advances towards it, if the Natives will not meet us half way, we cannot help it, let the Event lie at their own doors.

But after all, I see not how those Instances have any manner of relation to the *English* Chief Governours in *Ireland*; they were neither the Causers, Contrivers, nor Promoters of those Acts. The King and an *English* Parliament did it without consulting them; if they had, it is forty to one my Lord of *Ormond*, and the Council, whose Stake is so great in *Ireland*, would have hindred it as much as possible. Our Author's Argument proves indeed, That it is detrimental to *Ireland*, to be a subordinate Kingdom to *England*, (and 'tis plain, 'tis that he drives at, let him disguise it as much as he will) but the Conclusion he would prove, cannot at all be deduced from it; shortly I expect he will speak plainer, and in downright terms propose, That the two Kingdoms may be govern'd by different Kings; matters seem to grow ripe for such a disloyal Proposition.

If these Acts (and not the Subjection to an *English* King) were the Grievances, they would be so to the *British* there, as well as to the Natives: but though we wish them repealed, we do not repine. In the mean time, if the *British*, who are the most considerable Trading part of that Nation, and consequently feel the ill Effects of those Acts more sensibly, can be contented, why the Natives should not acquiesce in it (unless it be for the forementioned Reasons) I cannot see.

Our Author allows, that there are different ways of obeying the King: 'tis a Point gain'd for us, and proves there may be such a partiality exercised in executing his Majesty's Commands, as may destroy the very intent of them; and yet, taking the matter strictly [the King is obeyed] but a good Minister will consider his Master's Intentions, and not make use of a Word that may have a double Sense to the Ruin of a Kingdom, nor of a Latitude of Power, wherewith he is intrusted, to the Destruction of the most considerable Party in it: Far be it from us to think it was his Majesty's Intentions to depopulate a flourishing Country, to undo Multitudes of laborious thriving Families in it, to diminish and destroy his own Revenue, to put the Sword into Mad-men's Hands, who are sworn Enemies to the *British*: No! his Majesty, who is willing that Liberty of Trade as well as Conscience, should equally flourish in all parts of his Dominions, that recommends himself to his Subjects, by his Impartiality in distributing Offices of Trust; and from that Practice raises his greatest Argument to move his People to repeal the *Penal Laws*; never intended that some general Commands of his should be perverted to the destruction of that *People* his Intention is to protect. His Majesty (great as he is) cannot have two Consciences, one calculated for the Latitude of *England*, another for *Ireland*. We ought therefore to conclude (in respect to the King) that his Commands have been ill understood, and worse executed; and this may be done (as our Author confesses) and the King (undoubtedly obey'd;) but such an Obedience is no better than a Sacrifice of the best Subjects the King has in this Kingdom.

Our Author has given very good Reasons why the Natives may be well content with their present Governour, but I cannot forbear laughing at those he has found out to satisfy the poor *British* with my Lord *Tyrconnel's* most Excellent, Charitable, *English* Lady: His high-sounding Name *TALBOT*, in great Letters, a Name that no less frightens the poor *English* in *Ireland*, than it once did the *French*; a Name which because he is in possession of, I will not dispute his Title to, but I have been credibly informed, that he has no relation to that most Noble Family of *Shrewsbury* (tho' my Lord *Tyrconnel* presumes to bear the same Coat of Arms:) a Name, in short, which I hope in time *Vox & præterea nihil*.

A

A Second Reason is drawn from his [Education.] We have heard (and it has never yet been contradicted) that my Lord *Tyrconnel* from his Youth upwards, has constantly born Arms against the *British*: If our Author will assure us of the contrary, I am apt to believe his Excellency will give him no thanks, who lays the foundation of his Merit upon the Basis of his constant adherence to the *Irish* Party: What use of Consolation can be drawn from this Head by the *British*, is beyond my Skill to comprehend.

A third Reason is drawn from his Stake in *England*; the Author would do well to shew us, in what Country this lies, that we may know where to find Reprisals hereafter; for since he offers this for our Security, 'tis fit to enquire into the Title and Value of the Land, before we give so valuable a Consideration.

Thus this great heap of substantial Reasons, together with a large Panegyrick upon his Excellency's fair Face and good Shapes, [telling us by the bye, how he was not killed at *Drogheda*, because he run away,] is enough and more than enough to demonstrate, that [the *British* have not the least cause to be dejected, because they are sufficiently secure:] But I will agree with the Author in this, that he seems to have been reserved by Heaven against the most critical occasion, that should happen in this Age, as one of the Vials of God's Wrath to plague the People.

'Tis well known [Self-preservation is allowed by God and Man;] and since he tells us, we are [People of a contrary Interest,] he gives us right to provide for our selves, and our Families, as well as we may; 'tis like a generous Aggressor: First, he declares who are his Enemies, then gives them warning to put themselves in a posture of Defence. We are beholden to him for this hint; and, I hope, shall make a right use of it. 'Tis below me to take notice of the meanness of the Expression of [an honest Man's losing his Head in a Crowd,] and the Nonsense of the other, [The most Men bite at the Stone, &c.] Dogs indeed use to do so with us; but this is only to let the World know what Country-Man our Author is, and it may be 'tis the custom here for these Men to imitate those more rational Creatures.

Our Author seems sensible that many hard things have been done, which occasioned Clamours against the present Government; tho' I think our Grievances (how intolerable soever) have been born more silently than any People since the Creation: Since I do not remember on any Pamphlet has hitherto come out, to represent them; ours being of that nature, as stupify us, and take away the use of the Tongue and Pen: *Curæ leves loquuntur, ingentes stupent*: I say, he is not willing this Load of Calumny should rest on my Lord *Tyrconnel*, but casts it on his Majesty, imagining that the respect we bear, (and justly) to our King, ought to render us tongue-ty'd in relation to the Male-Administration of his Minister. But I have already shewn, how the King's Orders may be stretched, and perverted. The very best and most cautiously penn'd Laws have a double edge, and (if the Executive Power be lodged in ill hands) have the worst Effect, even to the Punishment of Well-doers, and the Encouragement of them that do ill; and I question not in the least, but this is our Case, and as little doubt that our Grievances would be redressed, did not one of his Majesty's most eminent Virtues interpose between us and his Grace, I mean his Constancy to his old Servants: and our Condition is so much the more deplorable, that his Majesty cannot be a Father of his Country without seeming to desert his Minister; but 'tis to be hoped, that at long run, the Groans of a distressed Nation will prevail over all private Considerations.

Whether the Employment his Majesty has given my Lord *Tyrconnel*, has not proved the occasion of the Augmentation of his Fortune, (as our Author insinuates it has not) shall neither prove the Subject of this Discourse, nor Object of our Envy. I shall only say, if the report be true, that my Lord owes all his Estate to the King's bounty, 'tis ungratefully done to rob his Majesty of the Honour and Thanks due to him, by denying it; much less is it our business to find fault with the Advancement of five *Relations*. In this point Authors differ, for some speak 55 at least: If there had not been the greatest Partiality in the World shewed, we should never have opened our Mouths, if in an Army of about 9000 *English* Officers and Soldiers, there be not 200 left, (in a Country where the *English* have so much cause to fear) and those turned out for the most part, without any cause assign'd, after the most ignominious disgraceful manner imaginable, stript naked in the Field, their Horses, Boots, Buff-coats, &c. taken from them, giving them Bills to receive so much Money in *Dublin*, as amounted to half the Value of their Equipage, and that not paid without Charge and Attendance; have they not reason to fear? If in a Country, whose Government was perfectly in the *English* Hands, so sudden an alteration was made, that both the Courts of Judicature, and Charters of their Corporations, were taken from them without any fault of theirs, have they not reason to complain, and be afraid? If those very Arms which are taken from them, be put into the hands of their sworn Enemies, and their just Debts paid after a new Method, by beating or killing the Creditors, when they demand their own; have they not reason to fear and desert the Kingdom?

If

If thefe and an hundred other things do not juftify the retreat of feveral of the *Britifh* into *England*, I know not what fhall be adjudged a fufficient Reafon. This, our Author would infinuate, is caufed by a fullen Combination ; as if the Gentry of a Nation could agree together, to do a thing fo contrary to their vifible Intereft, as defert their Houfes and E-ftates, to the lofs of one half of them, meerly out of Spite to the Government.

But becaufe our Author is fo good at his Narratives, and would induce the World to believe that there were but two Regiments disbanded [by his talking only of two] and in another place fpeaking of [fome Officers] that were Cafhiered : We fhall hereafter give you a faithful Account of the Proceedings in the Bufinefs of Disbanding ; and in the mean time affirm, that his whole Account of the Affair at *Mclingar* is moft unfincere. The *Englifh* Soldiers were given to underftand, that they were all to be turned out, and the only Grace his Excellency did them, was to declare before a long and tedious March, that fuch as had a mind or had Settlements in that Country, might better quit then, than hereafter. This is plainly fhewn by the turning out (afterwards) all thofe *Englifh*, who then actually continued in the Service ; they were glad that any would quit voluntarily, but thofe that did not, and after a publick Trial, were willing to ferve his Majefty, they foon after turned out. Thus the falfe glofs that our Author puts upon my Lord *Tyrconnel's* Speech is difcovered : And I affure the Reader, the Memoirs I have by me are from fuch unqueftionable Hands, and there are fo many hundred living Witneffes to the Truth of them, that our Author will not have the Impudence to deny what may be proved before his Majefty, if he require it. I fhall only take notice of the ill Application of our Author's Sea-Metaphor. Though in ftrefs of weather, the Owner is willing to make ufe of all Hands that may be helpful towards the faving of the Veffel, yet he takes care to call for none whofe practice it hath been to cut the Tacklings, and to fteer contrary to the Pilot's Directions ; he thinks fuch fafer by far fhut up under Hatches, than fet at liberty or employ'd to do mifchief. As for his fuppofition of 30000 Men to be fent out of *Ireland* into *Flanders*, I cannot tell what to make on't. Let them crack the Shell, that hope to find the Kernel in it. For my part I defpair ; though the readinefs of the *Englifh* Soldiers of *Ireland*, who at twenty four Hours warning came into *England* to ferve his Majefty in the time of *Monmouth's* Rebellion, ought to have been remembered to their advantage, and might ferve (to any unprejudiced Perfon) as a Patern of the Loyalty and good Inclinations of all the Proteftants in that Kingdom, if his Majefty had had occafion for them. Whether the Parliament will repeal the *Teft* for thofe feveral weighty Reafons our Author fays [are fitter for Contemplation than Difcourfe] though methinks it would be pleafant to fee a Houfe of Commons fit like the Brethren at a filent Meeting, is not my province to determine : As likewife, whether they will fo much confider that grand Reafon [the King will have it fo] (for his Confcience and theirs may differ) or what the Diffenters will do, I cannot tell. One thing I am fure of, there will be no fuch Stumbling-block in the way of the King's Defires, when they meet, as the prefent Condition of *Ireland* ; they will be apt (when his Majefty tells them they fhall have their equal fhares in employments, when they have repealed the Laws) to fay, Look at *Ireland*, fee what is done there, where the Spirit of Religion appears bare-faced ! and accordingly compute what may become of us when we have removed our own legal Fences, fince they now leap over thofe Hedges, what may we expect when they are quite taken away !

Poynings's Law is a great grievance to our Author, and here in one word, he difcovers that it is the dependance this Kingdom has on *England*, he quarrels at : 'Tis fit the Reader fhould underftand, that Law (enacted when *Poynings* was Lord Deputy) makes all the *Englifh* Acts of Parliament of force in *Ireland* ; we are therefore fo fond of that Law, and covet fo much to preferve our dependance on *England*, that all the Arguments our Author can bring, fhall not induce us to part with it.

I will not reflect in the leaft on the Courage of the *Irifh*, I know there are feveral brave Men among them, but they have had the Misfortune to fall under the Confideration of (as our Author foftens it, but the plain fenfe is, been beaten by) a warlike Nation ! And, I queftion not, unlefs they behave themfelves modeftly in their Profperity, they will again fall under the Confideration of the fame Nation : 'tis better we fhould live in peace and quietnefs, but the choice is in their hands ; and if they had rather come under our Confideration again than avoid it, let them look to the Confequence.

Another Advantage which may accrue to *Ireland*, by a Native, as a Governour, our Author reckons to be, *His perfonal knowledge of the* Tories, *and their Harbourers, and his being thereby better capacitated to fupprefs them*. Malicious People would be apt to infer from this Suggeftion, That his Excellency had occafion formerly to be familiarly acquainted with fuch fort of Cattle. I have heard indeed that one of our braveft *Englifh* Princes, *Henry* V. during the Extravagancies of his Youth, kept company with pub-

lick

lick Robbers, and often shar'd both in the Danger and Booty: but as soon as the Death of his Father made way for his Succession to the Crown, he made use of his former Acquaintance of their Persons and Haunts, to the extirpating and dissolving the greatest knot of Highway-men that ever troubled *England*. My Lord therefore (in imitation of this great Prince, no doubt) will make use of his Experience that way, to the same end: And I readily assent to the Author, that no *English* Governour can be so fit to clear that Kingdom of Tories, and that for the same Reason he gives us.

There are two other Advantages remaining; one is, his Excellency's having already made different Parties in that Kingdom, the Objects of his Love and Hatred, let the Offences of the one or the Merits of the other be ever so conspicuous: Whether the *British* can draw any comfort from his Excellency's knowledge of them this way, is fit to be debated. The other is, the probability of his getting the Statute for benefit of Clergy, in favour of Cow-stealers and House-robbers repealed; and where, by the way, there is a severe Rebuke given to our *English* Priests, for their ill placed Mercy to *Irish* Offenders: A Fault I hope they will be no more guilty of.

Whether these Advantages be so considerable as to move his Majesty to continue a Man (for other more weighty Reasons) absolutely destructive to this Kingdom, or whether some of them might not be performed by an *English* Governour, his Majesty is the only Judge: Only this I am sure of, the King (if he were under any Obligations to his Minister) has fully discharged them all, and has shew'd himself to be the best of Masters, in giving so great and honourable an Employment to his Creature, and continuing him in it so long, notwithstanding the Decrease of his own Revenue, and the other visible bad effects of his Management; the Impoverishment of that Kingdom, amounting to at least two Millions of Money: And his Majesty may be now at liberty (without the least imputation of Breach of Promise to his Servant) to restore us to our former flourishing Condition, by sending some *English* Noblemen among us, whose contrary Methods will, no doubt, produce different Effects.

To conclude; Methinks the comparison between his Majesty and *Philip* of *Macedon*, when he was drunk, is a little too familiar, not to say unmannerly; and that between *Antipater* and my Lord *Tyrconnel*, is as great a Complement to the latter.

But provided my Lord be commended, which was our Author's chief Design, he cares not though the comparison does not hold good in all points; 'tis enough that we know we are governed by such a Prince that neither practises such Debauches himself, nor allows of them in his Servants. But we are not beholden to the Author for the knowledge of this; should a Foreigner read his Pamphlet, or get it interpreted to him, he would be apt (and with reason) to conclude, that his Majesty as much resembled *Philip* in a Debauch, as my Lord *Tyrconnel* doth sober *Antipater*.

I have now done with all that seems of any weight in our Author's Pamphlet; and can see nothing in his Postscript that deserves an Answer. All that I will say, is, That his *Recipes* bear no proportion to our desperate Disease, and he will prove not to be a Physician, but a pretending Quack, who by ill-apply'd Medicines will leave us in a worse Condition than he found us.

I shall conclude with telling you, That your Letter, which enclosed the Pamphlet, whereof I have here given you my thoughts, was more than a Fortnight on the way, or else you had received this sooner. I am,

SIR,

Your most humble

Dublin, 1688.

Servant.

A

A PLAIN
ACCOUNT
OF THE
PERSECUTION
Laid to the CHARGE of the
Church of England.

THE Defire of Liberty to ferve God in that way and manner which Men judge to be moſt acceptable to him, is ſo Natural and Reaſonable, that they cannot but be extreamly provoked againſt thoſe who would force them to ſerve him in any other. But the conceit withal, which moſt Men have, that their Way of ſerving God is the only acceptable Way ; naturally inclines them, when they have Power, to uſe all Means to conſtrain all others to ſerve him in that way only. So that Liberty is not more deſired by all, at one time, than it is denied by the very ſame Perſons at another. Put them into different Conditions, and they are not of the ſame mind : but have different Inclinations, in one State, from what they have in another ; as will be apparent by a ſhort View of what hath paſſed in theſe Churches and Kingdoms, within our Memory.

II. Before the late Civil Wars, there were very grievous complaints made of the Biſhops ; that they preſſed the Ceremonies ſo ſtrictly, as to inflict heavy Cenſures upon thoſe called *Puritans*, who could not in Conſcience conform to them. Now no ſooner had thoſe very Perſons who thus complained, got their Liberty to do as they pleaſed, but they took it quite away from the other : and ſequeſter'd all thoſe who would not enter into their *Holy League and Covenant* ; for the reforming all things according to the Model which they propounded. Nay, they were not willing to bear with five Diſſenting Brethren among themſelves, who could not conform to *Presbyterial* Government. And when theſe Diſſenting Brethren, commonly known by the Name of *Independents*, had got a Party ſtrong enough, which carried all before them, they would not allow the uſe of the *Common-Prayer* in any Pariſh ; no not to the *King* himſelf in his own Chapel : nor grant to one of the old Clergy ſo much liberty as to teach a School, *&c.* Which things I do not mention (God knows) to reproach thoſe who were guilty of them, but only to put them in mind of their own Failings : that they may be humbled for them, and not inſult over the Church of *England*, nor ſeverely upbraid them with that, which, when time was, they acted with a higher hand themſelves. If I ſhould report all that the *Presbyterians* did here, and in *Scotland*, and all that the *Independents* did here and in *New-England* ; it would not be thought that I exceed the Truth, when I ſay they have been more guilty of this Fault, than thoſe whom they now charge with it. Which doth not excuſe the Church of *England*, it muſt be confeſſed, but doth in ſome meaſure mitigate her Fault. For the Conformable Clergy having met with ſuch very hard Uſage in that diſmal Time, wherein many of them were oppreſſed above meaſure ; no wonder if the Smart of it, then freſh in their Minds, ſomething imbittered their Spirits ; when God was pleaſed, by a wonderful Revolution, to put them into Power again.

III. Then a ſtricter *Act of Uniformity* was made, and ſeveral Laws purſuant to it, for the enforcing that Uniformity, by ſevere Penalties. But let it be remembred, that none were by thoſe Laws conſtrain'd to come to Church, but had liberty left them to ſerve God at home (and ſome Company with them) in their own Way. And let it be farther remembred, that the Reaſon why they were denied their Liberty of meeting in great Aſſemblies, was becauſe ſuch Aſſemblies were repreſented, as *greatly endangering the publick Peace and Safety* : as the Words are in the very firſt Act of this nature againſt *Quakers*, in the Year 1662. Let any one read the *Oxford Act*, (as it is commonly called) made in the Year 1665. and that at *Weſtminſter*, in the Year 1670. and he will find them intended againſt *Seditious Conventicles* ; that is, they who made them, were perſwaded by the *Jeſuit Intereſt* at firſt to look upon ſuch Meetings as

Nurſeries

Nurseries of Sedition, where bad *Principles* were infused into Mens Minds, destructive to the *Civil Government.* If it had not been for this, it doth not appear that the Contrivers of these Laws were inclined to such *Severities* as were thereby enacted ; but the *Nonconformists* might have enjoyed a larger Liberty in Religion. It was not Religion alone which was considered, and pretended, but the *publick Peace and Settlement,* with respect to which they were tied up so straitly in the exercise of their *Religion.* Which, to deal clearly, I do not believe would have taught *Rebellion* ; but this was constantly insinuated by the *Court-Agents* ; and it is no wonder if the *Parliament,* who remembred how the Ministers of that Persuasion (though indeed from the then Appearance of *Popery*) had been the principal Encouragers of that *Defensive War* against the King, were easily made to believe that they still retained the same *Principles,* and would propagate them, if they were suffered among the People. Certain it is also, that the Court made it their Care to have those Acts passed, though at the same time they hindred their Execution ; that they might keep up both Parties in the height of their Animosities ; and especially that they might make the Church of *England* be both hated and despised by the *Dissenters.*

IV. Thus things continued for some time, till wise Men began to see into the Secret ; and think of *Reconciliation.* But it was always hindred by the *Court,* who never thought of giving *Liberty* by a *Law,* but only by the *Prerogative,* which could as easily take it away. There was a time, for instance, when a *Comprehension,* &c. was projected by several great Men, both in *Church* and *State* ; for the taking as many as possible into Union with us ; and providing Ease for the rest. Which so nettled the late King, that meeting with the then Arch-bishop of *Canterbury,* he said to him (as I perfectly remember) *What, my Lord, you are for a Comprehension?* To which he making such a Reply as signified, he heard some were about it : *No,* said the King, *I will keep the Church of* England *pure and unmixed* ; that is, never suffer a Reconciliation with the *Dissenters.* And when the *Lords and Commons* also had not many years ago passed a Bill for the repealing of the most heavy of all the *Penal Laws* against *Dissenters,* viz. the Statute of 35 *Eliz.* 1. (which by the Parliament is made against the *wicked and dangerous Practices of Seditious Sectaries and disloyal Persons*) his late Majesty so dealt with the Clerk of the Parliament, that it was shuffled away, and could not be found ; when it was to have been presented to him, among other Bills for his Royal Consent unto it. A notable Token of the Abhorrence the Court then had of all *Penal Laws,* and of their great Kindness to *Dissenters* !

V. Who may remember, if they please, that as once there was a time, when the Court turned out, or chid those *Justices,* who were forward in the Execution of the Laws against *Nonconformists,* because they were then in so low a Condition, that the Court was afraid the Church of *England* might indeed be established in its Uniformity : So when the *Nonconformists* were by some Liberty grown stronger, and set themselves against the Court-Interest, in the Election of *Sheriffs,* and such like things ; then all those *Justices* were turned out who hung back, and would not execute the Laws against them ; and *Justices* pickt out for the purpose, who would do it severely. Nay, the Clergy were called upon, and had Orders sent them, to return the Names of all *Nonconformists* in their several Parishes ; that they might be proceeded against in the *Courts Ecclesiastical.* And here I cannot forget the Order made by the *Middlesex Justices,* at the Sessions at *Hicks's Hall, Jan.* 13. 1681. where they urge the Execution of the Act of 22 *C.* 2. against *Conventicles,* because in *all probability they will destroy both Church and State.* This was the reason which moved them to call upon *Constables,* and all other *Officers* to do their Duty in this matter: Nay, to call upon the B. of *London* himself, that *he would use his utmost endeavours, within his Jurisdiction, that all such Persons may be excommunicated.* This was a bold stroke, proceeding from an unusual degree of Zeal ; which plainly enough signifies, that the *Bishops* were not so forward as the *Justices* in the prosecuting of *Dissenters.* Who may do well to remember that the *House of Commons,* a little before this, had been so kind to them, that those *Justices* would not have dared to have been so severe as they were at *Hicks's Hall,* if they had not been set on by Directions from *White-Hall.* For in their *Order* they press the Execution of the Statute 1 *Eliz.* and 3 *Jac.* 1. for levying *Twelve-Pence a Sunday* upon all those that do not come to Church: Whereas the *House of Commons, Nov.* 6. 1680. had *Resolved,* Nemine Contradicente, *That it is the Opinion of this House, That the Acts of Parliament made in the Reign of Queen* Elizabeth, *and King* James, *against Popish Recusants, ought not to be extended against Protestant Dissenters.*

VI. Who should not forget how backward the Clergy of *London* especially, were to comply with this Design, of reviving the Execution of the Laws against them ; ' What Courses they took to save them from this Danger ! and what Hatred they incurred for being so kind to them ! Which in truth was Kindness to themselves ; for now they saw plainly that Nothing was intended but the Destruction of us both, by setting us, in our turns, one against the other. Many indeed were possessed with the old Opinion, that the Dissenters aimed at the Overthrow of the Government both in Church and State : which made them the more readily join with those who were employed to suppress them, by turning the Edge of the Laws upon them. But both these were most industriously promoted by

O o o o   the

'the Court; who laboured might and main to have this believed, that they who were
'called *Whigs*, intended the Ruin of the Church, and of the Monarchy too, and there-
'fore none had the Court-favour, but they alone who were for the ruining of them; all
'others were frown'd upon, and branded with the Name of *Trimmers*; who they adventu-
'red, at laft, to fay were worfe than *Whigs*, meerly becaufe they feeing through the Defign,
'defired thofe ugly Names of *Whig* and *Tory* might be laid afide; and perfuaded all to
'*Moderation, Love, Unity,* and *Peace.* If any Man had thefe dangerous Words in his
'Mouth, he had a mark fet upon him, and was lookt upon as an Enemy, as foon as he
'difcovered any Defires of Reconciliation. *No Peace with Diffenters* was then as much in
'fome Mens mouths, as *no Peace with Rome* had been in others. They were all voted
'to Deftruction; and it was an unpardonable Crime fo much as to mention an Accom-
'modation.

Such things as thefe ought not to be forgotten.

VII. But if they lift not to call them to mind, (though they be of frefh Memory) yet
let them at leaft confider what they have had at their Tongues end, ever fince they knew
any thing: That *the Church of* Rome *is a perfecuting Church, and the Mother of Perfecution.* Will they then be deluded by the prefent *Sham* of *Liberty of Confcience*; which they
of that Church pretend to give? It is not in their Power, no more than in their Spirit:
They neither will nor can give *Liberty of Confcience*, but with a defign to take all Liberty from us. That Church muft be obeyed; and there is no middle Choice among them,
between *Turn or Burn, Conform or be Undone.* What Liberty do they give in any Country
where their Power is eftablifhed? What Liberty can they give, who have determined that
Hereticks ought to be rooted out? Look into *France* (with which we have had the ftricteft
Alliance and Friendfhip a long time) and behold, how at this Moment they compel thofe
to go to Mafs, who they know abhor it as an abominable Idolatry. Such a violent Spirit now
acts them, that they ftick not to prophane their own moft *holy Mysteries,* that they may have
the Face of an *Univerfal Conformity* without the leaft *Liberty.* For the *New Converts,* as
they are called, poor Wretches! are known to be mere *outward Compliers,* in their Hearts
abominating that which they are forced externally to worfhip. They declare as much
by efcaping from this Tyranny over their Confciences, and bewailing their finful Compliance, whenfoever they have an Opportunity. And they that cannot efcape, frequently
proteft they have been conftrained to adore that, which they believe ought not to be adored. And when they come to die, refufe to receive the *Romifh Sacrament,* and thereupon
are dragg'd, when dead, along the Streets, and thrown like dead Dogs upon the Dunghils.
Unto what a height of Rage are the Spirits of the *Romifh Clergy* inflamed; that it
perfectly blinds their Eyes, and will not let them fee how they expofe the moft facred
thing in all their *Religion* (the *Holy Sacrament,* which they believe to be *Jefus Chrift* himfelf)
to be received by thofe who they know have no Reverence at all for it, but utterly abhor
it? For they force them by all manner of Violence, to adore the *Hoft* againft their Will,
and then to eat what they have adored; though they have the greateft reafon to believe,
that thofe poor Creatures do not adore it. That is, the Church of *Rome* will have her
Myfteries adored by all, though it be by Hypocrites. None fhall be excufed, but whether
they believe or not believe, they fhall be compelled to do as that Church doth. Nothing
fhall hinder it; for the Hatred and Fury wherewith they are now tranfported, is fo exceeding great, that it makes them (as I have faid) offer Violence even to their own Religion, rather than fuffer any body not to conform to it.

VIII. And affure your felves, they are very defirous to extend this Violence beyond the
bounds of *France.* They would fain fee *England* alfo in the fame Condition, the Bifhop of
Valence and *Die* hath told as much, in the Speech which he made to the *French King,* in
the Name of the Clergy of *France,* to congratulate his glorious Atchievements, in rooting out the Herefy of *Calvin.* In which he hath a moft memorable Paffage, for which
we are beholden to him, becaufe it informs us that they are not fatisfied with what their
King hath done there; but would have him think there is a further Glory referved for
him, of lending his help to make us fuch good Catholicks, as he hath made in *France.* This
is the bleffed Work they would be at, and if any among us be ftill fo blind as not to fee
it, we muft look upon it as the juft Judgment of God upon them for fome other Sins which
they have committed. They are deliver'd up to a reprobate Mind, which cannot difcern the
moft evident things. They declare to all the World, that they have been above fifty Years
crying out againft, they know not what. For they know not what Popery is (of which
they have feemed to be horribly afraid) if they believe that they of that Religion, either
can or will give any Liberty, when they have Power to eftablifh their Tyranny. It is no
better; St. *John* himfelf hath defcribed that Church under the Name of *Babylon,* that
cruel City, and of a BEAST, which, like a Bear, tramples all under its Feet; and of another *Beaft, which caufes as many as will not worfhip the Image of the Beaft, to be killed; and
that no man may buy or fell, fave fuch as have had his Mark;* i. e. are of his Religion,
Rev. 13. 1, 15, 16. This Character they will make good to the very end of their
Reign, as they have fulfilled it from the beginning. They cannot alter their Nature no
more

more than the *Ethiopian change his Skin, or the Leopard his Spots.* It ever was, since the rising of the *Beast*, and it ever will be till its fall, a bloody Church, which can bear no Contradiction to her Doctrine and Orders, but will endeavour to root out all those that oppose her from the Face of the Earth. Witness the barbarous *Crusado's* against the poor *Albigenses* in *France*: in one of which alone, *Bellarmine* himself saith, and not without Triumph, there were killed no less than one hundred thousand. Witness the horrible Butcheries committed in *France*, in *England*, and in the *Low-Countries* in the Age before us ; and in *Poland*, the Valleys of *Piedmont*, and in *Ireland* in this Age, upon those who had no other Fault but this, that they made the Holy Scriptures, not the *Roman Church*, the Rule of their Faith.

IX. ' But if you be ignorant of what hath been done and doing abroad, yet I hope you
' observe what they do here at home. What do you think of the *Declaration* which was
' very lately imposed to be read in all our Churches ? Which when several Bishops and
' their Clergy most humbly represented, they could not in Conscience publish to the Peo-
' ple in time of Divine Service ; this would not excuse them, their Petition was received
' with Indignation, and looked upon as a Libel ; the Bishops were prosecuted for it, and
' Inquiry is now ordered to be made after those who did not read it (as well as those that
' did) that they may be punished by the High Commissioners. Call you this Liberty of
' Conscience ? Or do you imagine you shall never have any thing imposed upon you to be
' read in your Congregations, which you cannot comply withal ? Consider, I beseech
' you, what will become of you when that time shall come ? What's the meaning of this,
' that ever they are look'd upon as Offenders, for following their Conscience, whose Ser-
' vices have been acknowledged to be so great, that they should never be forgotten ? It ought
' to teach Dissenters what they are to expect hereafter, when they have served them so
' far (by taking off the *Tests* and *Penal Laws*) as to enable them with safety to remember
' all their former pretended Transgressions. Let them assure themselves, the *Services* of
' the Church of *England* are not now more certainly forgotten than the *Sins* of *Dissenters*
' will hereafter, when they have got Power to punish them, be most certainly remember'd.
' Be not drawn in then by *deceitful Words*, to help forward your own Destruction. If you
' will not be assistant to it, they cannot do it alone ; and it will be very strange if you be
' persuaded to lend them your help, when the Deceit is so apparent. For what are all
' the present Pleas for *Liberty*, but so many infamous Libels upon the *Roman* Church,
' which denies all Men this Liberty ? While they declaim so loudly against *Persecution*,
' they most notoriously reproach *Popery*, which subsists by nothing but *Deceit* and *Cruel-*
' *ty*. And who can think that they would suffer their Church to be so exposed and reviled
' as it is by such Discourses, but with a Design to cheat heedless People into its Obedience ?
' For this end they can hear it proved, nay, prove it themselves to be an *Antichristian*
' *Church*, when they prove it is against *Christianity*, nay, against the Law of *Nature* and
' *Common Reason*, to trouble any body for his Opinion in Religion.

' X. Once more then, I beseech you, be not deceived by good Words, if you love your
' Liberty and your Life. Call to mind how our poor Brethren in *France* were lately de-
' luded by the repeated Protestations which their King made, he would observe the Edict
' of *Nantes* (which was the Foundation of their Liberty) even then, when he was about
' to overthrow it ; and by many Assurances which were given them by those who came to
' torment them, that the King *intended to reform the Church of* France, *as soon as he had*
' *united his Subjects*. What he had done already against the Court of *Rome*, they told them,
' was an Instance of it ; and they should shortly see other Matters. Such ensnaring
' Words they heard there daily from the Mouths of their armed Prosecutors, who were
' ready to fall upon them, or had begun to oppress them : And therefore they would be
' arrant Fools here, if they did not give good Words when they have no power to hurt
' us. But we shall be far greater Fools, if we believe they will keep their Word when
' they have got that Power; the greatest of all Fools if we give them that Power. They
' have no other way but this, to wheedle us out of our *Laws* and *Liberties*. Do but sur-
' render the one, I mean our Laws, and they will soon take away the other, our beloved
' *Liberties*. Be not tempted to make such a dangerous Experiment, but let the *Laws*
' stand as they are, because they are against them (as appears by their earnest Endeavours
' to repeal them) and be not used as Tools to take them away, because they have been
' grievous to you. They never can be so again. For can they, who now court you,
' have the face to turn them again upon you, after they have made all this Noise for Li-
' berty ? And the Church of *England*, you may be assured, will not any more trouble
' you : But when a Protestant Prince shall come, will join in the Healing of all our Breach-
' es, by removing of all things out of the way, which have long hindred that blessed
' Work. They cannot meet together in a Body to give you this Assurance, (how should
' they, without the King's Authority so to do?) but every particular Person that I have
' discoursed withal, which are not a few (and you yourselves would do well to ask them,
' when you meet them) profess that they see an absolute Necessity of making an end of
' these differences that have almost undone us : and will no longer contend to bring all

Men

'Men to one *Uniformity* ; but promote an *Uniform Liberty*. Do not imagine I intend to
'give meer *Words* : I mean honestly ; such a regular *Liberty*, as will be the Beauty and
'Honour, not the Blot and Discredit of our Religion. To such a *Temper* the Archbishop
'of *Canterbury*, with several other Bishops of his Province, and their Clergy, have openly
'declared they are willing to come. And the Bishops and Clergy of the Church of *Eng-
'land* have never been known to act deceitfully. Our Religion will not at any time allow
'them to *equivocate*, nor to give good Words without a Meaning, much less at such a
'time as this, when our Religion is in great danger, and we have nothing to trust unto
'but God's Protection of sincere Persons. *Let Integrity and Uprightness preserve us*, is their
'constant Prayer. They can hope for no Help from Heaven, if they should prevaricate
'with Men. God they know would desert them, if they should go about to delude their
'Brethren. And they are not so void of common Sense, as to adventure to incur his
'most high Displeasure, when they have nothing to rely upon but his Favour.
'In short, *Trust* to those who own you for their *Brethren*, as you do them ; for though
'they have been angry Brethren, yet there is hope of Reconciliation between such near Re-
'lations. But put no Confidence in those, who not only utterly disown any such Relation
'to you, but have ever treated you with an implacable Hatred, as their most mortal *Ene-
'mies*, unto whom it is impossible they should be reconciled.
Prov. 12. 19, 20. *The Lips of Truth shall be established for ever : but a lying Tongue
is but for a moment.*
Lying Lips are an Abomination to the Lord ; but they that deal truly are his Delight.

Abby *and other* Church-Lands, *not yet assured to such Possessors as are* Roman Catholicks. *Dedicated to the Nobility and Gentry of that Religion.*

SInce it is univerasally agreed on, that so great a matter as the total Alienation of all
the *Abby-Lands*, &c. in *England*, can never be made legal and valid ; and such as
will satisfy the reasonable Doubts and Scruples of a religious and conscientious Person, except it be confirm'd by the Supreme Authority in this Church ; 'tis evident that the Protestants, who assert the Church of *England* to be *Autokephalos*, and such as allows of no Foreign Jurisdiction or Appeals, having had these Lands confirmed to them by the King, as
Head of the Church, the Convocation, as the Church-Representative, and by the King
and Parliament as the Supreme Legislative Power in this Realm, have these Alienations
made as valid to them as any Power on Earth can make them : but the Members of the
Church of *Rome*, who maintain a Foreign and Supreme Juridiction, either in a General
Council, or in the Bishop of *Rome*, or both together, cannot have these Alienations confirm'd to them, without the Consent of one or both of these Superior Jurisdictions. If therefore I shall make it appear, that these Alienations in *England* were never confirm'd by either, I do not see how any *Roman Catholick* in *England* can, without Sacrilege, retain
them and his Religion together.
As to the first of these, since there hath been no Council from the first Alienation of
Abby-Lands in *England* to this day, that pretends to be General, but that of *Trent* ; we
need only look into that for the Satisfaction of such *Roman Catholicks* as esteem a General
Council above the Bishop of *Rome*. And I am sure that that Council is so far from confirming these *Abby-Lands* to the present Possessors, that it expresly denounceth them accur-
sed that detain them. *Sess. 22. Decret. de Ref. Cap. 11. Si quem*, &c. 'If Covetousness, the
'Root of all Evil, shall so far possess any Person whatsoever, whether of the Clergy or
'Laity, though he be an Emperor or a King, as that by Force, Fear or Fraud, or any
'Art or Colour whatsoever, he presume to convert to his own Use, and usurp the Jurisdicti-
'on, Goods, Estates, Fruits, Profits or Emoluments whatever, of any Church, or any
'Benefice, Secular or Regular, Hospital or Religious House, or shall hinder that the Pro-
'fits of the said Houses be not received by those to whom they do of right belong, let him
'lie under an *Anathema* till the said Jurisdiction, Goods, Estates, Rents and Profits, which he
'hath possessed and invaded, or which have come to him any manner of way, be restored
'to the Church ; and after that have Absolution from the *Bishop* of *Rome*.' So great a
Terror did this strike into the *English* Papists that were Possessors of Church-Lands, against
whom this *Anathema* seems particularly directed, that many of the zealous Papists began
to think of Restitution, and Sir *William Peters*, notwithstanding his private *Bull* of Absolution from Pope *Julius* the Fourth, was so much startled at it, that the very next Year he
endowed eight new Fellowships in *Exeter-College* in *Oxford*. Again, the same Council,
'*Sess. 25. Decret. de Ref. c. 20. Cupiens Sancta Synodus*, &c. Decreeth and commandeth,
'that all the Holy Canons, and General Councils, and Apostolick Sanctions in favour of
'Ecclesiastical Persons, and the Liberties of the Church, and against those that violate
'them, be exactly observed by every one ; and doth farther admonish the Emperor,
'Kings, Princes, and all Persons of what Estate soever, that they would observe the

Rights

' Rights of the Church, as the Commands of God, and defend them by their particular
' Patronage, nor suffer them to be invaded by any Lords or Gentlemen whatsoever ; but
' severely punish all those who hinder the Liberties, Immunities and Jurisdictions of the
' Church ; and that they would imitate those excellent Princes, who by their Authority
' and Bounty encreased the Revenues of the Church ; so far were they from suffering them
' to be invaded, and in this let every one sedulously perform his part, &c.' And now after
so full and express Declaration of the Council of *Trent*, I do not see how any of those *Roman
Catholicks*, who esteem a general Council to be the Supreme Authority in the Church,
and receive the *Trent* Council as such, can any way excuse themselves in point of Conscience
from those heavy Curses that are there denounc'd against all those that detain Church-
Lands, especially since the Papists themselves vehemently accuse King *Henry* the eighth
for sacrilegiously robbing of Religious Houses, and seizing of their Lands ; a great part
of which Lands are to this very day possess'd by Papists. Now though there may be
some Plea for the Pope's Authority, in the interim of a general Council, and in such things
wherein they have made no determination ; yet in this matter there is no colour for any
pretences, since the Council of *Trent* was actually assembled within few years after these
Alienations, and expresly condemned the Possessors of *Abby-Lands*, and after all this was
confirm'd and ratified by the Pope himself in his *Bulla super conf. gen. Concil. Trid. A. D.*
1564. And tho' we have here the Judgment of the infallible See, as to this matter, in the
Confirmation of the *Trent Council* ; yet because there be some that magnify the Pope's
extravagant and unlimited power over the Church, and pretend that he confirm'd the *Abby-
Lands* in *England* to the Lay-possessors of them, I shall shew, Secondly, That the Pope
neither hath, nor pretends to any such Power, nor did ever make use of it in this matter
under debate. Only I shall premise, that whereas some part of the Canon-Law seems to allow of such particular Alienations as are made by the Clerks and Members of the Church,
with the consent of the Bishop, yet such free consent was never obtained in *England* ; and
as to what was done by force, fraud, and violence, is of so little moment as to giving a
legal Title, that even the Alienations that were made by *Charles Martell*, who is among the
Papists themselves as infamous for Sacrilege as King *Henry* the Eighth, yet even his Acts
are said to be done by a Council of Bishops, as is acknowledg'd by Dr. *Johnston* in his assurance of *Abby-Lands*, p. 27. I shall proceed to shew, First, That the Pope hath no such
power as to confirm these Alienations, and this is expresly determined by the infallible
Pope *Damasus* in the Canon-Law, *Caus.* 12. 9. 2. c. 20. *The Pope cannot alienate Lands
belonging to the Church in any manner, or for any necessity whatsoever, both the buyer and
the seller lie under an* Anathema *till they be restored* ; so that any Church-man may oppose any
such Alienations, and again require the Lands and Profits so alienated. So that here we have
a full and express Determination of the infallible See. And tho' in answer to this it is
urged by Dr. *Johnston*, that this Canon is with small difference publish'd by *Binius* in the
Councils, and so as to confine it to the suburbicary Diocess of *Rome* ; yet that this Answer
is wholly trivial, will appear,

First, Because if the Bishop of *Rome* hath no Authority to confirm such Alienations in
his own peculiar Diocess where he hath most power, much less can he do it in the Provinces where his Power is less.

Secondly, That in all Ecclesiastical Courts of the Church of *Rome*, it is not *Binius*'s E-
dition of the Councils, but *Gratian*'s Collection of Canons, that is of Authority, in which
Book these words are as here quoted.

Thirdly, Since this Book of the Pope's Decree hath been frequently reprinted by the
Authority and Command of several Popes, and constantly used in their Courts ; this is
not to be looked upon as a Decree of Pope *Damasus* only, but of all the succeeding
Popes, and in the opinion of *F. Ellis*, (*Sermon before the King, Decem.* 5. 1686. *p.* 21.)
what is inserted in the Canon Law is become the whole Judgment of the whole Church.

Fourthly, It's absolutely forbid by Pope *Gregory* the Thirteenth, in his Bull prefixed
before the Canon-Law (*A. D.* 1580.) for any one to *add, or invert any thing in that Book*.

So that according to this express Determination in the Pope's own Law, the Bishops of
Rome have no power to confirm any such Alienations as have been made in *England* ; and
agreeable to all this, Pope *Julius* the Fourth (the very person that is pretended to have confirm'd these Alienations) declar'd to our *English* Ambassadors, that were sent upon that Errand, *That if he had Power to grant it, he would do it most readily, but his Authority was not
so large. F. Paul's H.* of Council of *Trent*, *Lond. A. D.* 1629. And therefore all Confirmations from the Bishop of *Rome*, are already prejudg'd to be invalid, and of no force at all.

Secondly, No Bishop of *Rome* did ever confirm them. The Breve of Pope *Julius* the
Third, which gave Cardinal *Pool* the largest Powers towards the effecting this, had this ex-
press limitation, *Salvo tamen in his (quibus propter rerum magnitudinem & gravitatem, hæc
Sancta sedes merito tibi videtur consulenda) nostro & præfatæ sedis beneplacito & confirmatione,*

P p p p   i. e.

i. e. ' Saving to us in these matters (in which by reason of their weight and greatness, this
' Holy See may justly seem to you, that of right it ought to be consulted) the good pleasure and confirmation of us and of the Holy See, which is the true *English* to that *Latin* ; and
that this whole Kingdom did then so understand these words, is evident from the Ambassadors that were sent to *Rome* the next Spring, *viz.* Viscount *Montacute,* Bishop of *Ely,*
and Sir *Edward Carn,* (these being one to represent every state of the Kingdom) to obtain of him a Confirmation of all those Graces which Cardinal *Pool* had granted. *Burnet's
H. Ref. p. 2. f. 300.* So that in the esteem of the whole Nation, what the Cardinal had
done, was not valid without the Confirmation of the Pope himself. Now this Pope *Julius,*
and the next *Marcellus,* both died before there is any Pretence of any Confirmation from
Rome ; but this was at length done by Pope *Paul* the Fourth, is pretended, and for proof
of it three things are alledged, First, The Journals of the House of Commons, where are
these words, *After which was read a Bill from the Pope's Holiness, confirming the doing of
my Lord Cardinal touching the assurance of Abby-Lands, &c.* Secondly, a Bull of the same
Pope to Sir *Will. Peters.* Thirdly, The Decrees of Cardinal *Pool,* and his Life by *Dudithius* : To all which I answer,

First, That it's confess'd on all hands, that there is no such Bull or Confirmation by
Pope *Paul* the Fourth, to be any where found in the whole World, nor any Copy or
Transcript of it, not in all the *Bullaria,* nor our own Rolls and Records, tho' it be a
matter of so great moment to the Roman Catholicks of *England* ; and what cannot be produced, may easily be denied. Nor can it be imagined that a Journal of Lay-Persons that
were parties concerned, or a private Bull to Sir *W. Peters,* or some hints in the Decrees and
Life of the Cardinal, will be of any moment in a Court at *Rome,* whensoever a matter of that
vast consequence, as all the *Abby-Lands* in *England,* shall come to be disputed ; especially
if it be observed, that this very Journal of the House of Commons is no publick Record,
but *hath past through private hands, hath been corrupted and defaced, and that in Passages of
the greatest moment,* as are the words of *W. Hakewell* Esq; in his Observation upon them
70 Years since, printed *A. D.* 1641. And whereas the Journals of the House of Lords
are true Records, and kept by their proper Officer ; there is not one word to be found of
any such confirmation.

Secondly, If there ever was any such Bull, it had this limitation in it, that the Possessors
of such Lands should bestow them all on Colleges, Hospitals, parochial Ministers, or o-
ther such like spiritual Uses : And this I prove,

First, Because the famous Instances that are usually given of the Pope's Alienations of
Church-Lands, were only a changing them from one religious Use to another. Thus when
Pope *Clement* the Fifth, *A. D.* 1307. suppreft the *Knights-Templars* in this Nation and
seiz'd all their Lands and Goods, he gave them all to the Hospitallers of St. *John* of *Jeru-
salem,* and that was ratified in Parliament, 17 *Edw.* Second ; which Act sets forth, *That
tho' those Lands were escheated to the Lords of the Fee by the said Dissolution, yet it was not lawful to detain them.* When Pope *Clement* the Seventh, *A. D.* 1528. gave Cardinal *Woolsey* a
Power to suppress several Monasteries ; he was to transfer all their Goods and Possessions
to his Collegiate Church at *Windsor* and to King's College in *Cambridge* ; and when the
same Pope gave the same Cardinal many other Religious Houses, it was for the endowing
Christ Church in *Oxford,* and his College in *Ipswich* : And to name no more, when
Pope *Alexander* the Seventh, *A. D.* 1655. suppressed the Order of the *Fratres Cruciferi,*
he disposed of all their Houses, Farms and Rights to such uses and pious works as he
thought fit. *Vide Bullar. Lugd. Vol. Ult. fol.* 220.

Secondly, When this very Pope was attended with the *English* Ambassadors that came
to his Confirmation, the Pope found fault with them, ' That the Church-yards were not
' restored, *saying* that it was by no means to be tolerated, and that it was necessary to ren-
' der all even to a Farthing, because the things that belong to God, can never be applied
' to human uses, and he that withholdeth the least part of them, is in a continual state of
' Damnation ; that if he had power to grant them, he would do it most readily,—but
' his Authority was not so large as that he might prophane the things that are dedicated to
' God ; and let *England* be assured that this would be *Anathema, &c. F. Paul's H.* of the
' *Council* of *Trent,* p. 392. *Sleidani Com.* p. 779. And all this was said by the Pope,
within four Months of the pretended Confirmation.

Thirdly, The private Bull to Sir *W. Peters* bears date within two Months after the pretended Confirmation, *vide* Sir *W. Dugdale's Eccl. Col. fol.* 207. The Title of which Bull is
this, ' *The Bull* of *Paul* the Fourth Bishop of *Rome,* in which he confirms to Sir *W. Peters*
' all and singular the Sales of several Mannors, *&c.* sometime belonging to Monasteries,
' which the said Sir *W. Peters* is ready to assign and demise to spiritual uses. *Then follows
the Bull it self, which saith,* ' That this Confirmation was humbly desired from us, and that
' there were reasonable Causes to persuade it, *viz.* a Petition exhibited by the said Sir *W.*
' *Peters,* that the Mannors, *&c.* belonging to certain Monasteries, and sold to him by King
Henry

' *Henry* the Eighth, which he is ready to assign and demise to spiritual uses, may be approved
' and confirmed to him; wherefore the said Pope doth acquit and absolve him, being in-
' clined by the said supplications, *&c.* By which Bull, Sir *W.* Peters had no power given
' him to keep those Lands or dispose of them to his Heirs, but only to distribute them to
' such Religious Uses as he thought best. Now it is a most improbable a thing, that Sir *W.*
' *Peters* should petition the Pope for a limited Dispensation, if the whole Nation, as is pre-
' tended, had been absolutely dispensed with but two Months before, without any limita-
' tion at all : So that either there was no such General Confirmation, or else it was limited,
' with the same restrictions as that to Sir *W. Peters, viz.* To bestow them upon spiritual
' Uses. And this is the only probable Reason why in *England* this Bull is wholly sup-
' press'd and lost.' In Confirmation of this, it may be observed, that *Cardinal Pool*, notwithstanding his Dispensation, earnestly exhorted all persons by the Bowels of Christ Jesus,
that not being unmindful of their Salvation, they would at least out of their Ecclesiastical Goods take care to encrease the Endowments of Parsonages and Vicarages, that the
Incumbents may be commodiously and honestly maintain'd according to their Quality and
Estate, whereby they may laudably exercise the Cure of Souls, and support the Incumbents
Burthens; and farther urg'd the Judgments that fell upon *Balthazar*, for converting the
holy Vessels to prophane uses.

Fourthly, Queen *Mary*, who best understood what had been done, after the time of this
pretended Confirmation from the Pope, restored all the Church-Lands that were then in
the Crown, saying, " That they were taken away contrary to the Law of God and of
" the Church, and therefore her Conscience did not suffer her to detain them, *&c.*" When
she gave them to the Pope and his Legate, to dispose of, to the Honour of God, *&c.* she
said, " She did it because she set more by the Salvation of her Soul than ten such King-
" doms." *Heylin's H. Ref.* p. 235. And to this Act of Restitution, she was vehemently
press'd by the Pope and his Legate, *F. Paul's H.* of the *C.* of *Trent*, p. 393. *Dudithius in
vita Poli*, p. 32. And these things thus restored by the Queen, were disposed of by the Legate to several Churches, *Dudithius ib.* From all which it's evident, that neither the Pope,
nor his Legate, nor Queen *Mary* knew of any such Confirmations of these Alienations as
would quiet the Conscience, without restoring them to the spiritual uses.

Fifthly, Queen *Mary*, not only did so her self, but press'd it vehemently upon her
Nobles and Parliament, that they would make full Restitution, *Heylin*, p. 237. *Sleidan*, p.
791. and several of them, as Sir *Thomas*, Sir *William Peters, &c.* who had swallowed the
largest morsels of those Lands, did make some sort of Restitution, tho' not to the Abbies
themselves, yet to Colleges and Religious Uses.

Sixthly, This very Pope *Paul* the Fourth, published a Bull, in which he threaten'd
Excommunication, to all manner of persons as kept any Church-Lands to themselves,
and to all Princes, Noblemen, and Magistrates, that did not forthwith put the same in
execution. *Heylin's H. Ref.* p. 238. So that by a new Decree he retrieved all those Goods
and Ecclesiastical Revenues which had been alienated from the Church, since the time of
Julius the Second, *Rycaut's Contin.* p. 112. So improbable a story is it, that this Pope
confirmed these Alienations in *England*. And whereas Dr. *Johnston*, p. 173. hath these
words, Mr. Fox *saith,* ' The Pope published a Bull in print against the restoring of Abby-
' Lands, which Dr. *Burnet* affirms also, Ap. fol. 403.' It is notoriously false, they both
asserting the contrary; Dr *Burnet's* Words in that very place are these; ' The Pope in
' plain terms refused to ratify what the Cardinal had done, and soon after set out a severe
' Bull, cursing and condemning all that held any Church-Lands.

Seventhly and lastly, The succeeding Popes have been clearly of this opinion. Pope
Pius the Fourth, who immediately succeeded this *Paul,* confirm'd the *Council* of *Trent*,
and therein damned all the detainers of *Church-Lands*; and tho' he was much importuned
to confirm some Alienations made by the King of *France* to pay the debts of the Crown,
yet he absolutely refused it, *F. Paul's H. C. Trent.* 713. Pope *Innocent* the Tenth, first
protested against the Alienations of *Church-Lands* in *Germany*, that were made at the
great Treaty of *Munster* and *Osnaburg. A. D.* 1648. and when that would not do, by his
Bull, *Nov.* 26. in the very same Year, damns all those that should dare to retain the
Church-Lands, and declares the Treaty void, *Instrumentum pacis,* &c. *& Innocentii* X. *me
declaratio nullitatis, Artic. &c.* and all their late Popes in the *Bulla cœnæ* do very solemnly ' Damn and Excommunicate all who usurp any Jurisdiction, Fruits, Revenues and E-
' moluments belonging to any Ecclesiastical Person upon account of any Churches, Mona-
' steries, or other Ecclesiastical Benefices, or who, upon any occasion or cause, sequester
' the said Revenues without the express Leave of the Bishop of *Rome*, or others, having
' lawful power to do it, *&c.* And tho' upon *Good-Friday* there is published a general Absolution, yet out of that are expresly excluded all those who possess any *Church-Lands* or
Goods, who are still left under the Sentence of Excommunication. *Toleti Instr. Sacerd.*
and his *Explicatio casuum in Bulla cœnæ Dni reserva.*   From

From which conſideration it's evident, that it never was the deſign of the Pope to con-firm the *Engliſh Church-Lands* to the Lay-poſſeſſors, but that he always urg'd the neceſſity of reſtoring of them to religious uſes ; in order to which, the Papiſts prevailed to have the ſtatute of *Mortmain* repealed for 20 Years. In Queen *Elizabeth's* Reign the factious party that was manag'd wholly by Romiſh Emiſſaries demanded to *have Abbies and ſuch Re-ligious Houſes reſtored for their Uſe* ; and A. D. 1585, *in their Petition to the Parliament, they ſet it down as a reſolute Doctrine, that things once dedicated to Sacred Uſes ought ſo to remain by the Word of God for ever, and ought not to be converted to any private Uſe. Biſhop* Bancroft's *Sermon at* P. C. A. D. 1588. *p.* 25. And that the *Church* of *Rome* is ſtill gaping after theſe Lands, is evident from many of their late Books, as the Religion of *M. Luther*, lately printed at *Oxford*, p. 15. *The Monks wrote Anathema upon the Regiſters and Donati-ons belonging to Monaſteries ; the weight and effect of which Curſes are both felt and dreaded to this day.* To this end, the *Monaſticon Anglicanum* is ſo diligently preſerved in the *Va-tican*, and other Libraries in the popiſh Countries ; and eſpecially this appears from the ob-ſtinate refuſal of this preſent Pope to confirm theſe Alienations, tho' it be a matter ſo much controverted, and which would be of that vaſt Uſe towards promoting their Religion in Kingdom.

If therefore the Biſhops of *Rome* did never confirm theſe Alienations of *Church-Lands*, but earneſtly and ſtrictly require their Reſtitution ; if they have declared in their Authen-tick *Canons*, that they have no power to do it, and both they and the laſt general *Council* pronounce an heavy *Curſe* and *Anathema* againſt all ſuch as detain them : Then let every one that poſſeſſeth theſe Lands, and yet own either of theſe Foreign Juriſdictions, con-ſider, that here is nothing left to excuſe him from Sacrilege, and therefore with his E-ſtate he muſt derive a curſe to his poſterity. There is ſcarcely any Papiſt but that is for-ward to accuſe King *Henry* the 8*th* of Sacrilege, and yet never reflects upon himſelf who quietly poſſeſſeth the Fruits of it, without Reſtitution ; either let them not accuſe him, or elſe reſtore themſelves. Now whatever opinions the Papiſts may have of theſe things in the time of health, yet I muſt deſire to remember what the *Jeſuits* propoſed to Cardinal *Pool* in Doctor *Pary's* Days, viz. *That if he would encourage them in* England, *they did not doubt but that by dealing with the Conſciences of thoſe who were dying, they ſhould ſoon recover the greateſt part of the Goods of the Church.* Dr. *Burnet's* Hiſt. Vol. 2. p. 328. Not to mention that whenſoever the Regulars ſhall grow numerous in *England*, and by conſe-quence burthenſome to the few Nobility and Gentry of that perſuaſion, they will find it neceſſary for them to conſent to a Reſtitution of their Lands, that they may ſhare the burthen among others. For ſo vaſt are the Burthens and Payments that that Religion brings with it, that it will be found at length an advantagious Bargain to part with all the *Church-Lands* to indemnify the reſt. And I am confident that the Gentry of *England* that are Papiſts, have found greater Burthens and Payments ſince their Religion hath been allow'd, than ever they did for the many years it was forbid ; and this charge muſt daily encreaſe, ſo long as their *Clergy* daily grows more numerous, and their few *Converts* are moſt of them of the meaneſt Rank, and ſuch as want to be provided for : And that it's no eaſy mat-ter to force *Converts*, may appear from that Excellent Obſervation of the great Emperor *Charles* the Fifth, who told Queen *Mary, That by endeavouring to compel others to his own Religion, he had tired and ſpent himſelf in vain, and purchas'd nothing by it, but his own diſho-nour.* Card. *Pool* in *Heylin's* Hiſt Ref. p. 217. And to conclude this Diſcourſe, had the Act of Pope *Julius* the Third by his Legate *Cardinal Pool*, in confirming the Alienation of *Church-Lands* in *England*, been as valid as is by ſome pretended, yet what ſhall ſecure us from an Act of Reſumption ? That very Pope, after that pretended Grant to *Cardinal Pool*, publiſhed a Bull, in which he excommunicated all that kept *Abby-Lands* or *Chu·ch-Lands, Burnet's* Hiſt. Vol. 2. p. 309. by which all former Grants, had there been any, were cancell'd. His Succeſſor, Pope *Paul* the Fourth, retrieved all the Goods and Eccle-ſiaſtical Revenues that had been alienated from the Church, ſince the time of *Julius* the Se-cond ; and the chief Reaſons that are given why the Popes may not ſtill proceed to an Act of Reſumption of theſe Lands in *England*, amount only to this, That they may ſtay for a fair opportunity, when it may be done without diſturbing the peace of the Kingdom. From all which it's evident, that the detaining of *Abby-Lands*, and other *Church-Lands*, from the Monks and Friars, is altogether inconſiſtent with the Doctrine and Principles of the *Romiſh* Religion.

The King's Power in Ecclesiastical Matters truely stated.

HIS present Majesty having erected an High-Commission *Court* to enquire of, and make redress in, Ecclesiastical Matters, &c.

Q. Whether such a *Commission*, as the Law now stands, be good or not?

And I hold that the *Commission* is not good. And to maintain my Opinion herein, I shall, in the first place, briefly consider, what Power the *Crown* of *England* had in Ecclesiastical or Spiritual Matters (for I take them to be synonymous Terms) before 17 *Car.* 1. *cap.* 11. And, *Secondly*, I shall particularly consider the Act of 17 *Car.* 1. *cap.* 11. And, *Thirdly*, I shall consider 13 *Car.* 2. *cap.* 12. And by that time I have fully considered these Acts of Parliament, it will plainly appear, that the *Crown* of *England* hath now no *Power* to erect such a *Court*.

I must confess, and do agree, That by the *Common Law* all Ecclesiastical Jurisdiction was lodged in the Crown ; and the *Bishops*, and all spiritual *Persons* derived their Jurisdiction from thence : And I cannot find that there were any attempts by the Clergy to divest the Crown of it till *William* the First's Time, and his Successors down to King *John*, the *Pope* obtained four *Points* of Jurisdiction. *First*, Sending of Legats into *England*. *Secondly*, Drawing of Appeals to the Court of *Rome*. *Thirdly*, Donation of Bishopricks and other Ecclesiastical Benefices. And *Fourthly*, Exemption of Clerks from the Secular *Power*. Which four Points were gained within an hundred and odd Years ; but with all the Opposition imaginable of the Kings and their People ; and the Kingdom never came to be absolutely enslaved to the Church of *Rome* till King *John*'s Time, and then both King and People were, and so continued to be in a great measure in *Henry* the Third's Time ; and so would in all likelihood have continued, had not wise *Edward* the first opposed the Pope's Usurpation, and made the Statute of *Mortmain :* But that which chiefly brake the Neck of this, was, That after the Pope and Clergy had endeavoured in *Edward* the Second's Time, and in the Beginning of *Edward* the Third, to usurp again ; *Edward* the Third did resist the Usurpation, and made the Statutes of Provisors, 25 *Ed.* 3. and 27 *Ed.* 3. And *Richard* the second backed those Acts with 16 *Rich.* 2. *cap.* 5. and kept the *Power* in the Crown by these Laws, which being interrupted by Queen *Mary* (a bloody Bigot of the Church of *Rome*) during her Reign, there was an Act made in 1 *Eliz. cap.* 1. which is intituled, *An Act to restore to the Crown the ancient Jurisdiction over the Estate Ecclesiastical and Spiritual, and abolishing all foreign Powers repugnant to the same :* From which Title I collect three things. *First*, That the Crown had anciently a Jurisdiction over the Estate Ecclesiastical and Spiritual. *Secondly*, That that Jurisdiction had for some time been at least suspended, and the Crown had not exercised it. *Thirdly*, That this Law did not introduce a new Jurisdiction, but restored the old ; but with restoring the old Jurisdiction to the Crown, gave a Power of delegating the Exercise of it. And as a Consequence from the whole, that all Jurisdiction that is lodged in the Crown, is subject nevertheless to the Legislative Power in the Kingdom.

Keeble's Stat.

I shall now consider what Power this Act of 1 *Eliz.* 1. declares to have been anciently in the Crown, and that appears from Sect. 16, 17, 18. of the same Act.

Section 16. Abolisheth all foreign Authority in Cases Spiritual and Temporal, in these Words : *And to the intent that all the usurped and foreign Power and Authority, Spiritual and Temporal, may for ever be clearly extinguished, and never be used or obeyed within this Realm, or any other your Majesty's Dominions or Countries,* (2.) *May it please your Highness, that it may be further enacted by the Authority aforesaid, that no foreign Prince, Person, Prelate, State or Potentate Spiritual or Temporal, shall at any time after the last Day of this Session of Parliament use, enjoy, or exercise any manner of Power, Jurisdiction, Superiority, Authority, Preheminence or Privilege Spiritual or Ecclesiastical within this Realm, or within any other your Majesty's Dominions or Countries that now be, or hereafter shall be, but from thenceforth the same shall be clearly abolished out of this Realm, and all other your Highness's Dominions for ever ; any Statute, Ordinance, Custom, Constitutions, or any other Matter or Cause whatsoever to the contrary in any wise notwithstanding.* And after the said Act hath abolished all foreign Authority, in the very next Section, Sect. 17. it annexeth all Ecclesiastical Jurisdiction to the Crown in these Words : *And that also it may likewise please your Highness, That it may be established and enacted by the Authority aforesaid, That such Jurisdictions, Privileges, Superiorities, and Preheminences, Spiritual and Ecclesiastical, as by any Spiritual or Ecclesiastical Power or Authority hath heretofore been, or may lawfully be exercised, or used for the Visitation of the Ecclesiastical State and Persons, and for Reformation, Order and Correction of the same ; and of all manner of Errors, Heresies, Schisms, Abuses, Offences, Contempts and Enormities, shall for ever, by Authority of this present Parliament, be united and annexed to the Imperial Crown of this Realm.* From these Words, That such Jurisdiction, &c. as by any Spiritual or Ecclesiastical Power or Authority had thentofore been exercised or used, were annexed to the Crown ; I observe, That the

four

four things aforesaid, wherein the Pope had incroached, were all restored to the Crown; and likewise all other Ecclesiastical Jurisdiction that had been exercised or used in this Kingdom, and did thereby become absolutely vested in the Crown.

Then *Section* 18. gives a Power to the Crown to assign Commissioners to exercise this Ecclesiastical Jurisdiction in these Words: *And that your Highness, your Heirs and Successors, Kings or Queens in this Realm, shall have full Power and Authority, by virtue of this Act, by Letters Patents under the Great Seal of* England, *to assign, name, and authorize, when, and as often as your Highness, your Heirs or Successors shall think meet and convenient, and for such, and so long time as shall please your Highness, your Heirs or Successors, such Person or Persons being natural born Subjects to your Highness, your Heirs or Successors, as your Majesty, your Heirs or Successors shall think meet to exercise, use, occupy and execute under your Highness, your Heirs and Successors, all manner of Jurisdictions, Privileges, and Preheminencies in any wise touching or concerning any Spiritual or Ecclesiastical Jurisdiction within these your Realms of* England *and* Ireland, *or any other your Highness's Dominions and Countries: (2.) And to visit, reform, redress, order, correct and amend all such Errors, Heresies, Schisms, Abuses, Offences, Contempts and Enormities whatsoever, which by any manner of Spiritual or Ecclesiastical Power, Authority or Jurisdiction can, or may lawfully be reformed, ordered, redressed, corrected, restrained and amended, to the pleasure of Almighty God, the increase of Virtue, and the conservation of Peace and Unity in this Realm: (3.) And that such Person or Persons so to be named, assigned, authorised and appointed by your Highness, your Heirs and Successors, after the said Letters Patents to him or them made and delivered, as is aforesaid, shall have full Power and Authority, by virtue of this Act, and of the said Letters Patents under your Highness, your Heirs and Successors, to exercise, use and execute all the Premisses, according to the Tenor and Effect of the said Letters Patents, any matter or cause to the contrary in any wise notwithstanding.*

So that, I take it, that all manner of Ecclesiastical Jurisdiction was in the Crown by the Common Law of *England,* and declared to be so by the said Act of 1 *Eliz.* 1. and by that Act, a Power given to the Crown to assign Commissioners to exercise this Jurisdiction; which was accordingly done by Queen *Elizabeth,* and a High Commission Court was by her erected; which sat and held Plea of all Causes, Spiritual and Ecclesiastical, during the Reign of Queen *Elizabeth,* King *James* the First, and King *Charles* the First, till the 17th Year of his Reign.

Which leads me to consider the Statute of 17 *Car.* 1. *cap.* 11. which Act recites the Title of 1 *Eliz. cap.* 1. and *Sect.* 18. of the same Act; and recites further, *Section* 2. That *whereas by colour of some Words in the aforesaid Branch of the said Act, whereby Commissioners are authorised to execute their Commission according to the Tenor and Effect of the King's Letters Patents, and by Letters Patents grounded thereupon, the said Commissioners have, to the great and insufferable Wrong and Oppression of the King's Subjects, used to fine and imprison them, and to exercise other authority, not belonging to Ecclesiastical Jurisdiction restored by that Act, and divers others great Mischiefs and Inconveniencies have also ensued to the King's Subjects, by occasion of the said Branch, and Commissions issued thereupon, and the Executions thereof: Therefore for the repressing and preventing of the foresaid Abuses, Mischiefs and Inconveniences in time to come,* (by *Sect.* 3. the said Clause in the said Act 1 *Eliz.* 1. is repealed with a *Non-obstante* to the said Act in these Words:) *Be it enacted by the King's most Excellent Majesty, and the Lords and Commons in this present Parliament assembled, and by the Authority of the same, That the aforesaid Branch, Clause, Article or Sentence contained in the said Act, and every Word, Matter and Thing contained in that Branch, Clause, Article or Sentence, shall from henceforth be repealed, annulled, revoked, annihilated and utterly made void for ever, any thing in the said Act to the contrary in any wise notwithstanding.*

And in *Sect.* 5. of the same Act, it is enacted, That from and after the first of *August* (in the said Act mentioned) all such Commissions shall be void, in these Words; *And be it further enacted, That from and after the said first Day of* August, *no new Court shall be erected, ordained or appointed within this Realm of* England, *or Dominion of* Wales, *which shall or may have the like Power, Jurisdiction or Authority as the said High Commission Court now hath, or pretendeth to have; but that all and every such Letters Patents, Commissions and Grants, made or to be made by his Majesty, his Heirs and Successors; and all Powers and Authorities, granted or pretended, or mentioned to be granted thereby; and all Acts, Sentences, and Decrees, to be made, by virtue or colour thereof, shall be utterly void, and of none effect.*

By which Act then, the Power of exercising Ecclesiastical Jurisdiction by Commissioners, under the Broad Seal, is so taken away, that it provides no such Power shall ever for the future be delegated by the Crown, or any Person or Persons whatsoever.

Let us then in the last place consider, whether the Act of 13 *Car.* 2. *cap.* 12. hath restored this Power or not.

And for this, I take it, that it is not restored by the said Act, or any Clause in it; and to make this evident, I shall first set down the whole Act, and then consider it in the several Branches of it, that relate to this Matter: The Act is Entituled,

An Act for explanation of a Clause contained in an Act of Parliament made in the 17th *Year of the late King* Charles, *Entituled, An Act for Repeal of a Branch of a Statute, in* Primo Elizabethæ, *concerning Commissioners for Causes Ecclesiastical.*

The Act itself runs thus ; *Whereas, in an Act of Parliament, made in the seventeenth Year of the late King* Charles, *Entituled, An Act for Repeal of a Branch of a Statute primo* Elizabethæ, *concerning Commissioners for Causes Ecclesiastical, it is (amongst other things) enacted, That no Archbishop, Bishop or Vicar-General, nor any Chancellor, nor Commissary of any Arch-Bishop, Bishop, or Vicar-General, nor any Ordinary whatsoever, nor any other Spiritual or Ecclesiastical Judge, Officer, or Minister of Justice, nor any other Person, or Persons whatsoever, exercising Spiritual or Ecclesiastical Power, Authority or Jurisdiction, by any Grant, Licence or Commission of the King's Majesty, his Heirs or Successors, or by any Power or Authority derived from the King, his Heirs or Successors, or otherwise, shall (from and after the first Day of August which then should be in the Year of our Lord God* 1641.) *award, impose or inflict any Pain, Penalty, Fine, Amercement, Imprisonment or other corporal Punishment upon any of the King's Subjects, for any Contempt, Misdemeanor, Crime, Offence, Matter or Thing whatsoever, belonging to Spiritual or Ecclesiastical Cognizance or Jurisdiction : (2.) Whereupon some doubt hath been made, that all ordinary Power of Coertion, and proceeding in Causes Ecclesiastical were taken away, whereby the ordinary Course of Justice in Causes Ecclesiastical hath been obstructed. (3.) Be it therefore declared and enacted by the King's most Excellent Majesty, by, and with the Advice and Consent of the Lords and Commons in this present Parliament assembled, and by the Authority thereof, That neither the said Act, nor any thing therein contained, doth or shall take away any ordinary Power or Authority from any of the said Arch-Bishops, Bishops, or any other Person or Persons named as aforesaid ; but that they and every of them, exercising Ecclesiastical Jurisdiction, may proceed, determine, sentence, execute and exercise all manner of Ecclesiastical Jurisdiction, and all Censures and Coertions appertaining and belonging to the same, before any making of the Act before recited, in all Causes and Matters belonging to Ecclesiastical Jurisdiction, according to the King's Majesty's Ecclesiastical Laws, used and practised in this Realm, in as ample Manner and Form as they did and might lawfully have done before making of the said Act.*

Sect. 2. *And be it further enacted by the Authority aforesaid, That the afore recited Act of* Decimo Septimo Car. *and all the Matters and Clauses therein contained (excepting what concerns the High Commission Court, or the new Erection of some such like Court by Commission) shall be and is hereby repealed to all intents and purposes whatsoever, any Thing, Clause or Sentence in the said Act contained to the contrary notwithstanding.*

Sect. 3. *Provided always, and it is hereby enacted, That neither this Act, nor any thing herein contain'd, shall extend, or be construed to revive, or give force to the said Branch of the said Statute made in the first Year of the Reign of the said late Queen* Elizabeth, *mentioned in the said Act of Parliament made in the seventeenth Year of the Reign of the said King* Charles ; *but that the said Branch of the said Statute, made in the said first Year of the Reign of the said late Queen* Elizabeth, *shall stand and be repealed in such sort as if this Act had never been made.*

Sect. 4. *Provided always, and it is hereby enacted, That it shall not be lawful for any Arch-Bishop, Bishop, Vicar-General, Chancellor, Commissary, or any other Spiritual or Ecclesiastical Judge, Officer or Minister, or any other Person having or exercising Spiritual or Ecclesiastical Jurisdiction, to tender or administer unto any Person whatsoever the Oath usually called* Ex Officio, *or any other Oath whereby such Person, to whom the same is tendred and administred, may be charged to confess or accuse, or to purge him or herself of any Criminal matter or thing, whereby he or she may be liable to Censure or Punishment ; any thing in this Statute, or any other Law, Custom or Usage heretofore to the contrary hereof, in any wise notwithstanding.*

Sect. 5. *Provided always, That this Act, or any Thing therein contained, shall not extend, or be construed to extend, to give unto any Arch-Bishop, Bishop, or any other Spiritual or Ecclesiastical Judge, Officer, or other Person or Persons aforesaid, any Power or Authority to exercise, execute, inflict or determine any Ecclesiastical Jurisdiction, Censure or Coertion, which they might not by Law have done before the Year of our Lord* 1639. (2.) *Nor to abridge or diminish the King's Majesty's Supremacy in Ecclesiastical Matters and Affairs, nor to confirm the Canons made in the Year* 1640. *nor any of them, nor any other Ecclesiastical Laws or Canons not formerly confirmed, allowed, or enacted by Parliament, or by the established Laws of the Land, as they stood in the Year of our Lord* 1639.

From the Title of the Act, and the Act itself considered, I gather,

First, That it is an explanatory Act of the 17th of Car. 1. as to one particular Branch of it, and not introductive of any new Law.

Secondly, That the Occasion of making it was not from any Doubt that did arise, Whether the High Commission Court were taken away ? or whether the Crown had Power to erect any such like Court for the future, *but from a Doubt that was made, that all ordinary Power of Coertion, and Proceedings in Causes Ecclesiastical was taken away, whereby Justice*

in

in *Ecclesiastical Matters was obstructed* ; and this doubt did arise from a Clause in 17 *Car.* 1. *cap.* 11. *Sect.* 4. herein mentioned to be recited in the said Act of 13 *Car.* 2. *cap.* 12.

Thirdly, That the Statute of 13 *Car.* 2. *cap.* 12. as appears upon the Face of it, was made to the intent the ordinary Jurisdiction which the Bishops and other Ecclesiastical *Persons* had always exercised under the Crown, might not be infringed ; but not to restore to the Crown the Power of delegating the Exercise of Ecclesiastical Jurisdiction by *Letters Patents* to Lay-Persons or any others; and as to this, nothing can be plainer, than the Words of the Act itself, *Sect.* 2.

Whereby 17 *Car.* 1. *is repealed, but takes particular care to except what concerned the High Commission Court, or the new Erection of some such Court by Commission.*

Neither did the Law-makers think this Exception in that Statute of 13 *Car.* 2. *cap.* 12. *Sect.* 2. to be sufficient ; but to put the Matter out of all doubt, in the third Section of the same Statute, *it is provided and enacted, That neither that Act, nor any thing therein contained, shall extend or be construed to revive, or give force to the Branch of* 1 *Eliz.* 1. *Sect.* 18. *but the same Branch should stand absolutely repealed.* And if so, then the Power of the Crown to delegate the Exercise of Ecclesiastical Jurisdiction is wholly taken away ; for it was vested in the Crown by 1 *Eliz.* 1. and taken away by 17 *Car.* 1. *cap.* 11. and is in no manner restored by 13 *Car.* 2. *cap.* 12. or any other.

But there may arise an Objection from the Words in the Statute of 13 *Car.* 2. *cap.* 12. that saith, That *that Act shall not extend to abridge or diminish the King's Majesty's Supremacy in Ecclesiastical Matters and Affairs.* Whence some Men would gather, that the same Power still remains in the Crown that was in it before, 17 *Car.* 1. *cap.* 11.

To which Objection I give this Answer, That every Law is to be so constructed, that it may not be *Felo de se*, and that for the Honour of the Legislators, Kings, Lords and Commons. Now I would appeal to the Gentlemen themselves, that assert this Doctrine, whether they can so construe the Act of 13 *Car.* 2. *cap.* 12. as they pretend to do, without offering Violence to their own Reason ? For when the 17 *Car.* 1. *cap.* 11. had absolutely repealed the Branch of 1 *Eliz.* 1. that vested the Power in the Crown of delegating the Exercise of Ecclesiastical Jurisdiction, and enacts, That no such Commission shall be for the future ; and the Act of 13 *Car.* 2. *cap.* 12. repeals the 17 *Car.* 1. *cap.* 12. except what relates to that particular Branch; there can no more of the King's Supremacy in Ecclesiastical Matters and Affairs, be saved by the saving in the 13 *Car.* 2. *cap.* 12. but what was left in the Crown by 17 *Car.* 1. *cap.* 11.

And now I hope I have sufficiently evinced, That all the Proceedings before the Ecclesiastical Commissioners are *CORAM NON JUDICE* ; and therefore have sufficient Reason to believe that the same would never have been set on foot by his present Majesty (who had always the Character of *JAMES the Just*, and hath promised upon his Royal Word, that he will invade no Man's Property) had he not been advised thereunto by them who are better versed in the Canons of the Church of *ROME*, than in the Laws that relate to the CROWN and CHURCH of *ENGLAND*.

A LETTER, *Writ by* Mijn Heer Fagel, *Pensioner of* Holland, *to Mr.* James Stewart, *Advocate ; giving an Account of the Prince and Princess of* Orange's *Thoughts concerning the Repeal of the Test, and Penal Laws.*

S I R;

I Am extream sorry, that my ill Health so long hindred me from answering those Letters, in which you so earnestly desired to know of me, what their *Highnesses* Thoughts are concerning the Repeal of the *Penal Laws*, and more particularly of that concerning the *Test:* I beg you to assure your self, that I will deal very plainly with you in this Matter, and without reserve, since you say that your *Letters* were writ by the King's knowledge and allowance. I must then first of all assure you very positively, that their *Highnesses* have often declared, as they did it more particularly to the Marquis of *Albeville*, his Majesty's *Envoy* Extraordinary to the *States*, that it is their Opinion, *That no Christian ought to be persecuted for his Conscience, or be ill used because he differs from the publick and established Religion* ; and therefore, they consent, that the *Papists* in England, Scotland and Ireland be suffered to continue in their *Religion*, with as much liberty as is allowed them by the *States* in these *Provinces* ; in which it cannot be denied that they enjoy a full Liberty of Conscience. And as for the Dissenters, their *Highnesses* do not only consent, but do heartily *approve* of their having an entire Liberty, for the full exercise of their *Religion*, without any trouble or hindrance ; so that none may be able to give them the least disturbance on that account.

And

And their Highneffes are very ready, in cafe his Majefty fhall think fit to defire it, to declare their willingnefs to concur in the fettling and confirming this Liberty, and as far as it lies in them, they will protect and defend it ; and according to the Language of Treaties, they will confirm it with their *Guaranty,* of which you made mention in yours.

And if his Majefty fhall think further to defire their concurrence in the repealing of the *Penal Laws,* they are ready to give it ; *provided always that thofe Laws remain ftill in their full vigour, by which the Roman Catholicks. are fhut out of both Houfes of Parliament, and out of all publick Employments, Ecclefiaftical, Civil and Military.* As likewife all thofe other Laws, which confirm the *Proteftant Religion,* and which fecure it againft all the attempts of the *Roman Catholicks.*

But their Highneffes cannot agree to the Repeal of the Teft, or of thofe other Penal Laws laft mentioned, that tend to the fecurity of the Proteftant Religion ; fince the *Roman Catholicks* receive no other Prejudice from thefe, than the being excluded from Parliaments, or from publick Employments. And that by them the Proteftant Religion is vered from all the Defigns of the *Roman Catholicks* againft it, or againft the publick Safety ; and neither the Teft, nor thefe other Laws, can be faid to carry in them any feverity againft the Roman Catholicks upon account of their Confciences : They are only Provifions qualifying Men to be Members of Parliament, or to be capable of bearing Office ; by which they muft declare before God and Men, that they are for the *Proteftant Religion.* So that indeed, all this amounts to no more than a fecuring the *Proteftant Religion* from any prejudices that it may receive from the *Roman Catholicks.*

Their Highneffes have ✦thought, and do ftill think, that more than this ought not to be asked, or expected from them ; fince by this means the *Roman Catholicks* and their Pofterity will be for ever fecured from all trouble in their Perfons or Eftates, or in the Exercife of their *Religion ;* and that the *Roman Catholicks* ought to be fatisfy'd with this, and not to difquiet the Kingdom becaufe they cannot be admitted to fit in Parliament, or to be in Employments, or becaufe thofe Laws in which the fecurity of the *Proteftant Religion* does chiefly confift, are not repealed, by which they may be put in a Condition to overturn it.

Their Highneffes do alfo believe, that the Diffenters will be fully fatisfy'd when they fhall be for ever covered from all danger of being difturbed, or punifhed for the free Exercife of their Religion, upon any fort of pretence whatfoever.

Their Highneffes having declared themfelves fo pofitively in thefe Matters, it feems very plain to me, that they are far from being any hindrance to the freeing Diffenters, from the Severity of *Penal Laws,* fince they are ready to ufe their utmoft Endeavours for the eftablifhing of it : Nor do they at all prefs the denying to the Roman Catholicks the Exercife of their *Religion,* provided it be managed modeftly, and without Pomp or Oftentation. As for my own part, I ever was and ftill am very much againft all thofe, who would perfecute any *Chriftian* becaufe he differs from the publick and eftablifhed *Religion :* And I hope by the Grace of God to continue ftill in the fame mind ; for fince that Light with which *Religion* illuminates our Minds, is according to my fnefe of things purely an Effect of the Mercy of God to us, we ought then, ¯as I think, to render to God all poffible Thanks for his Goodnefs to us ; and to have pity for thofe who are ftill fhut up in Error, even as God has pitied us : and to put up moft earneft Prayers to God, for bringing thofe into the way of Truth, who ftray from it, and to ufe all gentle and friendly Methods for reducing them to it.

But I confefs, I could never comprehend how any that profefs themfelves Chriftians, and that may enjoy their *Religion* freely, and without any difturbance, can judge it lawfull for them to go about to difturb the Quiet of any Kingdom or State, or to overturn Conftitutions, that fo they themfelves be admitted to Employments, and thofe *Laws* in which the Security and Quiet of the eftablifhed Religion confift, fhould be fhaken.

It is plain, that the *Reformed Religion,* is by the Grace of God, and by the *Laws* of the Land, enacted both by *King* and *Parliament ;* the publick and eftablifhed *Religion,* both in *England, Scotland* and *Ireland ;* and that it is provided by thofe *Laws,* that none can be admitted either to a place in *Parliament,* or any other publick Employment, except thofe that do openly declare that they are of the Proteftant Religion, and not Roman Catholicks : and it is alfo provided by thofe Laws, that the Proteftant Religion fhall be in all time coming, fecured from the Defigns of the *Roman Catholicks* againft it. In all which I do not fee, that thefe *Laws* contain any Severity, either againft the Perfons or Eftates of thofe that cannot take thofe *Tefts,* that are contrary to the *Roman Catholick Religion ;* all the Inconveniencies that can redound to them from thence, is, that their Perfons, their Eftates, or even the Exercife of their *Religion* being affured to them, only they can have no fhare in the Government, nor in Offices of Truft, as long as their Confciences do not allow them to take thefe *Tefts :* and they are not fuffered to do any thing that is to the prejudice of the *Reform'd Religion.*

Rrrr

Since,

Since, as I have already told you, their Highnesses are ready to concur with his Majesty for the Repeal of those *Penal Laws,* by which Men are made liable to Fines or other Punishments.

So I see there remains no difficulty concerning the repealing the *Penal Laws,* but only this, that some would have the *Roman Catholicks* rendered capable of all publick Trusts and Employments, and that by consequence, all those should be repealed, that have secured the Protestant Religion against the Designs of the *Roman Catholicks,* where others at the same time are not less earnest to have those *Laws* maintained in their full and due vigour ; and think, that the chief Security of the established *Religion* consists in the preserving of them sacred and unshaken.

It is certain, that there is no Kingdom, Commonwealth, or any constituted Body or Assembly whatsoever, in which there are not Laws made for the Safety thereof ; and that provide against all Attempts whatsoever, that disturb their Peace, and that prescribe the Conditions and Qualities that they judge necessary for all that shall bear Employments in that Kingdom, State or Corporation : And no Man can pretend, that there is any Injury done him, that he is not admitted to Employments when he doth not satisfy the Conditions and Qualities required.

Nor can it be denied, that there is a great difference to be observ'd in the Conduct of those of the *Reformed Religion,* and of the Roman Catholicks towards one another : The Roman Catholicks not being satisfy'd to exclude the *Reform'd* from all Places of Profit or of Trust, they do absolutely suppress the whole Exercise of that *Religion,* and persecute all that profess it ; and this they do in all those places where it is safe and without danger, to carry on that rigour. And I am sorry that we have at this present so many deplorable Instances of this Severity before our eyes, that is at the same time put in practice in so many different places.

I would therefore gladly see one single good Reason to move a Protestant that fears God, and that is concerned for his *Religion,* to consent to the repealing of those Laws that have been enacted by the Authority of *King* and *Parliament,* which have no other tendency but to the security of the *Reformed Religion,* and to the restraining of the Roman Catholicks from a capacity of overturning it ; these Laws inflict neither Fines nor Punishments, and do only exclude the Roman Catholicks from a share in the Government, who by being in Employments must needs study to encrease their Party, and to gain to it more Credit and Power ; which, by what we see every day, we must conclude, will be extreamly dangerous to the *Reformed Religion,* and must turn to its great prejudice : Since in all Places, those that are in publick Employments do naturally favour that *Religion* of which they are, either more or less. And who would go about to perswade me or any Man else to endeavour to move their Highnesses, whom God hath honoured so far as to make them the Protectors of his Church, to approve of, or to consent to things so hurtful, both to the *Reformed Religion,* and to the publick Safety ? Nor can I, Sir, with your good leave, in any way, grant what you apprehend, that no prejudice will thereby redound to the *Reformed Religion.*

I know it is commonly said, that the Number of the *Roman Catholicks* in *England* and *Scotland* is very inconsiderable ; and that they are possessed only of a very small number of the Places of Trust; tho' even as to this, the Case is quite different in *Ireland* : Yet this you must of necessity grant me, that if their numbers are small, then it is not reasonable that the publick Peace should be disturbed on the account of so few Persons, especially when so great a Favour may be offered to them ; such as the free Exercise of their *Religion* would be. And if their numbers are greater, then there is so much the more Reason to be afraid of them. I do indeed believe, that *Roman Catholicks,* as things at present stand, will not be very desirous to be in publick Offices and Employments, nor that they will make any attempts upon the *Reformed Religion,* both because this is contrary to Law, and because of the great Inconveniencies that this may bring at some other time both on their Persons and their Estates : Yet if the Restraints of the Law were once taken off, you would see them brought into the Government, and the chief Offices and Places of Trust would be put into their hands, nor will it be easy to his *Majesty* to resist them in this, how stedfast soever he may be ; for they will certainly press him hard in it, and they will represent this to the King, as a Matter in which his Conscience will be concerned ; and when they are possessed of the publick Offices, what will be left for the *Protestants* to do, who will find no more the support of the Law, and can expect little Encouragement from such Magistrates ? And on the other hand, the Advantages that the *Roman Catholicks* would find in being thus set loose from all restraints, are so plain, that it were a loss of time to go about the proving of it. I neither can nor will doubt of the sincerity of his Majesty's Intentions, and that he has no other Design before him in this Matter, but that all his Subjects may enjoy in all things the same *Rights* and *Freedom.*

But plain Reason, as well as the Experience of all Ages, the present as well as the past, shews, that it will be impossible for *Roman Catholicks* and *Protestants,* when they are mix'd together in Places of Trust and publick Employments, to live together peaceably, or to

maintain

maintain a good Correspondence together. They will be certainly always jealous of one another: For the Principles and the Maxims of both *Religions* are so opposite to one another, that in my opinion I do not see how it will be in the power of any Prince or King whatsoever, to keep down those Suspicions and Animosities which will be apt to arise upon all occasions.

As for that which you apprehend, that the *Dissenters* shall not be delivered from the *Penal Laws* that are made against them, unless at the same time the *Test* be likewise repealed: This will be indeed a great unhappiness to them; but the Roman Catholicks are only to blame for it, who will rather be content that they and their Posterity should lie still under the weight of the *Penal Laws,* and exposed to the hatred of the whole Nation; than be still restrained from a capacity of attempting any thing against the Peace and the Security of the *Protestant Religion:* And be deprived of that small Advantage (if it is at all to be reckoned one) of having a share in the Government and publick Employments; since in all Places of the World this has been always the Privilege of the *Religion* that is established by Laws. And indeed these Attempts of the *Roman Catholicks* ought to be so much the more suspected and guarded against by *Protestants,* in that they see the *Roman Catholicks,* even when liable to that Severity of *Penal Laws,* do yet endeavour to perswade his *Majesty,* to make the *Protestants,* whether they will or not, dissolve the Security which they have for their *Religion:* and to clear a Way for bringing in the *Roman Catholicks* to the Government, and to publick Employments, in which Case there would remain no relief for them, but what were to be expected from a *Roman Catholick* Government.

Such then will be very unjust to their *Highnesses,* who shall blame them for any Inconveniency that may arise from thence; since they have declared themselves so freely on this Subject, and that so much to the advantage even of the *Roman Catholicks.* And since the Settlements of Matters stick at this single Point, that their Highnesses cannot be brought to consent to things that are so contrary to *Laws* already in being, and that are so dangerous and so hurtful to the Protestant Religion, as the admitting of *Roman Catholicks* to a share in the Government, and to Places of Trust, and the repealing of those Laws, that can have no other effect but the securing of the *Protestant Religion,* from all the Attempts of the *Roman Catholicks* against it, would be.

You write, That *the Roman Catholicks in these Provinces are not shut out from Employments and Places of Trust*; but in this you are much mistaken. For our Laws are express, excluding them by name from all share in the Government, and from all Employments either of the Policy or Justice of our Country. It is true, I do not know of any express Law, that shuts them out of Military Employments; that had indeed been hard, since in the first Formation of our *State* they joined with us in defending our publick Liberty, and did us eminent Service during the Wars: therefore they were not shut out from those Military Employments, for the publick Safety was no ways endangered by this, both because their Numbers that served in our Troops were not great, and because the States could easily prevent any Inconvenience that might arise out of that; which could not have been done so easily, if the Roman Catholicks had been admitted to a share in the Government, and in the Policy or Justice of our *State.*

I am very certain of this, of which I could give very good Proofs, that there is nothing which their Highnesses desire so much, as that his *Majesty* may reign happily, and in an entire confidence with his Subjects; and that his Subjects being perswaded of his *Majesty's* fatherly Affection to them, may be ready to make him all the returns of Duty that are in their power. But their Highnesses are convinced in their Consciences, that both the Protestant Religion, and the Safety of the Nation, would be exposed to most certain Dangers, if either the *Tests,* or those other *Penal Laws,* of which I have made frequent mention, should be repealed; *Therefore they cannot consent to this, nor concur with his Majesty's Will; for they believe they should have much to answer for to God, if the consideration of any present Advantage should carry them to consent and concur in things, which they believe would be not only dangerous, but mischievous to the Protestant Religion.*

Their Highnesses have ever paid a most profound Duty to his Majesty, which they will always continue to do; for they consider themselves bound to it, both by the Laws of God and of Nature: But since the Matter that is now in hand, relates not to the making of *new Laws,* but to the total repealing of those already made both by *King* and *Parliament*; they do not see how it can be expected of them, that they should consent to such a *Repeal,* to which they have so just an aversion, as being a thing that is contrary to the Laws and Customs of all Christian *States,* whether *Protestants,* or *Papists,* who receive none to a share in the Government, or to publick Employments, but those who profess the publick and established *Religion,* and that take care to secure it against all Attempts whatsoever.

I do not think it necessary to demonstrate to you how much their Highnesses are devoted to his *Majesty,* of which they have given such real Evidences as are beyond all verbal ones; and they are resolved still to continue in the same Duty, and Affection; or rather to encrease it, if that is possible. I am, SIR,

Yours, &c.

Nov. 4. 1687.   *Reflections*

Reflections on Monsieur Fagel's Letter.

S I R,

I Shall endeavour to answer yours as fully and briefly as possible.

1. You desire to know whether the Letter I sent you be truly Monsieur *Fagel*'s or not.
2. Whether their Highnesses gave him Commission to write it.
3. How far the Dissenters may rely on their Highnesses word.
4. What effects it has on all sorts of People.

Sir, Roman Catholicks may be pardoned if they endeavour to make that Letter pass for an Imposture ; it is their Interest so to do, and they are seldom wanting to promote that, let the Methods be ever so indirect which they are forced to make use of : It does indeed spoil many hopeful Projects of theirs. But how any Protestant among us can really doubt the Truth of it, is strange to me. Some things carry their own Evidence along with them, I take this Letter to be one of that kind. I do not desire you to believe me upon my bare Affirmation that I know it to be genuine, (though this be most true) but shall offer my Reasons to convince you that it cannot be otherwise.

First, the Letter is like its Author, the Matter is weighty, the Reasoning solid, the Stile grave, full and clear, like that of a Lawyer : It has an Air all over, which as well shews the Religion and Temper of its Writer, as the Matter and Method of it does his Capacity and Judgment. Now all these Qualities make up the Character of Monst. *Fagel*.

Secondly, There are the same grounds to believe this Letter to be M. *Fagel*'s, as there are to believe any thing you have not seen, *viz*. The constant Asseverations of Persons of undoubted Credit that come from *Holland*, who all agree in it, and assure us of it. M. *Fagel* own'd it to several *English* Gentlemen, and many both here and in *Holland* knew two Months ago, that such a Letter was written ; a Forgery would before this time have been detected, especially such a one as ruins the Designs of the triumphing Party.

Thirdly, It was written by M. *Fagel*, in answer to Letters from Mr. *Stewart*, sent by his Majesty's special Orders, and Mr. *Stewart* had both an *English* and *Latin* Copy sent him : Therefore the *English* Copy is not called a Translation, but it is a sort of Original ; for you are not to doubt but the matter was ordered so, that her Royal Highness might peruse it as well as his Majesty.

In the next place you would know *whether their Highnesses gave order to Monsieur* Fagel *to write it*.

I wish, Sir, you would take the pains to read the Letter over again, and consider who this Monsieur *Fagel* is : He is Pensionary of *Holland*, and first Minister of State, rais'd to that Dignity by the Prince's Favour ; he answers Letters written to him, which are ordered by his Majesty to be communicated to their Highnesses. In his Answer, he gives an Account of their Highnesses Opinion about the Repeal of the Penal Laws and Test ; Matters of a National Concern, and of the greatest Importance. Now you must have a strange opinion of Monsieur *Fagel*, if you think him capable of so great Indiscretion (or rather Imposture) as to write such a Letter of his own Head. The Letter it self demonstrates, that whoever writ it is no Fool, and the Circumstances I have marked shew that he is no Knave. And indeed the Substance of it is not new, it only repeats to his Majesty the same Answer which the Prince and Princess had formerly given to his Majesty's Envoy there.

In short, you may leave the whole Matter to this plain Issue : If this Letter be a false one, it will be disowned ; if a true one, it will be owned. Their Highnesses love not to do things that will not bear the Light. It is evident, they did not intend the Matter of it should be a Secret, having told it to Monsieur *D'Albeville*, as often as he (in his discreet way) necessitated them to do it. But how it came to be printed, I cannot inform you justly ; however you shall have my Conjecture.

I remember, as soon as it was noised about Town, that Mr. *Stewart* had received a Letter of such a nature from Monsieur *Fagel*, care was taken that the Writer of the common News-Letters, which are dispersed over the Kingdom, should insert in them, that their Highnesses had declared themselves for the Repeal of the Test. This *Pia Fraus* might, I suppose, give occasion to the printing of the Letter, as the Wisdom and Policy of our States-men (in putting Mr. *Stewart* on writing such Letters) had procured it : I say *Letters*, for Monsieur *Fagel* had five or six on that Subject, before he answered ; so unwilling were they in *Holland* to return an Answer, since they could not give one that was pleasing, or do any thing that looked like meddling.

The third thing you desir'd to be satisfy'd in, is, *Whether the Dissenters may rely on their Highnesses Word*. I am as apt to mistrust Princes Promises, as you are. But shall now give you my Reasons, why I think the Dissenters may safely do it. And at the same time, because of the Affinity of the Matter, I will tell you why I think we may all rely on their Highnesses for

our

our *Civil Liberties*, as well as the Diſſenters may do for *Liberty of Conſcience*. Much of what I have to ſay, is equally applicable to them both; yet becauſe I know you have had an Account of her Royal Highneſs better than I can give you, I ſhall for the moſt part, ſpeak only of the Prince.

My firſt Reaſon is the certaineſt of all Reaſons, That it will be his Highneſs's Intereſt to ſettle Matters at home, which only can be done by a Legal Toleration or Comprehenſion in matters of Religion; and by reſtoring the Civil Liberties of the Nation, ſo much invaded of late. That this will be his Intereſt is evident, if his Deſigns lie abroad, as it is certain they do. Deſigns at home and abroad at the ſame time, are ſo inconſiſtent, that we ſee his Majeſty, tho' raiſed above his Fears at home by his late Victory; and invited abroad by all that can excite his Appetite for Glory, cannot reconcile them: The truth is, one that would undertake it, is in the ſame Condition with Officers that beat their Men to make them fight; they have Enemies before and behind.

But you may haply object, that Princes do not always follow their true Intereſts, of which it is not difficult, in this Age, to give ſeveral fatal Inſtances. I anſwer, that it is to be preſum'd that Princes, as well as other Men, will follow their Intereſts till the contrary appear; and if they be of an Age to have taken their Fold, and have till ſuch an Age kept firm to their Intereſts, the Preſumption grows ſtrong; but if their Inclinations, the Maxims of their Families, the Impreſſions of their Education, and all their other Circumſtances do ſide with their Intereſt, and lead them the ſame way, it is hardly credible they ſhould ever quit it. Now this being the preſent Caſe, we have all the certainty that can be had in ſuch Matters.

The Prince of *Orange* has above theſe 15 Years given ſo great Proofs of his Firmneſs and Reſolution as well as of his Capacity and Conduct in oppoſing the grand Raviſher (I may add the Betrayers too) of Liberty and Religion, that he is deſervedly (by all Impartial Men) owned to be the Head of the Proteſtant Intereſt: a Headſhip, which no Princes but the Kings of *England* ſhould have, and none but they would be without it.

Now one may rationally conclude, that when the Prince ſhall join to his preſent Poſſeſſion of this Headſhip, a more natural Title, by being in a greater Capacity to act, he will not degrade himſelf, nor lay aſide Deſigns and Intereſts, which ought to be the Glory of *England*, as they are indeed the Glory of his Family, acquired and derived to him by the Blood of his Anceſtors, and carried on and maintained by himſelf with ſo much Honour and Reputation.

I might add here, that the Prince is a Man of a ſedate, even Temper, full of Thoughts and Reflections; one that precipitates neither in thinking, ſpeaking, nor acting; is cautious in reſolving and promiſing, but firm to his Reſolutions, and exact in obſerving his Word. Inform yourſelf, and you'll find this a part of his Character, and conclude from hence what may be preſumed from his Inclinations.

Now as to the Maxims of his Family, let us compare them a little, where it may decently be done.

The *French* King broke his Faith to his Proteſtant Subjects, upon this ſingle Point of Vain-Glory, that he might ſhew the World he was greater than moſt of his Predeceſſors; who tho' they had the ſame Inclinations, were not potent enough to purſue them effectually, as he has done to the everlaſting Infamy of his Name and Reign. The Maxims of the *French* Kings have been, how to outvie each other in robbing their Neighbours, and oppreſſing their Subjects by Perfidiouſneſs and Cruelty. But thoſe of the Family of *Orange*, on the contrary, have been, to reſcue *Europe* from its Oppreſſors, and maintain the Proteſtant Intereſt, by Virtue, Truth, Honour and Reſolution; knowing that ſuch Methods are as neceſſary to make Proteſtant Princes and States flouriſh, as Vice and Oppreſſion are to maintain Popiſh Government.

No Popiſh Prince in *Europe* can pretend to have kept his Word to his Proteſtant Subjects, as the Princes of *Orange* have always done to their Popiſh Subjects at *Orange*, and elſewhere; and the Papiſts have often broke their Word to that Family, and have been and are its declared Enemies; and tho' the Prince's two great Grand-fathers, Admiral *Coligni*, and Prince *William*, were aſſaſſinated by the Authority, and with the Approbation of that whole Party, yet it cannot be made appear, that ever the Princes of that Family failed in keeping their Word, even to ſuch Enemies, or uſed their own Popiſh Subjects the worſe for it, in making diſtinction between them and their other Subjects, or influenced the States to uſe theirs ſo: I ſay, the States who allow their *R. C.* Subjects all the Privileges of their other Subjects, only they are kept by a Teſt from having any ſhare in the Government, which is truely a Kindneſs done them, conſidering that ill-natured Humour of deſtroying all thoſe that differ from them, which is apt to break out when that Religion is in Power.

Now the Church of *England* may juſtly expect all ſort of Protection and Countenance from the Succeſſors, when it is their Turn to give it; they have a legal Right to it, and impartial Diſſenters muſt acknowledge, that of late they have deſerved it.

S ſ ſ ſ
But

But as for the Proteſtant Diſſenters, I think no honeſt Man among them will apprehend, that their Highneſſes, who keep their word to their Popiſh Enemies, will break it to Proteſtant Subjects, tho' differing from the publick Eſtabliſhment.

The next thing I am to make good, is, That his Highneſs's Education muſt have infuſed ſuch Principles as ſide with his Intereſt: There muſt be a fatal Infection in the *Engliſh* Crown, if Matters miſcarry in his Highneſs's hands. His Veins are full of the beſt Proteſtant Blood in the World. The Reformation in *France* grew up under the Conduct and Influence of *Coligni.* Prince *William* founded the Government of the United *Netherlands* on the Baſis of Property and Liberty of Conſcience, his Highneſs was bred and lives in that State, which ſubſiſts and flouriſhes by adhering ſteadily to the Maxims of its Founder.

He himſelf, both in his publick and private Concerns, as well in the Government of his Family, and of ſuch Principalities as belong to him, as in that of the Army, and in the diſpenſing of that great Power which the States have given him, has as great regard to Juſtice, Virtue and true Religion, as may compleat the Character of a Prince, qualify'd to make thoſe he governs happy.

It does not indeed appear, that their Highneſſes have any ſhare of that devouring Zeal which hath ſo long ſet the World on fire, and tempted thinking Men to have a Notion of Religion itſelf like that we have of the ancient Paradiſe, as if it had never been more than an intended Bleſſing: but all who have the Honour to know their Highneſſes and their Inclinations in Matters of Religion, are fully ſatisfy'd that they have a truely Chriſtian Zeal, and as much as is conſiſtent with Knowledge and Charity.

As to his Highneſs's Circumſtances, they will be ſuch when his Stars make way for him, as may convince our Scepticks, that certain Perſons, Times and Things are prepared for one another. I know not why we may not hope, that as his Predeceſſors broke the Yoak of the Houſe of *Auſtria* from off the Neck of *Europe*; the Honour of breaking that of the Houſe of *Bourbon* is reſerved for him. I am confident, the Nation will heartily join with him in his juſt Reſentments. Reſentments which they have with ſo much Patience longed to find, and have miſſed with the greateſt Indignation in the Hearts of their Monarchs.

His Highneſs has at preſent a greater influence on the Councils of the moſt part of the *Princes* of *Chriſtendom*, than poſſibly any King of *England* ever had: And this acquired by the weight of his own perſonal Merit, which will no doubt grow up to a glorious Authority, when it is cloathed with Sovereign Power. May I here mention (to lay the Jealouſies of the moſt unreaſonable of your Friends) that his Highneſs will have only a borrowed Title, which we may ſuppoſe will make him more cautious in having Deſigns at home, and his wanting Children (to our great Misfortune) will make him leſs ſolicitous to have ſuch Deſigns.

But after all, it muſt be acknowledged, that in Matters of this nature, the Premiſes may ſeem very ſtrong, and yet the Concluſion not follow. Human Infirmities are great, Temptations to Arbitrarineſs are ſtrong, and often both the Spirit and Fleſh weak. Such fatal miſtakes have been made of late, that the Succeſſors themſelves may juſtly pardon Men's Jealouſies. A Widow that has had a bad Huſband, will cry on her Wedding-Day, though ſhe would be married with all her heart. But I am confident you will grant to me, that in the Caſe of the preſent Succeſſors, the Poſſibilities are as remote, and the Jealouſies as ill grounded, and that there is as much to ballance them, as ever there was to be found in the proſpect of any Succeſſors to the Crown of *England.* Now may I add, to conclude the Reaſons that I have given you, why we may depend on their Highneſſes, that I know conſiderable Men, who after great Enquiry and Obſervation, do hope that their Highneſſes (being every way ſo well qualify'd for ſuch an End) are predeſtinated (if I may ſpeak ſo) to make us happy, in putting an end to our Differences, and in fixing the Prerogative, and in recovering the Glory of the Nation, which is ſo much ſunk, and which now (when we were big with Expectations) we find ſacrificed to unhappy Partialities in Matters of Religion.

The laſt thing you deſire to know, is, *What Effect this Letter has had?* But it is not yet old enough for me to judge of that; I can better tell you what effects it ought to have. I find the moderate wiſe Men of all Perſwaſions are much pleaſed with it.

I know *Roman Catholicks*, that wiſh to God matters were ſettled on the Model given in it; they ſee the great Difficulty of getting the Teſt repealed: And withal, they doubt whether it is their Intereſt that it ſhould be repealed or not: They fear needy violent Men might get into Employments who would put his Majeſty on doing things that might ruin them and their Poſterity. They are certainly in the right of it. It is good to provide for the worſt. A Revolution will come with a Witneſs; and it is like it may come before the Prince of *Wales* be of Age to manage an unruly Spirit, that I fear will accompany it. Human Nature can hardly digeſt what it is already neceſſitated to ſwallow, ſuch Provocations even alter Men's Judgements. I find that Men, who otherwiſe hate ſeverity, begin to be of opinion that Queen *Elizabeth*'s Lenity to the R. C's proves now Cruelty to the Proteſtants. The whole body of Proteſtants in the Nation, was lately afraid of a *Popiſh Succeſſor*, and when they reflected on Queen *Mary's* Reign,

thought

thought we had already sufficient Experience of the Spirit of that Religion ; and took Self-preservation to be a good Argument for preventing a second Trial. But now a handful of *Roman Catholicks*, perhaps reflecting on Queen *Elizabeth*'s Reign, are not, it seems, afraid of *Protestant Successors*. But if some *Protestants* at that time, from an Aversion to the Remedy, hoped that the Disease was not so dangerous as it proves ; I am confident at present, all *Protestants* have agreed, that henceforward the Nation must be saved, not by Faith. And therefore I would advise the R. C's to consider, that *Protestants* are still Men ; that late Experiences at home, and the Cruelties of *Popish Princes* abroad has given a very terrible *Idea* of their Religion. That Opportunity is precious, and very slippery ; and if they let the present Occasion pass by, they can hardly ever hope that it will be possible for them to recover it. That their Fathers and Grand-fathers would have thought themselves in Heaven to have had such an Offer as this is, in any of the four last Reigns ; and therefore, they had better be contented with *Half a Loaf than no Bread*. I mean, it will be their Wisdom to embrace this Golden Occasion of putting themselves on a Level with all other *English* Men, at least as to their private Capacity, and to disarm once for all, the severity of those Laws ; which, if ever they should come to be in good earnest executed by a Protestant Successor, will make *England* too hot for them : And therefore I should particularly advise those among them, who have the Honour to approach his Majesty, to use their Credit to prevail with him to make this so necessary a Step in favour of the Nation ; since the Successors have advanced two Thirds of the Way for effecting so good and pious a Work. Then, and not till then, the R. C's may think themselves secured, and his Majesty may hope to be great, by translating Fear and Anger from the Breasts of his Subjects, to the Hearts of his own and the Nation's Enemies.

But if an evil Genius (which seems to have hovered over us now a long time) will have it otherwise ; if I were a R. C. I would meddle no more, but live quiet at home, and caress my Protestant Neighbours : and in so doing, I should think myself better secured against the Resentments of the Nation, than by all the Forces, Forts, Leagues, Guaranties, and even *Male Children*, that his Majesty may hope to leave behind him.

As for the Protestant Dissenters, I am confident the Body of them will continue to behave themselves like Men, who, to their great honour have ever preferred the Love of their Country and Religion to all Dangers and Favours whatsoever, but there are both weak and interested Men among all great Numbers : I would have them consider how much the state of things is altered, upon the coming out of this Letter ; for if hitherto they have been too forward in giving ear to Proposals on this Mistake, that they could never have such a favourable Juncture, for getting the Laws against them repealed : I hope now they are undeceived, since the Successors have pawn'd their Faith and Honour for it, which I take to be a better Security (as Matters go at present) than the so much talked of *Magna Charta* for Liberty of Conscience would be, tho' got in a legal Way : for our Judges have declared, That Princes can dispense with the Obligation of Laws, but they have not yet given their Opinion, that they can dispense with the Honour of their Word ; nor have their Highnesses any Confessor to supply such an Omission.

However, it is not to be charged on their Highnesses, if such a *Magna Charta* be not at present given them, provided the Test be let alone ; but I fear the *Roman Catholicks* Zeal will have all or nothing ; and the Test too must be repealed by wheedling the Dissenters to join with willing Sheriffs in violating the Rights of Elections, which are the Root of the Liberties of *England* ; a prudent way of recommending their Religion to all true *English Men*.

But if any of the Dissenters be so destitute of sense and honesty, as to prefer a *Magna Charta* so obtain'd, void and null in itself, to their own Honour and Conscience, to the Love and Liberties of their Country, to the present Kindness of all good Men, and their Countenance at another time ; and above all, to the Favour and Word of the Successors, who have now so generously declared themselves for them : We may pronounce, that they are Men abandoned to a reprobate Sense, who will justly deserve infamy and the hatred of the Nation at present, and its Resentments hereafter. Is it possible, that any Dissenter, who either deserves or loves the Reputation of an honest Man, can be prevailed with by any Pretences or Insinuations, how plausible soever, to make so odious and pernicious a Bargain, as that of buying a precarious pretended Liberty of Conscience, at the price of the Civil Liberties of their Country, and at the price of removing that, which under God is the most effectual Bar to keep us from the Dominion of a Religion, that would, as soon as it could, force us to abandon our own, or reduce us to the miserable Condition of those of our Neighbours, who are glad to forsake all they have in the World, that they may have their Souls and Lives for a Prey.

As for the Church of *England*, their Clergy have of late opposed themselves to *Popery*, with so much Learning, Vigour, Danger and Success, that I think all honest Dissenters will lay down their Resentments against them, and look on that Church, as the present

sent

fent Bulwark and Honour of the Proteftant Religion. I wifh thofe high Men among them, who have fo long appropriated to themfelves the Name and Authority of the Church of *England*, and have been made Inftruments to bring about Defigns, of which their prefent Behaviour convinces me, they were ignorant, as I fuppofe many of the Diffenters are, whofe turn it is now to be the Tools:

I fay, I wifh fuch Men would confider, to what a pafs they have brought Matters by their Violences, or rather the Violences of thofe whofe Property they were, and at length be wife: They cannot but be fenfible of the Advantages they receive by this Letter. I fuppofe they apprehend (I am fure they ought to do it) that the Ruin of their Church is refolved on: But if the Diffenters upon this Letter withdraw themfelves, the *R. C's* have neither Hearts to keep firm to fuch a Refolution, nor Hands to execute it.

Since therefore they themfelves have unhappily brought their Church into fuch Precipices by provoking the Diffenters, it is in a particular manner their Duty, as well as their Intereft, to endeavour to foften them, by affifting the Letter, and promoting the Defign of it.

But if the old *Leaven* ftill remain, and they continue to argue as formerly, if the Surplice be parted with, the Church of *England* is loft; if the Penal Laws be repealed, the Teft will follow: and comfort themfelves with this moft Chriftian Reflection, that the *R. C.* will not accept of what is offered them; fuch Men deferve all the Mifery that is preparing for them, and will perifh without Pity, and give thinking Men occafion to remember the Proverb, *Beat a Fool* (or a *Zealot*) *in a Mortar, yet his Foolifhnefs will not depart from him.* But the Diffenters ought not to be much concerned at this, they have their own Bigots, and the Church of *England* theirs, there will be Tools whilft there are Workmen.

This is a time for Wifdom to be juftified of her Children, when honeft Men ought to leave off minding the leffer Interefts of this or that particular Church, and join in fecuring the common Interefts of the Proteftant Religion. And to conclude, I would particularly beg of the Diffenters to make ufe of their beft Judgment on this fo critical an occafion, which they will do, in my Opinion, in keeping clofe to the Contents of this Letter, by endeavouring to obtain in a fair and legal way, fuch a Liberty to all Perfwafions, as is the natural Right of Free-men, and as our Proteftant Succeffors declare themfelves willing to join in; and if thofe who have an equal, nay, a greater Intereft than themfelves, will not agree to fuch a Liberty, becaufe they will be Mafters or nothing; the Diffenters will have the Comfort of having difcharged their own Confciences, as prudent Men and good Chriftians ought to do, and may fafely truft God with the Event.

Sir, I thought I had made an end, but looking your Letter over again, I find I have forgot to anfwer a Reafon or two you give, why you doubt whether the Letter be truly M. *Fagel's:* You are informed (you fay) that fuch and fuch Great Men doubted of it; but fome might as well pretend to doubt of the Truth of that Letter (tho' they knew it to be true) as believe her Majefty to be with Child almoft before fhe knew it herfelf; and that fhe was quick, when the Embryo, as Anatomifts fay, is not above an Inch long. I don't think that Popifh Succeffors, like certain Weeds, grow fafter than others: The Perfons you name may trim, and prefume on their Merit, left they might be thought capable of Refentment. A dangerous Reflection! I fay their Merit: You have feen a long Relation of the great Services fome (when they were in Power) did their Highneffes; it is bound up with a Relation of the true Caufes of their Sufferings for their (or rather their Highneffes) Religion. You know how even one of them the laft Summer pay'd them his Reverence with all the Refpect and Humility of a due Diftance, and with the fame Caution with which the invincible Monarch fights out of Cannon-Shot. But Sir, though the Character of a Trimmer be ordinarily the Character of a prudent Man, there are Times and Seafons when it is not the Character of an honeft Man.

I acknowledge, that fince their Highneffes Marriage, nothing has happened fo much for the Good of the Proteftant Intereft as this Letter of M. *Fagel's*; and if I had been either the Writer or Advifer of it, I fhould be very proud of it, and think the Nation much in my debt. But Sir, that was not a very good Reafon to make you doubt of it; for a good Caufe will have its Time, though not fo often as a bad one, which hath ordinarily the Majority on its fide.

I am confident at prefent that we have all the reafon in the World to expect it: for my own part, tho' I am neither young nor ftrong, I hope to live to fee a Day of Jubilee in *England* for all that deferve it; when honeft Men fhall have the fame Pleafure in thinking on thefe Times, that a Woman happily delivered hath in reflecting on the Pain and Danger fhe was in. But Knaves will remember them, as I am told, the Damned do their Sins, curfing both them and themfelves.

S I R,

January the 12th, 1688.   *I am yours.*

Animadverfions

Animadversions upon a pretended Answer to Mijn Heer Fagel's *Letter.*

S I R,

I Have been so far hitherto from thinking, that the pretended *Answer* to the Excellent *Letter of Mijn Heer Fagel* deserved a Reply, that I judged it would have been a disgrace offered to the Judgment of Persons of the most ordinary Intellectuals, as well as the witnessing not only a great measure of self-denial, but the submitting of my self to a severe mortification and penance, to bestow one upon it. For as it argues a mean Opinion of mankind, to believe that they should need any assistance, save what their own Reason furnisheth them with, in order to their preservation from being imposed upon, by so weak, foolish, incoherent and self-contradictious a Paper; so 'tis both the rendring one mean and cheap, and the inflicting upon himself a most uneasy chastisement, to waste his time and employ his thoughts in animadverting upon, and exposing so trifling and despicable an Author. But seeing I am told, that not only he who is commonly supposed to have had the presumption and indiscretion to write the *Answer*, has also the vanity to value himself upon it; but that there are others, whose wit, candor and ingenuity are much of a size with his, who do improve our silence in reference unto it, tho' arising from the contempt and neglect which all wise men have for it, to countenance themselves in a belief, and to obtrude an Opinion upon others, of it's containing something nervous and considerable; I shall therefore account my self, for once, so much a debtor both to the vain, and to the unwise, as to bestow a few such Reflections upon it, as may serve to rectify the Judgments of the one; and both to correct the folly, and to abate the pride and swelling confidence of the other. And indeed the Author's concealing his Name, may make us justly suspect, that we are not to look for truth, strength, nor candor in that Paper, especially when he writes not only in justification of the proceedings of his Majesty of *Great Britain*, which is enough to shield him from all severe Attacks, provided that he had conducted himself as became a wise and an honest man: But in that he enters the lists against a person of *Mijn Heer Fagel's* quality, and whose Letter not only had his Name affixed to it, and was beautified with all those impressions of Clearness, Gravity, Strength, Prudence and Religion, which became the greatness of the Subject, and whereunto the having been able to return an Answer, that had the umbrage and appearance of Reason, would have given a reputation to the Undertaker; but which had been also penned by the Command and Authority of their Serene Highnesses the *Prince* and *Princess* of *Orange*, in order to declare their Opinion in a matter of the greatest importance that ever *English* Protestants were concerned in, and from Principles of Conscience and Justice hath given that assurance and satisfaction, which all peaceable and good men either stood in need of, or could desire. And as this Author's venturing abroad in the fashion of an *Incognito*, was not without Reason, seeing he might thereby hope not only to treat *Mijn Heer Fagel* without regard to truth or ingenuity, but that with the less hazard both to his person and reputation, he might arraign the Justice and Fidelity of these States, and charge them with a violation of the Fundamental Articles, upon which their Government was at first erected; so that he must not take it amiss, if upon encountering him in the dark, I not only fail in paying him the deference which he may conceive due unto him, but handle him unsuitably to the Post he is said to possess. Tho' I am not without apprehension, that if he bear the Character which is vulgarly ascribed to him; and if the greatest indication of the wisdom and integrity of Princes, be the prudence and sincerity of their Ministers, but that we may thence come under a necessity of entertaining meaner thoughts than we otherwise would, both of the Moral and Intellectual Capacity of him, to whom this Gentleman is indebted both for his Titles, and the Function he is exalted unto. Whereas on the other hand, besides many signal Evidences, which have filled all *Europe* with admiration of the admirable Wisdom, inflexible Integrity, eminent Vertues, religious tho' calm and discreet Zeal, and steddy and impartial Justice of his Highness the Prince of *Orange*; our Ideas of him as a Person under whose Government, Conduct and Shadow all good men may promise themselves happiness, are not a little heightned by the consideration of the excellent Qualities of *Monsieur Fagel*, whose advancement as *Pensionary* of *Holland*, to the first Ministry in that State, is owing to the *Prince's* Grace and Recommendation. Which eminent Trust, as he hath all along discharged with Honour to his *Highness*, Reputation to himself, and to the Satisfaction of those who are interested

Tttt
rested

refted in the Affairs of that Republick; fo by nothing hath he more merited an univerfal Efteem and Praife from all Proteftants, and acquitted himfelf more worthily
towards God and their Serene *Highneſſes*, than by that *Letter* wherein he was honoured to declare their Thoughts, and in which he hath with fo much wifdom, moderation and convincing light, expreffed both their *Highneſſes* Sentiments, and his
own, as well concerning the *Engliſh* Laws, the Papifts may, and the Diffenters ought
to be favoured with the Repeal of, as concerning thofe, which no wife Non-conformift defires to have refcinded, and which to humour the Papifts with the Abrogation of, were no lefs than to expofe the Nation to ruin, and to lay the Reformed Religion open to be totally fubverted.

Now this excellent *Letter*, and which hath produced all the good Effects that honeft men long'd for, but knew not before how to compafs, our *Anonymous* Anfwerer
is pleafed with an Indignation and angry Refentment, and in hopes to exafperate his
Majefty of *Great Britain* againft their Serene Highneffes, to ftile a *kind of Manifefto in
reference to moſt important Affairs, which even Mr. Stewart*, who, in obedience to the
injunctions of his Sovereign, had with fo much importunity follicited their Highneffes
Opinion about the Repeal of the Penal and Teft Laws, he fays, *could not have expected*.
And of whom to teftify his exact and intimate knowledge, and to recompenfe him
for the unfortunate Service he had been employed in, and to encourage his readinefs
to future drudgery, he is pleafed by a Creation of his own, as being the Subftitute of
the Fountain of Honour, to confer the Title of *Dr.* upon. But certainly had this *Anonymous* Writer the fenfe and prudence of an ordinary man, he would not, under the
prefent conjuncture of Affairs, talk of *Manifeftos*, nor put people in mind of them at a
feafon, when moft perfons of all ranks and qualities are fo much difgufted, and when
they at *Whiteball* are fo lavifh in their provocations towards *fome*, who if they were
not ftrangely fortified againft all tincture of Refentment, are known to be capable of
doing them irreparable prejudice, and who by fuch a *Manifefto* as there is caufe enough
to emit, might not only difturb their proceedings, but with the greateft facility blow
up at once both all their hopes and projections. I would fain know of this modeft and
difcreet Gentleman, whether if their *Highneſſes* had ordered a Letter to be written,
declarative of their Opinion for the Abrogation of the *Teſts*, by what Name he would
have judged it worthy to be called, and whether if he had beftowed upon it the Title
of a *Manifefto*, he would have thereby intended to faften upon it an imputation of prefumption and reproach? All good men have reafon mightily to bewail their *Highneſſes*
condition, feeing according to this rate of proceeding towards them, it is in the power
of the Papal Ecclefiafticks in *England*, when they pleafe, to prevail upon the *King* to
reduce them to the uneafy circumftances, either of offending againft their Confciences,
or of difpleafing him. For there is no more requifite towards the bringing them into this unhappy *Dilemma*, but that *Father Peters*, or any other of the Tribe who have
an Afcendency over his Majefty, do perfuade him to defire their *Highneſſes* Thoughts,
in reference to fuch particulars, wherein it is neither confiftent with their Religious
Principles, nor agreeable with their Honour, to comply with his Majefty's Judgment
and Inclinations. For if in prudence they decline the returning of an Anfwer, they are
fure not only to be cenfured, as guilty of neglect, incivility and rudenefs, but they
do thereby adminifter an advantage to their Enemies, of diffufing reports to their prejudice thro' the Nation, as if they approved all thofe Court-methods, which for no
other reafon, fave upon the meer motives of refpect and wifdom, they avoided openly
to difallow. And if, on the other hand, they fuffer themfelves to be overcome by importunities, and thereupon give an Anfwer agreeable to the Dictates of their own
minds, but which is found to interfere with the prepoffeffions wherewith his Majefty is
imbued, then their Lot is, to have it called by the unkind and ignominious Title of a
Manifefto. One would think that *Letter* ought to have been mentioned by a fofter
name, if we do but confider it's being written not only with the utmoft modefty that
becomes the Relation their Highneffes ftand in to the King, and which is any ways
agreeable to their own quality, but that it is enforced with all the Reafons, that may
ferve to demonftrate that their opinion is the refult of conviction and judgment, and
not the effect of humour, nor a fentiment they are meerly determined unto by their
intereft. But we fee no Term is too hard to be beftowed upon a Paper that hath fo
much prejudiced the Priefts in their defigns, and laid fo great an obftruction in the
way of thofe methods, which they had propofed to themfelves, for the robbing *England* of the Proteftant Religion.

And whereas our Author tells us, that tho' Mr. *Stewart did not account himfelf obliged
to anfwer Monſieur* Fagel's *Letter, yet one who extremely efteems and honoureth Mr.* Stewart, *thinks the Publick too much concerned, not to have the weakneſs of the reafonings in it de-*
2   *tected,*

tected, and to have it made appear that the inferences deduced from them are no ways convincing. I can easily believe that Mr. *Stewart* did not judge himself obliged to answer the *Pensionary's Letter*, and all men do account it a piece of wisdom in him to forbear endeavouring it. For tho' he be much better qualified for such an Undertaking than our Author, yet he could not but be sensible that it was not to be attempted with any hope of success. And if our Author had been endow'd with any measure of discretion, he would have applied himself to any other Employment, rather than have betaken himself to writing, being a thing which Nature never intended him for, and especially upon a Subject so far above the reach of his Understanding, and against a discourse of that solid and well-digested Strength, that even the Reverend Fathers, whose *Letter-carrier* he used to be (if we be not strangely mistaken in the Gentleman) had so much wit as not to attack it: As knowing that notwithstanding all their Art and Sophistry, they must have come off baffled ; and that their false colours would have been easily detected, by the Beams of that Light, which dart themselves forth in all parts of that excellent Paper. And I dare farther say, that as Mr. *Stewart* will never much value himself, upon the being esteemed by one either of this Gentleman's Religious Principles, or of his intellectual Accomplishments ; so I can never think that he can be so much degenerated from what he formerly was, as to obtain the approbation of his mind, to return any considerable degree of honour to a Person who upon all accounts does so little merit it, unless it be that he may possibly challenge it by virtue of an undeserved Title, and of a Character that he is exceeding ill qualified for.

However, seeing Fools will be meddling, tho' they are sure to come by the worst, I shall reduce all I have to say in Castigation of this vain and presumptuous man, to the *seven* following heads. (1.) His Falsifications in reference to several parts of *Mijn Heer Fagel's Letter*. (2.) His Injustice to their Highnesses the *Prince and Princess* of *Orange*, and the hidden spleen he every where ventureth to express against them. (3.) His slanderous Calumnies against the States of these Provinces, and how he studies to excite their Roman Catholick Subjects to disturb the Peace and Tranquillity of this Country. (4.) His shameless Impudence in endeavouring to impose upon the World, as if the Protestant Dissenters in *England* were concluded by their Highnesses to stand hereafter involved in the same rank and condition with the Papists. (5.) His publishing the Villany of the Romish Church, and proclaiming the Injustice and Dishonour of the most eminent Papal Monarchs, while he pretends to commend and justify the proceeding of his Majesty of *Great Britain*. (6.) His egregious Ignorance in relation to Government, Laws, Customs, and matters of Fact. (*Lastly*) The signal Ingratitude of the Papists towards their Royal Highnesses for all that Grace, Favour and Ease, which they were willing to have allowed unto them.

As to the *first*, 'Tis known to be a received Principle among the *Casuists* of the *Society*, that it is at most but a venial sin, to detract from, misrepresent, and calumniate those whom they either take to be their Enemies, or do conceive to have done them any ways a prejudice. And tho' the Opinion authorising such a Practice, be condemned by a *Bull* of the present *Pope*, bearing Date *Anno* 1679, yet our Author is more a Vassal to the *Ignatian Order*, than upon the Authority of one whom the *Jesuits* do so little value, to forbear putting a Doctrine into exercise, which he hath been so well instructed in by these Reverend Fathers, and especially when he finds it so conducible to his Design and Interest. What can be remoter from Truth, as well as Ingenuity, than to charge *Monsieur Fagel with confining the name of Protestants in* England, *only to those of the conformable Communion, and with excluding the Dissenters from the glorious Privilege of that appellation?* For tho' it be true, that thro' the hatred and violence of the late King and his present Majesty to the Fanaticks, and by virtue of their Commands to a Company of mercenary, timorous and servile Justiciaries and Officers, it hath some time come to pass that the Laws which were originally enacted, and only intended against *Papists*, have been executed upon *Dissenters* ; yet all men know that to have been a perversion of Justice, seeing in all the Statutes, to the Penalties whereof they were made obnoxious, they are still considered and acknowledged for *Protestants*, and made liable to sufferings by no other Title than that of persons differing from the Church of *England*, in matter of *Discipline*, and about *Forms* and *Rites* of external Worship. Nor is there one word in *Mijn Heer Fagel's* Letter, whereby they are precluded from that Stile, or any ways represented as unworthy of it. While they stand obnoxious to several Laws, in which the Members of the Church of *England* have no concernment, nor are in any danger from ; it was impossible to avoid the giving them a name by which they might be distinguished from those of the Legal and National Communion. And so tender hath the *Pensionary* been of charactering them by any offensive or harsh denomination, that he hath not so much as once in his whole Letter called them *Fanaticks*, tho'

it

it be an appellation that hath been vulgarly affixed to them ; but he hath chofen always to denominate them by the name of *Diffenters*, which is not only the fofteft Term they can be defcribed by, but that which themfelves have elected as the ftile by which they are willing to be difcriminated from their fellow Proteftants, with whom they differ in fome few and little particulars.   And many of them being people, whofe Principles are coincident and agreeable with theirs of the legal Eftablifhment in *Holland*, in whofe Fellowfhip *Monfieur Fagel* is known to be ; it could not have entred into the thoughts of any fave one of our Author's Intellectuals and Integrity, either to charge upon him, or fo much as to imagine, that he fhould be fo injurious to himfelf and to the *Dutch* Churches, as to preclude thofe from the lift of Proteftants.   But whether this calumnious charge and falfification, be the fruit of an *Irifh* Underftanding, or of Papal Sincerity, or the effect of both, I fhall leave others to judge, who may poffibly know this Author, better than I pretend to do.   Only this I fhall add, that he proceeds with the fame wit and honefty as he hath begun.   For from their Highneffes declaring that they cannot agree to the Repeal of the *Tefts*, and *Monfieur Fagel's* thereupon faying, that thefe Laws inflict not any mulct or penalty upon the Roman Catholicks, but that they are only means of fecuring the Reformed Religion, thro' containing provifions by which men are to be accounted qualified for Members of Parliament, and to bear publick Offices ; our Author does by a ftrange kind of falfification and calumny, faften upon him his having affirmed, *That the Nonconformifts are to be accounted dangerous Enemies of the State, and not to be admitted into any publick Employments.* He muft either be of a very unufual and perverfe frame of mind, or extreamly ignorant of the nature of thofe Laws, and the Terms wherein they are enacted, otherways it is impoffible he fhould imagine how the *Diffenters* are capable of receiving prejudice by them.   Seeing all required by thofe Laws towards the qualifying perfons to fit in Parliament, and to exercife Offices in Church and State, is only to declare that they *do believe there is not any Tranfubftantiation in the Sacrament of the Lord's Supper, or in the Elements of Bread and Wine, at or after the Confecration by any perfons whatfoever ; and that the Invocation of the Virgin* Mary, *or any other Saint, and the Sacrifice of the Mafs, as they are now ufed in the Church of* Rome, *are Superftitious and Idolatrous.*   And this Declaration the Non-conformifts are of all people, the moft inclinable and forward to make, and therefore very far by virtue of thofe Statutes from ftanding incapable of any Truft, Office, and Employment, that other Subjects are admitted unto.   Nor hath there been a Proteftant Diffenter fince the firft hour that thefe Laws were enacted, that ever fcrupled to take the *Tefts*, or that was precluded from Office and Employment for refufing them.   But on the contrary, feveral of the moft famous Diffenters, fuch as Sir *John Hartop*, Alderman *Love*, and Mr. *Eyles*, perfons who at all times have kept at the greateft diftance from Communion with the Church of *England*, by reafon of her Forms and Ceremonies, are known to have chearfully made the Declaration contained in the *Teft* Laws, and thereupon to have fat as Members in divers Parliaments.   And as a further demonftration of the impudence and difhonefty of our Author in this particular, it is not unworthy of remark, that tho' the King hath taken upon him to difpenfe with the *Tefts*, and to prohibit the requiring them ; yet the Diffenters, who have fince that time been preferred to publick Trufts, continue ftill to take them, and go to the refpective Courts, where by Law the Declaration is enjoined to be exacted, and there demand the being admitted to make it.   Tho' in the mean feafon they cannot be unfenfible, that it is the thing in the world whereby they moft highly offend his Majefty ; it being both a proclaiming the Illegality of that Authority which he challengeth of difpenfing with Laws ; and a defeating, fo far as lieth in them, his great defign as well as artifice, for the introducing of Popery, which his Soul is fo much in travel with.   And were not this Author both a perfon of a moft depraved Confcience, and deftitute of all common fenfe, he would never have flandered *Monfieur Fagel*, and fo egregioufly perverted his plain meaning, as to tell us, that tho' he be a *Hollander and a Non-conformift, yet he thanks God for the Teft-Laws, by which his Non-conforming Brethren in* England, *of what degree and quality foever they be, ftand excluded from publick Employments.*   For every one that will be fo kind to himfelf, and fo juft to the *Penfionary*, as to read his Letter, will immediately difcern that there is not one word in it, upon which to fuperftruct this calumny and accufation ; feeing he therein affirms in repeated and emphatical Terms, that all contained in, and defigned by the *Teft* Laws, is *the fecuring the Reformed Religion, thro' the having provided, that none be allowed to fit in Parliament, nor admitted to publick Offices, except they declare that they are of the Reformed, and not of the Roman Catholick Religion.*   So that how *Monfieur Fagel's* Non-conforming Brethren in England fhould come to be affected by thefe Laws, fo as to receive any prejudice by them, is that which none but a perfon of our Author's wit, integrity and candor could have had the faculty either to conceive or alledge.   But

But that we may come to the *second particular*; there is the less reason to wonder at this Gentleman's calumniating *Mijn Heer Fagel*, and affixing dull, tho' malicious Forgeries of his own unto him, if we do but confider with what petulancy and injuftice he treats their *Serene Highneffes*, and at the gate of their own Court affumeth the confidence to mifreprefent, leffen and afperfe them. The nearnefs which thofe Princes ftand in to the afcending the *Englifh* Throne, and the joyful profpect which all Proteftants have of it, exciteth a difcontent and rage in our Author, which he knows not how either to fupprefs or govern. For not to mention what we learn of the kindnefs of Roman Catholicks to an Heir, profeffing the Reformed Religion, from the proceedings of *Sixtus Quintus*, and the Papifts in *France* towards *Henry* 4. we are fufficiently inftructed what good Will they bear to a Proteftant Succeffor, by the Bull which *Clement* 8. publifhed about the End of Queen *Elizabeth*'s Reign. For the Supream and Infallible Head does therein ordain, *That when it fhould happen to that miferable Woman to die, they fhould admit none to the Crown, quantumque propinquitate fanguinis niterentur, nifi ejufmodi effent qui fidem Catholicam non modo tolerarent, fed omni ope ac ftudio promoverent, & more majorum jurejurando fe id praeftituros fufciperent; whatfoever Right and Title they fhould have thereunto, by virtue of their next affinity in blood, unlefs they fhould firft fwear not only to tolerate, but to advance and eftablifh the Romifh Religion.* Nor can I avoid being filled with fear and reverence to the fafety of fome certain perfons, when I remember how Cardinal *Baronius* commends *Irene* for murdering the Emperor her Son, becaufe he was againft the Worfhip of Images, and not only calls it *Juftitiae zelum,* a righteous zeal, but adds, *Chriftum docuiffe, fummum pietatis genus effe in hoc adverfus filium effe fidelem, That Chrift hath taught the Perfection of Religion in fuch a cafe to confift in fidelity to the Church, tho' by deftroying one that was both her Son and her Sovereign.* 'Tis a high piece of injuftice in our Author towards their *Highneffes,* and calculated for no other end but to alienate his Majefty's affections from them, when he tells us, that *the thing aimed at in the writing of the Penfionary's Letter, as well as that purfued in the manner of publifhing it, was to obftruct the King's righteous and pious defigns, and to render them unpracticable.* For the Letter being written in obedience to the Command of their *Highneffes,* and to declare their Opinion in reference to the feveral matters, about which it treateth; it plainly follows, that tho' *Mijn Heer Fagel* be accountable for the manner of cloathing and delivering their thoughts, and for the Order and Method in which things are digefted, and poffibly for the Ratiocinations by which they are fupported and enforced, yet that the *Prince* and *Princefs* are the perfons who are alone refponfible for the End unto which it was intended. And it appears to have been fo far from their intentions, thereby to obftruct and defeat any pious and juft defigns of his Majefty; that nothing can be more vifible, than that as it is admirably adapted to the giving eafe and fecurity to all his Proteftant Subjects, fo it offereth means for relieving the Papifts from the fevere Laws to which they are liable, and for the granting them a Warranty in a legal way for the exercife of their Religion. Nor doth it difcourage any kind of favour towards them, fave that which the conceffion whereof, would not only be inconfiftent with the peace and fafety of thofe of the Reformed Religion in *England*; but which might enflame the Nation to fuch Refentments, as would in all likelihood both endanger his Majefty's Perfon and Crown, and come at laft to iffue in the reducement of the Roman Catholicks to worfe circumftances, than they have been hitherto acquainted with. But to proceed with our Author, to whom it is fo natural to act foolifhly, and with faucinefs and injuftice, that neither the Character he is faid to bear, nor the Quality of the Perfons of whom he fpeaks, can either reftrain his intemperance, or correct his rudenefs and indifcretion: For *Monfieur Fagel* having faid, that he believes there are many Roman Catholicks, who under the prefent ftate of Affairs, will not be very defirous to be in Publick Offices and Employments, nor ufe any attempts againft thofe of the Reformed Religion; and that not only becaufe they know it to be contrary to Law, but left it fhould at fome other time, prove prejudicial to their Perfons and States: Our Author is fo unjuft as well as imprudent, as to call this *a menacing not only of all the Nonconformifts and Roman Catholicks in* England, *but a threatning of his Majefty, and an infulting over him.* And from thence he takes occafion to add, *that he hopes God will enable his Majefty to reprefs and prevent the effects of thefe menaces, and furnifh him with means of mortifying thofe who do thus threaten and infult over him.* It certainly argues a ftrange weaknefs and diftemper of mind, to call fo modeft and foft an expreffion, both a *menacing of the King and of all his Catholick Subjects,* when I dare fay, it proclaimeth the fenfe of all among the Papifts who are endowed with any meafure of Wifdom, and is nothing elfe fave a Declaration of the meafure, by which they do at this day regulate and conduct themfelves. But the injuftice of our Author towards their *Highneffes* in his Reflections upon the forementioned expreffion of the *Penfio-*

nary's, is his intending them by the persons that do threaten his Majesty and insult over him. For did he take *Mijn Heer Fagel* for the only guilty person in reference to this Phrase which he miscalls a *Menace*, it would be a strange detracting in him from the Power and Glory of his Majesty of *Great Britain*, to wish him sufficient means whereby to shun the effects of a Gentleman's threatning, whose highest Figure in the World is meerly to be a Minister in a Republick. Nor would he bring down his Master to so low a level, as to make it the highest Object of his Hopes, concerning so great a Monarch, that he shall be able to mortify a Person, who, whatsoever his Merit be, yet his Fortune is to fill no sublimer a *Post*. So that it can be no other save the *Prince* and *Princess*, whom our Author, in his usual way of injustice, petulancy and indiscretion does here character, represent and intend. And what he thereupon means by the *King's having power in his hands, and by his hoping that God would furnish him with means by which he may mortify them*, is not a matter of difficult penetration, even by persons of the most ordinary capacities. For the several methods that have been projected, and are still carrying on, for the debarring them from the Succession to the Imperial Crowns of *England*, *Scotland* and *Ireland*, to which they have so Just and Hereditary a Right, are sufficient to detect unto us what our Author intends, and serve as a Key whereby to open the scope, and meaning of his Expressions. But whatsoever the Papal and Jesuitick Endeavours may be, for the obstructing and preventing their Ascending the Thrones of *Great Britain*, I dare say that all the effects they will have, will be only the discovering the folly and malice of those that attempt it, and that they can never be able to compass and accomplish it. For as their Highnesses have both that Interest in the Love and Veneration of all Protestants, and so indisputable a Title, that it is impossible they should be precluded either by *Force*, or in a way to which their Enemies may affix the Name of *Legal*; so there is no great cause to apprehend or fear, their being supplanted by the King's having Male Issue of a vigour to live, considering both his Majesty's Condition and the Queen's, which is such that they can never communicate *bona stamina vitæ*. And for the Papists being able to *Banter* a supposititious Brat upon the Nation, (tho' there are many among them villanous enough to attempt it) we have not only the watchfulness of Divine Providence to rely upon for preventing it, but there are many faithful and waking Eyes that will be ready and industrious to discover the Cheat. And if the People once perceive, that there hath been a contrivance carried on for putting so base an affront upon a noble and generous Kingdom, and of committing so horrid a wrong against such Vertuous and Excellent Princes; I do not know but that their Resentment of it may rise so high, as that all who are discovered to have been accessory unto it, may undergo the like fate that they of old did, who were found to have been conscious and contributory unto the thrusting the Eunuch *Smerdis* into the *Persian* Throne. Nor do I in the least doubt but that the same Righteous, Wise and Merciful God, who prevented the like villany when designed in the time of Queen *Mary*, and which was advanced so far, that some Priests had the wickedness and impudence, both to give Thanks in the publick Churches for her Majesty's safe delivery of a Prince, and also to describe the Beauty and Features of the *Babe*, tho' all she had gone with, amounted only to a *Tympany* of Wind and Water; I say that I do not question, but that the same God will out of his immense Grace and Sapience, find ways and methods, of which there are many within the Compass of his infinite Understanding, by which so hellish a piece of villany, if there be any such projected and promoting, may be brought into light and disappointed. And truly when I consider the Christian and Royal Vertues wherewith their Highnesses are imbued, and how they are furnished with all the Moral, Intellectual and Religious Accomplishments, that are requisite for adapting them to wield Scepters, and which render them not only so agreeable to the necessities and desires of all good people, but so admirably qualified to answer both the present Posture of Affairs in *Europe*, and the Exigencies of those that are oppressed and afflicted; I grow into a confidence, that as the Church of God both in *Britain* and elsewhere, and the circumstances in which so many Countries are involved, do bespeak and crave their Exaltation to the Thrones of the *British* Dominions, so that they are both destined of God unto them, and will in due time be safely conducted thither. Nor can I avoid pleasing my self with those joyful and hopeful thoughts, when I reflect upon the various steps of Divine Providence, by which they are brought into that nearness of legally inheriting these Crowns. Certainly there is a voice that speaketh loud to this purpose, not only in God's denying a Legitimate Issue to the late King, and in his taking away from time to time all the lawful Male Off-spring of his present Majesty, but in the uniting their *Highnesses* in Marriage, even to the crossing a certain Person's Inclinations, whom I forbear to name, as well as to the disgusting of a Neighbouring Monarch,

narch, and to the defeating the bufy endeavours of the Popifh Party. But I muft return to our Author, whofe Injuftice to their *Highneffes*, and his malice againft their Honour, Intereft and Reputation, knows neither end nor bounds. For upon *Monfieur Fagel's* having ask'd, Who would go about to advife him or any man elfe, to endeavour to perfuade their *Highneffes*, whom God has fo far honoured, as to make them Defenders of his Church, to approve and promote things fo dangerous and hurtful both to the reformed Religion, and to the publick Safety, as the Repealing of the *Teft*-Laws would be ; our Author does hereupon with his wonted Friendfhip, Equity and Candor to thofe excellent *Princes*, tell us, *that he hath not met with fo bold a Declaration as this of calling them the Protectors of God's Church, and that the afcribing it to them, is a detracting from the Honour of Kings and Monarchs, who will not abdicate from themfelves to any other fo glorious a Title.* And in purfuance of his rancour towards their *Highneffes*, he runs out in his way of Wit and Learning, into a moft filly and impertinent Difcourfe about the Nature of a Church, and accufeth the *Prince* and *Princefs*, as if by having this Character conferred upon them, they had a defign to ufurp from his Majefty of *Great Britain*, the ftile of Defenders of the Faith, and to challenge to themfelves *the being the Protectors of the Church of* England. Surely this Gentleman does by virtue of his *Popifh* Zeal and *Irifh* Underftanding, believe that no Titles are due to Princes in reference to the Church of God, but what are derived from the Papal Chair. Whereas I dare fay, that *Monfieur Fagel* in beftowing this Title upon their *Highneffes*, did not dream of the *Roman Pontiff*, but had been taught it by God Almighty, whom I take to be the fupream and true Fountain of Honour, who is pleafed to character fuch Princes as do cherifh and favour his Church, by the Name of *Nurfing Fathers and Nurfing Mothers*, which is the term that the *Penfionary* ufeth in reference to their *Highneffes*. And as it is their own Merit, which according to the Tenor of the Divine Creation, hath entitled them to this glorious ftile ; fo they are neither to be ridicul'd nor hector'd out of that duty, of countenancing and fupporting the Reformed Religion, nor to be deterred by bold and empty words from thofe compaffionate, generous and Princely Offices to fincere Orthodox Believers, by which they have deferved it. And while others glory in the enjoyment of the Titles of moft Chriftian and moft Catholick Kings, which their Vaffalage to the See of *Rome*, their contributing to the Exaltation of the Triple Crown, and their being the Pope's Executioners in the fhedding the Blood of Saints, hath procured unto them, 'tis enough for their *Highneffes* to be by the Suffrage of all true Proteftants, and that agreeably to the Doctrine and Authority of the Sacred Scriptures, had in efteem, and reverenced for *Nutritii* and Protectors of God's Church. Nor do they appropriate this ftile to themfelves, tho' they account it the brighteft among all their Titles ; but they acknowledge it to belong equally to many others, and are afflicted at nothing more, than that all Potentates may not juftly claim a fhare in it. And as the *Penfionary's* afcribing it unto their *Highneffes* was out of no defign to ufurp upon the King of *England's* Title of Defender of the Faith, nor to affix any Authority unto them over that Church ; fo it will be no prefumption to add, that all of the Reformed Religion in that Kingdom, how much foever differing in little and circumftantial things among themfelves, are yet fo far fenfible of the obligations they are under to their *Highneffes*, and of the benefits they have all the Affurance to expect from them hereafter, that without meaning ill either to the King or to any one elfe, they will unanimoufly join in ftiling them Defenders of the Chriftian Reformed Faith, and Protectors of God's Church profeffing the Proteftant Religion. And they will eafily know with whom they are to be angry, and againft whom to direct their Refentments. *Mijn Heer Fagel* had faid, that if the Diffenters cannot during his Majefty's Reign be eafed from the Penal Laws, unlefs the Tefts be alfo abrogated, that this will be an unhappinefs unto them, but for which the Roman Catholicks are only to be blamed, who chufe rather to be contented, that they and their Pofterity fhould remain ftill obnoxious to the Penal Laws, and expofed to the hatred of the whole Nation, than be reftrained from a capacity of attempting any thing againft the peace and fecurity of the Reformed Religion. Our Author, whofe envy and injuftice againft their Highneffes, is not yet fully fpent, doth in his imprudent and indifcreet way obtrude from hence upon the World, *that the Non-conformifts as well as the Roman Catholicks may hereby fee where their true Intereft ftands, and that they are extreamly obliged to thofe in whofe Name this advice is given, for the Confolation afforded them in the condition under which they are ftated by Law.* Which is as much as if he fhould harangue the Non-conformifts into difcontentment againft the *Prince* and *Princefs*, by affuring them that they are to hope for no relief againft the Penal Laws by any favour of theirs. Whereas the *Diffenters* are not only told that their *Highneffes* are willing to confent, but that they do fully ap-

prove,

prove, that they should have an entire Liberty for the full exercise of their Religion, without being obnoxious to receive any prejudice, trouble, or molestation upon that account. So that the heat which our Author would enflame the Dissenters unto against their *Highnesses*, ought to turn and spend itself against the Papists, who rather than part with the *Tests*, which the Non-conformists are as much concerned to have maintained as they of the National Communion can be, are resolved to keep all the Penal Laws in force, and to leave the Dissenters under the dread and apprehension of them. But this they may be fully persuaded of, that if they can escape the edge of them during this King's Reign, they will be in no danger of them, in case the Nation come once to be so happy as to see their Highnesses seated on the Throne. For as much as they have not only their word, which was hitherto never violated, laid to pledge for their relief and ease, but in that their Interest as well as their Principles will oblige them to be compassionate and tender to all sorts of Protestants; and if they cannot be so fortunate as to unite them, yet to exercise equal kindness and favour towards them.

Having examined what our Author in his impertinent way venteth in unjust Reflections against their Highnesses; and having in some measure chastned him for them, tho' not to the degree he does deserve; I come now in the *third place* to call him to an account for his calumniating the States of these Provinces, and for his endeavouring to possess the minds of their Popish Subjects with dissatisfaction and prejudice towards them. And if he be the person whom most men take him for, tho' he may have herein acted suitably to himself, yet he hath behaved disagreeably to his character, and unworthy of the *Post*, which his Master hath placed him in. Nor need we from henceforth to doubt, but that he does all the ill Offices he can between his Majesty of *Great Britain* and this Government, seeing he hath by slanders destitute of all Foundation, most maliciously studied to raise differences betwixt them and their own Subjects: And if the Intelligence which he transmits to *Whitehall*, be as equally distant from truth and sincerity, as the *Memoirs* are which he hath here published, we may easily conjecture what little credit ought to be given unto it, tho' at the same time we cannot but discern the end that it must be shapen and designed unto. Nor was there the least occasion administred by *Mijn Heer Fagel* in his *Letter*, by which our Author could be provoked to attack these *States*, with so much rudeness, injustice, and falshood, as he hath done in his *Answer*. For all that the *Pensionary* had said, and which it seems threw our Author into a raging fit, was only that their Highnesses could consent that the Papists in *England*, *Scotland* and *Ireland*, should be suffered to exercise their Religion with as much freedom, as is allowed them in these Provinces, in which they enjoy a full Liberty of Conscience. And as the time hath been, and may hereafter come, when the *English* Roman Catholicks would have thought, and may again account such a Liberty for a happiness; so I do not understand if the condition of the Roman Catholicks in these Countries, be as our Author describes it, with what consistency either to Reason or with themselves, the Papists in *England* should have so often heretofore in their Pleas for a Toleration, have made the Liberty vouchsafed their Brethren in these Provinces, not only a motive for their own being capable of Indulgence, but to have represented it as the largest measure of the freedom they desired, and which they would have been thankful for: Seeing this Gentleman according to his accustomed manner of truth and ingenuity takes upon him to assure us, *That as there can be no greater Persecution, than what the* Papists *undergo in the exercise of their Religion, in* Guelderland, Friesland, Zealand, *and the Province of* Groningue; *so that the Liberty which they even enjoy in* Holland, *is so mean and inconsiderable, that it doth not deliver them from being subject to daily fines and molestations.* Surely this man is either very unacquainted with what is done upon the account of Religion in other parts of the World, or else he must needs think, that the most brutal severities to some, are Acts of Merit; while gentle Restrictions upon others, are mortal Crimes, otherwise he could never write at this ignorant and extravagant rate, wherein all persons must discern his folly, as well as insincerity and neglect of truth. For we have too many deplorable evidences, daily before our Eyes, besides those which arrive with us by reports of unquestionable credit, of a stranger kind of *Persecution* exercised towards those of the Reformed Religion in *France* and *Piedmont*, than any which the Roman Catholicks in those Provinces can be alledged to be under, except it be by one of our Author's veracity and discretion. Neither needs there any other Refutation of the calumny with which he asperseth the Supream and Subordinate Magistrates of this Country in reference to the treating their Popish Subjects with horrid Severities, nor a clearer proof that those of the Romish Communion do esteem themselves to be in a condition of peace, freedom and ease under this Government, than

that

that of their behaviour during the late War carried on by the *French* King against these States, which he gave out both at *Rome* and at several other Courts in *Europe*, to have been undertaken in favour, and for the restoring of the Roman Catholick Religion. For had they lain under that grievous persecution, and those tragical hardships in the practice of it, which our Author would impose the belief of upon the World; they would not have failed to welcome that Monarch as their happy Deliverer, and would have united in a general Insurrection against the States, for their having been tyrannous over them. But instead of that, most of them acquitted themselves with the same Zeal for the support of this Government, and in defence of their Country, that other Subjects did. Which demonstrates beyond all controul, that they do not judge themselves to be in so wretched and miserable circumstances, as this bold and calumnious Person represents them to be. And whereas *Monsieur Fagel* in justification of the necessity of preserving the *Test-Laws* by which the Papists are precluded from Employments and Places of Trust, and to rectify a Mistake in Mr. *Stewart* about his conceiving the Roman Catholicks to continue capable of bearing publick Offices in this Commonwealth, had said, that by the Laws of this Republick they are expresly shut out from all the Employments both of Policy and Justice : Our Author does hereupon with the highest injustice, and with all the acrimony he can, accuse the States, not only *of departing from the express terms of the Pacification of* Gant, *but of violating the Articles of the Union at* Utrecht, *which was the foundation upon which this Government was both originally erected and doth still subsist.* And with his wonted degree of knowledge and prudence he further adds, *That the Provinces, and most of the Cities, would not have entered into the aforesaid Union, but upon condition that they of the Roman Catholick Religion should at all times possess the Government. And particularly that* Amsterdam *had it stipulated unto them, under the guaranty of the Prince of* Orange, *that none of the Reformed Religion should be allowed a Place to assemble in, either within the Walls or without, so far as the Jurisdiction of the City did extend.* One would have little expected, that a Person living in the Communion of the Romish Church, as our Author professeth himself to do, should upbraid these States with the violation of Articles, relating unto a Grant made unto any for their Security in the free Exercise of their Religion, at a season when Popish Sovereigns not only account it their glory to break all Laws, Oaths, and Edicts, by which Protestants had their Religion, together with many other Rights and Privileges, established and confirmed unto them, but who with a salvageness and barbarity, which scarce any Age can parallel, seek to extirpate their Religion and destroy them. And all this attempted and pursued against them, not only without their being guilty of any crime, by which they might have deserved to lose the favour of their Princes, and to forfeit protection in the free exercise of their Religion, and their safety as to their Persons and Estates, which had been sworn unto them, and secured by authentic Laws : But when one of the chiefest motives unto it, was their Loyalty, and the merit that they had laid upon their respective Sovereigns, which by a new way of gratitude was thought fit to be thus recompensed and rewarded. And if we be not, as I have formerly said, strangely deceived in the Person and Character of our Author, this charge upon the States of these Provinces is the effect of a most prodigious folly, as well as of inveterate malice, in that his Master contrary both to the Laws of the Realms, his often repeated Promises, and his Coronation Oath, assumes a Power of introducing those into Offices, who by the Statutes of the Land stand precluded from them, and of thrusting them out, who alone are the Persons that are legally capable of them. Which manner of proceeding in his Majesty, hath, besides the injustice that attends it towards all that are laid aside, a signal piece of ingratitude accompanying it to many of them, as having been the Persons whose Zeal for his Person brought him to the Throne, and whose Courage maintained him in it. But I shall not think it enough merely to have exposed his imprudence and indiscretion in the fore-mention'd accusation against the whole governing Body of this Country; but I shall likewise shew it to be false, slanderous, and unjust in every part and branch of it. And that I may act with more truth and candour than our Author hath done, I do acknowledge, that at the first commencement of the War against the King of *Spain*, for the defence of the Laws and Privileges of these and the neighbouring Provinces, that not only they of the Reformed Religion, but likewise the Roman Catholicks, took Arms and hazarded their Lives and Estates in that just quarrel : And I do also grant that thereupon there was Liberty of Conscience allowed and established by several Treaties, in the virtue of which, both Parties were to be equally tolerated, and the one not to disturb or disquiet the other. Nor was there ever any thing done by way of Ordinance or Law, to lessen or restrain the Liberty of the Papists, nor to abridge, much less deprive them, of any Power, Jurisdiction, and

Autho-

Authority that they poffeffed, fo long as they remained faithful in the common caufe, and behaved themfelves with Equity, Juftice, and Peace towards thofe who had withdrawn from the Roman Communion. But fuch was the afcendency of the Priefts over the Roman Catholicks, and fo powerful was their influence upon them, that in a little time they not only hindred and molefted the Proteftants in the exercife of their Religion, and committed many unjuft and cruel feverities againft them, but they proceeded to various attempts of betraying the Rights and civil Liberties of the whole Country, and of enflaving it both to the tyranny of the King of *Spain*, and to the bloody and cruel Inquifition. So that from hence it became a matter of neceffity rather than at firft of choice, that the Government fhould be difpofed into Proteftant hands ; and that the liberty of the Papifts, fhould have thofe limits and regulations given unto it, as might render it both confiftent with the Peace, Freedom, and Safety of thofe of the reformed Religion, and with the prefervation of the civil Rights and Privileges of thefe Provinces. This is the account, which all who have written with any knowledge and integrity of the Tranfactions of thofe Times, do give us of the many Changes and Revolutions that fell out in reference to Religion, till all matters both concerning it, and the political Government of thefe Countries, came to be eftablifhed in the form and* way, wherein they do ftill continue and fubfift. And this I do undertake to make good by all publick, authentick, and approved Hiftories, if our Author fhall have the confidence to infift upon the juftification of his criminations; and all that I fhall at prefent direct Men unto for the confirmation of what I have faid, is that admirable *Apology* of *William* I. Prince of *Orange*, whom his prefent *Highnefs* does in Wifdom, Steadinefs, and true temperate Chriftian Zeal fo fignally imitate, and which that great Prince, who was the firft and happy Founder of this Republick, publifhed in defence of himfelf, and of thofe actings, for which the flavifh and mercenary Factors of *Rome* and *Spain* had traduced and afperfed him. But let us advance to a particular Examination of thofe matters of Fact, upon which our Author challengeth thefe States *for violating their Faith*, with their *Roman Catholick Subjects*. And the things he is pleafed to fpecify, *are their departing from the terms of the Pacification of* Gant, *and their breaking the Articles of the Union agreed unto at U-trecht*, 1597. Nor am I unwilling to acknowledge, that foon after the *Pacification* concluded at *Gant*, there were feveral indecent and undifcreet things done contrary to the purport and tendency of it, both by thofe of the Romifh, and by them of the Reformed Religion ; which proceeded from the fuperftitious fury of the former, and the imprudent Zeal of the latter. Yet it is certain, that the ground of its coming to be rendered wholly ineffectual, arofe from a defign of the King of *Spain*'s, under the cloak and palliation of that Treaty, to fubvert the civil Rights and Privileges of all the Provinces, to the defence and prefervation of which the Roman Catholicks, as well as Proteftants, were fworn and bound by the faid *Pacification*. For after that *Philip* II. had in compliance with the neceffity of his Affairs, confented unto, and ratified all the Terms, Provifions, and Conditions, which both the Papifts and the Reformed had in that *Pacification*, League, and Confederacy, infifted upon, and agreed to adhere unto ; it was foon after difcovered by Letters intercepted to *Don John*, who was at that time conftituted Governor over the Low Countries, that all which *Philip* aimed at, was thro' the having rendered them fecure by the ratification of that Treaty, to take advantages whereby to enflave them, and under the Covert of it, to provide himfelf of means, by which he might be eftablifh'd in an unbounded Tyranny over them. So that by reafon of what was detected in thofe Letters, and from *Don John*'s proceeding to poffefs himfelf of *Namur*, and his endeavouring to corrupt and debauch the *German* Troops, which were in the States fervice, and paid by them, together with the defection of many of the Roman Catholicks from all the Terms of that Pacification ; the War came again to be reviv'd againft the King of *Spain*, and all that had been agreed unto at *Gant*, was rendered ineffectual and overthrown. And I would fain know of our learned and wife Author, how the States of the *Seven* Provinces are more guilty of the violation of that *Pacification* by making the Proteftant Religion to be that of the publick Eftablifhment, within their Territories and Jurifdiction ; than the King of *Spain*, and the States of the *Spanifh Netherlands*, are in their denying a Toleration of the Proteftant Religion in thofe Provinces ; feeing I am fure it was agreed and fworn unto in that *Pacification*. And as for the Union concluded at *Utrecht*, the terms whereof our Author upbraids thefe States with a departure from ; it will be no difficult matter to fhew how his knowledge and fincerity are in reference to this particular of one meafure and piece. For tho' diverfe of the Provinces, which entred into that Union, did thereby enjoy a Liberty of chufing and determining which of the two Religions fhould have the ftamp of the publick

efta-

establishment within their own Jurisdictions ; yet it was then and there ordained, that the Proteftant Religion alone should be publickly profefsed, and have the protection of the Laws in the Provinces of *Holland* and *Zealand*. And as the other Provinces were left to do, as they should judge beft for the peace and fafety of their refpective Territories, and the fupport and defence of the Union ; fo it is a thing wherein all that have written with any integrity, do agree, that the alterations which were afterwards made in thefe Provinces, or in reference unto them, concerning Religion, were either refolved and decreed in the provincial Affemblies of the States of thofe feveral Provinces, or elfe in the meetings of the States-General, where not only the Deputies of thofe feveral Provinces were prefent and confenting, but behoved to have the approbation of their Principals, in order to the rendring thofe alterations legal and binding. Nor is it unworthy to be obferved, that the chief occafion for shutting the Roman Catholicks out of the Government, and for depreffing the Romish Religion from being dominant, arofe from the Papifts themfelves ; in that not only contrary to their ftipulations and promifes, they were found in the virtue of a malice imbib'd from their Religion, to be upon all occafions committing violences and outrages againft the Reformed, but in that the Roman Catholick Magiftrates, and many others of that Communion, were difcovered to retain too great an inclination to *Spain*, and to be ready to abandon and betray the Freedom and civil Rights of their Country, inftead of continuing ftedfaft and faithful in the defence of them, as they had covenanted and fworn. In a word, as neither the Articles of the Union at *Utrecht*, nor any other terms agreed upon, before the abdication of the King of *Spain*, which was not until *Anno* 1581, can be called the fundamental Laws of the Government of this Republick, tho' they may be ftiled conditions upon which fuch and fuch Provinces affociated for mutual defence againft the *Spanish* Power and Tyranny ; fo it is undeniable, that by reafon of the many dangers they found themfelves expofed unto, and the hazards they had run of being betrayed again into the hands of the *Spaniard*, thro' their having fuffered the Magiftracy to remain any where in Papifts, and thro' their having allowed the Roman Catholick Religion to be publickly preached and exercifed, they thereupon reaffumed and gave a new frame unto their Union in the Year 1583. in which it was agreed and enacted by all the Provinces, that from that time forward, the Reformed Religion should alone be openly profeffed and preached, and that none but Proteftants should from that time be admitted to any Office of Policy and Juftice in the Government. And as this is the true fundamental Law upon which this State has fince fo happily fubfifted and flourished ; fo there can be nothing objected againft the Juftice of it, but what will lie againft all States of the World, who have always changed and moulded their Laws, as they have been neceffitated in order to felf-prefervation. And fo remote from all truth, is our Author's affirming the Roman Catholicks to have been upon thefe alterations brought under Perfecution ; that Sir *William Temple*, whom the World will much fooner believe than this Gentleman, tho' poffibly he may bear the fame character which that worthy Perfon once did, does affure us in his excellent *Obfervations upon the United Provinces of the* Netherlands, That *no Papift can here complain of being preffed in his Confcience, of being reftrained from his own manner of Worship in his Houfe, or obliged to any other abroad ; and that all fuch, who ask no more than to ferve God and fave their own Souls, have as much Freedom, Eafe, and Security as they can defire.* Yea, it is demonftrable, that the Roman Catholicks enjoy advantages under this Government, which they have not in Popish States. In that being fuffered to exercife their Religion fo far as is neceffary to attain all the ends of it, if it be capable of affording them any whereon they can hereafter find themfelves happy, they are delivered from the Tyranny of Priefts over their Perfons and Eftates, and hindred from being in a condition to do that ill to others, which the Doctrines of their Church would both tempt them unto and juftify them in. And as to that which our Author fays of the Injuftice done to the City of *Amfterdam*, and of the violating the Conditions towards the Roman Catholicks there, upon which under the guaranty of the Prince of *Orange* they came into the *Union* ; he is miftaken in that whole matter, and betrays only his ignorance, infidelity, or both. For the conditions which he mentioneth, were the refult of an Agreement made *Anno* 1578, when upon the *Naffovian* Army's coming before their City to attack them, they abandoned the Party and Intereft of the King of *Spain*, whom they had till that time adhered unto, and came into an alliance with the reft of the Towns of the Province, to oppofe him in defence of the Privileges of thefe Countries. And as this was a year before the *Union* concluded at *Utrecht*, into which *Amfterdam* entred at the fame time that *Gelderland, Zutphen, Holland, Zealand,* and *Utrecht* did ; fo they joined in the *Union* upon the fame Terms, that the other Towns
of

of their own Province had agreed unto. Nor could the Prince of *Orange* be *Guarantee* in reference to the conditions specified in the *Union*; forasmuch as tho' the Act of *Union* was signed *Jan.* 23, 1579, yet the Prince did not sign it till the *May* following. And that the Roman Catholick Magistrates came to be divested of the Government, contrary to the Articles made with them when they forsook the party of the King of *Spain*, they have none to blame for it but themselves, nor was there that injustice in it which our Author does imagine. For not being satisfied to remain disobedient and refractory to an Edict and Decree of the Arch-Duke *Matthias* and the Council of State, who Anno 1578 had appointed, that wheresoever there were a hundred Families of those professing the Reformed Religion, that they should there be allowed a Church or Chapel for the exercise of their Worship; they not only broke all their Capitulations made with the Protestants, thro' oppressing them in various, severe, unjust, methods, and in denying them a decent and convenient Place in which they might bury their Dead; but they were found to be still inclining to the *Spanish* Interest, and ready to espouse it upon the first convenient opportunity. And therefore the Protestants, who were by much the majority, partly to relieve themselves from the sufferings which were daily inflicted upon them contrary to Stipulations and Articles, and partly to prevent the mischiefs which would have ensued to the whole Country, should that City have been betrayed again into the power and hands of the *Spaniards*, assumed the Government to themselves, and eased the other party of the Trust, which they had so unwisely and unrighteously managed. Nor can our Author deny, but that since they took on them the ruling Authority, they have exercised it with all the moderation that can be expressed: And have been so far from returning to the Roman Catholicks, the like measures which themselves had met with, that they have in no one thing given them cause to complain, unless they should quarrel that they are kept out of capacity of doing the mischief, their Priests would otherways be ready to excite them unto, and which their Religion would countenance them in.

But it is now time that I should proceed to the *fourth* thing, for which I promised to call our *Anonymous* Answerer to an account. And were he not of a singular *Forehead*, and of a peculiar complexion from all others; he could not have had the impudence to endeavour to deceive the world into a belief, that the Protestant Dissenters in *England*, stand listed by their *Highnesses* into the same rank with the Papists, and that they are hereafter to expect, to be shut up into the same state and condition. Certainly he must either have an Antipathy woven into his nature against all truth and sincerity, or else thro' having long accustomed himself to the misreporting of Persons, and to the giving false representations of things, he must at last have acquired an incurable Habit; otherwise it were impossible to prevaricate to that degree from truth, in every thing he meddleth with, and which he undertaketh to say.

For *Mijn Heer Fagel* having declared, that the reason why their Highnesses cannot agree to the repeal of the Test-Laws, is, because they are of no other tendency, than to secure the Reformed Religion from the designs of the Roman Catholicks, and that they contain only conditions and provisions, whereby Men may be qualified to be Members of Parliament, and to bear publick Offices: Our Author hereupon tells us, *That the Nonconformists, as well as the Roman Catholicks, do apprehend that they receive a great deal of damage, by those Laws, and do account them extreamly prejudicial to their Persons and Families.* And whereas *Monsieur Fagel* had said, that he would be glad to hear one good Reason, whereby a Protestant fearing God, and concerned for his Religion, could be prevailed upon to consent to the repealing of these Laws which have been enacted by the Authority of King and Parliament, and that have no other tendency save the providing for the safety of the Reformed Religion, and the hindring Roman Catholicks from being in a capacity to subvert it: Our Author, in way of reflection upon this, tells us, *That it is not only a Childish Demand, but that it is to be hoped that the Pensionary will from hence be brought to acknowledge, how trifling and weak all those Reasons are, by which he would preclude the Nonconformists as well as the Roman Catholicks from publick Employments.* So that by these and many other Passages equally false and disingenuous in our Author's pretended Answer, which for brevity's sake I forbear to mention, it is apparent that he endeavours to persuade the world into a belief, that the Dissenters are stated by their *Highnesses* in the same rank and condition with the Papists, and are to expect to be treated in the same manner, in case it please the Almighty God to bring their Highnesses to the Throne. One would wonder at this sudden and strange change in the opinion and conduct of the Papists towards the Nonconformists; that they who were represented by them a while ago as unfit to live in his Majesty's Dominions, should now come to be accounted the King's best and most faithful Subjects, and worthy to be advanced to the chief Trusts and Employs.

2

ploys.

ploys. 'Tis but a few years since, that all the Laws enacted against them, were judged to be too few and gentle, and therefore they had Laws executed upon them, to which the Legislators had never made them obnoxious ; but now the Roman Catholicks are become so tender of their ease and safety, that out of pure kindness unto them, if any will be so foolish as to believe it, they must have Laws abrogated, which in the worst times, and during the most illegal and barbarous proceedures against them, they were never affected with nor suffered the least prejudice by. And whereas it was the only way for Persons heretofore to make their Court at St. *James's,* by declaiming against the Dissenters as Rebels and Traitors, and by putting them into a salvage Dress, to be run upon as beasts of prey ; it is now grown the only method of becoming gracious at *Whitehall,* to proclaim their Loyalty, and to cry them up for the only People in whom his Majesty, with safety to his Person and Crown, can repose a confidence. But under all the Shapes which the Papists do assume, they may be easily discovered to retain the same malice to the Reformed Religion, and only to act those various and opposite parts, in order the better to subvert it. And the Dissenters being harassed and oppressed before, and indulged and caressed now, was upon the same motive of hatred unto it, and in subserviency to its extirpation. The methods are altered, but the design is one, and tho' they have changed their Tools, yet they remain constant in the pursuance of the same end. While they of the Church of *England* were found compliant with the ways, which the Factors for *Rome* thought serviceable thereunto, they were not only the Favourites of the Court and of the whole Popish Party, but were gratified, at least as was pretended, with a rigorous execution of the penal Laws upon Dissenters. But there remaining several steps to be taken for the Introduction of Popery, and the extirpation of the Reformed Religion, which they of the national Communion would not go along with them in, they are forced to shift Instruments, and to betake themselves to the Nonconformists ; whose assistance the better to engage, they have not only suspended all the Penal Laws, to which the Dissenters were liable, but have endeavoured to fill them with jealousy and apprehension of danger from the Test-Acts, tho' at the same time they know that Nonconformists never either did, or could receive prejudice by them. Only they are sensible, that if they could work up that easy People into such a belief, they should thereby not only obtain their concurrence and abetment, for the rescinding of those Laws, that are at present the only great remaining fence about our Religion, and upon the abrogation whereof, nothing could hinder the Papists from getting into a condition to extirpate it ; but make them a formed and united Body with themselves against the *Prince* and *Princess* of *Orange,* who have with so much Wisdom, Courage, and Integrity, declared that they are against the having them repealed. And as the Dissenters cannot have so far renounced all regard both to honesty and to a good name, as to be fond of being herded with the Papists, or thank our Author for it ; so they must be become void of all sense and understanding, if they suffer themselves to be either wheedled or frighted into an opinion of their being subject to receive any damage by the Tests ; it being so expresly contrary both to the terms of those Laws, and to their own experience. Nor can they be so far abandoned of God, nor prove so treacherous to the Nation, Posterity, and the whole Protestant Interest thro' *Europe,* as to cooperate to the repeal of them, by destroying that great Fence about the Reformed Religion in *England,* and to put the Papists into capacity both of subverting it there and every where else. And setting aside a few mercenary fellows among them, there is no ground to fear, after we have had so many proofs of their zeal for the Protestant Religion and *English* Liberties, in the worst of times, and under the greatest temptations, that they should at this season, when all others behave themselves with so much Integrity and Courage, be accessory to so villanous a thing. The ill success which the Court hath met with in the several Towns and Cities, since the late Regulation of the Corporations, sufficiently shews, that the Dissenters who were put into Magistracy, in hopes by them to have compassed the packing of a Parliament, are no less careful of preserving the Test-Laws, than they of the Church of *England* Communion were, who were displaced to make way for them. And to discover the grossness of the abuse, which our Author, without regard to Truth or Ingenuity, endeavours to put upon them, as if they were judged by their Highnesses to be incapable of Trusts and Employments, or any ways concluded to stand under those restraints by the Test, which the Roman Catholicks do ; there is not one word in *Mijn Heer Fagel's* Letter, whereby they are said to be subject unto them, or by which there is any ground administred of fancying they are put into the same rank with the Papists, and whereby to fear that they may hereafter come to be treated accordingly. But instead of this, they are expresly told, that their

Highnesses do both allow and desire the abrogation of all the penal Laws against Dissenters, and the having them freed from the severity of them; and that they do not only consent, but heartily approve of their having an entire liberty granted them for the full exercise of their Religion, without any trouble or hindrance, or being left exposed to the least molestation or inconvenience upon that account. And to testify how far the Nonconformists are from being in the least menaced by those Laws, it is again declared, That the only reason why their *Highnesses* refuse to consent to the having them repealed, is, because that they have no other tendency, save to secure the Reformed Religion from the Designs of the Papists, by containing provisions, in the virtue of which, those only may be kept out of Office who cannot testify that they are of the Reformed, and not of the Roman Catholick Religion. Which as it is the highest evidence imaginable, of their own stedfastness and integrity in the Reformed Religion, and of the compassion and love which they equally bear to all who profess it, and how careful they will at all times be to have it maintained and supported; so it is the putting such a merit upon all Protestants, that it should engage their prayers for their happy exaltation to the Throne, and make them ambitious as well as willing and ready to hazard their Lives and Fortunes, for the securing the Succession unto them, if any should be so wicked as to go about to preclude them.

But I must pay a further attendance upon our Author, and accompany him to the *fifth* particular which I promised to consider; namely, that according to his own foolish and incoherent way of writing, while he pretends to commend and justify the proceeding of his Majesty of *Great-Britain*, he publisheth the villany of the Papal Church, and proclaims the dishonour and injustice of divers eminent Monarchs and Princes of the Romish Communion. His *Panegyricks* upon the King of *England*, are so many just *Satyrs* upon the Church of *Rome*, the Monarch of *France*, and the Duke of *Savoy*, &c. For if it be *becoming a Christian, to be of a contrary judgment to those who are for persecuting such as differ from the publick and established Religion; and if it be a sentiment worthy of a royal Mind, that none ought to be oppressed for their Consciences in divine Matters*; what characters of irreligion, ignominy, wickedness, are due unto them, who judge it to be meritorious to destroy sincere Christians, for no other pretended Crime, save that they cannot believe as the Pope and the Church of *Rome* do. Surely our Author must either be extremely ignorant of the Doctrine of his own Church, and of the bloody and barbarous practices pursuant thereunto, both at this day, and for many ages past; or else he must be the most unsincere miscreant that ever writ, or at best be guilty of the inconsistency and folly, as to continue in the Communion of a Church, whose Articles of Faith he condemns as Antichristian, and whose Practices according to the terms made necessary for Salvation, he abhorreth both as unworthy of royal Minds, and contrary to christian Piety. But tho' nothing can render a false Man honest, or a foolish Man wise, yet seeing nothing may be done towards the curing a Person's ignorance if he be teachable, or at least to shew his obstinacy, and that the fault is in his Will, not in his Understanding, if he will not learn and be convinced; I shall therefore both acquaint him a little with the Doctrine of that Church, and briefly put him in remembrance, how those of the Roman Fellowship have therefore persecuted Christians, and still continue so to do, only for differing from the publick and established Religion. As to the first, it is sufficiently known that according to the judgment of the Church of *Rome* we are Hereticks, and that Heresy being *Crimen læsæ Majestatis Divinæ*, we are therefore the worst of Traitors, and liable to the Penalties of the greatest High Treason. And thereupon we are not only declared to be infamous and sentenced to be depriv'd of all Honour and Dignity, and to be incapable of all Offices, and have our Estates confiscated and seized, but we are condemned to be burnt; and if that cannot conveniently be effected, it is both made lawful and meritorious to extirpate us by War or Massacre, as shall be best and most safe for the Church of *Rome*. In order whereunto, not only all Laws made for our Security are declared to be null, and that no Promises made unto us, ought to be kept; but all Princes, that neglect to destroy and extirpate us, are proclaimed to be deposed. And suitable hereunto has their carriage been for many ages, to such as differ from them in Articles of Faith, and will not join in their Superstitions and Idolatries. In proof whereof, I neither need to insist upon the infinite Murders, committed by the *Inquisition*, the most devilish Engine of Cruelty that ever the World was acquainted with, nor to reflect so far backward as the *Parisian* and *Irish* Massacres, or the infinite Slaughters perpetrated heretofore in *France*, *Germany*, and the *Low Countries*, &c. seeing we have such fresh and doleful evidences of the mercy and gentleness of the Papal Church, in the ungrateful, inhuman, perjurious, and salvage Persecutions executed so lately

in

in *France* and *Piedmont. If it be the effect of royal and paternal affection in the King of England to his Subjects, that all he endeavoureth, is to treat them as becomes a common Father, without making any distinction between one and another,* as our Author is pleased to call it in his Testimony concerning him ; what cruel Parents must many Princes of the Roman Communion be, who act with that difference towards their People, that while they cherish and embrace some, they tear out the Bowels, and suck the Blood of others ? And if no Society destitute of such tender and christian affections, can merit the name of a Church, we hence learn where to fasten the character of being the *Mother of Harlots.* In that we not only know whose Doctrine it is, that whom she cannot convert, she ought to destroy ; but that we have observ'd her, to have been in all Ages *drunk with the Blood of Saints.* All the commendations our Author bestows upon the King of *England,* are not only either so many accusations of his Majesty's insincerity in the Papal Faith, or infallible Indications that both the King (pardon the Expression) and his Minister, are hypocritical Dissemblers ; but they are stabbing and twinging Satyrs against Mother-Church, and the holy Father, and against his Britannick Majesty's dear Brother and Ally the *French* King. Nor can we be guilty either of Crime or Indecency, in the worst we can say of the Church of *Rome,* and the most Christian King ; seeing we have in equivalent terms a Precedent for it, both from so good a Catholick, and so wise a Minister of a great Monarch, as our honourable Author is.

And tho' I begin to grow weary of conversing with so impertinent a Man, yet I am bound to wait upon him a little longer, and while the Reader can reap no advantage by any thing he says, to see whether it be not possible to lay hold of an occasion from his ignorance and folly, to communicate things that may be more solid and instructive. The *sixth* thing therefore whereof I accused him, and for which I promised to call him to an account, is his egregious ignorance in relation to Government, Laws, Customs, and Matters of Fact : *Mijn Heer Fagel* tells us, that the *Test* Laws being enacted by King and Parliament for the security of the Reformed Religion, and the Roman Catholicks receiving no prejudice by them, but being merely restrained from getting into a condition to subvert it, therefore their *Highnesses* could not consent to their repeal. And he further adds, that there is no Kingdom, Common-wealth, or any constituted Body and Society, in which there are not Laws made for the safety thereof, which not only provide against all attempts that may disturb their peace, but which prescribe such conditions as they judge necessary, for the discerning who are qualified to bear Employments. To which he again subjoins, that there is a great difference between the conduct of these of the Reformed Religion towards Roman Catholicks, which is moderate, and only to prevent their getting into a capacity to do hurt ; and that of those of the Roman Catholick Religion towards the Reformed, who not being satisfied to exclude them from places of trust, do both suppress the whole exercise of their Religion, and severely persecute all that profess it. And he finally adds, that both Reason and the Experience of the present, as well as past Ages do shew, that it is impossible for Roman Catholicks, and those of the Reformed Religion, when joined together in places of Trust, and publick Employment, to maintain a good Correspondence, live in mutual peace, and to discharge their Offices quietly and to the publick good. Now from these several passages, which carry their own evidence along with them, our Author takes occasion both to vent his foolish and ridiculous Politicks, and to proclaim his ignorance in History and of the most obvious Matters of Fact. However, we shall have the patience to hearken to what he hath been pleased to say, and shall examine it piece by piece, as we go along. And the first thing he does, is to acquaint us with a mighty mystery of State, and which none but so great a Minister could have been able to have revealed ; namely, that tho' *the King and Parliament upon the first Revolution with respect to Religion, and the introducing and setting up the Reformed Religion, thought fit to make those Laws which they judged necessary for its preservation ; yet that it does not follow that his present Majesty and a Parliament would be of the same mind, but that they might enact Laws of a differing nature from the former, and re-establish Religion into the same State, in which it was before the Reformed Doctrine and Worship was set up.* We are much obliged to our Author for this discovery, though I must add, that this it is to trust a Fool with secrets, for he will sure to be blabbing. For tho' he subjoin, that he would not say that matters would be pushed so far ; yet he hath already told us enough, to make us understand both what his own hopes are, and what is designed by the Papal Party, if they could compass a Parliament of a Complexion and Temper to their mind. But there are two fatal things, which lie in their way. One is, that neither progressing nor closeting, bribing nor threatning,

ning, can prove effectual to give them the slenderest ground of confidence of their obtaining a Parliament of that mould and constitution. And the second is, that all the Members must take the Tests, before they can be a legal Parliament; and then there is little Probability, that they who can make the Declaration required in these Laws, will be inclinable to repeal them; especially at a season, when their own safety, as well as that of the Protestant Religion, renders it so necessary to have them maintained. Whatsoever any Body of Men, by what name soever they be called, or within what Walls soever they assemble, shall attempt to do, without first having taken the Tests, is *ipso facto* null and void in Law, and will serve to no legal purpose, but to make themselves obnoxious to the severest punishments, which the Justice of a provoked and betrayed Nation can be able to inflict upon them. So that we do not doubt what the King would do, for the re-establishing Popery, and banishing the Protestant Religion, could he get a Parliament to his mind; but our hope is, that he will not, and the better to prevent it, we will endeavour to keep our Test-Laws. But to go on with our Author, who with his accustomed ignorance, but personating here the wisdom of a *Solon* or a *Lycurgus*, takes upon him to instruct us, that *as nothing can be called the fundamental Law of a Kingdom or a Republick, but what was enacted at the commencement of that State or Society, before any alterations could fall out in it with reference to Religion, so nothing deserves the name of such a Law save that which is to the advantage and benefit of all the Subjects.* It were not amiss here to enquire, by what Authority our Author fastens on *Mijn Heer Fagel* this term of fundamental Law in reference to the Tests; seeing he never used it in his Letter, much less applied it to such a purpose. But falsifying is so natural to this Gentleman, that he could not avoid it, even when he might have been sensible, that he would not escape the being challenged for it. There is a Country in the world, that is said to bear no poisonous animal, nor had it need, seeing if any number of the Natives be of the mould and frame that some are, there are brutal and venomous Creatures enough in it, tho' there be neither Toad nor Serpent there. But may not the Test-Laws answer the end they were design'd unto, of being a fence about Religion, tho' they be none of the fundamental Laws of the Government? It is not the name that alone gives value to a Law; but the Sanction of the Legislative Authority, and the usefulness of it to the publick good. A Statute, that was occasioned by a necessity arising in reference to the publick Safety, ought as much to be stood by and upheld while that necessity continues, as if it were an original Law, and coæval with the Constitution. And if it was the indispensable dependance of the welfare and safety of the Community upon such and such Provisions at first, that gave them the Name of fundamental Laws; I am sure, that under our present Circumstances, we may call the Test-Laws absolutely needful, if we assume not the vanity to stile them Fundamental. Besides, I would fain know of our Author, that if all Laws lie exposed to an easy Abrogation, that are not coæval with the Kingdom; what will then become of the *Magna Charta* for Liberty of Conscience, which his Majesty not only promiseth, but undertakes to make irrepealable? And withal, may not some Laws be as necessary to the being and preservation of a State under the notion of Protestant, as others are to its being and subsistence under the consideration of an embodied and formed Society? Every Society is bound to use all necessary means to preserve itself, and while it maketh no Provisions in order thereunto, that derive inconvenience upon others, unless it be only to keep them from being able to do hurt; it would be a wickedness as well as a folly to neglect them. In a word, as the making no Laws necessary for the safety of a People under any knowledge of God they may be grown up into, but what were coæval with their first formation into a Kingdom or Republick, were the weakning and undermining the Security of the Christian Religion in all parts of the world where it hath obtained to be embraced and settled; so by the same reason that it is lawful to make Provisions for the preservation of Christianity in a State professing the Gospel of *Jesus Christ*, it is also lawful to make the like Provisions for the Security of the Reformed Religion in these Kingdoms and Common-wealths, which have judged it to be their Duty to God, and their Souls, to receive and establish it. And for our Author's saying, that no *Law deserves to be called Fundamental, save that which is to the benefit and advantage of all the Subjects*; it is wholly impertinent to the case for which it is alledged, and does no way attack or weaken what the *Pensionary* had said. For as the Laws contended for to be maintained, were never stiled fundamental; so many thousands may have benefit by a Law, whom nevertheless all persons of sense and wisdom will account unfit to be advanced to publick Trusts. As no Man will judge it unreasonable to require that all who are held capable of publick employments, should have

some

some degree of wit and understanding; so I think it is very reasonable that they should be qualified with so much honesty, as to be well affected to the Government as it is by Law established. And to speak properly, it is not the Law that makes the Papists uncapable of Offices and Employments, it only declares they shall not be admitted, because they were incapable before, and had made themselves unfit to be trusted, partly thro' their dependance upon a foreign power, that is at enmity with the State, and seeks to subvert it, and partly by reason of that principle which they are possessed with, of its being their duty to destroy us whensoever they can. And as it's a great favour vouchsafed by the Government, to suffer such to live under it, as stand so ill affected to it, and want only means to overthrow it; so if the Roman Catholicks will not be content with the first without the latter, it will be a great temptation upon the Kingdom to deprive them of the Privilege they have, because they would not be content with it, unless they might obtain that which the Nation could not grant, without being *Felo de se*, and without abandoning the means both of our safety here, and happiness hereafter. And whereas our Author takes the confidence to tell us, *That there are many States and Cities in* Germany, *where without the giving occasion to any disturbance, the Government is shared between Papists and Protestants, and where both those of the Roman Catholick and Reformed Religion, do equally partake in publick Trusts and Employments:* He must pardon me, if I not only say he is mistaken, but that it is a downright Falshood, and that herein he betrays his wonted ignorance, or at least gives us a new discovery of the insincerity that is natural to him. Nor would he have vented this in so general terms, but that he did foresee if he should have condescended to particulars, how easy it would have been for Persons of very ordinary acquaintance either with History or the World, to have both contradicted and refuted him. And if there were some one or other small City, where, by reason of the fewness of those of one Religion to exercise the Government, and to take care of the welfare of the Society, those of the other Religion are sometimes received into Employments, in order to prevent the Inconveniences which the want of a competent number of Magistrates would be attended with, and where the Jealousy and Fear of being swallowed up by some envious and potent Neighbour, may lay them under a necessity of agreeing better together than otherwise they would, or than the principles of some of them incline them unto; must we thence conclude that it ought to be so in a great Kingdom, where there is so vast a number of Protestants admirably qualified with Wisdom, Interest, and Estates, to discharge all the Offices of the Government, and to manage the universal Care of the Society, without running the hazard of the many mischiefs, that would accompany the taking the Papists into partnership with them? Nor could *Mijn Heer Fagel* in representing what is safe or unsafe to so great and noble a Nation, take notice of what is practised upon necessity in some mean Town or Corporation, (supposing that it were there as our Author alledgeth) without transgressing against all the Rules both of prudence and decency. But as the *Pensionary* had no where in his *Letter* affirmed, that there were not any States or Cities, in which the Protestants and Papists bear Office in Government together; but had only said, that Reason and Experience do shew us, how impossible it will be for them when joined together in places of Trust and publick Employments, to maintain a good Correspondence, and to live peaceably with one another; so this is found to be so just a truth, and so pertinently observed, that in all the places where it hath been practised (tho' not in *Germany*, as our Author ignorantly suggests) they have not only lived in continual heats and dissensions, but have often come to open Hostility against each other. Nor hath it meerly fallen out thus in private, and particular States within themselves, but the like evils have often followed and ensued where more States have associated into Union for the common preservation of the Generality; and where the Government hath been in some in the hands of Protestants, and in others executed by Roman Catholicks. Of this we have divers Examples in the *Cantons* of *Switzerland*, where thro' the Magistrates being in some *Cantons* of the Reformed, and in others of the Roman Catholick Religion, they have not only been often hindred from joining and acting vigorously, as they ought to have done, for the interest of all, and the benefit of the common Confederation and Union; but they have sometimes come to open ruptures, and have been embarked in War against one another. And forasmuch as our Author makes bold to say, *That there was never any Christian Kingdom, where the Religion that the Prince professeth, and which had in former ages been dominant, was so far laid aside and banished, that his Subjects professing the same with himself, were shut out and precluded from Trusts and Employments:* I will take the freedom to tell him, that it is so gross and palpable a

Zzzz False-

Falshood, that none but a Person of his ignorance and impudence would have had the face to have asserted it. For there are Christian Kingdoms that have done more than this amounts unto, and who to prevent the danger of having Papists preferred to Trusts and Employments, in case a Prince of their Religion should come to the Throne, have been so wise as to declare Roman Catholicks incapable either of obtaining or keeping the Sovereignty. And it was in the virtue of such a Law, and by reason of the dread of it, that *Christina* Queen of *Sweden*, upon the having taken up a resolution to turn Papist, chose to demit her Crown before she declared herself, as knowing that immediately after such a Declaration, she would have been deposed from the Throne, and possibly not have had so liberal an allowance assigned her afterwards, as by that conduct she did obtain. Nor is it unknown to any, except it be to such as our Author is for natural and acquired accomplishments, that there were not only Laws in *Scotland* for precluding a Popish Prince from coming to the Government, but that the same thing was employed in the *English Oaths* of *Allegiance* and *Supremacy*, as being Oaths of such a frame and nature that it had been most incongruous to impose them upon Subjects to a King of the Roman Catholick Religion. And tho' these two Nations did not improve the advantage which they had by means of their legal Provisions, to hinder the present King from inheriting the Crowns of the respective Realms; yet those Laws serve to inform us, how far some Christian Kingdoms thought it lawful to go, and to what height to act, not only against Popish Subjects, but against Catholick Princes themselves. Yea, the time was, that the very Papists were so far from condemning the having Men of their Religion debarred from Trusts and Employments in Protestant Kingdoms under a Popish Prince, that they made the *Test*-Laws by which they are shut out from Offices and declared incapable of them, the great Argument against the necessity of having the Bill passed for excluding the Duke of *York* from the Crown, and improved them as the main Engine for allaying the fears of the Nation, under the apprehensions they had of his being a Roman Catholick, and coming to the Throne. But by their different Language now from what it was then, all *Englishmen* understand how far they are to be believed in other cases: And whether the many Promises which they do make at this time, in order to a further design, and the putting a new Trick upon the Nation, ought to be depended on by them whom they have already deceived. And whereas upon *Mijn Heer Fagel*'s having observed that the conduct of Roman Catholicks is much more severe towards Protestants, than that of those of the Reformed Religion towards Papists, our Author is pleased to reply, *that in order to judge as we should of that different proceedure, we are to consider whether it be not less just, to banish a Religion that had been so long dominant as the Roman Catholick had been, than to withstand the introduction of a new Religion that would depress and supplant the old.* All I shall say in reference to this, is, that as it does not weaken, but in effect acknowledge what the *Pensionary* had said; so by justifying what the Papists did, to prevent the bringing in of the Protestant Religion, which he stiles new, he forewarns us what we are to expect they will be ready to do, for the re-introducing the Papal Religion, to which he gives the character of old. Nor is it at all pertinent to the present case, which of the Religions is the oldest, or which is the newest; but all contended for, is, that the methods of the one have been, and still are, more severe and sanguinary, than the methods of those of the other. And as we believe our Religion to be as ancient as *Jesus Christ* and his Apostles; so no prescription of time for Popery's having been in possession, can deprive that which has the Divine Authority to warrant it, from a right of re-entrance.

There remains only one thing to be spoken unto, of all that I undertook to discipline and correct our Author for, and that is the signal ingratitude of the Papists, and particularly of this Gentleman, to their Highnesses, for all that Liberty, Favour, and Ease which their Highnesses were willing to have had allowed unto them. And that we may the more fully have an Idea of their unthankfulness, we are to consider both the extent of that Liberty which their Highnesses were contented to have bestowed upon them, and the obligations they would have come under for the rendring it hereafter inviolable. And all this not only at a season, when many of the Papists carry it so undutifully towards their Highnesses, but at a time when they of the Reformed Religion are so inhumanly persecuted by several Popish Princes in other parts of the world. It had not been an unreasonable desire that before the Papists had been so importunate to have all Penal Laws against them in Protestant Nations rescinded and taken away; that they should have declared themselves, and improved their interest, for the Abrogation of all such Laws as are in force against those of the Reformed Religion in Popish Countries. And if their Highnesses
had

had infifted upon fuch a ftipulation, before they would have given their confent for the Repeal of the Penal Laws againft Roman Catholicks in *England*, it had been no more than what was agreeable to the Rules of Wifdom and Juftice. But their High-neffes not thinking it fit to fuffer their own mercy to be reftrained by reafon of the want of Chriftian bowels in others, took the firft opportunity put into their hands, of teftifying their readinefs to confent to the repeal of all thofe Laws againft Papifts in *England*, *Scotland*, and *Ireland*, by which they are made liable to fines or other punifhments : And that thofe which they cannot agree to the refcinding of, are only fuch by which the Reformed Religion is covered from the defigns of the Roman Catholicks againft it, and by which they are reftrained from getting into a condition to overturn it. One would think that this fhould have been received as a moft fpecial favour, and have obliged them to very hearty acknowledgments : Efpecially when the Prince and Princefs were willing to confirm both this and a Liberty for the private Exercife of their Religion with their Guaranty. But inftead of any Symptoms of gratitude, there is nothing to be heard of from many of them, or to be met with in our Anfwerer, but what proclaims their diffatisfaction, anger, and revenge. For befides all the ill returns, we have already taken notice of in this wrathful and unthankful Man ; he tells us, that all which their Highneffes declare themfelves ready to confent unto, amounts only *to the abolifhing fome cruel Laws, by which Romifh Ecclefiafticks ftood condemned to death, for no other reafon fave their being Priefts ; and in the virtue of which, other Perfons were banifhed and deprived of their Eftates, meerly for being Roman Catholicks ; all which was a higher degree of barbarity than was ever practifed among the moft falvage Nations.* Now not to trouble myfelf about what kind of entertainment, Romifh Priefts and Lay Papifts have met with among thofe Nations, which our Author ftiles Barbarous, tho' it will be found infinitely more fevere, than any thing that was ever inflicted upon them in *England*, *Scotland*, or *Ireland*, by reafon of their Religion, or upon the fcore of any ecclefiaftical Character ; I would only know of this modeft and veracious Gentleman, what he thinks of the barbarous and innumerable Cruelties, that were perpetrated in all ages and places heretofore, and which are at this day committed upon peaceable and fincere Chriftians, for no other crime but that they could not, and to this day cannot believe as the Church of *Rome* doth, nor continue in Communion with fo idolatrous and villanous a Society. Whatfoever meafure of feverity hath been any where exercifed towards Papifts, it was but according to the Precedents themfelves had fet, in their dealing with them whom they ftile Hereticks, and in which the Copy comes vaftly below the original. But then that which wholly alters the cafe, is, that whereas the Papifts perfecute and deftroy Chriftians, meerly upon the account of Religion ; there were never any fevere, much lefs fanguinary Laws enacted againft them, fave by reafon of their Crimes againft the State, and for being Enemies and Traitors to the Government. Popery was never perfecuted in *England* as it is a falfe and erroneous Belief ; but as it binds Men to the owning of a foreign, ufurped, and unlawful Jurifdiction. 'Tis neither for their believing Tranfubftantiation, nor for their worfhipping Images, that Papifts are adjudged to Penalties or Death ; but becaufe they adhere to a foreign Enemy, and are treacherous to their Country. Could they have been but good Subjects, their being bad Chriftians would never have prejudiced them. And indeed while they continue to hold that the Pope can depofe Proteftant Sovereigns, and abfolve Subjects from their Allegiance to them, and that it is lawful to cut the Throats of all whom they ftile Hereticks, and that all Laws made for our fecurity are null and void, as being enacted by an incompetent and unlawful Authority, it would feem according to the exact meafures of wifdom and reafon, that all lenity and favour towards them, were not only a fupererogating in Mercy, but an indifcretion in Policy. But then to let fuch into the Government, were plainly to betray the State, and wilfully to abandon both it and ourfelves to be deftroyed and ruined. Nor is there fo much danger in advancing Robbers and *Newgate* Felons to Employments, as there would be in preferring Papifts, efpecially if Jefuited and Bigotted, into civil Offices in a Reformed Kingdom. And therefore feeing they will not thankfully accept and quietly acquiefce in what is offered, and that rather from an exuberancy of Generofity and Mercy, than from maxims of prudence, and obligations arifing from duty ; it is beft to leave them, to fteer their own courfe, and to purfue thofe methods which will infallibly iffue in their difadvantage, to fay no worfe. All ways of Gentlenefs and Moderation towards them, do only encourage their making the bolder claims, and the proceeding further in their ufurpations. The giving them an Inch, provokes them to take an Ell, and they grow enraged becaufe we will not tamely fuffer it. If they act as they do, while the Chain

I

hangs

hangs ftill about their necks, what are we to expect if it fhould be wholly taken off, and they left loofe to exert the malignity which their Religion infpires them with? For not being contented to invade and ufurp all forts of employments and places of truft in defiance of the *Teft*-Laws; they have affumed that confidence, as to make thofe very Laws which were intentionally enacted and defigned to keep Papifts. out of Office and Power, the ground and occafion of incapacitating and fhutting out Proteftants. And whereas none are by Law to be admitted into Employments without making the Declarations contained in the *Tefts*; none are now to be continued, fave they who fhall both refufe to take them, and withal promife to give their votes for the Election of fuch Perfons into Parliament, as fhall be willing to abrogate and repeal them; which is not only fuch a piece of Chicanery in itfelf, but fuch an affault upon the Legiflative Authority, that it is hard to fpeak of it, without more than ufual emotion of mind, and the having one's indignation ftrangely excited and enflamed. However, all I fhall allow myfelf at prefent to fay, fhall be only to advife all forts of Perfons to take care what they do, there being no difpenfing Power lodged in the King, in reference to *Penal*, and much lefs in relation to the *Teft*-Laws. Of this we have a clear and uncontrolable proof in the proceedings of the Parliament, 1673, when the Houfe of Commons voted the Declaration of the late King for Liberty of Confcience, to be both a violation of the Laws of the Land, and an altering of the Legiflative Power. Which is the more remarkable, in that it was not only done by the moft obfequious Parliament that ever any King of *England* had, and of which many of the Members were his hir'd and brib'd *Penfioners*, but that they did thus adjudge, both after the King had acquainted them by a folemn Speech at the opening of the Seffion, that he was refolved to adhere to his Declaration, and had endeavoured to *hector* them into a departure from their Vote, by telling them in an Anfwer which he made to one of their Addreffes, that they had queftioned a Power in the Crown, which had never been difputed in the Reign of any of his Predeceffors, and which belonged unto him as a Prerogative infeparable from the Sovereignty. Yet notwithftanding both all this, and his applying himfelf in a Speech to the Houfe of Lords, to have engaged them to ftand by him againft the Commons, he was neceffitated upon the Commons infifting, that there was never any fuch Difpenfing Power vefted in the Crown, nor claimed or exercifed by any of his Predeceffors; and that the affuming it was a changing of the Conftitution, and an altering of the Legiflative Authority; and upon the Lords declining to ftand by him, and their advifing him to give liberty by way of Bill to be paffed into a Law: I fay, he was neceffitated to take his Declaration off from the File, tear the Seal from it, and to affure both Houfes in a Speech he made to them, *March* 8, that what he had done in taking upon him to fufpend the Penal Laws, fhould not for the future be drawn either into confequence or example. In brief, if the Papifts will not fo far confult their own intereft, and comply with our fafety, as to be contented with an Eafe from Penalties, and an Indulgence to be ratified into a Law, for the private exercife of their Religion; it is the indifpenfable duty of all Proteftants, of what party or perfuafion foever they be, to unite together in withftanding their endeavours and attempts for obtaining more. We have a laudable example in the carriage of all that pretended to Chriftianity, when they were brought into a condition fomewhat parallel with ours in one of the firft Centuries. For tho' the Orthodox had been perfecuted by the *Arians* under *Conftantius*, and fome of the *Arians* harfhly enough treated, at leaft, as they thought for a while under *Conftantine*; yet upon *Julian*'s coming to the Throne, both parties were fo far from embracing his offers in order to revenge their wrongs upon one another, that they refolved at that feafon, if not wholly to filence their Difputes, yet to forbear all thofe harfh Terms, that had enflamed their heats and animofities. To which I fhall add but this one thing more, and would beg of the Diffenters, that they may ferioufly confider it; namely, that as the *Donatifts* were the only party of Chriftians that made Addreffes to *Julian*, and received favours from him; fo they thereby became infamous, and were often afterwards reproached with it.

Thus, Sir, I have ftudied to do what you required of me; and if it be my misfortune not to have acquitted myfelf anfwerably to your expectations, yet the doing it as well, as the being bound up to an Author, that adminifters fo little occafion for valuable thoughts, would allow, gives me the fatisfaction of having approved myfelf,

S I R,

2

Your Obedient Servant.

Some Reflections *on* a Difcourfe, *called*, Good Advice to the Church of *England*, &c.

SIR,

I Have, at laft, procured a fight of the Book, ftiled, *Good Advice to the Church of* England, *Roman Catholick, and Proteftant Diffenter*; and of the *Three Letters from a Gentleman in the Country, to his Friend in* London; which, as they are written by one and the fame Perfon, fo he endeavours, in all of them, to make it appear to be the *Duty, Principles*, and *Intereft* of the parties mentioned, to *abolifh the Penal Laws* and *Tefts*. Now tho' I'm daily in expectation of feeing fuch an Anfwer return'd to thofe Papers, as will both give the Author caufe to wifh he had been otherways employed when he wrote them, and make the Court-faction afhamed of the Elogies they have heaped upon him for his fervice; yet it may not be amifs in the mean time, to fhew, in a very few Pages, that 'tis not any confiderable ftrength in thofe Difcourfes, which hath given them a Reputation, but the Intereft of fome to have every thing accounted unanfwerable that is publifhed in favour of their defigns, and the folly and weaknefs of others, which makes them believe that to be nervous, in whofe fuccefs they imagine their cafe to be wrapp'd up and involved.

I think it is univerfally acknowledged, and I'm fure it can be demonftratively proved, that they are written by a *Quaker*; and this ought to render us jealous both of the motives influencing unto it, and of the end to which they are defigned to be fubfervient. For firft, the affinity of feveral of the *Religious Principles* of that *Party*, with fome of the material *Doctrines* of the *Roman Church*, may, notwithftanding the Charity which we retain towards the Bulk of them, make us juftly apprehenfive, that one or more of their Leaders are entirely in the intereft of the *Church* of *Rome*. For as the Popifh Emiffaries know how to put themfelves into all fhapes, for the encreafing and heightning divifions among *Proteftants*, and for the expofing as well as fupplanting of our Religion; fo the defign promoted in the forefaid Papers, of deftroying all the *Legal Fences* againft *Popery*, and of letting the *Papifts* into the *Legiflative* and whole *Executive* Power of the Government, gives the World too much ground to fufpect out of whofe mint and forge writings of this ftamp and mettle do proceed. *Secondly*, It fhould not a little contribute to augment our Jealoufy, that they, who without being falfe to their Religious Tenets, cannot join to affift *Proteftants*, in cafe the *Papifts* fhould attempt to cut our Throats, or endeavour to impofe their Religion upon the Nation by *Military* Force, fhould, of all Men, ftudy to overthrow that fecurity which we have, by the *Teft*-Laws, whofe whole tendency is only to prevent the *Papifts* from getting into a condition to extirpate our Religion, and deftroy us. Is it not enough that they have robbed the Kingdom of the aid of fo many as they have leavened with their Doctrine, in cafe the King, upon defpairing to eftablifh *Popery* by a *Parliament*, fhould employ his *Janizaries* to compel us to receive it, and fhould fet upon the converting *Proteftants* in *England*, in the way that the *French Monarch* hath converted the *Hugonots*; but that over and above this, they fhould be doing all they can, to deprive us of all the Legal Security, whereby we may be preferved from the Power of the Papifts? Surely 'twere not Charity and Good-nature, but Stupidity and Folly, not to fufpect the tendency of fuch a defign, when we find it purfued and carried on by a Perfon that ftiles himfelf a *Quaker*.

But then, when befides this, we find that 'tis Mr. *William Pen*, who is the *Author* of thofe *Papers*, and the great Inftrument in advancing this projection, we have the more caufe to fufpect fome finiftrous thing at the bottom of it. For *firft*, he is under thofe Obligations to his Majefty, which, as they may put a biafs upon his Underftanding, fo they afford ground enough to *Proteftants* to look upon him no otherways than as one retained againft them. 'Twas thro' his prefent Majefty's Interceffion with the late King, that he obtained the *Proprietorfhip* of *Penfilvania*, and from his Bounty that he had the *Propriety* of *three* whole *Counties* bordering upon it, fuperadded thereunto. And as this cannot be but a ftrong Obligation upon fo grateful a Perfon as Mr. *Pen*, why he fhould effectually ferve the King, and make his will, in a very great degree, the meafure of his actings; fo it ought to be an inducement to others to be the more jealous of all he fays, and not to furrender themfelves too eafily either to his *Magifterial* Dictates upon the one hand, or to his fmooth Flatteries upon the other. He muft have either laid a mighty merit upon the two royal Brothers, of both whofe Religion we are at laft convinced, or he muft have come under Obligations, of doing them very confiderable fervice, in reference to that which they were moft fond of compaffing ; otherwife we have little caufe to think, that he would have been fingled out from all the reft of the Kingdom, to be made the object of fo fpecial favour, and of fo eminent liberality. For though there might be a debt owing to his Father Sir *William Pen*, yet they muft be extremely weak, who conceive there was no other motive to the forementioned Donation, fave Honour and Juftice in the two royal Brothers, for having it difcharged : Seeing many of the nobleft Families in *England*, who had fpent their Blood, and wafted their Eftates in fighting for the Crown, while Sir *William Pen* was all along engaged againft it, were not only left without all kind of Compenfation, for what they had eminently acted, and as eminently fuffered in behalf of the *Monarchy*, but could never get to be reimburfed one farthing of the vaft Sums, which they had lent the late King and his Father upon the fecurity of the royal Faith. *Secondly*, Mr. *Pen* hath too far detected himfelf in thefe very Difcourfes, not to give us ground to fufpect what they are calculated for, and whereunto they are fubfervient. For befides his juftifying the King's turning fo many Gentlemen of the Church of *England*, out of all Office and Employ, by faying, *They are not fit to be trufted, who are out of the King's Intereft* ; he further tells us, That *the King being mortal, it is not good fenfe, that he fhould leave the power in thofe hands, that to his face fhew their averfion to the Friends of his Communion, (Letter firft.)* For as this implies no lefs, than that they ought to have the whole legal and military Power of the *three Kingdoms* put into their hands, that they may be in a condition to preclude the right Heir from Succeffion to the Crown, or prefcribe fuch Laws to her as they pleafe, in cafe they fhould think fit to admit her ; fo a very fmall meafure of Underftanding will ferve to inftruct us, what the *Papifts* efteem to be an averfion to them, and in what manner, had they the power in their hands, they think themfelves obliged to treat us upon that account. And as we have had occafion to know too much of his *Majefty's* Temper and Defign, as well as to whofe Guidance he hath implicitly refigned himfelf, not to be fenfible what he efteems his *Intereft* ; fo we need no other evidence what it amounts unto *to be in it*, than the feeing fo many difplaced from all fhare in the adminiftration, whofe Quality gives them a Right, and their Abilities a Fitnefs for the chiefeft and moft honourable Trufts ; and whom as the King, by reafon of their fervices to himfelf as well as the *Crown*, cannot lay afide without the higheft ingratitude ; fo their known Loyalty to his Perfon, and Zeal for the grandeur of the *Monarchy* is fuch, that nothing could take them off from concurring in his Councils, and promoting his Defigns, but the conviction they are under, of their tendency to the fubverfion of Religion, and the altering of the legal Government.

And as we have reafon to fufpect what the forefaid Papers are intended to promote, both upon the account of the Author's being a *Quaker*, and becaufe not only of the many Obligations he is under to his Majefty, but his being fo entirely in his Intereft, as appears by his influence in Councils, the great ftroke he hath in all affairs, and from his being one of the King's principal Confidents ; fo upon looking into thofe Difcourfes, we find feveral things obtruded on us for truth, and propofed in order to wheedle and enfnare us into an abrogation of the Laws enacted for our fecurity, which to every one's knowledge are fo palpably falfe, that we have all the ground that may be, both to queftion and fufpect his fincerity, and to conclude, that his Mafters do not purpofe to confine themfelves within the bounds that he is pleafed to chalk out for them ; and which he undertakes they fhall be contented with for their allotment. For what can be remoter from Truth, than that the *Teft-Laws were defigned as a preamble to the Bill of Exclufion*, (as he phrafes it, *Letter firft*) and that *they were contrived to exclude the Duke of* York *from the Crown?* (as he expreffeth it, *p. 15, of his Good Advice*, &c.) When it is moft certain, that as the *Teft* in 73 was made long before there were, or could be any thoughts of it, and was enacted by a Parliament againft whofe Loyalty there can be no exception ; fo there was a claufe in the laft *Teft*-Act, by which it was provided, that he fhould not be obliged to take it. Again, what can be more repugnant to experience, than that *the King only defires eafe for thofe of his Religion*; (Good Adv. p. 44.) and that the *Papifts defire no more than a Toleration*, and are willing upon *thofe Terms, to make a perpetual peace with the Church of* England, (Good Advice, p. 17.) For do we not daily fee Proteftants turned out of all places of Truft, Authority, and Command ; and Papifts advanced into all Offices, military and civil ? Could the King have been contented with a Non-execution of the Laws againft thofe of his Communion, and could they have been fatisfied with fuch an Indulgence, and have modeftly improved it ; 'tis not improbable but that fuch a Behaviour, would have fo far prevailed upon the Ingenuity and Good-nature of the generality of Proteftants, that without needing to have been importuned, they would have repealed all the *Penal Laws*
.againft

againſt *Roman Catholicks.* But the methods which have been purſued by his Majeſty and them, ſhews, both that they aim at no leſs than the Domination, and that we muſt be very willing to be deceived, if we either credit Mr. *Pen,* or ſuffer ourſelves to be influenced by him, after his obtruding upon us for truths, matters, which our very ſenſes enable us to refute. It may juſtly make us queſtion his ſincerity, and beget a Suſpicion in all thinking people, of the ſiniſtrous deſign theſe *Papers* are adapted unto, when we find him endeavouring to cajole the Nation to an abrogation of the Laws, by which our Religion and Safety are ſecured, by telling us, That *the King's word is enough for us to rely upon,* if they were gone, (*Good Advice,* p. 49.) and *that he could eaſily pack a Parliament for repealing them, if he did not ſeek a more laſting and more agreeable ſecurity to his Friends,* (*Letter third,* p. 12.) and that if they were aboliſhed, *'tis below the Glory of our King, to uſe ways ſo unlike the reſt of his open and generous Principles, as to endeavour to get a* Parliament *afterwards returned, that is not duly choſen,* (*Letter ſecond,* p. 15.) and that *he is a Prince of that Honour, Conſcience, and generous Nature, as not by invading the Rights of the Church of* England, *to become guilty of an injuſtice and irreligion, he hath ſo often, ſo ſolemnly and earneſtly ſpoken againſt,* (*Letter ſecond,* p. 11.) He muſt needs take us to be ſtrangely unacquainted with the whole tenor of the *King's* Actings in *England,* as well as in *Scotland* and *Ireland,* and to be Perſons of very weak Underſtandings, and of an eaſy Belief, if he think we are to be impoſed upon, and decoy'd by ſuch Topicks as theſe, to aboliſh the *Teſts:* Or that after what we have ſeen and felt contradictory to thoſe *Panegyricks,* and inconſiſtent with thoſe beautiful and lofty Characters faſt-ned upon his Majeſty, we ſhould believe Mr. *Pen* to mean nothing but well and honeſt-ly towards the *Proteſtant* Intereſt, in what he ſo earneſtly ſoliciteth the Church of *England* and the Diſſenters in the forementioned *Papers* to concur and conſent unto.

I do acknowledge, that what he hath ſaid about Liberty, due to Men in matters of meer Religion, and by way of rebuke unto, and reflection upon the Wiſdom and Juſtice of thoſe, that either are, or have been for perſecution, is very ſtrong and convincing; but I muſt withal add, that it is all at this time very needleſs and impertinent. For the Church of *England* is ſo ſenſible of the iniquity, as well as folly of that method, that there is no ground to ſuſpect ſhe will ever be guilty of it for the future. They, whom no Arguments could heretofore convert, the Court (whoſe Tools they were in that miſchievous and unchriſtian work, and by whom they were inſtigated to all the ſeverities which they are now blamed for) by objecting it to them as their Reproach and Diſgrace, and by ſeeking to improve the reſentments of thoſe who had ſuffered by Penal Laws, to become an united party with the *Papiſts* for their ſubverſion, hath brought them at once to be aſhamed of what they did, and to reſolutions of promoting all Chriſtian Liberty for the time to come. And ſhould there be any peeviſh and ill-natur'd Eccleſiaſticks, who, upon a turn of affairs, would be ready to reaſſume their former principles, and purſue their wonted courſe; we may be ſecure againſt all fear of their being ſucceſsful in it, not only by finding the Majority, as well as the more learned, both of the dignified and inferior Clergy, unchangeably fixed and determined againſt it, but by having the whole Nobility and Gentry, and thoſe noble Princes whoſe right it will be next to aſcend the Throne, fully poſſeſſed with all the Generous and Chriſtian Purpoſes we can deſire, of making proviſion for Liberty of Conſcience by a Law. Nor can I forbear to ſubjoin how ſurpriſing it ought to be to all *Proteſtants,* that while Mr. *Pen* expreſſeth ſo much charity for the *Papiſts,* he entertaineth ſo little for the Church of *England.* He would perſuade us, that if the *Penal* and *Teſt-Laws* were abrogated, the *Papiſts* would be ſo far afterward from ſeeking to ſhake the Conſtitution of the *Church of England,* or from breaking in upon the Liberty that is now vouchſafed unto Diſſenters, or from endeavouring to make their Religion National; that they would not only be *contented with a bare Toleration,* but that upon their enjoyment of eaſe by Law, *they would turn good Countrymen, and come in to the Intereſt of the Kingdom,* (*Letter firſt*). Whereas at the ſame time, he would have us believe, that all the Proteſtations of thoſe in the Communion of the *Church of England* for exerciſing Moderation in time to come, are but the *Language of their fear, that their promiſes are not to be truſted,* (*Good Advice,* p. 54.) and that *the Diſſenters deſerve to be begged for Fools,* ſhould they be ſatisfied with any leſs aſſurance, *than the abolition of the Penal and Teſt-Laws,* (ibid. p. 55.) 'Tis enough, not only to excite our Jealouſy, but to ſtir up ſeverer paſſions, to be told at a ſeaſon when we know what the Catholicks are doing in *France,* and in moſt other places where they have any Power, that the *Papiſts through having burnt their fingers with perſecution, may be grown ſo wiſe as to do ſo no more;*
and

and yet to have it afferted in the fame Page, that they who can be prevailed upon to believe, *that the Church of* England *is forry for what fhe hath done, and that fhe will not be guilty of fuch a thing again, have little reafon to quarrel at the unaccountablenefs of Tranfubftantiation.* (*Good Advice,* p. 8.) Nor is it becoming one who ftiles himfelf a *Proteftant,* no more than it is confiftent with Truth, to extenuate our *being fcandaliz'd at the feverity upon Proteftants in* France, *by affirming, that he can parallel fome of the fevereft paffages in that Kingdom, out of the actions of fome Members of the Church of* England *in cool Blood,* (ibid. p. 7.) And tho' I have all the kindnefs imaginable for Mr. *Pen's* Perfon, and am loth to think otherways of him, as to his Religious Principles, than as his a-vowed profeffion difcovers him; yet thefe, and divers paffages more of that kind, to-gether with the acceffion he muft neceffarily have had to the apprehenfion and imprifon-ment of Mr. *Gray,* &c. for abandoning the *Benedictine Order;* are things I can neither reconcile to the title he affumes, nor to his many Difcourfes for repealing the *Teft-*Laws. And to fpeak freely, confidering the nature of our Laws againft *Papifts,* and that it was their manifold Treafons, and only our care to preferve ourfelves, that both gave the firft rife unto them, and has neceffitated their continuance; I know neither how to conftrue that Affertion of Mr. *Pen's* (Good Advice, p. 13.) that the *Principle which the Church of* England *acts by, juftifies the King of* France *and the Inquifition;* nor that other, (*Letter firft*) *of there having been eight times more Laws made for ruining Men for their Confcience, fince the Church of* England *came to be the National Eftablifhment, than were all the time that Popery was in the Chair.* Nor can this be defigned to any other end, but the giving the *Church of* Rome the commendation of Mercy and Moderation above a *Proteftant Church.* For as 'tis certain, that the *one Law* of burning and extir-pating Hereticks, was a thoufand fold worfe, and hath produced infinitely more fangui-nary Effects, than all the Laws and Rigours that the *Church* of *England* can be charged with; fo there is nothing can be falfer, than that either her Principle, or Practice, do parallel or juftify the barbarous and brutal feverities of the *French* King and the Inqui-fition.

Moreover, were all Proteftants agreed, that Liberty, in meer matters of Religion, fhould be immediately granted in a legal way; yet I do not fee how the Papifts fhould pretend to any benefit by it, or be able to lay a juft claim to a fhare in it. So that the foundation which Mr. *Pen* goes upon, of Men's having a Right to be indul-ged in matters of Religion, is too narrow to fupport the Structure he raifeth upon it. For though there may be fome things retained in Popery, which may be cal-led matters of Religion; yet in the bulk and complex of it, it is a Conjuration a-gainft all Religion, and a Confpiracy againft the Peace of Societies, and the Rights of Mankind. 'Tis one of the crimes, as well as the miferies of this Age, that out of a dread of fome, and in complacence to others, we have avoided reprefenting Popery in its native colours, and calling it by the names properly due unto it. But I have always thought, that 'tis better to fail in our Courtfhip to Men, than in our Duty to God, and Fidelity to the Intereft of *Jefus Chrift,* and the Safety of Mankind. Nor do I doubt but that they will be better approved in the great day of Account, who character Perfons, Doctrines, and Practices, as the Scripture doth, than they, who that they may accommodate themfelves unto, and be acceptable with the world, fpeak of them in a fofter ftile. Now if either Blafphemies againft God, or Tyrannies over Men; if either the defacing the Ideas of a Deity, or corrupting the Principles of Vertue, and moral Honefty; if either the fubverting the Foundations of natural *Re-ligion,* or the overthrowing the moft effential Articles of the Chriftian Faith; if either the moft avowed and bold affronts offered to heaven, or the bloodieft and moft bru-tal outrages executed againft the beft of Men; if all thefe be fufficient to preclude a party from the benefit of liberty due to People in Religious Matters, I am fure, none have reafon to challenge it in behalf of the *Papifts,* nor caufe to complain, if it be denied them. Can there be any thing more unreafonable, than that they fhould claim a *Toleration* in a *Proteftant State,* whofe Principles not only allow, but oblige them to deftroy us, as foon as their Power enables them to do it? Is not the Doctrine of the Pope's Supremacy, and his having a *Right* to *depofe Kings,* and abfolve Subjects from their Allegiance, together with that of breaking Faith to Hereticks, and the extirpa-ting all thofe who cannot believe as the Church of *Rome* doth, mighty inducements to thofe whom they have baptized with that Name, and to whom they long to ex-ercife that courtefy, for the *Repealing* of the *Penal* and *Teft-*Laws againft Papifts? Nor are thefe Principles falfely charged upon them, but they are the Oracular Deci-fions of their general *Councils* and *Popes,* whom they ftile infallible. So that Mr. *Pen's Book,* and *Letters,* which feem to have been written not fo much in favour

vour of Diſſenting *Proteſtants*, as of *Roman Catholicks*, can little advantage the latter, even allowing the Principle which he goes upon, and admitting all he hath ſaid for Mens Right to Liberty in meer matters of Religion, to be unanſwerable. And his telling us (*Good Adv.* p. 42.) *that Violence and Tyranny are not natural Conſequences of Popery*, does only diſcover his kindneſs to *Rome*, and the little Friendſhip and Care he hath for the Proteſtant Intereſt. For we know both the Principles of their Religion too well, and have at all times experienced, and do at this day feel the effects of them too ſenſibly, to be deluded by this kind of Sophiſtry, and impoſed upon by ſo palpable a Falſehood, to abandon the means of our ſafety. Whereſoever any *Popiſh* Rulers act with Gentleneſs and Moderation towards thoſe whom their Church hath declared *Hereticks*; 'tis either becauſe there are Political Reaſons for it, as might be eaſily ſhewed in reference to all thoſe States and Governments which he mentions, or becauſe there are ſome Princes of the *Roman Communion*, in whom the Dictates of Human Nature are more prevalent than thoſe of their Religion.

But ſhould the gentle Temper of the *Engliſh* Nation ſway them beyond the ſtrict obligations of duty, and make them willing to repeal the *Penal Laws* againſt Papiſts; yet to do it in their preſent circumſtances, and at ſuch a conjuncture as this, were the higheſt act of folly in the world, and a betraying both their own ſafety, and that of their Religion. Had the Roman Catholicks forbore to aſſume a liberty till it had been legally given them, they had been the more capable Objects of ſuch a Grace; but to beſtow it upon them after they have in contempt and defiance of all our Laws taken it, 'twere to juſtify their Uſurpation, and approve their Crime. Could they have been contented with the private practice of their Worſhip, and the non-exaction of the penalties to which our Statutes make them liable, without leaping into all Offices of Truſt and Command, and invading our Seats of Judicature, our Churches, and our Univerſities; their modeſty might have wrought much upon the generoſity and candor of all ſort of Proteſtants; but their audacious wreſting all power into their hands, and their laying aſide all thoſe that have either any zeal for our Civil Rights, or for the Proteſtant Religion, is enough to kindle our further indignation, inſtead of influencing us to thoughts of moderation and lenity. And ſhould we once begin to cancel our Laws, according to the meaſure and proportion, that they break them and uſurp upon them, no man can tell where that will terminate; and they will be ſure to turn it into an encouragement to further attempts. For having, in compliance with their Impudence, and to abſolve them from the guilt of their Crimes and Treaſons, abrogated the Laws againſt Popery; they will not fail, in a little while, to betake themſelves to the ſame Methods, for obtaining the abolition of all the Laws for Proteſtancy. 'Tis but for the King to declare, that he will have all his Subjects to be of his own Religion; and then by the Logick of the late Cant, which he uſed in his Speech to the Council at *Windſor*, *That they who are not for him, are againſt him*; we muſt immediately either turn Papiſts, or be put into the ſame Liſt with them, and be thought worthy of the ſame *Royal Diſpleaſure*, which they are become obnoxious unto, who cannot find it to be their duty and intereſt to deſtroy the *Teſts*. And Mr. *Pen*'s Argument of *being afraid of his Majeſty's and the Papiſts power, and yet to provoke it*, (Good Advice, p. 43.) will hold in the one caſe as well as in the other. Nor do I ſee but that the Court may improve another Topick of his againſt us (*Ibid.* p. 44.) viz. That we *were ill Courtiers by ſetting him up, firſt to give him Roaſt-meat, and then to beat him with the Spit*; by refuſing to be of his *Religion*. To which I may add, that the brutal Severities exerciſed towards Proteſtants in *France* and *Piedmont*, are but ill inducements to prevail upon a reformed Nation to give Liberty to Papiſts. 'Tis an Axiom founded in the Light of Nature, as well as an Oracle of Revelation, *That with what meaſure any do mete unto others, it ſhall be meaſured to them again; and that whatſoever any would that we ſhould do to them, they ſhould do ſo to us*. Would the Papiſts once perſuade Catholick Rulers to give Indulgence to thoſe of our Religion, it would be an argument that they acted ſincerely in their pleading againſt Penal Laws for matters of Religion; and would mightily prevail upon all of the reformed Communion to repeal ſuch Statutes as are enacted againſt them. But while they continue and increaſe their Perſecution againſt us in all places where they have power, I do not ſee how they can reaſonably expect that we ſhould believe them either to be juſt or honeſt, or to deſerve any meaſure of lenity. Reprizals are the only methods, whereby to bring them to peaceable and equal Terms. Had Proteſtant Princes and States given Papal Sovereigns to underſtand, that they would act upon the ſame ſquare that they do; and retaliate upon thoſe of the *Romiſh* Faith, whatſoever ſhould be inflicted becauſe of Religion upon thoſe of ours; I have ground to think that the *Clergy* in *France*

and

and *Savoy*, would have had more discretion, than to have been instrumental in stirring up the late Persecutions, and of instigating Rulers to such unparallelled Barbarities. 'Tis not many years since a Prince in *Germany* begun to treat *Protestants* with an unjust severity, and to banish them his Country, contrary to his word, and the Stipulation he had made with them ; but upon the Duke of *Brandenburg*'s both threatning and beginning to do so by the *Roman Catholicks* in his Dutchy of *Cleve*, the other Prince immediately forbare his rigour, and the *Protestants* had fair Quarter allowed them. And therefore if Mr. *Pen* and his Catholick Friends, in stead of reproaching the Church of *England of justifying by her principle the King of France and the Inquisition*, would prevail for the abolishing the one, and putting an end to Persecution by the other, they would thereby do more for inclining the Nations to tolerate Papists, than either by all their invidious *Satyrs* against the conformable Clergy, or by their *Panegyricks* upon a Popish Monarch, and the Roman Church. In the mean time, 'tis most unreasonable for them to demand or expect, and unwise as well as unseasonable, for *British Protestants* to consent to the Abrogation of the *Tests*, and the repealing of the *Penal-Laws* against Papists. Moreover, though 'tis possible that we might defend our selves against the dangers that might ensue upon it, had we a Prince of our own Religion on the Throne ; yet it would be to surrender our selves unto their power, and to expose our selves to their Discretion, should we venture to do it while a Papist of his Majesty's Humour hath the wielding of the Scepter. One of the main Arguments, by which Mr. *Pen* would persuade us against all apprehension of danger from the *Papists*, in case the *Test* and *Penal-Laws* were abolished, is the inconsiderableness of their number in comparison of *Protestants*, (*Good Advice*, p. 49.) And yet if there be so many ill men in the Nation, as he intimates, (*Letter 3d*, p. 12.) who being of no Religion, are ready, upon the motives of worldly Interest, to take upon them the profession of any, were it not for fear of being at one time or another called to an account ; I do not see but that as the Papists through having the King on their side, are already possessed of what he stiles the *Artificial* Strength of the Kingdom, why they may not, in a short while, were those Laws once destroyed, by which the atheistical and profane sort of Men are kept in awe, come to obtain too much of the *natural* strength of it, and raise their number to a nearer equality to that of Protestants. And though they should never multiply to any near proportion, yet we may easily imagine, what a few hands may be able to do, when authorized by a popish Sovereign, and seconded by a well-disciplin'd Army commanded by Roman Catholicks, could they once get to have a share in the Legislation, and to be legally stated in all places of Trust and Power. What need we had of a legal Security for our Religion, in case of a Papist's coming to inherit the Crown, not only the late King, who thorowly knew his Brother's temper and bigotry, but those loyal Zealots, who, with an unhappy vigour, opposed the Bill of Exclusion, were sensible of ; and therefore, besides all the Security which we have for our Religion by the Statutes in force, they offered many other provisions for its protection, and several of them very threatning to the Monarchy, which we might have had established into Laws, if through our pursuit of the point of Exclusion, we had not been so improvident as to despise and reject them. He that dares attempt so much as he hath done, in opposition unto, and defiance of all our Laws ; what will he not have the confidence to undertake, and be in a condition to accomplish, if these obstructions were out of his way. The *Penal Laws* cannot prejudice the Papists in this King's Reign, seeing he can connive at the non-execution of them ; and the Repeal of them now, cannot benefit the Papists when he is gone, because if they do not behave themselves modestly, we can either re-establish them, or enact others which they will be as little fond of. But their abrogation at this time, would infallibly prejudice us, and would prove to be the pulling up of the Sluices, and throwing down the Dikes, which stem the deluge that is breaking in upon us, and which hinder the threatning waves from overflowing us. And whereas Mr. *Pen* would obtrude upon weak and credulous Men, *That if these Laws were repealed, the King is willing to give us other for our security, and that he would only exchange the security, and not destroy it,* (*Letter 2d*, p. 11.) he must pardon us, if we do not easily believe him, after what we know of his Majesty's natural Genius, and religious Bigotry, and after what we have seen and experienced in the whole course of his Government. And if there be no other way of *giving the King an opportunity of keeping his word with the Church of England,* in preserving her, and maintaining our Religion, but the Repeating of the *Penal* and *Test Laws,* as he intimates unto us (*Good Adv.* p. 50.) we have not found the Royal

Faith

Faith so sacred and inviolable in other instances, as to rob our selves of a legal defence and protection, to depend upon the precarious one of a bare promise, which his *Ghostly* Fathers, whensoever they find it convenient, will tell him it was unlawful to make, and which he can have a Dispensation for the breaking of, at what time he pleaseth. Nor do we remember, that when he pledged his Faith unto us, in so many Promises, that the parting with our Laws was declared to be the condition, upon which he made, and undertook to perform them. Neither can any have the confidence to alledge it, without having recourse to the Papal Doctrine of *Mental Reservation.* Which being one of the Principles of that *Order*, under whose conduct he is, makes us justly afraid to rely upon his word without further Security. However, we do hereby see, with what little sincerity Mr. *Pen* writes, and what small regard he hath to his Majesty's honour, when he tells the Church of *England, That if She please,* and like the terms of giving up the *Penal* and *Test*-Laws against Papists, that then the *King will perform his word with her* (Good Adv. p. 17.) but that otherways, it is *She who breaks with him, and not he with her*, (ib. *p*. 44.)

Though something may be said, for the Repealing of all *Penal-Laws*, in reference to every persuasion that is called Religion, how incongruously soever it may claim that Name ; yet 'tis inconsistent with the safety of all Civil Government, and a plain betraying of the Civil Liberties, as well as the established Religion in *Great Britain*, not to allow the precluding those from places of Trust, of whose fidelity we can have no assurance. And therefore as all that Mr. *Pen* hath alledged for abolishing the *Tests* is miserably silly ; so he hath thereby too manifestly detected the small regard he bears to the safety of the Kingdoms and the Protestant Cause, not to be suspected in every thing else which he hath more plausibly and reasonably asserted. For as all Governments have an unquestionable Right to use means whereby to preserve themselves ; so 'tis not only lawful, but expedient, that they should have *Tests*, by which it may be known, who are fit to be trusted with the Legislative and Executive Power. Without this no Constitution can subsist, nor Subjects be in any security under it. Neither can any Reasons be advanced against the *Test*-Laws, but what are of equal force against exacting Oaths of Allegiance and Promises of Fidelity from those, whom the Government thinks meet to employ. One might think, that Mr. *Pen* should allow as much to the *Parliament* of *England*, as he challengeth to himself in his Government of *Pensilvania*. For I find, that not only such shall be precluded from a share in the Government there, *who shall either be convicted of ill Fame and unsober Conversation, or who shall not acknowledge* Jesus Christ *to be the Son of God, and Saviour of the World,* (*Chap.* 2d, *of their Constitutions and Laws*) but that *none shall be either chosen into Office, or so much as admitted to choose, but who solemnly declare and promise Fidelity to* William Pen *and his Heirs:* (*Chap.* 57.) This I take not only to be equivalent unto, but something more than our *Tests* do amount unto. For whereas there may be several whom the *Quakers* may judge Persons *of unsober Conversation* ; who may be true to the Civil Interest of their Country, and willing, to the utmost of their power, to preserve the Peace, and promote the Prosperity of it ; we have no ground to believe the like of *Papists*, in relation to the welfare and safety of a *Protestant* State. And that not only because they acknowledge a Foreign Jurisdiction inconsistent with, and paramount to ours ; but because they are obliged by the Principles of their Religion, whensoever they find themselves able, to destroy and extirpate us. I'm sure that the Motives which in 73, and 78, enforced to the Enacting of the *Test*-Laws, do at this Season plead more effectually for the continuing them. Nor had we so much cause then of being afraid of Popery, or to be apprehensive of having our Religion overturned by Papists, which were the Inducements to the making of those Laws, as we have ground to dread it at this time, and to be jealous of it under the present conjuncture. And the more that the *Roman Catholicks* and their *Advocates* press to have these Laws abolished, the more fear they excite in us of their design, if they knew how to effect it, and make us the more resolved to hazard all we have to maintain them. For as no Papist is prejudiced by them in his person or property ; so they are the most innocent and moderate security we can have for the preservation of our selves and of our Religion. Nor could any thing justify the Wisdom of the Nation in being without them so long, but that we were not till then suspicious of the Religion of the Regnant Prince, nor apprehensive before of the misfortune of having a Popish Successor. And whereas Mr. *Pen* tells us, that *it were ridiculous to talk of giving liberty of Conscience, and at the same time imagine that the Tests ought to be continued,* (Good Adv. *p.* 59.) we may not only reply, that Liberty of Conscience has no relation to Men's being admitted unto Civil Trusts, but that the same is practised in several States and Governments both Popish and Protestant ; and in *Pensilvania* itself, where

I

I suppose Liberty of Conscience is allowed. For as we find freedom vouchsafed to Men in matters of Religion, both in *Holland*, and in divers Protestant States in *Germany*, without their being capable of claiming a share in the Magistracy; so though the Protestant Religion be tolerated in *Collen*, yet it is with a preclusion of all of that Religion from Authority. Whatsoever else Mr. *Pen* says upon this head, is so despicably weak, that as I neither judge it worthy to be taken notice of, nor have room to do it; so I am confident, that be his Religion what it will, which by reason of his late Papers I have more reason to suspect than ever, he writes as much against his Conscience and Judgment, as against the Pattern and Example which he hath set us in *Pensilvania*.

I confess, the Dissenters are under more temptations than other Protestants, to wish for, and to endeavour the Abrogation of the Penal Laws. And as this makes them to be the more particularly applied unto by the Court for the promoting of it; so it renders them the more liable to be influenced by Discourses of the nature and complexion that Mr. *Pen's* are of. But I hope they will consider, that the preservation of the Protestant Religion to themselves, their Posterity, and the Kingdom, is more valuable than a little temporal ease, and which they only hold by the precarious tenure of the King's word. Surely they cannot be so infatuated, as to think that the Papists love them, or that they will trust them any longer, than they have occasion to use them. I would think, that it should both make them blush to find themselves coupled with *Roman Catholicks* in Courts and Employments, while their fellow Protestants are shut out; and make them jealous, that they are only made use of for some mischievous and sinistrous end. They can never hope to lay such a merit upon the Court, as the Church of *England* hath done; and her reward may forewarn them what they are to expect, when they have done the jobb that is allotted for them. His Majesty's sincerity in giving liberty to *dissenting Protestants*, may be easily guessed at, by his ordering 26 *poor Scots Dissenters* to be sent to the *Barbadoes* for Slaves; and this both since the emitting of his *First Proclamation for a Toleration*, and without the having any thing objected to them, but what concerned their Consciences, in matters of Religion. The Terms upon which Fanaticks are to enjoy his Majesty's favour, and how long they are to expect the continuance of that mighty Grace, we have declared by himself, as they stand recorded in my Lord *Melfort's Letter to the Prebyterian Ministers in Scotland*: Namely, *That he intends to continue their Liberty, if he have suitable encouragement and concurrence from them in their Doctrine and Practice, and if they concur with him in removing of the Penal Laws.* This is the Task that they are indulged and preferred for, and 'tis a wonder that they do not foresee that their destiny will be one and the same, in case they have once done it, as if they do it not. This is the Fountain of all his Majesty's friendship to them; and the glorious assertion of its having been always *his principle, that Conscience ought not to be constrained, and that none ought to be persecuted for meer matters of Religion,* is at last dwindled into this, that he will give them Liberty so long as they will concur and co-operate with him in his introducing of Popery, and till they have destroyed the Laws by which our own Religion is fenced about and defended. Certainly it is high time to consider, what this is which is exacted of them, and what hazard they not only expose the Nation and the Gospel unto, but what guilt they derive upon themselves if they undertake and pursue it. *Nor can they promote the repealing of the* Penal *Laws against* Papists, *and the* Test *Statutes, without running themselves under the guilt of perjury, and the making themselves chargeable before God, with all the Blood that was shed in the War between King* Charles I. *and the Parliament.* For as one of the Articles of the *Solemn League and Covenant* was, to endeavour to extirpate Popery; so the *countenance and incouragement which that Prince gave to Papists, was a main ingredient in the State of the Quarrel for which they drew their Swords against him, and in the assertion whereof so many thousands lost their lives.* Can they now be willing to act in direct opposition to that *Covenant*, which rather than renounce and disclaim the obligatory force of, many of them have suffered so much? or would they have the guilt of all the blood lie upon them, which was shed in the former long and fatal War? I'm persuaded that many, who are most forward, to pursue the Abrogation of the *Tests* and *Penal Laws* against Papists, never gave themselves leave to think what they are hurried unto. Mr. *Pen* tells them, he will beg them for Fools if they do it not, (*Good Advice*, pag. 54.) and I dare take upon me to say, that they are most execrable Knaves and Villains, if they do it. Is it possible they should be so deprived of all understanding, as not to perceive themselves meerly trick'd upon, and made use of for Tools to promote a Design which others have the wisdom and integrity not to be instrumental in; when *Jeffreys*, who a while ago said on the *Bench, Shew me a Fanatick, and I will shew you a Knave; and that 'twas impossible to be a Fanatick, and not to be a Rebel*; should now

caress

carefs them as his Majefty's beft and moft loyal Subjects, and tell them, upon their being advanced to Offices, That *he is glad to find honeft men come to be employed,* which was the compliment he lately beftowed upon Sir *John Shorter.* 'Tis likely they may be told, that if they will fall in with the Papifts for deftroying the Church of *England,* that they fhall be fecured from the Refentments of the next *Heir,* by having the Monarchy made diffolvable into a *Republick* upon his Majefty's Death. And this would feem to be what Mr. *Pen* intends, when he tells us, that fuch a *Bargain will be driven with the Kingdom, as will make the Church of* England *think that half a Loaf had been better than no Bread* ; (Good Adv. p. 43.) *and that one Year* will fhew *the Trick, and mightily deceive her, and the opportunity of her being preferved loft, and another Bargain driven mightily to her difadvantage,* (Ibid. p. 42.) But as it will be impoffible for Papifts and Diffenters, fhould they confpire together, to be able to effect it, confidering the intereft which her integrity in the Proteftant Religion, and her tendernefs for the Rights and Liberties of the Kingdoms, have juftly acquired unto her ; fo it were both the moft foolifh, as well as criminal thing, which any, pretending themfelves Proteftants, can be guilty of, to be in any meafure acceffory unto it. For as there is nothing in reference to their own Religious Liberties, and the Privileges of the Nation, which they may not undoubtedly expect, from her Juftice as well as from her Mercy and Moderation ; fo there is no means left within our view, either to give a lafting Peace and a firm Settlement to three diftracted Kingdoms, or to bring the Proteftant Intereft into fuch a condition, as may ballance the Papal Grandeur in *Europe,* and give check to the rage of Perfecution in all places, but her happy advancement to the Thrones of *Great Britain* and *Ireland,* when it fhall pleafe God to remove his Majefty. Until which time, I hope all who call themfelves Proteftants, will fubmit to the worft of fate, rather than to fall under the Curfe of this Age, and Ignominy with all that fhall come after, for becoming an united Party with the Church of *Rome,* in any of her Defigns, how plaufible foever they may appear.

The Ill Effects of Animofities.

TIS long fince the *Court of England,* under the Authority of the *late King* and his *Brother,* was embark'd in a defign of fubverting the *Proteftant Religion,* and of introducing and eftablifhing *Popery.* For the two *Royal Brothers* being in the time of their Exile feduced by the Careffes and Importunities of their Mother, allured by the promifes and favours of *Popifh* Princes, and being wheedled by the crafts and arts of Priefts and Jefuits, who are cunning to deceive, and know how to prevail upon perfons that were but weakly eftablifhed in the Doctrine, and wholly ftrangers to the Practice and Power of the Religion they were tempted from ; they not only abjured the reformed Religion, and became reconciled to the Church of *Rome* ; but by their Example, and the Influence which they had over thofe that depended upon them, both for prefent Subfiftence, and future Hopes, they drew many that accompanied them in their Banifhment, to renounce the Doctrine, Worfhip and Communion of the Church of *England,* though in the War between *Charles* the Firft and the Parliament, they had pretended to fight for them in equal conjunction with the prerogatives of the Crown. So that upon the Reftoration in the year 1660, they were not only moulded and prepared themfelves for promoting the Defires of the *Pope* and his Emiffaries, but they were furnifhed with a ftock of Gentlemen, out of whom they might have a fupply of Inftruments, both in Parliament and elfewhere, to co-operate with and under them in the methods that fhould be judged moft proper and fubfervient to the Extirpation of *Proteftancy,* and the bringing the Nation again into a Servitude to the Triple Crown. And befide the Obligations that the Principles of the Religion to which they had revolted, laid them under for eradicating the eftablifhed Doctrine and Worfhip, they had bound themfelves unto it, by all the Promifes and Oaths which perfons are capable of having prefcribed unto, and exacted of them.

Nor can any now disbelieve his late Majefty's having lived and died a Papift, who hath either heard what he both faid and did, when under the profpect of approaching Death, and paft hope of acting a part any longer on the prefent Stage, or who have feen and read the two Papers left in his Clofet, which have been fince publifhed to the World, and attefted for Authentick by the prefent King. And had we been fo juft to our felves, as to have examined the whole courfe of his Reign, both in his Alliances abroad, and his moft important Counfels and Actions at home ; or had we hearkned to the Reports of thofe who knew him at *Collen* and in *Flanders,* we had been long ago convinced of what Religion he was. Nor were his many repeated proteſtations of his Zeal for Proteſtancy, but in order to delude the Nation, till inſenſibly as to us, and with ſafety to himſelf, he had overturned the Religion which he pretended to own, and had introduced that which he inveighed againſt. And while with the higheſt aſſeverations he diſclaimed the being what he really was, and with moſt ſacred and tremendous Oaths profeſſed the being what he was not, his Religion might in the mean time have been traced through all the ſignal Occurrences of his Government, and have been diſcerned, written in Capital Letters, through all the material Affairs wherein he was engaged, from the Day he aſcended the Throne, till the Hour he left the World. His entring into two Wars againſt the *Dutch*, without any provocation on their part, or ground on his, ſave their being a Proteſtant State ; his being not only conſcious unto, but interpoſing his Commands, as well as Encouragements for the burning of *London*. His concurrence in all the parts of the Popiſh Plot, except that which the Jeſuits, with a few others, were involved in againſt himſelf ; his ſtifling that Conſpiracy, and delivering the Roman Catholicks from the Dangers into which it had caſt them. His being the Author of ſo many forged Plots, which he cauſed to be charged on Proteſtants. His conſtant Confederacies with *France*, to the diſobliging his people ; the betraying of *Europe* ; the neglect of the Reformed in that Kingdom, and the encouraging the Deſign carried on againſt them for their Extirpation. His entailing the Duke of *York* upon the Nation, contrary to the Deſires and Endeavours of three ſeveral Parliaments, and that not out of Love to his perſon, but Affection to Popery, which he knew that Gentleman would introduce and eſtabliſh. All theſe, beſides many other things which might be named, were ſufficient Evidences of the late King's Religion, and of the Deſign he was engaged in for the Subverſion of ours. So that it would fill a ſober perſon with amazement, to think, that after all this, there ſhould be ſo many ſincere Proteſtants and true *Engliſh* Men, who not only believed the late King to be of the reformed Religion, but with an unſatiableneſs thirſted after the Blood of thoſe that durſt otherwiſe repreſent him. And had it not been for his receiving Abſolution and Extream Unction from a Popiſh Prieſt at his Death ; and for what he left in writing in the two papers found in his *ſtrong Box*, he would have ſtill paſſed for a Prince who had lived and died a cordial and zealous Proteſtant ; and whoſoever had muttered any thing to the contrary, would have been branded for a Villain and an execrable Perſon. But with what a ſcent and odor muſt it recommend his Memory to them, to conſider his having not only lived and died in the Communion of the Church of *Rome*, in contradiction to all his publick Speeches, ſolemn Declarations, and higheſt Aſſeverations to his people in Parliament ; but his participating, from time to time, of the Sacrament, as adminiſtred in the Church of *England*, while, in the interim, he had abjured our Religion, ſtood reconciled to the Church of *Rome*, and had obliged himſelf by moſt ſacred Vows, and was endeavouring by all the Frauds and Arts imaginable, to ſubvert the eſtabliſhed Doctrine and Worſhip, and ſet up Hereſy and Idolatry in their room. And it muſt needs give them an abhorrent Idea and Character of Popery, and a loathſome repreſentation of thoſe truſted with the Conduct and Guidance of the Conſciences of Men in the Roman Communion, that they ſhould not only diſpenſe with, and indulge ſuch Crimes and Villanies, but proclaim them ſanctified and meritorious from the end which they are calculated for, and levelled at.

And for his dear Brother, and renowned Succeſſor, who poſſeſſed the Throne after him, I ſuppoſe his moſt partial Admirers, who took him for a Prince, not only merciful in his Temper, and imbued with all gracious Inclinations to our Laws, and the Rights of the Subject, but for one Orthodox in his Religion, and who would prove a zealous Defender of the Doctrine, Worſhip and Diſcipline of the Church eſtabliſhed by Law, are before this time both undeceived and filled with Reſentments for his having abuſed their Credulity, deceived their Expectations, and reproached all their Gloryings and Boaſtings of him. For as it would have been the greateſt Affront they could have put upon the King, to queſtion his being of the Roman Communion, or to detract from his Zeal for the introduction of Popery, notwithſtanding his own antecedent Proteſtations, as well as the many Statutes in force for the preſervation of the Reformed Religion ; ſo I muſt take the liberty to tell them, that his Apoſtacy is not of ſo late Date as the World is made commonly to believe. For though it was many Years concealed, and the contrary pretended and diſſembled ; yet it is moſt certain, that he abjured the Proteſtant Religion, ſoon after the Exilement of the Royal Family, and was reconciled to the Romiſh Church at *St. Germains* in *France*. Nor were ſeveral of the then ſuffering Biſhops and Clergy ignorant of this, though they had neither the Integrity nor Courage to give the Nation and Church warning of it. And within theſe five Years there was in the cuſtody of a very worthy and honeſt Gentleman, a Letter written to the late Biſhop of *D.*

2   by

by a Doctor of Divinity then attending upon the Royal Brothers, wherein the Apostacy of the then Duke of *York* to the See of *Rome*, is particularly related, and an Account given, how much the Dutchess of *Tremoville* (though without being herself observed) had heard the Queen Mother glorying of it, bewailed it as a dishonour unto the Royal Family, and as that which might prove of pernicious consequence to the Protestant Interest. But though the old Queen privately rejoiced and triumphed in it, yet she knew too well what disadvantage it might be, both to her Son, and to the Papal Cause in *Great Britain*, to have it at that Season communicated and divulged. Thereupon it remained a Secret for many Years, and by virtue of a Dispensation, he sometimes joined in all Ordinances with those of the Protestant Communion. But for all the Art, Hypocrisy and Sacrilege, by which it was endeavoured to be concealed, it might have been easily discerned, as manifesting itself in the whole Course of his Actions. And at last his own Zeal, the Importunity of the Priests, and the Cunning of the late King, prevailing over Reasons of State, he withdrew from all Acts of Fellowship with the Church of *England*. But neither that, nor his refusing the *Test* enjoined by *Law*, for distinguishing Papists from Protestants, though thereupon he was forced, both to resign his Office of Lord High Admiral, &c. nor his declining the Oath which the Laws of *Scotland*, for the securing a Protestant Governour, enjoin to be taken by the High Commissioner; nor yet so many Parliaments having endeavoured to get him excluded from Succession to the Crown, upon the account of having revolted to the See of *Rome*, and thereby become dangerous to the established Religion, could make impression upon a wilfully deluded and obstinate sort of Protestants, but in defiance of all means of Conviction, they would persuade themselves, that he was still a Zealot for our Religion, and a grand Patriot of the Church of *England*. Nor could any thing undeceive them, till upon his Brother's Death he had openly declared himself a Roman Catholick, and afterwards in the fumes and raptures of his Victory over the late Duke of *Monmouth*, had discovered and proclaimed his Intentions of overthrowing both our Religion and Laws. Yea, so closely had some sealed up their Eyes against all beams of Light, and hardned themselves against all Evidences from Reason and Fact, that had it pleased the Almighty God to have prospered the Duke of *Monmouth*'s Arms in the Summer 85, the present King would have gone off the Stage with the Reputation among them, of a Prince tender of the Laws of the Kingdom; and who, notwithstanding his own being a Papist, would have preserved the reformed Religion, and have maintained the Church of *England* in all her Grandeur and Rights. And though his whole Life had been but one continued Conspiracy against our Civil Liberties and Privileges, he had left the Throne with the Character, and under the Esteem of a Gentleman, that in the whole course of his Government would have regulated himself by the Rules of the Constitution, and the Statutes of the Realm.

Now among all the Methods fallen upon by the Royal Brothers, for the undermining and subverting our *Religion* and *Laws*, there is none that they have pursued with more Ardor, and wherein they have been more successful to the compassing of their Designs, than in their dividing *Protestants*, and alienating their Affections, and embittering their Minds from and against one another. And had not this lain under their prospect, and the means of effecting it appeared easy, they might have been *Papists* themselves, while in the mean time they had been dispensed with to protest and swear their being of the *Reformed Religion*, and they might have envied our Liberties, and bewailed their Restriction from arbitrary and despotical Power; but they never durst have entertained a Thought of subverting the *established Religion*, or of altering the Civil Government, nor would they ever have had the boldness to have attempted the introducing and erecting *Popery* and *Tyranny* in their room. And whosoever should have put them upon reducing the Nation to the Church of *Rome*, or upon rendring the Monarchy unlimited and independent on the Law, would have been thought to have laid a Snare for exposing the *Papists* to greater Severities than they were obnoxious unto before, and to have projected the robbing the Crown of the Prerogatives which belong unto it by the Rules of the Constitution, and to which it was so lately restored: And the despair of succeeding, would have rendred the Royal Brothers deaf to all Importunities from *Romish Emissaries*, and Court Minions. Neither the Promises and Oaths which they had made and taken beyond Sea, to introduce Popery, nor their Ambition to advance themselves beyond the restraint of Laws, and the Controul of Parliaments, would have prevailed upon them to have encounter'd the Hazards and Difficulties, which in case of the Union of *English Protestants*, must have attended and ensued upon Attempts and Endeavours of the one kind and of the other. Or should their beloved *Popery*, and their own Bigottedness in the *Romish Superstition*, have so far

trans-

transported them beyond the bounds of Wisdom and Discretion, as to have appeared possessed with an Intention of subverting the *Protestant Religion*, and of enslaving the Nation to the Superstition and Idolatry of *Rome*, they would have been made soon to understand, That the Laws which make it Treason to own the Jurisdiction of the *Pope*, or to seduce the meanest Subject to the Church of *Rome*, were not enacted in vain ; and that those, as well as many more, made for the Security of the *Protestant Religion*, and to prevent the growth and introduction of *Popery*, were not to be dallied and plaid withal. Or, should they have been so far infatuated and abandoned of all Understanding, as out of a foolish and haughty Affectation of being Absolute, to have attempted the Alteration of the Civil Government, they would have been immediately and unanimously told, That the People have the same Right to their Liberties, that the King hath to the Prerogatives of the Crown. And if they would not have been contented with what belongs unto the Prince, by the Common and Statute-Laws of the Realm, but had invaded the Privileges reserved unto the Subject ; they would have been made to know, that they might not only be withstood, in what they strove to usurp, contrary to *Magna Charta, the Petition of Right*, and other Laws of the Kingdom, but that thereby they forfeited, and might be disseized of what either appertained unto the Crown by fundamental Agreements, or hath been since settled upon the Monarch by Statute-Laws. Nor could any thing have emboldened his late Majesty and the present King to Enterprizes of the one kind or the other, but the prospect of begetting a Misunderstanding, Jealousy and Rancour among *Protestants*, and thereby both of making them instrumental to the ruin of one another, and contributary to the loss of *English* Liberty and the *reformed Religion*, which they equally value and esteem ; and to the setting up *Popery* and *Tyranny*, which the one detesteth and abhorreth no less than the other.

Though all *English Protestants* have ever been at an Accord in all the Essentials and Vitals of Religion, yet from the very beginning of the Reformation, there have been Differences among them concerning Ecclesiastical Government and Discipline, and about Forms, Rites and Ceremonies of Worship. And had they consulted either their Duty to God, or the common Interest of *Religion*, they might have found ways either for removing the occasions of them, or they ought to have lived together as Brethren, notwithstanding the differences which were among them in those things. But how much wiser are the Children of this World, than those of the Kingdom of God and of *Jesus Christ ?* For tho' the differences among the *Papists* do far exceed ours, both in their number, and in the Importance of those things wherein they disagree, yet they do mutually tolerate and bear with one another. The matters wherein they differ are neither made the Terms of their Church-Communion, nor the Grounds of mutual Excommunications and Persecutions.

But alas, one Party among us hath been always endeavouring to cut or stretch others to their own Size, and have made those things which themselves stile Indifferent, both the Qualifications for admission to the *Pastoral Office*, and the Conditions of Fellowship in the Ordinances of the Gospel. Nor is it to be expressed, what Advantages were hereby administred all along to the Common Enemy ; and what Sufferings peaceable and orthodox Christians were exposed unto from their peevish and angry Brethren. And though these things, with the Heats begotten among all, and the Calamities undergone by one side, were not the cause of that funestous War betwixt *Charles* the First and the *Parliament*, yet they were an occasion of diverting Thousands from the side which the persecuting Church-men espoused, and engaging them in the behalf of the *two Houses*, in the Quarrel which they begun and carried on against that *Prince*, for defence of the Civil Liberties, Privileges and Rights of the People ; but some of the Mitred Clergy were so far from being made wise by their own and the Nation's Sufferings, as upon their *Restoration* to hearken to moderate Counsels, and to decline their former Rigours and Severities, that they became the Tools and Instruments of the Court, not only for reviving, but for heightning and inflaming all the Differences which had formerly been among *English Protestants*. For the *Royal Brothers* finding nothing more adapted and subservient than this, to their Design of altering the Government, and subverting *Religion*, they animated those waspish and impolitick Ecclesiasticks, not only to pursue the *Restoration* of all those things which had given rise and occasion to former *Dissensions* and *Persecutions*, but to lay new Snares for alienating many persons of unspotted Lives and tender *Consciences*, from the Church, and of rendring them obnoxious to suffer in their Names, Persons and Estates. And what a satisfaction was it to the late King and his Brother, to find the old Episcopal Clergy prepared through Principles of revenge, as well as from love of Domination, Ambition and Covetousness, to fall in with the Design, not only of increasing Di-

I

visions among Protestants, both by making the Conditions of entring upon the Pastoral Function narrower, and for screwing Conformity with the Church in her Forms and Ceremonies of Worship, into Tests, for admission to Magistracy and Civil Trusts; but of obtaining several Laws against Dissenters, whereby the Penalties to which they foresaw that People would become liable, were rendred greater than they had been before, and their Sufferings made more merciless, inhuman and intolerable.

For though his late Majesty had, by a Declaration dated at *Breda*, promised Indulgence to all Protestants that would live peaceably under the Civil Government; yet it was never in his Thoughts to perform it: and the previous Obligations which he was under to the Church of *Rome*, had a virtue to supersede and cancel his Engagements to *English* Hereticks. And all he intended by that Declaration was only to wheedle and lull those into a tameness of admitting his Return into his Dominions, whom a jealousy of being afterwards persecuted for their Consciences, might have awakened to withstand and dispute it. And, to give him his due, he never judged himself longer bound to the Observation of Promises and Oaths made to his People, than, until without hazard to his Person and Government, he could violate and break them. Accordingly he was no sooner seated in the Throne of his Ancestors, and those whom he had been apprehensive of Resistance and Disturbance from, put out of Capacity and Condition of attempting any thing against him; but he thought himself discharged from every thing that the Royal Word and Faith of a Prince had been pledged and laid to stake for in that Declaration, and from that day forward acted in direct opposition to all the Parts and Branches of it. For having soon after his Return obtained a Parliament, moulded and adapted, both to his Arbitrary and *Popish* Ends, he immediately set all his Instruments at work for procuring of such Laws to be enacted, as might divide and weaken Protestants, and thereby make us, not only the more easy Prey to the *Papists*, but afford them an advantage through our Scuffles, of undermining our Religion with the less notice and observation.

How such persons came to be chosen, and to constitute the Majority of the House of Commons; who by their Actings have made themselves infamous and execrable to all Ages, were a matter too large to penetrate at present into the Reasons of; but that which my Theme conducts me to observe, is, That as they sacrificed the Treasure of the Nation to the profuseness and prodigality of the *Prince*, and our Rights and Liberties to his Ambition and arbitrary Will, so they both introduced and established those Things which have been a means of dividing us; and by many severe and repeated Laws, they subjected a great number of industrious *English*-Men and true Protestants, to Excommunications, Imprisonments, rigorous and multiplied Fines; and all this for Matters relating only to their Consciences, and for their Obedience to God in the Ordinances of his Worship and House. And notwithstanding the late King's often pretended compassion to the Dissenters, it will be hard to discern it, unless in Effects which proceed from very different and opposite Principles. The distance which he kept them from his Person and Favour; the influencing those Members of both Houses that depended upon him, to be the Authors and Promoters of Severities against them; the enjoining so often the Judges and Justices of Peace to execute the Laws upon them in their utmost rigour; the instigating the Bishops and Ecclesiastical Courts, if at any time they relented in their Prosecutions, to pursue them with fresh Citations and Censures; the arraigning them, not only upon the Statutes made intentionally against Dissenters, but upon those that were originally and solely enacted against the *Papists*: these, and other Proceedures of that nature, are the only Proofs and Evidences which I can find, of the late King's Bowels, Pity and Tenderness to them. And whereas the weak Church-men were imposed upon to believe, that all the Severity against the Non-conformists, was the Fruit of his Zeal for the Protestant Religion, and for the security of the Worship and Discipline established by Law; they might have easily discovered, if Passion, Prejudice, Wealth and Honour had not blinded them, that all this was calculated for Ends perfectly destructive to the Church, and inconsistent with the Safety and Happiness of all Protestants. For as his seeking oftner than once to have wriggled himself into a Power of superseding and dispensing with those Laws, and suspending their Execution, plainly shews, that he never intended the support and preservation of the Church by them; so his non-execution of the *Laws* against Papists; his conniving at their increase; his persuading those nearest unto him to reconcile themselves to the See of *Rome*, as he did, among others, the late D. of *Monmouth*; his countenancing the *Roman Catholicks* in their open and intolerable Insolencies; and his advancing them to the most gainful and *important Places* and *Trusts*, sufficiently declare, that he never had any love to *Protestants*, or care of the *Reformed Religion*; but that all his designs were of a contrary tendency, and his faireft Pretences for the Protection and Grandeur of the Church of *England*, adapted to other Ends.

Thus the *Royal Brothers*, having obtained fuch Laws to be enacted, whereby one *Party* of *Proteftants* was armed with means of oppreffing and perfecuting all others, neither the neceffity of their Affairs at any time fince, nor the Application and Interpofure of feveral Parliaments, for removing the Grounds of our Differences and Animofities, by an Indulgence to be paft into a *Law*, could prevail, either upon his late Majefty, or the prefent King, to forego the Advantage they had gotten of keeping us in mutual Enmity, and thereby of miniftring to their projection of fupplanting our Religion, and re-eftablifhing the Faith and Worfhip of the Church of *Rome*. Hereupon the laft King, not only refufed to confent to fuch Bills as divers late *Parliaments* had prepared for indulging Diffenters, and for bringing them into an Union of Counfels, and Conjunction of Intereft with thofe of the Church of *England*, for refifting the Confpiracies of the *Papifts* againft our legal Government and eftablifhed *Religion*; but he rejected an Addrefs for fufpending the Execution of the *Penal-Laws* againft Diffenters, which was offered and prefented unto him by that very *Parliament* which had framed and enacted thofe cruel and hard Laws.

And as the *Royal Brothers* have made it their conftant Bufinefs to cherifh a Divifion and Rancour among *Proteftants*, and to provoke one Party to perfecute and ruin another; fo nothing could more naturally fall in with the Defign of Arbitrarinefs, or be more fubfervient to the betraying the Nation to *Papal Idolatry* and Jurifdiction: For feveral *Penal Laws* againft a confiderable Body of People, do either expofe them againft whom they are enacted, to be deftroyed by the *Prince*, with whom the executive Power of the Law is trufted and depofited; or they prove a Temptation to fuch as are obnoxious, of refigning themfelves in fuch a manner to the Will and Pleafure of the Monarch, for the obtaining his connivancy at their violation of the Laws, as is unfafe and dangerous for the common Liberty and Good of the Kingdom. For in cafe the fupreme Magiftrate purfue an Intereft diftinct from, and deftructive to that of his People, they whom the Law hath made liable to be oppreffed, are brought under Inducements of becoming fo many *Partifans* for abetting him in his Defigns, in hopes of being thereupon protected from the *Penal Statutes*, the execution whereof is committed to him. And as it is not agreeable to the Wifdom and Prudence which ought to be among Men, nor to the Mercy and Compaffion which fhould be among Chriftians, for one party to furrender another into the hands and power of the Sovereign, to be impoverifhed and ruined by him at his pleafure; efpecially when thofe whom they thus give up to be thus treated and entertained, are at agreement with them in all the Effentials of Religion, equally zealous as themfelves for the Liberties of their Country; and who, for Sobriety in their Lives, Induftry in their Callings, and Ufefulnefs in the Commonwealth, are inferior to none of their Fellow-Subjects: So it is obvious to any, who give themfelves leave to think, that the King would long e'er this have been ftated in the Abfolutenefs that is afpired after, and both Church and State reduced to lie at the difcretion of the Monarch, provided the Non-conformifts, for procuring his Favour in non-execution of the Laws, had fuffered themfelves to be prevailed upon, and drawn over to ftand by and affift him in his *Popifh* and Defpotical Defigns.

But that honeft people, though hated and maligned by their Brethren, rather than be found aiding the King in his Ufurpations over the Kingdom, have chofen to undergo the utmoft Calamities they could be made fubject unto, either through the Execution of thofe Laws which had been made againft him, or through our Princes and their Minifters wrecking their Malice upon them in Arbitrary and Illegal Methods. But what the Royal Brothers could not work the afflicted and perfecuted Side unto, they found the Art to engage the other Side in, though not only excepted from all Obnoxioufnefs to thofe Laws, but ftrengthned and fupported by them. For as foon as the Court begun to defpair of prevailing upon Diffenters to become their Tools and Inftruments of enflaving the Nation, and of exalting the Monarchy to a defpotical Abfolutenefs, they applied to the Bigots of the Church of *England*, whom by gratifying with a vigorous Execution of the Laws upon Diffenters, they brought to abet, applaud and juftify them in all thofe Counfels and Ways, which have reduced us into that miferable Condition wherein we not long fince were. The Clergy being advanced to Grandeur and Opulency, things which many of them are fonder of, and lother to forego than Religion, and the Rights of the Nation; the Court made it their Bufinefs, to poffefs them with a Belief, that unlefs the Fanaticks were fuppreffed and ruined, they could not enjoy with Security their Dignities and Wealth. Whereupon not only the leffer Levites, but the

Superior Clergy having their Leſſon and Cue given them from *Whitehall* and *St. James's*, fell upon purſuing the Nonconformiſts with Eccleſiaſtical Puniſhments, and upon exciting and animating the Civil Officers againſt them. And under pretence of preſerving and defending the Church, they gave themſelves over to an implicit ſerving of the Court, and became not only Advocates but Inſtruments for the robbing of *Corporations* of their Charters, for impoſing Sheriffs upon the City of *London*, who had not been legally elected, and of fining and puniſhing Men arbitrarily for no Crime, ſave the having aſſerted their own and the Nation's Rights in modeſt and lawful ways. Poſterity will hardly believe that ſo many of the Prelatical Clergy, and ſo great a number of the Members of the Church of *England*, ſhould from an Enmity unto, and pretended Jealouſy of the Diſſenters, have become Tools under the late King for juſtifying the Diſſolution of ſo many Parliaments, the Invaſion made upon their Privileges, the ridiculing and ſtifling of the Popiſh Plot, the ſhamming of forged Conſpiracies upon Proteſtants, the condemning ſeveral to death for High-Treaſon, who could be rendred guilty by the Tranſgreſſion of no known Law, and finally for advancing a Gentleman to the Throne, who had been engaged in a Conjuration againſt Religion and the legal Government, and whom three ſeveral Parliaments would have therefore excluded from the Right of Succeſſion. And being ſeduced into an eſpouſal of the Intereſts of the Court againſt Religion, Parliaments and the Nation, it is doleful to conſider what Doctrines both from Pulpit and Preſs were thereupon brought forth and divulged : Such as *Monarchy's being a Government by Divine Right* ; *That it is in the Prince's power to rule as he pleaſeth* ; *That it is a Grace and Condeſcenſion in the King to give an Account of what he does* ; *That for Parliaments to direct, or regulate the Succeſſion, borders upon Treaſon, and is an Offence againſt the Law of Nature* ; *And that the only thing left to Subjects, in caſe the King will tyrannize over their Conſciences, Perſons and Eſtates, is tamely to ſuffer,* and, as ſome of them did abſurdly expreſs it, *to exerciſe Paſſive Obedience.* So that by corrupting the Minds and Conſciences of men with thoſe peſtilent and ſlaviſh Notions, they betrayed the Nation, both to the Miſchiefs which have already overtaken us, and to what further we were threatned with. Nor did theſe Doctrines tend meerly to the fettering and enfeebling the Spirits of Men, but they were a Temptation to the Royal Bothers to put in execution what they had been ſo long contriving, and travelling with, and were a kind of reprimanding them for being ignorant of their own Right and Power, and for not exerting it with that Vigour and Expedition which they might. I do acknowledge that there were many both of the Sacred Order, and of the Laick Communion of the Church of *England*, who were far from being infected with thoſe brutiſh Sentiments and Opinions, and who were as zealous as any for having the Monarchy kept within its ancient limits ; Parliaments maintained in their wonted Reverence and Authority ; the Subjects preſerved in the enjoyment of their immemorial Privileges ; and who were far from ſacrificing our Religion and Laws to Popery and Arbitrarineſs ; and from lulling us into a Tameneſs and Lethargy, in caſe the Court ſhould attempt the aboliſhing the eſtabliſhed Doctrine and Worſhip, and the ſubverting and changing the Civil Government. But alas ! beſides their being immediately branded with the Name of *Trimmer* and conformable *Fanaticks*, and regiſtred in the Kalender with thoſe that ſtood precluded the King's Favour, and merited his Animadverſion ; their Modeſty was ſoon drowned and ſilenced in the loud Noiſe of their clamorous Brethren, and their retiredneſs from Converſation, while the others frequented all places of Society and publick Concourſe, deprived the Nation of the benefit of their Example, and the happineſs of their Inſtructions. Nor have I mentioned the Extravagancies of any of the Eccleſiaſticks and Members of the Church of *England*, with a deſign either of reproaching and upbraiding them, or of provoking or exaſperating the Diſſenters to Reſentments ; but only to ſhew how fatal our Diviſions have been to us, what exceſſes they have occaſioned our being hurried and tranſported into, and what miſchievous Improvement our Enemies have made of them, to the ſupplanting and almoſt ſubverting of all that is valuable unto us, as we are *Engliſh*-Men, Chriſtians and Proteſtants.

And as our Animoſities, through our Diviſions, gave the Court an advantage of ſuborning that Party, which they pretended to befriend and uphold, into a Miniſtration to all their Counſels, and Projections againſt our Religion and Laws ; ſo by reaſon of the unnatural Heats wherewith Proteſtants have been enflamed and enraged againſt Proteſtants, many weak, ungrounded, and unſtable Souls, have been tempted to queſtion the Truth of our Religion, and to apoſtatize to the Church of *Rome*, and

and thereupon have become united in Inclination, Power and Endeavours with the Court, and our old Enemies the *Papifts*, for the Extirpation of Proteftancy, and the Alteration of the Government. As it hath been matter of Offence and Scandal to all Men, fo it hath been ground of ftumbling and falling unto many, to fee thofe who are profeffedly of the fame Religion, to be mutually embittered againft one another, and fo far tranfported with Malice and Rage, as to feek and purfue each other's Deftruction. For fuch a Carriage and Behaviour are fo contrary to the Spirit and Principles of Chriftianity, and to the Genius and Temper of true Religion, that it is no marvel if perfons ignorant of the Holy Scriptures, and ftrangers to the converting and comforting Vertue of the Doctrine of the Gofpel afferted in our Confeffions, and infifted upon by our Divines, fhould fufpect the Orthodoxy of that Religion which is accompanied with fo bitter Fruits, even in the Difpenfers of the Word as well as in others; and betake themfelves to the Communion of that Church, where how many and important foever their Differences be one with another, yet they do not break forth into thofe Flames of excommunicating and perfecuting each other, that ours have done. How have fome among us, through having their Spirits fretted and exafperated by the craft and cunning of our Enemies, not only loaded and ftigmatized their Brethren and Fellow-Proteftants with Crimes and Names, which, were they true, and deferved, would juftly render us a Loathing and an Abomination to Mankind; but have libelled and branded thofe whom God had honoured to be Inftruments of the Reformation, with Appellations and Characters fit to beget a Deteftation of their Doctrine as well as their Memory! The worft that the *Papifts* have forged and vomited out againft *Luther*, *Zwinglius*, *Calvin*, &c. hath been raked up and repeated, to the difparagement of the Reformation, and to the fcandalizing the Minds of weak Men againft it. And as the *Jefuits* and *Priefts* have improved thofe Slanders and Calumnies to the feduction of divers from the Church of *England*, and to a working them over to a Reconciliation with the Church of *Rome*; fo the Court hath thereby had an increafe of their Faction and Party againft our Religion and Liberties, and have been enabled to mufter Troops of *Janizaries* for their defpotical and unlimited Claim.

Nor have our Divifions, with the Heats, Animofities, Revilings and Perfecutions that have enfued thereupon, proved only an occafion of the Seduction of feveral from our Religion, and of their Apoftacy to *Popery*; but they have been a main fpring and fource of the Debauchery, Irreligion and Atheifm, which have over-fpread the Nation, and have brought fo many both to an indifferency and unconcernednefs for the *Gofpel*, and all that is vertuous and noble, and have difpofed them to fall in with thofe that could countenance and protect them in their Impiety and Profanenefs, and feed their Luxury and Pride with Honour and Gain. What a woful Scheme of Religion have we afforded the World! and how fhamefully have we painted forth and reprefented the Holy Doctrine of the bleffed *Jefus*, while we have not only lived in a direct oppofition to all the Commands of Meeknefs, Love and mutual Forbearance which our Religion lays us under the Authority of, but have neglected to practife Good Manners, to obferve the Rules of Civility, to treat one another with common Humanity, and to do as we would be done unto? While we have been more offended at what feemed to fupplant our Dominations and Grandeurs, than at what difhonoured God and reproached the *Gofpel*; while we weighed not fo much whether they whom we took into our Sacred Communion, as well as into our perfonal Friendfhip, were conformable in their Lives to the Scripture, as whether they complied with the Canons of the Church; while we reprobated all that were not of our way, though ever fo vertuous and devout, and fainted all that were, though ever fo wicked and profane; while we branded fuch for Fanaticks, whom we could juftly charge with nothing, fave the not admitting that into Religion, which came not from the Divine Author of it; and hugged thofe for good and orthodox Believers, that would fooner confult the Statute-Book for their Practice in the Worfhip of God, than the Bible; while we haled thofe to Prifon, and fpoiled them of their Eftates, to whom nothing could be objected, except their being too precife and confcientious, in avoiding that, through fear and apprehenfion of finning, which others had a liberty and latitude to do, as judging it lawful; and in the mean time efteemed thofe worthy of the chiefeft Trufts in the Church and Commonwealth, whofe Folly and Villanies made them unfit for Civil Societies; while they who lived moft agreeably to the Laws of God, and the Example of *Chrift*, were perfecuted as Enemies to Religion, and the Pefts of the Kingdom; and, in the interim, too many of the very Clergy were not only Countenancers of the moft profligate Perfons, as their beft Friends, but joined and affifted in fcandalous Debaucheries, under pretence of fuftaining the Honour of their

Tribe,

Tribe, and doing Service to the Church; I say, while these were the unhappy, but too obvious Fruits of our Divisions, and of the bitter Heats that accompanied them, how was the Reverence for the sacred Order lessened and diminished, the Veneration for Religion weakened and lost, the Shame and Dread of appearing prophane and wicked, removed and banished; and such who took the measures of Christianity from the Practices of those that were stiled Christians, rather than from the immaculate and holy Scriptures, tempted to think all Religion a Juggle, and Priesthood but an Artifice and Craft to compass Honour and Wealth. And though nothing but a shortness of Understanding, and an immoderate Love to their Lusts, could occasion the drawing such a Conclusion from the foregoing Premises, yet I must needs grant that there was too just a ground administred unto them of saying, that many did not believe that themselves, the Faith whereof they recommended to others. But that which I would more particularly observe, is, that it is from among those, who by the foregoing occasions have been tempted to Debauchery and Irreligion, that the *Romish* Emissaries have made the Harvest of Proselytes and Converts to the Church of *Rome*. For as they who fear not God, will be easily brought to imitate *Cæsar*; and such who are of no Religion, will in subserviency to secular Ends, assume the Mask and Profession of any; so Popery is extremely adapted to the Wishes and Desires of wicked and prophane Men, in that it provides for their living as enormously as they please here, and flatters them with hopes and assurances of Blessedness hereafter. They who can be ascertained of going to Heaven upon their confessing their Sins to a Priest, and their receiving Absolution, the Eucharist and extream Unction, need not look after Repentance towards God, Conversion to Holiness, nor a Life of Faith, Love, Mortification and Obedience, which the Protestant Religion, upon the Authority of the Gospel, obligeth them unto, in order to the obtaining of eternal Happiness. And as the late Apostates to Popery in *England*, are chiefly such who were notorious for Looseness, Prophaneness and Immorality, and were the Scandal of our Religion while they professed it; and while in our Church, were not properly of it: so it is from among Men of this stamp and character, that their late Majesties have found Persons assisting and subservient to their Despotical and Arbitrary Designs. *For whosoever takes a Survey of the Court-Faction, and considereth who have been the Advocates for Encroachments upon our Liberties, and Abetters of Usurpations over our Rights, they will find them to have been principally the profligate and debauched among the Nobility and Gentry, the mercenary, ignorant, and scandalous among the Clergy, the Off-scouring and such as are an Ignominy to Human Nature among the Yeomanry and Peasants.* And it was in order to this villanous End, that the Royal Brothers have endeavoured so industriously to debauch the Nation, and have made *Sensuality and Profaneness the Qualifications for Preferment, and the Badges of Loyalty.* And if among those that appear for the Preservation of the Liberties of their Country, there be any that deserve to be stiled Enemies to Religion and Virtue, as I dare affirm that they owe their Immoralities to Court-Education, Converse and Example; so I hope that though they have not hitherto been all of them so happy as to have left their Vices where they learned them, yet that they will not continue to disparage the good Cause, which they have espoused, with an unsuitable Life, nor give their Adversaries reason to say, that while they pretend to seek the Reformation of the State, they are both the Deriders of Sobriety and Virtue, without which no Constitution can long subsist, and guilty of such horrid Oaths, Cursing, Imprecations, Blasphemies and Uncleannesses, which naturally, as well as morally and meritoriously, dispose Nations to Subversion and Extirpation.

Finally, being through the bitter Effects which have ensued upon our Divisions, made apprehensive and jealous one of another, it hath from thence come to pass, that while *the Care of the Conformists hath been to watch against the growth of the Dissenters; and the Sollicitude of the Nonconformists hath been, how to prevent the Rage of the bigotted Church-men;* the Papists, in the mean time, without being heeded or observed, have both incredibly multiplied, and made considerable Advances in their designs of ruining us. For whensoever the Court was to take a signal step towards Popery and Arbitrary Power, there was a clamour raised of some menacing Boldness of the Dissenters. And if the Nation grew at any time alarmed, by reason of the Favour shewn to the Roman Catholicks, and of some visible Progress made towards the King's becoming Despotical, all was immediately hush'd with a shout and cry of the Government and Church's being in imminent hazard from the Dissenters. Yea, whensoever the Papists and their Royal Patrons stood detected, of having been conspiring against our Religion and Civil Liberties, all was diverted and stifled, by putting the Kingdom upon a false Scent, and by hounding out their Beagles upon the Nonconformists. So that the Eyes and Minds of Proteſtants being employed in reference to what was to be apprehended and feared from one another, the working of our Popiſh Enemies either eſcaped our Obſervation, or were heeded by moſt, only with a ſuperficial and unaffective Glance. And while our Church-men ſtood prepoſſeſſed by the Court, with a dread and jealouſy of the Diſſenters, all that was ſaid and written of a Conſpiracy carried on by the Papiſts againſt our *Laws* and *Religion,* was entertained and repreſented by the prejudiced Clergy, as an Artifice only of the Diſſenters for compaſſing an Indulgence from the Parliament, which in caſe ſuch a Plot had obtained the belief, that a Matter of ſo great Danger and Conſequence required, would have been eaſily granted, being the only rational Expedient for the preſervation of the eſtabliſhed Religion and the Legal Government. Nor did our Enemies queſtion but that having enflamed our Diviſions, and raiſed our Animoſities to ſo great a height, rather than the one Party would lay aſide their Severities, and the other let fall their Reſentments, we would even be contented to lie at their Mercy, and ſubmit our ſelves to the Pleaſure and Diſcretion of the Court and Papiſts. And there have not wanted ſome peeviſh, fooliſh, and ill Men of both Parties, who rather than ſacrifice their Spleen and Paſſion, and abandon their particular Quarrels for the Intereſt and Safety of the whole, have been inclined to ex-poſe the Proteſtant Religion and *Engliſh* Liberties, to the Hazards wherewith they were apparently threatned, and to ſuffer all Extremities, meerly to have the ſatisfaction of ſeeing thoſe whom they reſpectively hate, involved with them under the ſame Miſe-ries. But as this was ſuch a degree of Madneſs and Infatuation, as could proceed from nothing but brutiſh Rage, and argues no leſs than a Divine *Nemeſis*; ſo, I hope, they are but few that now ſtand infected with theſe paſſionate Sentiments and Inclinations, and remain thus hardned in their mutual Prejudices. And to thoſe I have nothing to ſay, nor the leaſt Advice to adminiſter, but ſhall leave them to their own Follies, as Perſons to whoſe Conviction no Diſcourſe, though ever ſo rational, can be adapted, and whom only Stripes can work upon.

'Tis to ſuch therefore as are capable of hearkning to Reaſon, and who are ready to embrace any Counſel that ſhall be found adjuſted to the common Intereſt, that I am to addreſs what remains to be repreſented and ſaid in the following Leaves. For all Parties of Proteſtants having ſeen how far our Enemies have improved our Diviſions and Ran-cours, to the compaſſing their wicked and ambitious Deſigns, and the robbing us of all that good and generous Men account valuable ; they are at laſt convinced of the ne-ceſſity we have been, and are reduced unto, of altering the meaſures of our acting to-wards one another, and both of laying aſide our Perſecutions, and of exchanging our Wranglings among our ſelves, into a joint contending for the Faith of the Goſpel, and the Rights of the Nation. For what the Gentleman, ſo lately in the Throne, intends and aims at, is not any longer matter of meer Suſpicion and Jealouſy, but of demon-ſtrable Evidence and unqueſtionable Certainty.

His Mask and Vizor of Zeal for the preſervation of the Church of *England*, and of tender regard for the Laws of the Land, were laid by and put off, and his Reſolutions of governing arbitrarily, and of introducing Popery, were become obvious to all Men, whom Reaſon and Senſe have not forſaken and left.

The Papiſts, whom it was thought much, a while ago, to ſee connived at in the ex-erciſe of their Worſhip in private Houſes, are allowed now to practiſe their Idolatry openly in our chief Towns, and in the Metropolitan City of the Kingdom to uſurp the publick Churches and Cathedrals. Thoſe Catholick Gentlemen, whom heretofore it was matter of ſurpriſe to ſee countenanced with the private Favour of the Prince, are now advanced to the ſupream Commands in the Army, and the principal Truſt in Civil Affairs. The Recuſant Lords, whoſe enlargement out of the *Tower* we could not but look upon as an unprecedented Violation, both of the Laws of the Land, and of the Rights and Juriſdiction of Parliament, being committed thither by the Authority of the Houſe of Lords, upon a Charge and Impeachment of High Treaſon, by the Commons of *England* in Parliament aſſembled, were now honoured to be Members of the Privy Council, and exalted to be chief Miniſters of State. They whom the Sta-tutes of the Realm make ſubject to the ſevereſt Penalties for Apoſtacy to *Rome,* are not only protected from the edge of the Laws, but maintained in Parochial Incumbencies, and Headſhips of Colleges.

Our Orthodox Clergy are not only inhibited to preach againſt Popery, but are il-legally reprimanded, ſilenced, and ſuſpended, for diſcharging that Duty which their Conſciences, Offices, Oaths, and the Laws of the Kingdom oblige them unto. And ſuch whom neither the Eccleſiaſtical nor *Weſtminſter* Courts can arraign and proceed againſt, we have a new Court of Inquiſition erected for the adjudging and puniſhing
of

of them. So that it is not the Diffenters who are the only Perfons to be ftruck at and ruined, but the Conformifts are to be treated after the fame manner, and to fhare in the common Lot whereunto all honeft and fincere Proteftants are deftined and defigned. Even they who were the Darlings of *Whitehall* and *St. James's*, and recompenfed with Honours and Titles for betraying the Rights and Privileges of Corporations, perfecuting Diffenters, and heading Addreffes, wherein Parliaments were reproached, the Courfe of Juftice againft Popifh Offenders was flandered, the illegal and arbitrary Proceedures of the Court applauded and juftified, and all that were zealous for our Laws and Liberties ftigmatized with the names of *Villains* and *Traitors*, are now themfelves, for but difcouraging Popifh Affemblies, and attempting to put the Laws in execution againft Priefts who had publickly celebrated Mafs, not only check'd and rebuked, but punifhed with Seizure and Imprifonment.

Nor are our Religion and Civil Liberties meerly fupplanted and undermined by illegal Tricks, gloffed over with the Varnifh of judicial Forms; but they are affaulted and battered in the face of the Sun, without fo much as palliation to give their Proceedures a plaufible figure. And the King being brought to a defpair of managing the Parliament to his barefaced Purpofe of Popery and Arbitrarinefs, and of prevailing with them to eftablifh Tyranny and Idolatry by Law, notwithftanding their having been as induftrioufly pack'd and chofen to anfwer fuch a Defign, as Art, Bribery and Authority could reach; and notwithftanding their having been obfequious in their firft Seffion to an excefs that has proved unfafe to themfelves and the Nation, he became refolved not to allow them to meet any more, but to fet up *a-la-mode de France*, and to have his perfonal Commands, feconded with the Affent of his *durante-bene-placito* Judges, to be acknowledged and obeyed for Laws. So that they who were formerly feduced into a good Opinion of him, are not only undeceived, but provoked to warm Refentments, for having had their credulity and eafinefs of belief fo grofly abufed. And as the converting fo vaft a number of well-meaning, but wofully deluded People, who had fuffered themfelves to be hoodwink'd, and fatally hurried to betray their Religion, Country and Pofterity, to the Ambition and Popifh Bigotry of the Court, was a defign becoming the Compaffion, Mercy and Wifdom of God; fo the Methods and Means whereby they are come to be enlightned and profelyted, are a fignal vindication of the Sapience and Righteoufnefs of God in all thofe tremendous fteps of his Providence, by which our Enemies have been emboldned to detect and difcover themfelves. For though their continuing fo long to have a good opinion of the prefent King, and their abetting him fo far in the undermining our Religion, and invading our Liberties, may feem to have proceeded not fo much from their Ignorance as from their Obftinacy and Malice; yet God, who penetrates into the Hearts of Men, may have difcovered fome degrees of Sincerity in their Pretenfions and Carriages, though accompanied with a great deal of Folly and Unmanlinefs. Nor are the Lord's ways like to ours, to give Perfons over as unteachable and irreclaimable, upon their withftanding every meafure of Light, and the refifting even thofe Means which were fufficient and proper for their Conviction; but he will try them by new and extraordinary Methods, and fee whether feeling and doleful Experience may not convert thofe, upon whom Arguments and Moral Evidence could make no impreffions. And there being among thofe formerly mifled and deluded Proteftants, many who retained a Love for their Country, a Care for their Pofterity, and a Zeal for the Gofpel and reformed Religion, even when their Actions imported the contrary, and feem'd to betray them; the fingling and weeding out fuch from among the Court-Faction and Party, is a compenfation both for the defeatment of all Endeavours, for the prevention of the Evils that have overtaken us, and for the Diftreffes and Calamities under which we do at prefent lie and groan. And if there be joy in Heaven upon the converfion of a Sinner, with what thankfulnefs to God, and joy in themfelves, fhould they who have fo many years wreftled againft the Encroachments of Popery and Arbitrarinefs, and who have deeply fuffered in their Names, Perfons and Eftates upon that account; welcome and embrace their once erring and mifled, but now enlightned, reclaimed and converted Brethren? And in ftead of remembring or upbraiding them with the oppofition and rancour which they expreffed againft our Perfons, Principles, and Ways,

let

I

let there be no Language heard from us, but what may declare the joy we have in our selves for their conversion, and the entire Trust and Confidence which we put in them.

The first Duty incumbent therefore upon Dissenters towards those of the Church of *England*, is to believe, that notwithstanding there have been many of them so long Advocates and Partisans for the Court, through ignorance of what was aimed at and intended, they are nevertheless as really concerned as any others, and as truly zealous for the preservation of the Protestant Religion, and for maintaining the legal Rights and Liberties of the Subject, and when occasion shall offer, will approve themselves accordingly. *'Tis a ridiculous, as well as mischievous Fancy, for one Party to confine all Religion only to themselves, or to circumscribe all the ancient English Ardor for the common Rights of the Nation, to such as are of their particular Fellowship and Persuasion; there being sincere Christians, and true Englishmen among those of all Judgments, and Societies of Protestants, and among none more than those of the Communion of the Church of* England. It were the height of Wickedness, as well as the most prodigious Folly, to imagine that the *Conformists* have abandon'd all Fidelity to God, and cast off all care of themselves and their Country, upon a mistaken Judgment of being Loyal and Obedient to the King. The contrary is plain enough; they knew as well as any, that the giving to *Cæsar* the Things that are *Cæsar's*, lay them under no Obligation of surrendring unto him the Things that are God's; nor of sacrificing unto the Will of the Sovereign the Privileges reserved unto the People by the Fundamental Rules of the Constitution, and by the Statutes of the Realm. And they understand, as well as others, that the Laws of the Land are the only Measures of the Prince's Authority, and of the Subjects Fealty; and where they give him no Right to Command, they lay them under no tye to Obey. And though here and there a Dissenter has written against Popery with good Success, yet they have been mostly Conformable Divines, who have triumphed over it in elaborate Discourses, and who have beaten the Romish Scriblers off the Stage. Nor can it be thought that they who have so accurately related and vindicated the History, and asserted and defended the Doctrine of the Reformation, should either tamely relinquish, or be wanting in all due and legal Ways to uphold and maintain it. And though some few of the Nonconformists have, with sufficient strength and applause, used their Pens against Arbitrariness, in detecting the Designs of the Royal Brothers; yet they who have generally, and with greatest Honour, appeared for our Laws and Legal Government, against the Invasions and Usurpations of the Court, have been Theologues and Gentlemen of the Church of *England*. Nor in case of further Attempts for altering the Constitution, and enslaving the Nation, will they shew themselves unworthy the having descended from Ancestors, whose Motto in the high Places of the Field was, *Nolumus Leges Angliæ mutari*: They who have so often justified the Arms of the *United Netherlands* against their Rightful Princes the Kings of *Spain*, and so unanswerably vindicated their casting off Obedience to those Monarchs, when they had invaded their Privileges, and attempted to establish the *Inquisition* over them, cannot be ignorant what their own Right and Duty is in behalf of the Protestant Religion and *English* Liberties; for the Security whereof, we have not only so many Laws, but the Coronation-Oaths, and Stipulations of our Kings.

And those Gentlemen of the Church of *England*, who appeared so vigorously in three Parliaments for excluding the Duke of *York*, from the Succession to the Crown, by reason of a Jealousy of what, through being a Papist, he would attempt against our Religion and Privileges, in case he were suffered to ascend the Throne; cannot be now to seek what becomes them towards him, having seen and felt what before they only apprehended and feared. For if the Law that entaileth the Succession upon the next of Kin, and obligeth the Subjects to admit and receive him, not only may, but ought to be dispensed with, in case the Heir, thro' having imbib'd Principles which threaten the Safety, and are inconsistent with the Happiness of the People, hath made himself incapable to inherit; we know, by a short Ratiocination, how far we stand bound to a Prince on the Throne, who by transgressing against the Laws of the Constitution, hath abdicated himself from the Government,

vernment, and ftands virtually depofed. For *whofoever fhall offer to rule Arbitrarily, does immediately ceafe to be King de jure, feeing by the Fundamental, Common, and Statute Laws of the Realm, we know none for fupreme Magiftrate and Governor, but a limited Prince, and one who ftands circumfcribed and bounded in his Power and Prerogative.*

And fhould the Diffenters entertain a belief that the Conformifts are lefs concerned and zealous than themfelves for the Proteftant Religion and Laws of the Kingdom, they would not only fin, and offend againft the Rules of Charity, but againft the Meafures of Juftice, and daily Evidences from Matters of Fact. For neither they, nor we, owe our Converfion to God, and our practical Holinefs to the Opinions about Difcipline, Forms of Worfhip, and Ceremonies, wherein we differ, but the Doctrines of Faith and Chriftian Obedience, wherein we agree. 'Tis not their being for a Liturgy, a Surplice, or a Bifhop, that hath heretofore influenced them to fubferve the Court in Defigns tending to Abfolutenefs, but they were feduced unto it, upon Motives whereof they are now afhamed; and the Ridiculoufnefs and Folly of which they have at laft difcover'd. Nor is *the multitude of profligate and fcandalous Perfons with which the Church of* England *is crowded,* any juft impeachment of the Purity of her Doctrine in the Vitals and Effentials of Religion, or of the Virtue and Piety of many of her Members. For as it is her being the only Society eftablifhed by Law that attracts thofe Vermin to her Bofom; fo it is her being reftrained by Law from debarring them, that keep them there to her reproach, and to the grief of many of her Ecclefiafticks. Neither is it the fault of the Church of *England,* that the Agents and Factors for Popery and Arbitrary Power, have chofen to pafs under the name of *her Sons;* but it proceeds partly from their Malice, as hoping by that means to difgrace her with all true *Englifhmen,* as well as with Diffenters; and partly from their Craft, in order thereby the better to conceal their Defign, and to fhroud themfelves from the Cenfure and Punifhment, which had it not been for that Mask, they would have been expofed unto, and have undergone. And I dare affirm, that befides the Obligations from Religion, which the Conformifts are equally under with Diffenters, for hindring the introduction of Popery, there are feveral Inducements from Intereft which fway them to prevent its eftablifhment, wherein the Diffenters are but little concerned. For though Popery would be alike afflictive to the Confciences of Proteftants of all Perfuafions, yet there are Gentlemen, and Minifters of the Church of *England,* whofe Livings, Revenues, and Eftates have been threatned in cafe it had come to be eftablifhed.

Nor would the moft loyal and obfequious Levites, provided they refolve to continue Proteftants, be willing that their Parfonages and Incumbencies, to which they have no lefs Right by Law, than the King hath to the Excife and Cuftoms, fhould be taken from them, and beftowed upon Romifh Priefts, by an Act of Defpotical Power, and of unlimited Prerogative. And for the Gentlemen, as I think few of them would hold themfelves obliged to part with their Purfes to Highway Padders, though fuch fhould have a Patent from the King to rob whomfoever they met upon the Road; fo there will not be many inclined to fuffer their Mannours and Abbey-Lands, to which they have fo good a Title, to be ravifhed from them, either by Monks or Janizaries, though authorized thereunto by the Priefts Commiffion. Even they who had formerly fuffered themfelves to be feduced, to prove in a manner Betrayers of the Rights and Religion of their Country, will now (being undeceived) not only in conjunction with others, withftand the Court in its profecution of Popifh and Arbitrary Defigns; but through a generous exafperation, for having been deluded and abufed, will judge themfelves obliged, in vindication for their Actings before, to appear for the Proteftant Religion, and the Laws of *England,* with a Zeal equal to that wherewith they contributed to the undermining and fupplanting of them. For they are not only become more fenfible than they were of the Mifchiefs of Abfolute Government, fo as for the future to prize and affert the Privileges referved unto the people by the Rules of the Conftitution, and chalked out for them in the Laws of the Land; but they have fuch a frefh view of Popery, both in its Herefies, Blafphemies, Superftitions, and Idolatries; and in the Treachery, Sanguinarinefs, Violence and Cruelty which the Papal Principles mould, influence, and oblige Men unto; that they not only entertain the greateft abhorrency and deteftation imaginable for it, but feem refolved not to cherifh in their Bofom, a Thing fo abominable to God, execrable to good Men, and deftructive to Human as well as to Chriftian Societies.

Nor are the Diſſenters meerly to believe that the Conformiſts are equally zealous as themſelves for the Reformed Religion, and *Engliſh* Rights, but they are to conſider them as the only great and united Body of Proteſtants in the Kingdom, with whom all other Parties compared bear no conſiderable proportion. For though the Nonconformiſts, conſidered abſtractly, make a vaſt number of honeſt and uſeful People, yet being laid in the Scale with thoſe of the Epiſcopal Communion, they are but few, and lie in a little room. And whoſoever will take the pains to ballance the one againſt the other, even where Diſſenters make the greateſt Figure, and may juſtly boaſt of their Multitude, they will ſoon be convinced that the number of the other doth far tranſcend and exceed them. And if it be ſo in Cities and Corporations, where the greateſt Bulk of Diſſenters are, it is much more ſo in Country Pariſhes, where the latter bear not the proportion of one to a hundred. Nor doth the Church of *England* more exceed the other Parties in her number, than ſhe doth in the quality of her Members. For whereas they who make up and conſtitute the ſeparate Societies, are chiefly Perſons of the middle Rank and Condition, the Church of *England* doth in a manner vouch and claim all the Perſons of Honour, of the Learned Profeſſions, and ſuch as have valuable Eſtates, for her Communicants. And though the other ſort are as neceſſary in the Common-wealth, and contribute as much to its Strength, Proſperity, and Happineſs, yet they make not that Figure in the Government, nor ſtand in that Capacity of having influence upon publick Affairs. For not only the Gentlemen of both the Gowns, who by reaſon of their Calling and Learning are beſt able to defend our Religion, and vindicate our Laws and Privileges with their Tongues and Pens, but they whoſe Eſtates, Reputation and Intereſt, recommend them to be elected Members of the great Senate of the Nation, as well as they, who, by reaſon of their Honours and Baronages, are hereditary Legiſlators, are generally, if not all, of the Communion of the Church of *England*. So, that they who conform to the eſtabliſhed Worſhip and Diſcipline, are to be look'd upon and acknowledged as the great Bulwark of the Proteſtant Religion in *England*, and the Hedge and Fence of our Civil Liberties and Rights.

And though it be true, that this great Breach made upon our Religion and Laws is fallen out under their hand, while the poor Diſſenters had neither acceſſion to, nor were in a condition to prevent it; yet ſeeing their own Conſciences do ſufficiently load and charge them for it with Shame and Ignominy, it were neither candid, nor at this Juncture ſeaſonable to upbraid it to them, or improve it to their Diſhonour and Reproach. For as they have tamely look'd on and connived till our Religion and Liberties are ſo far undermined and ſupplanted; ſo it is they alone who have been in a condition of ſtemming the Inundation of Idolatry and Tyranny, with which we were threatned, and of repairing our Breaches, and reducing the Prerogative to its old Channel, and making Popery ſneak and retreat into its holes and corners again. And ſhould the Church of *England* have been overthrown and devoured, what an eaſy Prey would the reſt have been to the Romiſh Cormorants! And could the King, under the Conduct of the Jeſuits, and with the Aſſiſtance of his *Myrmidons,* have diſſolved the eſtabliſhed Worſhip and Diſcipline, they of the Separation would have been in no capacity to ſupport the Reformed Religion, nor able to eſcape the common Ruin and Perſecution. 'Tis therefore the Intereſt, as well as the Duty of the Diſſenters, to help, maintain, and defend thoſe Walls, within the ſkreen and ſhelter whereof their own Huts and Cottages are built and ſtand. And the rather, ſeeing the Conformiſts are at laſt, though to their own Religion's and the Nation's expence, become ſo far enlightned, as to ſee a neceſſity of growing more amicable towards them, and, to enlarge the Terms of their Communion, grant an Indulgence to all Proteſtants that differ from them. And as we ought to admire the Wiſdom of God in thoſe Providences, by which Proteſtants are taught to lay aſide their Animoſities, and let fall their Perſecutions of one another; ſo it would be a Contradiction both to the Principles and repeated Proteſtations of Diſſenters, to aim at more than ſuch a Liberty as is conſiſtent with a National Eccleſiaſtick Eſtabliſhment. Yea, it were to proclaim themſelves both Villains and Hypocrites, not to allow their Fellow-Proteſtants the Exerciſe of their Judgments, with what further Profits and Emoluments the Law will grant them, provided themſelves may be diſcharged from all obnoxiouſneſs to Penalties and Cenſures upon the account of their Conſciences, and be admitted a free and publick Practice of their own reſpective Modes of Diſcipline, and be ſuffered to worſhip God in thoſe ways which they think he hath required and enjoined them. And were *England* immediately to be rendred ſo happy as to have a Proteſtant Prince or Princeſs (as we are not now quite out of hopes) aſcend the Throne, and to

enjoy

enjoy a Parliament duly chosen, and acting with freedom, no one Party of the Reformed Religion among us, must ever expect to be established and supported to the denial of Liberty to others, much less to be by Law empowered to ruin and destroy them. Should it please Almighty God to bring the Princess of *Orange* to the Crown, though the Church of *England* may in that case justly expect the being preserved and upheld as the National Establishment, yet all other Protestants may very rationally promise themselves an Indulgence ; and that not only from the Mildness and compassionate Sweetness of her Temper, but from the Influence which the Prince her Husband will have upon her, who, as he is descended from Ancestors, whose Glory it was to be the Redeemers of their Country from Papal Persecution and *Spanish* Tyranny ; so his Education, Generosity, Wisdom, and many Heroick Virtues, dispose him to embrace all Protestants with an equal Tenderness, and to erect his Interest upon the being Head and Patron of all that profess the Reformed Religion. Had the late Duke of *Monmouth* been victorious against the Forces of the present King, and inabled to have wrested the Scepter out of his Hand, though all Protestants might thereupon have expected, and would certainly have enjoyed an equal Freedom, without the liableness of any Party to penal Laws for matters of Religion ; yet he would have been careful, and I have reason to believe that it was his purpose to have had the Church of *England* preserved and maintained, and that she should have suffered no Alteration but what would have been to her Strength and Glory, through an enlargement of the Terms of her Communion, and what would have been to the Praise of her Moderation and Charity, through her being persuaded to bear with such as differ from her in little things, and could not prevail with themselves to partake with her in all Ordinances. Upon the whole, it is both the prudence and safety of Dissenters, as they would escape Extirpation themselves, and have Religion conveyed down to Posterity, to unite their Strength and Endeavours to those of the Church of *England* for the upholding her against the assaults of Popish Enemies, who pursue her Subversion. As matters have been circumstanced and stated in *England*, there hath not been an Affront or Injury offered or done unto her by the Court, which did not at the same time reach and wound the Dissenters. 'Tis not her being for Episcopacy, Ceremonies, and imposed Set-Forms of Worship, the things about which she and the Nonconformists differ, that she hath been, not long since, maligned and struck at by the Man in Power, and his Popish *Juncto* ; but it is for being Protestant, Reformed, and Orthodox, Crimes under the Guilt whereof Dissenters were equally concerned and involved. Being therefore in opposition to the common Cause of Religion, that the late Court of Inquisition was erected over her Ecclesiasticks, all Protestants jointly resented the Wrongs which she sustain'd, and not only to sympatize with those dignified and lower Clergy which were called to suffer, but to espouse her Quarrel with the same Warmth that we would our own.

And as we are to look upon those of the Episcopal Communion, to be the great Bulwark of the Protestant Religion and reformed Interest in *England* ; so it was farther incumbent on Dissenters towards them, and a Duty which they owe to God, the Nation and themselves, not to be accessary to any thing through which the legal Establishment of the Church of *England* might have been, by an Act of pretended Regal Prerogative, weakned and supplanted.

I never counsel the Dissenters to renounce their Principles, nor to participate with the Prelatical Church in all Ordinances, on the Terms to which they have straitned and narrowed their Communion. For while they remain unsatisfied of the lawfulness of those Terms and Conditions, they cannot do it without offending God, and contracting Guilt upon their Souls ; nor will they of the Church of *England* in Charity, Justice and Honesty, expect it from them. For whatsoever any Man believeth to be Sin, it is so to him, and will by God be imputed as such, till he be otherways enlightned and convinced ; nor are the Dissenters to be false and cruel to themselves, in order to be kind and friendly to them. But that which I would advise them unto, is, that after the maintaining the highest measure of Love to the conformable Congregations as Churches of Christ, and the esteeming their Members as Christian Protestant Brethren, notwithstanding the several Things wherein they judge them to err, and to be mistaken, that they would not by any Act and Transactions of theirs, betray them into a Despotical Power, nor directly nor indirectly acknowledge any Authority paramount unto, and superseding the Laws, by which the Church of *England* is established in its present Form, Order, and Mode of Jurisdiction, Discipline and external Worship.

Whatsoever

Whatsoever Ease arrived to the Dissenters, through the King's suspending the Execution of the Penal Laws, without their Address and Application, they might receive it with Joy and Humility in themselves, and with thankfulness to God, nor was there hereby any prejudice offered on their part, to the Authority of the Law, or Offence or Injury given or done to the conformable Clergy. Nor is it without grief and regret that the Church-men have been forced to behold the harrassing, spoiling, and imprisonment of the Nonconformists, while in the mean time the Papists were suffered to assemble to the Celebration of their Idolatrous Worship without Censure and Controul. And had it been in their power to remedy it, and give relief to their Protestant Brethren, they would with delight and readiness have embrac'd the occasion and opportunity of doing it. But alas! instead of having an advantage put into their hand, of contributing to the Relief of the Dissenters, which, I dare say, many of them ardently wish and desire, they were compelled, contrary to their Inclination, as well as their Interest, to become instrumental in persecuting and oppressing them. Nor does the late King covet a better and more legal advantage against the Conformists, than that they would refuse to pursue Dissenters, and decline molesting them with Ecclesiastical Censures and civil Punishments. So that their condition was to be pitied and bewailed, in that they were hindred from acting against the Papists, though both enjoin'd by Law, and influenced thereunto by Motives of Self-Preservation, as well as by ties of Conscience; while in the mean time they were forced to prosecute their Fellow-Protestants, or else to be suspended and deposed, and put out of their Offices and Employments. And tho' I believe that they would at last have more Peace in themselves, and be better accepted with God in the great Day of their Account, should they have refused to disturb and prosecute their Protestant Brethren, and scorn to be any longer Court-Tools for weakning and undermining the Reformed Cause and Interest; yet I could not but leave them to act in this as they should be persuaded in themselves, and as they judged most agreeable to the Principles of Wisdom and Conscience. In the Interim, the Dissenters have all the reason in the world to believe, that the Proceedings of the Clergy and Members of the Church of *England* against them, were not the Results of their Election and Choice, but the Effects of moral Compulsion and Necessity. Nor will any Dissenter that is prudent and discreet, blame them for a matter which they cannot help, but bear his Misfortune and Lot with Patience in himself, and with Compassion and Charity towards them; and have his Indignation raised only against that Court, which forced them to be instrumental in their Oppression and Trouble. The Protestant Dissenters could not be so far void of sense, as to think that the Person lately in the Throne bore them any good-will, but *his drift was to screw himself into a Supremacy and Absoluteness over the Law, and to get such an Authority confessed to be vested in him, as when he pleased he might subvert the Established Religion, and set up Popery.* For by the same Power that he can dispense with the penal Statutes against the Nonconformists, he may also dispense with those against the Roman Catholicks. And whosoever owneth that he hath a Right to do the first, doth in effect own that he hath a Right to do the last. For if he be allowed a Power for the superseding some Laws made in reference to Matters of Religion, he may challenge the like Power for the superseding others of the same kind. And then by the same Authority that he can suspend the Laws against Popery, he may also suspend those for Protestancy. And by the same Power that he can, in defiance of Law, indulge the Papists the Exercise of their Religion in Houses, he may establish them in the publick Celebration of their Idolatry in Churches and Cathedrals. Yea, whereas the Laws that relate to Religion are enacted by no less Authority, than those that are made for the Preservation of our Civil Rights, should the K. be admitted to have an Arbitrary Power over the one, it is very like that by the Logick of *Whitehall* he might have challenged the same Absoluteness over the other. *Nor do I doubt but that the* eleven Judges, *who gratified him with a Despoticalness over the former, would, when required, grant him the same over the latter.* I know the Dissenters have been under no small Temptations, both by reason of being hindred from enjoying the Ordinances of the Gospel, and because of many grievous Calamities which they suffer for their Nonconformity, of making Applications to the King for some Relief by his suspending the Execution of the Laws; but they must give me leave to add, that they ought not, for the obtaining of a little Ease, to have betrayed the Kingdom, and sacrifice the Legal Constitution of the Government to the Lust and Pleasure of a Popish Prince, whom nothing less would serve than being Absolute and Despotical. And had he once been in the quiet Possession of an Authority to dispense with the penal Laws, the Dissenters would not long have enjoyed the Benefit of it. Nor could they have denied him a Power of reviving the Execution of the Law, which is part of the Truft depofited with him as fupreme Magiftrate, who have granted him a Power of fufpending the Laws, which the Rules of the Government precluded him from.   And as he might, whenfoever he pleafed, caufe the Laws, to which they were obnoxious, to be executed upon them ; fo by virtue of having an Authority acknowledged in him of fuperfeding the Laws, he might deprive them of the Liberty of meeting together to the number of Five ; a Grace which the Parliament thought fit to allow them, under all the other Severities to which they were fubjected.   Nor needs there any further Evidence, that the Prince's challenging fuch a Power was an Ufurpation, and that the Subjects making any Application, by which it feem'd allowed to him, was a betraying the ancient legal Government of the Kingdom ; whereas the moft obfequious and fervile Parliament to the Court that ever *England* knew, not only denied this Prerogative to the late King *Charles,* but made him renounce it by revoking his Declaration of Indulgence which he had emitted *Anno* 1672.

And as it will be to the perpetual Honour of fome of the Diffenters, to have chofen rather to fuffer the Severities which the Laws make them liable unto, than by any Act and Tranfaction of theirs, to undermine and weaken either the Church or the State ; fo it will be a means both of endearing them, we hope, not only to the Prince of *Orange,* now by a miraculous Providence brought in amongft us, but to future Parliaments, and of bringing them and the Conformifts into an Union of Counfels and Endeavours againft Popery and Tyranny for ever ; which is at this feafon a thing fo indifpenfibly neceffary for their common Prefervation.   Efpecially when through a new and more threatning Alliance and Confederacy with *France,* than that in 72, the King had not only engaged to act by and obferve the fame Meafures towards Proteftants in *England,* which that Monarch had vouchfafed the World a Pattern and Copy of in his carriage towards thofe of the Reformed Religion in *France*; but had promifed to difturb the Peace and Repofe of his Neighbours, and to commence a War, in conjunction with that Prince, againft Foreign Proteftants.   For as the King's giving Liberty and Protection to the *Algerines* to frequent his Havens, and fell the Prizes which they take from the *Dutch,* is both a moft infamous Action for a Prince, pretending to be a Chriftian, and a direct Violation of his Alliance with the *States General*; fo nothing can be more evident, than that he thereby fought to render them the weaker for him to affault, and that he was refolved (if fome unforefeen and extraordinary Providence had not interpofed and prevented) to declare War againft them the next Summer ; in order whereunto great Remifes of Money were already ordered him from the *French* Court.   So that the Indulgence which he pretends to be inclinable to afford the Diffenters, was not an effect of Kindnefs and Good-will, but an Artifice whereby to oblige their Affiftance in deftroying thofe abroad of the fame Religion with themfelves.   Which if he could once compafs, it were eafy to forefee what Fate both the Diffenters, and they of the Communion of the Church of *England,* were to expect.   Who, as they would not then have known whither to retreat for fhelter ; fo they would have been deftitute of Comfort in themfelves, and deprived of Pity from others ; not only for having, through their Divifions, made themfelves a Prey to the Papifts at home, but for having been acceffary to the Ruin of the Reformed State abroad ; and which was the *Afilum* and Sanctuary of all thofe who were elfewhere oppreffed and perfecuted for Religion.

Gloria Deo Optimo, Maximo.
Honos Principi noftri celfiffimo, pientiffimo.

G g g g g

A Repre-

A Representation of the Threatning Dangers, Impending over Pro-
testants in Great Britain. *With an Account of the* Arbitrary
and Popish Ends, *unto which the* Declaration *for* Liberty of
Conscience *in* England, *and the* Proclamation *for a* Toleration *in* Scotland, *are designed.*

THey are great Strangers to the Transactions of the World, who know not how
many and various the Attempts of the *Papists* have been, both to hinder all
Endeavours towards a *Reformation*, and to overthrow and subvert it where *it* hath obtained and prevailed.   For beside the innumerable Executions and Murthers committed
by means of the *Inquisition* to crush and stifle the *Reformed Religion* in its Rise and Birth,
and to prevent its Succeeding and Settlement in *Spain, Italy,* and many other *Territories* ;
there is no *Kingdom* or *State,* where it hath so far prevailed as to come to be universally
received and legally established, but it hath been through strange and wonderful Con-
flicts with the Rage and Malice of the *Church* of *Rome.*   The Persecutions which the
Primitive Christians underwent by virtue of the *Edicts* of the *Pagan Emperors,* were not
more Sanguinary and Cruel, than what through the *Laws* and *Ordinances* of *Popish Princes,*
have been inflicted upon those, who have testified against the Heresies, Superstitions, and
Idolatries, and have withdrawn from the Communion of the *Papal Church.*   Nor were
the *Martyrs* that suffered for the Testimony of *Jesus* against *Heathenism,* either more
numerous or worthier of esteem for Virtue, Justice and Piety, than they who have been
slaughtered, upon no other Pretence, but for endeavouring to restore the *Christian Re-*
ligion to the Simplicity and Purity of its divine and first *Institution,* and to recover it
from the Corruptions, wherewith it was become universally tainted in Doctrine, Worship, and Discipline.   How have all the Nations in *Europe* been soak'd with the Blood
of Saints, through the barbarous Rage of *Popish Rulers,* whom the *Roman Bishops* and
Clergy stirred up and instigated, in order to support themselves in their secular Grandeur, and in their Tyranny over the Consciences of Men, and to keep the World in
Slavery under Ignorance, Errors, Superstition and Idolatry, which the reducing Christianity again to the Rule of the Gospel, would have redeemed Mankind from, and
been an effectual Means to have dissipated and subverted?   They of the *Roman Com-*
munion having strangely corrupted the Christian Religion in its Faith, Worship and
Discipline, and having prodigiously altered it, from what it was in the Doctrines and Institutions of our *Saviour* and his *Apostles* ; they found no other way whereby to sustain
their Errors and Corruptions, and to preserve themselves in the Possession of that Empire,
which they had usurped over Conscience, and in the Enjoyment of the Wealth and secular Greatness, by which working upon the Ignorance, Superstition, Lusts, and Prophaneness of People, they had skrewed and wound themselves into, but by adjudging
all who durst detect or oppose them, to Fire and Sword, or to Miseries, to which
Death in its worst shape were preferable.   Nor have they for the better obstructing the
Growth, and compassing the Extirpation of the *Reformed Religion,* omitted either the Arts
and Subtleties of *Julian,* or the Fury and Violence of *Galerius* and *Dioclesian.*   Whosoever hath not observed the Craft and Rage that hath been employed and exerted against
Protestants for these 170 Years, must have been very little conversant in Histories, and
strangely overlook'd the Conduct of Affairs in the World, and the Transactions in Churches
and States, during their own time.   And tho' the *Papists* do not think it fit, to put their
Maxims for preserving the *Catholick Religion,* and converting *Hereticks,* in execution at
all times, and in every place, yet some of their Writers are so ingenuous, as to tell us the
reason of it ; that they do not forbear it upon Principles of *Christianity* and *Good-Nature,* but
upon Motives of *Policy* and *Fear,* lest the cutting one of our Throats might endanger two
of their own. However, they have been careful not to suffer a period of *twenty Years* to lapse
since the beginning of the *Reformation,* without affording us in some place or another,
renewed Evidences of *Papal* Charity, and of the *Roman* Method of hindring the Growth
of Heresy, either by a Massacre, War, or Persecution, begun, and executed, upon no
other Account or Provocation, but merely that of our *Religion,* and because we cannot
believe and practise in the Matters of God, as they do.   And having obtained of late,
great Advantages for the pursuing their Malice against us, more boldly and avowedly
than at another Season, and that not only through a strange Concurrence and Conjunction of *Princes* in the *Papal* Communion, who are more intoxicated with their Superstitions

perftitions and Idolatries, or lefs wife, merciful, and humane, than fome of their Predeceffors of that Fellowfhip were, but through having obtained a *Prince* intirely devoted unto them, and under the implicit guidance of their Priefts, to be advanced unto a Throne, where fuch fometime ufed to fit, as were the Terror of *Rome*, the Safeguard of the *Reformed Religion*, and the Sanctuary of oppreffed *Proteftants* ; they have thereupon both affumed a Courage of ftirring up new and unprecedented Perfecutions in divers places, againft the moft ufeful, beft and loyalleft of Subjects, upon no other Charge or Allegation, but for diffenting from the *Tridentine* Faith, and denying Subjection to the Triple Crown, and are raifed into a Confidence of wholly Extirpating *Proteftancy*, and of re-eftablifhing the *Papal* Tyrannies and Superftition, in the feveral *Countries* whence they had been expelled, or ftood fo depreffed and difcountenanced, as that the Votaries and Partizans of their *Church* had not the Sway and Domination. Nor need we any other Conviction, both of their Defign, and of their Confidence of fucceeding in it, than what they have already done, and continue to purfue in *France, Hungary* and *Piedmont*, where their profpering to fuch a degree in their cruel and barbarous Attempts, not only gives them boldnefs of entertaining thoughts of taking the like Methods, and acting by the fame Meafure, in all places where they find Rulers at their beck, and under their influence, but to unite and provoke all *Popifh Monarchs* to enter into a holy War againft *Proteftants* every where, that by Conquering and Subduing thofe *States* and *Kingdoms*, where the *Reformed Religion* is received and eftablifhed, they may extirpate it out of the World, under the Notion of the *Northern* Herefy. If Principles of Humanity, Maxims of Intereft, Rules of Policy, Obligations of Gratitude, Ties of Royal and Princely Faith, or the repeated Promifes, Oaths, Edicts, and Declarations of Sovereigns, could have been a Security to *Proteftants*, for the Profeffion of their Faith, and Exercife of their Worfhip, in the forementioned Territories and Dominions, they had all that could be rationally defired, for their Safety and Protection, in the free and open Profeffion and Practice of their *Religion* ; whereas by a Violation of all that is Sacred among Men, of a binding Virtue unto Princes (except Chains and Fetters) or that confer a Right, Claim, and Security unto Subjects, the poor *Proteftants* in thofe Places have been, and ftill are, perfecuted with a Rage and Barbarity, which no Age can parallel, and for which it is difficult to find words proper and fevere enough, whereby to ftamp a Character of Infamy, upon the treacherous, cruel, and favage Authors, Promoters, and Inftruments of it. Nor does it proceed from a Malignancy of Nature peculiar to the *Emperor*, the *French King*, and the *Duke* of *Savoy*, above what it is in other *Princes* of the fame Communion, or that they are more regardlefs of Fame, and lefs concerned how future Generations will brand their Memories, than other *Papal Monarchs* feem to be, that they have fuffered themfelves to be prevailed upon, to violate the Promifes and Oaths they were bound by to their *Proteftant* Subjects ; feeing the *Emperor* is character'd for a Perfon of a meek and gentle Temper, and of the goodnefs of whofe Nature, there remain fome fhadows interwoven with the bloody ftreaks of the *Hungarian* Perfecution. And the *French King*, though he ftand not much commended for Sweetnefs and Benignity of Difpofition, is known to be unmeafurably ambitious, of having his name tranfmitted to Pofterity in Letters of Greatnefs and Honour, which his behaviour towards his Subjects of the *Reformed Religion* is no ways adapted unto, but calculated to make him hereafter lifted with *Nero* and *Julian*. As to the *Duke* of *Savoy*, there feems by the whole courfe of his other Actions, to be a certain Greatnefs of Mind in him, not eafily confifting with that favage and brutal Temper, which the Cruelties he hath exercifed upon the *Proteftants* in *Piedmont*, would intimate and denote. But it arifeth from the Mifchievoufnefs and Peftilency of their Religion, their Bigotry in it, and their having put themfelves fo entirely under the Conduct of the *Clergy*, particularly of the *Jefuits*, who are for the moft part a Set of Men, efpecially the latter, that through acting in the Profpect of no other Ends, but the Grandeur, Wealth, and Domination of the *Church* of *Rome*, do with an unlimited Rage, and a peculiar kind of Malice, perfecute all that have renounced Fellowfhip with it, and care not if they facrifice the Honour, Glory, and Safety of *Monarchs*, and bring their Kingdoms into Contempt and Defolation, by rendring them weak, poor, and difpeopled, provided they may wreek their Spleen and Revenge upon thofe, whofe Religion is not only diffonant from theirs, but fhould it prevail to be the Religion of the *Legiflators* and *Rulers* of Nations, thofe Springs of Wealth would be immediately dried up, by which their Superior *Clergy*, and all their Religious *Orders* are enriched and fed up in Idlenefs. And fhould the People come to be generally imbued with Principles of Gofpel-Light, and Liberty, they would immediately fhake off a blind and flavifh Dependance upon *Pope* and *Priefts*, and thereby fubvert the Foundation upon which the *Monarchick* Grandeur of the *Romifh Church* and

and their whole *Religion* is superstructed, and destroy the Engine by which they are inabled to lord it over the Bodies, Estates, and Consciences of Men. And if *Protestants* every where, especially under *Popish* Rulers, were not under a strange Infatuation, they would look for no fairer Quarter from *Papists*, than what their Brethren have met with in *France* and *Piedmont*, nor would they rely upon the Faith of any *King*, that stiles himself a *Roman Catholick*; seeing sacred Promises, tremendous Oaths, and the most authentick Declarations, are but *Papal* Arts, and Tricks sanctified at *Rome*, whereby to lull Subjects into a Security, and delude them into a neglect of all means, for preserving themselves, and their Religion, till their Rulers can be in a condition of obeying the *Decrees* of the *fourth Lateran Council*, that enjoins *Kings to destroy and extirpate Hereticks, under pain of Excommunication, and of having both their Subjects absolved from Allegiance to them, and their Territories given away to others*; and till without running any Hazard, they may comply with the *Ordinances* of the *Council* of *Constance*, which not only *releaseth them from all Obligation of keeping Faith to Hereticks, but requires them to violate it*; and accordingly made *Sigismond* break his *Faith* to *John Hus*, whom in defiance of the Security given him by that *King*, they caused to be condemned and burn'd. Nor is the Practice and late Example of the *Great Louis*, designed for less than a Pattern, by which all *Popish Princes* are to act, and his Proceedings are to be the Copy and Model, which they who would merit the name of Zealous *Catholicks*, and be esteemed dutiful *Sons* of the *Church*, are to transcribe and limn out in Lines of Force, Violence and Blood, and for the better corresponding with the *Original*, to employ *Dragoons* for *Missionaries*.

And tho' I will not say, but that there may be some *Popish Princes*, who through an extraordinary Measure of Good-nature, and from Principles of Compassion, woven into their Constitution, previously to all notices of Revelation, whether real or pretended, and who through Sentiments imbib'd from a generous Education, and their coming afterwards to be under the Influence and Managemeut of wise and discreet Counsellors, may be able to resist the malignant Impressions of their Religion, and so be preserved from the Inhumanities towards those of different Persuasions from them in the things of God, which their Priests would lay them under Obligations unto, by the Doctrines of the *Romish Faith*; yet there appears no reason why an understanding Man should be induced to believe, that the *King* of *England* is likely to prove a Prince of that great and noble Temper, there being more than enough, both to raise a Jealousy and beget a Persuasion, that there is not a *Monarch* among all those who are commonly stiled *Catholicks*, from whom *Protestants* may justly dread greater Severities than from *Him*, or look for worse or more barbarous Treatment. I am not ignorant, with what Candor we ought, by the Rules of Charity and good Manners, to speak of all Men, whatsoever their Religion is, nor am I unacquainted with what Veneration and Deference we are to discourse of Crowned Heads; but as I dare not give those flattering Titles unto any, of which there are not a few in some of the late *Addresses*, presented to the *King*, by an inconsiderable and foolish sort of *Dissenting* Preachers; so I should not know how to be accountable to God, my own Conscience, or the World, should I not in my Station, as a Protestant, and as a Lover of the Laws and Liberties of my Country, offer something whereby both to undeceive that weak and short-sighted People, whom their own being accommodated for a Season by the *Declaration* of *Indulgence*, hath deluded into an Opinion, that His Majesty cherisheth no thought of subverting our *Religion*, and also further to enlighten and confirm others, in the just Apprehensions they are possessed with, of the Design carrying on in *Great Britain* and *Ireland*, for the Extirpation of *Protestancy*, and that the late *Declaration for Liberty of Conscience*, is emitted in Subserviency thereunto, and calculated by the *Court*, toward the paving and preparing the way, for the more facile Accomplishment of it. And while *Mercenary Sycophants*, by their Flatteries infect and corrupt Princes, and by their representing them to the World, in Colours disagreeable from their Tempers and Dispositions, and in milder and fairer Characters, than any thing observable in them, either deserveth, or correspondeth with, to delude Subjects into such Opinions of them, as beget a neglect of Means for preserving themselves; 'tis become a necessary Duty, and an indispensible Service to Mankind, to deal plainly and above-board, that so by describing *Kings* as they are, and setting them in a true and just Light, we may prevent the People's being further imposed upon; or if through suffering themselves to be still deceived, they come to fall under Miseries and Persecutions, they may lay all their Distresses and Desolations at the door of their own Folly, in not having taken care, how to avoid what they were not only threatned with, but whereof they were warned and advertised. For as I am not of Sir *Roger l'Estrange*'s mind, *That if we cannot avoid being distrustful of our Safety, yet it is extremely vain, foolish,*

fooliſh, and extravagant to talk of it ; ſo I am very ſenſible how many of the *French Miniſters*, by painting forth their *King* more like a God than a Man, and by poſſeſſing their People with a belief of Wiſdom, Juſtice, Grace, and Mercy in him, of which they knew him deſtitute, they both emboldned *him* to attempt what he hath perpetrated, and laid them under Snares, which they knew not how to diſentangle themſelves from, in order to eſcape it. Nor would the *King* of *England* have acted with that neglect of the future ſafety of the *Papiſts*, nor have expoſed them to the Reſentment, and hereafter revenge of three Nations, by the arbitrary and illegal Steps he hath made in their favour, if he intended any thing leſs, than the putting *Proteſtants* for ever out of Capacity and Condition, of calling them to a Reckoning, and exacting an Account of them; which neither *he*, nor they about him, can have the weakneſs to think they have ſufficiently provided againſt, without compelling us by an order of *à la mode de France Miſſionaries* to turn *Catholicks*, or by adjudging us to *Mines* and *Galleys*, according to the *Verſailles* Precedent, for our heretical Stubbornneſs ; or which is the more expeditious way of *converting three Kingdoms*, to *murder* the *Proteſtant* Inhabitants, according to the Pattern, which his Loyal *Iriſh Catholicks* endeavoured to have ſet Anno 1641, for the *Converſion* of that Nation. Had his *Majeſty* been contented with the bare avowing, and publiſhing himſelf to be of the Communion of the *Church of Rome*, and of challenging a Liberty, though againſt Law, for the Exerciſe of his *Religion*, it might have awakened our Pity and Compaſſion, to ſee *him* embrace a *Religion*, where there are ſo many Impediments of Salvation, and in doing whereof, he was become obnoxious unto the Imprecation of his *Grandfather, who wiſhed the Curſe of God to fall upon ſuch of his Poſterity, as ſhould at any time turn Papiſts* ; but it would have raiſed no intemperate heats in the minds of any againſt him, much leſs have alienated them, from the Subjection and Obedience, which are due unto their *Sovereign*, by the Laws of the ſeveral *Kingdoms*, and the Fundamental Rules of the reſpective Conſtitutions. Or could *he* have been contented with waving the rigorous Execution of the Laws againſt *Papiſts*, of whatſoever Quality, Rank, or Order they were, and with the beſtowing perſonal and private Favours upon thoſe of his *Religion*, it would have been ſo far from begetting Rancour or Diſcontent in his *Proteſtant Subjects*, that they would not only have connived at and approved ſuch a Proceedure, and thoſe little Benignities and Kindneſſes ; but had the *Papiſts* quietly acquieſced in them, and modeſtly improved them, it might have been a means of reconciling the *Nation* to more Lenity towards them for the future, and might have influenced our *Legiſlators*, when God ſhall vouchſafe us a *Proteſtant* on the *Throne*, to moderate the Severities to which by the *Laws* in being, they are obnoxious, and to render their condition as eaſy and ſafe as that of other Subjects, and only to take care, for precluding them ſuch Places of Power and Truſt, as ſhould prevent their being able to hurt us, but could bring no damage or inconvenience upon themſelves. But the *King*, inſtead of terminating here, and allowing only ſuch Graces and Immunities to the *Papiſts*, as would have been enough for the placing them in the private Exerciſe of their *Religion*, with Security to them, and without any threatning Danger to us ; He hath not only ſuſpended all the *penal Laws* againſt *Roman Catholicks*, but *he* hath by an uſurped *Prerogative*, that is paramount to the *Rules* of the *Conſtitution*, and to all *Acts* of *Parliament*, diſpenſed with, and diſabled the *Laws* that enjoin the *Oath* of *Allegiance* and *Supremacy*, and which appoint and preſcribe the *Teſts*, that were the Fences, which the Wiſdom of the Nation had erected, for preſerving the *Legiſlative Authority*, ſecuring the *Government*, and keeping Places of Power, Magiſtracy, and Office, in the hands of *Proteſtants*, and thereby of continuing the *Proteſtant Religion*, and *Engliſh Liberties* to ourſelves, and the Generations that ſhall come after us. And as if this were not ſufficient, to awaken us to a conſideration of the danger we are in, of having our *Religion* ſupplanted and overthrown ; *he* hath not only advanced the moſt *violent Papiſts*, unto all Places of *Military* Command by Sea and Land, but hath eſtabliſhed many of them in the chief Truſts and Offices of *Magiſtracy* and *Civil Judicature*, ſo that there are ſcarce any continued in Power and Employment, ſave they who have either promiſed to turn *Roman Catholicks*, or who have engaged to concur and aſſiſt to the ſubverting our *Liberties* and *Religion*, under the Mask and Diſguiſe of *Proteſtants*. 'Tis already evident, that it is beyond the help and relief of all peaceable and civil means, to preſerve and uphold the *Proteſtant Religion* in *Ireland*, and that nothing but Force and an inteſtine War can retrieve it, and re-eſtabliſh it there, in any degree of Safety. Nor is it leſs apparent, from the arbitrary and tyrannous *Oath*, ordained to be required of his *Majeſty's Proteſtant Subjects* in *Scotland*, whereby they are to ſwear *Obedience to him without reſerve*, that our *Religion* is held only precariouſly in that Kingdom ; and that whenſoever *he* ſhall pleaſe to command the eſtabliſhment of *Popery*, and to enjoin the People to enter into the Communion of the *Church* of *Rome* he expects to have his Will immediately conformed unto, and not to be disputed or controlled. But lest what we are to expect from the *King*, as to the extirpation of the *Reformed Religion*, and the inflicting the utmost Severities upon his *Protestant Subjects*, that Papal Rage, armed with Power, can enable him unto, may not so fully appear, from what hath been already intimated, as either to awaken the *Dissenters* out of the *Lethargy*, into which the late *Declaration* hath cast them, or to quicken those of the *Church* of *England*, to that zealous Care, Vigilancy, and Use of all lawful means, for preserving themselves, and the *Protestant Religion*, that the impendent Danger, wherewith they are threatned, requires at their hands ; I shall give that farther Confirmation of it, from *Topicks* and Motives of Credibility, *Moral*, *Political*, and *Historical*, as may serve to place it in the brightest Light, and fullest Evidence, that a matter future and yet to come, which is only the Object of our prospect and dread, and not of our feeling and experience, is capable of.

It ought to be of weight upon the minds of all *English Protestants*, that the King of *Great-Britain*, is not only an open and avowed *Papist*, but as most *Apostates* use to be, a fiery *Bigot* in the *Romish Religion*, and who, as the *Leige Letter* from a *Jesuit* to a *Brother* of the *Order*, tells us, *is resolved either to convert* England *to Popery, or to die a Martyr*. Nor were the *Jewish* Zealots, of whose rageful transports, *Josephus* gives us so ample an Account, nor the *Dervises* among the *Turks* and *Indians*, of whose mad Attempts so many Histories make mention, more brutal in their Fanatical Heats, than a *Popish Bigot* useth to be, when favoured with Advantages, of exerting his Animosity against those who differ from him, if he be not carefully watched against, and restrained. Beside the innumerable Instances of the tragical Effects of *Romish Bigotry*, that are to be met with in Books of all kinds, we need go no farther for an Evidence of it, than to consult the Life of *Dominick*, the great Instigator and Promoter of the Massacre of the *Waldenses*, and the Founder of that *Order*, which hath the management of the bloody *Inquisition* ; together with the Life of *Henry* the Third, of *France*, who contrary to the Advice of *Maximilian* the *Emperor*, and the repeated Intreaties of the wisest of his own Counsellors, the *Chancellor de l' Hospital*, and the *President de Thou*, not only revived the War and Persecution against his *Reformed Subjects*, after he had seen what Judgments the like Proceedings had derived upon his Predecessors, and how prejudicial they had proved to the Strength, Glory, and Interest of his *Crown* and *Kingdom*, but he entred into a *League* with those that sought to depress, abdicate, and depose him, and became the head of a Faction for the destroying that part of his Subjects, upon whom alone he could rely for the defence of his Person, and support of his Dignity. Nor were the furies of the Duke *de Alva* heretofore, or the present barbarities of *Louis* the *Fourteenth*, so much the Effects of their haughty and furious Tempers, as of their *Bigotry* in their inhuman and sanguinary Religion. That the King of *England* is second to none, in a blind and rageful Popish Zeal, his Behaviour, both while a Subject, and since he arrived at the Crown, doth not only place it beyond the limits of a bare Suspicion, but affords us such Evidences of it, as that none in consistency with Principles of Wisdom, and Discretion, can either question or contradict it. To what else can we ascribe it, but to an excessive *Bigotry* ? that when the *Frigot*, wherein he was sailing to *Scotland*, Anno 1682, struck upon the Sands, and was ready to sink, he should prefer the Lives of one or two pitiful Priests, to those of Men of the greatest Quality, and receive those Mushrooms into the Boat, in which himself escaped, while at the same time, he refused to admit, not only his own *Brother-in-law*, but divers Noblemen of the supremest Rank and Character, to the benefit of the same means of Deliverance, and suffered them to perish, though they had undertaken that Voyage out of pure respect to his Person, and to put an Honour upon him, at a season, when he wanted not enemies. Nor can it proceed from any thing but a violent and furious *Bigotry*, that he should not only disoblige and disgust the two *Universities*, of whose Zeal to his service, he hath received so many seasonable and effectual Testimonies, but to the Violation both of the Laws of God and the King, offer force to their Consciences, as well as to their Rights and Franchises ; and all this in favour of *Father Francis*, whom he would illegally thrust into a *Fellowship* in *Cambridge*, and of Mr. *Farmer*, whom he would arbitrarily obtrude into the *Headship* of a *College* in *Oxford*, who, as they are too despicable to be owned, and stood for, in competition against two famous *Universities*, whose greatest crime hath been an excess of Zeal for his Person and Interest, when he was Duke of *York*, and a measure of Loyalty and Obedience unto him, since he came to the Crown, beyond what either the Rules of Christianity, or the Laws of the Kingdom, exact from them ; so he hath ways enough of expressing Kindness and Bounty, to those two little contemptible Creatures, and that in Methods as beneficial to them, as the Places into which he would thrust them, can be supposed to amount unto, and I'm sure with less Scandal

dal to himself, and less Offence to all Protestants, as well as without offering Injury to the Rights of the *University*, or of compelling those learned, grave, and venerable Men to perjure themselves, and act against their Duties and Consciences. The late Proceedings towards Dr. *Burnet*, are not only contrary to all the Measures of Justice, Law, and Honour, but argue a strange and furious *Bigotry* in his Majesty for Popery; there being nothing else into which a Man can resolve the whole Tenor of his present Actings against him; seeing, setting aside the Doctor's being a Protestant, and a Minister of the *Church* of *England*, and his having vindicated the *Reformation* in *England*, from the Calumnies and Slanders wherewith it was aspersed by *Sanders*, and others of the *Roman* Communion, and the approving himself in some other Writings, worthy of the Character of a *Reformed Divine*, and of that Esteem which the World entertains of him, for knowledge in History, and all other parts of good Learning; there hath nothing occurred in the whole Tenor and Trace of his Life, but what, instead of Rebuke and Censure, hath merited Acknowledgments, and the Retributions of Favour and Preferment from the Court. Whosoever considers his constant preaching up Passive Obedience to such a degree and height, as he hath done, may very well be surprised at the whole Method of their present Actings towards him, and at the same time that they find cause to justify the Righteousness of God, in making them the Instruments of his Persecution, whom in so many ways he had sought to oblige, they may justly conclude that none, save a *Bigotted Papist*, could be the Author of so insuitable, as well as illegal and unrighteous Returns. For as to all whereof he is accused, in the criminal *Letters* against him, bearing date the 19th of *April* 1687, I myself am both able to assert his Innocence, and dare assure the World, that none of the Persons whom he is charged to have conspired with against the King, would have been so far void of Discretion, (knowing his Principles) as to have transacted with him in matters of that kind; but whether his Letters since that, to the Earl of *Middletoun*, with the *Paper* inclosed in one of them, have administred any *Legal* Ground for their *Second Citation*, I shall not take upon me to determine; and will only say, that as I heartily wish, he had not in those *Letters* afforded them any probable Pretence for proceeding against him, so there are Excesses of Loyalty in them, to attone for the utmost Indiscretions, his words are capable of being wrested unto; nor can any thing but *Papal Malice* and *Romish Chicanery*, construe and pervert them, so far contrary to his Intentions, as to make Crimes, and much less to make Treasons of them. Now as nothing can be of more portentous *Omen* to *British* and *Irish Protestants*, than to have a *Popish Bigot* exalted to rule over them; so thro' a Concurrence of Ill-nature, and a deficiency in Intellectuals, met in him with this furious Zeal and *Bigotry*, they are the more to expect, whatsoever his Power enables him to inflict, that is severe and dreadful. 'Tis possible that a Ruler may be possessed with a fondness and valuation of Popery, as the only Religion wherein Salvation is to be obtained, and therefore in his private Judgment and Opinion, sentence all to eternal Flames, who cannot herd with him in the same Society; and yet he may, through a great measure of Humanity, and from an extraordinary Proportion of Compassion and Meekness, woven into his Nature, hate the imbruing his hands in their Blood, or treating those with any Harshness, whose supposed Misbelief is their only Crime; and that finding them in all other respects virtuous, peaceable, and industrious, he may leave them to the decretive Sentence of the sovereign and infallible Judge, without disturbing or meddling with them himself. Nor is it impossible, but that there may be a Prince so far *Bigotted* in Popery, as to have an Inclination and Propensity to force all under his Authority, to be of his Religion, or else to destroy and extirpate them; yet thro' being of that largeness of Understanding and Political Wisdom, as to be able to penetrate into the Hazards of attempting it, and to foresee the Consequences that may ensue upon it, in reference to the Peace and Safety of his Government, as well as the Wealth and Power of his Dominions, he may come to check and stifle his furious Inclinations, and chuse rather to leave his Subjects at quiet, than to impoverish, weaken, and dispeople his Country, either by destroying them, or by driving them to abandon his Territories, in order to find a shelter and sanctuary in other places. But where (as in the King of *England*) a small measure of Understanding, accompanied with a large share of a morose, fierce, and ill nature, and these attended with Insolency and Pride, as they usually are in weak and froward People, come to have a *Bigotry* in such a Religion as Popery, superadded to them, whose Doctrines and Principles instigate and oblige to Cruelty, towards all of other Persuasions; there Protestants do find nothing that may encourage to hope for Security and Protection under a Prince of that Temper and Complexion; but all that does affect and impress their Minds, bids them prepare for Persecution, and to look for the utmost Rigours and Severities that Pride, Malice, brutal Zeal, back'd and supported with Force and Power, can execute and inflict.

            And

I

And how much such a Prince's Religion proves too weak to restrain him from Uncleannesses, and other Immoralities, by so much the more is *he* to be dreaded, in that he thinks to compound for, and expiate Crimes of that nature, by his Cruelty to *Hereticks*, and *his* offering them up in Sacrifices of Attonement to the *Tripple Crown*. Nor are the Priests either displeased with, or careful to persuade Princes from Offences of that kind, though they know them to be great Provocations to God, and of mischievous Example to Subjects, seeing they are Masters of the Art of improving them, to the Service of *Holy Church*, and the advantage of the *Catholick Faith*. For instead of imposing upon those *Royal* Transgressors, the little and slavish *Penances* of Pilgrimages, Whippings, and **going** Bare-foot; they require them to make Satisfactions for those and the like crimes, by the pious and meritorious Acts of murdering *Protestants*, and of extirpating the *Northern Heresy*. And as one of the *French* Whores of State is reported to have been a Person that hath principally instigated to all the Cruelties against the *Reformed* in *France*; so no doubt but as she did it under the Influence and Conduct of her *Confessors*, to compensate for her Adulteries, so she advised and persuaded *Louis* to it upon motives of the same nature. Nor do they who have the guidance of Consciences at *Whitehall* want matter of the same kind to improve and work upon; and as there are of the licentious *Females*, that will be glad of attoning for their filthy Pollutions, by Acts so agreeable to the *Articles* of their *Religion*; so there are some, who as they have Influence enough upon the King, to counsel him to the like Methods, so they will find him sufficiently disposed to compound for his loathsom and promiscuons Scatterings, at a rate so suitable to his Temper, as well as to the Doctrines of the *Papal Faith*.

If any be deluded into a good Opinion of *his Majesty*, and brought to flatter themselves with expectations of their being protected in the Profession of the *Protestant* Religion, they may be easily undeceived, and prevailed upon to change their Sentiments, if they will but consider his Behaviour towards *Protestants* in the *Post* wherein he formerly stood, and what his carriage was to them, while he was fixed in a meaner and more subordinate Station than now he is. Though there have been many whose Behaviour in their private Condition, would have rendered them thought worthy to rule, if their actions, after their advancement to governing Power, had not confuted the Opinion entertained concerning them; yet here have been very few that have approved themselves Just and Merciful after their attaining to Sovereignty, whose Carriage in an inferior Station, had been to the damage and general hurt of Mankind, as far as their narrow Power and Interest would extend. It ought therefore to lay us under a Conviction, what we are to expect from *his Majesty* on the *Throne*, when we find the whole Thread and Series of his Conduct while a Subject, to have been a continued *Design* against our *Religion*, and an uninterrupted *Plot* for the subversion of our *Laws* and *Liberties*. 'Tis sufficiently known, how active he always was, to keep up and inflame the Differences among *Protestants*, and how he was both a great Promoter of all the severe Laws made against *Dissenters*, and a continual Instigator to the rigorous Execution of them: So that his affirming *it to have been ever his Judgment, that none ought to be oppressed and persecuted for matters of Religion*, nor to be hindered in worshipping God according to their several Persuasions; serves only to inform us, either with what little Honesty, Honour, and Conscience *he* acted, in concurring to the making of the foresaid *Laws*, or what small Faith and Credit is now to be given to his *Declaration*, and to what he hath, since the Emission of it, repeated both in his *Speech* to Mr. *Pen*, and in his *Letter* to Mr. *Alsop*. And to omit many other Instances of his Kindness and Benignity to the *Fanaticks*, whom he now so much hugs and caresseth, it may not be amiss to remember them, and all other *Protestants*, of that barbarous and illegal *Commission* issued forth by the *Council* of *Scotland*, while he, as the late King's *High Commissioner*, had the management of the affairs of that Kingdom; by which every *military Officer* that had command over twelve Men, was impowered to *impannel* Juries, try, condemn, and cause to be put to death, not only those who should be found to disclaim the King's Authority, but such as should refuse to acknowledge the King's new-modelled *Supremacy* over that *Church*; in the pursuance and execution of which *Commission*, some were shot to death, others were hang'd or drowned, and this not only during the continuance of the Reign of his late *Majesty*, but for above a Year and a half after the present *King* came to the Crown. But what need is there, of insisting upon such little Particulars, wherein he was at all times ready to express his Malice to *Protestants*, seeing we have not only Dr. *Oates*'s Testimony, and that of divers others, but most authentick proofs from Mr. *Coleman*'s *Letters*, of his having been in a Conspiracy several Years for the Subversion of our *Religion*, upon the meritorious and sanctified Motive of extirpating the *Northern Heresy*. Of which, beside all the Evidence that *four* successive

Parliaments arrived at, I know feveral, who, fince the Duke of *York* afcended the Throne, have had it confirmed unto them by divers foreign Papifts, that were lefs referved, or more ingenuous than many of that Communion ufe to be. To queftion the Exiftence of that Plot, and his prefent Majefty's having been acceffary unto, and in the Head of it, argues a ftrange *Effrontery* and Impudence, through cafting an afperfion of Weaknefs, Folly and Injuftice, not only upon thofe *Three Parliaments* that feemed to have retained fome Zeal for *Englifh* Liberties, but by faftning the fame Imputations upon the *Long Parliament*, which had fhewed itfelf at all times more obfequious to the Will of the Court, than was either for their own Honour, or the Safety and Intereft of the Kingdom, and who had expreffed a veneration for the *Royal Family*, that approached too much upon a degree of *Idolatry*. Whofoever confiders that train of Counfels, wherein the King was many Years engaged, and whereof we felt the woful Effects in the *Burning of London*, the frequent *Prorogations* and *Diffolutions of Parliaments*, the widening and *exafperating Differences* among *Proteftants*, the ftirring up and provoking *Civil Magiftrates*, and *Ecclefiaftical Courts*, to perfecute *Diffenters*, and the maintaining *Correfpondencies* with the *Pope* and *Catholick Princes* abroad, to the difhonour of the Nation, and danger of our Laws and Religion; cannot avoid being apprehenfive what we are now to look for at his hands, nor can he efcape thinking that he efteems his Advancement to the Crown, both a Reward from Heaven for what *he* hath done and plotted againft thefe three Kingdoms, and an Opportunity and Advantage adminiftred to him for the Perfecting and Accomplifhment of all thofe Defigns with which he hath been fo long big and in travel for the deftruction of our Religion, the Subverfion of our Laws, and the Re-eftablifhment of Popery in thefe Dominions.

The Conduct and Guidance under which his Majefty hath put himfelf, and the fiery Temper of that *Order* to whofe Government he hath refigned his Confcience, may greatly add to our Fears, and give us all the Jealoufy and Dread that we are capable of being impreffed with, in reference to matters to come, that there is nothing which can be fatal to our Religion or Perfons, that we may not expect the being called to conflict with and fuffer. For tho' moft of the Popifh *Ecclefiafticks*, efpecially the *Regulars*, bear an inveterate Malice to Proteftants, and hold themfelves under indifpenfible Obligations of eradicating whatfoever their *Church* ftiles *Herefy*, and have accordingly been always forward to ftir up and provoke Rulers, to the ufe and application of force for the deftruction of Proteftants, as a company of perverfe and obftinate *Hereticks*, adjudged and condemned to the Stake and Gibbet by the infallible *Chair*; yet of all Men in the Communion of the *Romifh Church*, and of their *Religious Orders*, the *Jefuits* are they who do moft hate us, and whofe Counfels have been moft fanguinary, and always tending to influence thofe Monarchs, whofe Confciences they had the guidance and conducting of, to the utmoft Cruelties and Barbarities towards us. What our Brethren have had meafured out to them in *France*, thro' *Father de la Chaife's* Influence upon that King, and thro' the bewitching Power and Domination he hath over him in the quality of his *Confeffor*, and as having the Direction of his Confcience, may very well alarm and inform us what we ought to expect from his Majefty of *Great-Britain*, who hath furrendered his Confcience to the Guidance of Father *Peters*, a Perfon of the fame Order, and of the like mifchievous and bloody Difpofition that the former is. 'Tis well obferved by the Author of the *Reafons againft repealing the Acts of Parliament concerning the Teft*, that *Cardinal Howard's* being of fuch a meek and gentle Temper, that is able to withftand the Malignity of his Religion, and to preferve him from concurring in thofe mifchievous Counfels which his Purple might feem to oblige him unto, is the reafon of his being fhut out from acquaintance with, and intereft in the *Englifh* Affairs tranfacted at *Rome*; and that whatfoever his Majefty hath to do in that *Court*, is managed by his Ambaffador under the fole Direction of the *Jefuits*. So that it is not without caufe, that the *Jefuit of Liege*, in his intercepted and lately printed Letter, tells a Brother of the *Order*, what a wonderful veneration the King hath for the Society, and with what profound Submiffion he receives thofe *Reverend Fathers*, and hearkens to whatfoever they reprefent. Nor is his Majefty's being under the Influence of the *Jefuits*, thro' having one of them for his *Confeffor*, and feveral of them for his *chief Counfellors*, and *principal Confidents*, the only thing, in this Matter, that awakens our Fear in what we are to expect from his armed Power, excited and ftirr'd up by that fiery *Tribe*; but there is another ground why we ought more efpecially to dread him, and that is, his being entred and enrolled into the *Order*, and become a Member of the Society, whereby he is brought into a greater Subjection and Dependance upon them, and ftands bound by *Ties* and *Engagements* of being obedient to the Commands of the *General* of the *Jefuits*, and that not only in Spirituals, but in whatfoever they fhall pretend to be fubfervient to the exaltation of the Church, and for upholding the Glory of the *triple Crown*. This is a Myftery which few are yet acquainted

with,

with, and which both his *Majesty*, and the *Order*, judge it their Interest to have industriously concealed, but whereof the World may e'er long receive that convictive Intelligence, that there will be no room left for suspecting the Truth of it, and whereof a *Jesuit*, in the late printed *Letter* from *Liege*, hath given us already sufficient Intimation, both in telling us, *That the King of* England *stiles himself a Son of the Society*; and how that he wrote to *Father de la Chaise, that he would account every Injury done to the Jesuits, to be a wrong committed against himself.* Neither is it so surprising, as it may seem at first view, that the King should list himself a Member of the *Order*, seeing there have been four other *Crowned Heads*, of whose Entrance and Matriculation into the *Society*, there is all the Evidence and Assurance imaginable. And tho' *one* of them is acknowledged to have been in the *Classis* of the *Directors*, while the other *three* are generally believed to have been in the *Form* of the *Directed*; yet such was the Power of the *Society* over them all, that a great part of the Cruelty exercised towards *Protestants* both in the last Age and in this, is to be ascribed to that implicit and blind *Obedience* which they were bound to yield to the Injunctions of the *Order*, and to the Commands of the *General. Philip the second*, of *Spain*, who was the first King that entred into the *Order*, and who did it upon Motives of Policy, in hopes by their means, to have compassed the *Universal Monarchy* which he was aspiring after, and who, thro' being in the *Classis* of *Directors*, had advantages of using and improving, and not of being in that degree of Servitude unto them which the others have been; yet to what *barbarous Cruelties* did they over-rule and instigate him, not only to the Destruction of unconceivable Numbers of his Subjects, whose only Crime was, that they could not believe as the Church of *Rome* doth, which issued in the depopulating some of his Dominions, and his being deposed from the Sovereignty in others; but to the sacrificing his Son and Heir Prince *Charles*, whom, to gratify the Society, he caused, upon an Accusation of his favouring the Low-Country *Hereticks*, and the being himself tainted with *Lutheranism*, to be murdered in his own Court and Palace. *Sigismond* of *Poland*, who was the second *Crowned Head* admitted into the *Order*, through complying with the Counsels, and serving the Wrath, Rage, and Passions of the *Jesuits*, in endeavouring to suppress *Religion* in *Swedeland*, to which he was *Heir*, and in striving to subvert their Civil Rights, drew upon himself the Resentment and Wrath of that Nation to such a degree, that they *abdicated him* and his Heirs from the Government, and advanced another to the Throne. *Casimire*, who was also King of *Poland*, is reckoned to be the third Sovereign Prince that entered into the *Society*; and he, through coming under the Domination of the *Jesuits*, and being bound to follow their Directions, and to execute whatsover the General of the *Order* thought fit to enjoin for the Promotion and Benefit of the Church, became not only an Instrument of a severe Persecution against all sorts of Dissenters from the *Romish Faith*, so that many were put to death, and more driven to abandon their Country; but through committing many things in the course of his Government, that were prejudicial to the Rights, and thereupon disgustful to the *Polish* Nobility, they conceived such an aversion and hatred for him, that to avoid the Effects of their Resentment and Indignation, he was forced to lay down his Crown, and to chuse to end his days in *France*, in no higher a Post, and under no more glorious a Character, than that of *Abbot* of *St. German*. There is a fourth Prince, and who is yet in being, that is generally believed to be enrolled into the *Order*, and the Persecution he hath carried on in *Hungary*, contrary to his natural Temper, and to all the Rules of Interest and Policy, and to the Violation of his Promises and Oaths for continuing unto them the liberty of their Religion, is both too probable an Evidence of it, and a strong Confirmation of the Cruelties which the *Jesuits* instigate Princes unto, over whom they have Influence, and whom they have wheedled into Engagements of obeying their Commands, and pursuing their Injunctions. And as the desolating of *Hungary*, thro' a long and bloody War, and the tempting the *Turks* to invade the *Austrian* Territories, are some of the Effects that have ensued upon the Emperor's complying with the fierce and heady Counsels of the *Jesuits*; so we have not seen all the Mischiefs that the Persecution, which they have engaged him in against *Protestants*, is like to issue in: tho' beside the disgusting several *Electoral* Princes and States in *Germany*, and the furnishing the *Ottoman* Potentate with Encouragements of continuing the War, there are wonderful Advantages afforded by it, to embolden the *French* King in his Encroachments upon the Empire, which otherways he would not have dared to attempt, and whereof the result at last may prove fatal to the *Imperial Dignity*, and to the whole House of *Austria*. Now what the *Protestants* in *Great-Britain* and *Ireland* ought to dread from the King, upon his being entred into a *Society* that hath breathed nothing but Fire and Blood since its first Institution, I leave to the serious Consideration of all Men who value their Lives, Liberties and Estates, and that do not think of renouncing their Religion, and turning Papists. Nor is it to be imagined that the King, before he can be supposed well settled on

the

the Throne, and while under a declining state of Body, as well as in an advanced Age, having the weight of *Four and Fifty* upon his Shoulders, beside something else that he is obliged to the Earl of *Southesk* for, which I shall not mention, would have taken so many bold, wide, and illegal steps for the supplanting our *Religion* and *Laws*, and for the Introduction and Establishment of *Popery* and *Tyranny*; and this not only to the losing and disobliging his former *Votaries* and *Partizans*, but to the strange alarming and disgusting most Persons of Honour, Quality and Interest in the three Kingdoms; were he not, beside the being under the sway of his own *Bigotry*, and the strong Ballance of a large Measure of Ill-nature, bound by Ties of implicit Obedience to the Commands of that extravagant and furious Society, to the promoting of whose Passions and Malice, rather than his own safety and glory, or the lasting benefit of the *Roman Catholicks* themselves, the whole course of his Government hitherto seems to have been shapen and adapted. The occasion and subject of the late Contest between *him* and the *Pope*, which hath made so great a noise not only at *Rome*, but through all *Europe*, may serve to convince us both of the extraordinary Zeal he hath for the *Society*, and of the transcendent Power they have over him, and that 'tis no wonder he should *exact an Obedience without reserve from his Subjects in* Scotland, seeing he himself yields an Obedience without reserve to the *Jesuits*. 'Tis known, how that by the Rules of their *Institution*, no *Jesuit* is capable of the Mitre; and that if the Ambition of any of them, should tempt him to seek or accept the Dignity of a *Prelate*, he must, for being capacitated thereunto, renounce his Membership in the *Order*. Yet so great is his Majesty's Passion for the Honour and Grandeur of the *Society*, and such is their Domination and absolute Power over him, that no less will serve him, neither would they allow him to insist upon less, than that the Pope should dispense with Father *Peters* being made a *Bishop*, without his ceasing to be a *Jesuit*, or the being transplanted into another *Order*. And this the old Gentleman at *Rome* hath been forced at last to comply with, and to grant a Dispensation, whereby Father *Peters* shall be capable of the *Prelature*, notwithstanding his remaining in the *Ignatian Order*; the Jesuits, through their Authority over the King, not suffering him to recede from his Demand, and his Majesty's Zeal for the Society, not permitting him to comply either with the Prayers, or the Conscience and Honour of the supreme Pontiff.

Not only the King's Unthankfulness unto, but his illegal Proceedings against, and his arbitrary invading the Rights of those who stood by him in all his Dangers and Difficulties, and who were the Instruments of preventing his Exclusion from the Crown, and the chief means both of his advancement to the Throne, and his being kept in it, are so many new Evidences of the ill will he bears to all *Protestants*, and what they are to dread from him, as occasions are administred of injuring and oppressing them; and may serve to convince all impartial and thinking People, that his *Popish Malice* to our *Religion*, is too strong for all Principles of *Honour* and *Gratitude*, and able to cancel the Obligations, which Friendship for his Person, and Service to his Interest, may be supposed to have laid him under to any heretofore. Had it not been for many of the *Church of England*, who stood up with a Zeal and Vigour for preserving the Succession in the right Line, beyond what Religion, Conscience, Reason or Interest could conduct them unto, he had never been able to have out-wrestled the endeavours of *Three Parliaments* for excluding him from the Imperial Crown of *England*: And had it not been for their abetting and standing by him with their Swords in their Hands, upon the Duke of *Monmouth*'s Descent into the Kingdom, *Anno* 1685, he could not have avoided the being driven from the Throne, and the having the Scepter wrested out of his Hand. Whosoever had the Advantage of knowing the Temper and Genius of the late King, and how afraid he was of embarking into any thing that might import a visible Hazard to the Peace of his Government, and draw after it a general Disgust of his Person; will be soon satisfied, that if all his Protestant Subjects had united in their Desires, and concurred in their Endeavours, to have had the Duke of *York* debarred from the Crown, that his late Majesty would not have once scrupled the complying with it, and that his Love to his Dear Brother, would have given way to the Apprehension and Fear of forfeiting a Love for himself in the hearts of his People, especially when what was required of him, was not an invasion upon the Fundamentals of the Constitution of the *English* Monarchy, nor dissonant from the Practice of the Nation in many repeated Instances. Nor can there be a greater Evidence of the present King's Ill-nature, Romish Bigotry, and prodigious Ingratitude, as well as of the Design he is carrying on against our *Religion* and *Laws*, than his Carriage and Behaviour towards the Church of *England*; tho' I cannot but acknowledge it a righteous Judgment upon them from God, and a just Punishment for their being not only so unconcerned for the Preservation of our Religion and Liberties, in avoiding to close with the only Methods that were adapted there-

2 unto,

unto, but for being so passionate and industrious to hasten the loss of them, through putting the Government into one's hands, who (as they might have foreseen) would be sure to make a Sacrifice of them to his beloved Popery, and to his inordinate Lust after despotical and arbitrary Power. And as the only Example bearing any Affinity to it, is that of *Louis* XIV, who in recompence to his *Protestant* Subjects for maintaining him on the Throne, when the late Prince of *Conde*, assisted by Papists, would have wrested the Crown from him, hath treated them with a Barbarity, whereof that of *Antiochus* towards the *Jews*, and that of *Dioclesian* and *Maximian* towards the primitive Christians were but scanty and imperfect Draughts; so there wants nothing for compleating the Parallel between *England* and *France*, but a little more time and a fortunate Opportunity, and then the deluded Church-men will find, that Father *Peters* is no less skilful at *Whitehall*, for transforming their Acts of Loyalty and Merit towards the King, into crimes and motives of their Ruin, than *Pere de la Chaise* hath shewn himself at *Versailles*; where, by an art peculiar to the *Jesuits*, he hath improved the Loyalty and Zeal of the *Reformed* in *France*, for the House of *Bourbon*, into a reason of alienating that Monarch from them, and into a ground of his destroying that dutiful and obedient People. It will not be amiss to call over some of his Majesty's Proceedings towards the Church of *England*, that from what hath been already seen and felt, both they and all *English* Protestants may the better know what they are to expect and look for hereafter. Tho' it be a Method very unbecoming a Prince, yet it shews a great deal of Spleen, to turn the former *Persecution of Dissenters* so maliciously upon the *Prelatical* and *Conforming Clergy*, as his Majesty doth in his Letter to Mr. *Alsop*, in stiling them *a party of Protestants, who think the only way to advance their Church, is by undoing those Churches of Christians that differ from them in smaller Matters.* Whereas the severity that the *Fanaticks* met with, had much of its original at Court, where it was formed and designed upon Motives of *Popery* and *Arbitrariness*; and the Resentment and revengeful Humour of some of the old Prelates, and other Church-men that had suffered in the late times, was only laid hold of, the better to justify and improve it. And tho' it be too true, that many of the dignified Rank, as well as of the little *Levites*, were both extremely fond of it, and contentiously pleaded for it; yet it is as true, that most of them did it not upon Principles of Judgment and Conscience, but upon inducements of Retaliation for conceived Injuries, and upon a belief of its being the most compendious Method to the next Preferment and Benefice, and the fairest way of standing recommended to the Favour of the two *Royal Brothers*. Nor is it unworthy of Observation, that some of the most virulent Writers against Liberty of Conscience, and others of the most fierce Instigators to the persecuting *Dissenters*, among whom we may reckon *Parker*, Bishop of *Oxford*, and *Cartwright*, Bishop of *Chester*, are, since addressing for the *Declaration of Indulgence*, become the means of being graciously looked upon at *Whitehall*, turned forward Promoters of it, tho' their Success in their *Diocesses* with their Clergy, hath not answered their Expectations and Endeavours. For as these two *Mitred Gentlemen* will fall in with and justify whatsoever the King hath a mind to do, if they may but keep their Sees, and enjoy their Revenues, which I dare say, that rather than lose, they will subscribe not only to the *Tridentine Faith*, but to the *Alcoran*; so it is most certain that they two, as well as the Bishop of *Durham*, have promised to turn *Roman Catholicks*; and that as *Crew* hath been several times seen assisting at the Celebration of the Mass, and that as *Cartwright* paid a particular respect to the *Nuncio* at his solemn entrance at *Windsor*, which some *Temporal Lords* had so much Conscience and Honour, as to scorn to do; so the Author of the *Liege Letter* tells us, that *Parker* not only extremely favours *Popery*, but that he brands in a manner all such for *Atheists*, who continue to plead for the Protestant Religion. 'Tis an act of the same Candor and Good-nature in the King with the former, and another Royal Effect of his *Princely Breeding*, as well as of his *Gratitude*, when he endeavours to cast a farther *Odium* upon the Church of *England*, and to exasperate the *Dissenters* against her, by saying in the forementioned Letter to Mr. *Alsop, That the reason why the Dissenters enjoyed not Liberty sooner, is wholly owing to the Sollicitation* of the conforming Clergy; whereas many of the learned and sober Men of the Church of *England* could have been contented that the *Non-conforming Protestants* should have had Liberty long ago, provided it had been granted in a legal way; and the chief Executioners of Severity upon them, were such of all Ranks, Orders, and Stations, as the Court both set on and rewarded for it. 'Tis not their Brethren's having Liberty, that displeaseth modest and good Men of the Church of *England*, but 'tis the having it in the virtue of an *Usurped Prerogative* over the Laws of the Land, and to the shaking all the legal Foundations of the Protestant Religion itself in the Kingdom. And had the *Declaration of Indulgence* imported only an Exemption of *Dissenters* and *Papists* from Rigours and Penalties, I know very few that would have been displeased at it; but the extending it to the removing all the Fences about the Reformed Doctrine

trine and Worfhip, and laying us open both to the tyranny of Papifts, and the being overflowed with a deluge of their Superftitions and Idolatries, as well as the defigning it for a means to overthrow the eftablifhed Church, is that which no wife *Diffenter* no more than a conformable man knows how to digeft. For I am not of Sir *R. L'Eftrange*'s mind, who after he hath been writing for many years againft *Diffenters*, with all the venom and malice imaginable, and to difprove the wifdom, juftice, and convenience of granting them liberty, hath now the impudence to publifh *that whatfoever he formerly wrote, bears an ex-* *act conformity to the prefent Refolutions of State, in that the Liberty now vouchfafed is an Act* *of Grace iffuing from the fupreme Magiftrate, and not a claim of right in the People.* And as to recited Expreffions of the King, they are only a papal trick whereby to keep up heats and animofities among Proteftants, when both the inward heats of men are much allay'd, and the external provocations to them are wholly removed; and they are merely *Jefuitick* methods by which our hatred of one another may be maintained, tho' the Laws enabling one party to perfecute the other, which was the chief fpring of all our mutual rancour and bitternefs, be fufpended. It would be the fport and glory of the *Ignatian Order*, to be able to make the difabling of *Penal Laws* as effectual to the fupporting differences among Proteftants, as the enacting and rigorous execution of them was to the firft raifing, and the continuing them afterwards for many years. And if the foregoing Topicks can fur-nifh the King arguments whereby to reproach the Ch. of *England*, when he thinks it fea-fonable, and for the intereft of *Rome* to be angry with them; I dare affirm he will ne-ver want pretences of being difcontented with, and of afperfing *Fanaticks*, when he finds the doing fo, to be for the fervice of the papal caufe. And if the forementioned Inftan-ces of his Majefty's behaviour to the Ch. of *England*, to which he ftands fo fuperlatively obliged, be neither teftimonies of his Ingenuity, evidences of his Gratitude, nor effects of common, much lefs royal Juftice; yet what remains to be intimated, does carry more vifible marks of his malice and defign both againft the legally eftablifhed Church and our Religion. For not being fatisfied with the fufpenfion of all thofe Laws, by which Proteftants, and they of the national Communion might feem to be injurious to Papifts in their Perfons and Eftates, fuch as the Laws which make thofe, who fhall be found to have taken Orders in the Church of *Rome*, obnoxious to death, or thofe other Statutes by which the King hath Power and Authority for levying two thirds of their Eftates that fhall be convicted of Recufancy; but by an ufurped Prerogative, and an abfolute Power he is pleafed to fufpend all the Laws by which they were only difabled from hurting us, thro' ftanding precluded from places of Power and Truft in the Government. So that the whole fecurity we have in time to come for our Religion, depends upon the tem-perate Difpofition and Good-nature of thofe *Roman Catholicks* that fhall be advanced to Offices and Employments, and does no longer bear upon the protection and fupport of the Law; and I think we have not had that experience of grace and favour from Papifts, as they may give us juft confidence of fair and candid treatment from them for the future. Now that we may be the better convinced, how little fecurity we have from his Majefty's Promife in his Declaration, of his protecting the *Archbifhops, Bifhops, and Clergy, and all other his Subjects of the Church of* England, *in the free exercife of their Re-ligion, as by Law eftablifhed, and in the quiet and full enjoyment of their Poffeffions, without any moleftation or difturbance whatfoever*, which is all the Tenure that is left us; 'tis not unworthy of obfervation, how that befide the fufpending the Bifhop of *London ab Officio*, and the Vice-Chancellor of *Cambridge*, both *ab Officio* and *Beneficio*, and this not only for Actions which the Laws of God and the Kingdom make their Duty, but thro' a fentence inflicted upon them by no legal Court of Judicature, but by five or fix mercenary Per-fons fupported by a tyrannous and arbitrary Commiffion, his Majefty, in his *Proclama-tion for Toleration in* Scotland, bearing date, *February* 12, doth, among many other Laws, cafs, difable, and difpenfe with the Laws enjoining the *Scots Teft*, tho' it was not only enacted by himfelf while he reprefented his Brother as his high Commiffioner, but hath been confirmed by him in Parliament fince he came to the Crown. Surely it is as eafy to depart from a Promife made in a Declaration, as 'tis to abfolve and difcharge himfelf from the obligation of a Law which he firft concurred to the enacting of, and gave the cre-ating Fiat unto as the late King's Commiffioner, and hath fince ratified in Parliament after he was come to the Throne. As there is no more infidelity, difhonour, and injuf-tice, fo there is lefs of abfolute power and illegality, in doing the one than the other. Nor is it poffible for a rational Man to place a confidence in his Majefty's Royal Word for the protection of our Religion, and the Church of *England* Men's enjoying their Poffeffions, feeing he hath not only departed from his Promife made to the Council im-mediately after his Brother's death, but hath violated his Faith given to the Parliament of *England* at their firft Seffion, which we might have thought would have been the more facred and binding, by reafon of the Grandeur, State, and Quality of the Affembly to which it was pledged.

Pref. to his Hift. of the Times, p. 8.

Kkkkk

If

If we confider how much *Proteftants* fuffered, what number of them was burnt at the Stake, as well as murdered in Goals, befide the vaft Multitudes, who to avóid the rage and power of their Enemies, were forced to abandon their Country, and feek for fhelter in foreign Parts, and what endeavours of all kinds were ufed for the extirpation of our Religion under Q. *Mary*; we may gather and learn from thence what is to be dreaded from *James* II. who is the next *Popifh* Prince to her, that, fince the Reformation, hath fat on the Throne of *England*. For tho' there be many things that adminifter grounds of Hope, that the *Papifts* will not find it fo eafy a matter to bring us in fhoals to the *Stake*, nor of that quick and eafy difpatch to fupprefs the *Proteftant Religion*, and fet up *Popery*, at this time, as they found it then; yet every thing that occurs to our Thoughts, or that can affeȼt our Underftandings, ferves not only to perfuade us into a belief that they will fet upon and endeavour it, but to work us up to an Affurance that his Majefty would take it for a diminution of his Glory, as well as reflection upon his Zeal for the Church of *Rome*, not to attempt what a Woman had both the Courage to undertake, and the Fortune to go thro' with. And there is withal a Concurrence of fo many things both abroad and at home at this Juncture, which if laid in the balance with the Motives to our hope of the *Papifts* mifcarrying, may juftly raife our Fears of their profpering to a very fad and uncomfortable height. Whofoever fhall compare thefe two Princes together, will find that there was lefs danger to be apprehended from *Mary*, and that not only upon the fcore of her *Sex*, but by reafon of a certain gentlenefs and goodnefs of Nature which all *Hiftorians* of Judgment and Credit afcribe unto her; than is to be expected from the prefent King, in whom a Sournefs of Temper, Fiercenefs of Difpofition, and Pride joined with a peevifhnefs of humour not to bear the having his Will difputed or controlled, are the principal Ingredients in his Conftitution, and which are all ftrangely heightned and enflamed by contracted diftempers of Body; and thro' furious Principles of Mind which he hath imbib'd from the *Jefuits*, who, of all Men, carry the Obligations arifing from the Doctrines of the *Popifh Religion*, to the moft outragious and inhuman Excelfes. Nor can I forbear to add, that whereas the Cruelty which that Princefs was hurried into, even to the making her Cities common Shambles, and her Streets Theatres of Murder for innocent Perfons, for which fhe became hated while fhe lived, and her Memory is render'd infamous to all Generations that come after, was wholly and entirely owing to her *Religion*, which not only proclaims it lawful, but a neceffary duty of Chriftianity, and an Act meriting a peculiar Crown of Glory in Heaven, to deftroy *Hereticks*; 'tis to be feared there will be found in the prefent King, a fpice of revenge againft us, as we are *Englifhmen*, as well as a meafure heaped up and running over of furious *Papal Zeal* againft us, as we are *Proteftants*. Befide the Wrath he bears unto us for our departure from the Communion of the *Romifh* Church, and our Rebellion againft the Triple Crown; the War wherein many of the Kingdom were engaged againft his *Father*, and the iffue of it in the Execution of that Monarch, is what he hath been heard to fay, *That he hopes to revenge upon the Nation.* And all that the City of *London* underwent thro' that dreadful *Conflagration* 1666, of which he was the great Author and Promoter, as well as the Refcuer and Protector of the *Varlets* that were apprehended in their fpreading and carrying on the fire, is but an Earneft in refpect of what is defigned farther to be paid them, for the having been the great Supporters of that War, both by continued Recruits of Men, and repeated Supplies of Treafure. Tho' it was Q. *Mary's* misfortune, and proved the mifery of *Proteftants*, that fhe was under the influence of *Popifh Bifhops*, and of *Religious* of feveral *Orders*, by whom fhe was whetted on and provoked to thofe Barbarities wherewith her Reign is ftain'd and reproach'd; yet fhe had no *Jefuits* about her, to whom all the other Orders are but punies in the arts of wheedling and frighting Princes forward to Cruelty: The Society being then but in its Infancy, and the diftance between its Inftitution, which was in 1540, and the time of her coming to the Crown, which was *Anno* 1553, not affording Seafon enough for their fpreading fo far abroad as they have fince done, nor for the perfecting themfelves to that degree in the methods of Butchery, and in the Topicks whereby to delude Monarchs, to ferve and promote their fanguinary Paffions, as they have in procefs of time attain'd unto. Nor have the Proteftants now any fecurity for their *Religion*, whereby it or themfelves may be preferv'd from the attempts of his Majefty for the Extirpation of both, but what our Predeceffors in the fame Faith had in the like kind, tho' not to the fame meafure and degree, when Queen *Mary* arrived at the Throne. For though our Religion was of late fenced about with more Laws, and we had *Royal Promifes* oftner repeated for the having it preferved, and ourfelves protected in the Profeffion of it; yet it is certain that it had not only received a legal Eftablifhment under K. *Edward* VI. but had the *Royal Faith* of Q. *Mary* laid to pledge in a *Promife* made to the Men of *Suffolk*, that nothing fhould be done towards its Subverfion, or whereby they might be hindred in the free Exercife of it. But as neither *Law* nor *Promife* could prove Reftraints upon *Mary*, to hinder her from *fubverting Religion*, and *burning*

Protef-

Proteſtants, ſo the Obligation of Gratitude that ſhe was under to the Men of *Suffolk,* for their coming in ſo ſeaſonably to her Aſſiſtance againſt the D. of *Northumberland,* who was in the field with an Army in the name of the Lady *Jane Gray,* whom the Council had proclaim'd Queen, could not excuſe them from ſharing in the Severity that others met with, it being obſerved that more of that County were burnt for Religion, than of any other *Shire* in *England.* And 'tis greatly to be feared, that this piece of her Example, will not eſcape being conformed unto by the King in his Carriage towards thoſe that eminent-ly ſerved *him,* as well as all the reſt of it in his Behaviour towards *Proteſtants* in gene-ral. Nor is it poſſible to conceive that the *Papiſts* living at that eaſe and quietneſs which they did under his late Majeſty, of whoſe being of their Religion they were not igno-rant, as appears by the Proofs they have vouchſafed the World of it ſince his Death, would have been in ſo many *Plots* for deſtroying him, and at laſt have haſtened him to his *Fathers,* as can be demonſtrated whenſoever it is ſeaſonable, had they not been aſſur'd of more to be attempted by his *Succeſſor* for the Extirpation of *Proteſtants,* than *Charles* could be wrought up unto, or prevailed upon to expoſe his Perſon and Crown to the danger and hazard of. For as it is not meerly a *Prince*'s being a *Papiſt,* and mild, gentle, and favourable to *Catholicks,* that will content the fiery Zealots of the *Roman Clergy* and the *Regular Orders,* but he muſt both gratify their Ambition in exalting them to a Con-dition above all others, and ſerve their inhuman Luſts and brutal Paſſions, in not ſuf-fering any to live in his Dominions that will not renounce the *Northern Hereſy* ; ſo it is not more incredible that they ſhould diſpatch a Prince by an infuſion in a Cup of *Tea* or *Cho-colate,* whom tho' they knew to be a *Papiſt,* yet they found too cold and ſlow in promo-ting their Deſigns ; than that they ſhould have murdered another by a *conſecrated Dag-ger* in the hand of *Ravilliac :* the one being both more eaſy to be detected, and likelier to derive an univerſal *Hatred* and *Revenge* upon them, than the other. And as the King's being conſcious of that *Parricide* committed upon his *Brother,* plainly tells us, that there is nothing ſo abominable and barbarous, which he hath not a Conſcience that will ſwal-low and digeſt ; ſo the Promotion of the *Catholick Cauſe* being the Motive to that horrid Crime, we may be ſure that what is hitherto done in favour of *Papiſts,* falls much ſhort of what is intended, there being ſomething more meritorious than all this amounts unto, needful to attone for ſo barbarous a Villany, which can be nothing elſe but the extirpa-ting the *Proteſtant Religion* out of the three Kingdoms. Nor is it probable that the pre-ſent King, who is repreſented for a Perſon ambitious of Glory, would loſe the Oppor-tunities wherewith the preſent poſture of Affairs in the World preſents him, of being the *Umpire* and *Arbiter* of Chriſtendom, and of giving check to the Grandeur and Uſurpa-tions of a neighbouring Monarch, to whom all *Europe* is in danger of becoming enſlav'd ; if he were not ſwallowed up in the thoughts of a Conqueſt over the Conſciences, Laws, and Liberties of his own People, and of ſubjugating his Dominions to the See of *Rome,* and had he not Hopes and Aſſurances of aid and aſſiſtance therein from that Monarch, as he is emboldned and encouraged thereunto by his Pattern and Example.

What the *Papiſts* have all along been endeavouring for the Subverſion of our *Religion,* during and under the Reigns of *Proteſtant Princes,* may yet farther inform and con-firm us, what they will infallibly attempt upon their having gotten one into the Throne, who is not only in all things of their own Faith, but of an Humour agreeable unto their Deſires, and of a Temper every way ſuited and adapted to their Deſigns. Tho' the *Proteſtant Religion* had obtained ſome entrance into ſeveral States and King-doms, and had made ſome conſiderable ſpread in *Europe,* before it came to be generally received, and eſtabliſhed upon Foundations of Law in *England* ; yet they other Coun-tries were little able to defend themſelves from the Power and Malice of the Church of *Rome,* and of *Popiſh* Princes, and many of them were very unſucceſsful in Endeavours of that nature, till *England,* in Queen *Elizabeth*'s time, by eſpouſing their Cauſe, and undertaking their Quarrel, not only wrought out their Safety, but made them flouriſh. This the Court of *Rome* and the Prieſts grew immediately ſenſible of, and have therefore moulded all their Counſels ever ſince againſt *England,* as being both the Bulwark of the Proteſtant Religion, and the Balance of *Europe.* All the late attempts for the extirpation of the Proteſtant Religion in *France* and elſewhere, are much to be aſcribed to the Confi-dence the *Papiſts* had in the late King and his Brother, of their giving no Diſcouragement nor Obſtruction to ſo *holy* a Deſign ; and thereupon as the firſt Edicts for infringing the Liberty, and weakning and oppreſſing Proteſtants in *France,* and the perſecution in *Hun-gary,* commenced and bore date with the Reſtoration of the Royal Family, and multipli-ed, and encreaſed from year to year as they grew into farther aſſurance of the *Royal Bro-thers* approving as well as conniving at what was done ; ſo that for the abolition of the Edict of *Nants,* and the total Suppreſſion of the Reform'd Religion in *France,* was emitted upon his preſent Majeſty's being exalted to the Throne, and the encouragement he gave

them

them to a Proceedure, which as he now justifies, he will hereafter imitate. It were to suppose *English* Protestants exceedingly unacquainted with the History of their own Nation, to give a long Deduction of what the Papists have attempted for the Extirpation of our Religion, while we had Princes on the Throne, whose belief and principles in Christianity, led them to assert and defend the *Reformation*, and who had courage as well as integrity, to punish those that conspired against it. Their many Conjurations against Queen *Elizabeth*'s Person, and their repeated Endeavours of bringing in *Foreigners*, and of betraying the Nation to the *Spaniards*, who were to convert the Kingdom, as they had done the *West-Indies*, by killing the Inhabitants; are sufficiently known to all who have allowed themselves leisure to read, or who have been careful to remember what they have been often told by those that have inspected the Memoirs of those times. The *Gunpowder-plot* with the Motives unto it, and the extent of the mischief it was shapen for, together with the insurrection they were prepared for, in case it had succeeded, and the foreign aid they had been solliciting and were promised, and all for the extirpation of *English Hereticks*; are things so modern, and which we have had so many times related to us by our Fathers, that it is enough barely to intimate them. The *Irish Massacre*, in which above 200,000 were murdered in cold Blood, and to which there was no provocation but that of hatred to our Religion, and furious Zeal to extirpate *Hereticks*, ought at this time to be more particularly reflected upon, as that which gives us a true scheme of the manner of the Church of *Rome*'s converting Protestant Kingdoms, and being the copy they have a mind to write after, and that in such Characters and Lines of Blood, as may be sure to answer the *Original*. At the season when they both entred upon and executed that hellish Conjuration, they were in a quiet and peaceable enjoyment of the private exercise of their Religion, yea had many publick meeting-places, thro' the means of the Queen and many great friends which they had at Court; and were neither disturbed for not coming to Church, nor suffered any severities upon the account of their Profession: but that would not satisfy, nor will any thing else, unless they may be allowed to cut the throats, or make Bonfires of all that will not join with them in a blind Obedience to the See of *Rome*, and of worshipping St. *Patrick*. The little harsh usages which the Papists at any time met with there or in *England*, they derived them upon themselves by their Crimes against the State, and for their Conspiracies against our Princes and their Protestant Subjects. For till the Pope had taken upon him to depose Q. *Elizabeth*, and absolve her Subjects from their *Allegiance*, and till the Papists had so far approved that Act of his Holiness, as to raise Rebellions at home, and enter into treasonable Confederacies abroad, there were no Laws, that could be stiled severe, enacted in *England* against Papists; and the making of them was the result of necessity, in order to preserve ourselves, and not from an inclination to hurt any for matters of mere Religion. Such hath always been the moderation of our Rulers, and so powerful are the incitements to lenity, which the generality of Protestants, thro' the influence and impression of their Religion, especially they of a more generous education, have been under towards those of the *Roman* Communion, that nothing but their unwearied restlessness to disturb the Government, and destroy Protestants, hath been the cause either of enacting those Laws against them that are stiled rigorous, or of their having been at any time put into execution. And notwithstanding that some such Laws were enacted as might appear to favour of severity, yet could they have but submitted to have dwelt peaceably in the Land, they would have found that their mere Belief, and the private practice of their Worship, would not have much prejudiced or endangered them; and that tho' the Laws had been continued unrepealed, yet it was only as a Hedge about us for our protection, and as Bonds of Obligation upon them to their good Behaviour. To which may be added, that more Protestants have suffered in one year, by the Laws made against Dissenters, and to the utmost height of the Penalties which the violation of them imported, and that by the instigation of Papists, and their influence over the late King, and his present Majesty, than there have Papists from the Beginning of Queen *Elizabeth*'s Reign, to this very day, tho' there was a difference in the punishments they underwent. However, we may from their many and repeated attempts against us, while we had Princes that both would and could chasten their insolencies, and inflict upon them what the Law made them obnoxious unto for their outrages, gather and conclude what we are now to expect, upon their having obtained a King imbu'd with all the persecuting and bloody Principles of Popery, and perfectly baptized into all the Doctrines of the *Councils* of *Lateran* and *Constance*. And it may strengthen our Faith, as well as increase our Fear, of what is purposed against and impends over us, in that they cannot but think that the suffering our Religion to remain in a condition to be at any time hereafter the Religion of the State, and of the universality of the People, may not only prove a means of retrieving Protestancy in *France*, and of assisting to

reveng:

✝

revenge the Barbarities perpetrated there upon a great and innocent People, but may leave the *Roman Catholicks* in *England* expoſed to the reſentment of the *Kingdom,* for what they have ſo fooliſhly and impudently acted both againſt our *Civil Rights,* and *Eſtabliſhed Religion,* ſince *James* II. came to the Crown ; and may alſo upon the Government's falling into good hands, and Magiſtrates coming to underſtand their true Intereſt, which is for an *Engliſh Prince* to make himſelf the Head of the *Proteſtant Cauſe,* and to eſpouſe their quarrel in all Places, give ſuch a Revolution in *Europe,* as will not only check the preſent Career of *Rome,* but cauſe them to repent the methods in which they have been engaged. Theſe things we may be ſure the Papiſts are aware of, and that having proceeded ſo far, they have nothing left for their ſecurity from Puniſhments becauſe of Crimes committed, but to put us out of all capacity of doing our ſelves Right and them Juſtice ; and he muſt be dull, who does not know into what that muſt neceſſarily hurry them.

It being then as evident as a matter of this nature is capable of, what we are to expect and dread from the King both as to our *Religion* and *Laws* ; we may do more than preſume that the late *Declaration for Liberty of Conſcience,* and the *Proclamation for a Toleration,* are not intended and deſigned for the benefit and advantage of the *Reformed Religion,* and that whatſoever motives have influenced to the granting and emitting of them, they do not in the leaſt flow or proceed from any kindneſs and good will to Proteſtant Diſſenters. And though many of thoſe weak and eaſy People may flatter themſelves with a belief of an intereſt in the *King's* favour, and ſuffer others to delude them into a perſuaſion of his bearing a gracious reſpect towards them ; yet it is certain, that they are the People in the world whom he moſt hates, and who when things are ripe for it, and that he hath abuſed their credulity into a ſerving his Ends as far as they can be prevailed upon, and as long as the preſent *Juggle* can be of any advantage for promoting the Papal Cauſe, will be ſure not only to have an equal ſhare in his diſpleaſure with their Brethren of the Church of *England,* but will be made to drink deepeſt in the cup of fury and wrath that is mingling and preparing for all Proteſtants. No provocation from their preſent behaviour, tho' it is ſuch as might warm a perſon of very cool temper, much leſs offences of another complexion adminiſtred by any of them, ſhall ever tempt me to ſay they deſerve it, or cauſe me to ravel into their former and paſt carriages, ſo as to faſten a blot or imputation upon the party or body of them, whatſoever I may be forced to do as to particular perſons among them. For as to the generality, I do believe them to be as honeſt, induſtrious, uſeful, and virtuous a people (tho' many of them be none of the wiſeſt nor of the greateſt proſpect) as any party of Men in the Kingdom, and that wherein ſoever their carriage (even abſtracting from their differences with their Fellow-Proteſtants in matters of Religion) hath varied from that of other Subjects ; they have been in the right, and have acted moſt agreeably to the Intereſt and Safety of the Kingdom. But it can be no reflection upon them, to recall into their memories, that the whole tenor of the *King's* actings towards them both when Duke of *York* and ſince *he* came to the Crown, hath been ſuch as might render it beyond diſpute, that they are ſo far from having any ſingular room in his favour, that he bears them neither pity nor compaſſion, but that they are the objects of his unchangeable indignation. For not to mention how the Perſecutions, that were obſerved always to relent both upon his being at any diſtance from the *late King,* and upon the abatement of his influence at any time in Counſels, were conſtantly revived upon his return to *Court,* and were carried on in degrees of ſeverity proportionable to the *figure* he made at *Whitehall,* and his *Brother's* diſpoſedneſs and inclination to hearken to him ; ſurely their memories cannot be ſo weak and untenacious, but they muſt remember how their ſufferings were never greater, nor the *Laws* executed with more ſeverity upon them, than ſince his *Majeſty* came to aſcend the *Throne.* As it is not many years ſince he ſaid publickly in *Scotland,* that it were well if all that part of the Kingdom, (which is above half of the Nation) where the Diſſenters were known to be moſt numerous, *were turned into a hunting Field* ; ſo none were favoured and promoted either *there* or in *England,* but ſuch as were taken to be the moſt fierce and violent of all others againſt *Fanaticks.* Nor were Men preferred either in Church or State for their Learning, Virtue or Merit, but for their paſſionate heats and brutal rigours to *Diſſenters.* And whereas the Papiſts from the very firſt day of his arrival at the Government, had beſide many other marks of *his Grace,* this ſpecial Teſtimony of it, of not having the *penal Statutes* to which they ſtood liable put in execution againſt them ; all the *Laws* to which the *Diſſenters* were obnoxious, were by his *Majeſty's* Orders to the *Judges, Juſtices* of the *Peace,* and all other *Officers Civil* and *Eccleſiaſtical,* moſt unmercifully executed. Nor was there the leaſt talk of lenity to *Diſſenters,* till the *King* found that he could not compaſs his Ends by the *Church* of *England,* and prevail upon the *Parliament* for repealing the *Teſts,* and cancelling the other

2

other *Laws* in force against *Papists*, which if they could have been wrought over unto, the *Fanaticks* would not only have been left pitiless, and continued in the Hands of the furious Church-men to exercise their Spleen upon, but would have been surrendred as a Sacrifice to new Flames of Wrath, if they of the Prelatical Communion had retained their wonted Animosity, and thought it for their Interest to exert it, either in the old or in fresh Methods. But that Project not succeeding, his *Majesty* is forced to shift Hands, and to use the Pretence of extending Compassion to *Dissenting Protestants*, that he may the more plausibly, and with the less Hazard, suspend and disable the *Laws* against *Papists*, and make way for their Admission into all Offices Civil and Military; which is the first Step, and all that he is in a Condition to take, for the *Subversion* of our *Religion*. And all the celebrated Kindness to *Fanaticks*, is only to use them as the *Cat*'s Paw, for pulling the Chesnut out of the Fire to the *Monkey*, and to make them *Stales*, under whose Shroud and Covert, the Church of *Rome* may undermine and subvert all the *legal Foundations* of our *Religion*; which to suffer themselves to be instrumental in, will not in the Issue turn to the Commendation of the *Dissenters Wisdom* or their *Honesty*. Nor is there more Truth in the *King*'s declaring it to *have been his constant Opinion that Conscience ought not to be constrained, nor People forced in Matters of mere Religion*, than there is of *Justice* in that malicious *Insinuation*, (in his Letter to Mr. *Alsop*) against the Church of *England*, *That should he see cause to change his Religion, he should never be of that Party of Protestants, who think their only way to advance their Church, is by undoing those Churches of Christians that differ from them in smaller Matters:* Forasmuch as he is in the mean time a Member of the most persecuting and bloody Society, that ever was cloathed with the name of a Church, and whose Cruelty towards Protestants he is careful not to arraign, by fastning his Offence at Severity upon Differences in *smaller Matters*, which he knows that those between *Rome* and us are not, nor so accounted of by any of the *Papal Fellowship*. It were to be wish'd that the *Dissenters* would reflect and consider, how when the *late King* had emitted a *Declaration of Indulgence*, *Anno* 1672, upon pretended Motives of *Tenderness* and *Compassion* to his *Protestant Subjects*, but in truth to keep all quiet at home, when in conjunction with *France*, he was engaged in an unjust War against a *Reformed State* abroad, and in order to steal a Liberty for the Papists to practise their Idolatries, without incurring a Suspicion himself, of being of the *Romish Religion*, and in hope to wind up the Prerogative to a paramount Power over the Law; and how when the *Parliament* condemned the Illegality of it, and would have the *Declaration* recalled, all his Kindness to *Dissenters* not only immediately vanished, but turned into that Rage and Fury, that tho' both that *Parliament* addressed for some Favour to be shew'd them, and another voted it a *betraying* of the *Protestant Religion* to continue the Execution of the *penal Laws* upon them, yet instead of their having any Mercy or Moderation exercised towards them, they were thrown into a *Furnace*, made seven times hotter than that wherein they had been scorched before. And without pretending to be a Prophet, I dare prognosticate and foretell, that whensoever the present *King* hath compassed the Ends, unto which this *Declaration* is designed to be subservient; namely, the placing the Papists both in the open Exercise of their Religion, and in all publick *Offices* and *Trusts*, and the getting a Power to be acknowledged vested in him over the *Laws*; that then, instead of the still Voice calmly whispered from *Whitehall*, they will both hear and feel the Blasts of a mighty rushing Wind, and that upon pretended Occasions arising from the Abuse of this *Indulgence*, or for some alledged Crimes wherein they and all other Protestants are to be involved, (tho' their supineness and excess of Loyalty continue to be their greatest Offences) this Liberty will not only be withdrawn, and the old Church of *England* Severities revived, but some of the new *à la mode de France* Treatments come upon the Stage, and be pursued against them, and all other perverse and obstinate *British Hereticks*.

The *Declaration for Liberty of Conscience*, being injurious to the Church of *England*, and not proceeding from any inward and real Good-will to the *Dissenters*; it will be worth our pains to inquire into, and make a more ample Deduction of the Reasons upon which it was granted, that the Grounds of emitting it being laid under every Man's view, they who have *addressed* may come to be asham'd of their Simplicity and Folly; they who have not, may be farther confirm'd both of the Unlawfulness and Inconveniency of doing it, and that all who preserve any regard to the *Protestant Religion* and the *Laws* of *England*, may be quickened to the use of all legal and due means for preventing the mischievous Effects which it is shapen for, and which the Papists do promise themselves from it. The *Motives* upon which His *Majesty* published the *Declaration*, may be reduced to *three*, of which, as I have already made some mention, so I shall now place every one of them in its several and proper light, and give such Proofs and Evidences of their being the great and sole *Inducements* for the *emitting* of it, that no rational Man shall be able, henceforth, to make a doubt of it. The first, is the *King*'s winding himself into a *Supremacy*

and

and *Abſoluteneſs* over the *Law*, and the getting it acknowledged, and calmly ſubmitted unto and acquieſced in by the *Subjeĉts*. The *Monarchy's* being *Legal* and not *Deſpotical*, bounded and regulated by *Laws*, and not to be exerciſed according to mere Will and Pleaſure, was that which he could not digeſt the thoughts of when a Subjeĉt, and had been heard to ſay, *That he had rather reign a day in that Abſoluteneſs that the French King doth, than an Age tied up and reſtrained by Rules as his Brother did*. And therefore to perſuade the Prince of *Orange* to approve what he had done, in *diſpenſing* with the *Laws*, and to obtain him and the Princeſs to join with His *Majeſty*, and to employ their Intereſt in the Kingdom for the *repealing the Teſt-Aĉts*, and the many other *Statutes* made againſt *Roman Catholicks*, he uſed this Argument in a Meſſage he ſent to their *Royal Highneſſes* upon that Errand, that the getting it done, would be greatly to the advantage, and *for the increaſe of the Prerogative*; but this, theſe two noble Princes, of whoſe Aſcent to the Throne all Proteſtants have ſo near and comfortable a Proſpeĉt, were too Generous, as well as Wiſe, to be wheedled with, as knowing that the Authority of the Kings and Queens of *England* is great enough, by the Rules of the *Conſtitution*, without graſping at a new Prerogative Power, which as the *Laws* have not veſted in them, ſo it would be of no uſe, but to enable them to do hurt. And indeed it is more neceſſary, both for the Honour and Safety of the *Monarch*, and for the Freedom and Security of the People, that the Prerogative ſhould be confined within its ancient and legal *Channels*, than be left to that illimited and unbounded Latitude, which the *late King* and his *preſent Majeſty* have endeavoured to advance and ſcrew it up unto. That both the *Declaration for Liberty of Conſcience in* England, and the *Proclamation for a Toleration in* Scotland, are calculated for raiſing the *Sovereign Authority* to a tranſcendent Power over the *Laws* of the two *Kingdoms*, may be demonſtrated from the Papers themſelves, which lay the *diſpenſing Power* before us in terms that import no leſs than his *Majeſty's* ſtanding free and abſolved from all Ties and Reſtraints, and his being cloathed with a Right of doing whatſoever he will. For if the Stile of *Royal Pleaſure* to ſuſpend the Execution of ſuch and ſuch *Laws*, and to forbid ſuch and ſuch *Oaths* to be required to be taken, and this in the virtue of no *Authority* declared by the *Laws* to be reſident in his *Majeſty*, but in the virtue of a certain vagrant and indeterminate thing called *Royal Prerogative*, as the Power exerciſed in the *Engliſh Declaration* is worded and expreſſed, be not enough to enlighten us ſufficiently in the matter before us; the *Stile of Abſolute Power, which all the Subjeĉts are to obey without reſerve*, whereby the King is pleaſed to chalk before us, the *Authority* exerted in the *Scots Proclamation*, for the *ſtopping, diſabling, and diſpenſing with* ſuch and ſuch *Laws* as are there referred unto, and for the *granting* the *Toleration* with the other *Liberties, Immunities*, and *Rights* there mentioned, is more than ſufficient to ſet the Point we are diſcourſing upon beyond all poſſibility of rational controll. As 'tis one and the ſame kind of *Authority* that is claimed over the *Laws* and *Subjeĉts* of both *Kingdoms*, tho' for ſome certain reaſons it may be more modeſtly deſigned and expreſſed in the *Declaration for a Liberty in* England, than it is in the *Proclamation* for a *Toleration in Scotland*; ſo the utmoſt that the *Czar* of *Moſco*, the Great *Mogul*, or the *Turkiſh Sultan* ever challenged over their reſpective Dominions, amounts only to an *Abſolute Power*, which the King both owns the Exertion of, and makes it the *Fountain* of all the *Royal Aĉts* exerciſed in the forementioned Papers. And as the improving this challenged *Abſolute Power* into an *Obligation* upon the *Subjeĉts* to obey his *Majeſty without reſerve*, is a *Paraphraſe* upon *deſpotical Dominion*, and an advancing it to a Pitch, above what any of the Ancient or Modern *Tyrants* ever dream'd of, and beyond what the moſt ſervile part of Mankind was ever acquainted with, till the preſent *French King* gave an Inſtance of it, in making his *mere Will and Pleaſure* to be the Ground and Argument upon which his Reformed Subjeĉts were to renounce their Religion, and to turn *Roman Catholicks*; ſo it is worth conſidering, whether His *Majeſty*, who glories to imitate that *Foreign Monarch*, may not, in a little time, make the like Application of this *Abſolute Power, which his Subjeĉts are bound to obey without reſerve*; and whether in that caſe, they who have *addreſſed* to thank him for his *Declaration*, and thereby juſtified the Claim of this *Abſolute Power*, being that upon which the *Declaration* is ſuperſtruĉted, and from which it emergeth, can avoid paying the Obedience that is demanded as a Duty in the Subjeĉt, inſeparably annexed thereunto. That which more confirms us is, that the *Engliſh Declaration* and the *Scots Proclamation*, are not only deſigned for the obtaining from the Subjeĉts an Acknowledgment of an abſolute Power veſted in the *King*, but that no leſs than the *Uſurpation* and *Exerciſe* of ſuch a Power, can warrant and ſupport them, are the many *Laws* and *Rights*, which a Juriſdiĉtion is challenged over and exerted in reference unto, in the Papers ſtiled by the forementioned Names. All confeſs a Royal Prerogative ſettled on the Crown, and appertaining to the Royal Office; nor can the

Supreme

Supreme Magistrate be executed and discharged to the Advantage and Safety of the Community, without a Power affixed unto it of superseding the Execution of some *Laws* at certain Junctures, nor without having an Authority over the Rights of particular Men in some incident cases; but then the received Customs of the respective Nations, and the universal Good, Preservation and Safety of the People in general, are the Measures by which this Prerogative in the Crown is to be regulated, and beyond which to apply or exert it, is an *Usurpation* and *Tyranny* in the *Ruler*. All the Power belonging to the *Kings* and *Queens* of England and *Scotland*, ariseth from an Agreement and Concession of the People, wherein it is *stipulated*, what *Rights*, *Liberties* and *Privileges* they reserved unto themselves, and what *Authority* and *Jurisdiction* they *delegated* and made over unto the *Sovereign*, in order to his being in a Condition to protect and defend them, and that they may the better live in Peace, Freedom and Safety, which are the *Ends* for which they have chosen *Kings* to be over them, and for the compassing whereof, they originally submitted unto, and pitched upon such a *Form* of *Civil Administration*. Nor are the *Opinions* of particular Men, of what Rank or Order soever they be, to be admitted as an Exposition of the Extent of this *Prerogative*, seeing they, through their Dependencies upon the *King*, and their Obnoxiousness to be influenced by selfish and personal *Ends*, may enlarge it beyond what is for the Benefit of the *Community*; but the immemorial course of *Administration*, with the Sense of the whole *Society* signified by their *Representatives* in *Parliament* upon emerging *Occasions*, are to be taken for the *Sense*, *Paraphrase* and *Declaration* of the *Limits* of this *Royal* and *Prerogative Power*; and for any to determine the Bounds of it from the Testimonies of *Mercenary Lawyers*, or *Sycophant Clergymen*, in Cases wherein the *Parliament* have, by their *Votes* and *Resolutions*, settled its *Boundaries*, is a Crime that deserves the severest *Animadversion*, and, which it is to be hoped, a true *English Parliament* will not let pass unpunished. Now a Power arising from *Royal Prerogative*, to suspend and disable a great number of *Laws* at once, and they of such a Nature and Tendency, as the great Security of the People consists in their being maintained, and which the whole *Community* represented in *Parliaments* have often disallowed and made void Princes meddling with, so as to interrupt their Execution and Course, is so far from being a Right inherent in the *Crown*, that the very pretending unto it, is a changing of the *Government*, and an overthrowing of the *Constitution*. *Fortescue* says, That *Rex Angliæ populum gubernat non merâ potestate Regiâ, sed politicâ; quia populus iis legibus gubernatur quas ipse fert;* *The King* of England *doth not so properly govern by a Power that is Regal, as by a Power that is Political, in that he is bound to rule by the Laws, which the People themselves chuse and enact.* And both *Bracton* and *Fleta* tell us, That *Rex Angliæ habet superiores, viz. legem per quam factus est Rex, ac Comites & Barones qui debent ei frænum ponere;* *The King* of England *hath for Superiors, both the Law by which he is constituted King, and which is the measure of his Governing Power; and the Parliament, which is to restrain him, if he do amiss.* And thereupon we have not only that other Saying of *Bracton*, That *Nihil aliud potest Rex, nisi id solum quod jure potest;* *The King can do nothing but what he can do by Law.* But we have that famous Passage in our *Parliament-Rolls, Non est ulla Regis prærogativa, quæ ex justitia & æquitate quicquam derogat;* *That there is no Prerogative belongs to the King, by which he can decline from acting according to Law and Justice.* So careful were our *Ancestors* both in *England* and *Scotland*, to preserve their *Laws* from being invaded and superseded by their *Kings*; that they have not only by divers *Parliamentary Votes* and *Resolutions*, and by several *Statutes*, declared all *Dispensations* by the *King*, from *Laws* enjoined by *Oaths*, to be *null* and *void*, and not admittable by the *Judges* or other *Executors* of *Law* and *Justice*; but they have often Impeached, Arraigned and Condemned those to one Penalty or another, that have been found to have counselled and advised *Kings* to an *Usurpation* of Power over the *Laws*, and to a Violation of established and enacted *Rules*. It would draw this Discourse to a length beyond what is intended, should I mention the several Laws against *Papists* as well as against *Dissenters*, that are *suspended, stop'd, disabled* and *dispensed* with, in the two fore-mentioned *Royal Papers*; and it would be an extending it much more, should I make the several *Reflections* that the matter is capable of, and which a Person of a very ordinary Understanding cannot be greatly to seek for: I shall therefore only take notice of two or three *Efforts* which occur there, of this Royal Prerogative and Absolute Power, which as they are very bold and ample Exertions of them for the first time, so should the next *Exercises* of them be proportionable, there will be nothing left us of the Protestant Religion, or of *English* Liberties, and we must be contented to be Papists and Slaves, or else to stand adjudged to *Tyburn* and *Smithfield*. One is the *suspending the Laws* which enjoin the *Oaths* of *Allegiance* and *Supremacy*, and the *prohibiting* that these *Oaths* be at any time hereafter required to be taken; by which single *Exercise* of *Royal Prerogative* and *Absolute Power*, the two *Kingdoms* are not only again subjected to a *Foreign Jurisdiction*, the Miseries whereof they

groaned

De Laudib.
Leg.Angl. c. 9.

Bract. l. 2. c.
16. Flet.l.2.
c. 17.

Lib.3. cap. 9.

Rot. Parl. 7.
Hen. 4. Num.
59.

groaned under for feveral Ages ; but as the *King* is hereby deprived of the greateft *Security* he had from his *Subjects*, both to himfelf and the *Government*, fo the *Crown* is robb'd of one of its chiefeft Jewels, namely, an *Authority* over all the *Subjects* ; which was thought fo effential to *Sovereignty* and *Royal Dignity*, that it was annexed to the *Imperial Crown* of *England*, and adjudged inherent in the *Monarch*, before the *Reformed Religion* came to be received and eftablifhed. And it concerns their *Royal Highnefses* of *Orange*, to whom the *Right* of fucceeding to the *Crown* of *Great Britain* unqueftionably belongs, to confider whether his Majefty may not, by the fame Authority whereby he alienates and gives away fo confiderable and inherent a *Branch* of the *Royal Jurifdiction*, transfer the *Succefsion* it felf, and difpofe the *Inheritance* of the *Crown* to whom he pleafeth. Nor will they about him, who thruft the laft King out of the Throne, to make room for his prefent Majefty, much fcruple to put a Proteftant Succeffor by it, if they can find another Papift as bigotted as this to advance unto it. However, were they on the *Throne* to-morrow, here is both a *Foreign Jurifdiction* brought in and fet up to rival and control theirs, and they are deprived of all means of being fecured of the *Loyalty* and *Fealty* of a great number of their *Subjects*. Nor will *His Majefty's certain Knowledge and long Experience* (whereof he boafts in the *Scots Proclamation*) *that the Catholicks, as it is their Principle to be good Chriftians, fo it is to be dutiful Subjects*, be enough for their *Royal Highnefses* to rely upon, their *Religion* obliging them to the contrary towards Princes, whom the Church of *Rome* hath adjudged to be *Hereticks*. A fecond Inftance wherein this pretended Royal Prerogative is exercifed paramount to all *Laws*, and which nothing but a claim of Abfolute Power in his Majefty can fupport, and an Acknowledgment of it by the Subjects, make them approve the *Declaration for Liberty of Confcience*, and the *Proclamation for Toleration* ; is the ftopping, difabling and fufpending the *Statutes* whereby the *Tefts* were enacted, and thereby letting the Papifts into all Benefices, Offices, and Places of Truft, whether Civil, Military, or Ecclefiaftick. I do not fpeak of fufpending the Execution of thofe *Laws*, whereby the being Priefts, or taking Orders in the Church of *Rome*, or the being reconciled to that Church, or the Papifts meeting to celebrate *Mafs*, were in one degree or another made punifhable, (tho' the King's difpenfing with them by a challenged Claim in the *Crown* be altogether *illegal*) for as divers of thefe *Laws* were never approved by any Proteftants, fo nothing would have juftified the making of them, but the many *Treafons* and *Confpiracies* that they were from time to time found guilty of againft the State. And as the Papifts, of all Men, have the leaft caufe to complain of the Injuftice, Rigor, and Severity of them, confidering the many *Laws*, more cruel and fanguinary, that are in force in moft Popifh Countries againft Proteftants, and thefe enacted and executed merely for their Opinions and Practices in the Matters of God, without their being chargeable with Crimes and Offences againft the Civil Government under which they live ; fo were it neceffary from Principles of Religion and Policy, to relieve the *Roman Catholicks* from the forementioned *Laws*, yet it ought not to be done but by the *Legiflative Authority* of the *Kingdoms* : and for the King to affume a Power of doing it, in the virtue of a pretended Prerogative, is both a high *Ufurpation* over the *Laws*, and a *Violation* of his *Coronation-Oath*. Nor is it any Commendation either of the Humanity of the Papifts, or of the Meeknefs and Truth of their Religion, that while they elfewhere treat thofe who differ from them in Faith and Worfhip with that Barbarity, they fhould fo clamoroufly inveigh againft the Severities which in fome Reformed States they are liable unto, and which their *Treafons* gave the Rife and Provocation unto at firft, and have been at all times the Motives to the Infliction of. But they alone would have the Allowance to be cruel, wherein they act confonantly to their own Tenets ; and I wifh that fome Provifion might be made for the future, for the Security of our Religion, and our Safety in the Profeffion of it, without the doing any thing that may unbecome the merciful Principles of Chriftianity, or be unfuitable to the meek and generous Temper of the *Englifh* Nation ; and that the Property of being *Sanguinary* may be left to the Church of *Rome*, as its peculiar Privilege and Glory, and as a more diftinguifhing *Character* than all the other Marks which fhe pretends unto. That which I am fpeaking of, is the fufpending the Execution of thofe *Laws*, by which the Government was fecured of the Fidelity of its Subjects, and by which they, in whom it could not confide, were merely fhut out from Places of Power and Truft, and were made liable to very fmall Damages themfelves, and only hindred from getting into a Condition of doing Mifchief to us. All Governments have a Right to ufe means for their own Prefervation, provided they be not fuch as are inconfiftent with the *Ends* of Government, and repugnant to the Will and Pleafure of the *Supreme Sovereign* of *Mankind* ; and it is in the power of the *Legiflative Affembly*, to declare who of the *Community* fhall be capable or incapable of thefe Imploys, and of poffeffing Offices, upon which the Peace, Welfare and Security of the whole Politick Body does depend. Without this, no Government could subsist, nor the People be in safety under it ; but the Constitution would be in constant danger of being subverted, and the Privileges, Liberties and Religion of the *Subjects* laid open to be overthrown. And should such a Power in *Legislators*, be, upon weak Suspicions and ill-grounded Jealousies, carried at any time too far, and some prove to be debarred from Trusts, whose being imployed would import no Hazard ; yet the worst of that, would be only a disrespect shewn to individual Persons, who might deserve more Favour and Esteem, but could be of no Prejudice to the *Society*, there being always a sufficient number of others, fit for the discharge of all *Offices*, in whom an entire Confidence may be reposed. And 'tis remarkable, that the *States General* of the *United Provinces*, who afford the greatest Liberty to all Religions, that any known State in *Europe* giveth ; yet they suffer no Papists to come into Places of *Authority* and *Judicature*, nor to bear any Office in the Republick, that may either put them into a Condition, or lay them under a Temptation of attempting any thing to the prejudice of Religion, or for the betraying the Liberty of the Provinces. And as 'tis lawful for any Government to preclude all such Persons from publick Trusts, of whose Enmity and Ill-will to the Establishment in Church or State, they have either a moral Certainty, or just Grounds of Suspicion ; so 'tis no less lawful to provide Tests for their Discovery and Detection, that they may not be able to mask and vizor themselves in order to getting into Offices, and thereupon of promoting and accomplishing their mischievous and malicious Intentions. Nor is it possible in such a case, but that the Tests they are to be tried by, must relate to some of those Principles by which they are most eminently distinguished from them of the National Settlement, and in reference whereunto they think it most piacular to dissemble their Opinion. Nor have the Papists cause to be offended, that the *Renouncing the Belief of Transubstantiation*, should be required as the distinguishing Mark, whereby, upon their refusal, they may be discerned, when all the Penalty upon their being known, is only to be excluded from a Share in the *Legislation*, and not to be admitted to Employments of Trust and Profit ; seeing it hath been, and still is their Custom, to require the *Belief of the Corporal Presence in the Sacrament*, as that upon the not Acknowledgment whereof, we are to be accounted *Hereticks*, and to stand condemned to be burnt, which is somewhat worse than the not being allowed to sit in the Two *Houses of Parliament*, or to be shut out from a *Civil* or *Military Office*. Neither are they required to Declare, much less to Swear, that the *Doctrine* of *Transubstantiation* is *false*, *or that there is no such thing as Transubstantiation*, (as is affirmed in a scurrilous Paper written against the Loyalty of the Church of *England*) but all that is enjoined in the *Test Acts*, is, that *I, A. B. do declare, that I do believe that there is not any Transubstantiation in the Sacrament of the Lord's Supper, or in the Elements of Bread and Wine, at or after the Consecration thereof by any Person whatsoever*. Tho' the Parliament was willing to use all the Care they could, for the discovering Papists, that the Provision for our Security, unto which those Acts were designed, might be the more effectual ; yet they were not so void of Understanding, as to prescribe a Method for it, which would have exposed them to the World for their Folly : 'Tis much different to say, swear, or declare, that *I do believe there is not any Transubstantiation*, and the saying or declaring that *there is not a Transubstantiation* ; the former being only expressive of what my Sentiment or Opinion is, and not at all affecting the Doctrine it self, to make, or unmake it, other than what it is, independently upon my Judgment of it ; whereas the latter does primarily *affect* the *Object* and the Determination of its Existence to such a Mode as I conceive it ; and there are a thousand things which I can say that I do not believe, but I dare not say that they are not. Now as 'tis the dispensing with these Laws that argues the King's assuming an absolute Power ; so the addressing by way of Thanks, for the *Declaration* wherein this Power is exerted, is no less than an owning and acknowledging of it, and that it rightfully belongs to him. There is a third thing which Shame or Fear would not suffer them to put into the *Declaration for Liberty of Conscience in* England, but which they have had the Impudence to insert into the *Proclamation for a Toleration in* Scotland, which as it carries *Absolute Power* written in the forehead of it, so it is such an unprecedented Exercise of *Despoticalness*, as hardly any of the *Oriental Tyrants*, or even the *French Leviathan* would have ventured upon. For having stop'd, disabled and suspended all *Laws* enjoining any Oaths, whereby our Religion was secured, and the Preservation of it to us and our Posterity was provided for ; he imposeth a new *Oath* upon his *Scots Subjects*, whereby they are to be bound to *defend and maintain him, his Heirs and lawful Successors, in the Exercise of their Absolute Power and Authority against all deadly*. The imposing an *Oath* upon *Subjects* hath been always look'd upon as the highest *Act* of *Legislative Authority*, in that it affects their Consciences, and requires the Approbation, or Disapprobation of their Minds and Judgments, in reference to whatsoever it is enjoined for ; whereas a *Law* that affects only Men's Persons, may be submitted unto, tho' in the mean time they think that which is enacted to be

be

be Unreaſonable and Unjuſt. And as it concerns both the Wiſdom and Juſtice of *Law-givers* to be very tender in ordaining *Oaths* that are to be taken by *Subjects*, and that not only from a care that they may not proſtitute the Name of *God* to Prophanation, when the matter about which they are impoſed, is either light and trivial, or dubious and un-certain ; but becauſe it is an Exerciſe of Juriſdiction over the Souls of Men, which is more than if it were only exerciſed over their *Goods, Bodies* and *Privileges* ; ſo never any of our Kings pretended to a Right of enjoining and requiring an *Oath* that was not firſt *enacted* and ſpecified in ſome *Law* ; and it would have been heretofore accounted a good Plea for refuſing ſuch or ſuch an *Oath*, to ſay there was no Statute that had required it. It was one of the Articles of High Treaſon (and the moſt material) charged upon the Earl of *Strafford*, that being *Lord Deputy of Ireland*, he required an *Oath* of the *Scots* who in-habited there, which no Law had ordained or preſcribed ; which may make thoſe Coun-ſellors who have adviſed the King to impoſe this new Oath, as well as all others that ſhall require it to be taken upon his Majeſty's bare Authority, to be a little apprehenſive, whether it may not at ſome time riſe in Judgment againſt them, and prove a Forfeiture of their Lives to Juſtice. And as the impoſing an Oath not warranted by *Law*, is an high *Act* of *Abſolute Power*, and in the King an altering of the Conſtitution ; ſo if we look into the *Oath* it ſelf, we ſhall find this *Abſolute Power* ſtrangely manifeſted and diſplayed in all the Parts and Branches of it, and the People required to ſwear themſelves his Majeſty's moſt obedient *Slaves* and *Vaſſals*. By one *Paragraph* of it, they are required to *ſwear that it is unlawful for Subjects, on any pretence, or for any cauſe whatſoever, to riſe in Arms againſt him, or any commiſſioned by him ; and that they ſhall never reſiſt his Power or Authority:* which as it may be intended for a foundation and means of keeping Men quiet when he ſhall break in upon their *Eſtates*, and overthrow their *Religion* ; ſo it may be deſigned as an Encouragement to his *Catholick Subjects*, to ſet upon the cutting *Proteſtants Throats*, when by this *Oath* their Hands are tied up from hindring them. It is but for the *Papiſts* to come *Authoriſed* with his *Majeſty's Commiſſion*, which will not be denied them for ſo meritorious a Work, and then there is no Help nor Remedy, but we muſt ſtretch out our Necks, and open our Breaſts to their conſecrated Swords and ſanctified Daggers. Nay, if the King ſhould transfer the Succeſſion to the Crown from the *Rightful Heir*, to ſome zealous *Ro-maniſt*, or *alienate* and diſpoſe of his *Kingdoms* in way of *Donation* and *Gift* to the *Pope*, or to the *Society* of the *Jeſuits* ; and for the better ſecuring them in the Poſſeſſion hereafter, ſhould inveſt and place them in the Enjoyment of them while he lives ; the *Scots* are bound, in the virtue of this *Oath*, tamely to look on, and calmly to acquieſce in it. Or ſhould his *Phyſicians* adviſe him to a nightly Variety of *Matrons* and *Maids*, as the beſt Re-medy againſt his malignant and venomous Heats ; all of that *Kingdom* are bound to ſurren-der their *Wives* and *Daughters* to him, with a dutiful Silence and a profound Veneration. And if by this *Oath* he can ſecure himſelf from the Oppoſition of his *Diſſenting Subjects*, in caſe, through recovery of their Reaſon, a Fit of ancient Zeal ſhould ſurprize them ; he is otherwiſe ſecured of an *Aſiatick* Tameneſs in his prelatical People, by a Principle which they have lately imbib'd, but neither learned from their Bibles, nor the Statutes of the Land. For the *Clergy*, upon thinking that the Wind would always blow out of one quarter, and being reſolved to make that a Duty by their Learning, which their Intereſt at that ſeaſon made convenient ; have preached up the *Doctrine of Paſſive Obedience* to ſuch a boundleſs height, that they have done what in them lies, to give up themſelves and all that had the Weakneſs to believe them, fettered and bound for *Sacrifices* to *Popiſh Rage* and *deſpotical Tyranny*. But for my ſelf (and I hope the like of many others) I thank God I am not tainted with that ſlaviſh and adulatory Doctrine, as having always thought that the firſt Duty of every Member of a *Body Politick*, is to the *Community*, for whoſe Safety good *Governors* are inſtituted, and that it is only to *Rulers*, as they are found to anſwer the main *Ends* they are appointed for, and to act by the legal Rules that are chalk'd out unto them. Whether it be from my Dullneſs, or that my Underſtanding is of a perverſer make than other Mens, I cannot tell ; but I could never yet be otherways minded, than that the *Rules* of the *Conſtitution*, and the *Laws* of the *Republick* or *Kingdom*, are to be the Meaſures both of the *Sovereign's Commands*, and of the *Subjects Obedience* ; and that as we are not to invade what by *Conceſſions* and *Stipulations* belongs unto the *Ruler*, ſo we may not only lawfully, but we ought to defend what is reſerved to our ſelves, if it be invaded and bro-ken in upon. And as without ſuch a Right in the *Subjects*, all *legal Governments*, and *mix'd Monarchies*, were but empty Names, and ridiculous Things ; ſo whereſoever the *Conſtitution* of a *Nation* is ſuch, there the *Prince*, who ſtrives to ſubvert the *Laws* of the *Society*, is the Traytor and Rebel ; and not the People who endeavour to preſerve and defend them. There is yet another Branch of the foreſaid *Oath*, that is of a much more unſeaſonable Strain than the former, which is, *That they ſhall, to the utmoſt of their Power, aſſiſt, defend and maintain him in the Exerciſe of this Abſolute Power and Authority* ;

which

which being tack'd *to our obeying without reserve,* make us the greatest *Slaves* that either are, or ever were in the Universe. Our *Kings* were heretofore bound to govern according to Law (and so is his present *Majesty,* if a *Coronation-Oath* and *Faith* to *Hereticks,* were not weaker than *Sampson*'s cords proved to be) but instead of that, here is a new *Oath* imposed upon the Subjects, by which they are bound to protect and defend the *King* in his *ruling arbitrarily.* It had been more than enough to have required only a calm submitting to the exercise of *Absolute Power ;* but to be enjoined to swear to *assist* and *defend* his *Majesty* and *Successors* in all things wherein they shall exert it, is a plain destroying of all *natural* as well as *civil Liberty,* and a robbing us of that freedom that belongs unto us, both as we are men and as we are born under a free and legal Government. For by this we become bound to drag our Brethren to the Stake, to cut their Throats, plunder their Houses, imbrue our hands in the Blood of our Wives and Children, if his *Majesty* please to make these the Instances wherein he will exert his *Absolute Power,* and require us to *assist him in the exercise of it.* As it was necessary to *cancel* all other *Oaths* and *Tests,* as being directly inconsistent with this ; so the requiring the *Scots* to swear this *Oath,* is the highest revenge he could take for their *Solemn League and Covenant,* and for all other *Oaths,* that Lust after *Arbitrariness* and *Popish Bigotry* will pronounce to have been injurious to the Crown. But no words are sufficient to express the mischiefs wrapt up in that new *Oath,* or to declare the abhorrency that all who value the *Rights* and *Liberties* of Mankind ought to entertain for it, nor to proclaim the Villany of those who shall by *Addresses* give thanks for the *Proclamation.* There may a *fourth* thing be added, whereby it will appear, that his *Majesty*'s assuming *Absolute Power,* stands recorded in Capital Letters in his *Declaration* for *Liberty of Conscience.* For not being contented to omit the requiring the *Oaths* of *Allegiance* and *Supremacy* and the *Test-Oaths* to be taken, nor being satisfied to suspend for a season the enjoining any to be demanded to take them ; he tells us that it is his *Royal Will and Pleasure* that the aforesaid *Oaths shall not at any time hereafter be required to be taken,* which is a full and direct *Repealing* of the Laws in which they are Enacted. It hath hitherto passed for an undoubted Maxim, that *eorum est tollere, quorum est condere, they can only abrogate Laws, who have Power and Authority to make them ;* and we have heretofore been made believe, that the *Legislative Power* was not in the King alone, but that the two *Houses* of *Parliament* had at least a share in it ; whereas here, by the disabling and suspending Laws for ever, the whole *Legislative Power* is challenged to be vested in the *King,* and at one dash the Government of *England* is subverted and changed. Tho' it hath been much disputed whether the *King* had a liberty of refusing to *assent* to *Bills* relating to the benefit of the Publick that had passed the two *Houses ;* and if there be any sense in those words of the *Coronation-Oath* of his being bound to *govern according to the Laws quas vulgus elegerit,* he had not ; yet none till now, that his Majesty doth it, had the impudence to affirm that he might *abrogate Laws* without the concurrence and assent of the *Lords* and *Commons.* For to say that Oaths enjoined by Laws to be required to be taken, *shall not at any time hereafter be required to be taken,* is a plain Cancelling and Repealing of these Laws, or nothing of this World ever was or is ; nor can the Wisdom of the Nation in Parliament assembled, find words more *emphatical* to declare their *Abrogation,* without saying so, which at this time it was necessary to forbear, for fear of alarming the Kingdom too far, before his Majesty be sufficiently provided against it. For admitting them to continue still in being and force, tho' the King may promise for the *non-execution* of them, during his own time, (which is even a pretty bold undertaking) yet he cannot assure us that the *Oaths shall not be required to be taken at any time hereafter,* unless he have promised for an eternal *Line* of *Popish Successors,* which God will not be so unmerciful as to plague us with ; or have gotten a Lease of a longer Life than *Methusalah*'s, which is much more than the full *Century* of years wished him in a late *Dedication,* by one that stiles himself an *Irishman ;* a thing he might have forborn telling us, because the Size of his Understanding fully declares it. However, here is such a stroke and exercise of *Absolute Power,* as dissolves the Government, and brings us all into a state of Nature, by discharging us from the ties, which by virtue of *Fundamental Stipulations* and *Statute Laws* we formerly lay under ; forasmuch as we know no *King* but a *King* by Law, nor no *Power* he hath but a *legal Power.* Which through disclaiming by a challenge that the whole Legislative Authority does reside in himself, he hath thrown the Gantlet to three *Kingdoms,* and provokes them to a tryal, whether he be ablest to maintain his *Absoluteness,* or they to justify their being a *free People.* And by virtue of the same *Royal Will and Pleasure,* that he annuls (which he calls suspending) the Laws enjoining the *Tests* and the *Oaths* of *Allegiance* and *Supremacy,* and commands that none of these Oaths and Declarations *shall at any time hereafter be required to be taken ;* he may in some following Royal Papers, give us *Whitehall* or *Hampton-Court* Edicts, conformable to those at *Versailles,* which at all times hereafter we shall be bound to submit unto, and stand obliged to be ruled

led by inſtead of the *Common Law* and *Statute Book.* Nor is the taking upon him to ſtamp us new *Laws*, excluſively of *Parliamentary* Concurrence, in the virtue of his *Royal Prerogative*, any thing more uncouth in it ſelf, or more diſagreeable to the *Rules* of the *Conſtitution*, and what we have been conſtantly accuſtomed unto, than the *caſſing, diſabling*, and abrogating ſo many old ones, which that *obſolete*, out of date, as well as ill-favoured thing upon *Monarchs*, called a *Parliament*, had a ſhare in the enacting of. I will not ſay that our *Addreſſers* were conſcious, that the getting an *Abſolute Power* in his *Majeſty*, to be owned and acknowledged, was one of the *Ends* for which the late *Declaration* was calculated and emitted ; but I think I have ſufficiently demonſtrated both that *ſuch a power* iſſueth and flows from, and that *ſuch a power* is plainly *exerciſed* in it. Which whether their coming now to be told and made acquainted with it, may make them repent what they have done, or at leaſt prevent their being acceſſory to the ſupport of this *Power* in other miſchievous effects that are to be dreaded from it, I muſt leave to time to make the diſcovery, it being impoſſible to foretel what a People fallen into a *phrenzy* may do in their *paroxiſms* of diſtraction and madneſs.

Nor was the *ſcruing himſelf* into the poſſeſſion of an *Abſolute Power*, and the getting it to be owned by at leaſt a part of the People, the only *Motive* to the publiſhing the *Declaration for Liberty of Conſcience* in *England*, and the *Proclamation for a Toleration* in *Scotland* ; but a *ſecond Inducement*, that ſway'd unto it, was the undermining and ſubverting the *Proteſtant Religion*, and the opening a door for the *introduction* and *eſtabliſhment* of *Popery*. Nor was it from any compaſſion to *Diſſenters*, that theſe *two Royal Papers* were emitted, but from his *Majeſty's* tender love to *Papiſts*, to whom as there ariſe many advantages for the preſent, ſo the whole benefit will be found to redound to them in the iſſue. We are told (as I have already mentioned) *that the King is reſolved to convert England, or to die a Martyr* ; and we may be ſure that if he did not think the *ſuſpending* the *penal Laws*, and the *diſpenſing* with requiring of the *Teſts*, and the granting *Liberty* and *Toleration*, to be means admirably adapted thereunto, he would not have acted ſo inconſiſtently with himſelf, nor in that oppoſition to his own *deſigns*, as to have diſabled theſe *Laws*, and vouchſafed the Freedom that reſults thereupon : Eſpecially when we are told by the *Liege Jeſuit*, that the King being *ſenſible of his growing old*, finds *himſelf* thereby obliged *to make the greater haſte, and to take the larger ſteps*, leſt through not living long enough to effect what he intends, he ſhould not only loſe the glory of *converting* three Kingdoms, but *ſhould leave the Papiſts in a worſe condition than he found them.* His *Highneſs* the *Prince* of *Orange* very juſtly concludes this to be the thing aim'd at by the preſent *Indulgence*, and therefore being deſired to approve the *Suſpenſion* of the *Teſt-Acts*, and to co-operate with *his Majeſty* for the obtaining their being *repealed* ; was pleaſed to anſwer, *That while he was, as well as profeſſeth himſelf, a Proteſtant*, he would *not act ſo unworthily as to betray the Proteſtant Religion*, which he neceſſarily muſt, if he ſhould do as he was deſired. Her *Royal Highneſs* the *Princeſs* of *Orange* has likewiſe the ſame apprehenſion of the tendency of the *Toleration* and *Indulgence*, and therefore was pleaſed to ſay. to ſome *Scots Miniſters* that did themſelves the honour, and performed the duty that became them, in going to wait upon *her*, that *ſhe* greatly commended *their* having *no acceſſion to the betraying of the Proteſtant Religion, by their returning home to take the benefit of the Toleration.* What an indelible Reproach will it be to a company of men, that pretend to *be ſet for the defence of the Goſpel*, and who ſtile themſelves *Miniſters of Jeſus Chriſt*, to be found betraying *Religion*, thro' juſtifying the *Suſpenſion* of ſo many *Laws* whereby it was *eſtabliſhed* and *ſupported*, and whereby the *Kingdoms* were *fenced* about, and guarded againſt *Popery* ; while theſe *two* noble *Princes*, to the neglect of *their* own Intereſt in His *Majeſty's* Favour, and to the provoking *him* to do *them* all the prejudice he can in their *Right of Succeſſion* to the *Imperial Crown* of *Great Britain*, do ſignify their open diſlike to that *Act* of the *King*, and that not only upon the account of its Illegality and Arbitrarineſs, but by reaſon of its tendency to ſupplant and undermine the *Reformed Religion*. And they are ſtrangely blind that do not ſee how it powerfully operates, and conduceth to the effecting of this, and that in more ways and methods than are eaſy to be recounted. For thereby our *Diviſions* are not only kept up at a time, when the united Counſels and Strength of all *Proteſtants* is too little againſt the craft and power of *Rome*.; but they who have *Addreſſed* to thank the *King* for his *Royal Papers*, are become a liſted and enrolled *Faction*, to abet and ſtand by the *King* in all that naturally follows to be done for the maintaining his *Declaration*, and juſtifying of the uſurped *Authority* from which it iſſues. 'Tis matter of a melancholy conſideration, and turns little to the credit of *Diſſenters*, that when they of the Church of *England*, who had with ſo great indiſcretion promoted things to that paſs, which an eaſy improvement of would produce what hath ſince enſued, are through being at laſt enlightned in the deſigns of the *Court*, come ſo far to recover

2

their wits, as that they can no longer do the service that they were wont, and which was still expected from them; there should be a new *Tribe* of men muster'd up to stand in their room, and who by their *Vows* and *Promises* made to their *King* in their *Addresses*, have undertaken to perform, what others have the Conscience and Honesty, as well as the Wisdom to refuse and decline. Nor are the *Divisions* among *Protestants* only hereby upheld and maintained; but our Animosities and Rancours are both continued and enflamed. For while they of the *established* way are provoked and exasperated to see all the *legal* Foundations both of the *Protestant Religion* and their *Church* subverted; the *Addressing Dissenters* are embolden'd to revenge themselves upon the National Clergy, in terms of the utmost Opprobry, Virulence, and Reproach, for their accession to the Sufferings which they had endured. Surely it would have been not only more *generous*, but much more *Christian*, to have made no other Retaliations but those of forgiveness and pardon for the injuries they had met with, and to have offered all the assistances they could give, to their *conformable Brethren*, for the stemming and withstanding the *deluge* of Popery and Tyranny that is impetuously breaking in upon the *Kingdoms*. And as this would have united all *Protestants* in bonds of forbearance and love, not to be dissolved through petty differences about Discipline, Forms of Worship, and a few Rites and Ceremonies; so it would, in the sense and judgment of all men, have given them a more triumphant Victory over those that had been their imprudent and peevish Enemies, than if they were to enjoy the spoils of the *conformable Clergy*, by being put into possession of their *Cures* and *Benefices*. The Relation I have stood in to the *Dissenting* Party, and the Kindness I retain for them above all other, make me heartily bewail their losing the happiest opportunity that ever was put into their hands, not only of improving the compassion, which their calamities had raised for them in the hearts of the generality, into friendship and kindness, but of acquiring such a merit upon the *Nation*, that the utmost favours which a true *English Protestant Parliament* could hereafter have shewed them, would have been accounted but slender as well as just Recompences. Nor can I forbear to say, that I had rather have seen the *Furnace* of Afflictions made hotter for them, though it should have been my own lot to be thrown into the most scorching flames, than to have beheld them guilty of those excesses of folly towards themselves, and of treachery to *Religion*, and the *Laws* of their *Country*, which their present ease, and a short opportunity afforded them of acquiring gain, have hurried and transported so many of them into. It plainly appears with what aspect upon our *Religion* the *Declaration for Liberty of Conscience* was emitted, if we do but observe the advantages the *Papists* have already reap'd by it. How is the whole Nation thereupon, not only overflow'd with swarms of *Locusts*, and all places filled with *Priests* and *Jesuits*, but the whole *executive Power* of the *Government*, and all preferments of Honour, Interest, and Profit, are put into *Roman Catholick* hands? So that we are not only exposed to the unwearied and restless importunities of *Seducers*, but thro' the advancement of *Papists* to all Offices *Civil* and *Military*, if not ecclesiastick; the *covetous* become brib'd, the timorous threatned, and the profane are baited with temptations suitable to their lusts; and they that stand resolved to continue honest, are laid open not only to the bold affronts of *Priests* and *Friers*, the insolencies of petulant *Popish Justices*, the chicaneries and oppressions of the *Arbitrary Commission-Court*, but to the rage of his *Majesty*, and the danger of being attack'd by his armed *Squadrons*. To which may be added, that by the same *Prerogative* and *Absolute Power* that his *Majesty* hath suspended the *Laws* made for the *Protection* of our *Religion*; he may disable and dispense with all the *Laws* by which it is set up and established. And as it will not be more *illegal* and *arbitrary* to make void the *Laws* for *Protestancy*, than to have suspended those against *Popery*; so I do not see how the *Addressers* that have approved the *one*, can disallow or condemn the *other*. For the *King* having obtained an acknowledgment of his *Absolute Power*, and of his *Royal Prerogative* paramount to *Laws*, on his exercising it in one instance; it now depends merely upon his own will (for any thing these thanksgiving Gentlemen have to say against it) whether he may not exert it in another, wherein they are not likely to find so much of their ease and gain.

There is a *third Inducement* to the emitting those Royal Papers, which tho' at the first view it may seem wholly to regard *Foreigners*, yet it ultimately terminates in the subversion of our *Religion* at home, and in the *King's* putting himself into a condition of exercising his *Absolute Power* in whatsoever Acts he pleaseth over his own *Subjects*, whether after the *French* fashion in commanding them to turn *Catholicks* because he will have it so, or after the manner of the *Grand Seignior* to require them to submit their *Necks* to the *Bow-string*; because he is jealous of them, or wants their Estates to pay his *Janizaries*. The *United Provinces* are they whom he bore a particular spleen and indignation unto, when he was a *Subject*, and upon whom, he is now in the *Throne*, he resolves

ſolves not only to wreck all his old Malice, but by *conquering* and *ſubduing* them (if he can) to ſtrengthen his *Abſoluteneſs* over his own People, and to pave his way for over-throwing the *Proteſtant Religion* in *Great Britain*, without lying open to the Hazards that may otherways attend and enſue upon the attempting of it. And inſtead of expecting nothing from him, but what may become a brave and generous Enemy, they ought to remember the Encouragement that he gave heretofore to two Varlets, to burn that part of their *Fleet* which belong'd to *Amſterdam* ; an Action as Ignominious as Fraudu-lent, and that might have been *Fatal* to all the Provinces, if, through a happy and ſea-ſonable Detection, and the Apprehenſion of one of the Miſcreants, it had not been prevented. He knows that the *States General* are not only zealous Aſſertors of the Pro-teſtant Religion, but always ready to afford a *Sanctuary* and a place of *Refuge* to thoſe, who being oppreſſed for the Profeſſion of it elſewhere, are forced to forſake their own *Coun-tries*, and to ſeek for Shelter and Relief in other Parts. And as he is not unſenſible, how eaſy the Withdrawment and Flight is into thoſe Provinces, for ſuch as are perſecuted in his Dominions ; ſo he is aware, that if Multitudes, and eſpecially Men of Condition and Eſtates, ſhould, for the avoiding his Cruelty, betake themſelves thither, that they would not be unthoughtful of all Ways and Means, whereby they might redeem their *Country* from *Tyranny*, and reſtore themſelves to the quiet Enjoyment of their *Eſtates* and *Liberties* at home. But that which moſt enrages him, is the *Figure* which the two Princes do make in that *State* (of whoſe Succeſſion to the Crown the Proteſtants in *Britain* have ſo near a Proſpect) and the Poſt which the Prince filleth in that Government ; ſo that he dare neither venture to *diſinherit Them*, nor impoſe upon them ſuch *Terms* and *Con-ditions*, as their Conſciences will not ſuffer them to comply with, while either theſe *States* remain free, or while ſuch *Engliſh* and *Scots*, as retain a Zeal for *Religion* and the ancient *Laws* and *Rights* of their reſpective *Countries*, can retreat thither under hopes of Admiſſion and Protection. And ſo closely are the *Intereſts* of all Proteſtants in *England* and *Scotland* woven and inlaid with the *Intereſt* of the *United Netherlands*, and ſuch is the ſingular regard that both the one and the other bear to the *Reformed Religion*, the *Liberty of Mankind*, and their ſeveral *Civil Rights* ; that it is impoſſible for his *Majeſty* to embark in a Deſign againſt the *One*, without reſolving at the ſame time upon the Ruin of the *Other*. Neither will the *One* be able to *ſubſiſt*, when once the *Other* is ſub-dued and enſlaved. As *Philip* the Second, of *Spain*, ſaw no way ſo compendious for the reſtoring himſelf to the Sovereignty and Tyrannous Rule over the *Dutch*, as the *ſubjugating* of *England* that help'd to ſupport and aſſiſt them, which was the ground of rigging out his formidable *Armado*, and of his Deſign againſt *England* in 1588 ; ſo his *Britiſh Majeſty* thinks no Method ſo expeditious for the enſlaving his own People, as the endeavouring firſt to *ſubdue* the *Dutch*. And as upon the one hand it would be of a threatning Conſequence to *Holland*, could the King ſubjugate his own People, extirpate the Proteſtant Religion out of his Dominions, and advance himſelf to a deſpotical Power ; ſo, upon the other hand, could he conquer the *Dutch*, we might with the greateſt cer-tainty *date* the woful *Fate* of *Great Britain*, and the loſs of all that is valuable to them as Men and Chriſtians, from the ſame Moment and Period of time. They are like the *Twins* we read of, whoſe *Deſtiny* was, to live and die together ; and which ſoever of the *two* is deſtroyed firſt, all the Hope and Comfort that the other can pretend unto, is to be laſt devoured. Now after the Advances which his *Majeſty* had made towards the enſla-ving his *Subjects*, and the *ſubverting* the *Reformed Religion* in his *Kingdoms*, he finds it ne-ceſſary, before he venture to give the laſt and fatal Stroke at home, and to enter upon the plenary Exerciſe of his *Abſolute Power*, in laying *Parliaments* wholly aſide, in can-celling all *Laws* to make way for *Royal Edicts* or *Declarations* of the Complexion of the former, and in commanding us to turn *Roman Catholicks*, or to be *Dragoon'd* ; I ſay, he thinks it needful, before he proceeds to theſe, to try whether he can *ſubdue* and *conquer* the *Dutch*, and thereby remove all hopes of Shelter, Relief, Comfort and Aſſiſtance from his own People, when he ſhall afterwards fall upon them. And how much ſoever the Court endeavours to conceal his Deſign, and ſtrives to complement the *States-General* into a Confidence that all *Alliances* between them and the *Crown* of *England* ſhall be maintained and preſerved ; yet they not only ſpeak their Intentions by ſeveral open and viſible Actions, but ſome of them cannot forbear to tell it, when their Blood is heated, and their Heads warm'd with a liberal Glaſs and a luſty Proportion of Wine. Thence it was that a *Governing Papiſt* lately told a Gentleman, after they two had drank hard together, *That they had ſome Work in* England *that would employ them a little time, but when that was over, they would make the* Dutch *fly to the end of the World to find a reſting-place.* *Delenda eſt Carthago* is engraven upon their Hearts, as being that, without which *Rome* cannot arrive at the *Univerſal Monarchy* that it aſpires after. It was upon a formed De-ſign of a War againſt the *United Provinces*, that the *King* hath for theſe two Years ſtirred up and incited, as well as countenanced and protected the *Algerines* in their Piracies, that through their weakening and spoiling the *Dutch* beforehand, it may be the more easy a matter for him to subdue them, when he shall think fit to begin his Hostilities. 'Tis in order to this, that he hath entred into new and secret Alliances with other Princes, the purport of which is boldly talk'd of in *London*, but whether believ'd at the *Hague*, I cannot tell. For as *Monsieur Barillon* and *Monsieur Bonrepos* present Transactions at *Whitehall* relate to something else than merely to the Affair of *Hudson's Bay* ; so Prince *George's* errand to *Denmark*, is of more importance than a bare Visit, or a naked Complement to his Brother. 'Tis upon this Design that all that great *Marine* Preparation hath been so long making in the several Ports of *England*; but to the hindring the execution whereof, some unexpected and not foreseen accidents have interposed. And it is in subserviency not to be disquieted at home, while he is carrying on this holy War abroad, that the *Declaration for Liberty of Conscience in England, and the Proclamation for a Toleration in Scotland*, are granted and published. 'Tis well enough known, how that after the *French King* had, among many other severities exercised against *Protestants*, made them uncapable of Employments and Commands ; yet to avoid the Consequences that might have ensued thereupon, while he was engaged in a War against the *Emperor*, the *King of Spain*, and the *States of Holland*, and to have the aid of his *Reformed Subjects*; he not only intermitted and abated in many other rigours towards them, but in *Anno* 1674, restored them to a capacity of being employed and preferred. And that this did not flow from any compassion, tenderness, or good-will towards them, his carriage since the issue of that War, and the miserable condition he hath reduc'd them to, does sufficiently testify and declare. Nor can we forget, how that the *late King*, after a rigorous execution of the *penal Laws* for several years against *Dissenters*; yet being to enter into an unjust War against the *United Provinces*, *Anno* 1672, not only forbore all proceedings of that kind, but published a *Declaration* for suspending the Execution of all those *Laws*, and for the allowing them liberty of assembling to worship God in their separate Meetings, without being hindred or disturbed. What Principle that proceeded from, and to what End it was calculated, appeared in his behaviour to them afterwards, when neither the danger the Nation was in from the *Papists*, nor the application of several *Parliaments*, could prevail for lenity towards them, much less for a *legal Repeal* of those impolitick and unreasonable Statutes. Nor does the present *Indulgence* flow from any kindness to *Fanaticks*, but it is only an artifice to stifle their Discontents, and to procure their assistance for the destroying of a *Foreign Protestant State*. And it may not be unworthy of observation, that as the *Declaration of Indulgence*, *Anno* 1672, bore date much about the same time with the *Declaration* of War against the *Dutch*; so at the very Season that his present *Majesty* emitted his *Declaration for Liberty of Conscience*, there were *Commissions* of *Reprisal* prepared and ready to be granted to the *English East-India Company* against the *Hollanders*, but which were suppressed upon the Court's finding that they whom the suspending the Execution of so many Laws, and the granting such Liberties, Rights and Immunities to the *Papists*, had disgusted and provoked, were far more numerous, and their resentments more to be apprehended, than they were, whose murmurings and discontents they had silenced and allay'd by the *Liberty* that was granted. Now as it will be at this juncture, when the *Protestant Interest* is so low in the World, and the *Reformed Religion* in so great danger of being destroyed, a most wicked as well as an imprudent Act, to contribute help and aid to the subjugating a People that are the chief *Protectors of the Protestant Religion* that are left ; and almost the only *Asserters* of the *Rights* and *Liberties of Mankind* ; so it may fill the *Addressers* with confusion and shame, that they should have not only justified an Act of His *Majesty*'s, that is plainly designed to such a mischievous End, but that they should by the Promises and Vows that they have made Him, have embolden'd His *Majesty* to continue his purposes and resolutions of a War against the *Dutch*; which as it must be funestous and fatal to the *Protestant Cause*, in case he should prosper and succeed ; so howsoever it should issue, yet the *Addressers*, who have done what in them lies to give encouragement unto it, will be held *Betrayers* of the *Protestant Religion*, both abroad and at home, and judged guilty of all the Blood of those of the same Faith with them that shall be shed in this Quarrel.

That *Liberty* ought to be allowed to men in matters of *Religion*, is no *Plea* whereby the *King's* giving it in an *illegal* and *arbitrary* manner, can be maintained and justified. Since ever I was capable of exercising any distinct and coherent acts of Reason, I have been always of that mind, that none ought to be persecuted for their Consciences towards God in matters of Faith and Worship. Nor is it one of those things that lie under the power of the *Sovereign* and *Legislative Authority*, to grant or not to grant ; but it is a Right settled upon Mankind antecedent to all *Civil Constitutions* and *Human Laws*, having its foundation in the *Law* of *Nature*, which no *Prince* or *State* can legitimately

mately violate and infringe. The Magistrate, as a CivilOfficer, can pretend nor claim no Power over a People, but what he either derives from the *Divine Charter*, wherein God, the Supreme Institutor of Magistracy, has chalk'd out the Duty of Rulers in general, or what the People, upon the first and original *Stipulation*, are supposed to have given him in order to the protection, peace and prosperity of the *Society*.   But as it does no where appear that God hath given any such Power to Governours, seeing all the Revelations in the Scripture, as well as all the Dictates of Nature, speak a contrary Language ; so neither can the People, upon their chusing such a one to be their Ruler, be imagined to tranfer and vest such a Power in him, forasmuch as they cannot divest themselves of a Power, no more than of a Right, of believing things, as they arrive with a Credibility to their several and respective Understandings.   As it is in no Man's power to believe as he will, but only as he sees cause ; so it is the most irrational Imagination in the World, to think they should transfer a Right to him whom they have chosen to govern them, of punishing them for what is not in their power to help.   Nor can any thing be plainer, than that God has reserved the *Empire* over *Conscience* to himself, and that he hath circumscribed the Power of all Human Governours to things of a civil and inferior nature.   And had God convey'd a Right unto Magistrates of commanding Men to be of this or that Religion, and that because they are so, and will have others to be of their mind ; it would follow, that the People may conform to whatsoever they require, tho' by all the Lights of Sense, Reason and Revelation, they are convinced of the Falshood of it : Seeing whatsoever the Sovereign *rightfully commands*, the *Subjects* may *lawfully obey*.   But tho' the prosecuting People, *for matters of meer Religion*, be repugnant to the Light of Nature, inconsistent with the Fundamental Maxims of Reason, directly contrary to the Temper and Genius, as well as to the Rules of the Gospel, and not only against the Safety and Interest of *Civil Societies*, but of a Tendency to fill them with Confusion, and to arm Subjects to the cutting one another's Throats ; yet Governors may both deny Liberty to those whose Principles oblige them to destroy those that are not of their mind, and may in some measure regulate the *Liberty* which they vouchsafe to others, whose Opinions, tho' they do not think dangerous to the Peace of the *Community*, yet through judging them erroneous and false, they conceive them dangerous to the Souls of Men. As there is a vast difference betwixt *tolerating* a Religion, and approving the Religion that is *tolerated* ; so what a *Government* doth not approve, but barely permits and suffers, may be brought under Restrictions as to time, place and number of those professing it, that shall assemble in one Meeting ; which it were an Undecency to extend to those of the justified and established way.   Now whatsoever *Restrictions* or *Regulations* are enacted, and ordained by the *Legislative Authority*, in reference to *Religions* or *religious Assemblies*, they are not to be stop'd, disabled or suspended, but by the same Authority that enacted and ordained them.   The King says very truly, *That Conscience ought not to be constrained, nor people forced in matters of meer Religion :*   But it does not from thence follow, (unless by the Logick of *Whitehall*) that without the concurrence of a Parliament, he should suspend and dispense with the Laws, and by a pretended Prerogative, relieve any from what they are obnoxious unto by the Statutes of the Realm.   His saying that the forcing People in matters of Religion, *spoils Trade, depopulates Countries, discourageth Strangers, and answers not the End of bringing all to an Uniformity, for which it was employ'd* ; would do well in a Speech to the Houses of Parliament, to persuade them to repeal some certain Laws ; or might do well to determine his Majesty to assent to such Bills as a Parliament might prepare and offer, for relieving Persons in matters of Conscience ; but does not serve for what it is alledged, nor can it warrant his suspending the Laws by his single Authority.   And by the way, I know when these very Arguments were not only despised by his Majesty, and ridiculed by those who took their *Cue* from Court, and had Wit to do it, as by the present Bishop of *Oxford*, in a very ill-natur'd Book, called *Ecclesiastical Polity* ; but when the daring to have mentioned them, would have provok'd the then Duke of *York's* Indignation, and have exposed the Party that did it, to discountenance and disgrace. The Question is not, what is convenient to be done in some measure and degree, and in reference to those whose Religion does not oblige them to destroy all that differ from them, when they have an opportunity for it ; but the Point in debate is, who hath the legal Power of doing it, and of fixing its Bounds and Limits.   It was never pretended that the King ought to be shut out from a share in *suspending* and *repealing Laws* ; but that the sole Right of doing it belongs to him, is what cannot be allowed, without changing the Constitution, and placing the whole Legislative Authority in his Majesty.   And as it is an *Usurpation* in the King to challenge it, and a *Treachery* in *English* Subjects to acknowledge it ; so the Inconveniencies that this or that Party are in the mean time exposed unto, through the *Laws* remaining in force, are rather to be endured, than that a Power of

giving

giving Eafe and Relief (farther than by Connivance) fhould be confeffed to refide in any *one,* in whom the Laws of the Community have not placed it. 'Tis better to undergo Hardfhips under the Execution of unjuft *Laws* ; than be releafed from our *Troubles,* by a Power ufurped over all Laws. For by the *one,* the *Meafures of Government,* as well as the Rights and Privileges of a Nation, are deftroyed; whereas by the other, only a part of the People are afflicted, and unduly dealt with. While we are governed by *Laws,* tho' feveral of them may be unjuft and inconvenient, yet we are under a Security as to all other things which thofe Laws have not made liable ; but when we fall under an illimited *Prerogative* and *Abfolute Power,* we have no longer a Title unto, or a Hedge about any thing, but all lies open to the Luft and Pleafure of him, in whom we have owned that Power to be feated. A *Liberty* is what *Diffenters* have a *Right* to *claim,* and which the *Legiflative Authority* is bound by the Rules of Juftice and Duty, as well as by *Principles* of *Wifdom* and *Difcretion,* to grant. And I am forry, that while they ftood fo fair to obtain it in a *Legal* and *Parliamentary* way, any of them by acknowledging a Right in another to give it, and that in a manner fo *fubverfive* of the Authority of *Parliaments,* fhould have rendred themfelves unworthy to receive it from them, to whom the Power of *Beftowing* it does belong. Not but that a *Toleration* will be always due to their Principles; but I know not whether the particular Men of thofe Principles, who have, by their *Addreffes,* betray'd the Kingdom, may not come to be judged to have forfeited all Share in it, for their Crime committed againft the Conftitution, and the whole Politick Society. Nor is there any thing more juft and equal, than that they who furrender and give away the Rights both of Legiflators and Subjects, fhould lofe all Grace and Favour from the former, and all Portion among the latter.

And how much foever fome Proteftant Diffenters may pleafe themfelves with the Liberty, that at prefent they enjoy in virtue of the two *Royal Papers* ; yet this may ferve to moderate them in their Tranfports of Gladnefs, that they have no folid Security for the Continuance of it. For fhould a *Parliament null* and make *void the Declaration for Liberty,* and *impeach the Judges* for declaring a power vefted in the King to fufpend fo many Laws, and for forbearing upon the *King's Mandate* to execute them ; the Freedom that the *Diffenters* poffefs, would immediately vanifh, and have much the fame Deftiny that the *Liberty* had, which was granted unto them by the *Declaration* of *Indulgence, Anno* 1672. Or fhould the *Parliament* be willing to grant Eafe and Indulgence to all Proteftants, by a Bill prepared for Repealing of all the Laws formerly made againft them, and fhould only be defirous to preferve in force the Laws relating to the *Oaths* of *Allegiance* and *Supremacy,* and the *Statutes* which enjoin the *Tefts,* of whofe Execution we never more wanted the Benefit, in order to our prefervation from *Popery,* and which an *English* Parliament cannot be fuppofed willingly to part with, at a time when our Lives, Eftates and Religion, are fo vifibly threatned to be fwallowed up, and deftroyed by the *Papifts :* In that cafe we may confidently believe, that the King, inftead either of *affenting* to fuch a Bill for feparate Favour to Proteftants, or perfevering in his Compaffion and Kindnefs of continuing the Sufpenfion of the Laws againft Diffenters, he would from an inveterate Enmity, as well as from a new-contracted Refentment, be ftirred up and enraged to the putting the Laws in execution with greater Rigour and Severity than hath been feen or felt heretofore. And all that the Addreffers would then reap by the *Declaration,* would be to undergo the furious Effects of Brutal Rage in their Perfecutors, and to be unpitied by the Kingdom, and unlamented by their Fellow-Proteftants. Or fhould his Majefty, in favour to his good *Catholicks,* refolve againft the Meeting of a *Parliament,* or to adjourn and prorogue them whenfoever he fhall find, that inftead of *confirming* what he hath done, they fhall make null his *Declaration,* vote his pretended Prerogative *Illegal* and *Arbitrary,* and fall upon thofe mercenary and perjured *Villains,* who have allowed him a *Power* tranfcendent to *Law* ; yet even upon that Suppofal, which is the beft that can be made, to fupport Mens hopes in the continuance of the prefent *Liberty,* the Proteftant Diffenters would have but flender Security ; all the Tenure they have for the Duration of their *Freedom,* being only precarious, and depending merely upon the *King's Word* and *Promife,* which there is fmall ground to rely upon. Nor can he be true to them, without being falfe to his *Religion,* which not only gives him leave to *break his Faith with Hereticks,* but obligeth him to it, and to deftroy them to boot ; and that both under the pain of Damnation, and of forfeiting his *Crown* and lofing his *Dominions.* And how far the *Promife* and *Royal Word* of a *Catholick Monarch* is to be trufted unto, and depended upon, we have a modern Proof and Evidence in the Behaviour of *Louis le Grand* towards his *Reformed Subjects,* not only in Repealing the many *Edicts* made and confirmed by himfelf, as well as his Anceftors, for the free Exercife of their Religion ; but in the Methods he hath always obferved

ferved, namely to promife them protection in the profeffion of their Faith, and practice of their Worfhip, when he was moft ftedfaftly refolved to fubvert their *Religion*, and was about making fome frefh advance, and taking fome new ftep for its Extirpation. Thus when he had firmly purpofed, not to fuffer a Minifter to continue a *year* in the Kingdom, he at the fame time publifhed an *Edict*, requiring Minifters to ferve but three Years in one Place, and not to return to the Church where they had firft *officiated*, till after the expiration of twenty Years. In the fame manner, when he had refolved, to repeal the Edict of *Nantes*, and had given injunction for the *Draught*, by which it was to be done, he, at the fame feafon, gave the Proteftants all affurances of Protection, and of the faid *Edict's* being kept inviolable. To which may be added, that fhameful and deteftable *Chicanery*, in paffing his Sacred and Royal Word, that no *violence* fhould be offered any for their *Religion*, tho' at that very moment, the *Dragoons* were upon their March, with orders of exercifing all manner of Cruelties and Barbarities, upon them. So that his Majefty of *Great Britain* hath a Pattern lately fent him, and that by the illuftrious Monarch whom he fo much admires, and whom he makes it his Ambition and Glory to imitate. Nor are we without proofs already, how infignificant the King's Promifes are, (except to delude) and what little confidence ought to be put in them. The difabling and fufpending the 13*th Statute* of his *late Parliament* in *Scotland*, wherein the *Teft* was confirmed, and his departing from all his Promifes regiftred in his *Letter*, as well as from thofe contained in the Speech made by the Lord Commiffioner, purfuant to the Inftructions which he had undoubtedly receiv'd, together with his having forgotten and receded from all his Promifes made to the *Church of England*, both when Duke of *York*, and fince he came to the Crown, are undeniable evidences, that his *Royal Word* is no more facred, nor binding, than that of fome other Monarchs ; and that whofoever of the Proteftants fhall be fo foolifh as to rely upon it, will find themfelves as certainly difappointed, and deceived, as they of the *Reformed Religion* elfewhere, have been. And while they of the *eftablifhed* Way, find fo fmall fecurity by the Laws, which the King is bound, by his *Coronation-Oath*, to obferve ; the *Diffenters* cannot expect very much, from a naked *Promife*, which as it hath not a folemn *Oath* to enforce it, fo 'tis both illegal in the making, and contrary to the principles of his *Religion* to keep. Nor is it unworthy of obfervation, that he hath not only departed from his Promifes made to the *Church of England*, but that we are told, in a late *Popifh* Pamphlet, intituled, *A new Teft of the Church of England's Loyalty*, publifhed (as itfelf fays) *by Authority*, that they were all *conditional*, (to wit, by virtue of fome Mental Refervation in his Majefty's Breaft) and that the *Conformable Clergy* having failed in performing the Conditions, upon which they were made, the *King* is abfolved, and difcharged, from all Obligation, of obferving them. The *Church of England*, (fays he) *muft give his Majefty leave not to nourifh a Snake in his Bofom, but rather to withdraw his Royal Protection, which was promifed, upon the account of her conftant fidelity.* Which as it is a plain threatning of all the *legal Clergy*, and a denunciation of the unjuft and hard meafure they are to look for; fo it fhakes the Foundation, upon which all credit unto, and reliance upon his Majefty's Word, can be any ways placed. For tho' *Threatnings* may have *tacit Referves*, becaufe the right of executing them refides in the *Threatner* ; yet *Promifes* are incapable of all *latent conditions*, becaufe every Promife vefts a Right in the *Promifee*, and that in virtue of the words in which it was made. But it is the lefs to be wondred at, if his Majefty fly to *Equivocations* and *mental Referves*, being both under the Conduct of that *Order*, and a Member of the *Society*, that firft taught and practifed this treacherous piece of *Chicanery*. However, it may inform the Diffenters, that if they be not able to anfwer the End, for which they are depended upon ; or be not willing in the manner and degree, that is expected; or if it be not for the Intereft of the Catholick Caufe, to have them indulged ; in all thefe cafes, and many more, the King may be pronounced acquitted, and difcharged from all the Promifes he hath given them, as having been meerly ftipulatory, and conditional. And as he will be fure then, *finem facere ferendæ alienæ perfonæ, to lay afide the difguife that he hath now put on* ; fo if they would reflect either upon his Temper, or upon his Religion, they might now know, *haud gratuitam in tanta fuperbia comitatem, that a perfon of his pride would not ftoop to fuch Flattery*, (as his Letter to Mr. *Alfop* expreffeth) *but in order to fome defign.* But what need other Proof of the fallacioufnefs of the two *Royal Papers*, and that no Proteftants can reafonably depend upon the *Royal Word*, there laid to pledge for the continuation of their Liberty, but to look into thefe two Papers themfelves, where we fhall meet expreffions, that may both detract from our belief of his Majefty's fincerity, and awaken us to a juft Jealoufy, that the Liberty, and Toleration, granted by them, are intended to be of no long ftanding and duration. For while he is pleafed to tell us, *that the granting his Subjects the free ufe of their Religion for the time to come, is an addition to the*

perfect

perfect Enjoyment of their Property, which has never been invaded by his Majesty since his coming to the Crown : He doth in effect say, that his Fidelity, Truth and Integrity, in what he grants, in reference to Religion, is to be measured and judged, by the Verity that is in what he tells us, as to the never having invaded our Property. And that I may borrow an Expression from Mr. *Alsop,* and to no less Person than to the *King* himself, namely, *That tho' we pretend to no refined Intellectuals, nor presume to philosophize upon Mysteries of Government, yet we make some pretence to the sense of Feeling, and whatever our Dullness be, can discern,* between what is exacted of us according to Law, and what we are robb'd of by an Excercise of arbitrary Power. For not to insist upon the violent seizure of Mens Goods, by Officers, as well as Soldiers, in all parts of *England,* which looks like an Invasion upon the Properties of the Subject ; nor to dwell upon his keeping an Army on foot in time of Peace, against the Authority, as well as without the Countenance of Law, which our *Ancestors* would have stiled an *Invasion* upon the whole Property of the *Kingdom ;* I would fain know, by what Name we are to call his levying the Customs, and the Additional Excise, before they were granted unto him by the Parliament ; all the legal Establishment of them upon the Nation, having been only, during the late King's Life, til' the Settlement of them upon the Crown was again renewed by Statute. It were also worth his Majesty's telling us, what *Titles* are due to the suspending the Vice-Chancellor of *Cambridge a Beneficio,* and the turning the President of *Magdalen's* in *Oxford,* out of his *Headship,* and the suspending Dr. *Fairfax* from his *Fellowship,* if there be not an *Invasion* upon our Property ; seeing every part of this is against all the known Laws of the Kingdom, and hath been done by no legal Court, but by a Set of mercenary Villains, armed with an arbitrary Commission, and who do as arbitrarily exercise it. And as the End unto which that *Inquisition* Court was instituted, was to rob us of our Rights and Privileges at the meer Pleasure of the King ; so the very Institution of it, is an Invasion both upon all our Laws, and upon the whole Property of the Nation, and is one of the highest Exercises of despotical Power, that it is possible for the most absolute and unlimited Monarch to exert. Among all the Rights reserved unto the Subjects by the Rules of the Constitution, and whereof they are secured by many repeated Laws and Statutes, there are none that have been hitherto less disputed, and in reference to which our Kings have been farther from claiming any Power and Authority, than those of levying Money without the Grant as well as the Consent of Parliament, and of *absolving* and *discharging Debtors* from paying their *Creditors,* and of *acquitting* them from being sued and imprisoned in case of Non-payment ; and yet in defiance of all Law, and to the subverting the Rights of the People, and the most essential Privilege and Jurisdiction of Parliaments, and to a plain changing the ancient legal Constitution into an *absolute* and *despotical* governing Power ; the King (they say) is assuming to himself an Authority, both of imposing a Tax of 5 *l.* *per Annum* upon every Hackney-Coach, and of releasing and discharging all Debtors, of whom their Creditors cannot claim and demand above 10 *l. Sterl.* which as they will be signal Invasions upon Property, and leading Cases for the raising Money in what other Instances he pleaseth, by a *Hampton Court* or a *Whitehall Edict,* without standing in need of a Parliament, or being obliged to a dependence upon their *Grant,* for all *Taxes* to be levied upon the Subjects, as his Predecessors have heretofore been ; so they may serve fully to instruct us what little Security either the Dissenters have, as to being long in the possession of their present Liberty, or Protestants in general of having a Freedom continued unto them of professing the reformed Religion, if we have nothing more to rely upon for preventing our being abridged and denied the Liberty of our Religion, than we have had for preserving our property from being invaded and broken in upon. We may subjoin to the Clause already mentioned, that other Expression which occurs in the foresaid Declaration, *viz.* That *as he freely gives them leave to meet and serve God after their own way and manner, so they are to take special care, that nothing be preached or taught among them, which may any ways tend to alienate the Hearts of the People from his Majesty or his Government :* Which words, as they import the price at which the Dissenters are to purchase their Freedom (whereof we shall discourse anon) so they admirably serve to furnish the King with a pretence of retrenching their Liberty whensoever he pleaseth ; nor are they inserted there for any other End, but that upon a plea of their having abused his *Gracious Indulgence, to the alienating the Hearts of his People from him,* they may be adjudged to have thereby deservedly forfeited, both all the Benefits of it, and of his Royal Favour. Nor is it possible for a Protestant Minister to preach one Sermon, which a Popish Critick, or a Romish Bigot, may not easily misconstrue and pervert, *to be an Alienation of the People's Hearts, from the King's Person and Government.* And of which, as we have heard many late Examples in *France,* so it will be easy to draw them into Precedent, and to imitate them in *England.* I might add the Observation of the ingenious *Author* of the *Reflections on his Majesty's Proclamation for a Toleration in* Scotland ; namely, that whereas the King gives all Assurance to his *Scots*

Subjects, that he will *not use invincible Necessity* against any Man, on the account of his Persuasion, he does thereby leave himself at a liberty of *Dragooning, Torturing, Burning,* and doing the utmost Violences, all these being vincible to a person of an ardent love to God, and of a lively Faith in *Jesus Christ* ; and which accordingly many Thousands have been triumphantly victorious over. Nor is it likely that this new and uncouth Phrase of *not using an invincible Necessity,* would have found room in a Paper of that nature, if it had not been first to conceal some malicious and mischievous Design, and then to justify the Consistency of its Execution, with what is promised in the Proclamation. Moreover, were there that Security intended by these two Royal Papers, that Protestant Dissenters might safely rely upon ; or did the King act with that Sincerity which he would delude his People into a Belief of, there would then be a greater agreeableness than there is, betwixt the *Declaration for Liberty of Conscience in England,* and the *Proclamation for a Toleration in Scotland.* The Principle that his Majesty pretends to act from, *That Conscience ought not to be constrained, and that none ought to be persecuted for meer matters of Religion,* would oblige him to act uniformly, and with an equal extension of favour to all his *Subjects,* whose Principles are the same, and against whom he hath no Exception, but in matters meerly Religious. Whereas the disparity of Grace, Kindness and Freedom, that is exercised in the *Declaration,* from that which is exerted in the *Proclamation,* plainly shews, that the whole is but a *Trick of State,* and done in subserviency to an end, which it is not yet seasonable to discover and avow. For his circumscribing the *Toleration* in *Scotland,* to such *Presbyterians* as he stiles Moderate, is not only a taking it off from its true Bottom, *matters of mere Religion,* and a founding it upon an *internal Quality* of the Mind, that is not discernable, but it implies the reserving a Liberty to himself, of withdrawing the Benefits of it from all *Scots Dissenters,* through fastning upon them a contrary *Character,* whensoever it shall be seasonable to revive Persecution. And even as it is now exerted to these *moderate ones,* it is attended with Restrictions, that his *Indulgence* in *England* is no ways clog'd with. All that the *Declaration* requires from those that are indulged, is, *That their Assemblies be peaceably, openly and publickly held, that all persons be freely admitted to them, that they signify and make known to some Justice of the Peace, what places they set apart for these uses ; and that nothing be preached or taught amongst them, which may any ways tend to alienate the Hearts of the People from the King or his Government :* Whereas the Proclamation not only restrains the Meetings of the *Scots Presbyterians* to *private Houses,* without allowing them either to build Meeting-Houses, or to use Out-houses or Barns ; but it prohibits the *hearing any Ministers,* save such as shall be willing to swear, *That they shall, to the utmost of their power, assist, defend and maintain the King, in the exercise of his absolute Power against all deadly.* Nor is it difficult to assign the reason of the Deformity that appears in his Majesty's present Actings towards his *Dissenting* Protestant Subjects in those two Kingdoms. For should there be no Restriction upon the *Toleration in Scotland,* to hinder the greatest part of the Presbyterians from taking the Advantage of it ; the Bishops and Conforming Clergy would be immediately forsaken by the generality, if not by all the People, and so an issue would not only be put to the Division among Protestants in that Kingdom, but they would become an united, and thereupon a formidable Body against *Popery,* which it is not for the Interest of the Roman Catholicks to suffer, or give way unto. Whereas the more unbounded the Liberty is, that is granted to Dissenters in *England,* the more are our Divisions not only kept up, but increased and promoted, (especially through this Freedom's arriving with them in an illegal way, without both the *Authority* of the *Legislative Power,* and the Approbation of a great part of the People) it being infallibly certain, that there is a vast number of all Ranks and Conditions, who do prefer the abiding in the Communion of the Church of *England,* before the joining in Fellowship with those of the *separate* and *dissenting Societies.* Upon the whole, this different Method of proceeding towards dissenting Protestants in *Matters merely Religious,* shews that all this *Indulgence* and *Toleration,* is a Trick to serve a present juncture of Affairs, and to advance a Popish and Arbitrary Design ; and that the *Dissenters* have no Security for the Continuance of their Liberty, but that when the Court and *Jesuitick* end is compassed and obtained, there is another Course to be steered towards them ; and instead of their hearing any longer of Liberty and Toleration, they are to be told, that it is the Interest of the Government, and the Safety and Honour of his Majesty, to have but *one Religion* in his Dominions, and that all must be Members of the Catholick Church ; and this because the King will have it so, which is the Argument that hath been made use of in the making so many Converts in *France.* They who now suffer themselves to be deluded into a Confidence in the Royal Word, will not only come to understand what Mr. *Coleman* meant, in his telling *Pere de la Chaise,* that the *Catholicks* in England *had a great work upon their hand, being about the Extirpation of that Heresy, which had born sway so long in this Northern part of the World* ; but they will also see and feel, how much of the Designs of *Rome* was represented in that passage of

P p p p p   the

the Pope's Nuncio's Letter, dated at *Bruſſels, Aug.* 9. 1674. wherein upon the Confidence which they placed in the Duke of *York,* which is not leſſened ſince he came to the Crown, he takes the confidence to write, *That they hoped ſpeedily to ſee the total and final Ruin of the Proteſtant Party.*

And as Proteſtant Diſſenters have no Security by the Declaration and Proclamation for the continuance of their Liberty, ſo they that have, by way of Thankſgiving, addreſſed to the King for thoſe Royal Papers, have not only acted very ill, in reference both to the Laws and Rights of the Kingdoms, and of Religion in general, but they have carried very unwiſely in relation to their own Intereſt, and the avoiding the Effects of that Reſentment, which moſt Men are juſtly poſſeſſed with, upon the illegal Emiſſion of theſe *Arbitrary* and *Prerogative Papers.* I ſhall not enter upon any long Diſcourſe, concerning this new Practice of *addreſſing* in general, it having been done elſewhere ſome years ago; but I ſhall only briefly intimate, that it was never in faſhion, unleſs either under a weak and precarious Government, or under one that took *illegal courſes,* and purſued a *different Intereſt* from that of the People and Community. As he who ruleth according to the ſtanding Laws of a Country over which he is ſet, needs not ſeek for an Approbation of his Actions from a part of his Subjects; the *Legality* of his Proceedings being the beſt *Juſtification* of him that governs, and giving the trueſt *Satisfaction* to them that are *ruled:* ſo he who enjoys the Love of his People, needs not look for Promiſes of being aſſiſted, ſtood by and defended, by any one Party or Faction among them; there being none from whom he can have the leaſt Apprehenſion of Oppoſition or Danger. It was the want of a *legal Title* in *Oliver Cromwel,* and his Son *Richard,* to the *Government,* that firſt begot this Device of *addreſſing,* and brought it upon the Stage in theſe *Britiſh* Nations; and it was the *arbitrary* Proceedures of the late King, as it is of his preſent Majeſty, and their acting upon a *diſtinct Bottom* from that of the Three Kingdoms, that hath revived, and does continue it. Nor is there any thing that hath rendred thoſe two *Princes* more contemptible abroad, and proclaimed them weaker at home, than their recurring unto, and ſolliciting the Flatteries and Aid of the mercenary, timorous, ſervile, and, for low and perſonal Ends, byaſs'd part of their Subjects; and thereby telling the World, that neither the Generality nor the moſt Honourable of their People, have been united in their Intereſt, nor Approvers of the Counſels that have been taken and purſued. And if any thing did ever caſt a Diſhonour upon the *Engliſh* Nation, it hath been that loathſome Flattery, and ſlaviſh Sycophancy, wherewith the *Addreſſers,* both now, and for ſome years paſt, have ſtuffed their Applications to the two *Royal Brothers.* The *Throne* that is ſuſtained and upheld by the *Pillars* of *Law* and *Juſtice,* needs not to hew out unto itſelf other *Supporters,* nor lean upon the crooked and weak Stilts of the inſignificant, and for the moſt part deceitful, as well as brib'd Vows, of a ſort of Men, who will be as ready upon the leaſt diſguſt, to cry *Crucify* to-morrow, as they were for being gratified, may be in their Luſts, Humours and Revenges, and at the beſt in ſome ſeparate Concern, to cry *Hoſanna* to-day. I ſhall decline proſecuting what concerns the Honour and Diſhonour of him, to whom the *Addreſſes* are made, or how politick or impolitick the countenancing and encouraging them is, and ſhall apply myſelf to this new *Sett* of *Addreſſers,* and endeavour to ſhew how fooliſhly as well as criminally they have acted. Nor is it an Argument either of their Prudence or Honeſty, or of their acting with any Conſiſtency to themſelves, that having ſo ſeverely inveighed againſt the *Addreſſes* that were in faſhion a few years ago, and having faſtened all the Imputations and Reproaches upon thoſe that were acceſſory to them, which that Rank of *Addreſſers* could be ſuppoſed to have deſerved; they now eſpouſe the Practice which they had condemned, and in reference to as arbitrary and unjuſtifiable an Act of his preſent Majeſty, as the moſt illegal one the late King was guilty of, or the worſt Exerciſe or Prerogative, for which any heretofore either commended, or promiſed to ſtand by him. For tho' the Matter and Subject of the Arbitrary Act of him now upon the Throne, be not, as to every Branch of it, ſo publickly ſcandalous, as ſome of the arbitrary Proceedings of the late King were, (as relating to a Favour which Mankind hath a juſt Claim unto) yet it is every way as illegal, being in reference to a Privilege, which his Majeſty hath no Authority to grant and beſtow. And were it not that there are many Diſſenters, who preſerve themſelves innocent at this Juncture, and upon whom the Temptation that is adminiſtred, makes no impreſſion; the World would have juſt ground to ſay, that the *Fanaticks* are not governed by Principles, but that the Meaſures they walk by, are what conduceth to their private and perſonal Benefit, or what lies in a Tendency to their Loſs and Prejudice: And that it was not the late King's uſurping and exerting an arbitrary and illegal Power that offended them, but that they were not the *Objects* in whoſe Favour it was exerciſed. 'Tis alſo an Aggravation of their *Folly,* as well as their *Offence,* that they ſhould revive a Practice which the Nation was grown aſham'd of, and whereof they who had been guilty begun to repent, through having ſeen that all the former *Declarations, Aſſurances* and *Promiſes* of the *Royal Brothers,* which tempted to Applications of that kind, were but ſo many Juggles, peculiar to the late *Breed* of the Family, for the deceiving of Mankind ; and that never one of them was performed and made good. But the Tranſgreſſion, as well as the Imprudence, of the preſent *Addreſſers,* is yet the greater, and they are the more criminal and inexcuſable before God and Men, in that they might have enjoyed all the Benefits of the *King's Declaration,* without acknowledging the Juſtice of the *Authority* by which it was granted, or making themſelves the Scorn and Contempt of all that are truly Honeſt and Wiſe, by their ſervile Adulations, and their Gratulatory Scriblers, unbecoming *Engliſh*-Men and *Proteſtants.* They had no more to do, but to continue their *Meetings,* as they had ſometimes heretofore uſed to do, without taking notice that the preſent Suſpenſion of the Laws, made their aſſembling together more ſafe, and freed them from Apprehenſions of Fines and Impriſonments. Nor could the King, how much ſoever diſpleaſed with ſuch a Conduct, have at this time ventured upon the expreſſing Diſpleaſure againſt them ; ſeeing as that would have been both to have proclaimed his Hypocriſy, in ſaying, *That Conſcience ought not to be conſtrained, nor People forced in matters of meer Religion,* and a diſcovering the villainous Deſign, in ſubſerviency to which the Declaration had been emitted ; ſo it were not poſſible for him, after what he hath publiſhed, to ſingle out the Diſſenters from amongſt other *Proteſtants* ; and to fall upon all, before Matters are more ripe for it, might be a means of the abortion of all his Popiſh Projections, and of ſaving the whole *Reformed* Intereſt in *Great Britain.* Neither would the Church of *England-men* have envied their Tranquillity, or have blamed their Carriage ; but would have been glad that their *Brethren* had been eaſed from Oppreſſions, and themſelves delivered from the grievous and diſhonourable Taſk of proſecuting them, which they had formerly been forced unto by *Court-Injunctions* and *Commands.* And as they would have, by a Conduct of this nature, had all the Freedom which they now enjoy, without the Guilt and Reproach which they have derived upon themſelves by *Addreſſing* ; ſo ſuch a *Carriage* would have wonderfully recommended them to the Favour of a true *Engliſh* Parliament, which tho' it would ſee cauſe to condemn the King's uſurping a Power of *ſuſpending* the Laws, and to make void his *Declaration* ; yet in gratitude to *Diſſenters* for ſuch a Behaviour, as well as in Pity and Compaſſion to them as *Engliſh* Proteſtants, ſuch a Parliament would not fail to do all it could, to give them relief in a legal way. Whereas if any thing enflame and exaſperate the Nation, to revive their Sufferings, it will ariſe from a Reſentment of the unworthy and treacherous Carriage of ſo many of them, in this critical and dangerous Juncture. But the *Terms,* which through their *Addreſſing,* they have owned the receiving their *Liberty* and *Indulgence* upon, does in a peculiar manner enhance their Guilt againſt God and their Country, and ſtrangely adds to the Diſguſt and Anger, which Lovers of *Religion,* and the Laws of the Nation have conceived againſt them. For it is not only upon the Acknowledgment of a Prerogative in the King over the Laws, that they have received, and now hold their *Liberty* ; but it is upon the Condition, *That nothing be preached or taught amongſt them, that may any ways tend to alienate the Hearts of the People from his Majeſty's Perſon and Government.* He muſt be of an Underſtanding very near allied unto, and approaching to that of an *Iriſh-man,* who does not know what the *Court-Senſe* of that Clauſe is ; and that his Majeſty thereby intends, that they are not to preach againſt *Popery,* nor to ſet forth the Doctrines of the *Romiſh* Church in *Terms* that may prevent the People's being infected by them, much leſs in Colours that may render them hated and abhorred. To accuſe the *King's Religion* of *Idolatry,* or to affirm the Church of *Rome* to be the *Apocalyptick Babylon,* and to repreſent the *Articles* of the *Tridentine Faith,* as faithful Miniſters of *Chriſt* ought to do, would be accounted an *alienating the Hearts of their Hearers from the King and his Government* ; which as they are in the foreſaid Clauſes required not to do, ſo they have, by their *Addreſſing,* confeſſed the *Juſtice* of the *Terms,* and have undertaken to hold their Liberty by that *Tenor:* And to give them their due, they have been very faithful hitherto, in conforming to what the King exacts, and in obſerving what themſelves have aſſented to the Equity of. For notwithſtanding all the Danger from Popery, that the *Nation* is expoſed unto, and all the Hazard that the *Souls* of Men are in, of being poiſoned with *Romiſh Principles* ; yet inſtead of *Preaching* or *Writing* againſt any of the *Doctrines* of the Church of *Rome,* they have agreed among themſelves, and with ſuch of their Congregations as approve their Proceedure, not ſo much as to mention them ; but to leave the *Province* of defending our *Religion,* and of detecting the Falſhood of *Papal Tenets,* to the Paſtors and Gentlemen of the Church of *England.* And being aſk'd (as I know ſome of them that have been) why they do not preach againſt *Antichriſt,* and confute the *Papal*

Doctrines; they very gravely reply, that by *preaching Christ*, they *preach* against *Anti-christ*; and that by *teaching the Gospel*, they *refute Popery*: which is such a piece of fraudulent and guileful Subterfuge, that I want Words to express the knavery and criminalness of it. What a reserve and change have I lived to see in *England*, from what I beheld a few years ago! It was but the other day that the *conformable Clergy* were represented by some of the *Dissenters*, not only as favourers of Popery, but as endeavouring to hale it in upon us by all the methods and ways that lay within their circle ; and yet now the whole *defence* of the reformed Religion, must be entirely devolved into their hands ; and when all the *Sluices* are pulled up, that had been made to hinder Popery from overflowing the *Nation*, they must be left alone to stem the Inundation, and prevent the Deluge. They among the *Fanaticks* that boasted to be the most avowed and irreconcileable Enemies of the Church of *Rome*, are not only become altogether silent, when they see the Kingdom pester'd with a *swarm* of busy and seducing *Emissaries* ; but are both turn'd Advocates for that Arbitrary Paper, whereby we are surrender'd as a Prey unto them, and do make it their business to detract from the Reputation, and discourage the Labours of the *National Ministers*, who with a *Zeal* becoming their *Office*, and a Learning which deserves to be admir'd, have set themselves in opposition to that *croaking Fry*, and have done enough by their excellent and inimitable Writings, to save People from being deluded or perverted, if either unanswerable confutations of Popery, or demonstrative defences of the Articles and Doctrines of the reformed Religion can have any efficacy upon the minds of Men. Among other fulsom Flatteries adorning a Speech made to his Majesty by an *Addressing Dissenter*, I find this hypocritical and shameful *Adulation* ; namely, *that if there should remain any seeds of Disloyalty in any of his Subjects, the transcendent goodness exerted in his Declaration, would mortify and kill them.* To which he might have added with more truth, that the same *transcendent Goodness* had almost destroyed all the seeds of their honesty, and mortified their care and concernment for the Interest of *Jesus Christ*, and for the Reformed Religion. Their old strain of zealous preaching against the Idolatry of *Rome*, and concerning *the coming out of Babylon my people*, are grown out of fashion with them in *England*, and are only reserved, and laid by, to recommend them to the kindness and acceptation of Foreign Protestants, when their occasions and conveniences draw them over to *Amsterdam*. Whoever comes into their *Assemblies*, would think, for any thing that he there hears delivered from their Pulpits, that *She* which was the *Whore of Babylon* a few years ago, was now become a *Chaste Spouse* ; and that what were heretofore the damnable *Doctrines* of *Popery*, were of late turned *innocent* and *harmless Opinions*. The King's Declaration would seem to have brought some of them to a *melius inquirendum* ; and as they are already arrived to believe a *Roman Catholick the best King*, that they may in a little time come to believe the *Papists* to be the best Christians. *The keeping back nothing that is profitable to such as hear them, and the declaring the whole Counsel of God*; that are the terms upon which they received their Commission from *Jesus Christ*, and wherein they have *Paul's* Practice and Example for a Pattern, would seem to be things under the *Power of the Royal Prerogative*, and that the King may supersede them by the Authority, by which he dispenses with the *Penal Statutes*. Which as it is very agreeable unto, and imported in his Majesty's Claim of being obeyed without *reserve*; so the owning this *absolute* Power, with that annex of challenged *obedience*, does acquit them from all obligations to the *Laws of Christ*, when they are found to interfere with what is required by the King. But whether *God's* Power or the *King's*, be *superior*, and which of the two can cassate the other's Laws, and whose wrath is most terrible, the Judgment-day will be able and sure to instruct them, if all means in this World prove insufficient for it. The *Addressers* know upon what *conditions* they hold their *Liberty*; and they have not only observed how several of the *National Clergy* have been treated for *preaching* against *Popery*, but they have heard how divers of the *reformed Ministers* in *France* (before the general Suppression) were dealt with for speaking against their *Monarch's Religion*; and therefore they must be pardoned, if they carry so as not to provoke his Majesty, tho' in the mean time, through their Silence, they both betray the *Cause* of their *Lord* and *Master*, and are unfaithful to the *Souls* of those, of whom they have taken upon them the spiritual Guidance. As for the Papers themselves, that are stiled by the name of *Addresses*, I shall not meddle with them, being as to the greatest part of them, fitter to be exposed and ridicul'd, either for their dullness and pedantry, or for the adulation and sycophancy with which they are fulsomly stuft, than to deserve any serious consideration, or to merit Reflections that may prove instrumentive to Mankind. Only, as that *Address* wherein his Majesty is thank'd for his restoring *God to his Empire over Conscience*; deserveth a rebuke for its Blasphemy ; so that other, which commends him for promising, *to force the Parliament to ratify his Declaration* (tho' by the way all he says is, *that he does not doubt of their concurrence*, which yet his ill success upon the Closetting so many Members, and his since dissolving that Parliament, shews that there was some cause for the

doubting

doubting of it) I say, that other Address merits a severe Censure for its Insolency against the *legislative Authority*. And the *Authors* of it ought to be punished for their crime committed against the *Liberty* and *Freedom* of the *two Houses*, and for encouraging the King to invade and subvert their most essential and fundamental Privileges; and without which, they can neither be a Council, Judicature, nor Lawgivers.

After all, I hope the Nation will be so ingenuous, as not to impute the Miscarriages of some of the *Non-conformists* to the whole *Party*, much less to ascribe them to the Principles of *Dissenters*. For as the *points* wherein they differ from the Church of *England*, are purely of another nature, and which have no relation to *Politicks*, so the influence that they are adapted to have upon Men as Members of *Civil Societies*, is to make them in a special manner regardful of the Rights and Franchises of the Community. But if some neither understand the tendency of their own Principles, nor are true and faithful unto them; these things are the personal faults of those men, and are to be attributed to their ignorance, or to their dishonesty; nor are their Carriages to be counted the effects of their *religious Tenets*, much less are others of the Party to be involved under the reproach and guilt of their imprudent and ill conduct. Which there is the more cause to acknowledge, because tho' the *Church of England* has all the reason of the world, to decline *Addressing*, in that all her *legal Foundation*, as well as *Security*, is shaken by the *Declaration*; yet there are some of her Dignitaries and Clergy, as well as divers of the Members of her Communion, who upon motives of Ambition, Covetousness, Fear, or Courtship, have enrolled themselves into the List of *Addressers*; and under pretence of giving thanks to the King for his promise of *protecting the Archbishops, Bishops, and Clergy, and all other of the Church of* England *in the free exercise of their Religion, as by Law established*; have cut the throat of their *Mother*, at whose breasts they have suck'd till they are grown fat, both by acknowledging the *usurped Prerogative* upon which the King assumes the Right and Authority of emitting the *Declaration*; and by exchanging the *legal* standing and security of their *Church*, into that precarious *one* of the *Royal Word*, which they fly unto as the *bottom of her Subsistence*, and trust to as the *Wall of her defence*. And as most of the Members of the separate *Societies*, are free from all accession to *addressing*, and the few that concurred were meerly drawn in by the wheedle and importunity of their Preachers; so they who are of the chiefest *Character*, and greatest reputation for Wisdom and Learning among the Ministers, have preserved themselves from all folly and treachery of that kind. The *Apostle* tells us, *that not many wise, not many noble are called*; which as it is verified in many of the *Dissenting Addressers*, so it may serve for some kind of Apology for their low and sneaking, as well as for their indiscreet and imprudent behaviour in this matter. And it is the more venial in some of them, as being not only a means of ingratiating themselves (as they fancy) with the King, who heretofore had no very good opinion of them; but as being both an easy and compendious method of *Atoning for Offences* against the *Crown*, of which they were strongly suspected; and a cheap and expenceless way of purchasing the pardon of their Relations, that had stood actually *accused of High Treason*. Nor is it to be doubted, but that as the King will retain very little favour and mercy for *Fanaticks*, when once he has served his Ends upon them; so they will preserve as little kindness for the Papists, if they can but obtain relief in a legal way. And as there is not a People in the Kingdom, that will be more *loyal* to Princes, while they continue so to govern as that Fealty by the Laws of God or Man remains due to them; so there are none, of what Principles or Communion soever, upon whom the Kingdom in its whole Interest come to lie at stake, may more assuredly and with greater confidence depend, than upon the generality of *Dissenting Protestants*, and especially upon those that are not of the *Pastoral Order*. The Severities that the *Dissenters* lay under before, and their deliverance from Oppression and Disturbance now, seconded with the *King's* expectation and demands of thanksgiving *Addresses*, were strong Temptations upon men void of generosity and greatness of Spirit, and who are withal of no great political Wisdom, nor of prospect into the Consequences of Councils and Tricks of State, to act as illegally in their *thanks*, as his Majesty had done in his *bounty*. So that whatsoever Animadversion they may deserve, should they be proceeded against according to their demerit; yet it is to be hoped, that both they, and the *Addressers* of the former stamp, may all find room in an *Act* of *Indemnity*, and that the *Mercy* of the *Nation* towards them, will triumph over and get the better of its *Justice*. As it would argue a strange and judicial infatuation, should they proceed to farther excesses, and think to escape the Punishment due to one Crime, by committing and taking sanctuary in another, thro' improving their Compliments into Actions of Treachery; so all their hope of Pardon, as well as of Lenity and Moderation, from a true *Protestant* and rightly constituted *Authority*, depends upon their conduct and behaviour henceforward, and their not suffering themselves to be hurried and deluded into a co-

2   Qqqqq   operation

operation with the Court for the obtaining of a Popifh Parliament. All their endeavours of that kind, would but more clearly detect, and manifeft, their treachery to *Religion* and the *Kingdom*, it not being in their power to out-vote the honeft *Englifh* part of the People, fo as to help the King to fuch a Houfe of Commons as he defires ; and were it poffible, that thro' their affiftance, in conjunction with violence and tricks, ufed in Elections and Returns by the Court, fuch a Houfe of Commons might be obtained, as would be ferviceable to Arbitrary and Papal Ends; yet neither the King nor they would be the nearer the compaffing what is aim'd at : it being demonftrable that the *Majority* of the Houfe of Lords, are never to be wrought over to juftify this *illegal Declaration*, or to grant the King a Power of *fufpending Laws* at his pleafure ; nor to give their *Affent* to a Bill for the *repealing* the *Teft-Acts*, and the *Statutes* that enjoin and require the *Oaths* of *Allegiance* and *Supremacy*. And if they fhould be fo far left of God, and betray'd by thofe among themfelves whom the Court hath gained, as to become guilty of fo enormous an Act of folly and villany; and fhould the Election of the next *Parliament, be the happy Juncture they wait for*, and the improving their Intereft, as well as the giving their own Votes for the Choice of Papifts in the Houfe of Commons, be what they mean *by an effential proof of their Loyalty, and of the fincerity of their humble Addreffes, and that whereby they intend to demonftrate, that the greateft thing they have promifed, is the leaft thing they will perform for his* Majefty's *fervice and fatisfaction:* as in that cafe, they will deferve to forfeit all hopes of being forgiven ; fo it would be an infidelity to God and Men, and a cruelty to our felves and our Pofterity, not to abandon them as *Betrayers of Religion* ; expunge them out of the Roll of *Proteftants* ; ftrip them of all that wherein *free Subjects* have a legal Right; and not to condemn them to the utmoft punifhments, which the *Laws* of the Kingdom adjudge the worft of Traitors and Malefactors unto. There are fome, who thro' hating of them, do wifh their mifcarrying and offending to fo unpardonable a degree, that they may hereafter be furnifhed with an advantage, both of ruining them and the whole diffenting Party for their fakes. But as the love that I bear unto them, and the perfuafion and belief I have of the truth of their *religious Principles*, do make me exceeding follicitous to have them kept and prevented from being hurried and tranfported into fo fatal and criminal a behaviour ; fo I defire to make no other excufe for my plain dealing towards them, but that of *Solomon*, who tells us, *that faithful are the wounds of a Friend, while the kiffes of an Enemy are deceitful* ; and that he *who rebukes a man, fhall find more favour afterwards than he who flattereth with his tongue.*

See Mr. Alfop's Speech to the King.

P O S T S C R I P T.

SInce the foregoing Sheets went to the Prefs, and while they were printing off, there is come to my hands a new *Proclamation* dated at *Windfor* the 28th of *June* 1687, for granting a further Liberty in *Scotland*, and which was publifhed there by an Order of the Privy Council of that Kingdom, bearing date at *Edinburgh* the 5th of *July*. This *Superfœtation* of one Proclamation after another in reference to the fame thing, is fo apportioned and parallel to the late *French* method of emitting Edicts in relation to thofe of the *Reformed Religion* in that Kingdom, that they feem to proceed out of one *Mint*, to be calculated for the fame end, and to be defigned for the compaffing and obtaining the like effects. For as foon as an *Alarm* was taken at the publifhing fome unreafonable and rigorous Edict, there ufed often to follow another of a milder ftrain, which was pretended to be either for the moderating the feverities of the former, or to remove and rectify what they were pleafed to call mifconftructions unduly put upon it ; but the true end whereof was only to ftifle and extinguifh the Jealoufies and Apprehenfions that the other had begotten and excited, and which, had they not been calmed and allay'd, might have awaken'd the Proteftants there to provide for their fafety by a timely withdrawing into other Countries, if they had not been provoked to generous endeavours of preventing the final fuppreffion of their Religion, and for obviating the ruin which that Court had projected againft them, and was haftning to involve them under. Nor does my fufpicion of his Majefty's purfuing the fame defign againft Proteftants, which the great *Louis* glories to have accomplifhed, proceed meerly from that Conjunction of Counfels that all the World obferves between *Whitehall* and *Verfailles* ; nor meerly from the King's abandoning his Nephew and Son-in-law the Prince of *Orange*, and not fo much as interpofing to obtain fatisfaction to be given him, for the many Injuries, Damages, Spoils and Robberies, as well as Affronts done him by that haughty Monarch, when one vigorous Application could not fail to effect it ; nor yet meerly from that

agree-

agreeableneſs in their proceedures, through the King of *England*'s imitating that foreign *Potentate*, and making the whole courſe that hath been taken in *France*, the *Pattern* of all his actings in *Great Britain*: But I am much confirmed in my fears and jealouſies, by remembring a Paſſage in one of Mr. *Coleman*'s *Letters*, who as he very very well knew what the then Duke of *York* had been for many years engaged in, againſt our Religion and Civil Liberties, and under what Vows and Promiſes he was, not to deſiſt from proſecuting what had been reſolved upon and undertaken; ſo he had the confidence to ſay, *that his Maſter's deſign, and that of the King of* France, *was one and the ſame*; and that this was no leſs, as he farther informs us, than the *extirpating the Northern Hereſy*. Had the King of *England* acted with ſincerity from that noble Principle, *that Conſcience ought not to be conſtrained, nor People forced in matters of meer Religion*, as he would delude weak and eaſy People to believe; and had not all his arbitrary and illegal Proceedings, in granting Liberty to diſſenting Proteſtants, been to ſubſerve and promote other Deſigns, which it is not yet ſeaſonable and convenient to diſcover and avow, he would have then acted with that conformity to the Principle he profeſſeth to be under the Influence and Government of, and with that conſonancy and harmonious agreeableneſs, in all the degrees of Indulgence, vouchſafed to thoſe of the Reformed Religion in *England* and *Scotland*, that differ from them of the eſtabliſhed Way, that there would have needed no ſecond *Proclamation* apporting new meaſures of Liberty, and favour to *Scots* Diſſenters, ſeeing they would have had it granted them at firſt in the ſame latitude and illimitedneſs, that it was beſtowed upon the *Engliſh* Non-conformiſts. But when Princes carry on and purſue miſchievous deſigns, under the palliations of Religion, publick Good, and the Right of Mankind; it comes often to paſs through adapting their methods to what they mean and intend, and not to what they pretend and give out, that their crafty projections by not being ſufficiently accommodated to their purpoſes, prove ineffectual to the compaſſing what was aimed at; and this forceth them to a new Game of Falſhood and Subtilty, but ſtill under the old varniſh and gloſs, and obligeth them to have recourſe to means that may be more proportioned than the former were, for their reaching the End that they ultimately drive at. Thence it is that thoſe Rulers, who are engaged in the Proſecution of wicked and unjuſtifiable Deſigns, are neceſſitated not only to apply themſelves to oppoſite Methods towards different *Parties*, and thoſe ſuch as muſt be ſuited and apportioned to their diſcrepant Intereſt, without the accommodating of which they can neither hope to mould them to that tame and ſervile Compliance, nor work them up to that active and vigorous abetting of their malicious and crafty Projections as is neceſſary for the rendring them ſucceſsful; but they are forced to vary their proceedings towards one and the ſame *Party*, and that as well when the ways they have acted in towards them are found inadequate to the end unto which they were calculated, as when the miſchief hid under them comes to be too ſoon diſcovered. This, weak and ſhort-ſighted People fancy to ariſe from an uncertainty in Princes Counſels, and from their being at no conſiſtency with themſelves; but they who can penetrate into Affairs, and that do conſider things more narrowly, can eaſily diſcern, that all this Variation, Diverſity, and ſhifting of Methods in Rulers Actings, proceed from other Cauſes, and that it is their Stability and Perſeverance in an illegal and wicked Deſign, that compels them to thoſe crooked and contrary Courſes, either for the gaining the unwary and ill-applied Concurrence of their Subjects, to the haſtning Diſtreſs and Deſolation upon themſelves, or for the throwing them into that Lethargy, and under that Supineneſs, as may hinder them from all Endeavours of obſtructing and diverting the Evils, that their Governours are ſeeking to bring upon them. Nor is there a more certain Indication of a Prince's being engaged in a Deſign, contrary to the good and happineſs of the Society, over which he is ſet; than his betaking himſelf to illegal ways, upon pretence of promoting the eaſe and benefit of his people; or according as he finds his Subjects to differ in their particular Intereſts, his applying himſelf to them in Methods, whereof the contrariety of the one to the other, renders them the more proper and adapted to enſnare the divided Factions, through accoſting each of them with ſomething that they are ſeverally fond of. *Legal Means* are always ſufficient to the purſuing and compaſſing *legal Ends*; and whatſoever is for the general good of the Community, may either be obtained by Courſes, wherein the Generality find their united Intereſt and common Felicity, or elſe by Application to a Parliament freely and duly choſen, which as it repreſents the whole Politick Society, ſo there may be expected moſt Compaſſion and Tenderneſs, as well as Wiſdom and Prudence, for redreſſing the Grievances, eaſing the Troubles, and providing for the Benefit and Safety of all that are wrapt up in and repreſented by them. And as every Prince, who ſincerely ſeeks and purſues the Advantage of his People, will ſo adjuſt and attemper all his Actions towards them, that his whole Carriage ſhall be uniform, and all the Exerciſes of his governing Power,

meet

meet in the benefit of the *Community*, as so many Lines from a *Circumference* uniting in their *Centre* ; so there needs no other proof that these *two* or *three* late Actions of his Majesty, which a foolish sort of Men are apt to interpret for Favours, and to account them effects of Compassion and Kindness ; are but to conceal his Malice, and to subserve as well as cover some fatal and pernicious Design that he is carrying on against his Protestant Subjects, than that while he is gratifying a few of them in one thing, he is at the same time robbing all of them of many ; and that while he is indulging the *Dissenters* with a freedom from the *penal Laws* for matters of Religion, he is invading the *Properties*, and subverting the *Civil Rights* of the three Nations, and changing the whole Constitution of the Government.   He that strips us of what belongs unto us as we are *English* and *Scots-men*, cannot mean honestly in the Favours he pretends to vouchsafe us as we are Christians ; nor can he that is endeavouring to enslave our Persons, and to subject our Estates to his arbitrary Lust and Pleasure, intend any thing else by this kindness granted to *Fanaticks* in matters of Religion, than the dividing them from the rest of the People, in what concerns the *Civil Interest* and external Happiness of the *Community*, and to render them an engaged Faction to assist and abet him in enthralling the Kingdoms.   Whosoever considers the whole Tenor of his Majesty's other Actings, in proroguing and dissolving *Parliaments*, when he finds them uncompliant with his Popish and despotical Ends ; his keeping on foot a formidable Army against all the Laws of the Land, and upon no other intention, but to maintain him in his Usurpations over our Rights, and to awe us into a tame and servile submission to his *Prerogative* Will ; his filling all places of *Judicature* with weak as well as treacherous persons, who instead of administring Justice may be the *Instruments of Tyranny* ; his robbing men of their Estates, by judicial *Forms*, and under pretence that *nullum tempus occurrit Regi*, after they have been quietly enjoyed by the Subjects for several hundred years ; his advancing none to Civil or Military Employs, but whom he hath some confidence in, as to the finding them ready to execute his despotical Injunctions ; and his esteeming no persons *loyal* and *faithful* to himself, save those who are willing to betray their Country, and be Rebels and Traitors against the *legal Constitution*: I say, whosoever considers all this, and a great deal more of the same hue and complexion, cannot imagine (unless he be under a judicial blindness and a strange infatuation) that any thing arriving from the King, tho' it may be a matter wherein they may find their present ease and advantage, should proceed from compassion and good-will to his Protestant Subjects, but that it must be only in order to promote a distinct interest from that of his People, and for the better and more easy accomplishing of some wicked and unjustifiable Design.   And tho' his Majesty would have us believe, that the reasons moving him to the emission of this *second Proclamation*, *were the sinistrous Interpretations which either have, or may be made, of some Restrictions in his former* ; yet it is not difficult, even without being of his Privy Council, to assign a truer motive, and a more real and effectual cause of it.   For as that of the 12th of *February* came forth attended with so many limitations, not easy to be digested by men of Wisdom or Honesty, left if it had been more unconfined and extensive, and should have opened a Door for all *Scots* Dissenters to have gone in and taken the benefit of it, the generality of Protestants in that Kingdom, abstracting from the Bishops, Curates, and a few others, should have joined in the *separate* Interest, and thereby have become an united Body against Popery ; but upon finding that hardly any would purchase their Freedom from the *penal Laws* at so dear a rate, as to do things so unbecoming Men and Christians, as the conforming to the *Terms* therein prescribed obliged them unto ; and as they of the *National Communion* were alarmed and disgusted, so few or none of the *Dissenting Fellowships* were pleased ; and that both were not only angry at the many illegal Favours, and threatning Advantages bestowed upon the Papists, but were grown so sensible of the Design carrying on against the Protestant Religion, and the Liberties and Privileges of the Subject, that tho' they could not renounce their respective Tenets in the matters wherein they differed, yet they were willing to stifle their Heats and Animosities, and to give that Encouragement, Aid and Assistance to one another, as was necessary for their common Safety: upon these *Considerations*, his Majesty (if he would have spoken sincerely) ought to have said, that he had published this new *Proclamation*, in order to hinder *Scots Protestants* from uniting, for their mutual defence against *Turkish* Tyranny, and *Romish* Idolatry, in hopes thereby to continue and exasperate their undue and passionate heats, and to keep them not only in divided and opposite interests, but to make them contribute to the suppressing and ruining each other, or at least to look on unconcernedly, till he have ripened his Designs against them both, and be prepared for extirpating the Reformed Religion, and for subverting the Fundamental as well as Statute Laws, and for bringing such to the Stake and Gibbet, as shall have the Integrity to assert the one, or the Courage to plead for the other.   And

yet

yet in his *laſt Proclamation*, wherein he grants a more illimited Freedom, than in the former, and promiſeth to protect *all in the Exerciſe of* Their *Proteſtant Religion*, as he diſdainfully and ignominiouſly calls it ; there is a Clauſe that may diſcourage all honeſt Men from owing their *Liberty* to the Authority that beſtows it, and from which it is derived and conveyed to them. For not being ſatisfied to ſuperſtruct his pretended Right, of *ſuſpending*, *ſtopping*, and *diſabling Laws*, upon his *Sovereign Authority* and *Prerogative Royal*, but as knowing that theſe give no ſuch Pre-eminence and Juriſdiction over the *Laws* of the *Kingdom*, he is pleaſed to challenge unto himſelf an *Abſolute Power*, as the Source and Spring of that exorbitant and paramount Claim, which he therein exerciſeth and exerts. And foraſmuch as *Abſolute Power* imports his *Majeſty*'s being looſe and free from all Ties and Reſtraints, either by *Fundamental Stipulations*, or ſuperadded *Laws* ; it is very natural to obſerve, that he allows the Government under which we were born, and to which we were ſworn and ſtood bound, to be hereby ſubverted and changed, and that thereupon we are not only abſolved and acquitted, from the Allegiance and Fealty, we were formerly under to his *Majeſty*, but are indiſpenſably obliged by the Ties and Engagements that are upon us, of maintaining and defending the Conſtitution and Government, to apply our ſelves to the uſe of all Means and Endeavours againſt him, as an Enemy of the People, and a Subverter of the legal Government, wherein all the Intereſt he had, or could lawfully claim, was an *Official Truſt*, and not an *Abſolute Power* or a *Deſpotical Dominion*, the firſt whereof he had depoſed and abdicated himſelf from, by challenging and uſurping the latter. And ſhould any *Scots Diſſenter*, either in his entrance upon the *Liberty* granted by this *Proclamation*, or in *addreſſing* by way of Thankfulneſs for it, take the leaſt notice of this Freedom's flowing from the King, which cannot be done, without *recognizing* this *Abſolute Power* in his *Majeſty* as the Fountain of it, he is to be look'd upon as the worſt of Traitors, and deſerves to be proceeded againſt both for his Acceſſion unto, and juſtifying the ſubverſion of the Laws, Liberties and Government of his Country, and for betraying the Rights of all Free-born Men. For thoſe few Reflections in the foregoing Sheets, which this new *Proclamation* may not only ſeem to render uſeleſs, and fruſtrate the end whereunto they were intended, but may make the publiſhing any Animadverſions upon that, which the King, by departing from, does himſelf cenſure and condemn, be eſteemed both a failure in Ingenuity and Candor, and a want of regard to thoſe Meaſures of Juſtice, which ought to be obſerved towards all Men, and more eſpecially towards Crowned Heads : I ſhall only ſay, that as the *Proclamation* arrived with me too late, to hinder and prevent the Communication of them to the Publick, ſo I have this farther to add, in juſtification of their being publiſhed, that it will thereby appear, that what his *Majeſty* ſtiles *Siniſtrous Interpretations made of ſome Reſtrictions mentioned in his former*, are no other than the juſt, natural, genuine, and obvious Conſtructions, which they lie open unto, and are capable of, and which a Man cannot avoid faſtening upon them, without renouncing all Senſe and Reaſon. And while the King continues to diſparage and aſperſe all ſober and judicious *Reflections* upon that Royal Paper, by charging upon them the unjuſt and reproachful Character of *Siniſtrous Interpretations* ; it is neceſſary, as well as equal, that the whole matter ſhould be plainly and impartially repreſented to the World, and that the Detection be remitted and left to the underſtanding and unbyaſs'd part of Mankind who are the Calumniators and Slanderers, they who accuſe the *Proclamation* of importing ſuch Principles, Conſequences, and Tendencies, or he and his *Miniſters*, who think they have avoided and anſwered the Imputations faſtned upon it, when they have loaded them with hard and uncivil Terms. For tho' he be pleaſed to aſſume to himſelf an *Abſolute Power*, *which all are bound to obey without reſerve* ; and in virtue of which he *ſuſpends*, *ſtops* and *diſables* what *Laws* he pleaſeth, yet I do not know but that his Intellectuals being of the Size of other Mens, and that ſeeing neither his Sovereignty, nor *Catholicalneſs*, have veſted in him an Inerrability, why we may not enter our Plea, and demur to the Dictates of his Judgment, tho' we know not how to withſtand the Efforts of his Power. Nor ſhall I ſubjoin any more, ſave that whereas his *Majeſty* declares ſo many Laws *to be diſabled to all intents and purpoſes*, he ought to have remembred, that beſide other *Intents* and *Purpoſes*, that ſeveral of them may hereafter ſerve unto, as the Papiſts may poſſibly come to have Experience ; there is one thing, in reference to which he cannot, even at preſent, hinder and prevent their Uſefulneſs and Efficacy, and that is, not only their raiſing and exciting all juſt Reſentments in the Minds of freeborn and generous Men, for his challenging a Power to *ſuſpend* and *caſſate* them, but their remaining and continuing *Monuments* of his Infidelity to the Truſt repoſed in him, of his departure from all Promiſes made at and ſince his entring upon the Government, and of his invading and ſubverting all the Rules of the Conſtitution.

The Declaration of His Highness William Henry *(by the Grace of God) Prince of* Orange, &c. *Of the Reasons inducing him to appear in Arms in the Kingdom of* England, *for Preserving of the Protestant Religion, and for Restoring the Laws and Liberties of* England, Scotland *and* Ireland.

IT is both certain and evident to all Men, that the publick Peace and Happiness of any State or Kingdom cannot be preserved, where the Laws, Liberties and Customs established, by the lawful Authority in it, are openly transgressed and annulled: More especially where the Alteration of *Religion* is endeavoured, and that a *Religion* which is contrary to Law is endeavoured to be introduced: Upon which those that are most immediately concerned in it, are indispensably bound to endeavour to preserve and maintain the established Laws, Liberties and Customs, and above all, the *Religion* and *Worship* of God that is established among them: And to take such an effectual Care, that the Inhabitants of the said State or Kingdom may neither be deprived of their *Religion*, nor of their Civil Rights. Which is so much the more necessary, because the Greatness and Security both of Kings, Royal Families, and all such as are in Authority, as well as the Happiness of their Subjects and People, depend, in a most especial manner, upon the exact Observation and Maintenance of these their Laws, Liberties and Customs.

Upon these grounds it is, that we cannot any longer forbear to declare, that to our great Regret, we see that those Counsellors, who have now the chief Credit with the King, have overturned the Religion, Laws and Liberties of those Realms; and subjected them in all things relating to their Consciences, Liberties and Properties, to Arbitrary Government; and that not only by secret and indirect ways, but in an open and undisguised manner.

Those evil Counsellors for the advancing and colouring this with some plausible Pretexts, did invent and set on foot, the King's *Dispensing Power*; by virtue of which, they pretend, that according to *Law*, he can *suspend* and *dispense* with the Execution of the *Laws*, that have been enacted by the Authority of the King and Parliament, for the Security and Happiness of the Subject, and so have rendered those Laws of no effect: Tho' there is nothing more certain, than that as no Laws can be made, but by the joint Concurrence of King and Parliament, so likewise Laws so enacted, which secure the publick Peace and Safety of the Nation, and the Lives and Liberties of every Subject in it, cannot be repealed or suspended, but by the same Authority.

For tho' the King may pardon the Punishment that a Transgressor has incurred, and to which he is condemned, as in the cases of *Treason* or *Felony*; yet it cannot be with any colour of Reason inferred from thence, that the King can entirely suspend the Execution of those Laws, relating to *Treason* and *Felony:* Unless it is pretended that he is cloathed with Despotick and Arbitrary Power, and that the Lives, Liberties, Honours and Estates of the Subjects, depend wholly on his Good-will and Pleasure, and are entirely subject to him; which must infallibly follow, on the King's having a Power to *suspend* the Execution of *Laws*, and to *dispense* with them.

Those evil Counsellors, in order to the giving some Credit to this strange and execrable Maxim, have so conducted the Matter, that they have obtained a Sentence from the Judges, declaring that this *Dispensing Power* is a Right belonging to the Crown; as if it were in the power of the Twelve Judges, to offer up the Laws, Rights and Liberties of the whole Nation to the King, to be disposed of by him arbitrarily, and at his Pleasure, and expresly contrary to Laws enacted, for the Security of the Subjects. In order to the obtaining this Judgment, those evil Counsellors did before-hand examine secretly the Opinion of the Judges, and procured such of them, as could not in Conscience concur in so pernicious a Sentence, to be turned out, and others to be substituted in their rooms, till by the Changes which were made in the Courts of Judicature, they at last obtained that Judgment. And they have raised some to those Trusts, who make open Profession of the Popish Religion, tho' those are by Law rendred incapable of all such Employments.

It is also manifest and notorious, that as his Majesty was, upon his coming to the Crown, received and acknowledged by all the Subjects of *England, Scotland* and *Ireland*, as their King, without the least Opposition, tho' he made then open Profession of the *Popish Religion*; so he did then promise, and solemnly swear, at his Coronation, that
he

he would maintain his Subjects in the free Enjoyment of their Laws, Rights and Liberties, and in particular, that he would maintain the *Church of* England *as it was eftablifhed by Law:* It is likewife certain, that there have been at divers and fundry times, feveral Laws enacted for the Prefervation of thofe Rights and Liberties, and of the Proteftant Religion: And among other Securities, it has been enacted, That all Perfons whatfoever, that are advanced to any Ecclefiaftical Dignity, or to bear Office in either Univerfity; as likewife all others, that fhould be put in any Employment, Civil or Military, fhould declare that they were not Papifts, but were of the Proteftant Religion, and that by their taking of the Oaths of *Allegiance* and *Supremacy,* and the *Teft*; yet thefe evil Counfellors have, in effect, annulled and abolifhed all thofe Laws, both with relation to Ecclefiaftical and Civil Employments.

In order to Ecclefiaftical Dignities and Offices, they have not only without any colour of Law, but againft moft exprefs Laws to the contrary, fet up a Commiffion of a certain number of Perfons, to whom they have committed the Cognizance and Direction of all Ecclefiaftical Matters; in the which Commiffion there has been and ftill is, one of His Majefty's Minifters of State, who makes now publick Profeffion of the Popifh Religion, and who at the time of his firft profeffing it, declared that for a great while before, he had believed that to be the only true Religion. By all this the deplorable State to which the Proteftant Religion is reduced is apparent, fince the Affairs of the Church of *England* are now put into the Hands of Perfons, who have accepted of a Commiffion that is manifeftly illegal, and who have executed it contrary to all Law; and that now one of their chief Members has abjured the *Proteftant Religion,* and declared himfelf a *Papift,* by which he is become incapable of holding any publick Employment: The faid Commiffioners have hitherto given fuch proof of their Submiffion to the Directions given them, that there is no reafon to doubt, but they will ftill continue to promote all fuch Defigns as will be moft agreeable to them. And thofe evil Counfellors take care to raife none to any Ecclefiaftical Dignities, but Perfons that have no Zeal for the Proteftant Religion, and that now hide their Unconcernednefs for it, under the fpecious Pretence of *Moderation.* The faid Commiffioners have fufpended the Bifhop of *London,* only becaufe he refufed to obey an Order that was fent him to fufpend a worthy Divine, without fo much as citing him before him, to make his own Defence, or obferving the common Forms of Procefs. They have turned out a Prefident, chofen by the Fellows of *Magdalen* College, and afterwards all the Fellows of that College, without fo much as citing them before any Court that could take legal Cognizance of that Affair, or obtaining any Sentence againft them by a Competent Judge. And the only reafon that was given for turning them out, was their refufing to chufe, for their Prefident, a Perfon that was recommended to them, by the Inftigation of thofe evil Counfellors; tho' the Right of a free Election belonged undoubtedly to them. But they were turned out of their Freeholds, contrary to Law, and to that exprefs Provifion in the *Magna Charta, That no Man fhall lofe Life or Goods, but by the Law of the Land.* And now thefe evil Counfellors have put the faid College wholly into the hands of Papifts, tho', as is above faid, they are incapable of all fuch Employments, both by the Law of the Land, and the Statutes of the College. Thefe Commiffioners have alfo cited before them all the Chancellors and Arch-deacons of *England,* requiring them to certify to them the Names of all fuch Clergy-men as have read the King's Declaration for *Liberty of Confcience,* and of fuch as have not read it; without confidering that the reading of it was not enjoined the Clergy by the Bifhops, who are their Ordinaries. The Illegality and Incompetency of the faid Court of the Ecclefiaftical Commiffioners was fo notorioufly known, and it did fo evidently appear, that it tended to the Subverfion of the Proteftant Religion, that the moft Reverend Father in God, *William* Archbifhop of *Canterbury,* Primate and Metropolitan of all *England,* feeing that it was raifed for no other end, but to opprefs fuch Perfons as were of eminent Virtue, Learning and Piety, refufed to fit or to concur in it.

And tho' there are many exprefs Laws againft all Churches or Chappels, for the Exercife of the Popifh Religion, and alfo againft all Monafteries and Convents, and more particularly againft the Order of the *Jefuits*; yet thofe evil Counfellors have procured orders for the building of feveral Churches and Chappels, for the Exercife of that Religion: They have alfo procured divers Monafteries to be erected, and in contempt of the Law, they have not only fet up feveral Colleges of *Jefuits,* in divers places, for the corrupting of the Youth, but have raifed up one of the *Order* to be a Privy-Counfellor and a Minifter of State. By all which they do evidently fhew, that they are reftrained by no Rules or Law whatfoever; but that they have fubjected the Honours and Eftates of the Subjects, and the eftablifhed Religion to a Defpotick Power, and to Arbitrary Government; in all which they are ferved and feconded by thofe Ecclefiaftical Commiffioners.

They

They have alfo followed the fame Methods with relation to Civil Affairs: For they have procured orders to examine all Lords-Lieutenants, Deputy-Lieutenants, Sheriffs, Juftices of Peace, and all others that were in any publick Employment, if they would concur with the King in the Repeal of the *Teft* and *Penal Laws*; and all fuch, whofe Confciences did not fuffer them to comply with their Defigns, were turned out, and others were put in their places, who they believed would be more compliant to them, in their defigns of defeating the Intent and Execution of thofe Laws, which had been made with fo much Care and Caution for the Security of the *Proteftant Religion.* And in many of thofe places they have put profeffed Papifts, tho' the Law has difabled them, and warranted the Subjects not to have any regard to their Order.

They have alfo invaded the Privileges, and feized on the Charters of moft of thofe Towns that have a right to be reprefented by their Burgeffes in Parliament ; and have procured Surrenders to be made of them, by which the Magiftrates in them have delivered up all their Rights and Privileges, to be difpofed of at the pleafure of thofe evil Counfellors ; who have thereupon placed new Magiftrates in thofe Towns, fuch as they can moft entirely confide in ; and in many of them they have put Popifh Magiftrates, notwithftanding the Incapacities under which the Law has put them.

And whereas no Nation whatfoever can fubfift without the Adminiftration of good and impartial Juftice, upon which Men's Lives, Liberties, Honours and Eftates do depend ; thofe evil Counfellors have fubjected thefe to an Arbitrary and Defpotick Power : In the moft important Affairs they have ftudied to difcover before-hand the Opinions of the Judges ; and have turned out fuch, as they found would not conform themfelves to their Intentions ; and have put others in their places, of whom they were more affured, without having any regard to their Abilities. And they have not ftuck to raife even profeffed Papifts to the Courts of Judicature, notwithftanding their Incapacity by Law, and that no regard is due to any Sentences flowing from them. They have carried this fo far, as to deprive fuch Judges, who in the common Adminiftration of Juftice, fhew that they were governed by their Confciences, and not by the Directions which the others gave them : By which it is apparent, that they defign to render themfelves the abfolute Mafters of the Lives, Honours and Eftates of the Subjects, of what Rank or Dignity foever they may be ; and that without having any regard either to the Equity of the Caufe, or to the Confciences of the Judges, whom they will have to fubmit in all things to their own Will and Pleafure ; hoping by fuch ways to intimidate thofe other Judges, who are yet in Imployment, as alfo fuch others as they fhall think fit to put in the rooms of thofe whom they have turned out; and to make them fee what they muft look for, if they fhould at any time act in the leaft contrary to their good liking; and that no Failings of that kind are pardoned in any Perfons whatfoever. A great deal of Blood has been fhed in many places of the Kingdom, by Judges governed by thofe evil Counfellors, againft all the Rules and Forms of Law ; without fo much as fuffering the Perfons that were accufed to plead in their own Defence.

They have alfo, by putting the Adminiftration of Juftice in the hands of Papifts, brought all the Matters of Civil Juftice into great Uncertainties ; with how much exactnefs and juftice foever thefe Sentences may have been given. For fince the Laws of the Land do not only exclude Papifts from all places of Judicature, but have put them under an Incapacity, none are bound to acknowledge or to obey their Judgments, and all Sentences given by them, are null and void of themfelves ; fo that all Perfons who have been caft in Trials before fuch Popifh Judges, may juftly look on their pretended Sentences, as having no more Force than the Sentences of any private and unauthorifed Perfon whatfoever. So deplorable is the cafe of the Subjects, who are obliged to anfwer to fuch Judges, that muft in all things ftick to the Rules which are fet them by thofe evil Counfellors, who as they raifed them up to thofe Employments, fo can turn them out of them at pleafure, and who can never be efteemed lawful Judges ; fo that all their Sentences are in the Conftruction of the Law, of no Force and Efficacy. They have likewife difpofed of all Military Employments in the fame manner : For tho' the Laws have not only excluded Papifts from all fuch Employments, but have in particular provided that they fhould be difarmed ; yet they, in contempt of thofe Laws, have not only armed the Papifts, but have likewife raifed them up to the greateft Military Trufts, both by Sea and Land, and that Strangers as well as Natives, and *Irifh* as well as *Englifh*, that fo by thefe means they have rendred themfelves Mafters both of the Affairs of the Church, of the Government of the Nation, and of the Courfe of Juftice, and fubjected them all to a Defpotick and Arbitrary Power, they might be in a capacity to maintain and execute their wicked Defigns, by the Affiftance of the Army, and thereby to enflave the Nation.

The

The difmal Effects of this Subverfion of the eftablifhed Religion, Laws and Liberties in *England,* appear more evidently to us, by what we fee done in *Ireland* ; where the whole Government is put into the hands of Papifts, and where all the Proteftant Inhabitants are under the daily Fears of what may be juftly apprehended from the Arbitrary Power which is fet up there ; which has made great Numbers of them leave that Kingdom, and abandon their Eftates in it, remembring well that cruel and bloody Maffacre which fell out in that Ifland in the year 1641.

Thofe evil Counfellors have alfo prevailed with the King to declare in *Scotland,* that he is cloathed with *Abfolute Power,* and that all the Subjects are bound *to obey him without referve* ; upon which he has affumed an Arbitrary Power, both over the Religion and Laws of that Kingdom ; from all which it is apparent, what is to be looked for in *England,* as foon as Matters are duly prepared for it.

Thofe great and infufferable Oppreffions, and the open Contempt of all Law, together with the Apprehenfions of the fad Confequences that muft certainly follow upon it, have put the Subjects under great and juft Fears ; and have made them look after fuch lawful Remedies as are allowed of in all Nations ; yet all has been without effect. And thofe evil Counfellors have endeavoured to make all Men apprehend the lofs of their Lives, Liberties, Honours and Eftates, if they fhould go about to preferve themfelves from this Oppreffion by Petitions, Reprefentations, or other means authorifed by Law. Thus did they proceed with the Archbifhop of *Canterbury,* and the other Bifhops, who having offered a moft humble Petition to the King, in Terms full of Refpect, and not exceeding the number limited by Law, in which they fet forth in fhort, the Reafons for which they could not obey that Order, which by the Inftigation of thofe evil Counfellors was fent them, requiring them to appoint their Clergy to read in their Churches the Declaration for *Liberty of Confcience* ; were fent to Prifon, and afterwards brought to a Trial, as if they had been guilty of fome enormous Crime. They were not only obliged to defend themfelves in that purfuit, but to appear before profeffed Papifts, who had not taken the Teft, and by confequence were Men whofe Intereft led them to condemn them ; and the Judges that gave their Opinions in their favour, were thereupon turned out.

And yet it cannot be pretended that any Kings, how great foever their Power has been, and how Arbitrary and Defpotick foever they have been in the Exercife of it, have ever reckoned it a Crime for their Subjects to come in all Submiffion and Refpect, and in a due Number, not exceeding the Limits of the Law, and reprefent to them the Reafons that made it impoffible for them to obey their Orders. Thofe evil Counfellors have alfo treated a Peer of the Realm as a Criminal, only becaufe he faid, that the Subjects were not bound to obey the Orders of a Popifh Juftice of Peace ; tho' it is evident, that they being by Law rendred incapable of all fuch Truft, no regard is due to their orders : This being the Security which the People have by the Law for their Lives, Liberties, Honours and Eftates, that they are not to be fubjected to the arbitrary Proceedings of Papifts, that are, contrary to Law, put into any Employments Civil or Military.

Both we our felves, and our Deareft and moft entirely Beloved Confort, the Princefs, have endeavoured to fignify in Terms full of Refpect to the King, the juft and deep Regret which all thefe Proceedings have given us ; and in compliance with his Majefty's Defires fignified to us, we declared both by word of mouth, to his Envoy, and in Writing, what our Thoughts were, touching the Repealing of the *Teft and Penal Laws* ; which we did in fuch a manner, that we hoped we had propofed an Expedient, by which the Peace of thofe Kingdoms, and a happy Agreement among the Subjects, of all Perfuafions, might have been fettled : but thofe evil Counfellors have put fuch ill Conftructions on thefe our good Intentions, that they have endeavoured to alienate the King more and more from us ; as if we had defigned to difturb the Quiet and Happinefs of the Kingdom.

The laft and great Remedy for all thofe Evils, is *the calling of a Parliament,* for fecuring the Nation againft the evil Practices of thofe wicked Counfellors ; but this could not be yet compaffed, nor can it eafily be brought about. For thofe Men apprehending, that a lawful Parliament being once affembled, they would be brought to an account for all their open Violations of Law, and for their Plots and Confpiracies againft the Proteftant Religion, and the Lives and Liberties of the Subjects, they have endeavoured, under the fpecious Pretence of *Liberty of Confcience,* firft to fow Divifions among Proteftants, between thofe of the Church of *England,* and the Diffenters : The Defign being laid to engage Proteftants, that are all equally concerned, to preferve themfelves from Popifh Oppreffion, into mutual Quarrellings ; that fo by thefe, fome Advantages might be given to them to bring about their Defigns ; and that both in the Election of the Members of Parliament, and afterwards in the Parliament it felf. For they fee well, that if all Proteftants could enter into a mutual good Underftanding one with another, and concur together in the preferving of their Religion, it would not be poffible for them to

compafs

compaſs their wicked ends. They have alſo required all Perſons in the ſeveral Counties of *England*, that either were in any Employment, or were in any conſiderable Eſteem, to declare before-hand, that they would concur in the Repeal of the *Teſt and Penal Laws*, and that they would give their Voices in the Elections to Parliament, only for ſuch as would concur in it. Such as would not thus pre-engage themſelves, were turned out of all Employments; and others who entered into thoſe Engagements were put in their places, many of them being Papiſts. And contrary to the Charters and Privileges of thoſe Boroughs, that have a Right to ſend Burgeſſes to Parliament, they have ordered ſuch Regulations to be made, as they thought fit and neceſſary, for aſſuring themſelves of all the Members that are to be choſen by thoſe Corporations; and by this means they hope to avoid that Puniſhment which they have deſerved; tho' it is apparent, that all the Acts made by Popiſh Magiſtrates, are null and void of themſelves; ſo that no Parliament can be lawful, for which the Elections and Returns are made by Popiſh Sheriffs and Mayors of Towns; and therefore as long as the Authority and Magiſtracy is in ſuch hands, it is not poſſible to have any lawful Parliament. And tho' according to the Conſtitution of the *Engliſh* Government, and Immemorial Cuſtom, all Elections of Parliament-men ought to be made with an entire Liberty, without any ſort of Force, or the requiring the Electors to chuſe ſuch Perſons as ſhall be named to them; and the Perſons thus freely elected, ought to give their Opinions freely, upon all Matters that are brought before them, having the Good of the Nation ever before their Eyes, and following in all things the Dictates of their Conſcience; yet now the People of *England* cannot expect a Remedy from a free Parliament, legally called and choſen. But they may perhaps ſee one called, in which all Elections will be carried by Fraud or Force, and which will be compoſed of ſuch Perſons, of whom thoſe evil Counſellors hold themſelves well aſſured, in which all things will be carried on according to their Direction and Intereſt, without any regard to the Good and Happineſs of the Nation. Which may appear evidently from this, that the ſame Perſons tried the Members of the laſt Parliament, to gain them to conſent to the Repeal of the *Teſt and Penal Laws*; and procured that Parliament to be diſſolved, when they found that they could not, neither by Promiſes nor Threatnings, prevail with the Members to comply with their wicked Deſigns.

But to crown all, there are great and violent Preſumptions, inducing us to believe, that thoſe evil Counſellors, in order to the carrying on of their ill Deſigns, and to the gaining to themſelves the more time for the effecting of them, for the encouraging of their Complices, and for the diſcouraging of all good Subjects, have publiſhed, that the *Queen* hath brought forth a *Son*; tho' there have appeared both during the *Queen's* pretended Bigneſs, and in the manner in which the Birth was managed, ſo many juſt and viſible Grounds of Suſpicion, that not only we our ſelves, but all the good Subjects of thoſe Kingdoms, do vehemently ſuſpect, that the pretended Prince of *Wales* was not born by the *Queen*. And it is notoriouſly known to all the World, that many both doubted of the Queen's Bigneſs, and of the Birth of the Child; and yet there was not any one thing done to ſatisfy them, or to put an end to their Doubts.

And ſince our Deareſt and moſt Entirely Beloved Conſort, the Princeſs, and likewiſe we our ſelves, have ſo great an Intereſt in this Matter, and ſuch a Right, as all the World knows, to the Succeſſion of the Crown; ſince alſo the *Engliſh* did in the Year 1672, when the States General of the *United Provinces* were invaded in a moſt unjuſt War, uſe their utmoſt Endeavours to put an end to that War, and that in oppoſition to thoſe who were then in the Government; and by their ſo doing, they run the hazard of loſing both the Favour of the Court, and their Employments: And ſince the *Engliſh* Nation has ever teſtified a moſt particular Affection and Eſteem both to our Deareſt Conſort the Princeſs, and to our ſelves, We cannot excuſe our ſelves from eſpouſing their Intereſts, in a matter of ſuch high Conſequence, and from contributing all that lies in us, for the maintaining both of the Proteſtant Religion, and of the Laws and Liberties of thoſe Kingdoms, and for the ſecuring to them the continual Enjoyment of all their juſt Rights. To the doing of which, we are moſt earneſtly ſolicited by a great many Lords, both Spiritual and Temporal, and by many Gentlemen and other Subjects of all Ranks.

Therefore it is, that we have thought fit to go over to *England*, and to carry over with us a Force, ſufficient, by the Bleſſing of God, to defend us from the Violence of thoſe evil Counſellors. And we being deſirous that our Intentions in this may be rightly underſtood, have for this end prepared this *Declaration*, in which as we have hitherto given a true Account of the Reaſons inducing us to it, ſo we now think fit to declare, that this our Expedition is intended for no other Deſign, but to have a free and lawful Parliament aſſembled as ſoon as is poſſible; and that in order to this, all the late Charters, by which

which the Elections of Burgeſſes are limited contrary to the ancient Cuſtom, ſhall be conſidered as null and of no force: And likewiſe all Magiſtrates who have been unjuſtly turned out, ſhall forthwith reſume their former Imployments, as well as all the Boroughs of *England* ſhall return again to their ancient Preſcriptions and Charters: And more particularly that the ancient Charter of the Great and famous City of *London* ſhall again be in force: And that the Writs for the Members of Parliament ſhall be addreſſed to the proper Officers, according to Law and Cuſtom. That alſo none be ſuffered to chooſe or to be choſen Members of Parliament, but ſuch as are qualified by Law: And that the Members of Parliament, being thus lawfully choſen, they ſhall meet and ſit in full Freedom, that ſo the two Houſes may concur in the preparing of ſuch Laws, as they upon full and free Debate ſhall judge neceſſary and convenient, both for the confirming and executing the Law concerning the *Teſt*, and ſuch other Laws as are neceſſary for the Security and Maintenance of the Proteſtant Religion; as likewiſe for making ſuch Laws as may eſtabliſh a good Agreement between the Church of *England*, and all Proteſtant Diſſenters, as alſo for the covering and ſecuring of all ſuch, who will live peaceable under the Government as becomes good Subjects, from all Perſecution, upon the account of their Religion, even *Papiſts* themſelves not accepted; and for the doing of all other things, which the Two Houſes of Parliament ſhall find neceſſary for the Peace, Honour and Safety of the Nation; ſo that there may be no more danger of the Nation's falling at any time hereafter, under *Arbitrary Government*. To this Parliament we will alſo refer the Enquiry into the Birth of the pretended Prince of *Wales*, and of all things relating to it, and to the Right of Succeſſion.

And we, for our part, will concur in every thing that may procure the Peace and Happineſs of the Nation, which a free and lawful Parliament ſhall determine; ſince we have nothing before our Eyes, in this our Undertaking, but the Preſervation of the Proteſtant Religion, the covering of all Men from Perſecution for their Conſciences, and the ſecuring the whole Nation the free Enjoyment of all their Laws, Rights and Liberties, under a Juſt and Legal Government.

This is the Deſign that we have propoſed to our ſelves, in appearing upon this occaſion in Arms: In the Conduct of which, we will keep the Forces under our Command, under all the Strictneſs of Martial Diſcipline; and take a ſpecial care, that the People of the Countries, through which we muſt march, ſhall not ſuffer by their means: And as ſoon as the State of the Nation will admit of it, we promiſe that we will ſend back all thoſe foreign Forces that we have brought with us.

We do therefore hope that all People will judge rightly of us, and approve of theſe our Proceedings: But we chiefly rely on the Bleſſing of God, for the Succeſs of this our Undertaking, in which we place our whole and only Confidence.

We do, in the laſt place, invite and require all Perſons whatſoever, all the Peers of the Realm, both Spiritual and Temporal, all Lords-Lieutenants, Deputy-Lieutenants, and all Gentlemen, Citizens, and other Commons of all Ranks, to come and aſſiſt us, in order to the executing of this our Deſign, againſt all ſuch as ſhall endeavour to oppoſe us; that ſo we may prevent all thoſe Miſeries which muſt needs follow, upon the Nation's being kept under Arbitrary Government and Slavery: And that all the Violences and Diſorders, which have overturned the whole Conſtitution of the *Engliſh* Government, may be fully redreſſed, in a *Free and Legal Parliament*.

And we do likewiſe reſolve, that as ſoon as the Nations are brought to a State of Quiet, we will take care that a Parliament ſhall be called in *Scotland*, for the reſtoring the ancient Conſtitution of that Kingdom, and for bringing the Matters of Religion to ſuch a Settlement, that the People may live eaſy and happy, and for putting an end to all the unjuſt Violences that have been in a courſe of ſo many Years committed there.

We will alſo ſtudy to bring the Kingdom of *Ireland* to ſuch a State, that the Settlement there may be religiouſly obſerved; and that the Proteſtant and *Britiſh* Intereſt there may be ſecured. And we will endeavour, by all poſſible means, to procure ſuch an Eſtabliſhment in all the Three Kingdoms, that they may all live in a happy Union and Correſpondence together; and that the Proteſtant Religion, and the Peace, Honour and Happineſs of thoſe Nations, may be eſtabliſhed upon laſting Foundations.

Given under our Hand and Seal, at our Court at the Hague, *the Tenth Day of* October, *in the Year* 1688.

William Henry, *Prince of* Orange.

By His Highneſs's Special Command,

C. HUYGENS.

His

His Highnefs's Additional Declaration.

AFter we had prepared and printed this our Declaration, we have underftood, that the Subverters of the Religion and Laws of thofe Kingdoms, hearing of our Preparations to affift the People againft them, have begun to retract fome of the Arbitrary and Defpotick Powers that they had affumed, and to vacate fome of their unjuft Judgments and Decrees. The Senfe of their Guilt, and the Diftruft of their Force, have induced them to offer to the City of *London*, fome feeming Relief from their great Oppreffions; hoping thereby to quiet the People, and to divert them from demanding a fecure Re-eftablifhment of their Religion and Laws under the fhelter of our Arms. They do alfo give out, that we intend to conquer and enflave the Nation: And therefore it is, that we have thought fit to add a few words to our Declaration.

We are confident, that no Perfons can have fuch hard thoughts of us, as to imagine that we have any other Defign in this Undertaking, than to procure a Settlement of the Religion, and of the Liberties and Properties of the Subjects upon fo fure a Foundation, that there may be no danger of the Nation's relapfing into the like Miferies at any time hereafter. And as the Forces that we have brought along with us, are utterly difproportioned to that wicked Defign of conquering the Nation, if we were capable of intending it, fo the great Numbers of the principal Nobility and Gentry, that are Men of eminent Quality and Eftates, and Perfons of known Integrity and Zeal both for the Religion and Government of *England*; many of them being alfo diftinguifhed by their conftant Fidelity to the Crown, who do both accompany us in this Expedition, and have earneftly folicited us to it, will cover us from all fuch malicious Infinuations. For it is not to be imagined, that either thofe who have invited us, or thofe that are already come to affift us, can join in a wicked Attempt of Conqueft, to make void their own lawful Titles to their Honours, Eftates and Interefts. We are alfo confident, that all Men fee how little weight there is to be laid, on all Promifes and Engagements that can be now made; fince there has been fo little regard had in time paft, to the moft folemn Promifes. And as that imperfect Redrefs that is now offered, is a plain Confeffion of thofe Violations of the Government that we have fet forth; fo the Defectivenefs of it is no lefs apparent, for they lay down nothing which they may not take up at pleafure; and they referve entire, and not fo much as mentioned, their Claims and Pretences to an Arbitrary and Defpotick Power; which has been the Root of all their Oppreffion, and of the total Subverfion of the Government. And it is plain, that there can be no Redrefs nor Remedy offered but in Parliament; by a Declaration of the Rights of the Subjects that have been invaded; and not by any pretended Acts of Grace, to which the Extremity of their Affairs has driven them. Therefore it is that we have thought fit to declare, that we will refer all to a free Affembly of the Nation, in a Lawful Parliament.

Given under our Hand and Seal, at our Court in the Hague, *the* 24th *Day of* October, *in the Year* 1688.

William Henry, *Prince of* Orange.

By His Highnefs's Special Command,

C. HUYGENS.

†						*By*

By his *Highness* William Henry, *Prince of* Orange, *a Declaration.   Printed in the Year* 1688.

WE have in the courfe of our whole Life, and more particularly by the apparent Hazards both by Sea and Land, to which we have fo lately expofed our Perfon, given to the whole World fo high and undoubted Proofs of our fervent Zeal for the Proteftant Religion, that we are fully confident no true *Englifhman* and good Proteftant can entertain the leaft Sufpicion of our firm Refolution, rather to fpend our deareft Blood and perifh in the Attempt, than not carry on the Bleffed and Glorious Defign which by the Favour of Heaven we have fo fuccefsfully begun, to refcue *England, Scotland* and *Ireland* from Slavery and Popery, and in a Free Parliament to eftablifh the Religion, the Laws, and the Liberties of thofe Kingdoms upon fuch a fure and lafting Foundation, that it fhall not be in the power of any Prince for the future to introduce Popery and Tyranny.

Towards the more eafy compaffing this great Defign, we have not been hitherto deceived in the juft Expectation we had of the Concurrence of the Nobility, Gentry, and People of *England* with Us, for the Security of their Religion, the Reftitution of the Laws, and the Re-eftablifhment of their Liberties and Properties: Great Numbers of all Ranks and Qualities having joined themfelves to us; and others at great diftances from us, have taken up Arms and declared for us. And, which we cannot but particularly mention, in that Army which was raifed to be the Inftrument of Slavery and Popery, may (by the fpecial Providence of God) both Officers and common Soldiers have been touched with fuch a feeling fenfe of Religion and Honour, and of true Affection for their native Country, that they have already deferted the illegal Service they were engaged in, and have come over to Us, and have given us full Affurance from the reft of the Army, that they will certainly follow this Example, as foon as with our Army we fhall approach near enough to receive them, without the hazard of being prevented and betray'd. To which end, and that we may the fooner execute this juft and neceffary Defign we are ingaged in for the publick Safety and Deliverance of thefe Nations, We are refolved, with all poffible diligence, to advance forward, that a Free Parliament may be forthwith called, and fuch Preliminaries adjufted with the King, and all things firft fettled upon fuch a foot according to Law, as may give us and the whole Nation juft reafon to believe the King is difpofed to make fuch neceffary Condefcenfions on his part, as will give entire Satisfaction and Security to all, and make both King and People once more happy.

And that we may effect all this, in the way moft agreeable to our Defires, if it be poffible without the Effufion of any Blood, except of thofe execrable Criminals who have juftly forfeited their Lives for betraying the Religion and fubverting the Laws of their native Country, We do think fit to declare, that as we will offer no Violence to any but in our own neceffary Defence; fo we will not fuffer any Injury to be done to the Perfon even of a Papift, provided he be found in fuch Place, and in fuch Condition and Circumftances as the Laws require. So we are refolved and do declare that all Papifts, who fhall be found in open Arms, or with Arms in their Houfes, or about their Perfons, or in any Office or Imployment Civil or Military upon any pretence whatfoever, contrary to the known Laws of the Land, fhall be treated by us and our Forces not as Soldiers and Gentlemen, but as Robbers, Free-booters and *Banditti*; they fhall be incapable of Quarter, and intirely delivered up to the Difcretion of our Soldiers. And We do further declare, that all Perfons who fhall be found any ways aiding and affifting to them, or fhall march under their Command, or fhall join with or fubmit to them in the Difcharge or Execution of their illegal Commiffions or Authority, fhall be looked upon as Partakers of their Crimes, Enemies to the Laws, and to their Country.

And whereas we are certainly informed that great Numbers of armed Papifts have of late reforted to *London* and *Weftminfter,* and parts adjacent, where they remain, as we have reafon to fufpect, not fo much for their own Security, as out of a wicked and barbarous Defign to make fome defperate Attempt upon the faid Cities, and their Inhabitants by Fire, or a fudden Maffacre, or both; or elfe to be the more ready to join themfelves to a Body of *French* Troops, defign'd, if it be poffible, to land in *England*, procured of the *French* King, by the Intereſt and Power of the Jeſuits in purſuance of the Engagements, which at the Inſtigation of that peſtilent Society, his moſt Chriſtian Majeſty, with one of his Neighbouring Princes of the ſame Communion, has entred into for the utter Extirpation of the Proteſtant Religion out of *Europe.* Tho' we hope we have taken ſuch effectual care to prevent the one, and ſecure the other, that by God's Aſſiſtance, we cannot doubt but we ſhall defeat all their wicked Enterprizes and Deſigns.

We cannot however forbear out of the great and tender Concern We have to preſerve the People of *England*, and particularly thoſe great and populous Cities, from the cruel Rage and bloody Revenge of the Papiſts, to require and expect from all the Lords-Lieutenants, Deputy-Lieutenants, and Juſtices of the Peace, Lord-Mayors, Mayors, Sheriffs, and all other Magiſtrates and Officers Civil and Military, of all Counties, Cities and Towns of *England*, eſpecially of the County of *Middleſex*, and Cities of *London* and *Weſtminſter*, and parts adjacent, that they do immediately diſarm and ſecure, as by Law they may and ought, within their reſpective Counties, Cities and Juriſdictions, all Papiſts whatſoever, as Perſons at all times, but now eſpecially moſt dangerous to the Peace and Safety of the Government, that ſo not only all Power of doing miſchief may be taken from them ; but that the Laws, which are the greateſt and beſt Security, may reſume their Force, and be ſtrictly executed.

And We do hereby likewiſe declare, that We will protect and defend all thoſe who ſhall not be afraid to do their Duty in Obedience to theſe Laws. And that for thoſe Magiſtrates and others, of what condition ſoever they be, who ſhall refuſe to aſſiſt Us, and in Obedience to the Laws to execute vigorouſly what we have required of them, and ſuffer themſelves at this Juncture to be cajoled or terrified out of their Duty, We will eſteem them the moſt criminal and infamous of all Men ; Betrayers of their Religion, the Laws, and their Native Country, and ſhall not fail to treat them accordingly ; reſolving to expect and require at their hands the Life of every ſingle Proteſtant that ſhall periſh, and every Houſe that ſhall be burnt or deſtroyed by their Treachery and Cowardiſe.

William Henry, Prince of *Orange.*

By his Highneſs's Special Command,

Given under our Hand and Seal at our Head-Quarters at Sherburn-*Caſtle, the* 28th *day of* November, 1688.

C. HUYGENS.

The following Paper was publiſhed by Mr. *Samuel Johnſon*, in the Year 1686, for which he was Sentenc'd by the Court of *King's-Bench*, (Sir *Edward Herbert* being Lord Chief Juſtice) to ſtand three times on the Pillory, and to be whipp'd from *Newgate* to *Tyburn:* Which barbarous Sentence was Executed.

An Humble and Hearty Addreſs to all the Engliſh Proteſtants *in this preſent Army.*

Gentlemen,

NExt to the Duty which we owe to God, which ought to be the principal Care of Men of your Profeſſion eſpecially, (becauſe you carry your Lives in your Hands, and often look Death in the Face ;) the ſecond Thing that deſerves your Conſideration, is, The Service of your Native Country, wherein you drew your firſt Breath, and breathed a free *Engliſh* Air. Now I would deſire you to conſider, how

how well you comply with these two main Points, by engaging in this present Service.

Is it in the Name of God, and for his Service, that you have joined your selves with *Papists* ; who will indeed fight for the *Mass-book*, but burn the *Bible*, and who seek to extirpate the *Protestant Religion* with *your Swords*, because they cannot do it with their *Own* ? And will you be aiding and assisting to set up *Mass-houses*, to erect that Popish Kingdom of Darkness and Desolation amongst us, and to train up all our Children in *Popery* ? How can you do these Things, and yet call your selves *Protestants* ?

And then what Service can be done your Country, by being under the Command of *French* and *Irish Papists*, and by bringing the Nation under a Foreign Yoke ? Will you help them to make forcible Entry into the Houses of your Country-men, under the name of *Quartering*, directly contrary to *Magna Charta* and the *Petition of Right* ? Will you be aiding and assisting to all the Murders and Outrages which they shall commit by their void Commissions ? Which were declared illegal, and sufficiently blasted by both Houses of Parliament, (if there had been any need of it) for it was very well known before, that a *Papist* cannot have a Commission, but by the Law is utterly disabled and disarmed. Will you exchange your Birth-right of *English Laws* and *Liberties* for *Martial* or *Club-Law*, and help to destroy all others, only to be eaten last your selves ? If I know you well, as you are *Englishmen*, you hate and scorn these Things. And therefore be not unequally yoaked with *Idolatrous* and *Bloody Papists. Be Valiant for the Truth, and shew your selves Men.*

The same Considerations are likewise humbly offered to all the *English Seamen* who have been the Bulwark of this Nation against *Popery* and *Slavery* ever since *Eighty Eight*.

Several Reasons for the Establishment of a standing Army, and dissolving the Militia. *By Mr.* S. Johnson.

1. BEcause the Lords-Lieutenants, Deputy-Lieutenants, and the whole *Militia*, that is to say, the Lords, Gentlemen, and Free-holders of *England*, are not fit to be trusted with their own Laws, Lives, Liberties and Estates, and therefore ought to have Guardians and Keepers assigned to them.

2. Because *Mercenary Soldiers*, who fight for twelve Pence a Day, will fight better, as having more to lose than either the Nobility or Gentry.

3. Because there are no *Irish Papists* in the *Militia*, who are certainly the best Soldiers in the World, for they have slain Men, Women, and Children, by Hundreds of Thousands at once.

4. Because the *Dragooners* have made more Converts than all the Bishops and Clergy of *France*.

5. The Parliament ought to establish one standing Army at the least, because indeed there will be need of Two, that one of them may defend the People from the other.

6. Because it is a thousand pities that a brave *Popish Army* should be a Riot.

7. Unless it be established by Act of Parliament, the Justices of Peace will be forced to suppress it in their own Defence ; for they will be loth to forfeit an hundred Pounds every day they rise, out of Complement to a *Popish Rout*. 13 *H.* 4. *c.* 7. 2 *H.* 5. *c.* 8.

8. Because a *Popish Army* is a *Nullity*. For all *Papists are utterly disabled* (and punishable besides) from bearing any Office in Camp, Troop, Band, or Company of Soldiers, and are so far disarmed by Law, that they cannot wear a Sword, so much as in their Defence, without the allowance of four Justices of the Peace of the County : And then upon a March they will be perfectly inchanted, for they are not able to stir above five Miles from their own Dwelling-house. 3 *Jac.* 5. *Sect.* 8. 27, 28, 29. 35 *Eliz.* 2. 3 *Jac.* 5. *Sect.* 7.

9. Because Persons utterly disabled by Law are utterly unauthorized ; and therefore the void Commissions of killing and slaying in the Hands of *Papists*, can only enable them to Massacre and Murder.

To the King's Most Excellent Majesty,

The Humble Petition of William Arch-bishop of Canterbury, and divers of the Suffragan Bishops of that Province (now present with him) in behalf of themselves, and others of their absent Brethren, and of the Clergy of their respective Dioceses;

Humbly sheweth,

THAT the great averseness they find in themselves to the distributing and publishing in all their Churches, your Majesty's late Declaration for *Liberty of Conscience,* proceeds neither from any want of Duty and Obedience to your Majesty, (our Holy Mother the Church of *England,* being both in her Principles and in her constant Practice unquestionably Loyal; and having, to her great Honour, been more than once publickly acknowledg'd to be so by your Gracious Majesty;) nor yet from any want of due Tenderness to Dissenters, in relation to whom they are willing to come to such a Temper as shall be thought fit, when that Matter shall be considered and settled in Parliament and Convocation. But among many other Considerations, from this especially, because that Declaration is founded upon such a dispensing Power, as has been often declared illegal in Parliament, and particularly in the years 1662, and 1672, and in the beginning of your Majesty's Reign; and is a Matter of so great Moment and Consequence to the whole Nation, both in Church and State, that your Petitioners cannot in Prudence, Honour, or Conscience, so far make themselves Parties to it, as the distribution of it all over the Nation, and the solemn Publication of it once and again, even in God's House, and in the time of his Divine Service, must amount to in common and reasonable Construction.

Your Petitioners therefore most Humbly and Earnestly beseech your Majesty, that you will be graciously pleased, not to insist upon their Distributing and Reading your Majesty's said Declaration.

And your Petitioners, as in Duty bound, shall ever Pray.

Will. *Cant.*	Tho. *Bathon. & Wellen.*
Will. *Asaph.*	Tho. *Peterburgen.*
Fr. *Ely.*	Jonath. *Bristol.*
Jo. *Cicestr.*	

His Majesty's Answer was to this effect.

I *Have heard of this before, but did not believe it. I did not expect this from the* Church *of England, especially from some of you. If I change my Mind, you shall hear from me; if not, I expect my Command shall be obeyed.*

The PETITION of the Lords Spiritual and Temporal for the Calling of a *Free Parliament:* Together with his Majesty's Gracious Answer to their Lordships.

To the KING's most Excellent Majesty,

The Humble Petition of the Lords Spiritual and Temporal, whose Names are subscribed.

May it please your Majesty,

WE your Majesty's most loyal Subjects, in a deep sense of the Miseries of a War now breaking forth in the Bowels of this your Kingdom, and of the Danger to which your Majesty's Sacred Person is thereby like to be exposed, and also of the Distractions of your People, by reason of their present Grievances; do think our selves bound in Conscience of the duty we owe to God, and our holy Religion, to your Majesty, jefty, and our Country, moft humbly to offer to your Majefty, that in our Opinion, the only vifible way to preferve your Majefty, and this your Kingdom, would be the Calling of a Parliament, regular and free in all its Circumftances.

> *We therefore do moft earneftly befeech your Majefty, That you would be gracioufly pleafed, with all fpeed, to call fuch a Parliament, wherein we fhall be moft ready to promote fuch Counfels and Refolutions of Peace and Settlement in Church and State, as may conduce to your Majefty's Honour and Safety, and to the quieting the Minds of your People: We do likewife humbly befeech your Majefty, in the mean time, to ufe fuch means for the preventing the Effufion of Chriftian Blood, as to your Majefty fhall feem moft meet.*

And your Petitioners fhall ever pray, *&c.*

W. *Cant.*	*Clare.*	*Rochefter.*	Fran. *Ely.*	*Paget.*
Grafton.	*Clarendon.*	*Newport.*	Tho. *Roffen.*	*Chandois.*
Ormond.	*Burlington.*	Nom. *Ebor.*	Tho. *Petriburg.*	*Offulfton.*
Dorfet.	*Anglefey.*	W. *Afaph.*	Tho. *Oxon.*	

Prefented by the Archbifhop of *Canterbury*, the Archbifhop of *York* elect, the Bifhop of *Ely*, and the Bifhop of *Rochefter*, the 17th of *November*, 1688.

His Majefty's moft gracious Anfwer.

My L O R D S,

WHat you ask of me, I moft paffionately defire : And I promife you, **upon the Faith of a King**, That I will have a Parliament, and fuch an one as you ask for, as foon as ever the Prince of *Orange* has quitted this Realm ; for, how is it poffible a *Parliament* fhould be *Free in all its Circumftances*, as you petition for, whilft an Enemy, is in the Kingdom, and can make a return of near an hundred Voices ?

The Lords Petition, with the King's Anfwer, may be printed, Novemb. 29. 1688.

The *P. O*'s Letter to the *Englifh* Army.

Gentlemen and Friends,

WE have given you fo full, and fo true an account of our Intentions, in this Expedition in our Declaration, that as we can add nothing to it, fo we are fure you can defire nothing more of us. We are come to preferve your Religion, and to reftore and eftablifh your Liberties and Properties ; and therefore we cannot fuffer ourfelves to doubt but that all true *Englifhmen* will come and concur with us, in our defire to fecure thefe Nations from P O P E R Y and S L A V E R Y. You muft all plainly fee, that you are only made ufe of as Inftruments to enflave the Nation, and ruin the Proteftant Religion; and when that is done, you may judge what ye yourfelves ought to expect, both from the cafhiering of all the Proteftant and *Englifh* Officers and Soldiers in *Ireland*, and by the *Irifh* Soldiers being brought over to be put in your places ; and of which you have feen fo frefh an inftance, that we need not put you in mind of it. You know how many of your Fellow-Officers have been ufed for their ftanding firm to the Proteftant Religion, and to the Laws of *England*, and you cannot flatter yourfelves fo far as to expect to be better ufed, if thofe who have broke their word fo often, fhould by your means be brought out of thofe Straits to which they are reduced at prefent. We hope likewife, that you will not fuffer yourfelves to be abufed by a falfe Notion of Honour, but that you will in the firft place confider, what you owe to Almighty God and your Religion, to your Country, to yourfelves, and to your Pofterity, which you, as Men of Honour, ought to prefer to all private Confiderations and Engagements whatfoever. We do therefore expect, that you will confider the Honour that is now fet before you, of being the Inftruments of ferving your Country, and fecuring your Religion, and we will ever remember the Service you fhall do us upon this occafion ; and will promife unto you, that we fhall place fuch particular Marks of our Favour on every one of you, as your Behaviour at this time fhall deferve of us and the Nation ; in which we will make a great Diftinction of thofe that fhall come feafonably to join their Arms with ours, and you fhall find us to be

Your well-wifhing, and affured Friend, W. H. P. O.

Prince

Prince George's *Letter to the King.*

S I R,

WITH a Heart full of Grief am I forced to write, what Prudence will not permit me to say to your face. And may I e'er find Credit with your Majesty, and Protection from Heaven, as what I now do, is free from Paffion, Vanity, or Defign, with which Actions of this nature are too often accompanied. I am not ignorant of the frequent Mischiefs wrought in the World by factious pretences of Religion ; but were not Religion the moft juftifiable Caufe, it would not be made the moft fpecious pretence. And your Majefty has always fhewn too uninterefted a Senfe of Religion, to doubt the juft Effects of it in one whofe Practices have, I hope, never given the World caufe to cenfure his real conviction of it, or his backwardnefs to perform what his Honour and Confcience prompt him to : How then can I longer difguife my juft Concern for that Religion in which I have been fo happily educated, which my Judgment throughly convinces me to be beft ; and for the Support of which I am fo highly interefted in my native Country ? And is not *England* now by the moft endearing Tie become fo ?

While the reftlefs Spirits of the Enemies of the *R E F O R M E D R E L I G I O N*, back'd by the cruel Zeal and prevailing Power of *France*, juftly alarm and unite all the Proteftant Princes of *Chriftendom*, and engage them in fo vaft an expence for the fupport of it, can I act fo degenerous and mean a part, as to deny my Concurrence to fuch worthy endeavours for difabufing of your Majefty by the Reinforcement of thofe Laws, and Eftablifhment of that Government, on which alone depends the well-being of your Majefty, and of the *P R O T E S T A N T R E L I G I O N* in *Europe ?* This, Sir, is that irrefiftible and only Caufe that could come in competition with my Duty and Obligations to your Majefty, and be able to tear me from you, whilft the fame Affectionate Defire of ferving you continues in me. Could I fecure your Perfon by the hazard of my Life, I fhould think it could not be better employed : And wou'd to God thefe your diftracted Kingdoms might yet receive that fatisfactory compliance from your Majefty in all their juftifiable pretenfions, as might upon the only fure Foundation, that of the Love and Intereft of your Subjects, eftablifh your Government, and as ftrongly unite the Hearts of all your Subjects to you, as is that of,

S I R,

Your Majefty's moft Humble, and moft Obedient
Son and Servant.

The Lord Churchill's *Letter to the King.*

S I R,

SInce Men are feldom fufpected of Sincerity, when they act contrary to their Interefts ; and though my dutiful Behaviour to your Majefty in the worft of Times, (for which I acknowledge my poor Services much over-paid) may not be fufficient to incline you to a charitable Interpretation of my Actions, yet I hope, the great advantage I enjoy under your Majefty, which I can never expect in any other Change of Government, may reafonably convince your Majefty and the World, that I am acted by a higher Principle, when I offer that violence to my inclination and intereft, as to defert your Majefty at a time when your Affairs feem to challenge the ftricteft Obedience from all your Subjects, much more from one who lies under the greateft perfonal Obligations imaginable to your Majefty. This Sir, could proceed from nothing but the inviolable Dictates of my *C O N S C I E N C E*, and a neceffary concern for my *R E L I G I O N*, (which no good Man can oppofe) and with which I am inftructed nothing ought to come in competition. Heaven knows with what partiality my dutiful Opinion of your Majefty hath hitherto reprefented thofe unhappy Defigns, which inconfiderate and felf-interefted Men have framed againft your Majefty's true Intereft and the Proteftant Religion. But as I can no longer join with fuch to give a pretence by Conqueft to bring them to effect, fo will I always with the hazard of my Life and Fortune (fo much your Majefty's due) endeavour to preferve your Royal Perfon and Lawful Rights, with all the tender Concern and dutiful Refpect that becomes, S I R,

Your Majefty's moft dutiful, and moft obliged Subject and Servant.

The

The Princefs Anne *of* Denmark's *Letter to the Queen.*

Madam,

I. Beg your pardon if I am fo deeply affected with the furprifing News of the Prince's being gone, as not to be able to fee you, but to leave this Paper to exprefs my humble Duty to the King and yourfelf ; and to let you know that I am gone to abfent myfelf, to avoid the King's Difpleafure, which I am not able to bear, either againft the Prince or myfelf: And I fhall ftay at fo great a diftance, as not to return before I hear the happy News of a Reconcilement. And as I am confident the Prince did not leave the King with any other Defign, than to ufe all poffible means for his Prefervation ; fo I hope you will do me the Juftice to believe, that I am uncapable of following him for any other end. Never was any one in fuch an unhappy Condition, fo divided between Duty and Affection, to a Father, and a Husband ; and therefore I know not what to do, but to follow one to preferve the other. I fee the general falling off of the Nobility and Gentry, who avow to have no other end, than to prevail with the King to fecure their Religion, which they faw fo much in danger by the *Violent Counfels of the Priefts* ; who, to promote their own Religion, did not care to what dangers they expofed the King : *I am fully perfuaded that the Prince of* Orange *defigns the King's fafety and prefervation,* and hope all things may be compofed without more Blood-fhed, by the calling a Parliament. God grant a happy end to thefe Troubles, that the King's Reign may be profperous, and that I may fhortly meet you in perfect peace and fafety ; till when, let me beg you to continue the fame favourable Opinion that you have hitherto had of,

Your moft obedient Daughter and Servant,

A N N E.

A Memorial of the Proteftants of the Church of *England,* Prefented to their Royal Highneffes the Prince and Princefs of *Orange.*

YOur Royal Highneffes cannot be ignorant that the Proteftants of *England,* who continue true to their Religion and the Government eftablifhed by Law, have been many ways troubled and vexed by reftlefs contrivances and defigns of the Papifts, under pretence of the Royal Authority, and things required of them unaccountable before God and Man ; ecclefiaftical Benefices and Preferments taken from them, without any other Reafon but the King's Pleafure ; that they have been fummoned and fentenced by ecclefiaftical Commiffioners, contrary to Law, deprived of their Birth-Right in the free Choice of their Magiftrates and Reprefentatives ; divers Corporations diffolved ; the legal Security of our Religion and Liberty, eftablifhed and ratified by King and Parliament, annull'd and overthrown by a pretended *Difpenfing Power* ; new and unheard of Maxims have been preached, as if Subjects had no right but what depends on the King's Will and Pleafure. The *Militia* put into the hands of Perfons not qualified by Law ; and a Popifh mercenary Army maintained in the Kingdom in time of Peace, abfolutely contrary to Law: The Execution of the Law againft feveral high Crimes and Mifdemeanors fuperfeded and prohibited ; the Statutes againft Correfpondence with the Court of *Rome,* Papal Jurifdiction, and Popifh Priefts, fufpended ; that in Courts of Juftice thofe Judges are difplaced, who dare acquit them whom the King would have condemned, as happened to Judge *Powel* and *Holloway* for acquitting the Seven Bifhops: Liberty of chufing Members of Parliament, notwithftanding all the Care taken, and Provifion made by Law on that behalf, wholly taken away by *Quo Warrantoes* ferved againft Corporations, and the three known Queftions. All things carried on in open view for the Propagation and Growth of Popery ; for which the Courts of *England* and *France* have fo long jointly laboured with fo much Application and Earneftnefs. Endeavours ufed to perfuade your Royal Highneffes to confent to Liberty of Confcience, and abrogating the Penal Laws and Tefts, wherein they fell fhort of their Aim.

That

That they moſt humbly implore the Protection of your Royal Highneſſes, as to the ſuſpending and encroachments made upon the Law for maintenance of the Proteſtant Religion, our civil and fundamental Rights and Privileges; and that your Royal Highneſs would be pleaſed to inſiſt, that the free Parliament of *England,* according to Law, may be reſtored, the Laws againſt Papiſts, Prieſts, Papal Juriſdiction, *&c.* put in execution, and the Suſpending and Diſpenſing Power declared null and void; the Rights and Privileges of the City of *London,* the free Choice of their Magiſtrates, and the Liberties as well of that as other Corporations reſtored, and all things returned to their ancient Channel, *&c.*

Admiral Herbert's *Letter to all Commanders of Ships and Seamen in his Majeſty's Fleet.*

Gentlemen,

I Have little to add to what his Highneſs has expreſs'd in general Terms, beſides laying before you the dangerous way you are at preſent in, where Ruin or Infamy muſt inevitably attend you, if you don't join with the *Prince* in the common Cauſe, for the Defence of your Religion and Liberties; for ſhould it pleaſe God, for the Sins of the *Engliſh* Nation, to ſuffer your Arms to prevail, to what can your Victory ſerve you, but to enſlave you deeper, and overthrow the true Religion, in which you have liv'd, and your Fathers died? Of which, I beg you, as a Friend, to conſider the Conſequences, and to reflect on the blot and infamy it will bring on you, not only now, but in all After-ages, That by your means the *Proteſtant Religion* was deſtroy'd, and your Country depriv'd of its ancient Liberties: And if it pleaſes God to bleſs the *Prince's* Endeavours with ſucceſs, as I don't doubt but he will, conſider then what their Condition will be that oppoſe him in this ſo good a Deſign, where the greateſt Favour they can hope for, is, their being ſuffered to end their Days in Miſery and Want, deteſted and deſpiſed by all good Men.

It is therefore, and for many more Reaſons, too long to inſert here, that I, as a true *Engliſhman* and your Friend, exhort you to join your Arms to the *Prince,* for the Defence of the common Cauſe, the Proteſtant Religion, and the Liberties of your Country. It is what I am well aſſured the major and beſt part of the Army, as well as the Nation, will do ſo ſoon as convenience is offered. Prevent them in ſo good an Action whilſt it is in your power; and may it appear, that as the Kingdom hath always depended on the Navy for its defence, ſo you will yet go further, by making it, as much as in you lies, the Protection of her Religion and Liberties; and then you may aſſure yourſelves of all Marks of Favour and Honour ſuitable to the Merits of ſo great and glorious an Action. After this, I ought not to add ſo inconſiderable a thing, as that it will for ever engage me to be in a moſt particular manner,

Your faithful Friend,

Aboard the Leyden
in the Gooree.

and humble Servant,

AR. HERBERT.

Lord Delamere's *Speech.*

TH E occaſion of this, is to give you my thoughts upon the preſent Conjuncture, which concerns not only you, but every Proteſtant, and Free-born Man of *England,* I am confident, that wiſhes well to the Proteſtant Religion and his Country; and I am perſuaded that every Man of you thinks both in danger, and now to lie at ſtake. I am alſo perſuaded, that every Man of you will rejoice to ſee Religion and Property ſettled; if ſo, then I am not miſtaken in my Conjectures concerning you. Can you ever hope for a better occaſion to root out *POPERY* and *SLAVERY,* than by joining with the *P.* of *O.* whoſe Propoſals contain and ſpeak the Deſires of every Man that loves his Religion and Liberty? And in ſaying this, I will invite you to nothing but what I will do myſelf; and I will not deſire any of you to go any further than I will move myſelf; neither will I put you upon any danger where I will not take ſhare in it. I propoſe this to you, not as you are my Tenants, but as my Friends, and as you are *Engliſhmen.*

men. No Man can love Fighting for its own fake, nor find any pleasure in danger. And you may imagine, I would be very glad to spend the rest of my days in peace, I having had so great a share in Troubles ; but I see all lies at stake, I am to chuse whether I will be a *Slave* and a *Papist*, or a *Protestant* and a *Freeman*; and therefore the Case being thus, I shall think my self false to my Country, if I sit still at this time. I am of Opinion, that when the Nation is delivered, it must be by Force or by Miracle : It would be too great a presumption to expect the latter, and therefore our Deliverance must be by Force, and I hope this is the time for it ; a Price is now put into our Hands, and if it miscarry for want of Assistance, our Blood is upon our own Heads ; and he that is passive at this Time, may very well expect that God will mock when the fear of Affliction comes upon him, which he thought to avoid by being indifferent.

If the King prevails, farewel Liberty of Conscience, which has hitherto been allowed, not for the sake of the Protestants, but in order to settle Popery. You may see what to expect if he get the better ; and he hath lately given you, of this Town, a taste of the Method, whereby he will maintain his Army. And you may see of what sort of People he intends his Army to confist ; and if you have not a mind to serve such Masters, then stand not by and see your Countrymen perish, when they are endeavouring to defend you.

I promise this on my Word and Honour, to every Tenant that goes along with me, that if he fall, I will make his Lease as good to his Family, as it was when he went from home. The thing then which I desire, and your Country does expect from you, is this, That every Man that hath a tolerable Horse, or can procure one, will meet me on *Boden*-Downs to-morrow, where I rendezvous : But if any of you is rendred unable by reason of Age, or any other just Excuse, then that he would mount a fitter Person, and put five Pounds in his Pocket. Those that have not, nor cannot procure a Horse, let them stay at home and assist with their Purses, and send it to me with a particular of every Man's Contribution. I impose on no Man, but let him lay his Hand on his Heart, and consider what he is willing to give to recover his Religion and Liberty ; and to such I promise, and to all that go along with me, that if we prevail, I will be as industrious to have him recompensed for his Charge and Hazard, as I will be to seek it for my self. This Advice I give to all that stay behind, That when you hear the Papists have committed any Out-rage, or any Rising, that you will get together ; for it is better to meet your Danger than expect it. I have no more to say, but that I am willing to lose my Life in the Cause, if God see it good, for I was never unwilling to die for my Religion and Country.

An Engagement of the Noblemen, Knights, and Gentlemen at Exeter, *to assist the Prince of* Orange, *in the Defence of the Protestant Religion, Laws, and Liberties of the People of* England, Scotland *and* Ireland.

WE do engage to Almighty God, and to his Highness the Prince of *Orange*, and with one another, to stick firm to this Cause, and to one another in the Defence of it, and never to depart from it, until our Religion, Laws, and Liberties are so far secured to us in a Free-Parliament, that we shall be no more in danger of falling under *Popery* and *Slavery*. And whereas we are engaged in the Common Cause under the Protection of the Prince of *Orange*, by which means his Person may be exposed to Danger, and to the desperate and cursed Designs of Papists, and other bloody Men, we do therefore solemnly engage to God and to one another, That if any such Attempts be made upon him, we will pursue not only those that made them, but all their Adherents, and all we find in Arms against us, with the utmost Severity of just Revenge in their Ruin and Destruction ; and that the executing any such Attempt (which God of his infinite Mercy forbid) shall not deprive us from pursuing this Cause which we do now undertake, but that it shall encourage us to carry it on with all the Vigour that so barbarous an Attempt shall deserve.

The

The Declaration of the Nobility, Gentry, and Commonalty at the Rendezvous at Nottingham, Nov. 22. 1688.

WE, the Nobility, Gentry, and Commonalty of these Northern Counties assembled together at *Nottingham*, for the Defence of the Laws, Religion, and Properties, according to those free-born Liberties and Privileges, descended to us from our Ancestors, as the undoubted Birth-right of the *Subjects* of this Kingdom of *England*, (not doubting but the Infringers and Invaders of our Rights will represent us to the rest of the Nation, in the most malicious dress they can put upon us) do here unanimously think it our Duty to declare to the rest of our *Protestant Fellow-Subjects*, the Grounds of our present Undertaking.

We are, by innumerable Grievances, made sensible, that the very Fundamentals of our Religion, Liberties, and Properties, are about to be rooted out by our late Jesuitical Privy-Council; as hath been of late too apparent, 1. By the King's dispensing with all the established Laws at his pleasure. 2. By displacing all Officers out of all Offices of Trust and Advantage, and placing others in their room that are known *Papists*, deservedly made incapable by the establish'd Laws of our Land. 3. By destroying the Charters of most Corporations in the Land. 4. By discouraging all Persons that are not *Papists*, preferring such as turn to *Popery*. 5. By displacing all honest and conscientious Judges, unless they would, contrary to their Consciences, declare that to be Law, which was merely arbitrary. 6. By branding all Men with the name of *Rebels*, that but offered to justify the Laws in a legal course against the arbitrary Proceedings of the King, or any of his corrupt Ministers. 7. By burthening the Nation with an Army, to maintain the violation of the Rights of the Subjects. 8. By discountenancing the Established Reformed Religion. 9. By forbidding the Subjects the benefit of petitioning, and construing them *Libellers*; so rendring the Laws a Nose of Wax, to serve their arbitrary Ends. And many more such-like, too long here to enumerate.

We being thus made sadly sensible of the Arbitrary and Tyrannical Government, that is, by the Influence of jesuitical Counsels, coming upon us, do unanimously declare, That not being willing to deliver our Posterity over to such a Condition of *Popery* and *Slavery*, as the aforesaid Oppressions inevitably threaten; we will, to the utmost of our power, oppose the same, by joining with the Prince of *Orange*, (whom we hope God Almighty hath sent to rescue us from the Oppressions aforesaid) and will use our utmost Endeavours for the recovery of our almost ruin'd Laws, Liberties, and Religion : And herein we hope all good *Protestant Subjects* will with their Lives and Fortunes be assistant to us, and not be bug-bear'd with the opprobrious Terms of *Rebels*, by which they would fright us, to become perfect Slaves to their tyrannical Insolencies and Usurpations : for we assure ourselves, that no rational and unbyassed Person will judge it Rebellion to defend our Laws and Religion, which all our Princes have sworn at their Coronations ; which Oath, how well it hath been observed of late, we desire a *Free Parliament* may have the Consideration of.

We own it Rebellion to resist a King that governs by Law, but he was always accounted a Tyrant that made his Will his Law ; and to resist such an one, we justly esteem no Rebellion, but a necessary Defence : And in this Consideration we doubt not of all honest Men's Assistance, and humbly hope for, and implore the great God's Protection, that turneth the Hearts of People as pleaseth him best ; it having been observed, that People can never be of one Mind without his Inspiration, which hath in all Ages confirmed that Observation, *Vox Populi est Vox Dei.*

The present restoring of Charters, and reversing the oppressing and unjust Judgment given on *Magdalen*-College Fellows, is plain, are but to still the People, like Plumbs to Children, by deceiving them for a while ; but if they shall by this Stratagem be fooled, till this present Storm that threatens the Papists, be past, as soon as they shall be resettled, the former Oppression will be put on with greater vigour : But we hope in vain is the Net spread in the sight of the Birds ; For (1.) the Papists old Rule is, *That Faith is not to be kept with Hereticks,* as they term *Protestants,* though the *Popish Religion* is the greatest Heresy. And (2.) Queen *Mary*'s so ill observing her Promises to the *Suffolk* Men that help'd her to the Throne : And above all, (3.) the Pope's dispensing with the breach of Oaths, Treaties, or Promises, at his pleasure, when it makes for the service of Holy Church, as they term it. These, we say, are such convincing Reasons to hinder us from giving Credit to the aforesaid Mock-Shews of Redress, that we think ourselves bound in Conscience to rest on no Security that shall not be approved by a *Freely elected Parliament*, to whom, under God, we refer our Cause.

His

His Grace the Duke of Norfolk's *Speech to the Mayor of* Norwich, *on the First of* December, *in the Market-place of* Norwich.

Mr. Mayor,

NOT doubting but you and the rest of your Body, as well as the whole City and Country, may be alarmed by the great Concourse of Gentry, with the numerous Appearance of their Friends and Servants, as well as of your own *Militia,* here this Morning, I have thought this the most proper Place, as being the most publick one, to give you an Account of our Intentions.

Out of the deep sense we had that in the present unhappy Juncture of Affairs, nothing we could think of was possible to secure the Laws, Liberties, and Protestant Religion, but a Free Parliament; WE ARE HERE MET TO DECLARE, That we will do our utmost to defend the same, by declaring for such a Free Parliament. And since his Majesty hath been pleased (by the News we hear this day) to order Writs for a Parliament to sit the Fifteenth of *January* next, I can only add, in the name of myself, and all these Gentlemen, and others here met, That we will ever be ready to support and defend the Laws, Liberties, and Protestant Religion. And so GOD SAVE THE KING.

To this the Mayor, Aldermen, and the rest of the Corporation, and a numerous Assembly, did concur with his Grace and the rest of the Gentry.

His Grace, at his lighting from his Horse, perceiving great numbers of common People gathering together, called them to him, and told them, he desired they would not take any occasion to commit any Disorder or Outrage, but go quietly to their Homes; and acquainted them that the King had ordered a Free Parliament to be called.

The Speech of the Prince of Orange, *to some principal Gentlemen of* Somersetshire *and* Dorsetshire, *on their coming to join his Highness at* Exeter, *the* 15th *of* Nov. 1688.

THO' we know not all your Persons, yet we have a Catalogue of your Names, and remember the Character of your Worth and Interest in your Country. You see we are come according to your Invitation, and our Promise. Our Duty to God obliges us to protect the Protestant Religion; and our Love to Mankind, your Liberties and Properties. We expected you that dwelt so near the Place of our Landing, would have joined us sooner, not that it is now too late, nor that we want your Military Assistance so much as your Countenance and Presence, to justify our declared Pretensions, rather than accomplish our good and gracious Designs. Tho' we have brought both a good Fleet, and a good Army, to render these Kingdoms happy, by rescuing all Protestants from Popery, Slavery, and Arbitrary Power; by restoring them to their Rights and Properties established by Law, and by promoting of Peace and Trade, which is the Soul of Government, and the very Life-blood of a Nation: yet we rely more on the Goodness of God and the Justice of our Cause, than on any human Force and Power whatever. Yet since God is pleased we shall make use of human Means, and not expect Miracles for our Preservation and Happiness; let us not neglect making use of this gracious Opportunity, but with Prudence and Courage put in execution our so honourable Purposes. Therefore, Gentlemen, Friends, and Fellow-Protestants, we bid you and all your Followers most heartily welcome to our Court and Camp. Let the whole World now judge, if our Pretensions are not just, generous, sincere, and above Price; since we might have even a Bridge of Gold to return back: But it is our Principle and Resolution, rather to die in a good Cause, than live in a bad one, well knowing that Virtue and true Honour is its own Reward, and the Happiness of Mankind our great and only Design.

The

The true Copy of a Paper delivered by the Lord Devonſhire, *to the* Mayor *of* Derby, *where he quartered the one and twentieth of* November, 1688.

WE the *Nobility* and *Gentry* of the *Northern Parts* of *England*, being deeply ſenſible of the Calamities that threaten theſe *Kingdoms*, do think it our Duty, as Chriſtians and good *Subjects*, to endeavour what in us lies, the healing of our preſent *Diſtractions*, and preventing greater: And as with grief we apprehend the ſaid Conſequences that may ariſe from the Landing of an *Army* in this *Kingdom* from *Foreign Parts*; ſo we cannot but deplore the Occaſion given for it, by ſo many Invaſions, made of late Years, on our *Religion* and *Laws*. And whereas we cannot think of any other Expedient to compoſe our Differences, and prevent Effuſion of Blood, than that which procured a Settlement in theſe *Kingdoms*, after the late Civil Wars, the *Meeting* and *Sitting* of a *Parliament*, freely and duly choſen, we think ourſelves obliged (as far as in us lies) to promote it; and the rather, becauſe the Prince of *Orange*, (as appears by his *Declaration*) is willing to ſubmit his own *Pretenſions*, and all other Matters, to their *Determination*: We *heartily Wiſh*, and *humbly Pray*, *That his Majeſty* would conſent to *this Expedient*, in order to a future Settlement; and hope that ſuch a Temperament may be thought of, as that the Army now on foot, may not give any Interruption to the proceeding of a Parliament. But if to the great Misfortune and Ruin of *theſe Kingdoms*, it ſhould prove otherwiſe, we further declare, that we will, to our utmoſt, defend the Proteſtant Religion, the Laws of the Kingdom, and the Rights and Liberties of the Subject.

A Letter from a Gentleman at King's Lynn, December 7. 1688, *to his Friend in* London.

SIR,

THE Duke of *Norfolk* came to Town on *Wedneſday* Night, with many of the chiefeſt of the County; and yeſterday in the Market-place received the Addreſs following, which was preſented by the Mayor, attended by the Body, and many hundreds of the Inhabitants.

To his Grace the moſt Noble Henry, *Duke of* Norfolk, *Lord Marſhal of* England.

My Lord,

THE daily Alarms we receive, as well from Foreign as Domeſtick Enemies, give us juſt Apprehenſions of the approaching Danger which we conceive we are in; and to apply with all earneſtneſs to your Grace as our great Patron, in all humble Confidence to ſucceed in our Expectations, that we may be put into ſuch a poſture by your Grace's Directions and Conduct, as may make us appear as zealous as any in the Defence of the *Proteſtant Religion*, the Laws, and ancient Government of this Kingdom: Being the deſire of many hundreds, who moſt humbly challenge a Right of your Grace's Protection.

His Grace's Answer.

Mr. Mayor,

I Am very much obliged to you, and the rest of your Body, and those here present, for your good Opinion of me; and the Confidence you have, that I will do what in me lies to support and defend the Laws, Liberties, and Protestant Religion, in which I will never deceive you.

And since the coming of the Prince of Orange *hath given us an opportunity to declare for the defence of them; I can only assure you, that no Man will venture his Life and Fortune more freely for the Defence of the Laws, Liberties, and Protestant Religion, than I will do; and with all these Gentlemen here present, and many more, will unanimously concur therein; and you shall see that all possible Care shall be taken, that such a Defence shall be made as you require.*

AFter which the Duke was, with his Retinue, received at the Mayor's House at Dinner, with great Acclamations; and his Proceedings therein have put our County into a Condition of Defence, of which you shall hear further in a little time, our *Militia* being ordered to be raised throughout the County.

Our Tradesmen, Seamen, and *Mobile*, have this morning generally put *Orange* Ribbon on their Hats, ecchoing *Huzza's* to the Prince of *Orange* and Duke of *Norfolk*.

All are in a hot Ferment: God send us a good Issue of it.

Lynn-Regis, Decemb. 10, 1688.

Sir,

BY mine of the 7th Instant, I gave you an Account of the Address of this Corporation to his Grace the Duke of *Norfolk*, and of his Grace's Answer thereto. Since which his Grace has sent for the Militia Troops, and put them in a posture of Defence, as appears by the ensuing Speech.

The Duke of *Norfolk*'s second Speech at *Lynn*.

I Hope you see I have endeavoured to put you in the posture you desired, by sending both for Horse and Foot of the Militia, and am very glad to see such an Appearance of this Town in so good a Condition. And I do again renew my former Assurances to you, that I will ever stand by you to defend the Laws, Liberties, and the Protestant Religion, and to procure a Settlement in Church and State, in concurrence with the Lords and Gentlemen in the North, and pursuant to the Declaration of the Prince of Orange.

And so God save the King.

The Declaration of the Lords Spiritual and Temporal, in and about the Cities of London *and* Westminster, *Assembled at* Guild-Hall, Dec. 1688.

WE doubt not but the World believes that in this great and dangerous Conjuncture, we are heartily and zealously concerned for the Protestant Religion, the Laws of the Land, and the Liberties and Properties of the Subject. And we did reasonably hope, that the King having issued his Proclamation and Writs for a Free Parliament, we might have rested secure under the Expectation of that Meeting: But his Majesty having withdrawn himself, and, as we apprehend, in order to his Departure out of this Kingdom, by the pernicious Counsels of Persons ill-affected to our Nation and Religion, we cannot, without being wanting to our Duty, be silent under those Calamities, wherein the Popish Counsels, which so long prevailed, have miserably

Y y y y y

rably

rably involved theſe Realms. We do therefore unanimouſly reſolve to apply our ſelves to his Highneſs the Prince of *Orange*, who with ſo great Kindneſs to theſe Kingdoms, ſo vaſt Expence, and ſo much Hazard to his own Perſon, hath undertaken, by endeavouring to procure a Free Parliament, to reſcue us, with as little Effuſion as poſſible, of Chriſtian Blood, from the imminent Dangers of Popery and Slavery.

And we do hereby Declare, That we will, with our utmoſt Endeavours, aſſiſt his Highneſs in the obtaining ſuch a Parliament with all ſpeed, wherein our Laws, our Liberties and Properties may be ſecured, the Church of *England* in particular ; with a due Liberty to Proteſtant Diſſenters, and in general the Proteſtant Religion and Intereſt over the whole World may be ſupported and encouraged, to the Glory of God, the Happineſs of the eſtabliſhed Government in theſe Kingdoms, and the Advantage of all Princes and States in Chriſtendom that may be herein concerned.

In the mean time, we will endeavour to preſerve, as much as in us lies, the Peace and Security of theſe great and populous Cities of *London* and *Weſtminſter*, and the Parts adjacent, by taking care to diſarm all Papiſts, and ſecure all Jeſuits and *Romiſh* Prieſts, who are in or about the ſame.

And if there be any thing more to be performed by us, for promoting his Highneſs's generous Intentions for the publick good, we ſhall be ready to do it as occaſion ſhall require.

W. Cant.	Suſſex.	P. Wharton.
Tho. Ebor.	Berkeley.	North and Grey.
Pembroke.	Rocheſter.	Chandos.
Dorſet.	Newport.	Montague.
Mulgrave.	Weymouth.	T. Jermyn.
Thanet.	P. Wincheſter.	Vaughan Carbery.
Carliſle.	W. Aſaph.	Culpeper.
Craven.	Fran. Ely.	Crewe.
Ailesbury.	Tho. Roffen.	Oſſulſton.
Burlington.	Tho. Petriberg.	

WHereas his Majeſty hath privately this Morning withdrawn himſelf, we the Lords Spiritual and Temporal, whoſe Names are ſubſcribed, being aſſembled at *Guild-hall* in *London*, having Agreed upon, and Signed a Declaration, intituled, *The Declaration of the Lords Spiritual and Temporal, in and about the Cities of* London *and* Weſtminſter, *aſſembled at* Guild-hall, 11th *December* 1688. Do deſire the Right Honourable the Earl of *Pembroke*, the Right Honourable the Lord Viſcount *Weymouth*, the Right Reverend Father in God the Lord Biſhop of *Ely*, and the Right Honourable the Lord *Culpeper*, forthwith to attend his Highneſs the Prince of *Orange* with the ſaid *Declaration* ; and at the ſame time acquaint his Highneſs with what we have further done at that Meeting. *Dated at* Guild-hall, *the* 11th *of* December, 1688.

A Paper delivered to his Highneſs the Prince of Orange, by the Commiſſioners ſent by his Majeſty to treat with him. And his Highneſs's Anſwer.

WHereas on the 8th of *December*, 1688. at *Hungerford*, a Paper ſigned by the Marquis of *Hallifax*, the Earl of *Nottingham*, and the Lord *Godolphin*, Commiſſioners ſent unto us from his Majeſty, was delivered to us in theſe Words following, *viz.*

Sir,

THE King commanded us to acquaint you, That he obſerveth all the Differences and Cauſes of Complaint alledged by your Highneſs ſeem to be referred to a Free Parliament.

His Majeſty, as he hath already declared, was reſolved before this to call one, but thought that in the preſent State of Affairs it was adviſable to defer it till things were more compos'd.

Yet ſeeing that his People ſtill continue to deſire it ; he hath put forth his Proclamation in order to it, and hath iſſued forth his Writs for the calling of it.

And to prevent any Cauſe of Interruption in it, he will conſent to every thing that can be reaſonably required for the Security of all thoſe that ſhall come to it. **His**

His Majeſty hath therefore ſent us to attend your Highneſs for the adjuſting of all Matters that ſhall be agreed to be neceſſary to the Freedom of Elections, and the Security of Sitting, and is ready immediately to enter into a Treaty in order to it.

His Majeſty propoſeth that in the mean time the reſpective Armies may be reſtrained within ſuch Limits, and at ſuch a Diſtance from *London*, as may prevent the Apprehenſions that the Parliament may in any kind be diſturbed, being deſirous that the Meeting of it may no longer be delay'd than it muſt be by the uſual and neceſſary Forms.

Hungerford,
Dec. 8. 88.   Signed, *Hallifax, Nottingham, Godolphin.*

We, with the Advice of the Lords and Gentlemen aſſembled with us, have, in Anſwer to the ſame, made theſe following Propoſals.

I. THat all Papiſts, and ſuch Perſons as are not qualified by Law, be Diſarmed, Disbanded, and Removed from all Employments, Civil and Military.

II. That all Proclamations which reflect upon us, or any that have come to us, or declared for us, be recalled ; and that if any Perſons for having ſo aſſiſted, have been committed, that they be forthwith ſet at liberty.

III. That for the Security and Safety of the City of *London*, the Cuſtody and Government of the Tower be immediately put into the Hands of the ſaid City.

IV. That if his Majeſty ſhall think fit to be at *London*, during the Sitting of the Parliament, that We may be there alſo, with equal Number of our Guards. Or if his Majeſty ſhall pleaſe to be in any place from *London*, at whatever diſtance he thinks fit, that We may be at a place of the ſame diſtance. And that the reſpective Armies do remove from *London* Thirty Miles, and that no more Foreign Forces be brought into the Kingdom.

V. That for the Security of the City of *London* and their Trade, *Tilbury* Fort be put into the Hands of the ſaid City.

VI. That to prevent the Landing of *French*, or other Foreign Troops, *Portſmouth* may be put into ſuch Hands, as by his Majeſty and Us ſhall be agreed upon.

VII. That ſome ſufficient part of the Publick Revenue be aſſigned us, for the maintaining of our Forces, until the Meeting of a Free Parliament. Given at *Littlecott*, the Ninth of *December* 1688.

W. H. *Prince of* Orange.

The Speech *of the Recorder of* Briſtol *to his Highneſs the Prince of* Orange, *Monday,* January *the* 7th, 1688. *The* Mayor, Recorder, Aldermen, *and* Commons *of the Principal Citizens of the City of* Briſtol, *waited upon the Prince of* Orange, *being introduced by his Grace the Duke of* Ormond, *their High-Steward, and the Earl of* Shrewsbury ; *where the Recorder ſpake to this Effect.*

May it pleaſe your Highneſs,

THE Reſtitution of our Religion, Laws and Liberties, and Freeing us from that Thraldom which hath rendred us for many years uſeleſs, and at laſt dangerous to the Common Intereſt of the Proteſtant World, by your Highneſs's ſingular Wiſdom, Courage and Conduct, are not only a ſtupendous Evidence of the Divine Favour and Providence for our Preſervation ; but will be, and ought to be an everlaſting Monument of your Highneſs's Magnanimity, and other the Heroick Virtues which adorn your great Soul, by whom ſuch a Revolution is wrought in this Nation, as is become the Joy and Comfort of the Preſent, and will be the Wonder of all Succeeding Ages.

In the Contrivance and Preparation of which great Work, your Highneſs (like the Heavens) did ſhed your propitious Influences upon us, whilſt we ſlept, and had ſcarce any proſpect from whence we might expect our Redemption.

But

But as ſince your happy Arrival in *England*, we did among the firſt, aſſociate our ſelves to aſſiſt and promote your Highneſs's moſt glorious Deſign, with our Lives and Fortunes; ſo we now think our ſelves bound in the higheſt Obligation of Gratitude, moſt humbly to preſent to your Highneſs our humble and hearty Thanks, for this our Deliverance from Popery and Arbitrary Power; and likewiſe, for declaring your gracious Intentions, That by the Advice of the Eſtates of this Kingdom, you will rectify the late Diſorders in the Government, both Eccleſiaſtical and Civil, according to the known Laws. The due and inviolable Obſervation of which, will, in our poor Opinion, be the only proper Means to render the Sovereign ſecure, and both Sovereign and Subject happy.

To which his Highneſs returned a moſt gracious Anſwer.

Guildhall,   *December the* 11th, 1688.
London.

By the Commiſſioners of Lieutenancy for the ſaid City.

Ordered,

THat Sir *Robert Clayton*, Kt. Sir *William Ruſſel*, Kt. Sir *Baſil Firebraſs*, Kt. and *Charles Duncomb*, Eſq; be a Committee from the ſaid Lieutenancy to attend his Royal Highneſs the Prince of *Orange*, and preſent to his Highneſs the Addreſs agreed by the Lieutenancy for that purpoſe: And that they begin their Journey to-morrow Morning.

By the Commiſſioners Command,

Geo. Evans, *Cl. Lieut.*London.

To His Highneſs the Prince of *Orange*,
The Humble Addreſs of the Lieutenancy of the City of London.

May it pleaſe Your Highneſs,

WE can never ſufficiently expreſs the deep Senſe we have conceived, and ſhall ever retain in our Hearts, That your Highneſs has expoſed your Perſon to ſo many Dangers, both by Sea and Land, for the Preſervation of the *Proteſtant Religion*, and the Laws and Liberties of this Kingdom; without which unparallel'd Undertaking we muſt probably have ſuffered all the Miſeries that *Popery* and *Slavery* could have brought upon us.

We have been greatly concerned, that before this time we have not had any ſeaſonable Opportunity to give your Highneſs and the World a real Teſtimony, that it has been our firm Reſolution to venture all that is Dear to us to attain thoſe glorious Ends which your Highneſs has propoſed for reſtoring and ſettling theſe Diſtracted Nations.

We therefore now unanimouſly preſent to your Highneſs our juſt and due Acknowledgments for the happy Relief you have brought unto us; and that we may not be wanting in this preſent Conjunction, we have put our ſelves into ſuch a Poſture, that (by the Bleſſing of God) we may be capable to prevent all ill Deſigns, and to preſerve this City in Peace and Safety till your Highneſs's happy Arrival.

We therefore humbly deſire that your Highneſs will pleaſe to repair to this City with what convenient ſpeed you can, for the perfecting the great Work which your Highneſs has ſo happily begun, to the general Joy and Satisfaction of us all.

December the 17th, 1688.

THE ſaid Committee this day made a Report to the Lieutenancy, that they had preſented the ſaid Addreſs to the Prince of *Orange*, and that his Highneſs received them very kindly.

December the 7th, 1688.

By the Lieutenancy.

Ordered,
That the ſaid Order and Addreſs be forthwith printed.

Geo. Evans.

To

To his Highnefs the Prince of Orange: *The Humble* Addrefs *of the Lord Mayor,* Aldermen *and* Commons *of the City of* London, *in Common Council affembled.*

May it pleafe your Highnefs,

WE taking into Confideration your Highnefs's fervent Zeal for the *Proteftant Religion,* manifefted to the World, in your many and hazardous Enterprizes; which it hath pleafed Almighty God to blefs you with miraculous Succefs: We render our deepeft Thanks to the Divine Majefty for the fame; and beg leave to prefent our moft humble Thanks to your Highnefs, particularly for your appearing in Arms in this Kingdom, to carry on and perfect your glorious Defign, to refcue *England, Scotland* and *Ireland* from Slavery and Popery, and in a free Parliament to eftablifh the Religion, the Laws, and the Liberties of thefe Kingdoms, upon a fure and lafting Foundation.

We have hitherto look'd for fome Remedy from thefe Oppreffions and imminent Dangers: We, together with our Proteftant Fellow-Subjects, laboured under, from his Majefty's Conceffions and Concurrences with your Highnefs's juft and pious Purpofes, expreffed in your gracious Declaration.

But herein finding our felves finally difappointed by his Majefty's withdrawing himfelf, we prefume to make your Highnefs our Refuge: And do, in the Name of this Capital C I T Y, implore your Highnefs's Protection; and moft humbly befeech your Highnefs to vouchfafe to repair to this C I T Y, where your Highnefs will be received with univerfal Joy and Satisfaction.

The Speech *of Sir* George Treby, *Kt. Recorder of the Honourable City of* London, *to his Highnefs the Prince of* Orange, Dec. 20. 1688.

May it pleafe Your Highnefs,

THE Lord Mayor being difabled by Sicknefs, your Highnefs is attended by the Aldermen and Commons of the Capital City of this Kingdom, deputed to congratulate your Highnefs upon this great and glorious Occafion.

In which, labouring for Words, we cannot but come fhort in Expreffion.

Reviewing our late Danger, we remember our Church and State, over-run by Popery and Arbitrary Power, and brought to the Point of Deftruction, by the Conduct of Men (that were our *true* Invaders) that brake the Sacred Fences of our Laws, and (which was worft) the very Conftitution of our Legiflature.

So there was no Remedy left but the *Laft.*

The only Perfon, under Heaven, that could apply this Remedy, was *Your Highnefs.*

You are of a *Nation,* whofe Alliances, *in all Times,* have been agreeable and profperous to us.

You are of a *Family* moft Illuftrious, Benefactors to Mankind. To have the Title of *Sovereign Prince, Stadtholder,* and to have worn the *Imperial* Crown, are among their *leffer* Dignities. They have long enjoyed a Dignity fingular and tranfcendent, *viz.* To be *Champions* of Almighty God, fent forth in feveral Ages, to vindicate his Caufe againft the greateft Oppreffions.

To this *Divine* Commiffion, our Nobles, our Gentry, and among them our brave *Englifh* Soldiers, rendred themfelves and their Arms upon your appearing.

GREAT SIR,

When we look back to the laft Month, and contemplate the *Swiftnefs* and *Fulnefs* of our prefent Deliverance, aftonifh'd, we think it miraculous.

Your Highnefs, led by the Hand of Heaven, and called by the *Voice* of the People, has preferved our deareft Interefts.

The *Proteftant Religion,* which is *Primitive* Chriftianity reftor'd.

Our *Laws,* which are our *ancient Title* to our Lives, Liberties and Eftates, and without which this World were a *Wildernefs.*

But what Retribution can we make to your Highnefs?

Z z z z z

Our

2

Our Thoughts are full charged with Gratitude.

Your Highnefs has a lafting Monument in the *Hearts,* in the *Prayers,* in the *Praifes* of all good Men among us. And late Pofterity will celebrate your ever-glorious Name, till Time fhall be no more.

Chapman, Mayor.

Cur' fpecial' tent' die Jovis xx. *die Decemb'* 1688. *Annoque RR. Jacobi Secundi Angl'* &c. *quarto.*

THIS Court doth defire Mr. *Recorder* to print his Speech this day made to the Prince of *Orange,* at the time of this Court's attending his Highnefs with the Deputies of the feveral Wards, and other Members of the Common Council.
Wagftaffe.

His Highnefs the Prince of *Orange*'s Speech to the *Scots* Lords and Gentlemen :

With their Advice, and his Highnefs's Anfwer. With a true Account of what paft at their Meeting in the Council-Chamber *at* Whitehall, January 7th, 168⅘.

His Highnefs the Prince of *Orange* having caufed advertife fuch of the *Scots* Lords and Gentlemen as were in Town, met them in a Room at *St. James's,* upon *Monday* the Seventh of *January,* at Three of the Clock in the Afternoon, and had this Speech to them.

My Lords and Gentlemen,

THE *only Reafon that induced me to undergo fo great an Undertaking, was, That I faw the Laws and Liberties of thefe Kingdoms overturned, and the* Proteftant Religion *in imminent Danger : And feeing you are here fo many Noblemen and Gentlemen, I have called you together, that I may have your Advice, what is to be done for fecuring the* Proteftant Religion, *and reftoring your Laws and Liberties, according to my* Declaration.

As foon as his Highnefs had retired, the Lords and Gentlemen went to the Council-Chamber at *Whitehall* ; and having chofen the Duke of *Hamilton* their Prefident, they fell a confulting, what Advice was fit to be given to his Highnefs in this Conjuncture : And after fome hours Reafoning, they agreed upon the Materials of it, and appointed the Clerks, with fuch as were to affift them, to draw up in Writing, what the Meeting thought expedient, to advife his Highnefs, and to bring it in to the Meeting the next Day in the Afternoon.

Tuefday, the Eighth Inftant, the Writing was prefented in the Meeting : And fome time being fpent in reafoning about the fitteft way of convening a General Meeting of the Eftates of *Scotland* ; at laft the Meeting came to agree in their Opinion, and appointed the Advice to be writ clean over, according to the Amendments. But as they were about to part for that Dyet, the Earl of *Arran* propofed to them, as his Lordfhip's Advice, that they fhould move the Prince of *Orange,* to defire the *King* to return and call a *Free Parliament,* which would be the beft way to fecure the Proteftant Religion and Property, and to heal all Breaches. This Propofal feemed to diffatisfy the whole Meeting, and the Duke of *Hamilton* their Prefident, Father to the Earl ; but they prefently parted.

Wednefday, the Ninth of *January,* they met at three of the clock in the fame Room, and Sir *Patrick Hume* took notice of the Propofal made by the Earl of *Arran,* and defired to know if there was any there that would fecond it : But none appearing to do it, he faid, That what the Earl had propofed, was evidently oppofite and inimicous to his Highnefs the Prince of *Orange*'s Undertaking, his Declaration, and the good Intentions of preferving the Proteftant Religion, and of Reftoring their Laws
and

and Liberties expreft in it ; and further, defired that the Meeting fhould declare this to be their Opinion of it. The Lord *Cardrofs* feconded Sir *Patrick's* Motion : It was anfwered by the Duke of *Hamilton,* Prefident of the Meeting, That their Bufinefs was to prepare an Advice to be offered to the Prince ; and the Advice being now ready to go to the Vote, there was no need that the Meeting fhould give their Senfe of the Earl's Propofal, which neither before nor after Sir *Patrick's* Motion, any had pretended to own or fecond ; fo that it was fallen, and out of doors ; and that the Vote of the Meeting, upon the Advice brought in by their Order, would fufficiently declare their Opinion: This being feconded by the Earl of *Sutherland,* the Lord *Cardrofs* and Sir *Patrick* did acquiefce in it ; and the Meeting voted unanimoufly the Advice following.

To His Highnefs the Prince of *Orange.*

WE the Lords and Gentlemen of the Kingdom of Scotland, *affembled at your Highnefs's defire, in this Extraordinary Conjuncture, do give your Highnefs our humble and hearty Thanks for your pious and generous* Undertaking, *for preferving of the* Proteftant Religion, *and reftoring the* Laws and Liberties *of thefe Kingdoms.*

In order to the attaining thefe Ends, our humble Advice and Defire is, That your Highnefs take upon you the Adminiftration of all Affairs both Civil and Military; the Difpofal of the Publick Revenues and Fortreffes of the Kingdom of Scotland, *and the doing every Thing that is neceffary for the Prefervation of the Peace of the Kingdom, until a general* Meeting *of the States of the Nation, which we humbly defire your Highnefs to call, to be holden at* Edinburgh *the Fourteenth day of* March *next, by your Letters or Proclamation, to be publifhed at the Market-crofs of* Edinburgh, *and other Head Burroughs of the feveral Shires and Stewartries, as fufficient Intimation to all concerned, and according to the Cuftom of the Kingdom: And that the Publication of thefe your Letters or Proclamation, be by the Sheriffs, or Stewart-Clerks, for the Free-holders, who have the value of Lands, holden according to Law, for making Elections ; and by the Town-Clerks of the feveral Burroughs, for the meeting of the whole Burgeffes of the refpective Royal Burroughs, to make their Elections at leaft Fifteen Days before the meeting of the Eftates at* Edinburgh; *and the Refpective Clerks to make Intimation thereof, at leaft Ten Days before the meetings for Elections : And that the whole Electors and Members of the faid Meeting at* Edinburgh, *qualified as above expreft, be Proteftants, without any other Exception or Limitation whatfoever ; to deliberate and refolve what is to be done for fecuring the Proteftant Religion, and reftoring the Laws and Liberties of the Kingdom, according to your Highnefs's Declaration. Dated at the Council-Chamber in* White-hall, *the Tenth Day of* January, 1689.

This Addrefs being fubfcribed by Thirty Lords, and about Eighty Gentlemen, was prefented in their prefence at *St. James's,* by the Duke of *Hamilton* their Prefident, to his Highnefs the Prince of *Orange,* who thanked them for the Truft they repofed in him, and defired time to confider of fo weighty an Affair.

Upon the Fourteenth of *January,* his Highnefs the Prince of *Orange* met again with the *Scots* Lords and Gentlemen at *St. James's* ; and fpoke to them as follows :

My Lords and Gentlemen,

IN purfuance of your Advice, I will, until the Meeting of the States in March next, give fuch Orders concerning the Affairs of Scotland, as are neceffary for the Calling of the faid Meeting, for the preferving of the Peace ; the applying of the publick Revenue to the moft preffing Ufes, and putting the Fortreffes in the Hands of Perfons, in whom the Nation can have a juft Confidence ; And I do further affure you, That you will always find me ready to concur with you in every Thing that may be found neceffary for fecuring the Proteftant Religion, and reftoring the Laws and Liberties of the Nation.

The Earl of *Crawfurd* defired of his Highnefs, That himfelf, the Earl of *Louthian,* and others, come to Town fince the Addrefs was prefented, might have an opportunity to fubfcribe it ; which was accordingly done. His Highnefs retired, and all fhewed great Satisfaction with his Anfwer.

The

The Emperor of Germany's *Account of K.* James's *Mifgovernment in joining with the King of* France (*the Common Enemy of Chriftendom*) *in his Letter to King* James, *viz.*

LEOPOLD, &c.

WE have received your Majefty's Letters, dated from *St. Germains* the fixth of *February* laft, by the Earl of *Carlingford,* your Envoy in our Court : By them we have underftood the Condition your Majefty is reduced to; and that you being deferted after the Landing of the Prince of *Orange,* by your Army, and even by your Domeftick Servants, and by thofe you moft confided in, and almoft by all your Subjects, you have been forced by a fudden Flight to provide for your own Safety, and to feek Shelter and Protection in *France :* Laftly, that you defire Affiftance from us for the recovering your Kingdoms. We do affure your Majefty, that as foon as we heard of this fevere Turn of Affairs, we were moved at it, not only with the common fenfe of Humanity, but with much deeper Impreffions fuitable to the fincere Affection which we have always born to you. And we were heartily forry, that at laft that was come to pafs, which (tho' we hoped for better things, yet) our own fad thoughts had fuggefted to us would enfue. If your Majefty had rather given Credit to the friendly Remonftrances that were made you, by our late Envoy the Count de *Kaunitz,* in our Name, than the deceitful Infinuations of the *French,* whofe chief aim was, by fomenting continual Divifions between you and your People, to gain thereby an Opportunity to infult the more fecurely over the reft of Chriftendom : And if your Majefty had put a ftop, by your Force and Authority, to their many Infractions of the Peace, of which by the Treaty of *Nimeguen* you are made the Guarantee, and to that end, entred into Confultations with us, and fuch others as have the like juft Sentiments in this matter ; We are verily perfuaded, that by this means you fhould have in a great meafure quieted the Minds of your People, which were fo much exafperated through their averfion to our Religion, and the publick Peace had been preferved as well in your Kingdoms as here in the *Roman* Empire. But now we refer it even to your Majefty, to judge what condition we can be in to afford you any Affiftance, we being not only engaged in a War with the *Turks,* but finding our felves, at the fame time unjuftly and barbaroufly attacked by the *French,* contrary to, and againft the Faith of Treaties, they then reckoning themfelves fecure of *England.* And *this ought not to be concealed, that the greateft Injuries which have been done to our Religion, have flowed from no other than the* French *themfelves ; who not only efteem it lawful for them, to make perfidious Leagues with the fworn Enemies of the Holy Crofs, tending to the deftruction both of us and of the whole Chriftian World,* in order to the checking our Endeavours which were undertaken for the Glory of God, and to ftop thofe Succeffes which it hath pleafed Almighty God to give us hitherto ; *but further have heaped one Treachery upon another, even within the Empire itfelf.* The Cities of the Empire which were furrendred upon Articles, figned by the *Dauphin* himfelf, have been exhaufted by exceffive Impofitions; and after their being exhaufted, have been plundered, and after plundering have been burned and razed. The Palaces of Princes, which in all times, and even in the moft deftructive Wars, have been preferved, are now burnt down to the ground. The Churches are robbed, and fuch as fubmitted themfelves to them are, in a moft barbarous manner, carried away as Slaves. In fhort, *It is become a Diverfion to them to commit all manner of Infolencies and Cruelties in many places, but chiefly in Catholick Countries, exceeding the Cruelties of the* Turks *themfelves ;* which having impofed an abfolute neceffity upon us to fecure our felves and the holy *Roman* Empire by the beft means we can think on, and that no lefs againft them than againft the *Turks ;* we promife our felves from your Juftice ready affent to this, That it ought not to be imputed to us, if we endeavour to procure, by a juft War, that fecurity to our felves which we could not hitherto obtain by fo many Treaties ; and that in order to the obtaining thereof, we take meafures for our mutual Defence or Prefervation, with all thofe who are equally concerned in the fame Defign with us. It remains that we beg of God that he would direct all things to his glory, and that he would grant your Majefty true and folid Comforts under this your great Calamity ; we embrace you with tender Affections of a Brother.

At Vienna *the 9th of* April, 1689.

The

The Declaration of the Lords Spiritual and Temporal, and Commons assembled at Westminster; *concerning the Misgovernment of King* James, *and filling up the Throne. Presented to King* William *and Queen* Mary, *by the Right Honourable the Marquess of* Hallifax, *Speaker to the House of Lords. With his Majesty's most gracious Answer thereunto.*

WHereas the late King *James* the Second, by the Assistance of divers Evil Counsellors, Judges, and Ministers employ'd by him, did endeavour to subvert and extirpate the Protestant Religion, and the Laws and Liberties of this Kingdom ;

By Assuming and Exercising a Power of dispensing with, and suspending of Laws, and the Execution of Laws, without consent of Parliament.

By Committing and Prosecuting divers Worthy Prelates, for humbly petitioning to be excused from concurring to the said assumed Power.

By issuing, and causing to be executed, a Commission under the great Seal, for erecting a Court called, *The Court of Commissioners for Ecclesiastical Causes.*

By levying Money for and to the use of the Crown, by pretence of Prerogative, for other time, and in other manner, than the same was granted by Parliament.

By raising and keeping a standing Army within this Kingdom, in the time of Peace, without consent of Parliament ; and Quartering Soldiers contrary to Law.

By causing several good Subjects, being Protestants, to be disarmed at the same time, when Papists were both armed and employ'd contrary to Law.

By violating the Freedom of Election of Members to serve in Parliament.

By Prosecutions in the Court of *King's Bench* for Matters and Causes cognizable only in *Parliament* ; and by divers other Arbitrary and Illegal Courses.

And whereas of late Years, partial, corrupt and unqualified Persons, have been returned and served on Juries in Trials, and particularly divers Jurors in Trials for High-Treason, which were not Freeholders :

And excessive Bail hath been required of Persons committed in Criminal Cases, to elude the Benefit of the Laws made for the Liberty of the Subjects :

And Excessive Fines have been imposed :

And illegal and cruel Punishments inflicted :

And several Grants and Promises made of Fines and Forfeitures before any Convictions or Judgment against the Persons upon whom the same were to be levied.

All which are utterly and directly contrary to the known Laws and Statutes, and Freedom of this Realm.

And whereas the said late K. *James* the Second having abdicated the Government, and the Throne being thereby vacant ;

His Highness the Prince of *Orange* (whom it hath pleased Almighty God to make the glorious Instrument of delivering this Kingdom from Popery and Arbitrary Power) did (by the Advice of the Lords Spiritual and Temporal, and divers principal Persons of the Commons) cause Letters to be written to the Lords Spiritual and Temporal, being Protestants, and other Letters to the several Counties, Cities, Universities, Burroughs, and Cinque-Ports, for the chusing of such Persons to represent them, as were of right to be sent to Parliament, to Meet and Sit at *Westminster* upon the 22d Day of *January* in this Year 1688, in order to such an Establishment, as that their Religion, Laws and Liberties, might not again be in danger of being subverted : Upon which Letters, Elections having been accordingly made ;

And thereupon the said Lords Spiritual and Temporal, and Commons, pursuant to their respective Letters and Elections, being now assembled in a full and free Representative of this Nation, taking into their most serious Consideration the best Means for attaining the Ends aforesaid, do in the first place (as their Ancestors in like Case have usually done) for the Vindicating and Asserting their Ancient Rights and Liberties, Declare,

That the pretended Power of suspending of Laws, or the Execution of Laws, by Regal Authority, without Consent of Parliament, is illegal.

That the pretended Power of dispensing with Laws, or the Execution of Laws, by Regal Authority, as it hath been assumed and exercised of late, is illegal.

That the Commission for erecting the late *Court of Commissioners for Ecclesiastical Causes*, and all Commissions and Courts of the like nature, are illegal and pernicious.

That levying of Money for, or to the Ufe of the Crown, by pretence of Prerogative, without grant of Parliament for longer time, or in other manner, than the fame is or fhall be granted, is illegal.

That it is the Right of the Subjects to petition the King, and all Commitments and Profecutions for fuch petitioning, are illegal.

That the raifing or keeping a ftanding Army, within the Kingdom in time of Peace, unlefs it be with Confent of Parliament, is againft Law.

That the Subjects which are Proteftants, may have Arms for their Defence, fuitable to their Condition, and as allowed by Law.

That Election of Members of Parliament, ought to be free.

That the Freedom of Speech, and Debates or Proceedings in Parliament, ought not to be impeached or queftioned in any Court or Place out of Parliament.

That exceffive Bail ought not to be required, nor exceffive Fines impofed, nor cruel and unufual Punifhments inflicted.

That Jurors ought to be duly empannell'd and return'd, and Jurors which pafs upon Men in Trials for High-Treafon ought to be Freeholders.

That all Grants and Promifes of Fines and Forfeitures of particular Perfons before Conviction, are illegal and void.

And that for Redrefs of all Grievances, and for the amending, ftrengthening and preferving of the Laws, Parliaments ought to be held frequently.

And they do claim, demand, and infift upon all and fingular the Premifes, as their undoubted Rights and Liberties; and that no Declarations, Judgments, Doings, or Proceedings, to the prejudice of the People in any of the faid Premifes, ought in any wife to be drawn hereafter into Confequence or Example.

To which Demand of their Rights they are particularly encouraged by the Declaration of his Highnefs the Prince of *Orange*, as being the only Means of obtaining a full redrefs and remedy therein.

Having therefore an entire Confidence, that his faid Highnefs the Prince of *Orange* will perfect the Deliverance fo far advanced by him, and will ftill preferve them from the Violation of their Rights, which they have here afferted, and from all other Attempts upon their Religion, Rights and Liberties:

The faid Lords Spiritual and Temporal, and Commons affembled at *Weftminfter*, do refolve,

That *William* and *Mary*, Prince and Princefs of *Orange*, be, and be declared, King and Queen of *England*, *France* and *Ireland*, and the Dominions thereunto belonging, to hold the Crown and Royal Dignity of the faid Kingdoms and Dominions, to them the faid Prince and Princefs, during their Lives, and the Life of the Survivor of them; and that the fole and full Exercife of the Regal Power be only in, and executed by the faid Prince of *Orange*, in the Names of the faid Prince and Princefs during their joint Lives; and after their Deceafes, the faid Crown and Royal Dignity of the faid Kingdoms and Dominions to be to the Heirs of the Body of the faid Princefs; and for default of fuch Iffue, to the Princefs *Anne* of *Denmark*, and the Heirs of her Body; and for default of fuch Iffue, to the Heirs of the Body of the faid Prince of *Orange*.

And the faid Lords Spiritual and Temporal, and Commons, do pray the faid Prince and Princefs of *Orange* to accept the fame accordingly.

And that the Oaths hereafter mentioned be taken by all Perfons, of whom the Oaths of Allegiance and Supremacy might be required by Law, inftead of them; and that the faid Oaths of Allegiance and Supremacy be abrogated.

I A. B. *do fincerely promife and fwear, That I will be Faithful, and bear true Allegiance to their Majefties King* WILLIAM *and Queen* MARY.

So help me God.

I A. B. *do fwear, That I do from my Heart Abhor, Deteft and Abjure, as Impious and Heretical, this damnable Doctrine and Pofition,* That Princes excommunicated or deprived by the Pope, or any Authority of the See of *Rome*, may be depofed or murdered by their Subjects, or any other whatfoever. *And I do declare, That no Foreign Prince, Perfon, Prelate, State, or Potentate, hath, or ought to have, any Jurifdiction, Power, Superiority, Pre-eminence, or Authority Ecclefiaftical or Spiritual, within this Realm.*

So help me God.

Jo. Browne, *Cleric' Parl.*

Die

Die Veneris 15 *Feb.* 1688.

His Majesty's Gracious *Answer*, to the *Declaration* of both *Houses.*

My Lords and Gentlemen,

THIS *is certainly the greatest proof of the Trust you have in Us, that can be given, which is the thing that maketh us value it the more ; and we thankfully accept what you have offered. And as I had no other Intention in coming hither, than to preserve your Religion, Laws and Liberties ; so you may be sure, That I shall endeavour to support them, and shall be willing to concur with any thing that shall be for the Good of the Kingdom, and to do all that is in my power to advance the Welfare and Glory of the Nation.*

Die Veneris 15 *Februarii* 1688.

ORdered by the Lords Spiritual and Temporal, assembled at *Westminster*, That his Majesty's Gracious Answer to the Declaration of both Houses, and the Declaration, be forthwith printed and published ; and that his Majesty's Gracious Answer this Day be added to the engrossed Declaration in Parchment, to be Enrolled in Parliament and Chancery.

Jo. Browne, Cleric'

Parliamentorum.

A PROCLAMATION

WHereas it hath pleased Almighty God, in his Great Mercy to this Kingdom, to Vouchsafe us a Miraculous Deliverance from Popery and Arbitrary Power; and that our Preservation is due, next under God, to the Resolution and Conduct of his Highness the Prince of ORANGE, whom God hath Chosen to be the Glorious Instrument of such an inestimable Happiness to us and our Posterity: and being highly sensible, and fully persuaded of the Great and Eminent Vertues of Her Highness the Princess of ORANGE, whose Zeal for the Protestant Religion, will, no doubt, bring a Blessing along with Her upon this Nation. And whereas the Lords and Commons now assembled at Westminster, have made a Declaration, and presented the same to the said Prince and Princess of ORANGE, and therein desired them to accept the Crown; who have accepted the same accordingly. We therefore, the Lords Spiritual and Temporal, and Commons, together with the Lord Mayor and Citizens of London, and others of the Commons of this Realm, do with a full Consent publish and proclaim, according to the said Declaration, WILLIAM and MARY, Prince and Princess of ORANGE, to be KING and QUEEN of England, France and Ireland, with all the Dominions and Territories thereunto belonging : Who are accordingly so to be Owned, Deemed, Accepted, and taken by all the People of the aforesaid Realms and Dominions, who are from henceforward bound to acknowledge and pay unto them all Faith and true Allegiance; beseeching God, by whom Kings Reign, to Bless King WILLIAM and Queen MARY with Long and Happy Years to Reign over Us.

God Save King *William* and Queen *Mary.*

Jo. Brown, *Cleric'*

Parliamentorum.

The

The Declaration of the Eſtates of Scotland *concerning the Miſgovernment of King* James *the Seventh, and filling up the Throne with King* William *and Queen* Mary.

THAT King *James* the Seventh had acted irregularly.

1. By his erecting publick Schools and Societies of the Jeſuits ; and not only allowing Maſs to be publickly ſaid, but alſo inverting Proteſtant Chapels and Churches to publick Maſs-houſes, contrary to the expreſs Laws againſt ſaying and hearing of Maſs.

2. By allowing Popiſh Books to be printed and diſperſed, by a Gift to a Popiſh Printer, deſigning him Printer to his Majeſty's Houſhold, College and Chapel, contrary to the Laws.

3. By taking the Children of Proteſtant Noblemen and Gentlemen, ſending them abroad to be bred Papiſts, making great Funds and Donations to Popiſh Schools and Colleges abroad, beſtowing Penſions on Prieſts, and perverting Proteſtants from their Religion, by Offers of Places, Preferments and Penſions.

4. By diſarming Proteſtants, while at the ſame time he employed Papiſts in the Places of greateſt Truſt, Civil and Military, ſuch as Chancellor, Secretaries, Privy Counſellors, and Lords of Seſſion ; thruſting out Proteſtants to make room for Papiſts, and intruſting the Forts and Magazines of the Kingdom in their hands.

5. By impoſing Oaths contrary to Law.

6. By giving Gifts and Grants for exacting of Money without Conſent of Parliament, or Convention of Eſtates.

7. By levying and keeping on foot a ſtanding Army in time of Peace, without conſent of Parliament ; which Army did exact Locality, free and day Quarters.

8. By employing the Officers of the Army, as Judges through the Kingdom, and impoſing them where there were held Offices and Juriſdictions, by whom many of the Lieges were put to death ſummarily without legal Trial, Jury or Record.

9. By impoſing exorbitant Fines to the Value of the Party's Eſtates, exacting extravagant Bail, and diſpoſing Fines and Forfeiture before any Proceſs or Conviction.

10. By impriſoning Perſons without expreſſing the Reaſon, and delaying to put them to Trial.

11. By cauſing purſue and forfault ſeveral Perſons upon ſtretches of old and obſolete Laws, upon frivolous and weak Pretences, upon lame and defective Probations ; as particularly the late Earl of *Argyle*, to the ſcandal and reproach of the Juſtice of the Nation.

12. By ſubverting the Right of the Royal Burroughs, the Third Eſtate of Parliament, impoſing upon them not only Magiſtrates, but alſo the whole Town Council and Clerks, contrary to the Liberties and expreſs Charters, without the pretence either of Sentence, Surrender or Conſent: So that the Commiſſioners to Parliament being choſen by the Magiſtrates and Councils, the King might in effect as well nominate that entire Eſtate of Parliament ; many of the ſaid Magiſtrates put in by him were avowed Papiſts ; and the Burghs were forced to pay Money for the Letters, impoſing theſe illegal Magiſtrates and Council upon them.

13. By ſending Letters to the chief Courts of Juſtice, not only ordering the Judges to ſtop and deſiſt *ſine die*, to determine Cauſes, but alſo ordering and commanding them how to proceed in Caſes depending before them, contrary to the expreſs Laws: And by changing the Nature of the Judges Gifts, *ad vitam aut culpam*, and giving them Commiſſions *ad bene-placitum*, to diſpoſe them to compliance by Arbitrary Courſes, turning them out of their Offices when they did not comply.

14. By granting perſonal Protections for Civil Debts, contrary to Law.

All which are utterly and directly contrary to the known Laws, Freedoms and Statutes of this Realm.

Therefore the Eſtates of the Kingdom of *Scotland* find, and declare, That King *James* the Seventh, being a profeſt Papiſt, did aſſume the Regal Power, and acted as a King, without ever taking the Oath required by Law ; and has, by Advice of evil and wicked Counſellors, invaded the Fundamental Conſtitution of the Kingdom, and altered it from a Legal, Limited Monarchy, to an Arbitrary and Deſpotick Power ; and hath exerciſed the ſame to the ſubverſion of the Proteſtant Religion, and the violation of the Laws and Liberties of the Kingdom: Inverting all the Ends of Government, whereby he hath forfeited the Right to the Crown, and the Throne is become vacant.

†

And

And whereas his Royal Highness, *William*, then Prince of *Orange*, now King of *England*, whom it hath pleased the Almighty God to make the glorious Instrument of delivering these Kingdoms from Popery and Arbitrary Power, did, by advice of several Lords and Gentlemen of this Nation, at *London*, for the time, call the Estates of this Kingdom, to meet the Fourteenth of *March* last, in order to such an Establishment, as that their Religion, Laws, and Liberties, might not be again in danger of being subverted : And the said Estates being now assembled, in a full and free Representative of this Nation, taking into their most serious Consideration, the best means for attaining the ends aforesaid, do in the first place, as their Ancestors in the like cases have usually done, for the vindicating and asserting their ancient Rights and Liberties, declare,

That by the Law of this Kingdom, no Papist can be King or Queen of this Realm, nor bear any Office whatsoever therein ; nor can any Protestant Successor exercise the Regal Power, until he or she swear the Coronation-Oath.

That all Proclamations asserting an absolute Power, to cass, annul, and disable Laws; the erecting Schools and Colleges for Jesuits ; the inverting Protestant Chapels and Churches to publick Mass-houses; and the allowing Mass to be said, are contrary to Law.

That the allowing Popish Books to be printed and dispersed, is contrary to Law.

That the taking the Children of Noblemen, Gentlemen, and others, sending and keeping them abroad to be bred Papists : The making Funds and Donations to Popish Schools and Colleges ; the bestowing Pensions on Priests, and the perverting Protestants from their Religion, by Offers of Places, Preferments, and Pensions, are contrary to Law.

That the disarming of Protestants, and employing Papists in the Places of greatest Trust, both civil and military ; the thrusting out Protestants, to make room for Papists, and the entrusting Papists with the Forts and Magazines of the Kingdom, are contrary to Law.

That the imposing Oaths without Authority of Parliament, is contrary to Law.

That the giving Gifts or Grants for raising of Money without the Consent of Parliament, or Convention of Estates, is contrary to Law.

That the employing Officers of the Army, as Judges through the Kingdom, or imposing them where there were several Offices and Jurisdictions, and the putting the Lieges to death summarily, and without legal Trial, Jury, or Record, are contrary to Law.

That the imposing extraordinary Fines, the exacting of exorbitant Bail, and the disposing of Fines and Forfaultures before Sentence, are contrary to Law.

That the imprisoning Persons, without expressing the reason thereof, and delaying to put them to Trial, are contrary to Law.

That the causing pursue and forfault Persons upon stretches of old and obsolete Laws, upon frivolous and weak Pretences, upon lame and defective Probation, as particularly the late Earl of *Argyle*, are contrary to Law.

That the nominating and imposing Magistrates, Councils, and Clerks, upon Burghs, contrary to the Liberties and express Charters, is contrary to Law.

That the sending Letters to the Courts of Justice, ordaining the Judges to stop or desist from determining Causes, or ordaining them how to proceed in Causes depending before them ; and the changing the Nature of the Judges Gifts *ad vitam aut culpam*, unto Commissions *Durante bene-placito*, are contrary to Law.

That the granting Personal Protections for civil Debts, is contrary to Law.

That the forcing the Lieges to depone against themselves in Capital Crimes, however the Punishment be restricted, is contrary to Law.

That the using Torture without Evidence, or in ordinary Crimes, is contrary to Law.

That the sending of an Army in a hostile manner upon any part of the Kingdom, in a peaceable time, and exacting of Locality, and any manner of free Quarter, is contrary to Law.

That the charging the Lieges with Law-burroughs at the King's instance, and the imposing of Bands without the Authority of Parliament, and the suspending the Advocates from their Employments for not compearing when such Bands were offered, were contrary to Law.

That the putting of Garrisons on private Men's Houses in a time of peace, without the consent of the Authority of Parliament, is contrary to Law.

That the Opinion of the Lords of Session in the two Causes following, were contrary to Law ; (*viz.*) 1. That the concerting the demand of a Supply for a forfaulted Person, although not given, is Treason. (2.) That Persons refusing to discover what are their private thoughts and judgments in relation to points of Treason, or other Men's actions, are guilty of Treason.

That

2

That the fining Husbands for their Wives withdrawing from the Church, was contrary to Law.

That Prelacy, and Superiority of any Office in the Church above Presbyters, is and hath been a great and unsupportable Grievance and Trouble to this Nation, and contrary to the Inclinations of the generality of the People ever since the Reformation, they having reformed from Popery by Presbyters, and therefore ought to be abolished.

That it is the Right and Privilege of the Subjects to protest for remand of Law to the King and Parliament, against Sentences pronounced by the Lords of Session, providing the same do not stop execution of the said Sentences.

That it is the Right of the Subjects to petition the King, and that all Imprisonments and Prosecutions for such Petitions, are contrary to Law.

That for redress of all Grievances, and for the amending, strengthning, and preserving of the Laws, Parliaments ought to be frequently called and allowed to sit, and the freedom of Speech and Debate secured to the Members.

And they do claim and demand and insist upon all and sundry the Premises, as their undoubted Right and Liberties, and that no Declarations, Doings, or Proceedings to the prejudice of the People in any of the said Premises, ought in any ways to be drawn hereafter in consequence and example ; but that all Forfaultures, Fines, Loss of Offices, Imprisonments, Banishments, Pursuits, Persecutions, and Rigorous Executions be considered, and the Parties seized, be redressed.

To which demand of the Rights, and redressing of their Grievances, they are particularly encouraged by his Majesty the King of *England*, his Declaration for the Kingdom of *Scotland*, of the   day of *October* last, as being the only means for obtaining a full Redress and Remead therein.

Having therefore an entire Confidence, That his said Majesty the King of *England*, will perfyte the Deliverance so far advanced by him, and will still preserve them from the violation of the Rights which they have here asserted, and from all other Attempts upon their Religion, Laws, and Liberties:

The said Estates of the Kingdom of *Scotland*, do resolve, That *William* and *Mary*, King and Queen of *England*, *France*, and *Ireland*, be, and be declared King and Queen of *Scotland* ; to hold the Crown and royal Dignity of the said Kingdom of *Scotland*, to them the said King and Queen during their Lives, and the longest Liver of them: And that the sole and full exercise of the Royal Power, be only in, and exercised by him the said King, in the Names of the said King and Queen, during their joint Lives: And after their deceases, the said Crown and Royal Dignity of the said Kingdom, to be to the Heirs of the Body of the said Queen. Which failing, to the Princess *Anne* of *Denmark*, and the Heirs of her Body: Which also failing, to the Heirs of the Body of the said *William*, King of *England*.

And they do pray the said King and Queen of *England*, to accept the same accordingly.

And that the Oath hereafter-mentioned, be taken by all Protestants of whom the Oath of Allegiance, and any other Oaths and Declarations might be required by Law instead thereof: And that the said Oath of Allegiance, and other Oaths and Declarations, may be abrogated.

I A. B. *Do sincerely promise and swear, That I will be faithful, and bear true Allegiance to their Majesties King* William *and Queen* Mary.

So help me God.

A Proclamation declaring *William* and *Mary* King and Queen of *England*, to be King and Queen of *Scotland*. Edinburgh, *April* 11. 1689.

𝖂Hereas, the Estates of this Kingdom of Scotland, by their Act of the Date of these Presents, have Resolved, That WILLIAM and MARY, King and Queen of England, France, and Ireland, be, and be declared King and Queen of Scotland, to hold the Crown and Royal Dignity of the said Kingdom of Scotland, to them the said King and Queen, during their Lives, and the longest Liver of them ; and that the sole and full Exercise of the Regal Power, be only in, and Exercised by the said King, in the Names of the said King and Queen, during their joint Lives. As also, the Estates having Resolved and Enacted an Instrument of Government, or Claim of
Right,

Right, to be presented with the Offer of the Crown, to the said King and Queen. They do Statute and Ordain, that William and Mary, King and Queen of England, France, and Ireland, be accordingly forthwith proclaimed King and Queen of Scotland, at the Mercat Cross of Edinburgh, by the Lyon King at Arms, or his Deputs, his Brethren Heraulds, Macers, and Pursevants, and at the Head-Burghs of all the Shires, Stewarties, Bailliaries, and Regalities within the Kingdom, by Messengers at Arms. Extracted forth of the Meeting of the Estates, by me,

Ja. Dalrymple, Cls.

God save King W I L L I A M and Queen M A R Y.

The Manner of the King and Queen taking the Scotish *Coronation-Oath.*

May, 11. 1689.

THIS Day being appointed for the publick Reception of the Commissioners, *viz.* The Earl of *Argyle*, Sir *James Montgomery* of *Skelmerly*, and Sir *John Dalrymple* of *Stair* younger, who were sent by the Meeting of the Estates of *Scotland*, with an Offer of the Crown of that Kingdom to their Majesties, they accordingly, at three of the clock, met at the Council-Chamber, and from thence were conducted by Sir *Charles Cotterel*, Master of the Ceremonies, attended by most of the Nobility and Gentry of that Kingdom, who reside in and about this Place, to the *Banquetting-House*; where the King and Queen came attended by many Persons of Quality, the Sword being carried before them by the Lord *Cardrosse*, (and their Majesties being placed on the Throne under a rich Canopy) they first presented a Letter from the Estates to his Majesty; then the Instrument of Government; thirdly, a Paper containing the Grievances, which they desired might be redressed; and lastly, an Address to his Majesty for turning the Meeting of the said Estates into a Parliament: All which being signed by his Grace the Duke of *Hamilton*, as President of the Meeting, and read to their Majesties, the King returned to the Commissioners the following Answer.

WHen I engaged in this Undertaking, I had particular Regard and Consideration for Scotland, and therefore I did emit a Declaration in relation to that as well as to this Kingdom, which I intend to make good and effectual to them. I take it very kindly that Scotland hath expressed so much Confidence in, and Affection to me: They shall find me willing to assist them in every thing that concerns the Weal and Interest of that Kingdom, by making what Laws shall be necessary for the security of their Religion, Property, and Liberty, and to ease them of what may be justly grievous to them.

After which, the Coronation-Oath was tendred to their Majesties, which the Earl of *Argyle* spoke Word by Word directly, and the King and Queen repeated it after him, holding their Right Hands up after the manner of taking Oaths in *Scotland*.

The Meeting of the Estates of *Scotland* did authorize their Commissioners to represent to his Majesty, That that Clause in the Oath in relation to the rooting out of Hereticks, did not import the destroying of Hereticks; and that by the Law of *Scotland*, no Man was to be persecuted for his private Opinion; and even obstinate and convicted Hereticks were only to be denounced Rebels or Outlawed, whereby their moveable Estates are confiscated. His Majesty, at the repeating that Clause in the Oath, *did declare, that he did not mean by these words, that he was under any Obligation to become a Persecutor.* To which the Commissioners made Answer, *That neither the Meaning of the Oath, or the Law of* Scotland *did import it.* Then the King replied, *That he took the Oath in that sense,* and called for *Witnesses,* the Commissioners, and others present; and then both their Majesties signed the said Coronation-Oath.

After which the Commissioners, and several of the *Scotish* Nobility, kissed their Majesties Hands.

The

*The Coronation-*O A T H *of* England.

The Arch-bishop or Bishop shall say,

WILL you solemnly promise and swear to govern the People of this Kingdom of *England,* and the Dominions thereto belonging, according to the Statutes in Parliament agreed on, and the Laws and Customs of the same?

The King and Queen shall say,
I solemnly promise so to do.

Archbishop or Bishop:
Will you, to your power, cause Law and Justice in Mercy to be executed in all your Judgments?

King and Queen.
I will.

Archbishop or Bishop,
Will you, to the utmost of your power, maintain the Laws of God, the true Profession of the Gospel, and the *Protestant* Reformed Religion, established by Law? And will you preserve, unto the Bishops and Clergy of this Realm, and to the Churches committed to their Charge, all such Rights and Privileges as by Law do or shall appertain unto them, or any of them?

King and Queen.
All this I promise to do.

(After this, the King and Queen laying his and her Hand upon the Holy Gospels, shall say,)

King and Queen,
The things which I have here before promised, I will perform and keep. *So help me God.*
(Then the King and Queen shall kiss the Book.)

---

*The Coronation-*O A T H *of* Scotland.

WE, *William* and *Mary,* King and Queen of *Scotland,* faithfully promise and swear, by this our Solemn Oath, in presence of the eternal God, that during the whole course of our Life, we will serve the same eternal God, to the uttermost of our power, according as he has required in his most holy Word, revealed and contained in the new and old Testament; and according to the same Word, shall maintain the true Religion of Christ Jesus, the preaching of his holy Word, and the due and right Ministration of the Sacraments, now received and preached within the Realm of *Scotland;* and shall abolish and gainstand all false Religion contrary to the same, and shall rule the People committed to our charge, according to the Will and Command of God, revealed in his aforesaid Word, and according to the laudable Laws and Constitutions received in this Realm, no ways repugnant to the said Word of the eternal God; and shall procure, to the utmost of our Power, to the Kirk of God, and whole Christian People, true and perfect Peace in all time coming. That we shall preserve, and keep inviolated the Rights and Rents, with all just Privileges of the Crown of *Scotland,* neither shall we transfer nor alienate the same; that we shall forbid and repress in all Estates and Degrees, Reif, Oppression, and all kind of wrong. And we shall command and procure that Justice and Equity in all Judgments be keeped to all Persons without exception, as the Lord and Father of all Mercies shall be merciful to us. And we shall be careful to root out all Hereticks and Enemies to the true Worship of God, that shall be convicted by the true Kirk of God, of the aforesaid Crimes, out of our Lands and Empire of *Scotland.* And we faithfully affirm the things above-written, by our solemn Oath.

God save King W I L L I A M and Queen M A R Y.

The

Proposals humbly offered to the Lords and Commons in the present Convention, *for settling of the Government,* &c.

My Lords and Gentlemen,

YOU are assembled upon Matters of the highest Importance to England, *and all Christendom ; and the result of your Thoughts, in this Convention, will make a numerous Posterity happy or miserable. If therefore I have met with any thing that I think worthy of your Consideration, I should think myself wanting in that duty which I owe to my Country and Mankind, if I should not lay it before you. If there be, as some say, certain Lineaments in the Face of Truth, with which one cannot be deceived, because they are not to be counterfeited; I hope, the Considerations which I presume to offer you, will meet with your Approbation: That, bringing back our Constitution to its first and purest Original, refining it from some gross Abuses, and supplying its Defects, you may be the joy of the present Age, and the Glory of Posterity.*

FIRST, 'Tis necessary to distinguish between *Power* itself, the *Designation* of the *Persons governing,* and the *Form* of *Government*: For,

1. All Power is from God, as the Fountain and Original.

2. The Designation of the Persons, and the Form of Government, is either, First, immediately from God, as in the case of *Saul* and *David,* and the Government of the *Jews*; or, secondly, from the Community, chusing some Form of Government, and subjecting themselves to it. But it must be noted, that though *Saul* and *David* had a Divine Designation, yet the People assembled; and in a general Assembly, by their Votes, freely chose them: Which proves, that there can be no orderly or lasting Government, without Consent of the People, tacit or exprefs'd; and God himself would not put Men under a Government without their consent. And in case of a Conquest, the People may be called *Prisoners* or *Slaves* (which is a State contrary to the nature of Man) but they cannot be properly Subjects, till their Wills be brought to submit to the Government : So that Conquest may *make way* for a Government, but it cannot constitute it.

Secondly, There is a supreme Power in every Community, essential to it, and inseparable from it; by which, if it be not limited immediately by God, it can form itself into any kind of Government. And in some extraordinary Occasions, when the Safety and Peace of the Publick necessarily require it, can supply the Defects, reform the Abuses, and re-establish the true Fundamentals of the Government ; by purging, refining, and bringing things back to their first Original : Which Power may be called, *The supreme Power Real.*

Thirdly, When the Community has made choice of some Form of Government, and subjected themselves to it, having invested some Person or Persons with the *supreme Power* ; the Power in those Persons may be called, *The supreme Power Personal.*

Fourthly, If this Form be a mixed Government of *Monarchy, Aristocracy,* and *Democracy* ; and for the easy Execution of the Laws, the *Executive Power* be lodg'd in a single Person, he has *a supreme Power Personal,* quoad hoc.

Fifthly, The *supreme Power Personal* of *England,* is in King, Lords, and Commons ; and so it was in effect agreed to, by King *Charles* the First, in his Answer to the nineteen Propositions, and resolved by the Convention of the Lords and Commons, in the Year 1660. And note, that the Acts of that Convention, tho' never confirmed by Parliament, have been taken for Law, and particularly by the Lord Chief Justice *Hales.*

Sixthly, The *supreme Power Personal* of *England,* fails three ways.

1. 'Tis dissolv'd : For two essential Parts fail. 1. A King. 2. A House of Commons ; which cannot be called according to Constitution, the King being gone, and the Freedom of Election being destroyed by the King's Encroachments.

2. The King has forfeited his Power several ways. Subjection to the Bishop of *Rome,* is the Subjection against which our Laws cry loudest : And even *Barclay,* that Monarchical Politician, acknowledges, That if a King alienate his Kingdom, or subject it to another, he forfeits it. And *Grotius* asserts, That if a King really attempt to deliver up, or subject his Kingdom, he may be therein resisted : And that, if the King have part of the *supreme Power,* and the People or Senate the other part, (the King in-

Cccccc
vading

vading that part which is not his) a juſt Force may be oppoſed, and he may loſe his Part of the Empire. *Grotius de Bello,* &c. *Cap.* 72. But that the King has *ſubjeſted the Kingdom to the Pope,* needs no proof ; that he has *uſurped an abſolute Power, ſuperior to all Laws,* made the People's ſhare in the legiſlative Power, impertinent and uſeleſs, and thereby invaded their juſt Rights, none can deny. 'Twere in vain to multiply Inſtances of his Forfeitures : And, if we conſider the Power exercis'd by him of late, it will moſt evidently appear, to all who underſtand the *Engliſh* Conſtitution, that it admits of no ſuch King, nor any ſuch Power.

3. The King has deſerted.

(1.) By incapacitating himſelf by a Religion inconſiſtent with the Fundamentals of our Government.

(2.) By forſaking the Power the Conſtitution allowed him, and uſurping a foreign one : So that tho' the Perſon remained, the King was gone long ago.

(3.) By perſonal withdrawing.

Seventhly, The *ſupreme Power Real* remains in the Community ; and they may act by their original Power : And tho' every particular Perſon is, notwithſtanding ſuch Diſſolution, Forfeiture, or Deſertion, ſubject to the Laws which were made by the *ſupreme Power Perſonal,* when in being ; yet the Community's Power is not bound by them, but is paramount to all Laws made by the *ſupreme Power Perſonal* : And has a full Right to take ſuch Meaſures for ſettling the Government, as they ſhall think moſt ſure and effectual, for the laſting Security and Peace of the Nation. For we muſt note, that it was the Community of *England,* which firſt gave Being to both King and Parliament, and to all the other parts of our Conſtitution.

Eighthly, The *moſt renowned Politician* obſerves, That thoſe Kingdoms and Republicks ſubſiſt longeſt that are often renewed, or brought back to their firſt Beginnings ; which is an Obſervation of ſelf-evident Truth, and implies, That the *ſupreme Power Real* has a right to renew, or bring back. And the moſt ingenious *Lawſon* obſerves, (in his *Politica*) that the Community of *England,* in the late times, had the greateſt Advantage that they or their Anceſtors had for many Ages, for this Purpoſe ; tho' God hid it from their Eyes : But the wonderful Concurrence of ſuch a Series of Providences, as we now ſee and admire, gives ground to hope, That the Veil is removed, and the Nation will now ſee the Things that concern their Peace.

Ninthly, The Acts done and executed by the *ſupreme Power Perſonal* (when in being) have ſo modell'd the Parts and Perſons of the Community, that the Original Conſtitution is the beſt, juſteſt, and the moſt deſirable. The *Royal Family* affords a Perſon that both Heaven and Earth point out for King. There are Lords, whoſe Nobility is not affected by the Diſſolution of the Government, and are the ſubject Matter of a Houſe of Lords ; and there are Places, which by Cuſtom or Charter, have right to chuſe Repreſentatives of the Commons.

Tenthly, There are inextricable Difficulties in all other Methods. For,

1. There is no Demiſe of the King, neither civil nor natural.

2. There is conſequently no Deſcent.

3. The Community only has a Right to take advantage of the King's Forfeiture or Deſertion.

4. Whatever other Power may be imagin'd in the two Houſes, as Houſes of Parliament, it cannot juſtify itſelf to the Reaſon of any, who underſtand the Bottom of our Conſtitution.

5. By this Method all *Popiſh Succeſſors* may be excluded ; and the Government ſecured, in caſe all the *Proteſtants* of the Family die without Iſſue : And this by the very Conſtitution of *England.* And the Queſtion can never ariſe about the Force or the Lawfulneſs of a Bill of Excluſion.

6. The Convention will not be obliged to take Oaths, &c.

Eleventhly, If theſe things be granted, and the Community be at liberty to act as above ; it will certainly be moſt adviſable, not only for the Security and Welfare of the Nation, but (if rightly underſtood) for the Intereſt of their Royal Highneſſes, to limit the Crown as follows : ———— To the Prince of *Orange* during his Life (yet with all poſſible Honour and Reſpect to the Princeſs, whoſe Intereſts and Inclinations are inſeparably the ſame with his) Remainder to the Princeſs of *Orange,* and the Heirs of her Body ; Remainder to the Princeſs of *Denmark,* and the Heirs of her Body ; Remainder to the Heirs of the Body of the Prince of *Orange* ; Remainder as an Act of Parliament ſhall appoint.

This will have theſe Conveniences among others.

1. Husband and Wife are but one Perſon in Law, and her Husband's Honour is hers.

2. It puts the preſent kingly Power into the beſt Hand in the World ; which (without flattery) is agreed on by all Men.

3. It

3. It afferts the above-faid Power in the Community.

4. It will be fome acknowledgment to the Prince for what he has done for the Nation: And it is worthy Obfervation, that before the *Theocracy* of the *Jews* ceafed, the manner of the Divine Defignation of their Judges, was by God's giving the People fome Deliverance by the hand of the Perfon, to whofe Government they ought to fubmit; and this even in that time of extraordinary Revelations. Thus *Othniel, Gideon, Jephthah, Sampfon,* and others were invefted by Heaven with the fupreme Authority: And tho' *Jofhua* had an immediate Command from God to fucceed *Mofes,* and an anointing to that purpofe, by the laying on of *Mofes*'s Hands; yet the Foundation of the People's Submiffion to him was laid in *Jordan.* And I challenge the beft Hiftorians to give an Inftance (fince that *Theocracy* ceafed) of a Defignation of any Perfon, to any Government, more vifibly divine than that which we now admire. If the hand of Providence (miraculoufly and timely difpofing natural Things, in every Circumftance to the beft advantage) fhould have any influence upon Men's Minds, moft certainly we ought not here to be infenfible. If *the Voice of the People, be the Voice of God,* it never fpoke louder: If a Nation of various Opinions, Interefts, and Factions, from a turbulent and fluctuating State, falls into a ferene and quiet Calm, and Men's Minds are ftrangely united on a fudden, it fhews from whence they are influenced. In a word, if the Hand of God is to be feen in human Affairs, and his Voice to be heard upon Earth, we cannot any where, fince the ceafing of Miracles, find a clearer, and more remarkable Inftance, than is to be obferved in the prefent Revolution. If one examines the pofture of foreign Affairs, making way for the Prince's Expedition, by fome fudden Events and Occurrences, which no human Wifdom or Power could have brought about; if one obferves that divine Influence which has directed all his Counfels, and crown'd his Undertakings, notwithftanding fuch innumerable Dangers and Difficulties, with conftant Honour and Succefs: If one confiders how happily and wonderfully both Perfons and Things are changed in a little time, and without Blood; it looks like fo many marks of God's Favour, by which he thinks fit to point him out to us in this extraordinary Conjuncture.

I will trouble you but with one Confideration more; which is, that the two things moft neceffary in this Affair, are Unanimity and Difpatch: For without both thefe, your Counfels will have little effect. In moft things 'tis good to be long in refolving; but in fome 'tis fatal not to conclude immediately: And Prefence of Mind is as great a Virtue, as Rafhnefs is a Vice. For the Turns of Fortune are fometimes fo quick, that if Advantage be not taken in the critical hour, 'tis for ever loft. But, I hope, your Lordfhips, and all thofe Gentlemen who compofe this Auguft Affembly, will proceed with fo much Zeal and Harmony, that the Refult of your prefent Confultations may be a lafting and grateful Monument to Pofterity, of your Integrity, Courage, and Conduct.

The late Honourable Convention *proved a* Legal Parliament.

I. THE neceffity of a Parliament agreed by the Lords and Commons voting that the Throne is vacant; for there being a Vacancy, there follows an immediate neceffity of fettling the Government, efpecially the Writs being deftroyed, and the great Seal carried away, put a period to all publick Juftice, and then there muft be a fupply by fuch means as the neceffity requires, or a failure of Government.

II. Confider the Antecedents to the calling the Convention; that is, about three hundred of the Commons, which is a majority of the fulleft Houfe that can be made; above fixty Lords, being a greater number, than any part divided amounted to at this great Meeting; the Lord-Mayor, Aldermen, and Common-Council of the City of *London,* by application to his then Highnefs the Prince of *Orange,* defired him to accept of the Adminiftration of publick Affairs, military and civil; which he was pleafed to do, to the great fatisfaction of all good People: and after that, his Highnefs was defired to iffue forth his circular Letters to the Lords, and the like to the Coroners, and in their abfence to the Clerks of the Peace, to elect Knights, Citizens, and Burgeffes. This was more than was done in fifty-nine, for the calling a Parliament in *April* 1660, for there the Summons was not real, but fictitious, *i. e.* in the names of the Keepers of the Liberties of *England,* a meer Notion fet up as a Form, there being no fuch Perfons, but a meer *Ens rationis,* impoffible really to exift: fo that here was much more done, than in 1659, and all really done which was poffible to be invented, as the Affairs then ftood. Befides, King *Charles* II. had not abdicated the Kingdom, but was willing to return, and was at *Breda,* whither they might have fent for Writs; and in the mean time have kept their form of Keepers of the Liberties, &c. But in the present case there was no King in being, nor any stile or form of Government, neither real, or notional left ; so that in all these respects, more was done before, and at the calling of this great Convention, than for calling that Parliament (for so I must call it) yet that Parliament made several Acts, in all thirty-seven, as appears by *Keeble's* Statutes, and several of them not confirmed ; I shall instance but in one, but it is one which there was occasion to use in every County of *England* ; I mean, the Act for confirming and restoring Ministers, being the 17th of that Sessions, all the Judges allowed of this as an Act of Parliament, tho' never confirmed, which is a stronger case than that in question; for there was only fictitious Summons, here a real one.

III. That, without the Consent of any Body of the People ; this, at the Request of a Majority of the Lords, more than half the number of the Commons duly chosen in King *Charles* the Second's time, besides the great Body of the City of *London*, being at least esteemed a fifth part of the Kingdom : yet after the King's Return, he was so well satisfied with the calling of that Parliament, that it was enacted by the King, Lords, and Commons, assembled in Parliament, that the Lords and Commons then sitting at *Westminster* in the present Parliament, were the two Houses of Parliament, notwithstanding any want of the King's Writs, or Writ of Summons, or any defect whatsoever; and as if the King had been present at the beginning of the Parliament. This I take to be a full Judgment in full Parliament of the case in question, and much stronger than the present case is ; and this Parliament continued till the 29th of *December* next following, and made in all, thirty-seven Acts, as above-mentioned.

The 13 *Caroli* 2. *chap.* 7. (a full Parliament called by the King's Writ) recites the other of 12 *Caroli* 2. and that after his Majesty's return, they were continued till the 29th of *December*, and then dissolved, and that several Acts passed ; this is the plain Judgment of another Parliament.

1. Because it says they were continued, which shews they had a real Being, capable of being continued ; for a Confirmation of a void Grant, has no effect, and Confirmation shews a Grant only voidable ; so the continuance there, shewed it at most but voidable ; and when the King came and confirmed it, all was good.

2. The dissolving it then, shews they had a being, for, as *ex nihilo nihil fit*, so *super nihil nil operatur*, as out of nothing, nothing can be made ; so upon nothing, nothing can operate.

Again, the King, Lords, and Commons, make the great Corporation or Body of the Kingdom, and the Commons are legally taken for the Free-holders, *Inst.* 4. *p.* 2. Now the Lords and Commons having proclaimed the King, the defect of this great Corporation is cured, and all the essential parts of this great Body politick united and made compleat, as plainly as when the Mayor of a Corporation dies, and another is chosen, the Corporation is again perfect ; and to say, that which perfects the great Body politick, should in the same instant destroy it ; I mean, the Parliament: is to make contradictions true, *simul & semel*, the perfection, and destruction of this great Body at one instant, and by the same Act.

Then if necessity of Affairs was a forcible Argument in 1660, a time of great peace, not only in *England*, but throughout *Europe*, and almost in all the World ; certainly 'tis of a greater force now, when *England* is scarce delivered from Popery and Slavery ; when *Ireland* has a mighty Army of Papists, and that Kingdom in hazard of final destruction, if not speedily prevented ; and when *France* has destroyed most of the Protestants there, and threatens the ruin of the *Low-Countries*, from whence God has sent the wonderful Assistance of our gracious, and therefore most glorious King : and *England* cannot promise safety from that Foreign Power, when forty days delay, which is the least can be for a new Parliament ; and considering we can never hope to have one more freely chosen, because first it was so free from Court-influence, or likelihood of all design, that the Letters of Summons issued by him, whom the great God in infinite Mercy raised to save us, to the hazard of his Life, and this done to protect the Protestant Religion, and at a time when the People were all concerned for one common interest of Religion and Liberty ; it would be vain when we have the best King and Queen the World affords, a full House of Lords, the most solemnly chosen Commons that ever were in the remembrance of any Man living, to spend Money and lose time (I had almost said, to despise Providence) and take great pains to destroy ourselves.

If any object Acts of Parliament mentioning Writs and Summons, &c.

I answer, the Precedent in 1660 is after all those Acts.

In private cases, as much has been done in point of necessity ; a Bishop Provincial dies, and *sede vacante* a Clerk is presented to a Benefice, the Presentation to the Dean and Chapter, is good in this case of necessity ; and if in a Vacancy by the Death of a Bishop

shop a Presentation shall be good to the Dean and Chapter, rather than a prejudice should happen by the Church lying void ; surely *à fortiori* ----- Vacancy of the Throne may be supplied without the formality of a Writ, and the great Convention turned to a real Parliament.

A Summons in all points is of the same real force as a Writ, for a Summons and a Writ differ no more than in name, the thing is the same in all substantial parts ; the Writ is recorded in Chancery, so are his Highness's Letters ; the proper Officer endorses the Return, so he does here, (for the Coroner, in defect of the Sheriff, is the proper Officer;) the People chuse by virtue of the Letters, *&c. & quæ re concordant, parum differunt*, they agree in Reality, and then what difference is there between the one and the other ?

Object. A Writ must be in Actions at Common Law, else all pleading after will not make it good, but Judgment given may be reversed by a Writ of Error.

Answ. The case differs, first, because Actions between party and party, are Adversary Actions, but Summons to Parliament are not so, but are Mediums only to have an Election.

2. In Actions at Law the Defendant may plead to the Writ, but there is no plea to a Writ for electing Members to serve in Parliament : and for this I have *Littleton's* Argument ; there never was such a Plea, therefore none lies.

Object. That they have not taken the Test.

Answ. They may take the Test yet, and then all which they do will be good ; for the Test being the distinguishing Mark of a Protestant from a Papist, when that is taken, the end of the Law is performed.

Object. That the Oaths of Allegiance and Supremacy ought to be taken, and that the new ones are not legal.

Answ. The Convention being the supreme Power, have abolished the old Oaths, and have made new ones; and as to the making new Oaths, the like was done in *Alfred's* time, when they chose him King, *vid.* Mirror of Justice, *Chap.* 1. For the Heptarchy being turned to a Monarchy, the precedent Oaths of the seven Kings, could not be the same King *Alfred* swore.

Many Precedents may be cited, where Laws have been made in Parliament, without the King's Writ to summon them, which for brevity's sake I forbear to mention.

For a farewel, the Objections quarrel at our happiness, fight against our safety, and aim at that which may endanger Destruction.

The Present Convention, a Parliament.

I. THAT the formality of the King's Writ of Summons is not so essential to an *English* Parliament, but that the Peers of the Realm, and the Commons, by their Representatives duly elected, may legally act as the great Council and Representative Body of the Nation, though not summoned by the King; especially when the circumstances of the time are such, that such Summons cannot be had ; will, I hope, appear by these following Observations.

First, The *Saxon* Government was transplanted hither out of *Germany,* where the meeting of the *Saxons* in such Assemblies was at certain fixed times, *viz.* at the New and Full Moon. But after their Transmigration hither, Religion changing, other things changed with it ; and the times for their publick Assemblies, in conformity to the great Solemnities celebrated by Christians, came to be changed to the Feasts of *Easter, Pentecost,* and the *Nativity.* The lower we come down in Story, the seldomer we find these general Assemblies to have been held ; and sometimes, (even very anciently) when upon extraordinary occasions, they met out of course, a *Precept,* an *Edict,* or *Sanction,* is mentioned to have issued from the King : But the times, and the very place of their ordinary Meeting having been certain, and determined in the very first and eldest times that we meet with any mention of such Assemblies, which times are as ancient as any Memory of the Nation itself ; hence I infer, that no Summons from the King can be thought to have been necessary in those days, because it was altogether needless.

Secondly, The Succession to the Crown, did not in those days, nor till of late years, run in a course of lineal Succession by right of Inheritance : But upon the death of a Prince, those Persons of the Realm that composed the then Parliament, assembled in order to the chusing of another. That the Kingdom was then Elective, though one

or

or other of the royal Blood was always chosen, but the next in lineal Succession very seldom, is evident from the Genealogies of the *Saxon* Kings, from an old Law made at *Calchuyth*, appointing how, and by whom Kings shall be chosen ; and from many express and particular Accounts, given by our old Historians, of such Assemblies held for electing of Kings. Now such Assemblies could not be summoned by any King ; and yet in conjunction with the King that themselves set up, they made Laws, binding the King and all the Realm.

Thirdly, After the death of King *William Rufus*, *Robert*, his elder Brother, being then in the *Holy Land*, *Henry*, the younger Son of King *William* the First, procured an Assembly of the Clergy and People of *England*, to whom he made large Promises of his good Government, in case they would accept of him for their King ; and they agreeing, that if he would restore to them the Laws of King *Edward the Confessor*, then they would consent to make him their King : He swore that he would do so, and also free them from some Oppressions, which the Nation had groaned under in his Brother's and his Father's time. Hereupon they chose him King, and the Bishop of *London*, and the Archbishop of *York*, set the Crown upon his Head : Which being done, a Confirmation of the *English* Liberties, passed the royal Assent in that Assembly, the same in substance, tho' not so large as King *John*'s, and King *Henry* the Third's *Magna Charta*'s afterwards were.

Fourthly, After that King's Death, in such another Parliament, King *Stephen* was elected, and *Mawd* the Empress put by, tho' not without some stain of perfidiousness upon all those, and *Stephen* himself especially, who had sworn in her Father's Life-time, to acknowledge her for their Sovereign after his decease.

Fifthly, In King *Richard* the First's time, the King being absent in the *Holy Land*, and the Bishop of *Ely*, then his Chancellor, being Regent of the Kingdom in his absence, whose Government was intolerable to the People, for his Insolence and manifold Oppressions, a Parliament was convened at *London*, at the instance of Earl *John*, the King's Brother, to treat of the great and weighty affairs of the King and Kingdom, in which Parliament this same Regent was deposed from his Government, and another set up, *viz.* the Archbishop of *Roan* in his stead. This Assembly was not convened by the King, who was then in *Palestine*, nor by any Authority deriv'd from him, for then the Regent and Chancellor must have called them together ; but they met, as the Historian says expresly, at the Instance of Earl *John*. And yet, in the King's absence, they took upon them to settle the publick Affairs of the Nation without him.

Sixthly, When King *Henry* III. died, his eldest Son, Prince *Edward*, was then in the *Holy Land*, and came not home till within the third year of his Reign ; yet, immediately upon the Father's death, all the Prelates and Nobles, and four Knights for every Shire, and four Burgesses for every Borough, assembled together in a great Council, and settled the Government till the King should return ; made a new Seal, and a Chancellor, &c.

I infer from what has been said, that Writs of Summons are not so essential to the being of Parliaments, but that the People of *England*, especially at a time when they cannot be had, may by Law, and according to our old Constitution, assemble together in a Parliamentary way without them, to treat of and settle the publick Affairs of the Nation. And that, if such Assemblies so convened, find the Throne vacant, they may proceed not only to set up a Prince, but with the Assent and Concurrence of such Prince, to transact all publick Business whatsoever, without a new Election ; they having as great Authority as the People of *England* can delegate to their Representatives.

II. The Acts of Parliament not formal nor legal in all their Circumstances, are yet binding to the Nation so long as they continue in force, and not liable to be questioned as to the Validity of them, but in subsequent Parliaments.

First, The two *Spencers*, *Temp. Edvardi Secundi*, were banished by Act of Parliament, and that Act of Parliament repealed by *Dures & Force* ; yet was the Act of Repeal a good Law, till it was annull'd, 1 *Ed.* 3.

Secondly, Some Statutes of 11 *Rich.* 2. and Attainders thereupon, were repealed in a Parliament, held *Ann.* 21. of that King, which Parliament was procured by forced Elections ; and yet the Repeal stood good, till such time as in 1 *Henry* 4. the Statutes of 11 *Rich.* 2. were revived, and appointed to be firmly held and kept.

Thirdly, The Parliament of 1 *Hen.* 4. consisted of the same Knights, Citizens, and Burgesses, that had served in the then last dissolved Parliament, and those Persons were by the King's Writs to the Sheriffs, commanded to be returned, and yet they passed Acts ; and their Acts, tho' never confirmed, continue to be Laws at this day.

Fourthly, Queen *Mary*'s Parliament that restored the Pope's Supremacy, was notoriously known to be pack'd, insomuch that it was debated in Queen *Elizabeth*'s time, whether or no to declare all their Acts void by Act of Parliament. That course was
then

2

then upon some prudential confiderations declined ; and therefore the Acts of that Parliament, not fince repealed, continue binding Laws to this day.

The reafon of all this, is, becaufe no inferior Courts have Authority to judge of the Validity or Invalidity of the Acts of fuch Affemblies, as have but fo much as a colour of Parliamentary Authority.

The Acts of fuch Affemblies being entred upon the Parliament Roll, and certified before the Judges of *Weftminfter-hall,* as Acts of Parliament, are conclufive and binding to them ; becaufe Parliaments are the only Judges of the Imperfections, Invalidities, Illegalities, &c. of one another.

The Parliament that called in King *Charles* the Second, was not affembled by the King's Writ, and yet they made Acts, and the Royal Affent was had to them ; many of which indeed were afterwards confirmed, but not all, and thofe that had no Confirmation, are undoubted Acts of Parliament without it, and have ever fince obtained as fuch.

Hence I infer that the prefent Convention may, if they pleafe, affume to themfelves a Parliamentary Power, and in conjunction with fuch King or Queen as they fhall declare, may give Laws to the Kingdom as a legal Parliament.

The Thoughts of a private Perfon, about the Juftice of the Gentlemen's Undertaking at York, Nov. 1688. *Wherein is fhewed, that it is neither againft Scripture, nor moral Honefty, to defend their juft and legal Rights, againft the illegal Invaders of them. Occafioned then by fome private Debates, and now fubmitted to better Judgments.*

The prefent Undertaking of the Gentlemen at *York, Nov.* 1688. taken into Confideration ; wherein is fhewed that it is neither againft Scripture, nor moral Honefty, to defend their juft and legal Rights againft the illegal and unjuft Invaders of them ; by way of Objection and Anfwer.

1. THat it is not againft Scripture is fhewed, Obj. 1, 2, 3.
    2. That it is not inconfiftent with the Frame of the Government in general, Obj. 4.
3. Not againft the Law, but the Law-breakers, Obj. 5.
4. Not Rebellion, Obj. 6.
5. No Ufurpation of the Power of the Sword, Obj. 7.
6. No unlawful Act in a moral Senfe, Obj. 8.
7. Not againft true Allegiance, Obj. 9.
8. Not againft the Declaration in a legal Senfe, Obj. 10.
9. Not againft political Power, but Force without political Power, Obj. 11.
10. Not againft any Royal Prerogative in general, Obj. 12.
11. Not againft the Supremacy, Obj. 13.
12. Not criminal Difobedience, Obj. 14.
13. Not incommodious or unfafe for the Publick, in refpect of the prefent and approaching Evils it removes, Obj. 15, 16.
14. No difparagement to the Frame of the Government, that cannot otherwife decide an obftinate difference between King and People, Obj. 17.
Laftly, The Conclufion, fhewing, that Non-refiftance of illegal Force, does in effect make all Monarchs arbitrary, and the People Slaves.

The

The Thoughts of a Private *Perſon*, &c.

MEN have three Rules to walk by, which we may call Laws, that is, *Nature*, *Reaſon*, and *Religion*; and anſwerable to theſe three, a Chriſtian hath three Principles, that is, *Senſitive*, *Rational*, and *Spiritual*, which I take to be the diſtinction that St. *Paul* makes, 1 *Theſ.* 5. 23. *I pray God your whole Spirit, Soul, and Body, be preſerved blameleſs, until the coming of our Lord Jeſus Chriſt.*

Nature conſiders all Men as ſingle Perſons, and directs them to Self-intereſt and Self-preſervation, as the chief end. *Reaſon* conſiders Men as ſociable Creatures, and directs them to unite the Government for the publick good (incluſive of their own Safety) as the chief end. And the *Spirit* conſiders Men as Candidates for Heaven, and directs them to live according to the Word of God, that they may attain eternal Happineſs, the chief end of Man. All theſe have the divine Warrant, and are of force where the Lower is not ſuperſeded by the Higher. A ſingle Perſon is not to expoſe himſelf to ruin, unleſs it be for the Publick Good ; and the Publick are not to expoſe themſelves to Beggary and Slavery, unleſs it be for the Kingdom of Heaven.

Now tho' theſe Rules may be conſidered ſeparate, and apart, yet they all ought to be in a Chriſtian Government. Laws for the publick Good, do not deſtroy the Law of Nature, but ſuperſede it for a greater Good ; and the Laws of God do not deſtroy the Law of Reaſon, but ſuperſede it for a higher end, and ſo make it ſtill more reaſonable to do ſo. Nothing therefore can juſtify a private Injury, but the publick Good ; and nothing can hinder the Publick Good from being carried on, but Sin. For theſe Laws are not deſtructive, but ſupportive of one another, and all ſupportive of Man. When a Man cannot defend himſelf, by the Method and Meaſures of the Publick, (as in caſe of ſudden Aſſaults) he may, by the Law of Nature, break the Peace, and ſmite his Adverſary, to ſave his own Life ; becauſe human Laws can reward no Perſon's obedience with ſo good a thing as Life ; and therefore, the Publick Good excepted, his Life is to be preferred before all forms of Law. But it is not ſo with the Laws of God ; for if I be urg'd to deny my Faith, or die, I muſt die, rather than break God's Law, becauſe God will give me a better Life, and an infinite Reward. Neceſſity can ſuſpend a poſitive Law of Man, that is merely ſuch, but it cannot ſuperſede what is eſtabliſhed by God or Nature ; an Act therefore that is civilly unlawful, may, notwithſtanding, be lawful ; becauſe it is not lawleſs, but under a more extenſive Law. If it be according to the Laws of God, or ſound Reaſon, the Conſcience is ſafe, and the Act commendable before God and good Men, tho' it be againſt the form of political Law : For tho' it be againſt the Form, it is not againſt the Reaſon of that Law ; and the Form not being extenſive enough of Man's ſafety, it muſt give place to neceſſity, and abſolve him of his duty, when his duty would deſtroy him.

The ſafety of Man ſhews us both the neceſſity and end of human Government ; for when private Perſons found they could not be ſafe, they were willing to enter into Compacts and Aſſociations, and repoſite their private Safety in the publick Intereſt. And therefore if after this Aſſociation, ſome of their Fellows will break the Covenants, and go about to deſtroy the reſt, it is lawful, both by the Laws of God and Man, for the injured to defend themſelves, and by the Laws and Compacts by them made, and conſented to, on both ſides, for the Publick Good : Otherwiſe it would be unlawful to reſiſt Injuſtice, and conſequently a Thief or a Robber.

Object. 1. *But you will ſay, in all Governments there are ſuperiors and inferiors, and God has made Obedience a part of Religion, and conſequently conducive to a higher end than the Publick Good ; and therefore if the Governors break the Laws, and introduce a Publick Evil for a private Intereſt, they muſt not be reſiſted upon pain of Damnation.*

Anſw. This were a good Plea, if it were true, but God is not the Patron of Injuſtice ; and therefore he gives no Prince or Potentate more Authority over the People, than the Tables of the Government expreſs, and of theſe there are diverſe degrees. Thoſe that are governed by the will of their Prince, whoſe Word is a Law, if he command their Perſons for Slaves, or Eſtates to ſerve his Ambition, they muſt obey, and God requires it of them, becauſe it is the Prince's Right. Arbitrary Princes have a political Power, to treat a Subject cruelly and inhumanly ; their immorality is an offence againſt God, not injuſtice to the Subject who had given up himſelf to be uſed at their diſcretion. But thoſe that are to rule by Laws made for the Publick Good, and ſuch as render the Subjects Freemen, not Slaves ; ſuch as ſecures their Religion, Liberty, and Property ; if theſe

Princes

†

Princes contrary to Law imprison their Persons, or seize their Estates, they do it unjustly, without God's Warrant, or any political Authority, and may be resisted; or else we might not resist the Devil, should he creep into the Court in a Jesuit's habit, and *Haman*-like, get a Commission to cut all our Throats.

If I be called to suffer for my Religion, or the Faith of Christ, I am bound to suffer upon a mighty reasonable account: For, 1. It is the best way to overcome, my Faith can triumph so by no other Victory as by Death, for that is a Victory never to be lost again. 2. Though I die, the Tyrant hath not his end, but is by that means utterly defeated of it. And 3. I shall be an infinite gainer by it, for I shall have an infinite Reward for what I suffer, and what I lose. But there is a vast difference between suffering for the Faith of Christ, and for the frame of a political Government; for if I may not resist, I am overcome. 2. If I am overcome, the Tyrant gets his End; namely, an Arbitrary Power. And 3. He has promis'd no Reward for such voluntary entering into Bondage, or owning an usurped Authority. The Church and the frame of the State stand upon two several Bottoms, God has promised to support the Church, and there needs no arm of flesh to defend it under the worst of Governments: But the frame of every Government is a human Structure; and though God does impower and authorize every Government, yet he has left the Choice of the several kinds to the parties, and has promised to bless them in the just Administration of their several Choices; but no where has he promised to support the particular frame they chose, that as their prudence raised it, or it must fall at every King's pleasure, and when they have chosen out the frame, God that approves it, grants neither the King nor the People greater privileges than the Frame it self expresses, which in divers Nations is different, some submitting to be governed by the will of him they voluntarily chuse: Others to one that will govern by Laws of their own making, and his approving: Others to one of their precedent King's Race or Line: Others to a Multitude: Others to a few of the best and presumptively wisest Persons. And every people's choice must be the measure of their Obedience; if they have made an ill Bargain they must stand to it, and if they have made a good one they may stand for it. If therefore any Governor challenge more of the Subject than is in the Submission, the Subjects may by the Laws of God and Man deny to yield it. And if the Prince deny to give the Subject as much as in the Grant, the Subject may challenge his Right; and if by Force or Fraud, contrary to the Frame of the Government, the Governor will force the Governed from his Right, the Obligation of subjection ceases so far, and he may defend himself from the oppression and injustice as well as he can.

Obj. 2. *But he must defend himself in God's way, his defence must be without Sin. And that is, either by Prayers to God, or Intreaties to the Prince, or by suffering; for the Scripture says,* All Power is of God, and they that resist the Power, resist the Ordinance of God, *Rom.* 13. 2. *And St.* Peter *gives Christians in charge,* that they submit to every Ordinance of Man for the Lord's sake.

Answ. All Powers indeed are of God, that is, every Government has God's Warrant to proceed according to the Frame of the Government, to the End of the Government, which is the publick Good. The Power is of God, but the Restraint of the Power is in the Frame of the Government, and the Frame is an human Ordinance or Structure, as the Apostle elegantly expresses it, ἀνθρωπίνη κτίσις; he therefore that resisteth the Governour, who proceeds according to the Frame of the Government, resisteth the Ordinance of God. But if the Governour proceed neither according to the Frame of the Government, nor to the End, but against it, such Process cannot be the Ordinance of God, unless God have two contradictory Ordinances, of force at one time in the same Government, and then the Command may be true and false, and the Subjects duty good and evil, and men would be perpetually distracted with serving two Masters. This would make the Government God's and the Devil's, and is no less than to put a blasphemous Juggle upon the Ordinance of God: which is always simple, and at one with it self. These Scriptures therefore cannot tie us to obey the Governour, contrary to the Government, because they tie us to obey the Government; and that this is all they tie us from resisting, is evident by the Reason St. *Paul* gives, which is, *because the Resisters resist the Ordinance of God.* And therefore it is warily exprest, if it were but as warily read; for it is not, whosoever resisteth the person or the will of the Governour, but whosoever resisteth the power (and that power is neither more nor less than the Frame of the Government expresses) resisteth the Ordinance of God, and to this Resistance the Penalty is annexed.

But it does not follow, because I may not resist the Ordinance of God, that I may not resist the powerless and inauthoritative, unjust Attempts of Superiours upon me,

for

for then a Soldier might not refift his Captain that would rob him, nor a married Man-fervant his Mafter that would force his Wife.

This I think evidences, That to refift a Superior and his evil Inftruments and Ac-complices, while they act contrary to the Frame of the Government, is not to refift the Power of God, or the Ordinance of God, but to keep off thofe who ufurp upon the Power of God, and the Frame of the Government, and the juft Rights of others. For I would fain know of the Doctors of Non-refiftance, whether the Act that contains the Teft, has the ftamp of God's Authority upon it or no; if it has not, the Power of the King and Parliament is no Power of God; if it has, then to refift that, is to refift the Ordinance of God: And thofe Commiffions that are contrary to it, have no power from God. If the affirmative be true, the negative is of no force. And there-fore to refift fuch Commiffions, is not to refift the Ordinance of God, unlefs God's Or-dinances be contradictory, and that would render God guilty of double dealing, as well as the Jefuits. Which being utterly impoffible, it muft be concluded, that the refift-ing fuch Commiffions, and the Inftruments acting by them, is not to refift lawful Au-thority, but to remove unlawful; not to do evil, but to hinder it; not to fin, but to prevent Sinners from doing Mifchief; and it would be very hard meafure for a Man to be damn'd for doing fuch a good Office. Bifhop *Bilfon*, therefore fpeaking of this Text, fays, *It is not refifting the King's Will againft Law, but according to Law, that is forbidden*. And both *Barclay*, and *Grotius* affirm, *That the People may in divers Cafes refift Kings that are tied to govern by Law, which they could not do, did they think thefe Scriptures for-bad all refiftance*.

Much indeed is faid from the Practice of the *Jews*, and the Primitive Chriftians, and the Subjection of Servants, but nothing to the purpofe; for their Cafe is not ours, more than their Frame of Government is ours; their Servants were Slaves, and their Kings and Emperors Wills were their Laws; their People had no *Magna Charta's* to fhow, nor fundamental Compacts, and fo could plead no Injuftice on any Command; the frame of the Government warranted all thofe Commands that had the Royal Pleafure: Their political Power was more extenfive than their moral Power. The People were wholly at the mercy of the Prince: All their Laws were Acts of Grace, not fundamen-tal Referves and inherent Rights; and therefore in Spirituals they had no Caufe to refift, and in Temporals they might not, as was obferved above. If they had been under limited Governments as we are, we might have heard of Blows as well as Words, St. *Paul* was never fo virulent with his Tongue, as when he was fmitten contrary to Law.

Obj. 3. *But the Perfon of the King is facred, and muft not be touched.*

Anfw. I fay fo too; but it is his juft Power that makes him fo. And therefore in dangerous times, he is to be counfelled and perfuaded to fecure himfelf, by keeping within the Sanctuary of the Laws, and holding them forth for the publick Good, by gaining the Affections of the People, and being content with that meafure of Power that is proper to the Government. For if he doth not, Right may and ought to be de-fended, and Refiftance (for the publick Good) of illegal commiffioned Forces, is not refifting the King's Perfon, but his Forces; not his Power, but his Force without Power. If none would execute the King's contradictory Commands, none would refift; and if he will againft all Juftice, Prudence and Perfuafions, join with wicked Men, and wilfully expofe himfelf to the mercy of blind Bullets, charge is to be given to all, that none kill him wittingly or wilfully; the hand that lifted him up may not pull him down: God forbid that any fhould think of killing him *de induftria*, or defpair of his repen-tance before God does; nothing paft can prejudice a Penitent before God, and I hope not before Men: thus the King's Perfon and Power will be fafe in the midft of a Civil War, not fo fafe as in peaceable times, but as fafe as can confift with the Subjects Right, when their Religion and Laws, Liberty and Property, are violently invaded. And therefore if any thing befall his Perfon by their hands, it is but a chance and accidental thing, which may happen alfo in peaceable times.

This fhows that refifting the King's illegal commiffion'd Forces, in defence of their own juft Rights, is not refifting the Ordinance of God, and confequently no Sin; and then the Confcience is not tied otherwife than the Laws of the Land, and the particular Frame of the Government ties it.

Obj. 4. *But to refift the King, or his Commiffioners, is againft the Frame of the Govern-ment, it being a Monarchy, and againft the Laws and Statutes of the Realm.*

Anfw. If it be fo, it is a great Sin; but as it is certain this is a Monarchy, fo it is cer-tain that it is limited in the Foundation, otherwife the King would have all the Legifla-tive Power, and the Parliament no Authority or Right but derived from him; and then

he

he muft be Arbitrary, and we Slaves, and all our Laws muft be Acts of Grace, not fundamental Rights: Not from any inherent Power referved at the Inftitution to ourfelves, and never fubmitted to the Princes, but from the gracious Condefcenfion of an Abfolute Monarch, which is contrary to the Story of all times, which fhows that the People ever claimed Liberty and Property, according to their ancient Laws and Cuftoms, not as a Gift, but as a Right inherent in themfelves, and never transferred, aliened, or conveyed to any King, but declared, recognized and confirmed to them by many.

I fhall therefore fuppofe (what I think none can upon fufficient grounds deny) that the King is bound by all the facred Ties of God and Man, to govern by the Laws, and not otherwife, neither by a foreign Law, nor by one of his own framing, nor by any Word or Will contrary to Law, feeing nothing can have the Force of Law here, but what has the joint Confent of King and Parliament, and that in a Parliamentary way ; and this fhows us the Terms of Submiffion that are fworn to on both fides. The King and the People by a joint confent make Laws, and make them the common Rule betwixt them, and the King fwears to obferve the Laws, and the People fwear to obey the King, and to leave the Execution of the Laws to the King, to be managed for the publick Good.

Therefore as long as he governs by Law, he and all his Minifters are fafe enough from Refiftance, the Refifter being liable to be punifhed both by God and Man ; and the fole Adminiftration being left to the King, fubjects all but himfelf to Criminal Procefs, and even himfelf to Civil : but his perfon and power are fafe in both, he may be fevere in the Execution of the Laws many times, but not unjuft ; as, if he will not fufpend a burthenfome Law, or revive an antiquated one, when the publick Good requires it ; this may render him uncharitable or imprudent, but he is fafe yet : for though he be bound to proceed according to Law, yet he is not tied to proceed always according to the beft Methods, when they are diverfe. But if he ftop the Courts of Juftice, erect new ones, or proceed contrary to Law, he acts without Authority, and againft his own Authority, and puts on a kind of a Vizard, that his Subjects can neither know him nor their Duty ; for it is the Laws that direct them to the perfon of the King, and their own Duty, without which they could know neither : And if the End be not the publick Good, it is downright Injuftice, as well as politically powerlefs. Neceffity indeed may juftify a political, unlawful Act, for the publick Good. As in cafe of an Invafion to burn a garifon rather than it fhould be a refuge for the Enemy, or to open Sluices and to drown part of the Country, for though thefe things have not the form of the Law, they have the reafon, and that is publick Good : And therefore it is not Law, but Neceffity, not the King's Command but publick Good, that warrants thefe Acts. And when Peace returns, the Injured are to have fatisfaction made by the Publick, not as of Charity, but as of Juftice ; which fhows that the Law looks upon it as a Trefpafs, juftified only by Neceffity and the publick Good. And the particular Perfons here, have reafon to be quiet and make no refiftance, becaufe they fhall reap double benefit by it ; one in the publick Good, and another from the publick Treafure. But it does not follow, that if the King, in an angry mood, fhould command his Guards to fire *Newmarket,* becaufe he had loft an Horce-race there, or had a mind to have a Bonfire, becaufe he had won one, that the Inhabitants might not refift them.

Obj. 5. *By what Law ? Not by the Law of the Land ?*

Anfw. Yes ; By the Law of the Land a Petty Conftable's Word would juftify Refiftance, better than the King's Commiffion could juftify the illegal Attempt. But fuppofe there were no Perfon that had the leaft Authority, and that the refiftance could not be within the prefcribed Form of Government ; yet becaufe the force is an unauthoritative force, and becaufe there is greater neceffity of the End of the Government than of the Form ; Men may by the Law of Nature and the Law of Reafon proceed to the End, not without all Form, but without the political Form, for thofe Proceedings that are according to Reafon, are not fimply under no Law, but under a more extenfive Law ; and that Law juftifies refiftance, even of Superiors, when there is no other way of defence left the People. If the Cafe will admit of Intreaties, or fober Counfels, or legal Appeals, they are to be ufed ; but if there be no room for thefe, or if they take no place, but illegal force be ufed, that force may, nay muft be refifted, or evil is confented to. For he that will not ferve the publick by that means, when there is no other, does actually confent to the ruin of it. He that has his Houfe on fire, and will not ftir to quench the flames, though he be able, is willing fure it fhould be burnt. The Rules of prudence indeed are to be obferved, for if there be no probability that refiftance will prevent the Evil, the attempt is Folly ; and if refiftance will do more harm than good, it

is

is inferviceable ; and if there be any other means effectual, it is unreasonable, for it ought to be the laft refuge ; and then if the Caufe be good, Neceffity juftifies proceeding to the End : Not by illegal means, but by fufpending the political Form, and appealing to the Reafon of Mankind, and introducing the Law of Nature. And this is no more than when Judgment at Common-Law is reverfed in Chancery, the Form of the Law gives place to Equity and found Reafon.

Obj. 6. *But is it Rebellion?*

Anfw. I anfwer, Rebellion is refifting the juft Power of the Government ; and if fo, then it is no Rebellion to refift the unjuft and ufurped Power, for then it would be Rebellion to refift Rebellion, and there could be no fuch thing as a juft defence againft the exorbitant Power of Princes ; and then the King might commiffion a Captain, or a Colonel, to roll up and down in the Country, and plunder, and it would be Rebellion in the *Poffe Com.* (at leaft in any private Family) to refift them. And a private Commiffion to cut our Throats, would tie our hands till the bufinefs were done. But the refifting fuch Force, as has neither moral nor political power, is no more Rebellion than to fight againft a wild Beaft, that came with Strength, but no Authority, to devour them. The *Papifts* indeed have taken up Arms, without and againft the juft power of this Land, not only againft the Form of Law, but to the overthrow of the Laws, and fundamental Rights of this Government, directly againft the Letter, the Power, and the End of the Law, which is as enflaving to the Subjects, as an ufurping Conqueft ; and it is no more Rebellion to refift them, than *Wat. Tyler* or *Jack Cade:* They are Rebels who arm againft the Government, not they that defend it by Arms.

Obj. 7. *But this is to ufurp the Power of the Sword, which by the Frame of the Government is wholly in the King's Hand.*

Anfw. The political Power of the Sword indeed is in the King, but that does not diveft the Subject of all defence by Arms, but only of fuch defence as is againft or inconfiftent with the political Power. If force be offered that wants political Power, whoever does it, does it but in the nature of a private Perfon, and private Perfons may refift fuch. The Right of Self-defence is a precedent Right to all Policy ; and every Man has fo much of it ftill, as is not given up unto the political Power he lives under. They therefore that have given themfelves up to be governed by Law only, have right to defend themfelves, not only againft the private Affailant, which is allowed in all Governments, but alfo againft illegal Force. And this Refiftance is no Ufurpation upon the Magiftrate's Power, becaufe it is an Act of Civil Authority, but of natural Right : And if thoufands join in the Attempt, they are all Voluntiers ; a Multitude, but no Body Corporate ; and fuch as challenge no Authority over thofe they refift, but deny Subjection to fuch unauthoritative Force : For fuch Force wanting political Power, has no Power but Strength, and Strength authorizes none to injure, but natural Right authorizes every one to defend himfelf ; fo that in this cafe, the Refifter has a moral Power or Warrant, but the illegal Invader none at all.

Obj. 8. *But the Refifters ought not to do an unlawful Act, to fupprefs fuch illegal Force.*

Anfw. I anfwer, That Act is not fimply unlawful that wants political Power ; the Law is made for the publick Good as the End, and therefore if the prefcribed Means be not fufficient for the End, the Law permits that other reafonable means be ufed, otherwife People might dwell upon the Shadow till they've loft the Subftance. The *Poffe Com.* ought not by the prefcribed Form of Law to go into another County ; but if the other County at that time had no Sheriff, whereby the Power of that County could not be raifed to defend it felf ; or if there were Ships in the Borders of the next County, to which the Plunderers might efcape if they were not hotly purfued, I queftion not but the *Poffe Com.* might do a commendable Act to purfue them, and take them in the next County. The Law was made for the publick Good, and not the publick Good for the Law ; and therefore when the Law cannot anfwer its own End, or prefcribes ineffectual Means, any juft and honeft Means may be ufed ; and this is not deftructive of the Law, but fuppletory ; not a violating the Form prefcribed, but an improving it : And though a Man may be called to account for doing a good Act in fuch a manner, I fuppofe it is but to know the Truth of the Matter, and to preferve the Reverence of the Laws ; for he is already cleared in his own Confcience, and in the Breafts of all good Men ; and a Pardon in that cafe does but declare it is fo, and ought of Right (not of Grace) to be granted. For it is not neceffary in refpect of any Crime, but in refpect of fome defect in the Law, which had not made fufficient provifion for the publick Good.

Obj. 9. *But it is againft true Allegiance, and an Oath muft be kept though it be to our own hurt.*

Anfw.

Anſw. True Allegiance muſt be proportioned to the Frame of the Government, and the End of that Frame. Therefore if the Frame be to reſtore arbitrary Power, the Subject cannot owe arbitrary Allegiance. Allegiance is more in ſome Places and leſs in others ; but no Man can owe ſo much Duty to his Prince, as not to have a *Salvo* for God and his Life ; and here we can owe none that is againſt our Laws and the publick Good, for that would deſtroy the Government. Our Allegiance therefore muſt be bounded by our Laws, and not by the King's Word, or Will : No Man can ſwear to obey the King's Word or Will ſimply, but according to Law. It would be Sin to tie our ſelves to think, or ſpeak, or do, what he would have us at large. Our Allegiance therefore muſt be ſuch as will conſiſt with the Frame of our Government, and that muſt be ſuch as is couched in the Body of our Laws. Other Allegiance there can be none, but what is wrapt up in Courteſies and Formalities. For it ſeems the King, as well as the People, is under the Law in ſome ſenſe, under the direction of it, though not under the conſtraint ; and therefore, at his Coronation, he does a kind of Fealty to the Laws and Government, and ſwears Allegiance to them, as to a ſupream Lord. The Oath is not only, *Will you grant the Laws, but will you grant and keep the Laws and Cuſtoms of* England? and the Anſwer is, *I grant and promiſe to keep them.* It is certain therefore, no Allegiance to the King can be againſt Law, to which he himſelf owes Allegiance.

The Caſe being thus far clear, That the Allegiance ſworn to, is no other but our legal Duty ; it does not hinder but that we may reſiſt illegal Force. When the King of the *Scots* ſwore Allegiance to our King, it did not deprive him of a juſt defence of his juſt Right, by taking up Arms if he were oppreſt. And the King of *England,* when he ſwore Allegiance to the King of *France,* made no ſcruple to take up arms againſt his Liege Lord, in defence of his juſt Rights : And the old Lawyers tell us, That the very Villain might in caſe of Rape and Murder arm againſt his Lord ; and if the Law arm a Villain againſt his Lord, Subjects are worſe than Villains, if they may not arm againſt their Sovereign Lord's illegal Forces, in defence of their Laws, Lives, Eſtates, and the publick Good. But what makes it moſt evident, is the Clauſe in King *Henry*'s Charter, which ſays, *If the King invade thoſe Rights, it is lawful for the Kingdom to riſe againſt him, and do him what injury they can, as though they owed him no Allegiance* ; the Words are theſe (if my Author fail me not) *Licet omnibus de Regno noſtro, contra nos inſurgere, & omnia agere quæ gravamen noſtrum reſpiciant, ac ſi nobis in nullo tenerentur.* Much to the ſame purpoſe is in King *John*'s Charter, which I find thus quoted : *Et illi Barones, cum communia totius terræ, diſtringent & gravabunt Nos, modis omnibus quibus poterunt ; ſcilicet per captionem caſtrorum, terrarum, poſſeſſionum, talibus modis quibus potuerint, donec fuerint emendatum, ſecundum Arbitrium eorum, ſalva Perſona noſtra & Reginæ noſtræ & Liberorum noſtrorum.* Much may be ſaid of this nature about the old Allegiance, which was all couched in Homage and Fealty ; but this is enough to ſhow that true Allegiance does not tie us from reſiſting illegal Force, and intolerable Incroachments upon our juſt Rights.

Obj. 10. *But ſuch Reſiſtance would be againſt the Declaration, which ſays, It is not lawful upon any pretence whatſoever to take up Arms againſt the King,* &c.

Anſw. The Latitude of the word Lawful cauſes the Scruple, which at firſt view ſeems to tell us, that it is ſinful upon any pretence whatſoever, to take up arms againſt the King, &c. But it is no good conſequence to ſay, that it is ſinful becauſe it is unlawful, unleſs the Diſcourſe be reſtrained to the Laws of God. I muſt confeſs it is politically unlawful for Subjects, in any Caſe, or for any Cauſe whatever, to take up arms againſt the King, and thoſe commiſſion'd by him ; becauſe ſuch a taking up arms here can have no political Authority : But it is morally lawful in all limited Governments to reſiſt that Force that wants political Power. The regal Power is irreſiſtible in all Perſons, from the King to the petty Conſtable ; but it does not hinder but that all theſe Perſons may be reſiſted, when they do what they have no political power to. They that have a limited power, and a preſcribed Duty, may either act againſt, or beyond their Commiſſion ; and when they ſo do, they may be reſiſted : For ſuch Acts have no political power in them, though the perſons have to other purpoſes. If a Commiſſion ſhould be granted to a Company of *Ruffians* to plunder and maſſacre, they might have ſomething more of the King's Affections, but no more of his Authority than private Robbers had ; and conſequently might be reſiſted with equal Honeſty. None therefore can make this Declaration in its full Latitude, but upon this preſumption,

that

That the King and his Minifters keep perpetually within the Bounds of the Law ; otherwife they declare the King has an arbitrary power, which is againft the fundamental Laws of this Land, and a kind of Treafon againft the State : For if he may not be refifted in any Cafe, he may be under fome moral reftraint, but under no political reftraint ; and confequently the political frame of the Government muft be arbitrary. The meaning therefore of this Declaration can be no other, but that a Man can have no civil power or authority in any Cafe to take up arms againft the King, &c. But this does not debar any man of the Natural Right of Self-defence, by private Arms againft inauthoritative Force.

Obj. 11. *To this fome reply, that feeing God hath placed the Governing (though limited) Power in the King's hand, no Man may, by any Natural Right or private Defence, refift his illegal Force ; God's Power muft not be refifted, though abufed.*

Anfw. There is a great difference between the abufe of power, and the want of power ; and therefore this argument either fuppofes the power greater than it is, or concludes ill. The King and Parliament have indeed an arbitrary power (I do not fay infinite, but as extenfive as the frame of Government will bear) and therefore if they make a very grievous Law (though they ought not, for they are under a moral reftraint, though no political) neither the King nor any of his Minifters may be refifted in the due Execution of it. But the King has no power to burden us beyond or againft Law ; and we may thank our own Weaknefs if ever he have Strength to do it. This fhows us there is a great difference betwixt the abufe of political power and the want of it. Abufed power muft not be refifted, but Force without power may. The political power of arbitrary Princes, is more extenfive than their moral power : And this ties the Subject to Non-refiftance, when he is immorally or unchriftianly ufed. They that fubject themfelves to another's Difcretion, diveft themfelves of all defence. But they that referve property and liberty to themfelves, may juftly defend them, when they are unjuftly invaded. Had the King an arbitrary power, which he did abufe to vex the *Proteftants,* I, for my part, fhould think my felf obliged to fuffer and not to refift, as I believe did all the Primitive Chriftians : but feeing he has no political power to ufe me as he lifts, and the moft abfolute Monarch has no moral power to do an unjuft Act to his Subject ; I fhould be a fenfelefs Fool, if without any Obligation either from God or Man, I fhould ftand Blows rather than withftand them. The truth is, Non-refiftance ftretch'd thus far, under his Government, would make us like the two Fools that went to the Field to fight with one Staff, with which *Vice Verfa,* he that had it, cudgell'd the other, who ftood all the while with his Hands in his pocket valiantly bearing all the Blows his Brother Fool thought good to lay on.

2. Others conclude otherwife againft this Doctrine, and fay, the King having the facred Power lodged in him, may not be refifted, though he act without, or againft that power, for reverence of that juft power of God that is in him.

This looks like a piece of Courtfhip to God, and fmells more of Superftition than Divinity : God requires no Honour to the prejudice of Juftice, or the advancement of Injuftice ; but this too devout kind of Reverence would inable a bad Prince to injure the Innocent, and would leave Juftice defencelefs on Earth. Juft power is a Sanctuary indeed, but the Sanctuary is of no larger extent than the power. This is evident by the Tenour of all Commiffions, the Granter muft have a competent power of what he grants, and that warrants the Executor to proceed to the End of the grant ; but the having power to one purpofe, cannot protect a Man from Refiftance, if he proceed to another. The Chimney-man that is irrefiftible in his Office, is refiftible if he gather the Corn in the Town-fields ; and the King that receives his Commiffion from the King of Heaven to execute the Law, and is therefore irrefiftible in the execution of it, is yet refiftible, if he fhut up all the Courts of Juftice, and abufe his Subjects contrary to Law : In this cafe he acts not by the power of God, but his own ; by an Arm of Flefh, or the Strength of wicked Men (not by any political power or moral power) but by the favage power of a Beaft, or the malicious power of Hell. And how any Honour fhould accrue to God by a voluntary fubmitting to fuch a power, is beyond my comprehenfion ; they are moft likely to honour God, that ftand up moft for his power, and will fubmit to no other.

I have brought in thefe two Objections here, becaufe the Declaration is the moft fpecious and obvious Plea for Non-refiftance, and is ufually back'd with one of thefe Conceits ; that either want of political power, is but abufe of political power ; or

that

that a limited political power is a Sanctuary for unlimited Actions in whomsoever it rests.

Obj. 12. *But to resist such Forces as are commission'd by the King, is against the Royal Prerogative of the Crown.*

Answ. The King has no Prerogative, (except such as are wrapt up in *honorary Formalities*) but what the Law gives him, we must not therefore presume a Prerogative, and then conclude it Law ; but first find the Law, and by it prove the Prerogative ; and when we have found the Prerogative, it must be measured by what the publick Good will bear, and not by what the Absoluteness of the Prerogative will admit : For no Prerogative can be used that is against the frame of the Government, or the publick Good. Interpretations of Law therefore ought rather to favour Liberty and Property than Prerogative ; because the benefiting of the Subject comes nearer to the End of the Government, than the excessive honouring the Prince. Honourary Prerogatives are in their degree necessary, and not superfluous ; there must be something to maintain the Reverence of Magistrates, but they ought to give way to publick Interest ; and the rest are nothing but powers placed in the King to do good with, and not good or ill as he pleases. A Prerogative therefore cannot destroy a Law, but it may supply its Defects, pardoning a condemn'd Innocent, or a hopeful Penitent, or dispensing with a Law, to one, that by particular Accident, the Law in its Rigour would undo : But no Prerogative can impower the King to destroy the people's liberty or property. That dispensing power, that like a State *Opium*, casts all the Laws asleep, and is an Engine of publick Mischief, is no Prerogative belonging to the Crown of *England*, but a Vice that does not belong to it. For it brings guilt upon the King, and damage upon the Subject, and is a real diminution of the Dignities of the Crown : For it, and such like, serve only to impower the King to do mischief with security ; that is, they give an Immunity from punishment, but not from guilt. As suppose the King, by such a claimed Prerogative, should shut up all the Courts of Justice, so that none should be had ; he might be free from punishment, but not from guilt ; he is clear by Necessity only, not by Right ; the Case transcends the Frame of the Government, none can judge him that has neither Equals nor Superiors, and so he escapes ; because he cannot be punished, not because he deserves it not. Thus the pretended Prerogative bespatters him, and so leaves him.

Obj. 13. *But it is against the Supremacy ; for the Supreme ought to have the Supreme Credit, both in judging what is Law, and what is for the publick Good.*

Answ. As the King is Supreme in the executive part, so the Parliament have a share in the Legislative, which I take to be the very Apex of Supremacy, and therefore they ought to have their share in interpreting Laws as well as the King, or his Judges ; because none knows the meaning so well as the Makers, if they be alive ; and if they be dead, none knows the publick Necessities so well ; none so unlikely to deceive, or be deceived, being so numerous ; none likely to be so faithful, and so unlikely to be corrupted, having so great an Interest in the publick good ; none like to be so effectual in working a compliance in the People's hearts, seeing it is in effect their own Determination : But yet they cannot do it without the King, for that would place his Parliament above himself.

The King indeed is Supreme in the legislative part as well as in the executive part, but he has not the whole Supremacy in the legislative part as he has in the executive : He is the Head of that Body in which he rests, but the Power (like the Soul of Man) is in the whole Body, though most eminently in the Head. The Parliament have their Existence, but not their Essence from him. When they are called together, they act by a proper and inherent Right of their own, and not by the King's Commission and Direction. It may be good Manners to fall upon what he directs them to first, but if any thing of greater moment require dispatch, they must wave a Complement to do a real kindness to the publick Interest ; which they could not do were they his Commissioners, and received their power to act by from him : It is unnatural for the Stream to stop the Fountain-head. But seeing they act by their own inherent Power, when met, they can restrain in the King, that he cannot make a Law without them, or give such an interpretation of any, either by himself or his Judges, as shall bind the Subject to follow, or is not reversible in Parliament ; for such Interpretation is

part

part of the legiſlative power, and that reſts in the King and Subjects *conjunctim*. Had the King Authority to bind his Interpretations for Law upon the Subject, he might at pleaſure elude any Law, and Law would be but a Sconce for arbitrary Power. The Opinion indeed of the Judges is reverend, but not irreverſible. None can finally bind an Interpretation on the Subject but thoſe that can make Law : Therefore if the King and Parliament differ about the ſenſe of a Law, it is not legally decided till both agree in one ſenſe. But that ſenſe that is really for the publick good has the Right of a Law, though not the Form ; and they that juſtify ſuch an Interpretation, are juſtifiable by the Law of Nature: for though it tranſcend the proceſs of Courts, and cannot have the force of a political Law, yet Reaſon (Mankind's prime Law) juſtifies Men to prefer a publick Good before a private Intereſt ; and what is for the publick good, they that feel are beſt able to judge.

Obj. 14. *But it is Diſobedience.*

Anſw. Diſobedience to a lawful Command is a grievous Crime, and a great Sin ; but it may be a great Duty to diſobey an unlawful Command. Obedience is due as far as the Law requires, and ſomething farther ; a particular perſon muſt ſuffer rather than the Honour and Majeſty of the Prince ſhould be brought into Contempt ; for though the Law does not bind to this, yet Conſcience and Reaſon do, the publick Intereſt muſt be promoted ; Scandal prevented, and the Government ſecured from Contempt, though it prejudice ſome particular perſon ; for ſuch Contempt may ariſe from a juſt refuſal of Obedience in ſome ſmall and ſingle Inſtances, and may be of worſe conſequence to the publick than a private Injury : but if the thing commanded tend to deſtroy the Government, or introduce a general Calamity, Diſobedience becomes a Duty, and ſuch Commands (in this Government) are morally, politically, and divinely powerleſs ; and the Diſobedient, in ſuch a Caſe, does the King as good Service, as he that diſcovers Treaſon ; for he gives him notice that his Foot is entering into a Snare, and that his preſervation ſtands in deſiſting, and repenting if he would but heed it : And if the Diſobedience be once good, the higher it goes the better it is, continuing ſtill good ; it is abſurd to go from good to worſe extenſively. Diſobedience that is good, is ſtill better as it is more likely to prevent the Evil : And then Diſobedience defenſive, is doubtleſs better than paſſive ; for that would introduce the Evil voluntarily, that is, they that were not willing to do it themſelves, were yet willing to let others do it ; and how far that can clear them, I ſee not. For though it is not a downright conſenting to ſubvert the Government, yet it is a conſenting that it ſhall be done, rather than they will run the hazard to defend it, or prevent it ; which is but, *Pilate*-like, to waſh the Hands of what their Hearts tell them they are acceſſary to.

Obj. 15. *But War is hurtful to the State.*

Anſw. The Arm that is broke cannot ſet it ſelf, nor can he that ſets it, ſet it by any natural Power, derived from the Spirits ; but by a violent diſturbing them again, the Bone-ſetter is often forced to pull them farther aſunder e'er he can join them well : and ſo it is when wicked Men have disjointed and broken the Bones of the State, the languiſhing Law cannot reſtore it ſelf ; nor can thoſe that ſeek to reſtore it, reſtore it without doing violence to its broken part ; but it is better to do that violence, than to let them grow crooked, or gangreen. He that has taken Poiſon, muſt ſuffer the Violence of a Vomit ; and they that are ſick, muſt be made ſicker oft before they can be well. The prejudice therefore the Government receives, by thoſe that go about to reſtore it, does no more denominate them Enemies to the State, than the little griping of Phyſick can denominate Phyſicians Enemies to Nature. The Evil proceeds from the Diſeaſe, not the Remedy ; and the Guilt is upon them that gave the Wound, not thoſe that dreſt it ; all the Anguiſh and Smart that follows the ſkilful Chirurgeon's Hand, is not to be attributed to the Chirurgeon, but to the wicked Aſſaſſine: and therefore though this Reſtoration have the Evil of a Civil War, yet the Guilt of all that Evil lies upon the Cauſers. Men are not bound to loſe their Right for fear of harming wicked Men, nor to ſave a leſs Good, by loſing a greater ; a ſhort Evil is to be choſen rather than a perpetual one : Men had better drudge to preſerve their own Freedom, than to enter into Bondage to drudge for others ; and the Patriots of our Country do well to bear the Burthen of a War, rather than to become Slaves themſelves, and leave Popery, Beggary and Slavery to their Poſterity.

Obj. 16.

Obj. 16. *But it is an unsafe and dangerous Medicine, it opens a Gap to the People to rebel at pleasure, and may indanger the change of the Government.*

Answ. A desperate Disease must have a desperate Cure ; but doing right can no way open to do wrong ; resisting illegal Forces, is hedging up a Gap, not making one. Raising of Men to take a Felon, will not excite the same Men to rise and seize an honest Man. We must not therefore forbear to take up Arms in a just Cause, lest it should incourage others to take up Arms in a bad Cause ; for then some that were breaking the Peace, and would not be quieted with Words, might not be resisted, lest it should teach the People to break the Peace ; but Blows bestowed on such Malefactors is no breach of Peace, and therefore can teach the People no such thing ; if they do ill by that Example, it is not long of the Copy, but of those that do not heed to write by it.

2. I know Men in Passion, and heightned with Success, and back'd with Strength, are apt to soar too high, and fall in love with new Inventions. But this hazard must be run, rather than a certain Change admitted. Resisting Illegalities, and Misgovernment, is the way to preserve Government ; and as long as the King is safe, and his just Power and Prerogatives, the Government is in no danger ; and there is not the least Colour imaginable that those that have surrendred their Offices and Honours, the Court and the King's Favour, for preserving the Government, and are now ready to hazard their Lives in defence of it, will ever alter it : No, their design is to preserve it ; a greater Evidence of which they could not give at present than to petition for a Free Parliament.

Obj. 17. *But this casts dirt upon the Frame of the Government, leaving room for perpetual quarrelling.*

Answ. 1. Neither this, nor any other Government that I know of, affords absolute means of Peace and Preservation : The Government is effectual enough so far as it reaches, but it is not extensive enough. If the Monarch were arbitrary, then no Cause could introduce Resistance ; the Nation might be at peace, but the Subjects could not be safe, and Liberty and Property would be lost : Therefore if Safety, Liberty and Property be worth the preserving, they must be defended when wicked Men would wrest them from us. The Constitution of this Government is such, that if the King and Parliament, or the King and the Subjects differ about fundamental Rights, they have no way to reconcile the Difference but by their own Consent. If the King without the Parliament could determine the Difference, he would be Arbitrary ; and if the People, or the Parliament, could determine it without him, they would be supream, and then it could be no Monarchy ; and if the Judges had the determining Power, they would get the Supremacy from both ; and if a Foreigner were to decide the Matter, he would seek his own Advantage ; so that they must either condescend for Peace sake to one another's Proposals, so as not to destroy the Government, or they must suffer the Grievance, and let the Quarrel fall for a time, till the injurious can be worn to a compliance, or they must fight it out ; for that is their going to law, the Soldiers are their Jury-men, and Victory is their Verdict. For the Question is not about breach of Government, but whether that be the Government, or no ; and seeing this Cause transcends the executive part of the Government, it cannot be decided by legal Progress, but by Law makers ; and if they cannot agree, Men are at liberty to join with that side they judge in the right : Reason and Conscience must be their Guide, the Law cannot, and they that proceed on this ground are their own Warrants on either side, for neither have a legal Power to determine the other. Therefore the Power of Judging is neither Authoritative nor Civil, and so argues no Superiority in those that judge, but only a Power residing in reasonable Creatures, or judging of their own Act, of which they never were divested by any lawful Authority, and therefore may lawfully use upon such Occasions ; and though the Government does not warrant a civil War, in such a case, yet the End and Reason of this Government does. For it being fram'd to prevent the exorbitant Power of the Prince, for the publick Good ; he that fights for the publick Good, against an usurped Power, or an arbitrary Invader of the Government's Rights, is justified by the design and intendment of the Frame, and consequently by the Equity of the Government, though not by any prescribed Form. For seeing many things are morally honest and profitable, that are not reduced into positive Laws, Men cannot proceed to those things (if at any time they become necessary) by prescribing Forms of Law, because they have none. And so, in this case, the Question being not about Breach of Law, but what is Law ; and the Law not able to satisfy both King and People, each claiming contrary Rights from the same Laws ; the Decision of this Case, though it be very good and profitable for this Nation, yet has no prescribed form of Law to direct us to ; and therefore both King and People are to proceed according to moral Honefty, to the end of the Government, that is, the publick Good.

The Conclufion of all which, is, That feeing the refifting of illegal and arbitrary Forces, in defence of the Laws and publick Intereft of theLand, is not againft the Scriptures, and confequently no Sin; nor againft moral Honefty, and confequently no Crime, (not a-gainft Law but Law-breakers, not againft true Allegiance, or any Prerogative of the Crown, no Rebellion, no Ufurpation of the Sword, nor criminal Difobedience, and not incommodious or unfafe for the publick, in refpect of the impendent Injuries and Hazards it removes) nor inconfiftent with the Frame of Government, which cannot otherwife decide an obftinate Difference betwixt King and People : I cannot but con-clude it is a very worthy and virtuous Act to be in Arms for defence of the Laws, the King's juft Rights, and the publick Good ; and confequently that thofe Gentlemen, who are in Arms for the defence of our Laws, Liberties, and Lives, againft illegal Forces, arbitrary Commands, and ufurped Powers, are in a virtuous Poft. For if the Subjects Right might not be defended by this means, it would be all loft ; it being all one, in thefe days, to have no Right, and to have no fufficient means to defend it. The Doc-trine of Non-refiftance plainly puts all we have into an ill King's hands, and the good ones will fcarce part with what they are apt to love fo dearly, and we parted with fo freely ; fhould we therefore preach this Doctrine to our Princes, and tell them that they might take what we have without danger or oppofition, we fhould teach them to try our Patience: if all muft be referr'd to their Confciences, they will foon (without the help of a Jefuit) find cafe enough and caufe enough to fecure that, and leave the ex-amination of them to the latter day; hatred of our Perfons, love of our Eftates, difguft at our Words or Actions, or diflike of our Religion, will foon judge us unworthy of our Liberty and Property, as well as it has already done of our Offices, Honours, and Preferments : Paffion and Scorn, Pride and Ambition, Covetoufnefs and Prodigality, would all prey upon what we had, with a quiet (though not with a good) Confcience ; but efpecially if the King were poor and neceffitous, either by wilful Profufenefs or Ne-gligence: for Nature would even tell him in fuch a Cafe, that we had all better want than he, and then farewell Property ; the worft you could do to him, was but to pet and cry a bit, and perhaps that might become a Pleafure to him too ; and then you had nothing to reft on, but that God would give you the Kingdom of Heaven, for beggar-ing your felves, impoverifhing the Church, and giving what you had to the Devil's Ser-vice ; an ill Ground for fuch coftly Hopes to ftand upon.

2. This Doctrine renders Government prejudicial to the greateft part of Mankind, depriving them of all juft Defence: For the illegal Force bars them of legal Defence ; and the Doctrine of Non-refiftance bars them of Corporal, and fo Man (under one of the beft Governments in the World) is left naked in the midft of favage Beafts, (for *homo lupus*) and muft not, though he be able, make any Defence for himfelf. Thus all the Rights of Society and Nature are facrificed to the Luft and Rage of a wicked King, and his evil Inftruments ; and the Body Politick is really in a worfe Condition than an unlimited Multitude, for they may defend themfelves (if they will) againft an Enemy ; but thefe have an Enemy, and may not defend themfelves, though in never fo juft a Caufe ; and what is worft of all, muft hold their own Hands whilft others cut their Throats.

Laftly, This Doctrine would make all Monarchs arbitrary Monarchs, and alike in effect ; for if the Subjects may not (nor ought if they were able) refift the Prince any further than by refufing to join with him, then he were Arbitrary, and might do what he pleas'd without oppofition, he had but moral Reftraint, and the moft abfolute Mo-narch had that upon him ; and all Limitations in the Fundamentals of Government would be idle and fuperfluous, becaufe they contained only fuch Rights as others might take from us at pleafure, and we might not defend or oppofe. But the end of limited Monarchies is, not that the Monarch might not lawfully or rightfully opprefs ; for an arbitrary Monarch is bound to all that: but the end of all Limitations in Government, is, that the Prince may want Means as well as Right to opprefs, that he may not be able to injure the Subject at all, either lawfully or unlawfully ; they are limited to govern by Laws, that they may want Means as well as Right to include the Subjects Property. But the Doctrine of Non-refiftance gives them Means for a Temptation, and is indeed but a fair Bait to draw them into a Snare.

An

An Enquiry *into the Measures of* Submission *to the* SUPREAM AUTHORITY: *And of the Grounds upon which it may be lawful or necessary for Subjects to defend their Religion, Lives and Liberties.*

THIS *Enquiry* cannot be regularly made, but by taking in the first place, a true and full view of the Nature of *Civil Society*, and more particularly of the Nature of *Supream Power*, whether it is lodged in one or more Persons?

I. It is certain, that the Law of Nature has put no difference nor subordination among Men, except it be that of Children to Parents, or of Wives to their Husbands ; so that with relation to the Law of Nature, all Men are born free: and this Liberty must still be supposed entire, unless so far as it is limited by Contracts, Provisions and Laws. For a Man can either bind himself to be a Slave, by which he becomes in the power of another, only so far as it was provided by the Contract ; since all that Liberty which was not expresly given away, remains still entire: so that the Plea for Liberty always proves it self, unless it appears that it is given up or limited by any special Agreement.

II. It is no less certain, that as the Light of Nature has planted in all Men a natural Principle of the Love of Life, and a Desire to preserve it ; so the common Principles of all Religion agree in this, that God having set us in this World, we are bound to preserve that Being, which he has given us, by all just and lawful Ways. Now this Duty of Self-preservation is exerted in Instances of two sorts ; the one is, in the resisting of violent Aggressors ; the other is, the taking of just Revenges of those, who have invaded us so secretly, that we could not prevent them, and so violently, that we could not resist them : In which Cases the Principle of Self-preservation warrants us, both to recover what is our own, with just Damages, and also to put such unjust Persons out of a capacity of doing the like Injuries any more, either to our selves, or to any others. Now in these Instances of Self-preservation, this difference is to be observed ; that the first cannot be limited by any slow Forms, since a pressing Danger requires a vigorous Repulse, and cannot admit of Delays ; whereas the second, of taking Revenges, or Reparations, is not of such haste, but that it may be brought under Rules and Forms.

III. The true and original Notion of *Civil Society* and *Government*, is, that it is a Compromise made by such a Body of Men, by which they resign up the right of demanding Reparations, either in the way of Justice against one another, or in the way of War against their Neighbours, to such a single Person, or to such a Body of Men as they think fit to trust with this. And in the management of this *Civil Society*, great distinction is to be made, between the Power of making Laws for the regulating the Conduct of it, and the Power of executing those Laws : The *Supream Authority* must still be supposed to be lodged with those who have the legislative Power reserved to them ; but not with those who have only the executive ; which is plainly a *Trust*, when it is separated from the legislative Power ; and all Trusts, by their Nature import, that those to whom they are given, are accountable, even though it should not be expresly specified in the words of the *Trust* it self.

IV. It cannot be supposed by the Principles of Natural Religion, that God has authorized any one Form of Government, any other way than as the general Rules of Order, and of Justice, oblige all Men not to subvert Constitutions, nor disturb the Peace of Mankind, or invade those Rights with which the Law may have vested some Persons : for it is certain, that as private Contracts lodge or translate private Rights, so the publick Laws can likewise lodge such Rights, Prerogatives, and Revenues, in those, under whose Protection they put themselves, and in such a manner, that they may come to have as good a Title to these, as any private Person can have to his Property : so that it becomes an Act of high Injustice and Violence, to invade these ; which is so far a greater Sin than any such Actions would be against a private Person, as the publick Peace and Order is preferable to all private Considerations whatsoever. So that in truth, the Principles of natural Religion, give those that are in Authority no Power at all, but they do only secure them in the possession of that which is theirs by Law. And as no Considerations of Religion can bind me to pay another more than I indeed owe him, but do only bind me more strictly to pay what I owe ; so the Considerations of Religion do indeed bring Subjects under stricter Obligations to pay all due Allegiance and Submission to their Princes, but they do not at all extend that Allegiance further than the Law carries it. And though a Man has no

divine

I

divine Right to his Property, but has acquired it by human Means, such as Succession, or Industry, yet he has a security for the Enjoyment of it from a Divine Right; so though Princes have no immediate Warrants from Heaven, either for their original Titles, or for the extent of them, yet they are secured in the possession of them by the Principles and Rules of Natural Religion.

V. It is to be considered, that as a private Person can bind himself to another Man's Service, by different Degrees, either as an ordinary Servant for Wages, or as one appropriate for a longer time, as an Apprentice; or by a total giving himself up to another, as in the case of Slavery; in all which Cases the general name of *Master* may be equally used: yet the degrees of his Power are to be judged by the nature of the Contract. So likewise Bodies of Men can give themselves up in different Degrees, to the Conduct of others; and therefore, though all those may carry the same name of *King*, yet every one's Power is to be taken from the Measures of that Authority which is lodged in him, and not from any general Speculations founded on some equivocal Terms, such as *King*, *Sovereign*, or *Supream*.

VI. It is certain, that God, as the Creator and Governour of the World, may set up whom he will, to rule over other Men: But this Declaration of his Will, must be made evident by Prophets, or by extraordinary Men sent from him, who have some manifest Proofs of the divine Authority that is committed to them on such Occasions; and upon such Persons declaring the Will of God, in favour of any others, that Declaration is to be submitted to, and obeyed. But this pretence of a divine Delegation, can be carried no further than to those who are thus expresly marked out, and is unjustly claimed by those who can prove no such Declaration to have been ever made in favour of them, or their Families. Nor does it appear reasonable to conclude from their being in possession, that it is the Will of God that it should be so; this justifies all Usurpers when they are successful.

VII. The Measures of Power, and by consequence of Obedience, must be taken from the express Laws of any State, or Body of Men, from the Oaths that they swear, or from immemorial Prescription, and a long Possession, which both give a Title, and in a long tract of Time make a bad one become good; since Prescription when it passes the Memory of Man, and is not disputed by any other Pretender, gives by the common sense of all Men a just and good Title: So upon the whole matter, the Degrees of all Civil Authority, are to be taken either from express Laws, immemorial Customs, or from particular Oaths, which the Subjects swear to their Princes; this being still to be laid down for a Principle, that in all the Disputes between *Power* and *Liberty*, *Power* must always be proved, but *Liberty* proves it self; the one being founded only upon positive Law, and the other upon the Law of Nature.

VIII. If from the general Principles of human Society, and natural Religion, we carry this matter to be examined by the Scriptures; it is clear that all the Passages that are in the *Old Testament*, are not to be made use of in this matter, of either side. For as the Land of *Canaan* was given to the Jews by an immediate Grant from Heaven, so God reserved still this to himself, and to the Declarations that he should make from time to time, either by his Prophets, or by the Answers that came from the Cloud of Glory that was between the Cherubims, to set up Judges or Kings over them, and to pull them down again as he thought fit. Here was an express Delegation made by God, and therefore all that was done in that Dispensation, either for or against Princes, is not to be made use of in any other State, that is founded on any other Bottom and Constitution; and all the Expressions in the *Old Testament* relating to the Kings, since they belong to Persons that were immediately designed by God, are without any sort of Reason applied to those, who can pretend to no such designation, either for themselves or for their Ancestors.

IX. As for the *New Testament*, it is plain, that there are no Rules given in it, either for the Forms of Government in general, or for the Degrees of any one Form in particular; but the general Rules of Justice, Order and Peace, being established in it upon higher Motives, and more binding Considerations, than ever they were in any other Religion whatsoever, we are most strictly bound by it, to observe the Constitution in which we are; and it is plain, that the Rules set us in the Gospel, can be carried no further. It is indeed clear from the *New Testament*, that the Christian Religion, as such, gives us no grounds to defend or propagate it by force. It is a Doctrine of the Cross, and of Faith, and Patience under it: And if by the Order of Divine Providence, and of any Constitution of Government, under which we are born, we are brought under Sufferings for our professing of it, we may indeed retire and fly out of any such Country, if we can; but if that is denied us, we must then, according to this Religion, submit to those Sufferings under which we may be brought, considering that

that God will be glorified by us in ſo doing, and that he will both ſupport us under our Sufferings, and gloriouſly reward us for them.

This was the ſtate of the Chriſtian Religion, during the three firſt Centuries, under Heathen Emperors, and a Conſtitution in which *Paganiſm* was eſtabliſhed by Law: But if by the Laws of any Government, the Chriſtian Religion, or any Form of it, is become a part of the Subjects Property, it then falls under another Conſideration, not as it is a *Religion,* but as it is become one of the principal Rights of the Subjects, to believe and profeſs it : and then we muſt judge of the Invaſions made on that, as we do of any other Invaſion that is made on our other Rights.

X. All the Paſſages in the *New Teſtament* that relate to Civil Government, are to be expounded as they were truly meant, in oppoſition to that falſe Notion of the Jews, who believed themſelves to be ſo immediately under the Divine Authority, that they could not become the Subjects of any other Power ; particularly of one that was not of their Nation, or of their Religion ; therefore they thought they could not be under the *Roman* Yoke, nor bound to pay Tribute to *Cæſar,* but judged that they were only ſubject out of fear, by reaſon of the force that lay on them, but not for Conſcience ſake : and ſo in all their diſperſion, both at *Rome* and elſewhere; they thought they were God's Freemen, and made uſe of this pretended Liberty as a Cloak of Maliciouſneſs. In oppoſition to all which, ſince in a courſe of many Years they had asked the Protection of the *Roman* Yoke, and were come under their Authority, our Saviour ordered them to continue in that, by his ſaying, *Render to* Cæſar *that which is* Cæſar's ; and both St. *Paul* in his Epiſtle to the *Romans,* and St. *Peter* in his general *Epiſtle,* have very poſitively condemned that pernicious Maxim ; but without any formal Declarations made of the Rules or Meaſures of Government. And ſince both the People and Senate of *Rome* had acknowledged the Power that *Auguſtus* had indeed violently uſurped, it became legal when it was thus ſubmitted to, and confirmed both by the Senate and People ; and it was eſtabliſhed in his Family by a long Preſcription, when thoſe *Epiſtles* were writ : ſo that upon the whole matter, all that is in the *New Teſtament* upon this Subject, imports no more, but that all Chriſtians are bound to acquieſce in the Government, and ſubmit to it, according to the Conſtitution that is ſettled by Law.

XI. We are then at laſt brought to the Conſtitution of our *Engliſh Government* ; ſo that no general Conſiderations from Speculations about Sovereign Power, nor from any Paſſages either of the *Old* or *New Teſtament,* ought to determine us in this matter ; which muſt be fixed from the Laws and Regulations that have been made among us. It is then certain, that with relation to the executive part of the Government, the Law has lodged that ſingly in the King ; ſo that the whole Adminiſtration of it is in him: but the legiſlative Power is lodged between the King and the two Houſes of Parliament ; ſo that the Power of making and repealing Laws, is not ſingly in the King, but only ſo far as the two Houſes concur with him. It is alſo clear, that the King has ſuch a determined extent of Prerogative, beyond which he has no Authority : as for inſtance, if he levies Money of his People, without a Law impowering him to it, he goes beyond the Limits of his Power, and asks that to which he has no right: ſo that there lies no obligation on the Subject to grant it ; and if any in his Name uſe Violence for the obtaining it, they are to be looked on as ſo many Robbers, that invade our Property, and they being violent Aggreſſors, the Principle of Self-preſervation ſeems here to take place, and to warrant as violent a Reſiſtance.

XII. There is nothing more evident, than that *England* is a free Nation, that has its Liberties and Properties reſerved to it by many poſitive and expreſs Laws : If then we have a right to our Property, we muſt likewiſe be ſuppoſed to have a right to preſerve it ; for thoſe Rights are by the Law ſecured againſt the Invaſions of the Prerogative, and by conſequence we muſt have a right to preſerve them againſt thoſe Invaſions. It is alſo evidently declared by our Law, that all Orders and Warrants that are iſſued out in oppoſition to them, are null of themſelves ; and by conſequence, any that pretend to have Commiſſions from the King, for thoſe ends, are to be conſidered as if they had none at all : ſince thoſe Commiſſions being void of themſelves, are indeed no Commiſſions in the Conſtruction of the Law ; and therefore thoſe who act in virtue of them, are ſtill to be conſidered as private Perſons who come to invade and diſturb us. It is alſo to be obſerved, that there are ſome Points that are juſtly diſputable and doubtful, and others that are ſo manifeſt, that it is plain that any Objections that can be made to them, are rather forced Pretences, than ſo much as plauſible Colours. It is true, if the Caſe is doubtful, the Intereſt of the publick Peace and Order ought to carry it ; but the Caſe is quite different when the Invaſions that are made upon Liberty and Property, are plain and viſible to all that conſider them.

XIII. The main and great Difficulty here, is, that though our Government does indeed affert the *Liberty of the Subject*, yet there are many exprefs Laws made, that lodge the Militia fingly in the King, that make it plainly unlawful upon any pretence whatfoever, to take Arms againft the King, or any commiffioned by him : And thefe Laws have been put in the form of an Oath, which all that have born any Employment either in Church or State have fworn ; and therefore thofe Laws, for the affuring our Liberties, do indeed bind the King's Confcience, and may affect his Minifters : yet fince it is a Maxim of our Law, that the King can do no wrong, thefe cannot be carried fo far as to juftify our taking Arms againft him, be the Tranfgreffions of Law ever fo many and fo manifeft. And fince this has been the conftant Doctrine of the Church of *England*, it will be a very heavy Imputation on us, if it appears, that though we held thofe Opinions as long as the Court and the Crown have favoured us, yet as foon as the Court turns againft us, we change our Principles.

XIV. Here is a true Difficulty of this whole Matter, and therefore it ought to be exactly confidered : 1. All general Words, how large foever, are ftill fuppofed to have a tacit exception, and referve in them, if the Matter feems to require it.   Children are commanded to obey their Parents in all things : Wives are declared by the Scripture to be fubject to their Husbands in all things, *as the Church is unto Chrift :* And yet how comprehenfive foever thefe Words may feem to be, there is ftill a referve to be underftood in them ; and though by our Form of Marriage, the Parties fwear to one another *till Death them do part*, yet few doubt but that this Bond is diffolved by Adultery, though it is not named ; for odious things ought not to be fufpected, and therefore not named upon fuch Occafions : But when they fall out, they carry ftill their own force with them. 2. When there feems to be a Contradiction between two Articles in the Conftitution, we ought to examine which of the two is moft evident, and the moft important, and fo we ought to fix upon it ; and then we muft give fuch an accommodating fenfe to that which feems to contradict it, that fo we may reconcile thofe together.   Here then are two feeming Contradictions in our Conftitution: The one is the *publick Liberty* of the Nation ; the other is the renouncing of all *Refiftance*, in cafe that were invaded. It is plain, that our *Liberty* is only a thing that we enjoy at the King's Difcretion, and during his Pleafure, if the other againft all Refiftance is to be underftood according to the utmoft extent of the Words.   Therefore fince the chief Defign of our whole Law, and of all the feveral Rules of our Conftitution, is to fecure and maintain our Liberty, we ought to lay that down for a Conclufion, that it is both the moft plain and the moft important of the two : And therefore the other Article againft *Refiftance*, ought to be fo foftned, as that it do not deftroy this.   3. Since it is by a Law that Refiftance is condemned, we ought to underftand it in fuch a fenfe, as that it does not deftroy all other Laws : And therefore the Intent of this Law, muft not only relate to the executive Power, which is in the King, and not to the Legiflature, in which we cannot fuppofe that our Legiflators, who made that Law, intended to give up that, which we plainly fee they refolved ftill to preferve entire, according to the ancient Conftitution. So then, the not refifting the King, can only be applied to the executive Power, that fo upon no pretence of ill Adminiftrations in the Execution of the Law, it fhould be lawful to refift him ; but this cannot with any reafon be extended to an Invafion of the *Legiflative Power*, or to a total *Subverfion of the Government.* For it being plain that the Law did not defign to lodge that Power in the King ; it is alfo plain, that it did not intend to fecure him in it, in cafe he fhould fet about it. 4. The Law mentioning the *King*, or thofe commiffionated by him, fhews plainly, that it only defigned to fecure the King in the executive Power ; for the word *Commiffion* neceffarily imports this, fince if it is not according to Law, it is no Commiffion ; and by confequence, thofe who act in virtue of it, are not commiffionated by the King in the fenfe of the Law. The King likewife imports a Prince cloathed by Law with the Regal Prerogative ; but if he goes to fubvert the whole Foundation of the Government, he fubverts that by which he himfelf has his Power, and by confequence he annuls his own Power ; and then he ceafes to be King, having endeavoured to deftroy that upon which his own Authority is founded.

XV. It is acknowledged by the greateft Afferters of Monarchical Power, that in fome Cafes a King may fall from his Power, and in other Cafes that he may fall from the Exercife of it. His deferting his people, his going about to enflave, or fell them to any other, or a furious going about to deftroy them, are in the opinion of the moft Monarchical Lawyers, fuch Abufes, that they naturally diveft thofe that are guilty of them, of their whole Authority. *Infancy* or *Phrenzy* do alfo put them under the Guardianfhip of others.   All the crowned Heads of *Europe* have, at leaft fecretly, approved of the putting the late King of *Portugal* under a Guardianfhip, and the keeping him ftill

Priſoner for a few Acts of Rage, that had been fatal to a very few Perſons: And even our *Court* gave the firſt countenance to it, though of all others the *late King* had the moſt reaſon to have done it at leaſt laſt of all; ſince it juſtified a younger Brother's ſupplanting the Elder: yet the evidence of the thing carried it even againſt Intereſt. Therefore if a King goes about to ſubvert the Government, and to overturn the whole Conſtitution, he by this muſt be ſuppoſed either to fall from his Power, or at leaſt from the Exerciſe of it, ſo far as that he ought to be put under Guardians; and according to the Caſe of *Portugal*, the next *Heir* falls naturally to be the Guardian.

XVI. The next thing to be conſidered, is to ſee in Fact whether the Foundations of this Government have been ſtruck at, and whether thoſe Errors, that have been perhaps committed, are only ſuch Malverſations, as ought to be imputed only to human Frailty, and to the Ignorance, Inadvertencies, or Paſſions to which all Princes may be ſubject, as well as other Men. But this will beſt appear if we conſider what are the fundamental Points of our *Government*, and the chief Securities that we have for our *Liberties*.

The Authority of the *Law* is indeed all in one word, ſo that if the *King* pretends to a power to *diſpenſe* with *Laws*, there is nothing left, upon which the *Subject* can depend; and yet as if *Diſpenſing Power* were not enough, if Laws are wholly ſuſpended for all time coming, this is plainly a repealing of them, when likewiſe the Men in whoſe hands the Adminiſtration of Juſtice is put by Law, ſuch as *Judges* and *Sheriffs*, are allowed to tread all Laws under foot, even thoſe that infer an Incapacity on themſelves if they violate them; this is ſuch a breaking of the whole Conſtitution, that we can no more have the Adminiſtration of Juſtice, ſo that it is really a Diſſolution of the *Government*; ſince all Trials, Sentences, and the Executions of them, are become ſo many unlawful Acts, that are null and void of themſelves.

The next thing in our *Conſtitution*, which ſecures to us our *Laws* and *Liberties*, is a *free* and *lawful Parliament*. Now not to mention the breach of the *Law* of *Triennial Parliaments*, it being above three years ſince we had a Seſſion that enacted any Law, Methods have been taken, and are daily taking, that render this impoſſible. *Parliaments* ought to be choſen with an entire Liberty, and without either Force or Preingagements: whereas if all Men are required beforehand to enter into Engagements how they will vote, if they are choſen themſelves, or how they will give their Voices in the electing of others; this is plainly ſuch a preparation to a Parliament, as would indeed make it no *Parliament*, but a *Cabal*; if one were choſen, after all that Corruption of Perſons, who had preingaged themſelves; and after the threatning and turning of all perſons out of Employments who had refuſed to do it; and if there are ſuch daily Regulations made in the Towns, that it is plain thoſe who manage them intend at laſt to put ſuch a number of Men in the Corporations, as will certainly chuſe the perſons who are recommended to them. But above all, if there are ſuch a number of Sheriffs and Mayors made over *England*, by whom the Elections muſt be conducted and returned, who are now under an Incapacity by Law, and ſo are no legal Officers, and by conſequence thoſe Elections that paſs under their Authority are null and void; if, I ſay, it is clear that things are brought to this, then the Government is diſſolved, becauſe it is impoſſible to have a *free and legal Parliament* in this ſtate of things. If then both the Authority of the Law, and the Conſtitution of the Parliament are ſtruck at and diſſolved, here is a plain Subverſion of the whole Government. But if we enter next into the particular Branches of the Government, we will find the like Diſorder among them all.

The *Proteſtant Religion*, and the *Church of England*, make a great Article of our Government, the latter being ſecured not only of old by *Magna Charta*, but by many ſpecial *Laws* made of late; and there are particular Laws made in K. *Charles* the Firſt's and the late King's time, ſecuring them from all *Commiſſions* that the King can raiſe for judging or cenſuring them: if then, in oppoſition to this, a *Court* ſo condemned is erected, which proceeds to judge and cenſure the Clergy, and even to diſſeiſe them of their Freeholds, without ſo much as the form of a Trial, though this is the moſt indiſpenſible Law of all thoſe that ſecures the Property of *England*; and if the King pretends that he can require the Clergy to publiſh all his Arbitrary Declarations, and in particular, one that ſtrikes at their whole Settlement, and has ordered Proceſs to be begun againſt all that diſobey'd this illegal Warrant, and has treated ſo great a number of the Biſhops as Criminals, only for repreſenting to him the Reaſons of their not obeying him; if likewiſe the King is not ſatisfied to profeſs his own Religion openly, though even that is contrary to Law, but has ſent Ambaſſadors to *Rome*, and received Nuncio's from thence, which is plainly Treaſon by Law; if likewiſe many *Popiſh Churches* and *Chappels* have been publickly opened;

if

if several *Colleges* of *Jesuits* have been set up in divers parts of the Nation, and one of the Order has been made a Privy-Counsellor, and a principal Minister of *State*; and if *Papists*, and even those who turn to that Religion, though declared Traitors by Law, are brought into all the chief Employments, both Military and Civil; then it is plain, that all the Rights of the *Church of England* and the whole Establishment of the *Protestant Religion* are struck at, and designed to be overturned; since all these things, as they are notoriously illegal, so they evidently demonstrate, that the great design of them all, is the rooting out of this *Pestilent Heresy*, in their stile, I mean the *Protestant Religion*.

In the next place, If in the whole Course of Justice, it is visible, that there is a constant practising upon the Judges, that they are turned out upon their varying from the Intentions of the Court, and if Men of no Reputation nor Abilities are put in their places; if an Army is kept up in time of Peace, and Men who withdraw from that illegal Service are hanged up as Criminals, without any colour of Law, which by consequence are so many Murders; and if the Soldiery are connived at, and encouraged in the most enormous Crimes, that so they may be thereby prepared to commit greater ones, and from single Rapes and Murders, proceed to a Rape upon all our Liberties and a destruction of the Nation: If, I say, all these things are true in fact, then it is plain, that there is such a dissolution of the Government made, that there is not any one part of it left sound and entire; and if all these things are done now, it is easy to imagine what may be expected, when *Arbitrary Power* that spares no Man, and *Popery* that spares no Heretick, are finally established: Then we may look for nothing but Gabelles, Tailles, Impositions, Benevolences, and all sorts of illegal Taxes, as from the other we may expect Burnings, Massacres, and Inquisitions. In what is doing in *Scotland*, we may gather what is to be expected in *England*; where if the King has over and over again declared, that he is vested with an *Absolute Power*, to which all are bound to *obey without reserve*, and has upon that annulled almost all the Acts of Parliament that passed in K. *James* Ist's Minority, though they were ratified by himself when he came to be of age, and were confirmed by all the subsequent Kings, not excepting the present; we must then conclude from thence, what is resolved on here in *England*, and what will be put in execution as soon as it is thought that the times can bear it. When likewise the whole Settlement of *Ireland* is shaken, and the Army that was raised, and is maintained by Taxes, that were given for an Army of *English Protestants*, to secure them from a new Massacre by the *Irish Papists*, is now all filled with *Irish Papists*, as well as almost all the other Imployments; it is plain, that not only all the *British Protestants* inhabiting that Island, are in daily danger of being butchered a second time, but that the Crown of *England* is in danger of losing that Island, it being now put wholly into the hands and power of the Native *Irish*, who as they formerly offered themselves up sometimes to the Crown of *Spain*, sometimes to the Pope, and once to the Duke of *Lorrain*; so are they perhaps at this present treating with another Court for the sale and surrender of the Island, and for the Massacre of the *English* in it.

If thus all the several Branches of our Constitution are dissolved, it might be at least expected, that one part should be left entire, and that is the *Regal Dignity*; and yet even that is prostituted, when we see a young *Child* put in the reversion of it, and pretended to be the *Prince* of *Wales*; concerning whose being born of the *Queen*, there appear to be not only no certain Proofs, but there are all the Presumptions that can possibly be imagined to the contrary. No Proofs were ever given either to the *Princess of Denmark*, or to any other *Protestant Ladies*, in whom we ought to repose any confidence, that the *Queen* was ever with Child; that whole matter being managed with so much Mysteriousness, that there were violent and publick Suspicions of it before the Birth. But the whole Contrivance of the Birth, the sending away the *Princess of* Denmark, the sudden shortning of the *Reckoning*, the *Queen*'s sudden going to *St. James's*, her no less sudden pretended *Delivery*; the hurrying the *Child* into another Room without shewing it to those present, and without their hearing it cry; and the mysterious Conduct of all since that time; no satisfaction being given to the *Princess of Denmark* upon her Return from the *Bath*, nor to any other *Protestant Ladies*, of the *Queen*'s having been really brought to bed: These are all such evident Indications of a base Imposture, in this matter, that as the *Nation* has the justest reason in the World to doubt of it, so they have all possible reason to be at no quiet till they see a *legal* and *free Parliament* assembled, which may impartially, and without either Fear or Corruption, examine that whole matter.

If all these Matters are true in fact, then I suppose no Man will doubt, that the whole Foundations of this Government, and all the most sacred Parts of it, are overturned. And as to the truth of all these Suppositions, that is left to every *Englishman*'s Judgment and Sense.

2

The Oaths of Allegiance and Supremacy, no Badges of Slavery.

THE ecclesiastical Jurisdiction of the Crown of *England,* having been invaded and broke in upon by the Power of the Court of *Rome,* in King *Henry* the Eighth's time, all Foreign Power was abolished, and the ancient legal Supremacy restor'd, and by many additional Acts corroborated. But all that was done of that kind, in King *Henry* the Eighth's time, was undone again in Queen *Mary's* ; and therefore in the first Year of Queen *Elizabeth's* Reign, an Act of Parliament was made, intitled, *All Ancient Jurisdiction restored to the Crown. A Repeal of divers Statutes, and Reviver of others ; and all foreign Power abolished.* Which Act recites, that *whereas, in the Reign of R. H. 8. divers good Laws were made and established, as well for the utter extinguishment and putting away of all usurped and foreign Powers and Authorities out of this Realm, as also for restoring and uniting to the imperial Crown of this Realm, the ancient Jurisdictions, Authorities, Superiorities, and Preheminences to the same of right belonging and appertaining ; by reason whereof, the Subjects of this Realm were kept in good order, and disburthened of divers great and intolerable Charges and Exactions, until such time as all the said good Laws and Statutes, by one Act of Parliament, made in the first and second Years of the Reigns of King* Philip *and Queen* Mary, *were clearly repealed and made void ; by reason of which Act of Repeal, the Subjects of* England *were eftsoons brought under an usurped foreign Power and Authority, and yet remained in that Bondage to their intolerable Charges :* And then enacts, *That for the repressing of the said usurped foreign Power, and the restoring of the Rights, Jurisdictions, and Preheminences, appertaining to the imperial Crown of this Realm, the said Act made in the first and second Years of the said late King* Philip *and Queen* Mary *(except as therein is excepted) be repealed, void, and of none effect.*

The said Act of *Primo Elizabethæ* proceeds, First, to revive by express words, many Statutes that had been made in King *Henry* the Eighth's time, and repealed in Queen *Mary's* ; and Secondly, to abolish all foreign Authority in these words ; (viz.) *And to the Intent that all usurped and foreign Power and Authority Spiritual and Temporal, may for ever be clearly extinguished, and never be used or obeyed within this Realm, &c.* May it please your Highness, *that it may be enacted, That no foreign Prince, Person, Prelate, State, or Potentate, Spiritual or Temporal, shall at any time after the last day of this Session of Parliament, use, enjoy, or exercise any manner of Power, Jurisdiction, Superiority, Authority, Preheminence, or Privilege, Spiritual or Ecclesiastical, within this Realm, &c. but the same shall be clearly abolished out of this Realm, &c. any Statute, Custom, &c. to the contrary notwithstanding.* Thirdly, The said Act restores, in the next Paragraph, *to the imperial Crown of this Realm, such Jurisdictions, Privileges, Superiorities, &c. Spiritual and Ecclesiastical, as by any Spiritual or Ecclesiastical Power, or Authority, had heretofore been, or might lawfully be exercised or used, &c.* Fourthly, the Act impowers the Queen to assign Commissioners to exercise Ecclesiastical Jurisdiction. And fifthly, *For the better observation and maintenance of this Act,* imposes upon *Ecclesiastical and Temporal Officers and Ministers,* &c. the Oath, commonly called the *Oath of Supremacy,* which runs thus ; *viz.*

The Oath of S U P R E M A C Y.

I A. B. *do utterly testify and declare, in my Conscience, that the Queen's Highness is the only supreme Governor of this Realm, and of all other her Highness's Dominions and Countries, as well in all spiritual or ecclesiastical Things, and Causes, as Temporal ; and that no foreign Prince, Person, Prelate, State, or Potentate, hath, or ought to have any Jurisdiction, Power, Superiority, Preheminence, or Authority, Ecclesiastical or Spiritual, within this Realm: And therefore I do utterly renounce and forsake all foreign Jurisdictions, Powers, Superiorities, and Authorities ; and do promise, that from henceforth, I shall bear Faith and true Allegiance to the Queen's Highness, her Heirs and lawful Successors ; and to my Power shall assist and defend all Jurisdictions, Privileges, Preheminences, and Authorities, granted, or belonging to the Queen's Highness, her Heirs and Successors ; or united and annexed to the imperial Crown of this Realm. So help me* God, *and the Contents of this Book.*

It cannot but be obvious to every impartial Peruſer of the Statute, eſpecially if he have the leaſt knowledge of what Condition the Government of this Nation was reduced to, by Papal Encroachments and Uſurpations;. That the makers of this Law, and the Senſe of this Oath, was no other in general, than that the People of this Realm ſhould *bear Faith and true Allegiance,* even in matters relating to ' Eccleſiaſtical Juriſdiction, ' to the Queen's Highneſs, her Heirs and lawful Succeſſors, and not to the Pope, or ' any foreign pretended Juriſdiction.

What the ſeveral ' Juriſdictions, Privileges, Preheminences, and Authorities, grant- ' ed or belonging to the Queen, her Heirs and Succeſſors, are in particular ; and what ' the Juriſdictions, Privileges, Preheminencies, and Authorities, united and annexed to ' the imperial Crown of this Realm, are in particular, is not material here to be diſ- courſed of ; though the ſeveral Statutes made in ' King *Henry* the Eighth's time, and ' King *Edward* the Sixth's, and reviv'd in Queen *Elizabeth*'s, will unfold many of them ; and clear the diſtinction, which the *O A T H* makes , betwixt ' Authorities granted or ' belonging to the King, and Authorities united and annexed to the imperial Crown ; and ' Mr. *Prynn*'s Hiſtory of the Pope's intolerable Uſurpations upon the Liberties of the ' Kings and Subjects of *England* and *Ireland* ;' together with ' Sir *Roger Twiſden*'s ' Hiſtorical Vindication of the Church of *England*, in point of Schiſm, ' will in a great meaſure acquaint the Curious how matters ſtood with us here, with reſpect to Church-Government, before the Pope had wreſted the Eccleſiaſtical Juriſdiction, almoſt wholly out of the hands of our Kings, our Parliaments, and Courts of Juſtice. In ſhort, thoſe Juriſdictions, &c. are ſuch, as the ancient Laws, Cuſtoms, and Uſages of the Realm, or latter Acts of Parliament have created, given, limited, and directed.

The makers of this Law did not deſign to impoſe upon the People of *England,* any new terms of Allegiance, but to ſecure the old ones, excluſive of any Pretences of the Pope, or See of *Rome.*

Nor are there any words in this Oath more ſtrong, more binding to Duty and Alle- giance, than the words which the old *Oath of Fealty* is conceived in ; which all Men were anciently obliged, and may yet be required to take to the King in the Court Leet, at twelve years of Age ; which runs thus ; *viz.*

You ſhall ſwear, that from this day forward, you ſhall be true and faithful to our ſove- reign Lord King James, *and his Heirs: And Faith and Truth ſhall bear of Life and Limb, and terrene Honour. And you ſhall not know nor hear of any ill or damage intend- ed to him, that you ſhall not defend. So help you Almighty God.*

This is as full and comprehenſive, as the Oath of Supremacy ; *I do promiſe, that I ſhall bear Faith and true Allegiance to the Queen's Highneſs, her Heirs, and lawful Succeſ- ſors ; and to my Power ſhall aſſiſt and defend all Juriſdictions,* &c. So that the true ſenſe and meaning of the Oath of Supremacy, is this ; *viz. I will be true and faithful to our ſovereign Lord the King, his Heirs, and lawful Succeſſors ; and will, to my Power, aſſiſt and defend all his Rights, notwithſtanding any pretence made by the Pope, or any other fo- reign Power, to exerciſe Juriſdiction within the Realm ; all which foreign Power, I utterly renounce, in Matters Eccleſiaſtical as well as Temporal.*

The *Oath of Allegiance* is appointed by the Act of 3 *Jac.* 1. *Chap.* 4. intitled, *An Act for diſcovering and repreſſing of Popiſh Recuſants.* It recites *the daily Experiences that many of his Majeſty's Subjects, that adhere in their Hearts to the Popiſh Religion, by the Infection drawn from thence, by the wicked and deviliſh Counſel of Jeſuits, Seminaries, and other like Perſons, dangerous to the Church and State, are ſo far perverted in the point of their Loy- alties, and due Allegiance to the King's Majeſty, and the Crown of* England, *as they are ready to entertain and execute any treaſonable Conſpiracies and Practices: and for the better trial how his Majeſty's Subjects ſtand affected in point of their Loyalties, and due Obedience,* Enacts, *that it ſhall be lawful for any Biſhop in his Dioceſe, or any two Juſtices of the Peace, whereof one to be of the* Quorum, *within the Limits of their Juriſdictions, out of the Seſſi- on, to require any Perſon of the age of eighteen Years, or above, which ſhall be convicted or indicted of Recuſancy, other than Noblemen,* &c. *or which ſhall not have received the Sacra- ment twice within the Year then next paſt, or any Perſon paſſing in or through the Country, unknown, that being examined upon Oath, ſhall confeſs, or not deny him or herſelf to be a Recuſant, and to take the Oath therein after expreſſed ;* viz. &c. *The Oath of Allegiance.*

So

So that by the occasion of imposing the *Oath*, and by the appointing it to be tendred only to Papists, or suspected Papists, it is apparent that the design of the Law-makers was to detect such Persons as were perverted, or in danger to be perverted in their Loyalty, by infection drawn from the *Popish Religion*.

The form of the Oath makes it yet more evident, being wholly level'd against any Opinion of the Lawfulness of deposing the King, or practising any Treason against him, upon pretence of his being excommunicated or deprived by the Pope, and against any Opinion of the Pope's Power, to discharge Subjects from their Oaths of Fidelity to their Princes. It runs thus ; *viz.*

I A. B. do truly and sincerely profess, testify, and declare, in my Conscience, before God and the World, that our Sovereign Lord King James, *is lawful and rightful King of this Realm, and of all his Majesty's Dominions and Countries : And that the Pope, neither of himself, nor by any Authority of the Church, or See of* Rome, *or by any other means, with any other, hath any Power or Authority to depose the King, or to dispose of any of his Majesty's Kingdoms or Dominions, or to authorize any foreign Prince to invade or annoy him, or his Countries, or to discharge any of his Subjects of their Allegiance, or Obedience to his Majesty, or to give licence or leave to any of them to bear Arms, raise Tumults, or to offer any Violence or Hurt to his Majesty's Royal Person, State, or Government, or to any of his Majesty's Subjects within his Majesty's Dominions.*

Also I do swear from my Heart, That, notwithstanding any Declaration or Sentence of Excommunication, or Deprivation made or granted, or to be made or granted by the Pope or his Successors, or by any Authority derived, or pretended to be derived from him or his See, against the said King, his Heirs and Successors, or any Absolution of the said Subjects from their Obedience, *I will bear Faith and true Allegiance to his Majesty, his Heirs, and Successors ; and him and them will defend to the uttermost of my Power, against all Conspiracies and Attempts whatsoever, which shall be made against his or their Persons, their Crown and Dignity, by reason or colour of any such Sentence or Declaration, or otherwise ; and will do my best endeavour to disclose, and make known unto his Majesty, his Heirs, and Successors, all Treasons and traitorous Conspiracies, which I shall know, or hear of, to be against him, or any of them.*

And I do further swear, That I do from my Heart abhor and detest, and abjure, as impious and heretical, this damnable Doctrine and Position, that Princes, which be excommunicated or deprived by the Pope, *may be deposed or murthered by their Subjects, or any other whatsoever.*

And I do believe, and in Conscience am persuaded, that neither the Pope, nor any Person whatsoever, hath Power to absolve me of this Oath, or any part thereof, which I acknowledge, by good and lawful Authority, to be lawfully administred unto me ; and I do renounce all Pardons and Dispensations to the contrary. And all these things I do plainly and sincerely acknowledge and swear, according to these express words by me spoken, and according to the plain and common Sense and Understanding of the same words, without any Equivocation, or mental Evasion, or secret Reservation whatsoever. And I do make this Recognition and Acknowledgment heartily, willingly, and truly, upon the true Faith of a Christian. So help me God.

And the Statute of 7 Jacobi cap. 6. recites ; ' That whereas, by a Statute made in the ' third Year of the said King's Reign, the Form of an Oath to be ministred and given ' to certain Persons in the same Act mentioned, is limited and prescribed, tending only ' to the Declaration of such Duty, as every true and well-affected Subject, not only by ' Bond of Allegiance, but also by the Commandment of Almighty God, ought to bear ' to the King, his Heirs and Successors ; which Oath, such as are *infected with Popish* ' *Superstition*, do oppugn with many false and unsound Arguments ; the just defence ' whereof, the King had therefore undertaken, and worthily performed, to the great ' contentment of all his Subjects, notwithstanding the Gainsayings of contentious Adver- ' saries : And to shew how greatly the King's loyal Subjects do approve the said Oath, ' they beseech his Majesty, that the said Oath be administred to all his Subjects.'

The *Pope*, and Authority of the See of *Rome*, run thro' the first Paragraph ; *Notwithstanding any Declaration, or Sentence of Excommunication, &c.* governs the second Paragraph : *Excommunicated and Deprived by the Pope*, are the material Words in the third Paragraph. The fourth is added *in majorem cautelam*, in opposition to the Popish Doctrine of *Dispensing* with Oaths, *absolving* Subjects from their *Allegiance, Equivocations, mental Evasions*, &c.

So

I

So that as the *Oath of Supremacy* did but enforce the ancient *Oath of Fealty*, with an acknowledgment of the Queen's supreme Authority, in Ecclesiastical Causes and Things, as well as temporal, and a Renunciation of all foreign Jurisdictions; so the *Oath of Allegiance* does but enforce the same old *Oath of Fealty*, by obliging the Subjects of *England*, exprefly to difown any lawful Authority in the Pope or See of *Rome*, to depofe, invade, or annoy the King, his Dominions, or Subjects. And, *notwithstanding any Sentence of Excommunication, Deprivation*, &c. *by the Pope*, &c. to bear Faith and true Allegiance to the King, his Heirs and lawful Succeffors; and to abjure that Pofition, That it is lawful to depofe Princes that are *Excommunicated or Depriv'd by the Pope*.

Whatever is added, in either Oath, over and above what was exprefs'd in the old *Oath of Fealty*, is but as explanatory of it, and branching it out into fuch Particulars, as time and occafion required.

So that the Oaths of Supremacy and Allegiance, not having altered the *Terms of Allegiance*, due from the People of *England* to their Princes, if their Princes, by ancient *Laws of the Realm*, and by the *Practice of our Forefathers*, were liable to be depofed by the great Councils of the Nation, for *Male-administration, Oppreffions*, and other *Exorbitances*, for not keeping their Coronation-Oaths, for *Insufficiency to govern*, &c. then they continue ftill liable to be depofed in like manner; the faid Oaths, or any Obligation contracted thereby, notwithstanding.

For the Practice of former times, I fhall begin with a very ancient Precedent in the Kingdom of the *Weft*-Saxons, viz.

Cudred, King of *Weft-Saxony*, being dead, *Sigebert* his Kinfman, fucceeded him in that Kingdom, and held it but a fmall time; for being puff'd up with Pride by the Succeffes of King *Cudred* his Predeceffor, he grew infolent, and became intolerable to his People. And when he evil intreated them all manner of ways, and either wrefted the Laws for his own ends, or eluded them for his own advantage; *Cumbra* one of his chief Officers, at the requeft of the whole People, intimated their Complaints to the Savage King. And becaufe he perfuaded the King to govern his People more mildly, and that laying afide his Barbarity, he would endeavour to appear acceptable to God and Man; the King immediately commanded him to be put to death, and increafing his Tyranny, became more cruel and intolerable than before: whereupon, in the beginning of the fecond Year of his Reign, becaufe he was arriv'd to an incorrigible pitch of Pride and Wickednefs, the NOBLES and the PEOPLE OF THE WHOLE KINGDOM affembled together, and upon MATURE DELIBERATION, did by UNANIMOUS CONSENT OF THEM ALL, drive him out of the Kingdom. In whofe ftead they chofe *Kenwolph*, an excellent Youth, and of the Royal Blood, to be King over the People and Kingdom of the *Weft-Saxons*. Collect. *p.* 769, 770. *ibid. p.* 795, 796.

Cudredo Rege Weft-Saxiæ defuncto, Sigebertus, Cognatus ejus, fibi in eodem Regno fuccefſit; brevi tamen tempore Regnum tenens, nam ex Cudredi *Regis Præceſſoris fui eventibus tumefactus, & infolens, intolerabilis fuis fuit; cum autem eos modis omnibus male tractaret, legefque vel ad commodum fuum depravaret, vel pro commodo fuo devitaret,* Cumbra Conful *ejus Nobiliſſimus prece totius populi Regi fero eorum querimonias intimavit. Et quia ipfe Regi fuaferat, ut leniùs Populum fuum regeret, & inhumanitate depofitâ Deo & hominibus amabilis appareret, Rex eum impiâ nece mox interfici jubens, populo fævior & intolerabilior quàm priùs fuam tyrannidem augmentavit; unde in principio fecundi Anni Regni fui cum incorrigibilis fuperbiæ & nequitiæ effet, Congregati funt PROCERES & POPULUS totius REGNI, & eum PROVIDA DELIBERATIONE à Regno UNANIMI CONSENSU OMNIUM expellebant. Cujus loco* Kenwolfum *juvenem egregium de Regiâ ftirpe oriundum, in Regem fuper Populum & Regnum* Weft-Saxiæ *elegerunt.* Collect. 769, 770. ibidem, p. 795, 796.

This Depofition of King *Sigebert*, appears to have been done in a formal and orderly Manner; viz. in a Convention of the *Proceres*, and the *Populus totius Regni*; and it was done *providâ deliberatione & unanimi Omnium Confenfu*, and confequently was not an Act of *Heat, Rebellion*, or *Tumultuary Infurrection* of the People: But was what the whole Nation apprehended to be *Legal, Juft*, and according to the *Conftitution of their Government*, and no breach of their Oaths of Allegiance.

Nor

Nor have we any reason to wonder that the *English* Nation should free themselves in such a manner from Oppreſſion, if we conſider that by an ancient poſitive Law, enacted in K. *Edward the Conf.* time, and confirmed by *William* the Conqueror, the Kings of *England* are liable to be depoſed, if they turn Tyrants.

The King, becauſe he is the Vicar of the Supreme King, is conſtituted to this end and purpoſe, that he may govern his earthly Kingdom, and the People of the Lord, and eſpecially to govern and reverence God's Holy Church, and defend it from Injuries, and root out, deſtroy, and wholly to extirpate all Wrong-doers. Which if he do not perform, HE SHALL NOT RETAIN SO MUCH AS THE NAME OF A KING. *And a little after*; The King muſt act all things according to Law, and by the Judgment of the *Proceres Regni*. For Right and Juſtice ought to reign in the Realm rather than a perverſe Will. It is the Law that makes Right; but Wilfulneſs, Violence, and Force, is not Right. The King ought above all things to fear and love God, and to keep his Commandments throughout his Kingdom. He ought alſo to preſerve, to cheriſh, maintain, govern, and defend againſt its Adverſaries, the Church within his Kingdom entirely and in all freedom, according to the Conſtitutions of the Fathers, and of his Predeceſſors, that God may be honoured above all things, and always be had before Men's Eyes. He ought alſo to ſet up good Laws and approv'd Cuſtoms, and to aboliſh evil ones, and put them away in his Kingdom. He ought to do right Judgment in his Kingdom, and maintain Juſtice by advice of the *Proceres Regni ſui*. All theſe things the King, in proper Perſon, looking upon, and touching the holy Goſpels, and upon the holy and ſacred Relicks, muſt ſwear in the Preſence of his People and Clergy to do, before he be crowned by the Archbiſhops and Biſhops of the Kingdom. *Lamb. of the ancient Laws of* England. *pag.* 142.

Rex autem, quia Vicarius ſummi Regis eſt, ad hoc eſt conſtitutus, ut Regnum terrenum & Populum Domini, & ſuper omnia ſanctam veneretur Eccleſiam ejus & regat, & ab injurioſis defendat, & maleficos ab eâ evellat & deſtruat, & penitus diſper. Quod niſi fecerit, nec nomen Regis in eo conſtabit. Et paulò poſt; Debet Rex omnia ritè facere in Regno, & per Judicium Procerum Regni. Debet enim jus & juſtitia magis regnare in Regno, quàm voluntas prava. Lex eſt ſemper quod Jus facit; voluntas autem, violentia & Vis non eſt Jus. Debet verò Rex Deum timere ſuper omnia & diligere, & mandata ejus per totum Regnum ſuum ſervare. Debet etiam ſanctam Eccleſiam Regni ſui cum omni integritate & libertate, juxta Conſtitutiones Patrum & Prædeceſſorum, ſervare, fovere, manutenere, regere, & contra inimicos defendere, ita ut Deus præ cæteris honoretur, & præ oculis ſemper habeatur. Debet etiam bonas Leges & Conſuetudines approbatas erigere, pravas autem delere, & omnes à Regno deponere. Debet judicium rectum in Regno ſuo facere, & juſtitiam per conſilium Procerum regni ſui tenere. Iſta verò debet omnia Rex in propriâ perſonâ, inſpectis & tactis ſacroſanctis Evangeliis, & ſuper ſacras & ſanctas reliquias coram Regno & Sacerdotio & Clero jurare, antequam ab Archiepiſcopis & Epiſcopis Regni coronetur. Lamb. de priſcis Anglorum Legibus, p. 142.

Another Inſtance of the Depoſition of a King of *England*, ſubſequent to this Law, we find in King *John*'s time, whoſe *Oppreſſions* and *Tyrannical Government*, our Hiſtories are full of. Of which take this following Account, out of a very ancient Hiſtorian.

Whereas the ſaid *John* had ſworn ſolemnly at his Coronation, as the manner is, that he would preſerve the Rights and Uſages of the Church and Realm of *England*; yet contrary to his Oath, he ſubjected, as far as in him lay, the Kingdom of *England*, which has always been free, and made it tributary to the Pope, without the Advice and Conſent of his Barons; ſubverting good Cuſtoms, and introducing evil ones, endeavouring by many Oppreſſions, and many ways, *to enſlave both the Church and Realm*, which

Cum præfatus Johannes in Coronatione ſuâ ſolenniter, prout moris eſt, juraſſet, ſe Jura & Conſuetudines Eccleſiæ & Regni Angliæ conſervaturum, contra juramentum ſuum abſque conſilio vel conſenſu Baronum ſuorum, idem Regnum, quod ſemper fuit liberum, quantum in ipſo fuit, Domino Papæ ſubjecit, & fecit tributarium, bonas conſuetudines ſubvertens, malas inducens, tam Eccleſiam quam Regnum multis oppreſſionibus multiſque modis ſtudens ancellare, quas oppreſſiones vos melius noſtis, quam nos, ut qui eas

Kkkkkk

which Oppreffions you know better than I, as having felt them by manifold Experience. For which Caufes, when after many Applications made, War was waged againft him by his Barons ; at laft, amongft other things it was agreed, with his exprefs Confent, that in cafe the faid *John* fhould return to his former Villanies, *the Barons fhould be at liberty to recede from their Allegiance to him*, never to return to him more. But he, after a few days, made his latter end worfe than his beginning, endeavouring not only to opprefs his Barons, but wholly to exterminate them ; who therefore in a GENERAL ASSEMBLY, and with the APPROBATION OF ALL THE REALM, adjudging him unworthy to be King, chofe US for their Lord and King. *Collect. p.* 1868, 1869. *Chron.* W. Thorn.

eas familiari senfiftis experimento. Pro quibus, cum post multas requisitiones guerra mota esset contra ipsum à Baronibus suis, tandem inter cætera de ejus expresso consensu, ità convenit, ut si idem Johannes ad flagitia prima rediret, ipse Barones ab ejus fidelitate recederent, nunquam ad eum postmodùm reversuri. Verùm ipse nihilominus paucis diebus evolutis, fecit novissima sua pejora prioribus, studens Barones suos non tantum opprimere, sed potiùs penitùs exterminare. Qui DE COMMUNI REGNI CONSILIO & APPROBATIONE ipsum Regno judicantes indignum, nos in Regem & Dominum elegerunt. Collect. 1868, 1869. Chron. *W. Thorn :* Lewis his Letter to the Abbot of St. *Auftin's,* Canterbury.

The next Inftance fhall be that of King *Edward* the Second ; the Record of whofe *Depofition*, if it were extant, would probably difclofe all the legal Formalities that were then accounted proper for the depofing an unjuft, oppreffive King : But they were cancell'd and embezled (as is highly probable from *Raftal's Stat. pag.* 170, 171, compar'd with the Articles exhibited in Parliament againft King *Richard* the Second, of which hereafter) in King *Richard* the Second's time, and by his Order : Yet the Articles themfelves are preferved in the *Collect.* and are as followeth ; *viz.*

Accorde eft que Sire Edward *Fitz aifnè du Roy ait le Goverment du Royalme & foit Roy couronne, pur les caufes que s' enfuent.*

1. *Pur ceo que la Perfon le Roy n' eft pas fuffifant de Governer. Car en tout fon temps il ad eftre mene & governe per auters que ly ont mavaifement confeillez, à defhonour de ly & deftruction de Saint Efglife, & de tout fon People fanz ceo que il le voufift veer ou conufter lequel il fuft bon ou mauvays ou remedie mettre, au faire le voufift quant il fuit requis par les grants & fages de fon Royalme, ou fouffrir que amende fuift faite.*

2. *Item, Par fon temps il ne fe voloit doner à bon counfel, ne le croire, ne à bon Goverment de fon Royalme, mes fe ad done tous jours as Ouvrages & Occupations nient Convenables enterleffant l'efploit des befoignes de fon Royalme.*

3. *Item, Par defaut de bon goverment ad il perdu le Royalme d' Efcoce, & auters Terres & Seigneuries en* Gafcoyne *&* Hyrland, *les queux fon Pere le leifa en pees & amiftè du Roy de* France, *& dets mults des auters Grants.*

4. *Item, Par fa fiertè & qualte & par mauvays counfel ad il deftruit Saint Efglife, & les perfons de Saint Efglife tenus en prifon les uns : & les auters en diftrefce, & auxynt plufors Grants & Nobles de fa terre mys à honteufe mort, enprifones, exulets & defheritez.*

5. *Item,*

It is accorded that Prince *Edward*, the King's eldeft Son, fhall have the Goverment of the Kingdom, and be crowned King for the Caufes following.

1. For that the Perfon of the King is infufficient to govern : for that during his whole Reign he has been led and governed by others, who have given him evil Counfel, to his Difhonour, and the Deftruction of Holy-Church, and of all his People ; he being unwilling to confider or know what was good or evil, or to provide remedy, even when it was required of him by the great and wife Men of his Realm, or fuffer any to be made.

2. Alfo, during all his time, he would neither hearken to, nor believe good Counfel, nor apply himfelf to the good Goverment of his Realm, but hath always given himfelf over to Things and Occupations altogether inconvenient, omitting in the mean time the neceffary Affairs and Bufinefs of the Kingdom.

3. Alfo, for want of good Government, he hath loft the Kingdom of *Scotland*, and other Lands and Territories in *Gafcoin* and *Ireland*, which his Father left him in peace and friendfhip with the *French* King, and with many other Grandees.

4. Alfo, By his Pride and Arrogance, and evil Counfel, he has deftroyed Holy-Church, imprifoning fome Perfons thereof, and put others in diftrefs. And alfo he hath put to a fhameful death, imprifoned and difinherited many of the Great Men, and Nobles of the Land.

5. Alfo,

5. *Item, Ld ou il eſt tenus par ſon ſerment à faire droit à toute il ne P ad pas volu faire, pur ſon propre proffitt & covetiſe de ly, & de ces maveis conſailires, que ount iſte pres de ly, ne ad garde les auters points del ſerment qu' il fiſt à ſon Coronement, ſi come il fueſt tenus.*

6. *Item, Il deguerpiſt ſon Royalme & fiſt tant come en ly fuſt que ſon Royalme & ſon People fuſt perduſt, & que pys eſt, pur la cruaute de ly & defaute de ſa perſonne il eſt trove incorrigible ſaunz eſperance de amendment, les queux choſes ſont ſi notoires, qu' ils ne pount eſte deſdits.*

For theſe Cauſes, *De conſilio & aſſenſu omnium Prælatorum, Comitum & Baronum & totius Communitatis Regni, amotus eſt à regimine Regni.* (Apolog. *Ade de Orleton* Collect. p. 2765, 2766.)

5. Alſo, Whereas he is bound by his Oath to adminiſter Juſtice to all, he would not do it, through his own Covetouſneſs, and that of evil Counſellors, that were about him ; neither hath he kept the other Points of the Oath, which he took at his Coronation, as he was bound.

6. Alſo, He hath waſted his Kingdom, and did what in him lay, that his Realm and People ſhould be deſtroyed ; and, which is worſe, by his Cruelty and perſonal Failings or Defects, he is found to be incorrigible, and paſt all hopes of amendment. All which things are ſo notorious, that they cannot be denied.

For theſe Cauſes, by advice and aſſent of all the Prelates, Earls and Barons, and of the whole Commonalty of the Kingdom, he was depoſed from the Government. (*Apology of* Adam de Orleton *Collect. p.* 2765, 2766.)

Theſe Proceedings againſt King *Edward* the Second, are no where extant but in that Author. Which is the leſs to be wondred at, if we conſider, that in King *Richard* the Second's time, the King's paraſitical Court-Favourites ſo influenced the Judges ; That to the Queſtion, *How he was to be puniſhed, that moved in the Parliament, that the Statute ſhould be ſent for, whereby* Edward, *the Son of King* Edward, *was another time indicted in the Parliament?* they anſwered, *That as well he that moved, as the other ; who, by force of the ſame motion, brought the ſaid Statute into the Parliament-Houſe, be as Criminals and Traitors, worthy to be puniſhed.* V. Raſtal's *Statutes,* 170, 171. (Tho' for that, and other extravagant, pernicious, and treaſonable Opinions delivered, thoſe Judges were ſeverely puniſhed, as is notoriouſly known.) And alſo, That it was afterwards one Article of Impeachment againſt King *Richard* the Second, *That he had cancell'd and raſed ſundry Records.*

In King *Richard* the Second's time, many Animoſities aroſe from time to time betwixt him and his Parliaments ; inſomuch, that in the eleventh Year of his Reign, the Parliament then ſitting at *London,* the King abſented himſelf from them, and ſtaid at *Eltham,* refuſing to come at them, and join with them in the Publick Affairs : Upon which Occaſion, *the Lords and Commons* ſent Meſſengers to him with an Addreſs ; which the Hiſtorian *H. Knighton* ſets forth at large, and which I will here give the Reader a Tranſcript of at large, becauſe it will afford many uſeful Inferences and Obſervations.

Salubri igitur uſi conſilio, miſerunt de communi Aſſenſu totius Parliamenti Dominum Thomam de Wodeſtoke Ducem Gloceſtriæ, & Thomam de Arundell Epiſcopum Elyenſem, ad regem apud Eltham, qui ſalutarent eum ex parte Procerum & Communium Parliamenti ſui, ſub tali ſenſu verborum ei referentes vota eorum.

Domine Rex, Proceres & Domini atque totus populus Communitatis Parliamenti veſtri, cum humillimâ ſubjectione ſe commendant excellentiſſimo Regalis Dignitatis veſtræ, cupientes proſperum iter invincibilis honoris veſtri contra inimicorum potentiam, & validiſſimum vinculum pacis & dilectionis cordis veſtri erga ſubditos veſtros, in augmentum commodi veſtri erga Deum, & ſalutem animæ veſtræ, & ad inedicibilem conſolationem totius Populi veſtri quem regis : Ex eorum parte hæc vobis intimamus, Quod ex antiquo Statuto habemus, & conſuetudine

Wherefore taking wholeſome Advice, they ſent by common Aſſent of the whole Parliament, the Lord *Thomas de Woodſtock,* Duke of *Gloceſter,* and *Thomas de Arundell,* Biſhop of *Ely,* to the King at *Eltham,* to ſalute him on behalf of the Lords and Commons of his Parliament, who expreſſed their Deſires to the King, to this effect.

Sir, *The Lords, and all the Commons of your Parliament,* have themſelves commended to your moſt excellent Majeſty, deſiring the Succeſs of your invincible Honour againſt the Power of your Enemies, and a moſt firm Bond of Peace and Love in your Heart towards your Subjects, for your good God-wards, and the good of your Soul ; and to the unſpeakable Comfort of all your People whom you govern : On whoſe behalf we intimate theſe things to you ; That it appears to us *by an ancient Statute, and* by

tudine laudabili & approbata, *cujus contrarietati dict non valebit, quod Rex noster convocare potest Dominos & Proceres Regni atque Communes semel in anno ad Parliamentum suam, tanquam ad summam curiam totius Regni, in quâ omnis æquitas relucere deberet absque qualibet scrupulositate vel nota, tanquam Sol in ascensu meridiei, ubi pauperes & divites pro refrigerio tranquillitatis & pacis, & repulsione injuriarum, refugium infallibile quærere possent ; ac etiam errata Regni reformare, & de Statu & Gubernatione Regis & Regni cum sapientiori consilio tractare, & ut inimici Regis & Regni intrinseci & hostes extrinseci destruantur & repellantur, quomodò convenientius & honorificentius fieri poterit cum salubri tractatu in eo disponere & prævidere; qualiter quæque onera incumbentia Regi & Regno levius ad ediam communitatis supportari poterunt. Videtur etiam iis, quod ex quo onera supportant incumbentia, habent etiam supervidere qualiter & per quos eorum bona & catalla expendantur. Dicunt etiam, quod habent ex antiquo Statuto, quod si Rex à Parliamento suo se alienaverit sua sponte, non aliqua infirmitate, aut aliqua alia de causa necessitatis, sed per immoderatam voluntatem protervè se subtraxerit per absentiam temporis quadraginta dierum, tanquam de vexatione populi sui, & gravibus eorum expensis non curans, extunc licitum omnibus & singulis eorum absque domigerio Regis redire ad propria, & unicuique eorum in patriam suam remeare : Et jam vos ex longiore tempore absentastis, & qua de causa nesciunt, venire renuistis.* Ad hæc Rex, *Jam plane consideramus, quod Populus noster atque Communes intendunt resistere, atque contra nos insurgere moliuntur ; & in tali infestatione melius nobis non videtur, quin cognatum nostrum Regem Franciæ, & ab eo consilium & auxilium petere contra insidiantes, & nos ei submittere potiùs quàm succumbere subditis nostris.* Ad hæc illi responderunt, *Non est hoc vobis sanum consilium, sed magis ducens ad inevitabile detrimentum ; nam Rex Franciæ capitalis inimicus vester est, & Regni vestri adversarius permaximus ; & si in terram Regni vestri pedem figeret potiùs, vos spoliare laboraret, & Regnum vestrum invadere, vosque à sublimitate Regalis solii expellere, quam vobis aliquatenùs manus adjutrices cum favore apponere ; si quod absit, ejus suffragio quandoque indigeretis. Ad memoriam igitur revocetis, qualiter avus vester* Edwardus *tertius Rex, & similiter pater* Edwardus *Princeps nomine ejus in sudore & angustiis in omni tempore suo per innumerabiles labores in frigori & calore certaverunt indefesse pro conquisitione Regni* Franciæ, *quod eis jure hæreditario attinebat, & vobis per successionem post eos. Reminiscemini quoque qualiter Domini regni & Proceres atque Communes innu-*

by laudable and approved *Usage*, which cannot be deny'd, that our King can call together the Peers of the Realm, and the Commons, once a Year to his Parliament, as to the supreme Court of the whole Kingdom, in which all Right and Justice ought to shine forth, without any doubt or stain, as the Sun at Noon-day, where Poor and Rich may find an infallible Refuge, to enjoy the Refreshments of Tranquility and Peace, and for repelling of Injuries ; where also Errors in Government are to be reformed, and the State and Government of King and Kingdom, treated upon by sage Advice, and the destroying and repelling of both intestine and foreign Enemies to the King and Kingdom, with most Convenience and Honour, may be debated upon, and provided for; as also in what manner the Charges incumbent upon the King and Kingdom, may be born with most ease to the Commonalty. They conceive likewise, that since they bear the incumbent Charges, it concerns them to inspect how and by whom their Goods and Chattels are expended. They say also, that it appears to them by an *ancient Statute*, that if the King absent himself from his Parliament voluntarily, not by reason of Sickness, or for any other necessary cause, but through an inordinate Will shall wantonly absent himself by the space of forty days, as not regarding the vexation of his People, and their great Expences, it shall then be lawful to all and singular of them, to return to their own homes without the King's leave : And you have now been longer absent, and have refused to come to them, for what cause they know not. *Then said the King,* I now plainly see, that my People and the Commons design to oppose me with Force, and are about to make an Insurrection against me : And, *if I be so infested, I think the best conrse I can take will be to* my Cousin the King of France, *and ask his Advice, and pray in aid of him against those that way-lay me, and rather to submit myself to him, than be foiled by my own Subjects. To which they replied, That Counsel is not for your good, but will inevitably turn to your ruin ; for the King of* France *is your capital Enemy, and the greatest Adversary that your Kingdom has ; and if he should set his foot within your Kingdom, he would rather endeavour to prey upon you, and invade your Realm, and to depose you from your Royal Dignity, than afford you any Assistance, if, which God forbid, you should stand in need of his help.* Call to mind therefore, how your Grandfather King *Edward* III. and your Father Prince *Edward* for him, fought indefatigably in Sweat and Sorrow all their days, and went through innumerable Hardships of Cold and Heat, to acquire the Kingdom of *France*, which by hereditary

innumerabiles tam de Regno Angliæ *quam* Franciæ, *Reges quoque & Domini de aliis Regnis atque populi innumerabiles in Guerrâ illâ mortem & mortis periculum sustinuerunt, bona quoque & catalla inæstimabilia & thesauros innumerabiles pro sustentatione hujus guerræ, Communes Regni hujus indefesse effuderunt. Et quod gravius dolendum est, jam in diebus vestris tanta onera iis imposita pro guerris vestris sustinendis, supportaverunt, quod ad tantam pauperiem incredibilem deducti sunt, quod nec reditus suos pro suis tenementis solvere possunt, nec Regi subvenire, nec vitæ necessaria sibi ipsis ministrare; & depauperatur Regia potestas, & Dominorum Regni, & magnatum infelicitas adducitur, atque totius populi debilitas. Nam Rex depauperari nequit, qui divitem habet populum; nec dives esse potest, qui pauperes habet communes. Et mala hæc omnia redundant non solum Regi, sed & omnibus & singulis Dominis & Proceribus Regni, unicuique in suo gradu. Et hæc omnia eveniunt per iniquos ministros Regis, qui malè gubernaverunt Regem & Regnum usque in præsens. Et nisi manus citius apponamus adjutrices, & remedii fulcimentum adhibeamus, Regnum* Angliæ *dolorose attenuabitur tempore, quo minus opinamur. Sed & unum aliud de nuncio nostro superest nobis ex parte populi vestri vobis intimare.* Habent enim EX ANTIQUO STATUTO, *& de facto non longe retroactis temporibus experienter quod dolendum est habito, si Rex,* EX MALIGNO CONSILIO QUOCUNQUE, *vel* INEPTA CONTUMACIA, *aut* CONTEMPTU, *seu* PROTERVA VOLUNTATE SINGULARI, *aut* QUOVIS MODO IRREGULARI, *se alienaverit à populo suo, nec voluerit per jura Regni, & Statuta ac laudabiles Ordinationes, cum salubri consilio Dominorum & Procerum Regni gubernari & regulari, sed capitose in suis insanis consiliis propriam voluntatem suam singularem proterve exercere, extunc licitum est iis, cum communi assensu & consensu Populi Regni ipsum* REGEM DE REGALI SOLIO ABROGARE, *& propinquiorem aliquem de stirpe Regiâ loco ejus in Regni solio sublimare.* H. Knighton, Collect. 2681.

reditary Right appertain'd to Them, and does now to You by Succession after them. Remember likewise, how innumerable Lords and Commons of both Realms, and Kings and Gentlemen of other Kingdoms, and People innumerable, perished, or hazarded perishing, in that War; and that the Commons of this Realm pour'd out Goods of inestimable value, and innumerable Sums of Money, for the carrying on of that same War; and, which is more to be lamented, they have now in your days undergone such heavy Taxes towards the maintaining of your Wars, that they are reduced to such incredible Poverty, that they cannot so much as pay their Rents for their Farms, nor aid the King, nor afford themselves Necessaries; and the King himself is impoverish'd, and the Lords become uneasy, and all the People faint; for a King cannot become poor, that has a rich People; nor can he be rich, whose People are poor. And all these Mischiefs redound not to the King only, but also to all and singular the Peers of the Realm, in proportion: And all these Mischiefs happen by means of the King's Evil Ministers, who have hitherto misgovern'd both the King and Kingdom; and if some course be not taken, the Kingdom of *England* will be miserably diminish'd sooner than we are aware. But there remains yet another part of our Message, which we have to impart to you on the behalf of your People. They find in an *antient Statute,* and it has been done in fact not long ago, That if the King, through any Evil Counsel, or foolish Contumacy, or out of Scorn, or some singular petulant Will of his own, or by any other irregular Means, shall alienate himself from his People, and shall *refuse to be govern'd and guided by the Laws of the Realm, and the Statutes and laudable Ordinances thereof,* together with the wholsom Advice of the Lords and great Men of his Realm, but persisting headstrong in his own hare-brain'd Counsels, shall petulantly prosecute his own singular humour, That then *it shall be lawful for them, with the common assent and consent of the People of the Realm, to depose that same King from his Regal Throne, and to set up some other of the Royal Blood in his room.* H. Knight. Coll. 2681.

No Man can imagine that the *Lords and Commons in Parliament* would have sent the King such a Message, and have quoted to him an old *Statute for deposing Kings* that would not govern according to Law, if the People of *England* had then apprehended that an Obedience *without reserve* was due to the King, or if there had not been such a Statute in being. And though the Record of that *Excellent Law* be lost, as the Records of almost all our Antient Laws are; yet is the Testimony of so credible an Historian, who lived when these things were transacted, sufficient to inform us, that such a Law was then known and in being, and consequently that the *Terms of English Allegiance,* according to the *Constitution of our Government,* are different from what some Modern Authors would persuade us they are.

This Difference betwixt the said King and his Parliament ended amicably betwixt them, in the punishment of many Evil Counsellors, by whom the King had been influenced to commit many *Irregularities in Government.*

But the Discontents of the People grew higher by his After-management of Affairs, and ended in the *Deposition* of that *King*, and setting up of another, who was not the next Heir in *Lineal Succession.*

The Articles against King *Richard* the Second may be read at large in *H. Knighton*, Collect. 2746, 2747, &c. and are yet extant upon Record. An Abridgment of them is in *Cotton's Records*, pag. 386, 387, 388. out of whom I observe these few, there being in all Thirty three.

The First was, *His wasting and bestowing the Lands of the Crown upon unworthy Persons, and overcharging the Commons with Exactions. And that whereas certain Lords Spiritual and Temporal, were assign'd in Parliament to intend the Government of the Kingdom, the King by a Conventicle of his own Accomplices endeavoured to impeach them of High-Treason.*

Another was, *For that the King by undue means procured divers Justices to speak against the Law, to the destruction of the Duke of* Glocester, *and the Earls of* Arundel *and* Warwick *at* Shrewsbury.

Another, *For that the King, against his own Promise and Pardon at a solemn Procession, apprehended the Duke of* Glocester, *and sent him to* Calice, *there to be choaked and murthered, beheading the Earl of* Arundel, *and banishing the Earl of* Warwick, *and the Lord* Cobham.

Another, *For that the King's Retinue, and a Rout gathered by him out of* Cheshire, *committed divers Murders, Rapes, and other Felonies, and refused to pay for their Victuals.*

Another, *For that the Crown of* England *being freed from the Pope, and all other Foreign Power, the King notwithstanding procured the Pope's Excommunication on such as should break the Ordinances of the last Parliament, in derogation of the Crown, Statutes and Laws of the Realm.*

Another, *That he made Men Sheriffs, who were not named to him by the Great Officers, the Justices and others of his Council ; and who were unfit, contrary to the Laws of the Realm, and in manifest breach of his Oath.*

Another, *For that he did not repay to his Subjects the Debts that he had borrowed of them.*

Another, *For that the King refused to execute the Laws, saying, That the Laws were in his Mouth and Breast, and that himself alone could make and alter the Laws.*

Another, *For causing Sheriffs to continue in Office above a Year, contrary to the tenor of a Statute-Law, thereby incurring notorious Perjury.*

Another, *For that the said King procured Knights of the Shires to be returned to serve his own Will.*

Another, *For that many Justices, for their good Counsel given to the King, were with evil Countenance and Threats rewarded.*

Another, *For that the King passing into* Ireland, *had carried with him, without the Consent of the Estates of the Realm, the Treasure, Reliques, and other Jewels of the Realm, which were used safely to be kept in the King's own Coffers from all hazard ; And for that the said King cancelled and razed sundry Records.*

Another, *For that the said King appear'd by his Letters to the Pope, to Foreign Princes, and to his Subjects, so variable, so dissembling, and so unfaithful and inconstant, that no Man could trust him, that knew him ; insomuch, that he was a Scandal both to himself and the Kingdom.*

Another, *That the King would commonly say amongst the Nobles, that all Subjects Lives, Lands and Goods were in his hands without any forfeiture ; which is altogether contrary to the Laws and Usages of the Realm.*

Another,

Another, *For that he suffered his Subjects to be condemned by Martial-Law, contrary to his Oath, and the Laws of the Realm.*

Another, *For that whereas the Subjects of* England *are sufficiently bound to the King by their Allegiance, yet the said King compell'd them to take new Oaths.*

These Articles, with some others, not altogether of so general a concern, being considered, and the King himself confessing his Defects, the same seemed sufficient to the *whole Estates* for the *King's Deposition,* and he was depos'd accordingly.

The Substance and Drift of all is, That our Kings were antiently liable to, and might lawfully be deposed for *Oppression* and *Tyranny,* for *Insufficiency to govern,* &c. in and by the great Council of the Nation, without any breach of the old *Oath of Fealty;* because (to say nothing of the nature of our *Constitution*) express and positive Laws warranted such Proceedings : And therefore, the Frame of our *Government* being the same still, and the *Terms of our Allegiance* being the same now that they were then, without any new Obligations superinduced by the *Oaths of Allegiance* and *Supremacy,* a King of *England* may legally at this day, for sufficient cause, be deposed by the *Lords and Commons* assembled in a *Great Council of the Kingdom,* without any breach of the present *Oaths of Supremacy or Allegiance. Quod erat demonstrandum.*

MANTISSA.

When *Stephen* was King of *England,* whom the People had chosen rather than submit to *Mawd,* tho the *Great Men* of the Realm had sworn Fealty to her in her Father's life-time, *Henry* Duke of *Anjou,* Son of the said *Mawd,* afterwards King *Henry* the Second, invaded the Kingdom *An. Dom.* 1153, which was towards the latter-end of King *Stephen's* Reign; and *Theobald* Archbishop of *Canterbury* endeavoured to mediate a Peace betwixt them, speaking frequently with the King in private, and sending many Messages to the Duke; and *Henry* Bishop of *Winchester* took pains likewise make them Friends. *Factum est autem, ut mense* Novembris, *in fine mensis,* EX PRÆCEPTO REGIS ET DUCIS, *convenirent apud* Wintoniam *Præsules & Principes Regni, ut & ipsi jam initæ paci præberent assensum, & unanimiter juramenti Sacramento confirmarent,* i.e. It came to pass, that in the Month of *November,* towards the latter end of the Month, *at the summons of the King and of the Duke,* the Prelats and Great Men of the Kingdom were assembled at *Winchester,* that they also might assent to the Peace that was concluded, and unanimously swear to observe it. Collect. pag. 1374, 1375.

In that *Parliament* the Duke was declared King *Stephen's* adopted Son, and Heir of the Kingdom, and the King to retain the Government during his Life.

I observe only upon this Authority, That there being a Controversy betwixt the King and the Duke, which could no otherwise be determined and settled but in a Parliament, the Summons of this Parliament were issued in the Names of both Parties concerned.

Quisquis habet aures ad audiendum, audiat.

F I N I S.